THE **MKTG** SOLUTION

Print + **Online**

MKTG¹⁰ delivers all the key terms and core concepts for the **Principles of Marketing** course.

MKTG Online provides the complete narrative from the printed text with additional interactive media and the unique functionality of **StudyBits**—all available on nearly any device!

What is a StudyBit™? Created through a deep investigation of students' challenges and workflows, the StudyBit™ functionality of **MKTG Online** enables students of different generations and learning styles to study more effectively by allowing them to learn their way. Here's how they work:

COLLECT WHAT'S IMPORTANT
Create StudyBits as you highlight text, images or take notes!

WEAK

FAIR

STRONG

UNASSIGNED

RATE AND ORGANIZE STUDYBITS
Rate your understanding and use the color-coding to quickly organize your study time and personalize your flashcards and quizzes.

StudyBit™

TRACK/MONITOR PROGRESS
Use Concept Tracker to decide how you'll spend study time and study YOUR way!

85%

PERSONALIZE QUIZZES
Filter by your StudyBits to personalize quizzes or just take chapter quizzes off-the-shelf.

CORRECT

INCORRECT

INCORRECT

INCORRECT

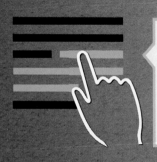

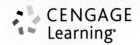
CENGAGE
Learning

MKTG10
Charles W. Lamb, Joseph F. Hair, Jr., Carl McDaniel

Vice President, General Manager, 4LTR Press:
Neil Marquardt

Product Director, 4LTR Press: Steven E. Joos

Product Manager: Laura Redden

Content/Media Developer: Daniel Celenza

Product Assistant: Lauren Dame

Marketing Manager: Jeff Tousignant

Marketing Coordinator: Casey Binder

Content Project Manager: Darrell E. Frye

Manufacturing Planner: Ron Montgomery

Production Service: Prashant Das,
MPS Limited

Sr. Art Director: Bethany Casey

Internal Design: Lou Ann Thesing/Thesing
Design

Cover Design: Curio Press, LLC/Lisa Kuhn

Cover Image: Bloomberg via Getty Images

Intellectual Property Analyst: Diane Garrity

Intellectual Property Project Manager:
Betsy Hathaway

Computer and tablet illustration:
©iStockphoto.com/furtaev

Smart Phone illustration: ©iStockphoto.com/
dashadima

Last ad: Shutterstock.com/Rawpixel.com

For product information and technology assistance, contact us at
Cengage Learning Customer & Sales Support, 1-800-354-9706
For permission to use material from this text or product,
submit all requests online at **www.cengage.com/permissions**
Further permissions questions can be emailed to
permissionrequest@cengage.com

Library of Congress Control Number: 2015960054

Student Edition ISBN: 978-1-305-63179-3

Student Edition with Online ISBN: 978-1-305-63182-3

Cengage Learning
20 Channel Center Street
Boston, MA 02210
USA

Cengage Learning is a leading provider of customized learning solutions with employees residing in nearly 40 different countries and sales in more than 125 countries around the world. Find your local representative at **www.cengage.com**.

Cengage Learning products are represented in Canada by Nelson Education, Ltd.

To learn more about Cengage Learning Solutions, visit **www.cengage.com**

Purchase any of our products at your local college store or at our preferred online store **www.cengagebrain.com**

Printed in the United States of America
Print Number: 01   Print Year: 2016

LAMB / HAIR / MCDANIEL

MKTG¹⁰

BRIEF CONTENTS

Bloomberg via Getty Images

iii

CONTENTS

Part 2
ANALYZING MARKET OPPORTUNITIES

Iea3a3/ShutterStock.com

Part 5
PROMOTION AND COMMUNICATION STRATEGIES

Part 6
PRICING DECISIONS

MKTG
ONLINE

ACCESS TEXTBOOK CONTENT ONLINE—
INCLUDING ON SMARTPHONES!

Includes Videos & Other Interactive Resources!

MANAGE MY COURSE ⌄   STUDENT

MKTG10

CHAPTER
1

An Overview of Marketing

CHAPTER
2

Strategic Planning for
Competitive Advantage

4LTR
PRESS

Access MKTG **ONLINE at www.cengagebrain.com**

1 | An Overview of Marketing

LEARNING OUTCOMES

After studying this chapter, you will be able to...

1-1 Define the term *marketing*

1-2 Describe four marketing management philosophies

1-3 Discuss the differences between sales and market orientations

1-4 Describe several reasons for studying marketing

After you finish this chapter go to **PAGE 13** for **STUDY TOOLS**.

Iofoto/Shutterstock.com

1-1 WHAT IS MARKETING?

What does the term *marketing* mean to you? Many people think *marketing* means personal selling. Others think it means advertising. Still others believe marketing has to do with making products available in stores, arranging displays, and maintaining inventories of products for future sales. Actually, marketing includes all of these activities and more.

Marketing has two facets. First, it is a philosophy, an attitude, a perspective, or a management orientation that stresses customer satisfaction. Second, marketing is an organization function and a set of processes used to implement this philosophy.

The American Marketing Association's definition of marketing focuses on the second facet. According to the AMA, **marketing** is the activity, set of institutions, and processes for creating, communicating, delivering, and exchanging offerings that

> "Marketing is too important to be left only to the marketing department."
>
> —DAVID PACKARD, COFOUNDER OF HEWLETT-PACKARD

have value for customers, clients, partners, and society at large.[1]

Marketing involves more than just activities performed by a group of people in a defined area or department. In the often-quoted words of David Packard, co-founder of Hewlett-Packard, "Marketing is too important to be left only to the marketing department." Marketing entails processes that focus on delivering value and benefits to customers, not just selling goods, services, and/or ideas. It uses communication, distribution, and pricing strategies to provide customers and other stakeholders with the goods, services, ideas, values, and benefits they desire when and where they want them. It involves

marketing the activity, set of institutions, and processes for creating, communicating, delivering, and exchanging offerings that have value for customers, clients, partners, and society at large

building long-term, mutually rewarding relationships when these benefit all parties concerned. Marketing also entails an understanding that organizations have many connected stakeholder "partners," including employees, suppliers, stockholders, distributors, and others.

Research shows that companies that consistently reward employees with incentives and recognition are those that perform best, while disgruntled, disengaged workers cost the United States economy upward of $350 billion a year in lost productivity.[2] In 2014, Google captured the number one position in *Fortune*'s "100 Best Companies to Work For" for the third year in a row. The company pays 100 percent of employees' health care premiums, offers paid sabbaticals, and provides bocce courts, a bowling alley, and twenty-five cafés—all for free. Google has also never had a layoff. One so-called Googler reported that "employees are never more than 150 feet away from a well-stocked pantry."[3]

One desired outcome of marketing is an **exchange**—people giving up something in order to receive something else they would rather have. Normally,

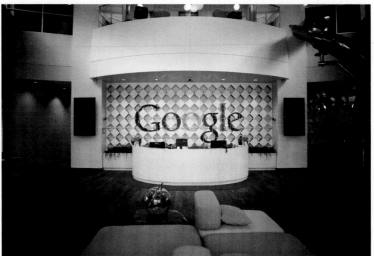

Zuma Press, Inc./Alamy

Google offers many amenities to its employees, part of the reason *Fortune* ranked it as the best company to work for in 2012, 2013, and 2014.

we think of money as the medium of exchange. We "give up" money to "get" the goods and services we want. Exchange does

exchange people giving up something in order to receive something else they would rather have

not require money, however. Two (or more) people may barter or trade such items as baseball cards or oil paintings.

An exchange can take place only if the following five conditions exist:

1. There must be at least two parties.

2. Each party has something that might be of value to the other party.

3. Each party is capable of communication and delivery.

4. Each party is free to accept or reject the exchange offer.

5. Each party believes it is appropriate or desirable to deal with the other party.[4]

Exchange will not necessarily take place even if all these conditions exist, but they must exist for exchange to be possible. For example, suppose you place an advertisement in your local newspaper stating that your used automobile is for sale at a certain price. Several people may call you to ask about the car, some may test-drive it, and one or more may even make you an offer. All five conditions that are necessary for an exchange to occur exist in this scenario. But unless you reach an agreement with a buyer and actually sell the car, an exchange will not take place.

Notice that marketing can occur even if an exchange does not occur. In the example just discussed, you would have engaged in marketing by advertising in the local newspaper even if no one bought your used automobile.

1-2 MARKETING MANAGEMENT PHILOSOPHIES

Four competing philosophies strongly influence an organization's marketing processes. These philosophies are commonly referred to as production, sales, market, and societal marketing orientations.

1-2a Production Orientation

A **production orientation** is a philosophy that focuses on the internal capabilities of the firm rather than on the desires and needs of the marketplace. A production orientation means that management assesses its resources and asks these questions: "What can we do best?" "What can our engineers design?" "What is easy to produce, given our equipment?" In the case of a service organization, managers ask, "What services are most convenient for the firm to offer?" and "Where do our talents lie?" The furniture industry is infamous for its disregard of customers and for its slow cycle times. For example, most traditional furniture stores (think Ashley or Haverty's) carry the same styles and varieties of furniture that they have carried for many years. They always produce and stock sofas, coffee tables, arm chairs, and end tables for the living room. Master bedroom suites always include at least a queen- or king-sized bed, two dressers, and two side tables. Regardless of what customers may actually be looking for, this is what they will find at these stores—and they have been so long-lived because what they produce has matched up with customer expectations. This has always been a production-oriented industry.

There is nothing wrong with assessing a firm's capabilities; in fact, such assessments are major considerations in strategic marketing planning (see Chapter 2). A production orientation falls short because it does not consider whether the goods and services that the firm produces most efficiently also meet the needs of the marketplace. Sometimes what a firm can best produce is exactly what the market wants. Apple has a history of production orientation, creating computers, operating systems, and other gadgetry because it can and hoping to sell the result. Some items have found a waiting market (early computers, iPod, iPhone). Other products, like the Newton, one of the first versions of a PDA, were simply flops.

In some situations, as when competition is weak or demand exceeds supply, a production-oriented firm can survive and even prosper. More often, however, firms that succeed in competitive markets have a clear understanding that they must first determine what customers want and then produce it, rather than focus on what company management thinks should be produced and hope that the product is something customers want.

1-2b Sales Orientation

A **sales orientation** is based on the belief that people will buy more goods and services if aggressive sales techniques are used and that high sales result in high profits. Not only are sales to the final buyer emphasized, but intermediaries are also encouraged to push manufacturers' products more aggressively. To sales-oriented firms, marketing means selling things and collecting money.

production orientation a philosophy that focuses on the internal capabilities of the firm rather than on the desires and needs of the marketplace

sales orientation the belief that people will buy more goods and services if aggressive sales techniques are used and that high sales result in high profits

LIGHTNING DOES NOT STRIKE TWICE

One of the dangers of a sales orientation is failing to understand what is important to the firm's customers. When that occurs, sales-oriented firms sometimes use aggressive incentives to drive sales. For example, after Apple received complaints about the $49 selling price of its Thunderbolt cable, the company reduced the cable's price to $39 and introduced a shorter $29 version. The company hoped to spark sales of the optical data transfer cable, compatible only with Apple's newest line of computers and laptops.[5]

JMiks/Shutterstock.com

"Josh Lowensohn, "Apple's Thunderbolt Cable Gets a Price Drop, Shorter Version," CNET, January 9, 2013, http://news.CNET.com/8301-13579_3-57563157-37/apples-thunderbolt-cable-gets-a-price-drop-shorter-version (Accessed January 10, 2015)."

The fundamental problem with a sales orientation, as with a production orientation, is a lack of understanding of the needs and wants of the marketplace. Sales-oriented companies often find that, despite the quality of their sales force, they cannot convince people to buy goods or services that are neither wanted nor needed.

1-2c Market Orientation

The **marketing concept** is a simple and intuitively appealing philosophy that articulates a market orientation. It states that the social and economic justification for an organization's existence is the satisfaction of customer wants and needs while meeting organizational objectives. What a business thinks it produces is not of primary importance to its success. Instead, what customers think they are buying—the perceived value—defines a business. The marketing concept includes the following:

- Focusing on customer wants and needs so that the organization can distinguish its product(s) from competitors' offerings

- Integrating all the organization's activities, including production, to satisfy customer wants

- Achieving long-term goals for the organization by satisfying customer wants and needs legally and responsibly

The recipe for success is to develop a thorough understanding of your customers and your competition, your distinctive capabilities that enable your company to execute plans on the basis of this customer understanding, and how to deliver the desired experience using and integrating all of the resources of the firm. For example, Kellogg's recently introduced Open for Breakfast, a forum the company uses to connect with consumers about what they are eating for breakfast. The program is also used to share stories about the foods the company makes and its pledge to care for the environment.[6]

Firms that adopt and implement the marketing concept are said to be **market oriented**, meaning they assume that a sale does not depend on an aggressive sales force but rather on a customer's decision to purchase a product. Achieving a market orientation involves obtaining information about customers, competitors, and markets; examining the information from a total business perspective; determining how to deliver superior customer value; and implementing actions to provide value to customers.

Some firms are known for delivering superior customer value and satisfaction. For example, in 2014, J.D. Power and Associates ranked Cadillac highest in customer satisfaction among luxury automotive brands, while Buick ranked

Oliver Hoffmann/Shutterstock.com

marketing concept the idea that the social and economic justification for an organization's existence is the satisfaction of customer wants and needs while meeting organizational objectives

market orientation a philosophy that assumes that a sale does not depend on an aggressive sales force but rather on a customer's decision to purchase a product; it is synonymous with the marketing concept

highest among mass-market brands.[7] Rankings such as these, as well as word-of-mouth from satisfied customers, drive additional sales for these automotive companies.

Understanding your competitive arena and competitors' strengths and weaknesses is a critical component of a market orientation. This includes assessing what existing or potential competitors intend to do tomorrow and what they are doing today. For example, BlackBerry (formerly Research in Motion) failed to realize it was competing against computer companies as well as telecom companies, and its wireless handsets were quickly eclipsed by offerings from Google, Samsung, and Apple. Had BlackBerry been a market-oriented company, its management might have better understood the changes taking place in the market, seen the competitive threat, and developed strategies to counter the threat. Instead, it reentered the market after a five-year slump with the wholly redesigned BlackBerry 10 operating system and sleek new flagship phones. These new products were fairly well received, but they failed to push Black-Berry back into the smartphone spotlight. By contrast, American Express's success has rested largely on the company's ability to focus on customers and adapt to their changing needs over the past 160 years.[8]

1-2d Societal Marketing Orientation

The **societal marketing orientation** extends the marketing concept by acknowledging that some products that customers want may not really be in their best interests or the best interests of society as a whole. This philosophy states that an organization exists not only to satisfy customer wants and needs and to meet organizational objectives but also to preserve or enhance individuals' and society's long-term best interests. Marketing products and containers that are less toxic than normal, are more durable, contain reusable materials, or are made of recyclable materials is consistent with a societal marketing orientation. The American Marketing Association's definition of marketing

LunaseeStudios/Shutterstock.com

recognizes the importance of a societal marketing orientation by including "society at large" as one of the constituencies for which marketing seeks to provide value.

Although the societal marketing concept has been discussed for more than thirty years, it did not receive widespread support until the early 2000s. Concerns such as climate change, the depleting of the ozone layer, fuel shortages, pollution, and health issues have caused consumers and legislators to become more aware of the need for companies and consumers to adopt measures that conserve resources and cause less damage to the environment.

Studies reporting consumers' attitudes toward, and intentions to buy, environmentally friendly products show widely varying results. A Nielsen study found that while eighty-three percent of consumers worldwide believe companies should have environmental programs, only twenty-two percent would pay more for an eco-friendly product. The key to consumer purchasing lies beyond labels proclaiming sustainability, natural ingredients, or "being green." Customers want sustainable products that perform better than their unsustainable counterparts.[9] Unilever, whose brands include Dove, Lipton, Hellmann's, and Ben & Jerry's, is one company that puts sustainability at the core of its business. It has promised both to cut its environmental footprint in half and to source all its agricultural products in ways that do not degrade the earth by 2020. The company also promotes the well-being of one billion people by producing foods with less salt and fat and has developed campaigns advocating hand washing and teeth brushing.[10]

1-2e Who Is in Charge?

The Internet and the widespread use of social media have accelerated the shift in power from manufacturers and retailers to consumers and business users. This shift began when customers began using books, electronics, and the Internet to access information, goods, and services. Customers use their widespread knowledge to shop smarter, leading executives such as former Procter & Gamble CEO A. G. Lafley to conclude that "the customer is boss."[11] Founder of Walmart and Sam's Club Sam Walton echoed this sentiment when he reportedly once said, "There is only one boss. The customer. And he can fire everybody in the company

societal marketing orientation the idea that an organization exists not only to satisfy customer wants and needs and to meet organizational objectives but also to preserve or enhance individuals' and society's long-term best interests

from the chairman on down, simply by spending his money somewhere else."[12] The following quotation, attributed to everyone from L.L.Bean founder Leon Leonwood Bean to Mahatma Gandhi, has been a guiding business principle for more than seventy years: "A customer is the most important visitor on our premises. He is not dependent on us. We are dependent on him. He is not an interruption in our work. He is the purpose of it. He is not an outsider in our business. He is part of it. We are not doing him a favor by serving him. He is doing us a favor by giving us an opportunity to do so."[13] And as Internet use and mobile devices become increasingly pervasive, that control will continue to grow. This means that companies must create strategy from the outside in by offering distinct and compelling customer value.[14] This can be accomplished only by carefully studying customers and using deep market insights to inform and guide companies' outside-in view.[15]

1-3 DIFFERENCES BETWEEN SALES AND MARKET ORIENTATIONS

The differences between sales and market orientations are substantial. The two orientations can be compared in terms of five characteristics: the organization's focus, the firm's business, those to whom the product is directed, the firm's primary goal, and the tools used to achieve the organization's goals.

1-3a The Organization's Focus

Personnel in sales-oriented firms tend to be inward looking, focusing on selling what the organization makes rather than making what the market wants. Many of the historic sources of competitive advantage—technology, innovation, economies of scale—allowed companies to focus their efforts internally and prosper. Today, many successful firms derive their competitive advantage from an external, market-oriented focus. A market orientation has helped companies such as Zappos.com and Bob's Red Mill Natural Foods outperform their competitors. These companies put customers at the center of their business in ways most companies do poorly or not at all.

CUSTOMER VALUE The relationship between benefits and the sacrifice necessary to obtain those benefits is known as **customer value**. Customer value is not simply a matter of high quality. A high-quality product that is available only at a high price will not

be perceived as a good value, nor will bare-bones service or low-quality goods selling for a low price. Price is a component of value (a $4,000 handbag is perceived as being more luxurious and of higher quality than one selling for $100), but low price is not the same as good value. Instead, customers value goods and services that are of the quality they expect and that are sold at prices they are willing to pay.

Value can be used to sell a Mercedes-Benz as well as a Tyson frozen chicken dinner. In other words, value is something that shoppers of all markets and at all income levels look for. Lower-income consumers are price sensitive, but they will pay for products if they deliver a benefit that is worth the money.[16] Conversely, wealthy customers with money to spend may value the social message of their purchases above all else. These shoppers are being courted by a new breed of social shopping sites. The basic premise is that a well-known fashion name (be it a fashion editor, elite socialite, or celebrity) moderates sites by handpicking pieces from favorite retailers, such as Barneys New York or Saks Fifth Avenue. Shoppers then purchase the curated items, and the site receives commission for each purchase. There are many of these sites; Moda Operandi has highlighted (and sold out of) woven skirts for $4,000 each, Motilo focuses on French fashion (including couture pieces), and *Fino File* is an online, shopable magazine, with pieces ranging from $80 tops to $1,000 boots. With reports of growing subscribers and sold-out merchandise, it is clear that these sites are attracting customers who value curated style.[17]

CUSTOMER SATISFACTION The customers' evaluation of a good or service in terms of whether that good or service has met their needs and expectations is called **customer satisfaction**. Failure to meet needs and expectations results in dissatisfaction with the good or service. Some companies, in their passion to drive down costs, have damaged their relationships with customers. Bank of America, Comcast, Dish Network, and AT&T are examples of companies where executives lost track of the delicate balance between efficiency and service.[18] Firms that have a reputation for delivering high levels of customer satisfaction do things differently from their competitors. Top management is obsessed with customer satisfaction, and employees throughout the organization understand the link between their job and satisfied customers. The

customer value the relationship between benefits and the sacrifice necessary to obtain those benefits

customer satisfaction customers' evaluation of a good or service in terms of whether it has met their needs and expectations

▶ **Offer products that perform:** This is the bare minimum requirement. After grappling with the problems associated with its Vista operating system, Microsoft listened to its customers and made drastic changes for Windows 7, which received greatly improved reviews. Microsoft's subsequent release, Windows 8, performed even better than Windows 7, but consumers were much slower to embrace the operating system's incremental improvements.

▶ **Earn trust:** A stable base of loyal customers can help a firm grow and prosper. To attract customers, online eyewear company Coastal.com offers a First Pair Free program, whereby new customers receive their first pair of prescription eyeglass for free. Moreover, Coastal.com offers 366-day returns and encourages its staff members to do whatever it takes to ensure that customers are delighted by a smooth and stress-free experience. Coastal.com's dedication to earning customers' trust is evident—in 2013, the company received the STELLA Service elite seal for excellence in outstanding customer service.[19]

▶ **Avoid unrealistic pricing:** E-marketers are leveraging Internet technology to redefine how prices are set and negotiated. With lower costs, e-marketers can often offer lower prices than their brick-and-mortar counterparts. The enormous popularity of auction sites such as eBay and the customer-bid model used by Priceline and uBid.com illustrates that online customers are interested in bargain prices. In fact, as smartphone usage grows, brick-and-mortar stores are up against customers who compare prices using their smartphones and purchase items for less online while standing in the store.

▶ **Give the buyer facts:** Today's sophisticated consumer wants informative advertising and knowledgeable salespeople. It is becoming very difficult for business marketers to differentiate themselves from competitors. Rather than trying to sell products, salespeople need to find out what the customer needs, which is usually a combination of friendliness, understanding, fairness, control, options, and information.[20] In other words, salespeople need

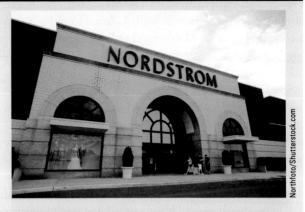

to start with the needs of the customer and work toward the solution.

▶ **Offer organization-wide commitment in service and after-sales support:** Upscale fashion retailer Nordstrom is widely known for its company-wide support system. If a customer finds that a competitor has reduced the price of an item also sold at Nordstrom, Nordstrom will match the other retailer's price and credit the customer's account—even long after the sale is made. Customer service agents at each of Nordstrom's 117 locations are knowledgeable and eager to assist customers before, during, or after a sale, and strive to make the return process as painless as possible. This attention to customer service is carried through to Nordstrom's online store as well: every order receives free shipping, as well as free return shipping. However and wherever they place their orders, customers know that Nordstrom will support them throughout—and long after—the checkout process.[21]

▶ **Co-create:** Some companies and products allow customers to help create their own experience. For example, Case-Mate, a firm that makes form-fitting cases for cell phones, laptops, and other personal devices, allows customers to design their own cases by uploading their own photos. Customers who do not have designs of their own can manipulate art from designers using the "design with" feature at case-mate.com. Either way, customers produce completely unique covers for their devices.

culture of the organization is to focus on delighting customers rather than on selling products.

Coming back from customer dissatisfaction can be tough, but there are some key ways that companies begin to improve customer satisfaction. Forrester Research discovered that when companies experience gains in the firm's Customer Experience Index (CxPi), they have implemented one of two major changes. Aetna, a major

health insurance provider, executed the first type of change—changing its decentralized, part-time customer service group into a full-time, centralized customer service team. Aetna's CxPi score rose six points in one year. Office Depot executed the second type of change—addressing customer "pain points" and making sure that what customers need is always available to them. By streamlining its supply chain and adding more stylish office products,

Office Depot satisfied business customers and female shoppers, increasing its CxPi by nine points.[22]

BUILDING RELATIONSHIPS Attracting new customers to a business is only the beginning. The best companies view new-customer attraction as the launching point for developing and enhancing a long-term relationship. Companies can expand market share in three ways: attracting new customers, increasing business with existing customers, and retaining current customers. Building relationships with existing customers directly addresses two of the three possibilities and indirectly addresses the other.

Relationship marketing is a strategy that focuses on keeping and improving relationships with current customers. It assumes that many consumers and business customers prefer to have an ongoing relationship with one organization rather than switch continually among providers in their search for value. Chicago-based software company 37signals decided to focus its marketing budget on helping current customers get more out of the software they already have rather than targeting new customers. The company would rather expand current customers' awareness of what is possible with its products than focus on short term sales.[23] This long-term focus on customer needs is a hallmark of relationship marketing.

Most successful relationship marketing strategies depend on customer-oriented personnel, effective training programs, employees with the authority to make decisions and solve problems, and teamwork.

Customer-Oriented Personnel For an organization to be focused on building relationships with customers, employees' attitudes and actions must be customer oriented. An employee may be the only contact a particular customer has with the firm. In that customer's eyes, the employee *is* the firm. Any person, department, or division that is not customer oriented weakens the positive image of the entire organization. For example, a potential customer who is greeted discourteously may well assume that the employee's attitude represents the whole firm.

Customer-oriented personnel come from an organizational culture that supports its people. Marriott, a multibillion dollar worldwide hotel chain, believes that treating employees well contributes to good customer service. The company has been among Fortune's "100 Best Companies to Work For" every year since the magazine introduced the list in 1998. For example, during the recent recession, Marriott ensured that all of its employees kept their benefits despite shorter shifts. For its focus on customer satisfaction, Marriott received the number three ranking on MSN.com's 2014 Customer Service Hall of Fame.[24]

Some companies, such as Coca-Cola, Delta Air Lines, Hershey, Kellogg, Nautilus, and Sears, have appointed chief customer officers (CCOs). These customer advocates provide an executive voice for customers and report directly to the CEO. Their responsibilities include ensuring that the company maintains a customer-centric culture and that all company employees remain focused on delivering customer value.

Marriott's customer-oriented focus is evident in initiatives like the Fairfield Inn & Suites "Some Like It Hot" food truck, which serves hot, made-to-order breakfasts to customers for free.

The Role of Training Leading marketers recognize the role of employee training in customer service and relationship building. Sales staff at the Container Store receive more than 240 hours of training and generous benefits compared to an industry average of 8 hours of training and modest benefits.

Empowerment In addition to training, many market-oriented firms are giving employees more authority to solve customer problems on the spot. The term used to describe this delegation of authority is **empowerment**. Employees develop ownership attitudes when they are treated like part-owners of the business and are expected to act the part. These employees manage themselves, are more likely to work hard, account for their own performance and that of the company, and take prudent risks to build a stronger business and sustain the company's success.

relationship marketing a strategy that focuses on keeping and improving relationships with current customers

empowerment delegation of authority to solve customers' problems quickly—usually by the first person the customer notifies regarding a problem

An emphasis on cooperation over competition can help a company's performance improve. That is why many companies have moved to using teams to get jobs done.

In order to empower its workers, the Ritz-Carlton chain of luxury hotels developed a set of twelve "Service Values" guidelines. These brief, easy-to-understand guidelines include statements such as "I am empowered to create unique, memorable and personal experiences for our guests" and "I own and immediately resolve guest problems." The twelve Service Values are printed on cards distributed to employees, and each day a particular value is discussed at length in Ritz-Carlton team meetings. Employees talk about what the value means to them and offer examples of how the value can be put into practice that day.[25]

Teamwork Many organizations that are frequently noted for delivering superior customer value and providing high levels of customer satisfaction, such as Southwest Airlines and Walt Disney World, assign employees to teams and teach them team-building skills. **Teamwork** entails collaborative efforts of people to accomplish common objectives. Job performance, company performance, product value, and customer satisfaction all improve when people in the same department or work group begin supporting and assisting each other and emphasize cooperation instead of competition. Performance is also enhanced when cross-functional teams align their jobs with customer needs. For example, if a team of

teamwork collaborative efforts of people to accomplish common objectives

telecommunications service representatives is working to improve interaction with customers, back-office people such as computer technicians or training personnel can become part of the team, with the ultimate goal of delivering superior customer value and satisfaction.

1-3b The Firm's Business

A sales-oriented firm defines its business (or mission) in terms of goods and services. A market-oriented firm defines its business in terms of the benefits its customers seek. People who spend their money, time, and energy expect to receive benefits, not just goods and services. This distinction has enormous implications. As Michael Mosley, director of office operations at health care provider Amedisys Home Health, notes, "We're in the business of making people better."[26] Answering the question "What is this firm's business?" in terms of the benefits customers seek, instead of goods and services, offers at least three important advantages:

- It ensures that the firm keeps focusing on customers and avoids becoming preoccupied with goods, services, or the organization's internal needs.

- It encourages innovation and creativity by reminding people that there are many ways to satisfy customer wants.

- It stimulates an awareness of changes in customer desires and preferences so that product offerings are more likely to remain relevant.

Because of the limited way it defines its business, a sales-oriented firm often misses opportunities to serve customers whose wants can be met through a wide range of product offerings instead of through specific products. For example, in 1989, 220-year-old Britannica had estimated revenues of $650 million and a worldwide sales force of 7,500. Just five years later, after three consecutive years of losses, the sales force had collapsed to as few as 280 representatives. How did this respected company sink so low? Britannica managers saw that competitors were beginning to use CD-ROMs to store huge masses of information but chose to ignore the new computer technology as well as an offer to team up with Microsoft. In 2012, the company announced that it would stop printing its namesake books and instead focus on selling its reference works to subscribers through its Web site and apps for tablets and smartphones.[27]

Having a market orientation and a focus on customer wants does not mean offering customers everything they want. It is not possible, for example, to profitably manufacture and market automobile tires that will last for 100,000 miles for twenty-five dollars. Furthermore, customers' preferences must be mediated by sound professional judgment as to how to deliver the benefits they seek. As Henry Ford once said, "If I had asked people what they wanted, they would have said faster horses."[28] Consumers have a limited set of experiences. They are unlikely to request anything beyond those experiences because they are not aware of benefits they may gain from other potential offerings. For example, before the Internet, many people thought that shopping for some products was boring and time-consuming but could not express their need for electronic shopping.

1-3c Those to Whom the Product Is Directed

A sales-oriented organization targets its products at "everybody" or "the average customer." A market-oriented organization aims at specific groups of people. The fallacy of developing products directed at the average user is that relatively few average users actually exist. Typically, populations are characterized by diversity. An average is simply a midpoint in some set of characteristics. Because most potential customers are not "average," they are not likely to be attracted to an average product marketed to the average customer. Consider the market for shampoo as one simple example. There are shampoos for oily hair, dry hair, and dandruff. Some shampoos remove the gray or color hair. Special shampoos are marketed for infants and elderly people. There are even shampoos for people with average or normal hair (whatever that is), but this is a fairly small portion of the total market for shampoo.

A market-oriented organization recognizes that different customer groups want different features or benefits. It may therefore need to develop different goods, services, and promotional appeals. A market-oriented organization carefully analyzes the market and divides it into groups of people who are fairly similar in terms of selected characteristics. Then the organization develops marketing programs that will bring about mutually satisfying exchanges with one or more of those groups. For example, Toyota developed a series of tongue-in-cheek videos and interactive Web pages featuring comedian Michael Showalter to advertise the 2013 Yaris subcompact sedan. Toyota used absurdist humor and an ironic slogan ("It's a car!") to appeal to Internet-savvy teens and young adults—a prime market for inexpensive subcompact cars.[29]

CUSTOMER RELATIONSHIP MANAGEMENT Beyond knowing to whom they are directing their products or services, companies must also develop a deeper understanding of their customers. One way of doing this is through *customer relationship management*.

Customer relationship management (CRM) is a company-wide business strategy designed to optimize profitability, revenue, and customer satisfaction by focusing on highly defined and precise customer groups. This is accomplished by organizing the company around customer segments, establishing and tracking customer interactions with the company, fostering customer-satisfying behaviors, and linking all processes of the company from its customers through its suppliers. The difference between CRM and traditional mass marketing can be compared to shooting a rifle versus a shotgun. Instead of scattering messages far and wide across the spectrum of mass media (the shotgun approach), CRM marketers now are homing in on ways to effectively communicate with each customer (the rifle approach).

Companies that adopt CRM systems are almost always market oriented, customizing product and service offerings based on data generated through interactions between the customer and the company. This strategy transcends all functional areas of the business, producing an internal system where all of the company's decisions and actions are a direct result of customer information. We will examine specific applications of CRM in several chapters throughout this book.

The emergence of **on-demand marketing** is taking CRM to a new level. As technology evolves and becomes more sophisticated, consumer expectations of their decision- and buying-related experiences have risen. Consumers (1) want to interact anywhere, anytime; (2) want to do new things with varied kinds of information in ways that create value; (3) expect data stored about them to be targeted specifically to their needs or to personalize their experiences; and (4) expect all interactions with a company to be easy. In response to these expectations, companies are developing new ways to integrate and personalize each stage of a customer's decision journey, which in turn should increase relationship-related behaviors. On-demand marketing delivers relevant experiences throughout the consumer's decision and buying process that are integrated across both physical and virtual environments. Trends such as the growth of mobile connectivity, better-designed Web sites, inexpensive communication through technology, and advances in handling big data have allowed companies to start designing

customer relationship management (CRM) a company-wide business strategy designed to optimize profitability, revenue, and customer satisfaction by focusing on highly defined and precise customer groups

on-demand marketing delivering relevant experiences, integrated across both physical and virtual environments, throughout the consumer's decision and buying process

on-demand marketing programs that appeal to consumers. For on-demand marketing to be successful, companies must deliver high-quality experiences across all touch points with the customer, including sales, service, product use, and marketing.

An example of on-demand marketing is Commonwealth Bank of Australia's new smartphone app that integrates and personalizes the house hunting experience. A prospective homebuyer starts by taking a picture of a house he or she likes. Using special software and location-based technology, the app finds the house and provides the list price and other information, connects with the buyer's financial data, and determines whether the buyer can be preapproved for a mortgage. This fast series of interactions decreases the hassle of searching real-estate agents' sites for a house and then connecting with agents, banks, and/or mortgage brokers—a process that traditionally takes up to a week.[30]

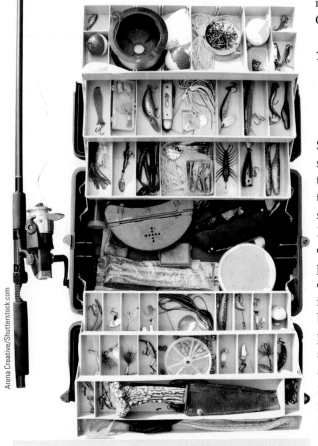

Arena Creative/Shutterstock.com

Using the correct tools for the job will help an organization achieve its goals. Marketing tools for success are covered throughout this book.

profits. Nonprofit organizations can and should adopt a market orientation. Nonprofit organization marketing is explored further in Chapter 12.

1-3e Tools the Organization Uses to Achieve Its Goals

Sales-oriented organizations seek to generate sales volume through intensive promotional activities, mainly personal selling and advertising. In contrast, market-oriented organizations recognize that promotion decisions are only one of four basic marketing mix decisions that must be made: product decisions, place (or distribution) decisions, promotion decisions, and pricing decisions. A market-oriented organization recognizes that each of these four components is important. Furthermore, market-oriented organizations recognize that marketing is not just a responsibility of the marketing department. Interfunctional coordination means that skills and resources throughout the organization are needed to create, communicate, and deliver superior customer service and value.

1-3d The Firm's Primary Goal

A sales-oriented organization seeks to achieve profitability through sales volume and tries to convince potential customers to buy, even if the seller knows that the customer and product are mismatched. Sales-oriented organizations place a higher premium on making a sale than on developing a long-term relationship with a customer. In contrast, the ultimate goal of most market-oriented organizations is to make a profit by creating customer value, providing customer satisfaction, and building long-term relationships with customers. The exception is so-called nonprofit organizations that exist to achieve goals other than

1-3f A Word of Caution

This comparison of sales and market orientations is not meant to belittle the role of promotion, especially personal selling, in the marketing mix. Promotion is the means by which organizations communicate with present and prospective customers about the merits and characteristics of their organization and products. Effective promotion is an essential part of effective marketing. Salespeople who work for market-oriented organizations are generally perceived by their customers to be problem solvers and important links to supply sources and new products. Chapter 18 examines the nature of personal selling in more detail.

1-4 WHY STUDY MARKETING?

Now that you understand the meaning of the term *marketing*, why it is important to adopt a marketing orientation, and how organizations implement this philosophy, you may be asking, "What's in it for me?" or "Why should I study marketing?" These are important questions whether you are majoring in a business field other than marketing (such as accounting, finance, or management information systems) or a nonbusiness field (such as journalism, education, or agriculture). There are several important reasons to study marketing: Marketing plays an important role in society, marketing is important to businesses, marketing offers outstanding career opportunities, and marketing affects your life every day.

1-4a Marketing Plays an Important Role in Society

The total population of the United States exceeds 320 million people.[31] Think about how many transactions are needed each day to feed, clothe, and shelter a population of this size. The number is huge. And yet it all works quite well, partly because the well-developed U.S. economic system efficiently distributes the output of farms and factories. A typical U.S. family, for example, consumes two and a half tons of food a year.[32] Marketing makes food available when we want it, in desired quantities, at accessible locations, and in sanitary and convenient packages and forms (such as instant and frozen foods).

1-4b Marketing Is Important to Businesses

The fundamental objectives of most businesses are survival, profits, and growth. Marketing contributes directly to achieving these objectives. Marketing includes the following activities, which are vital to business organizations: assessing the wants and satisfactions of present and potential customers, designing and managing product offerings, determining prices and pricing policies, developing distribution strategies, and communicating with present and potential customers.

All businesspeople, regardless of specialization or area of responsibility, need to be familiar with the terminology and fundamentals of accounting, finance, management, and marketing. People in all business areas need to be able to communicate with specialists in other areas. Furthermore, marketing is not just a job done by people in a marketing department. Marketing is a part of the job of everyone in the organization. Therefore, a basic understanding of marketing is important to all businesspeople.

1-4c Marketing Offers Outstanding Career Opportunities

Between one-fourth and one-third of the entire civilian workforce in the United States performs marketing activities. Marketing offers great career opportunities in such areas as professional selling, marketing research, advertising, retail buying, distribution management, product management, product development, and wholesaling. Marketing career opportunities also exist in a variety of nonbusiness organizations, including hospitals, museums, universities, the armed forces, and various government and social service agencies.

1-4d Marketing in Everyday Life

Marketing plays a major role in your everyday life. You participate in the marketing process as a consumer of goods and services. About half of every dollar you spend pays for marketing costs, such as marketing research, product development, packaging, transportation, storage, advertising, and sales expenses. By developing a better understanding of marketing, you will become a better-informed consumer. You will better understand the buying process and be able to negotiate more effectively with sellers. Moreover, you will be better prepared to demand satisfaction when the goods and services you buy do not meet the standards promised by the manufacturer or the marketer.

STUDY TOOLS 1

LOCATED AT BACK OF THE TEXTBOOK
☐ Rip out Chapter Review Card

LOCATED AT WWW.CENGAGEBRAIN.COM
☐ Review Key Terms Flashcards and create your own
☐ Track your knowledge & understanding of key concepts in marketing
☐ Complete practice and graded quizzes to prepare for tests
☐ Complete interactive content within the MKTG Online experience
☐ View the chapter highlight boxes within the MKTG Online experience

2 | Strategic Planning for Competitive Advantage

LEARNING OUTCOMES

After studying this chapter, you will be able to...

2-1 Understand the importance of strategic planning

2-2 Define strategic business units (SBUs)

2-3 Identify strategic alternatives and know a basic outline for a marketing plan

2-4 Develop an appropriate business mission statement

2-5 Describe the components of a situation analysis

2-6 Identify sources of competitive advantage

2-7 Explain the criteria for stating good marketing objectives

2-8 Discuss target market strategies

2-9 Describe the elements of the marketing mix

2-10 Explain why implementation, evaluation, and control of the marketing plan are necessary

2-11 Identify several techniques that help make strategic planning effective

Phase4Studios/Shutterstock.com

After you finish this chapter go to **PAGE 29** for **STUDY TOOLS.**

2-1 THE NATURE OF STRATEGIC PLANNING

Strategic planning is the managerial process of creating and maintaining a fit between the organization's objectives and resources and the evolving market opportunities. The goal of strategic planning is long-run profitability and growth. Thus, strategic decisions require long-term commitments of resources.

A strategic error can threaten a firm's survival. On the other hand, a good strategic plan can help protect and grow the firm's resources. For instance, if the March of Dimes had decided to focus only on fighting polio, the organization would no longer exist because polio is widely viewed as a conquered disease. The March of Dimes survived by making the strategic decision to switch to fighting birth defects.

Strategic marketing management addresses two questions: (1) What is the organization's main activity at a particular time? (2) How will it reach its goals? Here are some examples of strategic decisions:

- In an effort to halt decreasing sales and compete with other fast food and fast casual chains, McDonald's has unveiled plans to allow customers to customize their orders for the first time. The new offering, called Create a Taste, lets customers use their tablet computers to choose toppings for their sandwiches.[1]

- Coach, the iconic leather goods company that became successful with wallets and handbags, is making an effort to reinvent itself as a lifestyle brand. The company has introduced a variety of products, including

strategic planning the managerial process of creating and maintaining a fit between the organization's objectives and resources and the evolving market opportunities

footwear, women's apparel, jewelry, sunglasses, and watches. It even designed a luxury baseball glove for men.[2]

- Following founder Howard Schultz's vision of maintaining an entrepreneurial approach to strategy, Starbucks recently opened the Starbucks Reserve Roastery and Tasting Room in Seattle to appeal to upscale coffee lovers. The company also has plans to expand its food and beverage menu.[3]

All these decisions have affected or will affect each organization's long-run course, its allocation of resources, and ultimately its financial success. In contrast, an operating decision, such as changing the package design for Post Grape-Nuts cereal or altering the sweetness of a Kraft salad dressing, probably will not have a big impact on the long-run profitability of the company.

 2-2 STRATEGIC BUSINESS UNITS

Large companies may manage a number of very different businesses, called strategic business units (SBUs). Each SBU has its own rate

> "There are a lot of great ideas that have come and gone in [the digital advertising] industry. Implementation many times is more important than the actual idea."
>
> —DAVID MOORE, CEO OF 24/7 REAL MEDIA

of return on investment, growth potential, and associated risks, and requires its own strategies and funding. When properly created, an SBU has the following characteristics:

- A distinct mission and a specific target market
- Control over its resources
- Its own competitors
- A single business or a collection of related businesses
- Plans independent of the other SBUs in the total organization.

In theory, an SBU should have its own resources for handling basic business functions: accounting, engineering, manufacturing, and marketing. In practice, however, because of company tradition, management philosophy, and production and distribution economies, SBUs sometimes share manufacturing facilities, distribution channels, and even top managers.

strategic business unit (SBU) a subgroup of a single business or collection of related businesses within the larger organization

2-3 STRATEGIC ALTERNATIVES

There are several tools available that a company, or SBU, can use to manage the strategic direction of its portfolio of businesses. Three of the most commonly used tools are Ansoff's strategic opportunity matrix, the Boston Consulting Group model, and the General Electric model. Selecting which strategic alternative to pursue depends on which of two philosophies a company maintains about when to expect profits—right away or after increasing market share. In the long run, market share and profitability are compatible goals. For example, Amazon lost hundreds of millions of dollars its first few years, and the company posted quarterly net losses as recently as 2013. Amazon's primary goal is market share—not profit. It sacrifices short-term profit for long-term market share, and thus larger long-term profits.[4]

2-3a Ansoff's Strategic Opportunity Matrix

One method for developing alternatives is Ansoff's strategic opportunity matrix (see Exhibit 2.1), which matches products with markets. Firms can explore these four options:

- **Market penetration:** A firm using the **market penetration** alternative would try to increase market share among existing customers. FTR Energy Services, a division of Frontier Communications, introduced a Green-e certified energy service into New York, Ohio, and Indiana markets served by Frontier's telephone and broadband services. Though these markets were already served by separate, well-established energy companies, FTR Energy hoped to penetrate the energy market by allowing customers to lock in competitive rates and offering five percent cash back on energy usage.[5] Customer databases, discussed in Chapter 9, would help managers implement this strategy.

- **Market development: Market development** means attracting new customers to existing products. Ideally, new uses for old products stimulate additional sales among existing customers while also bringing in new buyers. McDonald's, for example, has opened restaurants in Russia, China, and Italy and is eagerly expanding into Eastern European countries. In the nonprofit arena, the growing emphasis on continuing education and executive development by colleges and universities is a market development strategy.

- **Product development:** A **product development** strategy entails the creation of new products for present markets. In January 2014, Beats Electronics launched Beats Music, a subscription-based streaming music service that offers advanced personalization systems and forward-thinking family sharing plans. Beats hopes this service's novel features, sleek design, and celebrity endorsements will catapult it to the front of the music streaming pack, which is currently fronted by competitors such as Spotify and Rdio.[6]

- **Diversification: Diversification** is a strategy of increasing sales by introducing new products into new markets. For example, UGG, a popular footwear

---

Exhibit 2.1 | ANSOFF'S OPPORTUNITY MATRIX

	Present Product	New Product
Present Market	*Market Penetration* — Starbucks sells more coffee to customers who register their reloadable Starbucks cards.	*Product Development* — Starbucks develops powdered instant coffee called Via.
New Market	*Market Development* — Starbucks opens stores in Brazil and Chile.	*Diversification* — Starbucks launches Hear Music and buys Ethos Water.

Source: Deckers Consumer Direct Corporation

UGG, a popular footwear brand, introduced an upscale men's footwear collection that was inspired by Jimi Hendrix and Jim Morrison.

---

market penetration a marketing strategy that tries to increase market share among existing customers

market development a marketing strategy that entails attracting new customers to existing products

product development a marketing strategy that entails the creation of new products for present markets

diversification a strategy of increasing sales by introducing new products into new markets

brand known for its casual boots, has introduced an upscale men's footwear collection. The shoes are inspired by rock'n'roll legends such as Jimi Hendrix and Jim Morrison, and are meant to appeal to new customers. "There are some UGG customers that will be interested in the Collection product, but it will also bring in new customers for us," says Leah Larson, UGG's vice president and creative director.[7] A diversification strategy can be risky when a firm is entering unfamiliar markets. However, it can be very profitable when a firm is entering markets with little or no competition.

2-3b The Innovation Matrix

Critics of Ansoff's matrix mention that the matrix does not reflect the reality of how businesses grow—that modern businesses plan growth in a more fluid manner based on current capabilities rather than the clear-cut sectors outlined by the opportunity matrix. To reflect this, Bansi Nagji and Geoff Tuff, global innovation managers at Monitor Group, have recently developed a system that enables a company to see exactly what types of assets need to be developed and what types of markets are possible to grow into (or create) based on the company's core capabilities, as shown in Exhibit 2.2.

The layout of the innovation matrix demonstrates that as a company moves away from its core capabilities (the lower left) it traverses a range of change and innovation rather than choosing one of the four sectors in Ansoff's matrix. These ranges are broken down into three levels:

1. **Core Innovation:** Represented by the yellow circle in Exhibit 2.2, these decisions implement changes that use existing assets to provide added convenience to existing customers and potentially entice customers from other brands. Packaging changes, such as Tide's laundry detergent pods, fall into this category.

2. **Adjacent Innovation:** Represented by the orange arc in Exhibit 2.2, these decisions are designed to take company strengths into new markets. This space uses existing abilities in new ways. For example, Botox, the popular cosmetic drug, was originally developed to treat intestinal problems and to treat crossed eyes. Leveraging the drug into cosmetic medicine has dramatically increased the market for Botox.

3. **Transformational Innovation:** Represented by the red arc in Exhibit 2.2, these decisions result in brand-new markets, products, and often new businesses. The company must rely on new, unfamiliar assets to develop the type of breakthrough decisions that fall in this category. The wearable, remote-controlled GoPro documentary video camera is a prime example of developing an immature market with a brand-new experience.[8]

2-3c The Boston Consulting Group Model

Management must find a balance among the SBUs that yields the overall organization's desired growth and profits with an acceptable level of risk. Some SBUs generate large amounts of cash, and others need cash to foster growth. The challenge is to balance the organization's portfolio of SBUs for the best long-term performance.

To determine the future cash contributions and cash requirements expected for each SBU, managers can use the Boston Consulting Group's portfolio matrix. The **portfolio matrix** classifies each SBU by its present or forecast growth and market share. The underlying assumption is that market share and profitability are strongly linked. The measure of market share used in the portfolio approach is *relative market share*, the ratio between the company's share and

> **portfolio matrix** a tool for allocating resources among products or strategic business units on the basis of relative market share and market growth rate

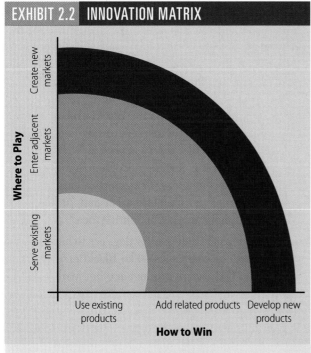

EXHIBIT 2.2 INNOVATION MATRIX

Where to Play:
- Create new markets
- Enter adjacent markets
- Serve existing markets

How to Win:
- Use existing products
- Add related products
- Develop new products

Based on Bansi Nagji and Geoff Tuff, "A Simple Tool You Need to Manage Innovation," *Harvard Business Review*, May 2012 http://hbr.org/2012/05/managing-your-innovation-portfolio/ar/1 (Accessed June 1, 2012).

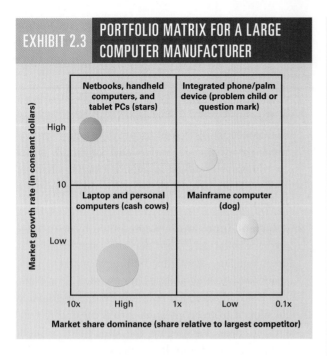

| EXHIBIT 2.3 | PORTFOLIO MATRIX FOR A LARGE COMPUTER MANUFACTURER |

Netbooks, handheld computers, and tablet PCs (stars)

Integrated phone/palm device (problem child or question mark)

Laptop and personal computers (cash cows)

Mainframe computer (dog)

Market growth rate (in constant dollars)

High
10
Low

10x High 1x Low 0.1x

Market share dominance (share relative to largest competitor)

the share of the largest competitor. For example, if a firm has a 50 percent share and the competitor has five percent, the ratio is 10 to 1. If a firm has a 10 percent market share and the largest competitor has 20 percent, the ratio is 0.5 to 1.

Exhibit 2.3 is a hypothetical portfolio matrix for a computer manufacturer. The size of the circle in each cell of the matrix represents dollar sales of the SBU relative to dollar sales of the company's other SBUs. The portfolio matrix breaks SBUs into four categories:

- **Stars:** A **star** is a fast-growing market leader. For example, the iPad is one of Apple's stars. Star SBUs usually have large profits but need lots of cash to finance rapid growth. The best marketing tactic is to protect existing market share by reinvesting earnings in product improvement, better distribution, more promotion, and production efficiency. Management must capture new users as they enter the market.

- **Cash cows:** A **cash cow** is an SBU that generates more cash than it needs to maintain its market share. It is in a low-growth market, but the product has a dominant market share. Personal computers and laptops are categorized as cash cows in Exhibit 2.3. The

basic strategy for a cash cow is to maintain market dominance by being the price leader and making technological improvements in the product. Managers should resist pressure to extend the basic line unless they can dramatically increase demand. Instead, they should allocate excess cash to the product categories where growth prospects are the greatest. For example, Heinz has two cash cows: ketchup and Weight Watchers frozen dinners.

- **Problem children:** A **problem child**, also called a **question mark**, shows rapid growth but poor profit margins. It has a low market share in a high-growth industry. Problem children need a great deal of cash. Without cash support, they eventually become dogs. The strategy options are to invest heavily to gain better market share, acquire competitors to get the necessary market share, or drop the SBU. Sometimes a firm can reposition the products of the SBU to move them into the star category. Elixir guitar strings, made by W. L. Gore & Associates, maker of Gore-Tex and Glide floss, were originally tested and marketed to Walt Disney theme parks to control puppets. After trial and failure, Gore repositioned and marketed heavily to musicians, who have loved the strings ever since.

- **Dogs:** A **dog** has low growth potential and a small market share. Most dogs eventually leave the marketplace. In the computer manufacturer example, the mainframe computer has become a dog. Another example is BlackBerry's smartphone line, which started out as a star for its manufacturer in the United States. Over time, the BlackBerry moved into the cash cow category, and then more recently, to a question mark, as the iPhone and Android-based phones captured market share. Even if it never regains its star status in the United States, BlackBerry has moved into other geographic markets to sell its devices. In parts of Africa, Blackberry is seen as a revolutionary company that is connecting people in a way that they have never been before. The company currently owns 48 percent of the mobile market and 70 percent of the smartphone market in South Africa.[9]

While typical strategies for dogs are to harvest or divest, sometimes companies—like BlackBerry—are successful with this class of product in other markets. Other companies may revive products that were abandoned as dogs. In early 2014, Church's Chicken brought its Purple Pepper dipping sauce back to the market using a "Back by Popular Demand" promotional campaign.[10]

After classifying the company's SBUs in the matrix, the next step is to allocate future resources for each. The four basic strategies are to:

star in the portfolio matrix, a business unit that is a fast-growing market leader

cash cow in the portfolio matrix, a business unit that generates more cash than it needs to maintain its market share

problem child (question mark) in the portfolio matrix, a business unit that shows rapid growth but poor profit margins

dog in the portfolio matrix, a business unit that has low growth potential and a small market share

- **Build:** If an organization has an SBU that it believes has the potential to be a star (probably a problem child at present), building would be an appropriate goal. The organization may decide to give up short-term profits and use its financial resources to achieve this goal. Apple postponed further work on the iPad to pursue the iPhone. The wait paid off when Apple was able to repurpose much of the iOS software and the iPhone's App Store for the iPad, making development less expensive and getting the product into the marketplace more quickly.[11]

- **Hold:** If an SBU is a very successful cash cow, a key goal would surely be to hold or preserve market share so that the organization can take advantage of the very positive cash flow. Fashion-based reality series *Project Runway* is a cash cow for the Lifetime cable television channel and parent companies Hearst and Disney. New seasons and spin-off editions such as *Project Runway: Under the Gunn* are expected for years to come.[12]

- **Harvest:** This strategy is appropriate for all SBUs except those classified as stars. The basic goal is to increase the short-term cash return without too much concern for the long-run impact. It is especially worthwhile when more cash is needed from a cash cow with long-run prospects that are unfavorable because of a low market growth rate. For instance, Lever Brothers has been harvesting Lifebuoy soap for a number of years with little promotional backing.

- **Divest:** Getting rid of SBUs with low shares of low-growth markets is often appropriate. Problem children and dogs are most suitable for this strategy. Nestle, for example, is in the process of selling its PowerBar SBU. Once the pioneering brand in the nutritional bar market, PowerBar has become an underperforming brand.[13]

2-3d The General Electric Model

The third model for selecting strategic alternatives was originally developed by General

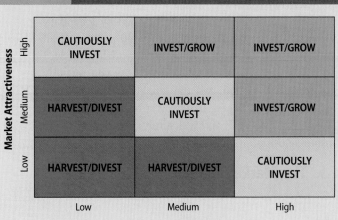

EXHIBIT 2.4 GENERAL ELECTRIC MODEL

	Low	Medium	High
High	CAUTIOUSLY INVEST	INVEST/GROW	INVEST/GROW
Medium	HARVEST/DIVEST	CAUTIOUSLY INVEST	INVEST/GROW
Low	HARVEST/DIVEST	HARVEST/DIVEST	CAUTIOUSLY INVEST

Market Attractiveness (vertical axis) / *Business Position* (horizontal axis)

Electric. The dimensions used in this model—market attractiveness and company strength—are richer and more complex than those used in the Boston Consulting Group model, but are harder to quantify.

Exhibit 2.4 presents the GE model. The horizontal axis, Business Position, refers to how well positioned the organization is to take advantage of market opportunities. Business position answers questions such as: Does the firm have the technology it needs to effectively penetrate the market? Are its financial resources adequate? Can manufacturing costs be held down below those of the competition? Can the firm cope with change? The vertical axis measures the attractiveness of a market, which is expressed both quantitatively and qualitatively. Some attributes of an attractive market are high profitability, rapid growth, a lack of government regulation, consumer insensitivity to a price increase, a lack of competition, and availability of technology. The grid is divided into three overall attractiveness zones for each dimension: high, medium, and low.

Those SBUs (or markets) that have low overall attractiveness (indicated by the red cells in Exhibit 2.4) should be avoided if the organization is not already serving them. If the firm is in these markets, it should either harvest or divest those SBUs. The organization should selectively maintain markets with medium attractiveness (indicated by the yellow cells in Exhibit 2.4). If attractiveness begins to slip, then the organization should withdraw from the market.

Conditions that are highly attractive—a thriving market plus a strong business position (the green cells in Exhibit 2.4)—are the best candidates for investment. For example, when Beats Electronics launched a new line of over-the-ear headphones in 2008, the consumer headphone market was strong but steady, led by inexpensive, inconspicuous earbuds. Four years later, the heavily branded and premium-priced Beats by Dr. Dre—helmed by legendary hip-hop producer Dr. Dre—captured 40 percent of all U.S. headphone sales, fueling market growth from $1.8 billion in 2011 to $2.4 billion in 2012. As you recently learned, Beats announced the launch of Beats Music in early 2014. This new market is growing quickly and is highly competitive, and will surely take Beats' strong business position to penetrate.[14]

2-3e The Marketing Plan

Based on the company's or SBU's overall strategy, marketing managers can create a marketing plan for individual products, brands, lines, or customer groups. **Planning** is the process of anticipating future events and determining strategies to achieve organizational objectives in the future. **Marketing planning** involves designing activities relating to marketing objectives and the changing marketing environment. Marketing planning is the basis for all marketing strategies and decisions. Issues such as product lines, distribution channels, marketing communications, and pricing are all delineated in the **marketing plan**. The marketing plan is a written document that acts as a guidebook of marketing activities for the marketing manager. In this chapter, you will learn the importance of writing a marketing plan and the types of information contained in a marketing plan.

2-3f Why Write a Marketing Plan?

By specifying objectives and defining the actions required to attain them, you can provide in a marketing plan the basis by which actual and expected performance can be compared. Marketing can be one of the most expensive and complicated business activities, but it is also one of the most important. The written marketing plan provides clearly stated activities that help employees and managers understand and work toward common goals.

Writing a marketing plan allows you to examine the marketing environment in conjunction with the inner workings of the business. Once the marketing plan is written, it serves as a reference point for the success of future

activities. Finally, the marketing plan allows the marketing manager to enter the marketplace with an awareness of possibilities and problems.

2-3g Marketing Plan Elements

Marketing plans can be presented in many different ways. Most businesses need a written marketing plan because a marketing plan is large and can be complex. Details about tasks and activity assignments may be lost if communicated orally. Regardless of the way a marketing plan is presented, some elements are common to all marketing plans. Exhibit 2.5 shows these elements, which include defining the business mission, performing a situation analysis, defining objectives, delineating a target market, and establishing components of the marketing mix. Other elements that may be included in a

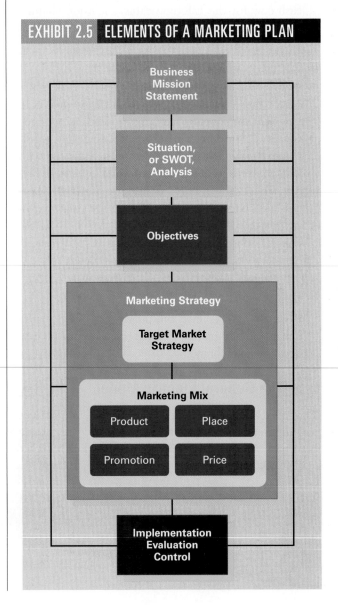

EXHIBIT 2.5 ELEMENTS OF A MARKETING PLAN

- Business Mission Statement
- Situation, or SWOT, Analysis
- Objectives
- Marketing Strategy
  - Target Market Strategy
  - Marketing Mix
    - Product
    - Place
    - Promotion
    - Price
- Implementation Evaluation Control

planning the process of anticipating future events and determining strategies to achieve organizational objectives in the future

marketing planning designing activities relating to marketing objectives and the changing marketing environment

marketing plan a written document that acts as a guidebook of marketing activities for the marketing manager

plan are budgets, implementation timetables, required marketing research efforts, or elements of advanced strategic planning.

2-3h Writing the Marketing Plan

The creation and implementation of a complete marketing plan will allow the organization to achieve marketing objectives and succeed. However, the marketing plan is only as good as the information it contains and the effort, creativity, and thought that went into its creation. Having a good marketing information system and a wealth of competitive intelligence (covered in Chapter 9) is critical to a thorough and accurate situation analysis. The role of managerial intuition is also important in the creation and selection of marketing strategies. Managers must weigh any information against its accuracy and their own judgment when making a marketing decision.

Note that the overall structure of the marketing plan (Exhibit 2.5) should not be viewed as a series of sequential planning steps. Many of the marketing plan elements are decided simultaneously and in conjunction with one another. Further, every marketing plan has different content, depending on the organization, its mission, objectives, targets, and marketing mix components. There is not one single correct format for a marketing plan. Many organizations have their own distinctive format or terminology for creating a marketing plan. Every marketing plan should be unique to the firm for which it was created. Remember, however, that although the format and order of presentation should be flexible, the same types of questions and topic areas should be covered in any marketing plan.

2-4 DEFINING THE BUSINESS MISSION

The foundation of any marketing plan is the firm's mission statement, which answers the question "What business are we in?" The way a firm defines its business mission profoundly affects the firm's long-run resource allocation, profitability, and survival. The mission statement is based on a careful analysis of benefits sought by present and potential customers and an analysis of existing and anticipated environmental conditions. The firm's mission statement establishes boundaries for all subsequent decisions, objectives, and strategies.

A mission statement should focus on the market or markets the organization is attempting to serve rather

Care must be taken when stating a business mission. Companies like Procter and Gamble have earned the right to be broad in their mission's wording.

than on the good or service offered. Otherwise, a new technology may quickly make the good or service obsolete and the mission statement irrelevant to company functions. Business mission statements that are stated too narrowly suffer from **marketing myopia**—defining a business in terms of goods and services rather than in terms of the benefits customers seek. In this context, *myopia* means narrow, short-term thinking. For example, Frito-Lay defines its mission as being in the snack-food business rather than in the corn chip business. The mission of sports teams is not just to play games but also to serve the interests of the fans.

Alternatively, business missions may be stated too broadly. "To provide products of superior quality and value that improve the lives of the world's consumers" is probably too broad a mission statement for any firm except Procter & Gamble. Care must be taken when stating what business a firm is in. For example, the mission of Ben & Jerry's centers on three important aspects of its ice cream business: (1) Product: "To make, distribute and sell the finest quality all natural ice cream and euphoric concoctions with a continued commitment to incorporating wholesome, natural ingredients and promoting business practices that respect the Earth and the Environment"; (2) Economic: "To operate the Company on a sustainable financial basis of profitable growth, increasing

mission statement a statement of the firm's business based on a careful analysis of benefits sought by present and potential customers and an analysis of existing and anticipated environmental conditions

marketing myopia defining a business in terms of goods and services rather than in terms of the benefits customers seek

value for our stakeholders and expanding opportunities for development and career growth for our employees"; and (3) Social: "To operate the Company in a way that actively recognizes the central role that business plays in society by initiating innovative ways to improve the quality of life locally, nationally, and internationally."[15] By correctly stating the business mission in terms of the benefits that customers seek, the foundation for the marketing plan is set. Many companies are focusing on designing more appropriate mission statements because these statements are frequently displayed on the companies' Web sites.

2-5 CONDUCTING A SITUATION ANALYSIS

Marketers must understand the current and potential environment in which the product or service will be marketed. A situation analysis is sometimes referred to as a **SWOT analysis**—that is, the firm should identify its internal strengths (**S**) and weaknesses (**W**) and also examine external opportunities (**O**) and threats (**T**).

When examining internal strengths and weaknesses, the marketing manager should focus on organizational resources such as production costs, marketing skills, financial resources, company or brand image, employee capabilities, and available technology. For example, when Dell's stock fell sharply throughout the mid-2010s, management needed to examine strengths and weaknesses in the company and its competition. Dell had a $6 billion server business (strength), but the shrinking PC market accounted for a significant 24 percent of sales (weakness). Competitors like IBM and Hewlett-Packard (HP) were moving heavily into software and consulting, so to avoid them, Dell moved into the enterprise IT and services market. The shift was not enough to offset poor sales in other areas, however, and in 2013, the company entered buyout talks with private investors such as Blackstone and company founder Michael S. Dell. Dell ultimately went private and continues to sell computers, software, and related services.[16] Another issue to consider in this section of the marketing plan is the historical background of the firm—its sales and profit history.

When examining external opportunities and threats, marketing managers must analyze aspects of the marketing environment. This process is called **environmental scanning**—the collection and interpretation of information about forces, events, and relationships in the external environment that may affect the future of the organization or the implementation of the marketing plan. Environmental scanning helps identify market opportunities and threats and provides guidelines for the design of marketing strategy. Increasing competition from overseas firms and the fast growth of digital technology essentially ended Kodak's consumer film business. After emerging from bankruptcy, Kodak has repositioned the firm as a smaller, business-to-business company that offers commercial printing and digital imaging services.[17] The six most often studied macroenvironmental forces are social, demographic, economic, technological, political and legal, and competitive. These forces are examined in detail in Chapter 4.

2-6 COMPETITIVE ADVANTAGE

Performing a SWOT analysis allows firms to identify their competitive advantage. A competitive advantage is a set of unique features of a company and its products that are perceived by the target market as significant and superior to those of the competition. It is the factor or factors that cause customers to patronize a firm and not the competition. There are three types of competitive advantage: cost, product/service differentiation, and niche.

Hydraulic fracturing is a competitive advantage for the United States in the global natural gas market.

SWOT analysis identifying internal strengths (S) and weaknesses (W) and also examining external opportunities (O) and threats (T)

environmental scanning collection and interpretation of information about forces, events, and relationships in the external environment that may affect the future of the organization or the implementation of the marketing plan

competitive advantage a set of unique features of a company and its products that are perceived by the target market as significant and superior to those of the competition

2-6a Cost Competitive Advantage

Cost leadership can result from obtaining inexpensive raw materials, creating an efficient scale of plant operations, designing products for ease of manufacture, controlling overhead costs, and avoiding marginal customers. Hydraulic fracturing (or fracking) is a controversial mining technique used to release petroleum, natural gas, and other valuable chemicals from layers of rock in the earth's crust. In the United States, fracking has revealed a vast supply of natural gas locked in shale rock, greatly reducing the cost of energy across the country and making the United States a primary player in the global natural gas market. According to George Blitz, vice president of energy and climate change at Dow Chemical Company, the shale gas boom has given the United States the biggest competitive advantage the industry has seen in several decades.[18] Having a **cost competitive advantage** means being the low-cost competitor in an industry while maintaining satisfactory profit margins. Costs can be reduced in a variety of ways:

- **Experience curves: Experience curves** tell us that costs decline at a predictable rate as experience with a product increases. The experience curve effect encompasses a broad range of manufacturing, marketing, and administrative costs. Experience curves reflect learning by doing, technological advances, and economies of scale. Firms like Boeing use historical experience curves as a basis for predicting and setting prices. Experience curves allow management to forecast costs and set prices based on anticipated costs as opposed to current costs.

- **Efficient labor:** Labor costs can be an important component of total costs in low-skill, labor-intensive industries such as product assembly and apparel manufacturing. Many U.S. publishers and software developers send data entry, design, and formatting tasks to India, where skilled engineers are available at lower overall cost.

- **No-frills goods and services:** Marketers can lower costs by removing frills and options from a product or service. Southwest Airlines, for example, offers low fares but no seat assignments or meals. Low costs give Southwest a higher load factor and greater economies of scale, which, in turn, mean lower prices.

- **Government subsidies:** Governments can provide grants and interest-free loans to target industries. Such government assistance enabled Japanese semiconductor manufacturers to become global leaders.

- **Product design:** Cutting-edge design technology can help offset high labor costs. BMW is a world leader in designing cars for ease of manufacture and assembly.

Reverse engineering—the process of disassembling a product piece by piece to learn its components and obtain clues as to the manufacturing process—can also mean savings. Reverse engineering a low-cost competitor's product can save research and design costs. The car industry often uses reverse engineering.

- **Reengineering:** Reengineering entails fundamental rethinking and redesign of business processes to achieve dramatic improvements in critical measures of performance. It often involves reorganizing functional departments such as sales, engineering, and production into cross-disciplinary teams.

- **Production innovations:** Production innovations such as new technology and simplified production techniques help lower the average cost of production. Technologies such as computer-aided design (CAD) and computer-aided manufacturing (CAM) and increasingly sophisticated robots help companies such as Boeing, Ford, and General Electric reduce their manufacturing costs.

- **New methods of service delivery:** Medical expenses have been substantially lowered by the use of outpatient surgery and walk-in clinics. Online-only magazines deliver great savings, and even some print magazines are exploring ways to go online to save material and shipping costs.

2-6b Product/Service Differentiation Competitive Advantage

Because cost competitive advantages are subject to continual erosion, product/service differentiation tends to provide a longer-lasting competitive advantage. The durability of this strategy tends to make it more attractive to many top managers. A **product/service differentiation competitive advantage** exists when a firm provides something that is unique and valuable to buyers beyond simply offering a lower price than that of the competition. Examples include brand names (Lexus), a strong dealer network (Caterpillar for construction work), product reliability (Maytag appliances), image (Neiman Marcus in retailing), or service

cost competitive advantage being the low-cost competitor in an industry while maintaining satisfactory profit margins

experience curves curves that show costs declining at a predictable rate as experience with a product increases

product/service differentiation competitive advantage the provision of something that is unique and valuable to buyers beyond simply offering a lower price than that of the competition

Customers have a loyalty to Caterpillar due to its strong network of dealerships.

Kevin Brine/Shutterstock.com

(Zappos). Uniqlo, a fast-fashion retailer with 840 stores in Japan and 1,170 stores outside Japan, is among the top five global clothing retailers. The company provides high-quality casual wear at reasonable prices. It differentiates itself from the competition in several ways. First, it develops and brands innovative fabrics like HeatTech, which turns moisture into heat and has air pockets in the fabric to retain that heat. HeatTech is thin and comfortable, and enables stylish designs different from the standard apparel made for warmth. Second, Uniqlo emphasizes the in-store experience, which involves carefully hiring, training, and managing all touchpoints with the customer. Every morning, for example, Uniqlo employees practice interacting with shoppers. Finally, the company has a recycling effort that moves millions of articles of discarded Uniqlo clothing to needy people around the world.[19]

2-6c Niche Competitive Advantage

A **niche competitive advantage** seeks to target and effectively serve a single segment of the market (see Chapter 8). For small companies with limited resources that potentially face giant competitors, niche targeting may be the only viable option. A market segment that has good growth potential but is not crucial to the success of major competitors is a good candidate for developing a niche strategy.

Many companies using a niche strategy serve only a limited geographic

niche competitive advantage the advantage achieved when a firm seeks to target and effectively serve a small segment of the market

sustainable competitive advantage an advantage that cannot be copied by the competition

market. Stew Leonard's is an extremely successful but small grocery store chain found only in Connecticut and New York. Blue Bell Ice cream is available in only about 26 percent of the nation's supermarkets, but it ranks as one of the top three best-selling ice creams in the country.[20]

The Chef's Garden, a 225-acre Ohio farm, specializes in growing and shipping rare artisan vegetables directly to its customers. Chefs from all over the world call to order or request a unique item, which is grown and shipped by the Chef's Garden. The farm provides personal services and specialized premium vegetables that aren't available anywhere else and relies on its customers to supply it with ideas for what they would like to be able to offer in their restaurants. The excellent service and feeling of contribution keep chefs coming back.[21]

2-6d Building Sustainable Competitive Advantage

The key to having a competitive advantage is the ability to sustain that advantage. A **sustainable competitive advantage** is one that cannot be copied by the competition. For example, Netflix, the online movie subscription service, has a steady hold over the movie rental market. No company has come close to the incomparable depth of titles available to be sent directly to homes or streamed online. Blockbuster tried to set up a similar online subscription service tied to new releases and Amazon.com offers free streaming to Prime members, but so far neither has been able to compete with the convenience and selection offered by Netflix. Netflix's 27.5 million subscribers have a twenty-eight-day delay on most of the latest movies, but Netflix says that only a couple hundred customers have complained about the delay. Redbox Instant, an up-and-coming streaming service from Verizon and Coinstar, builds on the popular Redbox kiosk-based rental service, allowing customers to stream movies *and* rent up to four physical DVDs for just $8 a month. Redbox Instant does not offer television shows, however—a key advantage of Netflix's service.[22] In contrast, when Datril was introduced into the pain-reliever market, it was touted as being exactly like Tylenol, only cheaper. Tylenol responded by lowering its price, thus destroying Datril's competitive advantage and ability to remain on the market. In this case, low price was not a sustainable competitive advantage. Without a competitive advantage, target customers do not perceive any reason to patronize an organization instead of its competitors.

The notion of competitive advantage means that a successful firm will stake out a position unique in some manner from its rivals. Imitation by competitors indicates

The ability to stream movies and rent up to four physical DVDs for just $8 a month is a compelling competitive advantage for Redbox Instant.

a lack of competitive advantage and almost ensures mediocre performance. Moreover, competitors rarely stand still, so it is not surprising that imitation causes managers to feel trapped in a seemingly endless game of catch-up. They are regularly surprised by the new accomplishments of their rivals.

Rather than copy competitors, companies need to build their own competitive advantages. The sources of tomorrow's competitive advantages are the skills and assets of the organization. Assets include patents, copyrights, locations, equipment, and technology that are superior to those of the competition. Skills are functions such as customer service and promotion that the firm performs better than its competitors. Marketing managers should continually focus the firm's skills and assets on sustaining and creating competitive advantages.

Remember, a sustainable competitive advantage is a function of the speed with which competitors can imitate a leading company's strategy and plans. Imitation requires a competitor to identify the leader's competitive advantage, determine how it is achieved, and then learn how to duplicate it.

 2-7 SETTING MARKETING PLAN OBJECTIVES

Before the details of a marketing plan can be developed, objectives for the plan must be stated. Without objectives, there is no basis for measuring the success of marketing plan activities.

A **marketing objective** is a statement of what is to be accomplished through marketing activities.

A strong marketing objective for Purina might be: "To increase sales of Purina brand cat food between January 1, 2016 and December 31, 2016 by 15 percent, compared to 2012 sales of $300 million."

Objectives must be consistent with and indicate the priorities of the organization. Specifically, objectives flow from the business mission statement to the rest of the marketing plan.

Carefully specified objectives serve several functions. First, they communicate marketing management philosophies and provide direction for lower-level marketing managers so that marketing efforts are integrated and pointed in a consistent direction. Objectives also serve as motivators by creating something for employees to strive for. When objectives are attainable

marketing objective a statement of what is to be accomplished through marketing activities

MARKETING OBJECTIVES SHOULD BE . . .

▸ **Realistic:** Managers should develop objectives that have a chance of being met. For example, it may be unrealistic for start-up firms or new products to command dominant market share, given other competitors in the marketplace.

▸ **Measurable:** Managers need to be able to quantitatively measure whether or not an objective has been met. For example, it would be difficult to determine success for an objective that states, "To increase sales of cat food." If the company sells one percent more cat food, does that mean the objective was met? Instead, a specific number should be stated, "To increase sales of Purina brand cat food from $300 million to $345 million."

▸ **Time specific:** By what time should the objective be met? "To increase sales of Purina brand cat food between January 1, 2016, and December 31, 2016."

▸ **Compared to a benchmark:** If the objective is to increase sales by 15 percent, it is important to know the baseline against which the objective will be measured. Will it be current sales? Last year's sales? For example, "To increase sales of Purina brand cat food by 15 percent over 2012 sales of $300 million."

and challenging, they motivate those charged with achieving the objectives. Additionally, the process of writing specific objectives forces executives to clarify their thinking. Finally, objectives form a basis for control: the effectiveness of a plan can be gauged in light of the stated objectives.

2-8 DESCRIBING THE TARGET MARKET

Marketing strategy involves the activities of selecting and describing one or more target markets and developing and maintaining a marketing mix that will produce mutually satisfying exchanges with target markets.

2-8a Target Market Strategy

A market segment is a group of individuals or organizations who share one or more characteristics. They therefore may have relatively similar product needs. For example, parents of newborn babies need formula, diapers, and special foods.

The target market strategy identifies the market segment or segments on which to focus. This process begins with a **market opportunity analysis (MOA)**—the description and estimation of the size and sales potential of market segments that are of interest to the firm and the assessment of key competitors in these market segments. After the firm describes the market segments, it may target one or more of them. There are three general strategies for selecting target markets.

Target markets can be selected by appealing to the entire market with one marketing mix, concentrating on one segment, or appealing to multiple market segments using multiple marketing mixes. The

characteristics, advantages, and disadvantages of each strategic option are examined in Chapter 8. Target markets could be eighteen- to twenty-five-year-old females who are interested in fashion (*Vogue* magazine), people concerned about sugar and calories in their soft drinks (Diet Pepsi), or parents without the time to potty train their children (Booty Camp classes where kids are potty trained).

Any market segment that is targeted must be fully described. Demographics, psychographics, and buyer behavior should be assessed. Buyer behavior is covered in Chapters 6 and 7. If segments are differentiated by ethnicity, multicultural aspects of the marketing mix should be examined. If the target market is international, it is especially important to describe differences in culture, economic and technological development, and political structure that may affect the marketing plan. Global marketing is covered in more detail in Chapter 5.

2-9 THE MARKETING MIX

The term marketing mix refers to a unique blend of product, place (distribution), promotion, and pricing strategies (often referred to as the four Ps) designed to produce mutually satisfying exchanges with a target market. The marketing manager can control each component of the marketing mix, but the strategies for all four components must be blended to achieve optimal results. Any marketing mix is only as good as its weakest component. For example, the first pump toothpastes were distributed over cosmetics counters and failed. Not until pump toothpastes were distributed the same way as tube toothpastes did the products succeed. The best promotion and the lowest price cannot save a poor product. Similarly, excellent products with poor placing, pricing, or promotion will likely fail.

Successful marketing mixes have been carefully designed to satisfy target markets. At first glance, McDonald's and Wendy's may appear to have roughly identical marketing mixes because they are both in the fast-food hamburger business. However, McDonald's has been most successful at targeting parents with young children for lunchtime meals, whereas Wendy's targets the adult crowd for lunches and dinner. McDonald's has playgrounds, Ronald McDonald the clown, and children's Happy Meals. Wendy's has salad bars, carpeted restaurants, and no playgrounds.

Style-photography/Shutterstock.com

marketing strategy the activities of selecting and describing one or more target markets and developing and maintaining a marketing mix that will produce mutually satisfying exchanges with target markets

market opportunity analysis (MOA) the description and estimation of the size and sales potential of market segments that are of interest to the firm and the assessment of key competitors in these market segments

marketing mix (four Ps) a unique blend of product, place (distribution), promotion, and pricing strategies designed to produce mutually satisfying exchanges with a target market

Variations in marketing mixes do not occur by chance. Astute marketing managers devise marketing strategies to gain advantages over competitors and best serve the needs and wants of a particular target market segment. By manipulating elements of the marketing mix, marketing managers can fine-tune the customer offering and achieve competitive success.

2-9a Product Strategies

Of the four Ps, the marketing mix typically starts with the product. The heart of the marketing mix, the starting point, is the product offering and product strategy. It is hard to design a place strategy, decide on a promotion campaign, or set a price without knowing the product to be marketed.

The product includes not only the physical unit but also its package, warranty, after-sale service, brand name, company image, value, and many other factors. A Godiva chocolate has many product elements: the chocolate itself, a fancy gold wrapper, a customer satisfaction guarantee, and the prestige of the Godiva brand name. We buy things not only for what they do (benefits) but also for what they mean to us (status, quality, or reputation).

Products can be tangible goods such as computers, ideas like those offered by a consultant, or services such as medical care. Products should also offer customer value. Product decisions are covered in Chapters 10 and 11, and services marketing is detailed in Chapter 12.

2-9b Place (Distribution) Strategies

Place, or distribution, strategies are concerned with making products available when and where customers want them. Would you rather buy a kiwi fruit at the 24-hour grocery store within walking distance or fly to Australia to pick your own? A part of this P—place—is physical distribution, which involves all the business activities concerned with storing and transporting raw materials or finished products. The goal is to make sure products arrive in usable condition at designated places when needed. Place strategies are covered in Chapters 13 and 14.

2-9c Promotion Strategies

Promotion includes advertising, public relations, sales promotion, and personal selling. Promotion's role in the marketing mix is to bring about mutually satisfying exchanges with target markets by informing, educating, persuading, and reminding them of the benefits of an organization or a product. A good promotion strategy, like using a beloved cartoon character such as SpongeBob SquarePants to sell gummy snacks, can dramatically increase sales. Each element of this P—promotion—is coordinated and managed with the others to create a promotional blend or mix. These integrated marketing communications activities are described in Chapters 16, 17, and 18. Technology-driven and social media aspects of promotional marketing are covered in Chapter 19.

2-9d Pricing Strategies

Price is what a buyer must give up in order to obtain a product. It is often the most flexible of the four Ps— the quickest element to change. Marketers can raise or lower prices more frequently and easily than they can change other marketing mix variables. Price is an important competitive weapon and is very important to the organization because price multiplied by the number of units sold equals total revenue for the firm. Pricing decisions are covered in Chapters 20 and 21.

The Game of Organizing E-Mail

E-mail has become a necessity for students and business professionals, as well as an integral part of many personal lives. With so much riding on e-mail, inboxes can overflow and important e-mails can fall by the wayside. One company is out to change that. Baydin is a software developer that sells Boomerang, a product that allows users to "snooze" e-mails. The user sets the time for the e-mail to reappear in the inbox, and Boomerang moves it into a folder out of the inbox until the specified time. To promote their e-mail management products for Outlook, Baydin also developed *The Email Game*. The game sets a timer for each message and accrues points for decisions made in a timely manner. Baydin guarantees the game will get you through your e-mail 40 percent faster or your money back.[23]

"How to Play the Email Game," The Email Game, http://emailgame.baydin.com/index.html (Accessed February 12, 2015).

2-10 FOLLOWING UP ON THE MARKETING PLAN

One of the keys to success overlooked by many businesses is to actively follow up on the marketing plan. The time spent researching, developing, and writing a useful and accurate marketing plan goes to waste if the plan is not used by the organization. One of the best ways to get the most out of a marketing plan is to correctly implement it. Once the first steps to implementation are taken, evaluation and control will help guide the organization to success as laid out by the marketing plan.

2-10a Implementation

Implementation is the process that turns a marketing plan into action assignments and ensures that these assignments are executed in a way that accomplishes the plan's objectives. Implementation activities may involve detailed job assignments, activity descriptions, time lines, budgets, and lots of communication. Implementation requires delegating authority and responsibility, determining a time frame for completing tasks, and allocating resources. Sometimes a strategic plan also requires task force management. A *task force* is a tightly organized unit under the direction of a manager who, usually, has broad authority. A task force is established to accomplish a single goal or mission and thus works against a deadline.

Implementing a plan has another dimension: gaining acceptance. New plans mean change, and change creates resistance. One reason people resist change is that they fear they will lose something. For example, when new-product research is taken away from marketing research and given to a new-product department, the director of marketing research will naturally resist this loss of part of his or her domain. Misunderstanding and lack of trust also create opposition to change, but effective communication through open discussion and teamwork can be one way of overcoming resistance to change.

Although implementation is essentially "doing what you said you were going to do," many organizations repeatedly experience failures in strategy implementation. Brilliant marketing plans are doomed to fail if they are not properly implemented. These detailed communications may or may not be part of the written marketing plan. If they are not part of the plan, they should be specified elsewhere as soon as the plan has been communicated. Strong, forward-thinking leadership can overcome resistance to change, even in large, highly integrated companies where change seems very unlikely.

2-10b Evaluation and Control

After a marketing plan is implemented, it should be evaluated. **Evaluation** entails gauging the extent to which marketing objectives have been achieved during the specified time period. Four common reasons for failing to achieve a marketing objective are unrealistic marketing objectives, inappropriate marketing strategies in the plan, poor implementation, and changes in the environment after the objective was specified and the strategy was implemented.

Once a plan is chosen and implemented, its effectiveness must be monitored. **Control** provides the mechanisms for evaluating marketing results in light of the plan's objectives and for correcting actions that do not help the organization reach those objectives within budget guidelines. Firms need to establish formal and informal control programs to make the entire operation more efficient.

Perhaps the broadest control device available to marketing managers is the **marketing audit**—a thorough, systematic, periodic evaluation of the objectives, strategies, structure, and performance of the marketing organization. A marketing audit helps management allocate marketing resources efficiently.

Although the main purpose of the marketing audit is to develop a full profile of the organization's marketing effort and to provide a basis for developing and revising the marketing plan, it is also an excellent way to improve communication and raise the level of marketing consciousness within the organization. It is a useful vehicle for selling the philosophy and techniques of strategic marketing to other members of the organization.

2-10c Post-audit Tasks

After the audit has been completed, three tasks remain. First, the audit should profile existing weaknesses and inhibiting factors, as well as the firm's strengths and the new opportunities available to it. Recommendations have to be judged and prioritized so that those with the potential to contribute most to improved marketing performance can be implemented first. The usefulness of the data also depends on the auditor's skill in interpreting and presenting the data so decision makers can quickly grasp the major points.

implementation the process that turns a marketing plan into action assignments and ensures that these assignments are executed in a way that accomplishes the plan's objectives

evaluation gauging the extent to which the marketing objectives have been achieved during the specified time period

control provides the mechanisms for evaluating marketing results in light of the plan's objectives and for correcting actions that do not help the organization reach those objectives within budget guidelines

marketing audit a thorough, systematic, periodic evaluation of the objectives, strategies, structure, and performance of the marketing organization

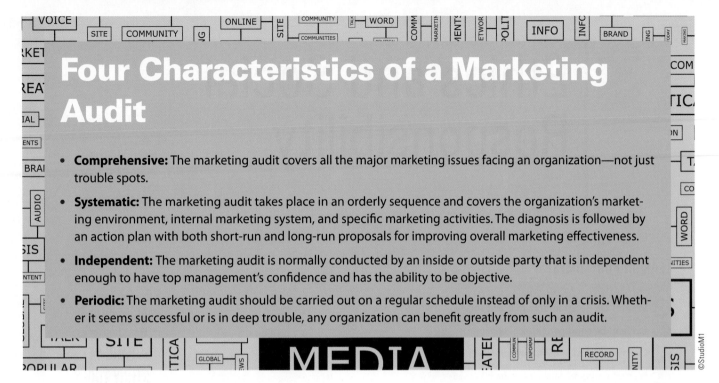

Four Characteristics of a Marketing Audit

- **Comprehensive:** The marketing audit covers all the major marketing issues facing an organization—not just trouble spots.

- **Systematic:** The marketing audit takes place in an orderly sequence and covers the organization's marketing environment, internal marketing system, and specific marketing activities. The diagnosis is followed by an action plan with both short-run and long-run proposals for improving overall marketing effectiveness.

- **Independent:** The marketing audit is normally conducted by an inside or outside party that is independent enough to have top management's confidence and has the ability to be objective.

- **Periodic:** The marketing audit should be carried out on a regular schedule instead of only in a crisis. Whether it seems successful or is in deep trouble, any organization can benefit greatly from such an audit.

©StudioM1

The second task is to ensure that the role of the audit has been clearly communicated. It is unlikely that the suggestions will require radical change in the way the firm operates. The audit's main role is to address the question "Where are we now?" and to suggest ways to improve what the firm already does.

The final post-audit task is to make someone accountable for implementing recommendations. All too often, reports are presented, applauded, and filed away to gather dust. The person made accountable should be someone who is committed to the project and who has the managerial power to make things happen.

2-11 EFFECTIVE STRATEGIC PLANNING

Effective strategic planning requires continual attention, creativity, and management commitment. Strategic planning should not be an annual exercise in which managers go through the motions and forget about strategic planning until the next year. It should be an ongoing process because the environment is continually changing and the firm's resources and capabilities are continually evolving.

Sound strategic planning is based on creativity. Managers should challenge assumptions about the firm and the environment and establish new strategies. For example, major oil companies developed the concept of the gasoline service station in an age when cars needed frequent and rather elaborate servicing. These major companies held on to the full-service approach, but independents were quick to respond to new realities and moved to lower-cost self-service and convenience store operations. Major companies took several decades to catch up.

Perhaps the most critical element in successful strategic planning is top management's support and participation. At Google, for example, top managers support their employees' strategic plans and even assist in entry-level employees' development as strategic planners. This has created a top-to-bottom culture of strategic excellence at Google.[24]

3 | Ethics and Social Responsibility

LEARNING OUTCOMES

After studying this chapter, you will be able to...

3-1 Explain the determinants of a civil society

3-2 Explain the concept of ethical behavior

3-3 Describe ethical behavior in business

3-4 Discuss corporate social responsibility

3-5 Describe the arguments for and against society responsibility

3-6 Explain cause-related marketing

After you finish this chapter go to **PAGE 44** for **STUDY TOOLS.**

3-1 DETERMINANTS OF A CIVIL SOCIETY

Have you ever stopped to think about the social glue that binds society together? That is, what factors keep people and organizations from running amok and doing harm, and what factors create order in a society like ours? The answer lies in **social control**, defined as any means used to maintain behavioral norms and regulate conflict.[1] **Behavioral norms** are standards of proper or acceptable behavior. Social control is part of your life at every level, from your family, to your local community, to the nation, to the global civilization. Several modes of social control are important to marketing:

1. **Ethics: Ethics** are the moral principles or values that generally govern the conduct of an individual or a group. Ethical rules and guidelines, along with customs and traditions, provide principles of right action.

2. **Laws:** Often, ethical rules and guidelines are codified into law. Laws created by governments are then enforced by governmental authority. This is how the dictum "Thou shall not steal" has become part of formal law throughout the land. Law, however, is not a perfect mechanism for ensuring good corporate and employee behavior. This is because laws often address the lowest common denominator of socially acceptable behavior. In other words, just because something is legal does not mean that it is ethical. For example, according to a recent study by Arizona State University, fast food restaurants disproportionally aim their child-focused marketing efforts at middle-income, rural, and predominately black communities.[2]

In a national study of more than 6,000 fast-food restaurants, researchers found that those situated in middle-income neighborhoods, rural communities, and predominately black neighborhoods were more likely to target children with ads featuring cartoon characters; displays on restaurant exteriors featuring movie, television, and sports stars; and indoor play areas and indoor displays of kids' meal toys. Overall, one-fifth of restaurants sampled in the study used one or more strategies targeting children. Fast-food companies in the U.S. spend nearly one-quarter of their marketing budgets to target kids age 2 to 17.[3] Is this ethical? What is your opinion?

3. **Formal and Informal Groups:** Businesses, professional organizations (such as the American Marketing Association and the American Medical Association), and clubs (such as Shriners and Ducks Unlimited) all have codes of conduct. These codes prescribe acceptable and desired behaviors of their members.

4. **Self-regulation:** Self-regulation involves the voluntary acceptance of standards established by nongovernmental entities, such as the American Association of Advertising Agencies (AAAA) or the National Association of Manufacturers. The AAAA has a self-regulation arm that deals with deceptive advertising. Other associations have regulations relating to child labor, environmental issues, conservation, and a host of other issues.

5. **The Media:** In an open, democratic society, the media play a key role in informing the public about the actions of individuals and organizations—both good and bad. The Children's Online Privacy Protection Act (COPPA) requires Web site operators to obtain verifiable consent from parents before collecting personal information about children under age thirteen. Recently, Yelp paid a $450,000 fine for collecting information on children under thirteen. Mobile app developer TinyCo was likewise fined $300,000.[4] Google has announced new versions of Chrome and YouTube tailored specifically for kids under the age of 13. To date, Google has not announced the safeguards it will use to meet COPPA standards. Since the vast majority of Google's revenue comes from advertising and the value of the company's ads is tied to its massive trove of user data,

social control any means used to maintain behavioral norms and regulate conflict

behavioral norms standards of proper or acceptable behavior. Several modes of social control are important to marketing

ethics the moral principles or values that generally govern the conduct of an individual or a group

COPPA compliance is very important to Google and advertisers alike.[5]

6. **An Active Civil Society:** An informed and engaged society can help mold individual and corporate behavior. The last state in the union to get a Walmart store was Vermont. Citizen campaigns against the big-box retailer were deciding factors in management's decision to avoid the state. The planned Keystone Pipeline has brought out environmentalists on one side of the debate and the petroleum industry on the other. Proponents argue that the oil pipeline snaking from Alberta, Canada, to Houston, Texas, will not only bring essential infrastructure to North American oil producers, but it will also provide jobs, long-term energy independence, and a boost to the economy.[6] TransCanada, proposed builder of the pipeline, says that it will be the safest and most advanced oil pipeline operation in North America. Opponents claim that the pipeline will create few post-construction jobs and will carry tar-sands oil (which is more hazardous than conventional oil). They argue that tar-sands refining has created toxic dust storms and that the pipeline would contribute little to U.S. energy independence.[7] The arguments on both sides are a product of an engaged and free society.

All six of the preceding factors—individually and in combination—are critical to achieving a socially coherent, vibrant, civilized society. These six factors (the social glue) are more important today than ever before due to the increasing complexity of the global economy and the melding of customs and traditions within societies.

PLEASE Take A Number

Sideways Design/Shutterstock.com

3-2 THE CONCEPT OF ETHICAL BEHAVIOR

It has been said that ethics is something everyone likes to talk about but nobody can define. Others have suggested that defining ethics is like trying to nail Jell-O to a wall. You begin to think that you understand it, but that is when it starts squirting out between your fingers.

Simply put, ethics can be viewed as the standard of behavior by which conduct is judged. Standards that are legal may not always be ethical, and vice versa. Laws are the values and standards enforceable by the courts. Ethics, then, consists of personal moral principles. For example, there is no legal statute that makes it a crime for someone to "cut in line." Yet, if someone does not want to wait in line and cuts to the front, it often makes others very angry.

If you have ever resented a line-cutter, then you understand ethics and have applied ethical standards in life. Waiting your turn in line is a social expectation that exists because lines ensure order and allocate the space and time needed to complete transactions. Waiting your turn is an expected but unwritten behavior that plays a critical role in an orderly society.

So it is with ethics. Ethics consists of those unwritten rules we have developed for our interactions with one another. These unwritten rules govern us when we are sharing resources or honoring contracts. "Waiting your turn" is a higher standard than the laws that are passed to maintain order. Those laws apply when physical force or threats are used to push to the front of the line. Assault, battery, and threats are forms of criminal conduct for which the offender can be prosecuted. But the law does not apply to the stealthy line-cutter who simply sneaks to the front, perhaps using a friend and a conversation as a decoy. No laws are broken, but the notions of fairness and justice are offended by one individual putting himself or herself above others and taking advantage of others' time and position.

Ethical questions range from practical, narrowly defined issues, such as a businessperson's obligation to be honest with customers, to broader social and philosophical questions, such as whether a company is responsible for preserving the environment and protecting employee rights. Many ethical dilemmas develop from conflicts between the differing interests of company owners and their workers, customers, and surrounding community. Managers must balance the ideal against the practical—that is, the need to produce a reasonable profit for the company's shareholders against honesty in business practices and concern for environmental and social issues.

3-2a Ethical Theories

People usually base their individual choice of ethical theory on their life experiences. The following are some of the ethical theories that apply to marketing.[8]

DEONTOLOGY The **deontological theory** states that people should adhere to their obligations and duties when analyzing an ethical dilemma. This means that a

deontological theory ethical theory that states that people should adhere to their obligations and duties when analyzing an ethical dilemma

person will follow his or her obligations to another individual or society because upholding one's duty is what is considered ethically correct. For instance, a deontologist will always keep his promises to a friend and will follow the law. A person who follows this theory will produce very consistent decisions because they will be based on the individual's set duties.

Note that deontological theory is not necessarily concerned with the welfare of others. For example, suppose a salesperson has decided that it is her ethical duty (and very practical!) to always be on time to meetings with clients. Today she is running late. How is she supposed to drive? Is the deontologist supposed to speed, breaking the law to uphold her duty to society, or is the deontologist supposed to arrive at her meeting late, breaking her duty to be on time? This scenario of conflicting obligations does not lead us to a clear, ethically correct resolution, nor does it protect the welfare of others from the deontologist's decision.

UTILITARIANISM The **utilitarian ethical theory** is founded on the ability to predict the consequences of an action. To a utilitarian, the choice that yields the greatest benefit to the most people is the choice that is ethically correct. One benefit of this ethical theory is that the utilitarian can compare similar predicted solutions and use a point system to determine which choice is more beneficial for more people. This point system provides a logical and rational argument for each decision and allows a person to use it on a case-by-case context.

There are two types of utilitarianism: act utilitarianism and rule utilitarianism. *Act utilitarianism* adheres exactly to the definition of utilitarianism as just described. In act utilitarianism, a person performs the acts that benefit the most people, regardless of personal feelings or societal constraints such as laws. *Rule utilitarianism*, however, takes into account the law and is concerned with fairness. A rule utilitarian seeks to benefit the most people but through the fairest and most just means available. Therefore, added benefits of rule utilitarianism are that it values justice and doing good at the same time.

As is true of all ethical theories, however, both act and rule utilitarianism contain numerous flaws. Inherent in both are the flaws associated with predicting the future. Although people can use their life experiences to attempt to predict outcomes, no human being can be certain that his predictions will be true. This uncertainty can lead to unexpected results, making the utilitarian look unethical as time passes because his choice did not benefit the most people as he predicted.

Another assumption that a utilitarian must make is that he has the ability to compare the various types of consequences against each other on a similar scale. However, comparing material gains such as money against intangible gains such as happiness is impossible because their qualities differ so greatly.

CASUIST The **casuist ethical theory** compares a current ethical dilemma with examples of similar ethical dilemmas and their outcomes. This allows one to determine the severity of the situation and to create the best possible solution according to others' experiences. Usually, one will find examples that represent the extremes of the situation so that a compromise can be reached that will include the wisdom gained from the previous situations.

One drawback to this ethical theory is that there may not be a set of similar examples for a given ethical dilemma. Perhaps that which is controversial and ethically questionable is new and unexpected. Along the same line of thinking, this theory assumes that the results of the current ethical dilemma will be similar to results in the examples. This may not be necessarily true and would greatly hinder the effectiveness of applying this ethical theory.

MORAL RELATIVISM **Moral relativism** is a belief in time-and-place ethics, that is, the truth of a moral judgment is relative to the judging person or group.[9] According to a moral relativist, for example, arson is not always wrong—if you live in a neighborhood where drug dealers are operating a crystal meth lab or crack house, committing arson by burning down the meth lab may be ethically justified. If you are a parent and your child is starving, stealing a loaf of bread is ethically correct. The proper resolution to ethical dilemmas is based upon weighing the competing factors at the moment and then making a determination to take the lesser of the evils as the resolution. Moral relativists do not believe in absolute rules. Their beliefs center on the pressure of the moment and whether the pressure justifies the action taken.

VIRTUE ETHICS Aristotle and Plato taught that solving ethical dilemmas requires training—that individuals solve ethical dilemmas when they develop and nurture a set of virtues.[10]

utilitarian ethical theory
ethical theory that is founded on the ability to predict the consequences of an action

casuist ethical theory
ethical theory that compares a current ethical dilemma with examples of similar ethical dilemmas and their outcomes

moral relativism an ethical theory of time-and-place ethics; that is, the belief that ethical truths depend on the individuals and groups holding them

A **virtue** is a character trait valued as being good. Aristotle taught the importance of cultivating virtue in his students and then having them solve ethical dilemmas using those virtues once they had become an integral part of his students' being through their virtue training.

Some modern philosophers have embraced this notion of virtue and have developed lists of what constitutes a virtuous businessperson. Some common virtues for business people are self-discipline, friendliness, caring, courage, compassion, trust, responsibility, honesty, determination, enthusiasm, and humility. You may see other lists of virtues that are longer or shorter, but here is a good start for core business virtues.

3-3 ETHICAL BEHAVIOR IN BUSINESS

Depending upon which, if any, ethical theory a businessperson has accepted and uses in his or her daily conduct, the action taken may vary. For example, faced with bribing a foreign official to get a critically needed contract or shutting down a factory and laying off a thousand workers, a person following a deontology strategy would not pay the bribe. Why? A deontologist always follows the law. However, a moral relativist would probably pay the bribe.

While the boundaries of what is legal and what is not are often fairly clear (for example, do not run a red light, do not steal money from a bank, and do not kill anyone), the boundaries of ethical decision making are predicated on which ethical theory one is following. The law typically relies on juries to determine if an act is legal or illegal. Society determines whether an action is ethical or unethical. A number of women have accused comedian Bill Cosby of sexual molestation and rape. Society would view this as unethical behavior, but at the time of this writing, Mr. Cosby had not been indicted. If he is subjected to a trial, a jury will determine if an illegal act was committed. In a business-related case, a federal prosecutor in San Francisco recently indicted Federal Express for shipping illegal prescription drugs. If successful, the case would extend a shipping company's responsibility from its own conduct to the conduct of its customers. This case raises a lot of questions about what a company can and should know about its customers.

What makes the Federal Express case different is that the company has chosen to fight it out in court. Businesspeople

Shipping companies may ultimately be responsible for the conduct of its customers.

generally argue that an indictment or a criminal charge can cause unacceptable damage, including the loss of operating licenses, government contracts, and customers. A company's only realistic choice may be to settle, even if it has a good chance of being acquitted. Some think this gives prosecutors too much power.[11] Consider the ethics of the FedEx case from a number of different perspectives.

Morals are the rules people develop as a result of cultural values and norms. Culture is a socializing force that dictates what is right and wrong. Moral standards may also reflect the laws and regulations that affect social and economic behavior. Thus, morals can be considered a foundation of ethical behavior.

Morals are usually characterized as good or bad. "Good" and "bad" have many different connotations. One such connotation is "effective" and "ineffective." A good salesperson makes or exceeds the assigned quota. If the salesperson sells a new computer system or HDTV to a disadvantaged consumer—knowing full well that the person cannot keep up the monthly payments—is that still a good salesperson? What if the sale enables the salesperson to exceed his or her quota?

"Good" and "bad" can also refer to "conforming" and "deviant" behaviors. A doctor who runs large ads offering discounts on open-heart surgery would be considered bad, or unprofessional, because he or she is not conforming to the norms of the medical profession. "Good" and "bad" also express the distinction between law-abiding and criminal behavior. And finally, different religions define "good" and "bad" in markedly different ways. A Muslim who eats pork would be considered bad by other Muslims, for example. Religion is just one of the many factors that affect a businessperson's ethics.

virtue a character trait valued as being good

morals the rules people develop as a result of cultural values and norms

3-3a Morality and Business Ethics

Today's business ethics actually consist of a subset of major life values learned since birth. The values businesspeople use to make decisions have been acquired through family, educational, and religious institutions.

Ethical values are situation specific and time oriented. Everyone must have an ethical base that applies to conduct in the business world and in personal life. One approach to developing a personal set of ethics is to examine the consequences of a particular act. Who is helped or hurt? How long do the consequences last? What actions produce the greatest good for the greatest number of people? A second approach stresses the importance of rules. Rules come in the form of customs, laws, professional standards, and common sense. "Always treat others as you would like to be treated" is an example of a rule.

A third approach to personal ethics emphasizes the development of moral character within individuals. In this approach, ethical development is thought to consist of three levels.[12]

- *Preconventional morality*, the most basic level, is childlike. It is calculating, self-centered, and even selfish, based on what will be immediately punished or rewarded. Fortunately, most businesspeople have progressed beyond the self-centered and manipulative actions of preconventional morality.

- *Conventional morality* moves from an egocentric viewpoint toward the expectations of society. Loyalty and obedience to the organization (or society) become paramount. A marketing decision maker operating at this level of moral development would be concerned only with whether a proposed action is legal and how it will be viewed by others.

- *Postconventional morality* represents the morality of the mature adult. At this level, people are less concerned about how others might see them and more concerned about how they see and judge themselves over the long run. A marketing decision maker who has attained a postconventional level of morality might ask, "Even though it is legal and will increase company profits, is it right in the long run? Might it do more harm than good in the end?"

3-3b Ethical Decision Making

Ethical questions rarely have cut-and-dried answers. Studies show that the following factors tend to influence ethical decision making and judgments:[13]

- **Extent of ethical problems within the organization:** Marketing professionals who perceive fewer ethical problems in their organizations tend to disapprove more strongly of "unethical" or questionable practices than those who perceive more ethical problems. Apparently, the healthier the ethical environment, the more likely it is that marketers will take a strong stand against questionable practices.

- **Top management's actions on ethics:** Top managers can influence the behavior of marketing professionals by encouraging ethical behavior and discouraging unethical behavior. Researchers found that when top managers develop a strong ethical culture, there is reduced pressure to perform unethical acts, fewer unethical acts are performed, and unethical behavior is reported more frequently.[14]

- **Potential magnitude of the consequences:** The greater the harm done to victims, the more likely that marketing professionals will recognize a problem as unethical.

- **Social consensus:** The greater the degree of agreement among managerial peers that an action is harmful, the more likely that marketers will recognize a problem as unethical. Research has found that a strong ethical culture among coworkers decreases observations of ethical misconduct. In companies with strong ethical cultures, 9 percent of employees observed misconduct, compared with 31 percent in companies with weaker cultures.[15]

- **Probability of a harmful outcome:** The greater the likelihood that an action will result in a harmful outcome, the more likely that marketers will recognize a problem as unethical.

- **Length of time between the decision and the onset of consequences:** The shorter the length of time between the action and the onset of negative consequences, the more likely that marketers will perceive a problem as unethical.

- **Number of people to be affected:** The greater the number of persons affected by a negative outcome, the more likely that marketers will recognize a problem as unethical.

As you can see, many factors determine the nature of an ethical decision. In October 2014, drugstore chain CVS ceased all sales of cigarettes and other tobacco products, becoming the first national pharmacy to do so.

CVS President and CEO Larry Merlo said that the decision better aligned the company with its purpose of improving customer health, and that it was simply the right thing to do.[16] Which of the above factors do you think contributed to CVS' decision?

In this February 2014 photo, cigarettes and other tobacco products can be seen on sale behind the counter at a New York City CVS location. As of October 1, 2014, CVS became the first chain of national pharmacies to remove cigarettes from its shelves.

3-3c Ethical Guidelines and Training

In recent years, many organizations have become more interested in ethical issues. One sign of this interest is the increase in the number of large companies that appoint ethics officers—from virtually none several years ago to over 40 percent of large corporations today.[17] In addition, many companies of various sizes have developed a **code of ethics** as a guideline to help marketing managers and other employees make better decisions. Creating ethics guidelines has several advantages:

- A code of ethics helps employees identify what their firm recognizes as acceptable business practices.

- A code of ethics can be an effective internal control of behavior, which is more desirable than external controls such as government regulation.

- A written code helps employees avoid confusion when determining whether their decisions are ethical.

- The process of formulating the code of ethics facilitates discussion among employees about what is right and wrong and ultimately leads to better decisions.

Ethics training is an effective way to help employees put good ethics into practice. The Ethics

code of ethics a guideline to help marketing managers and other employees make better decisions

GOOGLE'S CODE OF ETHICS

Google's now-famous guiding principle of personal conduct is simply "Don't be evil." This generally means providing Google users with unbiased access to information, focusing on user needs, and giving them the best products and services that the company can provide. Google's code of ethics is a means of putting "Don't be evil" into practice. A summary of the primary components of Google's code is as follows:

I. Serve Our Users
Our users value Google not only because we deliver great products and services, but because we hold ourselves to a higher standard in how we treat users and operate in general. This requires integrity, useful products, preserving privacy, security, freedom of expression, and being responsive to users.

II. Respect Each Other
We are committed to a supportive work environment where employees have the opportunity to reach their fullest potential. Each Googler is expected to do his or her utmost to create a respectful workplace culture that is free of harassment, intimidation, bias, and unlawful discrimination of any kind.

III. Avoid Conflicts of Interest
While working at Google, we have an obligation to always do what's best for the company and our users. When you are in a situation in which competing loyalties could cause you to pursue a personal benefit for you, your friends, or your family at the expense of Google or its users, you may be faced with a conflict of interest. All of us should avoid conflicts of interest and circumstances that reasonably present the appearance of a conflict.

IV. Preserve Confidentiality

V. Protect Google's Assets

IV. Ensure Financial Integrity and Responsibility
Financial integrity and fiscal responsibility are core aspects of corporate professionalism. This is more than accurate reporting of our financials, though that's certainly

important. The money we spend on behalf of Google is not ours; it's the company's, and ultimately, our shareholders'. Each person at Google—not just those in finance—has a role in making sure that money is appropriately spent, our financial records are complete and accurate, and internal controls are honored.

VII. **Obey the Law**
Each of Google's seven tenants of its code is followed by several pages of detail that fully explain the guiding principle. Space requirements don't allow reprinting the code in full.[18]

Resource Center's National Business Ethics Survey (NBES) found that 81 percent of companies provide ethics training. Coincidentally, the survey found that a historically low 41 percent of workers reported that they had observed misconduct on the job.[19] Still, simply giving employees a long list of *dos* and *don'ts* does not really help employees navigate the gray areas or adapt to a changing world market. In Carson City, Nevada, all governmental lobbyists are required to attend a course on ethics and policy before they can meet with lawmakers. The training outlines exactly how and when lobbyists are allowed to interact with lawmakers and how to report any money they spend. A clear understanding of ethical expectations is essential to an industry like lobbying, where illicit—often illegal—actions are taken to promote individual causes.

Do ethics training programs work? According to the NBES, it seems that they do. The number of employees who said they had felt pressure to commit an ethics violation—to cut corners or worse—dropped from 13 percent in 2011 to 9 percent in 2013.[20]

THE MOST ETHICAL COMPANIES Each year, *Ethisphere* magazine (targeted toward top management and focused on ethical leadership) examines more than 5,000 companies in thirty separate industries, seeking the world's most ethical companies. It then lists the top 100. The magazine uses a rigorous format to identify true ethical leadership. A few of the selected winners are shown in Exhibit 3.1.

ETHICS AND SMALL BUSINESS Large firms like those listed in Exhibit 3.1 often have ethics officers and extensive ethics training for employees. Small companies, however, are often on their own when facing ethical issues. Simply managing the business often demands extensive amounts of time for entrepreneurs, so ethics training and awareness may not be a priority. One area in which small firms sometimes suffer ethical lapses is in promotion. The Internet has changed promotional strategy because small companies can create their own ads and get them out quickly to the marketplace. A recent study found that the number of false advertising lawsuits involving small firms is continually rising.[21] One lawyer who represents small advertisers says, "In order to keep up with the big players, they feel like they have to exaggerate and they can get in trouble."[22] For example, Hello Products sells toothpaste in flavors such as "pink grapefruit" and "mojito mint." When this line of toothpastes launched, it was touted as "99% natural"

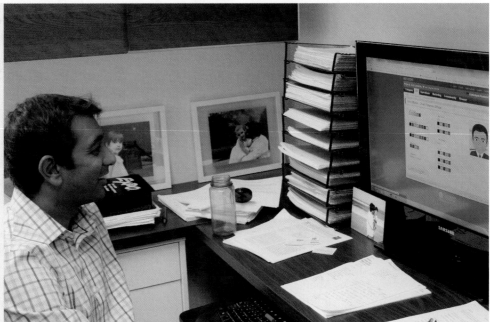

University of Virginia professor, Bobby Parmar, demonstrates BizHero, an online game that teaches business ethics and decision making.

AP Images/The Daily Progress/Nate Delesline III

EXHIBIT 3.1 SELECTED WINNERS OF THE WORLD'S MOST ETHICAL COMPANIES

Company	Industry
Rockwell Collins	Aerospace and Defense
Gap, Inc.	Apparel
Levi Strauss & Co.	Apparel
Cummins, Inc.	Automotive
Ford Motor Company	Autos
Accenture	Business Services
Dun & Bradstreet	Business Services
Manpower Group	Business Services
Dell Inc.	Computer Hardware
Intel Corporation	Computer Hardware
Google	Computer Services
Adobe Systems	Computer Software
Microsoft	Computer Software
Symantec	Computer Software
Colgate-Palmolive Company	Consumer Products
Kimberly-Clark Corporation	Consumer Products
Waste Management	Environmental Services
Kellogg Company	Food and Beverage
PepsiCo	Food and Beverage
L'OREAL	Health and Beauty
Cleveland Clinic	Healthcare Services
3M Company	Industrial Manufacturing
Deere & Company	Industrial Manufacturing
General Electric	Industrial Manufacturing
Time Warner	Media
Safeway	Retail Food Stores

Source: "2014 World's Most Ethical Companies," Ethisphere, http://ethisphere.com (Accessed January 20, 2015).

on the company's website and on the toothpaste packaging itself. After the firm delivered its first shipment, it received a letter from Procter & Gamble wanting Hello to retract its "99% natural" claim. Hello settled its dispute with P&G by agreeing to change the label to "Naturally Friendly." Hello ended up with 100,000 tubes that couldn't be sold. The firm ultimately gave them away on the streets of Manhattan hoping to get a little promotional mileage out of the old tubes.[23]

Foreign Corrupt Practices Act (FCPA) a law that prohibits U.S. corporations from making illegal payments to public officials of foreign governments to obtain business rights or to enhance their business dealings in those countries

corporate social responsibility (CSR) a business's concern for society's welfare

stakeholder theory ethical theory stating that social responsibility is paying attention to the interest of every affected stakeholder in every aspect of a firm's operation

3-3d Ethics in Other Countries

Studies suggest that ethical beliefs vary little from culture to culture. Certain practices, however, such as the use of illegal payments and bribes, are far more acceptable in some places than in others, though enforced laws are increasingly making the practice less accepted. One such law, the **Foreign Corrupt Practices Act (FCPA)**, was enacted because Congress was concerned about U.S. corporations' use of illegal payments and bribes in international business dealings. This act prohibits U.S. corporations from making illegal payments to public officials of foreign governments to obtain business rights or to enhance their business dealings in those countries. The act has been criticized for putting U.S. businesses at a competitive disadvantage. Many contend that bribery is an unpleasant but necessary part of international business, especially in countries such as China, where business gift giving is widely accepted and expected. But, as prosecutions under the FCPA have increased worldwide, some countries are implementing their own anti-bribery laws. For example, even though China is among the three countries with the most international corruption cases prosecuted under the FCPA, the country is working to develop its own anti-bribery laws.

3-4 CORPORATE SOCIAL RESPONSIBILITY

Corporate social responsibility (CSR) is a business's concern for society's welfare. This concern is demonstrated by managers who consider both the long-range best interests of the company and the company's relationship to the society within which it operates.

3-4a Stakeholders and Social Responsibility

An important aspect of social responsibility is **stakeholder theory**. Stakeholder theory says that social responsibility is paying attention to the interest of every affected stakeholder in every aspect of a firm's operation. The stakeholders in a typical corporation are shown in Exhibit 3.2.

- *Employees* have their jobs and incomes at stake. If the firm moves or closes, employees often face a severe hardship. In return for their labor, employees expect wages, benefits, and meaningful work. In return for their loyalty, workers expect the company to carry them through difficult times.

EXHIBIT 3.2 STAKEHOLDERS IN A TYPICAL CORPORATION

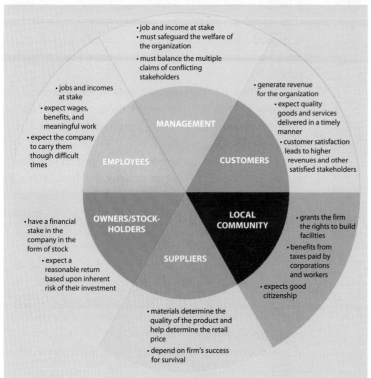

- job and income at stake
- must safeguard the welfare of the organization
- must balance the multiple claims of conflicting stakeholders

- jobs and incomes at stake
- expect wages, benefits, and meaningful work
- expect the company to carry them though difficult times

MANAGEMENT

EMPLOYEES

CUSTOMERS

- generate revenue for the organization
- expect quality goods and services delivered in a timely manner
- customer satisfaction leads to higher revenues and other satisfied stakeholders

OWNERS/STOCK-HOLDERS

LOCAL COMMUNITY

SUPPLIERS

- have a financial stake in the company in the form of stock
- expect a reasonable return based upon inherent risk of their investment

- grants the firm the rights to build facilities
- benefits from taxes paid by corporations and workers
- expects good citizenship

- materials determine the quality of the product and help determine the retail price
- depend on firm's success for survival

- *Management* plays a special role, as they also have a stake in the corporation. Like employees, managers have their jobs and incomes at stake. On the other hand, management must safeguard the welfare of the organization. Sometimes this means balancing the multiple claims of conflicting stakeholders. For example, stockholders want a higher return on investment and perhaps lower costs by moving factories overseas. This naturally conflicts with the interests of employees, the local community, and perhaps suppliers.

- *Customers* generate the revenue for the organization. In exchange, they expect high-quality goods and services delivered in a timely manner. Customer satisfaction leads to higher revenues and the ability to enhance the satisfaction of other stakeholders.

- *The local community*, through its government, grants the firm the right to build facilities. In turn, the community benefits directly from local taxes paid by the corporation and indirectly by property and sales taxes paid by the workers. The firm is expected to be a good citizen by paying a fair wage, not polluting the environment, and so forth.

- *Suppliers* are vital to the success of the firm. For example, if a critical part is not available for an assembly line,

then production grinds to a halt. The materials supplied determine the quality of the product produced and create a cost floor, which helps determine the retail price. In turn, the firm is the customer of the supplier and is therefore vital to the success and survival of the supplier. A supplier that fails to deliver quality products can create numerous problems for a firm. For example, Burger King stopped buying beef from an Irish supplier whose patties were found to contain traces of horse meat in Britain and Ireland.[24]

- *Owners* have a financial stake in the form of stock in a corporation. They expect a reasonable return based upon the amount of inherent risk on their investment. Sometimes managers and employees receive a portion of their compensation in company stock. When Apple launched its initial public stock offering, 30 Apple employees became instant millionaires.[25] Similarly, more than 10,000 Microsoft employees have become millionaires from their stock holdings.[26]

3-4b Pyramid of Corporate Social Responsibility

One theorist suggests that total corporate social responsibility has four components: economic, legal, ethical, and philanthropic. The **pyramid of corporate social responsibility** portrays economic performance as the foundation for the other three responsibilities (see Exhibit 3.3). At the same time that it pursues profits (economic responsibility), however, a business is expected to obey the law (legal responsibility); to do what is right, just, and fair (ethical responsibilities); and to be a good corporate citizen (philanthropic responsibility). These four components are distinct but together constitute the whole. Still, if the company does not make a profit, then the other three responsibilities are moot.

 ## ARGUMENTS FOR AND AGAINST SOCIAL RESPONSIBILITY

CSR can be a divisive issue. Some analysts believe that a business should focus on making a profit and leave social and environmental problems to nonprofit organizations and government. Economist

pyramid of corporate social responsibility a model that suggests corporate social responsibility is composed of economic, legal, ethical, and philanthropic responsibilities and that a firm's economic performance supports the entire structure

EXHIBIT 3.3

THE PYRAMID OF CORPORATE SOCIAL RESPONSIBILITY

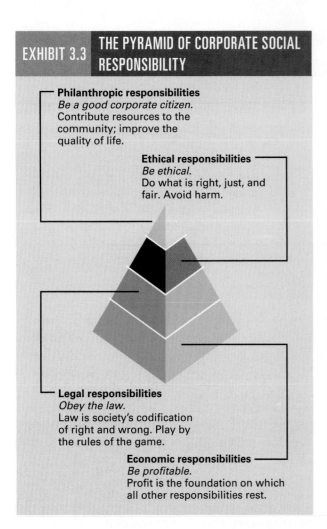

Philanthropic responsibilities
Be a good corporate citizen.
Contribute resources to the
community; improve the
quality of life.

Ethical responsibilities
Be ethical.
Do what is right, just, and
fair. Avoid harm.

Legal responsibilities
Obey the law.
Law is society's codification
of right and wrong. Play by
the rules of the game.

Economic responsibilities
Be profitable.
Profit is the foundation on which
all other responsibilities rest.

Recent research has found that being socially responsible and training front line employees about social responsibility can have a positive impact on the firm. In a business-to-business environment, researchers found that social responsibility activities can raise customer trust and identification with the firm. These factors, in turn, build customer loyalty, which often leads to higher profits.[28]

Another, more pragmatic, reason for being socially responsible is that if businesses do not act responsibly, then government will create new regulations and perhaps levy fines against them.

Finally, social responsibility can produce a direct profit. Smart companies can prosper and build value by tackling social problems. Starbucks rolled out a reusable plastic tumbler that customers could buy for $1 instead of using a disposable cardboard cup for each coffee they buy. Not only does the reusable tumbler reduce energy use, landfill waste, and litter, it saves Starbucks the cost of the disposable cups and encourages customers to buy their daily cup of coffee from the company. In 2015, Starbucks introduced a $30 double-walled tumbler made from recycled materials. Customers who brought the tumbler back to the store for refills received free coffee for a month.[29]

Milton Friedman believed that the free market, not companies, should decide what is best for the world.[27] Friedman argued that when business executives spend more money than necessary—to purchase delivery vehicles with hybrid engines, pay higher wages in developing countries, or even donate company funds to charity—they are spending shareholders' money to further their own agendas. It would be better to pay dividends and let the shareholders give the money away if they choose.

On the other hand, CSR has an increasing number of supporters based on several compelling factors. One is that it is simply the right thing to do. Some societal problems, such as pollution and poverty-level wages, have been brought about by corporations' actions; it is the responsibility of business to right these wrongs. Businesses also have the resources, so businesses should be given the chance to solve social problems. For example, businesses can provide a fair work environment, safe products, and informative advertising.

This reusable tumbler was purchased from a Starbucks location in the Chelsea neighborhood of New York City. Consumers have long criticized Starbucks' use of disposable containers, so the introduction of the reusable cup benefited both the company and its customers.

Richard B. Levine/Newscom

3-5a Sustainability

A popular theory in social responsibility is called **sustainability**. This refers to the idea that socially responsible companies will outperform their peers by focusing on the world's social and environmental problems and viewing them as opportunities to build profits and help the world at the same time.

Perhaps the company that most exemplifies the sustainability movement is Patagonia. The firm has recently launched a program called the Responsible Economy. Rick Ridgeway, Head of Sustainability for Patagonia, says, "Responsible Economy is about the role consumption plays in the continued decline of our planet's health."[30] Patagonia's goal is to get people to pay attention to environmental stress. Then, the company hopes, they will buy quality products that do not end up in a landfill after a few months.

Patagonia has placed ads on Black Friday—typically the busiest shopping day of the year—that read "don't buy our products." While this seems counterintuitive for a for-profit company, Patagonia has doubled in size and tripled its profits in recent years. CEO Rose Marcario says that the promotion has been very successful because what the ad *really* means is "don't buy more than you need" and "the more you consume, the more it strains the world's resources."[31] Marcario notes that Patagonia has released a film called "Worn Well" that stresses the durability of Patagonia's products and suggests that they can be handed down from generation to generation. Patagonia backs up this bold marketing strategy with a guarantee—if something happens, regardless of age, Patagonia will fix it for free.

Patagonia also funds various activities outside of the firm that support sustainability. Recently, the company paid for a documentary film called "Dam Nation," which advocates dam removal around the world. Marcario claims that there is a huge movement in China to dam virtually all natural rivers. This, she says, would mean less biodiversity.[32] Patagonia also announced a new $13 million project to put solar panels on homes in Hawaii because Marcario felt that solar infrastructure was not growing in Hawaii the way it should.[33]

Sustainability is not simply "green marketing," though environmental sustainability is an important component of the sustainability philosophy. An environmentally sustainable process contributes to keeping the environment healthy by using renewable resources and by avoiding actions that depreciate the environment.

3-5b Growth of Social Responsibility

The social responsibility of businesses is growing around the world. Companies around the globe are coming under increasing pressure from governments, advocacy groups,

DON'T BUY THIS JACKET

> Patagonia's decision to Responsible Economy is so strong that the company advises customers not to buy its products if they don't absolutely need to.

investors, prospective employees, current employees, and consumers to make their organizations more socially responsible. In turn, firms are seeing social responsibility as an opportunity. A recent global survey from the Nielsen Company, one of the world's largest marketing research firms, found that

sustainability the idea that socially responsible companies will outperform their peers by focusing on the world's social problems and viewing them as opportunities to build profits and help the world at the same time

55 percent of respondents around the world were willing to pay extra for products and services from companies providing positive social and environmental impact (see Exhibit 3.4).[34] More than half of the survey participants had bought at least one product or service in the past six months from a socially responsible company.[35]

UNITED NATIONS GLOBAL COMPACT

One way that U.S. firms can do more is by joining the United Nations Global Compact (UNGC). The UNGC, the world's largest global corporate citizenship initiative, has seen its ranks swell over the past few years. In 2001—the first full year after its launch—just sixty-seven companies joined, agreeing to abide by ten principles (see "The Ten Principles of the United Nation's Global Compact"). In 2015, there were more than 8000 business participants.[36]

Smaller companies that wish to join the social responsibility and sustainability movement are turning to the B Corp movement.[37] To become a B Corp Certified company, a firm must score at least 80 points on a 200-point assessment. Criteria include things like fair compensation

for workers, how much waste the company produces, and the company's work with local businesses. Firms such as Patagonia, Ben & Jerry's, online crafts marketplace Etsy, and cleaning products maker Method Products have qualified. New Seasons Market, a 13-store grocery chain in Oregon, stamps the B Corp logo on all of its grocery bags and gives employees B Corp badges to wear. The logo helps attract socially-minded shoppers and helps in recruiting new workers.

Fisherss/Shutterstock.com

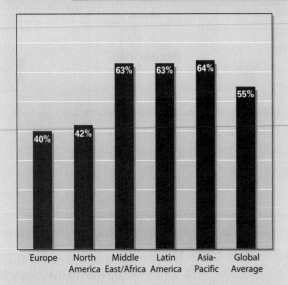

| EXHIBIT 3.4 | PERCENT OF RESPONDENTS WILLING TO PAY EXTRA FOR PRODUCTS AND SERVICES FROM COMPANIES COMMITTED TO POSITIVE SOCIAL AND ENVIRONMENTAL IMPACT |

Europe	North America	Middle East/Africa	Latin America	Asia-Pacific	Global Average
40%	42%	63%	63%	64%	55%

Source: "It Pays to Be Green: Corporate Social Responsibility Meets the Bottom Line," *Nielsen*, June 17, 2014, www.nielsen.com/us/en/insights/news/2014/it-pays-to-be-green-corporate-social-responsibility-meets-the-bottom-line.html (Accessed November 3, 2015).

THE TEN PRINCIPLES OF THE UNITED NATION'S GLOBAL COMPACT

Human Rights

▶ **Principle 1:** Businesses should support and respect the protection of internationally proclaimed human rights.

▶ **Principle 2:** Businesses should make sure that they are not complicit in human rights abuses.

Labor

▶ **Principle 3:** Businesses should uphold the freedom of association and the effective recognition of the right to collective bargaining.

▶ **Principle 4:** Businesses should uphold the elimination of all forms of forced and compulsory labor.

▶ **Principle 5:** Businesses should uphold the effective abolition of child labor.

▶ **Principle 6:** Businesses should uphold the elimination of discrimination in respect of employment and occupation.

Environment

▶ **Principle 7:** Businesses should support a precautionary approach to environmental challenges.

▶ **Principle 8:** Businesses should undertake initiatives to promote greater environmental responsibility.

▶ **Principle 9:** Businesses should encourage the development and diffusion of environmentally friendly technologies.

Anti-Corruption

▶ **Principle 10:** Businesses should work against corruption in all its forms, including extortion and bribery

Source: https://www.unglobalcompact.org/AboutThe GC/TheTenPrinciples/index.html

3-5c Green Marketing

An outgrowth of the social responsibility and sustainability movements is green marketing. **Green marketing** is the development and marketing of products designed to minimize negative effects on the physical environment or to improve the environment. One approach that firms use to indicate that they are part of the green movement is to use third-party eco-logos. Examples include the chasing-arrows recycling logo (the product is either recyclable or contains recycled materials); the Energy Star logo (the product is energy efficient); and Certified Organic (the U.S. Department of Agriculture created standards relative to soil quality, animal raising practices, pest and weed control, and the use of additives). These logos can enhance a product's sales and profitability.

Nearly four in 10 Americans (about 93 million people) say that they are dedicated to buying green products and services. Green purchasing is driven by young adults (age 18 to 34) and Hispanics; about half of the respondents in these groups report that they regularly seek out green products. Young adults are also more likely to be interested in a company's green practices and to avoid companies with poor environmental records.[38]

When a firm takes an action that is perceived as not environmentally friendly, it can create a significant amount of negative publicity. The *New Yorker* magazine recently ran a story about furniture and decorative accessories company Restoration Hardware. The article notes:

The first stirrings of dissent came from the UPS drivers. They began posting on Brown Café, an anonymous message board, about the thirty-three-hundred page catalogue bundles sent out by Restoration Hardware. "My building for the last few days is slammed with RF catalogues (17 pounds each) with another trailer full coming in next week," one wrote. One driver described orders to give the catalogues to passersby, if necessary, rather than return them to UPS distribution centers. "I see them all over my route in the recycle bins."

Then, customers rebelled. In Palo Alto, seven volunteers returned two thousand pounds of the catalogues to a Restoration Hardware store in one day, on hand trucks.

One page of the catalogue is devoted to Restoration Hardware's environmental impact. First, the company claims that sending out the catalogues all at once is more responsible than spreading them throughout the year. It does not acknowledge that, in 2003, when it mailed six catalogues annually, it used half as many total pages. Second, the company says that it purchases paper certified by the Programme for the Endorsement of Forest Certification. However, as *Business Week* explained, other retailers, such as Pottery Barn, buy paper from forests certified by the Forest Stewardship Council, which has stricter environmental standards. Third, Restoration Hardware points out that it purchases carbon offsets through UPS to fund conservation projects. Those offsets, while helpful, cover only the shipping, not the paper production, the most harmful of the process, because of the energy used to break down wood into pulp. The company responded to the *New Yorker's* questions about its environmental practices by emailing a press release containing information identical to what's in the catalogue.[39]

3-5d Leaders in Social Responsibility and Green Marketing

According to *Corporate Responsibility* magazine, the top four corporate citizens of 2014 were Bristol-Myers Squibb, Johnson & Johnson, Gap, and Microsoft.[40] Bristol-Myers Squibb currently funds more than 125 health care initiatives around the world. For example, it is a member of the Medicines Patent Pool in Geneva, Switzerland, which makes drugs available at low costs to people in the developing world with HIV/AIDS. The firm estimates that these projects are benefiting

Restoration Hardware, a furniture and decorating company, recently caught grief for overproducing their catalogs, thus causing them to develop a reputation of not being environmentally friendly.

Kevin Schafer/Moment Mobile/Getty Images

> **green marketing** the development and marketing of products designed to minimize negative effects on the physical environment or to improve the environment

more than 1 million people.[41] Johnson & Johnson has similarly partnered with 12 other companies to attack neglected tropical diseases in developing countries.[42] Gap runs a program that teaches basic skills like literacy, verbal communication, and health awareness to female garment workers in developing countries. So far, the program has reached 25,000 women. Gap is also expanding a youth program called This Way Ahead that offers job training and internships to underserved young people in New York City and San Francisco. In 2014, Microsoft donated $948 million in software and hardware to more than 86,000 nonprofits around the globe. The firm has made a three-year commitment to create opportunities for 300 million youths under the Microsoft Youth Spark initiative. The program focuses on education, employment, and entrepreneurship opportunities.[43]

3-6 CAUSE-RELATED MARKETING

A sometimes controversial subset of social responsibility is cause-related marketing. Sometimes referred to as simply "cause marketing," it is the cooperative efforts of a for-profit firm and a nonprofit organization for mutual benefit. The for-profit firm hopes to generate extra sales, and the nonprofit in turn hopes to receive money, goods, and/or services. Any marketing effort that targets social or other charitable causes can be referred to as cause-related marketing. Cause marketing differs from corporate giving (philanthropy), as the latter generally involves a specific donation that is tax deductible, whereas cause marketing is a marketing relationship not based on a straight donation.

Cause-related marketing is very popular and is estimated to generate about $7 billion a year in revenue. It creates good public relations for the firm and will often stimulate sales of the brand.[44] Nevertheless, the huge growth of cause-related marketing can lead to *consumer cause fatigue*. Researchers have found that businesses need to guard against being perceived as exploiting a cause simply to sell more of a product.[45]

Examples of cause-related marketing used by large companies are abundant. Clothing retailer H&M ran a promotion during the 2014 back-to-school sales period that promised that for every denim item purchased, the company would donate a new denim item to someone in need. The promotion was called "Wear Denim, Share Denim." Similarly, Starbucks recently launched "suspended coffee," a program where when customers bought coffee, they could support a fund that gives free coffee to people who cannot afford to pay. Quaker Oats recently created a contest called "Quaker Chewy for Charity." Every time a customer uploaded a photo or drawing of a customized lunch bag to Quaker's special Facebook app, could the company pledged to "show some lunch bag love" and send a 10 pound food donation to Food Banks Canada.[46]

Japan, Argentina, Australia, Russia, and France guarantee their citizens a respective 10, 14, 20, 28, and 30 paid vacation days per year. The United States is the only industrialized nation that does not require workplaces to offer paid vacation time. One in four working Americans, 28 million U.S. citizens, do not get any paid time off.

For Dallas-based Hotels.com, this legal status proved a great opportunity for cause-marketing. The company launched the Vacation Equality project, a website featuring an interactive map showing the number of vacation days granted to workers around the world as well as statistics on how paid vacation time benefits businesses and the economy. According to a Hotels.com/GfK phone survey, for example, 79 percent of Americans believe that vacation time positively affects their health and well-being.[47] The website included a digital petition asking the president to change the laws on guaranteed vacation time.

This cause-marketing campaign garnered 7.5 million total impressions and the petition received 17,120 signatures.[48] The primary benefit to Hotels.com was an improvement in brand image. A positive image is a huge factor in revenue growth for a .com organization.

cause-related marketing the cooperative marketing efforts between a for-profit firm and a nonprofit organization

STUDY TOOLS 3

LOCATED AT BACK OF THE TEXTBOOK
- ☐ Rip out Chapter Review Card

LOCATED AT WWW.CENGAGEBRAIN.COM
- ☐ Review Key Terms Flashcards and create your own
- ☐ Track your knowledge & understanding of key concepts in marketing
- ☐ Complete practice and graded quizzes to prepare for tests
- ☐ Complete interactive content within the MKTG Online experience
- ☐ View the chapter highlight boxes within the MKTG Online experience

MKTG ONLINE

STUDY YOUR WAY WITH STUDYBITS!

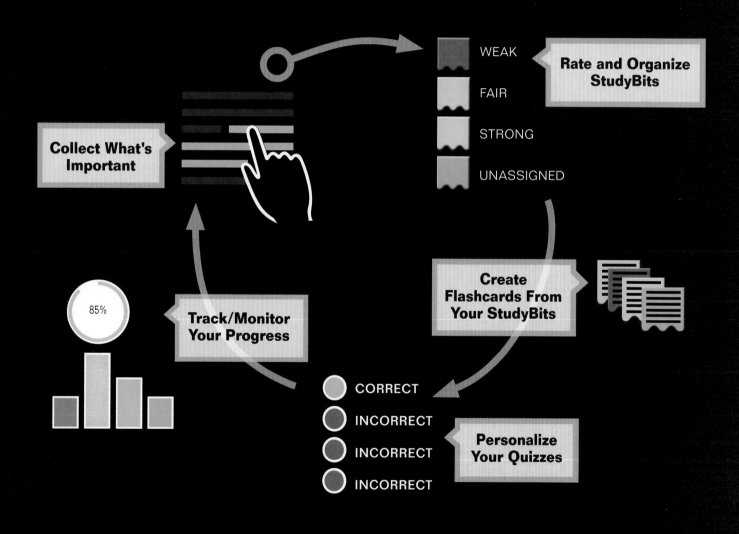

WEAK

FAIR

STRONG

UNASSIGNED

Rate and Organize StudyBits

Collect What's Important

Track/Monitor Your Progress

85%

CORRECT

INCORRECT

INCORRECT

INCORRECT

Personalize Your Quizzes

Create Flashcards From Your StudyBits

4LTR PRESS

4 | The Marketing Environment

LEARNING OUTCOMES

After studying this chapter, you will be able to...

4-1 Discuss the external environment of marketing and explain how it affects a firm

4-2 Describe the social factors that affect marketing

4-3 Explain the importance to marketing managers of current demographic trends

4-4 Explain the importance to marketing managers of growing ethnic markets

4-5 Identify consumer and marketer reactions to the state of the economy

4-6 Identify the impact of technology on a firm

4-7 Discuss the political and legal environment of marketing

4-8 Explain the basics of foreign and domestic competition

After you finish this chapter go to **PAGE 65** for **STUDY TOOLS.**

4-1 THE EXTERNAL MARKETING ENVIRONMENT

Perhaps the most important decisions a marketing manager must make relate to the creation of the marketing mix. Recall from Chapters 1 and 2 that a marketing mix is the unique combination of product, place (distribution), promotion, and price strategies. The marketing mix is, of course, under the firm's control and is designed to appeal to a specific group of potential buyers, or target market. A **target market** is a group of people or organizations for which an organization designs, implements, and maintains a marketing mix intended to meet the needs of that group, resulting in mutually satisfying exchanges.

target market a group of people or organizations for which an organization designs, implements, and maintains a marketing mix intended to meet the need of that group, resulting in mutually satisfying exchanges

Managers must alter the marketing mix because of changes in the environment in which consumers live, work, and make purchasing decisions. Also, as markets mature, some new consumers become part of the target market; others drop out. Those who remain may have different tastes, needs, incomes, lifestyles, and buying habits than the original target consumers. Technology, and the resulting change in buying habits, meant that consumers no longer have those "Kodak Moments" when taking pictures

Dmitrijs Dmitrijevs/Shutterstock.com

of a birthday party or an exceptional sunset. Digital photography has sent 35-millimeter film the way of the horse and buggy. Unfortunately, shifting technology ultimately led to the bankruptcy of Eastman Kodak.

Although managers can control the marketing mix, they cannot control elements in the external environment that continually mold and reshape the target market. Controllable and uncontrollable variables affect the target market, whether it consists of consumers or business purchasers. The uncontrollable elements in the center of the environment continually evolve and create changes in the target market. Think, for example, about how social media have changed your world. In contrast, managers can shape and reshape the marketing mix to influence the target market. That is, managers react to changes in the external environment and attempt to create a more effective marketing mix.

4-1a Understanding the External Environment

Unless marketing managers understand the external environment, the firm cannot intelligently plan for the future. Thus, many organizations assemble a team of specialists to continually collect and evaluate environmental information, a process called *environmental scanning*. The goal in gathering the environmental data is to identify future market opportunities and threats.

UNDERSTAND CURRENT CUSTOMERS You must first understand how customers buy, where they buy, what they buy, and when they buy. McDonald's had a rough year in 2014, suffering a net loss as customers moved on to different venues. While upcoming chains like Five Guys limit their offering to around a half dozen items, customers find the McDonald's menu confusing and too big. More upscale fast-casual restaurants like Chipotle Mexican Grill and Shake Shack are luring customers, particularly younger ones, by offering better quality food and the ability to customize their meals. For its part, McDonald's is in the process of changing its marketing mix to counter this trend and regain its lost market share around the globe.

In a brand-new McDonald's outlet near the company's headquarters in Oak Brook, Illinois, customers do not have to queue at the counter. They can go to a touch screen and build their own burger by choosing a bun, toppings, and sauces from a list of more than 20 ingredients including grilled mushrooms, guacamole, and caramelized onions. Customers then sit down and wait an average of seven minutes until a server brings their burgers to their table. The company is planning to roll out these "Create Your Taste" burgers in up to 2,000 restaurants by late 2015, and possibly more if they do well. McDonald's is also trying to engage with customers on social media and is working on a smartphone app as well as testing mobile-payment systems such as Apple Pay, Softcard, and Google Wallet.[1]

McDonald's is also changing its slogan of the past ten years from "I'm Lovin' It" to "Lovin' Beats Hatin'." The idea of the shift is to promote happiness over hate. So far, reaction to the new slogan has been underwhelming. The "It" in the old slogan can be tied back to McDonald's main product—food. Not so with the new slogan. The word "hatin'" is negative, and most advertisers try to avoid negative words in their slogans.[2] Clearly, McDonald's new slogan seems to have problems with both clarity (no ties to food) and likability.

Does McDonald's understand its current customers? By the time you read this text, you should be able to answer this question.

UNDERSTAND HOW CONSUMER DECISIONS ARE MADE Hotel chains like Hyatt, Holiday Inn, and Marriott must understand the decision process that consumers use when selecting a hotel. Boston research firm Chadwick Martin Bailey (CMB) found that mobile, social, and online factors influence leisure travelers very differently at different stages in the purchase process. Mobile devices play an important role in the initial research phase of hotel planning but are used sparingly to book hotel stays. More than 60 percent of travelers use a mobile device—47 percent use a smartphone—during their hotel purchase journey, but only 6 percent book their hotel via a smartphone. Mobile applications are used infrequently throughout the hotel purchase journey. In total, only 6 percent of shoppers use a mobile app.

Consumer reviews trump social media in influence, research, evaluation, and final decision making. Only 13 percent of bookers use social media during the purchase process versus the 59 percent who consult consumer reviews.

Price-comparison sites play an important role—even when they are not the final purchase location. Nearly half of travelers (49 percent) used a price-comparison site such as Expedia, Priceline, or Kayak. Thirty-six percent of those who use one or more of these sites ultimately book their stay with them.[3] The challenge for hotels, then, is to decide how to align their marketing budgets to intercept potential travelers and deliver the right promotion on the appropriate device and through the right channel.

IDENTIFY THE MOST VALUABLE CUSTOMERS AND UNDERSTAND THEIR NEEDS Often, 20 percent of a firm's customers produce eighty percent of the firm's revenue. An organization must understand what drives that loyalty and then take steps to ensure that those drivers are maintained and enhanced. Airlines use loyalty programs to satisfy and retain their best customers. For example, persons who fly more than 100,000 miles a year on American Airlines are called Executive Platinum members. They are granted priority boarding and seating, free domestic upgrades, no fees for checked luggage, coupons for international upgrades, and other benefits.

UNDERSTAND THE COMPETITION Successful firms know their competitors and attempt to forecast those competitors' future moves. Competitors threaten both a firm's market share and its profitability. With 55 million wireless customers and growing, T-Mobile is projected to overtake Sprint as the nation's third largest mobile carrier. What is behind this

This image of a T-Mobile store in Vienna, Switzerland, is a reminder that with 55 million wireless customers and growing, T-Mobile is projected to overtake Sprint as the third largest mobile carrier in the world-trailing Verizon and AT&T.

meteoric rise? After examining the competition, T-Mobile decided to be as different as possible from its rivals. As an innovation leader, T-Mobile is changing the way that carriers offer services. T-Mobile was first to eliminate monthly contracts and offer international data roaming at no extra cost. It was also the first to announce it would allow customers to roll over data capacity from month-to-month. The carrier still has a long way to go to overtake Verizon or AT&T, but its marketing strategy is fostering rapid growth.[4]

4-1b Environmental Management

No single business is large or powerful enough to create major change in the external environment. Thus, marketing managers are basically adapters rather than agents of change. For example, despite the huge size of firms like General Electric, Walmart, Apple, and Caterpillar, they do not control social change, demographics, or other factors in the external environment.

Just because a firm cannot fully control the external environment, however, does not mean that it is helpless. Sometimes a firm can influence external events. For example, extensive lobbying by FedEx has enabled it to acquire virtually all the Japanese routes it has sought. When a company implements strategies that attempt to shape the external environment within which it operates, it is engaging in **environmental management**. The factors within the external environment that are important to marketing managers can be classified as social, demographic, economic, technological, political and legal, and competitive.

 ## 4-2 SOCIAL FACTORS

Social change is perhaps the most difficult external variable for marketing managers to forecast, influence, or integrate into marketing plans. Social factors include our attitudes, values, and lifestyles. Social factors influence the products people buy; the prices paid for products; the effectiveness of specific promotions; and how, where, and when people expect to purchase products.

4-2a American Values

A *value* is a strongly held and enduring belief. During the United States' first 200 years, four basic values strongly influenced attitudes and lifestyles:

- **Self-sufficiency:** Every person should stand on his or her own two feet.

- **Upward mobility:** Success would come to anyone who got an education, worked hard, and played by the rules.

- **Work ethic:** Hard work, dedication to family, and frugality were moral and right.

- **Conformity:** No one should expect to be treated differently from anybody else.

These core values still hold for a majority of Americans today. A person's values are key determinants of what is important and not important, what actions to take or not to take, and how one behaves in social situations.

People typically form values through interaction with family, friends, and other influencers such as teachers, religious leaders, and politicians. The changing environment can also play a key role in shaping one's values.

Values influence our buying habits. Today's consumers are demanding, inquisitive, and discriminating. No longer willing to tolerate products that break down, they are insisting on high-quality goods that save time, energy, and often calories. U.S. consumers rank the characteristics of product quality as (1) reliability, (2) durability, (3) easy maintenance, (4) ease of use, (5) a trusted brand name, and (6) a low price. Shoppers are also concerned about nutrition and want to know what is in their food; many have environmental concerns as well.

4-2b The Growth of Component Lifestyles

People in the United States today are piecing together **component lifestyles**. A lifestyle is a mode of living; it is the way people decide to live their lives. With component lifestyles, people are choosing products and services that meet diverse needs and interests rather than conforming to traditional stereotypes.

In the past, a person's profession—for instance, banker—defined his or her lifestyle. Today, a person can be a banker and also a gourmet, fitness enthusiast, dedicated single parent, and Internet guru. Each of these lifestyles is associated with different goods and services and represents a target audience. Component lifestyles increase the complexity of consumers' buying habits. Each consumer's unique lifestyle can require a different marketing mix.

environmental management when a company implements strategies that attempt to shape the external environment within which it operates

component lifestyles the practice of choosing goods and services that meet one's diverse needs and interests rather than conforming to a single, traditional lifestyle

4-2c How Social Media Have Changed Our Behavior

In 2015, nearly half of the world's population—3 billion people—were on the Internet. Beyond accessing the Internet via computer, tablet, or smartphone, today there is much talk about the Internet of Things. In 2008, the number of "things" (clothing, thermostats, washing machines, fitness trackers, and lightbulbs, for example) connected to the Internet exceeded the number of people on earth. By 2020 there will be 50 billion connected tools, devices, and even cattle.[5] Yes, Dutch startup Sparked is developing a wireless sensor for cattle. When one is sick or pregnant, the sensor sends a message to the farmer. Similarly, Corventis makes a wireless cardiac monitor that doctors can use to monitor people for health risks in real time. And this is just the beginning—the Internet of Things has the potential to change life as we know it in nearly every area of life.

Social media are making profound changes in the way we obtain and consume information—consumers are interacting; sharing beliefs, values, ideas, and interests; and, of course, making purchases at a dizzying rate. These media have even played a major role in the beginnings of revolutions!

What exactly are social media? They are Web-based and mobile technologies that allow the creation and exchange of user-generated content. Social media encompasses a wide variety of content formats—you have most likely used sites such as Facebook, YouTube, Twitter, Tumblr, Instagram, and Pinterest, each of which serves a different function (see Chapter 18). These media have changed the way we communicate, keep track of others, browse for products and services, and make purchases. Social networking is part of regular life for people of all ages. Of the 3 billion Internet users, 2 billion use social media. From 2014 to 2015, 222 million people opened their first social media account.[6] Slightly more women than men use social media. At 89 percent, the heaviest users by age are 18- to 29-year-olds. Usage rates are lower among older age groups.[7]

More than one minute out of every five spent on the Internet worldwide is dedicated to social networking. Facebook, Instagram, Pinterest, LinkedIn, and Twitter are the most-used social networking sites worldwide. Facebook, by far, is the world's most popular, with more than 1.4 billion users. Sixty-six percent of Millennials around the world use Facebook.[8] A recent survey of persons using the Internet in America found:

- Multi-platform use is on the rise. Fifty-two percent of online adults now use two or more social media sites—a 10 percent increase since 2013.

- For the first time, more than half of all online adults 65 and older (56 percent) use Facebook. This represents 31 percent of all seniors.

- For the first time, roughly half of Internet-using young adults ages 18 through 29 (53 percent) use Instagram. Half of all Instagram users (49 percent) use the site daily.

- For the first time, the share of Internet users with college educations using LinkedIn reached 50 percent.

- Women dominate Pinterest. Forty-two percent of online women now use the platform, compared with 13 percent of online men.[9]

HOW FIRMS USE SOCIAL MEDIA Social networking has changed the game when it comes to opinion sharing. Now, consumers can reach many people at once with their views—and can respond to brands and events in real time. In turn, marketers can use social media to engage customers in their products and services. Marketers have learned that social media are not like network television, where a message is pushed out to a mass audience. Instead, social media enable firms to create conversations with customers and establish meaningful connections. In other words, social media marketing can humanize brands. Marketers for brands like Charmin tissues and Oreo cookies post custom videos about their products to Facebook and then invite feedback. Clearly it's a winning strategy—Facebook now attracts over a billion video views per day.[10]

A successful social media company requires creativity. For example, Airline WestJet recently asked travelers on one flight what they wanted for Christmas. While the passengers were airborne, WestJet shoppers raced to buy and wrap the requested items. These presents were then delivered to the recipients via the destination airport's baggage carousel. The campaign's YouTube video received more than 38 million views.[11] Most importantly, it created a positive image and goodwill for WestJet.

When fast-food chain Wendy's released the Pretzel Bacon Cheeseburger, it quickly became the chain's most successful product launch ever. Fans tweeted about their love for the new burger, and Wendy's turned the tweets (misspellings and all) into a series of silly love song music videos (including one staring Nick Lachey). In addition to being reported on all of the major news channels, the videos received 7.5 million Facebook views.[12]

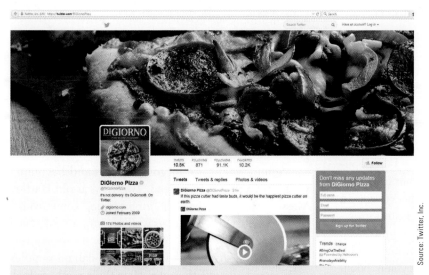

Source: Twitter, Inc.

DiGiorno has done a great job of using social media to convey their message as a brand.

On average, about 6,000 tweets are posted on Twitter every second. That equates to 350,000 tweets per minute and 500 million tweets (by 248 million unique users) per day. [13] Frozen pizza manufacturer DiGiorno has proven to be a master at making its tweets stand out from the crowd. The company frequently employs humor, Internet memes, and casual language to endear itself to customers. Here are a few winners:

KNOCK KNOCK who's there DELIVERY PIZZA delivery pizza who HAHAHA JK DELIVERY PIZZA WON'T BE HERE FOR HOURS
—DiGiorno Pizza (@DiGiornoPizza)

"I've got too much on my plate," said no one ever with pizza on their plate.
—DiGiorno Pizza (@DiGiornoPizza)

Keep Calm and Pizza O-WAIT WHAT THERE'S PIZZA OMG I'M SO FREAKING OUT ABOUT THIS
—DiGiorno Pizza (@DiGiornoPizza)

March madness was named after a guy who didn't eat pizza once in the month of march one time. True story
—DiGiorno Pizza (@DiGiornoPizza)[14]

Even though the topics are random, the tweets all relate back to pizza, cheese, or delivery. These tweets are often retweeted, which spreads the word to larger audiences.

DiGiorno also tweets at other Twitter users, replies to celebrities, and makes comments about live events. DiGiorno noticed that #SoundofMusicLive was trending and capitalized on the 18 million people watching the event by sending out a tweet using the hashtag. This

stunt is called "newsjacking" and it earned DiGiorno 2,000 new followers by the time the two hour special was over. The tweets included:

DOUGH a crust an unbaked crust RAY, a guy that likes pizza ME a pizza liked by a guy named ray FAH no idea what fah is SO so LA a city T tee
—DiGiorno Pizza (@DiGiornoPizza)

#TheSoundOFMusicLive Can't believe pizza isn't one of her favorite things smh
—DiGiorno Pizza (@DiGiornoPizza)

THE KITCHEN IS ALIVE, WITH THE SMELL OF FRESH-BAKED PIZZA #TheSoundOFMusicLive
—DiGiorno Pizza (@DiGiornoPizza)15

As its Twitter success continued, DiGiorno dropped the use of others' hashtags and created its own for college football. #DiGiorNOYOUDIDNT became an instant success as the company used it to make harmless, yet entertaining digs at teams. For example:

IS YOUR DEFENSE A DELIVERY PIZZA? BECAUSE IT LOOKS LIKE THEY'RE NOT SHOWING UP TONIGHT

#DiGiorNOYOUDIDNT

YO, THIS GAME IS LIKE A DIGIORNO PIZZA BECAUSE IT WAS DONE AFTER TWENTY MINUTES

#Super Bowl #SuperSmack #DiGiorNOYOUDIDNT
—DiGiorno Pizza (@DiGiornoPizza)[16]

We will explore social media marketing in greater depth in Chapter 18.

4-3 DEMOGRAPHIC FACTORS

Another uncontrollable variable in the external environment—also extremely important to marketing managers—is demography, the study of people's vital statistics, such as age, race and ethnicity, and location. Demographics are significant because the basis for any market is people.

> **demography** the study of people's vital statistics, such as age, race and ethnicity, and location

Demographic characteristics are strongly related to consumer buying behavior in the marketplace.

4-3a Population

People are directly or indirectly the basis of all markets, making population the most basic statistic in marketing. There are more than seven billion people alive today. China has the largest population with 1.39 billion persons; India is second with 1.23 billion.[17] The U.S. population is slightly over 318 million. Older Americans have moved to retirement communities like the Villages in Central Florida. This area is the nation's fastest growing metropolitan area. Midland and Odessa, in western Texas, are the second and third fastest growing areas in the country. Both cities have seen an employment boom in recent years amid new techniques to extract oil and natural gas. This growth may slow or stop in coming years as global oil prices tumbled in 2015.[18]

Rural areas away from the oil fields, meanwhile, posted their first-ever net loss of population in 2012. The populations of the United States' rural regions—from the Great Plains to the Mississippi delta to rural New England—are aging. These populations are not receiving many young transplants to replace those who die or migrate to urban areas. In many parts of the country, multigenerational households are increasingly common. More than 57 million people live in households with at least two adult generations. About 24 percent of young adults age 25 to 34 live in multiple generation households.[19]

Population is a broad statistic that is most useful to marketers when broken into smaller, more specific increments. For example, age groups present opportunities to focus on a section of the population and offer opportunities for marketers. These groups are called tweens, teens, Millennials (or Generation Y), Generation X, and baby boomers. Each cohort has its own needs, values, and consumption patterns.

TWEENS America's tweens (ages 8 to 12) are a population of more than twenty million. With access to information, opinions, and sophistication well beyond their years (and purchasing power to match), these young consumers are directly or indirectly responsible for sales of over $180 billion annually. Tweens themselves spend about $43 billion per year, and the remainder is spent by parents and family members for them.[20]

With such spending power, this age group is very attractive to many markets. One of the fastest growing tween markets is mobile games and other advertising- and microtransaction-based smartphone apps. In the United States, nearly 78 percent of tweens own a mobile phone and almost half (47 percent) have smartphones.[21] That number jumps to 75 percent among tweens in the United Kingdom, and 83 percent among tweens in Poland. Both boys and girls are playing mobile games to pass time in between classes and at home, and many marketers have tapped into this growing market by catering to tweens' desire for fast-paced, highly stylized games and apps.[22]

Some tweens are forgoing games and becoming young entrepreneurs instead. Twelve-year-old Hartley Messer's sleepover travel kit, for example, "comes with a super cute bag that's great as well as a super cool pencil case for school."[23]

Messer's prospects—young girls—dab on samples of creams and sniff their wrists as their mothers look on. "The Skinny Mini lip gloss is made to slide into your jeans or Lululemon pockets," adds Messer, who sells moisturizers, lip gloss, acne cream, and other products made by Willagirl Inc.

Known as "Willagirls," teens and tweens like Messer host Tupperware-like get-togethers at home, school, or just about anywhere 8- to 12-year-olds hang out. Invites typically are extended via text message, since "nobody uses email anymore," Messner says.[24]

Willagirl's young sales reps receive 25 percent of total sales for a potential monthly income of $320 to $3,500 according to a pamphlet sellers distribute at their parties. Party hosts also receive 15 percent of retail sales from the party in free products, plus one half-priced item if party sales exceed $400.

Founder and CEO Christy Prunier says Willagirl's sales reps don't buy their own inventory in advance. Instead, they take orders from customers, which the company fulfills as orders come in. They're never sitting on products," she says. "It's not work. It's what these girls like to do and their moms are thrilled that they're saving money and developing important skills."[25] They do, however, earn money by recruiting other sellers.

A *Quirk's* study on "global kids" found that tweens in 12 developed countries are surprisingly worldly and share much in common because of the Internet and social media. Global kids are plugging in at younger ages, and the vast majority frequently use electronic entertainment or communication devices including digital cameras (93 percent), video game consoles (84 percent), digital music players (78 percent), and cell phones (77 percent). According to the study, these kids are engaging in a wide range of activities, from playing games (92 percent) to doing schoolwork (76 percent) on these devices.

Global kids are active and grounded. They are highly engaged, very busy, and they value learning. When shown a list of more than 30 activities such as reading, camping, sports, and crafts, global kids said on average that they participated in 25 activities. And, in a world seemingly obsessed with money and celebrity, global kids placed "being smart" and "getting a good education" near the top of socially desirable attributes. In the United States, these attributes topped even fame and fortune. Globally, "getting a good education" and "being rich" are in a dead heat among tweens.[26]

TEENS There are approximately 25 million teenagers in the United States, and they spend approximately 72 hours per week tuned in electronically to television, the Internet, music, video games, and cell phones. About 95 percent of U.S. teens use the Internet. Of those online, approximately 90 percent use social media. They still prefer face-to-face communication to communicating electronically, however. Twenty-five percent of teens claim that social networking makes them less shy. Teens also note that networking enables them to keep in touch with friends that they can't see on a regular basis (89 percent); helps them get to know other students better (69 percent); and enables them to connect with people who share common interests (55 percent). Teens commonly use the following websites:

Facebook	90 percent
Twitter	49 percent
Tumblr	33 percent (more popular with girls)
4chan	23 percent (more popular with boys)
Pinterest	20 percent
Foursquare	12 percent

Sixty-two percent also go online to get the news and current events.[27]

In many households, teens are now passing technology down to their parents, not the other way around. Researchers have found that teens are commonly the ones telling their parents to buy smartphones and tablets and are often the driving force behind their families' technology upgrades.[28]

Teens command an immense amount of buying power. Worldwide, they spend approximately

Approximately 90 percent of teenagers that use the internet, also use some form of social media.

$819 billion every year.[29] In the United States and Canada, teens have almost $118 billion to spend.[30] Although much of that money comes from parents, teens make many shopping decisions. Seventy-one percent do at least some of the family shopping and 4 percent do all of the family shopping. Yet, only 13 percent are told what brands to buy.[31]

Twice a year, Piper Jaffary takes a survey of teen lifestyles and attitudes. Over a 27-year period, the firm has found several factors that remain the same. First, teens continue to seek peer affirmation. Second, their spending is mostly discretionary (as illustrated above). Third, they are early adopters of change. Some key findings from the most recent survey are that:

- Teen males are spending more—up 4 percent from fall 2013.

- For the first time in the survey history, food exceeded clothing as a percentage of teen spending.

- Top clothing brands continue to include Nike, Action Sports, Forever 21, American Eagle, Polo Ralph Lauren, and Hollister.

- At home, cable subscriptions are becoming less essential for teens while online streaming is more critical. Outside the home, IMAX continues to grow share among teens.

- Music listenership has grown for Pandora and local radio, largely at the cost of MP3s and CDs.

- Eighty-five percent of teen gamers play mobile games.[32]

MILLENNIALS **Millennials**, or **Generation Y**, are people born between 1979 and 1994. Initially, Millennials were a smaller cohort than baby boomers. However, due to immigration and the aging of the boomer generation, the seventy-seven million Gen Yers in the United States passed the boomers in total population in 2010. Millennials are currently in two different stages of the life cycle.

The youngest members of Gen Y, born in 1994, are just entering young adulthood. In contrast, the oldest Gen Yers, born in 1979, turned 37 years old in 2016. They have started their careers, and many have become parents for the first time, leading to dramatic lifestyle changes. They care for their babies rather than go out, and they spend money on baby products. Gen Yers already spend more than $200 billion annually; over their lifetimes, they will likely spend about $10 trillion. Many older Millennials graduated from college during the Great Recession and had difficulty finding good jobs. Almost a third still live at home with their parents. They also own the bulk of America's $1 trillion in student debt.[33] Younger Millennials do have several things in their favor. First, the recession is over and America is slowly recovering. Second, the size of the Millennial group is massive. There are more people in their 20s (44.5 million) than in their 30s, 40s, or 50s.[34] The sheer size of the 20-old group will create a significant amount of economic growth. This, in turn, will mean more and better jobs.

Millennials may be the most tech-savvy generation yet, spending more time surfing the Web and on social media than they do watching television, listening to radio, or reading newspapers, but they still use and value traditional media. Gen Yers expect brands to be on social media. They also like to use social media to share photos of things they are doing and keep up with people in their network. Fifty-one percent of Millennials have an Instagram account and 42 percent use Snapchat, a photo-sharing app. When it comes to daily use, photo-focused social applications are slightly more popular than their text-focused competitors; 31 percent of Millennials post on Instagram on a daily basis, while 29 percent tweet every day.[35]

As to the subject matter of Millennials' photos, clues can be found in where they spend their time and money: travel, outdoor activities, and experiences like concerts.[36]

Millennials are very aware of the data that sites like Instagram and others collect on them. One survey found that 52 percent of Gen Yers in the United States have no issue with brands and Web sites using data to provide a better customer experience.[37] This is in stark contrast to European Millennials—only 37 percent of Millennials in the United Kingdom and just 13 percent of Millennials in the Netherlands agree.[38]

GENERATION X **Generation X**—people born between 1965 and 1978—consists of fifty million U.S. consumers. It was the first generation of latchkey children—products of dual-career households or, in roughly half of the cases, of divorced or separated parents. Gen Xers often spent more time without adult support and guidance than any other age cohort. This experience made them independent, resilient, adaptable, cautious, and skeptical.[39]

Gen Xers are in their primary earning years and have acquired a disproportionate amount of spending power relative to the size of their group. They have an estimated 31 percent of total income dollars.[40] Gen Xers have higher average incomes than their Millennial and baby boomer counterparts. Higher incomes have contributed to Gen Xers' optimistic outlook on the future. Two-thirds are either "satisfied" or "very satisfied" with their lives, yet they are also concerned about crime, climate change, and their health.[41]

Saving money is a major priority for Gen Xers. About half note that providing for their children's college expenses is a major goal. They also want to become financially independent, buy or upgrade a home, and provide an estate for their heirs.[42] When asked, "what makes your generation unique?" Gen Xers responded:

- Technology use (12 percent)
- Work ethic (11 percent)
- Conservative/Traditional (7 percent)
- Smarter (6 percent)
- Respectful (5 percent)[43]

Gen Xers tend to be frugal and seek value when making purchases. They place a high value on education and knowledge and tend to do a significant amount of research before making a major purchase. Marketers need to provide a lot of accurate information about their products—particularly why their goods or services are a great value—to reach Gen Xers.

BABY BOOMERS There are approximately 75 million **baby boomers** (persons born between 1946 and 1964) in the United States. With average life expectancy at an all-time high of 77.4 years, more and more Americans over fifty consider middle age a new start on life. The size of the baby boom cohort group has

Millennials people born between 1979 and 1994

Generation X people born between 1965 and 1978

baby boomers people born between 1946 and 1964

been decreasing in size since 2012. The pace of this decline will accelerate as the baby boomers grow older. When the first baby boomers turned 65 in 2011, there were 77 million of them. In 2030, when the baby boomers will be between 66 and 84 years old, that number is projected to drop to 60 million.[44]

While baby boomers' current incomes are relatively low because many have retired, they accumulated a substantial amount of wealth over their working years. It is estimated that boomers control 67 percent ($28 trillion) of the country's wealth.[45] Baby boomers outspend other generations by an estimated $400 billion a year on consumer goods and services. They even outspend younger adults by 2:1 on a per-capita basis when making online purchases.[46] Boomers outspend other cohorts in categories such as gifts, personal care products, medical care, food away from home, and entertainment. Many boomers want to age in place, that is, not move to a retirement community. As a result, they often remodel their existing homes to the tune of around $25 billion per year.[47]

Like other cohort groups, boomers believe that price and quality are very important when making purchase decisions. Baby boomers tend to be influenced more by traditional advertising, sales reps, and word-of-mouth recommendations than other groups. Yet they are also very active in seeking product information online. Boomers tend to use laptops and tablets more than smartphones when conducting product research. While boomers make fewer product purchases online than do some other cohorts, the same is not true for services. Boomers now make 90 percent of their travel purchases online.[48]

Marketers targeting baby boomers must avoid the perception that boomers are old. Words such as "senior," "elderly," and "aged" can quickly drive away potential customers. Boomers today are active and feel entitled to enjoy the good life. Adult diaper company Depends targets consumers age 60 and older, yet the actors in its advertising are in their 40s and 50s.[49] Marketers can also subtly change their products and packaging to appeal to boomers. Depends are today sold as underwear rather than diapers, for example. Simplifying instructions for product assembly and use makes life easier for boomers. Enlarging font size may enable boomers to avoid reaching for their reading glasses. Realizing that holding up

Source: The Sherwin-Williams Company

a heavy paint can and reaching for your glasses at the same time can be tough, Sherwin Williams completely redesigned its can with a clean, crisp look and large fonts.[50]

 ## 4-4 GROWING ETHNIC MARKETS

The American demographic profile is rapidly changing as racial and ethnic groups continue to grow. The minority population today is about 118 million. By 2050, around one in three U.S. residents will be Hispanic. The United States will flip completely to a majority-minority makeup in 2041, meaning that whites of European ancestry will make up less than 50 percent of the population. Already, minorities make up about half of all Americans under the age of five.[51] As the demographic environment of America evolves, so too must the marketing mix change to reach growing target markets.

4-4a Marketing to Hispanic Americans

The term *Hispanic* encompasses people of many different backgrounds. Nearly 60 percent of Hispanic Americans are of Mexican descent. Puerto Ricans, the next largest group, make up just under ten percent of Hispanics. Other groups, including Central Americans, Dominicans, South Americans, and Cubans, each account for less than five percent of all Hispanics.

According to surveys, Hispanics believe that the number one way they contribute to American society is through their commitment to family. Over three-fourths say that the traditional family is the main building block of a healthy community.[52] Research has found that many adults who have been in the United States for a number of years become acculturated, but not to the mainstream U.S. culture. That is, they do not use much English for their everyday activities. Instead, they acculturate to the locally dominant Spanish-speaking Hispanic community, referred to as the primal 45-Latino society.[53] The primal culture tends to be regional. It differs widely enough that Latinos from one region may be unaware of the food, slang, and even music from another region. A good example is the difference in primal cultures between Los Angeles (which draws much of its influence from Mexico) and Miami (which draws much of its influence from Cuba). The same is true for brands purchased. Hispanics are more likely to purchase Jerritos soda if they are integrated into the primal Los Angeles culture than if they live elsewhere in the United States.[54]

Hispanic Millennials now account for 25 percent of all Hispanics living in the United States.[55] Many Hispanic Millennials were born in the United Sates or came when they were very young, and unlike older generations, they have become more acculturated into mainstream America. Hispanic Millennials are less likely than their peers to live at home with their parents. Of those who do live at home, 86 percent contribute to the family's finances. Moreover, they often act as language translators and cultural advisors to their Spanish-dominant family members. Normally, purchase decisions revolve around the Millennial son or daughter who is helping to interpret and manage bills.

Bilingual Hispanic Millennials share common behaviors and beliefs with both older Hispanics and their Millennial peers. They are more optimistic about politics and economics than non-Hispanic Millennials, and they have a stronger faith in the American dream. Bilingual Millennials also place more value on higher education.[56]

Hispanic Millennials in the U.S. are particularly prone to taking a bilingual, bicultural approach to their media consumption. Forty percent of Hispanic Millennials consume an equal amount of Spanish and English media.[57] Spending on Hispanic media now tops $8.3 billion in the United States.[58] The leading advertisers targeting Hispanics are Procter & Gamble, AT&T, and L'Oreal. The 2014 World Cup was very popular in the Hispanic market, and Kraft Foods targeted Hispanics with its "Flavor of the Championship" campaign. Throughout this campaign, Kraft used social media to suggest appropriate recipes for World Cup viewing parties. Finally, Hispanics, particularly Millennials, have embraced technology. They are more likely to download apps, chat, stream video, listen to music, and play games than non-Hispanics.[59]

4-4b Marketing to African Americans

There are approximately 44 million African Americans (14 percent of the country's population). They are young—53 percent are under the age of 35—giving them a strong influence on the latest trends, especially in regards to music and pop culture. Higher academic achievement has translated into increases in household income; 44 percent of all African American households now earn $50,000 or more and 23 percent earn more than $75,000. Higher household incomes, coupled with an overall population growth, are driving the substantial purchasing power of the African American consumer upwards. Total purchasing power is expected to reach $1.3 trillion within a few years.[60]

Black Americans want companies to recognize their unique culture. A recent study found that 87 percent feel that ethnic recognition is important, compared to 59 percent of the general population. Seventy-three percent of African American adults age 18 to 54 state that cultural/ethnic heritage is a critical part of their identity. Among African Americans age 18 to 54 with a household income greater than $50,000, 77 percent indicate that their heritage is an important part of who they are, as compared to 58 percent of the general population.[61]

Also compared to the general population, African Americans are 30 percent more likely to believe that diversity in advertising is important and 38 percent are more likely to make a purchase when advertisements include African American people. Further, 44 percent of African Americans are more likely to support companies that are owned by African Americans or other minority groups and 43 percent are more likely to purchase products endorsed by African American celebrities or musicians.[62]

Black Americans tend to be loyal to both brands and stores; they spend 18 percent more than the general population on store brands. African Americans also are more likely to patronize convenience, drug stores, and dollar stores than other groups. Relative to other cohorts, they spend more on groceries and hair care products.[63] Featuring nonwhite Americans has become a cornerstone of Cheerios' promotional strategy. A recent Honey Nut Cheerios commercial features musician Usher and Buzz Bee dancing and discussing heart health while Usher's song "She Came to Give It to You" plays in the background. Usher was chosen for the spot because of his broad appeal—he has more than 50.5 million Facebook fans.[64]

4-4c Marketing to Asian Americans

The Asian American population reached 19 million in 2015. U.S. births have been the primary driving force behind the increase in the Hispanic and African American populations. By contrast, Asian American population growth has been fueled primarily by immigration. Seventy-four percent of Asian Americans were foreign-born.[65] California and Hawaii are home to the largest Asian American populations. Asian Americans, who still represent only 6 percent of the U.S. population, have the highest average family income of all groups. At $67,000, it exceeds the average U.S. household income by roughly $15,000.[66] About 53 percent of Asian Americans over age 25 have at least a bachelor's degree.[67] Because Asian Americans are younger (the average age is 34), better educated, and have higher incomes than average, they are sometimes called a "marketer's dream." Asian Americans are heavy users of technology. Moreover, they are early adopters of the latest digital gadgets. They visit computer and consumer electronics Web sites 36 percent more often and spend 72 percent more time at these sites than the total population.[68] Because of their high level of education, Asian Americans are thriving in America's technology sector.

Women shop for symbolic Chinese New Year flowers at a New York City Chinatown flower market.

Although Asian Americans embrace the values of the larger U.S. population, they also hold on to the cultural values of their particular subgroup. Consider language: many Asian Americans, particularly Koreans and Chinese, speak their native tongue at home (though Filipinos are far less likely to do so). Cultural values are also apparent in the ways different groups make big-ticket purchases. In Japanese American homes, husbands alone make large purchase decisions nearly half the time; wives decide only about six percent of the time. In Filipino families, however, wives make these decisions a little more often than their husbands do, although, by far, most decisions are made by husbands and wives jointly or with the input of other family members.

Asian Americans like to shop at stores owned and managed by other Asian Americans. Small businesses such as flower shops, grocery stores, and appliance stores are often best equipped to offer the products that Asian Americans want. For example, at first glance, the Hannam Chain supermarket in Los Angeles's Koreatown seems like any other grocery store. But next to the Kraft American singles and the State Fair corn dogs are jars of whole cabbage kimchi. A snack bar in another part of the store cooks up aromatic mung cakes, and an entire aisle is devoted to dried seafood.

Asian Americans are big adopters of technology. More than 70 percent use smartphones—the highest rate of any ethnic group.[69] Social media continues to be a primary way to reach Asian Americans. Mobile chat apps like Kakao, Viber, Tango, WeChat and WhatsApp are also starting to become very popular in the Asian American community. Many Asian Americans use these apps to communicate with family and friends back in their home countries.

4-5 ECONOMIC FACTORS

In addition to social and demographic factors, marketing managers must understand and react to the economic environment. The three economic areas of greatest concern to most marketers are consumers' incomes, inflation, and recession.

4-5a Consumers' Incomes

As disposable (or after-tax) incomes rise, more families and individuals can afford the "good life." In recent years, however, average U.S. incomes have actually fallen. The annual median household income in the United States in 2015 was approximately $52,000, though the median household income varies widely from state to state. This means half of all U.S. households earned less, and the other half earned more. Census data shows that average family incomes, when adjusted for inflation (discussed later in the chapter), fell around eight percent between 2007 and 2012. However, it rose slightly in 2013 and 2014.[70] The unemployment rate was 5.6 percent in early 2015, which is the lowest it had been in six years. Scars from the Great Recession continue to affect the United States as 2.8 million people continue to suffer from long-term unemployment (defined as not having a job for 27 weeks or longer).[71]

Education is the primary determinant of a person's earning potential. For example, just 1 percent of workers with only a high school education earn over $100,000 annually. By comparison, 13 percent of college-educated workers earn six figures or more. People with a bachelor's degree take home an average of 38 percent more than those with just a high school diploma. Over a lifetime, an individual with a bachelor's degree will earn more than twice as much total income as a nondegree holder.[72]

In recent years, stores that cater to lower-income consumers—like Family Dollar and Dollar General—have done well. P&G has found that its typical middle-class customers are increasingly unwilling to spend their money on household staples with extra features, such as Tide with bleach. Many customers have switched to cheaper brands, while P&G brands like Bounce fabric softener and Bounty paper towels suffered. To regain market share, P&G has launched its bargain-priced Gain dish soap. The firm has also reduced some package sizes of Tide in order to sell them at Walmart for less than ten dollars.

4-5b Purchasing Power

Even when incomes rise, a higher standard of living does not necessarily result. Increased standards of living are a function of purchasing power. **Purchasing power** is measured by comparing income to the relative cost of a standard set of goods and services in different geographic areas, usually referred to as the *cost of living*. Another way to think of purchasing power is income minus the cost of living (i.e., expenses). In general, a cost of living index takes into account housing, food and groceries, transportation, utilities, health care, and miscellaneous expenses such as clothing, services, and entertainment. HomeFair.com's salary calculator uses these metrics when it determines that the cost of living in New York City is almost three times the cost of living in Youngstown, Ohio. This means that a worker living in New York City must earn nearly $279,500 to have the same standard of living as someone making $100,000 in Youngstown.

When income is high relative to the cost of living, people have more discretionary income. That means they have more money to spend on nonessential items (in other words, on wants rather than needs). This information is important to marketers for obvious reasons. Consumers with high purchasing power can afford to spend more money without jeopardizing their budget for necessities like food, housing, and utilities. They also have the ability to purchase higher-priced necessities—for example, a more expensive car, a home in a more expensive neighborhood, or a designer handbag versus a purse from a discount store.

4-5c Inflation

Inflation is a measure of the decrease in the value of money, generally expressed as the percentage reduction in value since the previous year, which is the rate of inflation. Thus, in simple terms, an inflation rate of five percent means you will need 5 percent more units of money than you would have needed last year to buy the same basket of products. If inflation is 5 percent, you can expect that, on average, prices have risen by about 5 percent since the previous year. Of course, if pay raises are matching the rate of inflation, then employees will be no worse off in terms of the immediate purchasing power of their salaries.

In times of low inflation, businesses seeking to increase their profit margins can do so only by increasing their efficiency. If they significantly increase prices, no one will purchase their goods or services. The Great Recession brought inflation rates to almost zero. In January 2015, the inflation rate was 0.8 percent.[73]

In creating marketing strategies to cope with inflation, managers must realize that, regardless of what happens to the seller's cost, the buyer is not going to pay more for a product than the subjective value he or she places on it. No matter how compelling the justification might be for a 10 percent price increase, marketers must always examine its impact on demand. Many marketers try to hold prices level for as long as is practical.

purchasing power a comparison of income versus the relative cost of a standard set of goods and services in different geographic areas

inflation a measure of the decrease in the value of money, expressed as the percentage reduction in value since the previous year

4-5d Recession

A **recession** is a period of economic activity characterized by negative growth. More precisely, a recession is defined as occurring when the gross domestic product falls for two consecutive quarters. Gross domestic product is the total market value of all final goods and services produced during a period of time. The official beginning of the Great Recession of 2008–2009 was December 2007. While the causes of the recession are very complex, this one began with the collapse of inflated housing prices. Those high prices led people to take out mortgages they could not afford from banks that should have known the money would not be repaid. By 2008, the recession had spread around the globe. A very slow economic recovery began in July 2009 and continues to this day.

4-6 TECHNOLOGICAL FACTORS

Technological success is based upon innovation, and innovation requires imagination and risk taking. Bringing new technology to the marketplace requires a corporate structure and management actions that will lead to success. Great corporate leaders must embed innovation into the lifeblood of the company. Managers should hire employees with a tolerance for risk. Then, workers must be told not to fear innovation failure. Not everything works the first time. Some of the greatest innovations in recent years, such as 3-D printing, hydraulic fracturing, social media, and the iPhone, all had setbacks before a successful product was created.

Shell, one of the world's largest oil producers, has created the Idea Factory, a technology-forward development platform consisting of four pillars. These are:

- *Game Changer:* This program works at the early or "blue sky" stage of innovation. If a start-up proves its concept, and it aligns with Shell's goals and passes a rigorous approval process, it qualifies for funding and technological help from Shell's engineers.

- *Shell Technology Ventures:* Shell's venture capital arm funds start-ups and entrepreneurs.

- *Shell Tech Works:* This program looks for technology created in other industries but that addresses areas that also apply to Shell.

- *Universities:* Shell collaborates with universities from around the world to complement its internal research and development department.

Some of the innovations that have come from Shell's Idea Factory include visualization tools to print 3-D pictures of rock and oil formations, solar power technologies that assist oil recovery, space robots, and the world's largest floating structure—a floating liquefaction plant for natural gas.[74]

4-6a Research

The United States, historically, has excelled at both basic and applied research. **Basic research** (or *pure research*) attempts to expand the frontiers of knowledge but is not aimed at a specific, pragmatic problem. Basic research aims to confirm an existing theory or to learn more about a concept or phenomenon. For example, basic research might focus on high-energy physics. **Applied research**, in contrast, attempts to develop new or improved products. The United States has dramatically improved its track record in applied research. For example, the United States leads the world in applying basic research to aircraft design and propulsion systems.

4-6b Stimulating Innovation

Companies attempting to innovate often limit their searches to areas they are already familiar with. This can help lead to incremental progress but rarely leads to a dramatic breakthrough. Companies are now using several approaches such as Shell's Idea Factory to keep innovation strong. These include:

- **Building scenarios:** Some firms use teams of writers to imagine detailed opportunities and threats for their companies, partners, and collaborators in future markets. With more than 1 billion smartphones in use around the world, more and

> **recession** a period of economic activity characterized by negative growth, which reduces demand for goods and services
>
> **basic research** pure research that aims to confirm an existing theory or to learn more about a concept or phenomenon
>
> **applied research** research that attempts to develop new or improved products

more companies are creating mobile-friendly sites and mobile apps. However, Senior Vice President at Forrester Research John Bernoff advises that simply cramming a piece of a Web site into a mobile experience is a recipe for disaster that will result in complaints and lost customers. Instead, he says, firms must identify mobile moments and context. A mobile moment is the point in time at which a customer pulls out a mobile device to get immediate access to the information that he or she wants.[75] Rob Moore, chief technical officer at Hertz, figured out number of key mobile moments during which he could make customers happier. For example, he found that customers preferred searching the lot for the best available car right from the airport bus. Krispy Kreme figured out that one of its key moments was right when fresh doughnuts came off of the line. To take advantage of this moment, the company built an app that lets customers know when hot doughnuts are available near them. Half a million downloads later, Krispy Kreme's same-store sales are up by double digits—without advertising.[76]

leedsn/ShutterStock.com

- **Enlisting the Web:** A few companies have created Web sites that act as literal marketplaces of ideas where innovators can go to look for help with scientific and business challenges.

- **Talking to early adopters:** Early adopters tend to be innovators themselves. They are risk takers and look for new things or wish for something better to help in daily tasks at home and work.

- **Using marketing research:** Firms find out what customers like and dislike about their products and competitors' products.

- **Creating an innovative environment:** Companies let employees know that they have the "freedom to fail." They create intranets to encourage sharing ideas. Most importantly, top management must lead by example to create an atmosphere where innovation is encouraged and rewarded.

- **Catering to entrepreneurs:** Policies that reserve blocks of time for scientists or engineers to explore

their own ideas have worked well at some companies. At 3M, scientists can spend fifteen percent of their time on projects they dream up themselves—a freedom that led to the development of the yellow Post-It note. Google is well known in the tech industry for its "20% time" policy, which grants employees a day a week to follow their entrepreneurial passions.[77]

Although developing new technology internally is a key to creating and maintaining a long-term competitive advantage, external technology is also important to managers for two reasons. First, by acquiring the technology, the firm may be able to operate more efficiently or create a better product. Second, a new technology may render existing products obsolete.

Radio frequency identification (RFID) chips were supposed to be a game changer for inventory tracking. Walmart tried using them, but was less than satisfied. JC Penney found that the chips interfered with existing anti-theft sensors. The company removed the anti-theft sensors, and shoplifting surged. Zara, a fashion chain that operates in 88 countries, claims to have learned from others' mistakes and is using RFID chips in a new way. A Zara employee suggested putting the RFID chips inside items' security tags. The security tag's plastic case protects the chip, preventing interference and allowing for reuse.

Before the new tags, taking inventory took 40 employees about five hours to complete. Now, ten employees walking down store aisles while waving pistol-like scanners can finish in half the time.[78] Each time a garment is sold, data from its chip prompts the stockroom to send out an identical item. Previously, store employees using paper sales reports restocked shelves a few times a day. If a customer can't find an item, a salesperson can point an iPod camera at a similar item's bar code and, using data gathered by the chips, see whether the desired item is available in the store, at a nearby Zara store, or online.[79]

4-7 POLITICAL AND LEGAL FACTORS

Business needs government regulation to protect innovators of new technology, the interests of society in general, one business from another,

and consumers. In turn, government needs business because the marketplace generates taxes that support public efforts to educate our youth, pave our roads, protect our shores, and the like.

Every aspect of the marketing mix is subject to laws and restrictions. It is the duty of marketing managers or their legal assistants to understand these laws and conform to them, because failure to comply with regulations can have major consequences for a firm. Sometimes just sensing trends and taking corrective action before a government agency acts can help avoid regulation.

4-7a Federal Legislation

Federal laws that affect marketing fall into several categories of regulatory activity: competitive environment, pricing, advertising and promotion, and consumer privacy. The key pieces of legislation in these areas are summarized in Exhibit 4.1. The primary federal laws that protect consumers are shown in Exhibit 4.2. The Patient Protection and Affordable Care Act, commonly called Obamacare, has had a significant impact on marketing. A few key provisions of the Act are that:

- Large employers must offer coverage to full-time workers.

- Workers cannot be denied coverage.

- A person cannot be dropped when he or she is sick.

- A worker cannot be denied coverage for a preexisting condition.

- Young adults can stay on their parents' plans until age 26.[80]

In 2010, Congress passed the Restoring American Financial Stability Act, which brought sweeping changes to bank and financial market regulations. The legislation created the Consumer Financial Protection Bureau (CFPB) to oversee checking accounts, private student loans, mortgages, and other financial products. The agency deals with unfair, abusive, and deceptive practices. Some groups have expressed concerns that the CFPB is assembling massive databases on credit cards, credit monitoring, debt cancellation products, auto loans, and payday loans. CFPB officials claim that they need the information to make effective rules and enforce those policies. One way or another, the CFPB has certainly had a significant impact on several United States businesses—the agency has recovered more than $1.6 billion from financial services firms in the name of wronged consumers.[81]

4-7b State and Local Laws

Legislation that affects marketing varies state by state. Oregon, for example, limits utility advertising to 0.5 percent of the company's net income. California has forced industry to improve consumer products and has enacted legislation to lower the energy consumption

EXHIBIT 4.1 PRIMARY U.S. LAWS THAT AFFECT MARKETING

Legislation	Impact on Marketing
Sherman Act of 1890	Makes trusts and conspiracies in restraint of trade illegal; makes monopolies and attempts to monopolize misdemeanors.
Clayton Act of 1914	Outlaws discrimination in prices to different buyers; prohibits tying contracts (which require the buyer of one product to also buy another item in the line); makes illegal the combining of two or more competing corporations by pooling ownership of stock.
Federal Trade Commission Act of 1914	Created the Federal Trade Commission to deal with antitrust matters; outlaws unfair methods of competition.
Robinson-Patman Act of 1936	Prohibits charging different prices to different buyers of merchandise of like grade and quantity; requires sellers to make any supplementary services or allowances available to all purchasers on a proportionately equal basis.
Wheeler-Lea Amendments to FTC Act of 1938	Broadens the Federal Trade Commission's power to prohibit practices that might injure the public without affecting competition; outlaws false and deceptive advertising.
Lanham Act of 1946	Establishes protection for trademarks.
Celler-Kefauver Antimerger Act of 1950	Strengthens the Clayton Act to prevent corporate acquisitions that reduce competition.
Hart-Scott-Rodino Act of 1976	Requires large companies to notify the government of their intent to merge.
Foreign Corrupt Practices Act of 1977	Prohibits bribery of foreign officials to obtain business.

EXHIBIT 4.2   PRIMARY U.S. LAWS PROTECTING CONSUMERS

Legislation	Impact on Marketing
Federal Food and Drug Act of 1906	Prohibits adulteration and misbranding of foods and drugs involved in interstate commerce; strengthened by the Food, Drug, and Cosmetic Act (1938) and the Kefauver-Harris Drug Amendment (1962).
Federal Hazardous Substances Act of 1960	Requires warning labels on hazardous household chemicals.
Kefauver-Harris Drug Amendment of 1962	Requires that manufacturers conduct tests to prove drug effectiveness and safety.
Consumer Credit Protection Act of 1968	Requires that lenders fully disclose true interest rates and all other charges to credit customers for loans and installment purchases.
Child Protection and Toy Safety Act of 1969	Prevents marketing of products so dangerous that adequate safety warnings cannot be given.
Public Health Smoking Act of 1970	Prohibits cigarette advertising on television and radio and revises the health hazard warning on cigarette packages.
Poison Prevention Labeling Act of 1970	Requires safety packaging for products that may be harmful to children.
National Environmental Policy Act of 1970	Established the Environmental Protection Agency to deal with various types of pollution and organizations that create pollution.
Public Health Cigarette Smoking Act of 1971	Prohibits tobacco advertising on radio and television.
Consumer Product Safety Act of 1972	Created the Consumer Product Safety Commission, which has authority to specify safety standards for most products.
Child Protection Act of 1990	Regulates the number of minutes of advertising on children's television.
Children's Online Privacy Protection Act of 1998	Empowers the FTC to set rules regarding how and when marketers must obtain parental permission before asking children marketing research questions.
Aviation Security Act of 2001	Requires airlines to take extra security measures to protect passengers, including the installation of stronger cockpit doors, improved baggage screening, and increased security training for airport personnel.
Homeland Security Act of 2002	Protects consumers against terrorist acts; created the Department of Homeland Security.
Do Not Call Law of 2003	Protects consumers against unwanted telemarketing calls.
CAN-SPAM Act of 2003	Protects consumers against unwanted e-mail, or spam.
Credit Card Act of 2009	Provides many credit card protections.
Restoring American Financial Stability Act of 2010	Created the Consumer Financial Protection Bureau to protect consumers against unfair, abusive, and deceptive financial practices.
Patient Protection and Affordable Care Act	Overhauled the U.S. healthcare system; mandated and subsidized health insurance for individuals.

of refrigerators, freezers, and air conditioners. Several states, including California and North Carolina, are considering levying a tax on all in-state commercial advertising.

Many states and cities are attempting to fight obesity by regulating fast-food chains and other restaurants. For example, California and New York have passed a law banning trans fats in restaurants and bakeries, New York City chain restaurants must now display calorie counts on menus, and Boston has banned trans fats in restaurants. New York City enacted a law prohibiting restaurants from selling soft drinks larger than 16 ounces, but the ban was overturned a day before it was to go into effect.

Consumer Product Safety Commission (CPSC) a federal agency established to protect the health and safety of consumers in and around their homes

4-7c Regulatory Agencies

Although some state regulatory bodies actively pursue violators of their marketing statutes, federal regulators generally have the greatest clout. The Consumer Product Safety Commission, the Federal Trade Commission, and the Food and Drug Administration are the three federal agencies most directly and actively involved in marketing affairs. These agencies, plus others, are discussed throughout the book, but a brief introduction is in order at this point.

CONSUMER PRODUCT SAFETY COMMISSION
The sole purpose of the **Consumer Product Safety Commission (CPSC)** is to protect the health and safety of consumers in and around their homes. The CPSC has the power to set mandatory safety standards for almost all products consumers use (about 15,000 items) and

can fine offending firms up to $500,000 and sentence their officers to up to a year in prison. It can also ban dangerous products from the marketplace. The CPSC oversees about 400 recalls per year. In 2008, Congress passed the Consumer Product Safety Improvement Act. The law is aimed primarily at children's products, which are defined as those used by individuals 12 years old or younger. The law addresses items such as cribs, electronics and video games, school supplies, science kits, toys, and pacifiers. The law requires mandatory testing and labeling and increases fines and prison time for violators.

FOOD AND DRUG ADMINISTRATION The **Food and Drug Administration (FDA)**, another powerful agency, is charged with enforcing regulations against selling and distributing adulterated, misbranded, or hazardous food and drug products. In 2009, the Tobacco Control Act was passed. This act gave the FDA authority to regulate tobacco products, with a special emphasis on preventing their use by children and young people and reducing the impact of tobacco on public health. Another recent FDA action is the "Bad Ad" program. It is geared toward health care providers to help them recognize misleading prescription drug promotions and gives them an easy way to report the activity to the FDA.

FEDERAL TRADE COMMISSION The **Federal Trade Commission (FTC)** is empowered to prevent persons or corporations from using unfair methods of competition in commerce. The FTC consists of five members, each holding office for seven years. Over the years, Congress has greatly expanded the powers of the FTC. Its responsibilities have grown so large that the FTC has created several bureaus to better organize its operations. One of the most important is the Bureau of Competition, which promotes and protects competition. The Bureau of Competition:

- reviews mergers and acquisitions, and challenges those that would likely lead to higher prices, fewer choices, or less innovation;

- seeks out and challenges anti-competitive conduct in the marketplace, including monopolization and agreements between competitors;

- promotes competition in industries where consumer impact is high, such as health care, real estate, oil and gas, technology, and consumer goods; and

- provides information and holds conferences and workshops for consumers, businesses, and policy makers on competition issues for market analysis.

The FTC's Bureau of Consumer Protection works for the consumer to prevent fraud, deception, and unfair business practices in the marketplace. The Bureau of Consumer Protection claims that it:

- enhances consumer confidence by enforcing federal laws that protect consumers;

- empowers consumers with free information to help them exercise their rights and to spot and avoid fraud and deception; and

- wants to hear from consumers who want to get information or file a complaint about fraud or identity theft.[82]

Another important FTC bureau is the Bureau of Economics. It provides economic analysis and support to antitrust and consumer protection investigations. Many consumer protection issues today involve the Internet.

4-7d Consumer Privacy

The popularity of the Internet for direct marketing, for collecting consumer data, and as a repository for sensitive consumer data has alarmed privacy-minded consumers. In 2003, the U.S. Congress passed the CAN-SPAM Act in an attempt to regulate unsolicited e-mail advertising. The act prohibits commercial e-mailers from using false addresses and presenting false or misleading information, among other restrictions.

Internet users who once felt fairly anonymous when using the Web are now disturbed by the amount of information marketers collect about them and their children as they visit various sites in cyberspace. The FTC, with jurisdiction under the Children's Online Privacy Protection Act, requires Web site operators to post a privacy policy on their home page and a link to the policy on every page where personal information is collected. An area of growing concern to privacy advocates is called *behavioral targeting*, which is discussed in more detail in Chapters 9 and 16. Behavioral targeting is used by researchers to better target advertising to Web surfers and users of search engines and social media.

Despite federal efforts, online tracking has become widespread and pervasive. A vast amount of personal data is collected through application software, commonly called *apps*. For example, some widely used apps on Facebook gather volumes of

Food and Drug Administration (FDA) a federal agency charged with enforcing regulations against selling and distributing adulterated, misbranded, or hazardous food and drug products

Federal Trade Commission (FTC) a federal agency empowered to prevent persons or corporations from using unfair methods of competition in commerce

information when they are downloaded. A Wall Street Journal analysis of the 100 most popular Facebook apps found that some seek e-mail addresses, current locations, and even sexual preferences. Information is collected not only from app users but also from their Facebook friends.

Successful tracking has created a $137 billion online-advertising business that is growing rapidly. There are more than 300 companies collecting data about users.[93] More than half the time, data collectors piggyback on each other. When a user visits a Web site that has a code for one type of tracking technology, the data collection triggers other tracking technologies that are not embedded on the site. Piggybacking means that Web sites really do not know how much data are being gathered about their users.

Acxiom uses more than 23,000 computer servers to collect, collate, and analyze consumer data. The firm has created the world's largest consumer database—the servers process more than fifty trillion data transactions a year. The database contains information on over 500 million consumers worldwide, with about 1,500 data points per person.[84] Acxiom customers include firms like E*Trade, Ford, Wells Fargo, Macy's, and many other major firms seeking consumer insights. Acxiom integrates online, mobile, and offline data to create in-depth consumer behavior portraits. The firm's proprietary software, PersonicX, assigns consumers to one of 70 detailed socioeconomic clusters. For example, the "savvy single" cluster includes mobile, upper-middle-class singles who do their banking online, attend pro sports events, are sensitive to prices, and respond to free-shipping offers.[85]

Many consumers don't want to be part of huge databases—they want their privacy back. Half of Americans are concerned about the wealth of personal data on the Internet.[86] Approximately 25 percent of American Internet users have downloaded privacy protection software.[87]

AVG PrivacyFix is a free program from antivirus software company AVG Technologies. The program's dashboard gives users a snapshot of what information they're actually sharing when they use social networks and services such as Facebook, LinkedIn, and Google. It pings users with a small red exclamation point if their privacy settings are weak and sends an alert when a visited website makes relevant changes to its privacy policies.[88]

Other products let people keep track of their personal data in other ways. Privowny, a free privacy toolbar for Firefox and Chrome, shows users which companies have their credit card numbers, phone numbers, and e-mail addresses. It also highlights sites that share user data.[89]

DuckDuckGo is a search engine that doesn't collect any information on its users and blocks all ad trackers from the search page.[90] Ixquick, another privacy-forward search engine, attracts more than 4 million users a day.[91]

4-8 COMPETITIVE FACTORS

The competitive environment encompasses the number of competitors a firm must face, the relative size of the competitors, and the degree of interdependence within the industry. Management has little control over the competitive environment confronting a firm.

4-8a Competition for Market Share and Profits

As U.S. population growth slows, global competition increases, costs rise, and available resources tighten,

A vending machine is a perfect example of competition for market share. Several brands are competing for the business of the person who has the munchies.

firms find that they must work harder to maintain their profits and market share, regardless of the form of the competitive market. Sometimes technology advances can usher in a whole new set of competitors that can change a firm's business model. For example, one of the United States' most competitive companies is Amazon. The firm has more than 245 million customers that rely on Amazon for everything from flat screen televisions to dog food.[92] The Reputation Institute has found Amazon to have the best reputation in America.[93] Amazon's success, spurred by extremely competitive prices, hurt Sears, JCPenney, Borders, and Best Buy, and even contributed to Circuit City's going out of business. At first glance, Google and Amazon don't seem to be competitors. Google is a search engine that sells ads and Amazon is a retailer that sells and delivers goods. However, Google is slowly getting into the market for on-demand goods and has launched a same-day delivery service called Google Express in several major markets. Google doesn't own massive warehouses like Amazon, but works with local retailers like Walgreens and Walmart. Conversely, people don't tend to think of Amazon as search engine, but if someone is looking for something to buy, she is probably looking on Amazon. Almost a third of people looking for something to buy start on Amazon.[94] Both companies already compete fiercely in the media streaming industry. Is this the beginning of the clash of the titans? Only time will tell.

4-8b Global Competition

Boeing is a very savvy international business competitor. Now Airbus, Boeing's primary competitor, is going to start assembling planes in the United States.

Many foreign competitors also consider the United States to be a ripe target market. Thus, a U.S. marketing manager can no longer focus only on domestic competitors. In automobiles, textiles, watches, televisions, steel, and many other areas, foreign competition has been strong. In the past, foreign firms penetrated U.S. markets by concentrating on price, but the emphasis has switched to product quality. Nestlé, Sony, and Rolls-Royce are noted for quality, not cheap prices. Global competition is discussed in much more detail in Chapter 5.

STUDY TOOLS 4

LOCATED AT BACK OF THE TEXTBOOK

☐ Rip out Chapter Review Card

LOCATED AT WWW.CENGAGEBRAIN.COM

☐ Review Key Terms Flashcards and create your own

☐ Track your knowledge & understanding of key concepts in marketing

☐ Complete practice and graded quizzes to prepare for tests

☐ Complete interactive content within the MKTG Online experience

☐ View the chapter highlight boxes within the MKTG Online experience

5 Developing a Global Vision

After you finish this chapter go to **PAGE 87** for **STUDY TOOLS.**

LEARNING OUTCOMES

After studying this chapter, you will be able to…

5-1 Discuss the importance of global marketing

5-2 Discuss the impact of multinational firms on the world economy

5-3 Describe the external environment facing global marketers

5-4 Identify the various ways of entering the global marketplace

5-5 List the basic elements involved in developing a global marketing mix

5-6 Discover how the Internet is affecting global marketing

5-1 REWARDS OF GLOBAL MARKETING AND THE SHIFTING GLOBAL BUSINESS LANDSCAPE

Today, global revolutions are underway in many areas of our lives: management, politics, communications, and technology. The word *global* has assumed a new meaning, referring to a boundless mobility and competition in social, business, and intellectual arenas. **Global marketing**—marketing that targets markets throughout the world—has become an imperative for business.

U.S. managers must develop a global vision not only to recognize and react to international marketing opportunities but also to remain competitive at home. Often a U.S. firm's toughest domestic competition comes from foreign companies. Consider the impact of Toyota and Honda on Ford and General Motors, for example. Moreover, a global vision enables a manager to understand that customer and distribution networks operate worldwide, blurring geographic and political barriers and making them increasingly irrelevant to business decisions. In summary, having a **global vision** means recognizing and reacting to international marketing opportunities, using effective global marketing strategies, and being aware of threats from foreign competitors in all markets.

World trade climbed from $200 billion in 1991 to more than $18 trillion in merchandise exports alone in 2015. Growth is not occurring evenly around the globe, however. In 2015, the United States was projected to

global marketing marketing that targets markets throughout the world

global vision recognizing and reacting to international marketing opportunities, using effective global marketing strategies, and being aware of threats from foreign competitors in all markets

grow by 3.2 percent. The European Union (discussed later in the chapter) was projected to grow 1.3 percent over the same span, while Japan was forecasted to grow just 0.8 percent due to struggles with economic policy. China's projected 2015 growth of 7.1 percent may seem gargantuan by comparison, but this actually represents the country's lowest growth rate in 15 years.[1] These low growth rates indicate that marketers are facing many challenges to their customary practices. Product development costs are rising, the life of products is getting shorter, and new technology is spreading around the world faster than ever. But marketing winners relish the pace of change instead of fear it.

Adopting a global vision can be very lucrative for a company. General Electric is involved in everything from private label credit cards to jet engines and health care equipment. There are now 24 countries outside of the United States where General Electric has annual sales of $1 billion or more. Today, the company has an order backlog of $244 billion.[2]

Despite the increasing availability of foreign customers, small businesses still account for only approximately 34 percent of U.S. exporting volume. Whether global business is daunting because of the various trade laws or tariffs, or because the markets are unfamiliar, small businesses are taking only slow, hesitant steps into the global market.

Of course, global marketing is not a one-way street whereby only U.S. companies sell their wares and services throughout the world. Foreign competition in the domestic market was once relatively rare but now is found in almost every industry. In fact, in many industries, U.S. businesses have lost significant market share to imported products. In electronics, cameras, automobiles, fine china, tractors, leather goods, and a host of other consumer and industrial products, U.S. companies have struggled at home to maintain their market shares against foreign competitors.

5-1a Importance of Global Marketing to the United States

Many countries depend more on international commerce than the United States does. For example, France, the United Kingdom, and Germany derive 28, 30, and 46 percent of their respective **gross domestic products (GDP)** from world trade—considerably more than the United States' 14 percent.[3] Gross domestic product is

gross domestic product (GDP) the total market value of all final goods and services produced in a country for a given time period

The Impact of Exports

Although some countries depend more on international commerce than the United States does, the impact of international business on the U.S. economy is still impressive:

- The United States exports about thirteen percent of its industrial production.[4]
- More than 11 million Americans hold jobs that are supported by exports.[5]
- Every U.S. state has realized net employment gains directly attributed to foreign trade.
- The United States exports more than $2.3 trillion in goods and services each year.[6]
- Every $1 billion in additional exports creates about 5,000 new U.S. jobs.[7]

the total market value of all final goods and services produced in a country for a given time period (usually a year or a quarter of a year). *Final* in this sense refers to final products that are sold, not to intermediate products used in the assembly of a final product. For example, if the value of a brake (an intermediate product) and that of a car (the final product) were both counted, the brake would be counted twice. Therefore, GDP counts only final goods and services in its valuation of a country's production.

The main types of goods that the United States exports are automobiles, agricultural goods, machines, airplanes, computers, chemicals, and petroleum products. Services that the United States exports are primarily educational, financial, legal, licensing-, and travel-related. When a foreign tourist visits the United States, all the money she spends while stateside is counted as a travel-related export. Why is this? Because she is buying a service product (travel) and is simply coming to the United States to pick it up!

Traditionally, only very large multinational companies have seriously attempted to compete worldwide. However, more and more small and medium sized companies have begun pursuing international markets, and some are even beginning to play a critical role in driving export growth. Today, a record 287,000 small and medium size firms export goods from the United States. The U.S. government is working with these firms to expand small business trade. The Export–Import bank of the United States, for example, helps thousands of small businesses obtain financing to expand their export sales. In 2014, the Export-Import Bank authorized $20.5 billion to support 164,000 U.S. jobs.[8]

outsourcing sending U.S. jobs abroad

In addition, the Small Business Administration backed more than 2,400 loans to 3,500 small businesses, supporting $3.4 billion in small business export sales.

JOB OUTSOURCING AND INSHORING The notion of **outsourcing** (sending U.S. jobs abroad) has been highly controversial for several decades. Many executives have said that it leads to corporate growth, efficiency, productivity, and revenue growth. Most companies see cost savings as a key driver in outsourcing. But outsourcing also has its negative side. For instance, Detroit has suffered as many factories in the auto industry have been shut down and relocated around the world. Ford manufactures the Fiesta compact sedan in several countries

Ford manufactures the Fiesta in several countries, but no Fiestas are being built in the United States.

Imports Can Help Too

Many people view exports as generally good for the United States and view imports as generally harmful to the United States. Indeed, waves upon waves of U.S. factories have had to close over the years because they could not compete with low-cost imports. China is widely known as the largest supplier of imports to the United States. Some claim that Chinese goods are so cheap because Chinese manufacturers pay their employees inhumane wages. Although China's wages are still relatively low, they have doubled since 2008. Further, nearly half of the United States' non-oil imports come from developed, high-wage countries like France, Germany, Ireland, and Switzerland. These countries all have higher average wages than does the United States, so low wages (and low prices) are only one factor driving the popularity of imports.[9]

While some employers can't compete with lower-cost imports, many U.S. workers actually owe their jobs to imports. Transportation workers move goods around the country. Workers for manufacturers, wholesalers, and retailers research and place orders with foreign suppliers for products ranging from paper boxes to computer servers.

More than 60 percent of U.S. imports are raw materials, components, and machinery used to make goods or grow crops.[10] American manufacturers use these imported inputs when locally produced substitutes are either not available or too expensive. Imported inputs thus keep American manufacturing competitive—both locally and globally.

©StudioM1

around the world—including Mexico—but no Fiestas are being built in the United States.

Recently, some companies have begun to suspect that outsourcing's negatives outweigh its positives. Improperly designed parts and products have caused production delays, and rising wages in the developing world have rendered American rates more competitive. Increased fuel and transportation costs associated with long-distance shipping, coupled with falling U.S. energy costs, have given impetus to **inshoring**, returning production jobs to the United States. Rapid consumer product innovation has led to the need to keep product designers, marketing researchers, logistics experts, and manufacturers in close proximity so that they can work quickly as a team. Thus, shrinking development and manufacturing timelines have further contributed to inshoring.

Walmart is also aiding the cause by promising to stock more "Made in the USA" goods. The firm plans to buy $50 billion of such goods as a start. This decision has already caused a ripple of effects. Redman & Associates, which manufactures battery-powered children's cars in China, recently announced a new factory in Rogers, Arkansas—not too far from Walmart's Bentonville, Arkansas headquarters.[11]

BENEFITS OF GLOBALIZATION Traditional economic theory says that globalization relies on

competition to drive down prices and increase product and service quality. Business goes to the countries that operate most efficiently and/or have the technology to produce what is needed. In summary, globalization expands economic freedom, spurs competition, and raises the productivity and living standards of people in countries that open themselves to the global marketplace. For less developed countries, globalization also offers access to foreign capital, global export markets, and advanced technology while breaking the monopoly of inefficient and protected domestic producers. Faster growth, in turn, reduces poverty, encourages democratization, and promotes higher labor and environmental standards. Though government officials in developing countries may face more difficult choices as a result of globalization, their citizens enjoy greater individual freedom. In this sense, globalization acts as a check on governmental power by making it more difficult for governments to abuse the freedom and property of their citizens.

Globalization deserves credit for helping lift many millions out of poverty and for improving standards of living of low-wage families. In developing countries around the world, globalization has created a vibrant middle class that has elevated the standard of living for hundreds of millions of people.

inshoring returning production jobs to the United States

5-2 MULTINATIONAL FIRMS

The United States has a number of large companies that are global marketers. Many of them have been very successful. A company that is heavily engaged in international trade, beyond exporting and importing, is called a **multinational corporation**. A multinational corporation moves resources, goods, services, and skills across national boundaries without regard to the country in which its headquarters is located.

Multinationals often develop their global business in stages. In the first stage, companies operate in one country and sell into others. Second-stage multinationals set up foreign subsidiaries to handle sales in one country. In the third stage, multinationals operate an entire line of business in another country. The fourth stage has evolved primarily due to the Internet and involves mostly high-tech companies. For these firms, the executive suite is virtual. Their top executives and core corporate functions are in different countries, wherever the firms can gain a competitive edge through the availability of talent or capital, low costs, or proximity to their most important customers.

A multinational company may have several worldwide headquarters, depending on where certain markets or technologies are located. Britain's APV, a maker of food-processing equipment, has a different headquarters for each of its worldwide businesses.

Many U.S.-based multinationals earn a large percentage of their total revenue abroad. Caterpillar, the construction-equipment company, receives 67 percent of its revenue from overseas markets, and General Electric earns 54 percent of its revenue abroad. Other large American exporters include General Motors, Ford, Hewlett-Packard, and IBM.

5-2a Are Multinationals Beneficial?

Although multinationals comprise far less than 1 percent of U.S. companies, they account for about nineteen percent of all private jobs, 25 percent of all private wages, 48 percent of total exports of goods, and a remarkable 74 percent of nonpublic research and development (R&D) spending.[12] For decades, U.S. multinationals have driven an outsized share of U.S. productivity growth, the foundation of rising standards of living for everyone.

multinational corporation a company that is heavily engaged in international trade, beyond exporting and importing

capital intensive using more capital than labor in the production process

The role of multinational corporations in developing nations is a subject of controversy. The ability of multinationals to tap financial, physical, and human resources from all over the world and combine them economically and profitably can benefit any country. They also often possess and can transfer the most up-to-date technology. Critics, however, claim that often the wrong kind of technology is transferred to developing nations. Usually, it is **capital intensive** (requiring a greater expenditure for equipment than for labor) and thus does not substantially increase employment. A "modern sector" then emerges in the nation, employing a small proportion of the labor force with relatively high productivity and income levels and with increasingly capital-intensive technologies. In addition, multinationals sometimes push for very quick production turn-around times, which has led to long hours and dangerous working conditions. In 2013, a Bangladesh garment factory collapsed and more than 1,100 people died as they rushed to meet production quotas for firms such as Benetton and Marks & Spencer.[13] Other critics say that the firms take more wealth out of developing nations than they bring in, thus widening the gap between rich and poor nations. The petroleum industry in particular has been heavily criticized in the past for its actions in some developing countries.

To counter such criticism, more and more multinationals are taking a proactive role in being good global citizens. Sometimes companies are spurred to action by government regulation; in other cases, multinationals are attempting to protect their good brand names. Some companies, such as Apple, Walmart, Calvin Klein, and Tommy Hilfiger, have begun conducting factory inspections to protect the health and safety of their workers. Coca-Cola has trained a half million women in 44 countries to

Coca-Cola has made an effort to provide opportunities for over half a million women in 44 countries.

Ellen Mack/Moment/Getty Images

become small-scale businesspeople. Coca-Cola has nurtured female owners of "sari-sari" convenience stores in the Philippines, farmers growing mangos in Kenya, and poor villagers building tiny recycling operations out of discarded bottles from trash heaps in Mexico.[14]

5-2b Global Marketing Standardization

Traditionally, marketing-oriented multinational corporations have operated somewhat differently in each country. They use a strategy of providing different product features, packaging, advertising, and so on. However, Ted Levitt, a former Harvard professor, has described a trend toward what he refers to as "global marketing," with a slightly different meaning.[15] He contends that communication and technology have made the world smaller so that almost all consumers everywhere want all the things they have heard about, seen, or experienced. Thus, he sees the emergence of global markets for standardized consumer products on a huge scale, as opposed to segmented foreign markets with different products. In this book, *global marketing* is defined as individuals and organizations using a global vision to effectively market goods and services across national boundaries. To make the distinction, we can refer to Levitt's notion as **global marketing standardization**.

Global marketing standardization presumes that the markets throughout the world are becoming more alike. Firms practicing global marketing standardization produce "globally standardized products" to be sold the same way all over the world. Most smartphones and tablets, for example, are standardized globally except for the languages displayed. These devices allow the user to switch easily from one language to another. Uniform production should enable companies to lower production and marketing costs and increase profits. Levitt has cited Coca-Cola, Colgate-Palmolive, and McDonald's as successful global marketers. His critics point out, however, that the success of these three companies is really based on variation, not on offering the same product everywhere. McDonald's, for example, changes its salad dressings and provides self-serve espresso for French tastes. It sells bulgogi burgers in South Korea and falafel burgers in Egypt. Further, the fact that Coca-Cola and Colgate-Palmolive sell some of their products in more than 160 countries does not signify that they have adopted a high degree of standardization for all their products globally. Only three Coca-Cola brands are standardized, and one of them, Sprite, has a different formulation in Japan.

Companies with separate subsidiaries in other countries can be said to operate using a multidomestic strategy. A **multidomestic strategy** occurs when multinational firms enable individual subsidiaries to compete independently in domestic markets. Simply put, multidomestic strategy is how multinational firms use strategic business units (see Chapter 2). Colgate-Palmolive uses both strategies: Axion paste dishwashing detergent, for example, was formulated for developing countries, and La Croix Plus detergent was custom made for the French market.

Nevertheless, some multinational corporations are moving beyond multidomestic strategies toward a degree of global marketing standardization. Colgate toothpaste and Nike shoes are marketed the same ways globally, using global marketing standardization.

5-3 EXTERNAL ENVIRONMENT FACED BY GLOBAL MARKETERS

A global marketer or a firm considering global marketing must consider the external environment. Many of the same environmental factors that operate in the domestic market also exist internationally. These factors include culture, economic development, the global economy, political structure and actions, demographic makeup, and natural resources.

5-3a Culture

Central to any society is the common set of values shared by its citizens that determines what is socially acceptable. Culture underlies the family, the educational system, religion, and the social class system. The network of social organizations generates overlapping roles and status positions. These values and roles have a tremendous effect on people's preferences and thus on marketers' options. A company that does not understand a country's culture is doomed to failure in that country. Cultural blunders lead to misunderstandings and often perceptions of rudeness or even incompetence. For example, when people in India shake hands, they sometimes do so rather limply. This is not a sign of weakness or disinterest; instead, a soft handshake conveys respect. Avoiding eye contact is also a sign of deference in India.

When eBay entered China in 2001, it did quite well because it had no competition. But when the Chinese

global marketing standardization production of uniform products that can be sold the same way all over the world

multidomestic strategy when multinational firms enable individual subsidiaries to compete independently in domestic markets

With a keen understanding of Chinese culture, Taobao proved to be stiff competition for eBay in China

competitor Taobao launched, eBay quickly lost ground. Its market share dropped from eighty percent to 7 percent in just five years. If you looked at eBay's site in China, you would recognize it—it looks very similar to eBay's United States site. This failure to adapt to Chinese culture led to eBay's decline: Americans do not want celebrity gossip or social interaction when they shop online, but the Chinese do.

Taobao is more than a one-stop shop for online shoppers—it is a social forum as well. The site features pictures and descriptions—very long descriptions—of products, but shoppers can also chat online about current trends, share shopping tips, and catch up on celebrity news at Taobao. Chinese shoppers are more inclined to follow fashion trends than American shoppers are, so Taobao lists trends in order of popularity, unlike eBay. Finally, when eBay entered China, it did not allow direct communication between buyers and sellers. As in the United States, all communication was handled by eBay's messaging system. This system was not well received in China because Chinese are much less likely than Americans to buy from strangers. Chinese Internet users expect Web sites to be much denser than many Western Internet users are used to. That is, Chinese Web sites tend to have more links, many more images, and longer page lengths than Western Web sites do. Eye-grabbing animations and floating images are common on Chinese sites. A page with less text, fewer embedded links, and nice imagery might be called "well-designed" by Western Internet users but "boring" by Chinese ones.

User experience issues also plague the digital divide between China and the West. In China, form fields like "first name," "middle name," and "last name" often confuse users. If you ask for name information this way in an online form, many Chinese users will be left scratching their heads. The simplest and most common approach to accommodate this cultural difference is to ask simply "name" instead of "first," "middle," and "last name." Similarly, addresses are not written in line with street names in Japan. For Japanese consumers, this small issue can make it incredibly hard to order products from Western Web sites.[16]

Language is another important aspect of culture that can create problems for marketers. Marketers must take care in translating product names, slogans, instructions, and promotional messages so as not to convey the wrong meaning. Free translation software, such as babelfish.com or Google Translate, allows users to input text in one language and output in another language. But marketers must take care using the software, as it can have unintended results—the best being unintelligible, the worst being insulting.

Each country has its own customs and traditions that determine business practices and influence negotiations with foreign customers. In many countries, personal relationships are more important than financial considerations. For instance, skipping social engagements in Mexico may lead to lost sales. Negotiations in Japan often include long evenings of dining, drinking, and entertaining, and only after a close personal relationship has been formed do business negotiations begin.

Making successful sales presentations abroad requires a thorough understanding of the country's culture. Germans, for example, do not like risk and need strong reassurance. A successful presentation to a German client will emphasize three points: the bottom-line benefits of the product or service, that there will be strong service support, and that the product is guaranteed. In southern Europe, it is an insult to show a price list. Without negotiating, you will not close the sale. The English want plenty of documentation for product claims and are less likely to simply accept the word of the sales representative. Scandinavian and Dutch companies are more likely to approach business transactions as Americans do than are companies in any other country.

5-3b Economic Factors

A second major factor in the external environment facing the global marketer is the level of economic development in the countries where it operates. In

PART ONE: The World of Marketing

general, complex and sophisticated industries are found in developed countries, and more basic industries are found in less developed nations. Average family incomes are higher in the more developed countries compared to the less developed countries. Larger incomes mean greater purchasing power and demand, not only for consumer goods and services, but also for the machinery and workers required to produce consumer goods.

According to the World Bank, the average *gross national income (GNI)* per capita for the world is $10,679.[17] GNI is a country's GDP (defined earlier) together with its income received from other countries (mainly interest and dividends) less similar payments made to other countries. The United States' GNI per capita is $53,470, but it is not the world's highest. That honor goes to Bermuda at $104,610. Of course, there are many very poor countries: Rwanda, $630; Afghanistan, $690; Ethiopia, $470; Liberia, $410; and Democratic Republic of Congo, $430.[18] GNI per capita is one measure of the ability of a country's citizens to buy various goods and services. A marketer with a global vision can use these data to aid in measuring market potential in countries around the globe.

Not only is per capita income a consideration when going abroad, but so is the cost of doing business in a country. Although it is not the same as the cost of doing business, we can gain insights into expenses by examining the cost of living in various cities.[19]

5-3c The Global Economy

A global marketer today must be fully aware of the intertwined nature of the global economy. In the past, the size of the U.S. economy was so large that global markets tended to move up or down depending on its health. It was said, "If America sneezes, then the rest of the world catches a cold." This is still true today. Slow growth in America—and even slower growth in Europe and Japan—have hampered global economic progress. Even China's astronomical growth rate is much lower today than in recent years. Unfortunately, politics is playing an increasingly important role in how multinational firms serve their markets in countries like China and Russia. Despite politics, the BRIC (Brazil, Russia, India, and China) countries will play an increasingly important role in the global economy for years to come. By 2020, Brazil's market will top $1.6 trillion. The consumer markets in India and China are together projected to top $10 trillion in 2020.[20]

There are more consumers trading up to higher-priced, higher-quality products in emerging markets than there are in developed nations. This holds especially true for big-ticket items like housing, cars, and large appliances. Seventy percent of consumers in China and 67 percent of consumers in India cite "brand name and reputation" as key reasons for trading up to higher-priced goods and services.[21]

About half of all Indians have a mobile subscription. In fact, more people in India have mobile phones than have toilets. The Indian middle class spends three hours a day on mobile—more time than they spend on TV. Clearly, targeting consumers via mobile is critical in India.[22]

5-3d Political Structure and Actions

Political structure is a fourth important variable facing global marketers. Government policies run the gamut from no private ownership and minimal individual freedom to little central government and maximum personal freedom. As rights of private property increase, government-owned industries and centralized planning tend to decrease. But a political environment is rarely at one extreme or the other. India, for instance, is a republic with elements of socialism, monopoly capitalism, and competitive capitalism in its political ideology.

A recent World Bank study found that less regulation fosters the strongest economies. The least regulated and most efficient economies are concentrated among countries with well-established common-law traditions, including Australia, Canada, New Zealand, the United Kingdom, and the United States. On par with the best performers are Singapore and Hong Kong. Not far behind are Denmark, Norway, and Sweden—social democracies that recently streamlined their business regulation. In the United States, starting a new business—the future lifeblood of any economy—on average takes 7 procedures, 25 days, and costs the entrepreneur 32 percent of income per capita in fees. While it takes as little as one procedure, half a day, and almost nothing in fees in New Zealand, a businessperson must wait 208 days in Suriname and 144 in Venezuela.[23]

It is not uncommon for international politics to affect business laws. China recently started investigating dozens of America's largest multinationals—companies structured to compete with other corporations, not governments. Among the investigated companies, Google left China after enduring cyber-attacks and governmental pressure to release user information. Apple CEO Tim Cook expressed "sincere apologies" in the wake of Beijing's media campaign against the company. Adobe shut down both its China headquarters and ended its research and development in the country.[24] Not all of

China's oversight is excessive, however. Mead Johnson and Abbott Laboratories were fined $110 million by Chinese authorities for price fixing. Glaxo Smith Kline was fined $490 million for bribing doctors to prescribe its drugs.[25] Walmart was fined $9.8 million for misleading pricing, selling poor quality products, and selling donkey meat that turned out to be fox. But Walmart is also doing something rare for a Western company: telling the Chinese government that it needs to clean up its *own* act.

In the U.S. and most other countries, manufacturers rather than retailers are responsible for ensuring product quality. In China, however, retailers are accountable. In 2014, Walmart executives met with China's Food and Drug Administration and urged officials to step up their inspections of food purveyors. Walmart later reported that it ended relationships with 300 suppliers in 2014 because they didn't pass the retailer's testing and safety standards. Those 300 suppliers had paperwork proving that they passed muster with local food watchdogs, however. Clearly, international business can be a proxy for political jousting when governments enter the mix.[26]

Russia has also directly attacked American companies in the wake of political disagreement. In 2014, Russia seized the Crimean peninsula, leading to an onslaught of sanctions from the European Union, the United States, and others. Russia fought back, banning these countries from selling billions of dollars worth of fruits, vegetables, fish, and meat to Russians. Russia then went after McDonald's, closing down a number of restaurants for "sanitary conditions."[27]

LEGAL CONSIDERATIONS As you can see, legal considerations are often intertwined with the political environment. In France, nationalistic sentiments led to a law that requires pop music stations to play at least forty percent of their songs in French (even though French teenagers love American and English rock and roll).

Many legal structures are designed to either encourage or limit trade:

- **Tariff:** a tax levied on the goods entering a country. Because a tariff is a tax, it will either reduce the profits of the firms paying the tariff

or raise prices to buyers, or both. Normally, a tariff raises prices of the imported goods and makes it easier for domestic firms to compete. In general, the U.S. economy is open to imports. America has tariffs on 1,000 product categories, but at a relatively low rate of 1.4 percent.[28] Exceptions to this are footwear and apparel, which carry a rate that is ten percent higher. In 2014, China and the U.S. slashed tariffs on a range of technology products. The agreement covered $1 trillion in trade and benefited companies like Apple, Intel, and Microsoft.[29] Nearly every piece of military gear that recruits get when they show up for training is made in the United States. The Pentagon recently conceded that even running shoes should be made domestically. New Balance will likely review the contract outlining production of up to 250,000 pairs of running shoes per year.[30]

- **Quota** a limit on the amount of a specific product that can enter a country. Several U.S. companies have sought quotas as a means of protection from foreign competition. The United States, for example, has a quota on raw cane sugar.

- **Boycott:** the exclusion of all products from certain countries or companies. Governments use boycotts to exclude companies from countries with which they have a political dispute. Several Arab nations have boycotted products made in Israel.

- **Exchange control:** a law compelling a company earning foreign exchange from its exports to sell it to a control agency, usually a central bank. A company wishing to buy goods abroad must first obtain a foreign currency exchange from the control agency. Some countries with foreign exchange controls are Argentina, Brazil, China, Iceland, India, North Korea, Russia, and Venezuela.

- **Market grouping (also known as a common trade alliance):** occurs when several countries agree to work together to form a common trade area that enhances trade opportunities. The best-known market grouping is the European Union (EU), which will be discussed later in this chapter.

- **Trade agreement:** an agreement to stimulate international trade. Not all government efforts are meant to stifle imports or investment by foreign corporations. The largest Latin American trade agreement is **Mercosur**, which includes Argentina, Bolivia, Brazil, Chile, Colombia, Ecuador, Paraguay, Peru, Uruguay,

Mercosur the largest Latin American trade agreement; includes Argentina, Bolivia, Brazil, Chile, Colombia, Ecuador, Paraguay, Peru, Uruguay, and Venezuela

NEW BALANCE'S STATESIDE STRIDE

New Balance is the only athletic shoe manufacturer that still operates factories in

Leonard Zhukovsky/Shutterstock.com

the United States. These plants produce about a quarter of the shoes that New Balance sells domestically—the rest are imported.

The company has invested in new machines and cut out waste at its U.S. plants, which together employ 1,350 people. But even in its most streamlined form, shoe making remains relatively labor-intensive. New Balance reports that despite its investments, it still costs 25 to 35 percent more to produce shoes in the United States than it does in Asia.

Why does New Balance continue to produce shoes in the United States. even though that means settling for less profit? The U.S. factories' flexibility allows the company to count turnaround times in days rather than weeks, making up for some of the company's higher costs. However, a push by rivals to do away with tariffs on imported running shoes—part of a larger trade deal—could finally tip the scales against New Balance's American strategy.

and Venezuela. The elimination of most tariffs among the trading partners has resulted in trade revenues of more than $16 billion annually. The economic boom created by Mercosur will undoubtedly cause other nations to seek trade agreements on their own or to enter Mercosur.

THE URUGUAY ROUND, THE FAILED DOHA ROUND, AND BILATERAL AGREEMENTS The **Uruguay Round** is a trade agreement that has dramatically lowered trade barriers worldwide. Adopted in 1994, the agreement has been signed by 159 nations. It is the most ambitious global trade agreement ever negotiated. The agreement has reduced tariffs by one-third worldwide—a move that has raised global income by

over $235 billion annually.[31] Perhaps most notable is the recognition of new global realities. For the first time, a trade agreement covers services, intellectual property rights, and trade-related investment measures such as exchange controls.

The Uruguay Round made several major changes in world trading practices:

- **Entertainment, pharmaceuticals, integrated circuits, and software:** The rules protect patents, copyrights, and trademarks for twenty years. Computer programs receive 50 years of protection, and semiconductor chips receive 10 years of protection. But many developing nations were given a decade to phase in patent protection for drugs. Also France, which limits the number of U.S. movies and television shows that can be shown, refused to liberalize market access for the U.S. entertainment industry.

- **Financial, legal, and accounting services:** Services came under international trading rules for the first time, creating a vast opportunity for these competitive U.S. industries. Now, it is easier for managers and key personnel to be admitted to a country. Licensing standards for professionals, such as doctors, cannot discriminate against foreign applicants. That is, foreign applicants cannot be held to higher standards than domestic practitioners.

- **Agriculture:** Europe is gradually reducing farm subsidies, opening new opportunities for such U.S. farm exports as wheat and corn. Japan and Korea are beginning to import rice. But U.S. growers of sugar and citrus fruit have had their subsidies trimmed.

- **Textiles and apparel:** Strict quotas limiting imports from developing countries are being phased out, causing further job losses in the U.S. clothing trade. But retailers are the big winners, because past quotas have added $15 billion a year to clothing prices.

- **A new trade organization:** The **World Trade Organization (WTO)** replaced the old **General Agreement on Tariffs and Trade (GATT)**, which was created in 1948. The WTO eliminated the extensive loopholes of which GATT members took advantage. Today, all WTO members must

Uruguay Round a trade agreement to dramatically lower trade barriers worldwide; created the World Trade Organization

World Trade Organization (WTO) a trade organization that replaced the old General Agreement on Tariffs and Trade (GATT)

General Agreement on Tariffs and Trade (GATT) a trade agreement that contained loopholes enabling countries to avoid trade-barrier reduction agreements

fully comply with all agreements under the Uruguay Round. The WTO also has an effective dispute settlement procedure with strict time limits to resolve disputes. Beijing recently lost a case on rare earth metals such as molybdenum and tungsten. The WTO charged that China's policies violated global trade rules and that Beijing was using export quotas to restrict trade. China claimed that the laws were for environmental protection. But the WTO said that this was an invalid reason for limiting exports.[32]

The latest round of WTO trade talks began in Doha, Qatar, in 2001. For the most part, the periodic meetings of WTO members under the Doha Round have been very contentious. One of the most contentious goals of the round was for the major developing countries, known collectively as BRIC (Brazil, Russia, India, and China), to lower tariffs on industrial goods in exchange for European and American tariff and subsidy cuts on farm products. Concerned that lowering tariffs would result in an economically damaging influx of foreign cotton, sugar, and rice, China and India demanded a safeguard clause that would allow them to raise tariffs on those crops if imports surged. A breakthrough came in 2014 when the United States and India reached an agreement over food security issues. Now India and the United States are looking forward to pushing the Doha Round to a conclusion.[33] Will it happen? Only time will tell.

Because many countries still view the Doha Round as virtually dead-in-the-water, several other coalitions have formed to negotiate alternative free-trade alliances. The Transatlantic Trade and Investment Partnership, which saw negotiations begin in 2013 and continue into 2015, is a proposed partnership between the United States and the European Union. The agreement would be a major benefit to Europe because of the continent's continued economic weakness.[34] A second set of negotiations are being conducted for the Trans-Pacific Partnership. The major goals of this partnership, formed by Australia, Brunei, Chile, Malaysia, New Zealand, Peru, Singapore,

The Doha Round suffers from fears of mass imports on agricultural goods that would economically stunt domestic producers.

Jim Barber/ShutterStock.com

Vietnam, and the United States, are to enhance trade and investment, promote innovation, and spur economic growth and development. The negotiations also center on control of data, intellectual property protection, and environmental and safety standards. The agreement, still being negotiated as of 2015, will cover about 40 percent of the world's gross domestic product and a third of all global trade.[35]

A third agreement, the Pacific Alliance, was signed in 2012 by Colombia, Chile, Peru, and Mexico to create a single region for the free movement of goods, services, investment, capital, and people. Full implementation of the Pacific Alliance, which created a market of 210 million people, began in 2014.[36] Costa Rica was recently accepted as a fifth member of the Alliance.

NORTH AMERICAN FREE TRADE AGREEMENT

At the time it was instituted, the **North American Free Trade Agreement (NAFTA)** created the world's largest free trade zone. Ratified by the U.S. Congress in 1993, the agreement includes Canada, the United States, and Mexico, with a combined population of 450 million. Since NAFTA's implementation in 1994, trade with Canada and Mexico has grown three and a half fold to $1.2 trillion. These countries now buy about one-third of U.S. merchandise exports.[37] The Act supports 14 million U.S. jobs.

The main impact of NAFTA was to open the Mexican market to U.S. companies. When the treaty went into effect, tariffs on about half the items traded

North American Free Trade Agreement (NAFTA) an agreement between Canada, the United States, and Mexico that created the world's then-largest free trade zone

across the Rio Grande disappeared. The pact removed a web of Mexican licensing requirements, quotas, and tariffs that limited transactions in U.S. goods and services. For instance, the pact allowed United States and Canadian financial-services companies to own subsidiaries in Mexico.

In August 2007, the three member countries met in Canada to tweak NAFTA but not make substantial changes. For example, the members agreed to further remove trade barriers on hogs, steel, consumer electronics, and chemicals. They also directed the North American Steel Trade Committee, which represents the three governments, to focus on subsidized steel from China.

DOMINICAN REPUBLIC–CENTRAL AMERICA FREE TRADE AGREEMENT The **Dominican Republic–Central America Free Trade Agreement (CAFTA–DR)** was instituted in 2005. Because it joined after the original agreement was signed, the Dominican Republic was amended to the original agreement title (Central America Free Trade Agreement, or CAFTA). Besides the United States and the Dominican Republic, the agreement includes Costa Rica, El Salvador, Guatemala, Honduras, and Nicaragua.

As of 2015, all consumer and industrial goods exported to CAFTA-DR countries are no longer subject to tariffs. Tariffs on agricultural goods will be phased out by 2020. The agreement also covers intellectual property rights, transparency, electronic commerce, and telecommunications. The CAFTA-DR countries comprise the 14th largest U.S. export market in the world. Today, the U.S. exports more than $30 billion in goods to the five Central American countries and Dominican Republic.[38]

EUROPEAN UNION The **European Union (EU)** is one of the world's most important free trade zones and now encompasses most of Europe. More than a free trade zone, it is also a political and economic community. As a free trade zone, it guarantees the freedom of movement of people, goods, services, and capital between member states. It also maintains a common trade policy with outside nations and a regional development policy. The EU represents member nations in the WTO. Recently, the EU also began venturing into foreign policy as well, getting involved in issues such as Iran's refining of uranium.

The European Union currently has twenty-eight member states: Austria, Belgium, Bulgaria, Croatia, Cyprus, the Czech Republic, Denmark, Estonia, Finland, France, Germany, Greece, Hungary, Ireland, Italy, Latvia, Lithuania, Luxembourg, Malta, Netherlands, Poland, Portugal, Romania, Slovakia, Slovenia, Spain, Sweden, and the United Kingdom. There are currently six candidate countries: Albania, Iceland, the Republic of Macedonia, Montenegro, Serbia, and Turkey. In addition, the western Balkan countries of Bosnia and Herzegovina and Kosovo are recognized as potential candidates.[39]

In early 2010, Greece entered a financial crisis that highlighted the challenges of a large currency union where member nations maintain responsibility for their own fiscal policies. Unable to devalue its currency to boost sales of products without injuring other member nations, Greece turned to member states for a bailout. In 2015, the anti-austerity Syriza party was elected in Greece. The newly elected officials vowed to have Greek debt forgiven and to enact a program of stimulus spending. The only leverage Greece has is to threaten to stop using the euro currency, an act that would cause a banking crises and a severe recession at home.[40]

The EU is the largest economy in the world (with the United States very close behind). The EU is also a huge market, with a population of nearly 500 million and a GDP of $18.4 trillion.[41] The United States and the EU have the largest bilateral trade and investment relationship in world history. Together, they account for almost half of the entire world GDP and nearly one-third of world trade flows. United States and EU companies have invested trillions of dollars in each other's economies, contributing to significant job growth on both sides of the Atlantic. The relationship between these two economic superpowers has also shaped the global economy as a whole—the United States and the EU are primary trade partners for almost every other country in the world.[42]

The EU is a very attractive market for multinational firms. But the EU presents marketing challenges because, even with standardized regulations, marketers will not be able to produce a single European product for a generic European consumer. With more than 14 different languages and individual national customs, Europe will always be far more diverse than the United States. Thus, product differences will continue to be necessary. Atag Holdings NV, a diversified Dutch company whose main business is kitchen appliances, was confident it could cater to both the "potato" and "spaghetti" belts—marketers' terms for

Dominican Republic-Central America Free Trade Agreement (CAFTA-DR) a trade agreement instituted in 2005 that includes Costa Rica, the Dominican Republic, El Salvador, Guatemala, Honduras, Nicaragua, and the United States

European Union (EU) a free trade zone encompassing 28 European countries

consumer preferences in northern and southern Europe. But Atag quickly discovered that preferences vary much more than that. Ovens, burner shape and size, knob and clock placement, temperature range, and colors vary greatly from country to country. Although Atag's kitchenware unit has lifted foreign sales to 25 percent of its total from 4 percent in the mid-1990s, it now believes that its diversified products and speed in delivering them—rather than the magic bullet of a Europroduct—will keep it competitive.

An entirely different type of problem facing global marketers is the possibility of a protectionist movement by the EU against outsiders. For example, European automakers have proposed holding Japanese imports at roughly their current ten percent market share. The Irish, Danes, and Dutch do not make cars and have unrestricted home markets; they would be unhappy about limited imports of Toyotas and Nissans. But France has a strict quota on Japanese cars to protect Renault and Peugeot. These local carmakers could be hurt if the quota is raised at all.

THE WORLD BANK, THE INTERNATIONAL MONETARY FUND, AND THE G-20 Two international financial organizations are instrumental in fostering global trade. The **World Bank** offers low-interest loans to developing nations. Originally, the purpose of the loans was to help these nations build infrastructure such as roads, power plants, schools, drainage projects, and hospitals. Now the World Bank offers loans to help developing nations relieve their debt burdens. To receive the loans, countries must pledge to lower trade barriers and aid private enterprise. In addition to making loans, the World Bank is a major source of advice and information for developing nations. The **International Monetary Fund (IMF)** was founded in 1945, one year after the creation of the World Bank, to promote trade through financial cooperation and eliminate trade barriers in the process. The IMF makes short-term loans to member nations that are unable to meet their budgetary expenses. It operates as a lender of last resort for troubled nations, such as Greece. In exchange for these emergency loans, IMF lenders frequently extract significant commitments from the borrowing nations to address the problems that led to the crises. These steps may include curtailing imports or even devaluing the currency. Greece, working with both the IMF and the EU, has raised taxes to unprecedented levels, cut government spending (including pensions), and implemented labor reforms such as reducing minimum wage as part of its austerity measures to receive loans from the IMF and the European Union.

The **Group of Twenty (G-20)** finance ministers and central bank governors was established in 1999 to bring together industrialized and developing economies to discuss key issues in the global economy. The G-20 is a forum for international economic development that promotes discussion between industrial and emerging-market countries on key issues related to global economic stability. By contributing to the strengthening of the international financial system and providing opportunities for discussion on national policies, international cooperation, and international financial institutions, the G-20 helps to support growth and development across the globe. The members of the G-20 are shown in Exhibit 5.1.

Artefficient/Shutterstock.com

EXHIBIT 5.1	MEMBERS OF THE G-20		
Argentina	European Union	Italy	South Africa
Australia	France	Japan	Republic of Korea
Brazil	Germany	Mexico	Turkey
Canada	India	Russia	United Kingdom
China	Indonesia	Saudi Arabia	United States

World Bank an international bank that offers low-interest loans, advice, and information to developing nations

International Monetary Fund (IMF) an international organization that acts as a lender of last resort, providing loans to troubled nations, and also works to promote trade through financial cooperation

Group of Twenty (G-20) a forum for international economic development that promotes discussion between industrial and emerging-market countries on key issues related to global economic stability

Members of the G-20 met in Brisbane, Australia in November 2014. The meeting focused on raising global growth to deliver better living standards and create high-quality jobs. In Brisbane, the G-20 set a goal to lift global GDP by two percent by 2018. This alone would add more than $2 trillion to the global economy and would create millions of new jobs.[43]

5-3e Demographic Makeup

The world's wealth is not evenly distributed. In fact, it is very highly concentrated. Only 0.7 percent of the world's population has assets valued at $1 million or more. This group owns an astounding 44 percent of all the world's wealth. The next 7.9 percent of the population owns an additional 41 percent of the world's wealth. That leaves 91.4 percent of the population controlling the remaining 14.7 percent of the wealth.[44] Two primary determinants of any consumer market are wealth and population.

China, India, and Indonesia are three of the most densely populated nations in the world. But that fact alone is not particularly useful to marketers. They also need to know whether the population is mostly urban or rural, because marketers may not have easy access to rural consumers. Belgium, for example, with about ninety percent of the population living in urban settings, is a more attractive market.

Another key demographic consideration is age. There is a wide gap between the older populations of the industrialized countries and the vast working-age populations of developing countries. This gap has enormous implications for economies, businesses, and the competitiveness of individual countries. It means that while Europe and Japan struggle with pension schemes and the rising cost of health care, countries like Brazil, China, and Mexico can reap the fruits of a *demographic dividend*. Caused by shifting birthrate trends, the demographic dividend results in a temporary bulge in the number of working-age people. This often leads to falling labor costs, a healthier and more educated population, and the entry of millions of women into the workforce. Population experts have estimated that one-third of East Asia's recent economic upswing can be attributed to a beneficial age structure. But the miracle occurred only because the governments had policies in place to educate their people, create jobs, and improve health.

5-3f Natural Resources

A final factor in the external environment that has become more evident in the past decade is the shortage of natural resources. For example, petroleum shortages have created huge amounts of wealth for oil-producing countries such as Norway, Saudi Arabia, and the United Arab Emirates. Both consumer and industrial markets have blossomed in these countries. Other countries—such as Indonesia, Mexico, and Venezuela—were able to borrow heavily against oil reserves in order to develop more rapidly. On the other hand, industrial countries such as Japan, the United States, and much of Western Europe experienced an enormous transfer of wealth to the petroleum-rich nations. The high price of oil has created inflationary pressures in petroleum-importing nations. Now, however, new technologies like fracking are facilitating the economic recovery of oil and gas from the tar sands of Canada and shale rock of America. This will significantly reduce U.S. demand for foreign oil.

Steep declines in the price of oil in 2014 and 2015 had a very negative impact on America's oil producers—particularly shale oil companies. Falling prices proved an economic boon to American consumers, however. Thanks to oil dropping to below $50 a barrel, the typical American household saved about $750 in 2015. People who depend upon home heating oil also saved around $750.[45]

Petroleum is not the only natural resource that affects international marketing. Warm climate and lack of water mean that many of Africa's countries will remain importers of foodstuffs. The United States, on the other hand, must rely on Africa for many precious metals. Vast differences in natural resources create international dependencies, huge shifts of wealth, inflation and recession, export opportunities for countries with abundant resources, and even a stimulus for military intervention.

The shortage of natural resources has become a major issue in the external environment in the last decade.

Kokhanchikov/Shutterstock.com

GLOBAL MARKETING BY THE INDIVIDUAL FIRM

A company should consider entering the global marketplace only after its management has a solid grasp of the global environment.

Companies decide to "go global" for a number of reasons. Perhaps the most important is to earn additional profits. Managers may believe that international sales will result in higher profit margins or more added-on profits. A second stimulus is that a firm may have a unique product or technological advantage not available to other international competitors. Such advantages should result in major business successes abroad. In other situations, management may have exclusive market information about foreign customers, marketplaces, or market situations not known to others. While exclusivity can provide an initial motivation for international marketing, managers must realize that competitors can be expected to catch up with the firm's information advantage. Finally, saturated domestic markets, excess capacity, and potential for economies of scale can also be motivators to go global. Economies of scale mean that average per-unit production costs fall as output is increased.

Many firms form multinational partnerships—called strategic alliances—to assist them in penetrating global markets; strategic alliances are examined in Chapter 7. Five other methods of entering the global marketplace are, in order of risk, exporting, licensing and franchising, contract manufacturing, joint venture, and direct investment (see Exhibit 5.2).

is currently the world's largest exporter, but the United States and Germany are not far behind.

Small companies comprise the majority of U.S. exporters. Businesses with fewer than 500 employees accounted for 294,589 of 301,238 U.S. exporters (about 98 percent) in 2012, the last year for which data is available.[46] Just over half were small manufacturers and wholesalers. Together they generated $460 billion in foreign trade—about 34 percent of total U.S. exports.

While paperwork is a headache for some small companies, it's not their biggest concern according to a survey of small businesses fielded by the National Small Business Association and the Small Business Exporters Association. Asked to identify the largest challenges to selling goods and services to foreign customers, 41 percent of respondents selected, "I worry about getting paid."[47]

"I think the biggest issue is getting a staff up overseas, as well as the cost of business travel, and of communication with far-flung clients," said Chris Coccio, chief executive of Sono-Tek Corp., which develops ultrasonic spray coating technology. Sono-Tek's primary overseas clients include contract manufacturers for electronic companies and medical firms. According to Coccio, about 60 percent of the company's roughly $10 million in annual revenue comes from sales to non-U.S. markets.[48]

Sono-Tek exports widely in Europe as well as to many parts of Asia (including China, Japan, and the Philippines). Its products can also be found in Mexico and Brazil. About 80 percent of the company's sales and marketing budget is spent on international sales, "so there clearly is extra cost per sales dollar," says Coccio.

5-4a Exporting

When a company decides to enter the global market, exporting is usually the least complicated and least risky alternative. **Exporting** is selling domestically produced products to buyers in other countries. A company can sell directly to foreign importers or buyers. China

exporting selling domestically produced products to buyers in other countries

EXHIBIT 5.2 — RISK LEVELS FOR FIVE METHODS OF ENTERING THE GLOBAL MARKETPLACE

On the whole, Coccio remains an advocate for exporting. "Without it, we would be one-third of our size," he says. Receiving payment is a regular concern when exporting goods, but "to deal with this our payment terms are front-end loaded with most of the payment prior to shipment."[49]

Instead of selling directly to foreign buyers, a company may decide to sell to intermediaries located in its domestic market. The most common intermediary is the export merchant, also known as a **buyer for export**, which is usually treated like a domestic customer by the domestic manufacturer. The buyer for export assumes all risks and sells internationally for its own account. The domestic firm is involved only to the extent that its products are bought in foreign markets.

A second type of intermediary is the **export broker**, who plays the traditional broker's role by bringing buyer and seller together. The manufacturer still retains title and assumes all the risks. Export brokers operate primarily in agricultural products and raw materials.

Export agents, a third type of intermediary, are foreign sales agents/distributors who live in the foreign country and perform the same functions as domestic manufacturers' agents, helping with international financing, shipping, and so on. The U.S. Department of Commerce has an agent/distributor service that helps about 5,000 U.S. companies each year find an agent or distributor in virtually any country of the world. A second category of agents resides in the manufacturer's country but represents foreign buyers. This type of agent acts as a hired purchasing agent for foreign customers operating in the exporter's home market.

5-4b Licensing and Franchising

Another effective way for a firm to move into the global arena with relatively little risk is to sell a license to manufacture its product to someone in a foreign country. **Licensing** is the legal process whereby a licensor allows another firm to use its manufacturing process, trademarks, patents, trade secrets, or other proprietary knowledge. The licensee, in turn, pays the licensor a royalty or fee agreed on by both parties.

A licensor must make sure it can exercise sufficient control over the licensee's activities to ensure proper quality, pricing, distribution, and so on. Licensing may also create a new competitor in the long run, if the licensee decides to void the license agreement. International law is often ineffective in stopping such actions. Two common ways of maintaining effective control over licensees are shipping one or more critical components from the United States and locally registering patents and trademarks to the U.S. firm, not to the licensee. Garment companies maintain control by delivering only so many labels per day; they also supply their own fabric, collect the scraps, and do accurate unit counts.

Franchising is a form of licensing that has grown rapidly in recent years. More than 400 U.S. franchisors operate more than 40,000 outlets in foreign countries, bringing in sales of more than $13 billion.[50] More than half of the international franchises are for fast-food restaurants and business services.

5-4c Contract Manufacturing

Firms that do not want to become involved in licensing or to become heavily involved in global marketing may engage in **contract manufacturing**, which is private label manufacturing by a foreign company. The foreign company produces a certain volume of products to specification, with the domestic firm's brand name on the goods. The domestic company usually handles the marketing. Thus, the domestic firm can broaden its global marketing base without investing in overseas plants and equipment. After establishing a solid base, the domestic firm may switch to a joint venture or direct investment.

5-4d Joint Venture

Joint ventures are somewhat similar to licensing agreements. In an international **joint venture**, the domestic firm buys part of a foreign company or joins with a foreign company to create a new entity. Thanks to a joint venture between General Electric and CFM International, workers assemble the best-selling aircraft engine in history in a huge factory just south of Paris. The engine's core, consisting of the

buyer for export an intermediary in the global market that assumes all ownership risks and sells globally for its own account

export broker an intermediary who plays the traditional broker's role by bringing buyer and seller together

export agent an intermediary who acts like a manufacturer's agent for the exporter; the export agent lives in the foreign market

licensing the legal process whereby a licensor allows another firm to use its manufacturing process, trademarks, patents, trade secrets, or other proprietary knowledge

contract manufacturing private label manufacturing by a foreign company

joint venture when a domestic firm buys part of a foreign company or joins with a foreign company to create a new entity

combustion chamber and related elements, is produced in a GE factory near Cincinnati, Ohio and shipped to France. Once the core arrives in France, engineers and technicians in blue overalls carefully marry the core to French-made turbo fans, turbines, and compressors. Combined, these parts form jet engines weighing two and a half tons each. Every month, about 65 of these engines are tested and shipped out. Like many successful joint ventures, one partner recently decided to acquire the other. General Electric made a $13.5 billion offer for CFM, and after much bickering with the French government, the deal was approved in November 2014.[51]

While this collaboration was successful, joint ventures can also be very risky. Many fail. Sometimes joint venture partners simply cannot agree on management strategies and policies. Often, joint ventures are the only way a government will allow a foreign company to enter its country. Joint ventures enable the local firm to acquire managerial skills and new technology.

5-4e Direct Investment

Active ownership of a foreign company or of overseas manufacturing or marketing facilities is called **direct foreign investment**. Direct foreign investment by U.S. firms is currently about $5.4 trillion.[52] Direct investors have either a controlling interest or a large minority interest in the firm. Thus, they have the greatest potential reward and the greatest potential risk. Because of problems with contract manufacturing and joint ventures in China, multinationals are going it alone. Today, nearly five times as much foreign direct investment comes into China in the form of stand-alone efforts as comes in for joint ventures.

A firm may make a direct foreign investment by acquiring an interest in an existing company or by building new facilities. It might do so because it has trouble transferring some resource to a foreign operation or getting that resource locally. One important resource is personnel, especially managers. If the local labor market is tight, the firm may buy an entire foreign firm and retain all its employees instead of paying higher salaries than competitors.

The United States is a popular place for direct investment by international companies. Foreign direct investment in the United States accounts for approximately $2.8 trillion.[53] The United States continues to receive more foreign investment flows than any country in the world. The United Kingdom is home to the largest investors in the United States, followed by Japan, the Netherlands, Canada, and France. U.S. affiliates of foreign firms employ more than 5.8 million people in the United States. These companies spend more than $50 billion on U.S. research and development and export over $345 billion worth of goods manufactured in the United States.[54]

5-5 THE GLOBAL MARKETING MIX

To succeed, firms seeking to enter into foreign trade must still adhere to the principles of the marketing mix. Information gathered on foreign markets through research is the basis for the four Ps of global marketing strategy: product, place (distribution), promotion, and price. Marketing managers who understand the advantages and disadvantages of different ways of entering the global market and the effect of the external environment on the firm's marketing mix have a better chance of reaching their goals.

The first step in creating a marketing mix is developing a thorough understanding of the global target market. Often this knowledge can be obtained through the same types of marketing research used in the domestic market (see Chapter 9). However, global marketing research is conducted in vastly different environments. Conducting a survey can be difficult in developing countries where telephone ownership is growing but is not always common and mail delivery is slow or sporadic. Drawing samples based on known population parameters is often difficult because of the lack of data. In some cities in Africa, Asia, Mexico, and South America, street maps are unavailable, streets are unidentified, and houses are unnumbered. Moreover, the questions a marketer can ask may differ in other cultures. In some cultures, people tend to be more private than in the United States and will not respond to personal questions on surveys. For instance, in France, questions about one's age and income are considered especially rude. In other situations, a question may simply not be relevant. A research company recently did an automobile-related study in Saudi Arabia. When asked for opinions about an advertisement that stressed fuel economy, a respondent was silent at first. Finally, he said, "Water is more expensive here than gas. We don't really think about fuel economy."[55]

5-5a Product Decisions

With the proper information, a good marketing mix can be developed. One important decision is whether to alter the product or the promotion for the global

direct foreign investment
active ownership of a foreign company or of overseas manufacturing or marketing facilities

marketplace. Other options are to radically change the product or to adjust either the promotional message or the product to suit local conditions.

ONE PRODUCT, ONE MESSAGE The strategy of global marketing standardization, which was discussed earlier, means developing a single product for all markets and promoting it the same way all over the world. For instance, P&G uses the same product and promotional themes for Head & Shoulders in China as it does in the United States. The advertising draws attention to a person's dandruff problem, which stands out in a nation of black-haired people. Head & Shoulders is now the best-selling shampoo in China despite costing over 300 percent more than local brands. Procter & Gamble markets its rich portfolio of personal-care, beauty, grooming, health, and fabric products in more than 180 countries. The firm has 20 brands that sell more than $1 billion annually around the world. Some brands, such as Duracell batteries, are heavily standardized. P&G has moved away from standardization for other brands, however. Its Axe line of male grooming products uses a constantly running sociological study in order to keep its video ads up to date with the latest trends among young men. Axe's promotion, bottle size, and pricing also change according to which country is being targeted.[56]

Global marketing standardization can sometimes backfire. Unchanged products may fail simply because of cultural factors. Any type of war game tends to do very poorly in Germany, even though Germany is by far the world's biggest game-playing nation. A successful game in Germany is highly detailed and has a thick rulebook. In Russia, Campbell's Soups failed because housewives prefer to make soup from scratch.

Sometimes the desire for absolute standardization must give way to practical considerations and local market dynamics. For example, because of the negative connotations of the word *diet* among European females, the European version of Diet Coke is Coca-Cola Light. Even if the brand name differs by market—as with Lay's potato chips, which are called Sabritas in Mexico—a strong visual relationship may be created by uniform application of the brandmark and graphic elements on packaging.

PRODUCT INVENTION In the context of global marketing, product invention can be taken to mean either creating a new product for a market or drastically changing an existing product. For example, more than 100 unique Pringles potato chip flavors have been invented for international markets. Prawn Cocktail (the United Kingdom), Seaweed (Japan), Blueberry (China), Cinnamon Sweet Potato (France), and Bangkok Grilled Chicken Wing (Thailand) are some of the many Pringles flavors available outside the United States.[57] Chinese consumers found Oreo cookies "too sweet," while Indian consumers said that they were "too bitter." In response, Kraft changed the recipe in each country and created a new Green Tea Oreo flavor for China.

PRODUCT ADAPTATION Another alternative for global marketers is to alter a basic product to meet local conditions. In India, Starbucks sells a tandoori paneer roll. KFC makes a "paneer zinger." Burger King sells its classic Whopper hamburger alongside a cheese-based Paneer King burger. This is largely how international food brands court India's 1.25 billion consumers—by playing to local tastes. But Domino's is doing more than simply creating new products in its attempt to woo Indian customers. It has reimagined everything about itself, from changing the flour it uses to maintaining a delicate balance between local tastes and Western influence. This dedication to adaptation has made Domino's India's largest international foreign-food chain; the company currently has 806 stores across 170 cities—more than twice as many as McDonald's.[58]

Pizza dough and toppings have much in common with Indian roti (flat bread) and subji (vegetables). Pizza also carries two important keystones of local Indian culture—shared plates and food that can be eaten with your hands. After eight months of research, Domino's introduced a small pizza called "Pizza Mania." It sells for 60 cents, is made in 2.5 minutes, and takes just six minutes to bake. The company also created a "cheese burst" (topped with chicken, salami, and classic Indian spices) and the "Taco Indiana" dish inspired by northern India's kebabs and parathas. In southern India, where pizza is less popular, research led to a spicy taw banana pizza.[59]

5-5b Promotion Adaptation

Another global marketing strategy is to maintain the same basic product but alter the promotional strategy. For example, bicycles are mainly pleasure vehicles in the United States, but in many parts of the world, they are a family's main mode of transportation. Thus, promotion in these countries should stress durability and efficiency. In contrast, U.S. advertising may emphasize escaping and having fun.

Language barriers, translation problems, and cultural differences have generated numerous headaches for international marketing managers. For example, a toothpaste claiming to give users white teeth was especially inappropriate in many areas of Southeast Asia, where the well-to-do chew betel nuts and black teeth are a sign of higher social status.

In many parts of the world, businesses market to customers via Web-connected smartphones by placing ads in everything from interactive games to graphics-laden productivity apps. Not so in rural India. To better reach the country's 833 million villagers, Unilever is delivering free Bollywood music and jokes to basic cell phones via old-fashioned phone calls. Users of Unilever's mobile phone music service listen to four product ads in between the popular tunes and cheesy jokes presented throughout each 15-minute program. Consumers like the offering; at least 2 million people subscribe to the free service.[60]

5-5c Place (Distribution)

Solving promotional and product problems does not guarantee global marketing success. The product must still get adequate distribution. For example, Europeans do not play sports as much as Americans do, so they do not visit sporting-goods stores as often. Realizing this, Reebok started selling its shoes in about 800 traditional shoe stores in France. In just one year, the company doubled its French sales.

Taiwanese convenience stores are quite different from what is found in the United States. Beyond the staple snacks, they provide an array of services including dry cleaning, train and concert ticket reservations, traffic fine and utility payment, hot sit-down meals, mail drop-off, and book pickup. They also deliver everything from refrigerators to multicourse banquets. As you might expect, heavy convenience store patronage is the norm in Taiwan.

Taiwan's major convenience store chains recently added seating areas to keep their customers around longer. This has resulted in convenience stores becoming popular hangouts for everyone from suited businesspeople conducting meetings to students using the stores' free wifi.[61]

Similarly, Starbucks targets white-collar consumers in China by providing larger eat-in areas with comfortable sofas, high-speed Internet access, and a business atmosphere. This allows Starbucks customers to sit in its coffee shops for casual business meetings.

In India's small cities, where eating out is often a family event, Domino's offers large dine-in spaces.

Its locations are situated exactly throughout the country; the pizza chain studies each neighborhood, its streets, and traffic flow before deciding to launch a new store. Then, each store's surrounding area is meticulously mapped (down to every intersection and traffic light) to find the fastest delivery routes. In India, Domino's still offers its "30 minute or it's free" policy—a promotion the company ended in America in 1993.[62]

In many developing nations, channels of distribution and the physical infrastructure are inadequate. South Africa has perhaps the best infrastructure in all of Africa, but even there distributing products in a safe and cost-effective way is a monumental task. Though *spazas* (informal convenience stores) comprise approximately thirty percent of South Africa's national retail market, no formal distribution system exists—many shop owners cannot even afford delivery vans. To counter this distributional hurdle, Nestlé established eighteen distribution centers to deliver Nespray, a mineral-rich milk powder, directly to the spazas scattered across rural South Africa.[63]

American companies importing goods from overseas facilities to the United States are facing other problems. Logistics has been a growing challenge for U.S. companies seeking to cut costs by shifting more production to countries where manufacturing is cheaper. Now, however, the rising costs for shipping goods are adding to their profit pressures. The surge in global trade in recent years has added to strains and charges for all forms of transport. As a result, some manufacturers are developing costly buffer stocks—which can mean setting up days' or weeks' worth of extra components—to avoid shutting down production lines and failing to make timely deliveries. Others are shifting to more expensive but more reliable modes of transport, such as airfreight, which is faster and less prone to delays than ocean shipping. Still others are inshoring as discussed earlier in the chapter.

5-5d Pricing

Once marketing managers have determined a global product and promotion strategy, they can select the remainder of the marketing mix. Pricing presents some unique problems in the global sphere. Exporters must not only cover their production costs but also consider transportation costs, insurance, taxes, and tariffs. When deciding on a final price, marketers must also determine how much customers are willing to spend on a particular product. Marketers also need to ensure that their foreign buyers will pay the price. Because developing nations lack mass purchasing power, selling to them often poses special pricing problems. Sometimes a product can be simplified in order to lower the price. A firm must not assume low-income countries are willing to accept lower quality, however. L'Oréal was unsuccessful selling cheap shampoo in India, so the company targets the rising class. It now sells a $17 Paris face powder and a $25 Vichy sunscreen. Both products are very popular.

Walmart's low-price business model has been slow to catch on with Chinese shoppers, many of whom like to shop for bargains online and in mom-and-pop stores.[64] Chinese consumers expect foreign retailers to offer the highest quality shopping environments, not the warehouse-like design common to United States Walmart stores. The company recently decided to close 29 underperforming stores in China.[65]

EXCHANGE RATES The **exchange rate** is the price of one country's currency in terms of another country's currency. If a country's currency *appreciates*, less of that country's currency is needed to buy another country's currency. If a country's currency *depreciates*, more of that currency will be needed to buy another country's currency.

How do appreciation and depreciation affect the prices of a country's goods? If, say, the U.S. dollar depreciates relative to the Japanese yen, U.S. residents will need to pay more dollars to buy Japanese goods. To illustrate, suppose the dollar price of one yen is $0.012 and that a Toyota is priced at ¥2 million. At this exchange rate, a U.S. resident pays $24,000 for a Toyota ($0.012 × ¥2 million = $24,000). If the dollar depreciates to $0.018 to ¥1, then the U.S. resident will need to pay $36,000 for the same Toyota.

As the dollar depreciates, the prices of Japanese goods rise for U.S. residents, so they buy fewer Japanese goods—thus, U.S. imports may decline. At the same time, as the dollar depreciates relative to the yen, the yen appreciates relative to the dollar. This means prices of U.S. goods fall for the Japanese, so they buy more U.S. goods—and U.S. exports rise.

Currency markets operate under a system of **floating exchange rates**. Prices of different currencies "float" up and down based on the demand for and the supply of each currency. Global currency traders create the supply of and demand for a particular country's currency based on that country's investment, trade potential, and economic strength. Sanctions imposed because of Russia's annexation of Crimea and its engagement in the Ukrainian conflict in 2014 and 2015 have resulted in the Russian ruble plunging in value. On August 3, 2014, the exchange rate was 35.75 rubles to the U.S. dollar. By January 29, 2015, the rate was 68.75 rubles to the dollar.[66]

DUMPING **Dumping** is the sale of an exported product at a price lower than that charged for the same or a like product in the "home" market of the exporter. This practice is regarded as a form of price discrimination that can potentially harm the importing nation's competing industries. Dumping may occur as a result of exporter business strategies that include (1) trying to increase an overseas market share, (2) temporarily distributing products in overseas markets to offset slack demand in the home market, (3) lowering unit costs by exploiting large-scale production, and (4) attempting to maintain stable prices during periods of exchange rate fluctuations.

Historically, the dumping of goods has presented serious problems in international trade. As a result, dumping has led to significant disagreements among countries and diverse views about its harmfulness. Some trade economists view dumping as harmful only when it involves the use of "predatory"

---

exchange rate the price of one country's currency in terms of another country's currency

floating exchange rates a system in which prices of different currencies move up and down based on the demand for and the supply of each currency

dumping the sale of an exported product at a price lower than that charged for the same or a like product in the "home" market of the exporter

---

If a country's currency depreciates, more of that currency will be needed to buy another country's currency.

OtnaYdur/Shutterstock.com

practices that intentionally try to eliminate competition and gain monopoly power in a market. They believe that predatory dumping rarely occurs and that anti-dumping rules are a protectionist tool whose cost to consumers and import-using industries exceeds the benefits to the industries receiving protection.

In January 2015, the United States Commerce Department declared anti-dumping duties for passenger and light truck tires imported from China. More than 30 different manufacturers were involved in dumping at various prices. The duty rates ranged from 19 to 88 percent.[67]

COUNTERTRADE Global trade does not always involve cash. Countertrade is a fast-growing way to conduct global business. In **countertrade**, all or part of the payment for goods or services is in the form of other goods or services. Countertrade is thus a form of barter (swapping goods for goods), an age-old practice whose origins have been traced back to cave dwellers. The U.S. Department of Commerce says that roughly thirty percent of all global trade is countertrade.[68] In fact, both India and China have made billion-dollar government purchasing lists, with most of the goods to be paid for by countertrade.

One common type of countertrade is straight barter. The Malaysian government purchased 20 diesel-electric locomotives from General Electric in exchange for a supply of 200,000 metric tons of palm oil. Sometimes, countertrades involve both cash and goods. General Motors sold locomotive and diesel engines to Yugoslavia in exchange for $4 million and Yugoslavian cutting tools.[69] Another form of countertrade is the compensation agreement. Typically, a company provides technology and equipment for a plant in a developing nation and agrees to take full or partial payment in goods produced by that plant. For example, General Tire Company supplied equipment and know-how for a Romanian truck tire plant. In turn, General Tire sold the tires it received from the plant in the United States under the Victoria brand name. Both sides benefit even though they do not use cash.

 ## 5-6 THE IMPACT OF THE INTERNET

In many respects, going global is easier than it has ever been before. Opening an e-commerce site on the Internet immediately puts a company in the international marketplace. Sophisticated language translation software can make any site accessible to people around the world. Global shippers such as UPS, FedEx, and DHL help solve international e-commerce distribution complexities. E4X Inc. offers software to ease currency conversions by allowing customers to pay in the currency of their choice. E4X collects the payment from the customer and then pays the site in U.S. dollars. Nevertheless, the promise of "borderless commerce" and the global "Internet economy" are still being restrained by the old brick-and-mortar rules, regulations, and habits. For example, Lands' End is not allowed to mention its unconditional refund policy on its e-commerce site in Germany because German retailers, which normally do not allow returns after 14 days, sued and won a court ruling blocking mention of it.

5-6a Social Media in Global Marketing

Because Facebook, YouTube, and other social media are popular around the world, firms both large and small have embraced social media marketing. Every passenger hopes for the opportunity to get a free upgrade to business class when flying. To help raise awareness of the launch of Air France's new business class cabins in Asia, Fred & Farid Shanghai created a social game in which travelers could compete to win a free upgrade to business class just prior to boarding. The agency transformed the boarding gates of Changi Airport in Singapore and Kansai Airport in Osaka, Japan into social gaming arenas where passengers could download a mobile game (similar to fruit ninja) and try to get a high score. Over 400 passengers were invited to compete against one another and monitor all the competitors on a large scoreboard during their wait.[70]

Fashion label H&M promoted its summer products on Twitter and Facebook using the hashtag #DivideOpinion. For each #DivideOpinion post, H&M captured a fashion item in two distinctive scenes (for example, a sheer lace top styled for both a romantic-inspired outfit and a street-style outfit) and asked its followers to reply with which look was better and why. The best responses received a trip to Los Angeles for each winner and a friend. With this campaign, H&M reinvented a popular idea often seen in fashion magazines for the mobile market. By comparing two products (rather than three or four) against one another, H&M was able to target mobile users who want quick snippets of information and whose screens do not allow for more than a couple of images at a time. This campaign was successful in its effort to drive excitement around H&M's summer fashions.[71]

Managers of global social media campaigns must always be aware of the cultures of the countries in

countertrade a form of trade in which all or part of the payment for goods or services is in the form of other goods or services

which they operate. Global energy drink giant Red Bull sparked a major spat with Kenyans after it posted a video that seemed to imply that Kenyans were backwards to Facebook. The video clip featured South African motorcycle rider Brian Capper, who started the video off by expressing his shock at how many people spoke English in Nairobi. "I've been blown away with the amount of people that speak English. I had absolutely no idea what to expect from that point of view; just about everybody I spoke to spoke English, which was really surprising for me," said the rider. "They are unbelievably knowledgeable … they know what's going on with the rest of the world."[72] Capper's comments did not go down well with many, as Red Bull's Facebook page quickly filled with angry comments such as:

> "Seems like a nice guy and cool video, but seriously, what era is he and the Red Bull crew living in! Surprised about the English and saying 3rd world country, eyes need to be open to 2015 Kenya! And the dude is from SA as well, so should really know better."
>
> "Don't you just love the ignorance of these people! Surprised that Kenyans speak English? We speak better English than you dude. All in all, great biking skills! Now go back to school."[73]

These reactions are reminiscent of a similar outcry after Korean Air termed Kenyans "primitive" in an online advertising campaign about the company's direct flights to Nairobi. The advertisement read in part: "Fly to Nairobi with Korean Air and enjoy the grand African savanna, the safari tour, and the indigenous people full of primitive energy." The words 'primitive energy' annoyed many Kenyans, who forced the airline to retract the ad and issue an apology on social media.[74]

STUDY TOOLS 5

LOCATED AT BACK OF THE TEXTBOOK

☐ Rip out Chapter Review Card

LOCATED AT WWW.CENGAGEBRAIN.COM

☐ Review Key Terms Flashcards and create your own

☐ Track your knowledge & understanding of key concepts in marketing

☐ Complete practice and graded quizzes to prepare for tests

☐ Complete interactive content within the MKTG Online experience

☐ View the chapter highlight boxes within the MKTG Online experience

6 | Consumer Decision Making

LEARNING OUTCOMES

After studying this chapter, you will be able to…

6-1 Explain why marketing managers should understand consumer behavior

6-2 Analyze the components of the consumer decision-making process

6-3 Explain the consumer's postpurchase evaluation process

6-4 Identify the types of consumer buying decisions and discuss the significance of consumer involvement

6-5 Identify and understand the cultural factors that affect consumer buying decisions

6-6 Identify and understand the social factors that affect consumer buying decisions

6-7 Identify and understand the individual factors that affect consumer buying decisions

6-8 Identify and understand the psychological factors that affect consumer buying decisions

After you finish this chapter go to **PAGE 113** for **STUDY TOOLS.**

6-1 THE IMPORTANCE OF UNDERSTANDING CONSUMER BEHAVIOR

Consumers' product and service preferences are constantly changing. Marketing managers must understand these desires in order to create a proper marketing mix for a well-defined market. So it is critical that marketing managers have a thorough knowledge of consumer behavior. **Consumer behavior** describes how consumers make purchase decisions and how they use and dispose of the purchased goods or services. The study of consumer behavior also includes factors that influence purchase decisions and product use.

consumer behavior
processes a consumer uses to make purchase decisions, as well as to use and dispose of purchased goods or services; also includes factors that influence purchase decisions and product use

Understanding how consumers make purchase decisions can help marketing managers in several ways. For example, if the product development manager for Trek bicycles learns through research that a more comfortable seat is a key attribute for purchasers of mountain bikes, Trek can redesign the seat to meet that criterion. If the firm cannot change the design in the short run, it can use promotion in an effort to change consumers' decision-making criteria. Trek, for example, could promote the ultra-light weight, durability, and performance of its current mountain bikes.

Buying a mountain bike, or anything else, is all about value. **Value** is a personal assessment of the net worth one obtains from making a purchase. To put it another way, value is what you get minus what you give up. When you buy something, you hope to get benefits like relief from hunger, durability, convenience, prestige, affection, happiness, a sense of belonging...the list goes on. In order to receive these benefits, you must give something up. You may sacrifice money, self-image, time, convenience, effort, opportunity, or a combination thereof. Value can also mean an enduring belief shared by a society that a specific mode of conduct is personally or socially preferable to another mode of conduct. This definition of "value" will be discussed later in the chapter.

Purchases are made based upon **perceived value**, which is what you *expect* to get. The actual value may be more or less than you expected. Recently, one of your authors bought a well-known brand of coffee maker with a thermal carafe. He likes to drink coffee all morning, but found that traditional coffee makers' heating elements tended to turn the coffee bitter and thick-tasting after a few hours. The thermal carafe has no such heating element, so the coffee stays fresh. That is, if the coffee actually makes it into the carafe. The carafe lid has a valve that lets the coffee drip into the carafe basin.

However, the valve tends to stick, and after about a week of use, the valve stuck during a fill-up and coffee went all over the kitchen counter. No value there! (For the curious, the author has moved on to a new traditional-style coffee maker.)

The value received from a purchase can be broken down into two categories. **Utilitarian value** is derived from a product or service that helps the consumer solve problems and accomplish tasks. Buying a washing machine and dryer gives you a convenient means of cleaning your clothes. Buying a new pair of eyeglasses lets you better view the computer screen. Utilitarian value, then, is a means to an end. Value is provided because the purchase allows something good to happen.

The second form of value is **hedonic value**. Hedonic value is an end in itself rather than as a means to an end. The purchase tends to give us good feelings, happiness, and satisfaction. The value is

value a personal assessment of the net worth one obtains from making a purchase, or the enduring belief that a specific mode of conduct is personally or socially preferable to another mode of conduct

perceived value the value a consumer *expects* to obtain from a purchase

utilitarian value a value derived from a product or service that helps the consumer solve problems and accomplish tasks

hedonic value a value that acts as an end in itself rather than as a means to an end provided entirely through the experience and emotions associated with consumption, not because another end is accomplished. Taking a ski vacation or a trip to the beach gives us hedonic value. Spending a day in a spa is a source of hedonic value. A coffee maker provides utilitarian value, but the coffee itself provides hedonic value.

Utilitarian and hedonic values are not mutually exclusive. In some cases, the purchase experience can give you both hedonic and utilitarian value. Morton's The Steakhouse is considered to be one of the top steak restaurant chains in America. Going to a Morton's and enjoying the atmosphere and a fine steak will give you hedonic value. At the same time, it satisfies your hunger pangs and thus provides utilitarian value. Some of the best consumer experiences are high in both utilitarian and hedonic value.[1]

Acquiring value comes from making a purchase. How does one go about making the decision to buy? We will explore this topic next.

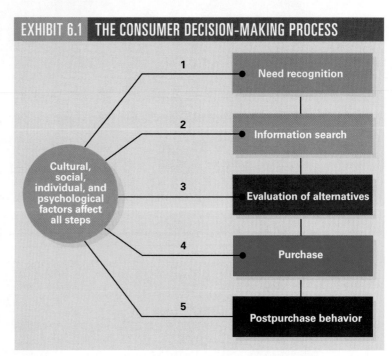

EXHIBIT 6.1 THE CONSUMER DECISION-MAKING PROCESS

Cultural, social, individual, and psychological factors affect all steps

1 Need recognition
2 Information search
3 Evaluation of alternatives
4 Purchase
5 Postpurchase behavior

6-2 THE CONSUMER DECISION-MAKING PROCESS

When buying products, particularly new or expensive items, consumers generally follow the consumer decision-making process shown in Exhibit 6.1: (1) need recognition, (2) information search, (3) evaluation of alternatives, (4) purchase, and (5) postpurchase behavior. These five steps represent a general process that can be used as a guide for studying how consumers make decisions. It is important to note, though, that consumers' decisions do not always proceed in order through all of these steps. In fact, the consumer may end the process at any time or may not even make a purchase. The section on the types of consumer buying decisions later in the chapter discusses why a consumer's progression through these steps may vary. We

begin, however, by examining the basic purchase process in greater detail.

6-2a Need Recognition

The first stage in the consumer decision-making process is need recognition. **Need recognition** is the result of an imbalance between actual and desired states. The imbalance arouses and activates the consumer decision-making process. A **want** is the recognition of an unfulfilled need and a product that will satisfy it. For example, have you ever gotten blisters from an old running shoe and realized you needed new shoes? Or maybe you have seen a new sports car drive down the street and wanted to buy it. Need recognition is triggered when a consumer is exposed to either an internal or an external **stimulus**, which is any unit of input affecting one or more of the five senses: sight, smell, taste, touch, and hearing. *Internal stimuli* are occurrences you experience, such as hunger or thirst. For example, you may hear your stomach growl and then realize you are hungry. *External stimuli* are influences from an outside source. In today's digital age, stimuli can come from a multitude of sources. Perhaps it was a YouTube video that created a purchase desire. Perhaps it was a Google search on a smartphone or an interactive advertisement playing on a large touch-enabled screen. Or perhaps it was a friend's video posted on Facebook using a new GoPro camera.

The imbalance between actual and desired states is sometimes referred to as the *want–got gap*. That is,

consumer decision-making process a five-step process used by consumers when buying goods or services

need recognition result of an imbalance between actual and desired states

want recognition of an unfulfilled need and a product that will satisfy it

stimulus any unit of input affecting one or more of the five senses: sight, smell, taste, touch, hearing

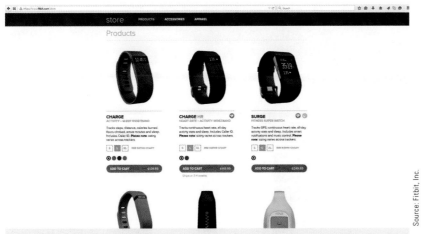

A want can be for a specific product, or it can be for a certain attribute or feature of a product.

there is a difference between what a customer has and what he or she would like to have. This gap does not always trigger consumer action. The gap must be large enough to drive the consumer to do something. Just because your stomach growls once does not mean that you necessarily will stop what you are doing and go eat.

A marketing manager's objective is to get consumers to recognize this want–got gap. Advertising, sales promotion, and social media often provide this stimulus. Surveying buyer preferences provides marketers with information about consumer needs and wants that can be used to tailor products and services. Marketing managers can create wants on the part of the consumer. An ad promoting a healthy, active lifestyle and the fun of fitness tracking may inspire you to purchase a wearable fitness tracker like a Fitbit Charge HR or a Runtastic Orbit. A want can be for a specific product, or it can be for a certain attribute or feature of a product. A runner may purchase the Orbit, for example, because the band pairs with the Runtastic app to display information about recent runs right on the wearer's wrist.

6-2b Information Search

After recognizing a need or want, consumers search for information about the various alternatives available to satisfy it. For example, you know you are interested in seeing a movie, but you are not sure what to see. So you visit the Rotten Tomatoes Web site to see what is getting great reviews by both critics and your peers on Facebook. This is a type of information search, which can occur internally, externally, or both. In an **internal information search**, the person recalls information stored in the memory. This stored information stems largely from previous experience with a product. For example, while traveling with your family, you may choose to stay at a hotel you have stayed in before because you remember that the hotel had clean rooms and friendly service.

In contrast, an **external information search** seeks information in the outside environment. There are two basic types of external information sources: nonmarketing-controlled and marketing-controlled. A **nonmarketing-controlled information source** is a product information source that is not associated with marketers promoting a product. These information sources include personal experiences (trying or observing a new product), personal sources (family, friends, acquaintances, and coworkers who may recommend a product or service), and public sources (such as Rotten Tomatoes, *Consumer Reports*, and other rating organizations that comment on products and services). Once you have read reviews on Rotten Tomatoes to decide which movie to see (public source), you may search your memory for positive theater experiences to determine where you will go (personal experience). Or you might rely on a friend's recommendation to try out a new theater (personal source). Marketers gather information on how these information sources work and use it to attract customers. For example, car manufacturers know that younger customers are likely to get information from friends and family, so they try to develop enthusiasm for their products via word of mouth and social media.

Living in the digital age has changed the way consumers get nonmarketing-controlled information. It can be from blogs, Amazon, social media, Web forums, or consumer opinion sites such as www.consumerreview.com, www.tripadvisor.com, or www.epinions.com. Eighty percent of U.S. consumers research electronics, computers, and media online before making an in-store purchase, and a quarter of shoppers utilize at least four sources for product information. To give you an idea of the number of searches this

internal information search
the process of recalling past information stored in the memory

external information search
the process of seeking information in the outside environment

nonmarketing-controlled information source a product information source that is not associated with advertising or promotion

implies, Google averages more than 12 billion searches a month.[2] This number is only going to expand.

The Internet has changed the quality of information available to make purchase decisions. In the past, consumers used quality proxies to help determine what to buy. A proxy could be a brand name ("it is made by Sony so it must be good"), price ("higher price meant higher quality"), or origin ("made in the USA is better"). Today, consumers can appraise a product based upon how it is evaluated by others. If you are looking for a hotel in New York City, for example, you can easily view a ranking of all New York hotels based upon thousands of reviews on Web sites like TripAdvisor. This provides much better information than simply relying on a brand name (such as Hilton) because you have the direct experience of others to guide you.[3] A word of caution, however: researchers using data from a large private label retailer's Web site found that approximately 5 percent of product reviews were submitted by people with no record of ever having purchased the products they were reviewing.[4] Expedia avoids this problem by only allowing customers who have purchased a service (such as a flight, car, or hotel room) to write a review. Similarly, Amazon identifies whether a review matches a confirmed transaction.

Social media are playing an ever-increasing role in consumer information search. Thirty percent of shoppers made a purchase via social media in 2014. Forty-four percent will discover new products via social networks, and 49 percent will make purchases based upon referrals from social media, recommendations from friends in their social networks, or promotions from brands that they follow on Facebook or Twitter.[5]

Although the use of a mobile device to make purchases is rising, consumers primarily use their smartphones and tablets to research products before buying. One survey found that 70 percent of respondents planned to research products on their mobile devices and then purchased them in-store.[6] In-store research and price comparisons conducted on mobile devices while shopping have become standard practice for many consumers.

The internet has changed the quality of information available to make purchase decisions.

Source: TripAdvisor

Not every information search is about comparing Product or Service Firm A with Product or Service Firm B. Yet, the online search can still influence purchase patterns. For example, a shopper may browse recipe Web sites or watch cooking demonstration videos before deciding on a dinner party menu. This research helps the shopper decide which ingredients to purchase at the supermarket.

A **marketing-controlled information source** is biased toward a specific product because it originates with marketers promoting that product. Marketing-controlled information sources include mass media advertising (radio, newspaper, television, and magazine advertising), sales promotion (contests, displays, premiums, and so forth), salespeople, product labels and packaging, and digital media. In 2016, the web influenced more than half of all retail transactions, representing sales of almost $2 trillion.[7]

The extent to which an individual conducts an external search depends on his or her perceived risk, knowledge, prior experience, and level of interest in the good or service. Generally, as the perceived risk of the purchase increases, the consumer enlarges the search and considers more alternative brands. For example, suppose that you want to purchase a surround-sound system for your home entertainment system. The decision is relatively risky because of the expense and technical nature of the surround-sound system, so you are motivated to search for information about models, prices, options, compatibility with existing entertainment products, and capabilities. You may decide to compare attributes of many speaker systems because the value of the time expended finding the

marketing-controlled information source a product information source that originates with marketers promoting the product

"right" stereo will be less than the cost of buying the wrong system.

A consumer's knowledge about the product or service will also affect the extent of an external information search. A consumer who is knowledgeable and well informed about a potential purchase is less likely to search for additional information. In addition, the more knowledgeable consumers are, the more efficiently they will conduct the search process, thereby requiring less time to search. For example, many consumers know that Spirit Airlines and other discount airlines have much lower fares, so they generally use the discounters and do not even check fares at other carriers.

The extent of a consumer's external search is also affected by confidence in one's decision-making ability. A confident consumer not only has sufficient stored information about the product but also feels self-assured about making the right decision. People lacking this confidence will continue an information search even when they know a great deal about the product. Consumers with prior experience in buying a certain product will have less perceived risk than inexperienced consumers. Therefore, they will spend less time searching and limit the number of products they consider.

A third factor influencing the external information search is product experience.

Radu Bercan/Shutterstock.com

experience. Consumers who have had a positive experience with a product are more likely to limit their search to items related to the positive experience. For example, when flying, consumers are likely to choose airlines with which they have had positive experiences, such as consistent on-time arrivals, and avoid airlines with which they have had a negative experience, such as lost luggage.

Finally, the extent of the search is positively related to the amount of interest a consumer has in a product. A consumer who is more interested in a product will spend more time searching for information and alternatives. For example, suppose you are a dedicated runner who reads jogging and fitness magazines and catalogs. In searching for a new pair of running shoes, you may enjoy reading about the new brands available and spend more time and effort than other buyers in deciding on the right shoe.

The consumer's information search should yield a group of brands, sometimes called the buyer's **evoked set** (or **consideration set**), which are the consumer's most preferred alternatives. From this set, the buyer will further evaluate the alternatives and make a choice. Consumers do not consider all brands available in a product category, but they do seriously consider a much smaller set. For example, from the many brands of pizza available, consumers are likely to consider only the alternatives that fit their price range, location, take-out/delivery needs, and taste preferences. Having too many choices can, in fact, confuse consumers and cause them to delay the decision to buy, or in some instances, cause them not to buy at all.

6-2c Evaluation of Alternatives and Purchase

After getting information and constructing an evoked set of alternative products, the consumer is ready to make a decision. A consumer will use the information stored in memory and obtained from outside sources to develop a set of criteria. Recent research has shown that exposure to certain cues in your everyday environment can affect decision criteria and purchase. For example, when NASA landed the *Pathfinder* spacecraft on Mars, it captured media attention worldwide. The candy maker Mars also noted a rather unusual increase in sales. Although the Mars bar takes its name from the company's founder and not the planet, consumers apparently responded to news about the planet Mars by purchasing more Mars bars.

The environment, internal information, and external information help consumers evaluate and compare alternatives. One way to begin narrowing the number of choices in the evoked set is to pick a product attribute and then exclude all products in the set that do not have that attribute. For example, assume Jane and Jill, both college sophomores, are looking for their first apartment. They need a two-bedroom apartment, reasonably priced and located near campus. They want the apartment to have a swimming pool, washer and dryer, and

evoked set (consideration set) a group of brands resulting from an information search from which a buyer can choose

covered parking. Jane and Jill begin their search with all fifty apartments in the area and systematically eliminate complexes that lack the features they need. Hence, they may reduce their list to ten apartments that possess all of the desired attributes. Now, they can use cutoffs to further narrow their choices. Cutoffs are either minimum or maximum levels of an attribute that an alternative must pass to be considered. Suppose Jane and Jill set a maximum of $1,000 per month for rent. Then all apartments with rent higher than $1,000 will be eliminated, further reducing the list of apartments from ten to eight. A final way to narrow the choices is to rank the attributes under consideration in order of importance and evaluate the products based on how well each performs on the most important attributes. To reach a final decision on one of the remaining eight apartments, Jane and Jill may decide proximity to campus is the most important attribute. As a result, they will choose to rent the apartment closest to campus.

If new brands are added to an evoked set, the consumer's evaluation of the existing brands in that set changes. As a result, certain brands in the original set may become more desirable. Suppose Jane and Jill find two apartments located an equal distance from campus, one priced at $800 and the other at $750. Faced with this choice, they may decide that the $800 apartment is too expensive given that a comparable apartment is cheaper. If they add a $900 apartment to the list, however, then they may perceive the $800 apartment as more reasonable and decide to rent it.

The purchase decision process described above is a piecemeal process. That is, the evaluation is made by examining alternative advantages and disadvantages along important product attributes. A different way consumers can evaluate a product is according to a categorization process. The evaluation of an alternative depends upon the particular category to which it is assigned. Categories can be very general (motorized forms of transportation), or they can be very specific (Harley-Davidson motorcycles). Typically, these categories are associated with some degree of liking or disliking. To the extent that the product can be assigned membership in a particular category, it will receive an evaluation similar to that attached to the category. If you go to the grocery store and see a new organic food on the shelf, you may evaluate it on your liking and opinions of organic food.

So, when consumers rely on a categorization process, a product's evaluation depends on the particular category to which it is perceived as belonging. Given this, companies need to understand whether consumers are using categories that evoke the desired evaluations. Indeed, how a product is categorized can strongly influence consumer demand. For example, what products come to mind when you think about the "morning beverages" category? To the soft drink industry's dismay, far too few consumers include sodas in this category. Several attempts have been made at getting soft drinks on the breakfast table, but with little success.

Brand extensions, in which a well-known and respected brand name from one product category is extended into other product categories, is one way companies employ categorization to their advantage. Brand extensions are a common business practice. For example, mixed martial arts promotional organization Ultimate Fighting Championship (UFC) has built its brand on pay-per-view events, cable and network television broadcasts, and merchandising. The UFC launched a 24-hour full-service gym in Long Island, New York. In addition to martial arts–themed activities, the UFC Gym features standard fitness equipment, a café, and signature classes like Hot Hula and Hi-Octane Conditioning.

TO BUY OR NOT TO BUY Ultimately, the consumer has to decide whether to buy or not buy. Specifically, consumers must decide:

1. Whether to buy
2. When to buy
3. What to buy (product type and brand)

The UFC Gym extends the Ultimate Fighting Championship's combative nature and gritty aesthetic into a new product category.

4. Where to buy (type of retailer, specific retailer, on-line or in store)

5. How to pay

As mentioned previously, technology has forever changed the way we make our purchase decisions. Imagine that Mike and Linda have just bought their first home and are now looking to purchase a washer and dryer. They start their journey by visiting several big-box retailers' Web sites. They identify three models they are interested in at one store's site and save them to a wish list. Because space in their starter home is limited—and because is the washer and dryer constitute a relatively big purchase in their eyes—they decide to see the items in person before deciding on which to buy.

The couple finds the nearest physical outlet on the retailer's Web site, gets directions using Google Maps, and then drives over to view the desired products. Even before they walk through the doors, a transmitter mounted at the retailer's entrance identifies Mike and Linda and sends a text message to their smartphones welcoming them and providing personalized offers and recommendations based on their unique histories with the store. In this case, they receive links to the wish list they created as well as updated specs and prices for the washers and dryers they had shown interest in (captured in their click trails on the store's Web site). Additionally, they receive notification of a sale ("15 percent off selected brand appliances—today only!") that applies to two of the items they had added to their wish list.

When Mike and Linda tap on their wish list in the store's app, they are provided with a store map directing them to the appliances section and a "call button" to speak with an expert. They meet with the salesperson, ask some questions, take some measurements, and close in on a particular brand and model of washer and dryer. Because the store employs sophisticated tagging technologies, information about the washer and dryer are automatically synced with other apps on the couple's smartphones. They scan reviews using the *Consumer Reports* app, share the appliance specs to their messaging apps and send them to their parents for advice, ask Facebook friends to weigh in on the purchase, and compare the retailer's prices against others. Mike and Linda also take advantage of a virtual designer feature in the retailer's mobile app that, with the entry of just a few key pieces of information, allows them to preview how the washer and dryer might look in their home.

All of the input is favorable, so the couple decides to take advantage of the 15 percent offer and buy the appliances. They use Mike's smartwatch to authenticate payment and walk out of the store with a date and time for delivery. A week later, on the designated day, they receive confirmation that a truck is in their area and that they will be texted within a half hour of arrival time ("No need to cancel other plans just to wait for your order to arrive!"). Three weeks after the appliances are delivered, the couple receives a message from the retailer with offers for other appliances and home-improvement services tailored toward first-year home owners ... and the cycle begins again.[8]

PLANNED VERSUS IMPULSE PURCHASE The previous example represents a *fully planned purchase* based upon a lot of information. People rarely buy a new washer and dryer simply on impulse. Often, consumers will make a *partially planned purchase* when they know the product category they want to buy (shirts, pants, reading lamp, car floor mats) but wait until they get to the store or go online to choose a specific style or brand. Finally, there is the *unplanned purchase*, which people buy on impulse. Research has found that 75 percent of adults in the United States have made an impulse purchase. We often think of impulse purchasing as buying inexpensive items at the grocery store checkout. This, however, is not always the case. In the survey above, 16 percent said that they spent $500 to $1,000 on impulse purchases while 10 percent spent more than $1,000.[9] The purchase may be in a planned category (for example, soup), but decisions regarding the brand (Campbell's), package (can), and type (tomato) are all made on impulse. Researchers using in-store video cameras observed that when shoppers make impulse buys, they tend to touch and examine the item more, stand further from the shelf, and are less likely to refer to their shopping lists, coupons, or in-store circulars.[10]

 6-3 POSTPURCHASE BEHAVIOR

When buying products, consumers expect certain outcomes from the purchase. How well these expectations are met determines whether the consumer is satisfied or dissatisfied with the purchase. For example, if a person bids on a used KitchenAid mixer from eBay and wins, she may have fairly low expectations regarding performance. If the mixer's performance turns out to be of superior quality, then the person's satisfaction will be high because her expectations were exceeded. Conversely, if the person bids on a new Kitchen Aid mixer expecting superior quality and performance, but the mixer breaks within one month, she will be very dissatisfied because her expectations were not met. Price often influences the level of expectations for a product or service.

For the marketer, an important element of any postpurchase evaluation is reducing any lingering doubts that the decision was sound. When people recognize inconsistency between their values or opinions and their behavior, they tend to feel an inner tension called **cognitive dissonance**. For example, suppose Angelika is looking to purchase an e-reader. After evaluating her options, she has decided to purchase an iPad, even though it is much more expensive than other dedicated e-readers. Prior to choosing the iPad, Angelika may experience inner tension or anxiety because she is worried that the current top-of-the-line technology, which costs much more than the middle-of-the-line technology, will be obsolete in a couple months. That feeling of dissonance arises as her worries over obsolescence battle her practical nature, which is focused on the lower cost of a Kindle Paperwhite and its adequate—but less fancy—technology.

Consumers try to reduce dissonance by justifying their decision. They may seek new information that reinforces positive ideas about the purchase, avoid information that contradicts their decision, or revoke the original decision by returning the product. In some instances, people deliberately seek contrary information in order to refute it and reduce dissonance. Dissatisfied customers sometimes rely on word of mouth to reduce cognitive dissonance by letting friends and family know they are displeased.

Marketing managers can help reduce dissonance through effective communication with purchasers. For example, a customer service manager may slip a note inside the package congratulating the buyer on making a wise decision. Postpurchase letters sent by manufacturers and dissonance-reducing statements in instruction booklets may help customers feel at ease with their purchase. Advertising that displays the product's superiority over competing brands or guarantees can also help relieve the possible dissonance of someone who has already bought the product. Apple's Genius Bar and customer service will ease cognitive dissonance for purchasers of an iPad because they know that the company is there to support them.

An excellent opportunity for a company to reduce (or if handled poorly, increase) cognitive dissonance is when a customer has a question or complaint and tries to contact the company. Too many firms view their contact centers as cost centers and every contact as a problem to be minimized by making it as hard as possible to speak to a customer representative. Have you ever gone through four or five automated sequences, pushing a series of buttons, only to be told, "We are experiencing a higher than normal call volume and you can expect a lengthy delay." Not only does this raise cognitive dissonance, it can also destroy brand loyalty. Marketing-oriented companies perceive the contact center as an opportunity to engage customers and reinforce the brand promise. At these companies, there is no long menu of buttons to push. Instead, a service rep answers on the first or second ring and is empowered to solve customer problems. A recent study found that positive contact experiences resulted in consumers being 15 times more likely to say that they would definitely buy again than those with negative contact experiences. Of four different channels for a company to interact with its customers, telephone was most effective. Eighty-six percent of respondents said that speaking on the phone with a service rep enabled them to resolve their issues. Chat earned a 70 percent success rate, e-mail 44 percent, and Facebook 27 percent.[11]

 ## 6-4 TYPES OF CONSUMER BUYING DECISIONS AND CONSUMER INVOLVEMENT

All consumer buying decisions generally fall along a continuum of three broad categories: routine response behavior, limited decision making, and extensive decision making (see Exhibit 6.2). Goods and services in these three categories can best be described in terms of five factors:

- Level of consumer involvement
- Length of time to make a decision
- Cost of the good or service
- Degree of information search
- Number of alternatives considered

The level of consumer involvement is perhaps the most significant determinant in classifying buying decisions. **Involvement** is the amount of time and effort a buyer invests in the search, evaluation, and decision processes of consumer behavior.

cognitive dissonance inner tension that a consumer experiences after recognizing an inconsistency between behavior and values or opinions

involvement the amount of time and effort a buyer invests in the search, evaluation, and decision processes of consumer behavior

EXHIBIT 6.2 CONTINUUM OF CONSUMER BUYING DECISIONS

	Routine	Limited	Extensive
Involvement	Low	Low to moderate	High
Time	Short	Short to moderate	Long
Cost	Low	Low to moderate	High
Information Search	Internal only	Mostly internal	Internal and external
Number of Alternatives	One	Few	Many

iStockphoto.com/Kickstand

Frequently purchased, low-cost goods and services are generally associated with **routine response behavior**. These goods and services can also be called *low-involvement products* because consumers spend little time on search and decision before making the purchase. Usually, buyers are familiar with several different brands in the product category but stick with one brand. For example, a person may routinely buy Tropicana orange juice. Consumers engaged in routine response behavior normally do not experience need recognition until they are exposed to advertising or see the product displayed on a store shelf. Consumers buy first and evaluate later, whereas the reverse is true for extensive decision making. A consumer who has previously purchased whitening toothpaste and was satisfied with it will probably walk to the toothpaste aisle and select that same brand without spending twenty minutes examining all other alternatives.

Limited decision making typically occurs when a consumer has previous product experience but is unfamiliar with the current brands available. Limited decision making is also associated with lower levels of involvement (although higher than routine decisions) because consumers expend only moderate effort in searching for information or in considering various alternatives. For example, what happens if the consumer's usual brand of whitening toothpaste is sold out? Assuming that toothpaste is needed, the consumer will be forced to choose another brand. Before making a final decision, the consumer will likely evaluate several other brands based on their active ingredients, their promotional claims, and the consumer's prior experiences.

Consumers practice **extensive decision making** when buying an unfamiliar, expensive product or an infrequently bought item. This process is the most complex type of consumer buying decision and is associated with high involvement on the part of the consumer. This process resembles the model outlined in Exhibit 6.1. These consumers want to make the right decision, so they want to know as much as they can about the product category and available brands. People usually experience the most cognitive dissonance when buying high-involvement products. Buyers use several criteria for evaluating their options and spend much time seeking information. Buying a home or a car, for example, requires extensive decision making.

The type of decision making that consumers use to purchase a product does not necessarily remain constant. For instance, if a routinely purchased product no longer satisfies, consumers may practice limited or extensive decision making to switch to another brand. And people who first use extensive decision making may then use limited or routine decision making for future purchases. For example, when a family gets a new puppy, they will spend a lot of time and energy trying out different toys to determine which one the dog prefers. Once the new owners learn

routine response behavior
the type of decision making exhibited by consumers buying frequently purchased, low-cost goods and services; requires little search and decision time

limited decision making the type of decision making that requires a moderate amount of time for gathering information and deliberating about an unfamiliar brand in a familiar product category

extensive decision making the most complex type of consumer decision making, used when buying an unfamiliar, expensive product or an infrequently bought item; requires use of several criteria for evaluating options and much time for seeking information

that the dog prefers a bone to a ball, however, the purchase no longer requires extensive evaluation and will become routine.

6-4a Factors Determining the Level of Consumer Involvement

The level of involvement in the purchase depends on the following factors:

- **Previous experience:** When consumers have had previous experience with a good or service, the level of involvement typically decreases. After repeated product trials, consumers learn to make quick choices. Because consumers are familiar with the product and know whether it will satisfy their needs, they become less involved in the purchase. For example, a consumer purchasing cereal has many brands to choose from—just think of any grocery store cereal aisle. If the consumer always buys the same brand because it satisfies his hunger, then he has a low level of involvement. When a consumer purchases a new category of cereal for the first time, however, it likely will be a much more involved purchase.

- **Interest:** Involvement is directly related to consumer interests, as in cars, music, movies, bicycling, or online games. Naturally, these areas of interest vary from one individual to another. A person highly involved in bike racing will be more interested in the type of bike she owns and will spend quite a bit of time evaluating different bikes. If a person wants a bike only for recreation, however, he may be fairly uninvolved in the purchase. He may just choose a bike from the most convenient location and in a reasonable price range.

- **Perceived risk of negative consequences:** As the perceived risk in purchasing a product increases, so does a consumer's level of involvement. The types of risks that concern consumers include financial risk, social risk, and psychological risk.

  - Financial risk is exposure to loss of wealth or purchasing power. Because high risk is associated with high-priced purchases, consumers tend to become extremely involved. Therefore, price and involvement are usually directly related: As price increases, so does the level of involvement. For example, someone who is purchasing a new car for the first time (higher perceived risk) will spend a lot of time and effort making this purchase.

  - Social risks occur when consumers buy products that can affect people's social opinions of them (for example, driving an old, beat-up car or wearing unstylish clothes).

  - Psychological risks occur if consumers believe that making the wrong decision might cause some concern or anxiety. For example, some consumers feel guilty about eating foods that are not healthy, such as regular ice cream rather than fat-free frozen yogurt.

- **Social visibility:** Involvement also increases as the social visibility of a product increases. Products often on social display include clothing (especially designer labels), jewelry, cars, and furniture. All these items make a statement about the purchaser and, therefore, carry a social risk.

High involvement means that the consumer cares about a product category or a specific good or service. The product or service is relevant and important, and means something to the buyer. High involvement can

Purchase involvement depends on level of interest. If this shopper is looking to use a bike as her main mode of transportation, then she is highly involved in this purchase decision.

yellowdog/Cultura RM/Alamy

take a number of different forms. The most important types are discussed below:

- *Product involvement* means that a product category has high personal relevance. Product enthusiasts are consumers with high involvement in a product category. The fashion industry has a large segment of product enthusists. These people are seeking the latest fashion trends and want to wear the latest clothes.

- *Situational involvement* means that the circumstances of a purchase may temporarily transform a low-involvement decision into a high-involvement one. High involvement comes into play when the consumer perceives risk in a specific situation. For example, an individual might routinely buy low-priced brands of liquor and wine. When the boss visits, however, the consumer might make a high-involvement decision and buy more prestigious brands.

- *Shopping involvement* represents the personal relevance of the process of shopping. Some people enjoy the process of shopping even if they do not plan to buy anything. For others, shopping is an enjoyable social activity. Many consumers also engage in **showrooming**—examining merchandise in a physical retail location without purchasing it, and then shopping online for a better deal on the same item.

- *Enduring involvement* represents an ongoing interest in some product, such as kitchen gadgets, or activity, such as fishing. The consumer is always searching for opportunities to consume the product or participate in the activity. Enduring involvement typically gives personal gratification to consumers as they continue to learn about, shop for, and consume these goods and services. Therefore, there is often linkage between enduring involvement, shopping, and product involvement.

- *Emotional involvement* represents how emotional a consumer gets during some specific consumption activity. Emotional involvement is closely related to enduring involvement because the things that consumers care most about will eventually create high emotional involvement. Sports fans typify consumers with high emotional involvement.

6-4b Marketing Implications of Involvement

Marketing strategy varies according to the level of involvement associated with the product. For high-involvement product purchases, marketing managers

Mikeledray/Shutterstock.com

Tide uses bright, eye-catching packaging to draw customers to what is otherwise a low-involvement product.

have several objectives. First, promotion to the target market should be extensive and informative. A good ad gives consumers the information they need for making the purchase decision and specifies the benefits and unique advantages of owning the product. For example, Ford has a vehicle with many custom options that is marketed to small business owners. One example of a recent print ad shows how one entrepreneur customized his Ford Transit to help improve the efficiency of his home theater and electronics installation business. Ford highlights the fact that unique businesses need unique and customizable transportation. The Transit comes in three body lengths, each offering a unique volume and payload capacity. There are also three different roof heights to choose from, and of course, several different engines.

For low-involvement product purchases, consumers may not recognize their wants until they are in the store. Therefore, in-store promotion is an important tool when promoting low-involvement products. Marketing managers focus on package design so the product will be eye-catching and easily recognized on the shelf. Examples of products that take this approach are Campbell's soups, Tide detergent, Velveeta cheese, and Heinz

showrooming the practice of examining merchandise in a physical retail location without purchasing it, and then shopping online for a better deal on the same item

ketchup. In-store displays also stimulate sales of low-involvement products. A good display can explain the product's purpose and prompt recognition of a want. Displays of snack foods in supermarkets have been known to increase sales many times above normal. Coupons, cents-off deals, and two-for-one offers also effectively promote low-involvement items.

Linking a product to a higher-involvement issue is another tactic that marketing managers can use to increase the sales or positive publicity of a relatively low-involvement product. In 2015, McDonald's tweaked its long-running advertising campaign from "I'm Lovin' It," which focused on McDonald's various menu items, to "Choose Lovin'." The notion of choosing love and offering love is a much more emotional and high-involvement message. The fast food chain randomly selected a million customers and let them pay for their meals with acts of love. Participants could do things like hug family members or call their moms and tell them that they loved them to "choose lovin'."[12]

Researchers have found that another way to increase involvement is to offer products on a "limited availability" basis. McDonald's, for example, has regularly cycled its McRib sandwich on and off its menu for more than 30 years. Marketers can use several ways to trigger limited availability, including daily specials (for example special soup *du jour*), day of the week (for example, Sunday brunch), promotional periods (for example, item availability for a limited time only), harvest time (for example, corn in the summer), and small production runs (for example, limited edition items). Limited availability creates a "get it now or never" mentality. Researchers have found that consuming such products leads to more consumer enjoyment than if the items were always available.[13]

It is important to understand that the consumer decision-making process does not occur in a vacuum. On the contrary, underlying cultural, social, individual, and psychological factors strongly influence the decision process. These factors have an effect from the time a consumer perceives a stimulus through postpurchase behavior. Cultural factors, which include culture and values, subculture, and social class, exert a broad influence over consumer decision making. Social factors sum up the social interactions between a consumer and influential groups of people, such as reference groups, opinion leaders, and family members. Individual factors, which include gender, age, family life cycle stage, personality, self-concept, and lifestyle, are unique to each individual and play a major role in the type of products and services consumers want. Psychological factors determine how consumers perceive and interact with their environments and influence the ultimate decisions consumers make. They include perception, motivation, and learning. Exhibit 6.3 summarizes these influences, and the following sections cover each in more detail.

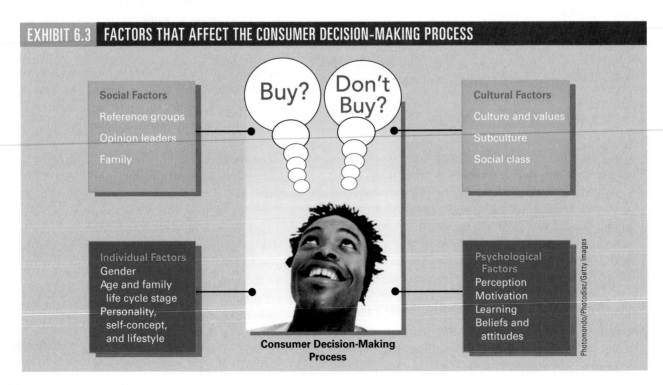

EXHIBIT 6.3 FACTORS THAT AFFECT THE CONSUMER DECISION-MAKING PROCESS

Social Factors
Reference groups
Opinion leaders
Family

Buy?

Don't Buy?

Cultural Factors
Culture and values
Subculture
Social class

Individual Factors
Gender
Age and family life cycle stage
Personality, self-concept, and lifestyle

Consumer Decision-Making Process

Psychological Factors
Perception
Motivation
Learning
Beliefs and attitudes

Photomondo/Photodisc/Getty Images

6-5 CULTURAL INFLUENCES ON CONSUMER BUYING DECISIONS

Of all the factors that affect consumer decision making, cultural factors exert the broadest and deepest influence. Marketers must understand the way people's culture and its accompanying values, as well as their subculture and social class, influence their buying behavior.

6-5a Culture and Values

Culture is the set of values, norms, attitudes, and other meaningful symbols that shape human behavior and the artifacts, or products, of that behavior as they are transmitted from one generation to the next. It is the essential character of a society that distinguishes it from other cultural groups. The underlying elements of every culture are the values, language, myths, customs, rituals, and laws that guide the behavior of the people.

Culture is pervasive. Cultural values and influences are the ocean in which individuals swim, and yet most are completely unaware that it is there. What people eat, how they dress, what they think and feel, and what language they speak are all dimensions of culture. Culture encompasses all the things consumers do without conscious choice because their culture's values, customs, and rituals are ingrained in their daily habits.

Culture is functional. Human interaction creates values and prescribes acceptable behavior for each culture. By establishing common expectations, culture gives order to society. Sometimes these expectations are enacted into laws. For example, drivers in our culture must stop at a red light. Other times these expectations are taken for granted: grocery stores and hospitals are open 24 hours, whereas banks are open only during "bankers' hours," typically nine in the morning until five in the afternoon.

Culture is learned. Consumers are not born knowing the values and norms of their society. Instead, they must learn what is acceptable from family and friends. Children learn the values that will govern their behavior from parents, teachers, and peers. As members of our society, they learn to shake hands when they greet someone, to drive on the right-hand side of the road, and to eat pizza and drink Coca-Cola.

Culture is dynamic. It adapts to changing needs and an evolving environment. The rapid growth of technology in today's world has accelerated the rate of cultural change. Our culture is beginning to tell us when it is okay to send a text message and when it is considered impolite. Assume that you are on a first date with someone in a nice, romantic restaurant and your date is talking to you about his or her favorite things to do. Pulling out your smartphone to check a text will probably lead to a very short date. Cultural norms will continue to evolve because of our need for social patterns that solve problems.

The most defining element of a culture is its values. Recall that "value" can refer to an enduring belief shared by a society that a specific mode of conduct is personally or socially preferable to another mode of conduct. People's value systems have a great effect on their consumer behavior. Consumers with similar value systems tend to react alike to prices and other marketing-related inducements. Values also correspond to consumption patterns. For example, Americans place a high value on convenience. This value has created lucrative markets for products such as breakfast bars, energy bars, and nutrition bars that allow consumers to eat on the go. Values can also influence consumers' television viewing habits or the magazines they read. For instance, people who strongly object to violence avoid crime shows and vegetarians avoid cooking magazines that feature numerous meat-based recipes.

6-5b Subculture

A culture can be divided into subcultures on the basis of demographic characteristics, geographic regions, national and ethnic background, political beliefs, and religious beliefs. A **subculture** is a homogeneous group of people who share elements of the overall culture as well as cultural elements unique to their own group. Within subcultures, people's attitudes, values, and purchase decisions are even more similar than they are within the broader culture. Subcultural differences may result in considerable variation within a culture in what, how, when, and where people buy goods and services.

Once marketers identify subcultures, they can design special marketing to serve their needs. The United States' growing Hispanic

> **culture** the set of values, norms, attitudes, and other meaningful symbols that shape human behavior and the artifacts, or products, of that behavior as they are transmitted from one generation to the next
>
> **subculture** a homogeneous group of people who share elements of the overall culture as well as unique elements of their own group

Bloody/Shutterstock.com

The popularity of biker events has created an opportunity for fans of Harley-Davidson to get together and create their own subculture.

arbitrator, and translator. This spouse compensates for her relative advantage in purchase decision making by giving up control in other decisions. Therefore, the immigrant spouse may gain greater influence in decisions relating to vacations, education, and food.[14]

6-5c Social Class

The United States, like other societies, has a social class system. A **social class** is a group of people who are considered nearly equal in status or community esteem, who regularly socialize among themselves both formally and informally, and who share behavioral norms.

A number of techniques have been used to measure social class, and a number of criteria have been used to define it. One view of contemporary U.S. status structure is shown in Exhibit 6.4.

As you can see from Exhibit 6.4, the upper and upper middle classes comprise the small segment of affluent and wealthy Americans. In terms of consumer buying patterns, the affluent are more likely to own their own homes and purchase new cars and trucks and are less likely to smoke. The very rich flex their financial muscles by spending more on vacation homes, jewelry, vacations and cruises, and housekeeping and gardening services. The most affluent consumers are more likely to attend art auctions and galleries, dance performances, operas, the theater, museums, concerts, and sporting events. What types of things do the wealthiest of the wealthy buy? The most expensive new car in the world is the Lamborghini Veneno. It goes from 0 to 60 miles per hour in 2.8 seconds and has a top speed of 221 mph. Only three of these cars are made a year at a price of $4,500,000 each.[15] Unfortunately, if you want one, you must get on a waiting list.

The majority of Americans today define themselves as middle class, regardless of their actual income or educational attainment. This phenomenon most likely occurs because working-class Americans tend to aspire to the middle-class lifestyle, while some of those who do achieve some affluence call themselves middle-class as a matter of principle.

The working class is a distinct subset of the middle class. Interest in organized labor is one of the most common attributes among the working class.

population has made South and Central American subcultures a prime focus for many companies, for example. Recall that marketing to Hispanics was discussed in Chapter 4.

In the United States alone, countless subcultures can be identified. Many are concentrated geographically. People who belong to the Church of Jesus Christ of Latter-Day Saints, for example, are clustered mainly in Utah; Cajuns are located in the bayou regions of southern Louisiana. Many Hispanics live in states bordering Mexico, whereas the majority of Chinese, Japanese, and Korean Americans are found on the West Coast. Other subcultures are geographically dispersed. Computer hackers, people who are hearing or visually impaired, Harley-Davidson bikers, military families, and university professors may be found throughout the country. Yet they have identifiable attitudes, values, and needs that distinguish them from the larger culture.

Today, America has a rapidly growing number of binational households. In such households, one spouse was born and raised in the United States while the other was originally from another country. This often creates cultural complexity in family purchase decision making. Researchers have found that the partner with the greatest cultural competence (knowledge of the customs of the country of residence) plays the family role of cultural bridge,

social class a group of people in a society who are considered nearly equal in status or community esteem, who regularly socialize among themselves both formally and informally, and who share behavioral norms

EXHIBIT 6.4 U.S. SOCIAL CLASSES

Upper Classes		
Capitalist class	1%	People whose investment decisions shape the national economy; income mostly from assets, earned or inherited; university connections
Upper middle class	14%	Upper-level managers, professionals, owners of medium-sized businesses; well-to-do, stay-at-home homemakers who decline occupational work by choice; college educated; family income well above national average
Middle Classes		
Middle class	33%	Middle-level white-collar, top-level blue-collar; education past high school typical; income somewhat above national average; loss of manufacturing jobs has reduced the population of this class
Working class	32%	Middle-level blue-collar, lower-level white-collar; income below national average; largely working in skilled or semi-skilled service jobs
Lower Classes		
Working poor	11–12%	Low-paid service workers and operatives; some high school education; below mainstream in living standard; crime and hunger are daily threats
Underclass	8–9%	People who are not regularly employed and who depend primarily on the welfare system for sustenance; little schooling; living standard below poverty line

This group often rates job security as the most important reason for taking a job. The working-class person depends heavily on relatives and the community for economic and emotional support.

Lifestyle distinctions between the social classes are greater than the distinctions within a given class. The most significant difference between the classes occurs between the middle and lower classes, where there is a major shift in lifestyles. Members of the lower class have annual incomes at or below the poverty level—$11,770 for individuals and $24,250 for families of four (as defined by the federal government).[16]

Social class is typically measured as a combination of occupation, income, education, wealth, and other variables. For instance, affluent upper-class consumers are more likely to be salaried executives or self-employed professionals with at least an undergraduate degree. Working-class or middle-class consumers are more likely to be hourly service workers or blue-collar employees with only a high school education. Educational attainment, however, seems to be the most reliable indicator of a person's social and economic status. Those with college degrees or graduate degrees are more likely to fall into the upper classes, while those with some college experience fall closest to traditional concepts of the middle class.

Marketers are interested in social class for two main reasons. First, social class often indicates which medium to use for promotion. Suppose an insurance company seeks to sell its policies to middle-class families. It might advertise during the local evening news because middle-class families tend to watch more television than other classes do. If the company wanted to sell more policies to upscale individuals, it might place an ad in a business publication like the *Wall Street Journal*. The Internet,

Knowing what products appeal to which social classes can help mareters determine where to best distribute their products.

long the domain of more educated and affluent families, has become an increasingly important advertising outlet for advertisers hoping to reach blue-collar workers and homemakers.

Second, knowing what products appeal to which social classes can help marketers determine where to best distribute their products. Affluent Americans, one-fifth of the U.S. population, have changed their buying habits since the Great Recession ended. They are now willing to spend more of their discretionary income on one-of-a-kind items. Full-priced and upscale retailers such as Neiman Marcus have experienced greater sales gains than have discount chains. Because many lower-income consumers are still struggling to recover from job loss, retailers such as Walmart are selling smaller packages of items because customers do not have enough cash to buy more standard-size products.

EXHIBIT 6.5 TYPES OF REFERENCE GROUPS

Reference groups

Direct Face-to-face membership
- **Primary** Small, informal group
- **Secondary** Large, formal group

Indirect Nonmembership
- **Aspirational** Group that someone would like to join
- **Nonaspirational** Group with which someone wants to avoid being identified

6-6 SOCIAL INFLUENCES ON CONSUMER BUYING DECISIONS

Many consumers seek out the opinions of others to reduce their search and evaluation effort or uncertainty, especially as the perceived risk of the decision increases. Consumers may also seek out others' opinions for guidance on new products or services, products with image-related attributes, or products for which attribute information is lacking or uninformative. Specifically, consumers interact socially with reference groups, opinion leaders, and family members to obtain product information and decision approval.

6-6a Reference Groups

People interact with many reference groups. A **reference group** consists of all the formal and informal groups that influence the buying behavior of an individual. Consumers may use products or brands to identify with or become a member of a group. They learn from observing how members of their reference groups consume, and they use the same criteria to make their own consumer decisions.

Reference groups can be categorized very broadly as either direct or indirect (see Exhibit 6.5). Direct reference groups are membership groups that touch people's lives directly. They can be either primary or secondary. A **primary membership group** includes all groups with which people interact regularly in an informal manner, such as family, friends, members of social media, and coworkers. Today, they may also communicate by e-mail, text messages, Facebook, Skype, or other social media as well as face-to-face. In contrast, people associate with a **secondary membership group** less consistently and more formally. These groups might include clubs, professional groups, and religious groups.

Consumers also are influenced by many indirect, nonmembership reference groups to which they do not belong. An **aspirational reference group** is a group a person would like to join. To join an aspirational group, a person must at least conform to the norms of that group. (A **norm** consists of the values and attitudes deemed acceptable by the group.) Thus, a person who

reference group all of the formal and informal groups in society that influence an individual's purchasing behavior

primary membership group a reference group with which people interact regularly in an informal, face-to-face manner, such as family, friends, and coworkers

secondary membership group a reference group with which people associate less consistently and more formally than a primary membership group, such as a club, professional group, or religious group

aspirational reference group a group that someone would like to join

norm a value or attitude deemed acceptable by a group

Members of the Hell's Angels biker gang protest in Oslo, Norway, against police bias towards motorcycle gangs.

professionals who take an interest in Harley-Davidson motorcycles, biker gangs serve as both an aspirational and a nonaspirational reference group. Though the professionals (derisively called RUBS—rich urban bikers—by hardcore Harley enthusiasts) aspire to the freedom, community, and tough posturing of biker gangs, they do not aspire to the perpetual life on the road, crime, or violence of gangs. Thus, a professional may buy a Harley because of the gangs, but he may intentionally buy a specific model not typically associated with those gangs.

Reference groups are particularly powerful in influencing the clothes people wear, the cars they drive, the electronics they use, the activities they participate in, the foods they eat, and the luxury goods they purchase. In short, the activities, values, and goals of reference groups directly influence consumer behavior. For marketers, reference groups have three important implications: (1) They serve as information sources and influence perceptions; (2) they affect an individual's aspiration levels; and (3) their norms either constrain or stimulate consumer behavior.

wants to be elected to public office may begin to dress more conservatively, as other politicians do. He or she may go to many of the restaurants and social engagements that city and business leaders attend and try to play a role that is acceptable to voters and other influential people.

Nonaspirational reference groups, or dissociative groups, influence our behavior when we try to maintain distance from them. A consumer may avoid buying some types of clothing or cars, going to certain restaurants or stores, or even buying a home in a certain neighborhood to avoid being associated with a particular group. For middle- and upper-middle-class

6-6b Opinion Leaders

Reference groups and social media groups (for example, your friends on Facebook) frequently include individuals known as group leaders, or **opinion leaders**—persons who influence others. Obviously, it is important for marketing managers to persuade such people to purchase their goods or services. They are often the most influential, informed, plugged-in, and vocal members of society. Technology companies have found that teenagers, because of their willingness to experiment, are key opinion leaders for the success of new technologies.

Opinion leadership is a casual phenomenon and is usually inconspicuous, so locating opinion leaders offline can be a challenge. An opinion leader in one field, such as cooking, may not be an opinion leader in another, such as sports. In fact, it is rare to find an opinion leader who spans multiple diverse domains. Thus, marketers often try to create opinion leaders. They may use high school cheerleaders to

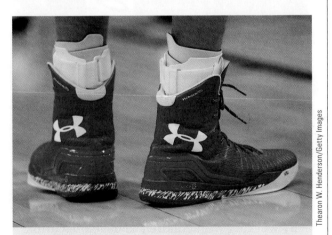

Professional athletes serve as opinion leaders when they choose a specific shoe they feel helps them perform at a high level.

nonaspirational reference group a group with which an individual does not want to associate

opinion leader an individual who influences the opinions of others

model new fall fashions or civic leaders to promote insurance, new cars, and other merchandise. On a national level, companies sometimes use movie stars, sports figures, and other celebrities to promote products, hoping they are appropriate opinion leaders. The effectiveness of celebrity endorsements varies, though, depending largely on how credible and attractive the spokesperson is and how familiar people are with him or her. Endorsements are most likely to succeed if a reasonable association between the spokesperson and the product can be established.

Increasingly, marketers are looking to social media to find opinion leaders, but the sheer volume of posts and platforms makes determining true opinion leaders challenging. So, marketers are focusing their attention on platforms such as Facebook, Pinterest, and Tumblr because those sites better identify the social trends that are shaping consumer behavior. With their unprecedented ability to network and communicate with each other, people often rely on each other's opinions more than marketing messages when making purchase decisions. And social media are becoming a key way that people communicate their opinions.

Social media have made identification of opinion leaders easier than ever before. Klout, for example, collects data from 13 social networks and search data from Bing and Google to measure a person's influence. The firm also looks at offline data such as how often the individual is mentioned in traditional media like magazines and newspapers. Klout then tabulates a score for each person ranging from 1 to 100.

Klout's Perks program has expanded from offering certain opinion leaders coupons and product samples to helping brands send out invitations for product launches, promotional events, and concerts. The company recently launched VIP Perks, a program that tracks opinion leaders' mobile devices to tell when they enter a store or restaurant. Marketers have used the program to offer social influencers with high Klout scores seat upgrades at Cirque Du Soleil shows and access to VIP airport lounges.[17] Research has found that when social media influencers purchase a new product, they tend to share this information right away with their social networks.[18]

6-6c Family

The family is the most important social institution for many consumers, strongly influencing values, attitudes, self-concept, and buying behavior. For example, a family that strongly values good health will have a

socialization process how cultural values and norms are passed down to children

grocery list distinctly different from that of a family that views every dinner as a gourmet event. Moreover, the family is responsible for the **socialization process**, the passing down of cultural values and norms to children. Children learn by observing their parents' consumption patterns, so they tend to shop in similar patterns.

Decision-making roles among family members tend to vary significantly, depending on the type of item purchased. Family members assume a variety of roles in the purchase process. *Initiators* suggest, initiate, or plant the seed for the purchase process. The initiator can be any member of the family. For example, Sister might initiate the product search by asking for a new bicycle as a birthday present. *Influencers* are members of the family whose opinions are valued. In our example, Mom might function as a price-range watchdog, an influencer whose main role is to veto or approve price ranges. Brother may give his opinion on certain makes of bicycles. The *decision maker* is the family member who actually makes the decision to buy or not to buy. For example, Dad or Mom is likely to choose the final brand and model of bicycle to

By working with children to develop a drink they like, Innocent Smoothies for kids can advertise kid-friendly flavors with healthy benefits, satisfying moms and kids.

buy after seeking further information from Sister about cosmetic features such as color and then imposing additional criteria of his or her own, such as durability and safety. The *purchaser* (probably Dad or Mom) is the one who actually exchanges money for the product. Finally, the *consumer* is the actual user—in this case, Sister.

Marketers should consider family purchase situations along with the distribution of consumer and decision-maker roles among family members. Ordinary marketing views the individual as both decision maker and consumer. Family marketing adds several other possibilities: sometimes more than one family member or all family members are involved in the decision, sometimes only children are involved in the decision, sometimes more than one consumer is involved, and sometimes the decision maker and the consumer are different people. In most households, when parental joint decisions are being made, spouses consider their partner's needs and perceptions to maintain decision fairness and harmony. This tends to minimize family conflict. When couples agree to narrow down their options before making a purchase, they are more likely to be satisfied with the eventual outcome and less likely to feel regret.

6-6d Individual Differences in Susceptibility to Social Influences

Social influence plays an important role in consumer behavior, but not all persons are equally influenced in their purchase decisions. Some have a strong need to build the images others have of them by buying products used by other members of their reference groups. Seeking approval of others through the "correct" product ownership is very important to these consumers. This is particularly true for conspicuous items (those that others can easily see) such as clothes, jewelry, cars, and even mobile devices. These individuals have a strong desire to avoid negative impressions in public settings. For example, wearing the wrong bather suit at the university swimming pool would be very distressing to this type of consumer.

Consumers differ in their feelings of connectedness to other consumers. A consumer with a **separated self-schema** perceives himself as distinct and separate from others. A person with a **connected self-schema** sees himself as an integral part of a group. Research has found that individuals who feel connected respond more favorably to advertisements that promote group belonging and cohesion.

The influence of other people on how a consumer behaves is strongest when that consumer knows or feels

that she is being watched. Researchers have found this to be especially true when individuals are consuming or buying personal products. Some people will not buy memberships to athletic clubs because they don't want to work out with (or even around) a group of people. They fear how they may appear to others.[19]

6-7 INDIVIDUAL INFLUENCES ON CONSUMER BUYING DECISIONS

While individuality impacts a person's susceptibility to social influences, factors such as gender, age, life cycle stage, personality, self-concept, and lifestyle also play important roles in consumer decision making. Individual characteristics are generally stable over the course of one's life. For instance, most people do not change their gender, and the act of changing personality or lifestyle requires a complete reorientation of one's life. In the case of age and life cycle stage, these changes occur gradually over time.

6-7a Gender

Physiological differences between men and women result in many different needs, such as with health and beauty products. Just as important are the distinct cultural, social, and economic roles played by men and women and the effects that these have on their decision-making processes. A recent survey found that 52 percent of women have purchased a product based upon a marketer's portrayal of women.[20] Messages and videos for companies such as Nike, Always, and Under Armour were perceived as very positive. The Dove "Real Beauty" campaign was named the number one ad of the 21st century by *Advertising Age*. Under Armour's "I Will What I Want" ad also fared well for its portrayal of women pushing back against the idea of perfection and simply embracing themselves (see an example at www.youtube.com/watch?v=ZY0cdXr_1MA).

Trends in gender marketing are influenced by the changing roles of men and women in society. For example, men used to rely on the women in their lives to shop for them. Today, however, more men are shopping for themselves. More than seventy percent of men shop online and about 48 percent shop

separated self-schema a perspective whereby a consumer sees himself or herself as distinct and separate from others

connected self-schema a perspective whereby a consumer sees himself or herself as an integral part of a group

from mobile devices. When doing so, men use smartphones twice as often as they use tablets. Men are price-conscious, often scanning QR codes rather than typing in URLs to retrieve promotional materials, coupons, and product information. In fact, a Harris Interactive poll found that, "men have become the chief coupon-cutters of the mobile era."[21]

6-7b Age and Family Life Cycle Stage

A consumer's age and family life cycle stage can have a significant impact on his or her behavior. How old a consumer is generally indicates what products he or she may be interested in purchasing. Consumer tastes in food, clothing, cars, furniture, and recreation are often age related.

Related to a person's age is his or her place in the family life cycle. As Chapter 8 explains in more detail, the *family life cycle* is an orderly series of stages through which consumers' attitudes and behavioral tendencies evolve through maturity, experience, and changing income and status. Marketers often define their target markets in terms of family life cycle, such as "young singles," "young married couples with children," and "middle-aged married couples without children." For instance, young singles spend more than average on alcoholic beverages, education, and entertainment. New parents typically increase their spending on health care, clothing, housing, and food and decrease their spending on alcohol, education, and transportation. Households with older children spend more on food, entertainment, personal care products, and education, as well as cars and gasoline. After their children leave home, spending by older couples on vehicles, women's clothing, and health care typically increases. For instance, the presence of children in the home is the most significant determinant of the type of vehicle that's driven off the new car lot. Parents are the ultimate need-driven car consumers, requiring larger cars and trucks to haul their children and all their belongings. It comes as no surprise, then, that for all households with children, SUVs rank either first or second among new-vehicle purchases, followed by minivans.

NONTRADITIONAL LIFE CYCLES Marketers should also be aware of the many nontraditional life cycle paths that are common today and provide insights into the needs and wants of such consumers as

Gelpi JM/Shutterstock.com

divorced parents, lifelong singles, and childless couples. Three decades ago, married couples with children under the age of 18 accounted for about half of U.S. households. Today, such families make up only 23 percent of all households, while people living alone or with nonfamily members represent more than thirty percent. Furthermore, according to the U.S. Census Bureau, the number of single-mother households grew by 25 percent over the last decade. The shift toward more single-parent households is part of a broader societal change that has put more women on the career track.

SINGLE PARENTS Careers often create a *poverty of time* for single parents. To cope with the dual demands of a career and raising children, single parents are always on the lookout for time saving products like quick-preparation foods and no-iron clothing. Rightly so, more and more marketers are catering to the single parent market. eTargetMedia maintains a list of over 9,500,000 active single parents that it rents out for both e-mail and postal advertising campaigns. The firm says that the list is ideal for offers pertaining to education, childcare, insurance, photo sharing, parenting magazines and books, camps, and children's recreation.[22]

LIFE EVENTS Another way to look at the life cycle is to look at major events in one's life over time. Life-changing events can occur at any time. A few examples are death of a spouse, moving, birth or adoption of a child, retirement, job loss, divorce, and marriage. Typically, such events are quite stressful, and consumers will often take steps to minimize that stress. Many times, life-changing events will mean new consumption patterns. For example, a recently divorced person may try to improve his or her appearance by joining a health club and dieting. Someone moving to a different city will need a new dentist, grocery store, auto service center, and doctor, among other things. Marketers realize that life events often mean a chance to gain a new customer. The Welcome Wagon offers free gifts and services for area newcomers. Lowe's sends out a discount coupon to those moving to a new community. And when you put your home on the market, you will quickly start receiving flyers from moving companies promising a great price on moving your household goods.

6-7c Personality, Self-Concept, and Lifestyle

Each consumer has a unique personality. **Personality** is a broad concept that can be thought of as a way of organizing and grouping how an individual typically reacts to situations. Thus, personality combines psychological makeup and environmental forces. It includes people's underlying dispositions, especially their most dominant characteristics. Although personality is one of the least useful concepts in the study of consumer behavior, some marketers believe personality influences the types and brands of products purchased. For instance, the type of car, clothes, or jewelry a consumer buys may reflect one or more personality traits.

Self-concept, or self-perception, is how consumers perceive themselves. Self-concept includes attitudes, perceptions, beliefs, and self-evaluations. Although self-concept may change, the change is often gradual. Through self-concept, people define their identity, which in turn provides for consistent and coherent behavior.

Self-concept combines the **ideal self-image** (the way an individual would like to be perceived) and the **real self-image** (how an individual actually perceives himself or herself). Generally, we try to raise our real self-image toward our ideal (or at least narrow the gap). Consumers seldom buy products that jeopardize their self-image. For example, someone who sees herself as a trendsetter would not buy clothing that does not project a contemporary image.

Human behavior depends largely on self-concept. Because consumers want to protect their identity as individuals, the products they buy, the stores they patronize, and the credit cards they carry support their self-image. No other product quite reflects a person's self-image as much as the car he or she drives. For example, many young consumers do not like family sedans like the Honda Accord or Toyota Camry and say they would buy one for their mom but not for themselves. Likewise, younger parents may avoid purchasing minivans because they do not want to sacrifice the youthful image they have of themselves just because they have new responsibilities. To combat decreasing sales, marketers of the Nissan Quest minivan decided to reposition it as something other than a "mom mobile" or "soccer mom car." They chose the ad copy "Passion built it. Passion will fill it up," followed by "What if we made a minivan that changed the way people think of minivans?"

Eurobanks/iStock/Thinkstock

By influencing the degree to which consumers perceive a good or service to be self-relevant, marketers can affect consumers' motivation to learn about, shop for, and buy a certain brand. Marketers also consider self-concept important because it helps explain the relationship between individuals' perceptions of themselves and their consumer behavior.

Many companies now use psychographics to better understand their market segments. For many years, marketers selling products to mothers conveniently assumed that all moms were fairly homogeneous and concerned about the same things—the health and well-being of their children—and that they could all be reached with a similar message. But recent lifestyle research has shown that there are traditional, blended, and nontraditional moms, and companies like Procter & Gamble and Pillsbury are using strategies to reach these different types of mothers. Psychographics is also effective with other market segments. Psychographics and lifestyle segmentation are discussed in more detail in Chapter 8.

6-8 PSYCHOLOGICAL INFLUENCES ON CONSUMER BUYING DECISIONS

An individual's buying decisions are further influenced by psychological factors: perception, motivation, and learning. These factors are what consumers use to interact with their world. They are the tools consumers use to recognize their feelings, gather and analyze information, formulate thoughts and opinions, and take action. Unlike the other three influences on consumer behavior, psychological influences can be affected by a person's environment because they are

personality a way of organizing and grouping the consistencies of an individual's reactions to situations

self-concept how consumers perceive themselves in terms of attitudes, perceptions, beliefs, and self-evaluations

ideal self-image the way an individual would like to be perceived

real self-image the way an individual actually perceives himself or herself

applied on specific occasions. For example, you will perceive different stimuli and process these stimuli in different ways depending on whether you are sitting in class concentrating on the instructor, sitting outside of class talking to friends, or sitting in your dorm room streaming a video.

6-8a Perception

The world is full of stimuli. A stimulus is any unit of input affecting one or more of the five senses: sight, smell, taste, touch, and hearing. The process by which we select, organize, and interpret these stimuli into a meaningful and coherent picture is called **perception**. In essence, perception is how we see the world around us. We act based upon perceptions that may or may not reflect reality. Suppose you are driving to the grocery and you see a house with smoke pouring from the roof. Your perception is that the house is on fire, so you quickly stop to warn any occupants and to call 911. As you approach the house, you hear laughter coming from the back yard. As you peek around the corner, you see a family burning a big pile of leaves and the wind carrying the smoke over the roof. There is no house fire. When you get to the grocery, you see a big, beautiful ripe pineapple and immediately put it in your cart. When you get home, you cut into the pineapple—only to find that it has a rotten core and is inedible. In both cases, you acted based upon perceptions that did not reflect reality.

People cannot perceive every stimulus in their environment. Therefore, they use **selective exposure** to decide which stimuli to notice and which to ignore. A typical consumer is exposed to nearly 3,000 advertising messages a day but notices only between 11 and 20.

The familiarity of an object, contrast, movement, intensity (such as increased volume), and smell are cues that influence perception. Consumers use these cues to identify and define products and brands. Double Tree hotels always have fresh chocolate chip cookies at the reception desk and the entire area smells like just-baked cookies. For most travelers, this cues feelings of warmth and comfort. Cutting-edge consumer research has found that a cluttered, chaotic environment results in consumers spending more. Why does this occur? The perception of a cluttered environment impairs self-control. Disorganized surroundings threaten one's sense of personal control, which in turn taxes one's self-regulatory abilities.[23]

The shape of a product's packaging, such as Coca-Cola's signature contour bottle, can influence perception. Color is another cue, and it plays a key role in consumers' perceptions. Packaged foods manufacturers use color to trigger unconscious associations for grocery shoppers who typically make their shopping decisions in the blink of an eye. Think of the red and white Campbell's soup can and the green and white Green Giant frozen vegetable box, for example.

Two other concepts closely related to selective exposure are selective distortion and selective retention. **Selective distortion** occurs when consumers change or distort information that conflicts with their feelings or beliefs. For example, suppose a college student buys a Dell tablet. After the purchase, if the student gets new information about an alternative brand, such as an Asus Transformer, he or she may distort the information to make it more consistent with the prior view that the Dell is just as good as the Transformer, if not better. Business travelers who are Executive Platinum frequent flyers on American Airlines may distort or discount information about the quality of United Airlines' business class service. The frequent flyer may think to herself, "Yes, the service is OK but the seats are uncomfortable and the planes are always late."

Selective retention is remembering only information that supports personal feelings or beliefs. The consumer forgets all information that may be inconsistent. After reading a pamphlet that contradicts one's political beliefs, for instance, a person may forget many of the points outlined in it. Similarly, consumers may see a news report on suspected illegal practices by their favorite retail store but soon forget the reason the store was featured on the news.

Which stimuli will be perceived often depends on the individual. People can be exposed to the same stimuli under identical conditions but perceive them very differently. For example, two people viewing a television commercial may have different interpretations of the advertising message. One person may be thoroughly engrossed by the message and become highly motivated to buy the product. Thirty seconds after the ad ends, the second person may not be able to recall the content of the message or even the product advertised.

perception the process by which people select, organize, and interpret stimuli into a meaningful and coherent picture

selective exposure a process whereby a consumer notices certain stimuli and ignores others

selective distortion a process whereby a consumer changes or distorts information that conflicts with his or her feelings or beliefs

selective retention a process whereby a consumer remembers only that information that supports his or her personal beliefs

MARKETING IMPLICATIONS OF PERCEPTION

Marketers must recognize the importance of cues, or signals, in consumers' perception of products. Marketing managers first identify the important attributes, such as price or quality, that the targeted consumers want in a product and then design signals to communicate these attributes. For example, consumers will pay more for candy in expensive-looking foil packages. But shiny labels on wine bottles signify less expensive wines; dull labels indicate more expensive wines. Marketers also often use price as a signal to consumers that the product is of higher quality than competing products. Of course, brand names send signals to consumers. The brand names of Close-Up toothpaste, DieHard batteries, and Caress moisturizing soap, for example, identify important product qualities. Names chosen for search engines and sites on the Internet, such as Yahoo!, Amazon, and Bing, are intended to convey excitement and intensity and vastness.

Consumers also associate quality and reliability with certain brand names. Companies watch their brand identity closely, in large part because a strong link has been established between perceived brand value and customer loyalty. Brand names that consistently enjoy high perceived value from consumers include Google, Disney, National Geographic, Mercedes-Benz, and Fisher-Price. Naming a product after a place can also add perceived value by association. Brand names using the words Santa Fe, Dakota, or Texas convey a sense of openness, freedom, and youth, but products named after other locations might conjure up images of pollution and crime. Marketing managers are also interested in the *threshold level of perception*, the minimum difference in a stimulus that the consumer will notice. This concept is sometimes referred to as the "just-noticeable difference." For example, how much would Apple have to drop the price of its 15-inch MacBook Pro with Retina display before consumers perceived it as a bargain—$100? $300? $500? Alternatively, how much could Hershey shrink its milk chocolate bar before consumers noticed that it was smaller, but selling for the same price?

Besides changing such stimuli as price, package size, and volume, marketers can change the product or attempt to reposition its image. But marketers must be careful when adding features. How many new services will discounter Target need to add before consumers perceive it as a full-service department store? How many sporty features will General Motors have to add to a basic two-door sedan before consumers start perceiving it as a sports car?

Marketing managers who intend to do business in global markets should be aware of how foreign consumers perceive their products. For instance, in Japan, product labels are often written in English or French, even though they may not translate into anything meaningful. Many Japanese associate foreign words on product labels with the exotic, the expensive, and high quality.

6-8b Motivation

By studying motivation, marketers can analyze the major forces influencing consumers to buy or not buy products. When you buy a product, you usually do so to fulfill some kind of need. These needs become motives when they are aroused sufficiently. For instance, suppose this morning you were so hungry before class that you needed to eat something. In response to that need, you stopped at Subway for a breakfast sandwich. In other words, you were motivated by hunger to stop at Subway. A **motive** is the driving force that causes a person to take action to satisfy specific needs.

Why are people driven by particular needs at particular times? One popular theory is **Maslow's hierarchy of needs**, illustrated in Exhibit 6.6, which arranges needs in ascending order of

> **motive** a driving force that causes a person to take action to satisfy specific needs
>
> **Maslow's hierarchy of needs** a method of classifying human needs and motivations into five categories in ascending order of importance: physiological, safety, social, esteem, and self-actualization

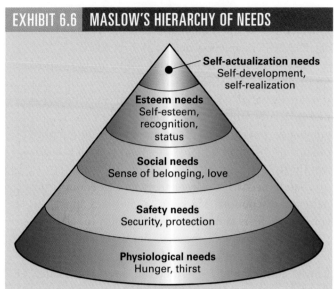

EXHIBIT 6.6   MASLOW'S HIERARCHY OF NEEDS

- **Self-actualization needs** Self-development, self-realization
- **Esteem needs** Self-esteem, recognition, status
- **Social needs** Sense of belonging, love
- **Safety needs** Security, protection
- **Physiological needs** Hunger, thirst

importance: physiological, safety, social, esteem, and self-actualization. As a person fulfills one need, a higher-level need becomes more important.

The most basic human needs—that is, the needs for food, water, and shelter—are *physiological*. Because they are essential to survival, these needs must be satisfied first. Ads showing a juicy hamburger or a runner gulping down Gatorade after a marathon are examples of appeals to satisfy the physiological needs of hunger and thirst.

Safety needs include security and freedom from pain and discomfort. Marketers sometimes appeal to consumers' fears and anxieties about safety to sell their products. For example, aware of the aging population's health fears, the retail medical imaging centers Heart Check America and HealthScreen America advertise that they offer consumers a full body scan for early detection of health problems such as coronary disease and cancer. Some companies or industries advertise to allay consumer fears. For example, in the wake of the September 11, 2001, terrorist attacks, the airline industry found itself having to conduct an image campaign to reassure consumers about the safety of air travel.

After physiological and safety needs have been fulfilled, *social needs*—especially love and a sense of belonging—become the focus. Love includes acceptance by one's peers, as well as sex and romantic love. Marketing managers probably appeal more to this need than to any other. Ads for clothes, cosmetics, and vacation packages suggest that buying the product can bring love.

Love is acceptance without regard to one's contribution. Esteem is acceptance based on one's contribution to the group. *Self-esteem needs* include self-respect and a sense of accomplishment. Esteem needs also include prestige, fame, and recognition of one's accomplishments. Montblanc pens, Mercedes-Benz automobiles, and Neiman Marcus stores all appeal to esteem needs.

The highest human need is *self-actualization*. It refers to finding self-fulfillment and self-expression, reaching the point in life at which "people are what they feel they should be." Maslow believed that very few people ever attain this level. Even so, advertisements may focus on this type of need. For example, American Express ads convey the message that acquiring an AmEx card is one of the highest attainments in life. The Centurion card, often called simply "the black card," requires a $5,000 initiation fee and carries an annual fee of $2,500.

6-8c Learning

Almost all consumer behavior results from **learning**, which is the process that creates changes in behavior through experience and practice. It is not possible to observe learning directly, but we can infer when it has occurred by a person's actions. For example, suppose you see an advertisement for a new and improved cold medicine. If you go to the store that day and buy that remedy, we infer that you have learned something about the cold medicine.

There are two types of learning: experiential and conceptual. *Experiential learning* occurs when an experience changes your behavior. For example, if the new cold medicine does not relieve your symptoms, you may not buy that brand again. *Conceptual learning*, which is not acquired through direct experience but based upon reasoning, is the second type of learning. Assume, for example, that you are standing at a soft drink machine and notice a new diet flavor with an artificial sweetener. Because someone has told you that diet beverages leave an aftertaste, you choose a different drink. You have learned that you would not like this new diet drink without ever trying it.

Reinforcement and repetition boost learning. Reinforcement can be positive or negative. If you see a vendor selling frozen yogurt (stimulus), buy it (response), and find the yogurt to be quite refreshing (reward), your behavior has been positively reinforced. On the other hand, if you buy a new flavor of yogurt and it does not taste good (negative reinforcement), you will not buy that flavor of yogurt again (response). Without positive or negative reinforcement, a person will not be motivated to repeat the behavior pattern or to avoid it. Thus, if a new brand evokes neutral feelings, some marketing activity, such as a price change or an increase in promotion, may be required to induce further consumption. Learning theory is helpful in reminding marketers that concrete and timely strategies are what reinforce desired consumer behavior.

Repetition is a key strategy in promotional campaigns because it can lead to increased learning. Most marketers use repetitive advertising so that consumers will learn what their unique advantage is over the competition. Generally, to heighten learning, advertising messages should be spread out over time rather than clustered together.

A related learning concept useful to marketing managers is **stimulus generalization**. In theory,

learning a process that creates changes in behavior, immediate or expected, through experience and practice

stimulus generalization a form of learning that occurs when one response is extended to a second stimulus similar to the first

stimulus generalization occurs when one response is extended to a second stimulus similar to the first. Marketers often use a successful, well-known brand name for a family of products because it gives consumers familiarity with and knowledge about each product in the family. Such brand name families spur the introduction of new products and facilitate the sale of existing items. OXO relies on consumers' familiarity with its popular kitchen and household products to sell office and medical supplies; Sony's film division relies on name recognition from its home technology, such as the PlayStation. Clorox bathroom cleaner relies on familiarity with Clorox bleach, and Dove shampoo relies on familiarity with Dove soap. Branding is examined in more detail in Chapter 10.

Another form of stimulus generalization occurs when retailers or wholesalers design their packages to resemble well-known manufacturers' brands. Such

Dcwcreations/Shutterstock.com

imitation conveys the notion that the store brand is as good as the national manufacturer's brand.

The opposite of stimulus generalization is **stimulus discrimination**, which means learning to differentiate among similar products. Consumers may perceive one product as more rewarding or stimulating, even if it is virtually indistinguishable from competitors. For example, some consumers prefer Miller Lite and others prefer Bud Light.

With some types of products—such as aspirin, gasoline, bleach, and paper towels—marketers rely on promotion to point out brand differences that consumers would otherwise not recognize. This process, called *product differentiation*, is discussed in more detail in Chapter 8. Usually, product differentiation is based on superficial differences. For example, Bayer tells consumers that it is the aspirin "doctors recommend most."

stimulus discrimination a learned ability to differentiate among similar products

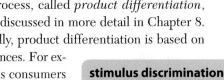

STUDY TOOLS 6

LOCATED AT BACK OF THE TEXTBOOK
☐ Rip out Chapter Review Card

LOCATED AT WWW.CENGAGEBRAIN.COM
☐ Review Key Terms Flashcards and create your own

☐ Track your knowledge & understanding of key concepts in marketing

☐ Complete practice and graded quizzes to prepare for tests

☐ Complete interactive content within the MKTG Online experience

☐ View the chapter highlight boxes within the MKTG Online experience

Business Marketing

LEARNING OUTCOMES

After studying this chapter, you will be able to...

7-1 Describe business marketing

7-2 Describe trends in B-to-B Internet marketing

7-3 Discuss the role of relationship marketing and strategic alliances in business marketing

7-4 Identify the four major categories of business market customers

7-5 Explain the North American Industry Classification System

7-6 Explain the major differences between business and consumer markets

7-7 Describe the seven types of business goods and services

7-8 Discuss the unique aspects of business buying behavior

Dusit/Shutterstock.com

After you finish this chapter go to **PAGE 130** for **STUDY TOOLS.**

7-1 WHAT IS BUSINESS MARKETING?

Business marketing (also called industrial, business-to-business, B-to-B, or B2B marketing) is the marketing of goods and services to individuals and organizations for purposes other than personal consumption. The sale of a personal computer (PC) to your college or university is an example of business marketing. A **business product**, or **industrial product**, is used to manufacture other goods or services, to facilitate an organization's operations, or to resell to other customers. A **consumer product** is bought to satisfy an individual's personal wants or needs. The key characteristic distinguishing business products from consumer products is intended use, not physical form.

business marketing (industrial, business-to-business, B-to-B, or B2B marketing) the marketing of goods and services to individuals and organizations for purposes other than personal consumption

business product (industrial product) a product used to manufacture other goods or services, to facilitate an organization's operations, or to resell to other customers

consumer product a product bought to satisfy an individual's personal wants or needs

How do you distinguish between a consumer product and a business product?

A product that is purchased for personal or family consumption or as a gift is a consumer good. If that same product, such as a PC or a cell phone, is bought for use

in a business, it is a business product. Some common items that are sold as both consumer goods and business products are office supplies (e.g., pens, paper, and staple removers). Some items, such as forklifts, are more commonly sold as business products than as consumer goods.

The size of the business market in the United States and most other countries substantially exceeds that of the consumer market. In the business market, a single customer can account for a huge volume of purchases. For example, IBM's purchasing department spends more than $40 billion annually on business products. Procter & Gamble, Apple, Merck, Dell, and Kimberly-Clark each spend more than half of their annual revenue on business products.[1]

Some large firms that produce goods such as steel, computer memory chips, or production equipment market exclusively to business customers. Other firms market to both businesses and to consumers. Hewlett-Packard marketed exclusively to business customers in the past but now markets laser printers and personal computers to consumers. Sony, traditionally a consumer marketer, now sells office automation products to businesses. Kodak used to sell its cameras exclusively to consumers, but has opted to sell its commercial printing services to businesses

> The key characteristic distinguishing business products from consumer products is intended use, not physical form.

since emerging from bankruptcy in 2013. All of these companies have had to make organizational and marketing changes to expand into the new market categories.

7-2 TRENDS IN B-TO-B INTERNET MARKETING

Over the past decade, marketers have become more and more sophisticated in their use of the Internet. Companies have had to transition from "We have a Web site because our customer does" to having a site that attracts, interests, satisfies, informs, and retains customers. B-to-B companies are increasingly leveraging the Internet as an effective sales and promotion platform (much like B-to-C companies have done for decades). B-to-B companies use the Internet in three major ways. First, they use their Web sites to facilitate communication and orders. Second, they use digital marketing to increase brand awareness. Third, they use digital marketing—primarily in the form of content marketing—to position their businesses as thought leaders and therefore generate sales leads. Companies selling to business buyers face the same challenges as all marketers, including determining the target market and deciding how best to reach it.

Most B-to-B companies see LinkedIn as the most beneficial platform through which to distribute content.

Source: LinkedIn

Every year, new applications that provide additional information about customers are developed. These applications often also lower costs, increase supply chain efficiency, or enhance customer retention, loyalty, and trust. Increasingly, business customers expect suppliers to know them personally, monitor people's movement within their company, and offer personal interaction through social media, e-mail, and personal mailers. As such, we have seen B-to-B marketers use technology like smartphones and tablets to facilitate orders and enhance customer experiences.

A few years ago, many people thought the Internet would eliminate the need for distributors. Why would customers pay a distributor's markup when they could buy directly from the manufacturer with a few mouse clicks? This has occurred less frequently than many expected because distributors often perform important functions such as providing credit, aggregating supplies from multiple sources, making deliveries, and processing returns. Many business customers, especially small firms, depend on knowledgeable distributors for information and advice that is not available to them online.

Social media usage has been the most pervasive B-to-B and B-to-C marketing trend of the past five years. Most companies use e-mail marketing, search engine optimization, paid search, and display advertising to pull customers to their Web sites. This field of marketing requires vigilant adjustment to keep track of new applications and platforms, as well as constant evaluation to determine whether these new avenues are beneficial to (or used by) customers. Generally, B-to-C marketers were faster to adopt social media as part of the promotional mix. B-to-B marketers did not initially see the value in these tools. However, that has changed as social media has become more popular.

Content marketing is a strategic marketing approach focused on creating and distributing valuable, relevant, and consistent content. The goal of this content is to attract and retain a clearly defined audience, and ultimately, drive profitable customer action. This strategy has played an important role for B-to-B marketers. Content marketing includes media such as videos, podcasts, webinars, blog posts, white papers, e-books, slide decks, and more. Sharing valuable insights and interesting content can position a company as a though leader in an area. A 2014 study by the Content Marketing Institute and MarketingProfs found that 86 percent of respondents use content marketing, but many struggle with developing effective content. More than 55 percent of respondents stated plans to increase their content marketing usage in 2015.[2] Most companies use content marketing to increase brand awareness and generate leads. Increasing engagement comes in at a close third. Interestingly, while most B-to-C companies favor Facebook as their primary social media platform, most B-to-B companies see LinkedIn as the most beneficial platform through which to distribute content. Regardless of the platform used, the key to social media-based content marketing for B-to-B marketers is to create compelling and useful content for customers. For example, HubSpot and Marketo develop white papers and e-books on topics such as generating leads through social media for customers and potential customers.

Content marketing a strategic marketing approach that focuses on creating and distributing content that is valuable, relevant and consistent.

As they build reputations in their business areas, many marketers use social media to increase awareness and build relationships and community. Social media platforms like YouTube, LinkedIn, Twitter, and Facebook provide great conversational platforms for doing just that. While building community is important, B-to-B marketers are also using social media to gather leads (as you may have gathered from the HubSpot and Marketo white paper example). Other goals include product promotion, traffic building, search engine optimization (SEO), competitive intelligence and listening, customer feedback and support, and product development.

As platforms such as mobile and streaming video grow, marketers must develop new ways to measure campaign effectiveness. For example, after using social analytics to determine the most effective hashtag from its "Internet of Everything" campaign, Cisco was able to increase usage of one particularly effective hashtag by 440

percent. Global information and measurement company Nielsen recently launched Nielsen Online Campaign Ratings, a "much-anticipated advertising measurement solution." [3] According to data collected through this new platform, less than half of all online advertisement impressions reach their intended audiences. Depending on the medium used, customer targeting varies between a 30 percent and 50 percent coverage rate. [4] Some metrics that are particularly useful for increasing the success of a social media campaign are awareness, engagement, and conversion. *Awareness* is the attention that social media attracts, such as the number of followers or fans. Awareness is generally used as the first step in the marketing funnel, and social media is often paired with paid digital media like display advertising and text-based ads to increase its effectiveness. *Engagement* refers to the interactions between the brand and the audience, such as comments, retweets, shares, and searches. The

The Top Social Media Tools for B-to-B Marketers

Twin Design/Shutterstock.com

BtoB Marketing Magazine surveyed hundreds of B-to-B marketers regarding their social media usage, and while LinkedIn, Facebook, and Twitter were used by the majority of respondents, LinkedIn was the most used social media tool overall (chosen by 94 percent of respondents). Runners up were Twitter (89 percent), Facebook (77 percent), YouTube (77 percent), and Google+ (61 percent). LinkedIn is so popular because it drives more traffic and leads than other platforms for B-to-B marketers. The company has only increased its favor among B-to-B marketers by adding new B-to-B-friendly features like sponsored company updates, groups connected to topics, products and services pages, and a thought leader blogging program. [5]

B-to-B marketers have begun making use of social advertising platforms such as advertisement exchanges on LinkedIn and promoted tweets on Twitter. Video, used for everything from product demonstrations to customer testimonials, is also proving to be an extremely compelling platform for many B-to-B marketers. After finding that attorney profiles were the most viewed parts of its Web site, for example, law firm Levenfeld Pearlstein decided to create a series of videos featuring attorney interviews. In these videos, attorneys answered questions about themselves and the firm, thereby telling a richer story about the company. [6]

purpose of engagement is to get customers to respond to brand-led posts and to start conversations themselves. *Conversions* occur when action is taken and include everything from downloading a piece of content (like a white paper) to actually making a purchase.[7] Each of these metrics affects the return on investment.

7-3 RELATIONSHIP MARKETING AND STRATEGIC ALLIANCES

H&R Block partnered with Arizona's private, Catholic school system in a marketing campaign highlighting the Private Education Tax Credit.

As explained in Chapter 1, relationship marketing is a strategy that entails seeking and establishing ongoing partnerships with customers. Relationship marketing has become an important business marketing strategy as customers have become more demanding and competition has become more intense. Loyal customers are also more profitable than those who are price sensitive and perceive little or no difference among brands or suppliers.

Relationship marketing is increasingly important as business suppliers use platforms like Facebook, Twitter, and other social networking sites to advertise themselves to businesses. Social networking sites encourage businesses to shop around and research options for all their needs. This means that, for many suppliers, retaining their current customers has become a primary focus, whereas acquiring new customers was the focus in the past. Maintaining a steady dialogue between the supplier and the customer is a proven way to gain repeat business.[8]

7-3a Strategic Alliances

A **strategic alliance**, sometimes called a **strategic partnership**, is a cooperative agreement between business firms. Strategic alliances can take the form of licensing or distribution agreements, joint ventures, research and development consortia, and partnerships. They may be between manufacturers, manufacturers and customers, manufacturers and suppliers, and manufacturers and channel intermediaries.

Business marketers form strategic alliances to strengthen operations and better compete. In 2013,

strategic alliance (strategic partnership) a cooperative agreement between business firms

news conglomerate Time formed a strategic alliance with wireless carrier Sprint. Under the partnership, Time's content would automatically be delivered to Sprint's SprintZone app, which comes preloaded on all Sprint devices. According to Cyrus Beagley, general manager of Time's Advertising Sales & Marketing Group, the purpose of the partnership was to "create a really compelling daily content snacking experience that leverages the breadth of our brands."[9]

Sometimes alliance partners are fierce competitors. Take, for example, the partnership between Amazon and Netflix. In 2014, Amazon introduced the Fire TV and the Fire TV Stick, both of which allow users to stream digital media to their home televisions. This product supports several media services, including Netflix, despite that Netflix offers competing services. Instead of trying to compete with Netflix, Amazon included its services in order to offer its customers a satisfactory product.[10]

Other alliances are formed between companies that operate in completely different industries. For example, tax preparation company H&R Block partnered with Arizona's private Catholic school system in a marketing campaign highlighting the Private Education Tax Credit, which allows low-income students to attend the state's high-performing Catholic schools. The partnership generated good publicity for H&R Block while effectively serving the schools' customers (the students' parents). In the first year of the partnership, H&R Block clients generated $167,000 in tax credit

EXHIBIT 7.1 STRATEGIC ALLIANCE: STARBUCKS AND GREEN MOUNTAIN

Gives		Gets	
Starbucks Branded Coffee Starbucks ground coffee has worldwide recognition and a strong market share.	→	**Market Share** Starbucks worldwide recognition allows Green Mountain to steal market share from other single-pod brands that don't carry Starbucks brand coffee.	
Starbucks Customers Starbucks customers are willing to brew at home and tend to be affluent.	→	**Stronger Brand Recognition** By offering the high-value Keurig brewing machine at Starbucks stores, Green Mountain is able to give its Keurig line stronger branding.	
Existing Green Mountain Customers Current Green Mountain customers own Keurig machines and brew single-pod coffee.	→	**Market Share** Focused access to Keurig machine users in homes and businesses increases Starbucks presence in those markets.	
Technology Keurig machines and single-pod brewing technology	→	**Expanded Product Offering** By selling Keurig machines and coffee pods in retail stores, Starbucks can offer more products and more ways to drink Starbucks coffee.	

gifts, sending ninety-two students to private Catholic schools.[11] Exhibit 7.1 demonstrates the benefits Starbucks and Green Mountain Coffee receive from each other through their strategic alliance.

For an alliance to succeed in the long term, it must be built on commitment and trust. **Relationship commitment** means that a firm believes an ongoing relationship with some other firm is so important that it warrants maximum efforts at maintaining it indefinitely.[12] A perceived breakdown in commitment by one of the parties often leads to a breakdown in the relationship.

Trust exists when one party has confidence in an exchange partner's reliability and integrity.[13] Some alliances fail when participants lack trust in their trading partners. Consider, for example, the failed partnership between Phones 4U, an independent phone retailer based in the United Kingdom, and Vodaphone, a British telecommunications company. While the two companies could have created a successful partnership, Vodaphone made the decision to cut ties with Phones 4U in 2014.[14] Vodaphone claimed that Phones 4U refused to improve upon the terms of their agreement when the contract came up for renewal, but Phones 4U believed that it was misled during negotiations and that cutting ties was an unfair decision. This decision forced Phones 4U to lay

off thousands of employees and left the company struggling to restructure its business.

7-3b Relationships in Other Cultures

Although the terms *relationship marketing* and *strategic alliances* are fairly new and popularized mostly by American business executives and educators, the concepts have long been familiar in other cultures. Businesses in China, Japan, Korea, Mexico, and much of Europe rely heavily on personal relationships.

In Japan, for example, exchange between firms is based on personal relationships that are developed through what is called *amae*, or indulgent dependency. *Amae* is the feeling of nurturing concern for, and dependence upon, another. Reciprocity and personal relationships contribute to *amae*. Relationships between companies can develop into a **keiretsu**—a network of interlocking corporate affiliates. Within a *keiretsu*, executives may sit on the boards of

relationship commitment a firm's belief that an ongoing relationship with another firm is so important that the relationship warrants maximum efforts at maintaining it indefinitely

trust the condition that exists when one party has confidence in an exchange partner's reliability and integrity

keiretsu a network of interlocking corporate affiliates

Wayne0216/Shutterstock.com; Jaimie Duplass/Shutterstock.com

their customers or their suppliers. Members of a *keiretsu* trade with each other whenever possible and often engage in joint product development, finance, and marketing activity. For example, the Toyota Group *keiretsu* includes 14 core companies and another 170 that receive preferential treatment. Toyota holds an equity position in many of these 170 member firms and is represented on many of their boards of directors.

Many firms have found that the best way to compete in Asian countries is to form relationships with Asian firms. For example, Google Enterprise has allied with several Asian tech companies to introduce its mapping and location-based services in new Asian markets. Through these partnerships, Google will bring its Maps platform to Ramco Services' cloud-based resource planning services (India), Hyundai and Kia Motors' navigation systems (South Korea), HSR International Realtors' property comparisons (Singapore), and Nintendo's Wii U video game console (Japan).[15]

Organizations like General Motors are OEMs because they buy business goods and incorporate them into the products they produce.

Linda Parton/Shutterstock.com

7-4 MAJOR CATEGORIES OF BUSINESS CUSTOMERS

The business market consists of four major categories of customers: producers, resellers, governments, and institutions.

7-4a Producers

The producer segment of the business market includes profit-oriented individuals and organizations that use purchased goods and services to produce other products, to incorporate into other products, or to facilitate the daily operations of the organization. Examples of producers include construction, manufacturing, transportation, finance, real estate, and food service firms. In the United States, there are more than thirteen million firms in the producer segment of the business market. Some of these firms are small, and others are among the world's largest businesses.

Producers are often called **original equipment manufacturers**, or **OEMs**. This term includes all individuals and organizations that buy business goods and incorporate them into the products they produce for eventual sale to other producers or to consumers. Companies such as

original equipment manufacturers (OEMs) individuals and organizations that buy business goods and incorporate them into the products they produce for eventual sale to other producers or to consumers

General Motors that buy steel, paint, tires, and batteries are said to be OEMs.

7-4b Resellers

The reseller market includes retail and wholesale businesses that buy finished goods and resell them for a profit. A retailer sells mainly to final consumers; wholesalers sell mostly to retailers and other organizational customers. There are approximately 1.5 million retailers and 500,000 wholesalers operating in the United States. Consumer product firms like Procter & Gamble, Kraft Foods, and Coca-Cola sell directly to large retailers and retail chains and through wholesalers to smaller retail units. Retailing is explored in detail in Chapter 14.

Business product distributors are wholesalers that buy business products and resell them to business customers. They often carry thousands of items in stock and employ sales forces to call on business customers. Businesses that wish to buy a gross of pencils or a hundred pounds of fertilizer typically purchase these items from local distributors rather than directly from manufacturers such as Empire Pencil or Dow Chemical.

7-4c Governments

A third major segment of the business market is government. Government organizations include thousands of federal, state, and local buying units. Collectively, these government units account for the greatest volume of purchases of any customer category in the United States.[16]

Companies like Kroger are resellers of products offered by P&G and Coca-Cola.

Marketing to government agencies can be an overwhelming undertaking, but companies that learn how the system works can position themselves to win lucrative contracts and build lasting, rewarding relationships.[17] Marketing to government agencies traditionally has not been an activity for companies seeking quick returns. The aphorism "hurry up and wait" is often cited as a characteristic of marketing to government agencies. Contracts for government purchases are often put out for bid. Interested vendors submit bids (usually sealed) to provide specified products during a particular time. Sometimes the lowest bidder is awarded the contract. When the lowest bidder is not awarded the contract, strong evidence must be presented to justify the decision. Grounds for rejecting the lowest bid include lack of experience, inadequate financing, or poor past performance. Bidding allows all potential suppliers a fair chance at winning government contracts and helps ensure that public funds are spent wisely.

FEDERAL GOVERNMENT Name just about any good or service and chances are that someone in the federal government uses it. The U.S. federal government buys goods and services valued at more than $875 billion per year, making it the world's largest customer.[18]

Although much of the federal government's buying is centralized, no single federal agency contracts for all the government's requirements, and no single buyer in any agency purchases all that the agency needs. We can view the federal government as a combination of several large companies with overlapping responsibilities and thousands of small independent units. One popular source of information about government procurement is *FedBizOpps*. Until recently, businesses hoping to sell to the federal government found the document (previously called *Commerce Business Daily*) unorganized, and it often arrived too late to be useful. The online version (www.cbd-net.com) is timelier and allows contractors to find leads using key word searches. Other examples of publications designed to explain how to do business with the federal government include *Doing Business with the General Services Administration*, *Selling to the Military*, and *Selling to the U.S. Air Force*.

STATE, COUNTY, AND CITY GOVERNMENT
Selling to states, counties, and cities can be less frustrating for both small and large vendors than selling to the federal government. Paperwork is typically simpler and more manageable than it is at the federal level. But vendors must decide which of the more than 89,000 government units are likely to buy their wares. State and local buying agencies include school districts, highway departments, government-operated hospitals, housing agencies, and many other departments and divisions.

7-4d Institutions

The fourth major segment of the business market consists of institutions that seek to achieve goals other than the standard business goals of profit, market share, and return on investment. This segment includes schools, hospitals, colleges and universities, churches, labor unions, fraternal organizations, civic clubs, foundations, and other so-called nonbusiness organizations. Some institutional purchasers operate similar to governments in that the purchasing process is influenced, determined, or administered by government units. Other institutional purchasers are organized more like corporations.[19]

7-5 THE NORTH AMERICAN INDUSTRY CLASSIFICATION SYSTEM

The **North American Industry Classification System (NAICS)** is an industry classification system introduced in 1997 to replace the standard industrial classification system (SIC). NAICS (pronounced *nakes*) is a system for classifying North American business establishments. The system, developed jointly by the United States, Canada, and Mexico, provides

> **North American Industry Classification System (NAICS)**
> a detailed numbering system developed by the United States, Canada, and Mexico to classify North American business establishments by their main production processes

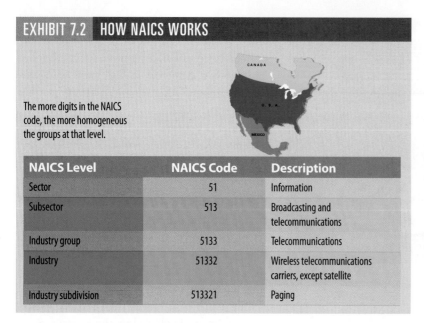

EXHIBIT 7.2 HOW NAICS WORKS

The more digits in the NAICS code, the more homogeneous the groups at that level.

NAICS Level	NAICS Code	Description
Sector	51	Information
Subsector	513	Broadcasting and telecommunications
Industry group	5133	Telecommunications
Industry	51332	Wireless telecommunications carriers, except satellite
Industry subdivision	513321	Paging

a common industry classification system for the North American Free Trade Agreement (NAFTA) partners. Goods- or service-producing firms that use identical or similar production processes are grouped together.

NAICS is an extremely valuable tool for business marketers engaged in analyzing, segmenting, and targeting markets. Each classification group is relatively homogeneous in terms of raw materials required, components used, manufacturing processes employed, and problems faced. Therefore, if a supplier understands the needs and requirements of a few firms within a classification, requirements can be projected for all firms in that category. The number, size, and geographic dispersion of firms can also be identified. This information can be converted to market potential estimates, market share estimates, and sales forecasts. It can also be used for identifying potential new customers. NAICS codes can help identify firms that may be prospective users of a supplier's goods and services. The more digits in a code, the more homogeneous the group. A sample of how NAICS codes function is listed in Exhibit 7.2. For a complete listing of all NAICS codes, see www.naics.com/search.htm.

7-6 BUSINESS VERSUS CONSUMER MARKETS

The basic philosophy and practice of marketing are the same whether the customer is a business organization or a consumer. Business markets do, however, have characteristics different from consumer markets.

derived demand the demand for business products

7-6a Demand

Consumer demand for products is quite different from demand in the business market. Unlike consumer demand, business demand is derived, inelastic, joint, and fluctuating.

DERIVED DEMAND The demand for business products is called **derived demand** because organizations buy products to be used in producing their customers' products. For instance, the number of drills or lathes that a manufacturing firm needs is derived from, or based upon, the demand for products that are produced using these machines. Following the Great Recession, California timber harvests fell by over 50 percent due to dramatic reductions in building construction. Since hitting a record low in 2009, the industry has rebounded each year, due in part to increased exports of whole logs to China and a slowly recovering construction industry in the United States.[20] Because demand is derived, business marketers must carefully monitor demand patterns and changing preferences in final consumer markets, even though their customers are not in those markets. Moreover, business marketers must carefully monitor their customers' forecasts because derived demand is based on expectations of future demand for those customers' products.

Some business marketers not only monitor final consumer demand and customer forecasts, but also try to influence final consumer demand. Aluminum producers use television and magazine advertisements to point out the convenience and recycling opportunities that aluminum offers to consumers who can choose to purchase soft drinks in either aluminum or plastic containers.

INELASTIC DEMAND The demand for many business products is inelastic with regard to price. *Inelastic demand* means that an increase or decrease in the price of the product will not significantly affect demand for the product. This will be discussed further in Chapter 19.

The price of a product used in the production of, or as part of, a final product is often a minor portion of the final product's total price. Therefore, demand for the final consumer product is not affected. If the price of automobile paint or spark plugs rises significantly, say, 200 percent in one year, do you think the number of new automobiles sold that year will be affected? Probably not.

Boeing's Big Blunder

The success or failure of one bid can make the difference between prosperity and bankruptcy. By early 2013, Boeing had delivered 50 of the 848 orders placed for its new, top-of-the-line 787 Dreamliner aircraft. But when reports of onboard fires and emergency landings began to emerge, all fifty Dreamliners were grounded pending investigation of a potentially faulty lithium-ion battery. These events spelled potential disaster for Boeing. The 848 orders were placed by just 56 customers, some ordering as many as 74 units. Each Dreamliner costs approximately $225 million, so a loss of even one of the orders would be devastating. Boeing pledged to fix the problem as quickly as possible and resume production and delivery, but irreparable damage may have already been done to the company's sales and image.[21]

Crowds look on as a Boeing 787 Dreamliner taxies to the runway at the Air-Venture airshow in Oshkosh, Wisconsin.

JOINT DEMAND **Joint demand** occurs when two or more items are used together in a final product. For example, a decline in the availability of memory chips will slow production of microcomputers, which will in turn reduce the demand for disk drives. Likewise, the demand for Apple operating systems exists as long as there is demand for Apple computers. Sales of the two products are directly linked.

FLUCTUATING DEMAND The demand for business products—particularly new plants and equipment—tends to be less stable than the demand for consumer products. A small increase or decrease in consumer demand can produce a much larger change in demand for the facilities and equipment needed to make the consumer product. Economists refer to this phenomenon as the **multiplier effect** (or **accelerator principle**).

Cummins Inc., a producer of heavy-duty diesel engines, uses sophisticated surface grinders to make parts. Suppose Cummins is using 20 surface grinders. Each machine lasts about 10 years. Purchases have been timed so two machines will wear out and be replaced annually. If the demand for engine parts does not change, two grinders will be bought this year. If the demand for parts declines slightly, only eighteen

grinders may be needed, and Cummins will not replace the worn ones. However, suppose that next year demand returns to previous levels plus a little more. To meet the new level of demand, Cummins will need to replace the two machines that wore out in the previous year, the two that wore out in the current year, plus one or more additional machines. The multiplier effect works this way in many industries, producing highly fluctuating demand for business products.

7-6b Purchase Volume

Business customers tend to buy in large quantities. Just imagine the size of Kellogg's typical order for the wheat bran and raisins used to manufacture Raisin Bran. Or consider that in 2013, the Chicago Transit Authority (CTA) began accepting bids to fulfill a purchase order of 846 new rail cars to replace its aging fleet. The purchase budget was estimated at $2 billion—quite a bit larger than the CTA's $2.25 ride fare.[22]

joint demand the demand for two or more items used together in a final product

multiplier effect (accelerator principle) phenomenon in which a small increase or decrease in consumer demand can produce a much larger change in demand for the facilities and equipment needed to make the consumer product

7-6c Number of Customers

Business marketers usually have far fewer customers than consumer marketers. The advantage is that it is a lot easier to identify prospective buyers, monitor current customers' needs and levels of satisfaction, and personally attend to existing customers. The main disadvantage is that each customer becomes crucial—especially for those manufacturers that have only one customer. In many cases, this customer is the U.S. government.

7-6d Concentration of Customers

Manufacturing operations in the United States tend to be more geographically concentrated than consumer markets. More than half of all U.S. manufacturers concentrate the majority of their operations in the following eight states: California, New York, Ohio, Illinois, Michigan, Texas, Pennsylvania, and New Jersey.[23] Most large metropolitan areas host large numbers of business customers.

7-6e Distribution Structure

Many consumer products pass through a distribution system that includes the producer, one or more wholesalers, and a retailer. In business marketing, however, because of many of the characteristics already mentioned, channels of distribution for business marketing are typically shorter. Direct channels, where manufacturers market directly to users, are much more common. The use of direct channels has increased dramatically in the past decade with the introduction of various Internet buying and selling schemes. One such technique is called a **business-to-business online exchange**, which is an electronic trading floor that provides companies with integrated links to their customers and suppliers. The goal of B-to-B exchanges is to simplify business purchasing and to make it more efficient. Alibaba.com is a B-to-B e-commerce portal based in China that allows companies from all over the world to purchase goods and services from Chinese suppliers. Recently, the Web site has begun expanding to include suppliers from countries outside of China, including the United States. Alibaba.com serves buyers in more than 190 countries worldwide and has suppliers representing more than 40 major product categories. The mission of Alibaba.com is to allow suppliers to reach a global audience and to help buyers quickly find the products and services they need.[24]

business-to-business online exchange an electronic trading floor that provides companies with integrated links to their customers and suppliers

reciprocity a practice whereby business purchasers choose to buy from their own customers

7-6f Nature of Buying

Unlike consumers, business buyers usually approach purchasing rather formally. Businesses use professionally trained purchasing agents or buyers who spend their entire career purchasing a limited number of items. They get to know the items and the sellers well. Some professional purchasers earn the designation of Certified Purchasing Manager (CPM) after participating in a rigorous certification program.

7-6g Nature of Buying Influence

Typically, more people are involved in a single business purchase decision than in a consumer purchase. Experts from fields as varied as quality control, marketing, and finance, as well as professional buyers and users, may be grouped in a buying center (discussed later in this chapter).

7-6h Type of Negotiations

Consumers are used to negotiating price on automobiles and real estate. In most cases, however, American consumers expect sellers to set the price and other conditions of sale, such as time of delivery and credit terms. In contrast, negotiating is common in business marketing. Buyers and sellers negotiate product specifications, delivery dates, payment terms, and other pricing matters. Sometimes these negotiations occur during many meetings over several months. Final contracts are often very long and detailed.

7-6i Use of Reciprocity

Business purchasers often choose to buy from their own customers, a practice known as **reciprocity**. For example, General Motors buys engines for use in its automobiles and trucks from BorgWarner, which in turn buys many of the automobiles and trucks it needs from General Motors. This practice is neither unethical nor illegal unless one party coerces the other and the result is unfair competition. Reciprocity is generally considered a reasonable business practice. If all possible suppliers sell a similar product for about the same price, does it not make sense to buy from those firms that buy from you?

7-6j Use of Leasing

Consumers normally buy products rather than lease them. But businesses commonly lease expensive equipment such as computers, construction equipment and vehicles, and automobiles. Leasing allows firms to reduce capital outflow, acquire a seller's latest products, receive better services, and gain tax advantages.

The leaser, the firm providing the product, may be either the manufacturer or an independent firm. The benefits to the leaser include greater total revenue from leasing compared to selling and an opportunity to do business with customers who cannot afford to buy.

7-6k Primary Promotional Method

Business marketers tend to emphasize personal selling in their promotion efforts, especially for expensive items, custom-designed products, large-volume purchases, and situations requiring negotiations. The sale of many business products requires a great deal of personal contact. Personal selling is discussed in more detail in Chapter 17.

 ## 7-7 TYPES OF BUSINESS PRODUCTS

Business products generally fall into one of the following seven categories, depending on their use: major equipment, accessory equipment, raw materials, component parts, processed materials, supplies, and business services.

7-7a Major Equipment

Major equipment includes capital goods such as large or expensive machines, mainframe computers, blast furnaces, generators, airplanes, and buildings. (These items are also commonly called **installations**.) Major equipment is depreciated over time rather than charged as an expense in the year it is purchased. In addition, major equipment is often custom designed for each customer. Personal selling is an important part of the marketing strategy for major equipment because distribution channels are almost always direct from the producer to the business user.

7-7b Accessory Equipment

Accessory equipment is generally less expensive and shorter-lived than major equipment. Examples include portable drills, power tools, microcomputers, and computer software. Accessory equipment is often charged as an expense in the year it is bought rather than depreciated over its useful life. In contrast to major equipment,

The market tends to set the price of raw materials, and individual producers have little pricing flexibility.

accessories are more often standardized and are usually bought by more customers. These customers tend to be widely dispersed. For example, all types of businesses buy microcomputers.

Local industrial distributors (wholesalers) play an important role in the marketing of accessory equipment because business buyers often purchase accessories from them. Regardless of where accessories are bought, advertising is a more vital promotional tool for accessory equipment than for major equipment.

7-7c Raw Materials

Raw materials are unprocessed extractive or agricultural products—for example, mineral ore, timber, wheat, corn, fruits, vegetables, and fish. Raw materials become part of finished products. Extensive users, such as steel or lumber mills and food canners, generally buy huge quantities of raw materials. Because there is often a large number of relatively small sellers of raw materials, none can greatly influence price or supply. Thus, the market tends to set the price of raw materials, and individual producers have little pricing flexibility. Promotion is almost always via personal selling, and distribution channels are usually direct from producer to business user.

major equipment (installations) capital goods such as large or expensive machines, mainframe computers, blast furnaces, generators, airplanes, and buildings

accessory equipment goods, such as portable tools and office equipment, that are less expensive and shorter-lived than major equipment

raw materials unprocessed extractive or agricultural products, such as mineral ore, lumber, wheat, corn, fruits, vegetables, and fish

7-7d Component Parts

Component parts are either finished items ready for assembly or products that need very little processing before becoming part of some other product. Caterpillar diesel engines are component parts used in heavy-duty trucks. Other examples include spark plugs, tires, and electric motors for automobiles. A special feature of component parts is that they can retain their identity after becoming part of the final product. For example, automobile tires are clearly recognizable as part of a car. Moreover, because component parts often wear out, they may need to be replaced several times during the life of the final product. Thus, there are two important markets for many component parts: the OEM market and the replacement market.

The availability of component parts is often a key factor in OEMs meeting their production deadlines. In September 2013, a massive fire at an SK Hynix factory in Wuxi, China halted the manufacture of much of the world's OEM-grade computer memory. This greatly reduced the availability of memory and sent the price of the remaining inventory through the roof. The price of a single stick of memory jumped nearly 42 percent overnight, forcing many OEMs to halt production while an alternate source could be found.[25]

The replacement market is composed of organizations and individuals buying component parts to replace worn-out parts. Because components often retain their identity in final products, users may choose to replace a component part with the same brand used by the manufacturer—for example, the same brand of automobile tires or battery. The replacement market operates differently from the OEM market, however. Whether replacement buyers are organizations or individuals, they tend to demonstrate the characteristics of consumer markets that were discussed in the previous section. Consider, for example, a replacement part for a piece of construction equipment such as a bulldozer or a crane. When a piece of equipment breaks down, it is usually important to acquire a replacement part and have it installed as soon as possible. Purchasers typically buy from local or regional dealers. Negotiations do not occur, and neither reciprocity nor leasing is usually an issue.

component parts either finished items ready for assembly or products that need very little processing before becoming part of some other product

processed materials products used directly in manufacturing other products

supplies consumable items that do not become part of the final product

business services expense items that do not become part of a final product

7-7e Processed Materials

Processed materials are products used directly in manufacturing other products. Unlike raw materials, they have had some processing. Examples include sheet metal, chemicals, specialty steel, treated lumber, corn syrup, and plastics. Unlike component parts, processed materials do not retain their identity in final products.

Timber, harvested from forests, is a raw material. Fluff pulp, a soft, white absorbent, is produced from loblolly pine timber by mills such as International Paper Co. The fluff pulp then becomes part of disposable diapers, bandages, and other sanitary products.[26]

Most processed materials are marketed to OEMs or to distributors servicing the OEM market. Processed materials are generally bought according to customer specifications or to some industry standard, as is the case with steel and plywood. Price and service are important factors in choosing a vendor.

7-7f Supplies

Supplies are consumable items that do not become part of the final product—for example, lubricants, detergents, paper towels, pencils, and paper. Supplies are normally standardized items that purchasing agents routinely buy. Supplies typically have relatively short lives and are inexpensive compared to other business goods. Because supplies generally fall into one of three categories—maintenance, repair, or operating supplies—this category is often referred to as MRO items. Competition in the MRO market is intense. Bic and Paper Mate, for example, battle for business purchases of inexpensive ballpoint pens.

7-7g Business Services

Business services are expense items that do not become part of a final product. Businesses often retain outside providers to perform janitorial, advertising, legal, management consulting, marketing research, maintenance, and other services. Contracting an outside provider makes sense when it costs less than hiring or assigning an employee to perform the task, when an outside provider is needed for particular expertise, or when the need is infrequent.

7-8 BUSINESS BUYING BEHAVIOR

As you probably have already concluded, business buyers behave differently from consumers. Understanding how purchase decisions are made in organizations is a first step in developing a business selling strategy. Business buying behavior has five important aspects: buying centers, evaluative criteria, buying situations, business ethics, and customer service.

7-8a Buying Centers

In many cases, more than one person is involved in a purchase decision. A salesperson must determine the buying situation and the information required from the buying organization's perspective to anticipate the size and composition of the buying center.[27]

A **buying center** includes all those people in an organization who become involved in the purchase decision. Membership and influence vary from company to company. For instance, in engineering-dominated firms like Bell Helicopter, the buying center may consist almost entirely of engineers. In marketing-oriented firms like Toyota and IBM, marketing and engineering have almost equal authority. In consumer goods firms like Clorox Corporation, product managers and other marketing decision makers may dominate the buying center. In a small manufacturing company, almost everyone may be a member.

The number of people involved in a buying center varies with the complexity and importance of a purchase decision. The average buying center includes more than one person and up to four per purchase.[28] The composition of the buying group will usually change from one purchase to another and sometimes even during various stages of the buying process. To make matters more complicated, buying centers do not appear on formal organization charts.

For example, even though a formal committee may have been set up to choose a new plant site, it is only part of the buying center. Other people, like the company president, often play informal yet powerful roles. In a lengthy decision-making process, such as finding a new plant location, some members may drop out of the buying center when they can no longer play a useful role. Others whose talents are needed then become part of the center. No formal announcement of "who is in" and "who is out" is ever made.

ROLES IN THE BUYING CENTER As in family purchasing decisions, several people may each play a role in the business purchase process:

- The *initiator* is the person who first suggests making a purchase.
- *Influencers/evaluators* are people who influence the buying decision. They often help define specifications and provide information for evaluating options.

Technical personnel are especially important as influencers.

- *Gatekeepers* are group members who regulate the flow of information. Frequently, the purchasing agent views the gatekeeping role as a source of his or her power. A secretary may also act as a gatekeeper by determining which vendors get an appointment with a buyer.

- The *decider* is the person who has the formal or informal power to choose or approve the selection of the supplier or brand. In complex situations, it is often difficult to determine who makes the final decision.

- The *purchaser* is the person who actually negotiates the purchase. It could be anyone from the president of the company to the purchasing agent, depending on the importance of the decision.

- *Users* are members of the organization who will actually use the product. Users often initiate the buying process and help define product specifications.

IMPLICATIONS OF BUYING CENTERS FOR THE MARKETING MANAGER Successful vendors realize the importance of identifying who is in the decision-making unit, each member's relative influence in the buying decision, and each member's evaluative criteria. Key influencers are frequently located outside of the purchasing department. Successful selling strategies often focus on determining the most important buying influences and tailoring sales presentations to the evaluative criteria most important to these buying center members. An example illustrating the basic buying center roles is shown in Exhibit 7.3.

Marketers are often frustrated by their inability to reach c-level (chief) executives who play important roles in many buying centers. Marketers who want to build executive-level contacts must become involved in the buying process early on. This is when eighty percent of executives get involved—when major purchase decisions are being made. Executives often ensconce themselves in the buying process because they want to understand current business issues, establish project objectives, and set the overall project strategy.[29] Senior executives are typically not involved in the middle phases of the buying process but often get involved again later in the process to monitor the deal's closing. Executives look for four characteristics in sales representatives:

- The ability to marshal resources
- An understanding of the buyer's business goals

buying center all those people in an organization who become involved in the purchase decision

EXHIBIT 7.3 BUYING CENTER ROLES FOR COMPUTER PURCHASES

Role	Illustration
Initiator	Division general manager proposes to replace company's computer network.
Influencers/evaluators	Corporate controller's office and vice president of information services have an important say in which system and vendor the company will deal with.
Gatekeepers	Corporate departments for purchasing and information services analyze company's needs and recommend likely matches with potential vendors.
Decider	Vice president of administration, with advice from others, selects vendor the company will deal with and system it will buy.
Purchaser	Purchasing agent negotiates terms of sale.
Users	All division employees use the computers.

- Responsiveness to requests
- Willingness to be held accountable

Some firms have developed strategies to reach executives throughout the buying process and during non-buying phases of the relationship. For example, FedEx Corp. has initiated a marketing effort called "access" aimed at c-level executives. It includes direct mail, e-mail, and a custom magazine prepared exclusively for c-level executives. It also hosts exclusive leadership events for these senior executives. Other firms have developed programs utilizing a combination of print, online, and events to reach the elusive c-level audience.[30]

View Apart/Shutterstock.com

Some firms have developed strategies to reach "c-level" executives, with FedEx leading the way.

7-8b Evaluative Criteria

Business buyers evaluate products and suppliers against three important criteria: quality, service, and price.

QUALITY In this case, *quality* refers to technical suitability. A superior tool can do a better job in the production process and superior packaging can increase dealer and consumer acceptance of a brand. Evaluation of quality also applies to the salesperson and the salesperson's firm. Business buyers want to deal with reputable salespeople and companies that are financially responsible. Quality improvement should be part of every organization's marketing strategy.

SERVICE Almost as much as they want satisfactory products, business buyers want satisfactory service. A purchase offers several opportunities for service. Suppose a vendor is selling heavy equipment. Prepurchase service could include a survey of the buyer's needs. After thorough analysis of the survey findings, the vendor could prepare a report and recommendations in the form of a purchasing proposal. If a purchase results, postpurchase service might consist of installing the equipment and training those who will be using it. Postsale services may also include maintenance and repairs.

Another service that business buyers seek is dependability of supply. They must be able to count on delivery of what was ordered when it is scheduled to be delivered. Buyers also welcome services that help them sell their finished products. Services of this sort are especially appropriate when the seller's product is an identifiable part of the buyer's end product.

PRICE Business buyers want to buy at low prices—at the lowest prices, under most circumstances. However, a buyer who pressures a supplier to cut prices to a point at which the supplier loses money on the sale almost forces shortcuts on quality. The buyer also may, in effect, force the supplier to quit selling to him or her. Then a new source of supply will have to be found.

7-8c Buying Situations

Often, business firms, especially manufacturers, must decide whether to make something or buy it from an outside supplier. The decision is essentially one of economics. Can an item of similar quality be bought at a lower price elsewhere? If not, is manufacturing it in-house the best use of limited company resources? For example, Briggs & Stratton Corporation, a major manufacturer of four-cycle engines, might be able to save $150,000 annually on outside purchases by spending $500,000 on the equipment needed to produce gas throttles internally. Yet Briggs & Stratton could also use that $500,000 to upgrade its carburetor assembly line, which would save $225,000 annually. If a firm does decide to buy a product instead of making it, the purchase will be a new buy, a modified rebuy, or a straight rebuy.

NEW BUY A **new buy** is a situation requiring the purchase of a product for the first time. For example, suppose a manufacturing company needs a better way to page its managers while they are working on the shop floor. Currently, each of the several managers has a distinct ring—for example, two short and one long—that sounds over the plant intercom whenever he or she is being paged by anyone in the factory. The company decides to replace its buzzer system of paging with hand-held wireless radio technology that will allow managers to communicate immediately with the department initiating the page. This situation represents the greatest opportunity for new vendors. No long-term relationship has been established for this product, specifications may be somewhat fluid, and buyers are generally more open to new vendors.

If the new item is a raw material or a critical component part, the buyer cannot afford to run out of supply. The seller must be able to convince the buyer that the seller's firm can consistently deliver a high-quality product on time.

MODIFIED REBUY A **modified rebuy** is normally less critical and less time-consuming than a new buy. In a modified rebuy situation, the purchaser wants some change in the original good or service. It may be a new color, greater tensile strength in a component part, more respondents in a marketing research study, or additional services in a janitorial contract.

Because the two parties are familiar with each other and credibility has been established, the buyer and seller can concentrate on the specifics of the modification. But in some cases, modified rebuys are open to outside bidders. The purchaser uses this strategy to ensure that the new terms are competitive. An example would be the manufacturing company buying radios with a vibrating feature for managers who have trouble hearing the ring over the factory noise. The firm may open the bidding to examine the price, quality, and service offerings of several suppliers.

STRAIGHT REBUY A **straight rebuy** is a situation vendors prefer. The purchaser is not looking for new information or other suppliers. An order is placed and the product is provided as in previous orders. Usually, a straight rebuy is routine because the terms of the purchase have been agreed to in earlier negotiations. An example would be the previously cited manufacturing company purchasing additional radios for new managers from the same supplier on a regular basis.

One common instrument used in straight rebuy situations is the purchasing contract. Purchasing contracts are used with products that are bought often and in high volume. In essence, the purchasing contract makes the buyer's decision making routine and promises the salesperson a sure sale. The advantage to the buyer is a quick, confident decision, and to the salesperson, reduced or eliminated competition. Nevertheless, suppliers must remember not to take straight rebuy relationships for granted. Retaining existing customers is much easier than attracting new ones.

7-8d Business Ethics

As we noted in Chapter 3, *ethics* refers to the moral principles or values that generally govern the conduct of an individual or a group. Ethics can also be viewed as the standard of behavior by which conduct is judged.

Although we have heard a lot about corporate misbehavior in recent years, most people, and most companies, follow ethical practices. To help achieve this, over half of all major corporations offer ethics training to employees. Many companies also have codes of ethics that help guide buyers and sellers. For example, Home Depot has a clearly written code of ethics available on its corporate Web site that acts as an ethical guide for all its employees.

7-8e Customer Service

Business marketers are increasingly recognizing the benefits of developing a formal system to monitor customer opinions and perceptions of the quality of customer service. Companies such as FedEx, IBM, and Oracle build their strategies not only around products but also around highly developed service skills.[31] These companies understand that keeping current customers satisfied is just as important as attracting new ones, if not

new buy a situation requiring the purchase of a product for the first time

modified rebuy a situation in which the purchaser wants some change in the original good or service

straight rebuy a situation in which the purchaser reorders the same goods or services without looking for new information or investigating other suppliers

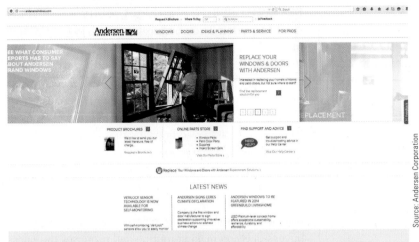

Source: Andersen Corporation

Andersen Windows and Doors assesses the loyalty of its trade customers by their willingness to carry its windows and doors.

more so. Leading-edge firms are obsessed not only with delivering high-quality customer service but also with measuring satisfaction, loyalty, relationship quality, and other indicators of nonfinancial performance. Delivering consistent, high-quality customer service is an important basis for establishing competitive advantage and differentiating one's company from competitors. Cisco Systems uses a Web-based survey to determine the presale and postsale satisfaction of customers.[32]

Most firms find it necessary to develop measures unique to their own strategies, value propositions, and target markets. For example, Andersen Corporation assesses the loyalty of its trade customers by their willingness to continue carrying its windows and doors, recommend its products to colleagues and customers, increase their volume with the company, and put its products in their own homes. Basically, each firm's measures should not only ask "What are your expectations?" and "How are we doing?" but should also reflect what the firm wants its customers to do.

Some customers are more valuable than others. They may have greater value because they spend more, buy higher-margin products, have a well-known name, or have the potential of becoming a bigger customer in the future. Some companies selectively provide different levels of service to customers based on their value to the business. By giving the most valuable customers

superior service, a firm is more likely to keep them happy, hopefully increasing retention of these high-value customers and maximizing the total business value they generate over time.

To achieve this goal, the firm must be able to divide customers into two or more groups based on their value. It must also create and apply policies that govern how service will be allocated among groups. Policies might establish which customers' phone calls get "fast tracked" and which customers are directed to use the Web and/or voice self-service, how specific e-mail questions are routed, and who is given access to online chat and who is not.

Providing different customers with different levels of service is a very sensitive matter. It must be handled very carefully and very discreetly to avoid offending lesser-value, but still important, customers.

STUDY TOOLS 7

LOCATED AT BACK OF THE TEXTBOOK

☐ Rip out Chapter Review Card

LOCATED AT WWW.CENGAGEBRAIN.COM

☐ Review Key Terms Flashcards and create your own

☐ Track your knowledge and understanding of key concepts in marketing

☐ Complete practice and graded quizzes to prepare for tests

☐ Complete interactive content within the MKTG Online experience

☐ View the chapter highlight boxes within the MKTG Online experience

MKTG ONLINE

PREPARE FOR TESTS ON THE STUDYBOARD!

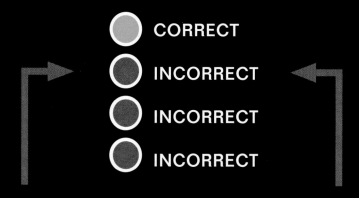

○ CORRECT
● INCORRECT
● INCORRECT
○ INCORRECT

Personalize Quizzes from Your StudyBits

Take Practice Quizzes by Chapter

CHAPTER QUIZZES
▶ Chapter 1
Chapter 2
Chapter 3
Chapter 4

4LTR PRESS

8 Segmenting and Targeting Markets

LEARNING OUTCOMES

After studying this chapter, you will be able to...

8-1 Describe the characteristics of markets and market segments

8-2 Explain the importance of market segmentation

8-3 Discuss the criteria for successful market segmentation

8-4 Describe the bases commonly used to segment consumer markets

8-5 Describe the bases for segmenting business markets

8-6 List the steps involved in segmenting markets

8-7 Discuss alternative strategies for selecting target markets

8-8 Explain how CRM can be used as a targeting tool

8-9 Explain how and why firms implement positioning strategies and how product differentiation plays a role

After you finish this chapter go to **PAGE 148** for **STUDY TOOLS.**

8-1 MARKETS AND MARKET SEGMENTS

The term *market* means different things to different people. We are all familiar with the supermarket, stock market, labor market, fish market, and flea market. All these types of markets share several characteristics. First, they are composed of people (consumer markets) or organizations (business markets). Second, these people or organizations have wants and needs that can be satisfied by particular product categories. Third, they have the ability to buy the products they seek. Fourth, they are willing to exchange their resources, usually money or credit, for desired products. In sum, a **market** is (1) people or organizations with (2) needs or wants and with (3) the ability and (4) the willingness to buy. A group of people or an organization that lacks any one of these characteristics is not a market.

> **market**
> people or organizations with needs or wants and the ability and willingness to buy

Within a market, a **market segment** is a subgroup of people or organizations sharing one or more characteristics that cause them to have similar product needs. At one extreme, we can define every person and every organization in the world as a market segment because each is unique. At the other extreme, we can define the entire consumer market as one large market segment and the business market as another large segment. All people have some similar characteristics and needs, as do all organizations.

From a marketing perspective, market segments can be described as somewhere between the two extremes. The process of dividing a market into meaningful, relatively similar, and identifiable segments, or groups, is called **market segmentation**. The purpose of market segmentation is to enable the marketer to tailor marketing mixes to meet the needs of one or more specific segments.

8-2 THE IMPORTANCE OF MARKET SEGMENTATION

Until the 1960s, few firms practiced market segmentation. When they did, it was more likely a haphazard effort than a formal marketing strategy. Before 1960, for example, the Coca-Cola Company produced only one beverage and aimed it at the entire soft drink market. Today, Coca-Cola offers more than a dozen different products to market segments based on diverse consumer preferences for flavors, calorie, and caffeine content. Coca-Cola offers traditional soft drinks, energy drinks (including POWERade), flavored teas, fruit drinks (Minute Maid), and water (Dasani).

Market segmentation plays a key role in the marketing strategy of almost all successful organizations and is a powerful marketing tool for several reasons. Most important, nearly all markets include groups of people or organizations with different product needs and preferences. Market segmentation helps marketers define customer needs and wants more precisely. Because market segments differ in size and potential, segmentation helps decision makers to more accurately define marketing objectives and better allocate resources. In turn, performance can be better evaluated when objectives are more precise.

Jax & Bones has successfully appealed to affluent customers with high-end pet products. For example, the company produces a $200 dog bed that

market segment
a subgroup of people or organizations sharing one or more characteristics that cause them to have similar product needs

market segmentation
the process of dividing a market into meaningful, relatively similar, and identifiable segments or groups

it sells in upscale retailers such as Bloomingdale's, Pottery Barn, and Barneys New York. The company's owner creates pet beds that reflect the latest colors, fabrics, textures, and styles. When memory foam became popular in human beds, Jax & Bones added memory foam to its beds. Last year, when gray, silver, and blue were popular in home design, these colors were incorporated into Jax & Bones' beds.[1]

8-3 CRITERIA FOR SUCCESSFUL SEGMENTATION

Marketers segment markets for three important reasons. First, segmentation enables marketers to identify groups of customers with similar needs and to analyze the characteristics and buying behavior of these groups. Second, segmentation provides marketers with information to help them design marketing mixes specifically matched with the characteristics and desires of one or more segments. Third, segmentation is consistent with the marketing concept of satisfying customer wants and needs while meeting the organization's objectives.

To be useful, a segmentation scheme must produce segments that meet four basic criteria:

1. **Substantiality:** A segment must be large enough to warrant developing and maintaining a special marketing mix. This criterion does not necessarily mean that a segment must have many potential customers. For example, marketers of custom-designed homes and business buildings, commercial airplanes, and large computer systems typically develop marketing programs tailored to each potential customer's needs. In most cases, however, a market segment needs many potential customers to make commercial sense. In the 1980s, home banking failed because not enough people owned personal computers. Today, a larger number of people own computers, and home banking is a thriving industry.

2. **Identifiability and measurability:** Segments must be identifiable and their size measurable. Data about the population within geographic boundaries, the number of people in various age categories, and other social and demographic characteristics are often easy to get, and they provide fairly concrete measures of segment size. Suppose that a social service agency wants to identify segments by their readiness to participate in a drug and alcohol program or in prenatal

care. Unless the agency can measure how many people are willing, indifferent, or unwilling to participate, it will have trouble gauging whether there are enough people to justify setting up the service.

3. **Accessibility:** The firm must be able to reach members of targeted segments with customized marketing mixes. Some market segments are hard to reach—for example, senior citizens (especially those with reading or hearing disabilities), individuals who do not speak English, and the illiterate.

4. **Responsiveness:** Markets can be segmented using any criteria that seem logical. Unless one market segment responds to a marketing mix differently than other segments, however, that segment need not be treated separately. For instance, if all customers are equally price conscious about a product, there is no need to offer high-, medium-, and low-priced versions to different segments.

8-4 BASES FOR SEGMENTING CONSUMER MARKETS

Marketers use segmentation bases, or variables, which are characteristics of individuals, groups, or organizations, to divide a total market into segments. The choice of segmentation bases is crucial because an inappropriate segmentation strategy may lead to lost sales and missed profit opportunities. The key is to identify bases that will produce substantial, measurable, and accessible segments that exhibit different response patterns to marketing mixes.

Markets can be segmented using a single variable, such as age group, or several variables, such as age group, gender, and education. Although it is less precise, single-variable segmentation has the advantage of being simpler and easier to use than multiple-variable segmentation. The disadvantages of multiple-variable segmentation are that it is often harder to use than single-variable segmentation; usable secondary data are less likely to be available; and as the number of segmentation bases increases, the size of individual segments decreases. Nevertheless, the current trend is toward using more rather than fewer variables to segment most markets. Multiple-variable segmentation is clearly more precise than single-variable segmentation.

Consumer goods marketers commonly use one or more of the following characteristics to segment markets: geography, demographics, psychographics, benefits sought, and usage rate.

segmentation bases (variables) characteristics of individuals, groups, or organizations

8-4a Geographic Segmentation

Geographic segmentation refers to segmenting markets by region of a country or the world, market size, market density, or climate. Market density means the number of people within a unit of land, such as a census tract. Climate is commonly used for geographic segmentation because of its dramatic impact on residents' needs and purchasing behavior. Snowblowers, water and snow skis, clothing, and air-conditioning and heating systems are products with varying appeal, depending on climate.

Consumer goods companies take a regional approach to marketing for four reasons. First, many firms need to find new ways to generate sales because of sluggish and intensely competitive markets. Second, computerized checkout stations with scanners give retailers an accurate assessment of which brands sell best in their region. Third, many packaged-goods manufacturers are introducing new regional brands intended to appeal to local preferences.

Fourth, a more regional approach allows consumer goods companies to react more quickly to competition. Macy's localizes the merchandising and shopping experience for every U.S. geographic region in which it operates. For example, Macy's stocks its downtown Chicago location to meet a high demand for women's shoes in larger sizes, while it stocks its Long Island location to meet high demand for electric coffee percolators. Men in some, but not all, of Macy's districts shop primarily for cuffed pants, so the company adjusts its product offerings accordingly.[2]

8-4b Demographic Segmentation

Marketers often segment markets on the basis of demographic information because it is widely available and often related to consumers' buying and consuming behavior. Some common bases of **demographic segmentation** are age, gender, income, ethnic background, and family life cycle.

AGE SEGMENTATION Marketers use a variety of terms to refer to different age groups. Examples include newborns, infants, young children, tweens, Millennials, Generation X, baby boomers, and seniors. Age segmentation can be an important tool, as a brief exploration of the market potential of several age segments illustrates.

Many companies have long targeted parents of babies and young children with products such as disposable diapers, baby food, and toys. Recently, other companies that have not traditionally marketed to young

children are developing products and services to attract this group. For example, high-intensity fitness company CrossFit recently developed a program for kids in an attempt to tackle childhood obesity. The coaches for these group fitness classes create special workouts and games like "Hungry, Hungry Hippos" and "Farmers and Lumberjacks" to make classes fun and kid-friendly.[3]

The tween and teenage cohort following the Millennials is sometimes called Generation Z. This group accounts for 25.9 percent of the U.S. population and contributes $44 billion to the U.S. economy.[4] Born after 1995, Gen Zers are incredibly tech savvy, have short attention spans, and do not distinguish between their online and offline friends. To reach this cohort, marketers must make sure that their brands are communicated consistently across different channels.[5] To attract Generation Z, Google is considering offering user accounts to children under the age of 13. These accounts will include a way for parents to control account usage. Similarly, Facebook allows teens age 13 to 17 to post publicly on its site.[6] In another effort to reach tween shoppers, Macy's joined with the ABC Family television network to offer apparel seen on the popular series *Pretty Little Liars*. While they shopped on the store's Web site for clothing, teens and tweens had the opportunity to chat live with one of the show's stars.[7]

The Millennial market makes up 25 percent of the adult population in the United States.[8] This group is the most educated, diverse, and technology-proficient generation ever. Most of their media consumption is online, including reading news and watching television shows. Millennials have formidable purchasing power, but they distrust advertising and are more likely to listen to their peers regarding product decisions.[9] The top brand attributes important to Millennials include trustworthiness, creativity, intelligence, authenticity, and confidence. Millennials are more likely than other generations to take a company's social responsibility into account before making a purchase decision.[10] Brands like TOMS Shoes and Warby Parker appeal to this group because they offer social value and align their brands with a higher purpose. These brands also invite participation and co-creation, both of which appeal to Millennials.[11]

geographic segmentation segmenting markets by region of a country or the world, market size, market density, or climate

demographic segmentation segmenting markets by age, gender, income, ethnic background, and family life cycle

Szefei/istock/Thinkstock

Generation X is smaller than both the Millennials and the baby boomers, making up only sixteen percent of the total population. Members of Generation X are at a life stage where they are often stuck between supporting their aging parents and young children (earning Gen X the nickname "the sandwich generation"). They grew up as *latchkey kids*, meaning that they spent time alone at home while their (often divorced) parents worked long into the night. They are the best-educated generation—29 percent have earned a bachelor's degree or better. They tend to be disloyal to brands and skeptical of big business. Many of them are parents, and they make purchasing decisions with thought for and input from their families.[12] Gen Xers desire an experience, not just a product. This desire has led to an increase in offbeat events such as Vancouver, Canada's Dine Out Vancouver food festival. More than a series of tastings and tours, the 17-day festival features experiences such as a drag queen cabaret and dinner show inspired by the film *The Birdcage*, a brunch crawl, the Grape Debate (where top wine experts debate contemporary topics), and prix fixe menus at more than 230 restaurants throughout the city.[13]

Recall from Chapter 4 that people born between 1946 and 1964 are often called baby boomers. Boomers make up 24.7 percent of the total population and they constitute almost one-third of the adult population. According to the U.S. Consumer Expenditure Survey, baby boomers outspend other generations by approximately $400 billion a year.[14] They are living longer, healthier, more active and connected lives, and will spend time and money doing whatever is necessary to maintain vitality as they age. This group spends more than other age brackets on dining out, housing, alcohol, and healthcare. Moreover, boomers' spending on vehicles is growing faster than any other demographic. Marketers should target boomers based on their core values, such as healthy eating and aging well. General Mills' Cheerios ads have long focused on heart health to reach boomers, for example.[15]

Consumers age seventy and older are part of the war generation and the Great Depression generation. Together, this group is often called the silent generation for its ability to quietly persevere through great hardships. The smallest generation of the last 100 years, members of this group tend to live modestly, save their money, and be civic minded. Many in this group view retirement not as a

Mayakova/Shutterstock.com

passive time, but as an active time they use to explore new knowledge, travel, volunteer, and spend time with family and friends.[16] However, as consumers age, they do require some modifications in the way they live and the products they purchase. According to gerontologist Stephen Golant, for example, aging individuals may need to install "well-placed handrails or grab bars, ramps, easy-access bathrooms, easy-access kitchens, stair lifts, widened doors or hallways, and modified sink faucets or cabinets" in their homes.[17]

GENDER SEGMENTATION In the United States, women make 85 percent of purchases of consumer goods each year.[18] They are an experienced purchasing group with the responsibility of purchasing the majority of household items. They also are increasingly part of what were once considered all-male markets, such as financial markets. Women tend to view money and wealth differently than men do. They do not seek to accumulate money for the sake of accumulation, but rather associate it with security, independence, and quality of life for themselves and their families. They also tend to research investments in-depth more than men do. Thus, financial advisors need to use different strategies to appeal to women.[19] Freshness Burger, Japan's biggest hamburger chain, recently unveiled a burger wrapper with the bottom half of a woman's face printed on it. As a woman eats a burger, she can cover the bottom half of her face with the wrapper, making it appear that she is not chowing down, but is instead smiling serenely. After Freshness Burger launched the wrapper, sales to women jumped more than 200 percent.[20] Marketers of products such as clothing, cosmetics, food, personal-care items, magazines, jewelry, and gifts still commonly segment markets by gender, and many of these marketers are going after the less-traditional male market. For example, Kraft used to target its Velveeta Shells and Cheese exclusively at busy moms. While conducting market research, Kraft "found a segment of men already making and cooking Shells and Cheese that we frankly weren't talking to," said Tiphanie Maronta, senior brand manager for Velveeta meals. To reach this new market, Kraft developed a series of humorous Eat Like That Guy You Know television ads that featured slacker heroes such as limo drivers and ham radio operators.[21] Similarly, Procter & Gamble sponsored "man-aisles" in some Walmart, Target, and Walgreen's stores in the U.S. and Canada.

These aisles group all men's products in one place and use shelf displays and small TV screens to guide men to skin-care items.[22]

INCOME SEGMENTATION Income is a popular demographic variable for segmenting markets because income level influences consumers' wants and determines their buying power. Many markets are segmented by income, including the markets for housing, clothing, automobiles, and food. Dollar stores, traditionally targeted at lower-income consumers, surged in growth as they began to target middle-income consumers during the Great Recession. In 2012, Dollar General announced that its fastest-growing customer segment was shoppers who earned more than $70,000 a year.[23] Wholesale clubs Costco and Sam's Club appeal to many income segments. High-income customers looking for luxury want outstanding customer service. Because they spend large amounts of money, luxury consumers expect to be treated extraordinarily well and to feel a personal connection to a product or brand. Luxury product showrooms and retail locations must constantly evolve to accommodate these customers' needs and to provide an exceptional, high-tech in-store experience.[24] On the other hand, some companies have found success in marketing to the very poor. People living in developing nations are emerging as reliable customers for multinational companies like Coca-Cola and McDonald's.[25]

ETHNIC SEGMENTATION In the past, ethnic groups in the United States were expected to conform to a homogenized, Anglo-centric ideal. This was evident both in how mass-produced products were marketed as well as in the selective way that films, television, advertisements, and popular music portrayed America's diverse population. Until the 1970s, ethnic foods were rarely sold except in specialty stores. Increasing numbers of ethnic minorities and increased buying power have changed this. Hispanic Americans, African Americans, and Asian Americans are the three largest ethnic groups in the United States. In the American Southwest, Caucasian populations comprise less than half the population and have become the minority to other ethnic groups combined. To meet the needs and wants of expanding ethnic populations, some companies, such as McDonald's and Kmart, make products geared toward specific ethnic groups. For example, Kmart has teamed up with Selena Gomez and Sofia Vergara, both popular Hispanic actors, to develop clothing lines that appeal to Latina consumers.[26] Many department stores carry Fashion Fair Cosmetics, a line of beauty products created specifically for (and marketed toward) African American women.[27]

FAMILY LIFE CYCLE SEGMENTATION The demographic factors of gender, age, and income often do not sufficiently explain why consumer buying behavior

Kmart has teamed up with Hispanic actress, Sofia Vergara, in order to appeal their clothing to Latina consumers.

varies. Frequently, consumption patterns among people of the same age and gender differ because they are in different stages of the family life cycle. The **family life cycle (FLC)** is a series of stages determined by a combination of age, marital status, and the presence or absence of children.

The life cycle stage consisting of the married-couple household used to be considered the traditional family in the United States. Today, however, married couples make up less than half of households, down from nearly eighty percent in the 1950s. Single adults are increasingly in the majority. Already, unmarried Americans make up 42 percent of the workforce, 40 percent of home buyers, and one of the most potent consumer groups on record. Exhibit 8.1 illustrates numerous FLC

family life cycle (FLC)
a series of stages determined by a combination of age, marital status, and the presence or absence of children

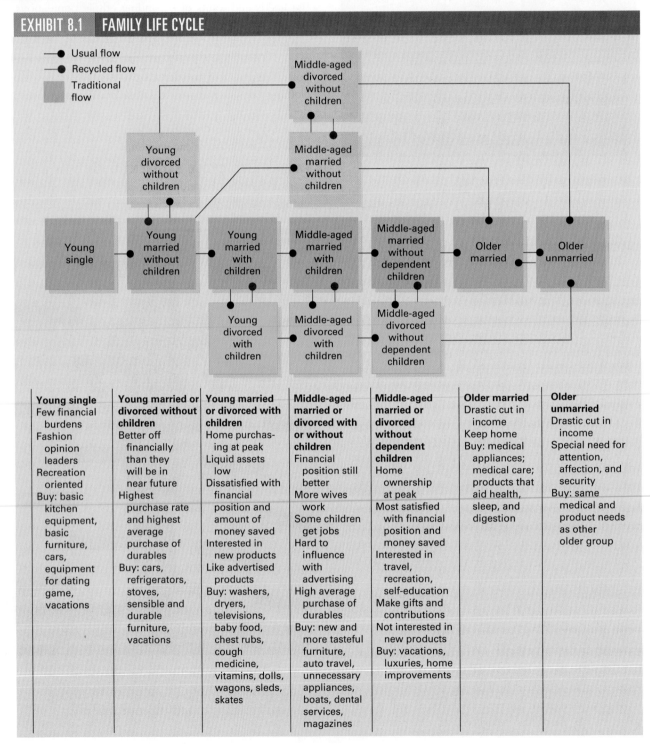

EXHIBIT 8.1 FAMILY LIFE CYCLE

Young single	Young married or divorced without children	Young married or divorced with children	Middle-aged married or divorced with or without children	Middle-aged married or divorced without dependent children	Older married	Older unmarried
Few financial burdens	Better off financially than they will be in near future	Home purchasing at peak	Financial position still better	Home ownership at peak	Drastic cut in income	Drastic cut in income
Fashion opinion leaders	Highest purchase rate and highest average purchase of durables	Liquid assets low	More wives work	Most satisfied with financial position and money saved	Keep home	Special need for attention, affection, and security
Recreation oriented	Buy: cars, refrigerators, stoves, sensible and durable furniture, vacations	Dissatisfied with financial position and amount of money saved	Some children get jobs	Interested in travel, recreation, self-education	Buy: medical appliances; medical care; products that aid health, sleep, and digestion	Buy: same medical and product needs as other older group
Buy: basic kitchen equipment, basic furniture, cars, equipment for dating game, vacations		Interested in new products	Hard to influence with advertising	Make gifts and contributions		
		Like advertised products	High average purchase of durables	Not interested in new products		
		Buy: washers, dryers, televisions, baby food, chest rubs, cough medicine, vitamins, dolls, wagons, sleds, skates	Buy: new and more tasteful furniture, auto travel, unnecessary appliances, boats, dental services, magazines	Buy: vacations, luxuries, home improvements		

patterns and shows how families' needs, incomes, resources, and expenditures differ at each stage. The horizontal flow shows the traditional FLC. The lower part of the exhibit gives some of the characteristics and purchase patterns of families in each stage of the traditional life cycle. The exhibit also acknowledges that about half of all first marriages end in divorce. If young marrieds move into the young divorced stage, their consumption patterns often revert to those of the young single stage of the cycle.

About four out of five divorced persons remarry by middle age and reenter the traditional life cycle, as indicated by the "recycled flow" in the exhibit. Consumers are especially receptive to marketing efforts at certain points in the life cycle. For example, baby boomers have increased needs for health care services, while families with babies need diapers, toys, and baby clothes.

8-4c Psychographic Segmentation

Age, gender, income, ethnicity, FLC stage, and other demographic variables are usually helpful in developing segmentation strategies, but often, they do not paint the entire picture. Demographics provide the skeleton, but psychographics add meat to the bones. **Psychographic segmentation** is market segmentation on the basis of the following psychographic segmentation variables:

- **Personality:** Personality reflects a person's traits, attitudes, and habits. Clothing is the ultimate personality descriptor. Fashionistas wear high-end, trendy clothes, and hipsters enjoy jeans and T-shirts with tennis shoes. People buy clothes that they feel represent their personalities and give others an idea of who they are.

- **Motives:** Marketers of baby products and life insurance appeal to consumers' emotional motives—namely, to care for their loved ones. Using appeals to economy, reliability, and dependability, carmakers like Subaru and Suzuki target customers with rational motives. Carmakers like Mercedes-Benz, Jaguar, and Cadillac appeal to customers with status-related motives.

- **Lifestyles:** Lifestyle segmentation divides people into groups according to the way they spend their time, the importance of the things around them, their beliefs, and socioeconomic characteristics such as income and education. For example, record stores specializing in vinyl are targeting young people who are listening to independent labels and often pride themselves on being independent of big business.

LEED-certified appliances appeal to environmentally conscious "green" consumers. PepsiCo is promoting its no-calorie, sugar-free flavored water, Aquafina FlavorSplash, to consumers who are health conscious.

- **Geodemographics: Geodemographic segmentation** clusters potential customers into neighborhood lifestyle categories. It combines geographic, demographic, and lifestyle segmentations. Geodemographic segmentation helps marketers develop marketing programs tailored to prospective buyers who live in small geographic regions, such as neighborhoods, or who have very specific lifestyle and demographic characteristics. College students, for example, often share similar demographics and lifestyles and tend to cluster around campus. Knowing this, marketing teams for startups and tech companies like Google often launch ambassador programs at insular college campuses. Student brand ambassadors for the Google Pizza Program bought pizza for their computer science peers during tough times and around deadlines. This helped the company create buzz and form ties with talented programmers. Through these programs, students are transformed into word-of-mouth marketers to their geodemographic peers.[28]

Psychographic variables can be used individually to segment markets or can be combined with other variables to provide more detailed descriptions of market segments. One approach is for marketers and advertisers to purchase information from a collector, such as eXelate Media, in order to reach the audience they want. eXelate, part of consumer research firm Nielsen, gathers information about Web-browsing habits through cookies placed on Web sites. Nielsen, using eXelate, organizes groups according to this information. One group, the "young digerati," includes 25- to 45-year-olds who:

- Are tech savvy

- Are affluent

- Live in trendy condos

- Read the *Economist*

- Have an annual income of $88,000

An automaker can purchase that list and the list of people who visit car blogs and then target ads to the young digerati interested in cars.[29]

psychographic segmentation segmenting markets on the basis of personality, motives, lifestyles, and geodemographics

geodemographic segmentation segmenting potential customers into neighborhood lifestyle categories

8-4d Benefit Segmentation

Benefit segmentation is the process of grouping customers into market segments according to the benefits they seek from the product. Most types of market segmentation are based on the assumption that this variable and customers' needs are related. Benefit segmentation is different because it groups potential customers on the basis of their needs or wants rather than on some other characteristic, such as age or gender. The snack-food market, for example, can be divided into six benefit segments: nutritional snackers, weight watchers, guilty snackers, party snackers, indiscriminate snackers, and economical snackers.

Customer profiles can be developed by examining demographic information associated with people seeking certain benefits. This information can be used to match marketing strategies with selected markets. Dish Network developed Sling TV, a streaming live television service that is available on devices such as gaming consoles and mobile devices, to appeal to people who want to get away from traditional TV sets and cable boxes. The service costs $20 a month for a basic package (additional channels can be purchased), and there are no set-up fees or commitments. Sling TV emphasizes family-friendly programming, which is especially attractive to families with young children.[30]

8-4e Usage-Rate Segmentation

Usage-rate segmentation divides a market by the amount of product bought or consumed. Categories vary with the product, but they are likely to include some combination of the following: former users, potential users, first-time users, light or irregular users, medium users, and heavy users. Segmenting by usage rate enables marketers to focus their efforts on heavy users or to develop multiple marketing mixes aimed at different segments. Because heavy users often account for a sizable portion of all product sales, some marketers focus on the heavy-user segment.

The **80/20 principle** holds that 20 percent of all customers generate 80 percent of the demand. Although the percentages usually are not exact, the general idea often holds true. Multinational corporations require vast amounts of computer storage, but these giant enterprises make up just a small percentage of the data storage market. When storage manufacturer Actifio found that eighty percent of its customers were midsize enterprises that bought computer storage in relatively modest batches of 100 terabytes (about 100,000 gigabytes), it developed the Actifio 100T, a storage appliance that allowed midsize enterprises to scale up to two petabytes (about two million gigabytes) of capacity. In this way, Actifio's 80 percent of low-demand customers could transition over time toward its 20 percent of high-demand customers.[31]

Developing customers into heavy users is the goal behind many frequency/loyalty programs like the airlines' frequent flyer programs. Most supermarkets and other retailers have also designed loyalty programs that reward the heavy-user segment with deals available only to them, such as in-store coupon dispensing systems, loyalty card programs, and special price deals on selected merchandise.

8-5 BASES FOR SEGMENTING BUSINESS MARKETS

The business market consists of four broad segments: producers, resellers, government, and institutions. (For a detailed discussion of the characteristics of these segments, see Chapter 7.) Whether marketers focus on only one or on all four of these segments, they are likely to find diversity among potential customers. Thus, further market segmentation offers just as many benefits to business marketers as it does to consumer product marketers.

8-5a Company Characteristics

Company characteristics, such as geographic location, type of company, company size, and product use, can be important segmentation variables. Some markets tend to be regional because buyers prefer to purchase from local suppliers, and distant suppliers may have difficulty competing in terms of price and service. Therefore, firms that sell to geographically concentrated industries benefit by locating close to their markets.

Segmenting by customer type allows business marketers to tailor their marketing mixes to the unique needs of particular types of organizations or industries. For example, the Amazon Webstore platform allows businesses

---

benefit segmentation the process of grouping customers into market segments according to the benefits they seek from the product

usage-rate segmentation dividing a market by the amount of product bought or consumed

80/20 principle a principle holding that 20 percent of all customers generate 80 percent of the demand

from single-person operations to multinational corporations to operate Amazon-hosted online shops. Entrepreneurs can easily set up templatized shops featuring products that are warehoused and fulfilled by Amazon, while enterprise-level corporations like Fruit of the Loom, Spalding, and Bacardi can use the platform to manage large-scale, customized Web stores. Amazon Webstore's Web site, http://webstore.amazon.com, caters to companies' diverse needs with an array of hosting packages and information pages segmented by both business size and business type.[32]

Volume of purchase (heavy, moderate, light) is a commonly used basis for business segmentation. Another is the buying organization's size, which may affect its purchasing procedures, the types and quantities of products it needs, and its responses to different marketing mixes. Banks frequently offer different services, lines of credit, and overall attention to commercial customers based on their size. Many products, especially raw materials like steel, wood, and petroleum, have diverse applications. How customers use a product may influence the amount they buy, their buying criteria, and their selection of vendors. For example, a producer of springs may have customers who use the product in applications as diverse as making machine tools, bicycles, surgical devices, office equipment, telephones, and missile systems.

8-5b Buying Processes

Many business marketers find it helpful to segment customers and prospective customers on the basis of how they buy. For example, companies can segment some business markets by ranking key purchasing criteria, such as price, quality, technical support, and service. Atlas Overhead Door has developed a commanding position in the industrial door market by providing customized products in just 4 weeks, which is much faster than the industry average of 12 to 15 weeks. Atlas's primary market is companies with an immediate need for customized doors.

The purchasing strategies of buyers may provide useful segments. Two purchasing profiles that have been identified are satisficers and optimizers. **Satisficers** contact familiar suppliers and place the order with the first one to satisfy product and delivery requirements. **Optimizers** consider numerous suppliers (both familiar and unfamiliar), solicit bids, and study all proposals carefully before selecting one.

The personal characteristics of the buyers themselves (their demographic characteristics, decision style, tolerance for risk, confidence level, job responsibilities, and so on) influence their buying behavior and thus offer a viable basis for segmenting some business markets.

8-6 STEPS IN SEGMENTING A MARKET

The purpose of market segmentation, in both consumer and business markets, is to identify marketing opportunities.

1. **Select a market or product category for study:** Define the overall market or product category to be studied. It may be a market in which the firm already competes, a new but related market or product category, or a totally new market.

2. **Choose a basis or bases for segmenting the market:** This step requires managerial insight, creativity, and market knowledge. There are no scientific procedures for selecting segmentation variables. However, a successful segmentation scheme must produce segments that meet the four basic criteria discussed earlier in this chapter.

3. **Select segmentation descriptors:** After choosing one or more bases, the marketer must select the segmentation descriptors. Descriptors identify the specific segmentation variables to use. For example, if a company selects demographics as a basis of segmentation, it may use age, occupation, and income as descriptors. A company that selects usage-rate segmentation needs to decide whether to go after heavy users, nonusers, or light users.

4. **Profile and analyze segments:** The profile should include the segments' size, expected growth, purchase frequency, current brand usage, brand loyalty, and long-term sales and profit potential. This information can then be used to rank potential market segments by profit opportunity, risk, consistency with organizational mission and objectives, and other factors important to the firm.

5. **Select markets:** Selecting markets is not a part of but a natural outcome of the

satisficers business customers who place an order with the first familiar supplier to satisfy product and delivery requirements

optimizers business customers who consider numerous suppliers (both familiar and unfamiliar), solicit bids, and study all proposals carefully before selecting one

TOO MANY COOKS

Campbell Soup Co. has classified home cooks into six distinct profile types: the passionate kitchen master, the familiar taste pleaser, the familiar taste pleaser (Mexican), the constrained wishful eater, the disciplined health manager, and the uninvolved quick fixer. The company uses these types as a foundation to develop and market new products and create recipes. For example, the passionate kitchen master loves to cook, usually has the time to do so, and knows how to make many dishes without a recipe. On the other end of the spectrum is the uninvolved quick fixer, who doesn't enjoy cooking and would be happy to snack all day. Campbell's develops unique approaches for each, as members of one market will not likely be persuaded to buy by a marketing mix targeted at the other. [33]

segmentation process. It is a major decision that influences and often directly determines the firm's marketing mix. This topic is examined in greater detail later in this chapter.

6. **Design, implement, and maintain appropriate marketing mixes:** The marketing mix has been described as product, place (distribution), promotion, and pricing strategies intended to bring about a mutually satisfying exchange relationship with a market. These topics are explored in detail in Chapters 10 through 20.

Markets are dynamic, so it is important that companies proactively monitor their segmentation strategies over time. Often, once customers or prospects have been assigned to a segment, marketers think their task is done. Once customers are assigned to an age segment, for example, they stay there until they reach the next age bracket or category, which could be ten years in the future. Thus, the segmentation classifications are static, but the customers and prospects are changing. Dynamic segmentation approaches adjust to fit the changes that occur in customers' lives. For example, American Eagle mainly targets 10-year-old boys and girls

target market a group of people or organizations for which an organization designs, implements, and maintains a marketing mix intended to meet the needs of that group, resulting in mutually satisfying exchanges

with its 77 kids stores. However, some segments are targeted by too many players, and choosing to enter those kinds of segments can be particularly challenging. For example, there are so many online fashion stores using flash sales to attract bargain hunters that *DailyWorth* put together a list of nine that it thinks are *actually* worth visiting. [34]

8-7 STRATEGIES FOR SELECTING TARGET MARKETS

So far, this chapter has focused on the market segmentation process, which is only the first step in deciding whom to approach about buying a product. The next task is to choose one or more target markets. A **target market** is a group of people or organizations for which an organization designs, implements, and maintains a marketing mix intended to meet the needs of that group, resulting in mutually satisfying exchanges.

Because most markets will include customers with different characteristics, lifestyles, backgrounds, and income levels, it is unlikely that a single marketing mix will attract all segments of the market. Thus, if a marketer wishes to appeal to more than one segment of the market, it must develop different marketing mixes. The three general strategies for selecting target markets—undifferentiated, concentrated, and multisegment targeting—are illustrated in Exhibit 8.2, which also illustrates the advantages and disadvantages of each targeting strategy.

8-7a Undifferentiated Targeting

A firm using an **undifferentiated targeting strategy** essentially adopts a mass-market philosophy, viewing the market as one big market with no individual segments. The firm uses one marketing mix for the entire market. A firm that adopts an undifferentiated targeting strategy assumes that individual customers have similar needs that can be met with a common marketing mix.

The first firm in an industry sometimes uses an undifferentiated targeting strategy. With no competition, the firm may not need to tailor marketing mixes to the preferences of market segments. Henry Ford's famous comment about the Model T is a classic example of an undifferentiated targeting strategy: "They can have their car in any color they want, as long as it's black." At one time, Coca-Cola used this strategy with a single

EXHIBIT 8.2 ADVANTAGES AND DISADVANTAGES OF TARGET MARKETING STRATEGIES

Targeting Strategy	Advantages	Disadvantages
Undifferentiated Targeting	• Potential savings on production/marketing costs	• Unimaginative product offerings • Company more susceptible to competition
Concentrated Targeting	• Concentration of resources • Can better meet the needs of a narrowly defined segment • Allows some small firms to better compete with larger firms • Strong positioning	• Segments too small or changing • Large competitors may more effectively market to niche segment
Multisegment Targeting	• Greater financial success • Economies of scale in producing/marketing	• High costs • Cannibalization

product and a single size of its familiar green bottle. Marketers of commodity products, such as flour and sugar, are also likely to use an undifferentiated targeting strategy.

One advantage of undifferentiated marketing is the potential for saving on production and marketing. Because only one item is produced, the firm should be able to achieve economies of mass production. Also, marketing costs may be lower when there is only one product to promote and a single channel of distribution. Too often, however, an undifferentiated strategy emerges by default rather than by design, reflecting a failure to consider the advantages of a segmented approach. The result is often sterile, unimaginative product offerings that have little appeal to anyone.

Another problem associated with undifferentiated targeting is that it makes the company more susceptible to competitive inroads. Hershey lost a big share of the candy market to Mars and other candy companies before it changed to a multisegment targeting strategy. Coca-Cola forfeited its position as the leading seller of cola drinks in supermarkets to PepsiCo in the late 1950s, when Pepsi began offering several sizes of containers.

You might think a firm producing a standard product such as toilet tissue would adopt an undifferentiated strategy. However, this market has industrial segments and consumer segments. Industrial buyers want an economical, single-ply product sold in boxes of a hundred rolls (or jumbo rolls a foot in diameter to use in public restrooms). The consumer market demands a more versatile product in smaller quantities. Within the consumer market, the product is differentiated with designer print or no print, as cushioned or noncushioned, and as economy priced or luxury priced. Undifferentiated marketing can succeed in certain situations, though. A small grocery store in a small, isolated town may define all of the people who live in the town as its target market. It may offer one marketing mix and generally satisfy everyone in town. This strategy is not likely to be as effective if there are three or four grocery stores in town.

8-7b Concentrated Targeting

With a **concentrated targeting strategy**, a firm selects a market **niche** (one segment of a market) for targeting its marketing efforts. Because the firm is appealing to a single segment, it can concentrate on understanding the needs, motives, and satisfactions of that segment's members and on developing and maintaining a highly specialized marketing mix. Some firms find that concentrating resources and meeting the needs of a narrowly defined market segment is more profitable than spreading resources over several different segments.

Intelligentsia Coffee & Tea, a Chicago-based coffee roaster/retailer, targets serious coffee drinkers with hand-roasted, ground, and poured super-gourmet

undifferentiated targeting strategy a marketing approach that views the market as one big market with no individual segments and thus uses a single marketing mix

concentrated targeting strategy a strategy used to select one segment of a market for targeting marketing efforts

niche one segment of a market

A bag of Intelligentsia coffee sits on a shelf before being shipped from the company's Chicago, Illinois headquarters

coffee or tea served by seriously educated baristas. The company also offers training classes for the at-home or out-of-town coffee aficionado. Starting price—$200 per class.

Small firms often adopt a concentrated targeting strategy to compete effectively with much larger firms. For example, Enterprise Rent-A-Car, number one in the car rental industry, started as a small company catering to people with cars in the shop. Some other firms use a concentrated strategy to establish a strong position in a desirable market segment. Porsche, for instance, targets an upscale automobile market through "class appeal, not mass appeal."

Concentrated targeting violates the old adage "Don't put all your eggs in one basket." If the chosen segment is too small or if it shrinks because of environmental changes, the firm may suffer negative consequences.

For instance, OshKosh B'gosh was highly successful selling children's wear in the 1980s. It was so successful, however, that the children's line came to define OshKosh's image to the extent that the company could not sell clothes to anyone else. Attempts at marketing older children's clothing, women's casual clothes, and maternity wear were all abandoned. Recognizing it was in the children's wear business, the company expanded into products such as kids' shoes, children's eyewear, and plush toys.

A concentrated strategy can also be disastrous for a firm that is not successful in its narrowly defined target market. Before Procter & Gamble (P&G) introduced Head & Shoulders shampoo, several small firms were already selling antidandruff shampoos. Head & Shoulders was introduced with a large promotional campaign, and the new brand captured over half the market immediately. Within a year, several of the firms that had been concentrating on this market segment went out of business.

8-7c Multisegment Targeting

A firm that chooses to serve two or more well-defined market segments and develops a distinct marketing mix for each has a **multisegment targeting strategy**. P&G offers 18 different laundry detergents, each targeting a different segment of the market. For example, Tide is a tough, powerful cleaner, and Era is good for stain treatment and removal. Zipcar, a membership-based car sharing company that provides car rentals to its members billable by the hour or day, shifted its targeting strategy from urban centers, adding services for business and universities like the University of Minnesota, which has five Zipcar stations located around its campus. On campuses across the nation, Zipcar targeting is further subdivided into faculty/staff and student markets.[35]

Multisegment targeting offers many potential benefits to firms, including greater sales volume, higher profits, larger market share, and economies of scale in manufacturing and marketing. Yet it may also involve greater product design, production, promotion, inventory, marketing research, and management costs. Before deciding to use this strategy, firms should compare the benefits and costs of multisegment targeting to those of undifferentiated and concentrated targeting.

Another potential cost of multisegment targeting is **cannibalization**, which occurs when sales of a new product cut into sales of a firm's existing products. For example, as sales of Apple's iPad mini have risen, sales of the 9.7-inch iPad have fallen—so much so that Sharp

multisegment targeting strategy a strategy that chooses two or more well-defined market segments and develops a distinct marketing mix for each

cannibalization a situation that occurs when sales of a new product cut into sales of a firm's existing products

Zipcar representative Travis Reik explains the car sharing process to University of Mississippi junior, Abby Oliver, shortly after Ole Miss accounced a partnership with the company.

Corp had to significantly cut back its production of the larger iPad's screens. Given that the tablet market continues to grow rapidly, this trend suggests that buyers may be choosing the less-expensive mini over the larger option—not opting for both, as Apple might have hoped.[36]

8-8 CRM AS A TARGETING TOOL

Recall from Chapter 1 that CRM entails tracking interactions with customers to optimize customer satisfaction and long-term company profits. Companies that successfully implement CRM tend to customize the goods and services offered to their customers based on data generated through interactions between carefully defined groups of customers and the company. CRM can also allow marketers to target customers with extremely relevant offerings. Birchbox, a company that creates custom boxes of beauty, grooming, and lifestyle product samples, uses CRM to personalize the customer experience. Birchbox reps get to know each customer via profile information, carefully monitoring product reviews, and general activity on the company's Web site. They then put together customized samples and editorial content that feels personal to customers. If a customer likes a sample, he can use Birchbox to buy the full product. [37]

As many firms have discovered, a detailed and segmented understanding of customers can be advantageous. There are at least four trends that will lead to the continuing growth of CRM: personalization, time savings, loyalty, and technology.

- **Personalization:** One-size-fits-all marketing is no longer relevant. Consumers want to be treated as the individuals they are, with their own unique sets of needs and wants. By its personalized nature, CRM can fulfill this desire.

- **Time savings:** Direct and personal marketing efforts will continue to grow to meet the needs of consumers who no longer have the time to spend shopping and making purchase decisions. With the personal and targeted nature of CRM, consumers can spend less time making purchase decisions and more time doing the things that are important to them.

- **Loyalty:** Consumers will be loyal only to those companies and brands that have earned their loyalty and reinforced it at every purchase occasion. CRM techniques focus on finding a firm's best customers, rewarding them for their loyalty, and thanking them for their business.

- **Technology:** Mass-media approaches will decline in importance as advances in market research and database technology allow marketers to collect detailed information on their customers. New technology offers marketers a more cost-effective way to reach customers and enables businesses to personalize their messages. For example, My.Yahoo.com greets each user by name and offers information in which the user has expressed interest. Similarly, RedEnvelope.com helps customers keep track of special occasions and offers personalized gift recommendations. With the help of database technology, CRM can track a business's customers as individuals, even if they number in the millions.

CRM is a huge commitment and often requires a 180-degree turnaround for marketers who spent the last half of the twentieth century developing and implementing mass-marketing efforts. Although mass marketing will probably continue to be used, especially to create brand awareness or to remind consumers of a product, the advantages of CRM cannot be ignored.

8-9 POSITIONING

Marketers segment their markets and then choose which segment, or segments, to target with their marketing mix. Then, based on the target market(s), they can develop the product's **positioning**, a process that influences potential customers' overall perception of a brand, product line, or organization in general. **Position** is the

Unique menu items help Kentucky Fried Chicken differentiate itself from other fast-food fried chicken restaurants.

place a product, brand, or group of products occupies in consumers' minds relative to competing offerings. Consumer goods marketers are particularly concerned with positioning. Coca-Cola has multiple cola brands, each positioned to target a different market. For example, Coca-Cola Zero is positioned on its bold taste and zero calories, Caffeine Free Coca-Cola is positioned as a no-caffeine alternative, and Tab is positioned as a cola drink for dieters.[38]

Positioning assumes that consumers compare products on the basis of important features. Marketing efforts that emphasize irrelevant features are therefore likely to misfire. For example, Crystal Pepsi and a clear version of Coca-Cola's Tab failed because consumers perceived the "clear" positioning as more of a marketing gimmick than a benefit.

Effective positioning requires assessing the positions occupied by competing products, determining the important dimensions underlying these positions, and choosing a position in the market where the organization's marketing efforts will have the greatest impact. In 2013, NBC Universal partnered with *Esquire* magazine to rebrand and reposition ailing cable television channel G4 as the Esquire Network. Transitioning away from a focus on nerd culture, video games, and immature humor, the channel was repositioned to target men age 18 to 49 who are upwardly mobile and highly educated—a demographic NBC Universal believes is underserved by current television offerings. While certain G4 programs like *American Ninja Warrior* were carried over to the new network, new programs focusing on cooking and travel were added to appeal to an older, more sophisticated demographic.[39] One positioning strategy that many firms use to distinguish their products from competitors is based on **product differentiation**. The distinctions between products can be either real or perceived. For example, Kentucky Fried Chicken differentiates itself from other fast-food fried chicken restaurants with its secret blend of eleven herbs and spices (perceived), as well as unique offerings like the Double Down, Famous Bowl, and Bucket & Bites Meal (real).[40] However, many everyday products, such as bleaches, aspirin, unleaded regular gasoline, and some soaps, are differentiated by such trivial means as brand names, packaging, color, smell, or "secret" additives. The marketer attempts to convince consumers that a particular brand is distinctive and that they should demand it.

Some firms, instead of using product differentiation, position their products as being similar to competing products or brands. Two examples of this positioning are

positioning developing a specific marketing mix to influence potential customers' overall perception of a brand, product line, or organization in general

position the place a product, brand, or group of products occupies in consumers' minds relative to competing offerings

product differentiation a positioning strategy that some firms use to distinguish their products from those of competitors

EXHIBIT 8.3

PERCEPTUAL MAP AND POSITIONING STRATEGY FOR SAKS DEPARTMENT STORES

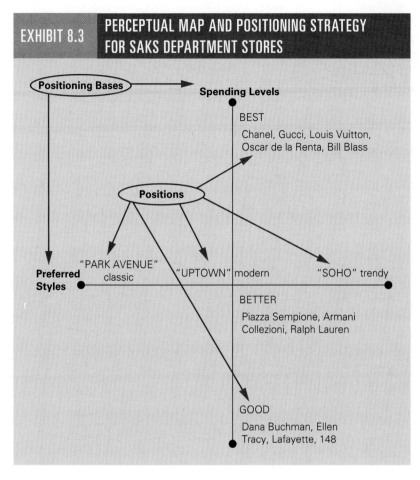

its products, Seventh Generation focuses on removing common toxins and chemicals from household products to make them safe for everyone in the household.

- **Price and quality:** This positioning base may stress high price as a signal of quality or emphasize low price as an indication of value. Neiman Marcus uses the high-price strategy; Walmart has successfully followed the low-price and value strategy. The mass merchandiser Target has developed an interesting position based on price and quality. It is an "upscale discounter," sticking to low prices but offering higher quality and design than most discount chains.

- **Use or application:** Stressing uses or applications can be an effective means of positioning a product with buyers. Danone introduced its Kahlúa liqueur using advertising to point out 228 ways to consume the product.

- **Product user:** This positioning base focuses on a personality or type of user. Gap Inc. has several different brands: Gap stores offer basic casual pieces, such as jeans and T-shirts, to middle-of-the-road consumers at mid-level prices; Old Navy offers low-priced, trendy casual wear geared to youth and college-age groups; and Banana Republic is a luxury brand offering fashionable, luxurious business and casual wear to twenty-five- to thirty-five-year-olds.[41]

- **Product class:** The objective here is to position the product as being associated with a particular category of products—for example, positioning a margarine brand with butter. Alternatively, products can be disassociated with a category.

- **Competitor:** Positioning against competitors is part of any positioning strategy. Apple positions the iPhone as cooler and more up-to-date than Windows-based smartphones, and Samsung positions the Galaxy series as cooler and more up-to-date than the iPhone.

- **Emotion:** Positioning using emotion focuses on how the product makes customers feel. A number of companies use this approach.

artificial sweeteners advertised as tasting like sugar and margarine as tasting like butter.

8-9a Perceptual Mapping

Perceptual mapping is a means of displaying or graphing, in two or more dimensions, the location of products, brands, or groups of products in customers' minds. For example, Saks Incorporated, the department store chain, stumbled in sales when it tried to attract a younger core customer. To recover, Saks invested in research to determine its core customers in its fifty-four stores across the country. The perceptual map in Exhibit 8.3 shows how Saks uses customer demographics such as spending levels and preferred styles to build a matrix that charts the best mix of clothes and accessories to stock in each store.

8-9b Positioning Bases

Firms use a variety of bases for positioning, including the following:

- **Attribute:** A product is associated with an attribute, product feature, or customer benefit. In engineering

perceptual mapping a means of displaying or graphing, in two or more dimensions, the location of products, brands, or groups of products in customers' minds

For example, Nike's "Just Do It" campaign did not tell consumers what "it" is, but most got the emotional message of achievement and courage. Luxury smartphone manufacturer Vertu shifted from a high-price message to an emotional one, positioning the $10,880 Ti model as the phone that will make "nothing else ever feel the same."[42]

8-9c Repositioning

Sometimes products or companies are repositioned in order to sustain growth in slow markets or to correct positioning mistakes. **Repositioning** is changing consumers' perceptions of a brand in relation to competing brands. For example, in its early years, the Hyundai brand was synonymous with cheap, low-quality cars. To reposition its brand, Hyundai redesigned its cars to be more contemporary-looking and started a supportive warranty program. Consumer perceptions changed because customers appreciated the new designs and were reassured of the cars' performance by the generous warranties. Today, Hyundai's brand reputation has vastly improved.[43]

STUDY TOOLS 8

LOCATED AT BACK OF THE TEXTBOOK

☐ Rip Out Chapter Review Card

LOCATED AT WWW.CENGAGEBRAIN.COM

☐ Review Key Terms Flashcards and create your own

☐ Track your knowledge and understanding of key concepts in marketing

☐ Complete practice and graded quizzes to prepare for tests

☐ Complete interactive content within the MKTG Online experience

☐ View the chapter highlight boxes within the MKTG Online experience

MKTG
ONLINE
REVIEW FLASHCARDS
ANYTIME, ANYWHERE!

Create Flashcards from Your StudyBits

Review Key Term Flashcards Already Loaded on the StudyBoard

4LTR PRESS

Access MKTG **ONLINE** at www.cengagebrain.com

9 | Marketing Research

IQoncept/Shutterstock.com

After you finish this chapter go to **PAGE 171** for **STUDY TOOLS.**

9-1 THE ROLE OF MARKETING RESEARCH

Marketing research is the process of planning, collecting, and analyzing data relevant to a marketing decision. The results of this analysis are then communicated to management. Thus, marketing research is the function that links the consumer, customer, and public to the marketer through information. Marketing research plays a key role in the marketing system. It provides decision makers with data on the effectiveness of the current marketing mix and insights for necessary changes. Furthermore, marketing research is a main data source for management information systems. In other words, the findings of a marketing research project become data for management decision making.

marketing research the process of planning, collecting, and analyzing data relevant to a marketing decision

Marketing research has three roles: descriptive, diagnostic, and predictive. Its *descriptive* role includes

gathering and presenting factual statements. For example, what is the historic sales trend in the industry? What are consumers' attitudes toward a product and its advertising? Its *diagnostic* role includes explaining data, such as

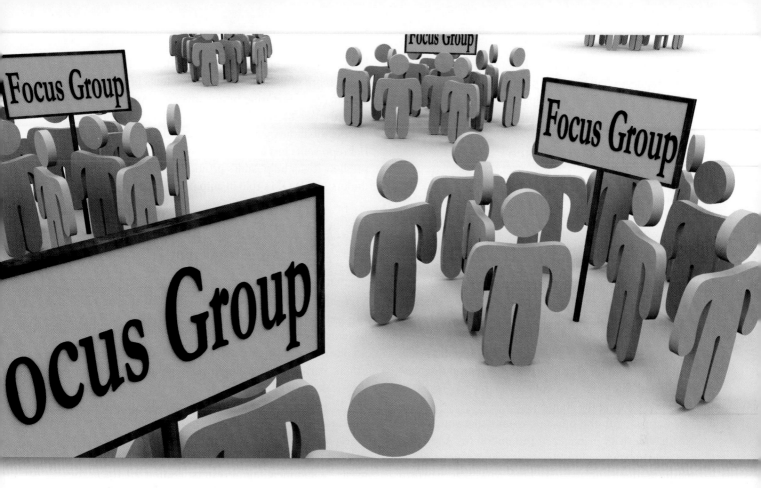

determining the impact on sales of a change in the design of the package. Its *predictive* function is to address "what if" questions. For example, how can the researcher use the descriptive and diagnostic research to predict the results of a planned marketing decision?

9-1a Management Uses of Marketing Research

Marketing research can help managers in several ways. First, it improves the quality of decision making, allowing marketers to explore the desirability of various alternatives before arriving at a path forward. Second, it helps managers trace problems. Was the initial decision incorrect? Did an unforeseen change in the external environment cause the plan to fail? How can the same mistake be avoided in the future? Questions like these can be answered through marketing research. Third, marketing research can help managers understand very detailed and complicated relationships. Most importantly, sound marketing research can help managers serve their customers accurately and efficiently. In order to be successful, manufacturers of fitness wearables like Activité Pop need to understand consumers' attitudes about their products. Marketing research has found that 80 percent of consumers have serious

concerns about wearable Internet-connected technology. However, half of these same consumers would be willing to share personal data collected through such devices if offered compensation such as a coupon or discount. Consumers also report that they would like information about better workouts to reach their goals (22 percent); the best foods to eat (22 percent); and coupons for fitness gear (19 percent).[1] This marketing research is critical for companies developing new fitness tracking devices.

Marketing research also helps managers gauge the perceived value of their goods and services, as well as the level of customer satisfaction. Such *satisfaction research* can be carried out at the individual product, product line, company, or industry level. Research has determined, for example, that the auto repair business needs an overhaul. According to a new consumer survey from AutoMD.com, most consumers (83 percent) feel overcharged in the auto repair process and rank the experience of going to the repair shop/dealership on par with going to the dentist—and women respondents actually *preferred* the dentist.[2] While women have a more negative view of the repair shop/service center experience than men do, consumers across the board report that a more transparent process would improve the experience. They also report that not knowing what a repair should cost is the biggest challenge in the process and that they want real apples-to-apples repair job quotes.

9-1b Understanding the Ever-Changing Marketplace

Marketing research helps managers understand what is going on in the marketplace and take advantage of opportunities. Now, with big data analytics (discussed later), we can understand the marketing environment like never before. Historically speaking, marketing research has been practiced for as long as marketing has existed. The early Phoenicians carried out market demand studies as they traded in the various ports of the Mediterranean Sea. Marco Polo's diary indicates he performed marketing research as he traveled to China. There is even evidence that the Spanish systematically conducted "market surveys" as they explored the New World, and there are examples of marketing research conducted during the Renaissance.

Returning to the present, assume that you are the North American manager of promotion for Audi. You are considering a significant increase in your social media budget and wonder both what role word of mouth (WOM) advertising plays in the promotion process and how Audi compares with other brands. The Foresight Research Word of Mouth Immersion Report provides insights into these questions. The report shows that among auto owners, MINI, Subaru, and Volvo owners stand out as the most likely to recommend their brands (all are 96 percent likely to do so). According to Nancy Walter, vice president of business development at Foresight, "Word of mouth is a prominent influencer in new auto purchases. Almost one-third of new auto buyers say they were moderately or completely influenced by it, and that can go as high as 45 percent for a highly-influenced brand like Audi."[3]

Foresight calls the consumers most likely to give advice *TalkersPlus*. These highly influential buyers comprise 15 percent of the buyer population but generate 59 percent of the WOM. They are most likely to be brand-loyal males who comment about their new vehicle purchases online. They spend $246 more on accessories and are more likely to be influenced by social media, use a mobile device, and attend motorsports events.

To put the giving and getting sides of WOM into perspective, Foresight developed the Amplifier Index, a measure that shows the strength of WOM for a brand, segment, or buyer characteristic. Audi's Amplifier Index score of 2.51, for example, reflects high levels of creating and nurturing brand advocacy. Audi beats out second-place Mercedes-Benz (at 2.14) and is more than double the industry average of 1.22. Although this material represents just a small section of the report, you can see how it can help Audi's promotion manager begin to understand WOM's role in auto purchases.

9-2 STEPS IN A MARKETING RESEARCH PROJECT

Virtually all firms that have adopted the marketing concept engage in some marketing research because it offers decision makers many benefits. Some companies spend millions on marketing research; others, particularly smaller firms, conduct informal, limited-scale research studies.

Whether a research project costs $200 or $2 million, the same general process should be followed. The marketing research process is a scientific approach to decision making that maximizes the chance of getting accurate and meaningful results. Exhibit 9.1 traces the seven steps in the research process, which begins with the recognition of a marketing problem or opportunity. As changes occur in the firm's external environment, marketing managers are faced with the questions "Should we change the existing marketing mix?" and, if so, "How?" Marketing research may be used to evaluate product, promotion, distribution, or pricing alternatives.

Biotechnology company Genentech gave its sales force iPads loaded with iDetail, an app that facilitates sales calls to the company's clients. Genentech quickly discovered, however, that many sales representatives chose not to use the tablets in their presentations. To find the root of the problem, the company turned to marketing research. This research found that the iDetail app was difficult to navigate and use, the font size was too small, and the prescription and safety information was difficult to find. The sales force also needed better information on how to effectively engage clients when using iDetail. Based on the findings of this market research, Genentech implemented additional training for sales reps using the iDetail app.[4]

The iDetail story illustrates an important point about problem/opportunity definition. The **marketing research problem** is information oriented. It involves determining what information is needed and how that information can be obtained efficiently and

marketing research problem determining what information is needed and how that information can be obtained efficiently and effectively

Source: Thingee Corporation

iDetail is an app that is designed to serve as an aid to companies and their sales force.

effectively. The **marketing research objective**, then, is the goal statement. The marketing research objective defines the specific information needed to solve the marketing problem and provides insightful

decision-making information. This requires specific pieces of information needed to solve the marketing research problem. Managers must combine this information with their own experience and other information to make proper decisions. Genentech's marketing research problem was to gather specific information about why a number of sales reps weren't using iDetail. The marketing research objective was to determine exactly what the company should do to solve the problem.

In contrast, the **management decision problem** is action oriented. Management problems tend to be much broader in scope and far more general than marketing research problems, which must be narrowly defined and specific if the research effort is to be successful. Sometimes several research studies must be conducted to solve a broad management problem. For Genentech, the management decision problem was determining how to make the sales force more effective.

9-2a Secondary Data

A valuable tool throughout the research process, particularly in the problem/opportunity identification stage, is **secondary data**—data previously collected for any purpose other than the one at hand. Secondary information originating within the company includes the company's' Web sites, annual reports, reports to stockholders, blogs, product testing results perhaps made available to the news media, YouTube videos, social media posts, and house periodicals composed by the company's personnel for communication to employees, customers, or others. Often, this information is incorporated into a company's internal database.

Innumerable outside sources of secondary information also exist, some in the forms of government departments and agencies (federal, state, and local) that compile and post summaries of business data. Trade and industry associations also publish secondary data.

EXHIBIT 9.1 THE MARKETING RESEARCH PROCESS

1. Identify and formulate the problem/opportunity.
2. Plan the research design and gather secondary data.
3. Specify the sampling procedures.
4. Collect primary data.
5. Analyze the data.
6. Prepare and present the report.
7. Follow up.

marketing research objective the specific information needed to solve a marketing research problem; the objective should be to provide insightful decision-making information

management decision problem a broad-based problem that uses marketing research in order for managers to take proper actions

secondary data data previously collected for any purpose other than the one at hand

Still more data are available in business periodicals and other news media that regularly publish studies and articles on the economy, specific industries, and even individual companies. The unpublished summarized secondary information from these sources corresponds to internal reports, memos, or special-purpose analyses with limited circulation. Competitive considerations in the organization may preclude publication of these summaries.

Secondary data save time and money if they help solve the researcher's problem. Even if the problem is not solved, secondary data have other advantages. They can aid in formulating the problem statement and suggest research methods and other types of data needed for solving the problem. In addition, secondary data can pinpoint the kinds of people to approach and their locations and serve as a basis of comparison for other data. The disadvantages of secondary data stem mainly from a mismatch between the researcher's unique problem and the purpose for which the secondary data were originally gathered, which are typically different. For example, a company wanted to determine the market potential for a fireplace log made of coal rather than compressed wood by-products. The researcher found plenty of secondary data about total wood consumed as fuel, quantities consumed in each state, and types of wood burned. Secondary data were also available about consumer attitudes and purchase patterns of wood by-product fireplace logs. The wealth of secondary data provided the researcher with many insights into the artificial log market. Yet nowhere was there any information that would tell the firm whether consumers would buy artificial logs made of coal.

The quality of secondary data may also pose a problem. Often, secondary data sources do not give detailed information that would enable a researcher to assess their quality or relevance. Whenever possible, a researcher needs to address these important questions: Who gathered the data? Why were the data obtained? What methodology was used? How were classifications (such as heavy users versus light users) developed and defined? When was the information gathered?

THE GROWING IMPORTANCE OF SOCIAL MEDIA
DATA Facebook owns and controls data collected from 890 million daily users and 1.4 billion monthly active users.[5] There are more than 284 million active Twitter users monthly, 80 percent of whom use mobile devices to tweet.[6] Instagram has over 300 million

big data the exponential growth in the volume, variety, and velocity of information and the development of complex, new tools to analyze and create meaning from such data

users. These Web sites' databases tell their marketers a lot about who you are and what you are like, though often on an anonymous basis.

In an effort to expand its information databases even further, Facebook now combines its social data with third-party information from data brokerages like Acxiom, Datalogix, and Alliance Data Systems. Using data collected from loyalty card programs and other mechanisms, these firms aggregate information about which items and brands consumers buy. Using software that obscures identifying information (such as e-mail addresses and phone numbers), they then combine their databases with Facebook's and group users based on certain combinations of data. This data includes the Web sites that Facebook members visit, e-mail lists they may have signed up for, and the ways they spend money, both online and offline—among many, many other metrics.[7] General Motors uses this new type of data synthesis to target younger buyers who might be interested in its Chevrolet Sonic. Pepsi uses it to show different ads based on whether a user regularly buys Pepsi, Diet Pepsi, or is a Pepsi switcher (that is, a person who tends to switch soda brands and is more price sensitive).

Another new Facebook tool allows advertisers to calculate their *return on investment* (total profit minus expenses divided by the investment made) on Facebook ads by tallying the actions taken by ad viewers. These actions include click-throughs, registrations, shopping cart checkouts, and other metrics. The tool also enables marketers to deliver ads to people who are most likely to make further purchases.[8]

Even photos shared on sites such as Flickr, Instagram, and Pinterest provide data for researchers. More than 20 billion photos have already been shared in Instagram, and users are adding about 60 million a day.[9] Companies like Ditto Labs and Piqora scan photos to glean insights about consumers. If a logo appears above a face, such as Smith ski goggles in a picture of a skier, the software logs the brand of apparel. Visual analysis can also show correlations between products, such as which beverages people drink while eating Kraft Macaroni and Cheese. Digital Labs' software can detect more than 3,000 different brand logos in pictures. Photos that were shot at a university, a bar, the beach, or a snowy mountain give clues about where and how customers use those brands.

THE INCREDIBLE WORLD OF BIG DATA **Big data** is
the exponential growth in the volume, variety, and velocity of information and the development of complex new tools to analyze and create meaning from such data.

In the past, the flow of data was slow, steady, and predictable. All data was quantitative (countable)—many firms collected sales numbers by store, by product line, and at most, perhaps by a few other measures. Today, data is constantly streaming in from social media, as well as other sources. Advanced big data databases allow the analysis of unstructured data such as e-mails, audio files, and YouTube videos.

In 2016, real-time advertising auctions are expected to account for a third of the $25 billion spent on digital display advertising in the United States.[10] Big data enables these auctions to take place in mere seconds. For example, suppose a bored woman sits waiting in an airline lounge. She scrolls through her iPhone and taps on a brightly colored icon to launch a free mobile game. In the instant before the app loads, predictive analytics firm Flurry collects data about the woman: here we have a new mother, business traveler, fashion follower, in her late 20s, and somewhere near JFK airport. Flurry then holds an automated auction among potential advertisers to fill an ad space that displays while the app is loading. In a fraction of a second, the mobile ad exchange picks the highest bidder with the best-fitting parameters, and the woman's screen flashes to an ad for Maui Jim sunglasses.[11]

Flurry provides an analytic tool that tells app developers how many people are using their apps. More than 540,000 apps now use the tool, which in turn funnels much of the user data back to Flurry. Flurry has a data pipe into more than 1.2 million mobile devices globally and pulls data from seven to ten apps per device. Flurry's analytic tool encrypts and combines identifying pieces of data to create anonymous IDs for each mobile device.[12] Mobile device users are then grouped into one of more than one hundred profiles such as "business traveler" or "sports fanatic."

Along with advanced data analysis tools came a software program called Hadoop, developed by Apache and named for a child's toy elephant. Traditionally, complex computer programs had to run on huge, expensive mainframe computers. Hadoop allows queries to be split up and run much more efficiently. Using Hadoop, different analytic tasks are distributed among numerous inexpensive computer servers, each of which solves part of the problem before reassembling the queries when the work is finished. Thus, with the aid of modern databases, software, and hardware, big data can be analyzed faster and cheaper than ever before.[13]

The ability to crunch numbers means nothing, however, if humans cannot use or even access that information. Most people cannot remember a string of numbers longer than their phone numbers. Modern databases sometimes contain billions of pieces of data, so the question quickly arose as to how big data could be presented in a meaningful way. The answer to this question is data visualization. An example of data visualization is shown in Exhibit 9.2. Visualization acts as an engine for bringing patterns to light—even the subtlest of patterns woven into the largest of data sets

Specialty women's apparel retailer Chicos uses big data analytics to find key brand influencers online and to determine how brand-related conversations impact sales. Sprint's Virgin Mobile uses analytics to tailor specific phone offers to particular customer types. For example, one effort promoted higher-end contract-free smartphones to individuals who could afford the monthly contractual plan but were likely to prefer the company's prepaid option. This offer resulted in increased customer retention and higher profits for Virgin Mobile. Online automotive market Edmunds.com uses big data analytics to help auto dealers predict how long a given car will remain on their lots. This helps dealers minimize the number of days a car remains unsold. Macy's adjusts pricing in near-real time for 73 million items based on demand and inventory. Walmart uses big data, including semantic search and synonym mining, to produce relevant search results for online shoppers. Semantic search improves purchase completion by 10 to 15 percent—a figure that is worth billions to Walmart.

One fast food chain is using cameras to determine what to display on its digital drive-through menu boards. When drive-through lines are longer, the menu board features products that can be served up quickly. When lines are shorter, the menu board features higher margin items that take longer to prepare. Similarly, the Los Angeles and Santa Cruz police departments are using big data to predict where crime will occur down to 500 square feet. Los Angeles has seen a 33 percent reduction in burglary and a 21 percent reduction in violent crime in areas where the software is being used.[14]

Big data analytics focuses very much on *what*. That is, its primary purpose is to uncover what patterns and relationships exist in this database. Often, the insights gained from *what* are all a marketer needs to create a strategy. Suppose that Amazon's analytic software uncovers that hundreds of online customers who bought *War and Peace* also bought *The Idiot*. Amazon can use this data to send promotional e-mails to customers who bought one book but not the other. *Why* never comes into play when sending out these promotional e-mails. Still, marketers often do need to understand why, and that is where traditional marketing research comes into play. If Mars launches a new type of chocolate bar and

EXHIBIT 9.2 **DATA VISUALIZATION (CONTAINS IMAGE OF SEARCHES IN CHINA)**

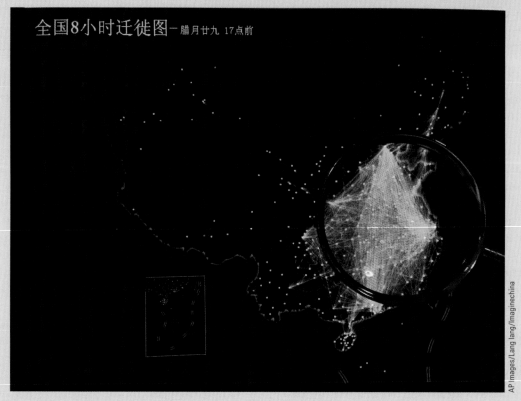

全国8小时迁徙图-腊月廿九 17点前

AP Images/Lang lang/Imaginechina

Baidu Migrate, an interactive heat map developed by China's largest search engine, uses smartphone data to visualize migration during the company's 40-day spring festival travel rush.

there are many initial purchases, but few repeat purchasers, then the driving question becomes "why?" In the following sections, we will return to the marketing research process to explain how such a question can be answered.

9-2b Planning the Research Design and Gathering Primary Data

Good secondary data and big data can help researchers conduct a thorough situation analysis. With that information, researchers can list their unanswered questions and rank them. Researchers must then decide the exact information required to answer the questions. The **research design** specifies which research questions must be answered,

research design specifies which research questions must be answered, how and when the data will be gathered, and how the data will be analyzed

primary data information that is collected for the first time; used for solving the particular problem under investigation

how and when the data will be gathered, and how the data will be analyzed. Typically, the project budget is finalized after the research design has been approved.

Sometimes research questions can be answered by gathering more secondary data; otherwise, primary data may be needed. **Primary data**, or information collected for the first time, are used for solving the particular problem under investigation. The main advantage of primary data is that they can answer specific research questions that secondary data cannot answer. Suppose that Olive Garden is considering discontinuing about a third of its menu and adding an equal number of new items. All of the new dishes have done very well in taste tests. The research question is whether or not to make such a major change in the menu. Primary data from a recent research project found that almost 70 percent of restaurant patrons won't try a new menu item (actual data). Of the 30 percent willing to try a new menu item, only 17 percent will order a completely new dish. Consumers tend to replace their preplanned menu items ("I'm going to have lasagna") with a new menu item only if the new

EXHIBIT 9.3 CHARACTERISTICS OF TRADITIONAL FORMS OF SURVEY RESEARCH

Characteristic	In-Home Personal Interviews	Mall Intercept Interviews	Central-Location Telephone Interviews	Self-Administered and One-Time Mail Surveys	Mail Panel Surveys	Executive Interviews	Focus Groups
Cost	High	Moderate	Moderate	Low	Moderate	High	Low
Time span	Moderate	Moderate	Fast	Slow	Relatively slow	Moderate	Fast
Use of interviewer probes	Yes	Yes	Yes	No	Yes	Yes	Yes
Ability to show concepts to respondent	Yes (also taste tests)	Yes (also taste tests)	No	Yes	Yes	Yes	Yes
Management control over interviewer	Low	Moderate	High	N/A	N/A	Moderate	High
General data quality	High	Moderate	High to moderate	Moderate to low	Moderate	High	Moderate
Ability to collect large amounts of data	High	Moderate	Moderate to low	Low to moderate	Moderate	Moderate	Moderate
Ability to handle complex questionnaires	High	Moderate	High, if computer aided	Low	Low	High	N/A

dish is the same type of food as the product they had originally planned to order.[15] Thus, Olive Garden replacing a third of its menu is not a good idea. Primary data are current, and researchers know the source. Sometimes researchers gather the data themselves rather than assign projects to outside companies. Researchers also specify the methodology of the research. Secrecy can be maintained because the information is proprietary. In contrast, much secondary data is available to all interested parties for relatively small fees or free.

Gathering primary data can be expensive; costs can range from a few thousand dollars for a limited survey to several million for a nationwide study. For instance, a nationwide, 15-minute telephone interview with 1,000 adult males can cost $50,000 or more for everything, including a data analysis and report. Because primary data gathering is so expensive, many firms do not bother to conduct in-person interviews. Instead, they use the Internet. Larger companies that conduct many research projects use another cost-saving technique. They *piggyback studies*, or gather data on two different projects using one questionnaire. Nevertheless, the disadvantages of primary data gathering are usually offset by the advantages. It is often the only way of solving a research problem. And with a variety of techniques available for research—including surveys, observations, and experiments—primary research can address almost any marketing question.

SURVEY RESEARCH The most popular technique for gathering primary data is **survey research**, in which a researcher either interacts with people or posts a questionnaire online to obtain facts, opinions, and attitudes. Exhibit 9.3 summarizes the characteristics of traditional forms of survey research.

In-Home Personal Interviews Although in-home personal interviews often provide high-quality information, they tend to be very expensive because of the interviewers' travel time and mileage costs. Therefore, they are rapidly disappearing from the American and European researchers' survey toolbox. They are, however, still popular in many less developed countries around the globe.

Mall Intercept Interviews The **mall intercept interview** is conducted in the common area of a shopping mall or in a market research office within the mall. To conduct this type of interview, the research firm rents office space in the mall or pays a significant daily fee. One drawback is that it is hard to get a representative sample of the population. One advantage is the ability of the

> **survey research** the most popular technique for gathering primary data, in which a researcher interacts with people to obtain facts, opinions, and attitudes
>
> **mall intercept interview** a survey research method that involves interviewing people in the common areas of shopping malls

interviewer to probe when necessary—a technique used to clarify a person's response and ask for more detailed information.

Mall intercept interviews must be brief. Only the shortest ones are conducted while respondents are standing. Often, researchers invite respondents into the office for interviews, which are still generally less than fifteen minutes long. The overall quality of mall intercept interviews is about the same as telephone interviews.

Marketing researchers use computer technology to speed the mall interview process. One technique is **computer-assisted personal interviewing**. The researcher conducts in-person interviews, reads questions to the respondent off a computer screen, and directly keys the respondent's answers into the computer. A second approach is **computer-assisted self-interviewing**. A mall interviewer intercepts and directs willing respondents to nearby computers. Each respondent reads questions off a computer screen and directly keys his or her answers into the computer. A third use of computer technology is fully automated self-interviewing. Respondents are guided by interviewers or independently approach a centrally located computer station

Tupungato/Shutterstock.com

or kiosk, read questions off a screen, and directly key their answers into the station's computer.

Telephone Interviews

Telephone interviews cost less than personal interviews, but cost is rapidly increasing due to respondent refusals to participate. Most telephone interviewing is conducted from a specially designed phone room called a **central-location telephone (CLT) facility**.

A CLT facility has many phone lines, individual interviewing stations,

headsets, and sometimes monitoring equipment. The research firm typically will interview people nationwide from a single location. The federal "Do Not Call" law does not apply to survey research.

Most CLT facilities offer computer-assisted interviewing. The interviewer reads the questions from a computer screen and enters the respondent's data directly into the computer, saving time. Hallmark Cards found that an interviewer administered a printed questionnaire for its Shoebox greeting cards in 28 minutes. The same questionnaire administered with computer assistance took only 18 minutes. The researcher can stop the survey at any point and immediately print out the survey results, allowing the research design to be refined as necessary.

MAIL SURVEYS Mail surveys have several benefits: relatively low cost, elimination of interviewers and field supervisors, centralized control, and actual or promised anonymity for respondents (which may draw more candid responses). A disadvantage is that mail questionnaires usually produce low response rates. The resulting sample may therefore not represent the surveyed population. Another serious problem with mail surveys is that no one probes respondents to clarify or elaborate on their answers. If a respondent uses the word "convenience," there is no way to clarify exactly what he means. Convenience could refer to location, store hours, or a host of other factors.

Mail panels offer an alternative to the one-shot mail survey. A mail panel consists of a sample of households recruited to participate by mail for a given period. Panel members often receive gifts in return for their participation. Essentially, the panel is a sample used several times. In contrast to one-time mail surveys, the response rates from mail panels are high. Rates of 70 percent (of those who agree to participate) are not uncommon.

Executive Interviews An **executive interview**

involves interviewing businesspeople at their offices concerning industrial products or services, a process that is very expensive. First, individuals involved in the purchase decision for the product in question must be identified and located, which can itself be expensive and time-consuming. Once a qualified person is located, the next step is to get that person to agree to be interviewed and to set a time for the interview. Finally, an interviewer must go to the particular place at the appointed time. Long waits are frequently encountered; cancellations are not uncommon. This type of survey requires the very best interviewers because they are frequently interviewing on topics that they know very little about.

Focus Groups A **focus group** is a type of personal interviewing. Often recruited by random telephone screening, seven to ten people with certain desired characteristics form a focus group. These qualified consumers are usually offered an incentive (typically $30 to $50) to participate in a group discussion. The meeting place (sometimes resembling a living room, sometimes featuring a conference table) has audiotaping and perhaps videotaping equipment. It also likely has a viewing room with a one-way mirror so that clients (manufacturers or retailers) can watch the session. During the session, a moderator, hired by the research company, leads the group discussion. Focus groups can be used to gauge consumer response to a product or promotion and are occasionally used to brainstorm new-product ideas or to screen concepts for new products. Focus groups also represent an efficient way of learning how products are actually used in the home. Lewis Stone, former manager of Colgate-Palmolive's research and development division, says the following about focus groups:

> If it weren't for focus groups, Colgate-Palmolive Co. might never know that some women squeeze their bottles of dishwashing soap, others squeeeeeze them, and still others squeeeeeeeeeze out the desired amount. Then there are the ones who use the soap 'neat.' That is, they put the product directly on a sponge or washcloth and wash the dishes under running water until the suds run out. Then they apply more detergent.

Stone was explaining how body language, exhibited during focus groups, provides insights into a product that are not apparent from reading questionnaires on habits and practices. Panelists' descriptions of how they perform tasks highlight need gaps, which can improve an existing product or demonstrate how a new product might be received.

QUESTIONNAIRE DESIGN All forms of survey research require a questionnaire. Questionnaires ensure that all respondents will be asked the same series of questions. Questionnaires include three basic types of questions: open-ended, closed-ended, and scaled-response (see Exhibit 9.4). An **open-ended question** encourages an answer phrased in the respondent's own words. Researchers get a rich array of information based on the respondent's frame of reference (What do you think about the new flavor?). In contrast, a **closed-ended question** asks the respondent to make a selection from a limited list of responses. Closed-ended questions can either be what marketing researchers call dichotomous (Do you like the new flavor? Yes or No.) or multiple choice. A **scaled-response question** is a closed-ended question designed to measure the intensity of a respondent's answer.

Closed-ended and scaled-response questions are easier to tabulate than open-ended questions because response choices are fixed. On the other hand, unless the researcher designs the closed-ended question very carefully, an important choice may be omitted. For example, suppose a food study asked this question: "Besides meat, which of the following items do you normally add to tacos that you prepare at home?"

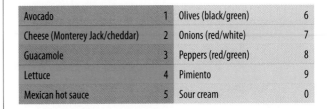

Avocado	1	Olives (black/green)	6
Cheese (Monterey Jack/cheddar)	2	Onions (red/white)	7
Guacamole	3	Peppers (red/green)	8
Lettuce	4	Pimiento	9
Mexican hot sauce	5	Sour cream	0

The list seems complete, doesn't it? However, consider the following responses: "I usually add a green, avocado-tasting hot sauce," "I cut up a mixture of lettuce and spinach," "I'm a vegetarian—I don't use meat at all," and "My taco is filled only with guacamole." How would you code these replies? As you can see, the question needs an "other" category.

A good question must be clear and concise and avoid ambiguous language. The answer to the question "Do you live within ten minutes of here?" depends on the mode of transportation (maybe the person walks), driving speed, perceived time, and other factors. Language should also be clear. As such, jargon should be avoided, and wording should be geared to the target audience. A question such as "What is the level of efficacy of your preponderant dishwasher powder?" would probably

EXHIBIT 9.4 TYPES OF QUESTIONS FOUND ON QUESTIONNAIRES FOR NATIONAL MARKET RESEARCH

Open-Ended Questions	Closed-Ended Questions	Scaled-Response Question
1. What advantages, if any, do you think ordering from a mail-order catalog offers compared to shopping at a local retail outlet? (*Probe:* What else?)	**Dichotomous** 1. Did you heat the Danish product before serving It? Yes..1 No..2 2. The federal government doesn't care what people like me think. Agree...1 Disagree 2	Now that you have used the rug cleaner, would you say that you . . . (*Circle one.*) Would definitely buy it...............1 Would probably buy it ....2 Might or might not buy it............3 Probably would not buy it...........4 Definitely would not buy it..........5
2. Why do you have one or more of your rugs or carpets professionally cleaned rather than cleaning them yourself or having someone else in the household clean them?	**Multiple Choice** 1. I'd like you to think back to the last footwear of any kind that you bought. I'll read you a list of descriptions and would like for you to tell me which category they fall into. (*Read list and circle proper category.*) Dress and/or formal.............................1	
3. What is it about the color of the eye shadow that makes you like it the best?	Casual..2 Canvas/trainer /gym shoes ....3 Specialized athletic shoes....................4 Boots..5 2. In the last three months, have you used Noxzema skin cream .... (*Circle all that apply.*) As a facial wash...................................1 For moisturizing the skin........................2 For treating blemishes ....3 For cleansing the skin...........................4 For treating dry skin..............................5 For softening skin.................................6 For sunburn..7 For making the facial skin smooth.............8	

be greeted by a lot of blank stares. It would be much simpler to say "Are you (1) very satisfied, (2) somewhat satisfied, or (3) not satisfied with your current brand of dishwasher powder?"

Stating the survey's purpose at the beginning of the interview may improve clarity, but it may also increase the chances of receiving biased responses. Many times, respondents will try to provide answers that they believe are "correct" or that the interviewer wants to hear. To avoid bias at the question level, researchers should avoid leading questions and adjectives that cause respondents to think of the topic in a certain way.

Finally, to ensure clarity, the interviewer should avoid asking two questions in one—for example, "How did you like the taste and texture of the Pepperidge Farm coffee cake?" This should be divided into two questions, one concerning taste and the other texture.

observation research a research method that relies on four types of observation: people watching people, people watching an activity, machines watching people, and machines watching an activity

mystery shoppers researchers posing as customers who gather observational data about a store

OBSERVATION RESEARCH In contrast to survey research, **observation research** entails watching what people do or using machines to watch what people do. Specifically, it can be defined as the systematic process of recording the behavioral patterns of people, objects, and occurrences without questioning them. A market researcher using the observation technique witnesses and records information as events occur or compiles evidence from records of past events. Carried a step further, observation may involve watching people or phenomena and may be conducted by human observers or machines. Examples of these various observational situations are shown in Exhibit 9.5.

Some common forms of people-watching-people research are one-way mirror observations, mystery shoppers, and behavioral targeting. A one-way mirror allows the researchers to see the participants, but the participants cannot see the researchers.

Mystery Shoppers **Mystery shoppers** are researchers posing as customers who gather observational data about a store (for example, are the shelves neatly stocked?) and collect data about customer/employee

EXHIBIT 9.5 OBSERVATIONAL SITUATIONS

Situation	Example
People watching people	Observers stationed in supermarkets watch consumers select frozen Mexican dinners; the purpose is to see how much comparison shopping people do at the point of purchase.
People watching an activity	An observer stationed at an intersection counts traffic moving in various directions.
Machines watching people	Movie or videotape cameras record behavior as in the people-watching-people example above.
Machines watching an activity	Traffic-counting machines monitor traffic flow.

interactions. The interaction is not an interview, and communication occurs only so that the mystery shopper can observe the actions and comments of the employee. Mystery shopping is, therefore, classified as an observational marketing research method even though communication is often involved. Restaurant chains like Subway use mystery shoppers to evaluate store cleanliness and quality of service.

Behavioral Targeting **Behavioral targeting (BT)**, sometimes simply called tracking, began as a simple process by placing cookies in users' browsers or mobile apps to track which Web sites they visited, how long they lingered, what they searched for, and what they bought. All of this information can be tracked anonymously—a "fly on the wall" perspective. While survey research is a great way to find out the "why" and the "how," behavioral targeting lets the researcher find out the "how much," the "how often," and the "where." Also, through **social media monitoring**, using automated tools to monitor online buzz, chatter, and conversations, a researcher can learn what is being said about the brand and the competition. Tracking is the basis for input into online databases. Companies like Tapad track customers across multiple devices—personal desktop computers, laptops, smartphones, and tablets, for example. If a customer is using multiple devices at the same time, Tapad knows, and knows what she is doing on each.

ETHNOGRAPHIC RESEARCH Ethnographic research comes to marketing from the field of anthropology. The technique is becoming increasingly popular in marketing research. **Ethnographic research**, or the study of human behavior in its natural context, involves observation of behavior and physical setting. Ethnographers directly observe the population they are studying. As "participant observers," ethnographers can use their intimacy with the people they are studying to gain richer, deeper insights into culture and behavior—in short, what makes people do what they do?

Managers at Cambridge SoundWorks recently faced a perplexing problem. Male customers stood wide-eyed and wallets-ready when sales reps showed off the company's hi-fi "blow-your-hair-back" stereo speakers in retail outlets across the country, but sales were slumping. Why didn't such unabashed enthusiasm for the product translate into more—and bigger ticket—sales?

To find out, the Andover, Massachusetts-based stereo equipment manufacturer and retailer hired research firm Design Continuum to follow a dozen prospective customers over the course of two weeks. After the two weeks were up, the researchers concluded that the high-end speaker market suffered from something they referred to as "the spouse acceptance factor." While men adored the big black boxes, women hated their unsightly appearance. Concerned about how speakers might look in the living room, women frequently talked their husbands out of buying the cool (but hideous) stereo equipment. Even those who purchased the products had trouble showing them off. Men would attempt to display the loudspeakers as trophies in their living rooms while women would hide them behind plants, vases, and chairs. "Women would come into the store, look at the speakers, and say, 'that thing is ugly,'" said principal at Design Continuum Ellen Di Resta. "The men would lose the argument and leave the store without a stereo. The solution was to give the target market what men and women *both* wanted: a great sound system that looks like furniture so you don't have to hide it."

Armed with this knowledge, Cambridge SoundWorks unveiled a new line of spouse-friendly speakers. The furniture-like Newton Series of speakers and home theater systems comes in an array of colors and finishes. The result? The Newton Series is the fastest-growing and best-selling product line in Cambridge SoundWorks' history.[16]

VIRTUAL SHOPPING

Advances in computer technology have enabled researchers to simulate an actual retail store environment on a computer screen. Depending on the type of simulation, a shopper can "pick up" a package by touching

behavioral targeting (BT) a form of observation marketing research that combines a consumer's online activity with psychographic and demographic profiles compiled in databases

social media monitoring the use of automated tools to monitor online buzz, chatter, and conversations

ethnographic research the study of human behavior in its natural context; involves observation of behavior and physical setting

Advances in computer technology have enabled researchers to simulate an actual retail store environment.

Sashkin/Shutterstock.com

its image on the monitor and rotate it to examine all sides. Like buying on most online retailers, the shopper touches the shopping cart to add an item to the basket. During the shopping process, the computer unobtrusively records the amount of time the consumer spends shopping in each product category, the time the consumer spends examining each side of a product, the quantity of the product the consumer purchases, and the order in which items are purchased.

A major apparel retailer using a computer simulated environment recently found that men have trouble putting outfits together. Men also hesitate to pick up clothing items because they can't fold them back the same way. With this knowledge, the apparel chain made two major changes: it began selling items together as complete outfit solutions and folded shirts and other clothes more simply. Sales of men's clothes increased by 40 percent.[17]

Virtual shopping research is growing rapidly. According to the United States Department of Agriculture, approximately 50,000 new consumer packaged goods are introduced each year.[18] All are vying for very limited retail shelf space. Any process, such as virtual shopping, that can speed product development time and lower costs is always welcomed by manufacturers. Some companies outside of retail have even begun experimenting with virtual shopping and other simulated environment

experiment a method of gathering primary data in which the researcher alters one or more variables while observing the effects of those alterations on another variable

sample a subset from a larger population

universe the population from which a sample will be drawn

tools—many telecom, financial, automotive, aviation, and fast-food companies are using such tools to better serve their customers.

EXPERIMENTS An **experiment** is a method a researcher can use to gather primary data. The researcher alters one or more variables—price, package design, shelf space, advertising theme, advertising expenditures—while observing the effects of those alterations on another variable (usually sales). The best experiments are those in which all factors except one are held constant. The researcher can then observe what changes in sales, for example, result from changes in the amount of money spent on advertising.

Holding all other factors constant in the external environment is a monumental and costly, if not impossible, task. Such factors as competitors' actions, weather, and economic conditions are beyond the researcher's control. Yet market researchers have ways to account for the ever-changing external environment. Mars, the candy company, was losing sales to other candy companies. Traditional surveys showed that the shrinking candy bar was not perceived as a good value. Mars wondered whether a bigger bar sold at the same price would increase sales enough to offset the higher ingredient costs. The company designed an experiment in which the marketing mix stayed the same in different markets but the size of the candy bar varied. The substantial increase in sales of the bigger bar quickly proved that the additional costs would be more than covered by the additional revenue. Mars increased the bar size—along with its market share and profits.

9-2c Specifying the Sampling Procedures

Once the researchers decide how they will collect primary data, their next step is to select the sampling procedures they will use. A firm can seldom take a census of all possible users of a new product, nor can they all be interviewed. Therefore, a firm must select a sample of the group to be interviewed. A **sample** is a subset from a larger population.

Several questions must be answered before a sampling plan is chosen. First, the population, or **universe**, of interest must be defined. This is the group from which the sample will be drawn. It should include all the people whose opinions, behavior, preferences, attitudes, and so on, are of interest to the marketer. For example, in a study whose purpose is to determine the market for a new canned dog food, the universe might be defined to include all current buyers of canned dog food.

SAMPLE

UNIVERSE

After the universe has been defined, the next question is whether the sample must be representative of the population. If the answer is yes, a probability sample is needed. Otherwise, a nonprobability sample might be considered.

PROBABILITY SAMPLES A **probability sample** is a sample in which every element in the population has a known statistical likelihood of being selected. Its most desirable feature is that scientific rules can be used to ensure that the sample represents the population.

One type of probability sample is a **random sample**—a sample arranged in such a way that every element of the population has an equal chance of being selected as part of the sample. For example, suppose a university is interested in getting a cross section of student opinions on a proposed sports complex to be built using student activity fees. If the university can acquire an up-to-date list of all the enrolled students, it can draw a random sample by using random numbers from a table (found in most statistics books) to select students from the list. Common forms of probability and nonprobability samples are shown in Exhibit 9.6.

NONPROBABILITY SAMPLES Any sample in which little or no attempt is made to get a representative cross section of the population can be considered a **nonprobability sample**. Therefore, the probability of selection of each sampling unit is not known. A common form of a nonprobability sample is the **convenience sample**, which uses respondents who are convenient or readily accessible to the researcher—for instance, employees, friends, or relatives.

Nonprobability samples are acceptable as long as the researcher understands their nonrepresentative nature. Because of their lower cost, nonprobability samples are sometimes used in marketing research.

TYPES OF ERRORS Whenever a sample is used in marketing research, two major types of errors may occur: measurement error and sampling error. **Measurement error** occurs when there is a difference between the information desired by the researcher and the information provided by the measurement process. For example, people may tell an interviewer that they purchase Crest toothpaste when they do not. Measurement error generally tends to be larger than sampling error.

Sampling error occurs when a sample somehow does not represent the target population. Sampling error can be one of several types. Nonresponse error occurs when the sample actually interviewed differs from the sample drawn. This error happens because the original people selected to be interviewed either refused to cooperate or were inaccessible.

Frame error, another type of sampling error, arises if the sample drawn from a population differs from the target population. For instance, suppose a telephone survey is conducted to find out Chicago beer drinkers' attitudes toward Coors. If a Chicago telephone directory is used as

probability sample a sample in which every element in the population has a known statistical likelihood of being selected

random sample a sample arranged in such a way that every element of the population has an equal chance of being selected as part of the sample

nonprobability sample any sample in which little or no attempt is made to get a representative cross section of the population

convenience sample a form of nonprobability sample using respondents who are convenient or readily accessible to the researcher—for example, employees, friends, or relatives

measurement error an error that occurs when there is a difference between the information desired by the researcher and the information provided by the measurement process

sampling error an error that occurs when a sample somehow does not represent the target population

frame error an error that occurs when a sample drawn from a population differs from the target population

EXHIBIT 9.6 TYPES OF SAMPLES

Probability Samples	
Simple Random Sample	Every member of the population has a known and equal chance of selection.
Stratified Sample	The population is divided into mutually exclusive groups (such as gender or age); then random samples are drawn from each group.
Cluster Sample	The population is divided into mutually exclusive groups (such as geographic areas); then a random sample of clusters is selected. The researcher then collects data from all the elements in the selected clusters or from a probability sample of elements within each selected cluster.
Systematic Sample	A list of the population is obtained—e.g., all persons with a checking account at XYZ Bank—and a skip interval is obtained by dividing the sample size by the population size. If the sample size is 100 and the bank has 1,000 customers, then the skip interval is 10. The beginning number is randomly chosen within the skip interval. If the beginning number is 8, then the skip pattern would be 8, 18, 28, ...
Nonprobability Samples	
Convenience Sample	The researcher selects the easiest population members from which to obtain information.
Judgment Sample	The researcher's selection criteria are based on personal judgment that the elements (persons) chosen will likely give accurate information.
Quota Sample	The researcher finds a prescribed number of people in several categories—e.g., owners of large dogs versus owners of small dogs. Respondents are not selected on probability sampling criteria.
Snowball Sample	Additional respondents are selected on the basis of referrals from the initial respondents. This method is used when a desired type of respondent is hard to find—e.g., persons who have taken round-the-world cruises in the last three years. This technique employs the old adage "Birds of a feather flock together."

the *frame* (the device or list from which the respondents are selected), the survey will contain a frame error. Not all Chicago beer drinkers have landline phones, and many phone numbers are unlisted. An ideal sample (in other words, a sample with no frame error) matches all important characteristics of the target population to be surveyed. Could you find a perfect frame for Chicago beer drinkers?

Random error occurs when the selected sample is an imperfect representation of the overall population. Random error represents how accurately the chosen sample's true average (mean) value reflects the population's true average (mean) value. For example, we might take a random sample of beer drinkers in Chicago and find that 16 percent regularly drink Coors beer. The next day, we might repeat the same sampling procedure and discover that 14 percent regularly drink Coors beer. The difference is due to random error. Error is common to all surveys, yet it is often not reported or is underreported. Typically, the only error mentioned in a written report is sampling error.

random error an error that occurs when the selected sample is an imperfect representation of the overall population

field service firm a firm that specializes in interviewing respondents on a subcontracted basis

9-2d Collecting the Data

Marketing research field service firms are used to collect some primary data. A **field service firm** specializes in interviewing respondents on a subcontracted basis. Many have offices, often in malls, throughout the country. A typical marketing research study involves data collection in several cities, which may require the marketer to work with a comparable number of field service firms. Besides conducting interviews, field service firms provide focus group facilities, mall intercept locations, test product storage, and kitchen facilities to prepare test food products.

9-2e Analyzing the Data

After collecting the data, the marketing researcher proceeds to the next step in the research process: data analysis. The purpose of this analysis is to interpret and draw conclusions from the mass of collected data. The marketing researcher tries to organize and analyze those data by using one or more techniques common to marketing research: one-way frequency counts, cross-tabulations, and more sophisticated statistical analysis. Of these three techniques, one-way frequency counts are the simplest. One-way frequency tables simply record the responses to a question. For example, the

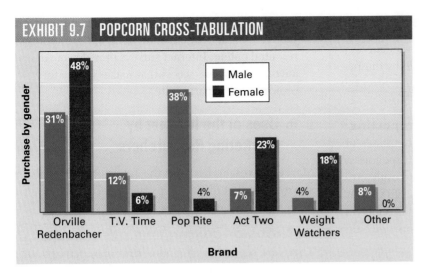

EXHIBIT 9.7   POPCORN CROSS-TABULATION

answers to the question "What brand of microwave popcorn do you buy most often?" would provide a one-way frequency distribution. One-way frequency tables are always done in data analysis, at least as a first step, because they provide the researcher with a general picture of the study's results. A **cross-tabulation** lets the analyst look at the responses to one question in relation to the responses to one or more other questions. For example, in Exhibit 9.7, what is the association between gender and the brand of microwave popcorn bought most frequently?

Researchers can use many other more powerful and sophisticated statistical techniques, such as hypothesis testing, measures of association, and regression analysis. A description of these techniques goes beyond the scope of this book but can be found in any good marketing research textbook. The use of sophisticated statistical techniques depends on the researchers' objectives and the nature of the data gathered.

9-2f Preparing and Presenting the Report

After data analysis has been completed, the researcher must prepare the report and communicate the conclusions and recommendations to management. This is a key step in the process. If the marketing researcher wants managers to carry out the recommendations, he or she must convince them that the results are credible and justified by the data collected.

Researchers are usually required to present both written and oral reports on the project. Today, the written report is often no more than a copy of the PowerPoint slides used in the oral presentation. Both reports should be tailored to the audience. They should begin with a clear, concise statement of the research objectives, followed by a complete but brief and simple explanation of the research design or methodology employed. A summary of major findings should come next. The conclusion of the report should also present recommendations to management.

Most people who enter marketing will become research users rather than research suppliers. Thus, they must know what to notice in a report. As with many other items we purchase, quality is not always readily apparent. Nor does a high price guarantee superior quality. The basis for measuring the quality of a marketing research report is the research proposal. Did the report meet the objectives established in the proposal? Was the methodology outlined in the proposal followed? Are the conclusions based on logical deductions from the data analysis? Do the recommendations seem prudent, given the conclusions?

9-2g Following Up

The final step in the marketing research process is to follow up. The researcher should determine why management did or did not carry out the recommendations in the report. Was sufficient decision-making information included? What could have been done to make the report more useful to management? A good rapport between the product manager, or whoever authorized the project, and the market researcher is essential. Often, they must work together on many studies throughout the year.

  THE PROFOUND IMPACT OF THE INTERNET ON MARKETING RESEARCH

More than 90 percent of U.S. marketing research companies conduct some form of online research. Paper questionnaires are going the way of the horse and buggy in marketing research Online survey research has replaced computer-assisted telephone interviewing as the most popular mode of data collection. The majority of online research is done through incentivized panels (discussed later in the chapter).

cross-tabulation a method of analyzing data that lets the analyst look at the responses to one question in relation to the responses to one or more other questions

9-3a Advantages of Internet Surveys

The huge growth in the popularity of Internet surveys is the result of the many advantages offered by the Internet. The specific advantages of Internet surveys, which are often sent to mobile devices, are many:

- **Rapid development, real-time reporting:** Internet surveys can be broadcast to thousands of potential respondents simultaneously. Respondents complete surveys simultaneously; then results are tabulated and posted for corporate clients to view as the returns arrive. The effect: survey results can be in a client's hands in significantly less time than would be required for traditional paper surveys.

- **Dramatically reduced costs:** The Internet can cut costs by 25 to 40 percent and provide results in half the time it takes to do traditional telephone surveys. Traditional survey methods are labor-intensive efforts incurring training, telecommunications, and management costs. Electronic methods eliminate these completely. While costs for traditional survey techniques rise proportionally with the number of interviews desired, electronic solicitations can grow in volume with little increase in project costs.

- **Personalized questions and data:** Internet surveys can be highly personalized for greater relevance to each respondent's own situation, thus speeding the response process.

- **Improved respondent participation:** Internet surveys take half as much time to complete as phone interviews, can be accomplished at the respondent's convenience (for example, after work hours), and are much more stimulating and engaging. As a result, Internet surveys enjoy much higher response rates.

- **Contact with the hard-to-reach:** Certain groups—doctors, high-income professionals, top management in Global 2000 firms—are among the most surveyed on the planet and the most difficult to reach. Many of these groups are well represented online. Internet surveys provide convenient anytime/anywhere access that makes it easy for busy professionals to participate.

9-3b Uses of the Internet by Marketing Researchers

Marketing researchers use the Internet to administer surveys, conduct focus groups, and perform a variety of other types of marketing research.

METHODS OF CONDUCTING ONLINE SURVEYS

There are several basic methods for conducting online surveys: Web survey systems, survey design and Web hosting sites, and online panel providers.

Web Survey Systems Web survey systems are software systems specifically designed for Web questionnaire construction and delivery. They consist of an integrated questionnaire designer, Web server, database, and data delivery program designed for use by nonprogrammers.

The Web server distributes the questionnaire and files responses in a database. The user can query the server at any time via the Web for completion statistics, descriptive statistics on responses, and graphical displays of data. Some popular online survey research software packages are Sawtooth CiW, Infopoll, SurveyMonkey, and SurveyPro.

Google Consumer Surveys Google, with more than a billion unique visitors worldwide, has entered the do-it-yourself Web survey arena. It does this in a rather unique manner; see www.google.com/insights/consumersurveys/home. Certain Web sites host premium content that usually requires a subscription or access fee. With Google Consumer Surveys, however, a visitor can gain access to the premium content by answering a couple of questions instead of paying the fee. Surveys are limited

iStockphoto.com/bgblue

to two questions. The first is typically a screening question such as, "Have you purchased anything online in the past ninety days?" The second question is more substantive, such as "Which promotion would you be most interested in—free shipping, 15% off, free returns, or saving $25 on your next purchase of $150?" Basic demographic and location information are inferred from Google's big data database. Google Consumer Surveys are fast and cheap, but some researchers have questioned the sampling methodology while others have suggested that the two-question format is too restrictive.[19]

Online Panel Providers Often, researchers use online panel providers for a ready-made sample population. Online panel providers such as Survey Sampling International and e-Rewards pre-recruit people who agree to participate in online market research surveys.

Some online panels are created for specific industries and may have a few thousand panel members, while the large commercial online panels have millions of people waiting to be surveyed. When people join online panels, they answer an extensive profiling questionnaire that enables the panel provider to target research efforts to panel members who meet specific criteria.

Some critics of online panels suggest that they are not representative of the target population. Others claim that offering incentives to join a panel leads to bias and misleading results. One such critic called online panels "a club of people who signed up to take point-and-click surveys for points redeemable for cash and gifts."[20] Online panel researchers contend that they use a number of interventions to detect poor quality online surveys. These include speed detection, straight-line response detection, challenge questions, IP address location checking, digital fingerprinting to identify multiple registrations, and analysis of aggregate responses.

ONLINE FOCUS GROUPS A number of research firms are currently conducting focus groups online. The process is fairly simple. The research firm builds a database of respondents via a screening questionnaire on its Web site. When a client comes to a firm with a need for a particular focus group, the firm goes to its database and identifies individuals who appear to qualify. It sends an e-mail to these individuals, asking them to log on to a particular site at a particular time scheduled for the group. Many times, these groups are joined by respondents on mobile devices. The firm pays them an incentive for their participation.

The firm develops a discussion guide similar to the one used for a conventional focus group, and a moderator runs the group by typing in questions online for all to see. The group operates in an environment similar to that of a chat room so that all participants see all questions and all responses. The firm captures the complete text of the focus group and makes it available for review after the group has finished.

Online focus groups also allow respondents to view things such as a concept statement, a mockup of a print ad, or a short product demonstration video. The moderator simply provides a URL for the respondents to go to in another browser window.

Benefits of Web Community Research

The popularity and marketing power of Web communities stems from several key benefits:

- Provide cost-effective, flexible research.
- Help companies create customer-focused organizations by putting employees into direct contact with consumers.
- Achieve customer-derived innovation.
- Establish brand advocates who are emotionally invested in a company's success.
- Engage customers in a space where they are comfortable, allowing clients to interact with them on a deeper level.
- Offer real-time results, enabling clients to explore ideas that normal time constraints prohibit.

More advanced virtual focus group software reserves a frame (section) of the screen for stimuli to be shown. Here, the moderator has control over what is shown in the stimulus area. Many online groups are now conducted with audio and video feeds as well. One advantage of this approach is that the respondent does not have to do any work to see the stimuli. There are many other advantages of online groups:

- **Better participation rates:** Typically, online focus groups can be conducted over the course of days; once participants are recruited, they are less likely to pull out due to time conflicts.

- **Cost-effectiveness:** Face-to-face focus groups incur costs for facility rental, airfare, hotel, and food. None of these costs is incurred with online focus groups.

- **Broad geographic scope:** Time is flexible online; respondents can be gathered from all over the world.

- **Accessibility:** Online focus groups allow access to individuals who otherwise might be difficult to recruit (for example, business travelers, senior executives, mothers with infants).

WEB COMMUNITY RESEARCH A Web community is a carefully selected group of consumers who agree to participate in an ongoing dialogue with a particular corporation. All community interaction takes place on a custom-designed Web site. During the life of the community—which may last anywhere from six months to a year or more—community members respond to questions posed by the corporation on a regular basis. In addition to responding to the corporation's questions, community members talk to one another about topics that are of interest to them. When Procter & Gamble was developing scents for a new product line, it asked members of its online community to record the scents that they encountered over the course of a day that made them feel good. By week's end, Procter & Gamble had received images, videos, and simple text tributes to cut grass, fresh paint, Play Dough, and other aromas that revealed volumes about how scent triggers not just nostalgia, but also feelings of competence, adventurousness, comfort, and other powerful emotions.[21]

9-4 THE GROWING IMPORTANCE OF MOBILE RESEARCH

Although desktop and laptop computers are the primary devices used for completing online research, the picture is changing rapidly. Mobile survey traffic now accounts

Nearly one in four mobile surveys are taken outside of the home—often at work.

for approximately 30 percent of interview responses. Nearly one in four mobile surveys are taken outside of the home—often at work.[22]

Mobile surveys are designed to fit into the brief cracks of time that open up when a person waits for a plane, is early for an appointment, commutes to work on a train, or stands in a line. Marketers strive to engage respondents "in the moment" because mobile research provides immediate feedback when a consumer makes a decision to purchase, consumes a product, or experiences some form of promotion. As new and better apps make the survey experience easier and more intuitive, the use of mobile surveys will continue to rise. As screen size decreases, so do survey completion rates. Seventy-six percent of surveys are completed on desktop; 70 percent on tablet; and 59 percent on mobile phone.[23] New responsive design technology automatically adjusts the content and navigation of a Web site to fit the dimensions and resolution of any screen it is viewed on.[24]

One advertiser wanted to conduct a survey on the televised advertisements that ran during the Super Bowl. The client wanted to measure real-time reactions, but most people do not sit in front of their desktop computers during the big game. They do, however, multitask using their smartphones. Respondents were recruited in advance of game day, and then during the game, surveys were pushed out in real time to collect feedback on commercials as they aired.[25]

An *ethnography shop-along* used to mean accompanying a participant on a shopping trip, but with today's mobile qualitative research tools, shop-alongs can be completely self-guided. Mondelez Canada recently set out to launch Potato Thins, a low-calorie snack food, in the United States. Potato Thins are packaged in a resealable pouch, differentiating the product and allowing customers to consume small portions of the bag at a time. Before the launch, Mondelez Canada set up a

Napporn/Shutterstock.com

research experiment to determine which grocery store shelf location would give Potato Thins the biggest boost. The key concern for Mondelez was to learn about shoppers' logic and motivations when it comes to in-store navigation and healthy snacking. Survey participants were sent on a "snacking safari" whereby they recorded their shopping and purchase habits by taking photos on their mobile devices. Researchers found that consumers demonstrated one of two distinct behaviors when shopping for snacks—hunting or browsing.

When hunting, consumers tended to ignore signage, as they knew which aisles to head for. When browsing, participants went up and down the aisles of the store, gathering the items they needed and keeping an eye out for new items.[26]

After the shopping safari, respondents were introduced to Potato Thins. Researchers asked whether they should be placed in the chip or cracker aisle, and the majority of participants picked the cracker aisle. One participant said, "I could see them in the snack food area, close to the chips. However, I would likely miss purchasing them, as I tend to avoid going down that aisle as it's too tempting and not healthy. So I suppose that it would be better to merchandise them close to the crackers." Researchers also concluded that the bag may look out of place on the chip aisle due to its size. One participant said, "The size of the package is quite small, so if you wanted to serve these rather than regular chips you would have to purchase quite a number of packages."[27]

 ## 9-5 SCANNER-BASED RESEARCH

Scanner-based research is a system for gathering information from respondents by continuously monitoring the advertising, promotion, and pricing they are exposed to and the things they buy. Scanner-based research also entails the aggregation of scanner data from retailers, analysis, and identification of sales trends by industry, company, product line, and individual brand. The variables measured are advertising campaigns, coupons, displays, and product prices. The result is a huge database of marketing efforts and consumer behavior.

The two major scanner-based suppliers are SymphonyIRI Group Inc. and the Nielsen Company. Each has about half of the market. However, SymphonyIRI is the founder of scanner-based research. SymphonyIRI's first product is called **BehaviorScan**. It delivers different TV advertisements to selected homes within the same market and then uses scanner purchase data

to analyze the impact of the advertising on consumers' actual buying behavior.[28]

Another SymphonyIRI's product is **InfoScan**, a scanner-based sales-tracking service for the consumer packaged-goods industry. Retail sales, detailed consumer purchasing information (including measurement of store loyalty and total grocery basket expenditures), and promotional activity by manufacturers and retailers are monitored and evaluated for all bar-coded products. Data are collected weekly from supermarkets, drugstores, and mass merchandisers.

Some companies have begun using neuromarketing to study microscopic changes in skin moisture, heart rate, brain waves, and other biometrics to see how consumers react to things such as package designs and ads. **Neuromarketing** is the process of researching brain patterns and measuring certain physiological responses to marketing stimuli. It is a fresh attempt to better understand consumers' responses to promotion and purchase motivations.

9-6 WHEN SHOULD MARKETING RESEARCH BE CONDUCTED?

When managers have several possible solutions to a problem, they should not instinctively call for marketing research. In fact, the first decision to make is whether to conduct marketing research at all.

Some companies have been conducting research in certain markets for many years. Such firms understand the characteristics of target customers and their likes and dislikes about existing products. Under these circumstances, further research would be repetitive and waste money. P&G, for example, has extensive knowledge of the coffee market. After it conducted initial taste tests with Folgers Instant Coffee, P&G went into national distribution without further research. Sara Lee followed the same strategy with its frozen croissants, as did Quaker Oats with Chewy Granola Bars. This tactic, however, can backfire. Marketers may think they understand a particular

---

scanner-based research a system for gathering information from a single group of respondents by continuously monitoring the advertising, promotion, and pricing they are exposed to and the things they buy

BehaviorScan a scanner-based research program that tracks the purchases of 3,000 households through store scanners in each research market

InfoScan a scanner-based sales-tracking service for the consumer packaged-goods industry

neuromarketing a field of marketing that studies the body's responses to marketing stimuli

market thoroughly and so bypass market research for a product, only to have the product fail and be withdrawn from the market.

If information were available and free, managers would rarely refuse more, but because marketing information can require a great deal of time and expense to accumulate, they might decide to forgo additional information. Ultimately, the willingness to acquire additional decision-making information depends on managers' perceptions of its quality, price, and timing. Research should be undertaken only when the expected value of the information is greater than the cost of obtaining it.

9-6a Customer Relationship Management

Recall from the beginning of the chapter that databases and big data play a key role in marketing decision making. A key subset of data management systems is a customer relationship management (CRM) system. CRM was introduced in Chapters 1 and 8. The key to managing relationships with customers is the CRM cycle (Exhibit 9.8).

To initiate the CRM cycle, a company must *identify customer relationships with the organization*. This may simply entail learning who the customers are or where they are located, or it may require more detailed information about the products and services they are using. Next, the company must *understand the interactions with current customers*. Companies accomplish this by collecting data on all types of communications a customer has with the company.

Using this knowledge of its customers and their interactions, the company then *captures relevant customer data on interactions*. Big data analytics are used not only to enhance the collection of customer data but also to *store and integrate customer data* throughout the company, and ultimately, to "get to know" customers on a more personal level. Customer data are the firsthand responses that are obtained from customers through investigation or by asking direct questions.

Every customer wants to be a company's main priority. Yet not all customers are equally important in the eyes of a business. Consequently, the company must *identify its profitable*

competitive intelligence (CI) an intelligence system that helps managers assess their competition and vendors in order to become more efficient and effective competitors

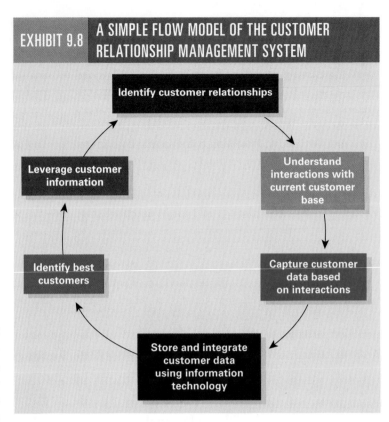

EXHIBIT 9.8 A SIMPLE FLOW MODEL OF THE CUSTOMER RELATIONSHIP MANAGEMENT SYSTEM

Identify customer relationships

Understand interactions with current customer base

Capture customer data based on interactions

Store and integrate customer data using information technology

Identify best customers

Leverage customer information

and unprofitable customers. Big data analytics compile actionable data about the purchase habits of a firm's current and potential customers. Essentially, analytics transform customer data into customer information a company can use to make managerial decisions. Big data analytics are examined in more detail in Chapter 14.

Once customer data are analyzed and transformed into usable information, the information must be *leveraged*. The CRM system sends the customer information to all areas of a business because the customer interacts with all aspects of the business. Essentially, the company is trying to enhance customer relationships by getting the right information to the right person in the right place at the right time.

9-7 COMPETITIVE INTELLIGENCE

Derived from military intelligence, competitive intelligence is an important tool for helping a firm overcome a competitor's advantage. Specifically, competitive intelligence can help identify the advantage and play a major role in determining how it was achieved. It also helps a firm identify areas where it can achieve its own competitive advantages.

Competitive intelligence (CI) helps managers assess their competitors and their vendors in order to become more efficient and effective competitors. Intelligence is analyzed information. It becomes decision-making intelligence when it has implications for the organization. For example, a primary competitor may have plans to introduce a product with performance standards equal to those of the company gathering the information but with a 15 percent cost advantage. The new product will reach the market in eight months. This intelligence has important decision-making and policy consequences for management. CI and environmental scanning (see Chapter 2) combine to create marketing intelligence.

The Internet is an important resource for gathering CI, but noncomputer sources can be equally valuable. Some examples include company salespeople, industry experts, CI consultants, government agencies, Uniform Commercial Code filings, suppliers, periodicals, the Yellow Pages, and industry trade shows.

STUDY TOOLS 9

LOCATED AT BACK OF THE TEXTBOOK
☐ Rip out Chapter Review Card

LOCATED AT WWW.CENGAGEBRAIN.COM
☐ Review Key Terms Flashcards and create your own

☐ Track your knowledge and understanding of key concepts in marketing

☐ Complete practice and graded quizzes to prepare for tests

☐ Complete interactive content within the MKTG Online experience

☐ View the chapter highlight boxes within the MKTG Online experience

10 | Product Concepts

Paket/Shutterstock.com

LEARNING OUTCOMES

After studying this chapter, you will be able to...

10-1 Define the term *product*

10-2 Classify consumer products

10-3 Define the terms *product item*, *product line*, and *product mix*

10-4 Describe marketing uses of branding

10-5 Describe marketing uses of packaging and labeling

10-6 Discuss global issues in branding and packaging

10-7 Describe how and why product warranties are important marketing tools

After you finish this chapter go to **PAGE 186** for **STUDY TOOLS**.

10-1 WHAT IS A PRODUCT?

The product offering, the heart of an organization's marketing program, is usually the starting point in creating a marketing mix. A marketing manager cannot determine a price, design a promotion strategy, or create a distribution channel until the firm has a product to sell. Moreover, an excellent distribution channel, a persuasive promotion campaign, and a fair price have no value when the product offering is poor or inadequate.

A **product** may be defined as everything, both favorable and unfavorable, that a person receives in an exchange. A product may be a tangible good like a pair of shoes, a service like a haircut, an idea like "don't litter," or any combination of these three. Packaging, style, color, options, and size are some typical product features. Just as important are intangibles such as service, the seller's image, the manufacturer's reputation, and the way consumers believe others will view the product.

To most people, the term *product* means a tangible good. However, services and ideas are also products. (Chapter 12 focuses specifically on the unique aspects of marketing services.) The marketing process identified in Chapter 1 is the same whether the product marketed is a good, a service, an idea, or some combination of these.

product everything, both favorable and unfavorable, that a person receives in an exchange

10-2 TYPES OF CONSUMER PRODUCTS

Products can be classified as either business (industrial) or consumer, depending on the buyer's intentions. The key distinction between the two types of products is their intended use. If the intended use is a business purpose, the product is classified as a business or industrial product. As explained in Chapter 7, a business product is used to manufacture other goods or services, to facilitate an organization's operations, or to resell to other customers. A consumer product is bought to satisfy an individual's personal wants or needs. Sometimes the same item can be classified as either a business or a consumer product, depending on its intended use. Examples include lightbulbs, pencils and paper, and computers.

We need to know about product classifications because business and consumer products are marketed differently. They are marketed to different target markets and tend to use different distribution, promotion, and pricing strategies.

Chapter 7 examined seven categories of business products: major equipment, accessory equipment, component parts, processed materials, raw materials, supplies, and services. This chapter examines an effective way of categorizing consumer products. Although there are several ways to classify them, the most popular approach

A marketing manager cannot determine a price, design a promotion strategy, or create a distribution channel until the firm has a product to sell.

includes these four types: convenience products, shopping products, specialty products, and unsought products. This approach classifies products according to how much effort is normally used to shop for them.

10-2a Convenience Products

A **convenience product** is a relatively inexpensive item that merits little shopping effort—that is, a consumer is unwilling to shop extensively for such an item. Candy, soft drinks, aspirin, small hardware items, dry cleaning, and car washes fall into the convenience product category.

Consumers buy convenience products regularly, usually without much planning. Nevertheless,

> **convenience product**
> a relatively inexpensive item
> that merits little shopping effort

consumers do know the brand names of popular convenience products, such as Coca-Cola, Bayer aspirin, and Old Spice deodorant. Convenience products normally require wide distribution in order to sell sufficient quantities to meet profit goals. For example, the gum brand Extra is available everywhere, including Walmart, Walgreens, gas stations, newsstands, and vending machines.

10-2b Shopping Products

A **shopping product** is usually more expensive than a convenience product and is found in fewer stores. Consumers usually buy a shopping product only after comparing several brands or stores on style, practicality, price, and lifestyle compatibility. They are willing to invest some effort into this process to get the desired benefits.

There are two types of shopping products: homogeneous and heterogeneous. Consumers perceive *homogeneous* shopping products as basically similar—for example, washers, dryers, refrigerators, and televisions. With homogeneous shopping products, consumers typically look for the lowest-priced brand that has the desired features. For example, they might compare Kenmore, Whirlpool, and General Electric refrigerators.

In contrast, consumers perceive *heterogeneous* shopping products as essentially different—for example, furniture, clothing, housing, and universities. Consumers often have trouble comparing heterogeneous shopping products because the prices, quality, and features vary so much. The benefit of comparing heterogeneous shopping products is "finding the best product or brand for me"; this decision is often highly individual. For example, it would be difficult to compare a small, private college with a large, public university, or IKEA with La-Z-Boy.

10-2c Specialty Products

When consumers search extensively for a particular item and are very reluctant to accept substitutes, that item is a **specialty product**. Omega watches, Rolls-Royce automobiles, Bose speakers, Ruth's Chris Steak House, and highly specialized forms of medical care are generally considered specialty products.

Consumers perceive houses as heterogeneous because of variety and differences.

Marketers of specialty products often use selective, status-conscious advertising to maintain a product's exclusive image. Distribution is often limited to one or a very few outlets in a geographic area. Brand names and quality of service are often very important.

10-2d Unsought Products

A product unknown to the potential buyer or a known product that the buyer does not actively seek is referred to as an **unsought product**. New products fall into this category until advertising and distribution increase consumer awareness of them.

Some goods are always marketed as unsought items, especially needed products we do not like to think about or care to spend money on. Insurance, burial plots, and similar items require aggressive personal selling and highly persuasive advertising. Salespeople actively seek leads to potential buyers. Because consumers usually do not seek out this type of product, the company must go directly to them through a salesperson, direct mail, or direct response advertising.

10-3 PRODUCT ITEMS, LINES, AND MIXES

Rarely does a company sell a single product. More often, it sells a variety of things. A **product item** is a specific version of a product that can be designated as a distinct offering among an organization's products. Campbell's Cream of Chicken soup is an example of a product item (see Exhibit 10.1).

A group of closely related product items is called a **product line**. For example, the column in Exhibit 10.1

shopping product a product that requires comparison shopping because it is usually more expensive than a convenience product and is found in fewer stores

specialty product a particular item for which consumers search extensively and are very reluctant to accept substitutes

unsought product a product unknown to the potential buyer or a known product that the buyer does not actively seek

product item a specific version of a product that can be designated as a distinct offering among an organization's products

product line a group of closely related product items

titled "Soups" represents one of Campbell's product lines. Different container sizes and shapes also distinguish items in a product line. Diet Coke, for example, is available in cans and various plastic containers. Each size and each container are separate product items.

An organization's **product mix** includes all the products it sells. All Campbell's products—soups, sauces, frozen entrées, beverages, and biscuits—constitute its product mix. Each product item in the product mix may require a separate marketing strategy.

In some cases, however, product lines and even entire product mixes share some marketing strategy components. UPS promotes its various services by demonstrating its commitment to its line of work with the tagline "We [heart] Logistics." Organizations derive several benefits from organizing related items into product lines:

- **Advertising economies:** Product lines provide economies of scale in advertising. Several products can be advertised under the umbrella of the line. Campbell's can talk about its soups being "M'm, M'm, Good!" and promote the entire line.

- **Package uniformity:** A product line can benefit from package uniformity. All packages in the line may have a common look and still keep their individual identities. Again, Campbell's soup is a good example.

- **Standardized components:** Product lines allow firms to standardize components, thus reducing manufacturing and inventory costs. For example, General Motors uses the same parts on many automobile makes and models.

- **Efficient sales and distribution:** A product line enables sales personnel for companies like Procter & Gamble to provide a full range of choices to customers. Distributors and retailers are often more inclined to stock the company's products if it offers a full line. Transportation and warehousing costs are likely to be lower for a product line than for a collection of individual items.

- **Equivalent quality:** Purchasers usually expect and believe

Dcwcreations/Shutterstock.com

product mix all products that an organization sells

EXHIBIT 10.1 CAMPBELL'S PRODUCT LINES AND PRODUCT MIX

	Width of the Product Mix				
DEPTH (Depth of the Product Lines)	**Soups**	**Sauces**	**Frozen Entrées**	**Beverages**	**Biscuits**
	Cream of Chicken	Cheddar Cheese	Macaroni and Cheese	Tomato Juice	Arnott's:
	Cream of Mushroom	Alfredo	Golden Chicken	V-Fusion Juices	Water Cracker
	Vegetable Beef	Italian Tomato	Fricassee	V8 Splash	Butternut Snap
	Chicken Noodle	Hollandaise	Traditional Lasagna		Chocolate Ripple
	Tomato				Spicy Fruit Roll
	Bean with Bacon				Chocolate Wheaten
	Minestrone				
	Clam Chowder				
	French Onion				
	and more				

Women's swimming suits are known for coming in wide varieties of styles from functional to poolside lounging.

Karkas/ShutterStock.com

that all products in a line are about equal in quality. Consumers expect that all Campbell's soups and all Gillette razors will be of similar quality.

Product mix width (or breadth) refers to the number of product lines an organization offers. In Exhibit 10.1, for example, the width of Campbell's product mix is five product lines. **Product line depth** is the number of product items in a product line. As shown in Exhibit 10.1, the sauces product line consists of four product items; the frozen entrée product line includes three product items.

Firms increase the *width* of their product mix to diversify risk. To generate sales and boost profits, firms spread risk across many product lines rather than depend on only one or two. Firms also widen their product mix to capitalize on established reputations. For example, in order to expand its portfolio of beverage-related businesses, Starbucks purchased specialty upscale tea retailer Teavana, which sells loose-leaf teas, tea accessories, and food items. With this purchase, Starbucks wants to position tea as it does coffee—as a luxury beverage rather than a commodity. [1]

Firms increase the *depth* of their product lines to attract buyers with different preferences, to increase sales and profits by further segmenting the market, to capitalize on economies of scale in production and marketing, and to even out seasonal sales patterns.

product mix width the number of product lines an organization offers

product line depth the number of product items in a product line

product modification changing one or more of a product's characteristics

planned obsolescence the practice of modifying products so those that have already been sold become obsolete before they actually need replacement

10-3a Adjustments to Product Items, Lines, and Mixes

Over time, firms change product items, lines, and mixes to take advantage of new technical or product developments or to respond to changes in the environment. They may adjust by modifying products, repositioning products, or extending or contracting product lines.

PRODUCT MODIFICATION Marketing managers must decide if and when to modify existing products. **Product modification** is a change in one or more of a product's characteristics:

- **Quality modification:** a change in a product's dependability or durability. Reducing a product's quality may let the manufacturer lower the price and appeal to target markets unable to afford the original product. Conversely, increasing quality can help the firm compete with rival firms. For example, Barnes & Noble offers a color version of its Nook that runs Android apps, allowing it to compete with tablet and netbook makers, such as Dell and Asus. Increasing quality can also result in increased brand loyalty, greater ability to raise prices, or new opportunities for market segmentation.

- **Functional modification:** a change in a product's versatility, effectiveness, convenience, or safety. In 2015, Cat's Pride introduced a new litter, Fresh & Light Ultimate Care, that has a unique ultra-lightweight formula that is good for both cats and their owners. It weighs half as much as traditional scoopable clay cat litters, has premium clumping ability, and features a dust-free formula. [2]

- **Style modification:** an aesthetic (how the product looks) product change rather than a quality or functional change. Clothing and auto manufacturers commonly use style modifications to motivate customers to replace products before they are worn out.

Planned obsolescence is a term commonly used to describe the practice of modifying products so that those that have already been sold become obsolete before they actually need replacement. For example, products such as printers and cell phones become obsolete because technology changes so quickly.

Some argue that planned obsolescence is wasteful; some claim it is unethical. Marketers respond that consumers favor style modifications because they like changes in the appearance of goods such as clothing and cars. Marketers also contend that consumers, not manufacturers and marketers, decide when styles are obsolete.

REPOSITIONING Repositioning, as Chapter 8 explained, involves changing consumers' perceptions of a brand. Known primarily for its fat-, sugar-, and salt-laden product offerings, McDonald has long fought to reposition itself as a healthy fast food alternative. The company recently announced that it would no longer market some of its less nutritional options to children, and would instead incorporate fruits and vegetables into combo meals for children and adults alike. Further, McDonald's announced that it would utilize menu boards and national television advertising to help consumers understand the nutritional choices available to them.[3] Changing demographics, declining sales, and changes in the social environment often motivate a firm to reposition an established brand. Retailer Target, for example, plans to reposition its brand toward Hispanic shoppers. The company's research showed that while only 38 percent of its shoppers said that the store was their favorite, 54 percent of Hispanic Millennials said that Target was their favorite store. Several departments, including the baby department, will be renovated to focus on marketing to Hispanic moms. Target also plans to be the first brand to launch a Spanish-language ad campaign on an English-language network.[4]

PRODUCT LINE EXTENSIONS A **product line extension** occurs when a company's management decides to add products to an existing product line in order to compete more broadly in the industry. Krispy Kreme recently developed a new series of ready-to-drink iced coffees that it plans to sell in Walmart stores that carry Krispy Kreme products. The drinks are relatively inexpensive, convenient, and are offered in the signature Krispy Kreme donut flavors. The company hopes to attract more coffee drinkers, as well as Walmart customers, to their products. In addition, Krispy Kreme will attempt to attract a bigger share of the home-brew consumer market by selling packages of its coffee blends at some Sam's Clubs locations in the Southeast.[5]

Krispy Kreme developed a line of beverages that it made available to sell in Walmart stores.

A company can add too many products, or demand can change for the type of products that were introduced over time. When this happens, a product line is overextended. Product lines can be overextended when:

- Some products in the line do not contribute to profits because of low sales or they cannibalize sales of other items in the line.

- Manufacturing or marketing resources are disproportionately allocated to slow-moving products.

- Some items in the line are obsolete because of new-product entries in the line or new products offered by competitors.

PRODUCT LINE CONTRACTION Sometimes marketers can get carried away with product extensions. (Does the world really need 31 varieties of Head & Shoulders shampoo?) Contracting product lines is a strategic way to deal with overextension. In March 2013, Internet pioneer Yahoo announced that it would be cutting seven products—the Yahoo BlackBerry app, Sports IQ, Yahoo Message Boards, Yahoo Avatars, Yahoo Clues, Yahoo App Search, and Yahoo Updates. "Ultimately, we're making these changes in an effort to sharpen our focus," said Jay Rossiter, Yahoo's executive vice president for platforms. "By continuing to hone in on our core products and experiences, we'll be able to make our existing products the very best they can be."[6]

Indeed, three major benefits are likely when a firm contracts an overextended product line. First, resources become

> **product line extension**
> adding additional products to an existing product line in order to compete more broadly in the industry

Brendan Howard/Shutterstock.com

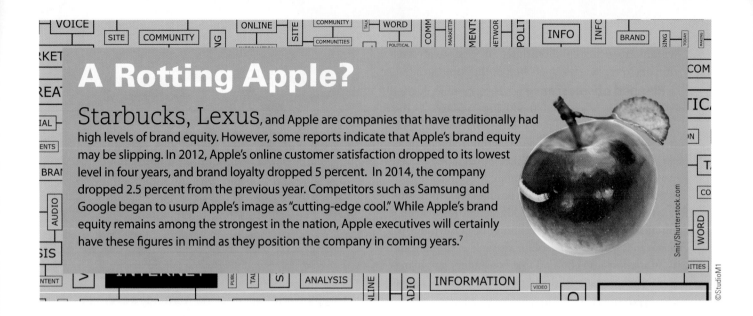

A Rotting Apple?

Starbucks, Lexus, and Apple are companies that have traditionally had high levels of brand equity. However, some reports indicate that Apple's brand equity may be slipping. In 2012, Apple's online customer satisfaction dropped to its lowest level in four years, and brand loyalty dropped 5 percent. In 2014, the company dropped 2.5 percent from the previous year. Competitors such as Samsung and Google began to usurp Apple's image as "cutting-edge cool." While Apple's brand equity remains among the strongest in the nation, Apple executives will certainly have these figures in mind as they position the company in coming years.[7]

concentrated on the most important products. Second, managers no longer waste resources trying to improve the sales and profits of poorly performing products. Third, new-product items have a greater chance of being successful because more financial and human resources are available to manage them.

10-4 BRANDING

The success of any business or consumer product depends in part on the target market's ability to distinguish one product from another. Branding is the main tool marketers use to distinguish their products from those of the competition.

A **brand** is a name, term, symbol, design, or combination thereof that identifies a seller's products and differentiates them from competitors' products. A **brand name** is that part of a brand that can be spoken, including letters (GM, YMCA), words (Chevrolet), and numbers (WD-40, 7-Eleven). The elements of a brand that cannot be spoken are called the **brand mark**—for example, the well-known Mercedes-Benz and Delta Air Lines symbols.

brand a name, term, symbol, design, or combination thereof that identifies a seller's products and differentiates them from competitors' products

brand name that part of a brand that can be spoken, including letters, words, and numbers

brand mark the elements of a brand that cannot be spoken

brand equity the value of a company or brand name

global brand a brand that obtains at least a one-third of its earnings from outside its home country, is recognizable outside its home base of customers, and has publicly available marketing and financial data

brand loyalty consistent preference for one brand over all others

10-4a Benefits of Branding

Branding has three main purposes: product identification, repeat sales, and new-product sales. The most important purpose is *product identification*. Branding allows marketers to distinguish their products from all others. Many brand names are familiar to consumers and indicate quality.

The term **brand equity** refers to the value of a company or brand name. A brand that has high awareness, perceived quality, and brand loyalty among customers has high brand equity—a valuable asset indeed. See Exhibit 10.2 for some classic examples of companies that leverage their brand equity to the fullest.

The term **global brand** refers to a brand that obtains at least one-third of its earnings from outside its home country, is recognizable outside its home base of customers, and has publicly available marketing and financial data. Yum! Brands, which owns Pizza Hut, KFC, and Taco Bell, is a good example of a company that has developed strong global brands. Yum! believes that it must adapt its restaurants to local tastes and different cultural and political climates. In Japan, for instance, KFC sells tempura crispy strips. In northern England, KFC focuses on gravy and potatoes, and in Thailand, it offers rice with soy or sweet chili sauce.

The best generator of *repeat sales* is satisfied customers. Branding helps consumers identify products they wish to buy again and avoid those they do not. **Brand loyalty**, a consistent preference for one brand over all others, is quite high in some product categories. More than half the consumers in product categories such as cigarettes, mayonnaise, toothpaste, coffee, headache remedies, bath soap, and ketchup are loyal to one brand. Many students go to college and purchase the same brands they used at home rather than

YUM! believes that it must adapt its restaurants to local tastes and different cultural and political climates.

EXHIBIT 10.2 THE POWER OF BRAND EQUITY

Product Category	Dominant Brand Name
Children's Entertainment	Disney
Laundry Detergent	Tide
Tablet Computer	Apple
Toothpaste	Crest
Microprocessor	Intel
Soup	Campbell's
Bologna	Oscar Meyer
Ketchup	Heinz
Bleach	Clorox
Greeting Cards	Hallmark
Overnight Mail	FedEx
Copiers	Xerox
Gelatin	Jell-O
Hamburgers	McDonald's
Baby Lotion	Johnson & Johnson
Tissues	Kleenex
Acetaminophen	Tylenol
Coffee	Starbucks
Information Search	Google

Source: Data from Chris Moorman.

choosing by price. Brand identity is essential to developing brand loyalty.

The third main purpose of branding is to *facilitate new-product sales*. Having a well-known and respected company and brand name is extremely useful when introducing new products.

10-4b Branding Strategies

Firms face complex branding decisions. Firms may choose to follow a policy of using manufacturers' brands, private (distributor) brands, or both. In either case, they must then decide among a policy of individual branding (different brands for different products), family branding (common names for different products), or a combination of individual branding and family branding.

MANUFACTURERS' BRANDS VERSUS PRIVATE BRANDS The brand name of a manufacturer—such as Kodak, La-Z-Boy, and Fruit of the Loom—is called a **manufacturer's brand**. Sometimes "national brand" is used as a synonym for "manufacturer's brand." This term is not always accurate, however, because many manufacturers serve only regional markets. Using "manufacturer's brand" precisely defines the brand's owner.

A **private brand**, also known as a private label or store brand, is a brand name owned by a wholesaler or a retailer. Target's Archer Farms brand is a popular private label, for example. Private labels are increasing in popularity and price as customers develop loyalties to store brands such as Archer Farms. According to research conducted in the United Kingdom, 44 percent of shoppers believe that private label brands are simply repackaged national brands. Fifty-nine percent believe that national brands are more expensive only because more money is spent advertising them. Seventy percent believe that private label foods are just as good or better than national brands.[8] Today, private label products have a 23 percent unit share and

manufacturer's brand the brand name of a manufacturer

private brand a brand name owned by a wholesaler or a retailer

EXHIBIT 10.3 COMPARISON OF MANUFACTURER'S AND PRIVATE BRANDS FROM THE RESELLERS PERSPECTIVE

Key Advantages of Carrying Manufacturers' Brands	Key Advantages of Carrying Private Brands
• Heavy advertising to the consumer by manufacturers such as Procter & Gamble helps develop strong consumer loyalties.	• A wholesaler or retailer can usually earn higher profits on its own brand. In addition, because the private brand is exclusive, there is less pressure to mark down the price to meet competition.
• Well-known manufacturers' brands, such as Kodak and Fisher-Price, can attract new customers and enhance the dealer's (wholesaler's or retailer's) prestige.	• A manufacturer can decide to drop a brand or a reseller at any time or even become a direct competitor to its dealers.
• Many manufacturers offer rapid delivery, enabling the dealer to carry less inventory.	• A private brand ties the customer to the wholesaler or retailer. A person who wants a DieHard battery must go to Sears.
• If a dealer happens to sell a manufacturer's brand of poor quality, the customer may simply switch brands and remain loyal to the dealer.	• Wholesalers and retailers have no control over the intensity of distribution of manufacturers' brands. Walmart store managers don't have to worry about competing with other sellers of Sam's American Choice products or Ol' Roy dog food. They know that these brands are sold only in Walmart and Sam's Club stores.

a nineteen percent dollar share of the food and beverage market.[9]

Retailers love consumers' greater acceptance of private brands. Because overhead is low and there are no marketing costs, private label products bring 10 percent higher profit margins, on average, than manufacturers' brands. More than that, a trusted store brand can differentiate a chain from its competitors. Exhibit 10.3 illustrates key issues that wholesalers and retailers should consider in deciding whether to sell manufacturers' brands or private brands. Many firms offer a combination of both.

Instead of marketing private brands as cheaper and inferior to manufacturers' brands, many retailers are creating and promoting their own **captive brands**. These brands carry no evidence of the store's affiliation, are manufactured by a third party, and are sold exclusively at the chains. This strategy allows the retailer to ask a price similar or equal to manufacturers' brands, and the captive brands are typically displayed alongside mainstream products. A recent study showed that 88 percent of consumers prefer store brands over name brands. These consumers believe that many store brands are just as good as, or better than, their favorite name brands.[10] For example, Simple Truth and Simple Truth Organic are Kroger's lines of natural and organic products designed to meet consumer desire for upscale brands. in 2014, these private brands accounted for $1.2 billion in sales for Kroger.[11]

captive brand a brand manufactured by a third party for an exclusive retailer, without evidence of that retailer's affiliation

individual branding using different brand names for different products

family branding marketing several different products under the same brand name

co-branding placing two or more brand names on a product or its package

INDIVIDUAL BRANDS VERSUS FAMILY BRANDS

Many companies use different brand names for different products, a practice referred to as **individual branding**. Companies use individual brands when their products vary greatly in use or performance. For instance, it would not make sense to use the same brand name for a pair of dress socks and a baseball bat. Procter & Gamble targets different segments of the laundry detergent market with Bold, Cheer, Dash, Dreft, Era, Gain, and Tide.

In contrast, a company that markets several different products under the same brand name is practicing **family branding**. Jack Daniel's family brand includes whiskey, coffee, barbeque sauce, heat-and-serve meat products like brisket and pulled pork, mustard, playing cards, and clothing lines.

CO-BRANDING **Co-branding** entails placing two or more brand names on a product or its package. Three common types of co-branding are ingredient branding, cooperative branding, and complementary branding. *Ingredient branding* identifies the brand of a part that makes up the product. For example, Church & Dwight co-branded an entire line of Arm & Hammer laundry detergents with OxiClean, a popular household cleaner and stain remover. OxiClean is also co-branded with Kaboom shower cleaner and Xtra detergent.[12] *Cooperative branding* occurs when two brands receiving equal treatment (in the context of an advertisement) borrow from each other's brand equity. A promotional contest jointly sponsored by Ramada Inn, American Express, and United Airlines used cooperative branding. Guests at Ramada who paid with an American Express card were automatically entered in a contest and were eligible to win more than 100 getaways for two at any Ramada in the continental United States

Craftsman and Harley-Davidson have partnered together to offer tool storage units.

- Shapes, such as the Jeep front grille and the Coca-Cola bottle.
- Ornamental colors or designs, such as the decoration on Nike tennis shoes, the black-and-copper color combination of a Duracell battery, Levi's small tag on the left side of the rear pocket of its jeans, or the cutoff black cone on the top of Cross pens.
- Catchy phrases, such as Prudential's "Own a Piece of the Rock," Mountain Dew's "This Is How We Dew," and Nike's "Just Do It!"
- Abbreviations, such as Bud, Coke, or the Met.

and round-trip airfare from United. In 2014, Bruegger's Bagels and Jamba Juice announced that five co-branded and co-operated locations would be opened across Florida. "Pairing Bruegger's Bagels with [Jamba Juice parent company] Great Service Restaurants is a fantastic match," said Paul Carolan, chief development officer for Le Duff America, which owns Bruegger's Bagels. "Great Service Restaurants shares our passion for community, quality, and providing exceptional guest experiences."[13] Finally, with complementary branding, products are advertised or marketed together to suggest usage, such as a spirits brand (Seagram's) and a compatible mixer (7Up).

Co-branding is a useful strategy when a combination of brand names enhances the prestige or perceived value of a product or when it benefits brand owners and users. Co-branding may also be used to increase a company's presence in markets where it has little room to differentiate itself or has limited market share. For example, Doc Popcorn and Dippin' Dots plan to join together to open their first co-branded store. The companies will sell sweet and savory flavors of popcorn as well as ice cream products under the same roof. This move will allow both brands to continue to grow domestically and internationally over the coming years. [14]

10-4c Trademarks

A **trademark** is the exclusive right to use a brand or part of a brand. Others are prohibited from using the brand without permission. A **service mark** performs the same function for services, such as H&R Block and Weight Watchers. Parts of a brand or other product identification may qualify for trademark protection. Some examples are:

- Sounds, such as the MGM lion's roar.

It is important to understand that trademark rights come from use rather than registration. An intent-to-use application is filed with the U.S. Patent and Trademark Office, and a company must have a genuine intention to use the mark when it files and must actually use it within three years of the granting of the application. Trademark protection typically lasts for ten years.[15] To renew the trademark, the company must prove it is using the mark. Rights to a trademark last as long as the mark is used. Normally, if the firm does not use it for two years, the trademark is considered abandoned, and a new user can claim exclusive ownership of the mark.

The Digital Millennium Copyright Act (DMCA) explicitly applies trademark law to the digital world. This law includes financial penalties for those who violate trademarks or register an otherwise trademarked term as a domain name. The DMCA has come under some criticism for its more restrictive provisions. In 2013, controversy erupted over the reinstitution of a section prohibiting individuals from unlocking their smartphones— a consumer who disables her phone's restriction to a specific carrier may be subject to a prison term of up to five years and a $500,000 fine.[16]

Companies that fail to protect their trademarks face the possibility that their product names will become generic. A **generic product name** identifies a product by class or type and cannot be trademarked. Former brand names that were not sufficiently protected by their owners and were subsequently declared to be generic product names

trademark the exclusive right to use a brand or part of a brand

service mark a trademark for a service

generic product name identifies a product by class or type and cannot be trademarked

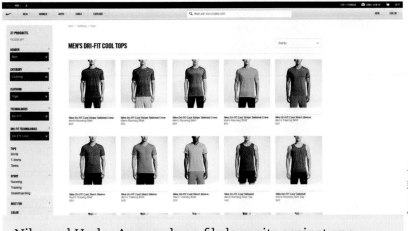

Nike and Under Armour have file lawsuits against one another in the recent past for trademark infringement; one instance being the use of the term "DRI-FIT".

Source: Nike, Inc.

by U.S. courts include aspirin, cellophane, linoleum, thermos, kerosene, monopoly, cola, and shredded wheat.

Companies such as Rolls-Royce, Cross, Xerox, Levi Strauss, Frigidaire, and McDonald's aggressively enforce their trademarks. Rolls-Royce, Coca-Cola, and Xerox even run newspaper and magazine ads stating that their names are trademarks and should not be used as descriptive or generic terms. In 2013, athletic apparel company Under Armour filed a trademark infringement lawsuit against Nike over the company's use of advertising phrases "I Will" and "Protect this house." According to Under Armour, Nike's use of phrases such as "I will protect my home court" in online and social media outlets infringed upon an Under Armour marketing campaign that used similar phrases. Ten years earlier, Nike filed a suit against Under Armour over the use of the term "DRI-FIT."[17]

To try to stem the number of trademark infringements, violations carry steep penalties. But despite the risk of incurring a penalty, infringement lawsuits are still common. Serious conflict can occur when brand names resemble one another too closely. Fashion brand Gucci has accused Guess of trademark violations for years. In 2015, a French court ruled in Guess's favor, finding that no trademark infringement, counterfeiting, or unfair competition between the two brands occurred. The court found that Guess had diluted Gucci's logos, not copied them. An American court ruled, however, that Guess was guilty of copying four of Gucci's five trademarked logos. This example also illustrates that there is no such thing as a global trademark. [18]

Companies must also contend with fake or unauthorized brands. Knockoffs of trademarked clothing lines are easy to find in cheap shops all over the world, and loose imitations are found in some reputable department stores as well. Today, whole stores are faked in China. Stores selling real iPhones and iPads in stores with sparse décor and bright lighting may seem like authentic Apple stores but are frequently imitating the real deal. Numerous fast-food restaurants have become victims of knockoff stores throughout China: Pizza Huh (Pizza Hut), Mak Dak (McDonald's), and Taco Bell Grande (Taco Bell) mimic the American chains' layouts and products. FBC, KFG, KLG, MFC, and OFC all lift Kentucky Fried Chicken's iconic logo, color scheme, and menu.[19]

In Europe, you can sue counterfeiters only if your brand, logo, or trademark is formally registered. Formal registration used to be required in each country in which a company sought protection. However, today a company can register its trademark in all European Union member countries with one application.

10-5 PACKAGING

Packages have always served a practical function— that is, they hold contents together and protect goods as they move through the distribution channel. Today, however, packaging is also a container for promoting the product and making it easier and safer to use.

10-5a Packaging Functions

The three most important functions of packaging are to contain and protect products; promote products; and facilitate the storage, use, and convenience of products. A fourth function of packaging that is becoming increasingly important is to facilitate recycling and reduce environmental damage.

CONTAINING AND PROTECTING PRODUCTS The most obvious function of packaging is to contain products that are liquid, granular, or otherwise divisible. Packaging also enables manufacturers, wholesalers, and retailers to market products in specific quantities, such as ounces.

Physical protection is another obvious function of packaging. Most products are handled several times between the time they are manufactured, harvested, or otherwise produced and the time they are consumed or used. Many products are also shipped, stored, and inspected several times between production and consumption. Some, like milk, need to be refrigerated. Others, like beer, are sensitive to light. Still others, like medicines and bandages, need to be kept sterile. Packages protect products from breakage, evaporation, spillage, spoilage, light, heat, cold, infestation, and many other conditions.

PROMOTING PRODUCTS Packaging does more than identify the brand, list the ingredients, specify features, and give directions. A package differentiates a product from competing products and may associate a new product with a family of other products from the same manufacturer. However, some products' packaging lacks useful information. The FDA is looking to remedy inconsistent and incomplete food packaging information by adding more facts to nutrition labels. These changes include listing the number of servings in each container and printing the calorie count for each serving in larger, bolder type. The FDA hopes that these changes will catch consumers' eyes and help them better manage their health.[20]

Mahathir Mohd Yasin/Shutterstock.com

Packages use designs, colors, shapes, and materials to try to influence consumers' perceptions and buying behavior. For example, marketing research shows that health-conscious consumers are likely to think that any food is probably good for them as long as it comes in green packaging. Packaging can also influence consumer perceptions of quality and/or prestige. England's Brothers Cider recently revamped its label and can designs in a move to reposition Toffee Apple Cider, Festival Pear Cider, and other cider flavors as premium adult beverages. The company replaced bright green bottles with tinted brown ones, and swapped colorful graphic labels for designs that employ a mix of classic and modern typefaces. To bolster its new prestigious image, Brothers rolled out its package redesign alongside a $7.6 million countrywide marketing push.[21]

FACILITATING STORAGE, USE, AND CONVENIENCE Wholesalers and retailers prefer packages that are easy to ship, store, and stock on shelves. They also like packages that protect products, prevent spoilage or breakage, and extend the product's shelf life.

Consumers' requirements for storage, use, and convenience cover many dimensions. Consumers are constantly seeking items that are easy to handle, open, and reclose, although some consumers want packages that are tamperproof or childproof. Research indicates that hard-to-open packages are among consumers' top

complaints—especially when it comes to clamshell electronics packaging. Indeed, Quora users voted clamshell packaging "the worst piece of design ever done." There is even a Wikipedia page devoted to "wrap rage," the anger associated with trying to open clamshells and other poorly designed packages.[22] As oil prices force the cost of plastics used in packaging skyward, companies such as Amazon, Target, and Walmart are pushing suppliers to do away with excessive and infuriating packaging. Such packaging innovations as zipper tear strips, hinged lids, tab slots, screw-on tops, simple cardboard boxes, and pour spouts were introduced to solve these and other problems. Easy openings are especially important for kids and aging baby boomers.

Some firms use packaging to segment markets. For example, a C&H sugar carton with an easy-to-pour, reclosable top is targeted to consumers who do not do a lot of baking and are willing to pay at least 20 cents more for the package. Different-sized packages appeal to heavy, moderate, and light users. Campbell's soup is packaged in single-serving cans aimed at the elderly and singles market segments. Packaging convenience can increase a product's utility and, therefore, its market share and profits.

FACILITATING RECYCLING AND REDUCING ENVIRONMENTAL DAMAGE One of the most important packaging issues today is eco-consciousness, a trend that has recently been in and out of consumer and media attention. Studies conflict as to whether consumers will pay more for eco-friendly packaging, though consumers repeatedly iterate the desire to purchase such products. A 2013 Harris Interactive study found that 78 percent of customers buy green products and services, up from sixty-nine percent in 2012. Twenty percent of respondents said that they purchased eco-friendly products to improve their health, while 47 percent reported that they did so to improve the environment.[23]

10-5b Labeling

An integral part of any package is its label. Labeling generally takes one of two forms: persuasive or informational. **Persuasive labeling** focuses on a promotional theme or logo, and consumer information is secondary. Note that the standard promotional claims—such as "new," "improved," and

> **persuasive labeling** a type of package labeling that focuses on a promotional theme or logo, and consumer information is secondary

CHAPTER 10: Product Concepts   183

THE DISAPPEARING PACKAGE

Some firms use innovative packaging to target environmentally concerned market segments. Package designer Aaron Mickelson's the Disappearing Package project showcased several inventive ways to make packaging more sustainable. Mickelson's designs include bar soap packaging that dissolves under shower water, trash bag packaging that doubles as a container and can be used as a trash bag itself, perforated tea bag booklets (eliminating the need for a box), and a rolled up tear-away detergent pod package with product information printed across the outside of the conjoined pods.[25]

Brand & product info are printed directly on the surface with soap-soluble ink.

Courtesy of Chapel House Photography

Aaron Mickelson's innovative packaging project included concepts such as this one—a reusable container with a soap-soluble label that rinsed off—allowing the container to be repurposed for other foods or household items.

"super"—are no longer very persuasive. Consumers have been saturated with "newness" and thus discount these claims.

Informational labeling, by contrast, is designed to help consumers make proper product selections and lower their cognitive dissonance after

the purchase. Most major furniture manufacturers affix labels to their wares that explain the products' construction features, such as type of frame, number of coils, and fabric characteristics. The Nutritional Labeling and Education Act of 1990 mandated detailed nutritional information on most food packages and standards for health claims on food packaging. An important outcome of this legislation has been guidelines from the Food and Drug Administration for using terms such as *low fat, light, reduced cholesterol, low sodium, low calorie, low carb,* and *fresh.* Getting the right information is very important to consumers, so some universities and corporations are working on new technologies to help consumers shop smart. For example, researchers at the Eindhoven University of Technology, the Universitá di Catania, CEA-Liten, and STMicroelectronics have developed a low-cost plastic converter that tests whether packaged foods are safe to eat. The converter then displays information about the food's freshness directly on its packaging, eliminating the need for "best before" dates that serve as cautious estimates at best. This not only reassures customers that they are buying fresh food; it prevents still-edible food from being thrown away once it is bought.[24]

GREENWASHING There are numerous products in every product category that use *greenwashing* to try and sell products. Greenwashing is when a product or company attempts to give the impression of environmental friendliness whether or not it is environmentally friendly.

As consumer demand for green products appeared to escalate, green certifications proliferated. Companies could create their own certifications and logos, resulting in more than 300 possible certification labels, ranging in price from free to thousands of dollars. Consumer distrust and confusion caused the Federal Trade Commission to issue new rules. Starting in late 2011, new regulations apply to labeling products with green-certification logos. If the same company that produced the product performed the certification, that relationship must be clearly marked. This benefits organizations such as Green Seal, which uses unbiased, third-party scientists and experts to verify claims about emissions or biodegradability, and hopes to increase consumer confidence in green products.[26]

10-5c Universal Product Codes

The **universal product codes (UPCs)** that appear on most items in supermarkets and other high-volume outlets were first introduced in 1974. Because the numerical codes appear as a series of thick and thin vertical lines, they are often called *bar codes.* The lines are read by computerized optical scanners that match codes with brand names, package sizes, and prices. They also print information on cash register tapes and help retailers rapidly and accurately prepare records of customer purchases, control inventories, and track sales. The UPC system and scanners are also used in scanner-based research (see Chapter 9).

 ## 10-6 GLOBAL ISSUES IN BRANDING AND PACKAGING

When planning to enter a foreign market with an existing product, a firm has three options for handling the brand name:

- **One brand name everywhere:** This strategy is useful when the company markets mainly one product and the brand name does not have negative connotations in any local market. The Coca-Cola Company uses a one-brand-name strategy in more than 195 countries around the world. The advantages of a one-brand-name strategy are greater identification of the product from market to market and ease of coordinating promotion from market to market.

- **Adaptations and modifications:** A one-brand-name strategy is not possible when the name cannot be pronounced in the local language, when the brand name is owned by someone else, or when the brand name has a negative or vulgar connotation in the local language. The Iranian detergent Barf, for example, might encounter some problems in the U.S. market.

- **Different brand names in different markets:** Local brand names are often used when translation or pronunciation problems occur, when the marketer wants the brand to appear to be a local brand, or when regulations require localization. Unilever's Axe line of male grooming products is called Lynx in England, Ireland, Australia, and New Zealand. PepsiCo changed the name of its eponymous cola to Pecsi in Argentina to reflect the way the word is pronounced with an Argentinian accent.

In addition to global branding decisions, companies must consider global packaging needs. Three aspects of packaging that are especially important in international marketing are labeling, aesthetics, and climate considerations. The major *labeling* concern is properly translating ingredient, promotional, and instructional information on labels. Care must also be employed in meeting all local labeling requirements. Several years ago, an Italian judge ordered that all bottles of Coca-Cola be removed from retail shelves because the ingredients were not properly labeled. Labeling is also harder in countries like Belgium and Finland, which require packaging to be bilingual.

Package *aesthetics* may also require some attention. Even though simple visual elements of the brand, such as a symbol or logo, can be a standardizing element across products and countries, marketers must stay attuned to cultural traits in host countries. For example, colors may have different connotations. Red is associated with witchcraft in some countries, green may be a sign of danger, and white may be symbolic of death. Such cultural differences could necessitate a packaging change if colors are chosen for another country's interpretation. In the United States, green typically symbolizes an eco-friendly product, but that packaging could keep customers away in a country where green indicates danger. Aesthetics also influence package size. Soft drinks are not sold in six-packs in countries that lack refrigeration. In some countries, products such as detergent may be bought only in small quantities because of a lack of storage space. Other products, such as cigarettes, may be bought in small quantities, and even single units, because of the low purchasing power of buyers.

Extreme climates and long-distance shipping necessitate sturdier and more durable packages for goods sold overseas. Spillage, spoilage, and breakage are all more important concerns when products are shipped long distances or frequently handled during shipping and storage. Packages may also need to ensure a longer product life if the time between production and consumption lengthens significantly.

10-7 PRODUCT WARRANTIES

Just as a package is designed to protect the product, a warranty protects the buyer and gives essential information about the product. A warranty confirms the quality or performance of a good or service. An **express warranty** is a written guarantee. Express warranties range from simple statements—such as "100-percent cotton" (a guarantee of quality) and "complete satisfaction guaranteed" (a statement of performance)—to extensive documents written in technical language. In contrast, an **implied warranty** is an unwritten guarantee that the good or service is fit for the purpose for which it was sold. All sales have an implied warranty under the Uniform Commercial Code.

warranty a confirmation of the quality or performance of a good or service

express warranty a written guarantee

implied warranty an unwritten guarantee that the good or service is fit for the purpose for which it was sold

Congress passed the Magnuson-Moss Warranty–Federal Trade Commission Improvement Act in 1975 to help consumers understand warranties and get action from manufacturers and dealers. A manufacturer that promises a full warranty must meet certain minimum standards, including repair "within a reasonable time and without charge" of any defects and replacement of the merchandise or a full refund if the product does not work "after a reasonable number of attempts" at repair. Any warranty that does not live up to this tough prescription must be "conspicuously" promoted as a limited warranty.

STUDY TOOLS 10

LOCATED AT BACK OF THE TEXTBOOK
☐ Rip out Chapter Review Card

LOCATED AT WWW.CENGAGEBRAIN.COM
☐ Review Key Terms Flashcards and create your own

☐ Track your knowledge and understanding of key concepts in marketing

☐ Complete practice and graded quizzes to prepare for tests

☐ Complete interactive content within the MKTG Online experience

☐ View the chapter highlight boxes within the MKTG Online experience

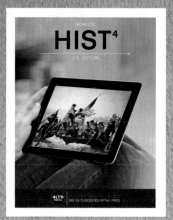

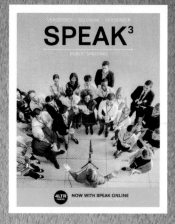

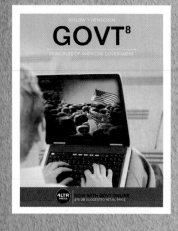

11 | Developing and Managing Products

LEARNING OUTCOMES

After studying this chapter, you will be able to…

11-1 Explain the importance of developing new products and describe the six categories of new products

11-2 Explain the steps in the new-product development process

11-3 Understand why some products succeed and others fail

11-4 Discuss global issues in new-product development

11-5 Explain the diffusion process through which new products are adopted

11-6 Explain the concept of product life cycles

After you finish this chapter go to **PAGE 203** for **STUDY TOOLS.**

Luminaimages/Shutterstock.com

11-1 THE IMPORTANCE OF NEW PRODUCTS

New products are important to sustain growth, increase revenues and profits, and replace obsolete items. Each year *Fast Company* rates and ranks its most innovative companies, based on the ability to buck tradition in the interest of reaching more people, building a better business, and spurring mass-market appeal for unusual or highly technical products or services. In 2015, the top five companies were Warby Parker, Apple, Alibaba, Google, and Instagram.[1] All of these firms have reputations for relying heavily on technology.

11-1a Introduction of New Products

Some companies spend a considerable amount of money each year developing new products. At Pfizer, the world's largest research-based pharmaceutical company, approximately $1.2 billion is spent on research and development for every new product released.[2] Other companies with large R&D spending include Toyota ($9.9 billion per year), IBM ($6.3 billion per year), and Procter & Gamble ($2 billion per year).[3]

Sometimes it is difficult to decide when to replace a successful product. Gillette Co. has a history of introducing new shaving systems (razors and accompanying blades) before the previous generation of products begins experiencing a sales decline. In fact, Gillette *expects* to cannibalize the sales of older models with its newer introductions. In early 2015, Apple reintroduced the MacBook line of laptops, effectively replacing the popular MacBook Air line. Apple executives agreed that the MacBook Air needed to be replaced to keep customers

satisfied, but the design of the new MacBook required complex decisions, tradeoffs, and risks. The new version features a retina display, thinner design, and a longer-lasting battery.[4] Clearly, the introduction of a new product is a monumental undertaking with a lot of open-ended questions—even for an established, multi-billion dollar company like Apple.

11-1b Categories of New Products

The term **new product** is somewhat confusing because its meaning varies widely. Actually, the term has several "correct" definitions. A product can be new to the world, to the market, to the producer or seller, or some combination of these. There are six categories of new products:

- **New-to-the-world products (also called *discontinuous innovations*):** These products create an entirely new market. For example, in early 2013, Taiwanese electronics company Polytron Technologies unveiled a completely transparent smartphone prototype. The device's new-to-the-world "Switchable Glass" technology employs liquid crystal molecules that display images only when electric current is run through them. Without power, the smartphone is completely see-through.[5] New-to-the-world products represent the smallest category of new products.

> **The average fast-moving consumer goods company introduces seventy to eighty new products per year.**

- **New product lines:** These products, which the firm has not previously offered, allow it to enter an established market. For example, Moleskine's first products were simple black-covered journals. Since then, the company has expanded into pens, travel bags, and even digital creative tools available on the iPhone and iPad.[6]

- Additions to existing product lines: This category includes new products that supplement a firm's established line. Fast-food restaurant chain Taco Bell and snack food manufacturer Frito-Lay have a longstanding partnership that has resulted in several product line additions. After the nacho cheese-flavored Doritos Locos taco proved to be the biggest launch in Taco Bell history, CEO Greg Creed announced that Cool Ranch– and

new product a product new to the world, the market, the producer, the seller, or some combination of these

New 2015 Ford F-150s feature high-strength, military-grade, aluminum-alloy bodies and beds.

Bill Pugliano/Getty Images

Flamas-flavored versions of the Doritos Locos taco would soon be added to Taco Bell's product line. Indeed, in March 2013, the Cool Ranch Doritos Locos taco was added to Taco Bell menus across America.[7]

- **Improvements or revisions of existing products:** The "new and improved" product may be significantly or only slightly changed. In May 2013, MillerCoors announced a new Miller Lite bottle that would only be available in bars and restaurants. According to the company, the new bottle shape featured "broad shoulders and a contoured grip." While the beer inside did not change, the revision was significant enough that the bottle could be called a new product.[8]

- **Repositioned products:** These are existing products targeted at new markets or market segments, or ones repositioned to change the current market's perception of the product or company, which may be done to boost declining sales. Mercedes is repositioning its ultra-luxurious Maybach line as a sub-brand to appeal to its most status-conscious customers. Although Mercedes is already known for luxurious vehicles, the Maybach line is intended to "set a new benchmark for exclusivity." The Mercedes-Maybach line will feature exceptionally comfortable and spacious seating and lavishly designed interiors.[9]

- **Lower-priced products:** This category refers to products that provide performance similar to competing brands at a lower price. The HP LaserJet Color MFP is a scanner, copier, printer, and fax machine combined. This new product is priced lower than many conventional color copiers and much lower than the combined price of the four items purchased separately.

new-product strategy a plan that links the new-product development process with the objectives of the marketing department, the business unit, and the corporation

11-2 THE NEW-PRODUCT DEVELOPMENT PROCESS

The management consulting firm Booz Allen Hamilton has studied the new-product development process for more than 30 years. Analyzing five major studies undertaken during this period, the firm has concluded that the companies most likely to succeed in developing and introducing new products are those that take the following actions:

- Make the long-term commitment needed to support innovation and new-product development.

- Use a company-specific approach, driven by corporate objectives and strategies, with a well-defined new-product strategy at its core.

- Capitalize on experience to achieve and maintain competitive advantage.

- Establish an environment—a management style, organizational structure, and degree of top management support—conducive to achieving company-specific new-product and corporate objectives.

Most companies follow a formal new-product development process, usually starting with a new-product strategy. Exhibit 11.1 traces the seven-step process, which is discussed in detail in this section. The exhibit is funnel-shaped to highlight the fact that each stage acts as a screen to filter out unworkable ideas.

11-2a New-Product Strategy

A **new-product strategy** links the new-product development process with the objectives of the marketing department, the business unit, and the corporation. A new-product strategy must be compatible with these objectives, and in turn, all three of the objectives must be consistent with one another.

A new-product strategy is part of the organization's overall marketing strategy. It sharpens the focus and provides general guidelines for generating, screening, and evaluating new-product ideas. The new-product strategy specifies the roles that new products must play in the organization's overall plan and describes the characteristics of products the organization wants to offer and the markets it wants to serve.

EXHIBIT 11.1 NEW-PRODUCT DEVELOPMENT PROCESS

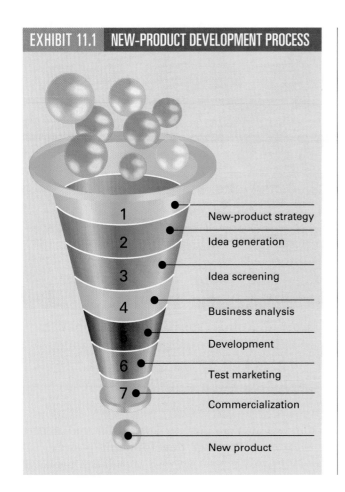

1 New-product strategy
2 Idea generation
3 Idea screening
4 Business analysis
5 Development
6 Test marketing
7 Commercialization

New product

11-2b Idea Generation

New-product ideas come from many sources, including customers, employees, distributors, competitors, research and development (R&D), consultants, and other experts.

CUSTOMERS The marketing concept suggests that customers' wants and needs should be the springboard for developing new products. Companies can derive insight from listening to Internet chatter or reading blogs, which often indicate early trends or areas consumers are interested in seeing develop or change. Another approach for generating new-product ideas is using what some companies are calling "customer innovation centers." The idea is to provide a forum for meeting with customers and directly involving them in the innovation process.

EMPLOYEES Sometimes employees know a company's products and processes better than anyone else. Many firms have formal and informal processes in place for employees to propose new product ideas. To encourage participation, some companies run contests, hold votes, and set up idea kiosks.[10]

PricewaterhouseCoopers uses a system called iPlace to encourage employee innovation. The system is so successful that 60 percent of employees participate in the idea-generation process; 140 of the 3,300 ideas have already been implemented.[11]

For Havianas Customers, Customization is Key

In the saturated summer sandals market, flip-flop manufacturer Havianas utilizes customization as a way to stand out. Havianas' online customization tool allows customers to combine different patterns and colors to create their own unique pairs of flip flops.[12]

Source: Havaianas

Some firms reward employees for coming up with creative new ideas. In an effort to encourage risk-taking through new ideas, companies like Google have begun implementing rewards for employees who fail after taking a big risk. Some of the most innovative Google ideas (such as driverless cars and Google glass) were developed through the Google X program. In order to promote innovative thinking and eliminate the fear of coming up with bad ideas among Google X employees, the company rewards failure. According to Google X employee Astro Teller, "You must reward people for failing. If not, they won't take risks and make breakthroughs. If you don't reward failure, people will hang on to a doomed idea for fear of the consequences. That wastes time and saps an organization's spirit."[13]

DISTRIBUTORS A well-trained sales force routinely asks distributors about needs that are not being met. Because they are closer to end users, distributors are often more aware of customer needs than are manufacturers. The inspiration for Rubbermaid's Sidekick, a litter-free lunch box, came from a distributor who suggested that the company place some of its plastic containers inside a lunch box and sell the box as an alternative to plastic wrap and paper bags.

COMPETITORS No firms rely solely on internally generated ideas for new products. As discussed in Chapter 9, a big part of any organization's marketing intelligence system should be monitoring the performance of competitors' products. One purpose of competitive monitoring is to determine which, if any, of the competitors' products should be copied. There is plenty of information about competitors on the Internet. Fuld & Company is a preeminent research and consulting firm in the field of competitive intelligence. Its clients include more than half of the U.S. *Fortune* 500 list and numerous international firms.[14]

Jack Burton Carpenter (center) speaks at the Vermont Ski and Snowboard Museum after Governor Peter Shumlin (right of center) signed a bill declaring skiing and snowboarding as the official state sports of Vermont.

other two ways are product development and product modification. **Product development** goes beyond applied research by converting applications into marketable products. Product modification makes cosmetic or functional changes to existing products. Many new-product breakthroughs come from R&D activities.

Founder and CEO of Burton Snowboards Jake Burton Carpenter believes that his company has been so successful because it invests considerably more in research and development than its competitors do. "We have to continue to make the best product out there," says Carpenter. "The minute we get beat on an innovation or make a mistake on quality we lose our lead."[15] While the United States is the global leader in research and development, this lead is beginning to slip. The United States' share has grown from 25 percent to 34 percent at the same time as China's share alone has jumped more than sevenfold to 15 percent. Still, the United States spends $429 billion per year on R&D—more than twice that spent by China ($208 billion) and nearly three times that spent by Japan ($147 billion).[16]

product development
a marketing strategy that entails the creation of marketable new products; the process of converting applications for new technologies into marketable products

RESEARCH AND DEVELOPMENT R&D is carried out in four distinct ways. You learned about basic research and applied research in Chapter 4. The

CONSULTANTS Outside consultants are always available to examine a business and recommend product ideas. Examples include the Weston Group, Booz Allen Hamilton, and Management Decisions Inc. Traditionally, consultants determine whether a company has a balanced portfolio of products and, if not, what new-product ideas are needed to offset the imbalance. For example, Continuum is an award-winning consultancy firm that designs new goods and services, works on brand makeovers, and conducts consumer research. Clients include PepsiCo, Moen, American Express, Samsung, Reebok, and Sprint.[17]

OTHER EXPERTS A technique that is being used increasingly to generate new product ideas is called "crowdsourcing." General information regarding ideas being sought is provided to a wide range of potential sources such as industry experts, independent researchers, and academics. These experts then develop ideas for the company. In addition to field experts, firms such as Quirky Inc. and General Electric Company have used crowdsourcing to generate ideas from the general public and freelance inventors. Lego is using crowdsourcing to develop new ideas for its building block sets. Lego fans and enthusiasts can suggest ideas for new concepts via "Lego Ideas," a program set up by the toymaker. In order to qualify for a review by the marketing team, users must submit photos and a description of their idea to the Lego Ideas Web site, where other users can view and vote to support the idea. If the idea receives support from 10,000 users, it is sent to the Lego marketing team.[18] For a more thorough discussion of crowdsourcing, see Chapter 18.

Creativity is the wellspring of new-product ideas, regardless of who comes up with them. A variety of approaches and techniques have been developed to stimulate creative thinking. The two considered most useful for generating new-product ideas are brainstorming and focus group exercises. The goal of **brainstorming** is to get a group to think of unlimited ways to vary a product or solve a problem. Group members avoid criticism of an idea, no matter how ridiculous it may seem. Objective evaluation is postponed. The sheer quantity of ideas is what matters. As noted in Chapter 9, an objective of focus group interviews is to stimulate insightful comments through group interaction. In the industrial market, machine tools, keyboard designs, aircraft interiors, and backhoe accessories have evolved from focus groups.

11-2c Idea Screening

After new ideas have been generated, they pass through the first filter in the product development process. This stage, called **screening**, eliminates ideas that are inconsistent with the organization's new-product strategy or are obviously inappropriate for some other reason. The new-product committee, the new-product department, or some other formally appointed group performs the screening review.

Concept tests are often used at the screening stage to rate concept (or product) alternatives. A **concept test** evaluates a new-product idea, usually before any prototype has been created. Typically, researchers get consumer reactions to descriptions and visual representations of a proposed product. Concept tests are considered fairly good predictors of success for line extensions. They have also been relatively precise predictors of success for new products that are not copycat items, are not easily classified into existing product categories, and do not require major changes in consumer behavior—such as Betty Crocker Tuna Helper. However, concept tests are usually inaccurate in predicting the success of new products that create new consumption patterns and require major changes in consumer behavior—such as microwave ovens, digital music players, and computers.

11-2d Business Analysis

New-product ideas that survive the initial screening process move to the **business analysis** stage, where preliminary figures for demand, cost, sales, and profitability are calculated. For the first time, costs and revenues are estimated and compared. Depending on the nature of the product and the company, this process may be simple or complex.

The newness of the product, the size of the market, and the nature of the competition all affect the accuracy of revenue projections. In an established market like soft drinks, industry estimates of total market size are available. Forecasting market share for a new entry in a new, fragmented, or relatively small niche is a bigger challenge.

Analyzing overall economic trends and their impact on estimated sales is especially important in product categories that are sensitive to fluctuations in the business cycle. If consumers view the economy as uncertain and risky, they will put off buying durable goods such as major home appliances, automobiles, and homes. Likewise, business buyers postpone major equipment purchases if they expect a recession.

brainstorming the process of getting a group to think of unlimited ways to vary a product or solve a problem

screening the first filter in the product development process, which eliminates ideas that are inconsistent with the organization's new-product strategy or are obviously inappropriate for some other reason

concept test a test to evaluate a new-product idea, usually before any prototype has been created

business analysis the second stage of the screening process where preliminary figures for demand, cost, sales, and profitability are calculated

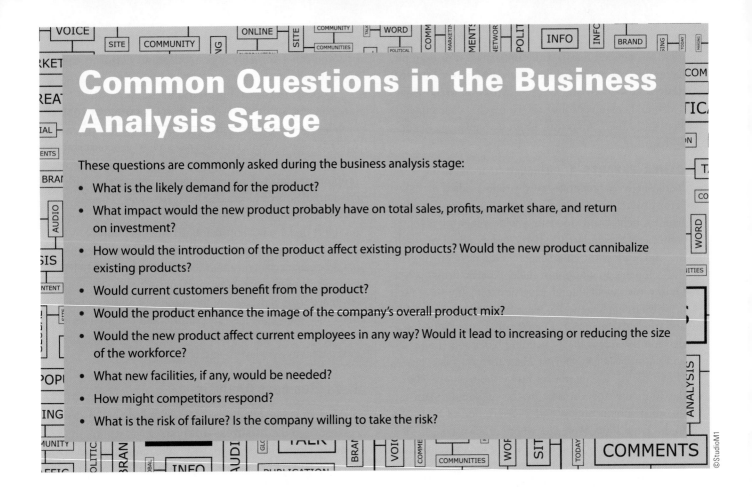

Common Questions in the Business Analysis Stage

These questions are commonly asked during the business analysis stage:

- What is the likely demand for the product?
- What impact would the new product probably have on total sales, profits, market share, and return on investment?
- How would the introduction of the product affect existing products? Would the new product cannibalize existing products?
- Would current customers benefit from the product?
- Would the product enhance the image of the company's overall product mix?
- Would the new product affect current employees in any way? Would it lead to increasing or reducing the size of the workforce?
- What new facilities, if any, would be needed?
- How might competitors respond?
- What is the risk of failure? Is the company willing to take the risk?

©StudioM1

Understanding the market potential is important because costs increase dramatically once a product idea enters the development stage.

11-2e Development

In the early stage of **development**, the R&D or engineering department may develop a prototype of the product. A process called 3D printing, or additive manufacturing, is sometimes used to create three-dimensional prototypes quickly and at a relatively low cost. During this stage, the firm should start sketching a marketing strategy. The marketing department should decide on the product's packaging, branding, labeling, and so forth. In addition, it should map out preliminary promotion, price, and distribution strategies. The feasibility of manufacturing the product at an acceptable cost should be thoroughly examined. The development stage can last a long time and thus be very expensive. It took ten years to develop Crest toothpaste, fifteen years to develop the Polaroid Colorpack camera and the Xerox copy

> **development** the stage in the product development process in which a prototype is developed and a marketing strategy is outlined

machine, 18 years to develop Minute Rice, and 51 years to develop the television. Video game developer Ubisoft took more than five years to develop open-world action game Watch Dogs and more than six years to develop racing game The Crew. The time invested in

Stefano Tinti/Shutterstock.com

3D Printing (or additive manufacturing) is sometimes used to create three-dimensional prototypes quickly and at a relatively low cost.

development, however, can often have a tremendous payoff. Watch Dogs broke launch day sales for Ubisoft, selling more than 4 million units during its first week.[19]

The development process works best when all the involved areas (R&D, marketing, engineering, production, and even suppliers) work together rather than sequentially, a process called **simultaneous product development**. This approach allows firms to shorten the development process and reduce costs. With simultaneous product development, all relevant functional areas and outside suppliers participate in all stages of the development process. Rather than proceeding through highly structured stages, the cross-functional team operates in unison. Involving key suppliers early in the process capitalizes on their knowledge and enables them to develop critical component parts.

The Internet is a useful tool for implementing simultaneous product development. On the Web, multiple partners from a variety of locations can meet regularly to assess new-product ideas, analyze markets and demographics, and review cost information. Ideas judged to be feasible can quickly be converted into new products. The best-managed global firms leverage their global networks by sharing best practices, knowledge, and technology.[20] Without the Internet, it would be impossible to conduct simultaneous product development from different parts of the world. Some firms use online brain trusts to solve technical problems. InnoCentive Inc. is a network of 80,000 self-selected science problem solvers in 173 countries. Its clients include NASA, *Popular Science*, and *The Economist*. When one of InnoCentive's partners selects an idea for development, it no longer tries to develop the idea from the ground up with its own resources and time. Instead, it issues a brief to its network of thinkers, researchers, technology entrepreneurs, and inventors around the world, hoping to generate dialogue, suggestions, and solutions.

Innovative firms are also gathering a variety of R&D input from customers online. Wheaties NEXT Challenge allowed customers to vote for which elite athlete would be featured on the next Wheaties cereal box by logging workouts through the MapMyFitness program. For each workout that was logged, a vote was cast for the participant's favorite Wheaties athlete. More than 71,000 people participated in the challenge.[21]

Laboratory tests are often conducted on prototype models during the development stage. User safety is an important aspect of laboratory testing, which actually subjects products to much more severe treatment than is expected by end users. The Consumer Product Safety Act of 1972 requires manufacturers to conduct a "reasonable testing program" to ensure that their products conform to established safety standards.

Many products that test well in the laboratory are also tried out in homes or businesses. Examples of product categories well suited for such use tests include human and pet food products, household cleaning products, and industrial chemicals and supplies. These products are all relatively inexpensive, and their performance characteristics are apparent to users. For example, P&G tests a variety of personal and home-care products in the community around its Cincinnati, Ohio, headquarters.

11-2f Test Marketing

After products and marketing programs have been developed, they are usually tested in the marketplace. **Test marketing** is the limited introduction of a product and a marketing program to determine the reactions of potential customers in a market situation. Test marketing allows management to evaluate alternative strategies and to assess how well the various aspects of the marketing mix fit together. Even established products are test marketed to assess new marketing strategies.

The cities chosen as test sites should reflect market conditions in the new product's projected market area. Yet no "magic city" exists that can universally represent market conditions, and a product's success in one city does not guarantee that it will be a nationwide hit. When selecting test market cities, researchers should therefore find locations where the demographics and purchasing habits mirror the overall market. The company should also have good distribution in test cities. Wendy's uses Columbus, Ohio as a test market for new burgers. Because the city has a nearly perfect cross-section of America's demographic breakdown, it is the perfect testing ground for new products. Most recently, Wendy's tested the reception of its Ciabatta Bacon Cheeseburger.[22] Moreover, test locations should be isolated from the media. If the television stations in a particular market reach a very large area outside that market, the advertising used for the test product may pull in many consumers from outside the market. The product may then appear more successful than it really is.

simultaneous product development a team-oriented approach to new-product development

test marketing the limited introduction of a product and a marketing program to determine the reactions of potential customers in a market situation

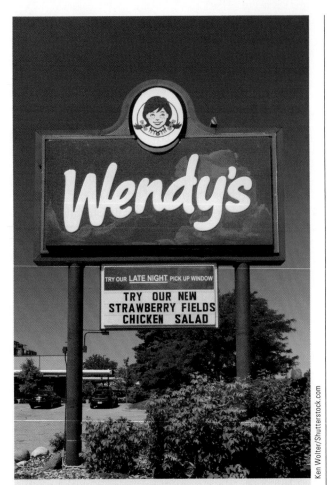

Wendy's uses Columbus, Ohio, as a test market for new burgers and menu items.

THE HIGH COSTS OF TEST MARKETING Test marketing frequently takes one year or longer, and costs can exceed $1 million. Some products remain in test markets even longer. In an effort to expand its product offerings, Starbucks launched the Dark Barrel Latte in select Ohio and Florida locations in September 2014. Some describe this new latte as having a taste similar to Guinness beer. As of this printing, the drink is yet to become more widely available.[23]

Despite the cost, many firms believe it is better to fail in a test market than in a national introduction. Because test marketing is so expensive, some companies do not test line extensions of well-known brands.

The high cost of test marketing is not just financial. One unavoidable problem is that test marketing exposes the new product and its marketing mix to competitors before its introduction. Thus, the element of surprise is lost. Competitors can also sabotage or "jam" a testing program by introducing their own sales promotion, pricing, or advertising campaign. The purpose is to hide or distort the normal conditions that the testing firm might expect in the market.

ALTERNATIVES TO TEST MARKETING Many firms are looking for cheaper, faster, safer alternatives to traditional test marketing. In the early 1980s, Information Resources Inc. pioneered one alternative: scanner-based research (discussed in Chapter 9). A typical supermarket scanner test costs about $300,000. Another alternative to traditional test marketing is **simulated (laboratory) market testing**. Advertising and other promotional materials for several products, including the test product, are shown to members of the product's target market. These people are then taken to shop at a mock or real store, where their purchases are recorded. Shopper behavior, including repeat purchasing, is monitored to assess the product's likely performance under true market conditions. Research firms offer simulated market tests for $25,000 to $100,000, compared to $1 million or more for full-scale test marketing.

The Internet offers a fast, cost-effective way to conduct test marketing. P&G uses the Internet to assess customer demand for potential new products. Many products that are not available in grocery stores or drugstores can be sampled from P&G's Web site devoted to samples and coupons, www.pgeveryday.com.[24]

Despite these alternatives, most firms still consider test marketing essential for most new products. The high price of failure simply prohibits the widespread introduction of most new products without testing.

11-2g Commercialization

The final stage in the new-product development process is **commercialization**, the decision to market a product. The decision to commercialize the product sets several tasks in motion: ordering production materials and equipment, starting production, building inventories, shipping the product to field distribution points, training the sales force, announcing the new product to the trade, and advertising to potential customers.

The time from the initial commercialization decision to the product's actual introduction varies. It can

simulated (laboratory) market testing the presentation of advertising and other promotional materials for several products, including a test product, to members of the product's target market

commercialization the decision to market a product

Ken Wolter/Shutterstock.com

range from a few weeks for simple products that use existing equipment to several years for technical products that require custom manufacturing equipment. And the total cost of development and initial introduction can be staggering.

 11-3 ## WHY SOME PRODUCTS SUCCEED AND OTHERS FAIL

Despite the amount of time and money spent on developing and testing new products, a large proportion of new product introductions fail. Products fail for a number of reasons. One common reason is that they simply do not offer any discernible benefit compared to existing products. Another commonly cited factor in new-product failures is a poor match between product features and customer desires. For example, there are telephone systems on the market with more than 700 different functions, although the average user is happy with just ten functions. Other reasons for failure include overestimation of market size, incorrect targeting or positioning, a price too high or too low, inadequate distribution, poor promotion, or simply an inferior product.

Estimates of the percentages of new products that fail vary. Many estimates range as high as 80 to 90 percent.[25] Failure can be a matter of degree, however. Absolute failure occurs when a company cannot recoup its development, marketing, and production costs—the product actually loses money for the company. A relative product failure results when the product returns a profit

but fails to achieve sales, profit, or market share goals. Examples of product failures in 2014 include the Amazon Fire Phone, detergent-free laundry systems, the Nike FuelBand, and Burger King's Satisfries, a healthier alternative to regular fries.[26]

High costs and other risks of developing and testing new products do not stop many companies, such as Newell Rubbermaid, Colgate-Palmolive, Campbell Soup Company, and 3M, from aggressively developing and introducing new products. These companies depend on new products to increase revenues and profits. The most important factor in successful new-product introduction is a good match between the product and market needs—as the marketing concept would predict. Successful new products deliver a meaningful and perceivable benefit to a sizable number of people or organizations and are different in some meaningful way from their intended substitutes.

NIKE+ FUELBAND SE
THE SMART, SIMPLE, AND FUN WAY TO GET MORE ACTIVE.

Source: Nike, Inc.

High costs of new products do not stop large companies from aggressively developing them, even if they fail.

11-4 GLOBAL ISSUES IN NEW-PRODUCT DEVELOPMENT

Increasing globalization of markets and competition provides a reason for multinational firms to consider new-product development from a worldwide perspective. A firm that starts with a global strategy is better able to develop products that are marketable worldwide. In many multinational corporations, every product is developed for potential worldwide distribution, and unique market requirements are satisfied during development whenever possible.

Some global marketers design their products to meet regulations in their major markets and then, if necessary, meet smaller markets' requirements country by country. Nissan develops lead-country car models that, with minor changes, can be sold in most markets. With this approach, Nissan has been able to reduce the number of its basic models from 48 to 18. Some products, however, have little potential for global market penetration without modification. Succeeding in some countries (such as China) often requires companies to develop products that meet the unique needs of these populations.[27] In other cases, companies cannot sell their products at affordable prices and still make a profit in many countries.

11-5 THE SPREAD OF NEW PRODUCTS

Managers have a better chance of successfully marketing products if they understand how consumers learn about and adopt products.

11-5a Diffusion of Innovation

An **innovation** is a product perceived as new by a potential adopter. It really does not matter whether the product is "new to the world" or some other category of new product. If it is new to a potential adopter, it is an innovation in this context. **Diffusion** is the process by which the adoption of an innovation spreads. Five categories of adopters participate in the diffusion process.

INNOVATORS Innovators are the first 2.5 percent of all those who adopt the product. Innovators are eager to try new ideas and products, almost as an obsession. In addition to having higher incomes, they are more worldly and more active outside their community than noninnovators. They rely less on group norms and are more self-confident. Because they are well educated, they are more likely to get their information from scientific sources and experts. Innovators are characterized as being venturesome.

EARLY ADOPTERS Early adopters are the next 13.5 percent to adopt the product. Although early adopters are not the very first, they do adopt early in the product's life cycle. Compared to innovators, they rely much more on group norms and values. They are also more oriented to the local community, in contrast to the innovators' worldly outlook. Early adopters are more likely than innovators to be opinion leaders because of their closer affiliation with groups. Early adopters are a new product's best friends. Because viral, buzz, and word-of-mouth advertising is on the rise, marketers focus a lot of attention identifying the group that begins the viral marketing chain—the influencers. Part of the challenge is that this group of customers is distinguished not by demographics but by behavior. Influencers come from all age, gender, and income groups, and they do not use media any differently than other users who are considered followers. The characteristic influencers share is their desire to talk to others about their experiences with goods and services. A desire to earn the respect of others is a dominant characteristic among early adopters.

EARLY MAJORITY The next 34 percent to adopt are called the early majority. The early majority weighs the pros and cons before adopting a new product. They are likely to collect more information and evaluate more brands than early adopters, thereby extending the adoption process. They rely on the group for information but are unlikely to be opinion leaders themselves. Instead, they tend to be opinion leaders' friends and neighbors. Consumers trust positive word-of-mouth reviews from friends, family, and peers.[28] In fact, 50 percent of purchase decisions are influenced by word-of-mouth, and 92 percent of consumers trust recommendations from friends and family more than any other form of advertising.[29] Product discussions often drive teen conversations, so word-of-mouth marketing is particularly powerful among this demographic. According to Lauren Hutter, group planning director at BBDO New York, "It's their countercultural currency . . . It's how to break into the group, how you bring something into the mix."[30]

While word-of-mouth marketing is important to teens, actually getting them to discuss products concretely can be difficult. According to Eric Pakurar, executive director and head of strategy at G2 USA, "They kind of

innovation a product perceived as new by a potential adopter

diffusion the process by which the adoption of an innovation spreads

ping-pong back and forth. They do a little research, then talk to their friends, and then do a little more research and check back with their friends and family."[31] Other groups, such as Millennials, also report word-of-mouth as the most important source of product information.[32] Many feel a responsibility to help friends and family make wise purchase decisions.

All word of mouth is not positive. Four out of five U.S. consumers report telling people around them about negative customer service experiences. Forty-two percent of consumers share customer service experiences on social media, roughly half of which is negative.[33] The early majority is an important link in the process of diffusing new ideas because they are positioned between earlier and later adopters. A dominant characteristic of the early majority is deliberateness.

LATE MAJORITY The late majority is the next 34 percent to adopt. The late majority adopts a new product because most of their friends have already adopted it. Because they also rely on group norms, their adoption stems from pressure to conform. This group tends to be older and below average in income and education. They depend mainly on word-of-mouth communication rather than on the mass media. The dominant characteristic of the late majority is skepticism.

LAGGARDS The final 16 percent to adopt are called laggards. Like innovators, laggards do not rely on group norms. Their independence is rooted in their ties to tradition. Thus, the past heavily influences their decisions. By the time laggards adopt an innovation, it has probably been outmoded and replaced by something else. For example, they may have bought their first color television set after flat screen televisions were already widely diffused. Laggards have the longest adoption time and the lowest socioeconomic status. They tend to be suspicious of new products and alienated from a rapidly advancing society. The dominant value of laggards is tradition. Marketers typically ignore laggards, who do not seem to be motivated by advertising or personal selling and are virtually impossible to reach online.

Note that some product categories may never be adopted by 100 percent of the population. The adopter categories refer to all of those who will eventually adopt a product, not the entire population.

11-5b Product Characteristics and the Rate of Adoption

Five product characteristics can be used to predict and explain the rate of acceptance and diffusion of a new product:

- **Complexity:** the degree of difficulty involved in understanding and using a new product. The more complex the product, the slower is its diffusion.

- **Compatibility:** the degree to which the new product is consistent with existing values and product knowledge, past experiences, and current needs. Incompatible products diffuse more slowly than compatible products.

- **Relative advantage:** the degree to which a product is perceived as superior to existing substitutes. Because it can store and play back thousands of songs, the iPod and its many variants have a clear relative advantage over the portable CD player.

- **Observability:** the degree to which the benefits or other results of using the product can be observed by others and communicated to target customers. For instance, fashion items and automobiles are highly visible and more observable than personal-care items.

- **"Trialability":** the degree to which a product can be tried on a limited basis. It is much easier to try a new toothpaste or breakfast cereal, for example, than a new personal computer.

11-5c Marketing Implications of the Adoption Process

Two types of communication aid the diffusion process: *word-of-mouth communication* among consumers and communication from marketers to consumers. Word-of-mouth communication within and across groups, including social media and viral communication, speeds diffusion. Opinion leaders discuss new products with their followers and with other opinion leaders. Marketers must therefore ensure that opinion leaders have the types of information desired in the media that they use. Suppliers of some products, such as professional and health care services, rely almost solely on word-of-mouth communication for new business.

Many large-scale companies like Procter & Gamble, Cisco Systems, and Salesforce.com seek out opinion leaders among their employees. Some companies conduct surveys to identify opinion leaders while others use technology to map connections between individuals and postings. Once identified, these influential employees are provided with specially tailored communication training and are invited to attend senior management briefings. The hope is that these opinion leaders will field co-workers' questions and build positive buzz. Influencers are frequently rewarded for their skills with promotions and other forms of recognition.[34]

The second type of communication aiding the diffusion process is *communication directly from the marketer to potential adopters*. Messages directed toward early adopters should normally use different appeals than messages directed toward the early majority, the late majority, or the laggards. Early adopters are more important than innovators because they make up a larger group, are more socially active, and are usually opinion leaders.

As the focus of a promotional campaign shifts from early adopters to the early majority and the late majority, marketers should study the dominant characteristics, buying behavior, and media characteristics of these target markets. Then they should revise messages and media strategy to fit. The diffusion model helps guide marketers in developing and implementing promotion strategy.

PRODUCT LIFE CYCLES

The product life cycle (PLC) is one of the most familiar concepts in marketing. Few other general concepts have been so widely discussed. Although some researchers and consultants have challenged the theoretical basis and managerial value of the PLC, many believe it is a useful marketing management diagnostic tool and a general guide for marketing planning in various life cycle stages.

The PLC is a biological metaphor that traces the stages of a product's acceptance, from its introduction (birth) to its decline (death). As Exhibit 11.2 shows, a product progresses through four major stages: introduction, growth, maturity, and decline.

The PLC concept can be used to analyze a brand, a product form, or a product category. The PLC for a product form is usually longer than the PLC for any one brand. The exception would be a

product life cycle (PLC)
a concept that provides a way to trace the stages of a product's acceptance, from its introduction (birth) to its decline (death)

product category all brands that satisfy a particular type of need

introductory stage the full-scale launch of a new product into the marketplace

brand that was the first and last competitor in a product form market. In that situation, the brand and product form life cycles would be equal in length. Product categories have the longest life cycles. A **product category** includes all brands that satisfy a particular type of need, such as shaving products, passenger automobiles, or soft drinks.

The time a product spends in any one stage of the life cycle may vary dramatically. Some products, such as fad items, move through the entire cycle in weeks. Fads are typically characterized by a sudden and unpredictable spike in sales followed by a rather abrupt decline. Examples of fad items are Silly Bandz, Beanie Babies, and Crocs. Other products, such as electric clothes washers and dryers, stay in the maturity stage for decades. Exhibit 11.2 illustrates the typical life cycle for a consumer durable good, such as a washer or dryer. In contrast, Exhibit 11.3 illustrates typical life cycles for styles (such as formal, business, or casual clothing), fashions (such as miniskirts or baggy jeans), and fads (such as leopard-print clothing). Changes in a product, its uses, its image, or its positioning can extend that product's life cycle.

The PLC concept does not tell managers the length of a product's life cycle or its duration in any stage. It does not dictate marketing strategy. It is simply a tool to help marketers forecast future events and suggest appropriate strategies.

11-6a Introductory Stage

The **introductory stage** of the PLC represents the full-scale launch of a new product into the marketplace. Computer databases for personal use, room-deodorizing

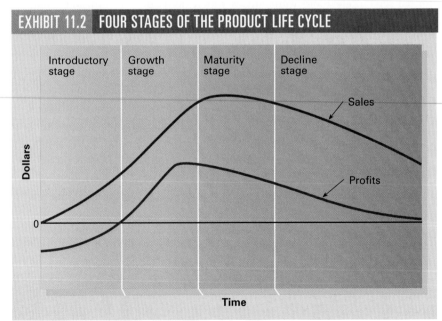

EXHIBIT 11.2 FOUR STAGES OF THE PRODUCT LIFE CYCLE

EXHIBIT 11.3 PRODUCT LIFE CYCLES FOR STYLES, FASHIONS, AND FADS

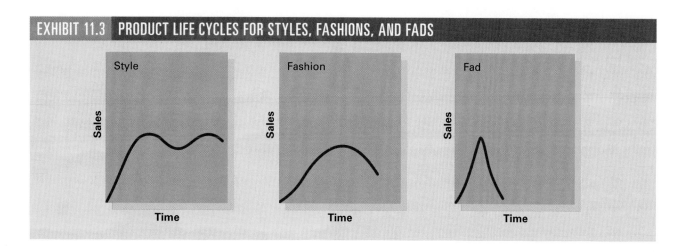

air-conditioning filters, and wind-powered home electric generators are all product categories that have recently entered the PLC. A high failure rate, little competition, frequent product modification, and limited distribution typify the introductory stage of the PLC.

Marketing costs in the introductory stage are normally high for several reasons. High dealer margins are often needed to obtain adequate distribution, and incentives are needed to get consumers to try the new product. Advertising expenses are high because of the need to educate consumers about the new product's benefits. Production costs are also often high in this stage, as product and manufacturing flaws are identified and corrected and efforts are undertaken to develop mass production economies.

Sales normally increase slowly during the introductory stage. Moreover, profits are usually negative because of R&D costs, factory tooling, and high introduction costs. The length of the introductory phase is largely determined by product characteristics, such as the product's advantages over substitute products, the educational effort required to make the product known, and management's commitment of resources to the new item. A short introductory period is usually preferred to help reduce the impact of negative earnings and cash flows. As soon as the product gets off the ground, the financial burden should begin to diminish. Also, a short introduction helps dispel some of the uncertainty as to whether the new product will be successful.

Promotion strategy in the introductory stage focuses on developing product awareness and informing consumers about the product category's potential benefits. At this stage, the communication challenge is to stimulate primary demand—demand for the product in general rather than for a specific brand. Intensive personal selling is often required to gain acceptance for the product among wholesalers and retailers. Promotion of convenience products often requires heavy consumer sampling and couponing. Shopping and specialty products demand educational advertising and personal selling to the final consumer.

11-6b Growth Stage

If a product category survives the introductory stage, it then advances to the **growth stage** of the life cycle. In this stage, sales typically grow at an increasing rate, many competitors enter the market, and large companies may start to acquire small pioneering firms. Profits rise rapidly in the growth stage, reach their peak, and begin declining as competition intensifies. Emphasis switches from primary demand promotion (e.g., promoting e-readers) to aggressive brand advertising and communication of the differences between brands (e.g., promoting Kindle versus Nook).

Distribution becomes a major key to success during the growth stage, as well as in later stages. Manufacturers scramble to sign up dealers and distributors and to build long-term relationships. Others are able to market direct to consumers using electronic media. Without adequate distribution, it is impossible to establish a strong market position.

As the economy recovers, more companies are entering the growth stage, and more workers are being hired. Because of this employment boom, staffing agencies are seeing a huge increase in revenues. On Assignment, a company that places temporary and permanent workers in several different industries, ranked third on *Fortune's* list of the fastest growing companies for 2014. In 2012, On Assignment acquired IT staffing agency ApexSystems,

growth stage the second stage of the product life cycle when sales typically grow at an increasing rate, many competitors enter the market, large companies may start to acquire small pioneering firms, and profits are healthy

becoming the second largest infotech staffing agency in the U.S. The company's stock rose 26.6 percent the day after the acquisition[35]

11-6c Maturity Stage

A period during which sales increase at a decreasing rate signals the beginning of the **maturity stage** of the life cycle. New users cannot be added indefinitely, and sooner or later the market approaches saturation. Normally, this is the longest stage of the PLC. Many major household appliances are in the maturity stage of their life cycles.

For shopping products such as durable goods and electronics, and many specialty products, annual models begin to appear during the maturity stage. Product lines are lengthened to appeal to additional market segments. Service and repair assume more important roles as manufacturers strive to distinguish their products from others. Product design changes tend to become stylistic (How can the product be made different?) rather than functional (How can the product be made better?).

As prices and profits continue to fall, marginal competitors start dropping out of the market. Dealer margins also shrink, resulting in less shelf space for mature items, lower dealer inventories, and a general reluctance to promote the product. Thus, promotion to dealers often intensifies during this stage in order to retain loyalty.

Heavy consumer promotion by the manufacturer is also required to maintain market share. Cutthroat competition during this stage can lead to price wars. Another characteristic of the maturity stage is the emergence of "niche marketers" that target narrow, well-defined, underserved segments of a market. Starbucks Coffee targets its gourmet line at new, young, affluent coffee drinkers, the only segment of the coffee market that is growing.

11-6d Decline Stage

A long-run drop in sales signals the beginning of the **decline stage**. The rate of decline is governed by how rapidly consumer tastes change or substitute products are adopted. Many convenience products and fad items lose their market overnight, leaving large inventories of unsold items, such as designer jeans. Others die more slowly. Landline telephone service

maturity stage a period during which sales increase at a decreasing rate

decline stage a long-run drop in sales

Goran Bogicevic/Shutterstock.com

Starbucks targets its gourmet line at new, young drinkers;—the only segment that is growing.

is an example of a product in the decline stage of the product life cycle. Nearly 40 percent of American homes do not have a landline, which represents a continued steady increase since 2010—and a steady drop in the use of landlines.[36] People abandoning landlines to go wireless and households replacing landlines with Internet phones have both contributed to this long-term decline.

Some firms have developed successful strategies for marketing products in the decline stage of the PLC. They eliminate all nonessential marketing expenses and let sales decline as more and more customers discontinue purchasing the products. Eventually, the product is withdrawn from the market.

11-6e Implications for Marketing Management

The new-product development process, the diffusion process, and the PLC concept all have implications for marketing managers. The funnel shape of Exhibit 11.1 indicates that many new product ideas are necessary to produce one successful new product. The new-product development process is sometimes illustrated as a decay curve with roughly half of the ideas approved at one stage rejected at the next stage. While the actual numbers vary widely among firms and industries, the relationship between the stages can be generalized. This reinforces the notion that an organized effort to generate many ideas from various sources is important for any firm that wishes to produce a continuing flow of new products.

The major implication of the diffusion process to marketing managers is that the message may need to

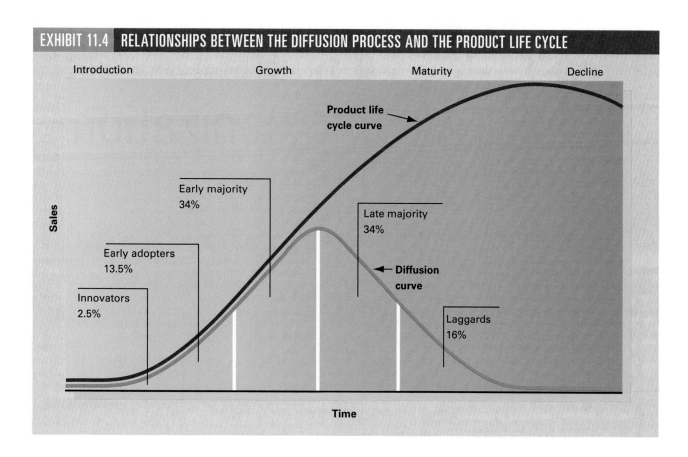

change over time. The targeted adopter and media may need to shift based on how various categories of adopters gather product information. A message developed for and targeted toward early adopters will not be perceived similarly by late majority adopters.

Exhibit 11.4 shows the relationship between the adopter categories and stages of the PLC. Note that the various categories of adopters buy products in different stages of the life cycle. Almost all sales in the maturity and decline stages represent repeat purchases.

STUDY TOOLS 11

LOCATED AT BACK OF THE TEXTBOOK
☐ Rip Out Chapter Review Card

LOCATED AT WWW.CENGAGEBRAIN.COM
☐ Review Key Terms Flashcards and create your own
☐ Track your knowledge and understanding of key concepts in marketing
☐ Complete practice and graded quizzes to prepare for tests
☐ Complete interactive content within the MKTG Online experience
☐ View the chapter highlight boxes within the MKTG Online experience

12 | Services and Nonprofit Organization Marketing

After you finish this chapter go to **PAGE 216** for **STUDY TOOLS.**

12-1 THE IMPORTANCE OF SERVICES

A service is the result of applying human or mechanical efforts to people or objects. Services involve a deed, a performance, or an effort that cannot be physically possessed. Today, the service sector substantially influences the U.S. economy. According to the Office of the United States Trade Representative, service industries accounted for 68 percent of U.S. gross domestic product (GDP) in 2014. These industries are responsible for four out of five U.S. jobs. Recent Census data shows that most service sectors reported revenue growth in 2014. The largest gains came in the real estate, administrative and support, and information services sectors.[1]

The marketing process described in Chapter 1 is the same for all types of products, whether they are goods or services. In addition, although a comparison of goods and services marketing can be beneficial, in reality it is hard to distinguish clearly between manufacturing and service firms. Indeed, many manufacturing firms can point to service as a major factor in their success. For example, maintenance and repair services offered by the manufacturer are important to buyers of copy machines. Nevertheless, services have some unique characteristics that distinguish them from goods, and marketing strategies need to be adjusted for these characteristics.

service the result of applying human or mechanical efforts to people or objects

12-2 HOW SERVICES DIFFER FROM GOODS

Services have four unique characteristics that distinguish them from goods. Services are intangible, inseparable, heterogeneous, and perishable.

12-2a Intangibility

The basic difference between services and goods is that services are intangible performances. Because of their **intangibility**, they cannot be touched, seen, tasted, heard, or felt in the same manner that goods can be sensed.

Evaluating the quality of services before or even after making a purchase is harder than evaluating the quality of goods because, compared to goods, services tend to exhibit fewer search qualities. A **search quality** is a characteristic that can be easily assessed before purchase—for instance, the color of an appliance or automobile. At the same time, services tend to exhibit more experience and credence qualities. An **experience quality** is a characteristic that can be assessed only after use, such as the quality of a meal in a restaurant. A **credence quality** is a characteristic that consumers may have difficulty assessing even after purchase because they do not have the necessary knowledge or experience. Medical and

consulting services are examples of services that exhibit credence qualities.

These characteristics also make it harder for marketers to communicate the benefits of an intangible service than to communicate the benefits of tangible goods. Thus, marketers often rely on tangible cues to communicate a service's nature and quality. For example, Travelers Insurance Company uses an umbrella symbol as a tangible reminder of the protection that insurance provides.

The facilities that customers visit, or from which services are delivered, are a critical tangible part of the total service offering. Messages about the organization are communicated to customers through such elements as the décor, the clutter or neatness of service areas, and the staff's manners and dress. Hotels know that guests form opinions quickly and are more willing than ever before to tweet them within the first fifteen minutes of

intangibility the inability of services to be touched, seen, tasted, heard, or felt in the same manner that goods can be sensed

search quality a characteristic that can be easily assessed before purchase

experience quality a characteristic that can be assessed only after use

credence quality a characteristic that consumers may have difficulty assessing even after purchase because they do not have the necessary knowledge or experience

their stay. Some hotels go to great lengths to make their guests feel at home right away. For example, employees at Ritz-Carlton hotels are trained to greet guests, bid them goodbye, and always address them by name. If a guest asks for directions to another part of the hotel, employees are required to escort them rather than pointing or giving complicated verbal directions.[2]

12-2b Inseparability

Goods are produced, sold, and then consumed. In contrast, services are often sold, produced, and consumed at the same time. In other words, their production and consumption are inseparable activities. This **inseparability** means that, because consumers must be present during the production of services like haircuts or surgery, they are actually involved in the production of the services they buy. That type of consumer involvement is rare in goods manufacturing.

Simultaneous production and consumption also means that services normally cannot be produced in a centralized location and consumed in decentralized locations, as goods typically are. Services are also inseparable from the perspective of the service provider. Thus, the quality of service that firms are able to deliver depends on the quality of their employees.

12-2c Heterogeneity

One great strength of McDonald's is consistency. Whether customers order a Big Mac in Chicago or Seattle, they know exactly what they are going to get. This is not the case with many service providers. Because services have greater **heterogeneity**, or variability of inputs and outputs, they tend to be less standardized and uniform than goods. For example, physicians in a group practice or barbers in a barbershop differ within each group in their technical and interpersonal skills. Because services tend to be labor intensive and production and consumption are inseparable, consistency and quality control can be hard to achieve.

Standardization and training help increase consistency and reliability. In the information technology sector, a number of certification programs are available to ensure that technicians are capable of working on (and within) complex enterprise software systems. Certifications such as the Cisco Certified Network Associate, CompTIA Security+, and Microsoft Certified Professional ensure a consistency of knowledge and ability among those who can pass these programs' rigorous exams.[3]

12-2d Perishability

Perishability is the fourth characteristic of services. **Perishability** refers to the inability of services to be stored, warehoused, or inventoried. An empty hotel room or airplane seat produces no revenue that day. The revenue is lost. Yet service organizations are often forced to turn away full-price customers during peak periods.

One of the most important challenges in many service industries is finding ways to synchronize supply and demand. The philosophy that some revenue is better than none has prompted many hotels to offer deep discounts on weekends and during the off-season.

12-3 SERVICE QUALITY

Because of the four unique characteristics of services, service quality is more difficult to define and measure than is the quality of tangible goods. Business executives rank the improvement of service quality as one of the most critical challenges facing them today.

12-3a Evaluating Service Quality

Research has shown that customers evaluate service quality by the following five components:

- **Reliability:** the ability to perform the service dependably, accurately, and consistently. Reliability is performing the service right the first time. This

Quality service is a must if a company wants to keep the customers coming back.

inseparability the inability of the production and consumption of a service to be separated; consumers must be present during the production

heterogeneity the variability of the inputs and outputs of services, which causes services to tend to be less standardized and uniform than goods

perishability the inability of services to be stored, warehoused, or inventoried

reliability the ability to perform a service dependably, accurately, and consistently

component has been found to be the one most important to consumers.

- **Responsiveness:** the ability to provide prompt service. Examples of responsiveness include calling the customer back quickly, serving lunch fast to someone who is in a hurry, or mailing a transaction slip immediately. The ultimate in responsiveness is offering service twenty-four hours a day, seven days a week.
- **Assurance:** the knowledge and courtesy of employees and their ability to convey trust. Skilled employees, who treat customers with respect and make customers feel that they can trust the firm, exemplify assurance.
- **Empathy:** caring, individualized attention to customers. Firms whose employees recognize customers and learn their specific requirements are providing empathy.
- **Tangibles:** the physical evidence of the service. The tangible parts of a service include the physical facilities, tools, and equipment used to provide the service, as well as the appearance of personnel.[4]

Overall service quality is measured by combining customers' evaluations for all five components.

12-3b The Gap Model of Service Quality

A model of service quality called the **gap model** identifies five gaps that can cause problems in service delivery and influence customer evaluations of service quality.[5] These gaps are illustrated in Exhibit 12.1.

- **Gap 1:** the gap between what customers want and what management thinks customers want. This gap results from a lack of understanding or a misinterpretation of the customers' needs, wants, or desires. A firm that does little or no customer satisfaction research is likely to experience this gap. To close gap 1, firms must stay attuned to customer wishes by researching customer needs and satisfaction.
- **Gap 2:** the gap between what management thinks customers want and the quality specifications that management develops to provide the service. Essentially, this gap is the result of management's inability to translate customers' needs into delivery systems within the firm. For example, KFC used to rate its managers according to "chicken efficiency," or how much chicken they threw away at closing; customers who came in late would either have to wait for chicken to be cooked or settle for chicken several hours old.

responsiveness the ability to provide prompt service

assurance the knowledge and courtesy of employees and their ability to convey trust

empathy caring, individualized attention to customers

tangibles the physical evidence of a service, including the physical facilities, tools, and equipment used to provide the service

gap model a model identifying five gaps that can cause problems in service delivery and influence customer evaluations of service quality

Has starbucks fallen into gap 3?

Starbucks used to stress the importance of "legendary service" during the company's extensive training program for new hires. However, a rash of labor cuts in recent years has both diminished the quality of Starbucks's barista training and forced employees to work longer hours with less help and resources—often resulting in a single stressed-out barista frantically working to serve a growing line of customers. The creeping incompetence, inaccuracy, and inattentiveness of Starbucks baristas was satirized in a Saturday Night Live skit in which even the automated Verismo espresso machine was neglectful and derisive toward its customers.[6]

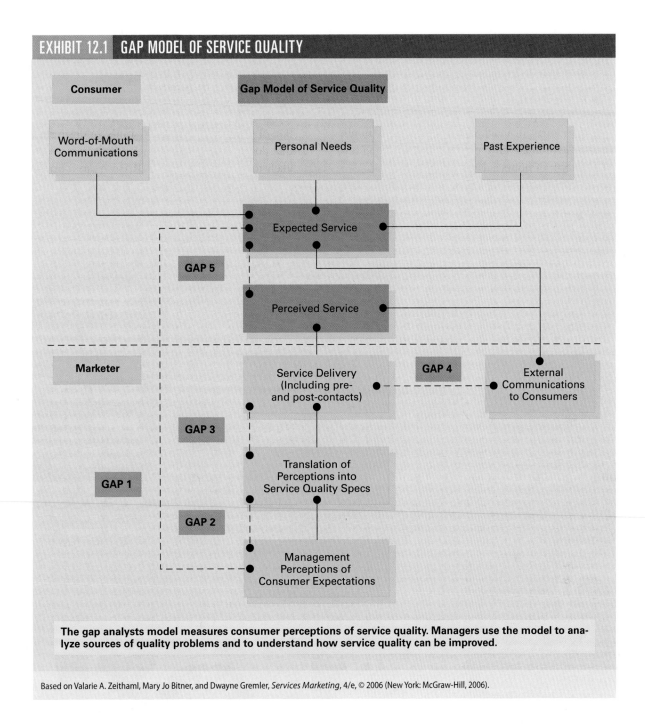

EXHIBIT 12.1   GAP MODEL OF SERVICE QUALITY

The gap analysts model measures consumer perceptions of service quality. Managers use the model to analyze sources of quality problems and to understand how service quality can be improved.

Based on Valarie A. Zeithaml, Mary Jo Bitner, and Dwayne Gremler, *Services Marketing*, 4/e, © 2006 (New York: McGraw-Hill, 2006).

- **Gap 3:** the gap between the service quality specifications and the service that is actually provided. If both gaps 1 and 2 have been closed, then gap 3 is due to the inability of management and employees to do what should be done. Management needs to ensure that employees have the skills and the proper tools to perform their jobs. Other techniques that help to close gap 3 are training employees so they know what management expects and encouraging teamwork.

- **Gap 4:** the gap between what the company provides and what the customer is told it provides. This is

clearly a communication gap. It may include misleading or deceptive advertising campaigns promising more than the firm can deliver or doing "whatever it takes" to get the business. To close this gap, companies need to create realistic customer expectations through honest, accurate communication about what the firms can provide.

- **Gap 5:** the gap between the service that customers receive and the service they want. This gap can be positive or negative. For example, if a patient expects to wait twenty minutes in the physician's office before

seeing the physician but actually waits only ten minutes, the patient's evaluation of service quality will be high. However, a 40-minute wait would result in a lower evaluation.

When one or more of these gaps is large, service quality is perceived as low. As the gaps shrink, service quality perception improves. In early 2013, Fifth Third Bank joined a growing number of financial institutions working quickly to close a persistent, gaping gap 1—customers' desire for full-featured mobile banking. To meet the needs of highly mobile, technologically tuned-in customers, Fifth Third launched a powerful mobile app whereby customers can view transactions, pay bills, transfer funds, or deposit checks simply by taking pictures of them with their smartphones. "The ways in which consumers interact with their bank are constantly evolving," said Larry McClanahan, vice president and director of Digital Delivery for Fifth Third Bank. "The enhancements we've made . . . reflect this shift in consumer preference and expectations."[7]

Several other companies consistently get their service quality right. According to MSN, the top five companies in terms of great customer service are:

1. Amazon
2. Hilton Worldwide
3. Marriott International
4. Chick-fil-A
5. American Express[8]

These companies have three core beliefs in common: good service starts at the top, service is seen as a continual challenge, and companies work best when people want to work for them.

12-4 MARKETING MIXES FOR SERVICES

Services' unique characteristics—-intangibility, inseparability of production and consumption, heterogeneity, and perishability—make marketing more challenging. Elements of the marketing mix (product, place, promotion, and pricing) need to be adjusted to meet the special needs created by these characteristics.

12-4a Product (Service) Strategy

A product, as defined in Chapter 10, is everything a person receives in an exchange. In the case of a service organization, the product offering is intangible and consists in large part of a process or a series of processes. Product strategies for service offerings include decisions on the type of process involved, core and supplementary services, standardization or customization of the service product, and the service mix.

SERVICE AS A PROCESS Two broad categories of things get processed in service organizations: people and objects. In some cases, the process is physical, or tangible, while in others the process is intangible. Based on these characteristics, service processes can be placed into one of four categories:

- *People processing* takes place when the service is directed at a customer. Examples are transportation services and health care.

- *Possession processing* occurs when the service is directed at customers' physical possessions. Examples are lawn care, dry cleaning, and veterinary services.

- *Mental stimulus processing* refers to services directed at people's minds. Examples are theater performances and education.

- *Information processing* describes services that use technology or brainpower directed at a customer's assets. Examples are insurance and consulting.[9]

Because customers' experiences and involvement differ for each of these types of services, marketing strategies may also differ. For example, people-processing services require customers to enter the *service factory*, which is a physical location, such as an aircraft, a physician's office, or a hair salon. In contrast, possession-processing services typically do not require the presence of the customer in the service factory. Marketing strategies for the former would therefore focus more on an attractive, comfortable physical environment and employee training on employee–customer interaction issues than would strategies for the latter.

CORE AND SUPPLEMENTARY SERVICE PRODUCTS The service offering can be viewed as a bundle of activities that includes the **core service**, which is the most basic benefit the customer is buying, and a group of **supplementary services** that support or enhance the core service. Exhibit 12.2 illustrates these concepts for a luxury hotel. The core service is providing bedrooms for rent which involves people processing. The supplementary services, some of which involve information processing, include food services, reservations, parking, phone, and television services.

> **core service** the most basic benefit the consumer is buying
>
> **supplementary services** a group of services that support or enhance the core service

EXHIBIT 12.2 | CORE AND SUPPLEMENTARY SERVICES FOR A LUXURY HOTEL

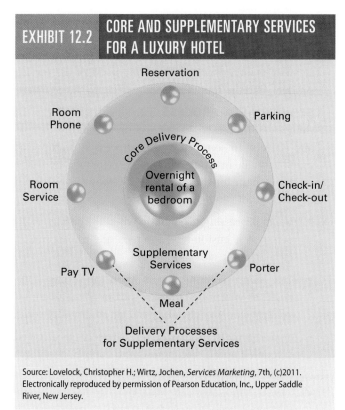

Source: Lovelock, Christopher H.; Wirtz, Jochen, *Services Marketing*, 7th, (c)2011. Electronically reproduced by permission of Pearson Education, Inc., Upper Saddle River, New Jersey.

In many service industries, the core service becomes a commodity as competition increases. Thus, firms usually emphasize supplementary services to create a competitive advantage. On the other hand, some firms are positioning themselves in the marketplace by greatly reducing supplementary services.

mass customization a strategy that uses technology to deliver customized services on a mass basis

CUSTOMIZATION/STANDARDIZATION An important issue in developing the service offering is whether to customize or standardize it. Customized services are more flexible and respond to individual customers' needs. They also usually command a higher price. Standardized services are more efficient and cost less.

Instead of choosing to either standardize or customize a service, a firm may incorporate elements of both by adopting an emerging strategy called **mass customization**. Mass customization uses technology to deliver customized services on a mass basis, which results in giving each customer whatever she or he asks for. Application Programming Interface (API) banking represents a new way to think about banking services and how to deliver these services to different customer groups. For example, API banking could allow a bank to offer Millennials a mobile banking app with tools to pay down student debt while offering Baby Boomers a similar app but with special services focused on retirement planning.[10]

THE SERVICE MIX Most service organizations market more than one service. For example, TruGreen offers lawn care, shrub care, carpet cleaning, and industrial lawn services. Each organization's service mix represents a set of opportunities, risks, and challenges. Each part of the service mix should make a different contribution to achieving the firm's goals. To succeed, each service may also need a different level of financial support. Designing a service strategy, therefore, means

Joleon Lescott and James Vaughn design customized Nike trainers in Liverpool, England's NikeTown iD Studio. Nike iD is an example of mass customization, employing technology to deliver customized shoes, apparel and bags on a mass basis.

deciding what new services to introduce to which target market, what existing services to maintain, and what services to eliminate.

12-4b Place (Distribution) Strategy

Distribution strategies for service organizations must focus on such issues as convenience, number of outlets, direct versus indirect distribution, location, and scheduling. A key factor influencing the selection of a service provider is *convenience*. An interesting example of this is Mac & Mia, a premium trunk club for children's clothing. This service targets parents of small children who have little or no time to shop. After a parent completes a style profile for his or her child at Mac & Mia's Web site, a company representative fills a box with a selection of hand-picked clothing and accessories and ships it out. Parents keep what they want and return what they don't within five days using an included prepaid envelope. The company provides busy parents an easy, fun, and convenient way to buy needed items for their kids.[11]

An important distribution objective for many service firms is the number of outlets to use or the number of outlets to open during a certain time. Generally, the intensity of distribution should meet, but not exceed, the target market's needs and preferences. Having too few outlets may inconvenience customers; having too many outlets may boost costs unnecessarily. Intensity of distribution may also depend on the image desired. Having only a few outlets may make the service seem more exclusive or selective.

The next service distribution decision is whether to distribute services to end users *directly* or *indirectly* through other firms. Because of the intangible nature of services, many service firms have to use direct distribution or franchising. Examples include legal, medical, accounting, and personal-care services. The newest form of direct distribution is the Internet. Most major airlines are now using online services to sell tickets directly to consumers, which results in lower distribution costs for the airlines. Other firms with standardized service packages have developed indirect channels using independent intermediaries. For example, Bank of America offers teller and loan services to customers in small satellite facilities at Albertsons grocery stores in Texas.

The *location* of a service most clearly reveals the relationship between its target market strategy and distribution strategy. For time-dependent service providers such as airlines, physicians, and dentists, *scheduling* is often a more important factor.

12-4c Promotion Strategy

Consumers and business users have more trouble evaluating services than goods because services are less tangible. In turn, marketers have more trouble promoting intangible services than tangible goods. Here are four promotion strategies they can try:

- **Stressing tangible cues:** A tangible cue is a concrete symbol of the service offering. To make their intangible services more tangible, hotels turn down the bedcovers and put mints on the pillows.

- **Using personal information sources:** A personal information source is someone consumers are familiar with (such as a celebrity) or someone they admire or can relate to personally. Service firms may seek to simulate positive word-of-mouth communication among present and prospective customers by using real customers in their ads.

- **Creating a strong organizational image:** One way to create an image is to manage the evidence, including the physical environment of the service facility, the appearance of the service employees, and the tangible items associated with a service (such as stationery, bills, and business cards). For example, McDonald's golden arches are instantly recognizable. Another way to create an image is through branding.

- **Engaging in postpurchase communication:** Postpurchase communication refers to the follow-up

Celebrity is a powerful promotional tool for services and nonprofits alike. Here, actor and Eastern Congo Initiative founder, Ben Affleck, testifies before a Senate Foreign Relations Committee hearing on the Congo.

activities that a service firm might engage in after a customer transaction. Postcard surveys, telephone calls, and other types of follow-up show customers that their feedback matters.

12-4d Price Strategy

Considerations in pricing a service are similar to the pricing considerations to be discussed in Chapter 19. However, the unique characteristics of services present two special pricing challenges.

First, in order to price a service, it is important to define the unit of service consumption. For example, should pricing be based on completing a specific service task (cutting a customer's hair), or should it be time based (how long it takes to cut a customer's hair)? Some services include the consumption of goods, such as food and beverages. Restaurants charge customers for food and drink rather than the use of a table and chairs.

Second, for services that are composed of multiple elements, the issue is whether pricing should be based on a "bundle" of elements or whether each element should be priced separately. A bundled price may be preferable when consumers dislike having to pay "extra" for every part of the service (e.g., paying extra for baggage or food on an airplane), and it is simpler for the firm to administer. Alternatively, customers may not want to pay for service elements they do not use. Many furniture stores now have "unbundled" delivery charges from the price of the furniture. Customers who wish to can pick up the furniture at the store, saving on the delivery fee.

Marketers should set performance objectives when pricing each service. Three categories of pricing objectives have been suggested:

- Revenue-oriented pricing focuses on maximizing the surplus of income over costs. This is the same approach that many manufacturing companies use. A limitation of this approach is that determining costs can be difficult for many services.

- Operations-oriented pricing seeks to match supply and demand by varying prices. For example, matching hotel demand to the number of available rooms can be achieved by raising prices at peak times and decreasing them during slow times.

- Patronage-oriented pricing tries to maximize the number of customers using the service. Thus, prices vary with different market segments' ability to pay, and methods of payment (such as credit) are offered that increase the likelihood of a purchase. Senior citizen and student discounts at movie theaters and restaurants are examples of patronage-oriented pricing.[12]

A firm may need to use more than one type of pricing objective. In fact, all three objectives probably need to be included to some degree in a pricing strategy, although the importance of each type may vary depending on the type of service provided, the prices that competitors are charging, the differing ability of various customer segments to pay, or the opportunity to negotiate price. For customized services (such as construction services), customers may also have the ability to negotiate a price.

 ## 12-5 RELATIONSHIP MARKETING IN SERVICES

Many services involve ongoing interaction between the service organization and the customer. Thus, they can benefit from relationship marketing, the strategy described in Chapter 1, as a means of attracting, developing, and retaining customer relationships. The idea is to develop strong loyalty by creating satisfied customers who will buy additional services from the firm and are unlikely to switch to a competitor. Satisfied customers are also likely to engage in positive word-of-mouth communication, thereby helping to bring in new customers.

Many businesses have found that it is more cost-effective to hang on to the customers they have than to focus only on attracting new ones. A bank executive, for example, found that increasing customer retention by two percent can have the same effect on profits as reducing costs by 10 percent.

Services that purchasers receive on a continuing basis (e.g., cable television, banking, insurance) can be considered membership services. This type of service naturally lends itself to relationship marketing. When services involve discrete transactions (e.g., in a movie theater, at a restaurant, or on public transportation), it may be more difficult to build membership-type relationships with customers. Nevertheless, services involving discrete transactions may be transformed into membership relationships using marketing tools. For example, the service could be sold in bulk (e.g., a theater series subscription or a commuter pass on public transportation). Or a service firm could offer special benefits to customers who choose to register with the firm (e.g., loyalty programs for hotels and airlines). The service firm that has a more formalized relationship with its customers has an advantage because it knows who its customers are and how and when they use the services offered.[13]

Relationship marketing can be practiced at four levels:

- **Level 1: Financial.** The firm uses pricing incentives to encourage customers to continue doing business with it. Frequent-flyer programs are an example of level 1 relationship marketing. This level of relationship marketing is the least effective in the long term because its price-based advantage is easily imitated by other firms.

- **Level 2: Social.** This level of relationship marketing also uses pricing incentives but seeks to build social bonds with customers. The firm stays in touch with customers, learns about their needs, and designs services to meet those needs. Level 2 relationship marketing is often more effective than level 1 relationship marketing.

- **Level 3: Customization**. A customization approach encourages customer loyalty through intimate knowledge of individual customers (often referred to as *customer intimacy*) and the development of one-to-one solutions to fit customers' needs.

- **Level 4: Structural.** At this level, the firm again uses financial and social bonds but adds structural bonds to the formula. Structural bonds are developed by offering value-added services that are not readily available from other firms.[14] The MGM Grand hotel in Las Vegas offers an entire floor of Stay Well suites that feature air purification systems to reduce allergens and toxins in the air; healthy energizing lighting developed to reduce jet lag and regulate circadian rhythms; and vitamin C-infused water in showers to neutralize chlorine and soften skin and hair.[15]

Companies like Google have designed and instituted a wide variety of programs such as flextime, on-site daycare and concierge service for their employees.

organic foods, free health and dental insurance, subsidized massages, nap pods, and on-site phycians.[16]

12-6 INTERNAL MARKETING IN SERVICE FIRMS

Services are performances, so the quality of a firm's employees is an important part of building long-term relationships with customers. Employees who like their jobs and are satisfied with the firm they work for are more likely to deliver superior service to customers. In other words, a firm that makes its employees happy has a better chance of retaining customers. Thus, it is critical that service firms practice **internal marketing**, which means treating employees as customers and developing systems and benefits that satisfy their needs. While this strategy may also apply to goods manufacturers, it is even more critical in service firms. This is because in service industries, employees deliver the brand promise—their performance as a brand representative—directly to customers. To satisfy employees, companies have designed and instituted a wide variety of programs such as flextime, on-site day care, and concierge services. Google offers its employees benefits such as free chef-prepared

12-7 NONPROFIT ORGANIZATION MARKETING

A nonprofit organization is an organization that exists to achieve some goal other than the usual business goals of profit, market share, or return on investment. Both nonprofit organizations and private-sector service firms market intangible products, and both often require the customer to be present during the production process. Both for-profit and nonprofit services vary greatly from producer to producer and from day to day, even from the same producer.

Few people realize that nonprofit organizations account for more than twenty percent of the economic activity in the United States. The cost of government (i.e., taxes), the predominant form of nonprofit organization, has become the biggest single item in the American family budget—more than housing, food, or health care. Together, federal, state, and local governments collect tax revenues that amount to more than one-third of the U.S. GDP. In addition to government entities, nonprofit organizations include hundreds of thousands of private museums, theaters, schools, and churches.

internal marketing treating employees as customers and developing systems and benefits that satisfy their needs

nonprofit organization an organization that exists to achieve some goal other than the usual business goals of profit, market share, or return on investment

12-7a What Is Nonprofit Organization Marketing?

Nonprofit organization marketing is the effort by nonprofit organizations to bring about mutually satisfying exchanges with target markets. Although these organizations vary substantially in size and purpose and operate in different environments, most perform the following marketing activities:

- Identify the customers they wish to serve or attract (although they usually use other terms, such as clients, patients, members, or sponsors)

- Explicitly or implicitly specify objectives

- Develop, manage, and eliminate programs and services

- Decide on prices to charge (although they use other terms, such as fees, donations, tuition, fares, fines, or rates)

- Schedule events or programs, and determine where they will be held or where services will be offered

- Communicate their availability through brochures, signs, public service announcements, or advertisements

Often, the nonprofit organizations that carry out these functions do not realize they are engaged in marketing.

12-7b Unique Aspects of Nonprofit Organization Marketing Strategies

Like their counterparts in business organizations, nonprofit managers develop marketing strategies to bring about mutually satisfying exchanges with target markets. However, marketing in nonprofit organizations is unique in many ways—including the setting of marketing objectives, the selection of target markets, and the development of appropriate marketing mixes.

OBJECTIVES In the private sector, the profit motive is both an objective for guiding decisions and a criterion for evaluating results. Nonprofit organizations do not seek to make a profit for redistribution to owners or shareholders. Rather, their focus is often on generating enough funds to cover expenses.

Most nonprofit organizations are expected to provide equitable, effective, and efficient services that respond to the wants and preferences of multiple constituencies. These include users, payers, donors, politicians, appointed officials, the media, and the general public. Nonprofit organizations cannot measure their success or failure in strictly financial terms.

Singer, Nick Lachey, volunteered his time at the Freestore Foodbank in Cincinnati, as he promoted the kick-off of The Everybody Wins Tour. Having a celebrity as a spokesperson is something that organizations regularly do to draw attention to their cause.

The lack of a financial "bottom line" and the existence of multiple, diverse, intangible, and sometimes vague or conflicting objectives make prioritizing objectives, making decisions, and evaluating performance hard for nonprofit managers. They must often use approaches different from the ones commonly used in the private sector.

TARGET MARKETS Three issues relating to target markets are unique to nonprofit organizations:

- **Apathetic or strongly opposed targets:** Private-sector organizations usually give priority to developing those market segments that are most likely to respond to particular offerings. In contrast, nonprofit organizations must often target those who are apathetic about or strongly opposed to receiving their services, such as vaccinations and psychological counseling.

- **Pressure to adopt undifferentiated segmentation strategies:** Nonprofit organizations often adopt undifferentiated strategies (see Chapter 8) by default. Sometimes they fail to recognize the advantages of targeting, or an undifferentiated approach may appear to offer economies of scale and low per-capita costs. In other instances, nonprofit organizations are pressured or required to serve the maximum number of people by targeting the average user.

- **Complementary positioning:** The main role of many nonprofit organizations is to provide services, with available resources, to those who are not adequately served by private-sector organizations. As a result, the nonprofit organization must often complement, rather

nonprofit organization marketing the effort by nonprofit organizations to bring about mutually satisfying exchanges with target markets

than compete with, the efforts of others. The positioning task is to identify underserved market segments and to develop marketing programs that match their needs rather than target the niches that may be most profitable. For example, a university library may see itself as complementing the services of the public library rather than as competing with it.

PRODUCT DECISIONS There are three product-related distinctions between business and nonprofit organizations:

- **Benefit complexity:** Nonprofit organizations often market complex behaviors or ideas. Examples include the need to exercise or eat right and the need to quit smoking. The benefits that a person receives are complex, long term, and intangible, and therefore are more difficult to communicate to consumers.

- **Benefit strength:** The benefit strength of many nonprofit offerings is quite weak or indirect. What are the direct, personal benefits to you of driving 55 miles per hour or donating blood? In contrast, most private-sector service organizations can offer customers direct, personal benefits in an exchange relationship.

- **Involvement:** Many nonprofit organizations market products that elicit very low involvement ("Prevent forest fires") or very high involvement ("Stop smoking"). The typical range for private-sector goods is much narrower. Traditional promotional tools may be inadequate to motivate adoption of either low- or high-involvement products.

PLACE (DISTRIBUTION) DECISIONS A nonprofit organization's capacity for distributing its service offerings to potential customer groups when and where they want them is typically a key variable in determining the success of those service offerings. For example, many large universities have one or more satellite campus locations to provide easier access for students in other areas. Some educational institutions also offer classes to students at off-campus locations through the use of interactive video technology or at home via the Internet.

The extent to which a service depends on fixed facilities has important implications for distribution decisions. Services like rail transit and lake fishing can be delivered only at specific points. Many nonprofit services, however, do not depend on special facilities.

PROMOTION DECISIONS Many nonprofit organizations are explicitly or implicitly prohibited from advertising, thus limiting their promotion options. Most federal agencies fall into this category. Other nonprofit organizations simply do not have the resources to retain advertising agencies, promotion consultants, or marketing staff.

Nonprofit organizations have a few special promotion resources to call on, however:

- **Professional volunteers:** Nonprofit organizations often seek out marketing, sales, and advertising professionals to help them develop and implement promotion strategies. In some instances, an advertising agency donates its services in exchange for potential long-term benefits. Donated services create goodwill; personal contacts; and general awareness of the donor's organization, reputation, and competency.

- **Sales promotion activities:** Sales promotion activities that use existing services or other resources are increasingly being used to draw attention to the offerings of nonprofit organizations. Sometimes nonprofit charities even team up with other companies for promotional activities.

- **Public service advertising:** A **public service advertisement (PSA)** is an announcement that promotes a program of a federal, state, or local government or of a nonprofit organization. Unlike a commercial advertiser, the sponsor of the PSA does not pay for the time or space. Instead, it is donated by the medium. PSAs are used, for example, to help educate students about the dangers of misusing and abusing prescription drugs, as well as where to seek treatment for substance abuse problems.

PRICING DECISIONS Five key characteristics distinguish the pricing decisions of nonprofit organizations from those of the profit sector:

- **Pricing objectives:** The main pricing objective in the profit sector is revenue or, more specifically, profit maximization, sales maximization, or target return on sales or investment. Many nonprofit organizations must also be concerned about revenue. Often, however, nonprofit organizations seek to either partially or fully defray costs rather than to achieve a profit for distribution to stockholders. Nonprofit organizations also seek to redistribute income—for instance, through taxation and sliding-scale fees. Moreover, they strive to allocate resources fairly among individuals or households or across geographic or political boundaries.

- **Nonfinancial prices:** In many nonprofit situations, consumers are not charged a monetary price but instead must absorb nonmonetary costs. The importance of those costs is illustrated by the large number of eligible citizens who do not take

> **public service advertisement (PSA)** an announcement that promotes a program of a federal, state, or local government or of a nonprofit organization

First Lady, Chirlane McCray announces a $78 million budget proposed by her husband, Mayor Bill de Blasio, for mental health services at a press conference at the Empire State Building.

advantage of so-called "free" services for the poor. In many public assistance programs, about half the people who are eligible do not participate. Nonmonetary costs include time, embarrassment, and effort.

- **Indirect payment:** Indirect payment through taxes is common to marketers of "free" services, such as libraries, fire protection, and police protection. Indirect payment is not a common practice in the profit sector.

- **Separation between payers and users:** By design, the services of many charitable organizations are provided for those who are relatively poor and are largely paid for by those who are better off financially. Although examples of separation between payers and users can be found in the profit sector (such as insurance claims), the practice is much less prevalent.

- **Below-cost pricing:** An example of below-cost pricing is university tuition. Virtually all private and public colleges and universities price their services below full cost.

12-8 GLOBAL ISSUES IN SERVICES MARKETING

The international marketing of services is a major part of global business, and the United States has become the world's largest exporter of services. Competition in international services is increasing rapidly, but many U.S. service industries have been able to enter the global marketplace because of their competitive advantages. U.S. banks, for example, have advantages in customer service and collections management.

For both for-profit and nonprofit service firms, the first step toward success in the global marketplace is determining the nature of the company's core products. Then, the marketing mix elements (additional services, place, promotion, pricing, and distribution) should be designed to take into account each country's cultural, technological, and political environment.

STUDY TOOLS 12

LOCATED AT BACK OF THE TEXTBOOK
☐ Rip out Chapter Review Card

LOCATED AT WWW.CENGAGEBRAIN.COM
☐ Review Key Terms Flashcards and create your own
☐ Track your knowledge and understanding of key concepts in marketing
☐ Complete practice and graded quizzes to prepare for tests
☐ Complete interactive content within the MKTG Online experience
☐ View the chapter highlight boxes within the MKTG Online experience

Supply Chain Management and Marketing Channels

LEARNING OUTCOMES

After studying this chapter, you will be able to...

13-1 Define the terms *supply chain* and *supply chain management* and discuss the benefits of supply chain management

13-2 Discuss the concepts of internal and external supply chain integration and explain why each of these types of integration is important

13-3 Identify the eight key processes of excellent supply chain management and discuss how each of these processes affects the end customer

13-4 Understand the importance of sustainable supply chain management to modern business operations

13-5 Discuss how new technology and emerging trends are impacting the practice of supply chain management

13-6 Explain what marketing channels and channel intermediaries are and describe their functions and activities

13-7 Describe common channel structures and strategies and the factors that influence their choice

13-8 Discuss omnichannel and multichannel marketing in both B-to-B and B-to-C structures and explain why these concepts are important

After you finish this chapter go to **PAGE 242** for **STUDY TOOLS.**

13-1 SUPPLY CHAINS AND SUPPLY CHAIN MANAGEMENT

Many modern companies are turning to supply chain management for competitive advantage. A company's **supply chain** includes all of the companies involved in the upstream and downstream flow of products, services, finances, and information, extending from initial suppliers (the point of origin) to the ultimate customer (the point of consumption). The goal of **supply chain management** is to coordinate and integrate all of the activities performed by supply chain members into a seamless process, from the source to the point of consumption, ultimately giving supply chain managers "total visibility and control" of the materials, processes, money, and finished products both inside and outside the company they work for. The philosophy behind

supply chain the connected chain of all of the business entities, both internal and external to the company, that perform or support the logistics function

supply chain management a management system that coordinates and integrates all of the activities performed by supply chain members into a seamless process, from the source to the point of consumption, resulting in enhanced customer and economic value

supply chain management is that by visualizing and exerting control over the entire supply chain, supply chain managers can balance supply and demand needs, maximize strengths, and increase efficiencies at each level of the chain. Understanding and integrating supply and demand-related information at every level enables supply chain managers to optimize their decisions, reduce waste, and respond quickly to sudden changes in supply or demand.

> In today's marketplace, products are being driven by customer demand, and businesses' need to balance demand with supply in order to ensure economic profits.

Supply chain management, when performed well, reflects a completely customer-driven management philosophy. In the mass production era, manufacturers produced standardized products that were "pushed" down through marketing channels to consumers, who were convinced by salespeople to buy whatever was produced. In today's marketplace, however, customers who expect to receive product configurations and services matched to their unique needs are driving demand. The focus of businesses has shifted to determining how products and services are being "pulled" into the marketplace by customers, and on partnering with members of the supply chain to enhance customer value. For example, when Rolls-Royce launched its Ad Personam customer value program, the company used a build-to-order system that allowed every customer to design his or her car with more than a million combinations of leather, fabric, wood, and paint.[1] This differed from the mass-manufacturing approach companies used historically, whereby a company's focus on efficiency determined a far narrower range of cars and custom options.

This reversal of the flow of demand from "push" to "pull" has resulted in a radical reformulation of traditional marketing, production, and distribution functions toward a philosophy of **supply chain agility**. Agile companies synchronize their activities through the sharing of supply and demand market information, spend more time than their competitors focusing on activities that create direct customer benefits, partner closely with suppliers and service providers to reduce customer wait times for products, and constantly seek to reduce supply chain complexity through the evaluation and reduction (or elimination) of stock-keeping units (SKUs) that customers aren't buying, among other strategies. By managing the product pipeline in this way, companies are able to reduce supply chain costs while at the same time offering better service levels, and in doing so, deliver more desirable products at better prices to customers.

13-1a Benefits of Effective Supply Chain Management

Supply chain management is a key means of differentiation for a firm, and therefore represents a critical component in marketing and corporate strategy. Companies that focus on supply chain management commonly report lower inventory, transportation, warehousing, and packaging costs; greater logistical flexibility; improved customer service; and higher revenues. Research has shown a clear relationship between supply chain performance

supply chain agility an operational strategy focused on creating inventory velocity and operational flexibility simultaneously in the supply chain

supply chain orientation a system of management practices that are consistent with a "systems thinking" approach

In a supply chain, agility which involves being flexible, like star athletes, allows companies to adapt to customer needs.

and both profitability and company value. Additionally, because well-managed supply chains are able to provide better value to customers with only marginal incremental expenditure on company assets, best-in-class supply chain companies such as Kimberly-Clark are becoming significantly more valuable investments for investors. Kimberly-Clark re-organized its supply chains by reducing distribution centers, increasing flexibility, and making its supply chain more "demand-driven." As a result, the company decreased forecasting errors by up to 35 percent each week, reduced fuel consumption by 2.4 million gallons per year, and reduced overall supply chain costs by millions of dollars per year[2]—all of which positively impact the company's bottom line.

13-2 SUPPLY CHAIN INTEGRATION

A key principle of supply chain management is that multiple entities (firms and/or their functional areas) should work together to perform tasks as a single, unified system, rather than as multiple individual units acting in isolation. Companies in a world-class supply chain combine their resources, capabilities, and innovations across multiple business boundaries so they are used for the best interest of the entire supply chain as a whole. The goal is that the overall performance of the supply chain will be greater than the sum of its parts.

As companies become increasingly focused on supply chain management, they come to possess a **supply chain orientation**. This means that they develop management practices that are consistent with a "systems thinking" approach. Supply chain oriented firms possess five characteristics that, in combination, set them apart from their partners:

1. *They are credible.* They have the capability to deliver on the promises they make.

2. *They are benevolent.* They are willing to accept short-term risks on behalf of others; are committed to others, and invest in others' success.

3. *They are cooperative.* They work with rather than against their partners when seeking to achieve goals.

4. *They have the support of top managers.* These managers possess the vision required to do things that benefit the entire supply chain in the short run so that they can enjoy greater company successes in the long run.

5. *They are effective at conducting and directing supply chain activity.* Thereby, they are better off in the long run financially than those who are not.

Management practices that reflect a highly coordinated effort between supply chain firms or across business functions within the same or different firms are "integrated." In other words, **supply chain integration** occurs when multiple firms or their functional areas in a supply chain coordinate business processes so they are seamlessly linked to one another. In a world-class supply chain, the customer may not know where the business activities of one company or business unit end and where those of another begin—each actor keeps their own interests in mind, but all appear to be reading from the same script, and from time to time, each makes sacrifices that benefit the performance of the system as a whole.

In the modern supply chain, integration can be either internal or external to a specific company or, ideally, both. From an internal perspective, the very best companies develop a managerial orientation toward **demand-supply integration (DSI).** Under the DSI philosophy, those functional areas in a company charged with creating customer demand (such as marketing, sales, or research/development) communicate frequently and are synchronized with the parts of the business charged with fulfilling the created demand (purchasing, manufacturing, and logistics). This type of alignment enhances customer satisfaction by ensuring that, for example, salespeople make promises to customers that can actually be delivered on by the company's logistics arm, or that raw materials being purchased actually meet customer specifications before they are placed into production. Simultaneously, the company gains efficiencies from ordering and using only those materials that lead directly to sales. In short, companies operating under a DSI philosophy are better at their business because all of the different divisions within the company "play from the same sheet of music."[3]

Additionally, the practice of world-class supply chain management requires that different companies act as if a single mission and leadership connect them. To accomplish this task across companies that have different ownership and interests, five types of external integration are sought by firms interested in providing top-level service to customers:[4]

- *Relationship integration* is the ability of two or more companies to develop social connections that serve to guide their interactions when working together. More specifically, relationship integration is the capability to develop and maintain a shared mental framework across companies that describes how they will depend on one another when working together. This includes the ways in which they will collaborate on activities or projects so that the customer gains the maximum amount of total value possible from the supply chain.

- *Measurement integration* reflects the idea that performance assessments should be transparent and measurable across the borders of different firms, and should also assess the performance of the supply chain as a whole while holding each individual firm or business unit accountable for meeting its own goals.

- *Technology and planning integration* refers to the creation and maintenance of information technology systems that connect managers across the firms in the supply chain. It requires information hardware and software systems that can exchange information when needed between customers, suppliers, and internal operational areas of each of the supply chain partners.

- *Material and service supplier integration* requires firms to link seamlessly to those outsiders that provide goods and services to them so that they can streamline work processes and thereby provide smooth, high-quality customer experiences. Both sides need to have a common vision of the total value creation process and be willing to share the responsibility for satisfying customer requirements to make supplier integration successful.

- *Customer integration* is a competency that enables firms to offer long-lasting, distinctive, value-added offerings to those customers who represent the greatest value to the firm or supply chain. Highly customer-integrated firms assess their own capabilities and then match them to customers whose

supply chain integration when multiple firms or business functions in a supply chain coordinate their activities and processes so that they are seamlessly linked to one another in an effort to satisfy the customer

demand-supply integration (DSI) a supply chain operational philosophy focused on integrating the supply-management and demand-generating functions of an organization

Relationally integrated supply chains have sets of rules, policies, and/or procedures that dictate how firms will work together and specify how conflicts among supply chain partners will be resolved.

desires they can meet and who offer large enough sales potential for the linkage to be profitable over the long term.

Success in achieving both the internal and external types of integration is very important. Highly integrated supply chains (those that are successful in achieving many or all of these types of integration) have been shown to be better at satisfying customers, managing costs, delivering high-quality products, enhancing productivity, and utilizing company or business unit assets, all of which translate into greater profitability for the firms and their partners working together in the supply chain.

Integration involves a balance between barriers and enablers. Companies that work closely with their suppliers encounter problems such as corporate culture, information hoarding, and trust issues. For example, Häagen-Dazs and General Mills share information with their vanilla suppliers to increase yields and improve sustainability practices, but at the same time, there is a danger. Giving supply chain partners this information enables those partners to share it with competitors. On the other hand, integration can be improved through long-term agreements, cross-organizational integrated product teams, and improved communication between partners. These factors all aid in integrating supply chain operations.[5]

13-3 THE KEY PROCESSES OF SUPPLY CHAIN MANAGEMENT

When firms practice good supply chain management, their functional departments or areas, such as marketing, research and development, and/or production, are integrated both within and across the linked firms. Integration, then, is "how" excellent supply chain management works. The business processes on which the linked firms work together represent the "what" of supply chain management—they are the objects of focus on which firms, departments, areas, and people work together when seeking to reduce supply chain costs or to generate additional revenues. **Business processes** are composed of bundles of interconnected activities that stretch across firms in the supply chain; they represent key areas that some or all of the involved firms are constantly working on to reduce costs and/or generate revenues for everyone throughout supply chain management. There are eight critical business processes on which supply chain managers must focus:

1. Customer relationship management
2. Customer service management
3. Demand management
4. Order fulfillment
5. Manufacturing flow management
6. Supplier relationship management
7. Product development and commercialization
8. Returns management[6]

13-3a Customer Relationship Management

The **customer relationship management (CRM) process** enables companies to prioritize their marketing focus on different customer groups according to each group's long-term value to the company or supply chain. Once higher-value customers are identified, firms should

business processes bundles of interconnected activities that stretch across firms in the supply chain

customer relationship management (CRM) process allows companies to prioritize their marketing focus on different customer groups according to each group's long-term value to the company or supply chain

focus more on providing customized products and better service to this group than to others. The CRM process includes customer segmentation by value and subsequent generation of customer loyalty for the most attractive segments. This process provides a set of comprehensive principles for the initiation and maintenance of customer relationships and is often carried out with the assistance of specialized CRM computer software. For example, C. H. Briggs, a specialty building materials distributor, integrated CRM software as part of an effort to serve its customers better. With this software, each company sales representative has access to every customer's purchasing history. With this information, representatives can shape the sales process for its most valuable customers and uncover opportunities to improve service for them, thereby optimizing decision-making throughout the company.[7]

Sales and Operations Planning quickly became a valuable asset to shoemaker, Red Wing Shoes—known for their rugged work boots.

13-3b Customer Service Management

Whereas the CRM process is designed to identify and build relationships with good customers, the customer service management process is designed to ensure that those customer relationships remain strong. The **customer service management process** presents a multi-company, unified response system to the customer whenever complaints, concerns, questions, or comments are voiced. When the process is well executed, it can have a strong positive impact on revenues, often as a result of quick positive response to negative customer feedback, and sometimes even in the form of additional sales gained through the additional customer contact. Customers expect service from the moment a product is purchased until it is disposed of, and the customer service management process allows for touch points between the buyer and seller throughout this life cycle. The use of customer care software enables companies to enhance their customer service management process. Dell's customer support software, Clear View, enables staff members at the tech company's customer service command centers to view information from Dell's internal systems (as well as that of its partners) in real-time. This information is combined with a geographical system that allows Dell to match each customer's complaint with the proper service dispatch center, making its response both rapid and effective.[8]

13-3c Demand Management

The **demand management process** seeks to align supply and demand throughout the supply chain by anticipating customer requirements at each level and creating customer-focused plans of action prior to actual purchases being made. At the same time, demand management seeks to minimize the costs of serving multiple types of customers who have variable wants and needs. In other words, the demand management process allows companies in the supply chain to satisfy customers in the most efficient and effective ways possible. Activities such as collecting customer data, forecasting future demand, and developing activities that smooth out demand help bring available inventory into alignment with customer desires.

Though it is very difficult to predict exactly what items and quantities customers will buy prior to purchase, demand management can ease pressure on the production process and allow companies to satisfy most of their customers through greater flexibility in manufacturing, marketing, and sales programs. One key way this occurs is through the sharing of customer demand forecasts and data during sales and operations planning (S&OP) meetings. During these meetings, the demand-generating functions of the business (marketing and sales) work together with the production side of the business (procurement, production, and

customer service management process presents a multi-company, unified response system to the customer whenever complaints, concerns, questions, or comments are voiced

demand management process seeks to align supply and demand throughout the supply chain by anticipating customer requirements at each level and creating demand-related plans of action prior to actual customer purchasing behavior

logistics) in a collaborative arrangement designed to both satisfy customers and minimize waste. When work boot manufacturer Red Wing Shoes implemented S&OP in 2013, it was able to reduce inventory by 27 percent while simultaneously increasing customer service rates by 8 to 10 percent, leading to significant costs savings that were passed along to customers.[9]

13-3d Order Fulfillment

One of the most fundamental processes in supply chain management is the order fulfillment process, which involves generating, filling, delivering, and providing on-the-spot service for customer orders. The **order fulfillment process** is a highly integrated process, often requiring persons from multiple companies and multiple functions to come together and coordinate to create customer satisfaction at a given place and time. The best order fulfillment processes reduce **order cycle time**—the time between order and customer receipt—as much as possible, while ensuring that the customer receives exactly what he or she wants. The shorter lead times are beneficial in that they allow firms to carry reduced inventory levels and free up cash that can be used on other projects. Overall, the order fulfillment process involves understanding and integrating the company's internal capabilities with customer needs, and matching these together so that the supply chain maximizes profits while minimizing costs and waste. Amazon now uses Kiva robots to help workers pack three to four times more orders per hour than before. These robots bring shelves of products to the human packers based on what is in each customer's order. The packers then pick out the correct items, pack them, and send the complete box off to another robot to be shipped. This process has greatly increased the speed of Amazon's order fulfillment process: recent research found that the work robots do at Amazon shaves more than an hour off the time needed to pick and pack the average order.[10]

order fulfillment process a highly integrated process, often requiring persons from multiple companies and multiple functions to come together and coordinate to create customer satisfaction at a given place and time

order cycle time the time delay between the placement of a customer's order and the customer's receipt of that order

manufacturing flow management process concerned with ensuring that firms in the supply chain have the needed resources to manufacture with flexibility and to move products through a multi-stage production process

supplier relationship management process supports manufacturing flow by identifying and maintaining relationships with highly valued suppliers

13-3e Manufacturing Flow Management

The **manufacturing flow management process** is concerned with ensuring that firms in the supply chain have the needed resources to manufacture with flexibility and to move products through a multi-stage production process. Firms with flexible manufacturing have the ability to create a wide variety of goods and/or services with minimized costs associated with changing production techniques. The manufacturing flow process includes much more than simple production of goods and services—it means creating flexible agreements with suppliers and shippers so that unexpected demand bursts can be accommodated, without disruptions to customer service or satisfaction.

The goals of the manufacturing flow management process are centered on leveraging the capabilities held by multiple members of the supply chain to improve overall manufacturing output in terms of quality, delivery speed, and flexibility, all of which tie directly to profitability. Depending on the product, supply chain managers may choose between a lean or agile supply chain strategy. In a lean supply chain, products are built before demand occurs, but managers attempt to reduce as much waste as possible. Lean supply chains first appeared within the Toyota Production System (TPS) as early as the 1950s. Agile strategies lie on the other end of the continuum—they prioritize customer responsiveness more so than waste reduction. Instead of trying to forecast demand and reduce waste, agile supply chains wait for demand to occur and use communication and flexibility to fill that demand quickly.[11]

13-3f Supplier Relationship Management

The **supplier relationship management process** is closely related to the manufacturing flow management process and contains several characteristics that parallel the customer relationship management process. The manufacturing flow management process is highly dependent on supplier relationships for flexibility. Furthermore, in a way similar to that found in the customer relationship management process, supplier relationship management provides structural support for developing and maintaining relationships with suppliers. Thus, by integrating these two ideas, supplier relationship management supports manufacturing flow by identifying and maintaining relationships with highly valued suppliers.

Just as firms benefit from developing close-knit, integrated relationships with customers, close-knit, integrated relationships with suppliers provide a means through which performance advantages can be gained. For example, careful management of supplier relationships is a key step toward ensuring that firms' manufacturing resources are utilized to their maximum potential. It is clear, then, that the supplier relationship management process has a direct impact on each supply chain member's bottom-line financial performance. In certain instances, it can be advantageous for the supply chain to integrate via a formal merger. American pharmaceutical company Bayer Health-Care recently purchased German-based Steigerwald Arzneimittelwerk, a partnering pharmacy supplier that specializes in herbal medicines. Purchasing a supplier gave Bayer HealthCare access to new medications. At the same time, purchasing a supplier based in Germany gave Bayer HealthCare enhanced access to European markets. Managing supplier relationships not only gave Bayer Health-Care better access to supplies, it also offered a chance to increase its customer base. The acquisition of one by the other simply sealed the deal by making the partnership permanent.[12]

Titus Green assembles a recycled iPhone at a Green Citizen recycling facility in Burlingame, California. Green Citizen collects and disposes old electronics in the San Francisco Bay area, tracking each device to ensure that it is recycled back into raw material or refurbished and resold.

13-3g Product Development and Commercialization

The **product development and commercialization process** (discussed in detail in Chapter 11) includes the group of activities that facilitate the joint development and marketing of new offerings among a group of supply chain partner firms. In many cases, more than one supply chain entity is responsible for ensuring new product success. Commonly, a multi-company collaboration is used to execute new-product development, testing, and launch, among other activities. The capability for developing and introducing new offerings quickly is key for competitive success versus rival firms, so it is often advantageous to involve many supply chain partners in the effort. The process requires the close cooperation of suppliers and customers, who provide input throughout the process and serve as advisers and co-producers for the new offering(s).

Designing a new product with the help of suppliers and customers can enable a company to introduce features and cost-cutting measures into final products. Customers provide information about what they want from the product, while suppliers can help to design for quality and manufacturability. Research has shown that when each supply chain partner shares responsibility for the design and manufacture of a new product, more obstacles can be identified early and opportunities for cost reduction are made possible. For example, Boeing involved a team of suppliers early in the development phase of its 787 Dreamliner aircraft, leading to a shift to a lighter composite material for the fuselage's outer shell. The lighter material is expected to make the aircraft substantially cheaper to operate on long haul flights.[13]

13-3h Returns Management

The final supply chain management process deals with situations in which customers choose to return a product to the retailer or supplier, thereby creating a reversed flow of goods within the supply chain. The **returns management process** enables firms to manage volumes of returned product efficiently while minimizing returns-related costs and maximizing the value of the returned assets to the firms

product development and commercialization process includes the group of activities that facilitates the joint development and marketing of new offerings among a group of supply chain partner firms

returns management process enables firms to manage volumes of returned product efficiently while minimizing returns-related costs and maximizing the value of the returned assets to the firms in the supply chain

in the supply chain. Returns have the potential to affect a firm's financial position in a major and negative way if mishandled. In certain industries, such as apparel e-retailing, returns can amount to as much as 40 percent of sales volume.

In addition to the value of managing returns from a pure asset-recovery perspective, many firms are discovering that returns management also creates additional marketing and customer service touch points that can be leveraged for added customer value above and beyond normal sales and promotion-driven encounters. Handling returns quickly creates a positive image, and gives the company an additional opportunity to please the customer, and customers who have positive experiences with the returns management process can become very confident buyers who are willing to reorder, since they know any problems they encounter with purchases will be quickly and fairly rectified. In addition, the returns management process allows the firm to recognize weaknesses in product design and/or areas for potential improvement through the direct customer feedback that initiates the process.

The mobile phone industry has been able to use returns management to its advantage. In a typical year, almost 100 million mobile phones are returned to manufacturers. With a return of between 35 and 75 percent of their original value in the secondary market, reselling 250,000 out of the 100 million returned phones would result in more than $20 million in additional revenue. Returns management also allows mobile phone companies to reclaim rare materials, such as gold, silver, and palladium. For example, reclaimed metals from one million mobile phones returned to one company brought in more than $2.8 million.[14]

 13-4 SUSTAINABLE SUPPLY CHAIN MANAGEMENT

In response to the need for firms to both reduce costs and act as leaders in protecting the natural environment, many are adopting sustainable supply chain management principles as a key part of their supply chain strategy. **Sustainable supply chain management** involves the integration and balancing of environmental, social, and economic thinking into all phases of the supply chain management process. In doing so,

sustainable supply chain management a supply chain management philosophy that embraces the need for optimizing social and environmental costs in addition to financial costs

the organization both better addresses current business needs and develops long-term initiatives that allow it to mitigate risks and avail itself of future opportunities in ways that preserve resources for future generations and ensure long-term viability. Such activities include environmentally friendly materials sourcing; the design of products with consideration given to their social and environmental impact; and end-of-life product management that includes easy recycling and/or clean disposal. By enacting sustainable supply chain management principles, companies can simultaneously generate cost savings, protect the Earth's natural resources, and ensure that socially responsible business practices are enacted.

UPS works continuously to develop a more sustainable supply chain. By integrating new transportation technology into its fulfillment networks, UPS mechanics and employees are able to facilitate package delivery in ways that are more fuel- and emissions-efficient—the proof lies in the more than 3 percent reduction in fuel use per package per year. UPS has logged more than 200 million miles on alternative fuel vehicles and offers carbon-neutral delivery in 36 countries.[15]

In addition to environmental sustainability, modern businesses are also balancing economic success with social sustainability practices like human rights, labor rights, employee diversity initiatives, and quality of life concerns. A common misconception surrounding both environmental and social sustainability is that their practice increases supply chain costs disproportionately, and therefore should be enacted only when business leaders are willing to act altruistically or for the purposes of good public relations. However, recent research on these subjects has demonstrated a strong business case for supporting many sustainability initiatives. As examples, the recycling of used pallets is both an environmentally sustainable practice and cheaper than purchasing new ones, and the employment of disabled workers in distribution operations ensures both social sustainability (via opportunities for economically disadvantaged people) and better overall performance for the employer. The benefits of social sustainability efforts have been demonstrated by retailers such as Lowe's Home Improvement and Walgreen Stores, where the hiring and training of disabled workers has increased productivity in the host facilities by up to 20 percent. These companies have found that disabled workers are far less likely to miss work and are often as effective at performing job tasks as their abled counterparts—while frequently exceeding them in terms of process execution and safety standards.[16]

13-5 TRENDS IN SUPPLY CHAIN MANAGEMENT

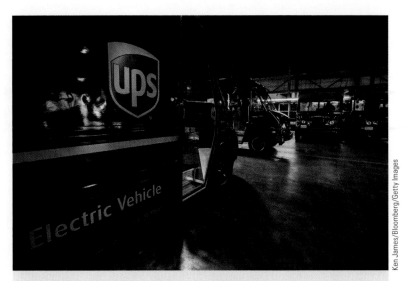

Several technological advances and business trends are affecting the job of the supply chain manager today. Some of the business trends that are affecting supply chain management include outsourcing logistics, maintaining a secure supply chain and minimizing supply chain risk, and maintaining a sustainable supply chain. While these trends exert pressure on managers to change the way their supply chains function, electronic distribution is being used and changed frequently to help make supply chain management more integrated and easier to track.

More than 100 new all-electric UPS delivery vehicles were deployed in February 2013, eliminating the use of 126,000 gallons of fuel per year.

13-5a Outsourcing Logistics Functions

Partnering organizations are becoming increasingly efficient at dividing responsibility for supply chain management. **Outsourcing**, or **contract logistics**, is a rapidly growing initiative in which a manufacturer or supplier turns over an entire logistical function (often buying and managing transportation, warehousing, and/or light postponed manufacturing) to an independent **third-party logistics company (3PL).** These service providers sell logistics solutions instead of physical products. Common 3PL products include warehouse space, transportation solutions, information sharing, manufacturing postponement, and enhanced technological innovations. When a firm's order fulfillment process is managed diligently, the amount of time between order placement and receipt of the customer's payment following order shipment (known as the *order-to-cash cycle*) is minimized as much as possible. Since many firms do not view order fulfillment as a core competency (versus, for example, product development or marketing), they often outsource this function to a 3PL that specializes in the order fulfillment process. The 3PL becomes a semi-permanent part of the firm's supply chain and is assigned to manage one or more specialized functions.[17] Other, more comprehensive partners, often known as **fourth-party logistics companies (4PLs) or logistics integrators**, create and manage entire solutions for getting products where they need to be, when they need to be there. Many times 3PLs and 4PLs provide a firm's only interaction with the customer, so they need to represent the needs and interests of the entire firm and supply chain. Developing and training these firms' employees to be empowered and to respond to the customer's needs in the best interest of the supply chain is becoming increasingly important.

Outsourcing enables companies to cut inventories, locate stock at fewer plants and distribution centers, and still provide the same level of service or even better. The companies then can refocus investment on their core business. In the hospitality industry, Avendra negotiates with suppliers to obtain virtually everything a hotel might need, from food and beverages to golf course maintenance. For example, by relying on Avendra to manage many aspects of the supply chain, companies like Fairmont Hotels & Resorts and Inter-Continental Hotels Group can concentrate on their core function—providing hospitality. The most progressive companies are engaging in vested outsourcing relationships, whereby both parties collaborate deeply to find mutually beneficial arrangements that allow both parties to "win" by reducing overall costs while achieving better performance.[18]

outsourcing (contract logistics) a manufacturer's or supplier's use of an independent third party to manage an entire function of the logistics system, such as transportation, warehousing, or order processing

third-party logistics company (3PL) a firm that provides functional logistics services to others

fourth-party logistics company (4PL or logistics integrator) a consulting-based organization that assesses another's entire logistical service needs and provides integrated solutions, often drawing on multiple 3PLs for actual service

Ken James/Bloomberg/Getty Images

North American companies have been outsourcing logistics and shipping to companies overseas.

products more closely to major demand centers, it also gives the supplier a chance to make its presence known at a local level. Mexican-based IT firm Rural Sourcing Inc. has long worked with customers in Mexico, but an influx of American partners has led the company to grow an average of 150 percent annually over the last four years.[19]

13-5b Public-Private Partnerships

Sometimes, the magnitude of a supply chain dilemma is too great for a company and its suppliers or outsourcing partners to handle alone. Increasingly, this is leading firms to work together with government agencies in the form of **public-private partnerships (PPPs)**. PPPs are critical to the satisfaction of both company and societal interests and provide a mechanism by which very-large scale problems or opportunities can be addressed.

Though it is often assumed that industries and governments work poorly together (or in fact work against one another) when problems common to both emerge, a number of successful PPPs have formed over the past decade to diminish the negative impacts of potentially hazardous supply chain situations. For

Because a logistics service provider is focused on logistical functions only, clients receive better service in a timely, efficient manner, thereby increasing their customers' satisfaction and boosting the perception of added value to a company's offerings. In many recent instances, North American companies have been **offshoring**, or outsourcing logistics to service providers located in countries with lower labor costs, such as Vietnam and Bangladesh. However, as fuel costs have risen and security issues become more prominent, many companies have begun to relocate outsourced operations closer to home. **Nearshoring** to locations such as Mexico or the Caribbean nations ensures low costs while reducing supply chain risk. Nearshoring not only allows a company to manufacture its

offshoring the outsourcing of a business process from one country to another for the purpose of gaining economic advantage

nearshoring the transfer of an offshored activity from a distant to a nearby country

public-private partnerships (PPPs) Critical to the satisfaction of both company and societal interests and provide a mechanism by which very-large scale problems or opportunities can be addressed

Efforts involving PPPs, like the Red Cross, will likely factor into the solution of future national and global supply chain.

example, immediately following the September 11, 2001, terror attacks on the United States, representatives from both industry and government collaborated to develop the Customs-Trade Partnership Against Terrorism (C-TPAT) in an effort to protect U.S.-based supply chains from terrorist disruption. The program currently has more than 10,000 company participants and has, in general terms, been successful at protecting cargo inbound for the United States while only minimally impacting the performance of its members' supply chains. Similarly, governmental agencies like the Federal Emergency Management Agency (FEMA) and non-government organizations like the Red Cross have benefitted from the inclusion of commercial logistics expertise in their disaster response systems.[20] Efforts involving.

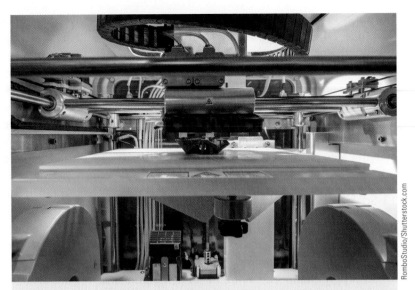

Using 3DP technology, objects are built to precise specifications using raw materials at or near the location where they will be consumed.

PPPs will likely factor into the solution of future national and global supply chain problems as well. For example, the dangerous combination of population growth and overuse of aging infrastructure has led to a situation whereby congestion and deterioration of roads imperils the timely shipment of goods. The U.S. Federal Highway Administration is openly soliciting proposals that would take some of the stress off of the U.S. highway network, including collaborating on building new toll roads and extending railways dedicated to cargo. These sorts of PPP-led advancements will play a critical role in the price of retail goods in upcoming years due to the costs associated with product and material delays.[21]

13-5c Electronic Distribution

Electronic distribution is the most recent development in the logistics arena. Broadly defined, **electronic distribution** includes any kind of product or service that can be distributed electronically, whether over traditional forms such as fiber-optic cable or through satellite transmission of electronic signals. Companies like E*TRADE, Apple (iTunes), and Movies.com have built their business models around electronic distribution.

In the near future, however, electronic distribution will not be limited only to products and services that are mostly composed of information that can therefore be easily digitized. Experiments with **three-dimensional printing (3DP)** have been successful in industries such as auto parts, biomedical, and even fast food. Using 3DP technology, objects are built to precise specifications using raw materials at or near the location where they will be consumed. Charge Bikes prints customized titanium bicycle parts based on customer specifications, thus reducing the need to transport complete frames around the world before they can be assembled and sold.[22] Shipping raw materials such as powdered titanium is cheaper than shipping finished bicycles because it can be packaged in a perfectly cubic container, making transportation much more efficient and cost effective. Powdered titanium is used only when it is needed, so virtually no waste is produced during printing. Web sites like 3DLT.com offer consumers templates for toys, dishes, and furniture that can be printed using the 3DP technology that is becoming increasingly available.[23]

Many industry experts project that 3DP (sometimes referred to as *additive manufacturing*) will radically transform the ways global supply chains work by changing the basic platforms of business. With 3DP, smaller, localized supply chains will become the norm and small manufacturers will produce many more

electronic distribution
a distribution technique that includes any kind of product or service that can be distributed electronically, whether over traditional forms such as fiber-optic cable or through satellite transmission of electronic signals

three-dimensional printing (3DP) the creation of three-dimensional objects via an additive manufacturing (printing) technology that layers raw material into desired shapes

custom products than ever before over very short lead times. And because such platforms will remove much of the need for transportation of finished goods to distribution centers and retailers, 3DP is expected to have a very positive impact on businesses' carbon footprints and the environment at large. At the same time, these platforms should make it possible to deliver unique goods more quickly, creating perceptions of better service.[24]

13-5d Global Supply Chain Management

Global markets present their own sets of challenges for supply chain managers. Strategically, there are many reasons why a company might wish to globalize its supply chain. The allure of foreign markets is strong, due to increasing demand for imported products worldwide. Cheap labor advantages and trade barriers/tariffs have encouraged firms to expand their global manufacturing operations. At the same time, globalization has brought about great uncertainty for modern companies, and specifically, their supply chains. Moving operations offshore exposes companies to risks associated with geopolitical conflict, foreign nationalization of assets and knowledge diffusion, and highly variable quality standards. Foreign suppliers are often less reliable, and due to the lengthening of the supply chain, variability in transportation service can lead to service failures. It is important to consider how sourcing and logistics will be impacted by supply chain globalization.

From a supply management standpoint, it often makes sense to procure goods and services from offshore suppliers. From an economic perspective, lower labor rates, government subsidies, and low materials costs are attractive, but are sometimes outweighed by the costs of quality variation and loss of intellectual property. Still, moving offshore also exposes the company to new technologies, introduces competition to domestic suppliers who have

become lackadaisical, and build brand equity. Companies moving offshore must carefully consider the pros and cons, and build supply management systems that can manage very diverse tasks. Logistically, it is critical for importers of all sizes to understand and cope with the legalities of trade in other countries. Shippers and distributors must be aware of the permits, licenses, and registrations they may need to acquire, and depending on the types of product they are importing, the tariffs, quotas, and other regulations that apply in each country. Sometimes, the complexities of handling overseas logistics are too great to overcome. As companies lengthen their global supply chains in search of cost advantages, other less obvious risks emanating from outside the immediate supply chain are also starting to come into play. Longer shipping lanes can expose shipments to natural disasters and extreme weather; political instability and trade restrictions can abruptly halt or slow shipments; fluctuations in currency values and border delays can diminish the value of products while they are on the path to the customer; and theft and piracy can present a greater threat due to increased time of exposure. For these reasons, many companies are now creating contingency plans so they can react quickly when something goes wrong.[25]

Indeed, as the world continues to globalize, supply chain management will undoubtedly continue to take on a globalized flavor. Worldwide, the resources needed to manufacture and sell increasingly demanded goods are becoming scarcer, and market boundaries are melting together. Free trade is expanding, and consumers in nations where demand has been traditionally low are viewing goods and placing orders via the Internet. Efforts to achieve world-class global supply chain management mean that the balancing of supply and demand—and the satisfaction of more and more customers worldwide—are becoming a reality for many companies.

egd/Shutterstock.com

Shippers and distributors must be aware of the permits, licenses, and registrations they may need to acquire, and depending on the types of product they are importing, the tariffs, quotas, and other regulations that apply in each country.

13-5e Supply Chain Analytics and Technology

In addition to outsourcing, globalization, PPPs, and 3D printing, other advancements in data and technology are beginning to exert an impact on the effectiveness and efficiency of the supply chain. First, a rapidly increasing prevalence of powerful computers and methods for capturing customer, supplier, and company information over the past two decades has resulted in the appearance of **big data**, a colloquial term for the explosive availability of data that has traditionally been hard to capture, store, manage, and analyze. The emergence of big data has presented both great opportunities and significant problems for supply chain managers. There is indeed more information available about supply chain operations than ever before, but the challenge of extracting usable date from this information is also very great. In order to harvest more useful information, many companies are using **cloud computing** to collaborate on big data projects and analyze findings in a quick and cost-effective manner.

As a result, many organizations are seeking to develop capabilities for **supply chain analytics**. Supply chain analytics programs that can interpret

Makeitdouble/Shutterstock.com

big data have great potential for improving supply chain operations. For example, the use of bigger and better data should allow supply chain forecasting to become more accurate; shipments to be re-routed in the event of traffic or bad weather; and warehouses to be stocked with exactly the products customers want (and none they don't want). Each of these ambitions, if realized, would offer lower prices for customers and lead to greater customer satisfaction.

Advanced technology enabled by big data is also improving supply chain operations. Fundamentally, the acquisition and analysis of big data allows a company to replace human reasoning with faster and more efficient decision making that is based on information rather than intuition. As a result, and combined with supply chain analytics, a company can automate many of its supply chain processes rather than using human labor. Many tasks that are done repetitively and require significant precision can be accomplished more cheaply and accurately by robots. For example, scientists at the University of California have developed robots—powered by cloud-based data about surgical patients—that are capable of performing basic hip and knee replacement surgery.[26] Cloud-based robots are already being used for large-scale production tasks like automobile and airplane manufacturing.

A final consideration related to technological advancement: sensory equipment that connects physical objects to decision-making analytics via the Internet is beginning to emerge. Recall the Internet of Things (IoT), which allows physical objects to relay specific information over the Internet without overt human interaction. The potential impact of the Internet of Things is tantalizing, but the technology is

Mr Aesthetics/Shutterstock.com

big data the rapidly collected and difficult-to-process large-scale datasets that have recently emerged, and which push the limits of current analytical capability

cloud computing the practice of using remote network servers to store, manage, and process data

supply chain analytics data analyses that support the improved design and management of the supply chain

currently in its infant stage. Connections between cargo vessels or trucks and transportation networks may eventually lead to the development of smart transportation modes that re-route in real time based on local traffic patterns, weather events, and accidents. Alternatively, the traffic grid could react to a need for emergency supplies by enabling a sequence of green stoplights along a critical emergency route. The possibilities are essentially endless for the IoT to positively impact the supply chain. Many companies have already launched projects related to the development of IoT-enabled supply chain management strategies.

 ## 13-6 MARKETING CHANNELS AND CHANNEL INTERMEDIARIES

A marketing channel can be viewed as a canal or pipeline through which products, their ownership, communication, financing and payment, and accompanying risk flow to the consumer. A **marketing channel** (also called a **channel of distribution**) is a business structure of interdependent organizations that reaches from the point of production to the consumer and facilitates the downstream physical movement of goods through the supply chain. Channels represent the "place" or "distribution" element of the marketing mix (product, price, promotion, and place), in that they provide a route for company products and services to flow to the customer. In essence, the marketing channel is the "downstream" portion of the supply chain that connects a producer with the customer. Whereas "upstream" supply chain members are charged with moving component parts or raw materials to the producer, members of the marketing channel propel finished goods toward the customer, and/or provide services that facilitate additional customer value.

Many different types of organizations participate in marketing channels. **Channel members** (also called *intermediaries*, *resellers*, and *middlemen*) negotiate with one another, buy and sell products, and facilitate the change of ownership between buyer and seller in the course of moving finished goods from the manufacturer into the hands of the final consumer. As products move toward the final consumer, channel members facilitate the distribution process by providing specialization and division of labor, overcoming discrepancies, and providing contact efficiency.

13-6a How Marketing Channels Work

According to the concepts of *specialization and division of labor*, breaking down a complex task into smaller, simpler ones and assigning these to specialists creates greater efficiency and lower average production costs via economies of scale. Marketing channels attain economies of scale through specialization and division of labor by aiding upstream producers (who often lack the motivation, financing, or expertise) in marketing to end users or consumers. In most cases, such as for consumer goods like soft drinks, the cost of marketing directly to millions of consumers—taking and shipping individual orders—is prohibitive. For this reason, producers engage other channel members such as wholesalers and retailers to do what the producers are not well suited to do. Some channel members can accomplish certain tasks more efficiently than others because they have built strategic relationships with key suppliers or customers or have unique capabilities. Their specialized expertise enhances the overall performance of the channel.

Because customers, like businesses, are specialized, they also rely on other entities for the fulfillment of most of their needs. Imagine what your life would be like if you had to grow your own food, make your own clothes, produce your own television shows, and assemble your own automobile! Luckily, members of marketing channels are available to undertake these tasks for us. However, not all goods and services produced by channel members exist in the form we'd most prefer, at least at first. Marketing channels are valuable because they aid producers in creating time, place, and exchange utility for customers, such that products become aligned with their needs. Producers, who sit at the top of the supply chain, provide **form utility** when they transform oats grown on a distant farm into the Cheerios that we like to eat for breakfast. **Time** and **place utility** are created by channel members, when, for example, a transport company hired by the producer physically moves boxes of cereal to a store near our homes in time for our next

marketing channel (channel of distribution) a set of interdependent organizations that eases the transfer of ownership as products move from producer to business user or consumer

channel members all parties in the marketing channel who negotiate with one another, buy and sell products, and facilitate the change of ownership between buyer and seller in the course of moving the product from the manufacturer into the hands of the final consumer

form utility the elements of the composition and appearance of a product that make it desirable

time utility the increase in customer satisfaction gained by making a good or service available at the appropriate time

place utility the usefulness of a good or service as a function of the location at which it is made available

Igor Strukov/Shutterstock.com

Sheila Fitzgerald/Shutterstock.com

MNStudio/Shutterstock.com

scheduled shopping trip. And the retailer, who is often the closest channel member to the customer, provides a desired product for some amount of money we are reasonably willing to give, creates **exchange utility** in doing so.

13-6b Functions and Activities of Channel Intermediaries

Intermediaries in a channel negotiate with one another, facilitate transfer of ownership for finished goods between buyers and sellers, and physically move products from the producer toward the final consumer. The most prominent difference separating intermediaries is whether they take title to the product. *Taking title* means they actually own the merchandise and control the terms of the sale—for example, price and delivery date. Retailers and merchant wholesalers are examples of intermediaries that take title to products in the marketing channel and resell them. **Merchant wholesalers** are organizations that facilitate the movement of products and services from the manufacturer to producers, resellers, governments, institutions, and retailers. All merchant wholesalers take title to the goods they sell, and most of them operate one or more warehouses where they receive finished goods, store them, and later reship them to retailers, manufacturers, and institutional clients. Since wholesalers do not dramatically alter the form of a good nor sell it directly to the consumer, their value hinges on their providing time and place utility and contact efficiency to retailers.

Other intermediaries do not take title to goods and services they market but do facilitate exchanges of ownership between sellers and buyers. **Agents and brokers** facilitate the sales of products downstream by representing the interests of retailers, wholesalers, and manufacturers to potential customers. Unlike merchant wholesalers, agents or

brokers only facilitate sales and generally have little input into the terms of the sale. They do, however, get a fee or commission based on sales volume. For example, grocery chains often employ the services of food brokers, who provide expertise for a range of products within a category. The broker facilitates the sale of many different manufacturers' products to the grocery chain by marketing the producers' stocks, but the broker never actually takes ownership of any food products.

Many different variations in channel structures are possible, with choices made based in large part on the numbers and types of wholesaling intermediaries that are most desirable. Generally, product characteristics, buyer considerations, and market conditions determine the types and number of intermediaries the producer should use, as follows:

- Customized or highly complex products such as computers, specialty foods, or custom uniforms are usually sold through an agent or broker, who may represent one or multiple companies. In contrast, standardized product such as soda or toothpaste are often sold through a merchant wholesaler and retailer channel.

- Buyer considerations such as purchase frequency or customer wait time influence channel choice. When there is no time pressure, customers may save money on books by ordering online and taking direct distribution from a wholesaler. However,

exchange utility the increased value of a product that is created as its ownership is transferred

merchant wholesaler an institution that buys goods from manufacturers and resells them to businesses, government agencies, and other wholesalers or retailers and that receives and takes title to goods, stores them in its own warehouses, and later ships them

agents and brokers wholesaling intermediaries who do not take title to a product but facilitate its sale from producer to end user by representing retailers, wholesalers, or manufacturers

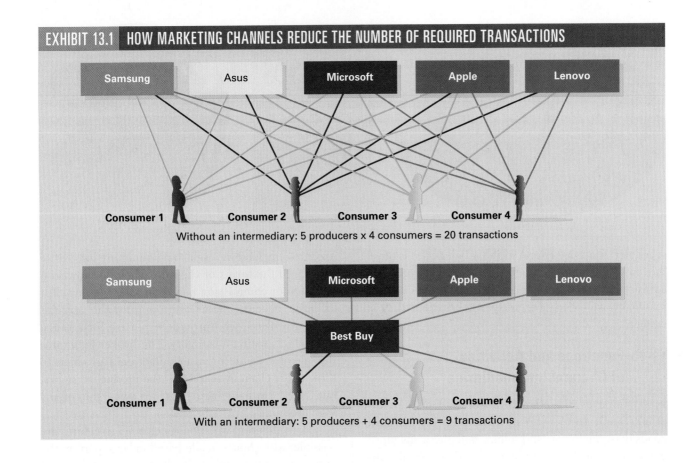

Without an intermediary: 5 producers x 4 consumers = 20 transactions

With an intermediary: 5 producers + 4 consumers = 9 transactions

if a book is needed immediately, it will have to be purchased at retail—at the school bookstore—and will include a markup.

- Market characteristics such as how many buyers are in the market and whether they are concentrated in a general location also influence channel design. In a home sale, the buyer and seller are localized in one area, which facilitates the use of a simple agent/broker relationship, whereas mass-manufactured goods such as automobiles may require parts from all over the world and therefore many intermediaries.

Retailers are those firms in the channel that sell directly to consumers as their primary function. A critical role fulfilled by retailers within the marketing channel is that they provide contact efficiency for consumers. Suppose you had to buy your milk at a dairy, your meat at a stockyard, and so forth. You would spend a great deal of time, money, and energy just shopping for just a few groceries. Retailers simplify distribution by reducing the number of transactions required by consumers, and by making an assortment of goods available in one location. Consider the example illustrated in Exhibit 13.1. Four consumers each want to buy a tablet computer. Without

retailer a channel intermediary that sells mainly to consumers

a retail intermediary like Best Buy, tablet manufacturers Samsung, Asus, Microsoft, Apple, and Lenovo would each have to make four contacts to reach the four consumers who are in the target market, for a total of twenty transactions. But when Best Buy acts as an intermediary between the producer and consumers, each producer needs to make only one contact, reducing the number to nine transactions. This benefit to customers accrues whether the retailer operates in a physical store location or online format.

13-6c Channel Functions Performed by Intermediaries

Intermediaries in marketing channels perform three essential functions that enable goods to flow between producer and consumer. *Transactional* functions involve contacting and communicating with prospective buyers to make them aware of existing products and to explain their features, advantages, and benefits. Intermediaries in the channel also provide *logistical* functions. Logistical functions typically include transportation and storage of assets, as well as their sorting, accumulation, consolidation, and/or allocation for the purpose of conforming to customer requirements. The third basic channel function, *facilitating*, includes research and financing.

Research provides information about channel members and consumers by getting answers to key questions: Who are the buyers? Where are they located? Why do they buy? Financing ensures that channel members have the money to keep products moving through the channel to the ultimate consumer. Although individual members can be added to or deleted from a channel, someone in the channel must perform these essential functions. Producers, wholesalers, retailers, or consumers can perform them, and sometimes nonmember channel participants such as service providers elect to perform them for a fee.

 ## 13-7 CHANNEL STRUCTURES

A product can take any of several possible routes to reach the final consumer. Marketers and consumers each search for the most efficient channel from many available alternatives. Constructing channels for a consumer convenience good such as candy differs from doing the same for a specialty good like a Prada handbag. Exhibit 13.2 illustrates four ways manufacturers can route products to consumers. When possible, producers use a **direct channel** to sell directly to consumers in order to keep purchase prices low. Direct marketing activities—including telemarketing, mail order and catalog shopping, and forms of electronic retailing such as online shopping and shop-at-home television networks—are good examples of this type of channel structure. There are no intermediaries. Producer-owned stores and factory outlet stores—like Sherwin-Williams, Polo Ralph Lauren, Oneida, and WestPoint Home—are also examples of direct channels.

By contrast, when one or more channel members are small companies lacking in marketing power, an *agent/broker channel* may be the best solution. Agents or brokers bring manufacturers and wholesalers together for negotiations, but they do not take title to merchandise. Ownership passes directly from the producer to one or more wholesalers and/or retailers, who sell to the ultimate consumer.

Most consumer products are sold through distribution channels similar to the other two alternatives: the retailer channel and the wholesaler channel. A *retailer channel* is most common when the retailer is large and can buy in large quantities directly from the manufacturer. Walmart, Sears, and car dealers are examples of retailers that often bypass a wholesaler. A *wholesaler channel* is commonly used for low-cost items that are frequently purchased, such as candy, cigarettes, and magazines.

13-7a Channels for Business and Industrial Products

As Exhibit 13.3 illustrates, five channel structures are common in business and industrial markets. First, *direct channels* are typical in business and industrial markets. For example, manufacturers buy large quantities of raw materials, major equipment,

> **direct channel** a distribution channel in which producers sell directly to consumers

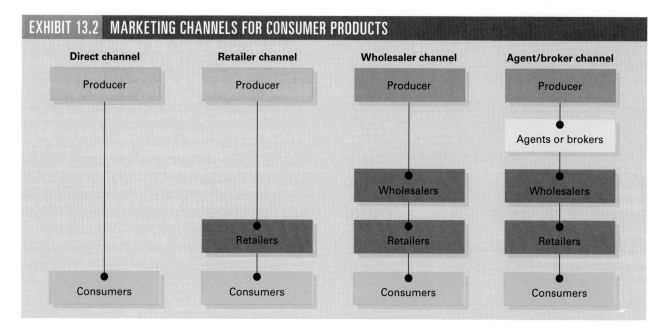

EXHIBIT 13.2 MARKETING CHANNELS FOR CONSUMER PRODUCTS

Direct channel	Retailer channel	Wholesaler channel	Agent/broker channel
Producer	Producer	Producer	Producer
			Agents or brokers
		Wholesalers	Wholesalers
	Retailers	Retailers	Retailers
Consumers	Consumers	Consumers	Consumers

EXHIBIT 13.3 CHANNELS FOR BUSINESS AND INDUSTRIAL PRODUCTS

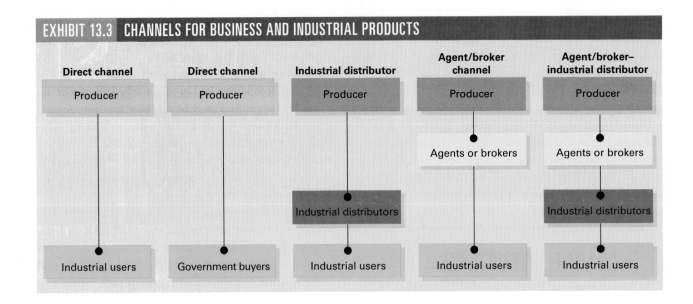

processed materials, and supplies directly from other producers. Manufacturers that require suppliers to meet detailed technical specifications often prefer direct channels. For instance, Apple uses a direct channel to purchase high-resolution retina displays for its innovative iPad tablet line. To ensure sufficient supply for iPad manufacturing, Apple takes direct shipments of screens from Sharp, LG, and Samsung.[27]

Alternatively, companies selling standardized items of moderate or low value often rely on *industrial distributors*. In many ways, an industrial distributor is like a supermarket for organizations. Industrial distributors are wholesalers and channel members that buy and take title to products. Moreover, they usually keep inventories of their products and sell and service them. Often small manufacturers cannot afford to employ their own sales force. Instead, they rely on manufacturers' representatives or selling agents to sell to either industrial distributors or users. Additionally, the Internet has enabled virtual distributors to emerge and has forced traditional industrial distributors to expand their business models. Many manufacturers and consumers are bypassing distributors and going direct, often via the Internet.

13-7b Alternative Channel Arrangements

Rarely does a producer use just one type of channel to move its product. It usually employs several different strategies, which include the use of multiple distribution, nontraditional channels, and strategic channel alliances. When a producer selects two or more channels to distribute the same product to target markets, this arrangement is called **dual or multiple distribution**. Dual or multiple distribution systems differ from single channel systems, and managers should recognize the differences. Multiple distribution channels must be organized and managed as a group, and managers must orchestrate their use in synchronization if whole system is to work well. As consumers increasingly embrace online shopping, more retailers are employing a multiple distribution strategy. This arrangement allows retailers to reach a wider customer base, but may also lead to competition between distribution channels through cannibalization (whereby one channel takes sales away from another). When multiple separate channels are used, they must all complement each other. Some customers use "showrooming" as a way of learning about products, but may then also shop as a way of making price comparisons. Regardless of which channel the customer chooses when making the final purchase, they should receive the same messages and "image" of the products.

The use of **nontraditional channels** may help differentiate a firm's product from the competition by providing additional information about products. Nontraditional channels include approaches such as mail-order television or video channels, or infomercials. Although nontraditional channels may limit a brand's coverage, they can give a producer serving a niche market a way to gain market access and customer attention without having to establish physical channel intermediaries and can also provide another sales avenue for larger firms.

dual distribution (multiple distribution) the use of two or more channels to distribute the same product to target markets

nontraditional channels non-physical channels that facilitate the unique market access of products and services

VERA BRADLEY

Vera Bradley signed a deal with Mitsubishi Corporation and its partner, Look, Inc., to distribute its handbags, luggage and accessories.

Furthermore, companies often form **strategic channel alliances** that enable them to use another manufacturer's already-established channel. Alliances are used most often when the creation of marketing channel relationships may be too expensive and time consuming. For example, U.S.-based Vera Bradley, Inc. signed a deal with Mitsubishi Corporation and its partner Look, Inc. to distribute the former's handbags, luggage, and accessories in the Japanese department stores and boutiques in their respective networks. This alliance helps Vera Bradley reach new markets in foreign cities and diversifies its revenue base, while minimizing its risks of going abroad.[28]

In addition to using primary traditional and nontraditional channels to flow products toward customer markets, many businesses also employ secondary channels, using either an active or passive approach. For example, though most automobile manufacturers sell their finished products to end users through networks of owned or franchised dealers, they also sell cars to rental agencies such as Enterprise or Hertz, who then rent them to potential customers. Similarly, fashion apparel companies might distribute their premium products, such as silk ties or branded watches, through primary channels such as department stores or specialty stores, while using an off-brand or discount outlet for distribution of low-end products. In each case, the goal of the company is the same: to engage a segment of customers who might otherwise never experience the product by offering it at a more easily affordable price or under trial conditions.

Marketers must also be aware, however, that some unintended secondary channels also exist. In some countries, **gray marketing channels** may be used to sell stolen or counterfeited products, which could detract from the profitability of the primary and secondary channels controlled by the business. Counterfeit products such as North Face outerwear, Rolex watches, and Prada handbags can be very difficult to distinguish from the real thing, and their presence provides unintended competition for the producer when such products are distributed through unauthorized intermediaries.

Along with marketing channels that move products downstream to end customers, retailers and manufacturers also manage channels that move products upstream, in the direction of the producer. These **reverse channels** enable consumers to return products to the retailer or manufacturer in the event of a product defect, or at the end of the product's useful life to the consumer. The retailers or manufacturers can then recycle the product and use components to manufacture new products, or refurbish and resell the same product in a secondary market. Several large companies, including Apple, Best Buy, and Walmart, offer opportunities to recycle items ranging from plastic bags and batteries to televisions and Christmas trees. Consumers and companies alike view reverse channels as not just a way to reduce the firm's environmental impact, but also as a means to gain some financial benefits as well.[29] For example, Apple will pay consumers for their old Apple products if they qualify for resale, or if their component parts are valuable for manufacturing new products.[30] **Drop and shop** programs use convenience to get consumers to recycle products, like batteries or cell phones, during a regular trip to the store.

13-7c Digital Channels

With technology changing rapidly, many companies are turning to digital channels to facilitate product

---

strategic channel alliance a cooperative agreement between business firms to use the other's already established distribution channel

gray marketing channels secondary channels that are unintended to be used by the producer, and which often flow illegally obtained or counterfeit product toward customers

reverse channels channels that enable customers to return products or components for reuse or remanufacturing

drop and shop a system used by several retailers that allow customers to bring used products for return or donation at the entrance of the store

A key advantage of Uber and similar apps is their frictionless payment interface.

distribution. **Digital channels** are pathways for moving product and information toward customers such that they can be sent and/or received with electronic devices, such as computers, smartphones, tablets, or video game consoles. Digital channels allow for either push- or pull-based information and product flows to occur, and sometimes simultaneously. For example, a downloaded video game or music file purchased by a customer can also include a digital ad for more games or a new music player.

In response to the growth of digital channels, customers are turning in droves to **M-commerce**, whereby a mobile device is used to assess, compare, and/or buy products. For example, suppose you need a ride from one point in Chicago to another. Instead of having to hail a cab or walk to the nearest elevated train station, you can use Uber's smartphone app to contact a local driver who will take you directly to your destination. A key advantage of Uber and similar apps is their frictionless payment interface. When you are done with your ride, you just get out of the car and walk away while the app charges your credit or debit card and pays the driver.[31] M-commerce is currently experiencing the largest growth in both retail and channel decision-making, in part because of its more than $20 billion annual revenue.

M-commerce also enables consumers using wireless mobile devices to connect to the Internet and shop. Essentially, M-commerce goes beyond text message advertisements to allow consumers to purchase goods and services using wireless mobile devices. M-commerce users adopt the new technology because it saves time and offers more convenience in a greater number of locations. The use of M-commerce has become increasingly important as users grow in both number and purchasing power. Consumers have become more reliant on digital technologies, as shown in the world's first fully digital generation, the Millennials, and firms that fail to react to this trend risk losing a rapidly growing group of M-commerce customers[32].

Many major companies, ranging from Polo Ralph Lauren to Sears, already offer shopping on mobile phones, and the growth potential is huge. Along with smartphone use, consumers are shopping with tablets just as much, if not more, than with company Web sites. One study even found that tablets accounted for twice as much in Web-based sales as smartphone purchases[33]. M-commerce in the United States will exceed $41 billion by 2017 and sales made on mobile devices on a global scale will exceed $110 billion in the same time frame.[34] In the United States, 87 percent of adults own a cellphone, 45 percent own a smartphone, 31 percent own a tablet, and 26 percent own an e-reader.[35] Fifty-five percent of adults use the Internet on their mobile devices, and 31 percent report that they go online with their mobile device more than they do with a desktop or laptop computer.[36] The gap between the number of smartphones owned and smartphones used for purchases is closing rapidly. During the holiday season, about 30 percent of smartphone owners check prices using some kind of price comparison app or read reviews online while inside a store, and almost 50 percent use their smartphones to call a friend or family member for purchase advice.[37] Overall, more than two-thirds of Americans use their mobile devices to obtain shopping information.[38]

Along with smartphone technology, companies are starting to look into other digital channels with which to connect with their customers. Social shopping allows multiple retailers to sell products to customers through social media sites. Aaramshop brings hundreds of neighborhood grocery stores to customers through Facebook. Customers makes their purchases online and their specific neighborhood stores take care of delivering the items directly to customers' homes.[39] Home delivery extends beyond groceries in many heavily populated

digital channels
electronic pathways that allow products and related information to flow from producer to consumer

M-commerce the ability to conduct commerce using a mobile device for the purpose of buying or selling goods or services

areas. In China and India, McDonald's has started delivering directly to its customers instead of making consumers come to them.

Firms are also using social media Web sites as digital channels—even in some cases without offering a purchasing opportunity. Companies create profiles on Web sites like Pinterest or Facebook and use them not only to give customers information about their products, but also to collect customer information. According to one recent study, 38 percent of all online customers follow at least one retailer on a social networking site. Many customers use these Web sites to find product information or get information on special deals, and those who follow a company's blog or profile on a social media site often end up clicking through to the firm's Web site.[40]

While some services group retailers together in order to bring products to customers, others allow consumers to combine and order larger amounts. Web sites like Groupon and Livingsocial give customers the opportunity to fulfill their individual needs at group prices. Many of these sites are organized and managed by intermediaries between manufacturers and customers, but others may be customer initiated or even created by firms to better promote their own products and manage demand.[41]

13-7d Factors Affecting Channel Choice

Marketing managers must answer many questions before choosing a marketing channel. A book manufacturer must decide, for example, what roles physical and electronic distribution will play in the overall marketing strategy and how these two paths will fare against each other. In addition, managers must decide what level of distribution intensity is appropriate and must ensure that the channel strategy they choose is consistent with product, promotion, and pricing strategies. The choice of channels depends on a holistic analysis of market factors, product factors, and producer factors.

MARKET FACTORS Among the most important market factors affecting distribution channel choices are market considerations. Specifically, managers should answer the following questions: Who are the potential customers? What do they buy? Where do they buy? When do they buy? How do they buy? Additionally, the choice of channel depends on whether the producer is selling to consumers directly, or through other industrial buyers, due to differences in the buying routines

of these groups. The geographic location and size of the market are also important factors guiding channel selection. As a rule, if the target market is concentrated in one or more specific areas, then direct selling through a sales force is appropriate, whereas intermediaries would be less expensive in broader markets.

PRODUCT FACTORS Complex, customized, and expensive products tend to benefit from shorter and more direct marketing channels. These types of products sell better through a direct sales force. Examples include pharmaceuticals, scientific instruments, airplanes, and mainframe computer systems. On the other hand, the more standardized a product is, the longer its distribution channel can be and the greater the number of intermediaries that can be involved without driving up costs. For example, with the exception of flavor and shape, the formula for chewing gum is fairly standard from producer to producer. As a result, the distribution channel for gum tends to involve many wholesalers and retailers.

The product stage in the life cycle is also an important factor in choosing a marketing channel. In fact, the choice of channel may change over the life of the product. As products become more common and less intimidating to potential users, producers tend to look for alternative channels. Similarly, perishable products such as vegetables and milk have a relatively short life span, and fragile products like china and crystal require a minimum amount of handling. Therefore, both require

Levi Strauss launched Signature, a line of low cost jeans available exclusively at Wal-Mart. According to the company, the Signature line offers superior fit, comfort, and style for less than $20.

fairly short marketing channels. Online retailers such as eBay facilitate the sale of unusual or difficult-to-find products that benefit from a direct channel.

PRODUCER FACTORS

Several factors pertaining to the producer itself are important to the selection of a marketing channel. In general, producers with large financial, managerial, and marketing resources are better able to perform their own marketing, and thus will use more direct channels. These producers have the ability to hire and train their own sales forces, warehouse their own goods, and extend credit to their customers. Smaller or weaker firms, on the other hand, must rely on intermediaries to provide these services for them. Compared to producers with only one or two product lines, producers that sell several products in a related area are able to choose channels that are more direct. Sales expenses then can be spread over more products.

A producer's desire to control pricing, positioning, brand image, and customer support also tends to influence channel selection. For instance, firms that sell products with exclusive brand images, such as designer perfumes and clothing, usually avoid channels in which discount retailers are present. Manufacturers of upscale products, such as Gucci (handbags) and Godiva (chocolates), may sell their wares only in expensive stores in order to maintain an image of exclusivity. Many producers have opted to risk their image, however, and test sales in discount channels. For example, Levi Strauss expanded its distribution network to include JCPenney, Sears, and Walmart.

Source: Spotify AB, Source: Gilt Groupe, Inc., Source: JackThreads, Source: Netflix, Inc.

13-7e Levels of Distribution Intensity

Organizations have three options for intensity of distribution: intensive distribution, selective distribution, or exclusive distribution. **Intensive distribution** is a form of distribution aimed at maximum market coverage. Here, the manufacturer tries to have the product available in every outlet where potential customers might want to buy it. If buyers are unwilling to search for a product, it must be made very accessible to buyers. The next level of distribution, **selective distribution**, is achieved by screening dealers and retailers to eliminate all but a few in any single area. Because only a few are chosen, the consumer must seek out the product. For example, HBO selectively distributes its popular television shows through a series of its own subscription-based channels (HBO, HBO on Demand, and HBO Go for mobile devices) and sells subscriptions or single episodes through Apple, Amazon.com, and Sony's online stores but does not stream them through Netflix or Hulu Plus. The most restrictive form of market coverage is **exclusive distribution**, which entails only one or a few dealers within a given area. Because buyers may have to search or travel extensively to buy the product, exclusive distribution is usually confined to consumer specialty goods, a few shopping goods, and major industrial equipment. Products such as Rolls-Royce automobiles, Chris-Craft powerboats, and Pettibone tower cranes are distributed under exclusive arrangements.

EMERGING DISTRIBUTION STRUCTURES In recent years, rapid changes in technology and communication have led to the emergence of new, experimental distribution methods and channel structures. For example, fashion flash sale sites like Gilt, JackThreads, and Ruelala have recently boomed in popularity. On these sites, new designer clothing items are made available every day—often at a discount from 15 to 80 percent, and always for an extremely limited time. The average fashion flash sale shopper is between 25 and 40 years of age and makes $100,000 a year—an ideal demographic for many marketers.

intensive distribution a form of distribution aimed at having a product available in every outlet where target customers might want to buy it

selective distribution a form of distribution achieved by screening dealers to eliminate all but a few in any single area

exclusive distribution a form of distribution that establishes one or a few dealers within a given area

Another emerging channel structure involves renting items that are usually only sold to end consumers. For example, some Web sites allow customers to rent and return high fashion products (renttherunway.com and fashionrenting.com), handbags and accessories (lovemeandleaveme.com), and even furniture (fashionfurniture.com). Rental versus retail channels open up an entirely new customer base for certain products that were once reserved for a much smaller group.

For many years, subscription services such as book-of-the-month clubs have provided customers products periodically over time. More recently, subscription services have expanded far beyond books and magazines to include clothing (bombfell.com), shoes (shoedazzle.com), crafting kits (craftaholicsanonymous.net), and wine (www.clubw.com). Many Web sites require subscriptions to view premium content, and streaming media services like Spotify, Netflix, and OnLive offer a wholly new type of subscription service.

Digital marketplaces like Steam and the Google Play Store constitute another recent trend in marketing channels. Digital licensing adds an interesting facet to customer sales; instead of selling a tangible product, digital marketplaces sell the rights to songs, movies, and television shows through their Web sites and applications. Instead of leaving home to purchase a physical album, game, or movie, consumers can select specific media and download them directly to their computers or mobile devices.

13-8 OMNICHANNEL VERSUS MULTICHANNEL MARKETING

Marketing channels are valuable because they provide a route for products and services to reach the customer. Customers have different preferences, however, as to which channels to use when browsing, seeking information, comparing products to one another, and making a purchase. A single customer may use different channels for each of these activities, including both traditional and digital channels! For example, a customer might first learn about a new smartwatch when browsing a catalog, then conduct research about it on the company's Web site. She might later go to a physical retail location to try out the product, before finally purchasing the device using a mobile app. Because of these varying preferences through different stages of the shopping cycle, many companies have begun to employ a multichannel marketing strategy, whereby customers are offered information, goods, services, and/or support through one or more synchronized channels. Recent studies have demonstrated that customers who use multiple channels when shopping become more engaged during the purchase process, and tend to spend more than customers who shop one channel only. The exception is when customers are buying simple, utilitarian products that are well known and intended for frequent use. Since customers are already familiar with these product types, single-channel designs are just as effective.[42]

Because consumers use multiple channels during the shopping experience, it has become important for channel members to create a seamless shopping

AND-ONE/iStock/Thinkstock

experience across all physical and digital channels. Facilitating such customer activities as checking a store's inventory online, purchasing an item through an app for in-store pickup, allowing online purchases to be returned in-store, and enabling mobile payment while shopping in-store are only a few strategies that producers and retailers are using to give customers the appearance that multiple channels are behaving as one.[43]

However, it is important to understand that the multichannel design does create redundancy and complexity in the firm's distribution system. Selling through multiple channels is typically accompanied by the construction of multiple, parallel supply chains, each with its own inventory, processes, and performance metrics. Multichannel systems typically have meant that each channel would operate different transportation and distribution systems, hold and account for its own inventory, and otherwise act as independent sales and profit centers, with little knowledge of the operations of the other. This proved problematic for one retailer who was selling its products both in physical stores and on its Web site. The company had a distribution center in Kentucky for its Internet retailing business, and another near Chicago for its physical stores located there. When a customer in Chicago visited the local store looking for a certain product, the shelves were empty, and he was directed to order products from the company's Web site if he wanted one in time for the holidays. He did so, and the product was shipped to his home—at significant expense—from the Kentucky distribution center, while unused product sat only miles from his home in the Chicago distribution center, waiting to be stocked on local store shelves.

Because of situations like these, many companies are transitioning to an omnichannel distribution operation that supports their multichannel retail operations and unifies their retail interfaces so that all customers receive equal and efficient service. For example,

retailers such as The Gap and Burberry allow customers to reserve items online for pickup in nearby stores, have employed a find-in-store feature on their Web sites that displays real-time stock information so customers can avoid unnecessary trips to the mall, and are beginning to provide in-store computer terminals or iPads for customers to search their Web sites for offerings the customer's local store may not carry. By making their inventory data available to customers in real-time, these retailers have effectively merged their multiple distribution channels in such a way that creates greater customer control over the shopping experience, leading to greater satisfaction and loyalty. We discuss further implications of this strategy in Chapter 15.

STUDY TOOLS 13

LOCATED AT BACK OF THE TEXTBOOK
☐ Rip out Chapter Review Card

LOCATED AT WWW.CENGAGEBRAIN.COM
☐ Review Key Terms Flashcards and create your own
☐ Track your knowledge and understanding of key concepts in marketing
☐ Complete practice and graded quizzes to prepare for tests
☐ Complete interactive content within the MKTG Online experience
☐ View the chapter highlight boxes within the MKTG Online experience

MKTG
ONLINE

ACCESS TEXTBOOK CONTENT ONLINE—
INCLUDING ON SMARTPHONES!

Includes Videos & Other
Interactive Resources!

MANAGE MY COURSE ⌄   STUDENT

MKTG10

CHAPTER
1

An Overview of Marketing

CHAPTER
2

Strategic Planning for
Competitive Advantage

4LTR
PRESS

Access MKTG ONLINE at www.cengagebrain.com

14 | Retailing

LEARNING OUTCOMES

After studying this chapter, you will be able to...

14-1 Explain the importance of the retailer within the channel and the U.S. economy

14-2 List and understand the different types of retailers

14-3 Explain why nonstore retailing is on the rise and list the advantages of its different forms

14-4 Discuss the different retail operations models and understand why they vary in strategy and format

14-5 Explain how retail marketing strategies are developed and executed

14-6 Discuss how services retailing differs from goods retailing

14-7 Understand how retailers address product/service failures and discuss the opportunities that service failures provide

14-8 Summarize current trends related to customer data, analytics, and technology

After you finish this chapter go to **PAGE 260** for **STUDY TOOLS.**

iStockphoto.com/kevinjeon00

14-1 THE IMPORTANCE OF RETAILING

Retailing represents all the activities directly related to the sale of goods and services to the ultimate consumer for personal, nonbusiness use. Retailing has enhanced the quality of our daily lives in countless ways. When we shop for groceries, hair care, clothes, books, or other products and services, we are doing business with **retailers**. The millions of goods and services provided by retailers mirror the diverse needs, wants, and trends of modern society. The U.S. economy depends heavily on the retail sector. Approximately two-thirds of the U.S. gross domestic product comes from retail activity, and retail sales account for nearly 30 percent of all consumer spending.[1]

retailing all the activities directly related to the sale of goods and services to the ultimate consumer for personal, nonbusiness use

retailer a channel intermediary that sells mainly to consumers

Retailing affects everyone, both directly and indirectly. The retailing industry is one of the largest employers in the United States, with almost 3.8 million U.S. retailers employing more than 29 million people—about one in five American workers. And the industry is expected to grow to more than 16 million by 2018.[2] In

addition, almost 10 percent of all businesses are classified as retailers.[3] Yet, retailing is still largely a mom-and-pop industry. Almost nine out of ten retail companies employ fewer than twenty employees, and according to the National Retail Federation, over 95 percent of all retailers operate just one store.[4] Most retailers are quite small, but a few giant organizations such as Walmart dominate the industry. Walmart's annual U.S. sales are greater than the combined sales of the four next largest U.S. retailers. As the retail environment changes, so too do retailers. Trends and innovations relating to customer data, social media, and alternative forms of shopping are constantly developing, and retailers have no choice but to react. The *best* retailers actually lead the way by anticipating change and developing new and exciting ways to interact with customers. We discuss each of these issues and more in this chapter.

 14-2 TYPES OF RETAILERS AND RETAIL OPERATIONS

Retail establishments can be classified in several ways, such as type of ownership, level of service, product assortment, and price. These variables can be combined in several ways to create numerous unique retail operating models. Exhibit 14.1 depicts the major types of retailers and classifies them by their key differentiating characteristics.

14-2a Ownership Arrangement

Depending on its ownership arrangement, a retailer can gain advantages from having a broad brand identity, or from having the freedom to take risks and innovate. Retail ownership takes one of three forms—they can be independently owned, part of a chain, or a franchise outlet.

- An **independent retailer** is owned by a person or group and is not operated as part of a larger network. Around the world, most retailers are independent, with each owner operating a singular store within a local community.

- A **chain store** is a group of retailers (of one or more brand names) owned and operated by a single organization. Under this form of ownership, a home office for the entire chain handles

independent retailer a retailer owned by a single person or partnership and not operated as part of a larger retail institution

chain store a store that is part of a group of the same stores owned and operated by a single organization

EXHIBIT 14.1 TYPES OF STORES AND THEIR CHARACTERISTICS

Type of Retailer	Level of Service	Product Assortment	Price	Gross Margin
Department store	Moderately high to high	Broad	Moderate to high	Moderately high
Specialty store	High	Narrow	Moderate to high	High
Supermarket	Low	Broad	Moderate	Low
Drugstore	Low to moderate	Medium	Moderate	Low
Convenience store	Low	Medium to narrow	Moderately high	Moderately high
Full-line discount store	Moderate to low	Medium to broad	Moderately low	Moderately low
Specialty discount store	Moderate to low	Medium to broad	Moderately low to low	Moderately low
Warehouse club	Low	Broad	Low to very low	Low
Off-price retailer	Low	Medium to narrow	Low	Low
Restaurant	Low to high	Narrow	Low to high	Low to high

retail buying; creates unified operating, marketing, and other administrative policies; and works to ensure consistency across different locations. The Gap and Starbucks are retail chains.

- A **franchise** is a retail business where the operator is granted a license to operate and sell a product under the brand name of a larger supporting organizational structure, such as Subway or Supercuts. Under this arrangement, a **franchisor** originates the trade name, product, methods of operation, and so on. A **franchisee**, in return, pays the franchisor for the right to use its name, product, and business methods, and takes advantage of the franchisor's brand equity and operational expertise. The most successful franchises are increasingly services retailers. Three of the top five franchises recognized by Entrepreneur Magazine are primarily service rather than goods providers.[5]

franchise a relationship in which the business rights to operate and sell a product are granted by the franchisor to the franchisee

franchisor the originator of a trade name, product, methods of operation, and the like that grants operating rights to another party to sell its product

franchisee an individual or business that is granted the right to sell another party's product

14-2b Level of Service

The service levels that retailers provide range from full-service to self-service. Some retailers, such as exclusive clothing stores, offer very high or even customized service levels. They provide alterations, credit, delivery, consulting, liberal return policies, layaway, gift-wrapping, and personal shopping. By contrast, retailers such as factory outlets and warehouse clubs offer virtually no service. After stock is set out for sale, the customer is responsible for any information gathering, acquisition, handling, use, and product assembly. At the extreme low end of the service continuum, a retailer may take the form of a product kiosk or vending machine.

14-2c Product Assortment

Retailers can also be categorized by the *width* and depth of their product lines. Width refers to the assortment of products offered; *depth* refers to the number of different brands offered within each assortment. Specialty stores such as Best Buy, Staples, and GameStop have the thinnest product assortments, usually carrying single or narrow product lines that are considerably deep. For example, a specialty pet store like PetSmart is limited to pet-related products, but may carry as many as twenty brands of dog food in a large variety of flavors, shapes, and sizes. On the other end of the spectrum, full-line discounters typically carry very wide assortments of merchandise that are fairly shallow.

Stores often modify their product assortments in order to accommodate factors in the external environment. Petitions started by concerned patrons in Australia and the United States caused major retailers to remove the Grand Theft Auto 5 video game and action figures from the popular television show Breaking Bad from store shelves. These patrons believed that the products' violent nature and association with the illegal drug culture were harmful to society.[6] Similarly, food products ranging from milk to vitamins to dog treats have been excluded from retail product lines in order to better ensure customer safety.

14-2d Price

Price is the fourth way to position retail stores. Traditional department stores and specialty stores typically charge the full "suggested retail price." In contrast, discounters, factory outlets, and off-price retailers use low prices and discounts to lure shoppers. The last column in Exhibit 14.1 shows the typical **gross margin**—how much the retailer makes as a percentage of sales after the cost of the goods sold is subtracted. (Margins will be covered in more detail in Chapter 19.) Today, prices in any store format might vary not just from day to day, but from minute to minute! Online retailers and traditional brick-and-mortar stores that have invested in electronic tagging systems are increasingly adopting dynamic pricing strategies that allow them to adjust to an item's surging popularity or slow movement in real time.[7]

14-2e Types of In-Store Retailers

Traditionally, retailers fall into one of several distinct types of retail stores, each of which features a product assortment, types of services, and price levels that align with the intended customers' shopping preferences. Recently, however, retailers began experimenting with alternative formats that blend the features and benefits of the traditional types. For instance, supermarkets are expanding their nonfood items and services, discounters are adding groceries, drugstores are becoming more like convenience stores, and department stores are experimenting with smaller stores. Nevertheless, many stores still fall into the traditional archetypes:

- **Department stores** such as JCPenney and Macy's carry a wide range of products and specialty goods, including apparel, cosmetics, housewares, electronics, and sometimes furniture. Each department acts as a separate profit center, but central management sets policies about pricing and the types of merchandise carried.

This December 2012 photo shows a wall that typically displays about 25 military-style rifles. Like many gun stores across American, Casper, Wyoming's Rocky Mountain Discount Sports sold out of firearms after the Sandy Hook shootings in Newtown, Connecticut.

- **Specialty stores** typically carry a deeper but narrower assortment of merchandise within a single category of interest. The specialized knowledge of their salesclerks allows for more attentive customer service. The Children's Place, Williams-Sonoma, and Foot Locker are well-known specialty retailers.

- **Supermarkets** are large, departmentalized, self-service retailers that specialize in food and some nonfood items. Some conventional supermarkets are being replaced by much larger *superstores*. Superstores offer one-stop shopping for food and nonfood needs, as well as services such as pharmacists, florists, salad bars, photo processing kiosks, and banking centers.

- **Drugstores** primarily provide pharmacy-related products and services, but many also carry an extensive selection of cosmetics, health and beauty aids, seasonal merchandise, greeting cards, toys, and some non-refrigerated

gross margin the amount of money the retailer makes as a percentage of sales after the cost of goods sold is subtracted

department store a store housing several departments under one roof

specialty store a retail store specializing in a given type of merchandise

supermarket a large, departmentalized, self-service retailer that specializes in food and some nonfood items

drugstore a retail store that stocks pharmacy-related products and services as its main draw

convenience foods. As other retailer types have begun to add pharmacies and direct mail prescription services have become more popular, drugstores have competed by adding more services such as 24-hour drive-through windows and low-cost health clinics staffed by nurse practitioners.

- A **convenience store** resembles a miniature supermarket but carries a much more limited line of high-turnover convenience goods. These self-service stores are typically located near residential areas and offer exactly what their name implies: convenient locations, long hours, and fast service in exchange for premium prices. In exchange for higher prices, however, customers are beginning to demand more from convenience store management, such as higher quality food and lower prices on staple items such as gasoline and milk.

- **Discount stores** compete on the basis of low prices, high turnover, and high volume. Discounters can be classified into several major categories:

  - **Full-line discount stores** such as Walmart offer consumers very limited service and carry a vast assortment of well-known, nationally branded goods such as housewares, toys, automotive parts, hardware, sporting goods, garden items, and clothing.

  - **Supercenters** extend the full-line concept to include groceries and a variety of services, such as pharmacies, dry cleaning, portrait studios, photo finishing, hair salons, optical shops, and restaurants. For supercenter operators such as Target,

Ken Wolter/Shutterstock.com

Sam's Club is an American chain of membership-only retail warehouse clubs owned and operated by Walmart.

customers are drawn in by food but end up purchasing other items from the full-line discount stock.

  - Single-line **specialty discount stores** such as Foot Locker offer a nearly complete selection of merchandise within a single category and use self-service, discount prices, high volume, and high turnover to their advantage. A **category killer** such as Best Buy is a specialty discount store that heavily dominates its narrow merchandise segment.

- A **warehouse club** sells a limited selection of brand name appliances, household items, and groceries. These are sold in bulk from warehouse outlets on a cash-and-carry basis to members only. Currently, the leading stores in this category are Sam's Club, Costco, and BJ's Wholesale Club.

- **Off-price retailers** such as TJ Maxx, Ross, and Marshall's sell at prices 25 percent or more below traditional department store prices because they buy inventory with cash and they don't require return privileges. These stores often sell manufacturers' overruns, irregular merchandise, and/

convenience store a miniature supermarket, carrying only a limited line of high-turnover convenience goods

discount store a retailer that competes on the basis of low prices, high turnover, and high volume

full-line discount store a discount store that carries a vast depth and breadth of product within a single product category

supercenter a large retailer that stocks and sells a wide variety of merchandise including groceries, clothing, household goods, and other general merchandise

specialty discount store a retail store that offers a nearly complete selection of single-line merchandise and uses self-service, discount prices, high volume, and high turnover

category killer a large discount store that specializes in a single line of merchandise and becomes the dominant retailer in its category

warehouse club a large, no-frills retailer that sells bulk quantities of merchandise to customers at volume discount prices in exchange for a periodic membership fee

off-price retailer a retailer that sells at prices 25 percent or more below traditional department store prices because it pays cash for its stock and usually doesn't ask for return privileges

or overstocks that they purchase at or below cost. A **factory outlet** is an off-price retailer that is owned and operated by a single manufacturer and carries one line of merchandise—its own. Manufacturers can realize higher profit margins using factory outlets than they would by disposing of the goods through independent wholesalers and retailers. **Used goods retailers** turn customers into suppliers: pre-owned items bought back from customers are resold to different customers. Used goods retailers can be either brick-and-mortar locations (such as Goodwill stores) or electronic marketplaces (such as eBay).

- **Restaurants** provide both tangible products—food and drink—and valuable services—food preparation and presentation. Most restaurants are also specialty retailers in that they concentrate their menu offerings on a distinctive type of cuisine—for example, Olive Garden Italian restaurants and Starbucks coffeehouses.

Laura Riquelme/Shutterstock.com

Tupperware, like the companies mentioned in the Direct Retailing section, directly markets itself to potential customers by offering a chance to purchase products inside the consumer's home.

14-3 THE RISE OF NONSTORE RETAILING

The retailing formats discussed so far entail physical stores where merchandise is displayed and to which customers must travel in order to shop. In contrast, **nonstore retailing** enables customers to shop without visiting a physical store location. Nonstore retailing adds a level of convenience for customers who wish to shop from their current locations. Due to broader changes in culture and society, nonstore retailing is currently growing faster than in-store retailing. The major forms of nonstore retailing are automatic vending, direct retailing, direct marketing, and Internet retailing (or *e-tailing*). In response to the recent successes seen by nonstore retailers, traditional brick-and-mortar retailers have begun seeking a presence in limited nonstore formats. For example, Target has begun to heighten its Internet presence by offering movies via streaming video. The new Target Ticket platform allows customers to purchase movies and popular television shows cheaply and without subscription fees, which allows Target to compete with services such as Apple's iTunes and Netflix.[8]

- **Automatic vending** entails the use of machines to offer goods for sale—for example, the soft drink, candy, or snack vending machines commonly found in public places and office buildings. Retailers are continually seeking new opportunities to sell via vending. As a result, modern vending machines today sell merchandise such as DVDs, digital cameras, perfumes, and even ice cream. A key aspect of their continuing success is the proliferation of cashless payment systems in response to consumers' diminishing preference for carrying cash.

- **Self-service technologies (SST)** comprise a form of automatic vending where services are the primary focus. Automatic teller machines, pay-at-the-pump gas stations, and movie ticket kiosks allow customers to make purchases that once required assistance from a company employee. However, as with any sort of self-service technology, automatic vending comes with failure risks due to human or technological error.

factory outlet an off-price retailer that is owned and operated by a manufacturer

used goods retailer a retailer whereby items purchased from one of the other types of retailers are resold to different customers

restaurant a retailer that provides both tangible products—food and drink—and valuable services—food preparation and presentation

nonstore retailing shopping without visiting a store

automatic vending the use of machines to offer goods for sale

self-service technologies (SST) technological interfaces that allow customers to provide themselves with products and/or services without the intervention of a service employee

Unless customers expect that they can easily recover from such errors, they may end up shopping elsewhere.

- **Direct retailing** representatives sell products door-to-door, in offices, or at in-home sales parties. Companies like Avon, Mary Kay, and The Pampered Chef have used this approach for years. Man Cave, a new home sales party developed for men, has been described as "like Mary Kay on steroids." Man Cave representatives invite male friends and family over for testosterone-fueled parties at which Man Cave products are used and Man Cave foods are eaten. Affiliates earn commissions for the sale of beer mugs, grilling tools, frozen steaks, and other Man Cave products.[9]

- **Direct marketing (DM)** includes techniques used to elicit purchases from consumers' homes, offices, and other convenient locations. Common DM techniques include telemarketing, direct mail, and mail-order catalogs. Shoppers using these methods are less bound by traditional shopping situations. Time-strapped consumers and those who live in rural or suburban areas are most likely to be DM shoppers because they value the convenience and flexibility it provides. DM occurs in several forms:

  - **Telemarketing** is a form of DM that employs outbound and inbound telephone contacts to sell directly to consumers. Telemarketing is a highly effective marketing technique; recent estimates indicate that 5,000 U.S. companies will spend over $15 billion on inbound and outbound calls by 2015.[10]

  - Alternatively, **direct mail** can be a highly efficient or highly inefficient retailing method, depending on the quality of the mailing list and the effectiveness of the mailing piece. With direct mail, marketers can precisely target their customers according to demographic,

direct retailing the selling of products by representatives who work door-to-door, office-to-office, or at home sales parties

direct marketing (DM) techniques used to get consumers to make a purchase from their home, office, or other nonretail setting

telemarketing the use of the telephone to sell directly to consumers

direct mail the delivery of advertising or marketing material to recipients of postal or electronic mail

microtargeting the use of direct marketing techniques that employ highly detailed data analytics in order to isolate potential customers with great precision

shop-at-home television network a specialized form of direct response marketing whereby television shows display merchandise, with the retail price, to home viewers

online retailing (e-tailing) a type of shopping available to consumers with personal computers and access to the Internet

geographic, and/or psychographic characteristics. Direct mailers are becoming more sophisticated in targeting the right customers. **Microtargeting** based on data analytics of census data, lifestyle patterns, financial information, and past purchase and credit history allows direct mailers to pick out those most likely to buy their products.[11] U.S. companies spend more than $45 billion annually on direct marketing—a larger share of advertising expenditures than any other media except television. More than $11.5 billion of that is spent on data and software solutions intended to heighten customer responsiveness.[12]

- **Shop-at-home television networks** such as HSN and QVC produce television shows that display merchandise to home viewers. Viewers can phone in their orders directly on toll-free lines and shop with their credit cards. The shop-at-home industry has quickly grown into a multi-billion-dollar business with a loyal customer following and high customer penetration.

- **Online retailing**, or **e-tailing**, enables a customer to shop over the Internet and have items delivered directly to her door. Global online shopping accounts for more than $1.3 trillion in sales today and is expected to reach $2.5 trillion by 2018.[13] Interactive shopping tools and live chats substitute for the in-store interactions with salespeople and product trials that customers traditionally use to make purchase decisions. Shoppers can look at a much wider variety of products online because physical space restrictions do not exist. While shopping, customers can take their time deciding what to buy.

In addition to retailer Web sites, consumers are increasingly using social media applications as shopping platforms. Social networking sites such as Facebook, Instagram, and Twitter enable users to immediately purchase items recommended by their social connections, a phenomenon known as *social shopping*. Companies are eager to establish direct linkages between social networking platforms and their own Web sites due to the belief that a product or service recommended by a friend will receive higher consideration from the potential customer.

 14-4 RETAIL OPERATIONS MODELS

The retail formats covered so far are co-aligned with unique operating models that guide the decisions made by their managers. Each operating

Back Stock   Floor Stock

model can be summarized as a set of guiding principles. For example, off-price retailers de-emphasize customer service and product selection in favor of lower prices, which are achieved through a greater focus on lean inventory management.

Alternatively, specialty shops generally adopt a high-service approach that is supported by an agile approach to inventory. By keeping a greater amount of **floor stock** (inventory displayed for sale to customers) and **back stock** (inventory held in reserve for potential future sale in a retailer's storeroom or stockroom) on hand, a broader range of customer demands can be accommodated. This operating model also implies higher prices for customers, however, so retail managers must make sure that they deliver on the promises their firms make to customers in order to secure their loyalty. At the same time, these retail managers must control demand via promotions and other sales events in order to sell off slow moving and perishable items, thereby making more room for items that are more popular.

These sorts of tradeoffs have been partially responsible for the recent emergence of hybrid retail operating models. As an example of a hybrid strategy, the Spanish women's fashion retailer Zara employs a specialty retail format with a twist: It uses a mass merchandising inventory strategy. Zara offers high quality products and excellent customer service to draw customers into its stores but never replenishes specific inventory items that are sold. Rather, its designers and buyers are continually introducing new products in small or medium quantities. Once a product sells out, a new one replaces it, allowing for a very lean operation. This strategy not only lowers inventory costs (and thereby increases profitability) but also creates an aura of exclusivity around each piece that the retailer sells: Each skirt, blouse, and accessory is effectively a limited edition item. This strategy also

has the ancillary benefit of driving customers back to the store in order to see what new products have arrived, and thus has the potential to increase repurchases.[14]

The tradeoffs inherent to retail operating models have both spurred the recent success of online-only retailers and led to a surge in online storefront development among retailers who have traditionally operated in physical formats only. A key advantage of online retail is that no physical retail store space is needed for displaying and selling merchandise. Lower cost remote distribution centers can be used since all of the showcasing occurs on the company's Web site. By moving online, a specialty store can gain the operational benefits of a mass merchandiser. It can showcase exclusive or trendy items in an almost-free space to potential customers located around the world, and can then fulfill demand from one of several localized distribution centers in a very short time. Fulfillment times are specified by the customer (according to their willingness to pay for greater shipping and delivery speed), and even this tradeoff is becoming less of a sticking point every year. Amazon's Prime subscription program, for example, includes free two-day shipping. The company recently revealed that it is experimenting with same day delivery via unmanned drones, and is already offering same-day delivery by traditional means within several limited geographic areas.[15] Startup company Deliv positioned itself in 2015 as a cutting-edge crowdsourced courier service. Deliv provides its more than 250 national and regional U.S. retail partners (such as Macy's and Footlocker) a means of competing with Amazon by offering same-day home delivery.[16] It will be very exciting to see

> **floor stock** inventory displayed for sale to customers
>
> **back stock** inventory held in reserve for potential future sale in a retailer's storeroom or stockroom

how these advances continue to change retail strategies and operations in the years to come.

Today, most retail stores remain operationally and tactically similar to those that have been in business for hundreds of years; with one or more physical locations that the customer must visit in order to purchase a stocked product, and with strategies in place to attract customers to visit. The sorts of differences we have described among retail operating models imply that managing one type of store instead of another can involve very different experiences. But most of the decisions that retail managers make can be distilled down to six categories of activity, referred to as the retailing mix. These categories, described in the next section, are relatively universal to all forms of retailing, but are applied in different ways based on the retail format.

14-5 EXECUTING A RETAIL MARKETING STRATEGY

Retail managers develop marketing strategies based on the goals established by stakeholders and the overall strategic plans developed by company leadership. Strategic retailing goals typically focus on increasing total sales, reducing costs of goods sold, and improving financial ratios such as return on assets or equity. At the store level, more tactical retailing goals include increased store traffic, higher sales of a specific item, developing a more upscale image, and creating heightened public awareness of the retail operation and its products or services. The tactical strategies that retailers use to obtain their goals include having a sale, updating décor, and launching a new advertising campaign. The key strategic tasks that precede these tactical decisions are defining and selecting a target market and developing the retailing mix to successfully meet the needs of the chosen target market.

14-5a Defining a Target Market

The first and foremost task in developing a retail strategy is to define the target market. This process begins with market segmentation, the topic of Chapter 8. Successful retailing has always been based on knowing the customer. Sometimes retailing chains flounder when management loses sight of the customers the stores should be serving. Customers' desires and preferences change over their personal and professional

> **retailing mix** a combination of the six Ps—product, promotion, place, price, presentation, and personnel—to sell goods and services to the ultimate consumer

lifespans, and it is important for retailers to be sensitive to these changes by migrating them to new and different products as their buying patterns evolve.

Target markets in retailing are often defined by demographics, geographic boundaries, and psychographics. For example, Blaze Pizza targets Millennial shoppers by providing a "build your own" pizza experience that mirrors the personal food design processes of Subway and Chipotle. This technique appeals to the Millennial psychographic characteristics of achievement and creativity.[17] Determining a target market is a prerequisite to creating the retailing mix. For example, Target's merchandising approach for sporting goods is to match its product assortment to the demographics of the local store and region.

14-5b Choosing the Retailing Mix

As previously noted, defining a retail operation entails combining the elements of the retailing mix to come up with a single retailing method to attract the target market. The **retailing mix** consists of six Ps: the four Ps of the marketing mix (*product, promotion, place,* and *price*) plus *presentation* and *personnel* (see Exhibit 14.2). The combination of the six Ps projects a store's (or Web site's) image and influences customers' perceptions. Using these impressions, shoppers position one store or Web site against another. Managers must make sure that the positioning is aligned with target customers' expectations.

PRODUCT The first element in the retailing mix is the product offering, also called the product assortment or merchandise mix. Developing a product offering is essentially a question of the width and depth of the product assortment. Price, store/Web site design, displays, and service are important to customers in determining where to shop, but the most critical factor is merchandise selection. This reasoning also holds true for online retailers. Amazon.com, for instance, offers enormous width in its product assortment with millions of different items, including books, music, toys, videos, tools and hardware, health and beauty aids, electronics, and software. Conversely, online specialty retailers such as Lemon and Mint and Bridge 55 focus on a single category of merchandise, hoping to attract loyal customers with a larger depth of products at lower prices and excellent customer service. Many online retailers purposely focus on single product line niches that could never attract enough foot traffic to support a traditional brick-and-mortar store. For instance, Web sites such as bugbitingplants.com and petflytrap.com sell and ship live carnivorous plants in the United States. After

EXHIBIT 14.2 THE RETAILING MIX

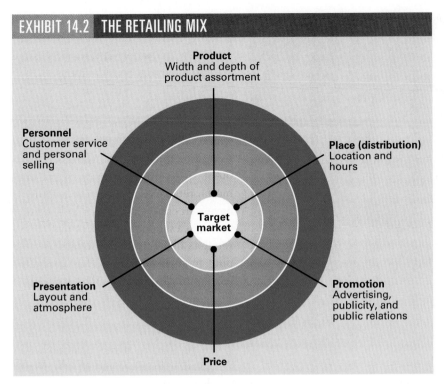

Product
Width and depth of product assortment

Personnel
Customer service and personal selling

Place (distribution)
Location and hours

Presentation
Layout and atmosphere

Promotion
Advertising, publicity, and public relations

Target market

Price

---

determining what products will satisfy target customers' desires, retailers must find sources of supply and evaluate the products. When the right products are found, the retail buyer negotiates a purchase contract.

PROMOTION Retail promotion strategy includes advertising, public relations and publicity, and sales promotion. The goal is to help position the store or Web site in customers' minds. Retailers design intriguing ads, stage special events, and develop promotions aimed at their target markets. Today's grand-openings are a carefully orchestrated blend of advertising, merchandising, goodwill, and glitter. All the elements of an opening—press coverage, special events, media advertising, and store displays—are carefully planned. Other promotions that are often used successfully include sales events, coupons, and discounts for certain products or customer groups. One risk associated with store promotions, however, is **brand cannibalization**: a situation whereby the promotion intended to draw in new customers simply shifts current customers from buying one brand to another brand. For example, when TGI Fridays began offering $10 appetizers to boost unit sales, sales of some main course items decreased.[18] Brand cannibalization is dangerous to the retailer for two reasons. First, the retailer incurs significant expense in executing the promotion itself. Second, the promotion creates inaccurate sales forecasts for both the promoted and cannibalized products, leading

to stockouts of the promoted brand and financial losses from discounting surplus inventory of the cannibalized brand. The latter types of losses can sometimes be significantly greater than the cost of the promotion itself. Therefore, retail managers should design their promotional activities carefully, with gaining new customers being the primary objective.

Much retail advertising is focused on the local level. Local advertising by retailers usually provides specific information about their stores, such as location, merchandise, hours, prices, and special sales. In contrast, national retail advertising generally focuses on image. For example, Target uses advertisements similar to designer fashion advertisements to depict high-quality goods. Paired with the ubiquitous red target and tag line "Expect more. Pay less," Target is demonstrating that it sells products that consumers normally aspire to own at prices they can afford.

Target's advertising campaigns also take advantage of cooperative advertising, another popular retail advertising practice. Traditionally, marketers would pay retailers to feature their products in store mailers, or a marketer would develop a television campaign for the product and simply tack on several retailers' names at the end. But Target's advertising uses a more collaborative trend by integrating products such as Tide laundry detergent or Coca-Cola into the actual campaign. Another common form of cooperative advertising involves promotion of exclusive products. For example, Target hires famous trendy designers for temporary partnerships, during which they develop reasonably priced product lines available exclusively at Target stores. Recently, Target teamed up with Neiman Marcus to offer a collection of holiday luxury items. These items were sold both at Target and Neiman Marcus stores, as well as on both stores' outlet Web stores.

PLACE The retailing axiom "location, location, location" has long emphasized the importance of place to the retail mix. The physical *location* decision is

> **brand cannibalization** the reduction of sales for one brand as the result of the introduction of a new product or promotion of a current product by another brand

The Victoria's Secret Fashion Show is a major part of the company's marketing strategy. Their "Angels" serve as key members of the company's marketing team.

important first because the retailer is making a large, semi-permanent commitment of resources that can reduce its future flexibility. Second, the physical location will almost inevitably affect the store's future growth and profitability. Many retailers work with consultants and/or city planners to determine the best sites for current sales as well as potential growth in the future.

Physical site location begins by choosing a community. Important factors to consider are the area's economic growth potential, the amount of competition, and geography. For instance, retailers like TJ Maxx and Walmart often build stores in new communities that are still under development. Fast-food restaurants tend to place a priority on locations with other fast-food restaurants because being located in clusters helps to draw customers for each restaurant. Even after careful research, however, the perfect location can be elusive in the face of changing markets. Mobile food trucks circumvent this problem by being able to relocate at will. By moving from spot to spot over the course of a day and parking outside events and heavily trafficked areas, mobile food trucks can maximize their exposure and adapt to changing markets.

After identifying a geographic region or community, retailers must choose a specific site. In addition to growth potential, the important factors to consider are neighborhood socioeconomic characteristics, traffic flows, land costs, zoning regulations, and public transportation. A particular site's visibility, parking, entrance and exit locations, accessibility, and safety and security issues are also important considerations.

A retailer should consider how its store fits into the surrounding environment. Retail decision makers probably would not locate a Dollar General store next door to a Neiman Marcus department store. Furthermore, brick-and-mortar retailers have to decide whether to have a freestanding unit or to become a tenant in a shopping center or mall. Large retailers like Target and sellers of shopping goods like furniture and cars often use an isolated, freestanding location. A freestanding store location may have the advantages of low site cost or rent and no nearby competitors. On the other hand, it may be hard to attract customers to a freestanding location, and no other retailers are around to share costs. To be successful, stores in isolated locations must become "destination stores." A **destination store** is a store consumers seek out and purposely plan to visit. Web sites can also be destinations for shoppers. Amazon is a destination Web site for a wide variety of products, and Google is a destination Web site for search information.

Freestanding units are increasing in popularity as brick-and-mortar retailers strive to make their stores more convenient to access, more enticing to shop, and more profitable. Freestanding sites now account for more than half of all retail store construction starts in the United States as more and more retailers are deciding not to locate in pedestrian malls. Perhaps the greatest reason for developing a freestanding site is greater visibility. Retailers often feel they get lost in huge shopping centers and malls, but freestanding units can help stores develop an identity with shoppers. Also, an aggressive expansion plan may not allow time to wait for shopping centers to be built. Drugstore chains like Walgreens have been purposefully relocating their existing shopping center stores to freestanding sites, especially street corner sites for drive-through accessibility.

Shopping centers first appeared in the 1950s when the U.S. population started migrating to the suburbs. The first shopping centers were *strip centers*, typically located along busy streets. They usually included a supermarket, a variety store, and perhaps a few specialty stores. Then *community shopping centers* emerged,

destination store a store that consumers purposely plan to visit prior to shopping

with one or two small department stores, more specialty stores, a couple of restaurants, and several apparel stores. These community shopping centers provided off-street parking and a broader variety of merchandise. *Regional malls* offering a much wider variety of merchandise started appearing in the mid-1970s. Regional malls are either entirely enclosed or roofed to allow shopping in any weather. Most are landscaped with trees, fountains, sculptures, and the like to enhance the shopping environment. They have acres of free parking. The *anchor stores* or *generator stores* (often major department stores) are usually located at opposite ends of the mall to create heavy foot traffic.

According to shopping center developers, *lifestyle centers* are emerging as the newest generation of shopping centers. Lifestyle centers typically combine outdoor shopping areas composed of upscale retailers and restaurants, with plazas, fountains, and pedestrian streets. They appeal to retail developers looking for an alternative to the traditional shopping mall, a concept rapidly losing favor among shoppers. Though shopping malls bring multiple retail locations together, location is often not the most important motivator for a customer to choose a specific store. Instead, most shoppers look for stores that guarantee product availability, more service employees, and time saving opportunities.

Many smaller specialty lines are opening shops inside larger stores to expand their retail opportunities without risking investment in a separate store. Toys"R"Us worked with Macy's to open stores-within-a-store at numerous Macy's locations. The 1,500-square-foot toy sections offered dolls, puzzles, and other potential stocking stuffers.[19] The Toys"R"Us modules reflect a popular trend of pop-up shops—tiny, temporary stores that stay in one location for only a few months. Pop-up shops help retailers reach a wide market while avoiding high rent at retail locations. They have become the marketing tool du jour for large companies.

PRICE Another important element in the retailing mix is price. Retailing's ultimate goal is to sell products to consumers, and the right price is critical to ensure sales. Because retail prices are usually based on the cost of the merchandise, an essential part of pricing is efficient and timely buying. Another pricing strategy is "value-based pricing," which focuses on the value of the product to the customer more than the cost of the product to the supplier. Price is also a key element in a retail store's positioning strategy. Higher prices often indicate a level of quality and help reinforce the prestigious image of retailers, as they do for Lord & Taylor and Neiman Marcus. On the other hand, discounters and off-price retailers, such as Target and TJ Maxx, offer a good value for the money.

PRESENTATION The presentation of a retail store helps determine the store's image and positions the retail store in consumers' minds. For instance, a retailer that wants to position itself as an upscale store would use a lavish or sophisticated presentation. The main element of a store's presentation is its **atmosphere**, the overall impression conveyed by a store's physical layout, décor, and surroundings. The atmosphere might create a relaxed or busy feeling, a sense of luxury or efficiency, a friendly or cold attitude, a sense of organization or clutter, or a fun or serious mood. Urban Outfitters stores, targeted to Generation Y consumers, use raw concrete, original brick, rusted steel, and unfinished wood to convey an urban feel. These are the most influential factors in creating a store's atmosphere:

- *Employee type and density:* Employee type refers to an employee's general characteristics—for instance, neat, friendly, knowledgeable, or service oriented. Density is the number of employees per thousand square feet of selling space. Whereas low employee density creates a do-it-yourself, casual atmosphere, high employee density denotes readiness to serve the customer's every whim.

- *Merchandise type and density:* A prestigious retailer like Nordstrom or Neiman Marcus carries the best brand names and displays them in a neat, uncluttered arrangement. Discounters and off-price retailers often carry seconds or out-of-season goods crowded into small spaces and hung on long racks by category—tops, pants, skirts, and so on—creating the impression that "We've got so much stuff, we're practically giving it away."

- *Fixture type and density:* Fixtures can be elegant (rich woods) or trendy (chrome and smoked glass); they can even consist of old, beat-up tables, as in an antiques store. The fixtures should be consistent with the general atmosphere the store is trying to create.

- *Sound:* Sound can be pleasant or unpleasant for a customer. Music can entice some customers to stay in the store longer and buy more or to eat quickly and leave a table for others. It can also control the pace of the store traffic, create an image, and attract or direct the shopper's attention.

- *Odors:* Smell can either stimulate or

atmosphere the overall impression conveyed by a store's physical layout, décor, and surroundings

detract from sales. Research suggests that people evaluate merchandise more positively, spend more time shopping, and are generally in a better mood when an agreeable odor is present. Retailers use fragrances as an extension of their retail strategy.

- *Visual factors:* Colors can create a mood or focus attention and therefore are an important factor in atmosphere. Red, yellow, and orange are considered warm colors and are used when a feeling of warmth and closeness is desired. Cool colors like blue, green, and violet are used to open up closed-in places and create an air of elegance and cleanliness. Many retailers have found that natural lighting, either from windows or skylights, can lead to increased sales. Outdoor lighting can also affect a customer's choice of retailer.

The **layout** of retail stores is also a key factor in their success. The goal is to use all of the store's space effectively, including aisles, fixtures, merchandise displays, and non-selling areas. In addition to making shopping easy and convenient for the customer, an effective layout has a powerful influence on traffic patterns and purchasing behavior. Layout also includes where products are placed in the store. Many technologically advanced retailers are using a technique called *market-basket analysis* to sift through the data collected by their point-of-purchase scanning equipment. The analysis looks for products that are commonly purchased together to help retailers find ideal locations for each product. Walmart uses market-basket analysis to determine where in the store to stock products for customer convenience. Kleenex tissues, for example, are in the paper-goods aisle and also beside the cold medicines.

Retailers can better acquire and use assets when they customize store layouts and merchandise mixes to the tastes of local consumer bases. For example, O'Reilly Auto Parts designs each of its retail outlets with the wants and needs of local auto drivers in mind, creating a neighborhood-specific strategy for each location. By customizing layout and product mix to the vehicles owned and operated in a particular area, the company can simultaneously provide greater levels of availability and reduce inventory, creating savings that the company passes along to customers.[20]

PERSONNEL People are a unique aspect of retailing. Most retail sales involve a customer–salesperson relationship, if only briefly. Sales personnel provide their customers with the amount of service prescribed by the retail strategy of the store.

layout the internal design and configuration of a store's fixtures and products

Retail salespeople serve another important selling function: They persuade shoppers to buy. They must therefore be able to persuade customers that what they are selling is what the customer needs. Salespeople are trained in two common selling techniques: trading up and suggestion selling. *Trading* up means persuading customers to buy a higher-priced item than they originally intended to purchase. To avoid selling customers something they do not need or want, however, salespeople should take care when practicing trading-up techniques. *Suggestion selling*, a common practice among most retailers, seeks to broaden customers' original purchases with related items. For example, if you buy a new printer at Office Depot, the sales representative will ask if you would like to purchase paper, a USB cable, and/or extra ink cartridges. Suggestion selling by sales or service associates should always help shoppers recognize true needs rather than sell them unwanted merchandise.

Providing great customer service is one of the most challenging elements in the retail mix because customer expectations for service vary greatly. What customers expect in a department store is very different from what they expect in a discount store. Customer expectations also change. Ten years ago, shoppers wanted personal, one-on-one attention. Today, many customers are happy to help themselves as long as they can easily find what they need.

14-6 RETAILING DECISIONS FOR SERVICES

The fastest-growing part of our economy is the service sector. Although distribution in the service sector is difficult to visualize, the same skills, techniques, and strategies used to manage inventory can also be used to manage service inventory, such as hospital beds, bank accounts, or airline seats. The quality of the planning and execution of distribution can have a major impact on costs and customer satisfaction.

Because service industries are so customer oriented, service quality is a priority. To manage customer relationships, many service providers, such as insurance carriers, physicians, hair salons, and financial services, use technology to schedule appointments, manage accounts, and disburse information. Service distribution focuses on four main areas:

- *Minimizing wait times:* Minimizing the amount of time customers wait in line is a key factor in maintaining the quality of service.

Quality of service is directly tied to how long people have to wait in line.

Andrey_Popov/Shutterstock.com

- *Managing service capacity:* If service firms don't have the capacity to meet demand, they must either turn down some prospective customers, let service levels slip, or expand capacity.

- *Improving service delivery:* Service firms are now experimenting with different distribution channels for their services. Choosing the right distribution channel can increase the times that services are available or add to customer convenience.

- *Establishing channel-wide network coherence:* Because services are to some degree intangible, service firms also find it necessary to standardize their service quality across different geographic regions to maintain their brand image.

14-7 ADDRESSING RETAIL PRODUCT/ SERVICE FAILURES

In spite of retailers' best intentions and efforts to satisfy each and every customer, all retailers inevitably disappoint a subset of their customers. In some cases, customer disappointment occurs by design. No retailer can be everything to every customer, and by making strategic decisions related to targeting, segmentation, and the retailing mix, retailers implicitly decide which customers will be delighted and which will probably leave the store unsatisfied. In other cases, service failures are unintentional. A product may be located where customers cannot easily find it (or it may remain in the stockroom, entirely out of customer view), or an employee may provide mistaken information about a product's features or benefits. Customers are generally indifferent to the reasons for retailer errors, and their

reactions to mistakes such as product stockouts and unexpectedly poor quality products can range widely. Some may simply leave the store, while others will respond with anger or even revenge behaviors intended to prevent other customers from visiting the store.[21]

The best retailers have plans in place not only to recover from inevitable lapses in service but perhaps even to benefit from them. For these top-performing stores, service recovery is handled proactively as part of an overarching plan to maximize the customer experience. Actions that might be taken include:

- Notifying customers in advance of stockouts and explaining the reasons why certain products are not available

- Implementing liberal return policies designed to ensure that the customer can bring back any item for any reason (if the product fails to work as planned, or even if the customer simply doesn't like it)

- Issuing product recalls in conjunction with promotional offers that provide future incentives to repurchase

In short, the best retailers treat customer disappointments as opportunities to interact with and improve relations with their customers. Evidence indicates that successful handling of such failures can sometimes yield even higher levels of customer loyalty than if the failure had never occurred at all.

14-8 RETAILER AND RETAIL CUSTOMER TRENDS AND ADVANCEMENTS

Though retailing has been around for thousands of years, it continues to change every day. Retailers are constantly innovating. They are always looking for new products and services (or ways to offer them) that will attract new customers or inspire current ones to buy in greater quantities or more frequently. Many of the most interesting and effective retail innovations that have recently taken hold are related to the use of purchase and shopping data to better understand customer wants and needs. Finding new and better ways to entice customers into a store—and then to spend more money once there—is another hotbed of innovation. This chapter concludes with an examination into emerging trends and recent advancements in retailing.

It is important to recognize that, fundamentally, retailers decide what to sell on the basis of what their target market wants to buy. They base these decisions on market research, past sales, fashion trends, customer requests, and other sources. Recently, the need for more and better information has led many retailers to use **big data analytics**, a process whereby retailers use complex mathematical models to make better product mix decisions. Dillard's, Target, and Walmart use big data analytics to determine which products to stock and at what prices, how to manage markdowns, and how to advertise to draw target customers. The data these and other companies collect at the point of sale and throughout their stores enable retailers and suppliers alike to gain better customer insights. For example, instead of simply unloading products into the distribution channel and leaving marketing, sales and relationship building to local dealers, auto manufacturers use Web sites to keep in touch with customers and prospects. They inquire about lifestyles, hobbies, and vehicle needs in an effort to develop long-lasting relationships in the hopes that these consumers will reward them with brand loyalty in the future.

Retailers are increasingly using **beacons**—devices that send out connecting signals to customers' smartphones and tablets. These devices recognize when a customer is in or near the store and indicate to an automated system that the customer is ripe to receive a marketing message via e-mail or text. Beacons can also notify sales associates to offer (or not offer) a coupon at the point of sale. Some retailers are using an app called Swarm to map customer foot traffic data, which they use to make better decisions about product placement within the floor grid. Carefully

Big retailers like Target use big data analytics to determine which products to stock and at what price.

designed beacons can even have an aesthetic appeal. At some retailers, cameras and beacons are built into mannequins located inside the store and in window displays. These beacons not only act as data collection devices, but also as primary displays for the clothing and jewelry that appeal to customers' eyes. [22]

14-8a Shopper Marketing and Analytics

Shopper marketing is an emerging retailing trend that employs market data to best serve customers as they prepare to make a purchase. Shopper marketing focuses first on understanding how a brand's target consumers behave as shoppers in different channels and formats, and then using this information in business-based strategies and initiatives that are carefully designed to deliver balanced benefits to all stakeholders— brands, channel members, and customers. It may sound simple, but it is anything but. Whereas brand manufacturers used to advertise widely and tried to ensure that their products were available wherever consumers shopped, now they are placing far more emphasis on partnering with specific retailers or Web sites. Brand manufacturers work with retailers on everything from in-store initiatives to customized retailer-specific products. Shopper marketing brings brand managers and account managers together to connect with consumers along the entire path-to-purchase,

big data analytics the process of discovering patterns in large data sets for the purposes of extracting knowledge and understanding human behavior

beacon a device that sends out connecting signals to customers' smartphones and tablets in order to bring them into a retail store or improve their shopping experience

shopper marketing understanding how one's target consumers behave as shoppers, in different channels and formats, and leveraging this intelligence to generate sales or other positive outcomes whether it be at home, on the go via mobile marketing, or in the store. Both manufacturers and retailers now think about consumers specifically while they are in shopping mode. They use **shopper analytics** to dig deeply into customers' shopping attitudes, perceptions, emotions, and behaviors—and are thereby able to learn how the shopping experience shapes these differences. More and more companies are conducting or participating in large-scale data analytics projects to better understand how shoppers think when they shop at a store or on a Web site and what factors influence their thought processes.

Shopper marketing is becoming increasingly popular as businesses see the implications of this new method of customer research. One implication is the strategic alignment of customer segments. Brands' core target consumers are compared to retailers' most loyal shoppers in an effort to find intersecting areas where brands and retailers can pool their resources. The ideal outcome is a more focused marketing effort and a three-way win for brands, channel members, *and* customers.

Shopper marketing also has significant implications for retailers' supply chains. As in-store initiatives become more unique and short-term and products become more customized, supply chains must react more quickly to customer demand changes. Thus, shopper marketing has increased the need for sophisticated analytics and metrics. As with many modern business efforts, shopper marketing forces managers to coordinate better, measure more, think more creatively, and move faster.

14-8b Future Developments in Retail Management

A retailing trend with great growth potential is the leveraging of technology to increase touchpoints with customers and thereby generate greater profitability. The use of mobile devices and social media while browsing, comparison shopping, and actually making a purchase is becoming extremely pervasive, leading retailers to rethink how they should appeal to shoppers in the decision-making mode. Recall that customers who "showroom" visit a physical retail store to examine product features or quality firsthand, but then eventually make the purchase online. This practice has motivated a showrooming response from retailers themselves, who reduce the amount of stock kept on hand, rent or lease smaller spaces, and ramp up their fulfillment capabilities at distribution centers. Showrooming and data analytics have even led to the development of virtual reality apps that enable customers to see themselves wearing articles of desired clothing without physically putting them on! These

Source: Toysrus.com

National toy store chain Toys'R'Us offers a click-and-collect service whereby customers can make purchases online and then pick their items up in-store.

shopper analytics searching for and discovering meaningful patterns in shopper data for the purpose of fine-tuning, developing, or changing market offerings

approaches have led some retailers to pursue a strategy of **retail channel omnification** (recall Chapter 13's discussion of omnichannel distribution operations). Retailers like Nordstrom used to treat their physical stores as entirely different businesses from their online stores, with each channel having a unique distribution system and a dedicated inventory. Now, retailers are combining these ventures into a single system that is responsible for delivering on customer demand regardless of whether it originated in a physical store or in cyberspace.[23] This single system avoids redundancies in inventory and transportation, saving costs and enabling retailers to offer competitive prices across their various outlets. Customers of Nordstrom, Nordstrom Rack, Nordstrom.com, hautelook.com, and nordstromrack.com can seamlessly transition between each of these channels when shopping, returning purchased goods or scheduling services such as alterations.

However, not all retailers are embracing omnification as the way of the future. The alternative strategy, **click-and-collect**, also enables customers to make their purchases online. Rather than waiting for orders to arrive at their homes, customers drive to physical stores to pick their orders up.[24] When retailers use this strategy, customers benefit from greater speed of delivery (in fact, they become the delivery vehicle), while retailers themselves benefit from the fact that customers must enter their stores in order to claim their purchases. Once inside, customers can be marketed to, increasing the likelihood that they will purchase add-on items or otherwise engage in impulse buying. It remains to be seen whether one or both of these strategies will stand the test of time, but it is certain that retailers are preparing for the inevitability of the Internet as an important shopping and purchasing medium for the foreseeable future.

retail channel omnification
the reduction of multiple retail channel systems into a single, unified system for the purpose of creating efficiencies or saving costs

click-and-collect the practice of buying something online and then traveling to a physical store location to take delivery of the merchandise

STUDY TOOLS 14

LOCATED AT BACK OF THE TEXTBOOK
☐ Rip out Chapter Review Card

LOCATED AT WWW.CENGAGEBRAIN.COM
☐ Review Key Terms Flashcards and create your own
☐ Track your knowledge and understanding of key concepts in marketing
☐ Complete practice and graded quizzes to prepare for tests
☐ Complete interactive content within the MKTG Online experience
☐ View the chapter highlight boxes within the MKTG Online experience

MKTG ONLINE

STUDY YOUR WAY WITH STUDYBITS!

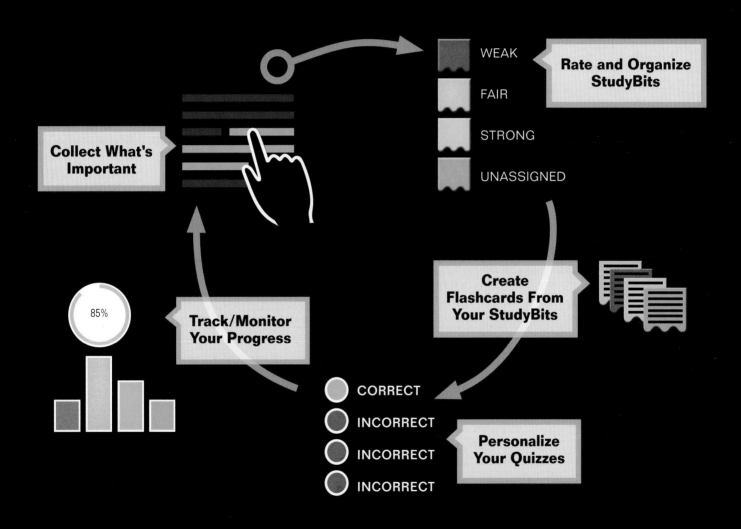

Rate and Organize StudyBits

WEAK
FAIR
STRONG
UNASSIGNED

Collect What's Important

Create Flashcards From Your StudyBits

Track/Monitor Your Progress

85%

CORRECT
INCORRECT
INCORRECT
INCORRECT

Personalize Your Quizzes

4LTR PRESS

15 | Marketing Communications

After you finish this chapter go to **PAGE 279** for **STUDY TOOLS.**

LEARNING OUTCOMES

After studying this chapter, you will be able to…

15-1 Discuss the role of promotion in the marketing mix

15-2 Describe the communication process

15-3 Explain the goals and tasks of promotion

15-4 Discuss the elements of the promotional mix

15-5 Discuss the AIDA concept and its relationship to the promotional mix

15-6 Discuss the concept of integrated marketing communications

15-7 Describe the factors that affect the promotional mix

15-1 THE ROLE OF PROMOTION IN THE MARKETING MIX

Few goods or services, no matter how well developed, priced, or distributed, can survive in the marketplace without effective **promotion**—communication by marketers that informs, persuades, and reminds potential buyers of a product in order to influence an opinion or elicit a response.

promotion communication by marketers that informs, persuades, and reminds potential buyers of a product in order to influence an opinion or elicit a response

promotional strategy a plan for the optimal use of the elements of promotion: advertising, public relations, personal selling, sales promotion, and social media

competitive advantage one or more unique aspects of an organization that cause target consumers to patronize that firm rather than competitors

Promotional strategy is a plan for the optimal use of the elements of promotion: advertising, public relations, personal selling, sales promotion, and social media. Promotion is a vital part of the marketing mix, informing consumers of a product's benefits and thereby positioning the product in the marketplace. As Exhibit 15.1 shows, the marketing manager determines the goals of the company's promotional strategy in light of the firm's overall goals for the marketing mix—product, place (distribution), promotion, and price. Using these overall goals, marketers combine the elements of the promotional strategy (the promotional mix) into a coordinated plan. The promotion plan then becomes an integral part of the marketing strategy for reaching the target market.

The main function of a marketer's promotional strategy is to convince target customers that the goods and services offered provide a competitive advantage over the competition. A **competitive advantage** is the set of unique features of a company and its products that are perceived by the target market as significant

and superior to those of the competition. Such features can include high product quality, rapid delivery, low prices, excellent service, or a feature not offered by the competition. Promotional strategies have changed a great deal over the years as many targeted customer segments have become more difficult to reach. Informative

EXHIBIT 15.1 ROLE OF PROMOTION IN THE MARKETING MIX

Overall marketing objectives

Promotional mix

- Advertising
- Public relations
- Sales promotion
- Personal selling
- Social media

Marketing mix

- Product
- Place (distribution)
- Promotion
- Price

Promotion plan

Target market

television advertisements are no longer enough, forcing marketers to think more creatively. Most modern campaigns utilize a variety of newer tactics—such as digital paid media, social media, and influencer marketing—in addition to more traditional media like television and print. Dodge, for example, chose fictitious *Anchorman* character Ron Burgundy (played by Will Ferrell) as its pitchman for the Durango SUV. The promotional strategy, which involved more than 80 Web and television ads, drove a 59 percent sales boost in the first month and an 80 percent increase in Web traffic for Dodge. Lower-level Web activities such as selecting automobile options and searching for a dealer rose more than 100 percent. Dodge's YouTube video views topped 15 million within two months, prompting guest appearances on several CNN programs and dozens of local newscasts in selected states. This campaign led some to feel that the Ron Burgundy character was overexposed, but the strategy proved extremely successful for Dodge.[1]

15-2 MARKETING COMMUNICATION

Promotional strategy is closely related to the process of communication. As humans, we assign meaning to feelings, ideas, facts, attitudes, and emotions.

Communication is the process by which meanings are exchanged or shared through a common set of symbols. When a company develops a new product, changes an old one, or simply tries to increase sales of an existing good or service, it must communicate its selling message to potential customers. Marketers communicate information about the firm and its products to the target market and various publics through their promotional programs.

15-2a Interpersonal Communication

Communication can be divided into two major categories: interpersonal communication and mass communication. **Interpersonal communication** is direct, face-to-face communication between two or more people. When communicating face-to-face, people see the other person's reaction and can respond almost immediately. Salespeople for French cosmetics store chain Sephora are trained on the company's most popular products, enabling them to assist customers and answer questions directly. A salesperson speaking directly with a customer is an example of an interpersonal marketing communication.

15-2b Mass Communication

Mass communication involves communicating a concept or message to large audiences. A great number of marketing communications are directed to consumers as a whole, usually through a mass medium such as television or newspapers. When a company advertises, it generally does not personally know the people with whom it is trying to communicate. Furthermore, the company often cannot respond immediately to consumers' reactions to its messages (unless they are using social media or other Internet-based marketing tools). Any clutter from competitors' messages or other distractions in the environment can reduce the effectiveness of the

Salespeople for Sephora are trained on the company's most popular products, this enables them to be more helpful to customers.

mass-communication effort. Continuing the previous example, Sephora uses many different mass media vehicles (including magazines, the Internet, and television) to reach its target audience.

15-2c The Communication Process

Marketers are both senders and receivers of messages. As *senders*, marketers attempt to inform, persuade, and remind the target market to take actions compatible with the need to promote the purchase of goods and services. As *receivers*, marketers listen to the target market in order to develop the appropriate messages, adapt existing messages, and spot new communication opportunities. In this way, most marketing communication is a two-way, rather than one-way, process. The two-way nature of the communication process is shown in Exhibit 15.2.

THE SENDER AND ENCODING The **sender** is the originator of the message in the communication process. In an interpersonal conversation, the sender may be a parent, a friend, or a salesperson. For an advertisement, press release, or social media campaign, the sender is the company or organization itself. It can sometimes be difficult to tell who the sender of a promotional message is, especially in the case of bold, avant-garde advertisements. Sometimes, senders intentionally cover up their identities in order to build buzz around an advertisement. For example, a video titled "Elevator Murder

communication the process by which we exchange or share meaning through a common set of symbols

interpersonal communication direct, face-to-face communication between two or more people

mass communication the communication of a concept or message to large audiences

sender the originator of the message in the communication process

EXHIBIT 15.2 **COMMUNICATION PROCESS**

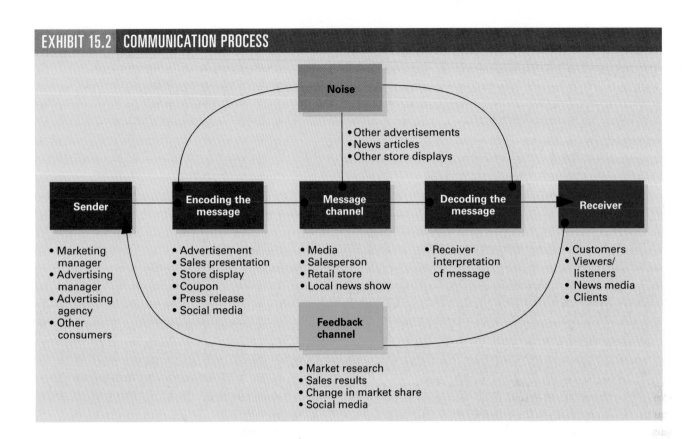

Experiment" recently went viral after mysteriously being uploaded to YouTube. In the video, the reactions of unsuspecting bystanders are secretly filmed as they witness a staged strangulation in a public New York City elevator. After the video went viral, it was revealed to be an advertisement for the Colin Farrell film *Dead Man Down*. The film's grim themes, extreme violence, and gritty settings were incorporated into the elevator prank video, which even used one of the film's plot points—murder in an elevator.

Encoding is the conversion of the sender's ideas and thoughts into a message, usually in the form of words or signs. A basic principle of encoding is that what the source says is not what matters, but what the receiver hears. In the case of "Elevator Murder Experiment," the video encoded sentiments such as "you won't know what to expect" and "difficult ethical choices will need to be made"—provocative selling points for a gruesome action thriller.[2] One way of conveying a message the receiver will hear properly is to use concrete words and pictures.

MESSAGE TRANSMISSION Transmission of a message requires a **channel**—a voice, radio, newspaper, computer, smartphone, or other communication medium. A facial expression or gesture can also serve as a channel. The *Dead Man Down's* marketing team used social media as the primary channel on which it distributed the advertisement. After marketers posted the video to YouTube, individuals fascinated by the social experiment ran with it. They shared the video with their friends in person, posted it to Facebook and Twitter, and shared it through several other unorthodox channels. Eventually, local and national media outlets published print articles and ran television segments about the video, creating new channels for the campaign as they did so.[3] The response to these viral activities clearly created a lot of free publicity.

Reception occurs when the message is detected by the receiver and enters his or her frame of reference. In a two-way conversation such as a sales pitch given by a sales representative to a potential client, reception is normally high. Similarly, when the message is a recommendation from a friend, the reception is high as well. By contrast, the desired receivers may or may not detect the message when it is mass communicated because most media are cluttered by **noise**—anything that interferes

encoding the conversion of a sender's ideas and thoughts into a message, usually in the form of words or signs

channel a medium of communication—such as a voice, radio, or newspaper—for transmitting a message

noise anything that interferes with, distorts, or slows down the transmission of information

with, distorts, or slows down the transmission of information. In some media overcrowded with advertisers, such as newspapers and television, the noise level is high and the reception level is low.

THE RECEIVER AND DECODING Marketers communicate their message through a channel to customers, or **receivers**, who will decode the message. It is important to note that there can be multiple receivers as consumers share their experiences and their recommendations online through social networks and other types of social media, as happened when the "Elevator Murder Experiment" video went viral. Online conversations are becoming an increasingly influential way to promote products and services. Indeed, this new empowerment of the receiver has transformed marketing and advertising. Receivers can easily share new information with their friends and followers on social media, and those new receivers can then share that information as well. This leads to a more diverse interrelationship between senders and receivers of social media messages. **Decoding** is the interpretation of the language and symbols sent by the source through a channel. Common understanding between two communicators, or a common frame of reference, is required for effective communication. Therefore, marketing managers must ensure a proper match between the message to be conveyed and the target market's attitudes and ideas.

Even though a message has been received, it may not necessarily be properly decoded because of selective exposure, distortion, and retention. When people receive a message, they tend to manipulate it to reflect their own biases, needs, experiences, and knowledge. Therefore, differences in age, social class, education, culture, and ethnicity can lead to miscommunication. Further, because people do not always listen or read carefully, they can easily misinterpret what is said or written. In fact, researchers have found that consumers misunderstand a large proportion of both printed and televised communications. YouTubers who watched the "Elevator Murder Experiment" and simply clicked away without absorbing that it was an advertisement for *Dead Man Down* received the message but could not decode it because they did not have adequate information. Bright colors and bold graphics have been shown to increase consumers' comprehension of marketing communication. Even these techniques are not foolproof, however.

receiver the person who decodes a message

decoding interpretation of the language and symbols sent by the source through a channel

feedback the receiver's response to a message

Marketers targeting consumers in foreign countries must also worry about the translation and possible miscommunication of their promotional messages by other cultures. Global marketers must decide whether to standardize or customize the message for each global market in which they sell.

FEEDBACK In interpersonal communication, the receiver's response to a message is direct **feedback** to the source. Feedback may be verbal, as in saying "I agree," or nonverbal, as in nodding, smiling, frowning, or gesturing. Feedback can also occur digitally, as in a Facebook like. Mass communicators are often cut off from direct feedback, so they must rely on market research, social media, or analysis of viewer responses for indirect feedback. They might use such measurements as the percentage of television viewers who recognized, recalled, or stated that they were exposed to the company's messages. Indirect feedback enables mass communicators to decide whether to continue, modify, or drop a message.

Some people who observed the video (receivers) found the "Elevator Murder Experiment" advertising stunt tasteless and macabre, while others praised it as an ingenious use of social media. YouTube users provided direct feedback by commenting on the video's page and clicking either the "Like" or "Dislike" button (the video garnered nearly 10,000 likes, versus approximately 700 dislikes). Regardless of receivers' responses and feedback, the video was effective, garnering more than 2.6 million views in just three days.[4]

With the increase in online advertising, marketers are able to get more feedback than before the Internet became such a driving social force. Using Web analytics, marketers can see how long customers stay on a Web site and which pages they view. Moreover, social media enable companies such as Dell and Comcast to provide instant feedback by responding to consumers' posts on Facebook and to complaints posted on Twitter.

The Internet and social media have had an impact on the communication model in two major ways. First, consumers are now able to become senders (as opposed to only brands being senders). A consumer who makes a recommendation on Facebook or Yelp is essentially a sender, meaning that the communication model is much more complicated today than it was just a few years ago. Second, the communication model shows the feedback channel as primarily impersonal and numbers driven. In the traditional communication process, marketers can see the results of customer behavior (for example, a drop or rise in sales) but are able to explain those

Social media enable companies to provide instant feedback by responding to consumers' posts on Twitter.

changes only by using their judgment. Today, customers use social media platforms like Facebook and Twitter to comment publically on marketing efforts. These platforms enable marketers to personalize the feedback channel by opening the door for direct conversations with customers. However, because social media conversations occur in real time and are public, any negative posts or complaints are highly visible. Thus, many companies have crisis communication strategies to deal with negative information and promote good brand reputations.

 ## 15-3 THE GOALS OF PROMOTION

People communicate with one another for many reasons. They seek amusement, ask for help, give assistance or instructions, provide information, and express ideas and thoughts. Promotion, on the other hand, seeks to modify behavior and thoughts in some way. For example, promoters may try to persuade consumers to eat at Burger King rather than at McDonald's. Promotion also strives to reinforce existing behavior—for instance, getting consumers to continue dining at Burger King once they have switched. The source (the seller) hopes to project a favorable image or to motivate purchase of the company's goods and services.

Promotion can perform one or more of four tasks: *inform* the target audience, *persuade* the target audience, *remind* the target audience, or *connect* with the audience. The ability to *connect* to consumers is one task that can be facilitated through social media. Often a marketer will try to accomplish two or more of these tasks at the same time.

15-3a Informing

Informative promotion seeks to convert an existing need into a want or to stimulate interest in a new product. It is generally more prevalent during the early stages of the product life cycle. People typically will not buy a product or service or support a nonprofit organization until they know its purpose and its benefits to them. Informative messages are important for promoting complex and technical products such as automobiles, computers, and investment services. For example, shortly after Google unveiled the Google Glass wearable computer and display, it released a series of commercials showing various practical uses for the device. A commercial titled "How It Feels" demonstrated point-of-view video and photo capture, messaging, video chatting, search, weather, mapping, and more. Even though it did not overtly explain the device's functions, the ad informed viewers how the device could record once-in-a-lifetime moments and provide the perfect solutions for life's little problems.[5] Informative promotion is also important for a "new" brand being introduced into an "old" product class. When the upstart video game console Ouya began its Kickstarter campaign, it used a video to inform backers about its unique benefits (such as its low cost, open development, free-to-play games, and Web-based game market).[6] When it launched, Ouya again used informative promotion to distinguish itself from seasoned competitors. New products cannot establish themselves against more mature products unless potential buyers are aware of them, value their benefits, and understand their positioning in the marketplace.

15-3b Persuading

Persuasive promotion is designed to stimulate a purchase or an action. Persuasion typically becomes the main promotion goal when the product enters the growth stage of its life cycle. By this time, the target market should have general product awareness and some knowledge of how the product can fulfill its wants. Therefore, the promotional task switches from informing consumers about the product category to persuading them to buy the company's brand rather than that of the competitor. At this time, the promotional message emphasizes the product's real and perceived competitive advantages, often appealing to emotional needs such as

#ALSICEBUCKETCHALLENGE

The ALS Association received a boost to awareness thanks to pro golfer Chris Kennedy kicking off the campaign.

and techniques can be too persuasive, causing consumers to buy products and services they don't really need.

15-3c Reminding

Reminder promotion is used to keep the product and brand name in the public's mind. This type of promotion prevails during the maturity stage of the life cycle. It assumes that the target market has already been persuaded of the merits of the good or service. Its purpose is simply to trigger a memory. Colgate toothpaste and other consumer products often use reminder promotion. Companies that produce products like automobiles and appliances advertise throughout the year in order to remind people about the brands when they are looking to purchase.

love, belonging, self-esteem, and ego satisfaction. For example, advertisers of Android-based smartphones try to persuade users to purchase their companies' devices instead of an iPhone (or even instead of another brand of Android phone). Advertising messages, therefore, highlight the unique technological benefits of Android phones such as a faster processors and larger screens.

Persuasion is important when the goal is to inspire direct action. In 2014, the ALS Association experienced a huge influx of donations through its "Ice Bucket Challenge" campaign. Pro Golfer Chris Kennedy kicked the vital hit off on his social network by pouring ice water over his head and then challenging others to do the same. The campaign spread all over Facebook and Twitter, was reported on cable television news shows, and eventually became part of popular culture. The effort raised $115 million, more than 20 times the usual donations received for that period of time. The "Ice Bucket Challenge" currently ranks as the largest social media fundraiser ever.[7] Persuasion can also be an important goal for very competitive mature product categories such as household items and soft drinks. In a marketplace characterized by many competitors, the promotional message often encourages brand switching and aims to convert some buyers into loyal users. Critics believe that some promotional messages

15-3d Connecting

The idea behind social media is to form relationships with customers and potential customers through technological ties such as Facebook, Twitter, YouTube, or other social media platforms. Indeed, some companies, such as Starbucks, have their own social networks that allow customers to share ideas, information, and feedback. By facilitating this exchange of information through a transparent process, brands are increasingly connecting with their customers in hopes they become brand advocates that promote the brand through their own social networks. Tools for connection include social networks, social games, social publishing tools, as well as social commerce. The ALS Association's "Ice Bucket Challenge" can also be considered an example of connecting since many people used videos posted to Facebook and Twitter to issue their challenges.

 ## THE PROMOTIONAL MIX

Most promotional strategies use several ingredients—which may include advertising, public relations, sales promotion, personal selling, and social media—to reach a target market. That combination is called the **promotional mix**. The proper promotional mix is the one that management believes will meet the needs of the target market and fulfill the organization's overall goals. Data plays a very important

promotional mix the combination of promotional tools—including advertising, public relations, personal selling, sales promotion, and social media—used to reach the target market and fulfill the organization's overall goals

role in how marketers distribute funding among their promotional mix tactics. The more funds allocated to each promotional ingredient and the more managerial emphasis placed on each technique, the more important that element is thought to be in the overall mix.

15-4a Advertising

Almost all companies selling a good or a service use advertising, whether in the form of a multi-million-dollar campaign or a simple classified ad in a newspaper. **Advertising** is any form of impersonal paid communication in which the sponsor or company is identified. Traditional media—such as television, radio, newspapers, magazines, pay-per-click online advertising, display advertising, direct mail, billboards, and transit advertising (such as on buses and taxis and at bus stops)—are most commonly used to transmit advertisements to consumers. Other options include Web sites, e-mail, blogs, videos, and interactive games. Marketers' budgets are shifting more and more toward these digital options (including

Helga Esteb/Shutterstock.com

Adverising can show up in any way, shape or form. Here, a movie premier backdrop is used to promote products and sponsors (pictured are Kimberly Williams-Paisley and Brad Paisley).

social media). However, as the Internet becomes a more vital component of many companies' promotion and marketing mixes, consumers and lawmakers are increasingly concerned about possible violations of consumers' privacy. Social networking sites like Facebook and Google+ are having to re-examine their privacy policies.

One of the primary benefits of advertising is its ability to communicate to a large number of people at one time. Cost per contact, therefore, is typically very low. Advertising has the advantage of being able to reach the masses (for example, through national television networks), but it can also be microtargeted to small groups of potential customers, such as television ads on a targeted cable network. Although the *cost per contact* in advertising is very low, the *total cost* to advertise is typically very high. This hurdle tends to restrict advertising on a national basis. Chapter 16 examines advertising in greater detail.

15-4b Public Relations

Concerned about how they are perceived by their target markets, organizations often spend large sums to build a positive public image. **Public relations** is the marketing function that evaluates public attitudes, identifies areas within the organization the public may be interested in, and executes a program of action to earn public understanding and acceptance. Public relations helps an organization communicate with its customers, suppliers, stockholders, government officials, employees, and the community in which it operates. Marketers use public relations not only to maintain a positive image but also to educate the public about the company's goals and objectives, introduce new products, and help support the sales effort.

A public relations program can generate favorable **publicity**—public information about a company, product, service, or issue appearing in the mass media as a news item. Social media sites like Twitter can provide large amounts of publicity quickly. Organizations generally do not pay for the publicity and are not identified as the source of the information, but they can benefit tremendously from it. However, although organizations do not directly pay for publicity,

advertising impersonal, one-way mass communication about a product or organization that is paid for by a marketer

public relations the marketing function that evaluates public attitudes, identifies areas within the organization the public may be interested in, and executes a program of action to earn public understanding and acceptance

publicity public information about a company, product, service, or issue appearing in the mass media as a news item

it should not be viewed as free. Preparing news releases, staging special events, and persuading media personnel to broadcast or print publicity messages costs money. Public relations and publicity are examined further in Chapter 16.

15-4c Sales Promotion

Sales promotion consists of all marketing activities—other than personal selling, advertising, and public relations—that stimulate consumer purchasing and dealer effectiveness. Sales promotion is generally a short-run tool used to stimulate immediate increases in demand. Sales promotion can be aimed at end consumers, trade customers, or a company's employees. Sales promotions include free samples, contests, premiums, trade shows, vacation giveaways, and coupons. It also includes experiential marketing whereby marketers create events that enable customers to connect with brands. Increasingly, companies such as LivingSocial and Groupon have combined social networks and sales promotions. Facebook is a growing platform through which companies run sweepstakes. For example, JPMorgan Chase ran a sweepstakes where Facebook users entered a drawing for a $1,000 grocery store gift card by "liking" the Chase Freedom Facebook page. In the past, Chase Freedom has run other Facebook sweepstakes where players could "like" the page to win $1 million. In addition to being entered into the large drawing, players were entered for a chance to win $500 every hour. The company runs this type of sweepstakes to educate potential customers about its cash-back rewards program available through the Chase Freedom credit card.[8]

Marketers often use sales promotion to improve the effectiveness of other ingredients in the promotional mix, especially advertising and personal selling. Research shows that sales promotion complements advertising by yielding faster sales responses. In many instances, more marketing money is spent on sales promotion than on advertising.

Many companies are using Facebook as a platform to run contests and promote their products and services.

Source: Facebook

15-4d Personal Selling

Personal selling is a purchase situation involving a personal, paid-for communication between two people in an attempt to influence each other. In this dyad, both the buyer and the seller have specific objectives they wish to accomplish. The buyer may need to minimize cost or assure a quality product, for instance, while the salesperson may need to maximize revenue and profits.

Traditional methods of personal selling include a planned presentation to one or more prospective buyers for the purpose of making a sale. Whether it takes place face-to-face or over the phone, personal selling attempts to persuade the buyer to accept a point of view. For example, a car salesperson may try to persuade a car buyer that a particular model is superior to a competing model in certain features, such as gas mileage. Once the buyer is somewhat convinced, the salesperson may attempt to elicit some action from the buyer, such as a test drive or a purchase. Frequently, in this traditional view of personal selling, the objectives of the salesperson are at the expense of the buyer, creating a win-lose outcome.

More current notions on personal selling emphasize the relationship that develops between a salesperson and a buyer. Initially, this concept was more typical in business-to-business selling situations, involving the sale of products like heavy machinery or computer systems. More recently, both business-to-business and business-to-consumer selling focus on building long-term relationships rather than on making a one-time sale.

Relationship selling emphasizes a win-win outcome and the accomplishment of mutual objectives that benefit both buyer and salesperson in the long term. Rather than focusing on a quick sale, relationship selling attempts to create a long-term, committed

sales promotion marketing activities—other than personal selling, advertising, and public relations—that stimulate consumer buying and dealer effectiveness

personal selling a purchase situation involving a personal, paid-for communication between two people in an attempt to influence each other

relationship based on trust, increased customer loyalty, and a continuation of the relationship between the salesperson and the customer. Personal selling, like other promotional mix elements, is increasingly dependent on the Internet. Most companies use their Web sites to attract potential buyers seeking information on products and services and to drive customers to their physical locations where personal selling can close the sale. Personal selling is discussed further in Chapter 17.

15-4e Content Marketing and Social Media

As promotional strategies change, and given brands' newfound ability to become publishers, content marketing has become a crucial part of promotion. Recall from Chapter 7 that content marketing entails developing valuable content for interested audience members and then using e-mail marketing, search engine optimization, paid search, and display advertising to pull customers to the company's Web site or social media channel so that they can learn about the brand or to make a purchase. Content created by brands is typically distributed through social media.

Recall that social media are promotion tools used to facilitate conversations and other interactions among people online. When used by marketers, these tools facilitate consumer empowerment. For the first time, consumers are able to speak directly to other consumers, the company, and Web communities. Social media include blogs, microblogs (such as Twitter), video platforms (such as You Tube, Twitch, and Vine), podcasting (online audio and video broadcasts), and social networks (such as Tumblr, Pinterest, Yik Yak, and Snapchat).

Initially, these tools were used primarily by individuals for self-expression. For example, a lawyer might develop a blog to talk about politics because that is her hobby. Or a college freshman might develop a profile on Facebook to stay in touch with his high school friends. But soon, businesses saw that these tools could be used to engage with consumers as well. Indeed, social media have become a "layer" in promotional strategy. Social media are ubiquitous—it just depends on how deep that layer goes for each brand. The rise of streaming video, for example, has created a completely new way for marketers to manage their image, connect with consumers, and generate interest in and desire for their companies' products. Now marketers are using social media as integral aspects of their campaigns and as a way to extend the benefits of their traditional media. Social media are discussed in more detail in Chapter 18.

15-4f The Communication Process and the Promotional Mix

The Internet has changed how businesses promote their brands. Traditionally, marketing managers have been in charge of defining the essence of the brand. This included complete brand control and mostly one-way communication between the brand and customers. All of the content and messages were focused on defining and communicating the brand value. The focus for many campaigns was pure entertainment, and the brand created all of the content for campaigns—from the Web site to television spots to print ads.

That approach has now changed. The consumer has much more control (which makes some brands quite nervous!). The communication space is increasingly controlled by the consumer, as is the brand message. Perception is reality as consumers have more control to adapt the brand message to fit their ideas. Instead of repetition, social media rely on the idea of customization and adaption of the message. Information is positioned as more valuable as opposed to being strictly entertaining. Probably the most important aspect is the idea of consumer-generated content, whereby consumers are able to both take existing content and modify it or to create completely new content for a brand. For example, Doritos has the "Crash the Super Bowl" promotion, where ordinary people are invited to create television commercials for Doritos that are then uploaded to www.crashthesuperbowl.com and voted on by millions of Doritos fans. The winning spots then run during the Super Bowl.

As a result of the impact of social media as well as the proliferation of new platforms, tools, and ideas, promotional tactics can also be categorized according to media type—paid, earned, or owned, as shown in Exhibit 15.3. **Paid media** is based on the traditional advertising model, whereby a brand pays for media space. Traditionally, paid media has included television, magazine, outdoor, radio, or newspaper advertising. Paid media also includes display advertising on Web sites, pay-per-click advertising on search engines, and even promoted tweets on Twitter. Paid media is quite important, especially as it migrates to the Web. Paid media is used with other media types to develop an integrated message strategy. **Earned media** is based on a public

paid media a category of promotional tactic based on the traditional advertising model, whereby a brand pays for media space

earned media a category of promotional tactic based on a public relations or publicity model that gets customers talking about products or services

CHAPTER 15: Marketing Communications 271

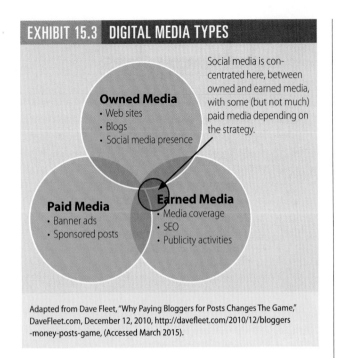

EXHIBIT 15.3 DIGITAL MEDIA TYPES

Owned Media
• Web sites
• Blogs
• Social media presence

Paid Media
• Banner ads
• Sponsored posts

Earned Media
• Media coverage
• SEO
• Publicity activities

Social media is concentrated here, between owned and earned media, with some (but not much) paid media depending on the strategy.

Adapted from Dave Fleet, "Why Paying Bloggers for Posts Changes The Game," DaveFleet.com, December 12, 2010, http://davefleet.com/2010/12/bloggers-money-posts-game, (Accessed March 2015).

for example, sharing a movie review on a social media site, is growing rapidly. Earned media is often created when people talk and share content on social media. Additionally, search engine optimization (SEO), whereby companies embed key words into content to increase their positioning on search engine results pages (SERPs), can also be considered earned media. **Owned media** is a new form of promotional tactic where brands are becoming publishers of their own content in order to maximize the brand's value to customers as well as increase their search rank in Google. Owned media includes the company's Web sites as well as its official presence on Facebook, Twitter, YouTube channels, blogs, and other platforms. This media is controlled by the brand but continuously keeps the customer and his or her needs in mind as it creates videos, blog posts, contests, photos, and other pieces of content. Owned media is often used as another term for content marketing, which is important to both B-to-B and B-to-C companies.

The elements of the promotional mix differ in their ability to affect the target audience. For instance, promotional mix elements may communicate with the consumer directly or indirectly. The message may flow one way or two ways. Feedback may be fast or slow, a little or a lot. Likewise, the communicator may have varying degrees of control over message delivery, content, and flexibility. Exhibit 15.4 outlines characteristics among the promotional mix elements with respect to mode of

relations or publicity model. The idea is to get people talking about the brand—whether through media coverage (as in traditional public relations) or through word of mouth (WOM). Word of mouth traditionally occurs face-to-face. Electronic word of mouth (EWOM),

owned media a new category of promotional tactic based on brands becoming publishers of their own content in order to maximize the brands' value to customers

EXHIBIT 15.4 CHARACTERISTICS OF THE ELEMENTS IN THE PROMOTIONAL MIX

	Advertising	Public Relations	Sales Promotion	Personal Selling	Social Media
Mode of Communication	Indirect and impersonal	Usually indirect and impersonal	Usually indirect and impersonal	Direct and face-to-face	Indirect but instant
Communicator Control over Situation	Low	Moderate to low	Moderate to low	High	Moderate
Amount of Feedback	Little	Little	Little to moderate	Much	Much
Speed of Feedback	Delayed	Delayed	Varies	Immediate	Intermediate
Direction of Message	One-way	One-way	Mostly one-way	Two-way	Two-way, multiple ways
Control over Message Content	Yes	No	Yes	Yes	Varies, generally no
Identification of Sponsor	Yes	No	Yes	Yes	Yes
Speed in Reaching Large Audience	Fast	Usually fast	Fast	Slow	Fast
Message Flexibility	Same message to all audiences	Usually no direct control over message audiences	Same message to varied targets	Tailored to prospective buyer	Some of the most targeted opportunities

communication, marketer's control over the communication process, amount and speed of feedback, direction of message flow, marketer's control over the message, identification of the sender, speed in reaching large audiences, and message flexibility.

From Exhibit 15.4, you can see that most elements of the promotional mix are indirect and impersonal when used to communicate with a target market, providing only one direction of message flow. For example, advertising, public relations, and sales promotion are generally impersonal, one-way means of mass communication. Because they provide no opportunity for direct feedback, it is more difficult to adapt these promotional elements to changing consumer preferences, individual differences, and personal goals.

Personal selling, on the other hand, entails direct two-way communication. The salesperson receives immediate feedback from the consumer and can adjust the message in response. Unlike other promotional tools, personal selling is very slow in dispersing the marketer's message to large audiences. Because a salesperson can communicate to only one person or a small group of persons at one time, it is a poor choice if the marketer wants to send a message to many potential buyers. Social media are also considered two-way communication, though not quite as immediate as personal selling. Social media can disperse messages to a wide audience and allow for engagement and feedback from customers through Twitter, Facebook, and blog posts.

15-5 PROMOTIONAL GOALS AND THE AIDA CONCEPT

The ultimate goal of any promotion is to get someone to buy a good or service or, in the case of nonprofit organizations, to take some action (for example, donate to a cause organization like Susan G. Komen). A classic model for reaching promotional goals is called the **AIDA concept**.[9] The acronym AIDA stands for *attention, interest, desire,* and *action*—the stages of consumer involvement with a promotional message. It mimics many "funnel-like" models that require audiences to move through a set of steps or stages.

15-5a The AIDA Model

This model proposes that consumers respond to marketing messages in a cognitive (thinking), affective (feeling), and conative (doing) sequence. First, a promotion manager may focus on attracting

a consumer's *attention* by training a salesperson to use a friendly greeting and approach or by using loud volume, bold headlines, movement, bright colors, and the like in an advertisement. Next, a good sales presentation, demonstration, or advertisement creates *interest* in the product and then, by illustrating how the product's features will satisfy the consumer's needs, arouses *desire*. Finally, a special offer or a strong closing sales pitch may be used to obtain purchase *action*.

The AIDA concept assumes that promotion propels consumers along the following four steps in the purchase-decision process:

1. **Attention:** The advertiser must first gain the attention of the target market. A firm cannot sell something if the market does not know that the good or service exists. When Apple introduced the iPad, it quickly became one of the largest electronics product launches in history. To create awareness and gain attention for its revolutionary tablet computer, Apple not only used traditional media advertising but also contacted influential bloggers and journalists so that they would write about the product in blogs, newspapers, and magazines. Because the iPad was a brand extension of the Apple computer, it required less effort than an entirely new brand would have. At the same time, because the iPad was an innovative new product

> **AIDA concept** a model that outlines the process for achieving promotional goals in terms of stages of consumer involvement with the message; the acronym stands for attention, interest, desire, and action

iStockphotos.com/Hocus-focus

The four steps of the AIDA process describe how consumers make purchases. These steps are:

1. **ATTENTION:** First, Apple uses a number of media outlets to gain the attention of the target market.

2. **INTEREST:** Next, it arranges iPad demonstrations and develops target messages to create interest among innovators and early adopters.

3. **DESIRE:** Then, Apple creates brand preference and convinces potential customers that they want the new iPad.

4. **ACTION:** Finally, having been attracted to the new iPad and convinced that they need it, customers purchase the iPad.

line, the promotion had to get customers' attention and create awareness of a new idea from an established company.

2. **Interest:** Simple awareness of a brand seldom leads to a sale. The next step is to create interest in the product. A print ad cannot tell potential customers all the features of the iPad. Therefore, Apple had to arrange iPad demonstrations and target messages to innovators and early adopters to create interest in the new tablet computer. To do this, Apple used both online videos on YouTube and personal demonstrations in Apple Stores. The iPad also received extensive media coverage from both online and traditional media outlets.

3. **Desire:** Potential customers for the Apple iPad may like the concept of a portable tablet computer, but they may not necessarily think that it is better than a laptop or smartphone. Therefore, Apple had to create brand preference with the iTunes Music Store, specialty apps, multiple functionality, and features such as better power management and a lighter weight unit. Specifically, Apple had to convince potential customers that the iPad was the best solution to their desire for a combination tablet computer and smartphone.

4. **Action:** Some potential target market customers may have been persuaded to buy an iPad but had yet to make the actual purchase. To motivate them to take action, Apple continued advertising to communicate the features and benefits more effectively. And the strategy worked—more than 250 million people own an iPad.[10.]

Most buyers involved in high-involvement purchase situations pass through the four stages of the AIDA model on the way to making a purchase. The promoter's task is to determine where on the purchase ladder most of the target consumers are located and design a promotion plan to meet their needs. For example, if Apple learned from its market research that many potential customers were in the desire stage but had not yet bought an iPad for some reason, it could place advertising on Facebook and Google, and perhaps in video games, to target younger individuals and professionals with messages motivating them to buy an iPad.

The AIDA concept does not explain how all promotions influence purchase decisions. The model suggests that promotional effectiveness can be measured in terms of consumers progressing from one stage to the next. However, the order of stages in the model, as well as whether consumers go through all steps, has been much debated. A purchase can occur without interest

or desire, perhaps when a low-involvement product is bought on impulse. Regardless of the order of the stages or consumers' progression through these stages, the AIDA concept helps marketers by suggesting which promotional strategy will be most effective.[11]

15-5b AIDA and the Promotional Mix

Exhibit 15.5 depicts the relationship between the promotional mix and the AIDA model. It shows that although advertising does have an impact in the later stages, it is most useful in gaining attention for goods or services. By contrast, personal selling reaches fewer people at first. Salespeople are more effective at creating customer interest for merchandise or a service and at creating desire. For example, advertising may help a potential computer purchaser gain knowledge about competing brands, but the salesperson may be the one who actually encourages the buyer to decide a particular brand is the best choice. The salesperson also has the advantage of having the computer physically there to demonstrate its capabilities to the buyer.

Public relations' greatest impact is as a method of gaining attention for a company, good, or service. Many companies can attract attention and build goodwill by sponsoring community events that benefit worthy causes such as an anti-bullying campaign or a global poverty program. Such sponsorships project a positive image of the firm and its products into the minds of consumers and potential consumers. Book publishers push to get their titles on the best-seller lists of major publications, such as *Publishers Weekly* or the *New York Times*. Book authors make appearances on talk shows and at bookstores to personally sign books and speak to fans. They also frequently engage with fans on social media like Facebook and Twitter.

Sales promotion's greatest strength is in creating strong desire and purchase intent. Coupons and other price-off promotions are techniques used to persuade

EXHIBIT 15.5	THE PROMOTIONAL MIX AND AIDA			
	Attention	**Interest**	**Desire**	**Action**
Advertising	●	●	○	●
Public Relations	●	●	○	●
Sales Promotion	○	○	●	●
Personal Selling	○	●	●	●
Social Media	●	●	○	○
● Very effective ○ Somewhat effective ● Not effective				

customers to buy new products. Frequent-buyer sales promotion programs, popular among retailers, allow consumers to accumulate points or dollars that can be redeemed for goods. Frequent buyer programs tend to increase purchase intent and loyalty and encourage repeat purchases.

Social media are a strong way to gain attention and interest in a brand, particularly if content goes viral. It can then reach a massive audience. Social media are also effective at engaging with customers and enabling companies to maintain interest in the brand if properly managed.

 ## 15-6 INTEGRATED MARKETING COMMUNICATIONS

Ideally, marketing communications from each promotional mix element (personal selling, advertising, sales promotion, social media, and public relations) should be integrated. That is, the message reaching the consumer should be the same regardless of whether it is from an advertisement, a salesperson in the field, a magazine article, a Facebook fan page, or a coupon in a newspaper insert.

From the consumer's standpoint, a company's communications are already integrated. Consumers do not think in terms of the five elements of promotion: personal selling, advertising, sales promotion, public relations, and social media. Instead, everything is an "ad." The only people who recognize the distinctions among these communications elements are the marketers themselves. Unfortunately, many marketers neglect this fact when planning promotional messages and fail to integrate their communication efforts from one element to the next. The most common rift typically occurs between personal selling and the other elements of the promotional mix.

This unintegrated, disjointed approach to promotion has propelled many companies to adopt the concept of **integrated marketing communications (IMC)**. IMC is the careful coordination of all promotional messages—traditional advertising, direct marketing, social media, interactive, public relations, sales promotion, personal selling, event marketing, and other communications—for a product or service to assure the consistency of messages at every contact point where a company meets the consumer. Following the concept of IMC, marketing managers carefully work out the roles that various promotional elements will play in the marketing mix. Timing of promotional activities is coordinated, and the results of each campaign are carefully monitored to improve future use of the promotional mix tools. Typically, a marketing communications director is appointed who has overall responsibility for integrating the company's marketing communications.

The IMC concept has been growing in popularity for several reasons. First, the proliferation of thousands of media choices beyond traditional television has made promotion a more complicated task. Instead of promoting a product just through mass-media options, like television and magazines, promotional messages today can appear in many varied sources.

Further, the mass market has also fragmented—more selectively segmented markets and an increase in niche marketing have replaced the traditional broad market groups that marketers promoted to in years past. Finally, marketers have slashed their advertising spending in favor of promotional techniques that generate immediate sales responses and those that are more easily measured, such as direct marketing. Online advertising has earned a bigger share of the budget as well due to its measurability. Thus, the interest in IMC is largely a reaction to the scrutiny that marketing communications has come under and, particularly, to suggestions that uncoordinated promotional activity leads to a strategy that is wasteful and inefficient.

 ## 15-7 FACTORS AFFECTING THE PROMOTIONAL MIX

Promotional mixes vary a great deal from one product and one industry to the next. Normally, advertising and personal selling are used to promote goods and services. These primary tools are often supported and supplemented by sales promotion. Public relations help develop a positive image for the organization and the product line. Social media have been used more for consumer goods, but business-to-business marketers are increasingly using these media. A firm may choose not to use all five promotional elements in its promotional mix, or it may choose to use them in varying degrees. The particular promotional mix chosen by a firm for a product or service depends on several factors: the nature of the product, the stage in the product life cycle, target market characteristics, the type of buying decision, funds available for promotion, and whether a push or a pull strategy will be used.

> **integrated marketing communications (IMC)** the careful coordination of all promotional messages for a product or a service to ensure the consistency of messages at every contact point at which a company meets the consumer

15-7a Nature of the Product

Characteristics of the product itself can influence the promotional mix. For instance, a product can be classified as either a business product or a consumer product. (Refer to Chapters 7 and 10.) As business products are often custom-tailored to the buyer's exact specifications, they are often not well suited to mass promotion. Therefore, producers of most business goods rely more heavily on personal selling than on advertising, but advertising still serves a purpose in the promotional mix. Advertising in trade media can also help locate potential customers for the sales force. For example, print media advertising often includes coupons soliciting the potential customer to "fill this out for more detailed information."

By contrast, because consumer products generally are not custom-made, they do not require the selling efforts of a company representative who can tailor them to the user's needs. Thus, consumer goods are promoted mainly through advertising or social media to create brand familiarity. Television and radio advertising, consumer-oriented magazines, and increasingly the Internet and other highly targeted media are used to promote consumer goods, especially nondurables. Sales promotion, the brand name, and the product's packaging are about twice as important for consumer goods as for business products. Persuasive personal selling is important at the retail level for goods such as automobiles and appliances.

The costs and risks associated with a product also influence the promotional mix. As a general rule, when the costs or risks of buying and using a product or service increase, personal selling becomes more important. Inexpensive items cannot support the cost of a salesperson's time and effort unless the potential volume is high. On the other hand, expensive and complex machinery, cars, and new homes represent a considerable investment. A salesperson must assure buyers that they are spending their money wisely and not taking an undue financial risk.

Social risk is an issue as well. Many consumer goods are not products of great social importance because they do not reflect social position. People do not experience much social risk in buying a loaf of bread. However, buying many specialty products such as jewelry and clothing involves a social risk. Many consumers depend on sales personnel for guidance in making the "proper" choice.

15-7b Stages in the Product Life Cycle

The product's stage in its life cycle is a big factor in designing a promotional mix (see Exhibit 15.6). During the *introduction stage*, the basic goal of promotion is to inform the target audience that the product is available. Initially, the emphasis is on the general product class—for example, smartphones. This emphasis gradually changes to gaining attention for a particular brand, such as Apple, Nokia, Samsung, Sony Ericsson, or Motorola. Typically, both extensive advertising and public relations inform the target audience of the product class or brand and heighten awareness levels. Sales promotion encourages early trial of the product, and personal selling gets retailers to carry the product.

When the product reaches the *growth stage* of the life cycle, the promotion blend may shift. Often a change is necessary because different types of potential buyers are targeted. Although advertising and public relations continue to be major elements of the promotional mix, sales promotion can be reduced because consumers need fewer incentives to purchase. The promotional strategy is to emphasize the product's differential advantage over the competition. Persuasive promotion is used to build and maintain brand loyalty during the growth stage. By this stage, personal selling has usually succeeded in getting adequate distribution for the product.

As the product reaches the *maturity stage* of its life cycle, competition becomes fiercer, and thus persuasive and reminder advertising are emphasized more strongly. Sales promotion comes back into focus as product sellers try to increase their market share.

All promotion, especially advertising, is reduced as the product enters the *decline stage*. Nevertheless, personal selling and sales promotion efforts may be maintained, particularly at the retail level.

Print media advertising often includes coupons soliciting the potential customer.

Stock Creative/Shutterstock.com

EXHIBIT 15.6 PRODUCT LIFE CYCLE AND THE PROMOTIONAL MIX

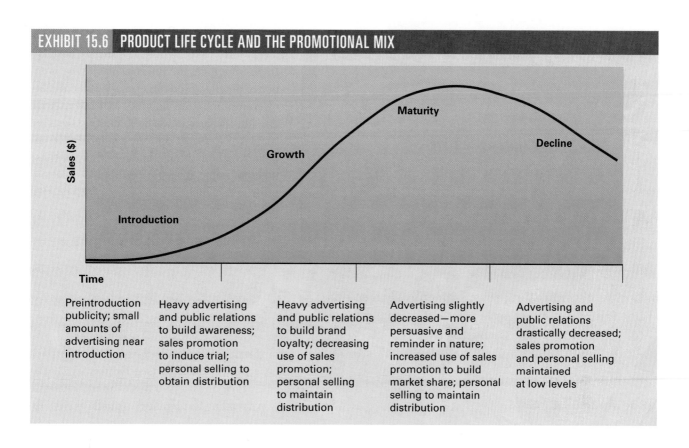

Preintroduction publicity; small amounts of advertising near introduction

Heavy advertising and public relations to build awareness; sales promotion to induce trial; personal selling to obtain distribution

Heavy advertising and public relations to build brand loyalty; decreasing use of sales promotion; personal selling to maintain distribution

Advertising slightly decreased—more persuasive and reminder in nature; increased use of sales promotion to build market share; personal selling to maintain distribution

Advertising and public relations drastically decreased; sales promotion and personal selling maintained at low levels

15-7c Target Market Characteristics

A target market characterized by widely scattered potential customers, highly informed buyers, and brand loyal repeat purchasers generally requires a promotional mix with more advertising and sales promotion and less personal selling. Sometimes, however, personal selling is required even when buyers are well informed and geographically dispersed. Although industrial installations may be sold to well-educated people with extensive work experience, salespeople must be present to explain the product and work out the details of the purchase agreement.

Often firms sell goods and services in markets where potential customers are hard to locate. Print advertising can be used to find them. The reader is invited to go online, call, or mail in a reply card for more information. As the online queries, calls, or cards are received, salespeople are sent to visit the potential customers.

15-7d Type of Buying Decision

The promotional mix also depends on the type of buying decision—for example, a routine decision or a complex decision. For routine consumer decisions like buying toothpaste, the most effective promotion calls attention to the brand or reminds the consumer about the brand. Advertising, and especially sales promotion, are the most productive promotion tools to use for routine decisions.

If the decision is neither routine nor complex, advertising and public relations help establish awareness for the good or service. Suppose a man is looking for a bottle of wine to serve to his dinner guests. As a beer drinker, he is not familiar with wines, yet he has read an article in a popular magazine about Silver Oak Cabernet and has seen an advertisement for the wine. He may be more likely to buy this brand because he is already aware of it. Online reviews are often important in this type of buying decision as well because the consumer has any number of other consumers' reviews easily accessible.

By contrast, consumers making complex buying decisions are more extensively involved. They rely on large amounts of information to help them reach a purchase decision. Personal selling is most effective in helping these consumers decide. For example, consumers thinking about buying a car typically research the car online using corporate and third party Web sites like Kelley Blue Book. However, few people buy a car without visiting the dealership. They depend on a salesperson to provide the information they need to reach a decision. In addition to online resources, print advertising may also be used for high-involvement purchase decisions because it can often provide a large amount of information to the consumer.

Despite a myriad of car advertisements, such as this one for Infiniti, most people rely on sales personnel for guideance when purchasing a car.

15-7e Available Funds

Money, or the lack of it, may easily be the most important factor in determining the promotional mix. A small, undercapitalized manufacturer may rely heavily on free publicity if its product is unique. If the situation warrants a sales force, a financially strained firm may turn to manufacturers' agents, who work on a commission basis with no advances or expense accounts. Even well capitalized organizations may not be able to afford the advertising rates of publications like *Time*, *Sports Illustrated*, and the *Wall Street Journal*, or the cost of running television commercials during *Modern Family*, *The Voice*, or the Super Bowl. The price of a high-profile advertisement in these media could support several salespeople for an entire year.

When funds are available to permit a mix of promotional elements, a firm will generally try to optimize its return on promotion dollars while minimizing the *cost per contact*, or the cost of reaching one member of the target market. In general, the cost per contact is very high for personal selling, public relations, and sales promotions like sampling and demonstrations. On the other hand, given the number of people national

push strategy a marketing strategy that uses aggressive personal selling and trade advertising to convince a wholesaler or a retailer to carry and sell particular merchandise

advertising and social media reach, they have a very low cost per contact. Usually, there is a trade-off among the funds available, the number of people in the target market, the quality of communication needed, and the relative costs of the promotional elements. There are plenty of low-cost options available to companies without a huge budget. Many of these include online strategies and public relations efforts, in which the company relies on free publicity.

15-7f Push and Pull Strategies

The last factor that affects the promotional mix is whether a push or a pull promotional strategy will be used. Manufacturers may use aggressive personal selling and trade advertising to convince a wholesaler or a retailer to carry and sell their merchandise. This approach is known as a **push strategy** (see Exhibit 15.7). The wholesaler, in turn, must often push the merchandise forward by persuading the retailer to handle the goods. The retailer then uses advertising, displays, and other forms of promotion to convince the consumer to buy the "pushed" products. Walmart uses aggressive discounts to push products out of its stores. For example, First Lady Michelle Obama praised the retailer for using drastically reduced prices to push fresh meat, produce, and other healthy options to consumers in low-income areas. The move proved to be a win-win strategy. Fresh foods generated 70 percent of Walmart's sales growth in recent

Lay's calls attention to its commitment to natural ingredients as a distinguishing attribute in order to help customers make a routine buying decision—purchasing Lay's snack food.

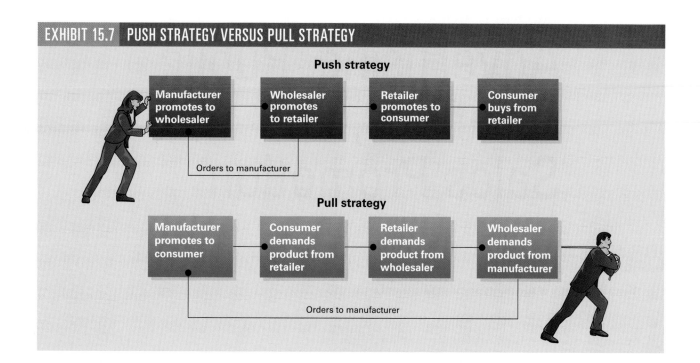

EXHIBIT 15.7 PUSH STRATEGY VERSUS PULL STRATEGY

Push strategy

Manufacturer promotes to wholesaler → Wholesaler promotes to retailer → Retailer promotes to consumer → Consumer buys from retailer

Orders to manufacturer

Pull strategy

Manufacturer promotes to consumer → Consumer demands product from retailer → Retailer demands product from wholesaler → Wholesaler demands product from manufacturer

Orders to manufacturer

years, and customers have saved more than $2.3 billion on fresh fruits and vegetables by shopping at Walmart.[12] This concept also applies to services.

At the other extreme is a **pull strategy**, which stimulates consumer demand to obtain product distribution. Rather than trying to sell to the wholesaler, the manufacturer using a pull strategy focuses its promotional efforts on end consumers or opinion leaders. Social media and content marketing are the most recent (and best) example of pull strategy. The idea is that social media content does not interrupt a consumer's experience with media (like a commercial interrupts your favorite television program). Instead, the content invites customers to experience it on social media or a Web site. Consumer demand pulls the product through the channel of distribution (see Exhibit 15.7). Heavy sampling, introductory consumer advertising, cents-off campaigns, and couponing are part of a pull strategy.

Rarely does a company use a pull or a push strategy exclusively. Instead, the mix will emphasize one of these strategies. For example, pharmaceutical companies generally use a push strategy (personal selling and trade advertising) to promote their drugs and therapies to physicians. Sales presentations and advertisements in medical journals give physicians the detailed information they need to prescribe medication to their patients. Most pharmaceutical companies supplement this push promotional strategy with a pull strategy targeted directly to potential patients through advertisements in consumer magazines and on television.

pull strategy a marketing strategy that stimulates consumer demand to obtain product distribution

STUDY TOOLS 15

LOCATED AT BACK OF THE TEXTBOOK

☐ Rip out Chapter Review Card

LOCATED AT WWW.CENGAGEBRAIN.COM

☐ Review Key Terms Flashcards and create your own

☐ Track your knowledge and understanding of key concepts in marketing

☐ Complete practice and graded quizzes to prepare for tests

☐ Complete interactive content within the MKTG Online experience

☐ View the chapter highlight boxes within the MKTG Online experience

16 Advertising, Public Relations, and Sales Promotion

LEARNING OUTCOMES

After studying this chapter, you will be able to…

16-1 Discuss the effects of advertising on market share and consumers

16-2 Identify the major types of advertising

16-3 Discuss the creative decisions in developing an advertising campaign

16-4 Describe media evaluation and selection techniques

16-5 Discuss the role of public relations in the promotional mix

16-6 Define and state the objectives of sales promotion and the tools used to achieve them

After you finish this chapter go to **PAGE 301** for **STUDY TOOLS.**

16-1 THE EFFECTS OF ADVERTISING

Advertising was defined in Chapter 15 as impersonal, one-way mass communication about a product or organization that is paid for by a marketer. It is a popular form of promotion, especially for consumer packaged goods and services. Increasingly, as more and more marketers consolidate their operations, advertising is seen as an international endeavor. Promotion makes up a large part of most brands' budgets. Typically, promotional spending is divided into *measured* and *unmeasured media*. Measured media ad spending includes network and cable TV, newspapers, magazines, radio, outdoor, and Internet (though paid search and social media are not included). Spending must be estimated for unmeasured media, which includes direct marketing, promotions, co-op, coupons, catalogs, product placement, and event marketing. Global advertising expenditures increase by almost 5 percent per year. In 2015, they reached almost $550 billion. The United States is, by far,

the largest spender ($182 billion, representing a full third of spending globally). China, Japan, Germany, and the United Kingdom round out the top five countries in terms of advertising spending. Latin America is the fastest growing market, recently increasing by almost 10 percent annually.[1]

The top 25 largest U.S. advertisers spend more than $50 billion each year. Procter & Gamble is by far the largest advertiser, spending almost $5 billion annually on its wide variety of brands. Telecommunications companies like AT&T ($3.3 billion) and Verizon ($2.4 billion) are other top spenders. Automotive companies also spend a great deal of money on advertising in the U.S.—GM alone spends $3.1 billion a year.[2]

Advertising and marketing services, agencies, and other firms that provide marketing and communications services employ millions of people across America. Just as the producers of goods and services need marketers to build awareness of their products, media outlets such as magazines and Web sites need marketing teams to coordinate with producers and transmit those messages to customers. The longer one thinks about the business of marketing, the more unique positions within the industry become apparent. One particular area that has continued to see rapid growth is the data side of marketing. Companies are collecting huge amounts of information and need skilled, creative, Web-savvy people to interpret the data coming in from Web, mobile, and other digital ad campaigns. One Microsoft study estimates that ninety percent of enterprise companies have a dedicated budget for addressing data analytics. Forty-nine percent of the demand for data analytics is driven by sales and marketing departments. According to IDC program vice president Dan Vesset, "A lot of the ultimate potential is in the ability to discover potential connections, and to predict potential outcomes in a way that wasn't really possible before. Before, you only looked at these things in hindsight."[3]

16-1a Advertising and Market Share

The five most valuable U.S. brands are Apple ($124 billion), Microsoft ($63 billion), Google ($57 billion), Coca-Cola ($56 billion), and IBM ($48 billion). These were all top brands the year before and all gained value, but Google jumped from fifth to third place. Most of these brands were built over many years by heavy advertising and marketing investments long ago. Google is the only exception—its brand value was built using digital platforms.[4] Today's advertising dollars for successful consumer brands are spent on maintaining brand awareness and market share.

New brands with a small market share tend to spend proportionately more for advertising and sales promotion than those with a large market share, typically for two reasons. First, beyond a certain level of spending for advertising and sales promotion, diminishing returns set in. That is, sales and market share improvements slow down and eventually decrease no matter how much is spent on advertising and sales promotion. This phenomenon is called the **advertising response function**. Understanding the advertising response function helps marketers use budgets wisely. A market leader like Johnson & Johnson's Neutrogena typically spends proportionately less on advertising than a newer line such as Unilever's Vaseline Spray & Go brand. Neutrogena has already captured the attention of the majority of its target market. It only needs to remind customers of its product.

The second reason new brands tend to require higher spending for advertising and sales promotion is that a certain minimum level of exposure is needed to measurably affect purchase habits. If Vaseline advertised its Spray & Go moisturizers in only one or two publications and bought only one or two television spots, it would not achieve the exposure needed to penetrate consumers' perceptual defenses and affect purchase intentions.

Eric Milos/Shutterstock.com

advertising response function a phenomenon in which spending for advertising and sales promotion increases sales or market share up to a certain level but then produces diminishing returns

16-1b The Effects of Advertising on Consumers

Advertising affects peoples' daily lives, informing them about products and services and influencing their attitudes, beliefs, and ultimately, their purchases. Advertising affects the television programs people watch, the content of the newspapers they read, the politicians they elect, the medicines they take, and the toys their children play with. Consequently, the influence of advertising on the U.S. socioeconomic system has been the subject of extensive debate in nearly all corners of society.

Interestingly, despite a proliferation of new technology options, consumers still spend a lot of time consuming traditional media (where much of advertising exists). The average person, for example, spends about 273 minutes a day watching television.[5] Americans report an average of 5.3 leisure hours a day, and most of it is spent watching TV. As a result, American consumers are exposed to thousands of advertising messages each year.[6]

Though advertising cannot change consumers' deeply rooted values and attitudes, advertising may succeed in transforming a person's negative attitude toward a product into a positive one. For instance, serious or dramatic advertisements are more effective at changing consumers' negative attitudes. Humorous ads, on the other hand, have been shown to be more effective at shaping attitudes when consumers already have a positive image of an advertised brand.

Advertising also reinforces positive attitudes toward brands. A brand with a distinct personality is more likely to have a larger base of loyal customers and market share. The more consistent a brand's personality, the more likely a customer will build a relationship with that brand over his or her lifetime. Consider Apple, for example. Sixty percent of iPhone users report they would switch to Apple's latest iPhone without considering any other options, admitting to "blind loyalty."[7] This is why market leaders spend billions of dollars annually to reinforce and remind their loyal customers about the benefits of their products.

Advertising can also affect the way consumers rank a brand's attributes. In years past, car ads emphasized such brand attributes as roominess, speed, and low maintenance. Today, however, car marketers have added technology, safety, versatility, customization, and fuel efficiency to the list.

16-2 MAJOR TYPES OF ADVERTISING

A firm's promotional objectives determine the type of advertising it uses. If the goal of the promotion plan is to improve the image of the company or the industry, **institutional advertising** may be used. In contrast, if the advertiser wants to enhance the sales of a specific good or service, **product advertising** should be used.

16-2a Institutional Advertising

Historically, advertising in the United States has been product and service oriented. Today, however, companies market multiple products and need a different type of advertising. Institutional advertising, or corporate advertising, is designed to establish, change, or promote the corporation's identity as a whole. It usually does not ask the audience to do anything but maintain a favorable attitude toward the advertiser and its goods or services. A beer company running a series of television spots advocating designated driving is an example of institutional advertising.

A form of institutional advertising called **advocacy advertising** is typically used to safeguard against negative consumer attitudes and to enhance the company's credibility among consumers who already favor its position. Corporations often use advocacy advertising to express their views on controversial issues. For example, in celebration of the one-year anniversary of New York's Marriage Equality Act, Nabisco's Oreo posted a gay pride-themed image (an Oreo cookie with six rainbow-colored layers of cream filling) on its Facebook page. Accompanying the image were the phrases "Pride" and "Proudly support love!" Responses to the images were mixed: "I'm never eating Oreos again. This is just disgusting," wrote one commenter, while another replied, "I didn't think it was possible for me to love Oreo's more than I already did!!" Though controversial, the post drew a considerable amount of support from fans, generating approximately 15,000 shares and 87,000 "likes."[9] Alternatively, a firm's advocacy campaign might react to criticism or blame, or to ward off increases in regulation, damaging legislation, or the unfavorable outcome of a lawsuit.

16-2b Product Advertising

Unlike institutional advertising, product advertising promotes the benefits of a specific good or service. The product's stage in its life cycle often determines which type of product advertising is used: pioneering advertising, competitive advertising, or comparative advertising.

PIONEERING ADVERTISING Pioneering advertising is intended to stimulate primary demand for a new product or product category. Heavily used during the introductory

institutional advertising
a form of advertising designed to enhance a company's image rather than promote a particular product

product advertising a form of advertising that touts the benefits of a specific good or service

advocacy advertising a form of advertising in which an organization expresses its views on controversial issues or responds to media attacks

pioneering advertising
a form of advertising designed to stimulate primary demand for a new product or product category

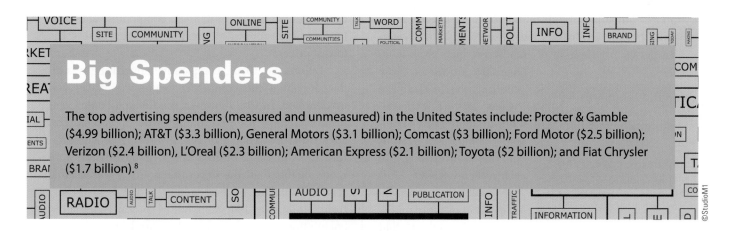

Big Spenders

The top advertising spenders (measured and unmeasured) in the United States include: Procter & Gamble ($4.99 billion); AT&T ($3.3 billion), General Motors ($3.1 billion); Comcast ($3 billion); Ford Motor ($2.5 billion); Verizon ($2.4 billion), L'Oreal ($2.3 billion); American Express ($2.1 billion); Toyota ($2 billion); and Fiat Chrysler ($1.7 billion).[8]

©StudioM1

stage of the product life cycle, pioneering advertising offers consumers in-depth information about the benefits of the product class. Pioneering advertising also seeks to create interest and, as such, can be quite innovative in its own right. For example, Motorola placed an ad for its new flagship smartphone, the Moto X, in *Wired*. The Moto X is highly customizable, featuring more than twenty different back plate and accent colors. Built in Austin, Texas, the Moto X is the first smartphone of its kind to be so customizable. Using an embedded LED array, microchip, and battery, the print ad allows the reader to push eleven different colored buttons, changing the color of the Moto X Smartphone pictured in the ad. A demonstration of the ad can be seen at www.youtube.com/watch?v=iMrZmSPpIRw.[10]

COMPETITIVE ADVERTISING Firms use competitive or brand advertising when a product enters the growth phase of the product life cycle and other companies begin to enter the marketplace. Instead of building demand for the product category, the goal of **competitive advertising** is to influence demand for a specific brand. Often, promotion becomes less informative and appeals more to emotions during this phase. Generally, this is where an emphasis on branding begins. Advertisements focus on showing subtle differences between brands, building recall of a brand name, and creating a favorable attitude toward the brand. GEICO uses competitive advertising that discusses the attributes of the brand, how little time it takes to get a quote, how much customers can save, and the ease of submitting a claim. All of its campaigns use humor to promote the brand above others in the industry but without actively comparing GEICO with other insurance companies.

COMPARATIVE ADVERTISING **Comparative advertising** directly or indirectly compares two or more competing brands on one or more specific attributes. Some advertisers even use comparative advertising against their own brands. Products experiencing slow growth or those entering the marketplace against strong competitors are more likely to employ comparative claims in their advertising. In contrast to GEICO's "Fifteen minutes can save you 15 percent or more on car insurance" tagline that

GEICO uses competitive advertising that discusses attributes of the brand.

Miro Vrlik Photography/Shutterstock.com

does not explicitly mention any other insurance company, 21st Century Insurance takes on its major competitors directly in its "Shopping Carts" television ad campaign. The ad features two cars, one labeled GEICO, the other 21st Century. As shopping carts pour down on the cars like rain, a voiceover explains that since both cars are covered, both get the same repairs.[11] Then the commercial goes on to explain that 21st Century Insurance customers who switch from GEICO save an average of $508 a year.[12] 21st Century is explicitly comparing its insurance rates with those of its main competitors and capitalizing on customers' desire for great coverage at the lowest prices.

Before the 1970s, comparative advertising was allowed only if the competing brand was veiled and unidentified. In 1971, however, the Federal Trade Commission (FTC) fostered the growth of comparative advertising by saying that the advertising provided information to the customer and that advertisers were more skillful than the government in communicating this information. Federal rulings prohibit advertisers from falsely describing competitors' products and allow competitors to sue if ads show their products or mention

competitive advertising
a form of advertising designed to influence demand for a specific brand

comparative advertising
a form of advertising that compares two or more specifically named or shown competing brands on one or more specific attributes

Make the RIGHT Choice!
Baked or Fried

Kellogg's pop·tarts Frosted Strawberry

TOTAL FAT	5g
SAT FAT	1.5g
TRANS FAT	0g
CHOLESTEROL	0mg
GOOD SOURCE OF VITAMINS AND MINERALS	7

Toaster Strudel Strawberry

TOTAL FAT	8g
SAT FAT	3.5g
TRANS FAT	1g
CHOLESTEROL	5mg
GOOD SOURCE OF VITAMINS AND MINERALS	0

Kellogg's pop·tarts toaster pastries

Always baked. Never fried.

What form of advertising is the Kellogg Company using in this Pop-Tarts advertisement? What does that say about the Pop-Tarts brand?

their brand names in an incorrect or false manner. FTC rules also apply to advertisers making false claims about their own products.

 16-3 CREATIVE DECISIONS IN ADVERTISING

Advertising strategies are typically organized around an advertising campaign. An **advertising campaign** is a series of related advertisements focusing on a common theme, slogan, and set of advertising appeals. It is a specific advertising effort for a particular product that extends for a defined period of time.

Before any creative work can begin on an advertising campaign, it is important to determine what goals or objectives the advertising should achieve. An **advertising objective** identifies the specific communication task that a campaign should accomplish for a specified target audience during a specified period. The objectives of a specific advertising campaign often

depend on the overall corporate objectives and the product being advertised.

The DAGMAR approach (Defining Advertising Goals for Measured Advertising Results) is one method of setting objectives. According to this method, all advertising objectives should precisely define the target audience, the desired percentage change in some specified measure of effectiveness, and the time frame in which that change is to occur.

Once objectives are defined, creative work can begin on the advertising campaign. Advertising campaigns often follow the AIDA model, which was discussed in Chapter 15. Depending on where consumers are in the AIDA process, the creative development of an advertising campaign might focus on creating attention, arousing interest, stimulating desire, or ultimately leading to the action of buying the product. Specifically, creative decisions include identifying product benefits, developing and evaluating advertising appeals, executing the message, and evaluating the effectiveness of the campaign.

16-3a Identifying Product Benefits

A well-known rule of thumb in the advertising industry is "Sell the sizzle, not the steak"—that is, in advertising, the goal is to sell the benefits of the product, not its attributes. Customers do not buy attributes, they buy benefits. An attribute is simply a feature of the product such as its easy-open package, special formulation, or new lower price. A benefit is what consumers will receive or achieve by using the product, such as convenience or ease of use. A benefit should answer the consumer's question "What's in it for me?" Benefits might be such things as pleasure, improved health, savings, or relief. A quick test to determine whether you are offering attributes or benefits in your advertising is to ask "So?" Consider this example:

- **Attribute:** "DogsBestFriend is an all-natural skin care lotion for dogs that combines traditional medicines and Nigella sativa seed oils with the newest extraction technology." "So . . . ?"

- **Benefit:** "So . . . DogsBestFriend acts as a natural replacement for hydrocortisone, antihistamines, and topical antibiotics that is powerful enough to combat inflammation, itching, and pain, yet safe enough to use on dogs of all ages."[13]

advertising campaign a series of related advertisements focusing on a common theme, slogan, and set of advertising appeals

advertising objective a specific communication task that a campaign should accomplish for a specified target audience during a specified period

16-3b Developing and Evaluating Advertising Appeals

An **advertising appeal** identifies a reason for a person to buy a product. Developing advertising appeals, a challenging task, is typically the responsibility of the creative team (e.g., art directors and copywriters) in the advertising agency. Advertising appeals typically play off consumers' emotions or address some need or want consumers have.

Advertising campaigns can focus on one or more advertising appeals. Often the appeals are quite general, thus allowing the firm to develop a number of subthemes or mini campaigns using both advertising and sales promotion. Several possible advertising appeals are listed in Exhibit 16.1.

Choosing the best appeal from those developed usually requires market research. Criteria for evaluation include desirability, exclusiveness, and believability. The appeal first must make a positive impression on and be desirable to the target market. It must also be exclusive or unique. Consumers must be able to distinguish the advertiser's message from competitors' messages. Most importantly, the appeal should be believable. An appeal that makes extravagant claims not only wastes promotional dollars but also creates ill will for the advertiser.

The advertising appeal selected for the campaign becomes what advertisers call its **unique selling proposition**. The unique selling proposition often becomes all or part of the campaign's slogan. High-end leather goods manufacturer Saddleback Leather uses its Web site to build brand personality and convey the company's unique selling proposition: its products are extremely tough and rugged—just like the consumers who buy them. First-person narratives recount trips to Mexican bullfighting rings, shark diving in Bora Bora, backpacking along the red sand dunes of Texas, and other adventures in exotic, often perilous locations. Of course, Saddleback Leather's messenger bags and luggage are up to the task, accompanying their sojourning owner everywhere he goes—even into the ocean. Saddleback Leather's slogan drives home its products' unique selling proposition: "They'll fight over it when you're dead."[14]

advertising appeal a reason for a person to buy a product

unique selling proposition a desirable, exclusive, and believable advertising appeal selected as the theme for a campaign

EXHIBIT 16.1 COMMON ADVERTISING APPEALS

Appeal	Goal
Profit	Lets consumers know whether the product will save them money, make them money, or keep them from losing money.
Health	Appeals to those who are body conscious or who want to be healthy; love or romance is used often in selling cosmetics and perfumes.
Fear	Can center around social embarrassment, growing old, or losing one's health; because of its power, requires advertiser to exercise care in execution.
Admiration	Frequently highlights celebrity spokespeople.
Convenience	Is often used for fast-food restaurants and microwave foods.
Fun and Pleasure	Are the keys to advertising vacations, beer, amusement parks, and more.
Vanity and Egotism	Are used most often for expensive or conspicuous items such as cars and clothing.
Environmental Consciousness	Centers around protecting the environment and being considerate of others in the community.

16-3c Executing the Message

Message execution is the way an advertisement portrays its information. In general, the AIDA plan (see Chapter 15) is a good blueprint for executing an advertising message. Any ad should immediately draw the reader's, viewer's, or listener's attention. The advertiser must then use the message to hold interest, create desire for the good or service, and ultimately motivate a purchase.

The style in which the message is executed is one of the most creative elements of an advertisement. Exhibit 16.2 lists some examples of executional styles used by advertisers. Executional styles often dictate what type of media is to be employed to convey the message. For example, scientific executional styles lend themselves well to print advertising, where more information can be conveyed. Testimonials by athletes are one of the more popular executional styles.

Injecting humor into an advertisement is a popular and effective executional style. Humorous executional styles are more often used in radio and television advertising than in print or magazine advertising, where humor is less easily communicated. Recall that humorous ads are typically used for lower-risk, low-involvement, routine purchases such as candy, cigarettes, and casual jeans than for higher-risk purchases or for products that are expensive, durable, or flamboyant.[15]

Sometimes an executional style must be modified to make a marketing campaign more effective. Nowhere

EXHIBIT 16.2 ELEVEN COMMON EXECUTIONAL STYLES FOR ADVERTISING

Executional Style	Description
Slice-of-Life	Depicts people in normal settings, such as at the dinner table or in their car. McDonald's often uses slice-of-life styles showing youngsters munching on french fries from Happy Meals on family outings.
Lifestyle	Shows how well the product will fit in with the consumer's lifestyle. As his Volkswagen Jetta moves through the streets of the French Quarter, a Gen X driver inserts a techno music CD and marvels at how the rhythms of the world mimic the ambient vibe inside his vehicle.
Spokesperson/ Testimonial	Can feature a celebrity, company official, or typical consumer making a testimonial or endorsing a product. Sheryl Crow represented Revlon's Colorist hair coloring, while Beyoncé Knowles was named the new face of American Express. Dell Inc. founder Michael Dell touts his vision of the customer experience via Dell in television ads.
Fantasy	Creates a fantasy for the viewer built around use of the product. Carmakers often use this style to let viewers fantasize about how they would feel speeding around tight corners or down long country roads in their cars.
Humorous	Advertisers often use humor in their ads, such as Snickers' "Not Going Anywhere for a While" campaign featuring hundreds of souls waiting, sometimes impatiently, to get into heaven.
Real/Animated Product Symbols	Creates a character that represents the product in advertisements, such as the Energizer Bunny or Starkist's Charlie the Tuna. GEICO's suave gecko and disgruntled cavemen became cult classics for the insurance company.
Mood or Image	Builds a mood or image around the product, such as peace, love, or beauty. De Beers ads depicting shadowy silhouettes wearing diamond engagement rings and diamond necklaces portrayed passion and intimacy while extolling that "a diamond is forever."
Demonstration	Shows consumers the expected benefit. Many consumer products use this technique. Laundry detergent spots are famous for demonstrating how their product will clean clothes whiter and brighter. Fort James Corporation demonstrated in television commercials how its Dixie Rinse & ReUse disposable stoneware product line can stand up to the heat of a blowtorch and survive a cycle in a clothes washer.
Musical	Conveys the message of the advertisement through song. For example, Nike's ads depicted a marathoner's tortured feet and a surfer's thigh scarred by a shark attack while strains of Joe Cocker's "You Are So Beautiful" could be heard in the background.
Scientific	Uses research or scientific evidence to give a brand superiority over competitors. Pain relievers like Advil, Bayer, and Excedrin use scientific evidence in their ads.

is this more evident than in the political realm, where advertisements for issues and candidates must account for ever-changing poll numbers and public sentiments. In Barack Obama's second presidential election, campaign advertisements taking aim at the president shifted in tone from sharply combative and accusatory to concerned—even mournful—about the state of the economy. According to Republican pollster Frank Luntz, focus group research revealed that ads that attacked Obama too personally turned people off in ways that kept them turned off. The Republican campaign shifted its executional style, opting for advertisements that appealed to citizens' worries and frustrations. In one ad, a forlorn-looking woman declares, "I supported President Obama because he spoke so beautifully. But since then, things have gone from bad to much worse."[16]

16-3d Post-Campaign Evaluation

Evaluating an advertising campaign can be the most demanding task facing advertisers. How can an advertiser assess if the campaign led to an increase in sales or market share or elevated awareness of the product? Many advertising campaigns aim to create an image for the good or service instead of asking for action, so their real effect is unknown. So many variables shape the effectiveness of an ad that advertisers often must guess whether their money has been well spent. Nonetheless, marketers spend considerable time studying advertising effectiveness and its probable impact on sales, market share, or awareness.

Testing ad effectiveness can be done before and/ or after the campaign. Before a campaign is released, marketing managers use pretests to determine the best advertising appeal, layout, and media vehicle. After advertisers implement a campaign, they use several monitoring techniques to determine whether the campaign has met its original goals. Even if a campaign has been highly successful, advertisers still typically do a post-campaign analysis to identify how the campaign might have been more efficient and what factors contributed to its success.

16-4 MEDIA DECISIONS IN ADVERTISING

A major decision for advertisers is the choice of **medium**—the channel used to convey a message to a target market. **Media planning**, therefore, is the series of decisions advertisers make regarding the selection and use of media, enabling the marketer to optimally and cost-effectively communicate the message to the target audience. Specifically, advertisers must determine which types of media will best communicate the benefits of their product or service to the target audience and when and for how long the advertisement will run.

Promotional objectives and the appeal and executional style of the advertising strongly affect the selection of media. Both creative and media decisions are made at the same time: creative work cannot be completed without knowing which medium will be used to convey the message to the target market. In many cases, the advertising objectives dictate the medium and the creative approach to be used. For example, if the objective is to demonstrate how fast a product operates, a television commercial that shows this action may be the best choice.

In 2015, U.S. advertisers spent about $180 billion on paid media monitored by national reporting services—newspapers, magazines, radio, television, the Internet, and outdoor/

medium the channel used to convey a message to a target market

media planning the series of decisions advertisers make regarding the selection and use of media, allowing the marketer to optimally and cost-effectively communicate the message to the target audience

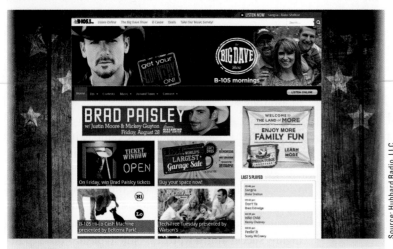

Future growth in advertising lies in the digital realm; this includes display ads, video ads, search ads and banner ads.

BEST OF THE BEST

According to *Advertising Age,* these are the best advertising campaigns in recent years:

1. Newcastle's "If We Made It"
2. Save the Children's "Most Shocking Second a Day"
3. Coca Cola Life's "Parents"
4. Wren's "First Kiss"
5. John Lewis' "Monty the Penguin"[17]

cinema.[18] The remainder was spent on unmonitored media such as direct mail, trade exhibits, cooperative advertising, brochures, coupons, catalogs, and special events. More than 38 percent of every media dollar goes toward television ads (cable, syndicated, spot, and network); almost 25 percent toward Internet ads; 12 percent toward newspaper ads; 10 percent toward magazine ads; 9 percent toward radio ads; and 5 percent toward outdoor/cinema ads.[19] But these traditional mass-market media are declining in usage as more targeted media are emerging. Future growth lies primarily in the digital realm, both in paid media (display ads, video ads, and search ads) and earned media (social media).

16-4a Media Types

Advertising media are channels that advertisers use in mass communication. The six major advertising media are newspapers, magazines, radio, television, the Internet, and outdoor media. Exhibit 16.3 summarizes the advantages and disadvantages of some of these major channels. In recent years, however, alternative media channels have emerged that give advertisers innovative ways to reach their target audience and avoid advertising clutter.

NEWSPAPERS Newspapers are one of the oldest forms of media. The advantages of newspaper advertising include geographic flexibility and timeliness. Although there has been a decline in circulation as well as in the number of newspapers, nationally, there are still several major newspapers including the *Wall Street Journal, USA Today,* the *New York Times,* the *Los Angeles Times,* and the *Washington Post.* But most newspapers are local. Because newspapers are generally a

EXHIBIT 16.3 ADVANTAGES AND DISADVANTAGES OF MAJOR ADVERTISING MEDIA

Medium	Advantages	Disadvantages
Newspapers	Geographic selectivity and flexibility; short-term advertiser commitments; news value and immediacy; year-round readership; high individual market coverage; co-op and local tie-in availability; short lead time	Little demographic selectivity; limited color capabilities; low pass-along rate; may be expensive
Magazines	Good reproduction, especially for color; demographic selectivity; regional selectivity; local market selectivity; relatively long advertising life; high pass-along rate	Long-term advertiser commitments; slow audience buildup; limited demonstration capabilities; lack of urgency; long lead time
Radio	Low cost; immediacy of message; can be scheduled on short notice; relatively no seasonal change in audience; highly portable; short-term advertiser commitments; entertainment carryover	No visual treatment; short advertising life of message; high frequency required to generate comprehension and retention; distractions from background sound; commercial clutter
Television	Ability to reach a wide, diverse audience; low cost per thousand; creative opportunities for demonstration; immediacy of messages; entertainment carryover; demographic selectivity with cable stations	Short life of message; some consumer skepticism about claims; high campaign cost; little demographic selectivity with network stations; long-term advertiser commitments; long lead times required for production; commercial clutter
Internet	Fastest-growing medium; ability to reach a narrow target audience; relatively short lead time required for creating Web-based advertising; moderate cost; ability to measure ad effectiveness; ability to engage consumers through search engine marketing, social media, display advertising, and mobile marketing	Most ad exposure relies on "click-through" from display ads; measurement for social media needs much improvement; not all consumers have access to the Internet, and many consumers are not using social media
Outdoor Media	Repetition; moderate cost; flexibility; geographic selectivity	Short message; lack of demographic selectivity; high "noise" level distracting audience

mass-market medium, however, they may not be the best vehicle for marketers trying to reach a very narrow market. Newspaper advertising also encounters distractions from competing ads and news stories. Therefore, one company's ad may not be particularly visible.

The main sources of newspaper ad revenue are local retailers, classified ads, and cooperative advertising. In **cooperative advertising**, the manufacturer and the retailer split the costs of advertising the manufacturer's brand. For example, Estée Lauder may split the cost of an advertisement with Macy's department store provided that the ad focuses on Estée Lauder's products. One reason manufacturers use cooperative advertising is the impracticality of listing all their dealers in national advertising. Also, cooperative advertising encourages retailers to devote more effort to the manufacturer's lines.

MAGAZINES Magazines are another traditional medium that has been successful. Some of the top magazines according to circulation include *AARP*, *Better Homes and Gardens*, *Reader's Digest*, *National Geographic*, and *Good Housekeeping*. However, compared to the cost of other media, the cost per contact in magazine advertising is usually high. The cost per potential customer may be much lower, however, because magazines are often targeted to specialized audiences and thus reach more potential customers.

RADIO Radio has several strengths as an advertising medium: selectivity and audience segmentation, a large out-of-home audience, low unit and production costs, timeliness,

Brian A Jackson/Shutterstock.com

cooperative advertising
an arrangement in which the manufacturer and the retailer split the costs of advertising the manufacturer's brand

and geographic flexibility. Local advertisers are the most frequent users of radio advertising, contributing over 75 percent of all radio ad revenue. Like newspapers, radio also lends itself well to cooperative advertising.

TELEVISION Television broadcasters include network television, independent stations, cable television, and direct broadcast satellite television. Network television reaches a wide and diverse market, and cable television and direct broadcast satellite systems, such as DIRECTV and DISH Network, broadcast a multitude of channels devoted to highly segmented markets. Because of its targeted channels, cable television is often characterized as "narrowcasting" by media buyers. DIRECTV is testing the ability to serve ads based on household data (as opposed to demographic and geographic data). To stay relevant amidst new technologies, DIRECTV and other television-focused companies are beginning to recognize the need for better audience targeting.[20]

Advertising time on television can be very expensive, especially for network and popular cable channels. Special events and first-run prime-time shows for top-ranked television programs command the highest rates for a typical commercial. For example, running a thirty-second spot during the sitcom *How to Get Away with Murder* on ABC costs $146,113, while running one during NFL Sunday Football costs $627,300. Cable programs like ESPN's *Monday Night Football* command similarly hefty price tags.[20] A thirty-second spot during the Super Bowl costs approximately $4.5 million.[21] Despite its high cost, many brands feel that a Super Bowl ad is a good investment given the earned media leading up to the game, during the game, and after the game.[22] An alternative to a commercial spot is the **infomercial**, a 30-minute or longer advertisement, which is relatively inexpensive to produce and air. Advertisers say the infomercial is an ideal way to present complicated information to potential customers, which other advertising vehicles typically do not allow time to do. Beachbody's P90X and Insanity exercise DVDs are advertised through infomercials.

infomercial a 30-minute or longer advertisement that looks more like a television talk show than a sales pitch

advergaming placing advertising messages in Web-based, mobile, console, or handheld video games to advertise or promote a product, service, organization, or issue

Probably the most significant trend of concern to television advertising is the rise in popularity of digital video recorders (DVRs) and on-demand viewing. For every hour of television programming, an average of 20 minutes is dedicated to nonprogram material (ads, public service announcements, and network promotions), so the popularity of DVRs among ad-weary viewers is hardly surprising. Like marketers and advertisers, networks are also highly concerned about ad skipping. If consumers are not watching advertisements, then marketers will spend a greater proportion of their advertising budgets on alternative media, and a critical revenue stream for networks will disappear.

THE INTERNET Online advertising has become a versatile medium to target specific groups. U.S. digital ad revenues exceed $50 billion annually and are expected to increase to $82 billion annually by 2018. This figure is projected to grow to more than $163 billion by 2016, at which point it will represent 26 percent of all advertising expenditures.[23] Online advertising includes search engine marketing (e.g., pay-per-click ads like Google AdWords), display advertising (e.g., banner ads, video ads), social media advertising (e.g., Facebook ads), e-mail marketing, and mobile marketing (including mobile advertising and SMS). Some online channels like Google offer the ability to *audience buy* (whereby advertisers can purchase ad space targeted to a highly specific group), but others, such as Turner Digital's FunnyOrDie.com, believe the complex cookie-based strategy poses too many risks.[24]

Popular Internet sites and search engines generally sell advertising space to marketers to promote their goods and services. Internet surfers click on these ads to be linked to more information about the advertised product or service. Both leading advertisers and companies whose ad budgets are not as large have become big Internet advertisers. Because of the relative low cost and high targetability, search engines generate nearly half of all Internet ad revenue. Display and banner ads are the next largest source of Internet revenue, followed by classifieds, mobile, and digital video.[25]

Another popular Internet advertising format is **advergaming**, whereby companies put ad messages in Web-based, mobile, console, or handheld video games to advertise or promote a product, service, organization, or issue. *Gamification*, the process of using game mechanics and a gaming mindset to engage an audience, is increasingly important for marketers to know about and utilize. Challenges, rewards, incentives, and competition are all important aspects in social media games like *Candy Crush Saga and Candy Crush Soda Saga*.[26] Some games amount to virtual commercials; others encourage players to buy in-game items and power-ups to advance; and still others allow advertisers to sponsor games or buy ad space for product placements. Many of these are social games, played on Facebook or mobile networks, where players can interact with one another. Social gaming has a huge audience—according to Facebook CEO Mark Zuckerberg, 235 million people play social games on Facebook every month. The Facebook gaming market is projected to more than double in the next three years, attracting 554 million people and generating $5.6 billion.[27]

More than three-fourths of Americans have mobile phones, and over one-third of those are smartphones. Fifty-five percent of mobile phone owners access the Web on their phones, making mobile Web sites and apps more important.[28] Mobile advertising has substantial upside potential given that there are more than six billion cell phone users in the world, and an increasing number of those users have smartphones or tablets with Internet access. Mobile advertising is finally reaching its tipping point, reaching almost $24 billion annually. This accounts for nearly all growth in digital advertising. The primary reason is that people are spending more of their time (19.4 percent) on mobile devices rather than on desktops and laptops.[29] As devices such as the iPad continue to grow in popularity, mobile advertising spending will continue to grow worldwide.

OUTDOOR MEDIA Outdoor or out-of-home advertising is a flexible, low-cost medium that may take a variety of forms. Examples include billboards, skywriting, giant inflatables, mini billboards in malls and on bus stop shelters, signs in sports arenas, and lighted moving signs in bus terminals and airports, as well as ads painted on cars, trucks, buses, water towers, manhole covers, drinking glass coasters, and even people, called "living advertising." The plywood scaffolding surrounding downtown construction sites often holds ads, which in places like Manhattan's Times Square, can reach over a million viewers a day.

Outdoor advertising reaches a broad and diverse market and is therefore ideal for promoting convenience products and services as well as directing consumers to local businesses. One of outdoor advertising's main advantages over other media is that its exposure frequency is very high, yet the amount of clutter from competing ads is very low. Outdoor advertising also can be customized to local marketing needs, which is why local businesses are the leading outdoor advertisers in any given region.

ALTERNATIVE MEDIA To cut through the clutter of traditional advertising media, advertisers are developing new media vehicles, like shopping carts in grocery stores, computer screen savers, interactive kiosks in department stores, advertisements run before movies at the cinema, posters on bathroom stalls, and *advertainments*—mini movies that promote a product and are shown online.

Marketers are looking for more innovative ways to reach captive and often bored commuters. For instance, subway systems are now showing ads via lighted boxes installed along tunnel walls. Other advertisers seek consumers at home. Some marketers have begun replacing hold music on customer service lines with advertisements and movie trailers. This strategy generates revenue for the company being called and catches undistracted consumers for advertisers. The trick is to amuse and interest this captive audience without annoying them during their ten- to fifteen-minute wait. After Yahoo! CEO Marissa Mayer called her company's on-hold message "garbage," audio production startup Jingle Punks hired Canadian rapper Snow (known for his 1992 hit "Informer") to write a humorous on-hold jingle for Yahoo! (you can hear the jingle at www.youtube.com /watch?v=vRmVDADlnOU). Yahoo! has yet to implement the jingle, however.[30]

PureSolution/Shutterstock.com

There are a number of factors to consider before committing to any sort of advertising medium; this includes flexibility of the medium, noise level, and the life span of the medium.

16-4b Media Selection Considerations

An important element in any advertising campaign is the **media mix**, the combination of media to be used. Media mix decisions are typically based on several factors: cost per contact, cost per click, reach, frequency, target audience considerations, flexibility of the medium, noise level, and the life span of the medium.

Cost per contact, also referred to as **cost per thousand (CPM)**, is the cost of reaching one member of the target market. Naturally, as the size of the audience increases, so does the total cost. Cost per contact enables an advertiser to compare the relative costs of specific media vehicles (such as television versus radio or magazine versus newspaper), or more specifically, within a media category (such as *People* versus *US Weekly*). Thus, an advertiser debating whether to spend local advertising dollars for television spots or radio spots could consider the cost per contact of each. Alternatively, if the question is which magazine to advertise in, she might choose the one with the greater reach. In either case, the advertiser can pick the vehicle with the lowest cost per contact to maximize advertising punch for the money spent. **Cost per click** is the cost associated with a consumer clicking on a display or banner ad. Although there are several variations, this option enables the marketer to pay only for "engaged" consumers—those who opted to click on an ad.

Reach is the number of target customers who are exposed to a commercial at least once during a specific period, usually four weeks. Media plans for product introductions and attempts at increasing brand awareness usually emphasize reach. For example, an advertiser might try to reach seventy percent of the target audience during the first three months of the campaign. Reach is related to a medium's ratings, generally referred to in the industry as *gross ratings points*, or *GRP*. A television program with a higher GRP means that more people are tuning in to the show and the reach is higher. Accordingly, as GRP increases for a particular medium, so does cost per contact.

Because the typical ad is short-lived, and often only a small portion of an ad may be perceived at one time, advertisers repeat their ads so that potential customers will remember the message. **Frequency** is the number of times an individual is exposed to a given message during a specific period. Advertisers use average frequency to measure the intensity of a specific medium's coverage. For example, Coca-Cola might want an average exposure frequency of five for its Powerade television ads. That means that each of the television viewers who saw the ad saw it an average of five times.

Media selection is also a matter of matching the advertising medium with the product's target market. If marketers are trying to reach teenage females, they might select *Teen Vogue* magazine. A medium's ability to reach a precisely defined market is its **audience selectivity**. Some media vehicles, like general newspapers and network television, appeal to a wide cross section of the population. Others—such as *Brides*, *Popular Mechanics*, *Architectural Digest*, *Lucky*, MTV, ESPN, and Christian radio stations—appeal to very specific groups.

The *flexibility* of a medium can be extremely important to an advertiser. For example, because of layouts and design, the lead time for magazine advertising is considerably longer than for other media types and so is less flexible. By contrast, radio and Internet advertising provide maximum flexibility. If necessary, an advertiser can change a radio ad on the day it is aired.

Noise level is the level of distraction experienced by the target audience in a medium. Noise can be created by competing ads, as when a street is lined with billboards or when a television program is cluttered with competing

media mix the combination of media to be used for a promotional campaign

cost per contact (cost per thousand or CPM) the cost of reaching one member of the target market

cost per click the cost associated with a consumer clicking on a display or banner ad

reach the number of target consumers exposed to a commercial at least once during a specific period, usually four weeks

frequency the number of times an individual is exposed to a given message during a specific period

audience selectivity the ability of an advertising medium to reach a precisely defined market

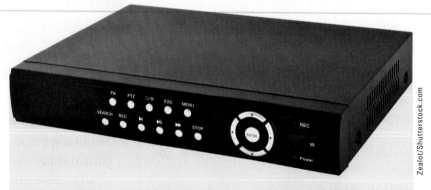

There are many ways for viewers to avoid watching commercials; this includes the use of a DVR.

Zealot/Shutterstock.com

ads. Whereas newspapers and magazines have a high noise level, direct mail is a private medium with a low noise level. Typically, no other advertising media or news stories compete for direct mail readers' attention.

Media have either a short or a long *life span*, which means that messages can either quickly fade or persist as tangible copy to be carefully studied. A radio commercial may last less than a minute, but advertisers can overcome this short life span by repeating radio ads often. In contrast, a magazine has a relatively long life span, which is further increased by a high pass-along rate.

Media planners have traditionally relied on the above factors in selecting an effective media mix, with reach, frequency, and cost often the overriding criteria. Well-established brands with familiar messages, however, probably need fewer exposures to be effective, while newer or unfamiliar brands likely need more exposures to become familiar. In addition, today's media planners have more media options than ever before. (Today, there are over 1,600 television networks across the country, whereas forty years ago there were only three.)

The proliferation of media channels is causing *media fragmentation* and forcing media planners to pay as much attention to where they place their advertising as to how often the advertisement is repeated. That is, marketers should evaluate reach *and* frequency in assessing the effectiveness of advertising. In certain situations, it may be important to reach potential consumers through as many media vehicles as possible. When this approach is considered, however, the budget must be large enough to achieve sufficient levels of frequency to have an impact. In evaluating reach versus frequency, therefore, the media planner ultimately must select an approach that is most likely to result in the ad being understood and remembered when a purchase decision is being made.

Advertisers also evaluate the qualitative factors involved in media selection. These include such things as attention to the commercial and the program, involvement, program liking, lack of distractions, and other audience behaviors that affect the likelihood that a commercial message is being seen and, hopefully, absorbed. While advertisers can advertise their product in as many media as possible and repeat the ad as many times as they like, the ad still may not be effective if the audience is not paying attention. Additional research highlights the benefits of cross-media advertising campaigns. According to Rick Mandler, VP of Digital Ad Sales at television network ABC, running an ad both on television and online delivers a lower median age, but delivers greater frequency and reach in the 18 to 24 age range, as well as greater overall reach for adults ages 18 to 49. ABC

Unified, a pioneering approach to cross-media advertising, is quickly gaining popularity among ABC's more than 200 advertisers.[31]

16-4c Media Scheduling

After choosing the media for the advertising campaign, advertisers must schedule the ads. A **media schedule** designates the medium or media to be used (such as magazines, television, or radio), the specific vehicles (such as *People* magazine, the show *Scandal* on television, or Rush Limbaugh's national radio program), and the insertion dates of the advertising.

There are four basic types of media schedules:

- A **continuous media schedule** allows the advertising to run steadily throughout the advertising period. Examples include Ivory soap and Charmin toilet tissue, which may have an ad in the newspaper every Sunday and a television commercial on NBC every Wednesday at 7:30 p.m. over a three-month time period. Products in the later stages of the product life cycle, which are advertised on a reminder basis, often use a continuous media schedule.

- With a **flighted media schedule**, the advertiser may schedule the ads heavily every other month or every two weeks to achieve a greater impact with an increased frequency and reach at those times. Movie studios might schedule television advertising on Wednesday and Thursday nights, when moviegoers are deciding which films to see that weekend.

- A **pulsing media schedule** combines continuous scheduling with flighted scheduling. It is continuous advertising that is simply heavier during the best sale periods. A retail department store may advertise on a year-round basis but place more advertising during certain sale periods such as Thanksgiving, Christmas, and back-to-school. Or beer may be advertised more heavily during the summer months and football

media schedule designation of the media, the specific publications or programs, and the insertion dates of advertising

continuous media schedule a media scheduling strategy in which advertising is run steadily throughout the advertising period; used for products in the later stages of the product life cycle

flighted media schedule a media scheduling strategy in which ads are run heavily every other month or every two weeks to achieve a greater impact with an increased frequency and reach at those times

pulsing media schedule a media scheduling strategy that uses continuous scheduling throughout the year coupled with a flighted schedule during the best sales periods

season given the higher consumption levels at those times.

- Certain times of the year call for a **seasonal media schedule**. Products like Sudafed cold tablets and Coppertone sunscreen, which are used more during certain times of the year, tend to follow a seasonal strategy.

Research comparing continuous media schedules and flighted ones suggests that continuous schedules are more effective than are flighted ones at driving sales through television advertisements. This research suggests that it may be important to reach a potential customer as close as possible to the time at which he makes a purchase. Therefore, the advertiser should maintain a continuous schedule over as long a period of time as possible. Often called *recency planning*, this theory of scheduling is now commonly used for scheduling television advertising for frequently purchased products such as Coca-Cola and Tide detergent. Recency planning's main premise is that advertising works by influencing the brand choice of people who are ready to buy. Mobile advertising may be one of the most promising tactics for contacting consumers when they are thinking about a specific product. For example, a GPS-enabled mobile phone can get text messages for area restaurants around lunchtime to advertise specials to professionals working in a big city.

Big Mama's and Papa's Pizzeria received more than $10 million in free publicity after Ellen DeGeneres placed an order with the restaurant during the 2014 Academy Awards broadcast.

 16-5 PUBLIC RELATIONS

Public relations is the element in the promotional mix that evaluates public attitudes, identifies issues that may elicit public concern, and executes programs to gain public understanding and acceptance. Public relations is a vital link in a forward-thinking company's marketing communication mix. Marketing managers plan solid public relations campaigns that fit into overall marketing plans and focus on targeted audiences. These campaigns strive to maintain a positive image of the corporation in the eyes of the public. As such, they should capitalize on the factors that enhance the firm's image and minimize the factors that could generate a negative image. The concept of earned media is based on public relations and publicity.

Publicity is the effort to capture media attention—for example, through articles or editorials in publications or through human-interest stories on radio or television programs. Corporations usually initiate publicity through press releases that further their public relations plans. A company about to introduce a new product or open a new store may send press releases to the media in the hope that the story will be published or broadcast. Savvy publicity can often create overnight sensations or build up a reserve of goodwill with consumers. Corporate donations and sponsorships can also create favorable publicity.

16-5a Major Public Relations Tools

Public relations professionals commonly use several tools, many of which require an active role on the part of the public relations professional, such as writing press releases and engaging in proactive media relations. Sometimes, however, these techniques create their own publicity.

NEW-PRODUCT PUBLICITY Publicity is instrumental in introducing new products and services. Publicity can help advertisers explain what's different about their new product by prompting free news stories or positive

seasonal media schedule a media scheduling strategy that runs advertising only during times of the year when the product is most likely to be used

public relations the element in the promotional mix that evaluates public attitudes, identifies issues that may elicit public concern, and executes programs to gain public understanding and acceptance

publicity an effort to capture media attention, often initiated through press releases that further a corporation's public relations plans

word of mouth about it. During the introductory period, an especially innovative new product often needs more exposure than conventional, paid advertising affords. Public relations professionals write press releases or develop videos in an effort to generate news about their new product. They also jockey for exposure of their product or service at major events, on popular television and news shows, or in the hands of influential people. Consider the publicity Apple generated for the release of the iPad Air, which included press coverage in traditional media as well as online blogs and forums. That was a small part of the entire marketing campaign.

PRODUCT PLACEMENT Marketers are increasingly using product placement to reinforce brand awareness and create favorable attitudes. **Product placement** is a strategy that involves getting one's product, service, or name to appear in a movie, television show, radio program, magazine, newspaper, video game, video or audio clip, book, or commercial for another product; on the Internet; or at special events. Including an actual product, such as a can of Pepsi, adds a sense of realism to a movie, television show, video game, book, or similar vehicle that cannot be created by a can simply marked "soda." Product placements are arranged through barter (trade of product for placement), through paid placements, or at no charge when the product is viewed as enhancing the vehicle it is placed in.

Global product placement expenditures total about $8 billion annually ($4.3 billion in the United States alone).[32] More than two-thirds of product placements are in movies and television shows, but placements in other alternative media are growing, particularly on the Internet and in video games. Digital technology now enables companies to "virtually" place their products in any audio or video production. Virtual placement not only reduces the cost of product placement for new productions but also enables companies to place their products in previously produced programs, such as reruns of television shows. Overall, companies obtain valuable product exposure, brand reinforcement, and increased sales through product placement.

CONSUMER EDUCATION Some major firms believe that educated consumers are more loyal customers. Financial planning firms often sponsor free educational seminars on money management, retirement planning, and investing in the hope that the seminar participants will choose the sponsoring organization for their future financial needs.

> **product placement** a public relations strategy that involves getting a product, service, or company name to appear in a movie, television show, radio program, magazine, newspaper, video game, video or audio clip, book, or commercial for another product; on the Internet; or at special events

The Many Duties of Public Relations Departments

Public relations departments may perform any or all of the following functions:

- **Press relations:** Placing positive, newsworthy information in the news media or in the hands of influential bloggers to attract attention to a product, a service, or a person associated with the firm or institution
- **Product publicity:** Publicizing specific products or services through a variety of traditional and online channels
- **Corporate communication:** Creating internal and external messages to promote a positive image of the firm or institution
- **Public affairs:** Building and maintaining local, national, or global community relations
- **Lobbying:** Influencing legislators and government officials to promote or defeat legislation and regulation
- **Employee and investor relations:** Maintaining positive relationships with employees, shareholders, and others in the financial community
- **Crisis management:** Responding to unfavorable publicity or a negative event placement, often at a much lower cost than in mass media like television ads

SPONSORSHIP Sponsorships are increasing both in number and as a proportion of companies' marketing budgets. Currently sitting at about $32 billion annually, U.S. sponsorship spending is likewise increasing.[33] Probably the biggest reason for the increasing use of sponsorships is the difficulty of reaching audiences and differentiating a product from competing brands through the mass media.

With **sponsorship**, a company spends money to support an issue, cause, or event that is consistent with corporate objectives, such as improving brand awareness or enhancing corporate image. The biggest category of sponsorships is sports, which accounts for almost 70 percent of spending in sponsorships and has seen steady growth in recent years.[34] Nonsports categories include entertainment tours and attractions, causes, arts, festivals, fairs and annual events, and association and membership organizations.

Although the most popular sponsorship events are still those involving sports, music, or the arts, companies have recently been turning to more specialized events such as tie-ins with schools, charities, and other community service organizations. Marketers sometimes even create their own events tied around their products. For example, energy drink manufacturer Red Bull hosted Stratos, a multimillion-dollar event where Austrian Felix Baumgartner skydived from the edge of space—nearly twenty-four miles above Earth's surface. Baumgartner became the first human to break the sound barrier in free fall, reaching 834 miles per hour before touching down safely in New Mexico. A major marketing victory for Red Bull, Stratos set its own record as the most-watched YouTube live stream of all time—more than eight million viewers tuned in to the event.[35]

Corporations sponsor issues as well as events. Sponsorship issues are quite diverse, but the three most popular are education, health care, and social programs. Firms often donate a percentage of sales or profits to a worthy cause favored by their target market.

EXPERIENTIAL MARKETING While the Internet enables consumers to connect with their favorite brands in a virtual environment, there is often nothing like experiencing the real thing live and in person. Experiential marketing involves engaging with consumers in a way that enables them to feel the brand—not just read about it. Experiential and event marketing have increased in recent years, with most of the growth coming from the world's largest brands. Examples of experiential marketing include American Express's Small Business Saturday, which promotes shopping at local businesses, and Clear Channel's effort to run a carnival-style dunk tank in New York City's Times Square.[36]

COMPANY WEB SITES Companies are increasingly using the Internet in their public relations strategies. Company Web sites are used to introduce new products; provide information to the media, including social media news releases; promote existing products; obtain consumer feedback; communicate legislative and regulatory information; showcase upcoming events; provide links to related sites (including corporate and non-corporate blogs, Facebook, and Twitter); release financial information; interact with customers and potential customers; and perform many more marketing activities. In addition, social media are playing a larger role in how companies interact with customers online, particularly through sites like Facebook, Yelp, or Twitter. Indeed, online reviews (good and bad) from opinion leaders and other consumers help marketers sway purchasing decisions in their favor.

16-5b Managing Unfavorable Publicity

Although marketers try to avoid unpleasant situations, crises do happen. In our free-press environment, publicity is not easily controlled, especially in a crisis.

Corporations sponsor events in an attempt to market their product. The yearly Rose Bowl game has been sponsored by companies like Citi and Northwestern Mutual.

sponsorship a public relations strategy in which a company spends money to support an issue, cause, or event that is consistent with corporate objectives, such as improving brand awareness or enhancing corporate image

Crisis management is the coordinated effort to handle the effects of unfavorable publicity, ensuring fast and accurate communication in times of emergency.

When the Villa Fresh Italian Kitchen ran "Dub the Dew," an online contest to name a green apple–flavored variety of Mountain Dew exclusive to the restaurant, it was not long before Internet trolls descended. These digital pranksters submitted absurd and offensive names (such as "diabeetus," "gushing granny," and "Hitler did nothing wrong"), and then voted their submissions to the top of the contest leaderboard en masse. The contest's Web site was quickly taken offline, and Mountain Dew tweeted that the contest "lost to the internet." In an attempt to manage the crisis, the Villa Fresh Italian Kitchen issued an apologetic statement: "'Dub the Dew,' a local market promotional campaign that was created by one of our customers—not Mountain Dew—was compromised. We are working diligently with our customer's team to remove all offensive content that was posted and putting measures in place to ensure this doesn't happen again."[37]

 ## 16-6 SALES PROMOTION

In addition to using advertising and public relations, marketing managers can use **sales promotion to increase the effectiveness of their promotional efforts.** Sales promotion consists of marketing communication activities other than advertising, personal selling, and public relations, in which a short-term incentive motivates consumers or members of the distribution channel to purchase a good or service immediately, either by lowering the price or by adding value.

Sales promotion is usually cheaper than advertising and easier to measure. A major national television advertising campaign often costs $10 million or more to create, produce, and place. In contrast, promotional campaigns using the Internet or direct marketing methods can cost less than half that amount. It is also very difficult to determine how many people buy a product or service as a result of radio or television ads. With sales promotion, marketers know the precise number of coupons redeemed or the number of contest entries received.

Sales promotion usually has more effect on behavior than on attitudes. Giving the consumer an incentive to make an immediate purchase is the goal of sales promotion, regardless of the form it takes. Sales promotion is usually targeted toward either of two distinctly different markets. **Trade sales promotion** is directed to members of the marketing channel, such as wholesalers and retailers. **Consumer sales promotion** is targeted to the ultimate consumer market. The objectives of a promotion depend on the general behavior of targeted customers Exhibit 16.4.

crisis management a coordinated effort to handle all the effects of unfavorable publicity or another unexpected unfavorable event

sales promotion marketing communication activities other than advertising, personal selling, and public relations, in which a short-term incentive motivates consumers or members of the distribution channel to purchase a good or service immediately, either by lowering the price or by adding value

trade sales promotion promotion activities directed to members of the marketing channel, such as wholesalers and retailers

consumer sales promotion promotion activities targeted to the ultimate consumer market

EXHIBIT 16.4 TYPES OF CONSUMERS AND SALES PROMOTION GOALS

Type of Buyer	Desired Results	Sales Promotion Examples
Loyal customers People who buy your product most or all of the time	Reinforce behavior, increase consumption, change purchase timing	• Loyalty marketing programs, such as frequent buyer cards or frequent shopper clubs • Bonus packs that give loyal consumers an incentive to stock up or premiums offered in return for proofs of purchase
Competitor's customers People who buy a competitor's product most or all of the time	Break loyalty, persuade to switch to your brand	• Sampling to introduce your product's superior qualities compared to their brand • Sweepstakes, contests, or premiums that create interest in the product
Brand switchers People who buy a variety of products in the category	Persuade to buy your brand more often	• Any promotion that lowers the price of the product, such as coupons, price-off packages, and bonus packs • Trade deals that help make the product more readily available than competing products
Price buyers People who consistently buy the least expensive brand	Appeal with low prices or supply added value that makes price less important	• Coupons, price-off packages, refunds, or trade deals that reduce the price of the brand to match that of the brand that would have been purchased

From *Sales Promotion Essentials*, 2nd ed., by Don E. Schultz, William A. Robinson, and Lisa A. Petrison, published by McGraw-Hill Education.

For example, marketers who are targeting loyal users of their product need to reinforce existing behavior or increase product usage. An effective tool for strengthening brand loyalty is the *frequent buyer program*, which rewards consumers for repeat purchases. Other types of promotions are more effective with customers who are prone to brand switching or with those who are loyal to a competitor's product. A cents-off coupon, free sample, or eye-catching display in a store will often entice shoppers to try a different brand.

Once marketers understand the dynamics occurring within their product category and determine the particular customers and behaviors they want to influence, they can then go about selecting promotional tools to achieve these goals.

16-6a Tools for Trade Sales Promotion

As we'll discuss in section 16-6b, consumer promotions pull a product through the channel by creating demand. However, trade promotions *push* a product through the distribution channel (see Chapter 13). When selling to members of the distribution channel, manufacturers use many of the same sales promotion tools used in consumer promotions, such as sales contests premiums and point-of-purchase displays. Several tools, however, are unique to manufacturers and intermediaries:

- **Trade allowances:** A **trade allowance** is a price reduction offered by manufacturers to intermediaries such as wholesalers and retailers. The price reduction or rebate is given in exchange for doing something specific, such as allocating space for a new product or buying something during special periods. For example, a local Best Buy outlet could receive a special discount for running its own promotion on Sony surround sound systems.

- **Push money:** Intermediaries receive **push money** as a bonus for pushing the manufacturer's brand through the distribution channel. Often the push money is directed toward a retailer's salespeople. LinoColor, the leading high-end scanner company, produces a Picture Perfect Rewards catalog filled with merchandise retailers can purchase with points accrued for every LinoColor scanner they sell.

- **Training:** Sometimes a manufacturer will train an intermediary's

trade allowance a price reduction offered by manufacturers to intermediaries such as wholesalers and retailers

push money money offered to channel intermediaries to encourage them to "push" products—that is, to encourage other members of the channel to sell the products

personnel if the product is rather complex—as frequently occurs in the computer and telecommunications industries. For example, representatives of major pharmaceutical companies receive extensive training because they need to provide accurate information to doctors and nurses.

- **Free merchandise:** Often a manufacturer offers retailers free merchandise in lieu of quantity discounts. Occasionally, free merchandise is used as payment for trade allowances normally provided through other sales promotions. Instead of giving a retailer a price reduction for buying a certain quantity of merchandise, the manufacturer may throw in extra merchandise "free" (i.e., at a cost that would equal the price reduction).

- **Store demonstrations:** Manufacturers can also arrange with retailers to perform an in-store demonstration. Food manufacturers often send representatives to grocery stores and supermarkets to let customers sample a product while shopping.

- **Business meetings, conventions, and trade shows:** Trade association meetings, conferences, and conventions are an important aspect of sales promotion and a growing, multi-billion-dollar market. At these shows, manufacturers, distributors, and other vendors have the chance to display their goods or describe their services to potential customers. Companies participate in trade shows to attract and identify new prospects, serve current customers, introduce new products, enhance corporate image, test the market response to new products, enhance corporate morale, and gather competitive product information.

Trade promotions are popular among manufacturers for many reasons. Trade sales promotion tools help manufacturers gain new distributors for their products, obtain wholesaler and retailer support for consumer sales promotions, build or reduce dealer inventories, and improve trade relations. Car manufacturers annually sponsor dozens of auto shows for consumers. The shows attract millions of consumers, providing dealers with increased store traffic as well as good leads.

16-6b Tools for Consumer Sales Promotion

Marketing managers must decide which consumer sales promotion devices to use in a specific campaign. The methods chosen must suit the objectives to ensure success of the overall promotion plan. The popular tools for consumer sales promotion, discussed in the following pages, have also been easily transferred to online versions to entice Internet users to visit sites, purchase products, or use services on the Web.

COUPONS AND REBATES A **coupon** is a certificate that entitles consumers to an immediate price reduction when the product is purchased. Coupons are a particularly good way to encourage product trial and repurchase. They are also likely to increase the amount of a product bought. Coupons can be distributed in stores as instant coupons on packaging, on shelf displays with pull-off coupon dispensers, and at cash registers, printed based on what the customer purchased; through freestanding inserts (FSIs); and through various Internet daily deal sites.

American Express is experimenting with Twitter to offer cardholders great deals at participating businesses.

FSIs, the promotional coupons inserts found in newspapers, are the traditional way of circulating printed coupons. FSIs are used to distribute approximately 80 percent of coupons. Such traditional types of coupon distribution, which also include direct mail and magazines, have been declining for several years, as consumers use fewer coupons. About 3 billion coupons are redeemed annually. Mobile coupons have a much higher redemption rate than paper coupons.[38]

The Internet is changing the face of coupons. In addition to Internet coupon sites such as Valpak.com and Coolsavings.com, and social coupon sites such as Groupon and LivingSocial, there are also deal sites like DealSurf.com that aggregate offers from different sites for convenience. While daily deal sites have been quite popular with consumers, sites like Groupon and LivingSocial are coming under some fire as many small businesses claim they lose money or drown under the flood of coupon redemptions. American Express is using Twitter to drive card use. After syncing their credit cards to their Twitter accounts, American Express customers can send tweets using an approved hashtag (or "cashtag") to pay for items purchased through third-party retailers. Cardholders can also receive automatic discounts from partner businesses on Twitter when they make purchases with their American Express cards.[39]

A **rebate** is similar to a coupon in that a rebate offers the purchaser a price reduction; however, because the purchaser must mail in a rebate form and usually some proof of purchase, the reward is not as immediate. Manufacturers prefer rebates for several reasons. Rebates allow manufacturers to offer price cuts to consumers directly. Manufacturers have more control over rebate promotions because they can be rolled out and shut off quickly. Further, because buyers must fill out forms with their names, addresses, and other data, manufacturers use rebate programs to build customer databases. Perhaps the best reason of all to offer rebates is that although rebates are particularly good at enticing purchase, most consumers never bother to redeem them—only about 40 percent of consumers eligible for rebates collect them.[40]

PREMIUMS A **premium** is an extra item offered to the consumer, usually in exchange for some proof that the promoted product has been purchased. Premiums reinforce the consumer's purchase decision, increase consumption, and persuade nonusers to switch brands. A longstanding example of the use of premiums is the McDonald's Happy Meal, which rewards children with a small toy. Premiums can also include more product for the regular price, such as two-for-the-price-of-one bonus packs or packages that include more of the product. Some companies attach a premium to the product's package, such as a small sample of a complementary hair product attached to a shampoo bottle.

LOYALTY MARKETING PROGRAMS A **loyalty marketing program** builds long-term, mutually beneficial relationships between a company and its key customers. One of the most popular types of loyalty programs, the **frequent buyer program**, rewards loyal consumers for making multiple purchases. The objective of loyalty marketing programs is to build long-term, mutually beneficial relationships between a company and its key customers.

iStockphoto.com/Magnez2

coupon a certificate that entitles consumers to an immediate price reduction when the product is purchased.

rebate a cash refund given for the purchase of a product during a specific period

premium an extra item offered to the consumer, usually in exchange for some proof of purchase of the promoted product

loyalty marketing program a promotional program designed to build long-term, mutually beneficial relationships between a company and its key customers

frequent buyer program a loyalty program in which loyal consumers are rewarded for making multiple purchases of a particular good or service

There are almost three billion loyalty program memberships in the United States; the average household has signed up for 18 programs.[41] Popularized by the airline industry through frequent-flyer programs, loyalty marketing enables companies to strategically invest sales promotion dollars in activities designed to capture greater profits from customers already loyal to the product or company. Co-branded credit cards are an increasingly popular loyalty marketing tool. Most department stores only offer loyalty programs if a customer opens their branded credit card. However, high-end chain Bloomingdales recently changed its rewards program to include anyone who will sign up. Members of the new Loyalist program receive one point for each dollar they spend and receive a $25 gift card after earning 5,000 points. While Bloomingdale's credit card holders receive more points per dollar spent, the company is hoping to monitor a greater number of its shoppers' spending habits by enabling non-cardholders to join Loyalist.[42]

Through loyalty programs, shoppers receive discounts, alerts on new products, and other types of enticing offers. In exchange, retailers are able to build customer databases that help them better understand customer preferences.

CONTESTS AND SWEEPSTAKES

Contests and sweepstakes are generally designed to create interest in a good or service, often to encourage brand switching. *Contests* are promotions in which participants use some skill or ability to compete for prizes. A consumer contest usually requires entrants to answer questions, complete sentences, or write a paragraph about the product and submit proof of purchase. Winning a *sweepstakes*, on the other hand, depends on chance, and participation is free. Sweepstakes usually draw about ten times more entries than contests do.

While contests and sweepstakes may draw considerable interest and publicity, generally they are not effective tools for generating long-term sales. To increase their effectiveness, sales promotion managers must make certain the award will appeal to the target market. Offering several smaller prizes to many winners

Baby formula companies like Enfamil, will send samples to expectant mothers or homes where baby's were recently born.

Source: Mead Johnson & Company

instead of one huge prize to just one person often will increase the effectiveness of the promotion, but there is no denying the attractiveness of a jackpot-type prize.

SAMPLING

Sampling allows the customer to try a product risk-free. In a recent study, in-store sampling proved to be the most successful promotional tactic when researchers introduced a new dairy product to grocery stores. In-store sampling events increased sales 116 percent, outperforming aisle displays (70 percent), ad circulars (63 percent), and temporary price reductions (48 percent).[43]

Samples can be directly mailed to the customer, delivered door-to-door, packaged with another product, or demonstrated or distributed at a retail store or service outlet. Sampling at special events is a popular, effective, and high profile distribution method that permits marketers to piggyback onto fun-based consumer activities—including sporting events, college fests, fairs and festivals, beach events, and chili cook-offs. Distributing samples to specific location types, such as health clubs, churches, or doctors' offices, is also one of the most efficient methods of sampling. Online sampling is catching up in popularity, however, with the growth of social media. Branded products not only run contests through Facebook, but also connect with fans, show

sampling a promotional program that allows the consumer the opportunity to try a product or service for free

commercials, and offer samples of new products in exchange for "liking" the brand.

POINT-OF-PURCHASE PROMOTION A **point-of-purchase (P-O-P) display** includes any promotional display set up at the retailer's location to build traffic, advertise the product, or induce impulse buying. P-O-P displays include shelf "talkers" (signs attached to store shelves), shelf extenders (attachments that extend shelves so products stand out), ads on grocery carts and bags, end-aisle and floor-stand displays, television monitors at supermarket checkout counters, in-store audio messages, and audiovisual displays. One big advantage of the P-O-P display is that it offers manufacturers a captive audience in retail stores. According to POPAI's Shopper Engagement Study, approximately 76 percent of all retail purchase decisions are made in-store. Fifty-seven percent of shoppers buy more than they anticipated once in the store, so P-O-P displays can be very effective.[44] Other strategies to increase sales include adding cards to the tops of displays, changing messages on signs on the sides or bottoms of displays, adding inflatable or mobile displays, and using signs that advertise the brand's sports, movie, or charity tie-in.

16-6c Trends in Sales Promotion

The biggest trend in sales promotion on both the trade and consumer side has been the increased use of the Internet. Social media-, e-mail-, and Web site–based promotions have expanded dramatically in recent years. Marketers are now spending billions of dollars annually on such promotions. Sales promotions online have proved both effective and cost-efficient—generating response rates three to five times higher than off-line promotions. The most effective types of online sales promotions are free merchandise, sweepstakes, free shipping with purchases, and coupons. One major goal of retailers is to add potential customers to their databases and expand marketing touch points.

Marketers have discovered that online coupon distribution provides another vehicle for promoting their products. The redemption rate of online coupons has been growing substantially while total coupon redemption has remained steady.[45] Online coupons can help marketers lure new customers, and with the speed of online feedback, marketers can track the success of a coupon in real time and adjust it based on changing market conditions.[46]

Online versions of loyalty programs are also popping up, and although many types of companies have these programs, the most successful are those run by hotel and airline companies. A final major trend in sales promotion is the utilization of sales promotions on social media and at the point of purchase. Google's Zero Moment of Truth (ZMOT) insights illustrate how important consumer feedback is to consumer purchases, highlighting the importance of behavioral data when serving up a targeted sales promotion.[47]

> **point of purchase (P-O-P) display** a promotional display set up at the retailer's location to build traffic, advertise the product, or induce impulse buying

STUDY TOOLS 16

LOCATED AT BACK OF THE TEXTBOOK
☐ Rip out Chapter Review Card

LOCATED AT WWW.CENGAGEBRAIN.COM
☐ Review Key Terms Flashcards and create your own
☐ Track your knowledge and understanding of key concepts in marketing
☐ Complete practice and graded quizzes to prepare for tests
☐ Complete interactive content within the MKTG Online experience
☐ View the chapter highlight boxes within the MKTG Online experience

17 | Personal Selling and Sales Management

LEARNING OUTCOMES

After studying this chapter, you will be able to...

17-1 Understand the sales environment

17-2 Describe personal selling

17-3 Discuss the key differences between relationship selling and traditional selling

17-4 List and explain the steps in the selling process

17-5 Understand the functions of sales management

17-6 Describe the use of customer relationship management in the selling process

After you finish this chapter go to **PAGE 320** for **STUDY TOOLS.**

17-1 THE SALES ENVIRONMENT

Many people around the world work in some form of selling. Traditionally, salespeople engage in direct face-to-face contact with customers. This can take place either at the salesperson's place of business or at a secondary location (such as when a salesperson travels door-to-door or meets a customer at her office or home). Salespeople can be consumer-focused (as in the case of retail) or business-focused.

In many cases, consumer-focused salespeople require customers to come directly to a retail store, shortening the sales process time. Even though many retailers use multiple customer relationship management processes (including information kiosks, Web sites, and self-check outs), one-to-one interactions are often key to retail success. Most major retailers use trained salespeople—not just order takers—to enhance the customer experience. Nordstrom's, for example, offers a retail management internship that provides both hands-on selling experience and classroom learning for students looking for careers in retail management and sales.[1] By having knowledgeable salespeople, retailers can help their customers select the products or services that are best for them.

As previously discussed, some consumer-focused salespeople travel to their customers' locations. For example, many home improvement and maintenance salespeople meet potential customers at their homes. Certain cosmetics, small appliances, and magazine subscriptions are sold directly to customers at their homes. These salespeople are considered direct salespeople. Companies such as CUTCO Cutlery, AVON, and Mary Kay Cosmetics have been very successful in direct selling.

Business-focused salespeople call on other companies to sell their products. These business-to-business salespeople often spend a good deal of time traveling

Angela Waye/Shutterstock.com

to customer locations to make sales calls, and the sales process generally takes a longer period of time. Often, business-to-business salespeople have more extensive sales training, are required to travel more, and receive a higher level of compensation.

The sales environment changes constantly as new competitors enter the market and old competitors leave. The ways that customers interact with salespeople and learn about products and suppliers are changing due to the rapid increase in new sales technologies. In order for companies to successfully sell products or services using a sales force, they must be very effective at personal selling, sales management, customer relationship management, and technology—all of which play critical roles in building strong long-term relationships with customers.

 ## 17-2 PERSONAL SELLING

As mentioned in Chapter 15, *personal selling* is a purchase situation involving a personal, paid-for communication between two people in an attempt to influence each other. In a sense, all businesspeople are salespeople. An individual may become a plant manager, a chemist, an engineer, or a member of any profession and yet still have to sell. During a job search,

applicants must "sell" themselves to prospective employers in an interview. Personal selling offers several advantages over other forms of promotion:

- Personal selling provides a detailed explanation or demonstration of the product. This capability is especially needed for complex or new goods and services.

- The sales message can be varied according to the motivations and interests of each prospective customer. Moreover, when the prospect has questions or raises objections, the salesperson is there to provide explanations and guidance. By contrast, advertising and sales promotion can respond only to the questions and objections that the copywriter *thinks* are important to customers.

- Personal selling should only be directed toward qualified prospects. Other forms of promotion include some unavoidable waste because many people in the audience are not prospective customers.

- Costs can be controlled by adjusting the size of the sales force (and resulting expenses) in one-person increments. On the other hand, advertising and sales promotion must often be purchased in fairly large amounts.

- Perhaps the most important advantage is that personal selling is considerably more effective than other forms of promotion in obtaining a sale and gaining a satisfied customer.

- Personal selling also has several limitations compared to other forms of promotion:

  - Cost per contact is much greater than for mass forms of communication, leading companies to be highly selective about where and when they use salespeople.

  - If the sales force is not properly trained, the message provided can be inconsistent and inaccurate. Continual sales force management and training are necessary.

  - Salespeople can convince customers to buy unneeded products or services. This can lead to increased levels of cognitive dissonance among buyers if a salesperson is being pushed to meet certain quotas.

Personal selling often works better than other forms of promotion given certain customer and product characteristics. Generally speaking, personal selling becomes more important as the number of potential customers decreases, as the complexity of the product increases, and as the value of the product grows (see Exhibit 17.1). For highly complex goods such as business jets and private communication systems, a salesperson is needed to determine the prospective customer's needs and wants, explain the product's benefits and advantages, and propose the exact features and accessories that will best meet the client's needs. Many upscale clothing retailers offer free personal shopping, whereby consultants select and suggest designer clothing they believe will fit the customer's style and specified need. Bloomingdales' personal shoppers help customers select gifts for others, provide guidance tailored to the individual's personal tastes, coordinate gift wrapping and alterations, help navigate the entire store from clothing to home goods, and even schedule reminders for special occasions.[2]

Technology plays an increasingly important role in personal selling. Instead of being handed traditional sales pamphlets and brochures, consumers are now able to easily learn about products and services by searching the Internet before entering a store. Many consumers compare product features, prices, and quality online before even deciding which store to visit. Even after entering a store, consumers use their smartphones to browse competitors' Web sites while evaluating products. In addition to their own research, consumers are being bombarded with in-store messages, coupons, and sale information using beacon technology like Apple's iBeacon. Suffice to say, consumers are more educated about products and services today than they've ever been before.

This shift in technology has changed the dynamic of how information is obtained. If salespeople do not stay well informed about the products they're selling, consumers may enter the store knowing even more than they do. This reduces the ability of the salesperson to build trust and confidence. Salespeople are increasingly turning to social media like LinkedIn, Facebook, blogs, and Twitter to help establish their expertise within a field. With more than 300 million members, LinkedIn positions itself as the world's largest professional network.[3] In addition to its networking function, LinkedIn offers sales solutions to help salespeople find prospects, qualify leads, and make product recommendations to decision makers.[4] LinkedIn also provides free advice on how to effectively sell using social media, including a six-step guide to aid salespeople in successful social selling.[5] LinkedIn also provides actionable social selling tips, making it a great resource for salespeople looking to harness the power of technology themselves.[6]

17-3 RELATIONSHIP SELLING

Historically, marketing theory and practice concerning personal selling have focused almost entirely on planned presentations to prospective customers for the sole purpose of making sales. Marketers were mostly concerned with making one-time sales and then moving on to the next prospect. Traditional personal selling methods attempted to persuade the buyer to accept a point of view or convince the buyer to take some action. Frequently, the objectives of the

EXHIBIT 17.1	COMPARISON OF PERSONAL SELLING AND ADVERTISING/SALES PROMOTION
Personal selling is more important if . . .	**Advertising and sales promotion are more important if . . .**
The product has a high value.	The product has a low value.
It is a custom-made product.	It is a standardized product.
There are few customers.	There are many customers.
The product is technically complex.	The product is easy to understand.
Customers are concentrated.	Customers are geographically dispersed.
Examples: Insurance policies, custom windows, airplane engines	**Examples:** Soap, magazine subscriptions, cotton T-shirts

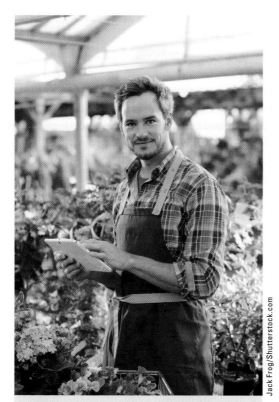
Technology is leading the way in selling in all forms of business.

Jack Frog/Shutterstock.com

consultative selling, is a multistage process that emphasizes personalization, win-win outcomes, and empathy as key ingredients in identifying prospects and developing them as long-term, satisfied customers. The focus, therefore, is on building mutual trust between the buyer and seller through the delivery of long-term, value-added benefits that are anticipated by the buyer.

Relationship or consultative salespeople, therefore, become consultants, partners, and problem solvers for their customers. They strive to build long-term relationships with key accounts by developing trust over time. The emphasis shifts from a one-time sale to a long-term relationship in which the salesperson works with the customer to develop solutions for enhancing the customer's bottom line. The end result of relationship selling tends to be loyal customers who purchase from the company time after time, often with an increased share-of-purchase. A relationship selling strategy focused on retaining customers is often less expensive to a company than having to constantly prospect for and sell to new customers. Relationship selling provides many advantages over traditional selling in the consumer goods market. Still, relationship selling is more often used in selling situations for industrial-type goods, such as heavy machinery and computer systems, and services, such as airlines and insurance, than in selling situations for consumer goods. Exhibit 17.2 lists the key differences between traditional personal selling and relationship or consultative selling.

salesperson were at the expense of the buyer, creating a win–lose outcome. Although this type of sales approach has not disappeared entirely, it is being used less and less often by professional salespeople.

By contrast, modern views of personal selling emphasize the relationship that develops between a salesperson and a buyer. **Relationship selling**, or

> **relationship selling (consultative selling)** a sales practice that involves building, maintaining, and enhancing interactions with customers in order to develop long-term satisfaction through mutually beneficial partnerships

EXHIBIT 17.2 KEY DIFFERENCES BETWEEN TRADITIONAL SELLING AND RELATIONSHIP SELLING

Traditional Personal Selling	Relationship or Consultative Selling
Sell products (goods and services)	Sell advice, assistance, and counsel
Focus on closing sales	Focus on improving the customer's bottom line
Limited sales planning	Consider sales planning as top priority
Spend most contact time telling customers about product	Spend most contact time attempting to build a problem-solving environment with the customer
Conduct "product-specific" needs assessment	Conduct discovery in the full scope of the customer's operations
"Lone wolf" approach to the account	Team approach to the account
Proposals and presentations based on pricing and product features	Proposals and presentations based on profit impact and strategic benefits to the customer
Sales follow-up is short term, focused on product delivery	Sales follow-up is long term, focused on long-term relationship enhancement

Source: Robert M. Peterson, Patrick, L. Schul, and George H. Lucas Jr., "Consultative Selling: Walking the Walk in the New Selling Environment, "*National Conference on Sales Management Proceedings*, March 1996; and Ari Walker, *7 Ways to Stop "Selling" and Start Building Relationships*, http://marketing.about.com/od/salestraining/a/stopselling .htm (Accessed March 2015).

17-4 STEPS IN THE SELLING PROCESS

Completing a sale requires multiple steps. The **sales process**, or **sales cycle**, is simply the set of steps a salesperson goes through to sell a particular product or service. The sales process can be unique for each product or service offered. The actual sales process depends on the features of the product or service, characteristics of customer segments, and internal processes in place within the firm (such as how leads are gathered).

Some sales take only a few minutes to complete, but others may take much longer. Sales of technical products like a Boeing or Airbus airplane and customized goods and services typically take many months, perhaps even years, to complete. On the other end of the spectrum, sales of less technical products like stationery are generally more routine and often take less than a day to complete. Whether a salesperson spends a few minutes or a few years on a sale, there are seven basic steps in the personal selling process:

1. Generating leads
2. Qualifying leads
3. Approaching the customer and probing needs
4. Developing and proposing solutions
5. Handling objections
6. Closing the sale
7. Following up

Like other forms of promotion, the steps of selling follow the AIDA concept discussed in Chapter 16. Once a salesperson has located and qualified a prospect with the authority to buy, he or she tries to get the prospect's attention. A thorough needs assessment turned into an effective sales proposal and presentation should generate interest. After developing the customer's initial desire (preferably during the presentation of the sales proposal), the salesperson seeks action in the close by trying to get an agreement to buy. Follow-up after the sale, the final step in the selling process, not only lowers cognitive dissonance (refer to Chapter 6) but also may open up opportunities for repeat business, cross-sales of related products and services, and new customer referrals.

Traditional selling and relationship selling follow the same basic steps. They differ in the relative importance placed on key steps in the process. Traditional selling efforts are transaction oriented, focusing on generating as many leads as possible, making as many presentations as possible, and closing as many sales as possible. Minimal effort is placed on asking questions to identify customer needs and wants or matching these needs and wants to the benefits of the product or service. Often, traditional selling efforts allow little time for following up and ensuring that customers are satisfied with the products or services they received. Again, these types of sales generally generate lower levels of customer satisfaction and can result in more win-lose transactions for salespeople.

By contrast, salespeople practicing relationship selling emphasize a long-term investment in the time and effort needed to uncover each customer's specific needs and wants and meet them with the product or service offering. By doing their homework up front, salespeople often create the conditions necessary for a relatively straightforward close. In general, customers are more satisfied, engage in more repeat business, and provide higher shares-of-purchase over longer periods of time with relationship salespeople. In the following sections, we will examine each step of the personal selling process.

17-4a Step 1: Generating Leads

Initial groundwork must precede communication between the potential buyer and the salesperson. **Lead generation**, or **prospecting**, is the

Julia Tim/Shutterstock.com

---

sales process (sales cycle) the set of steps a salesperson goes through in a particular organization to sell a particular product or service

lead generation (prospecting) identification of those firms and people most likely to buy the seller's offerings

identification of those firms and people most likely to buy the seller's offerings. These firms or people become "sales leads" or "prospects."

Sales leads can be obtained in many different ways, most notably through advertising, trade shows and conventions, social media, webinars, or direct mail and telemarketing programs. Favorable publicity also helps to create leads. Company records of past client purchases are another excellent source of leads. Many sales professionals are also securing valuable leads from their firm's Web site.

A basic unsophisticated method of lead generation is done through **cold calling**—a form of lead generation in which the salesperson approaches potential buyers without any prior knowledge of the prospects' needs or financial status. Although cold calling is still used in generating leads, many sales managers have realized the inefficiencies of having their top salespeople use their valuable selling time searching for the proverbial "needle in a haystack." Passing the job of cold calling to a lower-cost employee, typically an internal sales support person, allows salespeople to spend more time and use their relationship-building skills on prospects who have already been identified.

Another way to gather a lead is through a **referral**—a recommendation from a customer or business associate. The advantages of referrals over other forms of prospecting are highly qualified leads, higher closing rates, larger initial transactions, and shorter sales cycles. Referrals are often as much as ten times more productive in generating sales than are cold calls. Unfortunately, although many clients are willing to give referrals, most salespeople do not ask for them. Effective sales training can help to overcome this reluctance to ask for referrals. To increase the number of referrals, some companies even pay or send small gifts to customers or suppliers that provide referrals. Generating referrals is one area that social media and technology can usually make much more efficient.

Salespeople should build strong networks to help generate leads. **Networking** is using friends, business contacts, coworkers, acquaintances, and fellow members in professional and civic organizations to identify potential clients. Indeed, a number of national networking clubs have been started for the sole purpose of generating leads and providing valuable business advice. Increasingly, sales professionals are also using online networking sites like LinkedIn to connect with targeted leads and clients around the world, 24 hours a day.

17-4b Step 2: Qualifying Leads

When a prospect shows interest in learning more about a product, the salesperson has the opportunity to follow up, or qualify, the lead. Typically, unqualified prospects give vague or incomplete answers to a salesperson's specific questions, try to evade questions on budgets, and request changes in standard procedures like prices and terms of sale. In contrast, qualified leads are real prospects who answer questions, value the salesperson's time, and are realistic about money and when they are prepared to buy.

Lead qualification involves determining whether the prospect has three things:

1. **A recognized need:** The most basic criterion for determining whether someone is a prospect for a product is a need that is not being satisfied. The salesperson should first consider prospects who are aware of a need but should not disregard prospects who have not yet recognized that they have one. With a little more information about the product, they may decide they do have a need for it. Preliminary questioning can often provide the salesperson with enough information to determine whether there is a need.

2. **Buying power:** Buying power involves both authority to make the purchase decision and access to funds to pay for it. To avoid wasting time and money, the salesperson needs to identify the purchasing authority and his or her ability to pay before making a presentation. Organizational charts and information about a firm's credit standing can provide valuable clues.

3. **Receptivity and accessibility:** The prospect must be willing to see the salesperson and be accessible to the salesperson. Some prospects simply refuse to see salespeople. Others, because of their stature in their organization, will see only a salesperson or sales manager with similar stature.

Often the task of lead qualification is handled by

> **cold calling** a form of lead generation in which the salesperson approaches potential buyers without any prior knowledge of the prospects' needs or financial status
>
> **referral** a recommendation to a salesperson from a customer or business associate
>
> **networking** a process of finding out about potential clients from friends, business contacts, coworkers, acquaintances, and fellow members in professional and civic organizations
>
> **lead qualification** determination of a sales prospect's (1) recognized need, (2) buying power, and (3) receptivity and accessibility

a telemarketing group or a sales support person who prequalifies the lead for the salesperson. Prequalification systems free sales representatives from the time-consuming task of following up on leads to determine need, buying power and receptiveness. Prequalification systems may even set up initial appointments with the prospect for the salesperson. The result is more time for the sales force to spend in front of interested customers.

Companies are increasingly using their Web sites and other software to qualify leads. When qualifying leads online, companies want visitors to register, indicate the products and services they are interested in, and provide information on their time frames and resources. Leads from the Internet can then be prioritized (those indicating short time frames, for instance, are given a higher priority) and then transferred to salespeople. Enticing visitors to register also enables companies to customize future electronic interactions.

Personally visiting unqualified prospects wastes valuable salesperson time and company resources. Many leads often go unanswered because salespeople are given no indication as to how qualified the leads are in terms of interest and ability to purchase. Inside salespeople and sales support staff assess leads to maximize successful meetings, while CRM systems provide resources to increase lead follow-up rates. Still, according to Salisify, salespeople only follow up on 10 percent of leads.[7]

17-4c Step 3: Approaching the Customer and Probing Needs

Before approaching customers, the salesperson should learn as much as possible about the prospect's organization and its buyers. This process, called the **preapproach**, describes the "homework" that must be done by the salesperson before contacting the prospect. This may include visiting company Web sites, consulting standard reference sources such as Moody's, Standard & Poor's, or Dun & Bradstreet, or contacting acquaintances or others who may have information about the prospect. Reading the prospect's social media sites (following the company's Twitter feed and reading its Facebook page, for example) is a great way to get to know the company culture, become acquainted with customer needs, and learn more about daily activities.[8] Another preapproach task is to determine whether the actual approach should be a personal visit, a phone call, a letter, or some other form of communication. Note that the preapproach applies to most business-to-business sales and outside consumer sales, but it is usually not possible when consumers approach salespeople in the retail store environment.

During the sales approach, the salesperson either talks to the prospect or secures an appointment to probe the prospect further about his or her needs. Relationship selling theorists suggest that salespeople should begin developing mutual trust with their prospect during the approach. Salespeople must sell themselves before they can sell the product. Small talk that projects sincerity and some suggestion of friendship is encouraged to build rapport with the prospect, but remarks that could be construed as insincere should be avoided.

The salesperson's ultimate goal during the approach is to conduct a **needs assessment** to find out as much as possible about the prospect's situation. The salesperson should be determining how to maximize the fit between what he or she can offer and what the prospective customer wants. As part of the needs assessment, the consultative salesperson must know everything there is to know about the following:

- **The product or service:** Product knowledge is the cornerstone for conducting a successful needs analysis. The consultative salesperson must be an expert on his or her product or service, including technical specifications, features and benefits, pricing and billing procedures, warranty and service support, performance comparisons with the competition, other customers' experiences with the product, and current advertising and promotional campaign messages. For example, a salesperson who is attempting to sell a Canon copier to a doctor's office should be very knowledgeable about Canon's selection of copiers, their attributes, capabilities, technological specifications, and postpurchase servicing.

- **Customers and their needs:** The salesperson should know more about customers than he knows about himself. That's the secret to relationship and consultative selling, where the salesperson acts not only as a supplier of products and services but also as a trusted consultant and adviser. The professional salesperson brings each client business-building ideas and solutions to problems. For example, if the Canon salesperson is asking the "right" questions, then he or she should be able to identify copy-related areas where the doctor's office is losing or wasting money. Rather than just selling a copier, the Canon salesperson can act as a consultant on how the doctor's office can save money and time.

preapproach a process that describes the "homework" that must be done by a salesperson before he or she contacts a prospect

needs assessment a determination of the customer's specific needs and wants and the range of options the customer has for satisfying them

- **The competition:** The salesperson must know as much about the competitor's company and products as he or she knows about his or her own company. Competitive intelligence includes many factors: who the competitors are and what is known about them, how their products and services compare, advantages and disadvantages, and strengths and weaknesses. For example, if the competitor's Xerox copy machine is less expensive than the Canon copier, the doctor's office may be leaning toward purchasing the Xerox. But if the Canon salesperson can point out that the cost of long-term maintenance and toner cartridges is lower for the Canon copier, offsetting its higher initial cost, the salesperson may be able to persuade the doctor's office to purchase the Canon copier.

- **The industry:** Knowing the industry requires active research by the salesperson. This means attending industry and trade association meetings, reading articles published in industry and trade journals, keeping track of legislation and regulation that affect the industry, being aware of product alternatives and innovations from domestic and foreign competition, and having a feel for economic and financial conditions that may affect the industry. It is also important to be aware of economic downturns, as businesses may be looking for less expensive financing options.

Creating a *customer profile* during the approach helps salespeople optimize their time and resources. This profile is then used to help develop an intelligent analysis of the prospect's needs in preparation for the next step,

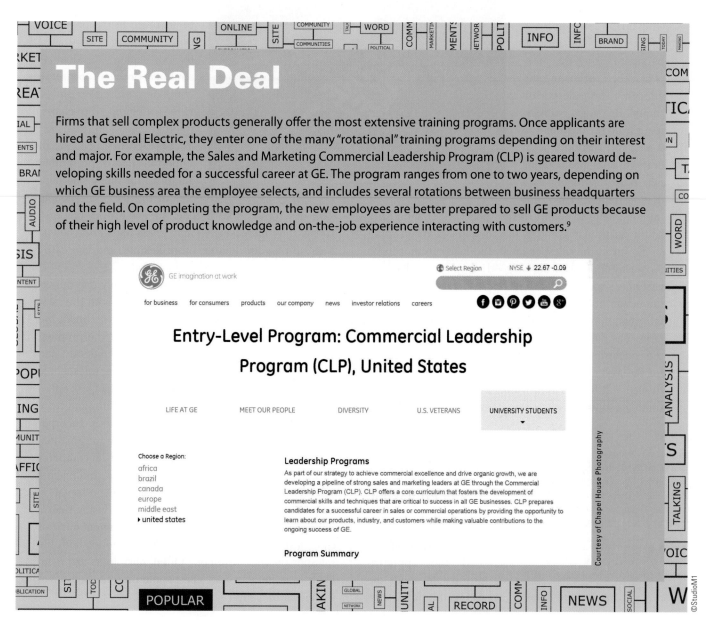

The Real Deal

Firms that sell complex products generally offer the most extensive training programs. Once applicants are hired at General Electric, they enter one of the many "rotational" training programs depending on their interest and major. For example, the Sales and Marketing Commercial Leadership Program (CLP) is geared toward developing skills needed for a successful career at GE. The program ranges from one to two years, depending on which GE business area the employee selects, and includes several rotations between business headquarters and the field. On completing the program, the new employees are better prepared to sell GE products because of their high level of product knowledge and on-the-job experience interacting with customers.[9]

Courtesy of Chapel House Photography

©StudioM1

developing and proposing solutions. Customer profile information is typically stored and manipulated using sales force automation software packages designed for use on laptop computers, smartphones, or tablets. Sales force automation software provides sales reps with a computerized and efficient method of collecting customer information for use during the entire sales process. Further, customer and sales data stored in a computer database can be easily shared among sales team members. The information can also be appended with industry statistics, sales or meeting notes, billing data, and other information that may be pertinent to the prospect or the prospect's company. The more salespeople know about their prospects, the better they can meet their needs.

A salesperson should wrap up the sales approach and need-probing mission by summarizing the prospect's need, problem, and interest. The salesperson should also get a commitment from the customer to some kind of action, whether it is reading promotional material or agreeing to a demonstration. This commitment helps to qualify the prospect further and justify additional time invested by the salesperson. When doing so, however, the salesperson should take care not to be too pushy or overbearing—a good salesperson will read a customer's social cues. The salesperson should reiterate the action he or she promises to take, such as sending information or calling back to provide answers to questions. The date and time of the next call should be set at the conclusion of the sales approach as well as an agenda for the next call in terms of what the salesperson hopes to accomplish, such as providing a demonstration or presenting a solution.

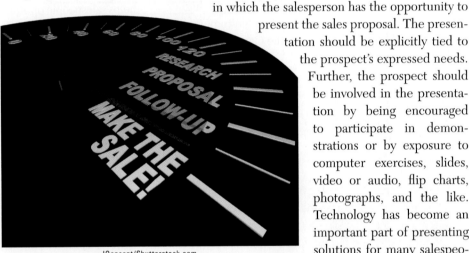
IQoncept/Shutterstock.com

the next step is to determine whether her company's products or services match the needs of the prospective customer. The salesperson then develops a solution, or possibly several solutions, in which the salesperson's product or service solves the client's problems or meets a specific need.

These solutions are typically presented to the client in the form of a sales proposal presented at a sales presentation. A **sales proposal** is a written document or professional presentation that outlines how the company's product or service will meet or exceed the client's needs. The **sales presentation** is the formal meeting in which the salesperson has the opportunity to present the sales proposal. The presentation should be explicitly tied to the prospect's expressed needs. Further, the prospect should be involved in the presentation by being encouraged to participate in demonstrations or by exposure to computer exercises, slides, video or audio, flip charts, photographs, and the like. Technology has become an important part of presenting solutions for many salespeople. In the past, salespeople took desktop PCs with them to make presentations. Today, they increasingly carry iPads and other tablets because they are lighter, more flexible, and can easily access information stored in the cloud.

Because the salesperson often has only one opportunity to present solutions, the quality of both the sales proposal and the presentation can make or break the sale. Salespeople must be able to present the proposal and handle any customer objections confidently and professionally. For a powerful presentation, salespeople must be well prepared, use direct eye contact, ask open-ended questions, be poised, use hand gestures and voice inflection, and focus on the customer's needs. Incorporating visual elements that impart valuable information, knowing how to operate the audio/visual or computer equipment being used for the presentation, and making sure the equipment works will make the presentation flow smoother. Nothing loses customers faster than a boring or ill-prepared presenter, and equipment mishaps can consume valuable (often limited) time for both the salesperson and customer. Often, customers are more likely to remember how salespeople present themselves than what they say.

17-4d Step 4: Developing and Proposing Solutions

Once the salesperson has gathered the appropriate information about the client's needs and wants,

17-4e Step 5: Handling Objections

Rarely does a prospect say "I'll buy it" right after a presentation. Instead, the prospect often raises objections or asks questions about the proposal and the product. The potential buyer may insist that the price is too high or that the good or service will not satisfy the present need.

One of the first lessons every salesperson learns is that objections to the product should not be taken personally as confrontations or insults. A good salesperson considers objections a legitimate part of the purchase decision. To handle objections effectively, the salesperson should anticipate specific objections (such as concerns about price), fully investigate the objection with the customer, be aware of what the competition is offering, and, above all, stay calm.

Often salespeople can use objections to close the sale. The customer may try to pit suppliers against each other to drive down the price, so the salesperson should be prepared to point out weaknesses in the competitor's offer and stand by the quality and value of his or her own proposal.

17-4f Step 6: Closing the Sale

At the end of the presentation, the salesperson should ask the customer how he or she would like to proceed. If the customer exhibits signs that he or she is ready to purchase, all questions have been answered, and objections have been met, then the salesperson can try to close the sale. Customers often give signals during or after the presentation that they are ready to buy or are not interested. Examples include changes in facial expressions, gestures, and questions asked. The salesperson should look for these signals and respond appropriately.

Closing requires courage and skill. A salesperson should keep an open mind when asking for the sale and be prepared for both a yes and a no. Often, a salesperson will be told no flat out. In such a case, the salesperson must be resilient and must be able to handle this type of rejection gracefully and effectively. The typical salesperson makes several hundred sales calls a year, many of which are repeat calls to the same client in an attempt to make a single sale. Building and developing a good relationship with the customer is very important. Often, if the salesperson has developed a strong relationship with the customer, only minimal efforts are needed to close a sale (increasing the salesperson's closure rate).

Closing and negotiating requires courage and skill. It is often a team effort when companies complete business deals.

Edhar/Shutterstock.com

Negotiation often plays a key role in the closing of the sale. **Negotiation** is the process during which both the salesperson and the prospect offer special concessions in an attempt to arrive at a sales agreement. For example, the salesperson may offer a price cut, free installation, or a trial order. Effective negotiators, however, avoid using price as a negotiation tool and are able to show increased value in their products or services. Because companies spend millions on advertising and product development to create value, when salespeople give in to price negotiations too quickly, it decreases the value of the product. Salespeople should also be prepared to ask for trade-offs and try to avoid giving unilateral concessions. Moreover, if the customer asks for a 5 percent discount, the salesperson should ask for something in return, such as higher volume or more flexibility in delivery schedules.

More and more U.S. companies are expanding their marketing and selling efforts into global markets. Salespeople selling in foreign markets should tailor their presentations and closing styles to each market. Different personalities and skills will be successful in some countries and absolute failures in others. For instance, if a salesperson is an excellent closer and always focuses on the next sale, doing business in Latin America might be difficult because people there want to take a long time building a personal relationship with their suppliers. Similarly, personal space and physical contact are treated differently in different cultures. In many European and South American cultures, it is customary to kiss a business associate on both cheeks instead of shaking hands.[10]

negotiation the process during which both the salesperson and the prospect offer special concessions in an attempt to arrive at a sales agreement

17-4g Step 7: Following Up

A salesperson's responsibilities do not end with making the sale and placing the order. One of the most important aspects of the job is **follow-up**—the final step in the selling process, in which the salesperson must ensure delivery schedules are met, goods or services perform as promised, and buyers' employees are properly trained to use the products.

In the traditional sales approach, follow-up with the customer is generally limited to successful product delivery and performance. A basic goal of relationship selling is to motivate customers to come back again and again by developing and nurturing long-term relationships. Exhibit 17.3 depicts the time involved in the sales process and how those elements relate to the traditional and relationship selling approaches.

Most businesses depend on repeat sales, and repeat sales depend on thorough and continued follow-up by the salesperson. When customers feel abandoned, cognitive dissonance arises and repeat sales decline. Today, this issue is more pertinent than ever because customers are far less loyal to brands and vendors. Buyers are more inclined to look for the best deal, especially when they experience poor postsale follow-up. Automated e-mail follow-up marketing—a combination of sales automation and Internet technology—is one tool that some marketers are using in an effort to enhance customer satisfaction and bring in more business. After the initial contact with a prospect, a software program automatically sends a series of personalized e-mail messages over a period of time. Another approach is to use contact software like GoTo-Meeting, which facilitates live face-to-face exchanges via video conferencing and direct access to cloud-based datacenters.

17-4h The Impact of Technology on Personal Selling

Will the increasingly sophisticated technology now available at marketers'

EXHIBIT 17.3 RELATIVE AMOUNT OF TIME SPENT IN THE KEY STEPS OF THE SELLING PROCESS

Source: Data from Robert M. Peterson, Patrick L. Schul, and George H. Lucas Jr., "Consultative Selling: Walking the Walk in the New Selling Environment," *National Conference on Sales Management Proceedings*, March 1996; and Mark Ellwood, *How Sales Reps Spend Their Time*, http://paceproductivity.com/files/How_Sales_Reps_Spend_Their_Time.pdf (Accessed March 2015).

fingertips eliminate the need for salespeople? Experts agree that a relationship between the salesperson and customer will always be necessary. Technology, however, can certainly help to improve that relationship. Cell phones, laptops, text messaging, e-mail, and electronic organizers allow salespeople to be more accessible to both clients and the company. Moreover, the Internet provides salespeople with vast resources of information on clients, competitors, and the industry.

E-business—buying, selling, marketing, collaborating with partners, and servicing customers electronically using the Internet—has had a significant impact on personal selling. Virtually all large companies and most medium and small companies are involved in e-commerce and consider it to be necessary to compete in today's marketplace. For customers, the Web has become a powerful tool, providing accurate and up-to-date information on products, pricing, and order status. The Internet also facilitates cost-effective processing of orders and service requests. Although on the surface the Internet might appear to be a threat to the job security of salespeople, the Web is actually freeing sales reps from tedious administrative tasks like shipping catalogs, placing routine orders, or tracking orders. This leaves them more time to focus on the needs of their clients.

follow-up the final step of the selling process, in which the salesperson ensures delivery schedules are met, goods or services perform as promised, and the buyers' employees are properly trained to use the products

17-5 SALES MANAGEMENT

There is an old adage in business that nothing happens until a sale is made. Without sales, there is no need for accountants, production workers, or even a company president. Sales provide the fuel that keeps the corporate engines humming. Companies such as Cisco Systems, International Paper, Johnson Controls, and thousands of other manufacturers would cease to exist without successful salespeople. Even companies such as Procter & Gamble and Kraft Foods, which mainly sell consumer goods and use extensive advertising campaigns, still rely on salespeople to move products through the channel of distribution. Thus, sales management must be one of every firm's most critical specialties. Effective sales management stems from a success-oriented sales force that accomplishes its mission economically and efficiently. Poor sales management can lead to unmet sales and profit objectives or even to the downfall of the corporation.

Just as selling is a personal relationship, so is sales management. Although the sales manager's basic job is to maximize sales at a reasonable cost while also maximizing profits, he or she also has many other important responsibilities and decisions:

1. Defining sales goals and the sales process
2. Determining the sales force structure
3. Recruiting and training the sales force
4. Compensating and motivating the sales force
5. Evaluating the sales force

17-5a Defining Sales Goals and the Sales Process

Effective sales management begins with a determination of sales goals. Without goals to achieve, salesperson performance would be mediocre at best, and the company would likely fail. Like any marketing objective, sales goals should be stated in clear, precise, and measurable terms and should always specify a time frame for their completion. Overall sales force goals are usually stated in terms of desired dollar sales volume, market share, and/or profit level. For example, a life insurance company may have a goal to sell $50 million in life insurance policies annually, to attain a twelve percent market share, and/or to achieve $1 million in profits.

Individual salespeople are also assigned goals in the form of quotas. A **quota** is a statement of the salesperson's sales goals, usually based on sales volume alone, but sometimes including other focuses such as key accounts (those with greatest potential), new account generation, volume of repeat sales, profit margin, and specific product mixes sold.

17-5b Determining the Sales Force Structure

Because personal selling is so costly, no sales department can afford to be disorganized. Proper design helps the sales manager organize and delegate sales duties and provide direction for salespeople. Sales departments are most often organized by geographic regions, product lines, marketing functions performed (such as account development or account maintenance), markets, industries, individual clients, or accounts. For example, the sales force for Hewlett-Packard (HP) could be organized into sales territories covering New England, the Midwest, the South, and the West Coast or into distinct groups selling different product lines. HP salespeople might also be assigned to specific industries or markets (such as the telecommunications industry), or to key clients (such as AT&T, Virgin Mobile, and Verizon).

Market or industry-based structures and key account structures are gaining popularity in today's competitive selling environment, especially with the emphasis on relationship selling. Being familiar with one industry or market allows sales reps to become experts in their

> **quota** a statement of the salesperson's sales goals, usually based on sales volume

Part of sales management is defining sales goals for the sales force.

iStockphoto.com/Hocus-focus

fields and thereby offer better solutions and service. Further, by organizing the sales force around specific customers, many companies hope to improve customer service, encourage collaboration with other arms of the company, and unite salespeople in customer-focused sales teams.

17-5c Recruiting and Training the Sales Force

Sales force recruitment should be based on an accurate, detailed description of the sales task as defined by the sales manager. For example, General Electric (GE) uses its Web site to provide prospective salespeople with explanations of different career entry paths and video accounts of what it is like to have a career at GE. Aside from the usual characteristics such as level of experience or education, what traits should sales managers look for in applicants?

- **Ego strength:** Great salespeople should have a strong, healthy self-esteem and the ability to bounce back from rejection.

- **Sense of urgency and competitiveness:** These traits push their sales to completion, as well as help them persuade people.

- **Assertiveness:** Effective salespeople have the ability to be firm in one-to-one negotiations, to lead the sales process, and to get their point across confidently without being overbearing or aggressive.

- **Sociable:** Wanting to interact with others is a necessary trait for great salespeople.

- **Risk takers:** Great salespeople are willing to put themselves in less-than-assured situations, and in doing so, often are able to close unlikely sales.

- **Capable of understanding complex concepts and ideas:** Quick thinking and comprehension allow salespeople to quickly grasp and sell new products or enter new sales areas.

- **Creativity:** Great salespeople develop client solutions in creative ways.

- **Empathetic:** Empathy—the ability to place oneself in someone else's shoes—enables salespeople to understand the client.

In addition to these traits, almost all successful salespeople say their sales style is relationship oriented rather than transaction oriented.[11]

After the sales recruit has been hired and given a brief orientation, initial training begins. A new salesperson generally receives instruction in company policies and practices, selling techniques, product knowledge, industry and customer characteristics, and nonselling duties such as filling out sales and market information reports and using a sales automation computer program. Continuous training then keeps salespeople up-to-date on changes in products and services, technology, the competitive landscape, and sales techniques, among other issues. Continuous training can occur during sales meetings, annual meetings, or during the course of everyday business.

Training can take place in a classroom environment, in the field, or using online modules. When conducting job training in the field via a live sales call, the trainer should be a more experienced salesperson or sales manager. This type of training provides real world experience for the trainee, but may reduce the effectiveness of the call because it often entails a reduced selling time. Another form of training involves the trainee working in inside sales, primarily phone-based sales, for an extended period of time before being given an outside territory to cover. This enables the trainee to develop selling skills with less-important and/or less-established accounts before facing the challenges of outside sales.

17-5d Compensating and Motivating the Sales Force

Compensation planning is one of the sales manager's toughest jobs. Only good planning will ensure that compensation attracts, motivates, and retains good salespeople. Generally, companies and industries with lower levels of compensation suffer higher turnover rates. This increases costs (including training and recruiting costs), decreases sales effectiveness, and harms relationship management. Therefore, compensation needs to be competitive enough to attract and motivate the best salespeople. Firms sometimes take profit into account when developing their compensation plans. Instead of paying salespeople on overall volume, they pay according to the profitability achieved from selling each product.

Still other companies tie a part of the salesperson's total compensation to customer satisfaction. As the emphasis on relationship selling increases, many sales managers believe that a portion of a salesperson's compensation should be tied to a client's satisfaction. To determine this, sales managers can survey clients on a salesperson's ability to create realistic expectations and his or her responsiveness to customer needs. At PeopleSoft, a division of Oracle, structure, culture, and strategies are all built around customer satisfaction. Sales force compensation is tied to both sales quotas and a satisfaction metric that enables clients to voice their opinions on the services provided.[12]

Although a compensation-based plan motivates a salesperson to sell, sometimes it is not enough to produce the volume of sales or the profit margin required by sales management. Sales managers therefore often offer rewards or incentives, such as recognition at ceremonies, plaques, and/or monetary-based rewards such as vacations, merchandise, pay raises, and cash bonuses. Cash awards are the most popular sales incentive and are used by virtually all companies. Mary Kay Cosmetics offers a unique type of incentive whereby salespeople can earn the use of different types of vehicles—from a lowly Ford Fiesta all the way up to the coveted pink Mary Kay Cadillac. To qualify for these vehicles, salespeople must reach certain sales quotas.[13]

Recognition and rewards may help increase overall sales volume, add new accounts, improve morale and goodwill, move slow items, and bolster slow sales. They can also be used to achieve short- and long-term objectives such as reducing overstocked inventory and meeting a monthly or quarterly sales goal. In motivating their sales force, however, sales managers must be careful not to encourage unethical behavior.

17-5e Evaluating the Sales Force

The final task of sales managers is evaluating the effectiveness and performance of the sales force. To evaluate the sales force, the sales manager needs feedback—that is, regular information from salespeople. Typical performance measures include sales volume, contribution-to-profit, calls per order, sales or profits per call, or percentage of calls achieving specific goals such as sales of products that the firm is heavily promoting.

Performance information helps the sales manager monitor a salesperson's progress through the sales cycle and pinpoint where breakdowns might be occurring. For example, by learning the number of prospects an individual salesperson has in each step of the sales cycle process and determining where prospects are falling out of the sales cycle, a manager can determine how effective a salesperson might be at lead generation, needs assessment, proposal generation, presenting, closing, and follow-up stages. This information can then tell a manager which sales skills might need to be reassessed or retrained. For example, if a sales manager notices that a sales rep seems to be letting too many prospects slip away after presenting proposals, it might mean he or she needs help with developing proposals, handling objections, or closing sales.

17-6 CUSTOMER RELATIONSHIP MANAGEMENT AND THE SALES PROCESS

As we have discussed throughout the text, customer relationship management (CRM) is the ultimate goal of a new trend in marketing that focuses on understanding customers as individuals instead of as part of a group. To do so, marketers are making their communications more customer specific using the CRM cycle, covered in Chapter 8, and by developing relationships with their customers through touch points and data mining. CRM was initially popularized as one-to-one marketing. But CRM is a much broader approach to understanding and serving customer needs than is one-to-one marketing.

Throughout the text, our discussion of a CRM system has assumed two key points. First, customers take center stage in any organization. Second, the business must manage the customer relationship across all points of customer contact throughout the entire organization. By identifying customer relationships, understanding the customer base, and capturing customer data, marketers and salespeople can leverage the information not only to develop deeper relationships but also to close more sales with loyal customers in a more efficient manner.

17-6a Identify Customer Relationships

Companies that have CRM systems follow a customer-centric focus or model. **Customer-centric** is an internal management philosophy similar to the marketing concept discussed in Chapter 1. Under this philosophy, the company customizes its product and service offering based on data generated through interactions between the customer and the company. This philosophy transcends all functional areas of the business, producing an internal system where all of the company's decisions and actions are a direct result of customer information.

Each unit of a business typically has its own way of recording what it learns, and perhaps even has its own customer information system. The departments' different interests make it difficult to pull all of the customer information together in one place using a common format. To overcome this problem, companies using CRM rely on knowledge

customer-centric a philosophy under which the company customizes its product and service offerings based on data generated through interactions between the customer and the company

management. **Knowledge management** is a process by which customer information is centralized and shared in order to enhance the relationship between customers and the organization. Information collected includes experiential observations, comments, customer actions, and qualitative facts about the customer.

As Chapter 1 explained, *empowerment* involves delegating authority to solve customers' problems. Usually, organizational representatives, salespeople for example, are able to make changes during interactions with customers through phone, fax, e-mail, social media, or face-to-face.

An **interaction** occurs when a customer and a company representative exchange information and develop learning relationships. With CRM, the customer—not the organization—defines the terms of the interaction, often by stating his or her preferences. The organization responds by designing products and services around customers' desired experiences. Social media have created numerous new ways for companies to interact with customers—see Chapter 18 for more on this topic.

The success of CRM—building lasting and profitable relationships—can be directly measured by the effectiveness of the interaction between the customer and the organization. In fact, what further differentiates CRM from other strategic initiatives is the organization's ability to establish and manage interactions with its current customer base. The more latitude (empowerment) a company gives its representatives, the more likely the interaction will conclude in a way that satisfies the customer.

EXHIBIT 17.4 CUSTOMER-CENTRIC APPROACH FOR MANAGING CUSTOMER INTERACTIONS

interaction the point at which a customer and a company representative exchange information and develop learning relationships

touch points areas of a business where customers have contact with the company and data might be gathered

knowledge management the process by which customer information is centralized and shared in order to enhance the relationship between customers and the organization

17-6b Understand Interactions of the Current Customer Base

The interaction between the customer and the organization is the foundation on which a CRM system is built. Only through effective interactions can organizations learn about the expectations of their customers, generate and manage knowledge about them, negotiate mutually satisfying commitments, and build long-term relationships.

Exhibit 17.4 illustrates the customer-centric approach for managing customer interactions. Following a customer-centric approach, an interaction can occur through different communication channels, such as a phone, the Internet, or a salesperson. Any activity or touch point a customer has with an organization, either directly or indirectly, constitutes an interaction.

Companies that effectively manage customer interactions recognize that data provided by customers affect a wide variety of **touch points**. In a CRM system, touch points are all areas of a business where customers have contact with the company and data might be gathered. Touch points might include: a customer registering for a particular service; a customer communicating with customer service for product information; a customer completing and returning the warranty information card for a product; or a customer talking with salespeople, delivery personnel, and product installers. Data gathered at these touch points, once interpreted, provide information that affects touch points inside the company. Interpreted information may be redirected to marketing research to develop profiles of extended warranty purchasers, to production to analyze recurring problems and repair components, to accounting to establish cost-control models for repair service calls, and to sales for better customer profiling and segmentation.

WEB-BASED INTERACTIONS Web-based interactions are an increasingly popular touch point for customers to communicate with companies on their own terms. Web users can evaluate and purchase products, make reservations, input preferential data, and provide customer feedback on services and products. Data from these Web-based interactions are then captured, compiled, and used to segment customers, refine marketing efforts, develop new products, and deliver a degree of individual customization to improve customer relationships.

SOCIAL CRM As social media have become more popular, many companies have begun to use these media for "social CRM." ZDNet journalist Paul Greenberg recently named Salesforce, Microsoft, Blackbaud, Xactly, Infusionsoft, Accenture, and EY as companies to watch in the field of social CRM.[14] Essentially, social CRM takes the most successful aspects of traditional CRM, such as behavioral targeting, and expands them to include ways to engage customers through social media. This new

paradigm includes a new customer recommendation value called the *net promoter score*. The net promoter score measures how much a customer influences the behavior of other customers through recommendations on social media. Its ultimate purpose is to gather all consumer interactions into a single database so that they can be analyzed and used to improve communication. Social CRM also enables marketers to focus more on the relationship aspect of CRM. For example, REI empowers customers to "carve your own adventure" through its YouTube channel. JetBlue uses Facebook and Twitter to provide advice and updates to travelers. To use social CRM effectively, companies must understand which sites customers use, whether they post opinions, and who the major influencers in the category are. They can then marry this information with behavioral data like purchases and purchase frequency.

POINT-OF-SALE INTERACTIONS Another touch point is through **point-of-sale interactions** in stores or at information kiosks. Many point-of-sale software programs enable customers to easily provide information about themselves without feeling violated. The information is then used for marketing and merchandising activities and to accurately identify the store's best customers and the types of products they buy. Data collected at point-of-sale interactions are also used to increase customer satisfaction through the development of in-store services and customer recognition promotions.

17-6c Capture Customer Data

Vast amounts of data can be obtained from the interactions between an organization and its customers. Therefore, in a CRM system, the issue is not how much data can be obtained, but rather what types of data should be acquired and how the data can effectively be used for relationship enhancement.

The traditional approach for acquiring data from customers is through channel interactions. Channel interactions include store visits, conversations with salespeople, interactions via the Web, traditional phone conversations, and wireless communications. In a CRM system, channel interactions are viewed as prime information sources based on the channel selected to initiate the interaction rather than on the data acquired. In some cases, companies use online chat to answer questions customers have about products they are looking for. For example, 24 Hour Fitness has an online chat window that opens when a

GET UNDER THE SKIN OF YOUR MAN.
TAKE OUR VALENTINE QUIZ.

MR. ACTION MR. SENSITIVE

MR. SMOOTH MR. EXTREME

Take our quiz to find the perfect products for your man and for your chance to WIN A ROMANTIC BREAK!

Go to
facebook.com/LorealParisUK

L'ORÉAL
MEN EXPERT

EXPERT AT BEING A MAN

This advertisement for L'Oreal directs a highly segmented group of customers to its Facebook page, where the company will continue to engage them through social CRM.

point-of-sale interactions a touch point in stores or information kiosks that uses software to enable customers to easily provide information about themselves without feeling violated

potential customer begins to review the Web site. If the visitor remains on the site, the online chat window asks if he or she needs help finding something specific.

Interactions between the company and the customer facilitate the collection of large amounts of data. Companies can obtain not only simple contact information (name, address, phone number) but also data pertaining to the customer's current relationship with the organization—past purchase history, quantity and frequency of purchases, average amount spent on purchases, sensitivity to promotional activities, and so forth.

In this manner, a large amount of information can be captured from one individual customer across several touch points. Multiply this by the thousands of customers across all of the touch points within an organization, and the volume of data can rapidly become unmanageable for company personnel. The large volume of data resulting from a CRM initiative can be managed effectively only through technology. Once customer data are collected, the question of who owns those data becomes extremely salient. In its privacy statement, Toysmart.com declared that it would never sell information registered at its Web site—including children's names and birth dates—to a third party. When the company filed for bankruptcy protection, it said that the information it collected constituted a company asset that needed to be sold off to pay creditors. Despite the outrage at this announcement, many dot-coms closing their doors found they had little in the way of assets and followed Toysmart's lead.

17-6d Leverage Customer Information

Data mining identifies the most profitable customers and prospects. Managers can then design tailored marketing strategies to best appeal to the identified segments. In CRM, this is commonly referred to as leveraging customer information to facilitate enhanced relationships with customers. Exhibit 17.5 shows some common CRM marketing database applications.

CAMPAIGN MANAGEMENT Through campaign management, all areas of the company participate in the development of programs targeted to customers. **Campaign management** involves monitoring and leveraging customer interactions to sell a company's products and to increase customer service. Campaigns are based directly on data obtained from customers through various interactions. Campaign management includes monitoring the success of the communications based on customer reactions through sales, orders, callbacks to the company, and so on. If a campaign appears unsuccessful, it is evaluated and changed to better achieve the company's desired objective.

Campaign management involves developing customized product and service offerings for the appropriate customer segment, pricing these offerings attractively, and communicating these offers in a manner that enhances customer relationships. Customizing product and service offerings requires managing multiple interactions with customers, as well as giving priority to those

campaign management
developing product or service offerings customized for the appropriate customer segment and then pricing and communicating these offerings for the purpose of enhancing customer relationships

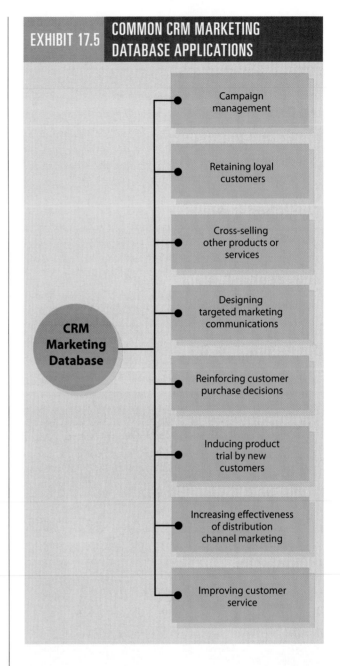

EXHIBIT 17.5 COMMON CRM MARKETING DATABASE APPLICATIONS

CRM Marketing Database

- Campaign management
- Retaining loyal customers
- Cross-selling other products or services
- Designing targeted marketing communications
- Reinforcing customer purchase decisions
- Inducing product trial by new customers
- Increasing effectiveness of distribution channel marketing
- Improving customer service

products and services that are viewed as most desirable for a specifically designated customer. Even within a highly defined market segment, individual customer differences will emerge. Therefore, interactions among customers must focus on individual experiences, expectations, and desires.

RETAINING LOYAL CUSTOMERS If a company has identified its best customers, then it should make every effort to maintain and increase their loyalty. When a company retains an additional five percent of its customers each year, profits will increase by as much as 125 percent. What's more, improving customer retention by a mere two percent can decrease costs by as much as ten percent.[15]

Loyalty programs reward loyal customers for making multiple purchases. The objective is to build long-term, mutually beneficial relationships between a company and its key customers. More than 4,000 small- and medium-sized businesses across thirty-five states have teamed up with reward management firm Belly to develop unique rewards programs, such as getting to throw eggs at a food truck after a specified number of purchases or having the owner of your favorite bagel store sing to you after buying 100 bagels. The individualized rewards reflect each business's personality and (ideally) those of its customers, making the rewards programs highly motivating.[16] In addition to rewarding good customers, loyalty programs provide businesses with a wealth of information about their customers and shopping trends, which can be used to make future business decisions.

CROSS-SELLING OTHER PRODUCTS AND SERVICES
CRM provides many opportunities to cross-sell related products. Marketers can use the database to match product profiles and consumer profiles so that they can cross-sell customers products that match their demographic, lifestyle, or behavioral characteristics. The financial services industry uses cross-selling better than most other industries do. Cross selling is a key part of Wells Fargo's strategy, for example, and is a large contributor to the company's success in the industry. After engaging with customers to determine their financial needs and aspirations, Wells Fargo reps work to determine how the company's wide range of products can synergize to meet or exceed those financial goals.[17]

Internet companies use product and customer profiling to reveal cross-selling opportunities while customers surf their sites. Past purchases, tracking programs, and the site a surfer is referred from give online marketers clues about the surfer's interests and what items to cross-sell. Amazon, for example, has used profiling to better meet customer needs for years. The company systematically compares individuals' shopping habits and online activities to other Amazon customers to make better tailored recommendations. Customers are also able to proactively rate products, review products, add products to wishlists, recommend products, and save products for a later purchase—all of which make for a more customized customer experience.[18]

A small company, such as this Gorilla Cheese food truck, may use the services of Belly to reward customers for their loyalty.

iStockphoto.com/Wdstock

DESIGNING TARGETED MARKETING COMMUNICATIONS Using transaction and purchase data, a database allows marketers to track customers' relationships to the company's products and services and modify the marketing message accordingly.

Customers can also be segmented into infrequent users, moderate users, and heavy users. A segmented communications strategy can then be developed based on which group the customer falls into. Communications to infrequent users might encourage repeat purchases through a direct incentive such as a limited-time price discount for ordering again. Online marketers for retailers like GNC and Newegg send out periodic e-mails with discounts to customers who made previous purchases. Communications to moderate users may use fewer incentives and more reinforcement of past purchase decisions. Communications to heavy users would be designed around loyalty and reinforcement of the purchase rather than around price promotions.

Source: General Nutrition Center

Online marketers for retailers like GNC will use email as a way to reach out to previous customers.

STUDY TOOLS 17

LOCATED AT BACK OF THE TEXTBOOK
☐ Rip Out Chapter Review Card

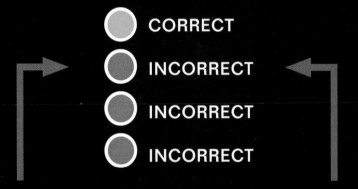

18 | Social Media and Marketing

LEARNING OUTCOMES

After studying this chapter, you will be able to…

18-1 Describe social media, how they are used, and their relation to integrated marketing communications

18-2 Explain how to create a social media campaign

18-3 Evaluate the various methods of measurement for social media

18-4 Explain consumer behavior on social media

18-5 Describe the social media tools in a marketer's toolbox and how they are useful

18-6 Describe the impact of mobile technology on social media

18-7 Understand the aspects of developing a social media plan

After you finish this chapter go to **PAGE 339** for **STUDY TOOLS.**

18-1 WHAT ARE SOCIAL MEDIA?

The most exciting thing to happen to marketing and promotion in recent years is the increasing use of online technology to promote brands, particularly using social media. Social media have changed the way that marketers can communicate with their brands—from mass messages to intimate conversations. As marketing moves into social media, marketers must remember that for most people, social media are meant to be a social experience, not a marketing experience. In fact, the term *social media* means different things to different people, though most people think it refers to digital technology. The American Bar Association uses a definition developed by social media expert Brian Solis. According to Solis, **social media** is "any tool or service that uses the Internet to facilitate conversations."[1] However, social media can also be defined relative to traditional advertising like

social media any tool or service that uses the Internet to facilitate conversations

Source: Twitter, Inc.

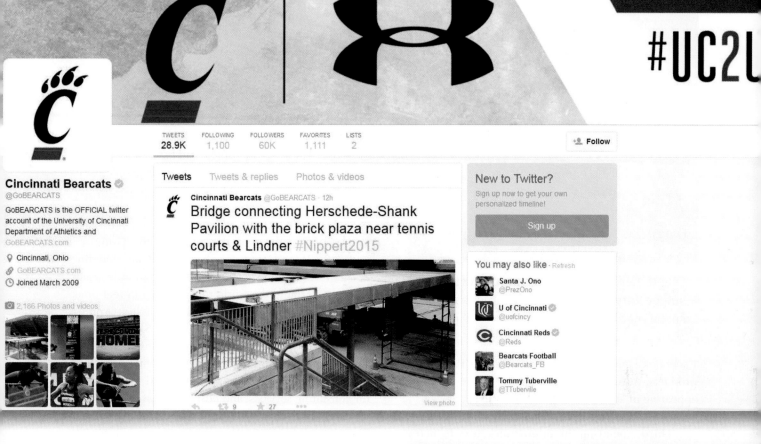

television and magazines: whereas traditional marketing media offer a mass media method of interacting with consumers, social media offer more one-to-one ways to meet consumers.

Social media have several implications for marketers and the ways that they interact with their customers. First, marketers must realize that they often do not control the content on social media sites. Consumers are sharing their thoughts, wishes, and experiences about brands with the world through social media. Because of this level of visibility and discussion, marketers must realize that having a great ad campaign is not enough—the product or service must be great, too.

Second, the ability to share experiences quickly and with such large numbers of people amplifies the impact of word of mouth in ways that can affect a company's bottom line. Singer Katy Perry has more than 66 million Twitter followers, and as such, has a very large reach.[2] YouTube is the company with the largest Twitter presence (more than 50 million followers), and

"Interaction and engagement [on social media] is something that you don't necessarily see in traditional media. That's why we [at Ford] continue to accelerate our digital advertising investment to more than 25% of our media dollars."[3]

—JIM FARLEY, FORD GLOBAL SALES AND MARKETING VICE PRESIDENT

Coca-Cola is the most liked brand on Facebook with almost 90 million fans.[4] The total reach of these brands is difficult to quantify, but it is unquestionably massive. Many companies use mascots to drive their marketing messages on social media. For example, Progressive auto insurance's perky saleswoman Flo has almost 5.5 million

Due to her more than 65 million Twitter followers, singer Katy Perry has a very large reach on social media.

Facebook fans that read her posts about Progressive products. According to the company, since Flo began appearing in ads, the company has seen yearly gains in the number of policies taken out.[5]

Third, social media allow marketers to listen. Domino's Pizza listened to what was being posted about its products (much of which was not nice) and decided to use that information to change its product. Social media, along with traditional marketing research, allowed Domino's to gain the insight needed to completely reinvent its pizza. Dell and Gatorade have taken social media monitoring to a whole new level as they literally put social media at the center of their marketing efforts. Premium sportswear company Lululemon was forced to acknowledge manufacturing problems after comments critical of the company's product quality were posted across its social media sites.[6]

Fourth, social media provide more sophisticated methods of measuring how marketers meet and interact with consumers than traditional advertising does. Currently, social media include tools and platforms like social networks, blogs, microblogs, and media sharing sites, which can be accessed through a growing number of devices including smartphones, e-readers, televisions, tablets, video game consoles, and netbooks. This technology changes daily, offering consumers new ways to experience social media platforms. As such, social media must constantly innovate to keep up with consumer demands.

Finally, social media allow marketers to have much more direct and meaningful conversations with customers. Social media offer a form of relationship building that will ultimately bring the customer and brand closer. Indeed, the culture of *participation* that social media foster may well prove to be a fifth "P" for marketing.

At the basic level, consumers of social media want to exchange information, collaborate with others, and have conversations. Social media are designed for people to socialize with each other. They have changed how and where conversations take place, even globalizing human interaction through rapidly evolving technology. Google+ Hangouts, a popular facet of the fledgling Google+ social network, allows individuals around the world to video chat in real time. Competing with products such as Apple's FaceTime and Microsoft's Skype, Hangouts offers unique innovations such as live streaming and recording. Various companies have used Hangouts to conduct team meetings and webinars, offer consulting services, and host live press conferences. Bakespace.com has successfully utilized Hangouts as a potent marketing platform. The company interacts with customers, shares recipes, and hosts chats with celebrity chefs using Hangouts. And as a chef might say, the proof is in the pudding—Bakespace.com has more than 450,000 people in its Hangouts circle, compared to just 14,000 fans on Facebook.[7] Clearly, conversations are happening online; it is up to the marketer to decide if engaging in those conversations will be profitable and to find the most effective method of entering the conversation.

Companies are beginning to understand the implications of their employees' activities on social media. In fact, there have been several examples of employees getting fired for airing their personal feelings on social media platforms. To combat this, many companies have begun developing social media policies as to what can be posted and what is inappropriate. Some companies have rules concerning corporate blogs, Facebook, Twitter, LinkedIn, comments, and even passwords. Adidas has adopted an "encouraging but strict" approach whereby employees may state their affiliation with Adidas but must also state that any personal views are just that—personal. Obviously, employees are still prohibited from sharing sensitive information. Similarly, Best Buy has a clear set of social media guidelines stating that any negative posts regarding religion, race, or ethnicity will not be tolerated.[8] Having a social media policy can certainly help mitigate risk, but it is not a guarantee that employees won't occasionally slip up.

Marketers are interested in online communication because it is wildly popular: brands, companies, individuals, and celebrities all promote their messages online. In fact, some social media are becoming so important that celebrities, sports stars, and even hotels are hiring coaches to help them strike the correct tone. Britney Spears, Carly Rae Jepsen, and Will.I.Am all have coaches that help them navigate the perilous landscape of Twitter. Coaches instruct clients on best practices and advise them how to leverage their personal brands in online spaces. They also monitor clients' Twitter feeds in real time, acting as editor, security guard, and advisor all at once. Some celebrities have social media advisors accompany them to galas and award shows, but coaches are often underutilized by the entertainment elite. As one celebrity coach noted, "It can get really busy if you're doing interviews on the red carpet, and it's just nice to have someone with you who can say, 'Hey, you should take a picture with your other-famous-person friend right now. Here you go, now you should tweet it.'"[9]

Some companies go so far as to require Facebook and Twitter training for high-profile employees. Approximately thirty percent of Adobe's employees have gone through some form of social media training. According to Cory Edwards, head of Adobe's Social Business Center of Excellence, Adobe's social media training "helps employees understand key principles such as disclosure and who to contact with questions. Guided by a set of core Adobe principles, the program aims to build employee social media fluency through awareness, empowerment, and excellence."[10]

18-1a How Consumers Use Social Media

Before beginning to understand how to leverage social media for brand building, it is important to understand which social media consumers are using and how they are using them. It is safe to assume that many of your customers are active on Facebook. Targeting can be accomplished by using less ubiquitous platforms. Qzone and Sina Weibo are two of the largest social media platforms in China, for example. Match.com, OkCupid, and Tinder are great platforms to reach young adult singles. Y8 and Big Fish Games offer a wide variety of social games. Teens tend to use platforms like Snapchat, Instagram, Twitch, Yik Yak, and Tumblr. While Facebook is used widely by older teens and adults, its popularity among younger consumers is decreasing.[11]

Videos are another of the most popular tools by which marketers reach consumers, and YouTube is by far the largest online video repository—it has more content than any major television network. Twitter's Vine, which limits videos to six seconds in length, is also widely popular. Flickr, Twitter, and blogs—all of which will be discussed in more detail later on—are some of the other most popular social media destinations among consumers. In 2015:

- Instagram grew by 50 percent to more than 300 million users; it is larger than Twitter and has one of the highest engagement levels of any social platform.
- Millennials spent more than two hours per day on their smartphones and used an average of six apps during that time.
- Facebook had more video views (12.3 billion) than YouTube (11.3 billion).
- Snapchat grew by 56 percent.[12]
- Tumblr added 120,000 new users per day.[13]

The bottom line, according to Universal McCann's Comparative Study on Social Media Trends, is that "if you are online, you are using social media."[14]

Increased usage of alternative platforms like smartphones and tablet computers has further contributed to the proliferation of social media usage. In the United States, ninety percent of American adults own a cell phone, while forty-five percent own a smartphone. These numbers jump to ninety-three percent and sixty-three percent for adults age eighteen to twenty-nine. Among all adults, 55 percent access the Internet on a mobile phone, and forty percent have accessed a social media Web site.[15] Tablet usage has hit critical mass among mobile surfers—one in four smartphone users owns a tablet as well. According to Mark Donovan, senior vice president of mobile at ComScore, "Tablets are one of the most rapidly adopted consumer technologies in history and are poised to fundamentally disrupt the way people engage with the digital world both on-the-go and perhaps most notably, in the home."[16] The overall impact of tablet computing on social media (and thus the discipline of marketing) is yet to be seen, but given the incredible impact that the smartphone has had in its short life span, tablets could indeed prove to be game changing.

SOCIAL COMMERCE A new area of growth in social media is **social commerce**, which combines social media with the

> **social commerce** a subset of e-commerce that involves the interaction and user contribution aspects of social online media to assist online buying and selling of products and services

basics of e-commerce. Social commerce is a subset of e-commerce that involves the interaction and user contribution aspects of social online media to assist online buying and selling of products and services.[17] Basically, social commerce relies on user-generated content on Web sites to assist consumers with purchases. Pinterest lets users collect ideas and products from all over the Web and "pin" favorite items to individually curated pinboards. Other users browse boards by theme, keyword, or product; click on what they like; and either visit the originating sites or re-pin the items on their own pinboards. Social commerce sites often include ratings and recommendations (as Amazon.com does) and social shopping tools (as Groupon does). In general, social commerce sites are designed to help consumers make more informed decisions on purchases and services.

Social commerce generated almost $24 billion in sales in 2014, with nearly half of all online sales coming through social media sites.[18] There are seven types of social commerce:

- Peer-to-peer sales platforms (like eBay and Etsy)
- Social networking Web sites driven by sales (like Pinterest and Twitter)
- Group buying platforms (like Groupon and Social Living)
- Peer recommendation sites (like Yelp and JustBoughtIt)
- User-curated shopping sites (like The Fancy and Lyst)
- Participatory commerce platforms (like Kickstarter and Threadless)
- Social shopping sites (like Motilo and GoTryItOn).[19]

As companies migrate to social commerce sites such as Pinterest, consumer interactions across the sites may change. One way that companies are leveraging Pinterest's user base is by running promotions. For example, Favorite Family Recipes offered two iPads as prizes for users who followed and pinned the logos of thirteen associated Pinterest boards.[20] This type of promotion can undermine the authenticity that many consumers rely on when using social commerce sites. However, some companies hope to cultivate authentic relationships by staying away from promotions. Whole Foods pins items that relate to the company's values but are not promotional or linked back to the Whole Foods site. Customers have built a relationship with Whole Foods based on upcycled products and recipes, rather than free products.[21]

18-1b Social Media and Integrated Marketing Communications

While marketers typically employ a social media strategy alongside traditional channels like print and broadcast, many budget pendulums are swinging toward social media. Forrester Research predicts that mobile marketing, social media, e-mail marketing, display advertising, and search marketing will grow to more than thirty-five percent of spending in the next few years, equaling spending on television today. The bulk of this budget will still go to search marketing and display advertising, but substantial investments will also be made in mobile marketing and social media.[22]

A unique consequence of social media is the widespread shift from one-to-many communication to many-to-many communication. Instead of simply putting a brand advertisement on television with

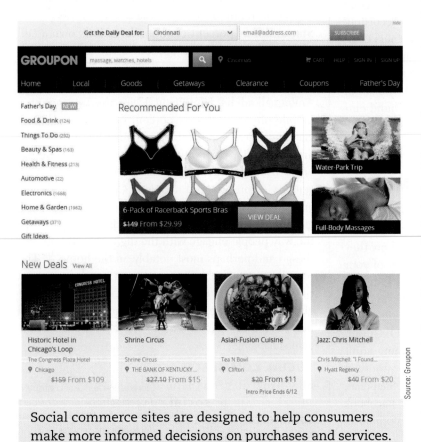

Source: Groupon

Social commerce sites are designed to help consumers make more informed decisions on purchases and services.

Talenthouse asks customers for their input when it comes to album art, performer wardrobes, etc. A winner is selected through social media voting.

Source: Talenthouse

no means for feedback, marketers can use social media to have conversations with consumers, forge deeper relationships, and build brand loyalty. Social media also allow consumers to connect with each other, share opinions, and collaborate on new ideas according to their interests.

With social media, the audience is often in control of the message, the medium, the response, or all three. This distribution of control is often difficult for companies to adjust to, but the focus of social marketing is unavoidably on the audience, and the brand must adapt to succeed. The interaction between producer and consumer becomes less about entertaining and more about listening, influencing, and engaging.

Using consumers to develop and market products is called **crowdsourcing**. Crowdsourcing describes how the input of many people can be leveraged to make decisions that used to be based on the input of only a few people.[23] Companies get feedback on marketing campaigns, new product ideas, and other marketing decisions by asking customers to weigh in. One company called Talenthouse is offering up the crowd to help musicians fulfill all sorts of needs—for example, someone to design album art or sew a dress for a lead singer. Talenthouse has users submit work to be voted on by Facebook and Twitter peers. The winner gets the job (though the musician has the final say in who wins). Some musicians see Talenthouse as a way to gain publicity or to help aspiring artists. English singer-songwriter Ellie Goulding set up a contest for Talenthouse competitors to submit a photograph that showed people connecting with music at a concert or festival. The winner received £1,000 (about $1,500), a new laptop, special promotion, and a job as the official photographer for an Ellie Goulding concert.[24] Crowdsourcing offers a way for companies to engage

heavy users of a brand and receive input, which in turn increases those users' brand advocacy and lessens the likelihood that a change will be disliked enough to drive away loyal customers.

18-2 CREATING AND LEVERAGING A SOCIAL MEDIA CAMPAIGN

Social media is an exciting new field, and its potential for expanding a brand's impact is enormous. Because the costs are often minimal and the learning curve is relatively low, some organizations are tempted to dive headfirst into social media. As with any marketing campaign, however, it is always important to start with a strategy. For most organizations, this means starting with a marketing or communications plan. Important evaluative areas such as situation analysis, objectives, and evaluation are still essential. It is important to link communication objectives (for example, improving customer service) to the most effective social media tools (for example, Twitter) and to be able to measure the results to determine if the objectives were met. It is also important to understand the various types of media involved.

The new communication paradigm created by a shift to social media marketing raises questions about categorization. In light of the convergence of traditional and digital media, researchers have explored different ways that interactive marketers can categorize media types, namely owned, earned, and paid media (recall these concepts from Chapter 15). The purpose of owned media is to develop deeper relationships with customers. A brand's Facebook presence, YouTube channel, Twitter presence, Pinterest presence, and presence on other social platforms constitute owned media. Additional content such as videos, webinars, recommendations, ratings, and blog posts are also considered owned media since they are sharable on social media platforms. In an interactive space, media are *earned* through word of mouth or online buzz about something the brand is doing. Earned media include viral videos, retweets, comments on blogs, and other forms of customer feedback resulting from a social media

crowdsourcing using consumers to develop and market products

Companies with an established brand recognition have deeper layers of social media—customers know and recognize instantly.

presence. When consumers pass along brand information in the form of retweets, blog comments, or ratings and recommendations, this is an example of earned media. In other words, the word of mouth is spread online rather than face-to-face. Paid media are similar to marketing efforts that utilize traditional media, like newspaper, magazine, and television advertisements. In an interactive space, paid media include display advertising, paid search words, and other types of direct online advertising.[25] Ads purchased on Facebook, for example, are considered paid media since the brand is paying for the text-based or visual ad that shows up on the right-hand side of Facebook profiles.

As a result, social media can really be thought of as an additional "layer" that many brands decide to develop. Some layers are quite deep—Doritos, Old Spice, and Nike can be said to have deeper layers of social media since these are brands that people talk about. Other brands, for example, many B-to-B brands, may have a more shallow social media layer and provide access on only one or two social media platforms. At the end of the day, it really depends on the type of product being sold and the customer's propensity to participate in social media.

To leverage all three types of media, marketers must follow a few key guidelines. First, they must maximize owned media by reaching out beyond their existing Web sites to create portfolios of digital touch points. This is especially true for brands with tight budgets, as the organization may not be able to afford much paid media. Second, marketers must recognize that public and media relations no longer translates into earned media. Instead, marketers must learn how to listen and respond to stakeholders. This will stimulate word of mouth. Finally, marketers must understand that paid media must serve as a catalyst to drive customer engagement and expand into emerging channels.[26] If balanced correctly, all three types of media can be powerful tools for interactive marketers.

18-2a The Listening System

The first action a marketing team should take when initiating a social media campaign is simple—it should just listen. Customers are on social media and assume that the brand is there as well. They expect a new level of engagement with brands. Developing an effective listening system is necessary to both understanding and engaging an online audience. Marketers must not only hear what is being said about the brand, the industry, the competition, and the customer, but they must also pay attention to who is saying what and act upon that information. The specific ways that customers and noncustomers rate, rank, critique, praise, deride, recommend, snub, and generally discuss brands are all important. Thus, social media have created a new method of market research: customers telling marketers what they want and need (and do not want and do not need).

Once a company has started listening, it typically wants to develop a more formalized approach. **Social media monitoring** is the process of identifying and assessing what is being said about a company, individual, product, or brand. It can involve sentiment analysis and *text mining* specific key words on social networking Web sites, blogs, discussion forums, and other social media. Negative comments and complaints are of particular importance, both because they can illuminate unknown brand flaws and because they are the comments that tend to go viral. Listening is important because consumers believe that if negative comments about a brand go unanswered, that brand is insincere, and consumers will

social media monitoring
the process of identifying and assessing what is being said about a company, individual, product, or brand

take their business elsewhere. Failure to respond to criticism typically leads to a larger crisis. Online tools such as Google Alerts, Google Blog Search, Twitter Search, Social Mention, Social Bakers and Socialcast are extremely helpful in monitoring social media. Larger companies typically use an enterprise system such as Salesforce.com's Radian6 CRM software to monitor social media.

18-2b Social Media Objectives

After establishing a listening platform, the organization should develop a list of objectives for its social media team to accomplish. These objectives must be developed with a clear understanding of how social media change the communication dynamic with and for customers. Remember, attempting to reach a mass audience with a static message will never be as successful as influencing people through conversation. Marketing managers must set objectives that reflect this reality. Here are some practical ideas that marketing managers should consider when setting social media objectives:

- **Listen and learn:** Monitor what is being said about the brand and competitors, and glean insights about audiences. Use online tools and do research to implement the best social media practices. If you have established a listening strategy, this objective should already be accomplished.

- **Build relationships and awareness:** Open dialogues with stakeholders by giving them compelling content across a variety of media. Engage in conversations, and answer customers' questions candidly. This will both increase Web traffic and boost your search engine ranking. This is where crowdsourcing can be useful for product development and communication campaign feedback.

- **Promote products and services:** The clearest path to increasing the bottom line using social media is to get customers talking about products and services, which ultimately translates into sales.

- **Manage your reputation:** Develop and improve the brand's reputation by responding to comments and criticism that appear on blogs and forums. Additionally, organizations can position themselves as helpful and benevolent by participating in other forums and discussions. Social media make it much easier to establish and communicate expertise.

- **Improve customer service:** Customer comments about products and services will not always be

positive. Use social media to search out displeased customers and engage them directly in order to solve their service issues.

 ## 18-3 EVALUATION AND MEASUREMENT OF SOCIAL MEDIA

Social media have the potential to revolutionize the way organizations communicate with stakeholders. Given the relative ease and efficiency with which organizations can use social media, a positive return on investment (ROI) is likely for many—if not most—organizations. A Forrester Research report found that ninety-five percent of marketers planned to increase or maintain their investments in social media. However, though they understand that it is a worthwhile investment, most marketers have not been able to figure out how to measure the benefits of social media.

As with traditional advertising, marketers lack hard evidence as to the relative effectiveness of these tools. Some marketers accept this unknown variable and focus on the fact that social media are less about ROI than about deepening relationships with customers; others work tirelessly to better understand the measurement of social media's effectiveness. A recent Ragan/NASDAQ OMX Corporate Solutions survey found that forty percent of marketers are unsure of what evaluative tools to use, and about seventy percent are only "somewhat satisfied" or "not satisfied at all" with how their companies measure social media. "I'm not sure what to measure or how," said one survey participant. "I know it's important, but I can't show my boss how many retweets a post received and expect him to care."[27]

While literally hundreds of metrics have been developed to measure social media's value, these metrics are meaningless unless they are tied to key performance indicators.[28] For example, a local coffee shop manager may measure the success of her social media presence by the raw number of friends on Facebook and followers on Twitter she has accumulated. But these numbers depend entirely on context. The rate of accumulation, investment per fan and follower, and comparison to similarly sized coffee shops are all important metrics to consider. Without context, measurements are meaningless. This is a hot topic, and several marketing blogs cover the areas of social media measurement. Jim Sterne's book *Social Media Metrics* is one of the best sources information on monitoring and using social media metrics.

SOCIAL BEHAVIOR OF CONSUMERS

Social media have changed the way that people interact in their everyday lives. Some say that social media have made people smarter by giving people (especially children) access to so much information and interactivity. Social media allow people to stay in touch in ways never before experienced. Social media have also reinvented civic engagement (recall that the ALS Association's "Ice Bucket Challenge" grew worldwide through social media like Facebook and Twitter). Social media have drastically changed the advertising business from an industry based on mass-media models (for example, television) to an industry based on relationships and conversations. This all has implications for how consumers use social media and the purposes for which they use those media.[29]

Once objectives have been determined and measurement tools have been implemented, it is important to identify the consumer the marketer is trying to reach. Who is using social media? What types of

Marcos Mesa Sam Wordley/Shutterstock.com

Social media has reinvented civic engagement—see the ALS Ice Bucket Challenge as a prime example.

WHICH METRICS ARE MOST EFFECTIVE?

Many social media marketers will simply need to start with good measurable objectives, determine what needs to be measured, and figure it out. Still, some social media metrics to consider include:

- **Buzz:** volume of consumer-created buzz for a brand based on posts and impressions, by social channel, by stage in the purchase channel, by season, and by time of day.

- **Interest:** number of "likes," fans, followers, and friends; growth rates; rate of virality or pass along; and change in pass along over time.

- **Participation:** number of comments, ratings, social bookmarks, subscriptions, page views, uploads, downloads, embeds, retweets, Facebook posts, pins, and time spent with social media platform.

- **Search engine ranks and results:** increases and decreases on searches and changes in key words.

- **Influence:** media mentions, influences of bloggers reached, influences of customers reached, and second-degree reach based on social graphs.

- **Sentiment analysis:** positive, neutral, and negative sentiment; trends of sentiment; and volume of sentiment.

- **Web site metrics:** clicks, click-through rates, and percentage of traffic.

social media do they use? How do they use social media? Are they just reading content, or do they actually create it? Does Facebook attract younger users? Do Twitter users retweet viral videos? These types of questions must be considered because they determine not only which tools will be most effective but also, more importantly, whether launching a social media campaign even makes sense for a particular organization.

Understanding an audience necessitates understanding how that audience uses social media. In *Groundswell*, Charlene Li and Josh Bernoff of

Forrester Research identify six categories of social media users:

1. **Creators:** Those who produce and share online content like blogs, Web sites, articles, and videos
2. **Critics:** Those who post comments, ratings, and reviews of products and services on blogs and forums
3. **Collectors:** Those who use RSS feeds to collect information and vote for Web sites online
4. **Joiners:** Those who maintain a social networking profile and visit other sites
5. **Spectators:** Those who read blogs, listen to podcasts, watch videos, and generally consume media
6. **Inactives:** Those who do none of these things[30]

A Forrester Research study determined that twenty-four percent of social media users function as creators, 36 percent function as critics, 23 percent function as collectors, 68 percent function as joiners, 73 percent function as spectators, and 14 percent function—or rather, do not function—as inactives.[31] Participation in most categories has slowed slightly, prompting analysts to recommend that marketers re-examine how they are engaging with their customers online.

Despite the apparent slowdown, research also shows that more social networking "rookies" are classified as joiners. Another bright spot is a new category, "conversationalists," or people who post status updates on social networking sites and microblogging services such as Twitter. Conversationalists represent 36 percent of users.[32] This type of classification gives marketers a general idea of who is using social media and how to engage them. It is similar to any type of market segmentation—especially the 80/20 rule. Those who are creating content and active on social media could be those consumers most likely to actively engage with a brand as well as actively post negative comments on social media. The critics and collectors make up most of this group. However, it is important not to miss the joiners and spectators, because they are eager to follow and act on the comments of their fellow customers.

18-5 SOCIAL MEDIA TOOLS: CONSUMER- AND CORPORATE- GENERATED CONTENT

Given that it is important for marketers to engage with customers on social media for the reasons mentioned earlier, there are a number of tools and platforms that can be employed as part of an organization's social media strategy. Blogs, microblogs, social networks, media creation and sharing sites, social news sites, location-based social networking sites, review sites, and virtual worlds and online gaming all have their place in a company's social marketing plan. These are all tools in a marketing manager's toolbox, available when applicable to the marketing plan but not necessarily to be used all at once. Because of the breakneck pace at which technology changes, this list of resources will surely look markedly different five years from now. More tools emerge every day, and branding strategies must keep up with the ever-changing world of technology. For now, the resources highlighted in this section remain a marketer's strongest set of platforms for conversing and strengthening relationships with customers.

18-5a Blogs

Blogs have become staples in many social media strategies and are often a brand's social media centerpiece. A **blog** is a publicly accessible Web page that functions as an interactive journal, whereby readers can post comments on the author's entries. Some experts believe that every company should have a blog that speaks to current and potential customers, not as consumers, but as people.[33] Blogs allow marketers to create content in the form of posts, which ideally build trust and a sense of authenticity in customers. Once posts are made, audience members can provide feedback through comments. Because it opens a dialogue and gives customers a voice, the comments section of a blog post is one of the most important avenues of conversation between brands and consumers.

Blogs can be divided into two broad categories: corporate and professional blogs, and noncorporate blogs such as personal blogs. **Corporate blogs** are sponsored by a company or one of its brands and are maintained by one or more of the company's employees. They disseminate marketing-controlled information and are effective platforms for developing thought leadership, fostering better relationships with stakeholders, maximizing search engine optimization, attracting new customers, endearing the organization with anecdotes and stories about brands, and providing an active forum for testing new ideas. Many companies, however, have moved

blog a publicly accessible Web page that functions as an interactive journal, whereby readers can post comments on the author's entries

corporate blogs blogs that are sponsored by a company or one of its brands and maintained by one or more of the company's employees

away from corporate blogs, replacing the in-depth writing and comment monitoring that come with blog maintenance with the quick, easy, and more social Facebook, Twitter, or Tumblr. Coca Cola, Walmart, and AllState operate some of the best big company corporate blogs. All are known for their creative and engaging content and the authenticity of their tone.[34]

On the other hand, **noncorporate blogs** are independent and not associated with the marketing efforts of any particular company or brand. Because these blogs contain information not controlled by marketers, they are perceived to be more authentic than corporate blogs. Mommy bloggers, women who review children's products and discuss family-related topics on their personal blogs, use noncorporate blogs. The goal of mommy blogs is to share parenting tips and experiences and become part of a community. Food blogs are especially popular, particularly those posting restaurant reviews, diet and exercise tips, and recipes.

Because of the popularity of these and other types of blogs, many bloggers receive products and/or money from companies in exchange for a review. Many bloggers disclose where they received the product or if they were paid, but an affiliation is not always clear. Because of this, bloggers must disclose any financial relationship with a company per Federal Trade Commission rules. Marketing managers need to understand the rules behind offering complimentary products to bloggers before using them as a way to capitalize on the high potential for social buzz; four out of five noncorporate bloggers post brand or product reviews. Even if a company does not have a formal social media strategy, chances are the brand is still out in the blogosphere, whether or not a marketing manager approached a blogger.

18-5b Microblogs

Microblogs are blogs that entail shorter posts than traditional blogs. Twitter, the most popular microblogging platform, requires that posts be no more than 140 characters in length. However, there are several other platforms, including Tumblr, Plurk, and, of course, Facebook's status updates. Unlike Twitter,

Some social media platforms allow users to post longer pieces of text, videos, images and links.

these platforms allow users to post longer pieces of text, videos, images, and links. While some microblogs (such as Tumblr) do not have text length limits, their multimedia-based cultures discourage traditional blog-length text posts. The content posted on microblogs ranges from five-paragraph news stories to photos of sandwiches with the ingredients as captions (scanwiches.com). While Tumblr is growing rapidly, Twitter, originally designed as a short messaging system used for internal communication, is wildly popular and is used as a communication and research tool by individuals and brands around the world. Twitter is effective for disseminating breaking news, promoting longer blog posts and campaigns, sharing links, announcing events, and promoting sales. By following, retweeting, responding to potential customers' tweets, and tweeting content that inspires customers to engage the brand, corporate Twitter users can lay a foundation for meaningful two-way conversation quickly and effectively. Celebrities also flock to Twitter to interact with fans, discuss tour dates, and efficiently promote themselves directly to fans. Research has found that when operated correctly, corporate Twitter accounts are well respected and well received. Twitter can be used to build communities, aid in customer service, gain prospects, increase awareness, and, in the case of nonprofits, raise funds.

The ways a business can use microblogs to successfully engage with customers are almost limitless. A wide variety of companies find Tumblr's easy and customizable format a great way to promote an individual brand. Mashable uses its Tumblr to give a glimpse inside the offices and share the company's sense of humor. Ace Hotel, located in New York, Portland, Seattle, and Palm

noncorporate blogs independent blogs that are not associated with the marketing efforts of any particular company or brand

microblogs blogs with strict post length limits

Springs, shows off its properties and local art exhibits on a spare, gallery-like Tumblr. Lure Fishbar shows off its delectable food on its Tumblr.[35]

18-5c Social Networks

Social networking sites allow individuals to connect—or network—with friends, peers, and business associates. Connections may be made around shared interests, shared environments, or personal relationships. Depending on the site, connected individuals may be able to send each other messages, track each other's activity, see each other's personal information, share multimedia, comment on each other's blog and microblog posts—or do all of these things. Depending on a marketing team's goals, several social networks might be engaged as part of a social media strategy: Facebook is the largest social network; Instagram and Snapchat are popular among younger audiences; LinkedIn is geared toward professionals and businesses who use it to recruit employees; and niche networks like Twitch, SoundCloud, Grindr, BlackPlanet, and ChristianMingle.com cater to specialized markets. There is a niche social network for just about every demographic and interest. Beyond those already established, an organization may decide to develop a brand-specific social network or community. Although each social networking site is different, some marketing goals can be accomplished on any such site. Given the right strategy, increasing awareness, targeting audiences, promoting products, forging relationships, highlighting expertise and leadership, attracting event participants, performing research, and generating new business are attainable marketing goals on any social network.

There is a niche social network for just about every demographic and interest.

EXHIBIT 18.1 FACEBOOK LINGO

Non-Individual (Usually Corporate)	Individual
Page	Profile
Fan of a page, tells fan's friends that the user is a fan, creates mini viral campaign	Friend a person, send private messages, write on the Wall, see friend-only content
Public, searchable	Privacy options, not searchable unless user enabled

FACEBOOK Facebook originated as a community for college students that opened to the general public as its popularity grew. It now has almost 1.5 billion monthly active users, making it the largest social networking site by far. Growth in new profiles is highest among baby boomers using Facebook as a way to connect with old friends and keep up with family. Facebook is popular not only with individuals, but also with groups and companies. How an individual uses Facebook differs from the way a group or company uses Facebook, as you can see in Exhibit 18.1. Individual Facebook users create profiles, while brands, organizations, and nonprofit causes operate as pages. As opposed to individual profiles, all pages are public and are thus subject to search engine indexing.

By maintaining a popular Facebook page, a brand not only increases its social media presence, it also helps to optimize search engine results. Pages often include photo and video albums, brand information, and links to external sites. One of the most useful page features is the Timeline. The Timeline allows a brand to communicate directly with fans via status updates, which enables marketers to build databases of interested stakeholders. When an individual becomes a fan of your organization or posts on your Timeline, that information is shared with the individual's friends, creating a mini viral marketing campaign. Other Facebook marketing tools include groups, applications, and ads. Facebook is an extremely important platform for social marketers.

Facebook has proved to be fertile ground for new marketing ideas and campaigns. Many companies use Facebook as a way to share photos of the business they are doing, whether that is images of the

social networking sites
Web sites that allow individuals to connect—or network—with friends, peers, and business associates

plant where the product is made or finished construction on a new project. Offering guides relevant to a company's product or service as a way to educate interested customers has worked well for Kitchen Cabinet Kings, which found that educated customers make more purchases. Threadless' Voting Hub Facebook page allows fans to share, promote, and vote on new t-shirt designs.[36]

LINKEDIN LinkedIn is used primarily by professionals who wish to build their personal brands online and businesses that are recruiting employees and freelancers. LinkedIn features many of the same services as Facebook (profiles, status updates, private messages, company pages, and groups) but is oriented around business and professional connections—it is designed to be information-rich rather than multimedia-rich. LinkedIn serves as a virtual rolodex, providing recruiters and job seekers alike a network to connect and conduct business. LinkedIn's question-and-answer forum, endorsement system, job classifieds platform, and acquisition of presentation-hosting Web site SlideShare set it apart from Facebook as a truly business-oriented space.[37] LinkedIn is the most effective social media platform for B-to-B marketing, as many use it for lead generation. Some companies use LinkedIn for recruiting, and others use it for thought leadership. Indeed, company pages on LinkedIn can serve as an effective hub for products and services, promotional videos, and company news.

media sharing sites Web sites that allow users to upload and distribute multimedia content like videos and photos

Video creation and distribution have gained popularity among marketers because of video's rich ability to tell stories.

18-5d Media Sharing Sites

Media sharing sites allow users to upload and distribute multimedia content like videos and photos. YouTube, Flickr, Pinterest, Instagram, Vine, and Snapchat are particularly useful to brands' social marketing strategies because they add a vibrant interactive channel on which to disseminate content. Suffice to say, the distribution of user-generated content has changed markedly over the past few years. Today, organizations can tell compelling brand stories through videos, photos, and audio.

Photo sharing sites allow users to archive and share photos. Flickr, Picasa, Twitpic, Photobucket, Facebook, and Imgur all offer free photo hosting services that can be utilized by individuals and businesses alike. Instagram is often used by brands to engage younger audience members. Snapchat is also useful, but since photos and videos are only visible for a few seconds, complex marketing messages cannot easily be conveyed.

Video creation and distribution have also gained popularity among marketers because of video's rich ability to tell stories. YouTube, the highest-trafficked video-based Web site and the third-highest-trafficked site overall, allows users to upload and stream their videos to an enthusiastic and active community.[38] YouTube is not only large (in terms of visitors), but it also attracts a diverse base of users: age and gender demographics are remarkably balanced.

Many entertainment companies and movie marketers have used YouTube as a showcase for new products, specials, and movie trailers. User-generated content can

Ask Me Anything

Politicians, celebrities, and business leaders from all walks of life have used Reddit's Ask Me Anything (AMA) series to promote their issues, projects, and products. After an AMA is posted, Reddit users ask questions—sometimes complex or controversial questions—and the poster answers them as he or she chooses. Some of the site's most popular AMAs have included Bill Gates, Molly Ringwald, Snoop Lion, Neil deGrasse Tyson, Louis C.K., and President Barack Obama.[39]

also be a powerful tool for brands that can use it effectively. While YouTube is still the champ, Vine is quickly becoming another popular platform for corporate promotion.

A podcast, another type of user-generated media, is a digital audio or video file that is distributed serially for other people to listen to or watch. Podcasts can be streamed online, played on a computer, uploaded to a portable media player, or downloaded onto a smartphone. Podcasts are like radio shows that are distributed through various means and not linked to a scheduled time slot. While they have not experienced the exponential growth rates of other digital platforms, podcasts have amassed a steadily growing number of loyal devotees. For example, Etsy, an online marketplace for handmade and vintage wares, offers a podcast series introducing favorite craftspeople to the world—driving business for those individuals.

Since location site technology is relatively new, many brands are still figuring out how to best utilize Foursquare.

18-5e Social News Sites

Social news sites allow users to decide which content is promoted on a given Web site by voting that content up or down. Users post news stories and multimedia on crowdsourced sites such as Reddit for the community to vote on. The more interest from readers, the higher the story or video is ranked. Marketers have found that these sites are useful for promoting campaigns, creating conversations around related issues, and building Web site traffic.

If marketing content posted to a crowdsourced site is voted up, discussed, and shared enough to be listed among the most popular topics of the day, it can go viral across other sites, and eventually, the entire Web. Social bookmarking sites such as Delicious and StumbleUpon are similar to social news sites but the objective of their users is to collect, save, and share interesting and valuable links. On these sites, users categorize links with short, descriptive tags. Users can search the site's database of links by specific tags or can add their own tags to others' links. In this way, tags serve as the foundation for information gathering and sharing on social bookmarking sites.[40]

18-5f Location-Based Social Networking Sites

Considered by many to be the next big thing in social marketing, location sites like Foursquare and Loopt should be on every marketer's radar. Essentially, **location-based social networking sites** combine the fun of social networking with the utility of location-based GPS technology. Foursquare, one of the most popular location sites, treats location-based micronetworking as a game: Users earn badges and special statuses based on their number of visits to particular locations. Users can write and read short reviews and tips about businesses, organize meet-ups, and see which Foursquare-using friends are nearby. Foursquare updates can also be posted to linked Twitter and Facebook accounts for followers and friends to see. Location sites such as Foursquare are particularly useful social marketing tools for local businesses, especially when combined with sales promotions like coupons, special offers, contests, and events. Location sites can be harnessed to forge lasting relationships with and deeply ingrained loyalty from customers.[41] For example, a local restaurant can allow consumers to check in on Foursquare using their smartphones and receive coupons for that day's purchases. Since the location site technology is relatively new, many brands are still figuring out how best to utilize Foursquare. Facebook added Places to capitalize on this location-based technology, which allows people to "check in" and share their location with their online friends. It will be interesting to see how use of this technology grows over time.

18-5g Review Sites

Individuals tend to trust other people's opinions when it comes to purchasing.

social news sites Web sites that allow users to decide which content is promoted on a given Web site by voting that content up or down

location-based social networking sites Web sites that combine the fun of social networking with the utility of location-based GPS technology

Giving marketers the opportunity to respond their customers directly and put their business in a positive light, is why review sites like Yelp have thrived.

According to Nielsen Media Research, more than seventy percent of consumers said that they trusted online consumer opinions. This percentage is much higher than that of consumers who trust traditional advertising. Based on the early work of Amazon.com and eBay to integrate user opinions into product and seller pages, countless Web sites allowing users to voice their opinions have sprung up across every segment of the Internet market. **Review sites** allow consumers to post, read, rate, and comment on opinions regarding all kinds of products and services. For example, Yelp, the most active local review directory on the Web, combines customer critiques of local businesses with business information and elements of social networking to create an engaging, informative experience. On Yelp, users scrutinize local restaurants, fitness centers, tattoo parlors, and other businesses, each of which has a detailed profile page. Business owners and representatives can edit their organizations' pages and respond to Yelp reviews both privately and publicly. Yelp even rewards its most popular (and prolific) reviewers with Elite status. Businesses like Worthington, Ohio's Pies & Pints will throw Elite-only parties to allow these esteemed Yelpers to try out their restaurant, hoping to receive a favorable review. A Tiki Beach Party for Yelp Elites at Montreal, Canada's Le Lab garnered thirteen reviews averaging five stars out of five.[42] By giving marketers the opportunity to respond to their customers directly and put their businesses in a positive light, review

sites certainly serve as useful tools for local and national businesses.

18-5h Virtual Worlds and Online Gaming

Virtual worlds and online gaming present additional opportunities for marketers to engage with consumers. These include massive multiplayer online games (MMOGs) such as *League of Legends*, *Destiny*, and *The Elder Scrolls Online* as well as online communities (or virtual worlds) such as *Second-Life*, *Poptropica*, and *Habbo Hotel*. Although virtual worlds are unfamiliar to and even intimidating for many traditional marketers, the field is an important, viable, and growing consideration for social media marketing. Consultancy firm KZero Worldwide reported that almost 800 million people participate in some sort of virtual world experience, and the sector's annual revenue approaches $1 billion. Some of the most popular and profitable games, including *Diamond Dash* and *Farm-Ville 2*, are built on the Facebook platform. Much of these games' revenue comes from in-game advertising—virtual world environments are often fertile grounds for branded content. Organizations such as IBM and the American Cancer Society have developed profitable trade presences in *Second Life*, but others have abandoned the persistent online community as its user base has declined—the average number of users logged into *Second Life* has dropped almost 25 percent in the last four years.[43]

One area of growth is social gaming. Nearly twenty-five percent of people play games like *Words with Friends* and *Trivia Crack*, either within social networking sites like Facebook or on mobile devices. Interestingly, the typical player is a forty-five-year-old woman with a full-time job and college education (while users who play on mobile devices tend to be younger). Women are most likely to play with real-world friends or relatives as opposed to strangers. Most play multiple times per week, and more than thirty percent play daily. Facebook is by far the largest social network for gaming, though hi5 is hoping to win over more users with its large variety of games. The top five games on Facebook are *Candy Crush Saga*, *FarmVille 2*, *Texas HoldEm Poker*, *Pet Rescue Saga*, and *Dragon City*.[44] King's *Candy Crush Saga* entices more than ninety-three million users a day. These games are attractive because they can be played in just five minutes, perhaps while waiting for the train.[45] Many mobile games use mobile ads to generate revenue for the game-makers. As long as the ads are not overly intrusive, most users opt to play the free game with ads over the paid version that does not have ads.

review sites Web sites that allow consumers to post, read, rate, and comment on opinions regarding all kinds of products and services

Another popular strategy is to give an ad-free game away for free and then charge small sums of money for in-game items and power-ups. These *microtransactions* account for 21 percent of all mobile profits.[46] Though *Kim Kardashian: Hollywood* is free to download and play, for example, the game has earned more than $200 million from in-game microtransactions.[47]

Another popular type of online gaming targets a different group—MMOGs tend to draw eighteen to thirty-four-year-old males. In MMOG environments, thousands of people play simultaneously, and the games have revenues of more than $400 billion annually. Regardless of the type of experience, brands must be creative in how they integrate into games. Social and real-world-like titles are the most appropriate for marketing and advertising (as opposed to fantasy games), and promotions typically include special events, competitions, and sweepstakes. In some games (like *The Sims*), having ads increases the authenticity. For example, Nike offers shoes in *The Sims Online* that allow the player to run faster.

 # 18-6 SOCIAL MEDIA AND MOBILE TECHNOLOGY

While much of the excitement in social media has been based on Web sites and new technology uses, much of the growth lies in new platforms. These platforms include the multitude of smartphones as well as iPads and other tablets. The major implication of this development is that consumers now can access popular Web sites like Facebook, Mashable, Twitter, and Foursquare from all their various platforms.

18-6a Mobile and Smartphone Technology

Worldwide, there are more than six billion mobile phones in use, seventeen percent of which are smartphones.[48] It is no surprise, then, that the mobile platform is such an effective marketing tool—especially when targeting a younger audience. Smartphones up the ante by allowing individuals to do nearly everything they can do with a computer—from anywhere. With a smartphone in hand, reading a blog, writing an e-mail, scheduling a meeting, posting to Facebook, playing a multiplayer game, watching a video, taking a picture, using GPS, and surfing the Internet might all occur during one ten-minute bus ride. Smartphone technology, often considered the crowning achievement in digital convergence and social media integration, has opened the door to modern mobile advertising as a viable marketing strategy.

Mobile advertising has grown as much as 80 percent per year in the U.S., but that rate is expected to slow to about 50 percent per year over the next few years. Digital advertising accounted for almost 34 percent of all U.S. ad spending in 2015, and mobile advertising alone made up about a third of that.[49] There are several reasons for the recent popularity of mobile marketing. First, an effort to standardize mobile platforms has resulted in a low barrier to entry. Second, especially given mobile marketing's younger audiences, there are more consumers than ever acclimating to once-worrisome privacy and pricing policies. Third, because most people carry their smartphones with them at all times, mobile marketing is uniquely effective at garnering customer attention in real time. Fourth, mobile marketing is measurable: metrics and usage statistics make it an effective tool for gaining insight into consumer behavior. Fifth, in-store notification technology such as Apple's iBeacon can send promotional messages based on real-time interactions with customers. Finally, mobile marketing's response rate is higher than that of traditional media types like print and broadcast advertisement. Some common mobile marketing tools include:

- **SMS (short message service):** 160-character text messages sent to and from cell phones. SMS is typically integrated with other tools.

- **MMS (multimedia messaging service):** Similar to SMS but allows the attachment of images, videos, ringtones, and other multimedia to text messages.

- **Mobile Web sites (MOBI and WAP Web sites):** Web sites designed specifically for viewing and navigation on mobile devices.

- **Mobile ads:** Visual advertisements integrated into text messages, applications, and mobile Web sites. Mobile ads are often sold on a cost-per-click basis.

- **Bluetooth marketing:** A signal is sent to Bluetooth-enabled devices, allowing marketers to send targeted messages to users based on their geographic locations.

- **Smartphone applications (apps):** Software designed specifically for mobile and tablet devices.

A popular use for barcode scanning apps is the reading and processing of Quick Response (QR) codes. When scanned by a smartphone's QR reader app, a QR code takes the user to a specific site with content about or a discount for products or services. Uses range from donating to a charity by scanning the code to simply checking out the company's Web site for more information. For example, Modify Watches offers a watch face with no hands. Instead it has a QR code that, when scanned, shows the correct time.[50]

Another smartphone trend is called "near field communication" (NFC), which uses small chips hidden in or behind products that, when touched by compatible devices, will transfer the information on the chip to the device. Barnes & Noble is hoping to work with publishers to ship hardcover books containing NFC chips to Barnes & Noble stores. The chips will be embedded with editorial reviews about that book from Barnes & Noble's Web site. When a NOOK user touches the hardcover with her NOOK, the book reviews will display on her tablet, helping her make a purchase decision.[51] The Samsung Galaxy S6 smartphone can track users' eye movements and shift screen content depending on where they are looking. While a relatively new technology, eye tracking has interesting implications for mobile marketing in the near future.[52]

Finally, mobile marketing is particularly powerful when combined with geo-location platforms such as Foursquare, whereby people can "check in" to places and receive benefits and special offers. These platforms allow retailers and other businesses to incentivize multiple visits, visits at certain times of the day, and positive customer reviews.

18-6b Apps and Widgets

Given the widespread adoption of Apple's iPhone, Android-based phones, and other smartphones, it is no surprise that millions of apps have been developed for the mobile market. Dozens of new and unique apps that harness mobile technology are added to mobile marketplaces every day. While many apps perform platform-specific tasks, others convert existing content into a mobile-ready format. Whether offering new or existing content, when an app is well branded and integrated into a company's overall marketing strategy, it can create buzz and generate customer engagement.

Web widgets, also known as gadgets and badges, are software applications that run entirely within existing online platforms. Essentially, a Web widget allows a developer to embed a simple application such as a weather forecast, horoscope, or stock market ticker into a Web site, even if the developer did not write (or does not understand) the application's source code. From a marketing perspective, widgets

allow customers to display company information (such as current promotions, coupons, or news) on their own Web sites or smartphone home screens. Widgets are often cheaper than apps to develop, can extend an organization's reach beyond existing platforms, will broaden the listening system, and can make an organization easier to find.[53]

Twin Design/Shutterstock.com

18-7 THE SOCIAL MEDIA PLAN

To effectively use the tools in the social media toolbox, it is important to have a clearly outlined social media plan. The social media plan is linked to larger plans such as a promotional plan or marketing plan and should fit appropriately into the objectives and steps in those plans (for more information, review Chapters 2 and 16). It is important to research throughout the development of the social media plan to keep abreast of the rapidly changing social media world. There are six stages involved in creating an effective social media plan:

1. **Listen to customers:** This is covered in more detail in section 18-2a.

2. **Set social media objectives:** Set objectives that can be specifically accomplished through social media, with special attention to how to measure the results. Numerous metrics are available, some of which are mentioned throughout the chapter.

3. **Define strategies:** This includes examining trends and best practices in the industry.

4. **Identify the target audience:** This should line up with the target market defined in the marketing plan, but in the social media plan, pay special attention to how that audience participates and behaves online.

5. **Select the tools and platforms:** Based on the result of Step 4, choose the social media tools and platforms that will be most relevant. These choices are based on the knowledge of where the target audience participates on social media.

6. **Implement and monitor the strategy:** Social media campaigns can be fluid, so it is important to keep a close eye on what is successful and what is not. Then, based on the observations, make changes as needed. It also becomes important,

EXHIBIT 18.2 | SOCIAL MEDIA TRENDS

Trend	Change	Where Is It Now?
Yik Yak	Anonymous geolocated messaging	
Microsoft Office 365, Google Drive	Integration with file hosting	
Ello	Challengers to Facebook's dominance	
Bing	Rewards program offers prizes for using Bing Search	
The Internet of Things	Integration into wearables, appliances, apparel, and more	
Apple Pay, Google Wallet, Bitcoin, and NFC-enabled payment options	Replace credit cards with various forms of digital payment	
Loot Crate, Trunk Club, and NatureBox	Online and subscription-based personal shopping	
Twitch, Meerkat, and Periscope	Live video streaming for everybody	
Tinder and Grindr	The mainstreaming of geolocated dating apps	

therefore, to go back to the listening stage to interpret how consumers are perceiving the social media campaign.

Listening to customers and industry trends, as well as continually revising the social media plan to meet the needs of the changing social media market, are keys to successful social media marketing. There are numerous industry leaders sharing some of their best practices, and sources such as *Fast Company* and the *Wall Street Journal* report regularly on how large and small companies are successfully using social media to gain market share and sales. A good example of using social media strategies is HubSpot, a company that practices what it preaches. HubSpot advocates the benefits of building valuable content online and then using social media to pull customers to its Web site. Social engine profiles have increased HubSpot's Web site traffic, which has made its lead generation program much more effective.

18-7a The Changing World of Social Media

As you read through the chapter, some of the trends that are noted may already seem ancient to you. The rate of change in social media is astounding—usage statistics change daily for sites like Facebook and Twitter. Some things that are in the rumor mill as we write this may have exploded in popularity; others may have fizzled out without even appearing on your radar. In Exhibit 18.2, we have listed some of the items that seem to be on the brink of exploding on to the social media scene. Take a moment to fill in the current state of each in the third column. Have you heard of it? Has it come and gone? Maybe it is still rumored, or maybe it has petered out. This exercise highlights not only the speed with which social media change but also the importance of keeping tabs on rumors. Doing so may give you a competitive advantage by being able to understand and invest in the next big social media site.

STUDY TOOLS 18

LOCATED AT BACK OF THE TEXTBOOK
☐ Rip out Chapter Review Card

LOCATED AT WWW.CENGAGEBRAIN.COM
☐ Review Key Terms Flashcards and create your own

☐ Track your knowledge and understanding of key concepts in marketing

☐ Complete practice and graded quizzes to prepare for tests

☐ Complete interactive content within the MKTG Online experience

☐ View the chapter highlight boxes within the MKTG Online experience

19 | Pricing Concepts

LEARNING OUTCOMES

After studying this chapter, you will be able to…

19-1 Discuss the importance of pricing decisions to the economy and to the individual firm

19-2 List and explain a variety of pricing objectives

19-3 Explain the role of demand in price determination

19-4 Understand the concepts of dynamic pricing and yield management systems

19-5 Describe cost-oriented pricing strategies

19-6 Demonstrate how the product life cycle, competition, distribution and promotion strategies, customer demands, the Internet and extranets, and perceptions of quality can affect price

19-7 Describe the procedure for setting the right price

19-8 Identify the legal constraints on pricing decisions

19-9 Explain how discounts, geographic pricing, and other pricing tactics can be used to fine-tune a base price

little Whale/Shutterstock.com

After you finish this chapter go to **PAGE 361** for **STUDY TOOLS.**

19-1 THE IMPORTANCE OF PRICE

Price means one thing to the consumer and something else to the seller. To the consumer, it is the cost of something. To the seller, price is revenue—the primary source of profits. In the broadest sense, price allocates resources in a free-market economy. Marketing managers are frequently challenged by the task of price setting, but they know that meeting the challenge of setting the right price can have a significant impact on the firm's bottom line. Organizations that successfully manage prices do so by creating a pricing infrastructure within the company. This means defining pricing goals, searching for ways to create greater customer value, assigning authority and responsibility for pricing decisions, and creating tools and systems to continually improve pricing decisions.

19-1a What Is Price?

Price is that which is given up in an exchange to acquire a good or service. Price also plays two roles in the evaluation of product alternatives: as a measure of sacrifice and as an information cue. To some degree, these are two opposing effects.

THE SACRIFICE EFFECT OF PRICE Price is, again, "that which is given up," which means what is sacrificed to get a good or service. In the United States, the sacrifice is usually money, but it can be other things as well. It may also be time lost while waiting to acquire the good or service. Price might also include lost dignity for individuals who lose their jobs and must rely on charity.

THE INFORMATION EFFECT OF PRICE Consumers do not always choose the lowest-priced product in a category, such as shoes, cars, or wine, even when the products are otherwise similar. One explanation of this behavior, based upon research, is that we infer quality information from price. That is, higher quality equals higher price. The information effect of price may also extend to favorable price perceptions by others because higher prices can convey the prominence and status of the purchaser to other people. Thus, both a Swatch and a Rolex can tell time accurately, but they convey different meanings. The price–quality relationship will be discussed later in the chapter.

> "Trying to set the right price is one of the most stressful and pressure-filled tasks of the marketing manager."

VALUE IS BASED UPON PERCEIVED SATISFACTION Consumers are interested in obtaining a "reasonable price." "Reasonable price" really means "perceived reasonable value" at the time of the transaction. When high-end housewares retailer Williams-Sonoma launched a $279 bread maker, the company garnered only mediocre returns. Undeterred, Williams-Sonoma released a second, slightly larger bread maker with similar features for $429. The more expensive model flopped, but when it was released, sales of the smaller, less expensive model skyrocketed. Though nothing changed about the smaller model's features or marketing mix, the $429 model affected people's perceptions, making the $279 model look like a much better value.

price that which is given up in an exchange to acquire a good or service

19-1b The Importance of Price to Marketing Managers

As noted in the chapter introduction, prices are the key to revenues, which in turn are the key to profits for an organization. **Revenue** is the price charged to customers multiplied by the number of units sold. Revenue is what pays for every activity of the company: production, finance, sales, distribution, and so on. What is left over (if anything) is **profit**. Managers usually strive to charge a price that will earn a fair profit.

Price × Units = Revenue

To earn a profit, managers must choose a price that is not too high or too low—a price that equals the perceived value to target consumers. If, in consumers' minds, a price is set too high, the perceived value will be less than the cost, and sale opportunities will be lost.

19-2 PRICING OBJECTIVES

To survive in today's highly competitive marketplace, companies need pricing objectives that are specific, attainable, and measurable. Realistic pricing goals then require periodic monitoring to determine the effectiveness of the company's strategy. For convenience, pricing objectives can be divided into three categories: profit oriented, sales oriented, and status quo.

19-2a Profit-Oriented Pricing Objectives

Profit-oriented pricing objectives include profit maximization, satisfactory profits, and target return on investment.

PROFIT MAXIMIZATION *Profit maximization* means setting prices so that total revenue is as large as possible relative to total costs. Profit maximization does not always signify unreasonably high prices, however. Both price and profits depend on the type of competitive environment a firm faces, such as whether it is in a monopoly position (being the only seller) or in a much more competitive situation. Also, remember that a firm cannot charge a price higher than the

product's perceived value. Sometimes managers say that their company is trying to maximize profits—in other words, trying to make as much money as possible. Although this goal may sound impressive to stockholders, it is not good enough for planning.

In attempting to maximize profits, managers can try to expand revenue by increasing customer satisfaction, or they can attempt to reduce costs by operating more efficiently. A third possibility is to attempt to do both. Some companies may focus too much on cost reduction at the expense of the customer. Lowe's lost market share when it cut costs by reducing the number of associates on the floor. Customer service declined—and so did revenue. When firms rely too heavily on customer service, however, costs tend to rise to unacceptable levels. United States' airlines used to serve full meals on two-hour flights and offered pillows and blankets to tired customers. This proved to be unsustainable. A company can maintain or slightly cut costs while increasing customer loyalty through customer service initiatives, loyalty programs, customer relationship management programs, and allocating resources to programs that are designed to improve efficiency and reduce costs.

Airlines use to offer full meals on flights of two hours or more. Now, you are lucky to get a drink and peanuts.

revenue the price charged to customers multiplied by the number of units sold

profit revenue minus expenses

SATISFACTORY PROFITS Satisfactory profits are a reasonable level of profits. Rather than maximizing profits, many organizations strive for profits that are satisfactory to the stockholders and management—in other words, a level of profits consistent with the level of risk an organization faces. In a risky industry, a satisfactory profit may be thirty-five percent. In a low-risk industry, it might be seven percent.

TARGET RETURN ON INVESTMENT The most common profit objective is a target **return on investment (ROI)**, sometimes called the firm's return on total assets. ROI measures management's overall effectiveness in generating profits with the available assets. The higher the firm's ROI, the better off the firm is. Many companies use a target ROI as their main pricing goal. In summary, ROI is a percentage that puts a firm's profits into perspective by showing profits relative to investment.

Return on investment is calculated as follows:

$$\text{Return on investment} = \frac{\text{Net profits after taxes}}{\text{Total assets}}$$

Assume that in 2017 Johnson Controls had assets of $4.5 million, net profits of $550,000, and a target ROI of ten percent. This was the actual ROI:

$$\text{ROI} = \frac{\$550,000}{\$4,500,000} = 12.2 \text{ percent}$$

As you can see, the ROI for Johnson Controls exceeded its target, which indicates that the company prospered in 2017.

Comparing the 12.2 percent ROI with the industry average provides a more meaningful picture, however. Any ROI needs to be evaluated in terms of the competitive environment, risks in the industry, and economic conditions. Generally speaking, firms seek ROIs in the ten to thirty percent range. In some industries, such as the grocery industry, however, a return of under five percent is common and acceptable.

A company with a target ROI can predetermine its desired level of profitability. The marketing manager can use the standard, such as ten percent ROI, to determine whether a particular price and marketing mix are feasible.

In addition, however, the manager must weigh the risk of a given strategy even if the return is in the acceptable range.

19-2b Sales-Oriented Pricing Objectives

Sales-oriented pricing objectives are based on market share as reported in dollar or unit sales. Firms strive for either market share or to maximize sales.

EXHIBIT 19.1 TWO WAYS TO MEASURE MARKET SHARE (UNITS AND REVENUE)

Company	Units Sold	Unit Price	Total Revenue	Unit Market Share	Revenue Market Share
A	1,000	$1.00	$1,000	50	25
B	200	4.00	800	10	20
C	500	2.00	1,000	25	25
D	300	4.00	1,200	15	30
Total	2,000		$4,000		

MARKET SHARE **Market share** is a company's product sales as a percentage of total sales for that industry. Sales can be reported in dollars or in units of product. It is very important to know whether market share is expressed in revenue or units because the results may be different. Consider four companies competing in an industry with 2,000 total unit sales and total industry revenue of $4,000 (see Exhibit 19.1). Company A has the largest unit market share at fifty percent, but it has only twenty-five percent of the revenue market share. In contrast, Company D has only a fifteen percent unit share but the largest revenue share: thirty percent. Usually, market share is expressed in terms of revenue and not units.

Many companies believe that maintaining or increasing market share is an indicator of the effectiveness of their marketing mix. Larger market shares have indeed often meant higher profits, thanks to greater economies of scale, market power, and ability to compensate top-quality management. Conventional wisdom also says that market share and ROI are strongly related. For the most part they are; however, many companies with low market share survive and even prosper. To succeed with a low market share, companies often need to compete in industries with slow growth and few product changes—for instance, industrial supplies. Otherwise, they must vie in an industry that makes frequently bought items, such as consumer convenience goods.

The conventional wisdom about market share and profitability is not always reliable, however. Because of extreme competition in some industries, many market share leaders either do not reach their target ROI or actually lose money. Procter & Gamble switched from market share

return on investment (ROI) net profit after taxes divided by total assets

market share a company's product sales as a percentage of total sales for that industry

The 5.7 inch Galaxy Round, released in October 2013, iterates on Samsung's Galaxy Note line of phablets by introducing a curved display.

to ROI objectives after realizing that profits do not automatically follow from a large market share.

SALES MAXIMIZATION Rather than strive for market share, sometimes companies try to maximize sales. A firm with the objective of maximizing sales ignores profits, competition, and the marketing environment as long as sales are rising.

If a company is strapped for funds or faces an uncertain future, it may try to generate a maximum amount of cash in the short run. Management's task when using this objective is to calculate which price–quantity relationship generates the greatest cash revenue. Sales maximization can also be effectively used on a temporary basis to sell off excess inventory. It is not uncommon to find Christmas cards, ornaments, and other seasonal items discounted at 50 to 70 percent off retail prices after the holiday season has ended.

Maximization of cash should never be a long-run objective because cash maximization may mean little or no profitability.

19-2c Status Quo Pricing Objectives

Status quo pricing seeks to maintain existing prices or to meet the competition's prices. This third category of pricing objectives has the major advantage of requiring little planning. It is essentially a passive policy.

Often, firms competing in an industry with an established price leader simply meet the competition's prices. These industries typically have fewer price wars than those with direct price competition. In other cases, managers regularly shop competitors' stores to ensure that their prices are comparable.

Status quo pricing often leads to suboptimal pricing. This occurs because the strategy ignores customers' perceived value of both the firm's goods or services and those offered by its competitors. Status quo pricing also ignores demand and costs. Although the policy is simple to implement, it can lead to a pricing disaster.

19-3 THE DEMAND DETERMINANT OF PRICE

After marketing managers establish pricing goals, they must set specific prices to reach those goals. The price they set for each product depends mostly on two factors: the demand for the good or service and the cost to the seller for that good or service. When pricing goals are mainly sales oriented, demand considerations usually dominate. Other factors, such as distribution and promotion strategies, perceived quality, needs of large customers, the Internet, and the stage of the product life cycle, can also influence price.

19-3a The Nature of Demand

Demand is the quantity of a product that will be sold in the market at various prices for a specified period. The quantity of a product that people will buy depends on its price. The higher the price, the fewer goods or services consumers will demand. Conversely, the lower the price, the more goods or services they will demand.

Supply is the quantity of a product that will be offered to the market by a supplier or suppliers at various prices for a specified period. At higher prices, manufacturers earn more capital and can produce more products.

19-3b Elasticity of Demand

To appreciate the concept of demand , you should understand elasticity. **Elasticity of demand** refers to consumers' responsiveness or sensitivity to changes in price. **Elastic demand** is a situation in which consumer

---

status quo pricing a pricing objective that maintains existing prices or meets the competition's prices

demand the quantity of a product that will be sold in the market at various prices for a specified period

supply the quantity of a product that will be offered to the market by a supplier at various prices for a specified period

elasticity of demand consumers' responsiveness or sensitivity to changes in price

elastic demand a situation in which consumer demand is sensitive to changes in price

demand is sensitive to price changes. Conversely, **inelastic demand** means that an increase or a decrease in price will not significantly affect demand for the product.

FACTORS THAT AFFECT ELASTICITY

Several factors affect elasticity of demand, including the following:

- **Availability of substitutes:** When many substitute products are available, the consumer can easily switch from one product to another, making demand more elastic. The same is true in reverse: A person with complete renal failure will pay whatever is charged for a kidney transplant because there is no substitute.

- **Price relative to purchasing power:** If a price is so low that it is an inconsequential part of an individual's budget, demand will be inelastic. If the price of pepper doubles, for example, people won't stop putting pepper on their eggs or buying more when they run out.

- **Product durability:** Consumers often have the option of repairing durable products (like cars and washing machines) rather than replacing them, thus prolonging their useful life. In other words, people are sensitive to the price increase, and demand is more elastic.

- **A product's other uses:** The greater the number of different uses for a product, the more elastic demand tends to be. If a product has only one use, as may be true of a new medicine, the quantity purchased probably will not vary as price varies. A person will consume only the prescribed quantity, regardless of price. On the other hand, a product like steel has many possible applications. As its price falls, steel becomes more economically feasible in a wider variety of applications, thereby making demand relatively elastic.

Examples of both elastic and inelastic demand abound in everyday life. The slow recovery of the housing market following the Great Recession was in part a function of elasticity of demand. Housing prices dropped forty percent or more in cities like Phoenix, Las Vegas, and Miami. Ultimately, these low prices began bringing buyers back into the marketplace. On the other hand, demand for tickets to certain sporting and

Everett Collection/Shutterstock.com

The Rolling Stones are still selling out concerts with tickets priced at up to $400.

concert events is highly inelastic. The Rolling Stones are still selling out concerts with tickets priced at up to $400. Hershey, maker of Kisses, Milk Chocolate bars, and other classic candies, recently raised a majority of its products' prices by 8 percent. Chocolate consumption has historically been very inelastic; people tend to indulge even when prices spike.[1]

19-4 THE POWER OF DYNAMIC PRICING AND YIELD MANAGEMENT SYSTEMS

When competitive pressures are high, a company must know when it can raise prices to maximize its revenues. More and more companies are turning to **dynamic pricing** to help adjust prices. Dynamic pricing is most useful when two product or service characteristics co-exist. First, the product/service expires at a given point in time. Airline flights and vacant hotel rooms eventually lose their ability to make money, as do products with "sell before" dates such as meat and dairy items. Second, capacity is fixed well in advance and can only be increased at a high cost. For example, Delta has eight flights a day to Chicago. To increase

inelastic demand a situation in which an increase or a decrease in price will not significantly affect demand for the product

dynamic pricing a strategy whereby prices are adjusted over time to maximize a company's revenues

Dynamic Pricing to the Extreme

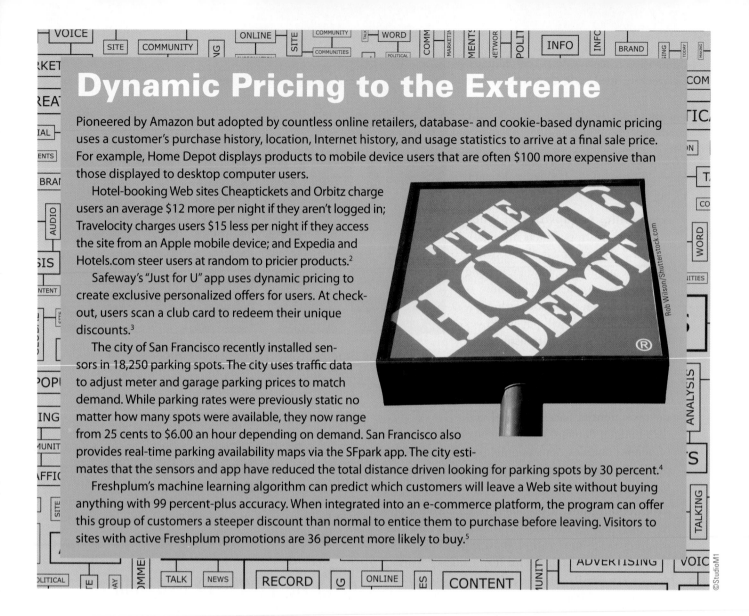

Pioneered by Amazon but adopted by countless online retailers, database- and cookie-based dynamic pricing uses a customer's purchase history, location, Internet history, and usage statistics to arrive at a final sale price. For example, Home Depot displays products to mobile device users that are often $100 more expensive than those displayed to desktop computer users.

Hotel-booking Web sites Cheaptickets and Orbitz charge users an average $12 more per night if they aren't logged in; Travelocity charges users $15 less per night if they access the site from an Apple mobile device; and Expedia and Hotels.com steer users at random to pricier products.[2]

Safeway's "Just for U" app uses dynamic pricing to create exclusive personalized offers for users. At checkout, users scan a club card to redeem their unique discounts.[3]

The city of San Francisco recently installed sensors in 18,250 parking spots. The city uses traffic data to adjust meter and garage parking prices to match demand. While parking rates were previously static no matter how many spots were available, they now range from 25 cents to $6.00 an hour depending on demand. San Francisco also provides real-time parking availability maps via the SFpark app. The city estimates that the sensors and app have reduced the total distance driven looking for parking spots by 30 percent.[4]

Freshplum's machine learning algorithm can predict which customers will leave a Web site without buying anything with 99 percent-plus accuracy. When integrated into an e-commerce platform, the program can offer this group of customers a steeper discount than normal to entice them to purchase before leaving. Visitors to sites with active Freshplum promotions are 36 percent more likely to buy.[5]

that number to twelve flights would probably be very expensive. A Hyatt hotel in Denver has 120 rooms available for February twenty-sixth. To increase the number to 160 would involve huge construction costs.

Developed in the airline industry, **yield management systems (YMS)** use complex mathematical software to profitably fill unused capacity. The software employs techniques such as discounting early purchases, limiting early sales at these discounted prices, and overbooking capacity. One of the key inputs in airlines' yield management systems is what has been the historical pattern of demand for a specific flight.

Now dynamic pricing and YMS are spreading beyond service industries as their popularity increases. The lessons of airlines and hotels are not entirely applicable to other industries, however, because plane seats and hotel beds are perishable—if they go empty, the revenue opportunity is lost forever. So it makes sense to slash prices to move toward capacity if it's possible to do so without reducing the prices that other customers pay. Cars and steel are not so perishable, but the capacity to make them is. An underused factory is a lost revenue opportunity. So it makes sense to cut prices to use up capacity if it is possible to do so while getting other customers to pay full price.

19-5 THE COST DETERMINANT OF PRICE

Sometimes companies minimize or ignore the importance of demand and decide to price their products largely or solely on the basis of costs.

yield management systems (YMS) a technique for adjusting prices that uses complex mathematical software to profitably fill unused capacity by discounting early purchases, limiting early sales at these discounted prices, and overbooking capacity

Prices determined strictly on the basis of costs may be too high for the target market, thereby reducing or eliminating sales. On the other hand, cost-based prices may be too low, causing the firm to earn a lower return than it should. Nevertheless, costs should generally be part of any price determination, if only as a floor below which a good or service must not be priced in the long run.

The idea of cost may seem simple, but it is actually a multifaceted concept, especially for producers of goods and services. A **variable cost** is a cost that varies with changes in the level of output; an example of a variable cost is the cost of materials. In contrast, a **fixed cost** does not change as output is increased or decreased. Examples include rent and executives' salaries. Costs can be used to set prices in a variety of ways. While markup pricing is relatively simple, break-even pricing uses more complicated concepts of cost.

19-5a Markup Pricing

Markup pricing, the most popular method used by wholesalers and retailers to establish a selling price, does not directly analyze the costs of production. Instead, **markup pricing** uses the cost of buying the product from the producer, plus amounts for profit and for expenses not otherwise accounted for. The total determines the selling price.

A retailer, for example, adds a certain percentage to the cost of the merchandise received to arrive at the retail price. An item that costs the retailer $1.80 and is sold for $2.20 carries a markup of forty cents, which is a markup of twenty-two percent of the cost ($0.40 ÷ $1.80). Retailers tend to discuss markup in terms of its percentage of the retail price—in this example, eighteen percent ($0.40 ÷ $2.20). The difference between the retailer's cost and the selling price (forty cents) is the gross margin.

The formula for calculating the retail price given a certain desired markup is as follows:

$$\text{Retail price} = \frac{\text{Cost}}{1 - \text{Desired return on Sales}}$$

$$= \frac{\$1.80}{1.00 - 0.18}$$

$$= \$2.20$$

If the retailer wants a 30 percent return, then:

$$\text{Retail price} = \frac{\$1.80}{1.00 - 0.30}$$

$$= \$2.57$$

The reason that retailers and others speak of markups on selling price is that many important figures in financial reports, such as gross sales and revenues, are sales figures, not cost figures.

To use markup based on cost or selling price effectively, the marketing manager must calculate an adequate gross margin—the amount added to cost to determine price. The margin must ultimately provide adequate funds to cover selling expenses and profit. Once an appropriate margin has been determined, the markup technique has the major advantage of being easy to employ.

Markups are often based on experience. For example, many small retailers markup merchandise 100 percent over cost. (In other words, they double the cost.) This tactic is called **keystoning**. Some other factors that influence markups are the merchandise's appeal to customers, past response to the markup (an implicit demand consideration), the item's promotional value, the seasonality of the good, its fashion appeal, the product's traditional selling price, and competition. Most retailers avoid any set markup because of such considerations as promotional value and seasonality.

19-5b Break-Even Pricing

Now, let's take a closer look at the relationship between sales and cost. **Break-even analysis** determines what sales volume must be reached before the company breaks even (its total costs equal total revenue) and no profits are earned.

The typical break-even model assumes a given fixed cost and a constant average variable cost (total cost divided by quantity of output). Suppose that Universal Sportswear, a hypothetical firm, has fixed costs of $2,000 and that the cost of labor and materials for each unit produced is fifty cents. Assume that it can sell up to 6,000 units of its product at $1 without having to lower its price.

Exhibit 19-2a illustrates Universal Sportswear's break-even point. As Exhibit 19.2b indicates, Universal Sportswear's total variable costs increase by fifty cents every time a new unit is produced, and total fixed costs remain constant at $2,000 regardless of the level of output. Therefore, for 4,000 units of output, Universal Sportswear has $2,000 in fixed costs and

variable cost a cost that varies with changes in the level of output

fixed cost a cost that does not change as output is increased or decreased

markup pricing the cost of buying the product from the producer, plus amounts for profit and for expenses not otherwise accounted for

keystoning the practice of marking up prices by 100 percent, or doubling the cost

break-even analysis a method of determining what sales volume must be reached before total revenue equals total costs

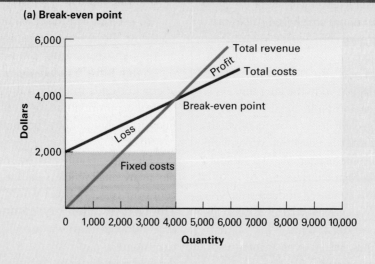

(a) Break-even point

(b) Costs and revenues

Output	Total fixed costs	Average variable costs	Total variable costs	Average total costs	Average revenue (price)	Total revenue	Total costs	Profit or loss
500	$2,000	$0.50	$ 250	$4.50	$1.00	$ 500	$2,250	($1,750)
1,000	2,000	0.50	500	2.50	1.00	1,000	2,500	(1,500)
1,500	2,000	0.50	750	1.83	1.00	1,500	2,750	(1,250)
2,000	2,000	0.50	1,000	1.50	1.00	2,000	3,000	(1,000)
2,500	2,000	0.50	1,250	1.30	1.00	2,500	3,250	(750)
3,000	2,000	0.50	1,500	1.17	1.00	3,000	3,500	(500)
3,500	2,000	0.50	1,750	1.07	1.00	3,500	3,750	(250)
*4,000	2,000	0.50	2,000	1.00	1.00	4,000	4,000	0
4,500	2,000	0.50	2,250	0.94	1.00	4,500	4,250	250
5,000	2,000	0.50	2,500	0.90	1.00	5,000	4,500	500
5,500	2,000	0.50	2,750	0.86	1.00	5,500	4,750	750
6,000	2,000	0.50	3,000	0.83	1.00	6,000	5,000	1,000

*Break-even point

$2,000 in total variable costs (4,000 units × $0.50), or $4,000 in total costs.

The advantage of break-even analysis is that it provides a quick estimate of how much the firm must sell to break even and how much profit can be earned if a higher sales volume is obtained. If a firm is operating close to the break-even point, it may want to see what can be done to reduce costs or increase sales.

Break-even analysis is not without several important limitations. Sometimes it is hard to know whether a cost is fixed or variable. If labor wins a tough guaranteed-employment contract, are the resulting expenses a fixed cost? More important than cost determination is the fact that simple break-even analysis ignores demand. How does Universal Sportswear know it can sell 4,000 units at $1? Could it sell the same 4,000 units at $2 or even $5?

19-6 OTHER DETERMINANTS OF PRICE

Other factors besides demand and costs can influence price. For example, the stages in the product life cycle, the competition, the product distribution strategy, the promotion strategy, guaranteed price matching,

demands of large customers, and the perceived quality can all affect pricing.

19-6a Stages in the Product Life Cycle

As a product moves through its life cycle (see Chapter 11), the demand for the product and the competitive conditions tend to change:

- **Introductory stage:** Management usually sets prices high during the introductory stage. One reason is that it hopes to recover its development costs quickly. In addition, demand originates in the core of the market (the customers whose needs ideally match the product's attributes) and thus is relatively inelastic. On the other hand, if the target market is highly price sensitive, management often finds it better to price the product at the market level or lower. When companies introduce highly innovative products such as consumer electronics, medical devices, and pharmaceuticals, they must properly estimate the elasticity or demand for those products. This is particularly true today, when some life cycles are measured in months, not years.

- **Growth stage:** As the product enters the growth stage, prices generally begin to stabilize for several reasons. First, competitors have entered the market, increasing the available supply. Second, the product has begun to appeal to a broader market. Finally, economies of scale are lowering costs, and the savings can be passed on to the consumer in the form of lower prices.

- **Maturity stage:** Maturity usually brings further price decreases as competition increases and inefficient, high-cost firms are eliminated. Distribution channels become a significant cost factor, however, because of the need to offer wide product lines for highly segmented markets, extensive service requirements, and the sheer number of dealers necessary to absorb high-volume production. The manufacturers that remain in the market toward the end of the maturity stage typically offer similar prices. At this stage, price increases are usually cost initiated, not demand initiated. Nor do price reductions in the late phase of maturity stimulate much demand. Because demand is limited and producers have similar cost structures, the remaining competitors will probably match price reductions.

- **Decline stage:** The final stage of the life cycle may see further price decreases as the few remaining competitors try to salvage the last vestiges of demand. When only one firm is left in the market, prices begin to stabilize. In fact, prices may eventually rise dramatically if the product survives and moves into the specialty goods category, as horse-drawn carriages and vinyl records have.

19-6b The Competition

Competition varies during the product life cycle, of course, and so at times it may strongly affect pricing decisions. Although a firm may not have any competition at first, the high prices it charges may eventually induce another firm to enter the market.

One way to counter a competitor's prices is through price matching. Recall that showrooming is inspecting a product in a retail store and then buying it online. Seventy-two percent of male buyers and 56 percent of female buyers engage in showrooming when buying electronics. Forty-seven percent of female buyers engage in showrooming when buying apparel, clothing, and accessories. Four out of ten showrooming consumers plan to buy online from the outset but want to check the product out in person before ordering.[6] Fed up with losing sales, Best Buy announced in late 2013 that it would match the prices of all local competitors as well as online retailers such as Amazon, Apple, and Walmart.com. By 2015, Best Buy's sales had increased significantly.

Another way that Best Buy gets around price matching problems is to carry exclusive versions of products that have similar specifications to ones carried in other stores but have different model or serial numbers. Best

Sergey Yechikov/Shutterstock.com

In late 2013, Best Buy announced it would match the prices of its major competitors, Amazon, Apple, and Walmart.com.

Buy's premium collection of laptops, which includes approximately thirty popular models from brands such as Dell and Samsung, are carried exclusively and therefore cannot be price matched.

19-6c Distribution Strategy

An effective distribution network can sometimes overcome other minor flaws in the marketing mix. For example, although consumers may perceive a price as being slightly higher than normal, they may buy the product anyway if it is being sold at a convenient retail outlet.

Adequate distribution for a new product can often be attained by offering a larger-than-usual profit margin to distributors. A variation on this strategy is to give dealers a large trade allowance to help offset the costs of promotion and further stimulate demand at the retail level.

19-6d The Impact of the Internet and Extranets

The Internet, **extranets** (private electronic networks), and wireless setups are linking people, machines, and companies around the globe—and connecting sellers and buyers as never before. These links are enabling buyers to quickly and easily compare products and prices, putting them in a better bargaining position. At the same time, the technology allows sellers to collect detailed data about customers' buying habits, preferences, and even spending limits so that sellers can tailor their products and prices.

USING SHOPPING BOTS A shopping bot is a program that searches the Web for the best price for a particular item that you wish to purchase. Bot is short for robot. Shopping bots theoretically give pricing power to the consumer. The more information that the shopper has, the more efficient his or her purchase decision will be.

There are two general types of shopping bots. The first is the broad-based type that searches (trawls) a wide range of product categories such as Google Shopping, Nextag, and PriceGrabber. These sites operate using a Yellow Pages type of model in that they list every retailer they can find. The second is the niche-oriented type that searches for prices for only one type of product such as consumer electronics (CNET), event tickets (Seat-Geek), or travel-related services (Kayak).

Shopping bots have been around for quite some time, and security protocols have been developed by some Internet

> **extranet** a private electronic network that links a company with its suppliers and customers

retailers to limit bot trawls. Still, shopping bots remain a powerful and impactful marketing tool to this day.

INTERNET AUCTIONS The Internet auction business is huge. Among the most popular consumer auction sites are the following:

- **www.ubid.com:** Offers a large range of product categories. "My page" consolidates all of the user's activity in one place.

- **www.ebay.com:** The most popular auction site.

- **www.bidz.com:** Buys closeout deals in very large lots and offers them online in its no-reserve auctions.

Even though consumers are spending billions on Internet auctions, business-to-business auctions are likely to be the dominant form in the future. Recently, Whirlpool began holding online auctions. Participants bid on the price of the items that they would supply to Whirlpool but with a twist: they had to include the date when Whirlpool would have to pay for the items. The company wanted to see which suppliers would offer the longest grace period before requiring payment. Five auctions held over five months helped Whirlpool uncover savings of close to $2 million and more than doubled the grace period.

Whirlpool's success is a sign that the business-to-business auction world is shifting from haggling over prices to niggling over parameters of the deal. Warranties, delivery dates, transportation methods, customer support, financing options, and quality have all become bargaining chips.

Source: eBay, Inc.

Ebay is the most popular internet auction site.

19-6e Promotion Strategy

Price is often used as a promotional tool to increase consumer interest. In many cases, consumer perceptions of a store's prices are more impactful than the actual prices themselves. Walmart, for example, has always promoted low prices. Many consumers view Target as a higher priced store than Walmart even though a recent study tracking prices on 55 items, both food and nonfood, revealed that Target's prices are consistently as low as or lower than Walmart's.[7] At the other end of the spectrum, Whole Foods is perceived as significantly more expensive than other grocery stores despite having prices that are largely in line with competitors. Whole Foods has made a concerted effort to change its pricing image by promoting lower prices and adding new lower-priced options. Similarly, Nordstrom is perceived as a pricier alternative to Macy's even though it has similar prices in many categories and lower prices in other categories. Clearly, price promotion alone does not always create a low price image. Upscale ambiance, expensive specialty offerings, premier locations, a high level of service, and a lack of price matching contribute to a high price image as well.[8]

Often, the amount saved is the most important information when promoting a discount. For example, starting with a retail price of $80, a 40 percent discount creates a savings of $32 for a net sale price of $58. Of these four numbers—80, 40, 32, and 58—the most effective one to promote is the absolute savings of $32.[9]

19-6f Demands of Large Customers

Manufacturers find that their large customers such as department stores often make specific pricing demands that the suppliers must agree to. Department stores are making greater-than-ever demands on their suppliers to cover the heavy discounts and markdowns on their own selling floors. They want suppliers to guarantee their stores' profit margins, and they insist on cash rebates if the guarantee is not met. They are also exacting fines for violations of ticketing, packing, and shipping rules. Cumulatively, the demands are nearly wiping out profits for all but the very biggest suppliers, according to fashion designers and garment makers.

Walmart is the largest retailer in the world, and the company uses that size to encourage companies to meet its needs. When Walmart decided that its grocery department needed to have everyday low prices instead of periodic rollbacks, it talked to its major suppliers, such as ConAgra, General Mills, and McCormick & Co., to discuss the possibility of offering a consistently lower price to drive business. Some companies, like ConAgra, are struggling to lower costs while grain and other ingredients are steadily increasing in price. Other companies, like Kraft, have been steadily lowering costs and are having an easier time meeting Walmart's demands. Walmart's demands are not all about keeping prices low, however. The company recently instituted a policy requiring suppliers to evaluate and disclose the full environmental costs of their products.[10] The risk of not working with Walmart? Either your product is important enough to drive traffic that Walmart keeps the item, or you lose the world's biggest sales outlet.

19-6g The Relationship of Price to Quality

As mentioned at the beginning of the chapter, when a purchase decision involves uncertainty, consumers tend to rely on a high price as a predictor of good quality. Reliance on price as an indicator of quality seems to occur for all products, but it reveals itself more strongly for some items than for others. Among the products that benefit from this phenomenon are coffee, aspirin, shampoo, clothing, furniture, whiskey, education, and many services. In the absence of other information, people typically assume that prices are higher because the products contain better materials, because they are made more carefully, or, in the case of professional services, because the provider has more expertise. A 2014 MIT study found that passengers of premier airlines like Delta and United Airlines complain about service failures ten times more often than do customers of low-cost airlines like Frontier and Southwest. Customers expect more from higher-cost airlines, so they are more likely to become upset when their expectations are not met.[11]

Customers expect more from higher-cost airlines.

Researchers have found that price promotions of higher priced, higher quality brands tend to attract more business than do similar promotions of lower priced and lower quality brands. Higher prices increase expectation and set a reference point against which people can evaluate their consumption experiences (as was demonstrated in the recent airliner example). A bad experience with a higher priced product tends to increase the level of disappointment.[12] Finally, products that generate strong emotions, such as perfumes and fine watches, tend to get more "bang for the buck" in price promotions.[13]

19-7 HOW TO SET A PRICE ON A PRODUCT

Setting the right price on a product is a four-step process, as illustrated in Exhibit 19.3 and discussed throughout this chapter:

1. Establish pricing goals.

2. Estimate demand, costs, and profits.

3. Choose a price strategy to help determine a base price.

4. Fine-tune the base price with pricing tactics.

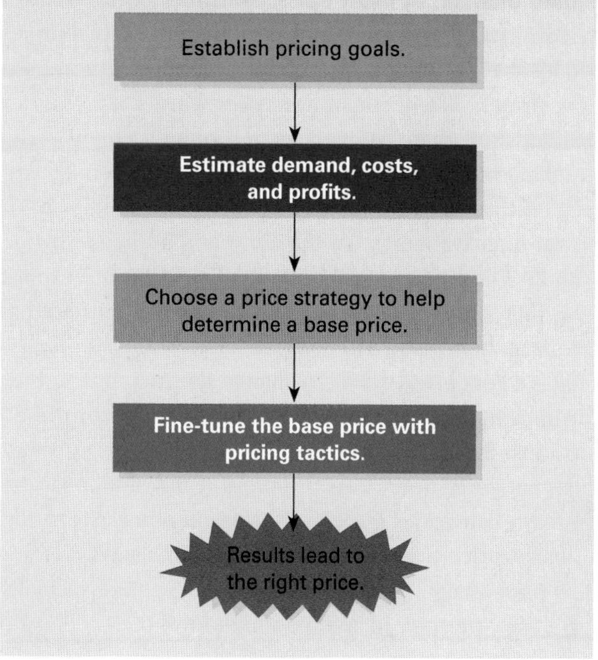

19-7a Establish Pricing Goals

The first step in setting the right price is to establish pricing goals. Recall that pricing objectives fall into three categories: profit oriented, sales oriented, and status quo. These goals are derived from the firm's overall objectives. A good understanding of the marketplace and of the consumer can sometimes tell a manager very quickly whether a goal is realistic.

All pricing objectives have trade-offs that managers must weigh. A profit maximization objective may require a bigger initial investment than the firm can commit to or wants to commit to. Reaching the desired market share often means sacrificing short-term profit because without careful management, long-term profit goals may not be met. Meeting the competition is the easiest pricing goal to implement. But can managers really afford to ignore demand

EXHIBIT 19.3 STEPS IN SETTING THE RIGHT PRICE ON A PRODUCT

Establish pricing goals.

↓

Estimate demand, costs, and profits.

↓

Choose a price strategy to help determine a base price.

↓

Fine-tune the base price with pricing tactics.

↓

Results lead to the right price.

and costs, the life cycle stage, and other considerations? When creating pricing objectives, managers must consider these trade-offs in light of the target customer, the environment, and the company's overall objectives.

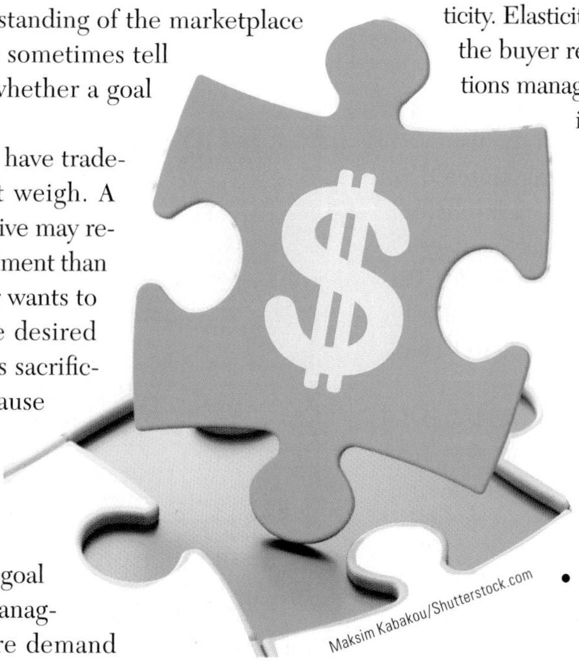

19-7b Estimate Demand, Costs, and Profits

Recall that total revenue is a function of price and quantity demanded and that quantity demanded depends on elasticity. Elasticity is a function of the perceived value to the buyer relative to the price. The types of questions managers consider when conducting marketing research on demand and elasticity are key. Some questions for market research on demand and elasticity are:

- What price is so low that consumers would question the product's quality?

- What is the highest price at which the product would still be perceived as a bargain?

- What is the price at which the product is starting to be perceived as expensive?

- What is the price at which the product becomes too expensive for the target market?

Maksim Kabakou/Shutterstock.com

After establishing pricing goals, managers should estimate total revenue at a variety of prices. This usually requires marketing research. Next, they should determine corresponding costs for each price. They are then ready to estimate how much profit, if any, and how much market share can be earned at each possible price. Managers can study the options in light of revenues, costs, and profits. In turn, this information can help determine which price can best meet the firm's pricing goals.

19-7c Choose a Price Strategy

The basic, long-term pricing framework for a good or service should be a logical extension of the pricing objectives. The marketing manager's chosen **price strategy** defines the initial price and gives direction for price movements over the product life cycle.

The price strategy sets a competitive price in a specific market segment based on a well-defined positioning strategy. Changing a price level from premium to super premium may require a change in the product itself, the target customers served, the promotional strategy, or the distribution channels.

A company's freedom in pricing a new product and devising a price strategy depends on the market conditions and the other elements of the marketing mix. If a firm launches a new item resembling several others already on the market, its pricing freedom will be restricted. To succeed, the company will probably have to charge a price close to the average market price. In contrast, a firm that introduces a totally new product with no close substitutes will have considerable pricing freedom.

The conventional wisdom is that store brands such as Target's Archer Farms and Kroger's Simple Truth should be priced lower than manufacturer's national brands. In fact, private label products are priced an average of twenty-nine percent less than their national brand counterparts.[14] However, savvy retailers doing pricing strategy research have found that store brands do not necessarily have to be cheap. When store brands are positioned as gourmet or specialty items, consumers will even pay more for them than for gourmet national brands.

Companies that do serious planning when creating a price strategy usually select from three basic approaches: price skimming, penetration pricing, and status quo pricing.

PRICE SKIMMING **Price skimming** is sometimes called a "market-plus" approach to pricing because it denotes a high price relative to the prices of competing products. The term *price skimming* is derived from the phrase "skimming the cream off the top." Companies often use this strategy for new products when the product is perceived by the target market as having unique advantages. Often companies will use skimming and then lower prices over time. This is called "sliding down the demand curve." Manufacturers sometimes maintain skimming prices throughout a product's life cycle. A manager of the factory that produces Chanel purses (retailing for over $2,000 each) told one of your authors that it takes back unsold inventory and destroys it rather than selling it at a discount.

Price skimming works best when there is strong demand for a good or service. Apple, for example, uses skimming when it brings out a new iPhone or iPad. As new models are unveiled, prices on older versions are normally lowered. Firms can also effectively use price skimming when a product is well protected legally, when it represents a technological breakthrough, or when it has in some other way blocked the entry of competitors. Managers may follow a skimming strategy when production cannot be expanded rapidly because of technological difficulties, shortages, or constraints imposed by the skill and time required to produce a product (such as fine china, for example).

A successful skimming strategy enables management to recover its product development costs quickly. Even if the market perceives an introductory price as too high, managers can lower the price. Firms often believe it is better to test the market at a high price and then lower the price if sales are too slow. Successful skimming strategies are not limited to products. Well-known athletes, lawyers, and celebrity hairstylists are experts at price skimming. Naturally, a skimming strategy will encourage competitors to enter the market.

PENETRATION PRICING **Penetration pricing** is at the opposite end of the spectrum from skimming. Penetration pricing means

Sheila Fitzgerald/Shutterstock.com

---

price strategy a basic, long-term pricing framework that establishes the initial price for a product and the intended direction for price movements over the product life cycle

price skimming a pricing policy whereby a firm charges a high introductory price, often coupled with heavy promotion

penetration pricing a pricing policy whereby a firm charges a relatively low price for a product when it is first rolled out as a way to reach the mass market

charging a relatively low price for a product when it is first rolled out as a way to reach the mass market. The low price is designed to capture a large share of a substantial market, resulting in lower production costs. If a marketing manager has made obtaining a large market share the firm's pricing objective, penetration pricing is a logical choice.

Penetration pricing does mean lower profit per unit, however. Therefore, to reach the break-even point, it requires a higher volume of sales than would a skimming policy. The recovery of product development costs may be slow. As you might expect, penetration pricing tends to discourage competition.

A penetration strategy tends to be effective in a price-sensitive market. Price should decline more rapidly when demand is elastic because the market can be expanded through a lower price. The ultra-low-cost airline Spirit is now the most profitable U.S. airline. Its cut-rate fares include little more than a seat—nearly everything else is sold à la carte (adding an average $54.00 to the ticket price). The only complimentary item in the cabin is ice. If you want water with your ice, it costs $3.00. Yet this airline maintains the highest load numbers in the industry and it continues its rapid growth. Clearly, price matters.[15]

If a firm has a low fixed cost structure and each sale provides a large contribution to those fixed costs, penetration pricing can boost sales and provide large increases in profits—but only if the market size grows or if competitors choose not to respond. Low prices can attract additional buyers to the market. The increased sales can justify production expansion or the adoption of new technologies, both of which can reduce costs. And, if firms have excess capacity, even low-priced business can provide incremental dollars toward fixed costs.

Penetration pricing can also be effective if an experience curve will cause costs per unit to drop significantly. The experience curve proposes that per-unit costs will go down as a firm's production experience increases. Manufacturers that fail to take advantage of these effects will find themselves at a competitive cost disadvantage relative to others that are further along the curve.

The big advantage of penetration pricing is that it typically discourages or blocks competition from entering a market. The disadvantage is that penetration means gearing up for mass production to sell a large volume at a low price. If the volume fails to materialize, the company will face huge losses from building or converting a factory to produce the failed product.

STATUS QUO PRICING The third basic price strategy a firm may choose is status quo pricing. Recall that this pricing strategy means charging a price identical to or very close to the competition's price. Although status quo pricing has the advantage of simplicity, its disadvantage is that the strategy may ignore demand or cost or both. If the firm is comparatively small, however, meeting the competition may be the safest route to long-term survival.

19-8 THE LEGALITY OF PRICE STRATEGY

As mentioned in Chapter 4, some pricing decisions are subject to government regulation. Among the issues that fall into this category are unfair trade practices, price fixing, price discrimination, and predatory pricing.

19-8a Unfair Trade Practices

In more than half of the United States, **unfair trade practice acts** put a floor under wholesale and retail prices. Selling below cost in these states is illegal. Wholesalers and retailers must usually take a certain minimum percentage markup on their combined merchandise cost and transportation cost. The most common markup figures are 6 percent at the retail level and 2 percent at the wholesale level. If a specific wholesaler or retailer can provide conclusive proof that operating costs are lower than the minimum required figure, lower prices may be allowed.

The intent of unfair trade practice acts is to protect small local firms from giants like Walmart, which operates very efficiently on razor-thin profit margins. State enforcement of unfair trade practice laws has generally been lax, however, partly because low prices benefit local consumers.

19-8b Price Fixing

Price fixing is an agreement between two or more firms on the price they will charge for a product. Suppose two or more executives from competing firms meet to decide how much to charge for a product or to decide

unfair trade practice acts laws that prohibit wholesalers and retailers from selling below cost

price fixing an agreement between two or more firms on the price they will charge for a product

which of them will submit the lowest bid on a certain contract. Such practices are illegal under the Sherman Act and the Federal Trade Commission Act. Offenders have received fines and sometimes prison terms. Price fixing is one area where the law is quite clear, and the U.S. Justice Department's enforcement is vigorous.

19-8c Price Discrimination

The Robinson-Patman Act of 1936 prohibits any firm from selling to two or more different buyers, within a reasonably short time, commodities (not services) of like grade and quality at different prices where the result would be to substantially lessen competition. The act also makes it illegal for a seller to offer two buyers different supplementary services and for buyers to use their purchasing power to force sellers into granting discriminatory prices or services.

The Robinson-Patman Act provides three defenses for a seller charged with price discrimination (in each case the burden is on the seller to prove the defense):

- **Cost:** A firm can charge different prices to different customers if the prices represent manufacturing or quantity discount savings.

- **Market conditions:** Price variations are justified if designed to meet fluid product or market conditions. Examples include the deterioration of perishable goods, the obsolescence of seasonal products, a distress sale under court order, and a legitimate going-out-of-business sale.

- **Competition:** A reduction in price may be necessary to stay even with the competition. Specifically, if a competitor undercuts the price quoted by a seller to a buyer, the law authorizes the seller to lower the price charged to the buyer for the product in question.

19-8d Predatory Pricing

Predatory pricing is the practice of charging a very low price for a product with the intent of driving competitors out of business or out of a market. Once competitors have been driven out, the firm raises its prices. This practice is illegal under the Sherman Act and the Federal Trade Commission Act. To prove predatory pricing, the Justice Department must show that the predator—the destructive company—explicitly tried to ruin a competitor and that the predatory price was below the predator's average variable cost.

Prosecutions for predatory pricing suffered a major setback when a federal judge threw out a predatory pricing suit filed by the Department of Justice against

American Airlines went after low-cost competitors in the Dallas area by using predatory pricing.

American Airlines. The Department of Justice argued that the definition should be updated and that the test should be whether there was any business justification, other than driving away competitors, for American's aggressive pricing. Under that definition, the Department of Justice attorneys thought they had a great case. Whenever a fledgling airline tried to get a toehold in the Dallas market, American would meet its fares and add flights. As soon as the rival retreated, American would jack its fares back up.

Under the average variable cost definition, however, the case would have been almost impossible to win. The reason is that, like a high-tech industry, the airline industry has high fixed costs and low marginal costs. Once a flight is scheduled, the marginal cost of providing a seat for an additional passenger is almost zero. Thus, it is very difficult to prove that an airline is pricing below its average variable cost. The judge was not impressed by the Department of Justice's argument, however, and kept the average variable cost definition of predatory pricing.

19-9 TACTICS FOR FINE-TUNING THE BASE PRICE

After managers understand both the legal and the marketing consequences of price strategies, they should set a **base price**—the general price level at which the company expects

> **predatory pricing** the practice of charging a very low price for a product with the intent of driving competitors out of business or out of a market

> **base price** the general price level at which the company expects to sell the good or service

to sell the good or service. The general price level is correlated with the pricing policy: above the market (price skimming), at the market (status quo pricing), or below the market (penetration pricing). The final step, then, is to fine-tune the base price.

Fine-tuning techniques are approaches that do not change the general price level. They do, however, result in changes within a general price level. These pricing tactics allow the firm to adjust for competition in certain markets, meet ever-changing government regulations, take advantage of unique demand situations, and meet promotional and positioning goals. Fine-tuning pricing tactics include various sorts of discounts, geographic pricing, and other pricing strategies.

19-9a Discounts, Allowances, Rebates, and Value-Based Pricing

A base price can be lowered through the use of discounts and the related tactics of allowances, rebates, low or zero percent financing, and value-based pricing. Managers use the various forms of discounts to encourage customers to do what they would not ordinarily do, such as paying cash rather than using credit, taking delivery out of season, or performing certain functions within a distribution channel. The following are the most common tactics:

- **Quantity discounts:** When buyers get a lower price for buying in multiple units or above a specified dollar amount, they are receiving a **quantity discount**. A **cumulative quantity discount** is a deduction from list price that applies to the buyer's total purchases made during a specific period; it is intended to encourage customer loyalty. In contrast, a **noncumulative quantity discount** is a deduction from list price that applies to a single order rather than to the total volume of orders placed during a certain period. It is intended to encourage orders in large quantities.

- **Cash discounts:** A **cash discount** is a price reduction offered to a consumer, an industrial user, or a marketing intermediary in return for prompt payment of a bill. Prompt payment saves the seller carrying charges and billing expenses and allows the seller to avoid bad debt.

- **Functional discounts:** When distribution channel intermediaries, such as wholesalers or retailers, perform a service or function for the manufacturer, they must be compensated. This compensation, typically a percentage discount from the base price, is called a **functional discount** (or **trade discount**). Functional discounts vary greatly from channel to channel, depending on the tasks performed by the intermediary.

- **Seasonal discounts:** A **seasonal discount** is a price reduction for buying merchandise out of season. It shifts the storage function to the purchaser. Seasonal discounts also enable manufacturers to maintain a steady production schedule year-round.

- **Promotional allowances:** A **promotional allowance** (also known as a **trade allowance**) is a payment to a dealer for promoting the manufacturer's products. It is both a pricing tool and a promotional device. As a pricing tool, a promotional allowance is like a functional discount. If, for example, a retailer runs an ad for a manufacturer's product, the manufacturer may pay half the cost.

- **Rebates:** A **rebate** is a cash refund given for the purchase of a product during a specific period. The advantage of a rebate over a simple price reduction for stimulating demand is that a rebate is a temporary inducement that can be taken away without altering the basic price structure. A manufacturer that uses a simple price reduction for a short time may meet resistance when trying to restore the price to its original, higher level.

- **Zero percent financing:** To get consumers into automobile showrooms, manufacturers sometimes offer zero percent financing, which enable purchasers to borrow money to pay for new cars with no interest charge. This tactic creates a huge increase in sales, but is not without its costs. A five-year interest-free car loan typically represents a loss of more than $3,000 for the car's manufacturer.

quantity discount a price reduction offered to buyers buying in multiple units or above a specified dollar amount

cumulative quantity discount a deduction from list price that applies to the buyer's total purchases made during a specific period

noncumulative quantity discount a deduction from list price that applies to a single order rather than to the total volume of orders placed during a certain period

cash discount a price reduction offered to a consumer, an industrial user, or a marketing intermediary in return for prompt payment of a bill

functional discount (trade discount) a discount to wholesalers and retailers for performing channel functions

seasonal discount a price reduction for buying merchandise out of season

promotional allowance (trade allowance) a payment to a dealer for promoting the manufacturer's products

rebate a cash refund given for the purchase of a product during a specific period

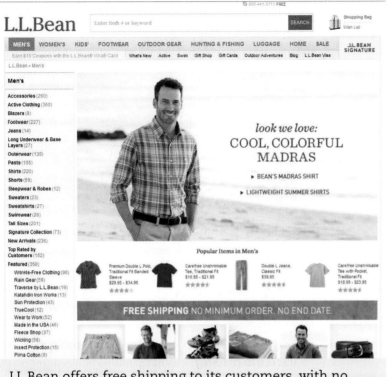

LL Bean offers free shipping to its customers, with no minimum amount.

- **Free shipping:** Free shipping is another method of lowering the price for purchasers. Zappos, Nordstrom, and L.L. Bean offer free shipping with no minimum order amount. However, since shipping is an expense to the seller, it must be built into the cost of the product. Amazon spends about $6.6 billion on shipping but brings in only about $3.1 billion in payments for shipping.[16] Amazon, Best Buy, and Gap recently raised their minimum order requirements to receive free shipping. Based on a study of 113 major retailers, a customer must spend an average of $82 on merchandise to qualify for free shipping.[17]

VALUE-BASED PRICING **Value-based pricing**, also called *value pricing*, is a pricing strategy that has grown out of the quality movement. Value-based pricing starts with the customer, considers the competition and associated costs, and then determines the appropriate price. The basic assumption is that the firm is customer driven, seeking to understand the attributes customers want in the goods and services they buy and the value of that bundle of attributes to customers. Because very few firms operate in a pure monopoly, however, a marketer using value-based pricing must also determine the value of competitive offerings to customers. Customers determine the value of a product (not just its price) relative to the value of alternatives. In value-based pricing, therefore, the price of the product is set at a level that seems to the customer to be a good price compared with the prices of other options.

Research has found that loyal customers become even more loyal when they receive discounts. Also, customers who are loyal because of superior service and quality are less likely to bargain over price.[18]

19-9b Geographic Pricing

Because many sellers ship their wares to a nationwide or even a worldwide market, the cost of freight can greatly affect the total cost of a product. Sellers may use several different geographic pricing tactics to moderate the impact of freight costs on distant customers. The following methods of geographic pricing are the most common:

- **FOB origin pricing:** **FOB origin pricing**, also called FOB factory or FOB shipping point, is a price tactic that requires the buyer to absorb the freight costs from the shipping point ("free on board"). The farther buyers are from sellers, the more they pay, because transportation costs generally increase with the distance merchandise is shipped.

- **Uniform delivered pricing:** If the marketing manager wants total costs, including freight, to be equal for all purchasers of identical products, the firm will adopt uniform delivered pricing, or "postage stamp" pricing. With **uniform delivered pricing**, the seller pays the actual freight charges and bills every purchaser an identical, flat freight charge. This is sometimes called *postage stamp pricing* because a person can send a letter across the street or across the country for the same price.

- **Zone pricing:** A marketing manager who wants to equalize total costs among buyers within large geographic areas—but not necessarily all of the seller's

value-based pricing setting the price at a level that seems to the customer to be a good price compared to the prices of other options

FOB origin pricing a price tactic that requires the buyer to absorb the freight costs from the shipping point ("free on board")

uniform delivered pricing a price tactic in which the seller pays the actual freight charges and bills every purchaser an identical, flat freight charge

market area—may modify the base price with a zone-pricing tactic. **Zone pricing** is a modification of uniform delivered pricing. Rather than using a uniform freight rate for the entire United States (or its total market), the firm divides it into segments or zones and charges a flat freight rate to all customers in a given zone.

- **Freight absorption pricing:** In **freight absorption pricing**, the seller pays all or part of the actual freight charges and does not pass them on to the buyer. The manager may use this tactic in intensely competitive areas or as a way to break into new market areas.

- **Basing-point pricing:** With **basing-point pricing**, the seller designates a location as a basing point and charges all buyers the freight cost from that point, regardless of the city from which the goods are shipped. Thanks to several adverse court rulings, basing-point pricing has waned in popularity. Freight fees charged when none were actually incurred, called *phantom freight*, have been declared illegal.

19-9c Other Pricing Tactics

Unlike geographic pricing, other pricing tactics are unique and defy neat categorization. Managers use these tactics for various reasons—for example, to stimulate demand for specific products, to increase store patronage, and to offer a wider variety of merchandise at a specific price point. Such pricing tactics include a single-price tactic, flexible pricing, professional services pricing, price lining, leader pricing, bait pricing, odd–even pricing, price bundling, and two-part pricing.

SINGLE-PRICE TACTIC

A merchant using a **single-price tactic** offers all goods and services at the same price (or perhaps two or three prices). Dollar Tree and Dollar Bill chains sell everything for $1 or less. Such a strategy can be quite

Pavel L Photo and Video/Shutterstock.com

Flexible pricing allows a seller to close a sale with price-conscious consumers.

successful. The 280-store chain 99 Cents Only sold for $1.6 billion.[19]

FLEXIBLE PRICING **Flexible pricing** (or **variable pricing**) means that different customers pay different prices for essentially the same merchandise bought in equal quantities. This tactic is often found in the sale of shopping goods, specialty merchandise, and most industrial goods except supply items. Car dealers and many appliance retailers commonly follow the practice. It allows the seller to adjust for competition by meeting another seller's price. Thus, a marketing manager with a status quo pricing objective might readily adopt the tactic. Flexible pricing also enables the seller to close a sale with price-conscious consumers.

The obvious disadvantages of flexible pricing are the lack of consistent profit margins, the potential ill will of high-paying purchasers, the tendency for salespeople to automatically lower the price to make a sale, and the possibility of a price war among sellers.

PROFESSIONAL SERVICES PRICING Professional services pricing is used by people with lengthy experience, training, and often certification by a licensing board—for example, lawyers, physicians, and family counselors. Professionals sometimes charge customers at an hourly rate, but sometimes fees are based on the solution of a problem or performance of an act (such as an eye examination) rather than on the actual time involved.

Those who use professional pricing have an ethical responsibility not to overcharge a customer. Because demand is sometimes highly inelastic, such as when a person requires heart surgery to survive, there may be a temptation to charge "all the traffic will bear."

PRICE LINING When a seller establishes a series of prices for a type of merchandise, it creates a price line. **Price lining** is the practice of offering a product line with several items at specific price points. Wireless providers use price lining for cell phones that are purchased with a two-year contract. The top tier is usually priced at $299 (the highest the market will pay), and subsequent tiers are $249, $199, $149, $99, and $49.

Price lining reduces confusion for both the salesperson and the consumer. The buyer may be offered a wider variety of merchandise at each established price. Price lines may also enable a seller to reach several market segments. For buyers, the question of price may be quite simple: all they have to do is find a suitable product at the predetermined price. Moreover, price lining is a valuable tactic for the marketing manager, because the firm may be able to carry a smaller total inventory than it could without price lines. The results may include fewer markdowns, simplified purchasing, and lower inventory carrying charges.

Price lines also present drawbacks, especially if costs are continually rising. Sellers can offset rising costs in three ways. First, they can begin stocking lower-quality merchandise at each price point. Second, sellers can change the prices, although frequent price line changes confuse buyers. Third, sellers can accept lower profit margins and hold quality and prices constant. This third alternative has short-run benefits, but its long-run handicaps may drive sellers out of business.

LEADER PRICING **Leader pricing** (or **loss-leader pricing**) is an attempt by the marketing manager to attract customers by selling a product near or even below cost in the hope that shoppers will buy other items once they are in the store. This type of pricing appears weekly in the newspaper advertising of supermarkets. Leader pricing is normally used on well-known items that consumers can easily recognize as bargains.

Leader pricing is not limited to products. Health clubs offer a one-month free trial as a loss leader.

BAIT PRICING In contrast to leader pricing, which is a genuine attempt to give the consumer a reduced price, bait pricing is deceptive. **Bait pricing** tries to get consumers into a store through false or misleading price advertising and then uses high-pressure selling to persuade them to buy more expensive merchandise. You may have seen this ad or a similar one:

REPOSSESSED . . . Singer slant-needle sewing machine . . . take over 8 payments of $5.10 per month . . . ABC Sewing Center.

This is bait. When a customer goes in to see the machine, a salesperson says that it has just been sold or else shows the prospective buyer a piece of junk. Then the salesperson says, "But I've got a really good deal on this fine new model." This is the switch that may cause a susceptible consumer to walk out with a $400 machine. The Federal Trade Commission considers bait pricing a deceptive act and has banned its use in interstate commerce. Most states also ban bait pricing, but sometimes enforcement is lax.

ODD-EVEN PRICING **Odd-even pricing** (or **psychological pricing**) means pricing at odd-numbered prices to connote a bargain and pricing at even-numbered prices to imply quality. For years, many retailers have priced their products in odd numbers—for example, $99.95—to make consumers feel they are paying a lower price for the product. Even-numbered pricing is often used for "prestige" items, such as a fine perfume at $100 a bottle or a good watch at $1,000. The demand curve for such items would also be sawtoothed, except that the outside edges would represent even-numbered prices and, therefore, elastic demand.

PRICE BUNDLING **Price bundling** is marketing two or more products in a single package for a special price. For example, Microsoft offers "suites" of software that bundle spreadsheets, word processing, graphics, e-mail, Internet access, and groupware for networks of microcomputers. Price bundling can stimulate demand for the bundled items if the target market perceives the price as a good value.

Services like hotels and airlines sell a perishable commodity (hotel rooms and airline seats) with relatively fixed costs. Bundling can be an important income stream for these businesses because the variable costs tend to be low—for instance, the cost of cleaning a hotel room. To account for this variability, hotels sometimes charge a resort fee that covers things like use of the gym, pool, and WiFi.

Bundling is also widely used in the telecommunications industry.

---

price lining the practice of offering a product line with several items at specific price points

leader pricing (loss-leader pricing) a price tactic in which a product is sold near or even below cost in the hope that shoppers will buy other items once they are in the store

bait pricing a price tactic that tries to get consumers into a store through false or misleading price advertising and then uses high-pressure selling to persuade consumers to buy more expensive merchandise

odd-even pricing (psychological pricing) a price tactic that uses odd-numbered prices to connote bargains and even-numbered prices to imply quality

price bundling marketing two or more products in a single package for a special price

Companies offer local service, long distance, DSL Internet service, wireless, and even cable television in various bundled configurations. Telecom companies use bundling as a way to protect their market share and fight off competition by locking customers into a group of services. For consumers, comparison shopping may be difficult since they may not be able to determine how much they are really paying for each component of the bundle.

You inevitably encounter bundling when you go to a fast food restaurant. McDonald's Happy Meals and Value Meals are bundles, and customers can trade up these bundles by super sizing them. Super sizing provides a greater value to the customer and creates more profits for the fast food chain.

TWO-PART PRICING **Two-part pricing** means establishing two separate charges to consume a single good or service. Consumers sometimes prefer two-part pricing because they are uncertain about the number and the types of activities they might use at places like an amusement park. Also, the people who use a service most often pay a higher total price. Two-part pricing can increase a seller's revenue by attracting consumers who would not pay a high fee even for unlimited use. For example, a health club might be able to sell only 100 memberships at $700 annually with unlimited use of facilities, for a total revenue of $70,000. However, it could sell 900 memberships at $200 with a guarantee of using the racquetball courts ten times a month. Every use over ten would require the member to pay a $5 fee. Thus, membership revenue would provide a base of $180,000, with some additional usage fees throughout the year.

HamsterMan/Shutterstock.com

> **two-part pricing** a price tactic that charges two separate amounts to consume a single good or service
>
> **consumer penalty** an extra fee paid by the consumer for violating the terms of the purchase agreement

PAY WHAT YOU WANT To many people, paying what you want or what you think something is worth is a very risky tactic. Obviously, it would not work for expensive durables like automobiles. Imagine someone paying $1 for a new BMW! Yet this model has worked in varying degrees in digital media marketplaces, restaurants, and other service businesses. One of your authors has patronized a restaurant close to campus that asks diners to pay what they think their meals are worth. After several years, the restaurant is still in business. The owner says that the average lunch donation is around $8 for lunch. Social pressures can come into play in a "pay what you want" environment because an individual does not want to appear poor or cheap to his or her peers.

19-9d Consumer Penalties

More and more businesses are adopting **consumer penalties**—extra fees paid by consumers for violating the terms of a purchase agreement. Airlines often charge a fee for changing a return date on a ticket. Businesses impose consumer penalties for two reasons: they will allegedly (1) suffer an irrevocable revenue loss and/or (2) incur significant additional transaction costs should customers be unable or unwilling to complete their purchase obligations. For the company, these customer payments are part of doing business in a highly competitive marketplace. With profit margins in many companies increasingly coming under pressure, organizations are looking to stem losses resulting from customers not meeting their obligations. Some medical professionals charge a penalty fee if you don't show up for an appointment. However, the perceived unfairness of a penalty may affect some consumers' willingness to patronize a business in the future.

STUDY TOOLS 19

LOCATED AT BACK OF THE TEXTBOOK
☐ Rip out Chapter Review Card

LOCATED AT WWW.CENGAGEBRAIN.COM
☐ Review Key Terms Flashcards and create your own

☐ Track your knowledge & understanding of key concepts in marketing

☐ Complete practice and graded quizzes to prepare for tests

☐ Complete interactive content within the MKTG Online experience

☐ View the chapter highlight boxes within the MKTG Online experience

ENDNOTES

1

1. "Definition of Marketing," *American Marketing Association*, www.marketingpower.com/AboutAMA/Pages/DefinitionofMarketing.aspx (Accessed January 26 , 2015).

2. Lydia Dishman, "Secrets of America's Happiest Companies," *Fast Company*, January 10, 2013, www.fastcompany.com/3004595/secrets-americas-happiest-companies (Accessed January 26, 2015).

3. "Fortune 100 Best Companies to Work For," *CNN*, http://money.cnn.com/magazines/fortune/best-companies/ (Accessed January 25, 2015).

4. Philip Kotler and Kevin Lane Keller, *A Framework for Marketing Management*, 5th ed. (Upper Saddle River, NJ: Prentice Hall, 2011), 4–5.

5. Josh Lowensohn, "Apple's Thunderbolt Cable Gets a Price Drop, Shorter Version," *CNET*, January 9, 2013, http://news.*CNET*.com/8301-13579_3-57563157-37/apples-thunderbolt-cable-gets-a-price-drop-shorter-version (Accessed January 10, 2015).

6. Mark J. Miller, "Kellogg's is Open for Breakfast – and Your Opinion on its Brands," *Brand Channel*, January 20, 2015, www.brandchannel.com/home/post/2015/01/20/150120-Kellogg-Open-for-Breakfast (Accessed February 20, 2015).

7. "2014 U.S. Customer Service Index (CSI) Study," *J.D. Power and Associates*, January 26, 2015, http://www.jdpower.com/press-releases/2014-us-customer-service-index-csi (Accessed February 20, 2015).

8. Ian Paul, "RIM at CES: 5 Things to Know about BlackBerry 10," *PC World*, January 10, 2013, www.pcworld.com/article/2024740/rim-at-ces-5-things-to-know-about-blackberry-10.html (Accessed January 26, 2015).

9. "The 'Green' Gap between Environmental Concerns and the Cash Register," *Nielsen Wire*, August 31, 2011, http://blog.nielsen.com/nielsenwire/global/the-green-gap-between-environmental-concerns-and-the-cash-register (Accessed January 25, 2015).

10. Marc Gunther, "Unilever's CEO has a green thumb," *Fortune*, June 10, 2013, 125–130, http://connection.ebscohost.com/c/articles/89584471/unilevers-ceo-has-green-thumb (Accessed January 28, 2015).

11. A.G. Laffey and Ron Charon, cited in George S. Day and Christine Moorman, *Strategy from the Outside In: Profiting from Customer Value*, (New York City, NY: McGraw-Hill, 2010), 235.

12. Day and Moorman, 261–262.

13. "The Customer Is Not an Interruption in Our Work; He Is the Purpose of It," *Quote Investigator*, August 2, 2012, http://quoteinvestigator.com/2012/08/02/gandhi-customer (Accessed January 28, 2015).

14. Day and Moorman, 4.

15. *Ibid.*

16. "Using Advertising to Engage the Price Sensitive Consumer," *Dunnhumby*, http://info.dunnhumby.com/pricesensitivity2013 (Accessed January 29, 2015).

17. Eric Wilson, "Social Shopping: Everybody Wants In," *New York Times*, March 25, 2012, www.nytimes.com/imagepages/2012/03/25/fashion/25SOCIALSHOP_GRAPHIC.html?scp=1&sq=social%20shopping&st=cse (Accessed January 28, 2015).

18. Douglas A. McIntyre, Alexander Kent, Alexander E.M. Hess, Thomas C. Frolich and Ashley C. Allen, "Customer Service Hall of Shame," http://finance.yahoo.com/news/customer-hall-shame-161938050.html (Accessed January 29, 2015).

19. "Coastal.com Receives STELLAService Elite Seal for Outstanding Customer Service," *Fort Mill Times*, January 2, 2013, http://www.businesswire.com/news/home/20130102005748/en/Coastal.com-Receives-STELLAService-Elite-Seal-Outstanding-Customer (Accessed January 28, 2015).

20. Rosa Say, "The Six Basic Needs of Customers," *Lifehack*, April 27, 2013, www.lifehack.org/articles/work/the-six-basic-needs-of-customers.html (Accessed February 11, 2015).

21. Matt Granite, "Who Has the Best Customer Service," *WTSP*, January 11, 2013, www.wtsp.com/news/article/291523/397/Who-has-the-best-customer-service (Accessed January 28, 2015).

22. Harley Manning, "How The 'Most Improved' Companies Raised Their Customer Experience Game Last Year," *Harley Manning's Blog*, April 25, 2011, http://blogs.forrester.com/harley_manning/11-04-25-how_the_most_improved_companies_raised_their_customer_experience_game_last_year (Accessed January 29, 2015).

23. Jason Fried, "Marketing Without Marketing," *INC.*, December 2013/January 2014, 116.

24. Douglas A. McIntyre, Alexander Kent, Alexander E.M. Hess, Thomas C. Frolich and Ashley C. Allen, "Customer Service Hall of Shame."

25. David Kirkaday, "12 Service Values Ritz Carlton Uses (And You Can Too)," http://www.davidkirkaldy.com/12-service-values-ritz-carlton-uses-and-you-can-too/ (Accessed January 28, 2015).

26. Nicole Singleton, "'We're in the Business of Making People Better,'" *The Blount Countian*, January 2, 2013, http://www.blountcountian.com/news/2013-01-02/News/Were_in_the_business_of_making_people_better.html (Accessed January 30, 2015).

27. Shalini Ramachandran and Jeffrey A. Trachtenberg, "End of Era for Britannica," *Wall Street Journal*, March 14, 2013, http://online.wsj.com/news/articles/SB10001424052702304450004577280143364147250 (Accessed January 30, 2015).

28. Ekaterina Walter, "The Simple Secret of Business Innovation and Personal Growth," *Forbes*, November 26, 2013, http://www.forbes.com/sites/ekaterinawalter/2013/11/26/the-simple-secret-of-business-innovation-and-personal-growth/ (Accessed February 1, 2015).

29. "Yaris—It's a Car!" *Toyota*, www.toyota.com/itsacar (Accessed January 31, 2015).

30. Peter Dahlstrom and David Edelman, "The Coming Era of 'On-Demand' Marketing," *McKinsey*, April 2013, www.mckinsey.com/insights/marketing_sales/the_coming_era_of_on-demand_marketing (Accessed January 31, 2015).

31. U.S. Census Bureau, "U.S. & World Population Clocks," January 31, 2015, www.census.gov/main/www/popclock.html (Accessed February 20, 2015).

32. Nina Golgowski, "Average American Consumes One Ton of Food a Year While Equating a Gallon of Soda a Week," *Daily Mail*, January 1, 2012, www.dailymail.co.uk/news/article-2080940/Average-American-consumes-ton-food-year-equating-gallon-soda-week.html (Accessed January 14, 2014).

2

1. Dale Buss, "McDonald's Trims Menu, Expands Customization to Turn Around Brand," *Brand Channel*, December 11, 2014, www.brandchannel.com/home/post/2014/12/11/141211-McDonalds-DIY-Burgers.aspx?utm_campaign=141211-McDonalds-DIY-Burgers&utm_source=newsletter&utm_medium=email (Accessed February 8, 2015)

2. Barry Silverstein, "Coach Stretches Itself Thin with Brand Extensions as Sales Continue to Fall," *Brand Channel*, October 23, 2013, www.brandchannel.com/home/post/Coach-Brand-Struggles-102313.aspx (Accessed February 8, 2015).

3. Dale Buss, "Starbucks Goes Back to the Bean in 'Big Bet' on Upscale Coffee Lovers," *Brand Channel*, December 5, 2014, www.brandchannel.com/home/post/141205-Starbucks-Roastery.aspx (Accessed February 8, 2015).

4. Dan Caplinger, "Why Amazon.com, Zynga, and Deckers Outdoor Soared Today," *The Motley Fool*, October 25, 2013, http://www.fool.com/investing/general/2013/10/25/why-amazoncom-zynga-and-deckers-outdoor-soared-tod.aspx (Accessed February 11, 2015).

5. Troy L. Smith, "Frontier Inks Partnership to Provide Green Electricity," *Rochester Business Journal*, December 18, 2012, www.rbj.net/article.asp?aID=193463 (Accessed February 10, 2015).

6. Casey Newton, "Image Is Everything: Beats Music Bets on Style and Celebrity to Take On iTunes," *The Verge*, January 21, 2014, www.theverge.com/2014/1/21/5327594/image-is-everything-beats-music-bets-style-and-celebrity-take-on-itunes (Accessed February 11, 2015).

7. David Lipke, "Ugg Goes Upscale with Men's Collection Line," *Women's Wear Daily*, March 28, 2012, www.wwd.com/menswear-news/clothing-furnishings/ugg-goes-upscale-with-mens-collection-line-5833195 (Accessed February 10, 2015).

8. "GoPro Hero 3 HD Camera Picked as Top Device in 2013 according to iTrustNews," *PRWeb*, January 5, 2013, www.prweb.com/releases/prwebgopro-hero-3/gopro-hero-hd/prweb10293699.htmp (Accessed February 10, 2015).

9. Douglas Imaralu, "Can Africa Save Blackberry?" *Ventures*, May 30, 2014, www.ventures-africa.com/2014/05/can-africa-save-blackberry/ (Accessed February 8, 2015).

10. "Church's Chicken Purple Pepper Sauce Back by Popular Demand and Brand New Honey Buffalo BBQ Sauce to Complement Church's Fan Favorite Chicken Strips," *Restaurant News Release*, January 13, 2014, www.restaurantnewsrelease.com/churchs-chicken-purple-pepper-sauce-back-by-popular-demand-and-brand-new-honey-buffalo-bbq-sauce-to-complement-churchs-fan-favorite-tender-strips/8534625/ (Accessed February 12, 2015).

11. Peter Burrows and Jim Aley, "Why the iPad's Success May Spell the End of the Computer Industry as We Know It," *Bloomberg Businessweek*, March 26–April 1, 2012, 4–5. http://magsreview.com/bloomberg-businessweek/bloomberg-businessweek-march-26-2012/3264-nice-try.html (Accessed February 10, 2015).

12. Dave Walker, "'Under the Gunn,' Starring 'Project Runway's' Tim Gunn, Debuts on Lifetime," *NOLA*, January 16, 2014, http://www.nola.com/tv/index.ssf/2014/01/under_the_gunn_starring_projec.html (Accessed February 12, 2015).

13. Dale Buss, "To Stay Fit and Nimble in Slow Market, Nestle Plans to Shed Underperforming Brands," *Brand Channel*, October 4, 2013, www.brandchannel.com/home/post/2013/10/04/Nestle-Underperforming-Brands-100413.aspx (Accessed February 10, 2015).

14. Matthew Garrahan, "Dr Dre Beats New Paths in Music," *Financial Times*, January 11, 2013, www.ft.com/intl/cms/s/2/70a003d4-5bd7-11e2-bf31-00144feab49a.html (Accessed February 15, 2015); Todd Martens, "Beats Aligns with TopSpin, Picks Daisy Subscription Service Chief," January 10, 2013, www.latimes.com/entertainment/envelope/cotown/la-et-ct-beats-partners-with-topspin-daisy-subscription-service-20130110,0,305852.story (Accessed January 10, 2014).

15. "Ben & Jerry's Ice Cream - Ben & Jerry's Mission Statement," Ben & Jerry's, www.benjerry.com/activism/mission-statement (Accessed February 10, 2015).

16. Damon Poeter, "Report: Dell 'In Talks' to Go Private," *PC Magazine*, January 14, 2013, www.pcmag.com/article2/0,2817,2414282,00.asp (Accessed February 11, 2015); Donna Guglielmo, "Dell Officially Goes Private: Inside the Nastiest Tech Buyout Ever," *Forbes.com*, October 30, 2013, www.forbes.com/sites/connieguglielmo/2013/10/30/you-wont-have-michael-dell-to-kick-around-anymore/ (Accessed February 12, 2015).

17. Sheila Shayon, "Kodak Emerges from Bankruptcy with Focus on Digital Imaging, Commercial Printing," *Brand Channel*, April 9, 2013, www.brandchannel.com/home/post/2013/09/04/Kodak-Emerges-From-Bankruptcy (Accessed February 12, 2015).

18. Meg Handley, "Should the U.S. Export Natural Gas?," *U.S. News & World Report*, January 10, 2013, www.usnews.com/news/articles/2013/01/10/should-the-us-export-natural-gas (Accessed February 12, 2015).

19. David Aaker, "Why Uniqlo is Winning," *Marketing News*, January 2015, p. 24.

20. "Blue Bell History," www.bluebell.com/the_little_creamery/our_history.html (Accessed February 12, 2015).

21. "Our Story," *The Chef's Garden*, www.chefs-garden.com/our-story (Accessed January 5, 2014); "Research and Development," *The Chef's Garden*, www.chefs-garden.com/research-and-development (Accessed February 12, 2015).

22. Claire Atlinson, "Redbox Instant to Allow Subscribers to Stream Movies Straight to TVs," *New York Post*, January 10, 2013, www.nypost.com/p/news/business/up_stream_swim_SbrwwvfABL6e2EDfPJ7n2H (Accessed February 12, 2015).

23. "How to Play the Email Game," *The Email Game*, http://emailgame.baydin.com/index.html (Accessed February 12, 2015).

24. "Does Google's Lean Management Structure Make Them Even More Competitive?" *Collaboration*, February 23, 2014, www.collaboration-llc.com/blog/2014/02/23/does-googles-lean-management-structure-make-them-even-more-competitive/ (Accessed February 13, 2015).

3

1. "Social Control: From Hunter Gatherer Bands to the United Nations." *Anthropology Now*, April 17, 2014, http://anthropologynow.wordpress.com/tag/social-control (Accessed January 16, 2015).

2. "Fast-Food Marketers Target Kids in Certain Socioeconomic Groups More Than Others Study Shows." *Marketing News*, January 2015, 4.

3. *Ibid.*

4. Kimberlee Morrison, "Yelp Pays $450,000 FTC fine for COPPA Violation," *Social Times*, September 22, 2014, www.adweek.com/socialtimes/yelp-pays-450000-ftc-fine-coppa-violation/204977 (Accessed January, 14, 2015).

5. "Google to Launch Kid-Friendly Versions of Chrome, YouTube, Others in 2015," *Ars Technica*, December 3, 2014, http://arstechnica.com/gadgets/2014/12/google-to-launch-kid-friendly-versions-of-chrome-youtube-others-in-2015/ (Accessed January 13, 2015).

6. "Keystone XL Pipeline Project," *TransCanada*, http://keystone-xl.com/?gclid=CI-bwr3_mMMCFUok7A.od.xQAJw (Accessed January 13, 2015).

7. Rose Ann DeMoro, "10 Reasons to Oppose the Keystone XL Pipeline," *Huffington Post*, April 20, 2014, www.huffingtonpost.com/rose-ann-demoro/10-reasons-to-oppose-the-_1_b_4791713.html (Accessed January 13, 2015).

8. Catherine Rainbow, "Descriptions of Ethical Theories and Principles," *Davidson College*, www.bio.davidson.edu/people/kabernd/indep/carainbow/Theories.htm (Accessed January 10, 2015). Reprinted with permission.

9. "Relativism," *Vocabulary.com*, www.vocabulary.com/dictionary/relativism (Accessed January 20, 2014).

10. "Virtue Ethics," *Ethics*, http://ethicsmorals.com/ethicsvirtue.html (Accessed January 10, 2015).

11. "A Mammoth Guilt Trip," *The Economist*, August 20, 2014, 21-24.

12. "Moral Development: Lawrence Kohlberg and Carol Gilligan," *Academia.edu*, www.academia.edu/7829090/Moral_Development_Lawrence_Kohlberg_and_Carol_Gilligan (Accessed January 11, 2015).

13. Anusorn Singhapakdi, Scott Vitell, and Kenneth Kraft, "Moral Intensity and Ethical Decision Making of Marketing Professionals," *Journal of Business Research*, 36, no. 3, (1996): 245–255; Ishmael Akaah and Edward Riordan, "Judgments of Marketing Professionals about Ethical Issues in Marketing Research: A Replication and Extension," *Journal of Marketing Research*, 26, no. 1, (1989): 112–120; see also Shelby Hunt, Lawrence Chonko, and James Wilcox, "Ethical Problems of Marketing Researchers," *Journal of Marketing Research*, 21, no. 3, (1984): 309–324; Kenneth Andrews, "Ethics in Practice," *Harvard Business Review*, September 1989, 99–104; Thomas Dunfee, Craig Smith, and William T. Ross, Jr., "Social Contracts and Marketing Ethics," *Journal of Marketing*, 63, no. 3, (1999): 14–32; Jay Handelman and Stephen Arnold, "The Role of Marketing Actions with a Social Dimension: Appeals to the Institutional Environment," *Journal of Marketing*, 63, no. 3 (1999): 33–48; David Turnipseed, "Are Good Soldiers Good? Exploring the Link between Organizational Citizenship Behavior and Personal Ethics," *Journal of Business Research*, 55, no. 1, (2002): 1–15; and O.C. Ferrell, John Fraedrich, and Linda Ferrell, *Business Ethics: Ethical Decision Making and Cases*. 10th ed. (Stamford, CT: Cengage Learning) 2015, 128-137.

14. "A Strong Ethical Culture Is Key to Cutting Misconduct on the Job," *Ethics Resource Center*, June 23, 2010, http://ethics.org/news/strong-ethical-culture-key-cutting-misconduct-job (Accessed January 12, 2015); "Workplace Ethics in Transition," *Ethics.org*, www.ethics.org/resource/webcasts (Accessed January 12, 2015).

15. *Ibid.*

16. Brittany Umar, "CVS Says Not Selling Cigarettes Is the Right Thing to Do," *The Street*, February 5, 2014, www.thestreet.com/video/12310460/cvs-says-quitting-selling-cigarettes-is-the-right-thing-to-do.html (Accessed February 13, 2014).

17. Author's estimate.

18. "Code of Conduct," *Google*, http://investor.google.com/corporate/code-of-conduct.html (Accessed January 21, 2015).

19. Joe Mont, "Ethics Survey Finds Historically Low Rate of Workplace Misdeeds," *Compliance Week*, February 4, 2014, www.complianceweek.com/ethics-survey-finds-historically-low-rate-of-workplace-misdeeds/article/332690/ (Accessed January 19, 2015).

20. Joe Mont, "Ethics Survey Finds Historically Low Rate of Workplace Misdeeds."

21. "For Small Firms, New Perils in Ad Claims," *Wall Street Journal*, May 15, 2014, B5.

22. *Ibid.*

23. *Ibid.*

24. "Burger King Drops Supplier Linked to Horsemeat," *Times Union*, www.timesunion.com/news/ (accessed January 19, 2015).

25. "Apple IPO Makes Instant Millionaires," *EDN*, December 12, 2014, www.edn.com/electronics-blogs/edn-moments/44032761/ (Accessed January 16, 2015).

26. "Here's What You Don't Know About Microsoft, Today's Best Dow Stock," *The Motley Fool*, March 18, 2014, www.fool.com/investing/general/2014/03/18 (Accessed January 16, 2015).

27. "The Benefits and Costs of Socially Responsible Investing," *Morningstar*, January 7, 2015, http://news.morningstar.com/articlenet/article.aspx?id=679225.

28. Christian Homburg, Marcel Stierl, and Torsten Bornemann, "Corporate Social Responsibility in Business-to-Business Markets: How Organizational Customers Account for Supplier Corporate Social Responsibility Engagement," *Journal of Marketing*, November 2013, 53-72; Daniel Korschun, C.B. Bhattacharya, and Scott Swain, "Corporate Social Responsibility, Customer Orientation, and the Job Performance of Frontline Employees," *Journal of Marketing*, May 2014, 20-37.

29. "Made Greener Coffee Refill Tumbler, 16 fl. oz." *Starbucks*, http://store.starbucks.com/made-greener-coffee-refill-tumbler/011039302, default.pd.html (Accessed January 18, 2015).

30. "Questions for Rick Ridgeway," *Fortune*, September 16, 2013, 25.

31. Danielle Sacks, "Any Fight Worth Fighting – That's the Attitude We Take," *Fast Company*, February 2015, 34-36.

32. *Ibid.*

33. *Ibid.*

34. "It Pays to be Green: Corporate Social Responsibility Meets the Bottom Line," *Nielsen*, June 17, 2014, www.nielsen.com/us/en/insights/news/2014 (Accessed January 19, 2015).

35. *Ibid.*

36. "UN Global Compact Participants," *United Nations,* www.unglobalcompact.org/Participant-sandStakeholders/index.html (Accessed January 19, 2015).

37. "Certified B Corporations," *B Corporation,* www.bcorporation.net (Accessed January 18, 2015).

38. "Marketing to the Green Consumer," *Mintel,* www.mintel.com/marketing-to-the-green-consumers-us-March-2014 (Accessed January 18, 2015). To better understand the notion of "greenness" see: Andrew Gershoff and Judy Frels, "What Makes It Green? The Role of Centrality of Green Attributes in Evaluations of the Greenness of Products," *Journal of Marketing,* January 2015, 97-110.

39. Amy Merrick, "Restoration Hardware's Mail-Order Extravaganza," August 7, 2014, *New Yorker,* www.newyorker.com/business/currency/restoration-hardwares-mail-order-extravaganza (Accessed January 17, 2015); Barbara Wood, "Residents Return Stacks of Catalogs to Palo Alto Restoration Hardware," June 18, 2014, *Palo Alto Online,* www.paloaltoonline.com/news/2014/06/18/drowning-in-restoration-hardware-catalogs (Accessed January 17, 2015); Ben Elgin, "Cataloging Restoration Hardware's Cleanup of Its 17-Pound Delivery," June 20, 2014, *Bloomberg Business,* www.bloomberg.com/bw/articles/2014-06-20/inside-restoration-hardwares-messy-cleanup-of-its-17-pound-catalog-delivery (Accessed January 17, 2015); "Weaker Certification Schemes," March 3, 2014, *Greenpeace,* www.greenpeace.org/international/en/campaigns/forests/solutions/alternatives-to-forest-destruc/Weaker-Certification-Schemes/ (Accessed January 17, 2015).

40. "CR's 100 Best Corporate Citizens 2014," *CR Magazine,* www.thecro.com/files/100bestlist.pdf (Accessed January 18, 2015).

41. "Bristol-Myers Squibb Corporate Responsibility Report," *Bristol-Myers Squibb,* www.bms.com/Documents/foundation/BMS-Corporate-Responsibility-Report.pdf (Accessed January 18, 2015).

42. "Sustainability Report," *Johnson & Johnson,* www.jnj.com/sites/default/files/JNJ-Citizenship-Sustainability-Highlights-Report.pdf (Accessed January 18, 2015).

43. "2014 Citizenship Report," *Microsoft,* www.microsoft.com/About/corporatecitizenship/en-us/reporting (Accessed January 19, 2015).

44. Andrew Czaplewski, Eric Olson, and Peggy McNulty, "Going Green Puts Chipotle in the Black," *Marketing News,* March 2014, 31-37; "Good Business," *Marketing News,* July 2014, 27-29.

45. Michelle Andrews, Xueming Luo, Zheng Fang, and Jaakko Aspara, "Cause Marketing Effectiveness and the Moderating Role of Price Discounts," *Journal of Marketing,* November 2014, 120-142.

46. "Cause Related Marketing on Facebook: 3 Companies Doing Back to School Right," *Social Media Today,* September 3, 2014, www.socialmediatoday.comcontent/ (Accessed January 14, 2015).

47. "The Right to R&R", *Marketing News,* November 2014, 12-14.

48. *Ibid.*

4

1. "When the Chips Are Down," Economist, January 10, 2015, www.economist.com/node/21638115/print (Accessed January 29, 2015).

2. "Why Consumers are Hatin' McDonald's New Slogan," *CBS,* October 29, 2014, www.cbsnews.com/news (Accessed January 20, 2015).

3. "Travelers Research Hotels With Smartphones But Don't Book With Them," *Quirk's Marketing Research Review,* October 2014, 8.

4. "T-Mobile Continues to Steal Customers from Rivals," *CNET,* January 7, 2015, www.cnet.com/news/t-mobile-continues-to-steal-customers-from-rivals (Accessed January 20, 2015).

5. "Internet of Things (IoT)," *Cisco,* www.cisco.com/web/solutions/trends/iot/overview.html (Accessed February 23, 2015).

6. "Digital Social & Mobile Worldwide in 2015," *Wearesocial.net,* January 21, 2015, http://wearesocial.net/blog/2015/01 (Aaccessed January 21, 2015).

7. "Social Networking Fact Sheet," *Pew,* www.pewinternet.org/fact-sheets/ (Accessed January 21, 2015).

8. "Digital Social & Mobile Worldwide in 2015."

9. "Social Media Update 2014," *Pew,* January 9, 2015, www.pewinternet.org/2015/01/09/social-media-update-2014/ (Accessed January 21, 2015).

10. Heidi Cohen, "Video Becomes the Content of Choice," *Video Media Examiner,* www.videomediaexaminer.com/social-media-marketing-predictions-for-2015 (Accessed January 21, 2015).

11. "Social Media Campaign on the Year: WestJet Christmas Miracle," *CIO,* www.cio.com/article/2369784/social-media/155992-14-Must-See-Social-Media-Marketing-success-stories.html (Accessed January 21, 2015).

12. "Wendy's Pretzel Bacon Cheeseburger Love Songs," *CIO,* www.cio.com/article/2369784/social-media/155992-14-Must-See-Social-Media-Marketing-success-stories.html (Accessed January 21, 2015).

13. Lindsey Havansek, "It's Not Social Media Marketing, It's DiGiorno," *Social Media Today,* January 21, 2015, www.socialmediatoday.com/content/its-not-social-media-marketing-its-digiorno (Accessed January 21, 2015).

14. *Ibid.*

15. *Ibid.*

16. *Ibid.*

17. "Top Population by Country," *Photius,* www.photius.com/rankings/world2050_rank.html (Accessed January 21, 2015).

18. "Fracking and Retirees Drive U.S. Population Growth," *Businessweek,* March 27, 2014, www.businessweek.com/articles/2014-03-27 (Accessed January 21, 2015).

19. "Proof Young Americans Are Still Hurting From the Recession," *Huffington Post,* September 16, 2004, www.huffingtonpost.com/2014/09/16/multigenerational-homes-pew_N_5594440.html (Accessed January 21, 2015).

20. "Tweens By the Numbers: A Rundown of Recent Stats," *Chicago Now,* February 20, 2014, www.chicagonow.com/tween-us/2014/12 (Accessed January 22, 2015).

21. *Ibid.*

22. Jon Louis, "Tweens and Pre-Tweens Fastest Growing Users of Mobile Games & Facebook App," *Avant,* May 7, 2013, http://blog.avantexperience.com/tweens-and-pre-tweens-fastest-growing-users-of-mobile-games-facebook-app/ (Accessed January 22, 2015).

23. "Move Over Avon Lady, the Tweens Are Here," *Wall Street Journal,* June 17, 2014, B1-B2.

24. "Children Around the World Are Connected, Informed, and Concerned," *Quirk's Marketing Research Review,* November 2013, 16.

25. "The Digital World of Teens," *Pinterest,* www.pinterest.com/pin/16466354861535005 (Accessed January 22, 2015).

26. *Ibid.*

27. *Ibid.*

28. "Why Teens Are the Most Elusive and Valuable Customers in Tech," *Inc.,* www.inc.com/issie-lapowsky/inside-massive-tech-land-grab-teenabers.html (Accessed January 22, 2015).

29. Ian Johnston, "Consumer Buying Behavior of Teenagers & How to Market to Them," *AZCentral,* http://yourbusiness.azcentral.com/consumer-buying-behavior-teenagers-market-27398.html (Accessed September 22, 2014).

30. *Ibid.*

31. http://www.posttrib.chicagotribune.com/lifestyles/29705481-423 (Accessed January 22, 2015).

32. "Piper Jaffray Completes 27th Semi-Annual Taking Stock With Teens Marketing Research Project," *Piper Jaffray,* April 9, 2014, www.piperjaffray.com/2col.aspx?id=287&releaseid=1917315&title=Piper+Jaffray+completes+27th+semi-annual+Taking+stock+with+teens+Market+Research+Project (Accessed January 22, 2015).

33. "The 23-Year-Olds Will Save America," *Businessweek,* June 30 – July 6, 2014, 14–16.

34. *Ibid.*

35. "A Life Well Photographed," *Marketing News,* May 2014, 12-13; "Millennials-Best Friends, Gurus and One-Night Stands," *Quirk's Marketing Research Review,* February 2014, 28–31.

36. *Ibid.*

37. "With Millennials, Trust Opens Doors," *Quirk's Marketing Research Review,* October 2014, 12–14.

38. *Ibid.*

39. Dune Lawrence and Nora Zimmett, "Generation X Stymied by Boomers," *Bloomberg,* September 15, 2013, www.bloomberg.com/news/2011/09/15/generation-x-stymied-by-baby-boomers-refusing-to-give-up-jobs.html (Accessed January 22, 2015).

40. Rieva Lesonsky, "Gen X: How to Market to the Forgotten Generation," *American Express,* September 15, 2014, www.AmericanExpress.com/us/small-business/openforum/articles/gen-x-how-to-market-to-the-forgotten-generation (Accessed January 22, 2015).

41. *Ibid.*

42. *Ibid.*

43. "Generation X: America's Neglected Middle Child," *Pew,* June 5, 2014, www.pewresearch.org/fact-tank/2014/06/05/generation-x-america's-neglected-middle-child/ (Accessed January 22, 2015).

44. "The Baby Boom Cohort in the United States: 2012 to 2060," *United States Census Bureau,* May 2014, www.census.gov/prod/2014pubs/p25-1141.pdf (Accessed January 22, 2015).

45. "Resources: 50+Facts & Fiction," *Immersion Active,* November 12, 2014, www.immersionactive.com/resources/50-plus-facts-and-fiction/ (Accessed January 22, 2015).

46. *Ibid.*

47. *Ibid.*

48. "Are They Really Different?" *Quirk's Marketing Research Review,* February 2014, 32-36.

49. "4 Tips for Marketing to Baby Boomers in the Digital Age," *Contently,* July 16, 2014, www.contently.com/strategist/2014/07/16/4-tips-for-marketing-to-baby-boomers-in-the-digital-age/ (Accessed January 23, 2015).

50. *Ibid.*

51. "Are You Ready For the 'Majority-Minority Demographic?" *Media Post,* April 10, 2014, www.mediapost.com/publications/article/223044/are-you-ready-for-the-majority-minority-demographis.html (Accessed January 23, 2015).

52. "Focus on Faith and Family," *Quirk's Marketing Research Review,* February 2013, 16.

53. "Looking From a Different Perspective," *Quirk's Marketing Research Review,* August 2014, 46, 64–66.

54. *Ibid.*

55. "A One-Two Punch," *Marketing News,* December 2014, 12–13

56. *Ibid.*

57. *Ibid.*

58. "Ad Ages' 2014 Hispanic Fact Pack Is Out Now," *Advertising Age,* July 29, 2014, http://adage.com/article/hispanic-marketing/ad-age-s-2014-hispanic-fact-pack/294335/ (Accessed January 23, 2015).

59. *Ibid.*

60. "Connecting Through Culture: African Americans Favor Diverse Advertising," *Nielsen,* October 20, 2014, www.nielsen.com/us/en/insights/news/2014/connecting-through-culture-african-americans-favor-diverse-advertising.html (Accessed January 23, 2015).

61. *Ibid.*

62. *Ibid.*

63. "How Blacks Are Influencing Media, Marketing and Advertising," *BET,* www.bet.com/news/national/photos/Nielsen-company/ (Accessed January 23, 2015).

64. "Usher's Honey Nut Commercial Knows Its Audience," *Businessweek,* August 21, 2014, www.businessweek.com/articles/2014-08-21/ushers-honey-nut-cheerios-commercial-knows-its-audience (Accessed January 23, 2015).

65. "U.S. Hispanic and Asian Populations Growing, But For Different Reasons," *Pew,* June 26, 2014, www.pewresearch.org/fact-tank/2014/06/26 (Accessed September 23, 2014).

66. "Median Household Income in the United States in 2013, by Race or Ethnic Group (in U.S. Dollars)," *The Statistics Portal,* www.statista.com/statistics/233324/median-household-income-in-the-united-states-by-race (Accessed January 23, 2015).

67. Author's projection; "14 Important Statistics About Asian Americans," *Asian Nation,* www.asian-nation.org/14-statistics.shtml (Accessed January 23, 2015).

68. "State of the Asian American Consumer: Growing Market, Growing Impact Report," *Nielsen,* www.nielsen.com/asians (Accessed January 23, 2015).

69. "What's Next in Advertising to Asian Americans?" *Asian Fortune News,* April 30, 2014, http://asianfortunenews.com/2014/04/what's-next-in-advertising-to-asian-americans (Accessed January 23, 2015).

70. "Incomes End a 6-Year Decline, Just Barely," *Wall Street Journal,* September 17, 2014, A2.

71. "Labor Force Statistics From the Current Population Survey," *Bureau of Labor Statistics,* www.bls.gov/cps (Accessed January 23, 2015).

72. "Fast Facts: Income of Young Adults," *Institute of Education Sciences,* http://nces.ed.gov/fastfacts/display.asp?id=77 (Accessed January 23, 2015).

73. "Current US Inflation Rates: 2014-2015," *U.S. Inflation Calculator,* www.usinflationcalculator.com/inflation/current-inflation-rates/ (Accessed January 24, 2015).

74. "Innovation: A Look Inside the Idea Factory," *Wired,* www.wired.co.uk/promotions/shell-lets-go/innovation/the-idea-factory (Accessed January 24, 2015).

75. Josh Bernoff, "Strategic Thinking for the Mobile Mind Shift," *Marketing News,* July 2014, 24–25.

76. *Ibid.*

77. "20 Tips on Google's 20 Percent Time in Your Classroom," *Learning Personalized,* www.learningpersonalized.com/2015/01/06/20-tips-on-googles-20-percent-time-in-your-classroom/ (Accessed January 24, 2015).

78. "Zara Builds Its Business Around RFID," *Wall Street Journal,* September 19, 2014, B1-B2.

79. *Ibid.*

80. "Benefits of ObamaCare: Advantage of ObamaCare," *Obamacare Facts,* http://obamacarefacts.com/benefitsofobamacare/ (Accessed January 24, 2015).

81. "CFPB-2014 in Review–And What's Ahead for 2015," *Paul Hastings,* January 20, 2015, www.paulhastings.com/publications (Accessed January 24, 2015).

82. "Bureau of Consumer Protection," *Federal Trade Commission,* www.ftc.gov/about-ftc/bureaus-offices/bureau-consumer-protection (Accessed January 24, 2015).

83. "US Total Media Ad Spend Inches Up, Pushed by Digital," *eMarketor,* www.emarketor.com/Article/10101 (Accessed January 24, 2015).

84. Natasha Singer, "Mapping, and Sharing, the Consumer Genome," *New York Times,* June 16, 2012, www.nytimes.com/2012/06/17/technology/acxiom-the-quiet-giant-of-consumer-database-marketing.html; "Acxiom InfoBase Consumer List Mailing List," *NextMark,* http://Lists.nextmark.com/market?page=order/online/datacard&id=131838 (Accessed January 24, 2015).

85. "Personic X Lifestage Analysis," *Lab 3 Marketing,* http://Lab3marketing.com/direct-marketing/data-analytics/personicX-lifestage-analysis (Accessed January 24, 2015).

86. "Give Me Back My Privacy," *Wall Street Journal,* March 24, R1-R2.

87. *Ibid.*

88. "AVG PrivacyFix," *AVG,* www.avg.com/ww-en/privacyfix (Accessed January 24, 2015).

89. "Privowny," *Privowny,* http://privowny.com (Accessed January 24, 2015).

90. "DuckDuckGo," *DuckDuckGo,* https://duckduckgo.com (Accessed January 24, 2015).

91. http://2015newyear.org/tag/startpage-ixquick-passed-4-million-daily-searches-on-monday (Accessed January 24, 2015).

92. Daniel Kline, "How Many Customers Does Amazon Have?" *The Motley Fool,* May 24, 2014, www.fool.com/investing/general/2014/05/24/how-many-customers-does-amazon-have.aspx (Accessed January 25, 2015).

93. Susan Adams, "America's Most Reputable Companies, 2014," *Forbes,* May 13, 2014, www.forbes.com/sites/susanadams/2014/05/13/americas-most-reputable-companies-2014/ (Accessed January 25, 2015).

94. "Google Thinks Amazon Is Its Biggest Competitor," *Slate,* www.slate.com/articles/business/moneybox/2014/10/google_amazon_competition_how_amazon_prime_delivery_hurts_google_s_ad_business.html (Accessed January 25, 2015).

5

1. "2015 Global Economic Outlook: Better Than 2014 – But Not By Much," *Bloomberg Businessweek,* November 6, 2014, wwwbusinessweek.com/articles/2014-11-06/2015-global-economic-outlook-better-than-2014-but-not-by-much (Accessed January 25, 2015).

2. "GE Works," *GE,* February 27, 2014, www.ge.com/ar2013/pdf/GE_AR13.pdf (Accessed January 25, 2015).

3. "Exports of Goods and Services (% of GDP)," *The World Bank,* www.data.worldbank.org/indicator/NE.EXP.GNFS.2S (Accessed January 25, 2015).

4. "U.S. Exports 1950-2015," *Trading Economics,* www.tradingeconomics.com/united-states/exports (Accessed January 25, 2015).

5. "Export-Related Jobs," *International Trade Administration,* September 2014, www.trade.gov/MAS/IAN/employment (Accessed January 25, 2015).

6. "Exports of Goods and Services," *International Trade Administration,* www.trade.gov/MAS/IAN/employment (Accessed January 25, 2015).

7. "U.S. Exports Reach $2.37 Trillion, Set New Record for Fourth Straight Year," *United States Department of Commerce,* February 6, 2014, www.commerce.gov/news/press-releases/2014/02/06/us-exports-reach-23-trillion-2013-set-record-fourth-straight-year (Accessed January 25, 2015).

8. "Ex-ImBank Finishes Fiscal Year Strong, Providing Over 20.5 Billion to Finance US Small Business Exports and Supporting Over 160,000 American Jobs," *Export-Import Bank of the United States,* November 5, 2014, www.exim.gov/newsandevents/releases/2014/Fiscal/Year/Strong.cfm (Accessed January 25, 2015).

9. "Five Myths about Imports," *Wall Street Journal,* May 20, 2014, A11.

10. *Ibid.*

11. "Pitching to Walmart: Made in U.S.," *Wall Street Journal,* October 7, 2013, B1, B2.

12. Aaron Flaaen, "Multinational Firms in Context," *Federal Reserve Bank of Atlanta,* August 30, 2013, www.frbatlanta.org/documents/news/conferences/13rdc/s1_p1_intl_topics_Flaaen.pdf (Accessed January 26, 2015).

13. "Bangladesh Factory Collapse," *Huffington Post,* January 11, 2015, www.huffingtonpost.com/news/bangladesh-factory-collapse (Accessed January 26, 2015).

14. "As Foreign Aid Dries Up, Companies Take the Lead in Global Development," *Fortune,* July 24, 2014, 46.

15. Theodore Levitt, "The Globalization of Markets," *Harvard Business Review,* May 1983, 92–100.

16. "The Gentle Art of Crossing Borders," *Marketing Insights,* July/August 2014, 10-11.

17. "Gross National Income Per Capita," *The World Bank,* December 16, 2014, http://data.world.bank.org/data-catalog/GNI-per-capita-Atlas-and-PPR-table (Accessed March 19, 2015).

18. *Ibid.*

19. "The 10 Most Expensive Cities in the World," *Business Insider,* March 3, 2015, www.businessinsider.com/most-expensive-cities-2014 (Accessed January 26, 2015).

20. "In Search of the Middle," *Marketing News,* August 2014, 24.

21. *Ibid.*

22. *Ibid.*

23. "Doing Business 2014: Understanding Regulations for Small and Medium-Size Enterprises," *The World Bank,* http://openknowledge.worldbank.org/bitstream/handle/10986/16204/19984.pdf?sequence=1 (Accessed January 17m 2015).

24. "The New Cold War on Business," *Fortune,* October 8, 2014, 77-80.

25. "Beijing Pulls Back the Welcome Mat," *Fortune*, October 8, 2014, 88-92.

26. "Wal-Mart Fights Back in China," *Wall Street Journal*, April 14, 2014, A1-A14.

27. "The Putin Paradox," *Fortune*, October 8, 2014, 82-86.

28. "Five Myths about Imports," A11.

29. "Tariff Deal Is Big Step for Trade, Tech Firms," *Wall Street Journal*, November 12, 2014, B1, B4.

30. "New Balance, Saucony Vying for Soles of Military Recruits," *Boston Globe*, www.bostonglobe.com/business101/06/2015/new-balance-saucony-two-way-race-build-all-american-shoe/cqH1DMoyFKbninQ7Y9E5N/story.html (Accessed January 29, 2015).

31. "Uruguay Found Final Act Should Produce Overall U.S. Gains," *U.S. Government Accountability Office*, www.gao.gov/products/GAO/GGD-94-836 (Accessed January 29, 2015).

32. "Beijing Faces Setback in Rare-Earth Spat," *Wall Street Journal*, March 27, 2014, A12.

33. "After U.S. Deal, India to Push for Doha Agenda at WTO in 2015," *India Times*, December 18, 2014, http://articles.economictimes.indiatimes.com/2014-12-18/news/57196109_1_doha-round-trade-facilitation-agreement-doha-agenda (Accessed January 29, 2015).

34. "For a Fair, Transparent and Effective ISDS in TTIP," *EurActive*, January 16, 2015, http://euractiv.com/sections/trade-society/fair-transparent-and-effective-isds-ttip-311339 (Accessed January 29, 2015).

35. "Trades Big Breakout," *Politico*, January 2, 2015, www.politico.com/story/2015/01/trade-outlook-2015-113793.html (Accessed January 29, 2015).

36. "Most Dynamic Latin Countries Forge New Trade Accord," *Wall Street Journal*, February 11, 2014, A10.

37. "NAFTA Triumphant: Assessing Two Decades of Gains in Trade, Growth, and Jobs," *U.S. Chamber of Commerce*, www.uschamber.com/sites/default/files/legacy/reports/1112_INTL_NAFTA_20years.pdf (Accessed January 20, 2015).

38. "Dominican Republic-Central America-United States Free Trade Agreement (CAFTA-DR)," *Export.gov*, http://export.gov/FTA/cafta-dr/index.asp (Accessed March 19, 2015).

39. "Countries," *European Union*, http://europa.eu/about-eu/countries/index_en.htm (Accessed January 28, 2015).

40. "Why the Greek Elections Might be the Beginning of the End for the Euro," *Fortune*, January 26, 2015, http://fortune.com/2015/01/26/greek-elections-euro-end/ (Accessed January 28, 2015).

41. "2014 Autumn Economic Forecast: Slow Recovery with Very Low Inflation," *Europea*, November 4, 2014, http://europea.eu/rapid/press-release_IP_14_1362_en.htm (Accessed January 29, 2015).

42. "Countries and Regions: United States," *European Commission*, January 9, 2013, http://ec.europa.eu/trade/creating-opportunities/bilateral-relations/countries/united-states/ (Accessed January 29, 2015).

43. "G20 Leaders' Communique Brisbane Summit, 15-16 November 2014," *G-20*, https://g20.org/wp-content/uploads/2014/12/brisbane_g20_leaders_summit_communique1.pdf (Accessed January 29, 2015).

44. "Global Wealth," *Economist*, October 18, 2014, 93.

45. "Lower Oil Prices Provide Benefits to US Workers," *New York Times*, January 17, 2015, www.nytimes.com/2015/01/18/business/economy/lower-oil-prices-offer-a-bonanza-to-us-workers.html?_r=o (Accessed January 29, 2015).

46. "The Costs of Expanding Overseas," *Wall Street Journal*, February 27, 2014, B6.

47. *Ibid*.

48. *Ibid*.

49. *Ibid*.

50. Author's estimate.

51. "Exhibit A in GE's Case for Alston Deal," *New York Times*, May 23, 2014, www.nytimes.com/2014/05/26/business/international/generalelectric_joint_venture_in_France.html (Accessed January 29, 2015).

52. "Direct Investment Positions: Country and Industry Detail, July 2014, *Bureau of Economic Analysis*, www.bea.gov/scb/pdf/2014/07%20July/0714_direct_investment_positions.pdf (Accessed January 30, 2015).

53. "2015 Select USA Investment Summit is Now Open for Business," *United States Department of Commerce*, January 8, 2015, www.commerce.gov/blog/category/138 (Accessed January 30, 2015).

54. *Ibid*.

55. "The Gentle Art of Crossing Borders," *American Marketing Association*, July/August 2014, www.ama.org/publications/MarketingInsights/Pages/gentle-art-crossing-borders.aspx (Accessed January 30, 2015).

56. "How Procter & Gamble is Conquering Emerging Markets," *The Motley Fool*, www.fool.com/investing/general/2013/10/27/how-procter-gamble-is-conquering-emerging-markets.aspx (Accessed January 30, 2015).

57. "What is Selling Where? Pringles Chips," *Wall Street Journal*, April 24, 2013, D3

58. "How Domino's Won India," *Fast Company*, February 2015, 54.

59. *Ibid*.

60. "Pick Up. Your Ad Is Calling," *Business Week*, April 21-27, 2014, 19.

61. "How Convenient: In Taiwan, the 24/7 Store Does It All," *Wall Street Journal*, May 17-18, 2014, A1, A9.

62. "How Domino's Won...," 56.

63. "A Continent Goes Shopping," *The Economist*, August 18, 2013, www.economist.com/node/21560582 (Accessed January 30, 2015).

64. "Why Wal-Mart Hasn't Conquered Brazil," *Business Week*, May 8, 2014, 25.

65. *Ibid*.

66. "Russian Rubles to 1 US Dollar," *Exchange-rates.org*, January 29, 2015, www.exchange-rates.org/history/RUB/USD/T (Accessed January 30, 2015).

67. "Commerce Department Declares Anti-dumping Duties," *TireReview.com*, January 21, 2015, www.tirereview.com/commerce-department-declares-anti-dumping-duties/ (Accessed January 30, 2015).

68. "Suggested Reading about Countertrade," *Exporter-Sources.com*, http://exporters-sources.com/suggested-reading-about-countertrade (Accessed January 30, 2015).

69. "Countertrade," *All About Countertrade*, http://allaboutcountertrade.blogspot.com (Accessed January 30, 2015).

70. "Air France Launches the Upgrade Challenge Social Game," *Creative Guerrilla Marketing*, January 28, 2015, www.creativeguerrillamarketing.com/guerrilla-marketing/air-france-launches-the-upgrade-challenge-social-game/ (Accessed January 30, 2015).

71. "H&M Pushes Sales With Versatility Campaign on Twitter, Facebook," *Mobile Commerce Daily*, July 8, 2014, www.mobilecommercedaily.com/hm-pushes-sales-with-versatility-campaign-on-twitter-facebook/ (Accessed January 31, 2015).

72. "Red Bull Ad Sparks Social Media Outburst From Kenyans," *Jambonewspot*, January 15, 2015, www.jambonewspot.com/video-redbull-ad-sparks-social-media-outburst-kenyans/ (Accessed January 31, 2015).

73. *Ibid*.

74. *Ibid*.

6

1. The material on hedonic and utilitarian value was partially adapted from Barry Babin and Eric Harris, *CB* 6th ed., Cengage Learning, 2015, 28–29.

2. Craig Smith, "By the Numbers: 60 Amazing Google Search Statistics and Facts," *Expanded Ramblings*, January 22, 2015, http://expandedramblings.com/index.php/by-the-number-a-gigantic-list-of-google-stats-and-facts/ (Accessed February 17, 2015).

3. "Dethroning the Brand," *Marketing News*, December 2014, 14.

4. Eric Anderson and Duncan Simester, "Reviews Without a Purchase: Low Ratings, Loyal Customers, and Deception," *Journal of Marketing Research*, June 2014, 249–269.

5. "Good Tidings For Retail," *Marketing News*, December 2014, 14.

6. *Ibid*.

7. Edwin von Bommel, David Edelman, and Kelly Ungerman, "Digitizing the Consumer Decision Journey," *McKinsey*, June 2014, www.mckinsey.com/insights/marketing_sales/digitizing_the_consumer_decision_journey/ (Accessed February 17, 2015).

8. von Bommel, et al, "Digitizing the Consumer Decision..."

9. "Survey: 3 in 4 Americans Make Impulse Purchases," *CreditCards.com*, November 23, 2014, www.creditcards.com/credit-card-news/impulse-purchase-survey.php (Accessed February 17, 2015).

10. Sam Hui, Yanliu Huang, Jacob Suher, and Jeff Inman, "Deconstructing the First Moment of Truth: Understanding Unplanned Consideration and Purchase Conversion Using In-Store Video Tracking," *Journal of Marketing Research*, August 2013, 445–462.

11. Crystal Collier and Gavin Sinter, "Meet Them Where They Want To Be," *Quirk's Marketing Research Review*, October 2014, 58–62.

12. "McDonald's Ad Campaign Banks On A New Payment Method: Love," *Christian Science Monitor*, February 2, 2015, www.csmonitor.com/Business/The-Bite/2015/0202/McDonald-s-ad-campaign-banks-on-a-new-payment-method-love (Accessed February 18, 2015).

13. Julio Sevilla and Joseph Redden, "Limited Availability Reduces the Rate of Satiation," *Journal of Marketing Research*, April 2014, 205–217.

14. Samantha Cross and Mary Gilly, "Cultural Competence and Cultural Compensatory Mechanisms in Binational Households," *Journal of Marketing*, May 2014, 121–139.

15. "Most Expensive Cars in the World: Top 10 List 2014-2015," *The Supercars*, www.thesupercars.org/top-cars/most-expensive-cars-in-the-world-top-10-list/ (Accessed February 18, 2015).

16. "2015 Poverty Guidelines," January 22, 2015, *United States Department of Health and Human*

Services, http://aspe.hhs.gov/poverty/15poverty.cfm (Accessed February 18, 2015).

17. "Sphere of Influence," *Marketing News*, November 2014, 16–17.

18. Hans Risselada, Peter Verdoef, and Tammo Bijmolt, "Dynamic Effects of Social Influence and Direct Marketing on the Adoption of High-Technology Products," *Journal of Marketing*, March 2014, 52–68.

19. This section was partially adapted from Babin and Harris, 156–157.

20. "Is Women's Empowerment Marketing the New 'Pink It and Shrink It'?" *Entrepreneur*, February 9, 2015, www.entrepreneur.com/article /242677 (Accessed February 20, 2015).

21. "Industry Statistics Shows Growth in Men Engaging in Online Shopping," *Mobile Commerce Insider*, June 18, 2013, www.mobilecommerceinsider .com/topics/mobileecommerceinsider/articles /342484-industry-statistics-show-growth-men -engaging-online-shopping.html (Accessed January 29, 2014).

22. "Reach Over 45 Million American Families," *eTarget Media*, www.etargetmedia.com/family -lists.html (Accessed February 20, 2015).

23. "Messes and Wrong Guesses," *Wall Street Journal*, February 15-16, 2014, C4.

7

1. Michael D. Hutt and Thomas W. Speh, *Business Marketing Management*, 12th ed. (Boston: Cengage, 2017).

2. Jeffrey Cohen "20 Most Important Stats from the 2015 B2B Content Marketing Report," *Social Media B2B*, October 6, 2014, www.socialmediab2b .com/2014/10/b2b-content-marketing-report -statistics-2015.com (Accessed February 20, 2015).

3. Autumn Truong, "5 B2B Social Media Lessons Cisco Learned in 2014," *Social Media B2B*, January 20, 2015 www.socialmediab2b.com (Accessed February 20, 2015).

4. "Online Measurement," *Nielsen*, www.nielsen. com/us/en/nielsen-solutions/nielsen-measurement /nielsen-online-measurement.html (Accessed March 22, 2015).

5. "2014 Social Media Benchmarking Report," *B2B Marketing Magazine*, www.b2bmarketing.net /magazine (Accessed February 27, 2015).

6. Jeffrey Cohen, "7 Examples of B2B Content Marketing," *Social Media B2B*, September 18, 2013, www.socialmediab2b.com/category/social -media-101/ (Accessed February 19, 2015).

7. Chris Lee, "Why Online Marketing Is as Simple as Five-a-side Football," *Econsultancy*, February 1, 2013, http://econsultancy.com/us/blog/62018-why -online-marketing-is-as-simple-as-five-a-side-football (Accessed March 22, 2015).

8. "The Best Repeat Business Practices," *eLocal. com*, March 8, 2012, www.elocal.com/content /home-expert-network/repeat-business-practices -2547 (Accessed March 22, 2015).

9. TJ Raphael, "Time Inc. Forms Strategic Alliance with Sprint Nextel Corp.," *Folio*, May 7, 2013, www.foliomag.com/2013/time-inc-forms-strategic -alliance-sprint-nextel-corp (Accessed March 22, 2015).

10. Eric Griffin, "12 Amazon Fire TV Tips for Streaming Fans," *PC Mag*, February 19, 2015, www.pcmag.com/slideshow/story/332129/12 -amazon-fire-tv-tips-for-streaming-fans (Accessed March 22, 2015).

11. "H&R Block Saluted for Partnership with Arizona Catholic Schools," *Ahwatukee Foothills News*, February 6, 2013, www.ahwatukee.com /money/article_bb3dc05e-6f26-11e2-b270 -001a4bcf887a.html (Accessed March 22, 2015).

12. Robert M. Morgan and Shelby D. Hunt, "The Commitment-Trust Theory of Relationship Marketing," *Journal of Marketing*, 58, no. 3, 1994, 23.

13. *Ibid*.

14. Nils Pratley, "Phones 4U Has Only Itself to Blame," *The Guardian*, September 15, 2014, www.theguardian.com/business/nils-pratley-on -finance/2014/sep/15/phones-4u-administrators (Accessed March 22, 2015).

15. Jamie Yap, "Maps, LBS Bolster Google Enterprise's Asia Roadmap," *ZDNet*, February 1, 2013, www.zdnet.com/maps-lbs-bolster-google -enterprises-asia-roadmap-7000010671/ (Accessed March 22, 2015).

16. "Doing Business with the US Government," *iSquare*, September 19, 2013, www.isquare.com /fhome18.cfm (Accessed March 22, 2015).

17. Hutt and Speh, 7.

18. *Ibid*.

19. *Ibid*.

20. "California Timber Industry Bussing Post-Recession," *Lake Tahoe News*, March 22, 2013, www.laketahoenews.net/2013/03/california-timber -industry-buzzing-post-recession/ (Accessed March 22, 2015).

21. Alan Levin and Susanna Ray, "Boeing 878 Dreamlines Is Grounded Worldwide by Regulators," *Bloomberg*, January 17, 2013, www.bloomberg .com/news/2013-01-16/boeing-787-dreamliner-fleet -grounded-by-u-s-after-emergency.html (Accessed March 22, 2015).

22. Jon Hilkevitch, "CTA to Spend $2 Billion for 846 New Rail Cars," *Chicago Tribune*, February 6, 2013, www.chicagotribune.com/news/local/breaking /chi-cta-to-spend-2-billion-for-846-new-rail-cars -20130206,0,1482382.story (Accessed March 22, 2015).

23. Hutt and Speh, 6.

24. Paul Demery, "Alibaba.com Looks for Growth Among U.S. Suppliers," *Internet Retailer*, February 4, 2015, www.internetretailer.com/2015/02/04 /alibabacom-looks-growth-among-us-suppliers (Accessed March 22, 2015).

25. Cyril Kowaliski, "SK Hynix Fire Sends Memory Prices Soaring," *The Tech Report*, Septermber 24, 2013, http://techreport.com/news/25416/sk-hynix -fire-sends-memory-prices-soaring (Accessed March 22, 2015).

26. Cameron McWhirter, "Chinese Diapers Save U.S. Paper Mill," *The Wall Street Journal*, August 13, 2012, B1.

27. Hutt and Speh, 52.

28. *Ibid*.

29. Stuart Leung, "Selling to Executives: Bringing Your Sales "A" Game to the C-Level," *SalesForce Blog*, February 24, 2014, http://blogs.salesforce.com /company/2014/02/selling-to-c-level-executives .html (Accessed March 22, 2015).

30. *Ibid*.

31. Hutt and Speh, 231.

32. *Ibid*.

8

1. "Biting Off the High End of the Market," *Inc.*, February 2015, 25.

2. Halah Touryalai, "How Macy's Is Winning the Retail Battle," *Forbes*, December 24, 2013, www.forbes.com/sites/halahtouryalai/2013/12/24 /how-macys-is-winning-the-retail-battle-hint-it -knows-which-u-s-cities-love-cuffed-pants (Accessed February 2, 2015).

3. Rebecca Spera, "CrossFit for Kids Focuses on Fun," *ABC*, January 21, 2015, http://abc13.com /health/crossfit-for-kids-focuses-on-fun/482997/ (Accessed February 26, 2015).

4. Sheila Shayton, "Never Mind Millennials – Gen Z May be the Hardest Marketing Nut to Crack," *Brand Channel*, August 20, 2014, www.brandchannel .com/home/post/2014/08/20/140820-Gen-Z -Marketing (Accessed February 21, 2015).

5. Christine Birkner, "Z Marks the Spot," *Marketing News*, December 2013, 14, www.ama.org /publications/MarketingNews/Pages/generation -z-digital-channels-innovation.aspx (Accessed February 21, 2015).

6. Sheila Shayton, "Never Mind Millennials–Gen Z May be the Hardest Marketing Nut to Crack."

7. Christine Birkner, "Attention, Shoppers," *Marketing News*, December 2013, 26–33, www .ama.org/publications/MarketingNews/Pages /tweens-consumer-research-brand-management .aspx (Accessed February 21, 2015).

8. "Who are Millennials?" *Millennial Marketing*, http://www.millennialmarketing.com/who-are -millennials/ (Accessed February 23, 2015).

9. Tom Ryan, "Are Retailers Ready for the Millennial Takeover?" *RetailWire*, November 4, 2013, www.retailwire.com/discussion/17128 /are-retailers-ready-for-the-millennial-takeover (Accessed February 22, 2015).

10. "Which Brand Attributes Matter Most to Millennials?" *RetailWire*, September 29, 2014, www .retailwire.com/discussion/17807/which-brand -attributes-matter-most-to-millennials (Accessed February 21, 2015).

11. Jeff Fromm, "'Idea brands' Will Win Big with Millennials: Here's How to Attract Them," *Retail Customer Experience*, September 5, 2013, www.retailcustomerexperience.com/blog _print/11101 (Accessed February 21, 2015).

12. William F. Schroer, "Generations X, Y, Z and the Others," *The Social Librarian*, www.socialmarketing .org/newsletter/features/generation3.htm (Accessed February 22, 2015).

13. "Save the Date: Vancouver Turns Into Culinary Central During Dine Out Vancouver Festival 2015," *Tourism Vancouver*, www.tourismvancouver.com /articles/view/SAVE-THE-DATE-VANCOUVER -TURNS-INTO-CULINARY-CENTRAL-DURING -DINE-OUT-VANCOUVER-FESTIVAL-2015/652 /541/ (Accessed February 22, 2015).

14. Janet Eveleth, "Baby Boomers Are Shopping and Spending," *Examiner*, July 11, 2013, www .examiner.com/article/baby-boomers-are-shopping -and-spending (Accessed February 22, 2015).

15. Christine Birkner, "Senior Moment," *Marketing News*, September 2014, 12-13.

16. S. E. Smith, "What Is the Silent Generation?" *wiseGEEK*, January 23, 2013, www.wisegeek.com /what-is-the-silent-generation.htm (Accessed February 1, 2014).

17. Stephen M. Golant, "Aging in the American Suburbs: A Changing Population," *Aging Well*, www.agingwellmag.com/news/ex_06309_01.shtml (Accessed February 22, 2015).

18. Lauren Stiller Rikleen, "Not Buying Offensive Super Bowl Ads," *Boston Globe*, February 4, 2013, http://bostonglobe.com/opinion/2013/02/04 /not-buying-offensive-super-bowl-ads /1eNEMBDxLyLWFnHS7jKI2I/story.html (Accessed February 22, 2015).

19. "Men, Women and Money: How We View Finances Differently," *TransAmerica*, www.transamerica.com/yourlife/retirement/education/men-women-money-how-we-view-finances-differently (Accessed February 23, 2015).

20. Renee Montagne, "Japanese Burger Chain Finds Way to Appeal to Women," *NPR*, November 5, 2013, www.npr.org/2013/11/05/243185594/japanese-burger-chain-finds-way-to-appeal-to-women (Accessed February 22, 2015).

21. Annie Marie Cheker, "Groceries Become a Guy Thing," *Wall Street Journal*, October 16, 2013, http://online.wsj.com/news/articles/SB10001424052702303680045791394229728916331330 (Accessed February 23, 2015).

22. Ana Swanson, "What Super Bowl Manvertising Says About Men's New Role in America," *The Washington Post*, February 2, 2015, www.washingtonpost.com/blogs/wonkblog/wp/2015/02/02/what-super-bowl-manvertising-says-about-mens-new-role-in-america (Accessed February 26, 2015).

23. Marylouise Smith, "Dollar Stores Making a Buck in the Lebanon Valley," *Lebanon Daily News*, March 9, 2013, www.ldnews.com/ci_22749059/dollar-stores-making-buck-lebanon-valley (Accessed February 23, 2015).

24. Erin Shea, "How Luxury Retailers Can Take On Showrooming Threat," *Luxury Daily*, January 29, 2013, www.luxurydaily.com/how-luxury-retailers-can-take-on-threat-of-showrooming (Accessed February 22, 2015).

25. Judy Bankman, "Junk Food Marketing Makes Big Moves in Developing Countries," *Civil Eats*, October 2, 2013, http://civileats.com/2013/10/02/junk-food-marketing-makes-big-moves-in-developing-countries/ (Accessed February 23, 2015).

26. Breanne L. Heldman, "Adam Levine and Nicki Minaj Designing Clothes for Kmart," *Yahoo*, January 15, 2013, http://omg.yahoo.com/blogs/celeb-news/adam-levine-nicki-minaj-designing-clothes-kmart-194136723.html (Accessed February 23, 2015).

27. "Find a Store Near You," *Fashion Fair*, www.fashionfair.com/wtb2.php (Accessed February 23, 2015)

28. "Why You Need a Brand Ambassador Program (And 4 Companies that Are Doing it Right)," April 3, 2014, http://thenextweb.com/entrepreneur/2014/04/03/need-brand-ambassador-program-4-companies-right (Accessed February 23, 2015).

29. Laurie Sullivan, "Nielsen Taps eXelate's Data Pipeline," *MediaPost*, August 27, 2013, www.mediapost.com/publications/article/207917/nielsen-taps-exelates-data-pipeline.html (Accessed February 23, 2015); "The Start-Up Hunter," *Nielsen*, June 27, 2013, www.nielseninnovate.com/start-hunter (Accessed February 23, 2015).

30. Will Greenwald, "Sling TV," *PC Magazine*, February 17, 2015, www.pcmag.com/article2/0,2817,2475619,00.asp (Accessed February 26, 2015).

31. Joseph F. Kovar, "Actfio Looks to Simplify Storage Product Line, Channel Program," *CRN*, February 1, 2013, www.crn.com/news/storage/240147697/actifio-looks-to-simplify-storage-product-line-channel-program.htm (Accessed February 23, 2015).

32. "Amazon Webstore," *Amazon*, http://webstore.amazon.com/ (Accessed February 23, 2015).

33. Sarah Nassuer, "If Your Fridge Could Talk…" *Wall Street Journal*, December 17, 2014, D1, D2.

34. Amy Ahlberg, "9 Shopping Sites for Every Type of Fashionista," *DailyWorth*, April 24, 2013, www.dailyworth.com/posts/1823-9-shopping-sites-worth-visiting/4 (Accessed February 24, 2015).

35. Janice Bitters, "Mpls. To Expand Car Sharing," *Minnesota Daily*, February 13, 2013, www.mndaily.com/2013/02/13/mpls-expand-car-sharing (Accessed February 25, 2015).

36. Erik Sherman, "Is iPad Mini Cannibalizing its Bigger Sibling?" *CBS*, January 18, 2013, www.cbsnews.com/8301-505124_162-57564708/is-ipad-mini-cannibalizing-its-bigger-sibling (Accessed February 25, 2015).

37. Laura Fagan, "How Birchbox Used CR to Successfully Scale Their Business," April 1, 2014, http://blogs.salesforce.com/company/2014/04/birchbox.html (Accessed February 24, 2015).

38. "All Brands," *Coca-Cola*, www.thecoca-colacompany.com/brands/brandlist.html (Accessed February 24, 2015).

39. Jeanine Poggi, "Can Esquire's Brand Make a TV Channel a Hit?" *Advertising Age*, http://adage.com/article/media/nbc-universal-rebrands-g4-esquire-network/239727/ (Accessed February 25, 2015).

40. "Nutrition Guide," *Kentucky Fried Chicken*, January 22, 2013, www.kfc.com/nutrition/pdf/kfc_nutrition.pdf (Accessed February 25, 2015).

41. "Our Brands," *Gap Inc.*, www.gapinc.com/content/gapinc/html/aboutus/ourbrands.html (Accessed February 24, 2015).

42. Lara O'Reilly, "Vertu Shifts from Bling to Emotional Positioning," *MarketingWeek*, February 12, 2013, www.marketingweek.co.uk/news/vertu-shifts-from-bling-to-emotional-positioning/4005671.article (Accessed February 23, 2015).

43. Susan Gunelius, "Kia Rolls Out Brand Repositioning Ad Campaign," *Corporate Eye*, January 9, 2015, www.corporate-eye.com/main/kia-rolls-out-brand-repositioning-ad-campaign (Accessed February 26, 2015).

9

1. "Internet of Things Study Highlights Our Conflicted Relationship with Privacy," *Quirk's Marketing Research Review*, October 2014, 10.

2. "The Auto Repair Process Needs an Overhaul," *Quirk's Marketing Research Review*, August 2014, 14–15.

3. "Report Identifies Auto Marques with Gabbiest Owners," *Quirk's Marketing Research Review*, January 2015, 19.

4. A Detailed Exploration," *Quirk's Marketing Research Review*, October 2014, 30–34.

5. "By the Numbers? 200+ Amazing Facebook Users Statistics," *Expanded Ramblings*, February 3, 2015, http://expandedramblings.com/index.php/by-the-numbers-17-amazing-facebook-stats/ (Accessed February 22, 2015).

6. "30+ # Twitter Marketing Stats: 2015 - #infographic," *Digital Information World*, January 24, 2015, www.digitalinformationworld.com/2015/01/twitter-marketing-stats-and-facts-you-should-know.html (Accessed February 22, 2015).

7. "Buy Signal: Facebook Widens Data Targeting," *Wall Street Journal*, April 10, 2013, B4.

8. "Zuckerberg's New Tools," *Marketing Insights*, Spring 2013, 5.

9. "Smile! Marketers Are Mining Selfies," *Wall Street Journal*, October 10, 2014, B1–B2.

10. Parmy Olson, "We Know Everything," *Forbes*, November 18, 2013, 68-70.

11. *Ibid.*

12. "Adopt the Industry Standard, For Free," *Flurry*, www.flurry.com/solutions/analytics (Accessed February 22, 2015).

13. "What is Apache Hadoop?" *Apache*, www.hadoop.apache.org/#What+Is+Apache+Hadoop%3F (Accessed February 23, 2015).

14. "Ten Big Data Case Studies in a Nutshell," *SearchCIO*, http://searchcio.techtarget.com/opinion/Ten-big-data-case-studies-in-a-nutshell (Accessed February 23, 2015).

15. "More of the Same Please, *Quirk's Marketing Research Review*, March 2014, 14.

16. Carl McDaniel and Roger Gates, *Marketing Research*, 10th ed., Wiley, 2015, 171.

17. "The Science of Shopping," *Indiana University*, http://Kelley.iu.edu/Marketing/Research/Labs/shopability1.htmp (Accessed February 24, 2015).

18. "Viva Vantage Named 2015 Product of the Year," *PR Newswire*, www.prnewswire.com/news-releases/viva-vantage-named-2015-product-of-the-year-30032887/html (Accessed February 25, 2015).

19. "Google Consumer Surveys," *Google*, www.google.com/insights/consumersurveys/how (Accessed February 25, 2015).

20. "Election Reopens Debate Over Online Polling," *National Journal*, www.nationaljournal.com/politics/election-reopens-debate-over-online-polling-10121130 (Accessed February 24, 2015).

21. "Character Counts, Characters Count," *Quirk's Marketing Research Review*, July 2013, 48–51.

22. "Brand + TV + iPad: The New Research Triangle," *Quirk's Marketing Research Review*, March 2014, 36–41.

23. "Screen Size Correlates with Completion Rates," *Quirk's Marketing Research Review*, April 2014, 8.

24. "Easy Answers," *Quirk's Marketing Research Review*, February 2015, 32–36.

25. "Instant Insight," *Marketing News*, February 2013, 46–49.

26. "That's the Spot" *Quirk's Marketing Research Review*, July 2014, 38–45.

27. *Ibid.*

28. "Behavior Scan CPG TV Ad Testing," *IRI Worldwide*, www.iriworldwide.com/ProductSolutions/AllProductsDetail/productID/29.aspx (Accessed February 25, 2015).

10

1. Jessica Whol, "Starbucks Rolling Out Upscale Teavana Tea Cafes," April 29, 2014, http://articles.chicagotribune.com/2014-04-29/business/ct-starbucks-teavana-0429-biz-20140429_1_tazo-ceo-howard-schultz-seattle-based-coffee-chain (Accessed March 19, 2015).

2. "Cat's Pride Launches Fresh & Light Ultimate Care – Performance Based Litter That is 'Light Done Right,'" *The Herald Online*, March 3, 2015, www.heraldonline.com/incoming/article12692651.html (Accessed March 19, 2015).

3. Stephanie Strom, "McDonald's Moves toward a Healthier Menu," *New York Times*, September 27, 2013, www.bostonglobe.com/business/2013/09/26/mcdonald-moves-toward-healthier-menu/6Ez4YH7zEOZCIK3oS31S1N/story.html (Accessed February 9, 2014).

4. Sarah Halzach, "Target's New Strategy: We Need More Than Just Minivan Moms," *Washington Post*, March 4, 2015, www.washingtonpost.com/news/business/wp/2015/03/04/targets-new-strategy-we-need-more-than-just-minivan-moms (Accessed March 19, 2015).

5. "Krispy Kreme Hopes Iced Beverages Bring Bigger Share of Coffee Market," *Journal Now*, February 18, 2014, www.journalnow.com/business

/business_news/local/article/f55f0020-8dc7-11e3 (Accessed March 19, 2015).

6. Sam Laird, "Yahoo Killing Message Boards Site and Other Products," *Mashable*, March 2, 2013, http://mashable.com/2013/03/01/yahoo-kills -properties (Accessed February 9, 2014).

7. Ashraf Eassa, "Google Stole Apple's Mojo," *Seeking Alpha*, March 3, 2013, http://seekingalpha .com/article/1242371-google-stole-apple-s-mojo (Accessed February 9, 2014); Darcy Travlos, "Is Apple Losing Its Brand Equity?" *Forbes*, January 19, 2013, www.Forbes.com/sites/darcytravlos /2013/01/19/is-apple-losing-its-brand-equity (Accessed February 9, 2015); Jordan Kahn, "Despite Declining Sales, Samsung Somehow Beats Apple in Cell Phone Customer Satisfaction," *9 to 5 Mac*, December 31, 2014, http://9to5mac .com/2014/12/31/samsung-vs-apple-customer -satisfaction (Accessed March 19, 2015).

8. Pat Reynolds, "Shoppers Believe Private Label = National Brands in Different Packaging," *Packaging World*, February 26, 2013, www.packworld.com /venue/private-label/shoppers-believe-private-label -national-brands-different-packaging (Accessed February 9, 2014).

9. Domenick Celentano, "Private Label 2013 Trends—Strong Growth—Affordable, High Quality," *About.com*, http://foodbeverage.about.com/od /StartingAFoodBusiness/a/Strong-Growth-In-Private -Label-Brands-Private-Label-Manufacturers -Association.htm (Accessed February 9, 2014).

10. Christine Birkner, "Losing the Label, August 2014, *Marketing News*, 10-11.

11. Keith Nunes, "Kroger Succeeding with Simple Truth," *Meat+Poultry*, March 9, 2015, www .meatpoultry.com/articles/news_home/Trends/2015 /03/Kroger_succeeding_with_Simple.aspx?ID =%7B45586455-1818-4988-A981-FEA683EF49DA %7D&cck=1 (Accessed match 19, 2015).

12. "Brands & Products: Brand Browser," *Church & Dwight*, www.churchdwight.com/brands-and -products/brand-browser.aspx (Accessed February 9, 2014).

13. "Bruegger's Bagels Co-branding with Jamba Juice," *Fast Casual*, February 12, 2014, www .fastcasual.com/article/227795/Bruegger-s-Bagels -co-branding-with-Jamba-Juice (Accessed February 17, 2014).

14. "Doc Popcorn, Dippin' Dots to Debut First Co-Brand Store," *Business Wire*, February 10, 2015, www.businesswire.com/news/home /20150210005273/en/Doc-Popcorn-Dippin'-Dots -Debut-Co-Brand-Store (Accessed match 19, 2015).

15. T. Thompson, "What Is the Difference between a Copyright, Trademark, and Patent?" *WiseGEEK*, February 9, 2013, www.wisegeek.com/what-is-the -difference-between-a-copyright-trademark-and -patent.htm (Accessed February 9, 2014).

16. Edward Wyatt, "F.C.C. Backs Consumers in Unlocking of Cellphones," *New York Times*, March 4, 2013, www.nytimes.com/2013/03/05/technology /fcc-urges-a-right-to-unlock-cellphones.html (Accessed February 9, 2014).

17. Monte Burke, "Under Armour Files Lawsuit against Nike for Trademark Infringement," *Forbes*, February 21, 2013, www.forbes.com/sites /monteburke/2013/02/21/under-armour-files -lawsuit-against-nike-for-trademark-infringement (Accessed February 9, 2014).

18. Chantal Fernandez, "Gucci Loses Trademark Infringement Case Against Guess in France," *Fashionista*, February 2, 2015, http://fashionista.com /2015/02/french-court-rejects-gucci-trademark -claims-against-guess-paris-france (Accessed

March 19, 2015); "Counterfeit Combat," *Inc.*, March 2015, 68–69.

19. "11 Ridiculous Fast Food Chain Ripoffs in China," *Hardware Zone*, http://forums.hardwarezone .com.sg/eat-drink-man-woman-16/11-ridiculous -fast-food-food-chain-ripoffs-china-4281444.html (Accessed February 9, 2014).

20. Molly Soat, "Misunderstood Measures," *Marketing News*, January 2015, 18-19.

21. Gemma Charles, "Brothers Cider Unveils Premium Packaging," *Marketing*, February 28, 2013, www.marketingmagazine.co.uk/news /1172938/Brothers-Cider-unveils-new-premium -packaging (Accessed February 9, 2014).

22. Nathan Rao, "'Wrap Rage' Soars Over Packaging We Can't Open," *Express*, January 28, 2014, www.express.co.uk/news/uk/456493/Wrap-Rage -soars-over-packaging-we-can-t-open (Accessed February 17, 2014).

23. "U.S. Consumers Increase 'Green' Purchases; But Are They Willing to Pay More?" *PR Newswire*, June 5, 2013, www.prnewswire.com/news-releases /us-consumers-increase-green-purchases-but -are-they-willing-to-pay-more-210221081.html (Accessed February 17, 2014).

24. "New Packaging to Monitor Food Freshness," *Health24*, February 28, 2013, www.health24.com /Diet-and-nutrition/News/New-packaging-to-monitor -food-freshness-20130228 (Accessed February 10, 2014).

25. Adele Peters, "The Disappearing Package: From Dissolving Wrappers to Products that Package Themselves," *GOOD*, January 31, 2013, www.good.is/posts/the-disappearing-package-from -dissolving-wrappers-to-products-that-package -themselves (Accessed February 10, 2014).

26. "About Green Seal," *Green Seal*, www .greenseal.org/AboutGreenSeal.aspx (Accessed February 10, 2014).

11

1. "The World's 50 Most Innovative Companies," *Fast Company*, www.fastcompany.com/section /most-innovative-companies-2015 (Accessed April 21, 2015).

2. "Phases of Development," *Pfizer*, www.pfizer .com/research/clinical_trials/phases_of_development (Accessed April 21, 2015).

3. "10 Companies Spending Most on R&D in the World," *Rediff*, March 15, 2013, www.rediff.com /business/slide-show/slide-show-1-10-companies -spending-most-on-r-and-d-in-the-world/20130315 .htm (Accessed April 21, 2015).

4. Dieter Bohn, "Hands-on With the new 12-inch MacBook with Retina Display," *The Verge*, March 9, 2015, www.theverge.com/2015/3/9/8173685 /macbook-retina-display-usb-type-c-hands-on -video (Accessed April 21, 2015).

5. Amar Toor. "Has the Transparent Smartphone Finally Arrived?" *The Verge*, February 15, 2013, www.theverge.com/2013/2/15/3966950/will-we-see -a-transparent-phone-polytron-prototype-display (Accessed April 21, 2015).

6. "Moleskine World," *Moleskine*, www.moleskine .com/moleskine_world (Accessed April 21, 2015).

7. Ben Popken, "Taco Bell's Cool Ranch Tacos: Co-branding Genius," *Today*, January 10, 2013, http://lifeinc.today.com/_news/2013/01/10/16430586 -taco-bells-cool-ranch-tacos-co-branding-genius (Accessed April 21, 2014).

8. Rick Armon, "Miller Lite Releases New Bottle in Bars and Restaurants," *Ohio Breweries*, May 11,

2013, www.ohio.com/blogs/the-beer-blog/the-beer -blog-1.273124/miller-lite-releases-new-bottle-in -bars-and-restaurants-1.396902 (Accessed April 21, 2015).

9. Steven J. Erwing, "Mercedes Renames Utility Vehicles, Repositions Maybach as Sub-brand," *Autoblog*, November 11, 2014, www.autoblog.com /2014/11/11/mercedes-name-changes-gl-maybach/ (Accessed April 21, 2015).

10. Jacob Morgan, "Five Uncommon Internal Innovation Examples," *Forbes*, April 8, 2015, www .forbes.com/sites/jacobmorgan/2015/04/08/five -uncommon-internal-innovation-examples/ (Accessed April 21 ,2015).

11. Rachel Emma Silverman, "For Bright Ideas, Ask the Staff," *Wall Street Journal*, October 17, 2011, B7.

12. Michelle Greenwald, "NikeID, Coca-Cola Freestyle and Other Brands Mastering Infinite Customization," *Forbes*, October 8, 2014, www .forbes.com/sites/michellegreenwald/2014/10/08 /infinite-customization-12-category-examples-6 -key-questions-to-ask/ (Accessed April 21, 2015).

13. Tyler Falk, "How Google's Secretive Lab Innovates: Rewarding Failure," *ZDNet*, January 27, 2014, www.zdnet.com/article/how-googles-secretive -lab-innovates-reward-failure/ (Accessed April 21, 2015).

14. "Fuld & Company Is the World's Preeminent Research and Consulting Firm in the Field of Competitive Intelligence," *Fuld & Company*, www.fuld.com/company (Accessed April 21, 2015).

15. Liz Welch, "Success, One Board at a Time," *Inc.*, March 2014, 24–25.

16. David Kramer, "US Seeing Its Lead in R&D Slipping Against Other Nations," *Physicstoday*, February 2014, http://scitation.aip.org/content/aip /magazine/physicstoday/news/10.1063/PT.5.1010 (Accessed April 21, 2015).

17. "Company Profile," *Continuum*, http:// continuuminnovation.com/about/company-profile (Accessed April 21, 2015).

18. Jen Hansegard, "Lego's Plan to Find the Next Big Hit: Crowdsource It," *Wall Street Journal*, February 25, 2015, http://blogs.wsj.com/digits /2015/02/25/legos-plan-to-find-the-next-big-hit -crowdsource-it/ (Accessed April 21, 2015).

19. Eddie Makuch, "Ubisoft's Open-world Racer The Crew Has Been in Development for Six Years," *Gamespot*, May 15, 2014, www.gamespot.com /articles/ubisoft-s-open-world-racer-the-crew-has -been-in-development-for-six-years/1100-6419658/ (Accessed April 21, 2015); Eddie Makuch, "Watch Dogs Sells 4 Million Copies in First Week, Needs 2 Million More to Match Assassin's Creed Lifetime Tally," *Gamespot*, June 3, 2014, www.gamespot .com/articles/watch-dogs-sells-4-million-copies-in -first-week-needs-2-million-more-to-match-assassin -s-creed-s-lifetime-tally/1100-6420059/ (Accessed April 21, 2015).

20. Michael D. Hutt and Thomas W. Speh, *Business Marketing Management*, 12th ed. (Cincinnati: Cengage Learning, 2015).

21. "Wheaties™ Fans Select Anthony Pettis as America's NEXT Bow Chanpion," *PR Newswire*, September 3, 2014, www.prnewswire.com/news -releases/wheaties-fans-select-anthony-pettis-as -americas-next-box-champion-273732841.html (Accessed April 21, 2015).

22. Mary Vanac, "Meet Wendy's Ciabatta Bacon Cheeseburger," *Columbus Dispatch*, January 27, 2014, www.dispatch.com/content/blogs/the-bottom -line/2014/01/wendys-bringing-bacon-cheeseburger -back-with-ciabatta-bun.html (Accessed April 21, 2015).

23. John Dodge, "Dark Barrel Latte: Starbucks Has No Immediate Plan To Serve Beer-Flavored Drink In Chicago," *CBS Chicago*, September 24, 2014, http://chicago.cbslocal.com/2014/09/24/dark-barrel-latte-starbucks-has-no-immediate-plan-to-serve-beer-flavored-drink-in-chicago/ (Accessed April 21, 2015).

24. "P&G Everyday," *Procter & Gamble*, www.pgeveryday.com/pgeds/index.jsp (Accessed April 21, 2015).

25. Copernicus Marketing Consulting and Research, "Top 10 Reasons for New Product Failure," *Green-Book*, www.greenbook.org/marketing-research.cfm/top-10-reasons-for-new-product-failure (Accessed April 21, 2015).

26. Sage McHugh, "8 Biggest Product Fails of 2014,"*Alternet*, December 5, 2014 www.alternet.org/economy/8-biggest-product-fails-2014 (Accessed April 21, 2015).

27. Alex Pigliucci, "Wealth Management for China's Richest: An Industry with a Great Future," *Forbes*, January 28, 2013, www.Forbes.com/sites/Forbesleadershipforum/2013/01/28/wealth-management-for-chinas-richest-an-industry-with-a-great-future/ (Accessed April 21, 2015).

28. Susan Gunelius, "Data Proves Word-of-Mouth Marketing Works—Infographic," *Newstex*, February 12, 2014, http://newstex.com/2014/02/12/data-proves-word-of-mouth-marketing-works-infographic/ (Accessed April 21, 2015).

29. *Ibid*.

30. Mercedes Cardona, "Word-of-mouth Drives Teen Conversations," *Direct Marketing News*, July 1, 2012, www.dmnews.com/word-of-mouth-drives-teen-conversions/article/247170 (Accessed April 21, 2015).

31. *Ibid*.

32. "Millennials Depend on Word-of-Mouth More than Boomers," *RetailWire*, January 21, 2014, www.retailwire.com/discussion/17280/millennials-depend-on-word-of-mouth-more-than-boomers (Accessed April 21, 2015).

33. "Survey Reveals U.S. Consumers Feel Businesses Lead in Recognizing the Value of Listening to Feedback," *BusinessWire*, January 28, 2014, www.businesswire.com/news/home/20140128005598/en/Survey-Reveals-U.S.-Consumers-Feel-Businesses-Lead (Accessed April 21, 2015).

34. Rachael Feintzeig, "Boss's Next Demand: Make Lots of Friends," *Wall Street Journal*, February 12, 2014, B1.

35. Vivian Giang, "100 Fastest-Growing Companies," *Fortune*, http://fortune.com/100-fastest-growing-companies/on-assignment-3/ (Accessed April 21, 2015).

36. Robert Channick, "40% of Homes Now Without a Landline" *Chicago Tribune*, July 8, 2014, www.chicagotribune.com/business/breaking/chi-landlines-survey-20140708-story.html (Accessed April 21, 2015).

12

1. Aidan Smith, Roderick Asekhauno, Harold Laney, and Rebecca Hutchins, "Quarterly Estimates for Selected Service Industries 4th Quarter 2014," *U. S. Census Bureau*, www.census.gov/services/qss/qss-current (Accessed March 11, 2015); "Services," *Office of the United States Trade Representative*, August 28, 2014, https://ustr.gov/issue-areas/services-investment/services (Accessed March 11, 2015).

2. Flavio Martins, "Demystifying the Ritz-Carlton Secret of Legendary Customer Service," *Customer Think*, February 1, 2015, http://customerthink.com/demystifying-the-ritz-carlton-secret-of-legendary-customer-service (Accessed April 24, 2015).

3. Ed Jones, "Top 10 IT Certifications to Target in 2015," *Cloud Computing Intelligence*, January 5, 2015, www.cloudcomputingintelligence.com/item/1733-the-top-it-certifications-to-target-in-2015 (Accessed April 24, 2015).

4. Dwayne Gremler, Mary Jo Bitner, and Valarie Zeithaml, *Services Marketing* (New York: McGraw-Hill, 2012).

5. *Ibid*.

6. Simon Dumenco, "Venti, Venti Annoying: So How Does Starbucks Misspell Your Name?" *Advertising Age*, March 5, 2013, http://adage.com/article/the-media-guy/starbucks-pop-song-head/240104 (Accessed February 21, 2015).

7. Jim Harger, "New App Lets Fifth Third Bank Customers Deposit Checks via their Smartphones," *Michigan Live*, February 7, 2013, www.mlive.com/business/west-michigan/index.ssf/2013/02/new_app_lets_fifth_third_bank.html (Accessed February 24, 2015).

8. Douglas A. McIntyre, Alexander Kent, Alexander E.M. Hess, Thomas C. Frohlich, and Ashley C. Allen, "Customer Service Hall of Fame, http://247wallst.com/special-report/2014/07/18/customer-service-hall-of-fame, (Accessed March14, 2015).

9. Much of the material in this section is based on Christopher H. Lovelock and Jochen Wirtz, *Services Marketing*, 7th ed. (Upper Saddle River, NJ: Prentice Hall, 2011).

10. Zac Townsend, "Era of Mass Customization in Banking," *Bank Innovation*, April 17, 2014, http://bankinnovation.net/2014/04/era-of-mass-customization-in-banking (Accessed March 16, 2015).

11. Wendy Donahue, "Mac & Mia Trunk Club for Kids Makes Shopping Easy for Busy Moms," *The Charlotte Observer*, February 11, 2015, www.charlotteobserver.com/incoming/article10430567.html (Accessed April 24, 2015).

12. Lovelock and Wirtz, *Services Marketing*.

13. *Ibid*.

14. Much of the material in this section is based on Dwayne Gremler, Mary Jo Bitner, and Valarie Zeithaml, *Services Marketing*, (New York: McGraw-Hill), 2012.

15. Mia Taylor, "5 Hotels Opening in 2015 that Embody Latest Travel Trends," *MainStreet*, December 24, 2014, www.mainstreet.com/article/5-hotels-opening-in-2015-that-embody-latest-travel-trends (Accessed March 17, 2015).

16. "100 Best Companies to Work For 2015," *Fortune*, http://fortune.com/best-companies/ (Accessed April 14, 2015).

13

1. Hannah Elliott, "Rolls Royce's Bespoke Program Puts Virtually No Limits on Customization," *Pittsburgh Post-Gazette*, February 20, 2015.

2. Heather Clancy, "Kimberly-Clark Makes Sense of Demand," *Consumer Goods Technology*, October 11, 2012, http://consumergoods.edgl.com/case-studies/Kimberly-Clark-Makes-Sense-of-Demand82520 (Accessed February 2015).

3. Mark A. Moon, *Demand and Supply Integration: The Key to World-Class Demand Forecasting*. New York: Financial Times Press, 2013.

4. Much of this section is based on material adapted from Donald J. Bowersox, David J. Closs, and Theodore P. Stank, *21st Century Logistics: Making Supply Chain Integration a Reality*, Oak Brook, IL: Council of Logistics Management, 1999; Barbara Flynn, Michiya Morita, and Jose Machuca, *Managing Global Supply Chain Relationships: Operations, Strategies and Practices*, Business Science, Hershey, New York, 2010; and David Sims, "Integrated Supply Chains Maximize Efficiencies and Savings," *ThomasNet*, July 23, 2013, http://news.thomasnet.com/imt/2013/07/23/integrated-supply-chains-maximize-efficiencies-and-savings (Accessed March 2015).

5. Häagen-Dazs and General Mills to Help Smallholder Vanilla Farmers Increase Yields and Improve Sustainability Practices in Madagascar," *CSRwire*, February 20, 2013, www.csrwire.com/press_releases/35228-H-agen-Dazs-and-General-Mills-to-Help-Smallholder-Vanilla-Farmers-Increase-Yields-and-Improve-Sustainability-Practices-in-Madagascar (Accessed January 2015).

6. Much of this and the following sections are based on material adapted from the edited volume Douglas M. Lambert, ed., *Supply Chain Management: Processes, Partnerships and Performance*, Sarasota, FL: Supply Chain Management Institute, 2004; and "The Supply Chain Management Processes," *Supply Chain Management Institute*, www.ijlm.org/Our-Relationship-Based-Business-Model.htm (Accessed March 2015).

7. "C.H. Briggs Builds a Better Relationship with its Customers," *IBM*, October 16, 2012, www-01.ibm.com/software/success/cssdb.nsf/CS/STRD-8YWGWZ (Accessed March 2015).

8. James A. Cooke, "Inside Dell's Global Command Centers," *DC Velocity*, September 24, 2012, www.dcvelocity.com/articles/20120924-inside-dells-global-command-centers (Accessed January 2015).

9. Stephanie Grothe, "How They Did It: Red Wing Shoes' Journey to S&OP," *Supply Chain Management Review*, May/June 2014.

10. John Letzing, "Amazon Adds That Robotic Touch," *Wall Street Journal*, March 20, 2012, http://online.wsj.com/article/SB1000142405270230472440457729190324479621 4.htm (Accessed March 2015); Donna Tam, "Meet Amazon's Busiest Employee – The Kiva Robot," *CNET*, November 20, 2014, http://www.cnet.com/news/meet-amazons-busiest-employee-the-kiva-robot/ (Accessed March 2015).

11. Tony Hines, *Supply Chain Strategies: Demand Driven and Customer Focused*, 2nd ed., New York: Routledge, 2013.

12. "Bayer HealthCare to Purchase Pharmacy Supplier Steigerwald Arzneimittelwerk," *Zenopa*, May 17, 2013, www.zenopa.com/news/801587313/bayer-healthcare-to-purchase-pharmacy-supplier-steigerwald-arzneimittelwerk (Accessed March 3, 2015).

13. Kenneth J. Petersen, Robert Handfield, and Gary Ragatz, "Supplier Integration into New Product Development: Coordinating Product, Process, and Supply Chain Design," *Journal of Operations Management*, 23, no. 3-4, (2005): 371-388; and Stephen Trimble, "Analysis: US South Rises on Airbus, Boeing Expansion," *Flight Global*, www.flightglobal.com (Accessed February 2015).

14. Curtis Greve and Jerry Davis, "Recovering Lost Profits by Improving Reverse Logistics," *UPS*, www.ups.com/media/en/Reverse_Logistics_wp.pdf (Accessed February 2015).

15. UPS, "Logistics of Sustainability," *Compass*, Spring 2012, 10.

16. Steve Szilagyi, keynote address, *Warehousing Education and Research Council* Annual Conference, Atlanta GA, May 2012; and Judy Owen, "Lowe's Ramps Up Disability Inclusion," *Forbes*, April 2013.

17. Martin Christopher, *Logistics and Supply Chain Management*, 4th ed. (New York: Prentice Hall/Financial Times, 2010).

18. Kate Vitasek and Karl Manrodt, *Vested: How P&G, McDonalds, and Microsoft are Redefining Winning in Business Relationships* (New York: Palgrave MacMillan, 2012).

19. Dinah Wisenberg Brin, "Need Technology Experts? Try Rural America," *CNBC*, February 20, 2013, www.cnbc.com/id/100470457 (Accessed March 2015).

20. Wesley S. Randall, "Public-Private Partnerships in Supply Chain Management," *Journal of Business Logistics*, December 2013.

21. "Federal Highway Administration," *U.S. Department of Transportation*, www.fhwa.dot.gov/ (Accessed March 3, 2015).

22. "Printing Titanium Bicycle Parts. A Charge Bikes Collaboration with EADS," *Vimeo*, August 14, 2012, http://vimeo.com/47522348 (Accessed January 2015).

23. "Home," *3DLT*, www.3dlt.com (Accessed March 2015).

24. Hans-Georg Kaltenbrunner, "How 3D Printing is Set to Shake Up Manufacturing Supply Chains," *The Guardian*, November 25, 2014.

25. J. Paul Dittmann, *Managing Risk in the Global Supply Chain*, Global Supply Chain Institute: Knoxville, TN, 2014.

26. John Markoff, "New Research Center Aims to Develop Second Generation of Surgical Robots," *The New York Times*, October 23, 2014.

27. Eric Savitz, "Apple Screens for iPad3 in Short Supply," *Forbes*, March 1, 2012, 9.

28. "Vera Bradley Strikes International Agreement," *Inside Indiana Business*, June 4, 2014, www.insideindianabusiness.com/newsitem.asp?id=65477 (Accessed March 3, 2015).

29. "Takeback Programs," *South Carolina Department of Health and Environmental Control*, www.scdhec.gov/environment/lwm/recycle/e-cycle/takeback_programs.htm (Accessed February 2015).

30. "Frequently Asked Questions About the Apple Recycling Program," *Apple*, www.apple.com/recycling/includes/recycling-faq.html (Accessed January 2015).

31. Aaron Strout, "Frictionless Mobile Commerce: 5 Examples of Companies that are Leading," *Marketing Land*, www.marketingland.com (Accessed January 2015).

32. Alex Hamilton, "M-Commerce Causing Sales Figures to Explode," *TechRadar*, www.techradar.com (Accessed February 2015).

33. "Retailers Leveraging Tablets to Elevate Brand, Boost Sales," *Retailing Insight*, http://retailinginsight.com/industrynews8.html, Accessed January 2015.

34. "What Is the Size of the M-Commerce Market In the US?" *Quora*, www.quora.com/Mobile-Commerce-1/What-is-the-size-of-the-m-commerce-market-in-the-US (Accessed January 2015).

35. Joanna Brenner, "Pew Internet: Mobile," *Pew Mobile*, September 13, 2013, http://pewinternet.org/Commentary/2012/February/Pew-Internet-Mobile.aspx (Accessed January 2015).

36. Ibid.

37. Aaron Smith, "In-store Mobile Commerce During the 2012 Holiday Shopping Season," *Pew Internet*, January 31, 2013, http://pewinternet.org/Reports/2013/in-store-mobile-commerce.aspx (Accessed January 2015).

38. Ibid.

39. Jack Uldrich, "The Future of Retail Isn't So Foreign," *Jump the Curve*, January 30, 2013, http://jumpthecurve.net/retail-marketing/the-future-of-retail-isnt-so-foreign/ (Accessed January 2015).

40. "Survey Finds Consumers Using Pinterest to Engage With Retailers More Than Facebook, Twitter," *Retailing Insight*, http://retailinginsight.com/industrynews9.html (Accessed January 2015).

41. Wang, J. J., Zhao, X., and Li, J. J. (2013). "Group Buying: A Strategic Form of Consumer Collective," *Journal of Retailing* 89(3), 338-351.

42. Taurn Kushwaha and Venkatesh Shankar, "Are multichannel customers really more valuable? The moderating role of product category characteristics," *Journal of Marketing*, 77, no. 4, 67-85.

43. Jennifer Lonoff Schiff, "Eight Ways to Create a Successful Multichannel Customer Experience," *CIO Magazine*, February 23, 2015.

14

1. "Monthly & Annual Retail Trade," *United States Census Bureau*, March 12, 2015, www.census.gov/retail (Accessed February 2015).

2. "Retail's Impact Report," *National Retail Federation*, www.nrf.com/advocacy/retails-impact (Accessed March 2015).

3. C. Brett Lockard and Michael Wolf, "Occupational Employment Projections to 2020," *Bureau of Labor Statistics Monthly Labor Review*, 135, no. 1, (2012): 84–108.

4. "Retail Firms by Employment Size," *National Retail Federation*, www.nrf.com (Accessed February 2015).

5. Jason Daley, "The 2015 Franchise 500," *Entrepreneur*, December 16, 2014.

6. Paul Tassi, "GTA 5 and the Ethics of Mass Murder," *Forbes*, December 11, 2014; "Toys R Us Pulls Breaking Bad Dolls After Florida Mom's Petition," *Tampa Bay Times*, October 21, 2014, www.tampabay.com/features/media/toys-r-us-pulls-breaking-bad-dolls-after-florida-moms-petition-w-video/2203155 (Accessed March 13, 2015).

7. Susan Johnston, "Beware These Online Retail Pricing Strategies," *US News and World Report*, June 24, 2013.

8. Alaric Dearment, "Target Tackles Movie Streaming," *Retailing Today*, September 25, 2013, http://retailingtoday.com/article/target-tackles-movie-streaming (Accessed February 2015).

9. "Man Cave – Home Parties for Men," *Man Cave*, www.mancaveworldwide.com (Accessed March 2015).

10. "Telemarketing in the 21st Century," *BusinessTM*, http://businesstm.com/home-based/telemarketing-in-the-21st-century.html (Accessed January 2015).

11. Tianyi Jiang and Alexander Tuzhilin, "Dynamic Microtargeting: Fitness-based Approach to Predicting Individual Preferences," *Knowledge and Information Systems* 19, no. 3, (2009): 337–60.

12. Al Urbanski, "Big Money for Big Data: Marketers will Spend $11.5B in 2015," *Direct Marketing News*, www.dmnews.com (Accessed February 2015).

13. "Market Research on Digital Media, Internet Marketing," *eMarketer*, www.emarketer.com (Accessed March 2015).

14. Ashley Lutz, "Zara's Genius Business Model Could Destroy JCPenney and Sears," *Business Insider*, March 4, 2013, www.businessinsider.com/zaras-genius-business-model-2013-3 (Accessed April 1, 2015).

15. Harry McCracken, "Amazon Holiday Delivery Woes: Send in the Drones," *Time*, December 26, 2013. http://techland.time.com/2013/12/26/amazon-holiday-delivery-woes-send-in-the-drones/ (Accessed March 2015).

16. Lydia Dishman, "The Entrepreneur Who Is Beating Amazon at Same-day Delivery," *Fast Company*, www.fastcompany.com/3042207/strong-female-lead/the-entrepreneur-who-is-beating-amazon-at-same-day-delivery (Accessed March 13, 2015).

17. Sarah Favot, "Two Build-your-own Pizza Restaurants Opening in Monrovia," *Pasadena Star-News*, March 21, 2014.

18. Gabrielle Karol, "TGI Fridays Offering $10 Unlimited Appetizers Promotion," *Fox Business*, July 7, 2014, www.foxbusiness.com/industries/2014/07/07/tgi-fridays-offering-10-unlimited-appetizers-promotion/ (Accessed January 2015).

19. Tiffany Hsu, "Toys R Us to Open Holiday Pop-up Shops in Macy's," *Los Angeles Times*, October 10, 2012, http://articles.latimes.com/2012/oct/10/business/la-fi-mo-toys-r-us-holiday-popup-macys-20121010 (Accessed January 2015).

20. Adam Blair, "The Drive to Localize," *RIS News*, May 7, 2011, http://risnews.edgl.com/retail-news/The-Drive-to-Localize72436 (Accessed March 2015).

21. Haithem Zourrig, Jean-Charles Chebat, and Roy Toffoli, "Consumer Revenge Behavior: A Cross-Cultural Perspective," *Journal of Business Research* 62, no. 10, (2009): 995–1001.

22. Christopher Ratcliff, "iBeacons: The Hunt for Stats," *Econsultancy.com*, August 26, 2014; Rachel Abrams, "Psst! It's Me, the Mannequin," *New York Times*, 2015, A8.

23. Ben Kersey, "Wal-Mart Tries a Blended Channel Approach to Survive in a Digital World," *The Verge*, November 23, 2012, www.theverge.com/2012/11/23/3681694/walmart-hybrid-model (Accessed January 2015).

24. Stuart Miller, "Customers Have High Expectations for Click and Collect," *Real Business*, November 28, 2013, http://realbusiness.co.uk/article/24866-customers-have-high-expectations-for-click-and-collect (Accessed March 2015).

15

1. McCarthy, Michael, "Sick of Ron Burgundy? Durango Certainly Isn't," *Advertising Age*, December 9, 2013, http://adage.com/article/news/sick-ron-burgundy-durango/245586/ (Accessed March 2015).

2. Michael Blaustein, "Watch: Ad for Colin Farrell Movie Goes Too Far with 'Elevator Murder' Video," *New York Post*, March 5, 2013, www.nypost.com/p/entertainment/movies/watch_marketing_elevator_collin_NOOBhxqXYHO3QXW8W4SjII (Accessed March 2015); Emily Verona, "True Detective Season 2 News: HBO Hit Giving Colin Farrell's Career A Boost?," *Enstarz*, January 19, 2015, www.enstarz.com/articles/60607/20150119/true-detective-season-2-news-hbo-hit-giving-colin-farrells-career-a-boost-video.htm (Accessed March 2015).

3. Ibid.

4. "Elevator Murder Experiment," *YouTube*, March 4, 2013, www.youtube.com/watch?v=qo6Jzh7SHRA (Accessed March 2015).

5. Steve Dent, "Google Glass' Now-like UI Finally Revealed, Just Accept and Say 'Ok,'" *Engadget*, February 20, 2013, www.engadget.com/2013/02/20/google-glass-how-it-feels-video (Accessed March 2015).

6. Jared Newman, "Ouya Ships March 28 to Kickstarter Backers, More Exclusives Coming," *TIME*, March 1, 2013, http://techland.time.com/2013/03/01/ouya-ships-march-28-to-kickstarter-backers-more-exclusives-coming (Accessed March 2015).

7. Ice Bucket Challenge, *ALS Association*, www.alsa.org/fight-als/ice-bucket-challenge.html (Accessed March 2015).

8. Andrew Johnson, "As Card Firms Try Social Media, Critics Keep Watch," *Wall Street Journal*, March 23, 2012, http://online.wsj.com/article/SB10001424052702304724404577297860607013698.html (Accessed March 2015); "Chase Freedom," *Facebook*, www.facebook.com/ChaseFreedom (Accessed March 2015).

9. The AIDA concept is based on the classic research of E. K. Strong Jr. as theorized in *The Psychology of Selling and Advertising* (New York: McGraw-Hill, 1925) and "Theories of Selling," *Journal of Applied Psychology*, 9, 1925, 75–86; "AIDA Communications Model Attention, Interest, Desire and Action," *Learn Marketing*, www.learnmarketing.net/AIDA.html (Accessed March 2015).

10. "How Many People in America Own an iPad?" *Answers*, http://wiki.answers.com/Q/How_many_people_in_America_own_an_iPad?#slide=2 (Accessed March 2015).

11. Thomas E. Barry and Daniel J. Howard, "A Review and Critique of the Hierarchy of Effects in Advertising," *International Journal of Advertising*, 9, 1990, 121–135.

12. Diana Reese, "Why Is Michelle Obama Praising Wal-Mart in Springfield, Mo.?" *Washington Post*, March 1, 2013, www.washingtonpost.com/blogs/she-the-people/wp/2013/03/01/why-is-michelle-obama-praising-walmart-in-springfield-mo (Accessed March 2015).

16

1. "Marketers" *Advertising Age 2015 Edition Marketing Fact Pack*, December 29, 2014, 6.

2. *Ibid.*

3. Darryl K. Taft, "IBM's Not-so-secret Weapon: Big Data," *eWeek*, February 26, 2013, www.eweek.com/database/ibms-not-so-secret-weapon-big-data-marketing (Accessed March 2015).

4. "The World's Most Valuable Brands," *Forbes*, www.forbes.com/powerful-brands/ (Accessed March 2015).

5. "How Americans Use Leisure Time," *Advertising Age 2015 Edition Marketing Fact Pack*, December 29, 2014, 31.

6. "Time Spent Using Media," *Advertising Age 2015 Edition Marketing Fact Pack*, December 29, 2014, 17.

7. Matthew Sparkes, "iPhone Owners Admit Having 'Blind Loyalty' to Apple," *Telegraph*, February 12, 2014, www.telegraph.co.uk/technology/apple/10632787/iPhone-owners-admit-having-blind-loyalty-to-Apple.html (Accessed February 18, 2014).

8. "25 largest US Advertisers," *Advertising Age 2015 Edition Marketing Fact Pack*, December 29, 2014, 8.

9. David Griner, "Oreo Surprises 26 Million Facebook Fans with Gay Pride Post," *Adweek*, June 25, 2012, www.adweek.com/adfreak/oreo-surprises-26-million-facebook-fans-gay-pride-post-141440 (Accessed March 2015).

10. Oussama Jebali, "First Interactive Print Ad Featuring LED Light and Battery by Motorola," *Esprit Mobile*, January 21, 2014, http://espritmobile .com/first-interactive-print-ad-featuring-led-light-and-battery-by-motorola/ (Accessed March 2015).

11. "'Shopping Carts' Commercial—21st Century Auto Insurance: Same Great Coverage for Less," *YouTube*, February 22, 2012, www.youtube.com/watch?v=CDoAmgIfj_U (Accessed March 2015).

12. *Ibid.*

13. John Babish, "Ithaca, NY Company, Bionexus, Introduces First Natural Skin Care Lotion for Dogs Containing Standardized Nigella Sativa Extracts," *PRNewswire*, April 17, 2012, www.facebook.com/permalink.php?id=118344488181338&story_fbid=419853818042564 (Accessed March 2015).

14. "Bag Designer Uses Video to Teach Counterfeiters," *Will Video For Food*, January 19, 2014, http://willvideoforfood.com/2014/01/19/bag-designer-uses-video-to-teach-counterfeiters/ (Accessed March 2015); "The Saddleback Story," *Saddleback Leather*, www.saddlebackleather.com/Saddleback-Story (Accessed March 2015).

15. Lauren Cleave, "What Do We Really Think about Humour in Advertising?" http://adgrad.co.uk/?author=4 (Accessed March 2015).

16. Neil King Jr., "Anti-Obama Ads Take Elegiac Tone," *Wall Street Journal*, May 4, 2012, http://online.wsj.com/article/SB10001424052702303877604577383950339656854.html (Accessed March 2015).

17. "The Best Ads of 2014," *Adweek*, www.adweek.com/news-gallery/advertising-branding/10-best-ads-2014-161692 (Accessed March 2015).

18. "Media – Share of Ad Spending by Medium," *Advertising Age 2015 Edition Marketing Fact Book*, December 29, 2014, 16.

19. *Ibid.*

20. Alex Kantrowitz, "$70 Billion TV Ad Market Easing into Digital Direction," *Advertising Age*, October 14, 2013, http://adage.com/article/media/70-billion-tv-ad-market-eases-digital-direction/244699/ (Accessed March 2015).

21. Jeanine Poggi, "TV Ad Prices: Football Is Still King," Advertising Age, October 20, 2013, http://adage.com/article/media/tv-ad-prices-football-king/244832/ (Accessed March 2015).

22. Jeanine Poggi, "Most Pricey TV Buy: A Spot in NFL," *Advertising Age*, February 28, 2015, http://gaia.adage.com/images/bin/pdf/TV_pricing_chart_for_web.pdf (Accessed March 19, 2015).

23. Ingrid Lunden, "Digital Ads Will Be 22% Of All U.S. Ad Spend In 2013, Mobile Ads 3.7%; Total Global Ad Spend In 2013 $503B," *TechCrunch*, September 20, 2013, http://www.convergemg.com/digital-ads-will-be-22-of-all-u-s-ad-spend-in-2013-mobile-ads-3-7-total-global-ad-spend-in-2013-503b/ (Accessed March 2015).

24. David Kaplan, "For Turner Digital, Audience Buying Risk Outweighs Reward," *AdExchanger*, October 9, 2012, www.adexchanger.com/online-advertising/for-turner-digital-audience-buying-risk-outweighs-reward (Accessed March 2015).

25. "IAB Internet Advertising Revenue Report: 2012 Full Year Results," *PricewaterhouseCoopers*, April 2013, www.iab.net/media/file/IAB_Internet_Advertising_Revenue_Report_FY_2012.pdf (Accessed March 2015).

26. "Most popular Facebook Games in February 2015," *Statista*, www.statista.com/statistics/267003/most-popular-social-games-on-facebook-based-on-daily-active-users/ (Accessed March 2015).

27. "Facebook vs. Non-Facebook Social Network Gaming Ecosystem and Market Analysis 2013 - 2018," *MarketWatch*, February 4, 2014, www.marketwatch.com/story/facebook-vs-non-facebook-social-network-gaming-ecosystem-and-market -analysis-2013-2018-2014-02-04 (Accessed March 2015).

28. Joanna Brenner, "Pew Internet: Mobile," *Pew Research Center*, January 31, 2013, http://pewinternet.org/Commentary/2012/February/Pew-Internet-Mobile.aspx (Accessed March 2015).

29. Alex Kantrowitz, "Mobile Ad Revenue Explodes, Finally," *Advertising Age*, December 16, 2013, 6.

30. Owen Thomas, "New Marissa Mayer's Complaint about Yahoo's Hold Music Has Turned into a Music Video," *Business Insider*, February 4, 2013, www.businessinsider.com/yahoo-earnings-hold-music-video-snow-rapper-2013-2 (Accessed March 2015).

31. John Moulding, "ABC Proves the Value of the Unified TV/Digital Ad Buy," *Videonet*, October 23, 2013, www.v-net.tv/abc-proves-the-value-of-the-unified-tvdigital-ad-buy/ (Accessed March 2015).

32. Kathy Crosett, "Online Product Placement to Increase," *Ad-ology*, January 10, 2013, www.marketingforecast.com/archives/22200 (Accessed March 2015).

33. "US Ad Spending Forecast from Zenith Optimedia," *Advertising Age 2015 Edition Marketing Fact Pack*, December 29, 2014, 14.

34. *Ibid.*

35. Jennifer Wang, "10 Marketing Masterworks," *Entrepreneur*, February 18, 2013, www.entrepreneur.com/article/225462 (Accessed March 2015).

36. Edmund Lawler, "The Rise of Experiential Marketing," *Advertising Age*, November 18, 2013, C1–C2.

37. Philip Caulfield, "Web Pranksters Hijack Restaurant's Mountain Dew Naming Contest," *New York Daily News*, August 15, 2012, www.nydailynews.com/news/national/web-pranksters-hijack-mountain-dew-online-crowdsourced-naming-effort-new-green-apple-flavored-soda-article-1.1136204 (Accessed March 2015).

38. "Inmar 2014 Coupon Trends – Year End 2013," *Inmar*, February 2014, http://go.inmar.com/rs/inmar/images/Inmar_2014_Coupon_Trends_Report.pdf (Accessed March 2015).

39. Caitlin McGarry, "Pay by Hashtag: Twitter Wants to Get Inside your Wallet," *TechHive*, January 24, 2014, www.techhive.com/article/2090822/pay-by-hashtag-twitter-wants-to-get-inside-your-wallet.html (Accessed March 2015); Andrew R. Johnson, "@AmericanExpress Tries #Deals via Twitter," *Wall Street Journal*, March 7, 2012, www.wsj.com/articles/SB10001424052970204781804577267402969728444 (Accessed March 2015).

40. Donna L. Montaldo, "How to Avoid the Rebate Rip-off," *About.com*, http://couponing.about.com/od/bargainshoppingtips/a/hub_rebate.htm (Accessed March 2015).

41. Martin Moylan, "Retailers' Loyalty Programs Popular with Consumers," *Minnesota Public Radio*, January 2, 2013, http://minnesota.publicradio.org/display/web/2013/01/02/business/retail-rewards-programs (Accessed March 2015).

42. Elizabeth Holmes, "At Bloomies, Loyalty for All," *Wall Street Journal*, February 24, 2012, B5.

43. Kelly Short, "Study Shows In-store Sampling Events Outperform Other Top In-store Marketing Tactics," *Interactions*, February 28, 2013, www.interactionsmarketing.com/news/?p=352 (Accessed March 2015).

44. Jim Tierney, "Study Shows Most Customers Make Purchase Decisions In the Store," *Loyalty360*, November 11, 2013, http://loyalty360.org/resources/article/study-shows-most-customers-make-purchase-decisions-in-the-store (Accessed March 2015).

45. Don Davis, "Consumers Redeem 141% More Digital Coupons in 2013," *Internet Retailer*, January 16, 2014, www.internetretailer.com/2014/01/16/consumers-redeem-141-more-digital-coupons-2013 (Accessed March 2015).

46. Rachel King, "Google Trying out Real-time, Targeted Digital Coupons with Zavers," *ZDNet*, January 11, 2013, www.zdnet.com/google-trying-out-real-time-targeted-digital-coupons-with-zavers-7000009722/ (Accessed March 2015).

47. "Zero Moment of Truth (ZMOT)," *Google*, www.thinkwithgoogle.com/collections/zero-moment-of-truth.html (Accessed March 2015).

17

1. "Nordstrom Careers," *Nordstrom*, http://about.nordstrom.com/careers/ (Accessed March 2015).

2. "Personal Shoppers," *Bloomingdales*, www1.bloomingdales.com/about/shopping/personal.jsp (Accessed March 2015).

3. "What is LinkedIn?" *LinkedIn*, www.linkedin.com/static?key=what_is_linkedin&trk=hb_what (Accessed March 2015).

4. "Sales Navigator Product Datasheet," *LinkedIn*, https://business.linkedin.com/sales-solutions/site-forms/sales-navigator-datasheet (Accessed March 2015); "Featured Statistics – Brands," *Socialbakers*, www.socialbakers.com/statistics/facebook/pages/total/brands/ (Accessed April 7, 2015).

5. Alex Hisaka, "The 6-step Guide to Successful Social Selling on LinkedIn – Sales Solutions Blog," *LinkedIn*, January 22, 2015, http://sales.linkedin.com/blog/the-6-step-guide-to-successful-social-selling-on-linkedin/ (Accessed March 2015).

6. "Social Selling Tips: 10 Actionable Sale Tips LinkedIn Sales Solutions," *LinkedIn*, https://business.linkedin.com/sales-solutions/resources/social-selling/top-sales-tips (Accessed March 2015).

7. "Lead Qualification Response Management Teleservices," *Salesify*, www.salesify.com/lead-qualification (Accessed March 2015).

8. Kim Garst, "Find Prospects on Social Media and Turn Them into Customers," *Huffington Post*, February 18, 2014, www.huffingtonpost.com/kim-garst/find-prospects-on-social-_b_4785711.html (Accessed March 2015).

9. "Leadership Program," *General Electric*, www.ge.com/careers/students/clp/index.html (Accessed March 2015).

10. Linda Ray, "Examples of Cultural Differences in Business," *Demand Media*, http://smallbusiness.chron.com/examples-cultural-differences-business-21958.html (Accessed March 2015).

11. Weitz, B., Castleberry, S., and Tanner, J., *Selling*, Notebooks, 8th edition, 2014.

12. "Oracle PeopleSoft Applications," *Oracle*, www.oracle.com/us/products/applications/peoplesoft-enterprise/overview/index.htm (Accessed March 2015).

13. Peter Criscione, "Mary Kay's Top Salespeople are Pretty in Pink," *Brampton Guardian*, February 25, 2014, www.mississauga.com/news-story/4384280-mary-kay-s-top-salespeople-are-pretty-in (Accessed March 2015).

14. Paul Greenberg, "CRM Watchlist 2014 Winners: Upgraded to a Suite," *ZDNet*, February 17, 2014, www.zdnet.com/article/crm-watchlist-2014-winners-upgraded-to-a-suite-part-i/#! (Accessed March 2015).

15. "Revise Your Merchandising Strategy to Retain Customers in 2014," *Quantisense*, February 13, 2014, www.quantisense.com/blog/revise-your-merchandising-strategy-to-retain-customers-in-2014 (Accessed March 2015).

16. Heather Clancy, "7 Apps to Take Your Customer Loyalty Program Mobile," *ZDNet*, January 27, 2014, www.zdnet.com/7-apps-to-take-your-customer-loyalty-program-mobile-7000025654/ (Accessed February 19, 2014); Jessica Bruder, "A Customer Loyalty Program (From Some of the Folks Who Brought You Groupon)," *New York Times*, February 21, 2012, http://boss.blogs.nytimes.com/2012/02/21/a-customer-loyalty-program-from-some-of-the-folks-who-brought-you-groupon (Accessed March 2015).

17. Saul Perez, "Why Cross-Selling is Part of Wells Fargo's Strategy," *Market Realist*, October 10, 2014, http://finance.yahoo.com/news/why-cross-selling-part-wells-130018022.html;_ylt=aolevx (Accessed March 2015).

18. "About Recommendations," *Amazon*, www.amazon.com/gp/help/customer/display.html/ref=help_search_1-1?ie=UTF8&nodeId=16465251&qid=1426340118&sr=1-1 (Accessed March 2015).

18

1. "Social Media and the New Reality for Law Practice," *LegalWire*, February 24, 2013, www.legalwire.co.uk/?dt_portfolio=legal-profession-2-0-social-media-and-the-new-reality-for-law-firms (Accessed March 2015).

2. "Twitter: Most Followers," *FriendOrFollow*, http://friendorfollow.com/twitter/most-followers/ (Accessed March 2015).

3. Shanyndi Raice, Mike Ramsey, and Sam Schechner, "Facebook Gains Two Big Advertisers' Support," *Wall Street Journal*, June 20, 2012, B6.

4. "The 10 Most Liked Brands on Facebook; *Mashable*, September 6, 2013, http://mashable.com/2013/09/06/facebook-brands-likes/ (Accessed March 2015).

5. "Flo, the Progressive Girl," *Facebook*, www.facebook.com/flotheprogressivegirl (Accessed March 2015); Dale Buss, "Progressive Just Keeps Going with the Flo, Refreshing Its Effective Mascot," *Brandchannel*, November 5, 2013, www.brandchannel.com/home/post/2013/11/05/Progressive-Flo-110513.aspx (Accessed March 2015).

6. Lululemon Practiced Text Book Crisis PR During Yoga Pants Frenzy," *PR Daily*, www.prdaily.com/Main/Articles/Lululemon_practiced_textbook_crisis_PR_during_yoga_14137.aspx# (Accessed March 2015).

7. David Moth, "Six Brands that Have Been Busy Experimenting with Google Hangouts," *Econsultancy*, http://econsultancy.com/us/blog/62774-six-brands-that-have-been-busy-experimenting-with-google-hangouts (Accessed March 2015).

8. "5 Terrific Examples of Company Social Media Policies," *HireRabbit*, http://blog.hirerabbit.com/5-terrific-examples-of-company-social-media-policies/ (Accessed March 2015).

9. Tessa Stuart, "Secrets of a Celebrity Twitter Coach," *BuzzFeed*, February 19, 2013, www.buzzfeed.com/tessastuart/secrets-of-a-celebrity-twitter-coach (Accessed March 2015).

10. Cory Edwards, "A Shift in Social Media Training for Employees," *Adobe*, December 17, 2013, http://blogs.adobe.com/digitalmarketing/social-media/a-social-shift-in-social-media-training-for-employees/ (Accessed March 2015).

11. Parmy Olson, "Teenagers Say Goodbye to Facebook and Hello to Messenger Apps," *The Guardian*, November 9, 2013, www.theguardian.com/technology/2013/nov/10/teenagers-messenger-apps-facebook-exodus (Accessed March 2015).

12. "Useful Social Media Statistics for 2015," *Our Social Times*, December 22, 2014, http://oursocialtimes.com/8-useful-social-media-statistics-for-2015/ (Accessed April 7, 2015).

13. *Ibid.*

14. "SBANC Newsletter—June 5th, 2012," *International Council for Small Business*, June 5, 2012, www.icsb.org/article.asp?messageID=983 (Accessed March 2015).

15. Joanna Brenner, "Pew Internet: Mobile," *Pew Research Center*, January 31, 2013, http://pewinternet.org/Commentary/2012/February/Pew-Internet-Mobile.aspx (Accessed March 2015).

16. Steven Musil, "U.S. Tablet Usage Hits 'Critical Mass' ComScore Reports," *CNET*, June 10, 2012, http://news.cnet.com/8301-13579_3-57450079-37/u.s-tablet-usage-hits-critical-mass-comscore-reports (Accessed March 2015).

17. Sid Gandotra, "Why Social Commerce Matters," *Social Media Today*, November 6, 2012, http://socialmediatoday.com/sid-gandotra/974961/social-commerce-socialmedia-ecommerce (Accessed March 2015).

18. Janessa Rivera, "Gartner Says CRM Will Be at the Heart of Digital Initiatives for Years to Come," *Gartner*, February 12, 2014, www.gartner.com/newsroom/id/2665215 (Accessed March 2015).

19. Lauren Indvik, "7 Species of Social Commerce," *Mashable*, May 10, 2013, http://mashable.com/2013/05/10/social-commerce-definition/ (Accessed April 7, 2015).

20. "Giveaway!!! Pin it to Win it! An iPad Mini for Two Lucky Winners!!!" *Favorite Family Recipes*, March 10, 2013, www.favfamilyrecipes.com/2013/03/giveaway-pin-it-to-win-it-an-ipad-mini-for-two-lucky-winners.html (Accessed March 2015); Lauren Indvik, "How Brands Are Using Promotions to Market on Pinterest," *Mashable*, March 7, 2012, http://mashable.com/2012/03/07/pinterest-brand-marketing (Accessed March 2015).

21. *Ibid.*

22. "Complimentary White Paper: Forrester's US Interactive Marketing Forecast through 2016," *Adobe Marketing Cloud*, http://success.adobe.com/en/na/programs/products/digitalmarketing/migration12/1208_21408_forrester_interactive_marketing_forecast.html (Accessed March 2015).

23. Eric Mosley, "Crowdsource your Performance Reviews," *Harvard Business Review*, June 15, 2013, http://blogs.hbr.org/cs/2012/06/crowdsource_your_performance_r.html (Accessed March 2015).

24. "Photograph for Ellie Goulding with HP Connected Music," *Talenthouse*, www.talenthouse.com/photograph-for-ellie-goulding-and-hp-connected-music#description (Accessed March 2015).

25. "Paid Media Marketing," *Greenlight*, www.greenlightdigital.com/paid-media (Accessed March 2015).

26. *Ibid.*

27. Russell Working, "Most Unhappy with Social Media Measurement, Survey Says," *Ragan Communications*, www.ragan.com/Main/Articles/Most_unhappy_with_social_media_measurement_survey_45919.aspx (Accessed March 2015).

28. "Key Performance Indicators," *Intrafocus*, June 2013, www.intrafocus.com/wp-content/uploads/2014/06/Key-Performance-Indicators.docx (Accessed March 2015).

29. Andy Williams, "How Social Media Has Changed the Way We Complain," *Koozai*, February 25, 2013, www.koozai.com/blog/branding/reputation-management/how-social-media-has-changed-the-way-we-complain (Accessed March 2015); Bob Fine, "How Social Media Has Changed Politics: It's Not Just Tactics," *The Social Media Monthly*, January 18, 2013, http://thesocialmediamonthly

.com/how-social-media-has-changed-politics-its-not-just-tactics (Accessed March 2015); "How Social Media Has Changed the Way We Communicate," *Information Gateway*, January 24, 2013, www.informationgateway.org/social-media-changed-communicate (Accessed March 2015).

30. Charlene Li and Josh Bernoff, *Groundswell: Winning in a World Transformed by Social Technologies*, revised ed. (Boston: Harvard Business Press, 2011).

31. Gina Sverdlov, "Global Social Technographics Update: US and EU Mature, Emerging Markets Show Lots of Activity," *Forrester*, January 4, 2012, http://blogs.forrester.com/gina_sverdlov/12-01-04-global_social_technographics_update_2011_us_and_eu_mature_emerging_markets_show_lots_of_activity (Accessed March 2015); "What's the Social Technographics Profile of Your Customer?" *Forrester Empowered*, http://empowered.forrester.com/tool_consumer.html (Accessed March 2015).

32. Paige ONeil, "Forrester: Social Media Use in US and EU Maturing, More Passive Than Emerging Markets," http://paigeoneill.com/2012/01/05/forrester-social-media-use-in-us-and-eu-maturing-more-passive-than-emerging-markets/ (Accessed March 2015).

33. Shanna Mallon, "Should Every Company Have a Blog?" *The Media Revolution*, January 30, 2014, www.blogworld.com/2014/01/30/should-every-company-have-a-blog/ (Accessed March 2015).

34. Mark Schaefer, "The 10 Best Big Company Blogs in the World," *Businesses Grow*, January 12, 2015, www.businessesgrow.com/2015/01/12/best-company-blogs/ (Accessed March 2015).

35. Lauren Drell, "The Quick and Dirty Guide to Tumblr for Small Business," *Mashable*, February 18, 2012, http://mashable.com/2012/02/18/tumblr-small-biz-guide (Accessed March 2015).

36. Chris Erasmus, "The Voting Hub Facebook Page," *Threadless*, February 16, 2014, www.threadless.com/forum/post/990069/the_voting_hub_facebook_page/ (Accessed March 2015).

37. Josh Bersin, "Facebook Vs. LinkedIn—What's the Difference?" *Forbes*, May 21, 2012, www.forbes.com/sites/joshbersin/2012/05/21/facebook-vs-linkedin-whats-the-difference (Accessed March 2015).

38. "Top Sites," *Alexa*, www.alexa.com/topsites (Accessed March 2015).

39. Rob Walker, "How Reddit's Ask Me Anything Became Part of the Mainstream Media Circuit," *Yahoo*, March 13, 2013, http://news.yahoo.com/how-reddit-s-ask-me-anything-became-part-of-the-mainstream-media-circuit--130755591.html (Accessed March 2015); "Top Scoring Links: IAmA," *Reddit*, www.reddit.com/r/IAmA/top/ (Accessed March 2015).

40. Tony Nguyen, "The Importance of Social Bookmarking and RSS in SEO," *Business Review Center*, October 18, 2012, http://businessreviewcenter.com/social-bookmarking-and-rss (Accessed March 2015).

41. Jordan Slabaugh, "4 Ways to Get Customers on Your Side," *iMedia Connection*, January 29, 2014, www.imediaconnection.com/content/35808.asp (Accessed March 2015).

42. "Yelp Elite Event: Tiki Beach Party at Le Lab" *Yelp*, www.yelp.com/biz/yelp-elite-event-tiki-beach-party-at-le-lab-montr%C3%A9al (Accessed March 2015).

43. "Second Life Grid Survey—Economic Metrics," *GridSurvey*, March 15, 2013, http://gridsurvey.com/economy.php (Accessed March 2015).

44. Emanuel Maiberg, "Top 25 Facebook Games of May 2013," *Inside Social Games*, May 1, 2013, www.insidesocialgames.com/2013/05/01/the-top-25-facebook-games-of-may-2013/ (Accessed March 2015).

45. Eddie Makuch, "93 Million People Play Candy Crush Saga Daily—Do You?" *Gamespot*, February 18, 2014, www.gamespot.com/articles/93-million-people-play-candy-crush-saga-daily-do-you/1100-6417819/ (Accessed March 2015).

46. Chelsea Stark, "Microtransactions and Digital Sales Are Dominating Game Developers' Profits," *Mashable*, January 15, 2015, http://mashable.com/2015/01/15/game-developer-survey-2015/ (Accessed April 7, 2015).

47. Paul Tassl, "Kim Kardashian May Make $85 Million From Her Video Game," *Forbes*, July 17, 2014, www.forbes.com/sites/insertcoin/2014/07/17/kim-kardashian-may-make-85-million-from-her-video-game/ (Accessed April 7, 2015).

48. "Global Mobile Statistics 2013 Part A: Mobile Subscribers; Handset Market Share; Mobile Operators," *mobiThinking*, March 2013, http://mobithinking.com/mobile-marketing-tools/latest-mobile-stats/a (Accessed March 2015).

49. Ingrid Lunden, "Digital Ads Will Be 22% Of All U.S. Ad Spend In 2013, Mobile Ads 3.7%; Total Global Ad Spend In 2013 $503B," *TechCrunch*, September 1, 2013, http://techcrunch.com/2013/09/30/digital-ads-will-be-22-of-all-u-s-ad-spend-in-2013-mobile-ads-3-7-total-gobal-ad-spend-in-2013-503b-says-zenithoptimedia/ (Accessed March 2015).

50. "Modify QR Code Watch—Because Simply Reading Time on Your Watch Is Soooo 2011," *Modify Watches* February 23, 2012, www.modifywatches.com/blog/qr-code-watch (Accessed March 2015).

51. "The Samsung Galaxy Tab 4 NOOK 7.0," *Barnes and Noble*, www.barnesandnoble.com/p/samsung-galaxy-tab-4-nook-7-inch-barnes-noble/1119732448 (Accessed March 2015).

52. "The Next Big Thing is Almost Here – Samsung Galaxy S6," *T-Mobile*, www.t-mobile.com/cell-phones/samsung-galaxy-s-6-edge.html (Accessed March 2015).

53. Daniel Howley, "The Best iPhone Widgets You're Not Using," January 24, 2015, www.yahoo.com/tech/the-best-iphone-widgets-youre-not-using-108954809304.html (Accessed March 2015).

19

1. "Hershey Price Hike Tests Theory That Americans Love Chocolate at Any Price," *Wall Street Journal*, July 18, 2014, http://blog.wsj.com/moneybeat/2014/07/18/hershey-price-hike-tests-theory-that-americans-love-chocolate-at-any-price/html (Accessed February 26, 2015).

2. "Can You Trust That Web Price?" *Wall Street Journal*, October 23, 2014, B1.

3. "Personalized Pricing," *Business Week*, January 2, 2014, 47–48; Koert van Ittersum, Brian Wansink, Joost Pennings, and Daniel Sheehan, "Smart Shopping Carts: How Real Time Feedback Influences Spending," *Journal of Marketing*, November 2013, 21–36.

4. "SFPark Called a Success, Will Expand Throughout the City," June 21, 2014, *SFGate*, www.sfgate.com/bayarea/article/SFpark-called-a-success-willexpand-throughout-5568645.php (Accessed February 26, 2015).

5. "How Much Did You Pay For That Lipstick?" *Forbes*, April 14, 2015, 46–49.

6. "Best Buy Put Off By Showrooming, Guarantees Low Price," *Market Realist*, January 19, 2015, http://marketrealist.com/2015/01/best-buy-put-off-by-showrooming-guarantees-low-price/ (Accessed February 26, 2015).

7. Ryan Hamilton and Alexander Chernev, "Low Prices Are Just the Beginning: Price Image in Retail Management," *Journal of Marketing*, November 2013, 1–20.

8. *Ibid*.

9. Keith Coulter and Anne Roggeveen, "Price Number Relationships and Deal Processing Fluency: The Effects of Approximation Sequence and Number Multiples," *Journal of Marketing Research*, February 2014, 69–82.

10. "Developing a Sustainable Standard for Products," *Walmart*, http://corporate.walmart.com/global-responsibility/environment-sustainability/sustainability-index (Accessed February 26, 2015).

11. Jennifer Chu, "Flying the Not-so-friendly Skies" *MIT*, January 30, 2014, http://web.mit/edu/newsoffice/2014/flying-the-not-so-friendly-skies-0130.html (Accessed February 26, 2015).

12. Aylin Aydini, Marco Bertini, and Anja Lambrecht, "Price Promotion for Emotional Impact," *Journal of Marketing*, July 2014, 80–96.

13. Ayelet Eneezy, Uri Eneezy, and Dominique Olié Lauga, "A Reference-Dependent Model of the Price-Quality Heuristic," *Journal of Marketing Research*, April 2014, 153–164.

14. "Future of Private Labels Looks Bright," *McLoone*, January 31, 2014, www.mccloone.com/blog/future-of-private-labels-looks-bright/ (Accessed February 27, 2015).

15. "Spirit Airlines: The Power of a Clear Strategy," *Strongbrands*, February 2, 2015, http://timcalkins.com/branding-insights/spirit-airlines-power-clear-strategy/ (Accessed February 28, 2015).

16. "Free Shipping Is Getting More Expensive," *Wall Street Journal*, October 22, 2014, www.wsj.com/articles/free-shipping-is-going-to-cost-you-more-1414003507 (Accessed February 28, 2015).

17. *Ibid*.

18. Jan Wieseke, Sascha Alavi, and Johannes Habel, "Willing to Pay More, Eager to Pay Less: The Role of Consumer Loyalty in Price Negotiations," *Journal of Marketing*, November 2014, 17–37.

19. "The Psychology Behind the Sweet Spots of Pricing," *Fast Company*, www.fastcompany.com/1826172/psychology-behind-sweet-spots-pricing (Accessed February 28, 2015).

INDEX

advertising spending by, 283
use of social CRM by, 317
Labeling, 183–184
Labor costs, 23
Laffey, A.G., 6
Laggards, 199
Language
global marketing considerations, 72
promotion adaptation, 84
Late majority, 199
Laws, 30
Layout, retail operations, 256
Lead generation, 306–307
Lead qualification, 307–308
Leader pricing, 359
Lean supply chains, 224
Learning, influence of on consumer
buying behavior, 112–113
Leasing, use of in B-to-B market,
124–125
Legal factors, 22, 60–61
consumer privacy, 63–64
federal legislation, 61
global marketing and, 74–79
regulatory agencies, 62–63
state and local laws, 61–62
Legal responsibility, 39–40
Lego, use of crowdsourcing by, 193
Levels of distribution intensity, 240–241
Lever Brothers, 19
Licensing, global marketing and, 81
Life events, influence of on consumer
buying decisions, 108
Lifestyle, influence of on consumer
buying decisions, 109
Lifestyle centers, 255
Limited availability, consumer
involvement and, 100
Limited decision making, 97
LinkedIn, 50, 334
use of for B-to-B content
marketing, 116
use of for personal selling, 304
Livingsocial, 239, 299
Lobbying, 295
Local community, corporate social
responsibility to, 39
Local governments, marketing to, 121
Local laws, 61–62
Location-based social networking sites,
335, 338
Logistical functions, 234
Logistics integrators, 227
Loss-leader pricing, 359
Lowe's Home Improvement, social
sustainability efforts of, 226

Lower class, consumer buying behavior
of, 103
Loyalty marketing programs,
299–300, 319
Lululemon, 324

M

M-commerce, 238–239
Mac & Mia, distribution strategy of, 211
Macroenvironmental factors, 22
Macy's
market segmentation strategies, 135
pricing image of, 351
Magazines, advertising in, 289
Mail surveys, 158
Major equipment (installations), 125
Mall intercept interviews, 157–158
Man Cave, 250
Management, corporate social
responsibility to, 39
Management decision problem, 153
Manufacturers' vs. private brands,
179–180
Manufacturing flow management
process, 224
Marcario, Rose, 41
March of Dimes, strategic planning
of, 14
Marcosur, 74–75
Market, definition of, 132
Market attractiveness, 19–20
Market development, 16
Market factors, distribution channel
choice and, 239
Market grouping, 74
Market opportunity analysis (MOA), 26
Market orientation, 5–6
defining the business's primary goal, 12
defining the firm's business, 10–11
efforts to reduce cognitive
dissonance, 96
organizational focus, 7–10
target customers, 11–12
tools used with, 12
Market penetration, 16
Market research
analyzing the data, 164–165
data collection, 164
deciding when to conduct, 169–170
following up, 165
impact of Internet on, 165–168
importance of mobile research,
168–169
preparing and presenting the
report, 165

scanner-based, 169
specifying the sampling procedures,
162–164
Market segmentation
criteria for, 134
importance of, 133–134
steps in, 141–142
Market segments, 133
Market share, 343–344
advertising and, 282
Market-based analysis, 256
Marketing
B-to-B, 114–115 (See also B-to-B
marketing)
cause-related, 44
creating and leveraging social media
campaigns, 327–328
definition of, 2–3
experiential, 296
gender and, 107–108
green, 43–44
implications of involvement,
99–100
management philosophies, 4–7
metrics for social media, 330
omnichannel vs. multichannel,
241–242
primary U.S. laws affecting, 61–62
reasons for studying, 13
ROI for use of social media, 329
sales vs. market orientations, 7–12
social class and consumer buying
behavior, 103–104
use of social media for, 50–51
Marketing audit, 28
characteristics of, 29
Marketing channels, 232
functioning of, 232–233
transaction reduction due to use
of, 234
Marketing choice, factors affecting
choice of, 239–240
Marketing communication, 263–267
designing, 320
integrated, 275
Marketing concept, 5
Marketing databases, 318
Marketing managers, importance of
price to, 342
Marketing mix (four Ps), 26–27, 46
effect of social factors on, 49–51
global, 82–86
role of promotion in, 263
services, 209–212
Marketing myopia, 21
Marketing objectives, 25–26

CHAPTER OUTLINE

WHAT'S INSIDE:

Key topics in this chapter: definition of marketing, concept of exchange, the four marketing orientations, the marketing concept, introduction to relationship marketing, comparison of sales and marketing orientations, customer relationship management, and explanation of why marketing is relevant to your students.

LEARNING OUTCOMES

1-1 Define the term *marketing*

1-2 Describe four marketing management philosophies

1-3 Discuss the differences between sales and market orientations

1-4 Describe several reasons for studying marketing

DISCUSSION QUESTIONS

1. Name a company you think might be successfully following a production orientation. Why might a firm in this industry be successful following such an orientation?

2. Can the marketing concept reach a point of diminishing returns? That is, is there a point at which marketers can offer too much choice to too many consumers (try to satisfy too many needs/wants), or is the proliferation of product choices indicative of successful implementation of the marketing concept?

3. Are customer satisfaction and customer value interdependent or mutually exclusive? Can satisfaction occur simultaneously with low customer value?

4. Why would a course in marketing be helpful even if you don't pursue marketing as a career?

ASSIGNMENTS

1. Have students draft a response to the adage "People don't know what they want—they only want what they know." Direct students to address the extent to which they think marketers shape consumer wants.

2. Have students draft a response to any of the discussion questions above.

ETHICS EXERCISE

Rani Pharmaceuticals is the maker of several popular drugs used to treat high blood pressure and arthritis. Over time, the company has developed a positive relationship with many of the patients who use its medications through a quarterly newsletter that offers the latest information on new medical research findings and general health and fitness articles. The company has just been acquired by a group of investors who also own Soothing Waters Hot Tubs and Spas. The marketing director for Soothing Waters would like to use Rani's mailing list for a direct-mail promotion.

QUESTIONS

1. What should Rani Pharmaceuticals do?

2. Do you think it is ethical to use customer information across multiple divisions of the same company? Explain.

CHAPTER PREP 1

KEY TERMS

3. To which marketing management philosophy do you think the marketing director for Soothing Waters subscribes? Explain.

4. Does the AMA Statement of Ethics address the use of customer information by multiple divisions of the same company? Go to www.marketingpower.com and review the statement. Then write a brief paragraph on how the AMA Statement of Ethics relates to Rani Pharmaceuticals' dilemma.

ADDITIONAL EXAMPLE

The Walt Disney Company recently announced that it will be implementing firm advertising rules on its television channels, radio stations, and Web sites. Disney will ban all ads for junk food on its media networks, hoping to get kids to eat better by removing the temptation of junk food advertising. The new rules will make Disney a pioneer in recognizing the force of advertising on consumer behavior. Disney will evaluate a company's broad offerings, beyond the specific product it hopes to advertise on one of Disney's channels.

Products such as Kraft's Capri Sun and Oscar Mayer Lunchables do not meet Disney's nutrition standards. Capri Sun has too much sugar, and Lunchables has high sodium content. Cereal with more than 10 grams of sugar or a meal with more than 600 calories will not meet nutrition standards and cannot be advertised. Companies like McDonald's, which is involved in the advertising initiative as part of its support for First Lady Michelle Obama's campaign to curb childhood obesity, may not make Disney's cut. The rules take effect in 2015, and until then, Disney hopes that with the desire to keep kids interested in their products through advertising, companies will reformulate products to meet nutrition standards.

"Disney's New Diet for Kids: No More Junk Food Ads," *Yahoo!*, June 5, 2012, http://finance.yahoo.com/news/disneys-diet-kids-no-more-junk-food-ads-222602295.html (Accessed March 25, 2013).

NEW TO MKTG10 CHAPTER 1

MKTG10	Section
New Kellogg's example	1-2a
Updated J.D. Power and Associates customer satisfaction rankings	1-2a
37signals example	1-3a
Updated Marriott example	1-3a

CHAPTER OUTLINE

WHAT'S INSIDE:

Key topics in this chapter: strategic planning process, defining business missions, Ansoff's matrix, portfolio matrix, the Boston Consulting Group model, the General Electric model, sustainable competitive advantage, defining target markets, and marketing mix.

LEARNING OUTCOMES

2-1 Understand the importance of strategic planning

2-2 Define strategic business units (SBUs)

2-3 Identify strategic alternatives and know a basic outline for a marketing plan

2-4 Develop an appropriate business mission statement

2-5 Describe the components of a situation analysis

2-6 Identify sources of competitive advantage

2-7 Explain the criteria for stating good marketing objectives

2-8 Discuss target market strategies

2-9 Describe the elements of the marketing mix

2-10 Explain why implementation, evaluation, and control of the marketing plan are necessary

2-11 Identify several techniques that help make strategic planning effective

DISCUSSION QUESTIONS

1. Is it possible to achieve sustainable competitive advantage, or is sustainable competitive advantage theoretical only? Name a company that has done so and outline how. (You may want to fuel discussion by asking students whether Apple, Netflix, Starbucks, Walmart, or another popular and successful company has a sustainable competitive advantage.)

2. Can a company be successful without using a portfolio matrix as a strategic planning tool?

3. Which element of the marketing mix is the most compelling for customers?

ASSIGNMENT

Have students find a current article of substance in the business press (the *Wall Street Journal, Fast Company, Business 2.0, Fortune, Bloomberg Businessweek, Inc.*) that discusses topics covered to date. Although students will have learned enough terminology for the exercise, you may suggest that they read through the table of contents at the beginning of this book to become familiar with the concepts that will be presented later in the course.

Students should:

1. Write a one-paragraph summary of the key points in the article, then write a list of the terms or concepts critical

CHAPTER PREP 2

KEY TERMS

to understanding the article. Provide definitions of those terms. If a term or concept that is central to the article is unfamiliar, use the textbook as a reference tool. Relate these key points to the concepts in the text by citing page numbers.

2. Identify how the strategic elements of target market and marketing mix are relevant to the article.

Note: If students submit work electronically, you can use their examples in your next lecture for Chapter 2 or as an intro to Chapter 3.

ADDITIONAL EXAMPLE

In the early days of video games, gaming wasn't exactly a social affair. Sure, you could spend hours playing the same game, but it was with two or three other players at most. And, of course, the earliest consoles were great at video games, but there were no other social features built into them. Now, gaming has been completely transformed by online networks and social media. The video game market is filled with smartphones, tablets, laptops, social networking Web sites, and other highly-connected ways to play.

Within this evolving marketplace—where success is seen by companies that emphasize mobility and multi-connectivity—Nintendo adapted a seemingly outdated strategy with the release of the Wii U, which focuses primarily on games. Instead of selling its new console as a multimedia device that gives users a wide range of entertainment options and a high level of social connectivity, Nintendo is hoping to reestablish its competitive advantage by leaning on users' love of The Legend of Zelda, Super Mario Bros., Donkey Kong, Metroid, and other first-party franchises. According to Nintendo of America President Reggie Fils-Aime, this strategy is based on the company's belief that what consumers want is games, not all of the other trappings: "When you talk to players and understand what they want, it can only be delivered through a dedicated gaming device." Early Wii U sales indicate otherwise, however. Only 64,000 Wii Us were sold in February 2013, compared to 302,000 sales of Microsoft's nearly ten-year-old Xbox 360 console.

Jamin Warren, "Not Your Childhood's Video-Game System," *Fast Company*, November 2012, 70-72; Matt Peckham, "What's Going On with Nintendo's Wii U?" *TIME*, March 15, 2013, http://techland.time.com/2013/03/15/whats-going-on-with-nintendos-wii-u (Accessed March 25, 2013).

NEW TO MKTG10 CHAPTER 2

MKTG10	Section
McDonald's example	2-1
Starbucks example	2-1
Updated BlackBerry example	2-3c
Updated Dell example	2-5
Uniqlo example	2-6b

CHAPTER OUTLINE

WHAT'S INSIDE:

Key topics for this chapter: determinants of a civil society, ethical theories, arguments for and against social responsibility, ethical behavior and its place in business, how companies are expected to be socially responsible, and cause-related marketing.

LEARNING OUTCOMES

3-1 Explain the determinants of a civil society

3-2 Explain the concept of ethical behavior

3-3 Describe ethical behavior in business

3-4 Discuss corporate social responsibility

3-5 Describe the arguments for and against society responsibility

3-6 Explain cause-related marketing

DISCUSSION QUESTIONS

1. Is sustainability a viable concept for American businesses? Explain your answer.

2. Why are free and uncontrolled media important in a country? How does that affect ethical responsibilities?

ASSIGNMENTS

1. On the Web site of a company of your choice, look for information about that firm's efforts to be socially responsible. Look for things such as news releases, company information, and community programs. Describe the various activities you find and explain why you think the company is involved with them.

2. Do the activities described on the Web site seem consistent with the company's products? Why or why not? (For example, a shoe company may sponsor a race that raises money to help prevent a disease. Racers may use that company's running shoes; therefore, the race would be consistent with the company's products.)

3. Evaluate the effectiveness of the information in terms of presentation, impact, and if it will help to sell the company's products. Support any claims you make.

4. Does the information you collected during this activity change your evaluation of the company? If so, explain your reasons.

Your goal for this assignment is to evaluate how firms are being socially responsible. Limit your answers to one page and provide a printout of the Web site you visited

GROUP ACTIVITY

Task: This exercise is great for large classes. Have students bring in three cans of the same type of food (for example, peas)—one from a large manufacturer, one private label/house brand, and one generic. Each can is worth five points. Have students write a paper (one to three pages), comparing and contrasting the packaging strategy of each can. The paper is worth ten points. Encourage students to address such topics as:

- Size and pricing
- Use of color
- What attracted them to each can
- Strong and weak points of each label
- Which package was the most efficient and effective and why

CHAPTER PREP 3

KEY TERMS

Then encourage each student to design his or her own label and discuss why it is better than the other labels. This is worth an additional five points. After the project is completed, donate the food to a food bank to encourage social responsibility.

ADDITIONAL EXAMPLE

In the wake of a national campaign focusing on ammonia-spritzed lean finely textured beef—otherwise known as pink slime—media attention turned to another ethically questionable food-processing product. Transglutaminase, or meat glue, is a white powder used to bind scraps of beef that would have otherwise been discarded. Composite pieces of meat are coated in meat glue, reshaped, and resold as complete cuts of meat such as filet mignon steaks. Because meat glue becomes transparent when cooked, it is virtually undetectable by the average consumer. While the USDA ensures that meat glue is safe, California State Senator Ted Lieu believes that tighter regulations should be placed on the additive: "They should look at not just whether the meat glue itself is harmful, but the entire process of when you combine meats together."

Filets and other pieces of meat sold commercially must be appropriately labeled if they contain transglutaminase. However, the cuts of meat sold in bulk to restaurants and catering services often contain meat glue—a detail that goes unmentioned on most menus. According to Dr. Betsy Booren, Director of Scientific Affairs for the American Meat Institute, consumers should take responsibility for finding out where their food is coming from. Senator Lieu contends that ethical restaurants and food service providers need to be transparent about their use of food additives like meat glue and pink slime.

Amy Powell, "'Meat Glue' Scandal: California Lawmaker Urges USDA to Investigate," *ABC News*, May 2, 2012, http://abclocal.go.com/kabc/story?section=news /consumer&id=8646215 (Accessed May 3, 2012).

NEW TO MKTG10 CHAPTER 3

MKTG10	Section
Updated content and new key terms on social control and behavioral norms	3-1
fast food targeting example	3-1
New content and examples on COPPA	3-1
Keystone XL Pipeline example	3-1
Updated content on moral relativism	3-2a
Bill Cosby and Federal Express examples	3-3
Googles Code of Ethics box	3-3c
Updated content on ethics training	3-3c
Updated Exhibit 3.1: Selected Winners of the World's Most Ethical Companies	3-3c
New section: Ethics and Small Business	3-3c
Burger King example	3-4a
Apple and Microsoft examples	3-4a
New content on social responsibility	3-5
Updated Starbucks example	3-5
Updated Patagonia example	3-5a
Updated data on social responsibility	3-5b
New Exhibit 3.4: Percent of Respondents Willing to Pay Extra for Products and Services from Companies Committed to Positive Social and Environmental Impact	3-5b
New box: The Ten Principles of the United Nation's Global Compact	3-5b
New content on B Corp Certified companies	3-5b
Completely revamped section on green marketing with new content, examples, and quotes	3-5c
New Section 3-5d: Leaders in Social Responsibility and Green Marketing	3-5d
New content on cause-related marketing	3-6
H&M, Quaker Oats, and Hotels.com examples	3-6

CHAPTER PREP

The Marketing Environment

4

WHAT'S INSIDE:

Key topics in this chapter: understanding and managing the external environment; dealing with social change, including American values; demography, especially descriptions of generational groups; effect of ethnic markets and their increasing buying power; economic factors; the effect of social media; how changing political and legal factors affect the marketing mix; and competitive factors in the external environment.

LEARNING OUTCOMES

4-1 Discuss the external environment of marketing and explain how it affects a firm

4-2 Describe the social factors that affect marketing

4-3 Explain the importance to marketing managers of current demographic trends

4-4 Explain the importance to marketing managers of growing ethnic markets

4-5 Identify consumer and marketer reactions to the state of the economy

4-6 Identify the impact of technology on a firm

4-7 Discuss the political and legal environment of marketing

4-8 Explain the basics of foreign and domestic competition

DISCUSSION QUESTIONS

1. Are all generations the same? The baby boomers challenged societal and cultural norms when they were young. How is that different from today?

2. Does the idea of changing competition really matter? After all, companies will always have to react to competition, which is a fact of free markets.

3. Are there too many or not enough regulations governing marketing activities? Defend your answer.

ASSIGNMENT

Assign students to work individually or in teams to create a dining guide of ethnic restaurants in your area. The finished guide

will be descriptive only; it is not meant to be a rating guide. Details are in the Instructor Manual.

ADDITIONAL EXAMPLE

In 2011, pop music sensation One Direction became the first English music group to reach the number one spot on the Billboard 200 chart with a debut album. Assembled by Simon Cowell in 2010 and introduced on Cowell's *The X Factor* television series, One Direction quickly amassed tween fans in England and the United States through a unique interactive marketing campaign. According to the campaign's narrative, a One Direction superfan who went by the moniker "1DCyberpunk" stole the band's laptop, promising only to give it back when fans proved their support by completing a series of social media–based challenges. Active

WWW.CENGAGE.COM/LOGIN

CHAPTER PREP 4

KEY TERMS

participants were rewarded with exclusive content and events, culminating in a massive online album listening party during which the laptop was finally returned.

The fifty-day campaign was developed by marketing firm AIS in conjunction with One Direction's record label, Syco. According to AIS Creative Director Richard Coggin, "Syco had a lot of great content—videos, merchandise, singles, albums, lyrics, running orders, signed photos, radio and TV appearances—and our brief was to glue it all together and engage the fans on a daily basis. Filtered through 1DCyberpunk, the content became more valuable and sought-after." Though complex and often difficult to manage, the campaign was a success, netting 200,000 participants, 12 trending topics on Twitter, and more than 2.5 million views on YouTube. Perhaps most importantly, it laid the foundation for a passionate U.S. fan base that was desperate to see the band in their home country, buy the debut album, and send One Direction to the top of the charts.

Emma Hall, "U.K. Boy Band One Direction Rises Via Social Media," *Advertising Age,* April 12, 2012, http://adage.com/article/global -news/u-k-boy-band-direction-rises-social -media/234105 (Accessed March 25, 2013).

NEW TO MKTG10 CHAPTER 4

MKTG10	Section
McDonald's example	4-1a
Hotel chain and price-comparison website examples	4-1a
T-Mobile example	4-1a
Updated content and data on social media usage	4-2c
Updated content and data on overall Internet usage	4-2c
Completely revamped section: How Firms Use Social Media	4-2c
New data and content on population	4-3a
Updated content and data on tweens	4-3a
Updated content and data on teens	4-3a
Updated content and data on Millennials	4-3a
Updated content and data on Generation X	4-3a
Updated content and data on baby boomers	4-3a
Updated data on the American demographic profile	4-4
Updated content and data on Hispanic Americans	4-4a
Updated content and data on African Americans	4-4a
Updated content and data on Asian Americans	4-4a
Updated data on the Great Recession and unemployment	4-5a
New content on mobile moments and smartphone usage	4-6b
New examples on Hertz and Krispy Kreme	4-6b
Updated content on RFID chip usage	4-6b
Zara example	4-6b
New content on the Patient Protection and Affordable Care Act	4-7a
Updated Exhibit 4.2: Primary U.S. Laws Protecting Consumers	4-7a
AVG Technologies example	4-7d
Google and Amazon examples	4-8a

WHAT'S INSIDE:

Key topics in this chapter: importance of trade, external environments in the global marketplace, trade agreements, methods of going global, and creating a global marketing mix.

LEARNING OUTCOMES

5-1 Discuss the importance of global marketing

5-2 Discuss the impact of multinational firms on the world economy

5-3 Describe the external environment facing global marketers

5-4 Identify the various ways of entering the global marketplace

5-5 List the basic elements involved in developing a global marketing mix

5-6 Discover how the Internet is affecting global marketing

DISCUSSION QUESTIONS

1. On the whole, are multinationals beneficial or harmful to developing nations? Explain.

2. How involved should governments be in regulating foreign trade? Are free markets better than regulated markets, or vice versa?

3. Is it feasible for all companies to be global marketers? Do certain industries seem better suited for global marketing than others? Why or why not?

ASSIGNMENTS

1. The activity on "reverse" international marketing from Chapter 5 Instructor's Manual can be given as an assignment.

2. Have students write a paragraph discussing the role of purchasing power in global marketing decisions. Perhaps frame the exercise with this contextual example: When IKEA entered the Chinese market, it dropped the prices on its products significantly—but only in that market. Prices in Europe, the United States, and other Asian countries stayed the same. Do students think that is justifiable? What, if anything, do students expect to be the impact on customers in other countries?

ADDITIONAL EXAMPLE

Prolonged success for auto manufacturers is likely to come from their ability to sell cars in rapidly developing countries like Russia, Brazil, India, and Indonesia. However, selling cars in these emerging markets can be complicated, especially for foreign companies. Nissan is one company that has struggled to expand into emerging markets: its overall share of auto sales is 6 percent, but its share in Brazil is just 1.2 percent. With the goal of increasing its global reach, Nissan announced that it would revive the Datsun brand name and develop six new vehicles specifically designed for emerging markets' growing middle classes. The company aimed to produce modern, stylish cars that appealed to consumers visually, and more importantly, fit into their budgets.

In bringing back the Datsun brand, Nissan in effect created a distinctive identity for the unique set of cars that comprised its new global venture. The emerging middle class wants cars, but it can't afford to spend $15,000

CHAPTER PREP 5

to $20,000 on a family sedan. Thus, automobile companies like Nissan need to create small, extremely affordable cars; to do so, they must often take a bare bones approach. That means no air conditioning, no passenger air bags, and no power windows. While Datsun will provide entry into the market, the Nissan brand will continue to be sold as upscale, feature-rich cars. According to Ammar Master, an analyst at LMC Automotive in Bangkok, "Datsun could bring in volumes at the lower end of the market...While the Nissan brand will continue to move upmarket."

Source: Caroline Winter, "Behind the Birth, Death, and Rebirth of Datsun," *Bloomberg Businessweek*, March 21, 2012, www.businessweek.com/articles/2012-03-21 /behind-the-birth-death-and-re-birth-of-datsun (Accessed March 25, 2013); Chester Dawson, "For Datsun Revival, Nissan Gambles on $3000 Model," *Wall Street Journal*. October 1, 2012, http://online.wsj.com/article /SB10000872396390443890304578009284279919750 .html (Accessed March 25, 2013); Siddharth Philip, Anna Mukai, and Yuki Hagiwara, "Nissan Revives Datsun After Three Decades to Boost Sales," *Bloomberg*, March 21, 2012, www.bloomberg.com/news/2012-03-20/nissan -to-revive-datsun-brand-after-three-decades-to-boost -sales.html (Accessed March 25, 2013).

NEW TO MKTG10 CHAPTER 5

MKTG10	Section
Updated data on world trade	5-1
General Electric example	5-1
New content on GDP	5-1a
New example on the Export-Import Bank of the United States	5-1a
New box: Imports Can Help Too	5-1a
New Coca-Cola example	5-2a
New content on Chinese Internet trends	5-3a
New data on GNI	5-3b
New content on the global economy	5-3c
New content on how politics affects economic law	5-3d
New content, data, and examples on tariffs	5-3d
New examples on U.S., Chinese, and Indian relations	5-3d
Updated content on the Transatlantic Trade and Investment Partnership	5-3d
Updated data on NAFTA	5-3d
Updated content on CAFTA-DR	5-3d
Greece's Syriza party example	5-3d
Updated content on the G-20	5-3d
Updated data on world demographics	5-3e
New oil cost example	5-3e
New content, data, and examples on exporting	5-4a
General Electric and CFM International example	5-4d
New data on direct investment	5-4e
New example on the cost of gas in Saudi Arabia	5-5
Procter & Gamble example	5-5a
Fast food and Domino's examples	5-5a
New Unilever example	5-5b
Taiwanese convenience store and Starbucks examples	5-5c
New example on Russia's annexation of Crimea	5-5d
U.S. Commerce Department example	5-5d
New Malaysian government and General Electric example	5-5d
Completely revamped section: Social Media in Global Marketing	5-6a

CHAPTER OUTLINE

WHAT'S INSIDE:

Key topics in this chapter: consumer decision-making process, culture, opinion leaders, education and income, perception, motivation, beliefs, and attitudes.

LEARNING OUTCOMES

6-1 Explain why marketing managers should understand consumer behavior

6-2 Analyze the components of the consumer decision-making process

6-3 Explain the consumer's postpurchase evaluation process

6-4 Identify the types of consumer buying decisions and discuss the significance of consumer involvement

6-5 Identify and understand the cultural factors that affect consumer buying decisions

6-6 Identify and understand the social factors that affect consumer buying decisions

6-7 Identify and understand the individual factors that affect consumer buying decisions

6-8 Identify and understand the psychological factors that affect consumer buying decisions

DISCUSSION QUESTIONS

1. Why doesn't the type of decision-making process a consumer uses stay constant?

2. Is there a correlation between the level of cognitive dissonance a consumer experiences and the number of choices on the market for the product purchased? Explain.

3. Can anyone become an opinion leader? Why or why not?

4. Can marketers ever truly overcome negative attitudes toward a product?

ASSIGNMENTS

1. Have students review the main concepts in this chapter and create a checklist that itemizes them. Direct students to comb through magazines and newspapers for advertisements that illustrate each concept. To get a wide variety of ads, they should look through several magazines. Suggest that students use the campus library periodical room as a source for diverse ads. Have students select an ad that illustrates multiple concepts from the chapter and label it accordingly, or write a paragraph explaining how the ad illustrates the concepts.

2. Have each student select a product such as athletic shoes or jeans and determine the way in which their selection of that particular brand reflects their self-concept. Then have them determine a slogan and sketch a print ad that would appeal to consumers who seek to express this same self-concept through their product purchase.

CHAPTER PREP 6

KEY TERMS

ADDITIONAL EXAMPLE

In February 2013, Netflix debuted *House of Cards*, a smoldering political drama starring Kevin Spacey and featuring direction by Hollywood heavyweights like David Fincher and Joel Schumacher. The streaming video service made all 13 episodes of the original series' first season available at once—a bold strategy in a television industry seemingly pulled in opposite directions by tradition and technological advancement. *House of Cards* proved an instant hit among critics and Netflix customers alike—according to a Cowen and Co. survey, 86 percent of subscribers said that the availability of *House of Cards* made them less likely to cancel their subscriptions. A majority of respondents also said, however, that they would cancel their subscription if Netflix raised its $7.99-a-month price.

According to Netflix CEO Reed Hastings, *House of Cards* "met all of (our) expectations." Netflix quickly made plans to follow the series with a broader lineup of exclusive shows, including Tina Fey-helmed sitcom *The Unbreakable Kimmy Schmidt*, gothic horror series *Hemlock Grove*, cult classic *Arrested Development*, and science-fiction epic *Sense8*. Although such programming is proving popular—to say the least—among subscribers, the company has no plans to abandon its role as a hub for licensed television shows and movies. "I don't want you guys to think that suddenly we're the original content company," said Hastings. "It's phenomenally successful for us, but it's not the center of the company."

David Lieberman, "'House of Cards' Was 'a Great Success' Netflix Chief Says," *Deadline*, February 25, 2013, www.deadline.com/2013/02/netflix-reed-hastings-says-house-cards-success (Accessed March 27, 2013); Emma Roller, "House of Cards Is Paying Off for Netflix," *Slate*, February 21, 2013, www.slate.com/blogs/moneybox/2013/02/21/house_of_cards_netflix_subscribers_say_the_series_will_make_them_less_likely.html (Accessed March 27, 2013); Maria Sciullo, "Netflix Debuts Original Series 'House of Cards,'" *Pittsburgh Post-Gazette*, February 1, 2013, www.post-gazette.com/stories/ae/tv-radio/netflix-debuts-original-series-house-of-cards-672954 (Accessed March 27, 2013) "Wachowskis to Make Sci-fi Series for Netflix," *Miami Herald*, March 27, 2013, www.miamiherald.com/2013/03/27/3309370/wachowskis-to-make-sci-fi-series.html (Accessed March 27, 2013).

NEW TO MKTG10 CHAPTER 6

MKTG10	Section
New Trek example	6-1
New content on value and new key terms: perceived, utilitarian, and hedonic value	6-1
Updated content on external stimuli	6-2a
Fitness tracker example	6-2a
Updated content and examples on the Internet and social media	6-2b
Updated e-commerce data	6-2b
New extended example on the buying process	6-2c
New data on impulse purchases	6-2c
Kindle Paperwhite example	6-2c
New content on the handling of cognitive dissonance	6-2c
Ford Transit example	6-4b
McDonald's example	6-4b
New content on binational households	6-5b
Lamborghini Veneno example	6-5c
Klout example	6-6b
New section: Individual Differences in Susceptibility to Social Influences	6-6d
New key terms: separated self-schema and connected self-schema	6-6d
Ad portrayal of women example	6-7a
New content on perception	6-8a
Apple example	6-8a
American Express example	6-8b

WHAT'S INSIDE:

Key topics in this chapter: business versus consumer markets, business customers, business products, business buying behavior, and business buying situations.

LEARNING OUTCOMES

7-1 Describe business marketing

7-2 Describe trends in B-to-B Internet marketing

7-3 Discuss the role of relationship marketing and strategic alliances in business marketing

7-4 Identify the four major categories of business market customers

7-5 Explain the North American Industry Classification System

7-6 Explain the major differences between business and consumer markets

7-7 Describe the seven types of business goods and services

7-8 Discuss the unique aspects of business buying behavior

DISCUSSION QUESTIONS

1. Why is relationship marketing an important way to promote in business marketing?

2. Even though some airlines target business clientele, is the decision to use these carriers more like a business purchasing decision or a consumer purchasing decision? Explain.

ASSIGNMENTS

1. Have students write a paragraph responding to this question: Why is Internet marketing especially important in business marketing?

2. Have students pick a product and determine its NAICS code. They should turn in the product, the code, and a review of how easy (or difficult) it was it to trace the groups and sectors.

ADDITIONAL EXAMPLE

IBM's Watson is a supercomputer with a unique capability—it can understand and respond to natural language. IBM showcased this amazing computing ability on the game show *Jeopardy*, where Watson faced Ken Jennings, the holder of the longest winning streak in *Jeopardy* history, and Brad Rutter, who holds the record for the most amount of money won on *Jeopardy*. It was no contest—Watson won the two-day contest by a landslide.

IBM has its sights set on two areas for Watson: health care and investment. In health care, Watson can access millions of recent research and journal articles. What would take a doctor endless hours to read and comprehend, Watson can do in a matter of minutes. Watson is capable of parsing patient and family histories, clinical data, and drug treatment options, making it an invaluable asset not only when diagnosing a patient, but also in understanding the full range of treatments available.

CHAPTER PREP 7

KEY TERMS

Citigroup became the first company to purchase Watson for financial services. Citigroup will use Watson to analyze customers' needs so that it can facilitate their interactions with the company's automated banking system. According to Citigroup executives, Watson will be deployed to present a "customer interaction solution," which will "assist decision makers in identifying opportunities, evaluating risks, and exploring alternatives."

Within IBM, hopes are quite high for Watson. By strategically deploying its vast computing power, company leaders hope that Watson will contribute a significant portion to the company's $16 billion of revenues in analytics. Industry analysts at CLSA, meanwhile, estimate that by 2015, Watson will contribute $2.65 billion in revenue through the services it provides to other companies.

Doug Henschen, "IBM's Watson Could Be Healthcare Game Changer," *InformationWeek*, February 11, 2013, www.informationweek.com/software/business -intelligence/ibms-watson-could-be-healthcare-game -cha/240148273 (Accessed March 26, 2013); Mark Hachman, "IBM's Watson Hired by Citigroup," *PC Magazine*, March 6, 2012, www.pcmag.com/article2 /0,2817,2401203,00.asp (Accessed March 26, 2013); Rachel King, "IBM's Watson Being Put to the Test in Healthcare," *ZDNet*, September 24, 2012, www.zdnet.com/ibms-watson -being-put-to-the-test-in-healthcare-7000004725 (Accessed March 26, 2013); Steve Lohr, "I.B.M.'s Watson Goes to Medical School," *New York Times*, October 30, 2012, http://bits.blogs.nytimes.com/2012/10/30/i-b-m -s-watson-goes-to-medical-school (Accessed March 26, 2013).

NEW TO MKTG10 CHAPTER 7

MKTG10	Section
Updated Kodak example	7-1
New learning outcome: Describe trenda in B-to-B Internet marketing	7-2
Completely revamped section: Trends in B-to-B Internet Marketing	7-2
New box: The Top Social Media Tools for B-to-B Marketers	7-2
Amazon Fire TV example	7-3a
Vodaphone and Phones 4U example	7-3a
Alibaba.com example	7-6e

CHAPTER OUTLINE

WHAT'S INSIDE:

Key topics in this chapter: criteria for segmenting markets, segmentation bases, steps in segmenting a market, targeting strategies, one-to-one marketing, and repositioning.

LEARNING OUTCOMES

8-1 Describe the characteristics of markets and market segments

8-2 Explain the importance of market segmentation

8-3 Discuss the criteria for successful market segmentation

8-4 Describe the bases commonly used to segment consumer markets

8-5 Describe the bases for segmenting business markets

8-6 List the steps involved in segmenting markets

8-7 Discuss alternative strategies for selecting target markets

8-8 Explain how CRM can be used as a targeting tool

8-9 Explain how and why firms implement positioning strategies and how product differentiation plays a role

DISCUSSION QUESTIONS

1. Are college students a viable potential market for Mercedes? Why or why not?

2. Is it ethical for companies to avoid certain segments? For example, many brands do not target low-income consumers. Is that unethical?

ASSIGNMENTS

Have students visit the following Web site: www.claritas.com/MyBestSegments/Default .jsp?ID=20. Have students click on the "ZIP Code Look-Up" button and type in their ZIP Code. The database will generate many cluster descriptions based on the ZIP Code. Depending on the functionality of the Web site at the time students access the database, you may need to refine the instructions. For example, they may need to reenter their ZIP Code multiple times to read all the cluster descriptions. Then have them do the following:

1. Pick a product category, such as automobiles, athletic shoes, beverages, or health and beauty products. Then think about which products in that category would appeal to each of the clusters generated by your ZIP Code search. For example, a car that appeals to a cluster titled "Young Bohemians" may not be the car of choice for the cluster "Pools and Patios." If your search generated only one cluster type, you may wish to enter other ZIP Codes for your area of town or for your region.

2. Create a perceptual map for the product you chose. Write a short statement that describes the overall position of each product with an explanation of why you located it where you did on the perceptual map.

CHAPTER PREP 8

KEY TERMS

ADDITIONAL EXAMPLE

Long associated with biker culture, Harley-Davidson evokes images of carefree, rebellious, even lawless riders wearing long beards and leather vests, cruising across the country while living by their own rules. The company's typical customer is a 47-year-old white man, and while Harley-Davidson has an extremely loyal customer base, its brand has little cachet with people outside of this demographic. Such a limited (and rapidly aging) market does not bode well for the company's future.

In a bid to solidify its future, Harley-Davidson is looking to expand its customer base. According to CEO Keith Wandell, the company aims to boost the number of riders and consumers outside of the company's core customer group of white men over the age of 35 by marketing its motorcycles and accessories to women. This extended campaign consists of numerous programs, social events, Web sites, and design changes, all expressly aimed at making the Harley-Davidson experience seem like an attractive and thrilling hobby for women. For example, the company hosts a series of garage parties throughout its nationwide network of dealers. The parties are a social gathering for women, where they can sip on wine and enjoy appetizers while motorcycle enthusiasts share about the thrills of riding a Harley.

Even as it expands its customer base to a new market segment, Harley-Davidson is taking care not to alienate its core male customer base or to dilute its rebellious image. To maintain its appeal to white, middle-aged riders, Harley recently introduced the three-wheel Ultra Classic Trike, which was designed to be easier to control for older people who may have a reduced sense of balance. In a similar vein, Harley-Davidson's marketing chief, Mark-Hans Richer, said "We're trying to be our thing to more people."

Alexandra Straub, "Harley Party Helps Introduce Women to Bikes," *The Gazette*, February 24, 2013, www.montrealgazette.com/Harley+party+helps+introduce+women+bikes/8009187/story.html (Accessed March 26, 2013); Barbara Vilacis, "Harley Celebrates Women Riders," *Ultimate Motorcycling*, May 3, 2012, www.ultimatemotorcycling.com/2012/harley-celebrates-women-riders (Accessed March 26, 2013); Rich Rovito, "Harley-Davidson Launches Women Riders Month," *The Business Journal*, May 4, 2012, www.bizjournals.com/milwaukee/blog/2012/05/harley-davidson-launches-women-riders.html (Accessed March 26, 2013).

NEW TO MKTG10 CHAPTER 8

MKTG10	Section
Jax & Bones example	8-2
CrossFit Kids example	8-4b
New content and data on Generation Z	8-4b
New content on Millennials	8-4b
New content on Generation X	8-4b
General Mills example	8-4b
New content on gender segmentation	8-4b
Procter & Gamble example	8-4b
Google Pizza Program example	8-4c
Sling TV example	8-4d
New box: Too Many Cooks	8-6
Birchbox example	8-8
Hyundai example	8-9c

CHAPTER OUTLINE

WHAT'S INSIDE:

Key topics in this chapter: the marketing research process, primary and secondary data, sampling procedures, measurement errors, impact of the Internet and mobile research, scanners, the CRM cycle, and competitive intelligence.

LEARNING OUTCOMES

9-1 Define marketing research and explain its importance to marketing decision making

9-2 Describe the steps involved in conducting a marketing research project

9-3 Discuss the profound impact of the Internet on marketing research

9-4 Describe the growing importance of mobile research

9-5 Discuss the growing importance of scanner-based research

9-6 Explain when marketing research should be conducted

9-7 Explain the concept of competitive intelligence

DISCUSSION QUESTIONS

1. What is a potential downfall of mall intercept interviews? What is a potential downfall of computer-assisted self-interviewing? Is it possible for a marketing study to be completely error-proof?

2. Why is competitive intelligence so hot in today's business environment?

3. Do you see any disadvantages to scanner-based marketing research?

ASSIGNMENTS

BuzzBack asked 532 teen respondents to conjure up healthy new foods they'd gobble up. The following are two of their ideas:

1. A breakfast shake for teens. Something easy that tastes good, not necessarily for dieters like Slim Fast, etc. Something to balance you off in the morning. –Male, age 18.

2. Travel fruit. Why can't fruit be in travel bags like chips or cookies? Canned fruit is too messy. Maybe have a dip or something sold with it, too. –Female, age 17.

Have students choose one of these suggestions for healthy snack concepts and imagine that their company is interested in turning the idea into a new product and wants to conduct market research before investing in product development. Students should design a marketing research plan that will give company managers the information they need before engaging in new-product development of the idea.

ADDITIONAL EXAMPLE

Though it has been in production since 1983, Unilever's Axe body fragrance skyrocketed from a small European brand to a $2.5 billion global enterprise in recent years. Axe holds 76 percent of the body fragrance market, and grew 13.6 percent in 2012 alone. Without question, the key to Axe's success has been its excellence in marketing. As other companies do, Axe sponsors events and places advertisements that are aimed at

CHAPTER PREP 9

KEY TERMS

connecting with young men. Axe, however, takes things a step further by tying all of its marketing efforts to an incredible level of research.

Axe's core target demographic is men age twenty to twenty-five. It does not try to "age" with the group, meaning that it does not chase its customers as they age. The company operates a relentless research system that focuses squarely on this segment, tracking fads, trends, likes and dislikes, interests, and relationship patterns. Axe marketers know that what appealed to the 20 to 25 demographic 5 years ago will not appeal to the current 20 to 25 group, and that whatever is popular now will likely be out of style in another five years.

Axe's research skills have led to a significant shift in its advertising strategy. Early on, marketers found that males

and females would often spend time in separate groups. This knowledge led to advertising that focused on how guys could use Axe to get close to girls. In one commercial, a cheerleader, driven insane by Axe, tackles a football player wearing the fragrance. Recently, however, researchers found that males and females are spending more time together. Axe shifted its advertising strategy, playing to both men and women. The newer commercials show women being more demanding, telling males to groom themselves better and females to take charge of the budding romance.

Jason Feifer, "Axe's Highly Scientific Typically Outrageous and Totally Irresistible Selling of Lust," *Fast Company*, August 8, 2012, www.fastcompany.com/3000041/axes-highly-scientific-typically-outrageous-and-totally-irresistible-selling-lust (Accessed March 26, 2013).

NEW TO MKTG10 CHAPTER 9

MKTG10	Section
Fitness wearable example	9-1a
New content and data on satisfaction research	9-1a
New auto repair industry example	9-1a
New content, data, and examples on social media and word of mouth advertising	9-1b
Genentech example	9-2
New content and data on secondary data	9-2a
New Instagram and Flurry examples	9-2a
Macy's example	9-2a
Olive Garden example	9-2b
Cambridge SoundWorks example	9-2b
New content on computer simulated environments	9-2b
Updated box: Benefits of Web Community Research	9-3b
Updated data on mobile research	9-4
New Mondelez Canada example	9-4
Updated content on BehaviorScan	9-5

CHAPTER OUTLINE

WHAT'S INSIDE:

Key topics in this chapter: consumer product types; product items, lines, and mixes; branding and trademarks; and packaging, labeling, and warranties.

LEARNING OUTCOMES

10-1 Define the term *product*

10-2 Classify consumer products

10-3 Define the terms *product item*, *product line*, and *product mix*

10-4 Describe marketing uses of branding

10-5 Describe marketing uses of packaging and labeling

10-6 Discuss global issues in branding and packaging

10-7 Describe how and why product warranties are important marketing tools

DISCUSSION QUESTIONS

1. Is it possible to make a homogeneous shopping product into a heterogeneous shopping product? Push students to think about flat-panel televisions and front-loading washers.

2. Walgreens includes advertisements for its store brand on its Web site, runs ads in weekly flyers, and promotes its store brand products (such as Wal-zyr, the Zyrtec alternative) on endcaps in stores. How might this affect Walgreens's relationship with manufacturer's brand suppliers? Do you think this increases the cost of the store brand items?

3. Is it possible for marketers to reconcile the desires of consumers looking for the "next big thing" with those of consumers who like their product or service how it is? Explain.

ASSIGNMENTS

1. How does Hormel use its Web site (www.hormel.com) to promote its brands? Is the site designed more to promote the company or its brands? Check out the Spam Web site at www.spam.com. How do you think Hormel is able to sustain this brand, which is often the punch line to a joke?

ETHICS EXERCISE

A product that a potential buyer knows about but is not actively seeking is called an unsought product. Is the marketing of unsought products unethical? Discuss your answer in terms of the AMA Statement of Ethics, found at www.marketingpower.com.

CHAPTER PREP 10

KEY TERMS

ADDITIONAL EXAMPLE

Arizonian entrepreneur David Elliott recently sued Google Inc. to have the Internet advertising and search giant stripped of its eponymous trademark. Elliott claimed that the word *Google* had become a generic term meaning simply "to search on the Web," and like thermos, aspirin, and zipper, it should no longer belong to any one company. As evidence of this, Elliott's lawyer, Richard M. Wirtz, cited the American Dialect Society's decision to declare the verb *google* the word of the decade for 2000 to 2009.

Elliott's legal action against Google came only after the tech company filed—and won—a trademark infringement lawsuit against Elliott himself. In the suit, Google claimed that 750 Internet sites registered to Elliott used the term *Google* illegally. All 750 Web sites, featuring domain names such as googledonaldtrump.com and googlegaycruises.com were forfeited to Google. According to *paidContent* blogger Jeff John Roberts, Elliott's countersuit won't succeed as long as "Google can show that consumers still associate the word with the company."

Chris Matyszczyk, "Man Sues to Make 'Google' Ordinary Word," *CNET*, May 27, 2012, http://news.cnet.com/8301-17852_3-57442273-71/man-sues-to-make-google-ordinary-word/ (Accessed March 26, 2013); Jeff John Roberts, "Man Sues to Have 'Google' Declared a Generic Word," *paidContent*, May 25, 2012, http://paidcontent.org/2012/05/25/man-sues-to-have-google-declared-a-generic-word/ (Accessed March 26, 2013).

NEW TO MKTG10 CHAPTER 10

MKTG10	Section
Updated Teavana example	10-3a
Cat's Pride example	10-3a
Target example	10-3a
Krispy Kreme example	10-3a
New data on private brands	10-4b
Doc Popcorn and Dippin' Dots example	10-4b
Gucci and Guess example	10-4c
FDA food labeling example	10-5a

CHAPTER OUTLINE

WHAT'S INSIDE:

Key topics in this chapter: types of new products, new-product development process, test marketing, diffusion, and product life cycles.

LEARNING OUTCOMES

11-1 Explain the importance of developing new products and describe the six categories of new products

11-2 Explain the steps in the new-product development process

11-3 Understand why some products succeed and others fail

11-4 Discuss global issues in new-product development

11-5 Explain the diffusion process through which new products are adopted

11-6 Explain the concept of product life cycles

DISCUSSION QUESTIONS

1. If a product makes it through a rigorous development process, will it be a sure success? Why or why not?

2. Can actual test marketing be replaced by virtual test marketing using the Internet or other software applications? Why or why not?

3. Can you think of product categories in the maturity stage that are poised to be reinvented? Explain your answer.

ASSIGNMENT

Have students compile a list of 100 new products. Consider tabulating television ads for new products. A trip to the grocery store could probably yield the entire list, but the list would be limited to consumer products. Next, have students make a table with six columns labeled as follows: new-to-the-world products, new-product line, addition to existing product line, improvement/revision of existing product line, repositioned product, and lower-priced product. Once they have set up the table, students should place each of their 100 new products into one of the six categories. Tabulate the results at the bottom of each column. What conclusions can they draw from the distribution of their products? Consider adding results together with the whole class to get a larger and more random sample.

ADDITIONAL EXAMPLE

It has been more than a decade since America Online (AOL) has been even a minor player in the Internet world. However, in an effort to reposition itself as a major player in the online world, AOL recently unveiled Alto, a new product that it hopes will revolutionize e-mail. In general, nearly all e-mail platforms have the same layout. In Alto, the e-mail inbox list is located on a small vertical column on the left third of the page, while the other two-thirds of the page are occupied by what AOL calls "stacks." Messages and multimedia are instantly categorized and sorted into visual stacks according to their content. Daily deals, social notifications, business transactions, photos, and attachments each have their own stacks, and users can create their own customized

CHAPTER PREP 11

KEY TERMS

stacks as well. Instead of a bloated inbox, then, Alto provides a simplified, organized, visually dominated e-mail experience.

Alto does not require users to sign up for yet another e-mail address (though the option to create an @altomail.com address is available). Instead, users can simply sign into Alto using their existing credentials for Gmail, Yahoo, .me, and other accounts. According to David Temkin, AOL's senior vice president of mobile and mail, Alto is fully intended to be a disruptive and innovative product in a market that has grown somewhat complacent. As Temkin says, "Email hasn't had a serious rethink really since Gmail came out. We wanted to take a swing at that and

not be tethered by the existing 20 million or so people using AOL Mail." Early reviews of Alto are quite positive, though the product certainly faces an uphill battle in the crowded e-mail market.

Adam Bluestein, "AOL's Alto Reimagines the Email Experience with a Twitter, Pinterest, Gmail Mashup," *Fast Company*, October 18, 2012, www.fastcompany .com/3001755/aols-alto-reimagines-email-experience -twitter-pinterest-gmail-mashup (Accessed March 26, 2013); Caitline McGarry, "AOL's Alto Adds Visual Organization to E-mail," *PCWorld*, October 18, 2012, www.pcworld.com/article/2012220/aol-s-alto-adds -visual-organization-to-e-mail.html (Accessed March 26, 2013); Julianne Pepitone, "AOL Unveils Alto, an Email Service that Syncs 5 Accounts," *CNN*, October 18, 2012, http://money.cnn.com/2012/10/18/technology/aol-alto -email/index.html (Accessed March 26, 2013).

NEW TO MKTG10 CHAPTER 11

MKTG10	Section
Updated list of the most innovative companies	11-1
Apple example	11-1a
Mercedes Maybach example	11-1b
Havianas box	11-2b
Lego example	11-2b
Ubisoft example	11-2e
Wheaties NEXT example	11-2e
Starbucks example	11-2f
Updated list of product failures	11-3
On Assignment example	11-6b

CHAPTER OUTLINE

WHAT'S INSIDE:

Key topics in this chapter: characteristics of services, the gap model of service quality, marketing mixes for services, nonprofit organization marketing, and global issues in services marketing.

LEARNING OUTCOMES

12-1 Discuss the importance of services to the economy

12-2 Discuss the differences between services and goods

12-3 Describe the components of service quality and the gap model of service quality

12-4 Develop marketing mixes for services

12-5 Discuss relationship marketing in services

12-6 Explain internal marketing in services

12-7 Describe nonprofit organization marketing

12-8 Discuss global issues in services marketing

DISCUSSION QUESTIONS

1. Is there a risk to having an overwhelmingly service-oriented economy? Explain.

2. Are you more or less willing to give a service or a product a second chance after a bad experience? Explain your answer.

ASSIGNMENT

More than 25 years ago, Tim and Nina Zagat began publishing leisure guides containing reviews of restaurants. Today, the Zagat guides also rate hotels, entertainment, nightlife, movies, shopping, and music. In your opinion, are Zagat survey guides goods or services? Explain your reasoning.

ETHICS EXERCISE

Web sites such as www.cancerpage.com offer cancer patients sophisticated medical data and advice in exchange for personal information that is then sold to advertisers and business partners and used by the Web sites to create products to sell to patients. Some argue that cancer patients visiting these sites are willingly exchanging their personal information for the sites' medical information. Others contend that this kind of exchange is unethical.

QUESTIONS

1. Is this practice ethical?

2. Does the American Marketing Association (AMA) Statement of Ethics have anything to say about this issue? Go to www.marketingpower.com/AboutAMA/Pages/Statement%20of%20Ethics.aspx and review the statement. Then write a brief paragraph on what the AMA Statement of Ethics contains that relates to this situation.

ADDITIONAL EXAMPLE

Livestrong is currently one of the most visible and active charities in the world. It is consistently praised as resoundingly efficient and accountable; Charity Navigator

KEY TERMS

recently gave Livestrong a rating of four stars (its highest) and a score of 64 out of 70 for its financial responsibility and its transparency. However, all is not well at Livestrong. For years, cyclist and cancer survivor Lance Armstrong has been the face of Livestrong—a living symbol of the organization's commitment to empowering cancer patients to live to the fullest. Hundreds and thousands of individuals have given to Livestrong or bought a yellow wristband because they were inspired by Armstrong's bravery in overcoming cancer and reaching the pinnacle of sporting success.

However, Armstrong is now a tainted symbol. After a thorough investigation, the U.S. Anti-Doping Agency presented a mountain of evidence showing that Armstrong not only used performance-enhancing drugs during his career, but that he was in charge of a systematic doping program that pressured teammates to use drugs as well. Based on this evidence (and later confirmed by Armstrong's own admission), the USADA banned Armstrong from competing in any of its events, and the International Cycling Union stripped him of all seven of his Tour de France titles. Armstrong was now no longer a symbol of triumph or perseverance; in most eyes, he was simply a cheater who got caught.

In the midst of this professional disgrace, Armstrong decided that he would step down as chairman of Livestrong. Though he would continue to be a member of Livestrong's board, he would no longer have a role as its public face as he did for the past 15 years. This of course, was a huge blow to the organization, which lost its founder—and its best fundraiser.

Brent Schrotenboer, "USADA Release Massive Evidence vs. Lance Armstrong," *USA Today*, October 11, 2012, www.usatoday.com/story/sports/cycling/2012/10/10/lance-armstrong-usada-reasoned-decision-teammates-doping/1624551/ (Accessed March 26, 2013); David Wharton and Lance Pugmire, "USADA Report Details Case against Lance Armstrong," *Los Angeles Times*, October 11, 2012, http://articles.latimes.com/2012/oct/11/sports/la-sp-armstrong-doping-20121011 (Accessed March 26, 2013); "Factbox: State of the Lance Armstrong Foundations' Finances," *Chicago Tribune*, October 17, 2012, http://articles.chicagotribune.com/2012-10-17/business/sns-rt-us-cycling-armstrong-finances-bre89g21g-20121017_1_testicular-cancer-lance-armstrong-foundation-austin (Accessed March 26, 2013); Krishnadev Calamur, "Lance Armstrong Admits to Using Performance-enhancing Drugs," *NPR*, January 17, 2013, www.npr.org/blogs/thetwo-way/2013/01/17/169650077/lance-armstrong-to-admit-to-using-performance-enhancing-drugs (Accessed March 26, 2013); "Lance Armstrong Foundation," *Charity Navigator*, www.charitynavigator.org/index.cfm?bay=search.summary&orgid=6570 (Accessed March 26, 2013); Lance Pugmire, "Lance Armstrong Quits Livestrong Post, Loses Endorsement Deals," *Los Angeles Times*, October 18, 2012, http://articles.latimes.com/2012/oct/18/sports/la-sp-lance-armstrong-20121018 (Accessed March 26, 2013); "Where The Money Goes," *Livestrong*, October 31, 2012, www.livestrong.org/What-We-Do/Our-Approach/Where-the-Money-Goes (Accessed March 26, 2013).

NEW TO MKTG9 CHAPTER 12

MKTG10	Section
Updated U.S. Census data	12-1
Updated Ritz-Carlton example	12-2a
Updated content on the gap model of service quality	12-3b
Updated list of top customer service companies	12-3b
Application Programming Interface example	12-4a
Mac & Mia example	12-4b
Updated content on relationship marketing	12-5

CHAPTER OUTLINE

WHAT'S INSIDE:

Key topics in this chapter: supply chain management, supply chain integration, the key processes needed for successful supply chain management, the impacts of sustainability and new technology, distribution channels, channel relationships, channel intermediaries, multichannel and omnichannel marketing, and new developments in channel management.

LEARNING OUTCOMES

13-1 Define the terms *supply chain* and *supply chain management*, and discuss the benefits of supply chain management

13-2 Discuss the concepts of internal and external supply chain integration and explain why each of these types of integration is important

13-3 Identify the eight key processes of excellent supply chain management and discuss how each of these processes affects the end customer

13-4 Understand the importance of sustainable supply chain management to modern business operations

13-5 Discuss how new technology and emerging trends are impacting the practice of supply chain management

13-6 Explain what marketing channels and channel intermediaries are and describe their functions and activities

13-7 Describe common channel structures and strategies and the factors that influence their choice

13-8 Discuss omnichannel and multichannel marketing in both B-to-B and B-to-C structures and explain why these concepts are important

DISCUSSION QUESTIONS

1. Which, if any, supply chain functions can be performed over the Internet? Why do you think so?

2. How does the implementation of supply chain management result in enhanced customer value?

3. Which, if any, marketing channel functions can be performed over the Internet? Why do you think so?

ASSIGNMENTS

1. Pick a product with which you are very familiar or that you anticipate being able to research easily.

2. Map the supply chain of your product as far back as is feasible.

3. Identify the mode of transportation used between each stage in the channel.

4. Identify by name and location the component parts of the product, if any.

CHAPTER PREP 13

KEY TERMS

ADDITIONAL EXAMPLE

Luxury athletics and yoga apparel retailer Lululemon Athletica has had great success in its less than twenty years of operation. With more than 200 retail locations, the company netted a 51.4 percent growth in revenue from fiscal year 2010 to 2011 and projected a more than 10 percent growth in the first quarter of fiscal year 2012. While the company has made its name on high-quality, high-cost apparel for fitness enthusiasts—a pair of yoga pants can cost as much as $100—a recent manufacturing error shook consumer confidence and gave rise to quality control problems in the company's supply chain.

In March 2013, Lululemon was forced to recall its signature "Luon" yoga pants after finding they were so sheer that they were practically see-through. The recall of the nylon and Lycra-blend Luon pants followed a similar event in 2012, when several of the company's swimsuits and light-colored pants were found to be too sheer. According to RBC Capital Markets analyst Howard Tubin, Lululemon's fabric errors may simply represent a growing pain for the rapidly expanding company. "They tried to get in front of this by not letting the merchandise stay on store shelves and they're working with vendors to try to figure out how this happened," said Tubin. "They're probably handling it the best way they can." Citing Lululemon's fourth manufacturing snafu in one year, Credit Suisse analyst Christian Buss struck a slightly less forgiving tone: "Their supply chain hasn't kept up with the demand that they have for their product, and their quality control processes have been proven inadequate."

"Lululemon Athletica Inc. Announces Fourth Quarter and Full Year Fiscal 2011 Results," *Lululemon*, March 22, 2012, www.lululemon.com/media/index.php?id=219 (Accessed March 27, 2013); "Lululemon: Yoga Demonstration Not Required for Returns," *CBS*, March 27, 2013, www.cbsnews.com/8301-201_162-57576590/lululemon-yoga-demonstration-not-required-for-returns (Accessed March 27, 2013); Wendy Kaufman, "Lululemon's Too-sheer Yoga Pants Reveal Problems in Company's Supply Chain," *NPR*, March 20, 2013, www.npr.org/2013/03/20/174867737/lululemons-too-sheer-yoga-pants-reveal-problems-in-companys-supply-chain (Accessed March 27, 2013).

NEW TO MKTG10 CHAPTER 13

MKTG10	Section
Chapter 13 has been built from the ground up with all new content, examples, key terms, and data. The chapter focuses on social chain management and marketing channels, two concepts that were presented in separate chapters in previous editions.	13-1

CHAPTER OUTLINE

WHAT'S INSIDE:

Key topics in this chapter: classifying retailers, types of retailers, nonstore retailing, franchising, defining target markets, retailing mix and strategy, addressing retailing failures, shopper marketing and analytics, and trends in retail management.

LEARNING OUTCOMES

14-1 Explain the importance of the retailer within the channel and the U.S. economy

14-2 List and understand the different types of retailers

14-3 Explain why nonstore retailing is on the rise and list the advantages of its different forms

14-4 Discuss the different retail operations models and understand why they vary in strategy and format

14-5 Explain how retail marketing strategies are developed and executed

14-6 Discuss how services retailing differs from goods retailing

14-7 Understand how retailers address product/service failures and discuss the opportunities that service failures provide

14-8 Summarize current trends related to customer data, analytics, and technology

DISCUSSION QUESTIONS

1. Should a company ever knowingly engage in brand cannibalization? When might brand cannibalization actually benefit a company?

2. How is contemporary retailing different from retailing 100 years ago? Fifty years ago? Twenty years ago? Five years ago?

ASSIGNMENT

Instruct your class to choose an optimal location for a new retail establishment that appeals to college students—such as a bar, bike shop, or pizzeria. Divide the class into "location consultant groups" while you act as the client. Each store should have three or four groups looking for a location (have more than one type of store for larger classes). Groups should draft a report entailing a description, square footage, leasing terms or price, and justification for the selection of the site. The group offering the site that is selected by the client (instructor) receives bonus points.

ADDITIONAL EXAMPLE

It is common knowledge among consumers and retailers alike that apparel prices tend to be marked up artificially. Years of coupons and promotions have trained customers to wait for price reductions, only shopping at department stores when special sales are available. During the Great Recession, consumer confidence dropped and spending slowed dramatically. As the economy has improved, department stores such as Macy's

CHAPTER PREP 14

KEY TERMS

and JCPenney have begun looking for ways to increase customer spending. Many department stores have once again turned to steep sales and special coupons, further encouraging the cycle of regular (lukewarm) business and sale-time frenzy.

Taking a different route, JCPenney moved to reduce the artificial markup so common to department store apparel. Borrowing Walmart's long-time "everyday low prices" strategy, JCPenney hoped to spur demand and reduce off-sale shopper apathy with basic contemporary apparel, promotions such as "Best Price Fridays," and special month-long values. Customers accustomed to receiving a coupon before shopping did not respond well to the new retail strategy, however, and JCPenney incurred substantial losses. The company launched an informative marketing campaign extolling the great values available without needing coupons or special sales, but the public remained unmoved. In April 2013, JCPenney ousted the man behind the change, Ron Johnson, as CEO and promised a return to coupon-based sales.

Dana Mattioli, "Penney to Tweak Message, but Not Its Strategy," *Wall Street Journal*, June 19, 2012, http://online.wsj.com/article/SB10001424052702303703004577476830407027186.html (Accessed March 26, 2013).

NEW TO MKTG10 CHAPTER 14

MKTG10	Section
New data on retailing	14-1
Updated content on franchising	14-2a
New Grand Theft Auto and Breaking Bad example	14-2c
New content on price	14-2d
Updated content on department stores and convenience stores	14-2e
New content on automatic vending	14-3
New data on microtargeting and online retailing	14-3
New Amazon Prime and Deliv examples	14-4
New Blaze Pizza example	14-5a
New O'Reilly Auto Parts example	14-5b
New content and key term for beacons	14-8
Updated content on virtual reality showrooming	14-8b
New Nordstrom example	14-8b

CHAPTER OUTLINE

WHAT'S INSIDE:

Key topics in this chapter: role of promotion, communication process, the AIDA concept, goals of promotion, and integrated marketing communication.

LEARNING OUTCOMES

15-1 Discuss the role of promotion in the marketing mix

15-2 Describe the communication process

15-3 Explain the goals and tasks of promotion

15-4 Discuss the elements of the promotional mix

15-5 Discuss the AIDA concept and its relationship to the promotional mix

15-6 Discuss the concept of integrated marketing communications

15-7 Describe the factors that affect the promotional mix

DISCUSSION QUESTIONS

1. Why is understanding the target market a crucial aspect of the communication process?

2. How do the different stages of consumer involvement in the AIDA process affect the promotional mix?

3. Under what situations would a push strategy be used? What about a pull strategy?

ASSIGNMENTS

Present students with the following scenario: As the promotional manager for a new line of cosmetics targeted to preteen girls, you have been assigned the task of deciding which promotional mix elements—advertising, public relations, sales promotion, personal selling, and social media—should be used in promoting it. Your budget for promoting the preteen cosmetics line is limited. Ask students to write a promotional plan explaining their choice of promotional mix elements given the nature of the product, the stage in the product life cycle, target market characteristics, type of buying decision, available funds, and pull or push strategy.

ONLINE

How does a Web site's ease of use affect its ability to create attention, interest, desire, and action? Have students visit the kitchen and bath pages of Kohler's site (www.kohler .com) and determine how successful the company is at moving consumers through the AIDA process.

ADDITIONAL EXAMPLE

Brewing companies face a changing, challenging market. Large brewers like AB InBev, MillerCoors, and Heineken still hold the majority of market share around the world, but their sales are beginning to slip due to competition from wine, hard liquor, and consumers' rapidly growing preference for artisanal craft beers. Even in this declining market, there is one exception—MillerCoors's

CHAPTER PREP 15

KEY TERMS

Coors Light. This beer recently overtook Bud Light as the second-best selling beer in the United States and is the only top-ten selling beer to post consistent growth in the past decade. This has contributed to sustained success for MillerCoors, which has seen revenues climb 4.3 percent in the past year to $2.2 billion.

What is the secret to the success of Coors Light? It's not a change in the product, since the beer tastes the same and is manufactured the same way as it has been for decades. The success of Coors Light can be wrapped up in one word: cold. It's the core message of the promotional campaign surrounding Coors Light; that it is the coldest, most refreshing beer in the market. According to CEO Andrew England,

"We literally said, 'Okay, we're going to do nothing but focus around cold.'"

On one level, MillerCoors' focus on cold is a bit silly, since any beer of any brand will only be as cold as the refrigerator in which it's stored. Yet, the campaign has worked, as evidenced by the growing sales of Coors Light. According to Tom Pirko, president of the consulting firm Bevmark, the irrationality of the promotion is what makes it such a great marketing strategy. "What they have is this Pavlovian thing, where an image goes deep into your psyche," he says. "It's emotional, not intellectual."

Nicholas Kusnetz, "MillerCoors Took Taste Out Of The Equation And Made Cold Unique," *Fast Company*, September 12, 2012, www.fastcompany.com/3000877/millercoors-took-taste-out-equation-and-made-cold-unique (Accessed March 26, 2013).

NEW TO MKTG10 CHAPTER 15

MKTG10	Section
Updated content on competitive advantage	15-1
Updated content on encoding	15-2c
New ALS Association example	15-3b
New content on reminding	15-3c
New section: Content Marketing and Social Media	15-4e
New content on word of mouth and content marketing	15-4f
New content on the AIDA concept	15-5

CHAPTER PREP   16
Advertising, Public Relations, and Sales Promotion

WHAT'S INSIDE:

Key topics in this chapter: effects of advertising, advertising strategies, DAGMAR approach, creative decisions, media selection decisions, alternative media, public relations, sponsorship, crisis management, consumer sales promotion tools, and trade sales promotion.

LEARNING OUTCOMES

16-1 Discuss the effects of advertising on market share and consumers

16-2 Identify the major types of advertising

16-3 Discuss the creative decisions in developing an advertising campaign

16-4 Describe media evaluation and selection techniques

16-5 Discuss the role of public relations in the promotional mix

16-6 Define and state the objectives of sales promotion and the tools used to achieve them

DISCUSSION QUESTIONS

1. Even though advertising is expensive, can it be considered an investment?

2. Should advertising to children be even more restricted than it is at present? Explain your answer.

- Is there a "best" position in a commercial session? Why?
- How well do the commercials fit with the program? Do the programs and the products have similar target markets?

ASSIGNMENTS

Ask students to watch one hour of prime-time television and answer the following questions. They will need a watch or clock with a second hand and undivided attention during commercials.

- In a one-hour (full 60-minute) period, how many minutes were devoted to advertising? How were they distributed throughout the hour?
- How many commercials were 60 seconds long? 45 seconds? 30 seconds? 15 seconds?
- Was the same product advertised more than once during the hour? Were the commercials identical?

ONLINE

How easy is it to find out about advertising options on the Internet? Ask students to find and explore two large companies' advertiser Web pages. Have students find out what kind of information each company requires from potential advertisers and send an e-mail to each company requesting information. Have students compare the material they receive.

ADDITIONAL EXAMPLE

Product placement is nearly ubiquitous in movies today. Heineken recently paid nearly $45 million to MGM and Sony Pictures entertainment so that it could be prominently featured in the twenty-third installation

CHAPTER PREP 16

KEY TERMS

of the James Bond film franchise, *Skyfall*. This amount, nearly one-third of the entire production budget, meant that James Bond would no longer suavely approach a bar and order a martini, shaken not stirred, as he's done for more than forty years. Instead, he would now order a Heineken beer. Luxury automaker Acura signed a multi-year, multi-picture deal with Marvel Studios to have its cars featured in comic book–based films like *Iron Man 3*, *Thor: The Dark World*, and *The Avengers 2*.

However, not all is great with having a product featured prominently in a movie. Take, for example, the Robert Zemeckis-directed film *Flight*. Throughout the movie, both before and after he crashes an airplane, Denzel Washington's character is shown drinking heavily, with the Budweiser logo displayed prominently. This came as quite a surprise to parent company Anheuser-Busch InBev, which was not given any form of advance notice that its product would appear in the movie. "We would never condone the misuse of our products, and have a long history of promoting responsible drinking and preventing drunk driving," said Anheuser-Busch Vice President Rob McCarthy. "It is disappointing that Image Movers, the production company, and Paramount chose to use one of our brands in this manner." The company asked Paramount Studios to blur out or remove digitally the Budweiser logo from all DVDs, television presentations, and online streams of the movie.

Guy Lodge, "The Skyfall's the Limit on James Bond Marketing," *The Guardian*, October 23, 2012, www .guardian.co.uk/film/filmblog/2012/oct/23/skyfall -marketing-james-bond (Accessed March 25, 2013); Joe Flint and Mark Olsen, "Budweiser in 'Flight' Leaves Anheuser-Busch with a Bad Aftertaste," *Los Angeles Times*, November 6, 2012, www.latimes.com/entertainment /envelope/cotown/la-et-ct-budweiser-flight -20121106,0,1130173.story (Accessed March 25, 2013); John Pearley Huffman, "Driving the Avengers Acura NSX Roadster," *Edmunds*, April 16, 2012, www.edmunds.com /car-reviews/features/driving-the-avengers-acura-nsx -roadster.html (Accessed March 25, 2013).

NEW TO MKTG10 CHAPTER 16

MKTG10	Section
New content, examples, and data on measured and unmeasured media	16-1
Updated data on the most valuable U.S. brands	16-1a
New example on TV viewership	16-1b
Updated data on the top advertising spenders	16-2
Updated box: Best of the Best	16-4
Updated data on ad spending	16-4
Updated content and data on television ad costs	16-4a
Updated data on Internet ad spending	16-4a
New data on sponsorship	16-5a

CHAPTER OUTLINE

WHAT'S INSIDE:

Key topics in this chapter: the sales environment, personal selling, relationship versus traditional selling, the steps in the selling process, the sales management process, and the role of CRM in personal selling.

LEARNING OUTCOMES

17-1 Understand the sales environment

17-2 Describe personal selling

17-3 Discuss the key differences between relationship selling and traditional selling

17-4 List and explain the steps in the selling process

17-5 Understand the functions of sales management

17-6 Describe the use of customer relationship management in the selling process

DISCUSSION QUESTIONS

1. How is relationship selling tied to the marketing concept?

2. In today's culture of self-service, is personal selling destined for extinction? Explain your answer.

3. Discuss the role of personal selling in promoting products. What advantages does personal selling offer over other forms of promotion?

ASSIGNMENT

You are a new salesperson for a well-known medical software company, and one of your clients is a large group of physicians. You have just arranged an initial meeting with the office manager. Develop a list of questions you might ask at this meeting to uncover the group's specific needs.

ADDITIONAL EXAMPLE

Many companies are looking for better ways to protect their customers' information. This is particularly true of banks and online stores like eBay. One way eBay is working to protect its customers is by using their information to help identify fraud. Using big data, eBay is able to process large amounts of transaction information and product descriptions to detect sellers who are attempting fraud. According to eBay, fraud has decreased significantly since the company began implementing security measures based on big data. Ford uses data collected from 4 million cars to improve in-car features, such as voice recognition and vehicle safety. For example, in-car sensors relay information to Ford about how customers drive and how they use various features in the car. Customers can use the remote management system that provides Ford with information to receive notifications about any malfunctions or maintenance needs, such as brake pads that need to be replaced.

CHAPTER PREP 17

KEY TERMS

Michael Hickins, "For Some, Security is a Starting Point for Big Data," *Wall Street Journal*, May 3, 2012, http://blogs.wsj.com/cio/2012/05/03/for-some-security-is-a-starting-point-for-big-data/ (Accessed March 26, 2013); Rachel King, "Ford Gets Smarter about Marketing and Design," *Wall Street Journal*, June 20, 2012, http://blogs.wsj.com/cio/2012/06/20/ford-gets-smarter-about-marketing-and-design/ (Accessed March 26, 2013).

NEW TO MKTG10 CHAPTER 17

MKTG10	Section
Updated and reorganized learning outcome list	17-1
New section on the sales environment	17-1
New content on the limitations of personal selling	17-2
Bloomingdales example	17-2
New content on technology and personal selling	17-2
New LinkedIn example	17-2
New content on relationship selling	17-3
Updated content on the selling process	17-4
Removed content on cold calling	17-4a
New data on CRM and qualifying leads	17-4b
Canon example	17-4c
Updated content on closing the sale	17-4f
New content on training	17-5c
Updated PeopleSoft example	17-5d
Mary Kay Cosmetics example	17-5d
Wells Fargo example	17-6d
New Amazon example	17-6d

CHAPTER OUTLINE

WHAT'S INSIDE:

Key topics in this chapter: types of social media and how marketers use them, methods for companies to listen to buzz about the brand, tools to measure social media campaigns, who uses social media and how, mobile technology and how marketers are using it, and creating a social media plan.

LEARNING OUTCOMES

18-1 Describe social media, how they are used, and their relation to integrated marketing communications

18-2 Explain how to create a social media campaign

18-3 Evaluate the various methods of measurement for social media

18-4 Explain consumer behavior on social media

18-5 Describe the social media tools in a marketer's toolbox and how they are useful

18-6 Describe the impact of mobile technology on social media

18-7 Understand the aspects of developing a social media plan

DISCUSSION QUESTIONS

1. Do you see any disadvantages to brands participating in social media? How does marketing affect the way you interact with social media? Give specific examples for three platforms.

2. As a consumer of mobile marketing, what is your reaction to mobile ads? What are some of the most effective ads? The least? How do they differ?

demographic the company is trying to target or, if they aren't sure, explain why it is ineffective.

2. Divide students into groups of three or four. Have each group develop a social media strategy for a company of their choice. They should evaluate their target audience and choose their media accordingly. Each group should target as many demographics as possible with a variety of social media. Have each group write a brief paper explaining why the choices were made and develop samples of each type of social media used.

ASSIGNMENTS

1. Have students choose a company they are interested in and research that company's social media strategy. They should use specific references to tools covered in the chapter. After detailing the company's social media strategy, students should evaluate each aspect of the campaign based on their social media usage. If they think an aspect is ineffective, have them brainstorm the

ADDITIONAL EXAMPLE

Kickstarter is a Web site that enables independent creative professionals to raise funds for lofty commercial projects. Entrepreneurial artisans ask for pledges at fixed price points in exchange for tiered thank-you gifts—for example, a handwritten note for a $1.00 pledge, a copy of the final product for a $25.00 pledge, and a

CHAPTER PREP 18

home-cooked dinner for a $10,000 pledge. After being approved for a Kickstarter campaign, an entrepreneur must meet or exceed her total fundraising goal within a set timeframe. If she cannot reach her goal, she loses all of the funds pledged to that point. Everything from board games to luxury underwear lines to stand-up comedy tours have been successfully funded through Kickstarter, as artisans have appealed to friends, family, and complete strangers from around the world to endow their dreams.

Amanda Palmer, lead vocalist and pianist of offbeat rock group The Dresden Dolls, became the fastest ever entrepreneur to reach a Kickstarter goal in May 2012 when her campaign to finance a new independent solo album topped $100,000 in just four hours.

Palmer was able to raise more than $250,000 in the first day alone after writing about the campaign on her blog, posting it to Facebook, and tweeting about it with her husband, author Neil Gaiman, to their combined 2.25 million Twitter followers. According to Reuters finance blogger Felix Salmon, "While Kickstarter was originally embraced by the undiscovered and impecunious, its greatest potential, in the music industry, is actually with established acts who already have a large following."

SOURCE: Katie McLeod, "Amanda Palmer's Online Fundraising Efforts Explode," *The Boston Globe*, May 1, 2012, www.boston.com/ae/music/blog/2012/05 /amanda_palmers.html (Accessed March 26, 2013); Felix Salmon, "Kickstarter's Growing Pains," *Reuters*, May 1, 2012, http://blogs.reuters.com/felix-salmon/2012/05/01 /kickstarters-growing-pains/ (Accessed March 26, 2013).

NEW TO MKTG10 CHAPTER 18

MKTG10	Section
Updated content and data on social media	18-1
Updated content on popular social media platforms	18-1a
New data on social media usage	18-1a
New content on the types of social commerce	18-1a
New ALS Association example	18-4
Coca-Cola, Walmart, and AllState examples	18-5a
Updated social networks	18-5c
Updated Facebook data	18-5c
Updated LinkedIn data	18-5c
Updated content on popular online games	18-5h
New content on microtransactions	18-5h
Updated data on mobile advertising	18-6a
Updated Exhibit 18.2: Social Media Trends	18-7a

WHAT'S INSIDE:

Key topics in this chapter: basic pricing concepts; formulas for revenue, profit, elasticity of demand, break-even point, fixed cost contribution, and markup pricing; supply and demand; dynamic pricing; how to set a base price; laws affecting pricing practices; and discounts and refinements.

LEARNING OUTCOMES

19-1 Discuss the importance of pricing decisions to the economy and to the individual firm

19-2 List and explain a variety of pricing objectives

19-3 Explain the role of demand in price determination

19-4 Understand the concepts of dynamic pricing and yield management systems

19-5 Describe cost-oriented pricing strategies

19-6 Demonstrate how the product life cycle, competition, distribution and promotion strategies, customer demands, the Internet and extranets, and perceptions of quality can affect price

19-7 Describe the procedure for setting the right price

19-8 Identify the legal constraints on pricing decisions

19-9 Explain how discounts, geographic pricing, and other pricing tactics can be used to fine-tune a base price

DISCUSSION QUESTIONS

1. If a firm can increase its total revenue by raising its price, shouldn't it do so? Explain your answer.

2. Why is it important for managers to understand the concept of break-even points? Are there any drawbacks to using break-even analysis?

3. How important is it for a company to estimate ROI before launching a new product? What does a target ROI enable that company to do?

4. How does the stage of a product's life cycle affect price? Give some examples.

5. The U.S. Postal Service regularly raises the price of a first-class stamp but continues to operate in the red year after year. Is uniform delivered pricing the best choice for first-class mail? Explain your answer.

6. If price fixing results in a lower price to the consumer (the companies involved only want to build share), should it be illegal? Why or why not?

ASSIGNMENTS

The Instructor Manual contains a detailed assignment in step-by-step form that requires students to calculate a price–quality correlation using a simple and inexpensive product—canned goods. High school algebra is all that is required to perform the calculations. A worksheet and nine simple steps lead students through the process of determining if price is a good determinant of quality for canned vegetables (or fruit).

By Vaughn Judd, Auburn University

CHAPTER PREP 19

KEY TERMS

ONLINE

Which automakers are currently offering rebates? Have students visit Edmunds' Web site (www.edmunds.com) for information on national and regional incentives, rebates, and leases. Ask students: What effect do you think rebates and incentives have on overall operation costs and company financial performance?

ADDITIONAL EXAMPLE

In an effort to stem their losses and gain an advantage over their Internet competitors, Target and Best Buy recently announced that they would match the prices offered by a number of popular online retailers such as Amazon.com and Walmart.com. According to Target CEO Gregg Steinhafel, the price-match move was intended to show consumers that Target should be their preferred shopping destination. "We're already rock solid in price. But if periodically some competitor has a lower price, this gives our guests the ability to know 'I can do all of my one-stop shopping in Target.'"

On the surface of things, the price-match policies seem to favor consumers, since they can physically check out a product and get the lowest price. However, a number of exceptions to both policies made them difficult and frustrating to use. For example, shoppers have to ask for the price cuts and show proof of the lower price to an in-store employee. "Can you imagine," asked CEO of CFI Group Sheri Petras, "being on the checkout line at Target with 20 items and you're scanning products on your phone to find out the gum is 12 cents less at Amazon? Can you imagine standing behind that person in line?"

Many retail experts believe that, far from increasing physical store sales, such price-matching policies may actually do the opposite. They suggest that it is simply too difficult to match Internet prices since they fluctuate so much. Moreover, they argue that even with a price-match, there simply is not enough motivation for customers to drive to the store, wait in line, and hope that an employee doesn't make them the exception to the rule.

Ann Zimmerman, "We Promise to Match Prices*," *Wall Street Journal*, October 18, 2012, B1, B4; Ann Zimmerman and Elizabeth Holmes, "Target Vows Price Match," *Wall Street Journal*, October 17, 2012, B6; Tom Gara, "Best Buy's Online Price Matching: There Is a Catch," *Wall Street Journal*, October 12, 2012, http://blogs.wsj.com/corporate-intelligence/2012/10/12/best-buys-online-price-matching-there-is-a-catch (Accessed March 26, 2013).

NEW TO MKTG9 CHAPTER 19

MKTG10	Section
Chapter 19 has been built from the ground up with all new content, examples, key terms, and data. The chapter focuses on pricing concepts and setting the right price, two concepts that were presented in separate chapters in previous editions.	19-1

MKTG
ONLINE
REVIEW FLASHCARDS ANYTIME, ANYWHERE!

Create Flashcards from Your StudyBits

Review Key Term Flashcards Already Loaded on the StudyBoard

4LTR PRESS

Access MKTG ONLINE at www.cengagebrain.com

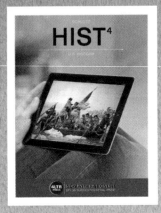

THE PROMO SOLUTION

Every 4LTR Press solution includes:

Visually Engaging Textbook

Online Study Tools

Tear-out Review Cards

Interactive eBook

STUDENT RESOURCES:
- Interactive eBook
- Auto-Graded Quizzes
- Flashcards
- Media Quizzing
- KnowNOW!
- Career Transitions
- Games: Crossword Puzzles, Beat the Clock, & Quiz Bowl
- PowerPoint® Slides
- Videos
- Review Cards

Students sign in at **www.cengagebrain.com**

INSTRUCTOR RESOURCES:
- All Student Resources
- Engagement Tracker
- First Day of Class Instructions
- LMS Integration
- Instructor's Manual
- Test Bank
- PowerPoint® Slides
- Instructor Prep Cards

Instructors sign in at **www.cengage.com/login**

"Both the printed book and digital add-ons were outstanding!!! Loved the book for the rich visual content and the easily understandable text."

– **Amit Bitnun**, Student, *Seneca College*

JULY 2010
4LTR Press adds eBooks in response to a 10% uptick in digital learning preferences.

Engagement Tracker launches, giving faculty a window into student usage of digital tools.

1 out of every 3 (1,400) schools has adopted a 4LTR Press solution.

AUGUST 2010

750,000 students are IN.

NOVEMBER 2010
Third party research confirms that 4LTR Press digital solutions improve retention and outcomes.

IN 2011
60 unique solutions across multiple course areas validates the 4LTR Press concept.

CourseMate
Students access the 4LTR Press website at 4x's the industry average.

APRIL 2011
1 out of every 2 (2,000) schools has a 4LTR Press adoption.

IN 2011
2,000

AUGUST 2011
Over 1 million students are IN.

We're always evolving. Join the 4LTR Press In-Crowd on Facebook at www.facebook.com/4ltrpress

2012 AND BEYOND

SOUTH-WESTERN
CENGAGE Learning

PROMO2
Thomas C. O'Guinn, Chris T. Allen, and Richard J. Semenik

Vice President of Editorial, Business:
Jack W. Calhoun

Publisher: Erin Joyner

Director, 4LTR Press: Neil Marquardt

Executive Editor: Mike Roche

Developmental Editor: Julie Klooster

Editorial Assistant: Megan Fischer

Marketing Manager: Gretchen Swann

Marketing Coordinator: Leigh T. Smith

Sr. Content Project Manager: Tim Bailey

Media Editor: John Rich

Manufacturing Planner: Ron Montgomery

Sr. Marketing Communications Manager:
Jim Overly

Editorial and Production Service: Integra

Sr. Art Director: Stacy Jenkins Shirley

Cover and Internal Designer: KeDesign,
Mason, OH

Sr. Rights AcquistionSpecialist, Images:
Deanna Ettinger

Rights Specialist, Text: Sam A. Marshall

Cover Images: © Jason Lugo, © PeskyMonkey,
© VikaValter, © Jacob Wackerhausen and
GETTY IMAGES: Creative/Photographer's
Choice RF

ExamView® is a registered trademark of eInstruction Corp. Windows is a registered trademark of the Microsoft Corporation used herein under license. Macintosh and Power Macintosh are registered trademarks of Apple Computer, Inc. used herein under license.

Library of Congress Control Number: 201194505

Student Edition Package ISBN 13: 978-1-133-62617-6
Student Edition Package ISBN 10: 1-133-62617-3
Student Edition ISBN 13: 978-1-133-37245-5
Student Edition ISBN 10: 1-133-37245-7

South-Western Cengage Learning
5191 Natorp Boulevard
Mason, OH 45040
USA

Cengage Learning products are represented in Canada by Nelson Education, Ltd.

For your course and learning solutions, visit **www.cengage.com.**

Purchase any of our products at your local college store or at our preferred online store **www.cengagebrain.com.**

Printed in the United States of America
1 2 3 4 5 6 7 16 15 14 13 12

Brief Contents

Contents

PART 1
THE PROCESS OF BRAND PROMOTION IN MARKETING

Yuri Arcurs/Shutterstock.com

Andrew Lever/Shutterstock.com

PART 2
UNDERSTANDING THE MARKET AND ENVIRONMENT FOR PROMOTING BRANDS

Fotocrisis/Shutterstock.com

Monkey Business Images/Shutterstock.com

michaeljung/Shutterstock.com

Courtesy of Mövenpick-Holding, Switzerland.

Haywiremedia/Shutterstock.com

PART 3
THE TOOLS, EVALUATION, AND MEASUREMENT OF BRAND PROMOTION

Pete Saloutos/Shutterstock.com

Gilian McGregor/Shutterstock.com

Photo by Jeff Greenberg/Thomson Learning (now Cengage Learning).

Rafael Ramirez Lee/Shutterstock.com

R. Gino Santa Maria/Shutterstock.com

Sean Prior/Shutterstock.com

Ronen/Shutterstock.com

The World of Integrated Marketing Communication

Learning Outcomes

After studying this chapter, you should be able to:

LO 1 Define promotion and integrated marketing communication (IMC).

LO 2 Discuss a basic model of communication.

LO 3 Describe the different ways of classifying audiences for promotion and IMC.

LO 4 Explain the key role of IMC as a business process.

> "Customers must recognize that you stand for something."
>
> —Howard Schultz

AFTER YOU FINISH THIS CHAPTER GO TO PAGE 21 FOR STUDY TOOLS

Sound Familiar?

It's a Friday night, and you just battled your way through an online quiz in Anthropology that had to be submitted by 11 PM, and you beat the deadline by a couple of hours. Feeling pretty good about the quiz (and suddenly having a little free time on Friday night), you check Facebook and Twitter to see who's attending what parties and concerts that night. You notice that some friends you haven't seen for a while are having a party, so you text two of your buddies to ask if they want to hit the party. Then you click to the Ticketmaster website (www.ticketmaster.com) because Redeye Empire from Vancouver is coming to the big arena on campus (you signed up for the Ticketmaster "performer alert" service and got an email this afternoon), and you want to snag a couple of tickets as soon as possible. Your buddies text back and say they are up for the party and will be at your place in half an hour. Before they arrive, you have just enough time to download the new Redeye Empire album from cdbaby (http://www.cdbaby.com) and set your Slingbox (www.slingmedia.com) so that you can check the NBA scores on SportsCenter from the Internet on your cell phone while you're at the party. (A Slingbox is a device that lets you access your television or TiVo from your computer or cell phone. Check out their website on the opposite page.)

Does this scenario sound familiar? If you're into keeping up with your friends and your interests, then it probably does. And you and your friends represent a huge challenge for companies that want to reach you with their promotional messages. For the last 50 years, firms have primarily been using television, radio, newspapers, magazines, and other traditional media to send messages to consumers about the companies' brands. However, the imaginary "you" in this scenario encountered little, if *any*, mass media advertising, even though you bought concert

What do you think?

I'm in control when I see or hear advertising.

1   2   3   4   5   6   7
STRONGLY DISAGREE   STRONGLY AGREE

Find out what others think at CourseMate for PROMO2.

tickets and a CD and accessed television programming on the Internet. Instead, a whole series of individually controlled information sources let you access all the information *you* wanted to see—not just information some company wanted you to see or hear.[1]

So, what are companies going to do to reach you with messages about their products and brands? They will still try to reach you and every other consumer around the globe who is acquiring information in new ways. But rather than relying as much on the old style of mass media, companies are turning to a wide range of new promotional techniques that complement their mass media advertising.[2]

The New World of Integrated Marketing Communication

As the world of promotion undergoes enormous change, companies are trying to keep up with how and where consumers want to receive information about brands. While they have not abandoned mass media, marketers are supplementing and supporting traditional communication channels with new ways to reach consumers. Consumer preferences and new technology are reshaping the communication environment. The lines between information, entertainment, and commercial messages are blurring. As one analyst put it, "The line of demarcation was obliterated years ago, when they started naming ballparks after brands."[3] Companies are turning to branded entertainment, the Internet, influencer marketing, and other communication techniques to reach consumers and get their brand messages across. *Advertising Age* calls this new world of advertising "Madison and Vine," as Madison Avenue advertising agencies attempt to use Hollywood entertainment-industry techniques to communicate about their brands.[4]

But no matter how much technology changes or how many new media are available for delivering messages, it's still all about the brand. As consumers, we know what we like and want, and advertising—regardless of the method—helps expose us to brands that can meet our needs. Even Heinz ketchup—which, according to chief marketing officer Brian Hansberry, is "in every household" with "higher household penetration than salt and pepper"—has to remind consumers why they value it. Conversely, a brand that does *not* meet our needs will not succeed—no matter how much is spent on advertising or brand communication. That's a painful lesson U.S. automakers learned over decades of declining market share.

LO 1 Promotion via Integrated Marketing Communication

You see advertising every day, even if you try to avoid most of it. It's just about everywhere because it serves so many purposes. To the CEO of a multinational corporation, like Pepsi, advertising is an essential marketing tool that helps create brand awareness and brand loyalty. To the owner of a small retail shop, advertising is an invitation that brings people into the store. To a website manager, it's a tool to drive traffic to the URL.

While companies believe in and rely heavily on advertising, it is only a single technique in a bigger process, the marketing activity known as promotion. As a business process, promotion is relied on by companies big and small to build their brands—the central theme of this book. As we will show, successful marketers do more than pay for advertising and other promotional activities; they plan how

CONSUMER PREFERENCES AND NEW TECHNOLOGY ARE **RESHAPING THE COMMUNICATION ENVIRONMENT.**

to combine them to strengthen their brands. These efforts at promotion and integrated marketing communication are keys to building awareness and preference for brands.

Promotion

As described later in this chapter, marketing encompasses activities such as designing products, setting a price, making the products available to customers, and promoting them, the topic of this book. **Promotion** is the communications process in marketing that is used to create a favorable predisposition toward a brand of product or service, an idea, or even a person. Most often, it involves promotion for a brand of product or service.

Promotion includes planning and carrying out a variety of activities, selected from a wide range of possibilities. Together these activities for a brand form its **promotional mix**, a blend of communications tools used by a firm to carry out the promotion process and to communicate directly with audiences. Here is a list of the most prominent tools:

- Advertising in mass media (television, radio, newspapers, magazines, billboards)
- Sales promotions (coupons, premiums, discounts, gift cards, contests, samples, trial offers, rebates, frequent-user programs, trade shows)
- Point-of-purchase (in-store) advertising
- Direct marketing (catalogs, telemarketing, email offers, infomercials)
- Personal selling
- Internet advertising (banners, pop-ups/pop-unders, websites)
- Social media
- Blogs
- Podcasting
- Event sponsorships
- Branded entertainment (product placement in television programming, webcasts, video games, and films), also referred to as "advertainment"
- Outdoor signage
- Billboard, transit, and aerial advertising
- Public relations
- Influencer marketing (peer-to-peer persuasion)
- Corporate advertising

promotion the communications process in marketing that is used to create a favorable predisposition toward a brand of product or service

promotional mix a blend of communications tools used to carry out the promotion process and to communicate directly with an audience

Image courtesy of The Advertising Archives.

No one grows Ketchup like Heinz.

To remind consumers that Heinz ketchup is a product the company has "cared for from seed to plate," the company's advertising combines the "No one grows Ketchup like Heinz" slogan with images of fresh tomatoes.[5]

Notice that this list includes various types of advertising, one of the most widely used promotional tools. Simply defined, **advertising** is a paid, mass-mediated attempt to persuade. This definition is loaded with distinctions.

First, advertising is *paid* communication by a company or organization that wants its information disseminated (see Exhibit 1.1). In advertising language, the company or organization that pays for advertising is called the **client** or **sponsor**. If a communication is *not paid for*, it's not advertising. *Publicity* is not advertising because it is not paid for. For the same reason, public service announcements (PSAs) are not advertising either, even though they look and sound like ads.

Second, advertising is *mass mediated*. This means it is delivered through a communication medium designed to reach more than one person, typically a large number—or mass—of people. Advertising is widely disseminated through traditional and new media:

- Television
- Radio
- Newspapers
- Magazines
- Direct mail
- Billboards
- Websites
- Podcasts

The mass-mediated nature of advertising creates a communication environment where the message is not delivered face to face. This distinguishes advertising from *personal selling* as a form of communication.

Third, all advertising includes an *attempt to persuade*. Put bluntly, ads are designed to get someone to do something. The ad informs the consumer for some purpose, and that purpose is to get the consumer to like the brand and, because of that liking, to eventually buy the brand.

Integrated Marketing Communication

Imagine how much more impact a promotional effort can have if ads, salespeople, point-of-purchase signs, and other communications send a consistent message, rather than work independently. Beginning in about 1990, many marketers embraced the concept of *integrated marketing communication (IMC)*. IMC attempts to coordinate promotional efforts so that messages are synergistic. But the reality of promotional strategies in the 21st century demands that the emphasis on *communication* give way to an emphasis on the *brand*. Recent research and publications on IMC are recognizing that, in effective marketing communications, the brand plays a central role.[6]

Exhibit 1.1
Is It an Ad?

What You See	Advertisement?
Will Smith appears on the *Late Show with David Letterman* to promote his newest movie.	**No**, it's publicity. The producer or film studio did not pay the *Late Show with David Letterman* for airtime. Rather, the show gets an interesting and popular guest, the guest star gets exposure, and the film gets plugged.
A film studio produces and runs ads on television and in newspapers for the newest Will Smith movie.	**Yes**. This communication is paid for by the studio and placed in media to reach consumers.
Trojan pays for print media to run a message that tells readers to "Get Real" and use a condom.	**Yes**. Trojan paid the print media to run an ad intended to increase demand for condoms, including Trojan condoms.
The United Kingdom's Health Education Authority prepares a message that urges readers to wear a condom; print media run the message.	**No**, it's a public service announcement. It is not paid for by an advertiser but offered in the public interest.

© Cengage Learning 2011

As a result, marketers have begun using a brand-oriented approach: **integrated marketing communication (IMC)**, defined as the process of using a wide range of promotional tools working together to create widespread brand exposure. IMC retains the goal of coordination and synergy of communication, but the emphasis is on the brand, not just the communication. With a focus on building brand awareness, identity, and ultimately preference, the IMC perspective recognizes that coordinated promotional messages need to have brand-building effects in addition to their communication effects.

Just as the definition of promotion was loaded with meaning, so too is the definition of integrated marketing communication. First, IMC is a *process*. It has to be. It is complicated and needs to be managed in an integrated fashion.

Second, IMC uses a *wide range of promotional tools* that have to be evaluated and scheduled. These communications tools, listed in the description of the promotional mix, include advertising, direct marketing, sales promotion, event sponsorships, point-of-purchase displays, public relations, and personal selling. In IMC, all of these varied and wide-ranging tools allow a marketer to reach target customers in different ways with different kinds of messages to achieve broad exposure for a brand.

Third, the definition of IMC highlights that all of these tools need to *work together*. That is, they need to be integrated to create a consistent and compelling impression of the brand. Having mass media advertising send one message and create one image and then having personal selling deliver another message will confuse consumers about the brand's meaning and relevance.

Finally, the definition of IMC specifies that all of the promotional efforts undertaken by a firm are designed to create *widespread exposure for a brand*. Unless consumers are reached by these various forms of messages, they will have a difficult time understanding the brand and deciding whether to use it regularly.

Advertising in IMC

As we noted, advertising is the most-used tool in the promotion mix, so IMC often relies heavily on advertising. An advertising plan combines advertisements in an advertising campaign. An **advertisement** refers to a specific message that someone or some organization has placed to persuade an audience. An **advertising campaign** is a series of coordinated advertisements that communicate a reasonably cohesive and integrated theme. The theme may be made up of several claims or points but should advance an essentially singular theme. Successful advertising campaigns can be developed around a single advertisement placed in multiple media, or, like the ads for Altoids shown on the next page, they can be made up of several different advertisements with a similar look, feel, and message. Advertising campaigns can run for a few weeks or for many years.

The advertising campaign is, in many ways, the most challenging aspect of advertising execution. It requires a keen sense of the complex environments within which a company must communicate to different audiences. One factor is that audience members have been accumulating knowledge from previous ads for a particular brand. Consumers interpret new ads through their experiences with a brand and previous ads for the brand. Even ads for a new brand or a new product are situated within audiences' broader knowledge of products, brands, and advertising. After years of viewing ads and buying brands, audiences bring a rich history and knowledge base to every communications encounter.

When marketers combine advertising campaigns with other promotional tools such as contests, a website, event sponsorship, and point-of-purchase displays, all aimed at building and maintaining brand awareness, they are using integrated marketing communication. BMW did just that when the firm (re)introduced the Mini Cooper automobile to the U.S. market. The IMC campaign used billboards, print ads, an interactive website, and "guerrilla" marketing (a Mini was mounted on top of a Chevy Suburban and driven around New York City). Each part of the campaign was coordinated with all the others.[7] Without coordination among these various promotional efforts, the consumer will merely encounter a series of unrelated (and often confusing) communications about a brand.

As consumers encounter a daily blitz of commercial messages and appeals, brands and brand identity offer them a way to cope with the overload of information. Brands and the images they project allow consumers to quickly identify and evaluate the relevance of a brand to their lives and value systems. The marketer who does not use IMC as a way to build brand exposure and meaning for consumers will, frankly, be ignored.

> **integrated marketing communication (IMC)** the use of a wide range of promotional tools working together to create widespread brand exposure
>
> **advertisement** a specific message that an organization has placed to persuade an audience
>
> **advertising campaign** a series of coordinated promotional efforts, including advertisements, that communicate a single theme or idea

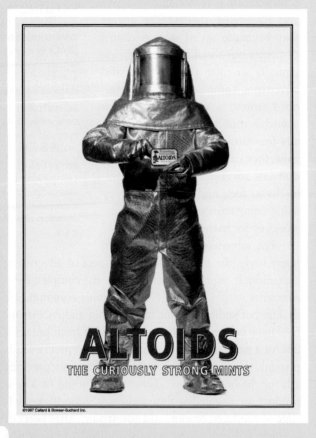

Notice the similar look and feel in this well-connected and well-executed advertising campaign.

LO 2 Mass-Mediated Communication

Promotion occurs through various forms of communication, and advertising is a particular type: mass-mediated communication (meaning it occurs not face to face but through a medium, such as magazines or the Internet). Therefore, to understand promotion, you must understand something about communication in general and about mass communication in particular. To help with gaining this understanding, let's consider a contemporary model of mass communication.

While there are many valuable models, Exhibit 1.2 presents a contemporary model of mass-mediated communication. This model shows mass communication as a process where people, institutions, and messages interact. It has two major components, each representing quasi-independent processes: *production* and *reception*. Between these are the mediating (interpretation) processes of *accommodation* and *negotiation*.

Production of the Content

Moving from left to right in the model, the first element is the process of communication production, where the content of any mass communication is produced. An advertisement, like other forms of mass communication, is the product of institutions (such as networks, corporations, advertising agencies, and governments) interacting to produce content (for example, what you watch on television or read in a magazine). The creation of the advertisement is a complex interaction of several variables:

- The company's message

- The company's expectations about the target audience's desire for information

- The company's assumptions about how the audience will interpret the words and images in an ad

- The rules and regulations of the medium that transmits the message

Advertising is rarely (if ever) the product of any one individual. Rather, it is a collaborative (social) product between people receiving a message and the institutions (companies and media companies) that send them that message.

Accommodation, Negotiation, and Reception

Continuing to the right in the model, the mediating processes of accommodation and negotiation lie between the production and reception phases. Accommodation and negotiation are the ways in which consumers interpret ads. Audience members have some ideas about how the company wants them to interpret the ad (we all know the rules of advertising—somebody is trying to persuade us to buy something). And consumers also have their own needs, agendas, and preferred interpretations. They also know about the way other consumers think about this product and this message because brands have personalities and send social signals. Given all this, consumers who see an ad arrive at an interpretation of the ad that makes sense to them, serves their needs, and fits their personal history with a product category and a brand.

This whole progression of consumer receipt and interpretation of a communication is usually wholly incompatible with the way the company wants consumers to see an ad! In other words, the receivers of the communication must *accommodate* these competing forces, meanings, and agendas and then *negotiate* a meaning, or an interpretation, of the ad. That's what makes communication an inherently *social* process: What a message means to any given consumer is a function not of an isolated solitary thinker but of an inherently social being responding to what he or she knows about the producers of the message (the companies), other receivers of it (peer groups, for example), and the social world in which the brand and the message about it resides. This interpretation happens very fast and without much contemplation, but it does happen. The level of conscious interpretation might be minimal (mere recognition) or it might be extensive (thoughtful, elaborate processing of an ad), but there is *always* interpretation.

Limits of Mass-Mediated Communication

The processes of production and reception are partially independent. Although the producers of a message can control the placement of a message in a medium, they cannot control or even closely monitor the circumstances that surround reception and interpretation of the ad. Audience members are exposed to advertising outside the direct observation of the company and are capable of interpreting advertising any way they want. (Of course, most audience interpretations are not completely off the wall, either.) Likewise, audience members have little control over or input into the actual production of the message—the company developed a message that audience members are *supposed* to like. As a result, producers and receivers are "imagined," in the sense that the two don't have significant direct contact with each other but have a general sense of what the other is like.

Exhibit 1.2
Mass-Mediated Communication

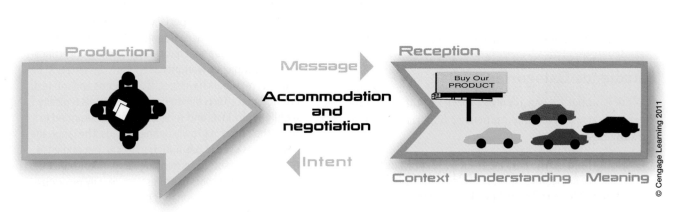

© Cengage Learning 2011

The communication model in Exhibit 1.2 underscores a critical point: No ad contains a single meaning for all audience members. An ad for a pair of women's shoes means something different for women than it does for men. Nevertheless, although individual audience members' interpretations will differ to some extent, they may be close enough to the company's intent to make the ad effective. When members of an audience are similar in their background, social standing, and goals, they generally yield similar enough meaning from an ad for it to accomplish its goals.

LO 3 Audiences for Promotion

In the language of promotion, an **audience** is a group of individuals who receive and interpret advertisements and other promotional messages sent from companies. The audience could be made up of household consumers, college students, or businesspeople. Any large group of people can be an audience.

A **target audience** is a particular group of consumers singled out by an organization for an advertising campaign or promotion strategy. These target audiences are singled out because the firm has discovered that audience members like or might like the product category. Target audiences are always *potential* audiences because a company can never be sure that the message will actually get through to them as intended.

Audience Categories

While companies can identify dozens of different target audiences, five broad audience categories are commonly described:

- **Household consumers** are the most conspicuous audience in that most mass media advertising is directed at them. McDonald's and State Farm have products and services designed for the consumer market, so their advertising targets household consumers. In the approximately 116 million U.S. households, there are about 307 million household consumers.[8] Total yearly retail spending by these households exceeds \$5 trillion in the United States.[9] This huge audience is typically where the action is in advertising. Under the very broad heading of "consumer advertising," companies can make very fine audience distinctions—for example, men aged 25 to 45, living in metropolitan areas, with incomes greater than \$50,000 per year.

- **Members of business organizations** are the focus of advertising for firms that produce business and industrial goods and services, such as office equipment and data storage. While products and services targeted to this audience often require personal selling, advertising is used to create awareness and a favorable attitude among potential buyers. Not-for-profit organizations such as universities, some research laboratories, philanthropic groups, and cultural organizations represent an important and separate business audience for advertising.

- **Members of a trade channel** include retailers (like Best Buy for consumer electronics), wholesalers (like Castle Wholesalers for construction tools), and distributors (like Sysco Food Services for restaurant supplies). They are a target audience for producers of both household and business goods and services. In the case of household goods, for example, Microsoft needs adequate retail and wholesale distribution through trade channels for the Xbox or else the brand will not reach target customers. The promotional tool used most often to communicate with this group is personal selling because this target audience represents a relatively small, easily identifiable group. When advertising also is directed at this target audience, it can serve an extremely useful purpose, as we will see later in the section on IMC as a business process.

- **Professionals** form a special target audience defined as doctors, lawyers, accountants, teachers, or any other professional group that has special training or certification. This audience warrants a separate classification because its members have specialized needs and interests. Promotional efforts directed to professionals typically highlight products and services uniquely designed to serve their more narrowly defined needs. The language and images used in promoting to this target audience often rely on esoteric terminology and unique circumstances that members of professions readily recognize. Advertising to professionals is predominantly carried out

Tatiana Popova/Shutterstock.com

through trade publications. **Trade journals** are magazines published specifically for members of a trade and carry highly technical articles.

- **Government officials and employees** constitute an audience in themselves due to the large dollar volume of buying that federal, state, and local governments do. Government organizations from universities to road maintenance operations buy huge amounts of various types of products. Producers of items such as office furniture, construction materials, and business services all target government organizations. Promotion to this target audience is dominated by direct mail, catalogs, and web advertising.

Audience Geography

Audiences for promotional messages also can be broken down by geographic location. Because of cultural differences that often accompany geographic location, very few messages can be effective for all consumers worldwide, and many are directed to one of the more limited geographic areas:

- **Global promotion** involves messages used worldwide with only minor changes. The few messages that can use global promotion are typically for brands that are considered citizens of the world and whose manner of use does not vary tremendously by culture. Using a Sony television or taking a trip on Singapore Airlines doesn't change much from culture to culture or from geographic location to geographic location. Firms that market brands with global appeal try to develop and place messages with a common theme and presentation in all markets around the world where the firm's brands are sold. Thus, global placement is possible only when a brand and the messages about that brand have a common appeal across cultures.

- **International promotion** occurs when firms prepare and place different messages in different national markets outside their home market. Often, each international market requires unique or original promotion due to product adaptations or message appeals tailored specifically for that market. Unilever prepares different

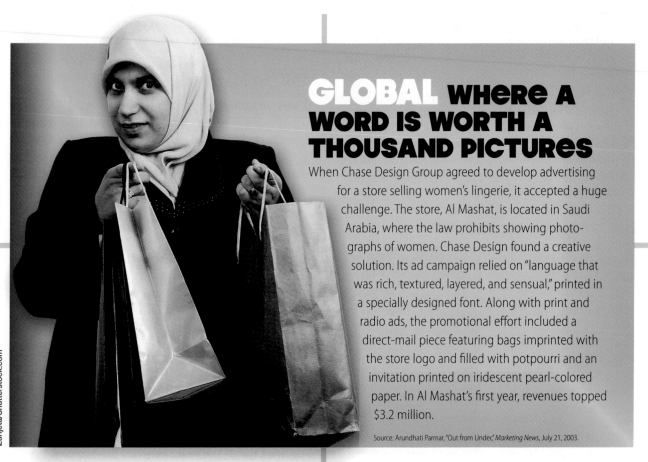

Zurijeta/Shutterstock.com

GLOBAL WHERE A WORD IS WORTH A THOUSAND PICTURES

When Chase Design Group agreed to develop advertising for a store selling women's lingerie, it accepted a huge challenge. The store, Al Mashat, is located in Saudi Arabia, where the law prohibits showing photographs of women. Chase Design found a creative solution. Its ad campaign relied on "language that was rich, textured, layered, and sensual," printed in a specially designed font. Along with print and radio ads, the promotional effort included a direct-mail piece featuring bags imprinted with the store logo and filled with potpourri and an invitation printed on iridescent pearl-colored paper. In Al Mashat's first year, revenues topped $3.2 million.

Source: Arundhati Parmar, "Out from Under," *Marketing News*, July 21, 2003.

versions of messages for its laundry products for nearly every international market because consumers in different cultures approach the laundry task differently. Consumers in the United States use large and powerful washers and dryers and a lot of hot water. Households in Brazil use very little hot water and hang clothes out to dry.

- **National promotion** reaches all geographic areas of one nation. It is the kind of promotion we see most often in the mass media in the U.S. market. As the box on the previous page highlights, national promotion is appropriate where a product category or promotional effort must be tailored to the unique situation of a particular culture. Organizations that promote their brand in several nations may combine different national-promotion efforts to engage in international promotion.

- **Regional promotion** is carried out by producers, wholesalers, distributors, and retailers that concentrate their efforts in a relatively large, but not national, geographic region. Albertson's, a regional grocery chain, has stores in 31 Western, Northwestern, Midwestern, and Southern states. Because of the nature of the firm's markets, it places messages only in regions where it has stores.

- **Local promotion**, much like regional promotion, is directed at an audience in a single trading area, either a city or state. For example, Daffy's is a discount clothing retailer with stores in the New York/New Jersey metropolitan area, and it uses local promotion to reach that market. Retailers like Daffy's use all types of local media to reach customers.

- **Cooperative promotion** (or **co-op promotion**) is a team approach to promotion in which national companies share promotion expenses in a market with local dealers to achieve specific objectives. For example, TUMI luggage and one of its retailers, Shapiro, have run co-op promotions that describe the benefits of TUMI's Safecase briefcase for carrying a laptop computer and also indicate that this product is available at Shapiro stores. If consumers respond by visiting Shapiro to buy the Safecase, then both promoters benefit.

LO 4 IMC as a Business Process

Besides being a communication process, promotion—especially in the context of integrated marketing communication (IMC)—is very much a business process, too. For multinational organizations like Microsoft, as well as for small local retailers, promotion within the framework of IMC is a basic business tool that is essential to retaining current customers and attracting new customers.

IMC in Marketing

Every organization *must* make marketing decisions. There simply is no escaping the need to develop brands, price them, distribute them, and advertise and promote them to a target audience. As organizations carry out these activities, IMC helps them do so in a way that achieves profitability and other goals.

Daffy's, a clothing retailer with several shops in the New York/ New Jersey metropolitan area, services a local geographic market, so it communicates through local advertising.

WHEN A CLOTHING STORE HAS A SALE ON SELECTED MERCHANDISE, WHY IS IT ALWAYS MERCHANDISE YOU'D NEVER SELECT?

At Daffy's you'll find 40-70% off all our clothes, every day 5th Ave. & 18th St., Madison Ave. & 44th St.

DAFFY'S CLOTHES THAT WILL MAKE YOU, NOT BREAK YOU.™

Courtesy of Daffy's.

Exhibit 1.3
The Marketing Mix

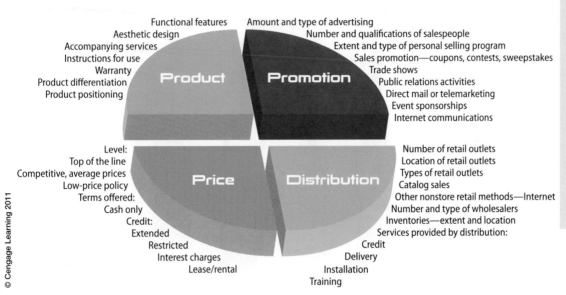

Functional features
Aesthetic design
Accompanying services
Instructions for use
Warranty
Product differentiation
Product positioning

Product

Amount and type of advertising
Number and qualifications of salespeople
Extent and type of personal selling program
Sales promotion—coupons, contests, sweepstakes
Trade shows
Public relations activities
Direct mail or telemarketing
Event sponsorships
Internet communications

Promotion

Level:
Top of the line
Competitive, average prices
Low-price policy
Terms offered:
Cash only
Credit:
Extended
Restricted
Interest charges
Lease/rental

Price

Number of retail outlets
Location of retail outlets
Types of retail outlets
Catalog sales
Other nonstore retail methods—Internet
Number and type of wholesalers
Inventories—extent and location
Services provided by distribution:
Credit
Delivery
Installation
Training

Distribution

© Cengage Learning 2011

Promotion in the Marketing Mix

A formal definition of marketing reveals that promotion is one of the primary marketing tools available to any organization: "**Marketing** is the process of planning and executing the conception, pricing, promotion, and distribution of ideas, goods, and services to create exchanges that satisfy individual and organizational objectives."[10]

Marketing people assume a wide range of responsibilities in an organization related to conceiving, pricing, promoting, and distributing goods, services, and even ideas. These four areas of responsibility and decision making in marketing are referred to as the **marketing mix**. The word *mix* is used to describe the blend of strategic emphasis on the product versus its price versus its promotion versus its distribution when a brand is marketed to consumers. This blend, or mix, results in the overall marketing program for a brand.

Exhibit 1.3 identifies factors typically considered in each area of the marketing mix. Decisions under each of the marketing mix areas can directly affect promotional messages. Thus, a firm's promotional effort must be consistent with and complement the overall marketing mix strategy. As we saw earlier, IMC is a process that helps companies meet that objective, with an eye toward strengthening their brands.

Looking specifically at promotional tools such as advertising, the role of IMC in the marketing mix is to communicate to a target audience the *value* a brand has to offer. Value consists of more than simply the tangible aspects of the brand itself. Indeed, consumers look for value in the brand, but they also demand such benefits as convenient location, credit terms, warranties and guarantees, and delivery. In addition, consumers may look for brands that satisfy a wide range of emotional values such as security, belonging, affiliation, excitement, and prestige. Think about the fact that a $16,000 Ford Focus can get you from one place to another in pretty much the same way as a $120,000 BMW M5. Emotionally, however, driving the BMW would deliver something extra—more thrill and style. People look for more than function in a brand; they often buy the emotional kick that a brand and its features provide.

Because consumers search for such diverse values, marketers must determine which marketing mix ingredients to emphasize and how to blend the mix elements in just the right way to attract customers. These marketing mix decisions play a significant role in determining the message content and media placement of advertising and other brand-related messages.

Supporting Brand Management

When embedded in IMC, promotion plays a critical role in brand development and management. To appreciate its role, we need a formal understanding of what a brand is. A **brand** is a name, term, sign, symbol, or any other feature that identifies one seller's good or service as distinct from those of other sellers.[11] A brand is in many ways the most precious business asset owned by a firm. It allows a firm to communicate consistently and efficiently with the market.

Business Week magazine in conjunction with Interbrand, a marketing analysis and consulting firm, has attached a dollar value to brand names based on a combination of sales, earnings, future sales potential, and intangibles other than the brand that drive sales. Often, the brand name is worth much more than the annual sales of the brand. In a recent year, Coca-Cola was identified as the most valuable brand in the world, with an estimated worth of almost $70 billion, even though sales of branded Coca-Cola products were only about $31 billion that year.[12]

Lack of effective marketing communication can leave a brand at a serious competitive disadvantage. Staples, the office supply retailer, was struggling with an outdated advertising campaign featuring the tagline "Yeah, we've got that." Customers were complaining that items were out of stock and sales staff didn't care. So the company's vice president of marketing, Shira Goodman, determined that shoppers wanted an "easier" shopping experience with well-stocked shelves and helpful staff. Once those operational changes were made, Staples introduced the "Staples: That Was Easy" campaign, featuring big red "Easy" push buttons that were available for sale at the stores. Clear, straightforward ads and customers spreading the word (called "viral" marketing) by putting their "Easy" buttons on display in offices across the country helped make Staples the runaway leader in office retail.[13]

For every organization, promotion supports brand development and management in five important ways:

1. **Information and persuasion**. Target audiences learn about a brand's features and benefits through the message content of advertising and, to a lesser extent,

THE CREST BRAND WAS ORIGINALLY ASSOCIATED WITH TOOTHPASTE; ADVERTISING HELPED THE COMPANY EXTEND THE BRAND TO THIS LINE OF TOOTHBRUSHES. HOW DID THE CREST NAME HELP WITH BRAND EXTENSION?

AP Photo/PRNewsFoto.

other promotional tools used in the IMC effort. Advertising has the best capability to inform or persuade target audiences about the values a brand has to offer. No other variable in the marketing mix is designed to accomplish this communication. Branding is crucial to the $190 billion cell phone market as Verizon, Sprint Nextel, T-Mobile, and AT&T compete for over 300 million wireless subscribers.[14] Marketing a cellular-service brand helps consumers distinguish why they should choose a particular service provider when the decision is complex and several providers offer essentially the same product.

2. **Introduction of new brands or brand extensions**. Advertising is absolutely critical when organizations introduce a new brand or extensions of existing brands to the market. For example, to introduce consumers to the idea of staying cozy in winter by wearing a blanket with sleeves, the president of Snuggie used low-budget cable-TV ads that urged consumers to place an order right away. As orders came in, demonstrating a demand for the product, stores became willing to put Snuggies on their shelves.[15] A **brand extension** is an adaptation of an existing brand to a new product area. For example, the Snickers Ice Cream Bar is a brand extension of the original Snickers candy bar. When brand extensions are brought to market, advertising attracts attention to the brand—so

A BRAND IS IN MANY WAYS THE MOST PRECIOUS BUSINESS ASSET OWNED BY A FIRM.

much so that researchers now suggest that "managers should favor the brand extension with a greater allocation of the ad budget."[16] In IMC, the advertising campaign works in conjunction with other promotional activities such as sales promotions and point-of-purchase displays.

3. **Building and maintaining brand loyalty**. One of the most important assets a firm can have is **brand loyalty**, which occurs when a consumer repeatedly purchases the same brand to the exclusion of competitors' brands. This loyalty can result because of habit, the prominence of a brand in the consumer's memory, barely conscious associations with brand images, or the attachment of some fairly deep meanings to a brand. The most important influence on building and maintaining brand loyalty is a brand's features, but promotion also plays a key role in the process by reminding consumers of the brand's values—tangible and intangible. Promotions such as frequent-buyer programs can give customers an extra incentive to remain brand loyal. When a firm creates and maintains positive associations with the brand in the minds of consumers, the firm has developed **brand equity**.[17] While development of brand equity occurs over long periods of time, short-term advertising activities are key to long-term success.[18] For example, Kraft defended its Miracle Whip brand against a new campaign by competitor Unilever for Imperial Whip by investing heavily in television advertising just before Unilever lowered prices on the Imperial Whip brand.[19]

4. **Creating an image and meaning for a brand**. Because advertising can communicate how a brand addresses certain needs and desires, it plays an important role in attracting customers to brands that appear to be useful and satisfying. But advertising can go further. It can help link a brand's image and meaning to a consumer's social environment and to the larger culture, and in this way, it actually delivers a sense of personal connection for the consumer. To advertise its prenatal vitamins, Schiff communicates with ads whose message is about love, not just the health advantages of using a nutritional supplement during pregnancy.

5. **Building and maintaining brand loyalty in the trade**. You might expect wholesalers, retailers, distributors, and brokers to be too practical to be brand loyal, but they will favor one brand over others given the proper support from a manufacturer. Advertising, particularly when integrated with other brand promotions, is an area where support is welcome. Marketers can provide the trade with sales training programs, collateral advertising materials, point-of-purchase advertising displays, premiums (giveaways like key chains or caps), and traffic-building special events. These promotional efforts are important because trade buyers can be a key to the success of new brands or brand extensions. To introduce a brand, marketers depend on cooperation among wholesalers and retailers in the trade channel. Research also shows that retailer acceptance of a brand extension is key to the success of the new product.[20] IMC is essential because the trade is less responsive to advertising messages than to other forms of promotion, such as displays, contests, and personal selling.

Implementing Market Segmentation, Differentiation, and Positioning

The third role for IMC in marketing is helping the firm implement market segmentation, differentiation, and positioning. **Market segmentation** is the process of breaking down a large, widely varied (heterogeneous) market into submarkets, or segments, that are more similar (homogeneous) than

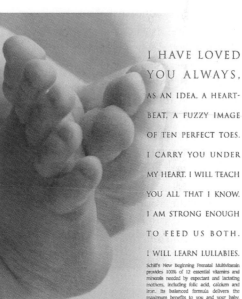

I HAVE LOVED YOU ALWAYS, AS AN IDEA, A HEARTBEAT, A FUZZY IMAGE OF TEN PERFECT TOES. I CARRY YOU UNDER MY HEART. I WILL TEACH YOU ALL THAT I KNOW. I AM STRONG ENOUGH TO FEED US BOTH. I WILL LEARN LULLABIES.

Schiff's New Beginning Prenatal Multivitamin provides 100% of 12 essential vitamins and minerals needed by expectant and lactating mothers, including folic acid, calcium and iron. Its balanced formula delivers the maximum benefits to you and your baby.

Benefits Beyond Your Daily Requirements. Schiff

Weider Nutrition International Copyright © 1995.

The message mines associations related to love and caring for an unborn or recently born child. Even the slogan for the brand, "Benefits Beyond Your Daily Requirements," plays on the notion that a vitamin is more than a vehicle for dosing up on folic acid. What meanings do you find in this message?

differentiation
creation of a perceived difference, in the consumer's mind, between an organization's brand and the competition's

positioning designing a product or service to occupy a distinct and valued place in the target consumer's mind and then communicating this distinctiveness

external position competitive niche pursued by a brand

dissimilar in terms of what the consumer is looking for. Underlying the strategy of market segmentation are two variables: consumers differ in their wants, and the wants of one person can differ under various circumstances. Thus, the market for automobiles can be divided into submarkets for different types of automobiles based on the needs and desires of various groups of buyers. Identifying those groups, or segments, of the population who want and will buy large or small, luxury or economy models is an important part of basic marketing strategy. In addition to needs, markets are often segmented on characteristics of consumers such as age, marital status, gender, and income. For example, Bayer has four different versions of its basic aspirin brand: regular Bayer for headache relief; Bayer Enteric Safety Coated 81 mg aspirin for people with cholesterol and heart concerns; Women's Bayer, which includes a calcium supplement; and Children's Bayer, which is lower dose and chewable. The role of IMC in market segmentation is to develop messages that appeal to the wants and desires of different segments and then to transmit those messages via appropriate media.

Differentiation is the process of creating a perceived difference, in the mind of the consumer, between an organization's brand and the competition's. This definition emphasizes that brand differentiation is based on *consumer perception*. Perceived differences can be tangible features or related to image or style. A $20 Timex and a $12,000 Fendi watch tell you the same time of day, but the consumers who pay extra for a Fendi are looking for a different degree of style and the experience of making a fashion statement or impressing a gift recipient with a prestigious brand. The differentiation works only if consumers *perceive* a difference between brands. Differentiation is one of the most critical of all marketing strategies. Perceiving a firm's brand as distinctive and attractive gives consumers a reason to choose that brand over a competitor or to pay more for the "better" or "more meaningful" brand. Advertising can help create

a difference in the mind of the consumer between an organization's brand and its competitors' brands. To do this, the ad may emphasize performance features or create a distinctive image for the brand. Either way, the goal is to develop a message that is different and unmistakably linked to the organization's brand.

Positioning is the process of designing a brand so that it can occupy a distinct and valued place in the target consumer's mind relative to other brands and then communicating this distinctiveness through advertising. Positioning, like differentiation, depends on a perceived image of tangible or intangible features. Consumers create a *perceptual space* in their minds for all the brands they might consider purchasing. A perceptual space describes how one brand is seen on any number of dimensions—such as quality, taste, price, or social display value—in relation to those same dimensions for other brands.

There are two positioning decisions for a brand:

1. **External position**—the niche the brand will pursue relative to all the competitive brands on the market.

Advertising is a key tool in a marketing strategy of differentiation. How does this ad differentiate Fendi watches from lower-priced brands?

Courtesy of Taramask S.A. Switzerland.

2. **Internal position**—the niche the brand will occupy with regard to the other similar brands within the firm.

With the external-positioning decision, a firm tries to create a distinctive *competitive* position based on design features, pricing, distribution, or promotion or advertising strategy. For example, BMW's 550i is priced around $100,000, while the Chevrolet Cobalt aims for the budget-conscious consumer with a base price of about $15,000. Effective internal positioning involves either developing vastly different products within the firm's own product line or creating advertising messages that appeal to different consumer needs and desires. Procter & Gamble does both to position its many laundry detergent brands. One P&G brand is advertised as being effective on kids' dirty clothes, while another brand is portrayed as effective for preventing colors from running.

The methods and strategic options available to an organization with respect to market segmentation, product differentiation, and positioning will be fully discussed in Chapter 4.

Enhancing Revenues and Profits

Many people believe that the fundamental purpose of marketing can be stated quite simply: to generate revenue. Marketing is the only part of an organization that has revenue generation as its primary purpose. In the words of highly regarded management consultant and scholar Peter Drucker, "Marketing and innovation produce results: all the rest are 'costs.'"[21] The "results" Drucker refers to are revenues. The marketing process is designed to generate sales and therefore revenues for the firm.

Creating sales as part of the revenue-generating process is where promotion plays a significant role. As we have seen, the promotional mix communicates persuasive information to audiences based on the values created in the marketing mix related to the product, its price, or its distribution. This communication highlights brand features—price, emotion, or availability—and attracts a target market. In this way, promotional messages make a direct contribution to the marketing goal of revenue generation. Although promotion *contributes* to the process of creating sales and revenue, it cannot be solely responsible for creating sales and revenue—it's not that powerful. Some organizations mistakenly see advertising or promotion as a panacea—the salvation for an ambiguous or ineffective overall marketing strategy. However, sales occur when a brand has a well-conceived and complete marketing mix.

The effect of promotion on profits comes about when it gives an organization greater flexibility in the price it charges for a product or service. Advertising can help create pricing flexibility in two ways:

1. Contributing to economies of scale
2. Helping create inelasticity of demand

When an organization creates large-scale demand for its brand, the quantity of product produced increases, and **economies of scale** lead to lower unit production costs. Cost of production decreases because fixed costs (such as rent and equipment costs) are spread over a greater number of units produced. Promotion contributes to demand stimulation by communicating to the market about the features and availability of a brand. By stimulating demand, advertising then contributes to the creation of economies of scale, which ultimately translates into higher profits per unit.

Brand loyalty, discussed earlier, brings about the other important source of pricing flexibility, **inelasticity of demand**, a situation in which consumers are relatively insensitive to price increases for the brand. When consumers are less price sensitive, firms have the flexibility to raise prices and increase profit margins. For example, Louis Vuitton, the maker of luxury handbags ($1,000 per bag or more) and other luxury items, enjoys an operating margin of 45 percent.[22] Advertising contributes directly to brand loyalty, and thus to inelasticity of demand, by persuading and reminding consumers of the satisfactions and values related to a brand. This business benefit of advertising was recently supported by a large research study in which companies that built strong brands and raised prices were more profitable than companies that cut costs as a way to increase profits—by nearly twice the profit percentage.

Promotion Objectives

An important set of decisions in IMC involves what the promotional objectives are supposed to achieve. For example, should the message increase demand for an entire product category or just a particular brand? Do you want the audience to act immediately or develop positive associations that will shape future decisions? In an integrated strategy, answering such questions will shape the kinds of messages you create and the elements you choose to include in the promotional mix.

> **internal position** niche a brand occupies with regard to the company's other, similar brands
>
> **economies of scale** lower per-unit production costs resulting from larger volume
>
> **inelasticity of demand** low sensitivity to price increases; may result from brand loyalty

Primary versus Selective Demand Stimulation

Promotional messages may stimulate either primary or selective demand. In **primary demand stimulation**, a company is trying to create demand for an entire product *category*. Primary demand stimulation is challenging and costly, and research evidence suggests that it is likely to have an impact only for products that are totally new, not for brand extensions or mature product categories. An example of effective primary demand stimulation was the introduction of the VCR to the consumer market in the 1970s. With a product that is totally new to the market, consumers need to be convinced that the product category itself is valuable and that it is, indeed, available for sale. When the VCR was first introduced in the United States, RCA, Panasonic, and Quasar ran primary demand stimulation advertising to explain to household consumers the value and convenience of taping television programs with this new product—something no one had ever done before at home.

For organizations that have tried to stimulate primary demand in mature product categories, typically trade associations, the results have been dismal. The National Fluid Milk Processor Promotion Board has tried using advertising to stimulate primary demand for the product category of milk. While the multibillion-dollar "mustache" campaign is popular and wins awards, milk consumption has *declined* every year during the time of this campaign.[23] Even if the attempts at primary demand have reduced the overall decline in milk consumption (which can't be determined), this result is still not very impressive. This should come as no surprise, though. Research over decades has clearly indicated that attempts at primary demand stimulation in mature product categories (orange juice, beef, pork, and almonds have also been tried) have never been successful.[24]

While some corporations have tried primary demand stimulation, the true power of advertising is shown when it functions to stimulate demand for a particular company's brand. In this approach, known as **selective demand stimulation**, the objective of the promotion is to point out a brand's unique benefits compared with the competition. For example, advertising for Tropicana orange juice notes that the brand offers a calcium-fortified option that can help keep bones strong.

Direct- versus Delayed-Response Promotion

Another promotion decision involves how quickly we want consumers to respond. **Direct-response promotion** asks consumers to act immediately. Examples include ads that direct you to "call this toll-free number" or "mail your $19.95 before midnight tonight." In many cases, direct-response promotion is used for products that consumers are familiar with, that do not require inspection at the point of purchase, and that are relatively low cost. However, the proliferation of toll-free numbers, websites that provide detailed information, and the widespread use of credit cards have been a boon to direct response for higher-priced products, such as exercise equipment.

Delayed-response promotion relies on imagery and message themes that emphasize the brand's benefits and satisfying characteristics. Rather than trying to stimulate an immediate action from an audience, delayed-response promotion attempts to develop awareness and preference for a brand over time. In

The National Fluid Milk Processor Promotion Board uses the famous milk mustache ads in an effort to build primary demand for milk, not for a particular brand.

general, delayed-response promotion attempts to create brand awareness, reinforce the benefits of using a brand, develop a general liking for the brand, and create an image for a brand. When a consumer enters the purchase process, the information from delayed-response promotion comes into play. Most advertisements we see on television and in magazines are of the delayed-response type. When McDonald's runs television ads during prime time, the company doesn't expect you to leap from your chair to go out and buy a Big Mac, but the company does hope you'll remember the brand the next time you're hungry.

Promoting the Company or the Brand

Promotional messages can be developed to build a favorable attitude toward either a brand or the image of the company itself. **Brand advertising**, as we have seen throughout this chapter, communicates the specific features, values, and benefits of a particular brand offered for sale by a particular organization.

Corporate advertising is meant to create a favorable attitude toward a company as a whole. Prominent uses of corporate advertising include BP's "Beyond Petroleum" and General Electric's "Ecomagination" campaigns. Similarly, Philips, the Dutch electronics and medical device conglomerate, turned to corporate advertising to unify the image of its brand name across a wide range of superior technologies.[25] Corporate campaigns have been designed to generate favorable public opinion toward the corporation as a whole, which can also affect the company's shareholders. When they see good corporate advertising, it instills confidence and, ultimately, long-term commitment to the firm and its stock. We'll consider this type of advertising in detail in Chapter 13.

Another form of corporate advertising is carried out by members of a trade channel, mostly retailers. When corporate advertising takes place in a trade channel, it is referred to as *institutional advertising*. Retailers such as Nordstrom and Walmart advertise to persuade consumers to shop at their stores. While these retailers may occasionally feature a particular manufacturer's brand in the advertising, the main purpose of the advertising is to get the audience to shop at their stores.

Economic Impact of Promotion

Promotion not only has an important impact on the individual business organizations that pay for it, but it also has effects across a country's entire economic system. These effects may seem far removed from marketing decisions, but they help shape public attitudes toward businesses and marketers.

Impact on Gross Domestic Product

The **gross domestic product (GDP)** is the measure of the total value of goods and services produced within an economic system. As a part of the marketing mix, promotion increases GDP indirectly by working with product, pricing, and distribution decisions to stimulate sales. When sales of products such as DVDs or alternative energy sources grow, producers have to make more of these products. In addition, the greater demand helps to fuel housing starts and corporate investment in finished goods and capital equipment. Consequently, GDP is affected by promotion, especially when it involves sales of products in new, innovative product categories.[26]

Impact on Business Cycles

Promotion can have a stabilizing effect on downturns in business activity. There is evidence that many firms increase advertising during times of recession in an effort to spend their way out of a business downturn.

Impact on Competition

Promotion is alleged to stimulate competition and therefore motivate firms to strive for better products, better production methods, and other competitive advantages that ultimately benefit the economy as a whole. Additionally, when promotion serves as a way to enter new markets, it fosters competition across the economic system.

Promotion is not universally hailed as a stimulant to competition. Critics point out that the amount of advertising dollars needed to compete effectively in many industries is often prohibitive. This requirement makes advertising a barrier to entry into an industry;

Valentyn Volkov/Shutterstock.com

brand advertising advertising that communicates a brand's features, values, and benefits

corporate advertising advertising intended to establish a favorable attitude toward a company

gross domestic product (GDP) the total value of goods and services produced within an economic system

value perception that a product or service provides satisfaction beyond the cost incurred to acquire it

symbolic value nonliteral meaning of a product or service, as perceived by consumers

that is, a firm may be able to compete in an industry in every way except spending enough on the advertising needed to compete. If this occurs, promotion can actually decrease the overall amount of competition in an economy.[27]

Impact on Prices

One of the widely debated effects of promotion has to do with its effect on the prices consumers pay for products and services. Some say that the millions or even billions of dollars spent on advertising are added to the prices for the products and services advertised. However, this relationship is not necessarily true.

First, across all industries, advertising costs incurred by firms range from about 2 percent of sales in the automobile and retail industries up to 30 percent of sales in the personal care and luxury products businesses.[28] Exhibit 1.4 shows the ratio of advertising to sales for three firms in different industries. Notice that there is no consistent and predictable relationship between advertising spending and sales. Different products and different market conditions demand that firms spend different amounts of money on advertising. These same conditions make it difficult to identify a predictable relationship between advertising and sales.

It is true that the cost of advertising is built into product costs, which are ultimately passed on to consumers. But this effect on price must be judged against a couple of cost savings that lower the price. First, there is the reduced time and effort a consumer has to spend in searching for a product or service. Second, economies of scale, discussed earlier, have a direct impact on cost and then on prices. When economies of scale lower the unit cost of production by spreading fixed costs over a large number of units produced, the cost reduction can be passed on to consumers in terms of lower prices, as firms search for competitive advantage with lower prices. Nowhere is this effect more dramatic than the price and performance of personal computers. In the early 1980s, an Apple IIe computer that ran at about 1 MHz and had 64K of total memory cost more than $3,000. Today, a Dell computer with multiple times the power, speed, and memory costs only about $800.

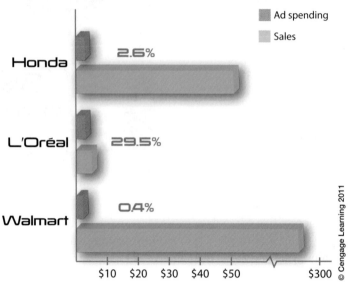

Exhibit 1.4
Ad Spending as a Percent of Sales

Honda — 2.6%
L'Oréal — 29.5%
Walmart — 0.4%

Ad spending
Sales

$10 $20 $30 $40 $50 $300

© Cengage Learning 2011

Impact on Value

The password for successful marketing is *value*. In modern marketing and advertising, **value** refers to consumers' perception that a brand provides satisfaction beyond the cost incurred to obtain that brand. The value perspective of the modern consumer is based on wanting every purchase to be a "good deal." Promotion can add value to the consumption experience. Consider the effect of branding on bottled water. Promotion helps create enough value in the minds of consumers that they (we) will *pay* for water that comes free out of the tap.

Promotion also affects a consumer's perception of value by contributing to the symbolic value and social meaning of a brand. **Symbolic value** refers to what a product or service means to consumers in a nonliteral way. For example, branded clothing such as Guess? jeans or Doc Martens shoes can symbolize self-concept for some consumers. In reality, all branded products rely, to some extent, on symbolic value; otherwise, they would not be brands but just unmarked commodities (like potatoes).

Social meaning refers to what a product or service means in a societal context. For example, social class is marked by various products that are used and displayed to signify class membership. An example is United Airlines' Connoisseur Class aimed at international business travelers. Often, the product's connection to a social class addresses a need within consumers to move up in class.

hifashion/Shutterstock.com.

Researchers from various disciplines have long argued that objects (brands included) are never just objects. They take on meaning from culture, society, and consumers.[29] It is important to remember that these meanings often become just as much a part of the brand as the product's physical features. Because the image of a brand is developed through promotion, it contributes directly to consumers' perception of the value of the brand. The more value consumers see in a brand, the more they are willing to pay to acquire the brand. If consumers value the image of a Nissan coupe or a Four Seasons hotel stay, then they will pay a premium to acquire that value.

CONCLUSION: PROMOTION MATTERS

When you get involved with brand promotion, you're not just selling goods that you hope consumers need. You're helping to make consumption experiences more valuable. You're contributing to the efficiency of trade, potentially making products more affordable. You're keeping competitors on their toes, so everyone gets better at serving customers. And especially when promotion is part of a careful IMC effort, you're helping your company or clients achieve strategic goals. The remaining chapters in this part and Part 2 will prepare you for this role by introducing you to how the promotion industry works and how buyers make decisions. Then the chapters in Part 3 explore how a variety of promotional tools can be used in a complete, effective IMC campaign. For the creative thinker, the possibilities are endless. And changes such as the ones described at the beginning of this chapter are making the industry more exciting than it ever has been. Welcome to the world of brand promotion!

STUDY TOOLS CHAPTER 1

Located at back of the textbook

- **Rip out Chapter in Review Card.**

Located at www.cengagebrain.com

- **Review Key Terms Flashcards (Print or Online).**
- **Complete the Practice Quiz to prepare for tests.**
- **Play "Beat the Clock" and "Quizbowl" to master concepts.**
- **Complete "Crossword Puzzle" to review key terms.**
- **Watch videos on IBM and McDonald's for real company examples.**
- **Find additional examples that support integrated marketing communication in the online examples. Examples include: Cadillac, Victoria's Secret, Exide, and Colgate.**

When you see a Coke cup on the judges' desk, does it make you want to drink a Coke?

Coca-Cola and *American Idol* team up to target consumers.

AP Photo/Michael Becker/Fox/PictureGroup.

Learning Outcomes

After studying this chapter, you should be able to:

LO 1 Discuss important trends transforming the promotion industry.

LO 2 Describe the promotion industry's size, structure, and participants.

LO 3 Summarize what advertising and promotion agencies do and how they are compensated.

LO 4 Identify experts who help plan and execute integrated marketing communication campaigns.

LO 5 Discuss the role played by media organizations in IMC campaigns.

> "Any damn fool can put on a deal, but it takes genius, faith, and perseverance to create a brand."
>
> —David Ogilvy

AFTER YOU FINISH THIS CHAPTER GO TO PAGE 43 FOR STUDY TOOLS

Welcome to the Power Struggle

There have always been power struggles in the promotion industry: brand versus brand; one agency versus another; agency versus media company; big advertiser with lots of money versus big retailer with lots of money. But those old-style power struggles were child's play compared with the 21st-century power struggle. Consumers, who on average encounter between 1,000 and 5,000 advertising messages every day,[1] are tired of the barrage of ads and try to avoid most of them. So today's power struggle is about how the promotion industry can adapt to the new technologies consumers are using to gain more control over their information environment.

From Facebook to YouTube to millions of blogs, consumers are seeking out information environments where *they* control their exposure to information rather than an advertiser or media company being in control. They are insisting on the convenience and appeal of their PC, iPod, and TiVo or Slingbox (as we saw in Chapter 1). This so-called mass collaboration by consumers is such a dramatic change from traditional information flow techniques that marketers, advertising and promotion agencies, and media companies are struggling to reinvent themselves.[2] Coca-Cola and American Idol are teaming up to do just that.

The traditional approach to promotion was for a marketer, like Nike or American Express, to work with an advertising agency, like Leo Burnett or J. Walter Thompson, which would develop television, radio, newspaper, magazine, or billboard ads. Then the marketer and its agency would buy media time or space to place the ads so that consumers would see and hear them. This still happens—a lot. Major media rake in about $450 billion worldwide in a year, and individual media companies like Hearst Corp. generate several billion dollars in annual revenue.[3] But even as marketers, agencies, and media companies try to reach control-seeking

What do you think?

Featuring a brand in a TV show can be as creative as a great TV commercial.

| 1 | 2 | 3 | 4 | 5 | 6 | 7 |

STRONGLY DISAGREE   STRONGLY AGREE

Find out what others think at CourseMate for PROMO2.

23

consumers, some very smart people think the industry is on the cusp of even more dramatic changes.[4]

While the traditional structure of the promotion industry may be changing, the *goal* has not changed: The brand still needs to be highlighted. The change in consumer orientation will make product branding *more* important as consumers choose what persuasive messages they want to receive and where they want to receive them.

As marketers, agencies, and their media partners struggle with how to meet enduring goals in this new environment, some think the answer is to go with the flow and invite consumers to contribute to brand content (for example, by sponsoring competitions for the best consumer-created ad).[5] Others, like Coca-Cola, respond to consumers' impatience with advertisements by using subtler and seemingly more natural ways to make brands part of consumers' daily lives. Part of Coke's approach: pay $20 million to have Coke cups on the judges' desks during Fox Network's *American Idol* program.[6] Other marketers are paying video game developers to insert their branded products into their games, reaching millions or tens of millions of players.[7]

Big media companies are adapting, too. NBC Universal, often referenced as the "classic" big media company with the deepest roots in the old media structure, is wooing advertisers by offering to help prepare advertising with the network's vast digital studio resources.[8] MTV Networks is offering new-media distribution like broadband channel MotherLoad, which is associated with Comedy Central programming.[9]

With much of the consumer control exerted online, marketers are trying harder to be where consumers are going and be a part of what they are doing. In 2009, for example, advertisers said they were spending significantly less to advertise in traditional media, and most were shifting the bulk of the money saved to digital brand promotion.[10] That's not just a matter of posting an ad in a new place, such as a popular website; rather, marketers are inviting consumers to "like" the brand on Facebook and download branded apps for their smart phones. Instead of brands interrupting what consumers are doing (watching a sitcom, reading a magazine), brands engage consumers by being part of what they are doing (building connections on Facebook, playing games on their mobile devices).

Alex Staroseltsev/Shutterstock.com

GLOBAL RICH SOIL FOR AGENCY GROWTH

- Hispanic agencies in the United States that develop campaigns for Spanish-speaking consumers have been enjoying double-digit growth. As Hispanic online spending has risen above $150 million a year, more of these agencies are starting interactive units.

- China is struggling to keep up with the need for advertising and promotional materials fueled by that country's dramatic economic growth. For some agencies in China, finding enough talent to hire is a "crisis."

- In Europe, Amsterdam has emerged as a hot agency market. Why? The city itself is artistic, easily attracts creative talent, and features broad diversity.

Sources: Laurel Wentz, "Look at Them Grow: U.S. Hispanic Agencies Thrive," *Advertising Age*, December 4, 2006, 31; Laurel Wentz and Normandy Madden, "China's Ad World: A New Crisis Every Day," *Advertising Age*, December 11, 2006, 6; and Jack Ewing, "Amsterdam's Red-Hot Ad Shops," *BusinessWeek*, December 18, 2006, 52.

Hewlett-Packard's chief marketing officer, Michael Mendenhall, calls this change a "move from interruptive to engagement," and he says marketers "can do that more effectively in the digital space."[11]

If you consider changes in technology, economic conditions, culture, lifestyles, and business philosophies, one or more of these broad business and societal forces are always affecting the effort to promote brands and communicate messages about what the brands stand for. Change in the promotion industry is nothing new, but the pace and complexity of the change are more challenging than the industry has ever faced. As you read about the structure of the industry, notice how the players are being shaped by—but also shaping—this change.

LO 1 Promotion Industry Trends

Often advertisers struggle with whether to use traditional mass media, like television and radio, which have wide reach, or to use newer, highly targeted media like personalized emails and social networking. But in the end, what is important is not the technology itself but rather the need to focus on the brand, its image, and a persuasive, integrated presentation of that brand to the target market. The choice of the Web or television should be based on which medium is likely to achieve the right persuasive impact.

Nevertheless, to understand the promotion industry, we need to know what is happening in it today.

Narrower Media Control

Consolidation has been taking place among media organizations, so control over media outlets is in fewer hands. Historically, there has been a legal limit on how much control any one media company could seize. But in 2003, the Federal Communications Commission (FCC) relaxed a decades-old rule that restricted media ownership. Now a single company can own television stations that reach up to 45 percent of U.S. households—up from the 35 percent specified in the old rule. In addition, the FCC voted to lift all "cross-ownership" restrictions, ending a ban on one company owning both a newspaper and broadcast station in a city.[12]

The consolidation is not restricted to television. Media companies of all types tend to pursue more and more "properties" if they are allowed to, thus creating what are now referred to as "multiplatform" media organizations.[13] Consider the evolution of media giant News Corp. and its holdings, which include television networks (Fox), newspapers (more than 20 worldwide, including the *Wall Street Journal*), in-store and at-home promotional materials (News America Marketing Group), satellite (Sky Italia), and cable systems (Fox News). Besides cultivating a Web presence by creating sites affiliated with other media, such as Fox News and the *Wall Street Journal*, News Corp. has experimented with investments in Internet-only media outlets including MySpace and Hulu. News Corp.'s worldwide media holdings generate more than $30 billion in revenue and reach every corner of the earth. As big as News Corp. is, the ultimate multiplatform may be Disney, which owns the ABC broadcasting network and the ESPN cable network group, plus 10 other cable stations, over 30 radio stations, video on demand, books, magazines, and the Disney Interactive Media Group, which creates a parenting website, websites that offer exploration of "virtual worlds," and video games for play on computers, game consoles, and mobile devices.

Media Clutter

Even though media companies and advertising agencies have been consolidating into fewer large firms, the number of media options has grown, giving marketers more ways to *try* to reach consumers than ever before. In television alone, the options have multiplied. In 1994, the consumer had access to about 27 television channels. Today, the average U.S. household has access to well over 100 channels. That means consumers are harder to find. In 1995, it took three well-placed TV spots to reach 80 percent of women television viewers. By 2003, it took 97 spots to reach them.[14]

The types of media also have proliferated with the introduction of cable television channels, direct-marketing technology, Web options, and alternative new media (podcasting, for example). New and

Not to be outdone, the Web has its own media conglomerates. InterActiveCorp (IAC) has amassed a media empire of Internet sites that include Ask.com, Match.com, Urbanspoon, and Dictionary.com. Together, these sites generate about $1.6 billion in revenue, which makes IAC nearly as big as better-known Internet merchants, but much more diversified.

increased media options have resulted in so much clutter that the probability of any one message breaking through and making a real difference continues to diminish.

As marketers struggle to stand out amid the clutter, they are losing faith in advertising alone. Promotion options such as online communication, brand placement in film and television, point-of-purchase displays, and sponsorships are more attractive to advertisers. For example, advertisers on the Super Bowl, notorious for its clutter and outrageous ad prices (about $3 million for a 30-second spot), use integrated marketing communication to ensure that attention begins well before game day. Up to two months ahead of the game, marketers announce their purchase of advertising time, hoping to spur some early publicity. Then at their own websites or on YouTube, they post video clips from the ad or behind-the-scenes video about making the ad, so curious consumers will check it out and spread the word. After the game, companies post the ads online for further viewing,

typically with applications that let viewers easily post the ad on their Facebook and Twitter pages. In 2010, Snickers created a micro-site featuring its Super Bowl ad. Viewers loved the scenes of Betty White playing football in the mud, and the ad became wildly popular—so much so that the veteran actress found she was a star once again.[15]

As marketers focus on integrating more tools within the overall promotional effort in an attempt to reach more consumers in different ways, traditional media expenditures are falling. Consider the decisions by Johnson & Johnson. In 2007, J&J announced that it had shifted $250 million in spending from traditional media—television, magazines, and newspapers—to "digital media," including the Internet and blogs.[16]

Advertisers are shifting spending out of traditional media because they are looking to the full complement of promotional opportunities in sales promotions (like the Miller chairs), event sponsorships, new-media options, and public relations as means to support and enhance the primary advertising effort for brands. Some advertisers are enlisting the help of Hollywood talent agencies in an effort to get their brands featured in television programs and films. The payoff for strategic placement in a film or television show can be huge. Getting Coca-Cola placed on *American Idol*, as we talked about earlier, is estimated to be worth up to $20 million in traditional media advertising.[17] This topic also is covered in Chapter 12, where we consider branded entertainment in detail.

Consumer Control

Historically, advertisers controlled information and the flow of information as a one-way mode of communication through mass media. But today's consumers are in greater control of the information they receive about product categories and the brands within those categories. The simplest and most obvious example is when consumers visit Internet sites *they* choose to visit for either information or shopping. But it gets a lot more complicated from there. **Blogs**—or websites frequented by individuals with common interests where they can post facts, opinions, and personal experiences—are emerging as new and sophisticated sources of product and brand information. Once criticized as the "ephemeral scribble" of 13-year-old girls and the babble of techno-geeks, blogs are gaining greater sophistication and organization. Web-based service firms like Blogdrive, Feedster, and Blogger are making blogs easier to use and accessible to the masses.

Another way in which consumers exert control over the messages they receive is by using digital video recorders (DVRs) like TiVo and controllers like Slingbox. Marketers initially reacted to this trend with fear, expecting that consumers would use DVRs as a way to fast-forward through ads. In fact, as the penetration of DVRs into U.S. households has

neared 40 percent, marketers are finding that households seem to be using DVRs as a way to watch more TV than ever, because they can watch shows at a convenient time. And they don't necessarily fast-forward through the ads—especially not young viewers, who may be using ad time to multitask by checking texts or Facebook posts.[18] In sum, the use of DVRs is a lot more complex than marketers had assumed.

Marketers and marketing professionals must adapt to consumers' control over the information they choose to receive. One adaptation is to be more creative with messages. For example, marketers are weaving ad stories into television stories, as when zombie attack rescuers arrived in a Toyota Corolla during the drama *The Walking Dead* or when Unilever products are tied into the story line of *Mad Men*. When skillfully done and entertaining in their own right, these ads hold viewers' attention—in fact, some viewers even use their DVRs to replay ads they enjoy.[19] Another technique—less creative but certainly effective—is to run advertising messages along the bottom of the programming. Finally, TiVo has introduced a service that sounds crazy: ads on demand.[20] The premise is that consumers about to buy expensive items like cars or resort vacations may want to watch information about alternative brands.

Web 2.0

Recently, consumer control has moved to a whole new level of collaboration via Web 2.0. A phrase coined by O'Reilly Media in 2004, *Web 2.0* refers to a second generation of Web-based use and services—such as social networking sites and wikis—that emphasize online collaboration and sharing among users. O'Reilly Media used the phrase as a title for a series of conferences, and it has since become widely adopted.

> **blog** personal journal on a website that is frequently updated and intended for public access

MARKETERS AND MARKETING PROFESSIONALS **MUST ADAPT** TO CONSUMERS' CONTROL OVER THE INFORMATION **THEY CHOOSE TO RECEIVE.**

social media highly accessible Web-based media that allow the sharing of information among individuals and between individuals and groups

crowdsourcing online distribution of tasks to groups (crowds) of experts, enthusiasts, or general consumers

Consumers' sharing and collaboration often involve the use of **social media**, highly accessible Web-based media that allow the sharing of information among individuals and between individuals and groups. Social media, discussed more fully in Chapter 13, have become the most significant form of consumer control over information creation and communication. Facebook has more than 350 million users worldwide, and Twitter has more than 50 million users.[21] Marketers can participate by setting up Facebook pages and sending 140-character messages, called tweets, to people who sign up to be followers on Twitter. Just three months after Honda started a Facebook page, 2 million people had signed up to be "friends" of the brand.[22]

When consumers use social media and other Web 2.0 applications, they are publishing their own thoughts and ideas. This opens for marketers the possibility of **crowdsourcing**, the online distribution of tasks to groups (crowds) of experts, enthusiasts, or general consumers.[23] The goal is that, as users of a product recommend innovations, they will become more committed to the brand. Dell, for example, launched its "Idea Storm" website to invite computing ideas, and Starbucks created "MyStarbucksIdea" to invite recommendations for new products and services that it might offer in its stores. Ford built interest in its Fiesta compact by inviting consumers to apply to be "agents" who would receive a Fiesta they would drive for six months in exchange for blogging about their experiences. Out of the 4,000 people who applied, Ford chose 100. Their videos and commentaries were posted online for consumers to view and share.

For years to come, these trends and the changes they bring about will force advertisers to think differently about the promotional mix and IMC. Similarly, advertising agencies will need to think about the way they

serve their clients and the way communications are delivered to audiences. Big clients such as Procter & Gamble and Miller Brewing Company are already demanding new and innovative programs to enhance the impact of their advertising and promotional dollars.

LO 2 Industry Scope and Structure

The promotion industry plays a significant role in the economy. More than $300 billion is spent in the United States alone on various categories of advertising, with nearly $600 billion spent worldwide. Spending on all forms of promotion including advertising exceeds a trillion dollars.[24]

Promotional efforts are a significant expense for many individual firms. The top U.S. advertisers spend billions of dollars a year on advertising alone. To keep this in perspective, however, these amounts need to be measured against revenues. Procter & Gamble spent about $4.8 billion on advertising in 2008, but this amount represented just under 7 percent of its sales.[25]

Overall, the 100 leading advertisers in the United States spent just over $105 billion on advertising in 2006, which was a healthy 3.1 percent increase over 2005.[26] While this is good news for ad agencies, there is no doubt that this rapidly increasing spending is related to increased clutter. Advertising may be quickly becoming its own worst enemy.

Who is spending all these ad dollars, and where are they spending that money? The structure of the industry tells us *who* does *what, in what order*, during the brand promotion process. The promotion industry is actually a collection of a wide range of talented people, all of whom have special expertise and perform a wide variety of tasks in planning, preparing, and placing promotional messages. Exhibit 2.1

Naiyyer/Shutterstock.com.

shows the structure of the promotion industry by identifying the participants in the process.

Exhibit 2.1 demonstrates that *marketers* (such as Kellogg) can employ the services of *advertising and promotion agencies* (such as Grey Global Group) that may or may not contract for specialized services with various *external facilitators* (such as Simmons Market Research Bureau), which results in advertising and other promotional messages being transmitted with the help of various *media organizations* (such as the TBS cable network) to one or more *target audiences* (like you).

Note the options available in Exhibit 2.1. Marketers do not always need to employ the services of advertising agencies, nor do agencies always seek the services of external facilitators. Some marketers deal directly with media organizations for placement of their advertisements or implementation of their promotions. In the case of traditional advertising, this happens either when a marketer has its own internal advertising/promotions department that prepares all the materials for the process or when media organizations (especially radio, television, and newspapers) provide technical assistance in the preparation of materials. Also, interactive media formats provide advertisers the opportunity to work directly with entertainment programming firms, such as Walt Disney and LiveNation, to provide integrated programming that features brand placements in films and television programs or at entertainment events. And, as you will see, many of the new-media agencies provide the creative and technical assistance advertisers need to implement campaigns through new media.

Marketers

The first participants in the promotion industry are the marketers. From the local pet store to multinational corporations, organizations of all types and sizes seek to benefit from the effects of advertising and other elements of the promotional mix. **Marketers** are business, not-for-profit, and government organizations that use advertising and other promotional techniques to communicate with target markets and to stimulate awareness and demand for their brands. Marketers are also referred to as **clients** by their advertising and promotion agency partners. Different types of marketers use advertising somewhat differently, depending on the type of product or service they market.

Manufacturers and Service Firms

The most prominent users of promotion are large national manufacturers of consumer products and services, which often spend hundreds of millions of dollars annually. Procter & Gamble and Merrill Lynch have national or global markets for their products

Exhibit 2.1
Structure of the Promotion Industry

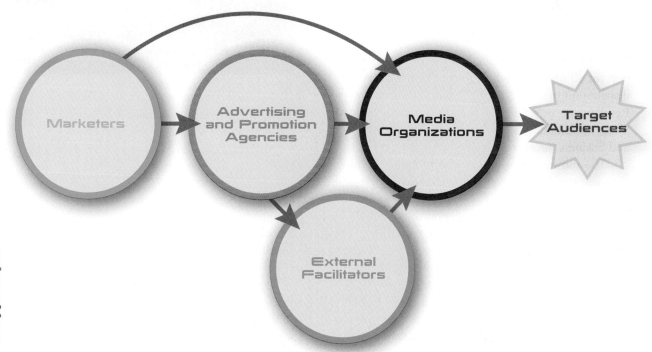

trade reseller
organization in the marketing
channel of distribution that
buys products to resell to
customers

and services. The use of advertising, particularly mass media advertising, by these firms is essential to creating awareness and preference for their brands.

But advertising is useful not just to national or multinational firms; regional and local producers of household goods and services also rely heavily on advertising. For example, regional dairy companies typically sell milk, cheese, and other dairy products in several states. These firms often use ads placed in newspapers and regional editions of magazines. Further, couponing and sampling are ways to communicate with target markets with IMCs that are well suited to regional application. Local producers of products are relatively rare, but local service organizations are common. Medical facilities, auto dealers, and arts organizations are examples of local service providers that use advertising to create awareness and stimulate demand. What car dealer in America has not advertised a holiday event or used a remote local radio broadcast to attract attention?

Firms that produce both business goods and services also may promote their products on global, national, regional, and local levels. IBM (computer and business services) and Deloitte (accounting and consulting services) are examples of global companies that produce business goods and services. At the national and regional levels, firms that supply agricultural and mining equipment and repair services are common users of promotion, as are consulting and research firms. At the local level, firms that supply janitorial, linen, and bookkeeping services use advertising to companies in their area.

Trade Resellers

The term **trade reseller** is simply a general description for all organizations in the marketing channel of distribution that buy products to resell to customers. Resellers can be retailers, wholesalers, or distributors. Their customers may include household consumers and business buyers at all geographic market levels.

The most visible reseller advertisers are retailers that sell in national or global markets. Walmart and McDonald's are examples of global retail companies that use various forms of promotion to communicate with customers. Regional retail chains, typically grocery chains such as Albertson's or department stores such as Dillard's, serve multistate markets and use advertising suited to their regional customers. At the local level, small retail shops of all sorts rely on newspaper, radio, television, and billboard advertising and special promotional events to reach a relatively small geographic area.

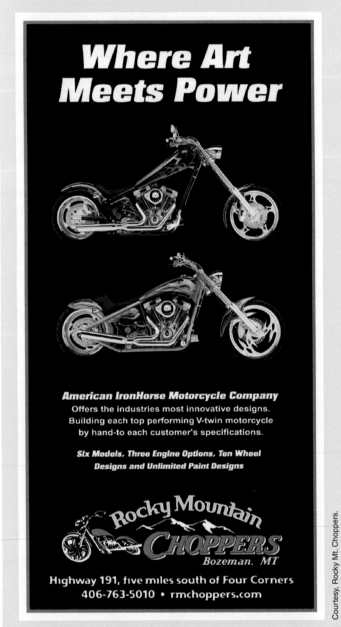

Where Art Meets Power

American IronHorse Motorcycle Company
Offers the industries most innovative designs.
Building each top performing V-twin motorcycle
by hand-to each customer's specifications.

*Six Models, Three Engine Options, Ten Wheel
Designs and Unlimited Paint Designs*

Rocky Mountain CHOPPERS
Bozeman, MT
Highway 191, five miles south of Four Corners
406-763-5010 • rmchoppers.com

Advertising is not reserved for manufacturers like Ford and giant retail chains like Target. Here, Rocky Mountain Choppers offers customized motorcycles to bikers in Montana.

Wholesalers and distributors, such as Ideal Supply (a company that supplies contractors with blasting and surveying equipment), are a completely different breed of reseller. Technically, these types of companies deal only with business customers because their position in the distribution channel dictates that they sell products either to producers (who buy goods to produce other goods) or to retailers (who resell goods to household consumers). Occasionally, an organization will call itself a wholesaler and sell to the public. Such an organization is actually operating as a retail outlet.

Wholesalers and distributors have little need for mass media advertising over media such as television and radio. Rather, they use trade publications, directory advertising such as the Yellow Pages and trade directories, direct mail, and their websites as their main advertising media.

Federal, State, and Local Governments

Government bodies may not seem to need advertising, but various agencies invest millions of dollars in advertising annually. The U.S. government often ranks as one of the 50 largest spenders on advertising in the United States, with expenditures typically exceeding $1 billion annually.[27] If you add in other IMC expenses, including brochures, recruiting fairs, and the personal selling expense of recruiting offices, the U.S. government easily spends well over $2 billion annually. The federal government's spending on advertising and promotion is concentrated in two areas: armed-forces recruiting and social issues. The U.S. government's broad-based advertising for military recruiting includes the U.S. Army's "Army Strong" campaign, which uses television, magazines, newspapers, and interactive games (America's Army) hosted at the Army recruiting website (www.goarmy.com).[28]

Social and Not-for-Profit Organizations

Advertising by social organizations at the national, state, and local levels is common. The Nature Conservancy, United Way, American Red Cross, and art organizations use advertising to raise awareness of their organizations, seek donations, and attempt to shape behavior (deter drug use or encourage breast self-examinations, for example). Organizations such as these use both the mass media and direct mail to promote their causes and services. Unique organizations such as historical societies and charities serve every state. Social organizations in local communities represent a variety of special interests, from computer clubs to food banks. The advertising used by social organizations has the same fundamental purpose as the advertising carried out by major multinational corporations: to stimulate demand and disseminate information. While big multinationals might use national or even global advertising, local organizations rely on advertising through local media to reach local audiences.

If these categories of marketers sound familiar, it's because, in Chapter 1, we identified the same groups

as distinct audiences for promotional messages. Firms are targets for marketing as well as marketers themselves.

The Marketer's Role in IMC

Very few of the marketers just discussed have the employees or financial resources to strategically plan and then totally prepare effective advertising or IMC programs. Most turn to advertising and promotion agencies, which play an important role in the promotion industry. But the marketer does play an important role before enlisting the services of an agency. For the agency to do its job effectively, marketers have to be prepared for their interaction with an agency. Marketers must:

- Fully understand and describe the value that the firm's brand provides to users.
- Fully understand and describe the brand's position in the market relative to competitive brands.
- Describe the firm's objectives for the brand in the near term and long term (e.g., brand extensions, international market launches).
- Identify the target markets that are most likely to respond favorably to the brand.
- Identify and manage the supply chain/distribution system that will most effectively reach the target markets.
- Be committed to using advertising and other promotional tools as part of the organization's overall marketing strategy to grow the brand.

Once a marketer has fulfilled these six responsibilities, then and *only* then is it time to enlist the services of an agency for help in effectively and creatively developing the market for the brand. While an agency can work with a marketer to help define and refine these factors, it is a mistake for a marketer to enter a relationship with an agency (of any type) without first preparing for a productive partnership.

LO 3 Advertising and Promotion Agencies

When you need to devise an advertisement or fully integrated marketing communication, no source will be more valuable than the advertising or promotion agency you work with. Advertising and promotion agencies are a critical link in the IMC process and give it the essential creative firepower. Marketers are fortunate to have a full complement of agencies that specialize in every detail of advertising and promotion.

Advertising Agencies

Most marketers choose to enlist the services of an advertising agency. An **advertising agency** is an organization of professionals who provide creative and business services to clients in planning, preparing, and placing advertisements. The reason so many firms rely on advertising agencies is that agencies house a collection of professionals with specialized talent, experience, and expertise that simply cannot be matched by in-house talent.

Advertising agencies are located in most big cities and small towns in the United States. Many agencies are global businesses. In a recent year, the biggest firms globally were WPP (based in London), Omnicom Group (New York), Interpublic Group (New York), Publicis Groupe (Paris), and Dentsu (Tokyo).[29]

Many types of agency professionals help advertisers in the planning, preparation, and placement of advertising and other promotional activities. Exhibit 2.2 lists some of the most widespread agency positions. As this list suggests, some advertising agencies can provide advertisers with a host of services, from campaign planning through creative concepts to e-strategies to measuring effectiveness. Also, because an agency is a business, agencies have CEOs, CFOs, and CTOs. Salaries in the positions listed range from about several million a year for a big agency chief executive officer to about $50,000 a year for a media planner.[30] Of course, those salaries change depending on whether you're in a big urban market or a small regional market.

It is up to the marketer to dig deep into an agency's background and determine which agency or set of multiple agencies will fulfill the company's marketing needs. Several different types of agencies are available, offering varying degrees of expertise and services:

- A **full-service agency** typically includes an array of advertising professionals to meet all the promotional needs of their clients. Often, such an agency will also offer global contacts. Giant full-service agencies like Omnicom Group and Dentsu employ hundreds or even thousands of people. Smaller shops can be full service with just a few dozen employees and serve big clients. Crispin Porter + Bogusky, a highly creative shop in Miami, has produced full-service, highly creative campaigns for Burger King and Mini USA.[31] Likewise, you don't have to be a big corporation with an ad budget in the hundreds of millions to hire a full-service agency. Cramer-Krasselt, a midsize agency, has built a stable of international clients one small to medium account at a time.[32]

- A **creative boutique** typically emphasizes creative concept development, copywriting, and artistic services. A marketer can employ this alternative for the strict purpose of infusing greater creativity into the message theme or individual advertisement. As one advertising expert put it, "If all clients want are ideas, lots of them, from which they can pick and mix to their hearts' delight, they won't want conventional, full-service agencies. They all want fast, flashy, fee-based idea factories."[33] Creative boutiques are these idea factories. Some large global agencies such as McCann-Erickson Worldwide and Leo Burnett have set up creative-only project shops that mimic the services provided by creative boutiques, with mixed results. The creative boutique's greatest advantage, niche expertise, may be its greatest liability as well. As firms search for IMC programs and make a commitment to IMC campaigns, the creative boutique may be an extra expense that they feel they cannot afford. Still, the creative effort is so essential to effective brand building that creativity will rise to prominence in the process, and creative boutiques are well positioned to deliver that value.

- **Digital/interactive agencies** help advertisers prepare communications for new media such as the Internet, podcasting, interactive kiosks, CDs, and interactive

ADVERTISING AND PROMOTION AGENCIES ARE A **CRITICAL LINK** IN THE IMC PROCESS AND GIVE IT THE **ESSENTIAL CREATIVE FIREPOWER.**

Courtesy, Bluestreak.

Digital/interactive agencies specialize in developing banner ads and corporate websites. An example is Bluestreak, whose goal is to provide the infrastructure so that marketers and their agencies can create online campaigns that meet goals for consumers to click on links and then make purchases.

television. These agencies focus on ways to use Web-based solutions for direct marketing and target market communications. Interactive agencies do work for Oracle, Nintendo, and the U.S. Army. Today, even a midsize full-service agency will offer digital and interactive services to clients. This being the case, many firms have consolidated all their IMC needs, including interactive media, with their main full-service agency. Digital/interactive agencies (for example, 24/7 Real Media) also have taken over a wide range of e-commerce activities that formerly required specialized agency services. The future for digital and interactive agencies may be the *virtual agency*—a website where users who pay a flat fee can make their own TV, print, radio, and interactive ads (for example, see **www.pick-n-click.com**). The idea is being brought "mainstream" by Zimmerman agency (part of the Omnicom Group) as a way for multiunit businesses, like franchises and car dealers, to respond quickly and specifically to varying geographic or competitive needs.[34]

- An **in-house agency** is often referred to as the advertising department in a firm and takes responsibility for the planning and preparation of advertising materials. This option has the advantage of greater coordination and control in all phases of the advertising and promotion process. Some prominent marketers that do most of their work in-house are Calvin Klein and Revlon. The marketer's own personnel have control over and knowledge of marketing activities, such as product development and distribution tactics. Another advantage is that the firm can essentially keep for itself any commissions an external agency would have earned. While the advantages of doing advertising work in-house are

in-house agency
advertising department of a marketer's own firm

Exhibit 2.2
Advertising Agency Positions

Account planners	Creative directors
Marketing specialists	Sales promotion and event planners
Account executives	Copywriters
Media buyers	Direct marketing specialists
Art directors	Radio and television producers
Lead account planners	Web developers
Chief executive officers (CEOs)	Researchers
Chief financial officers (CFOs)	Interactive media planners
Chief technology officers (CTOs)	Artists, graphic designers
Public relations specialists	Technical staff—printers, film editors, and so forth

© Cengage Learning 2011.

media specialist
organization that specializes in buying media time and space and that offers media strategy consulting to agencies and advertisers

promotion agency
specialized agency that handles promotional efforts

direct-marketing agency or **direct-response agency**
agency that maintains large databases of mailing lists and may design direct-marketing campaigns

database agency
agency that helps customers construct databases of target customers, merge databases, develop promotional materials, and execute direct-marketing campaigns

fulfillment center
operation that ensures consumers receive products ordered in response to direct marketing

infomercial long advertisement that resembles a talk show or product demonstration

consumer sales promotion sales promotion that is aimed at consumers and focuses on price-off deals, coupons, sampling, rebates, and premiums

trade-market sales promotion sales promotion that is designed to motivate distributors, wholesalers, and retailers to stock and feature a firm's brand in their merchandising programs

event-planning agency agency that finds locations, secures dates, and assembles a team of people to pull off a promotional event

attractive, there may be a lack of objectivity, which could constrain the execution of all phases of the advertising process. Also, an in-house agency could not match the breadth and depth of talent available in an external agency.

- While not technically agencies, **media specialists** are organizations that specialize in buying media time and space and that offer media strategy consulting to advertising agencies and advertisers. Although media-buying services have been a part of the advertising industry structure for many years, media planning is a recent addition to these specialists' services. An example is Starcom MediaVest Group (**www.smvgroup.com**), a subsidiary of Paris-based Publicis Groupe. Starcom encompasses an integrated network of nearly 6,200 contact architects specializing in media management, Internet and digital communications, response media, entertainment marketing, sports sponsorships, event marketing, and multicultural media. Strategic coordination of media and promotional efforts has become more complex because of the proliferation of media options and extensive use of promotional tools beyond advertising. Marketers are finding that a firm that buys space can provide keen insights into the media strategy as well. Also, because media specialists buy media in large quantities, they often can negotiate a much lower cost than an agency or marketer could. Furthermore, media specialists often have time and space in inventory and can offer last-minute placement of advertisements.

Promotion Agencies

While advertisers often rely on an advertising agency as a steering organization for their promotional efforts, many specialized agencies, known as **promotion agencies**, also enter the process. This is because advertising agencies, even full-service

agencies, will concentrate more on the advertising and often provide only a few key ancillary services for other promotional efforts. This is particularly true in the current era, in which new media are offering many different ways to communicate to target markets. Promotion agencies can handle everything from sampling to event promotions to in-school promotional tie-ins.

- **Direct-marketing agencies** (sometimes also called **direct-response agencies**) provide a variety of direct-marketing services. Direct-marketing agencies and **database agencies** maintain and manage large databases of mailing lists. They also can design direct-marketing campaigns that use mail or telemarketing or direct-response campaigns that use all forms of media. These agencies help advertisers construct databases of target customers, merge databases, develop promotional materials, and then execute the campaigns. In many cases, the agencies maintain **fulfillment centers**, which ensure that customers receive the product ordered through direct mail. Many of these agencies are set up to provide creative and production services to clients. These firms will design and help execute direct-response advertising campaigns using traditional media such as radio, television, magazines, and newspapers. Some firms can prepare **infomercials**: 5- to 60-minute information programs that promote a brand and offer direct purchase to viewers.

- *Sales promotion agencies* design and then operate contests, sweepstakes, special displays, or coupon campaigns for advertisers. When these agencies specialize in **consumer sales promotions**, they focus on price-off deals, coupons, sampling, rebates, and premiums. Other firms specialize in **trade-market sales promotions** designed to help advertisers use promotions aimed at wholesalers, retailers, vendors, and trade resellers. These agencies are experts in designing incentive programs, trade shows, sales force contests, in-store merchandising, and point-of-purchase materials.

- **Event-planning agencies** and organizers are experts in finding locations, securing dates, and putting together a team of people to pull off a promotional event: audiovisual people, caterers, security experts, entertainers, celebrity participants, or whoever is necessary to make the event come about. The event-planning organization often takes over advertising the event and making sure the press provides coverage (publicity) of the event. When an advertiser sponsors an entire event, such as a PGA golf tournament, managers will work closely with the event-planning agencies. If a marketer is just one of several sponsors of an event, such as a NASCAR race, then it has less control over planning. Like sales promotion, event sponsorship can be targeted to household consumers or the trade market.

- *Design firms* provide experts who do not get nearly enough credit in the advertising and promotion process: designers and graphics specialists. If you take a job in advertising or promotion, your designer will be one of your first and most important partners. While **designers** are rarely involved in strategy planning, they are intimately involved in the execution of the advertising or IMC effort. Most basically, they help a firm create a **logo**—the graphic mark that identifies a company—and other visual representations that promote an identity for a firm. This mark will appear on everything from advertising to packaging to the company stationery, business cards, and signage. Beyond the logo, graphic designers will design most of the materials used in supportive communications such as the package design, coupons, in-store displays, brochures, outdoor banners for events, newsletters, and direct-mail pieces. One of the largest consumer package goods firms recently increased its commitment to design across all aspects of its marketing and promotion, claiming that design was critical to "winning customers in the store."[35]

- **Public relations firms** manage an organization's relationships with the media, the local community, competitors, industry associations, and government organizations. Their tools include press releases, feature stories, lobbying, spokespersons, and company newsletters. Some of these firms, including PR Newswire (**www .prnewswire.com**), will handle putting all of a firm's news releases online. Most marketers prefer not to handle their own public relations tasks. One reason is that public relations requires highly specialized skills and talent not normally found in an advertising firm. Also, because managers are so close to public relations problems, they may not be capable of handling a situation, particularly a negative one, with measured public responses. For these reasons, marketers and advertising agencies turn to public relations firms. In a search of more and distinctive visibility, marketers have been turning to public relations firms to achieve film and television placements.[36] William Morris, originally a talent agency and now a public relations firm, served client Anheuser-Busch by getting Budweiser accepted as the first beer advertiser on the Academy Awards.

> **designer** specialist involved in execution of creative ideas and efforts by designing logos and other visual promotional pieces
>
> **logo** graphic mark that identifies a company
>
> **public relations firm** firm that handles an organization's needs regarding relationships with the local community, competitors, industry associations, and government organizations

HOW MANY BRANDS CAN YOU RECOGNIZE JUST FROM THEIR LOGOS? WHICH LOGOS DO YOU EXPECT TO FIND WHEN YOU SEE A PRO GOLFER?

Carlos E. Santa Maria/Shutterstock.com

Agency Services

As suggested by the many types of firms, advertising and promotion agencies offer a wide range of services. Therefore, before hiring any agency, marketers need to identify the particular services they need and then negotiate with the agency to reach an agreement on the services to be provided. Exhibit 2.3 shows where to find each of the main types of services in a typical full-service advertising agency that also provides a significant number of IMC services.

In practice, however, many agencies, large and small, have been flattened under economic pressures, and many big agencies have consolidated all forms of production under one manager. Where there used to be print production, film/video production, radio production, and retail advertising, now there is just "production." Thus, although the services indicated by the positions shown in Exhibit 2.3 are representative, any one agency and its menu of services may be quite different.

Account Services

Account services entail identifying the benefits a brand offers, the brand's target audiences, and the best competitive positioning, and then developing a complete promotion plan. These services are offered by managers who have titles such as account executive, account supervisor, or account manager and who work with clients to determine how the brand can benefit most from promotion. In some cases, account services in an agency can provide basic marketing and consumer behavior research, but, in general, the client should bring this information to the table. Knowing the target segment, the brand's values, and the positioning strategy is really the marketer's responsibility (more on this in Chapters 4 and 5).

Account services managers also work with the client in translating cultural and consumer values into advertising and promotional messages through the creative services in the agency. Finally, they work with media services to develop an effective media strategy for determining the best vehicles for reaching the targeted audiences. One of the primary tasks

Exhibit 2.3
Structure of a Full-Service Ad Agency

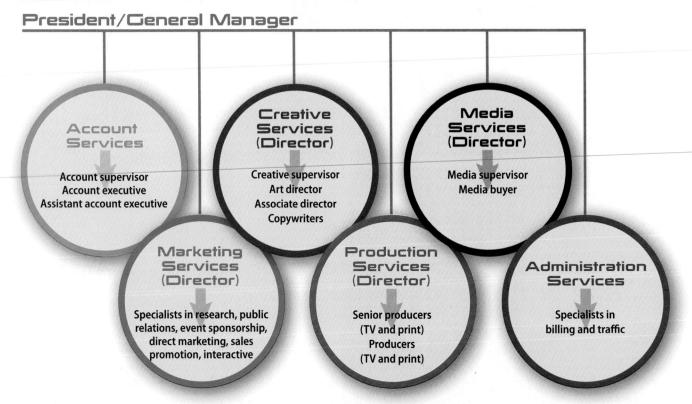

© Cengage Learning 2011.

Advertising agencies' greatest contribution to the promotion process may be their creative prowess. Here, FJCandN, a regional agency, implores marketers to "aim higher" (by working with its creative people, of course).

account planner
person in an advertising agency who synthesizes all relevant consumer research and uses it to design an advertising strategy

creative services
group in an advertising agency that develops the message to be delivered through advertising, sales promotion, direct marketing, event sponsorship, or public relations

in account services is to keep the various agency teams' creative, production, and media on schedule and within budget.

Marketing Research Services

Research conducted by an agency for a client usually consists of the agency locating studies (conducted by commercial research organizations) that have bearing on a client's market or advertising and promotion objectives. The research group will help the client interpret the research and communicate these interpretations to the creative and media people. If existing studies are not sufficient, research may be conducted by the agency itself. As mentioned in the account services discussion, some agencies can assemble consumers from the target audience to evaluate different versions of proposed advertising and determine whether messages are being communicated effectively.

Many agencies have established the position of **account planner** to coordinate the research effort. An account planner's stature in the organization is on par with that of an account executive. The account planner

is assigned to clients to ensure that research input is included at each stage of development of campaign materials. Some agency leaders, like Jay Chiat of Chiat/Day, think account planning has been the best new business tool ever invented.[37] Others are a bit more measured in their assessment. Either way, agencies understand that research, signaled by the appointment of an account planner, is the key to successful promotional campaigns.

Creative Services

The **creative services** group in an agency comes up with the concepts that express the value of a company's brand in interesting and memorable ways. In simple terms, the creative services group develops the message that will be delivered though advertising, sales promotion, direct marketing, event sponsorship, or public relations.

Clients will push their agencies hard to come up with interesting and expressive ways to represent the brand. Geoffrey Frost, vice president of consumer communications for Motorola's Personal Communications Sector, expressed his company's approach to demanding creative excellence by saying, "What we've challenged the agencies to do was to help us to figure out how to position Motorola as the company that has really figured out the future."[38] That statement beautifully captures the kind of creative services advertisers seek from their agencies.

The creative group in an agency will typically include a creative director, art director, illustrators or designers, and copywriters. In specialized promotion agencies, event planners, contest experts, and interactive media specialists will join the core group.

Production Services

Production services include producers (and sometimes directors) who take creative ideas and turn them into advertisements, direct-mail pieces, or events materials. Producers generally manage and oversee the endless details of production of the finished advertisement or other promotion material. Advertising agencies maintain the largest and most sophisticated creative and production staffs.

Media Planning and Buying Services

The service of media planning and buying was described earlier as being available from a specialized agency. Full-service advertising agencies also provide **media planning and buying services** similar to those of the specialized agencies. The central challenge is to determine how a client's message can most effectively and efficiently reach the target audience. Media planners and buyers examine an enormous number of options to put together an effective media plan within the client's budget. But media planning and buying is much more than simply buying ad space, timing a coupon distribution, or scheduling an event. A wide range of media strategies can be implemented to enhance the impact of the message. Most large agencies, such as Omnicom, Chiat/Day, and Fallon McElligott, set up their own interactive-media groups years ago in response to client demands that the Internet media option be included in nearly every IMC plan.

The three positions typically found in the media area are media planner, media buyer, and media researcher. These people are critically important because they provide services where most of the client's money is spent.

Administrative Services

Like other businesses, agencies have to manage their business affairs. Agencies have personnel departments, accounting and billing departments, and sales staffs that go out and sell the agency to clients. Most important to clients is the traffic department, which is responsible for monitoring projects to be sure that deadlines are met. Traffic managers make sure the creative group and media services are coordinated so that deadlines for getting promotional materials to printers and media organizations are met. The job requires tremendous organizational skills and is critical to delivering the other services to clients.

Agency Compensation

The way agencies get paid is somewhat different from the way other professional organizations are compensated. While accountants, doctors, lawyers, and consultants often work on a fee basis, advertising agencies often base compensation on a commission or markup system. Promotion agencies occasionally work on a commission basis, but more often they work on a fee or contract basis.

With cost pressure affecting all businesses and other organizations today, the atmosphere surrounding agency compensation is becoming tenser. Clients are demanding more services at lower cost. Some are including "procurement officers" in planning meetings with agencies. In response, some agencies bring their own financial executives. TBWA, an agency under the Omnicom umbrella, even created the position of chief compensation officer, responsible for the agency's financial discussions with clients.[39]

Commissions

The traditional method of agency compensation is the **commission system**, which is based on the amount of money the advertiser spends on media. Under this method, an agreed-upon percent of the total amount billed by a media organization is retained by the advertising or promotion agency

pollix/Shutterstock.com.

Exhibit 2.4
Agency Commissions: An Example

Marketer's cost of airtime = $1,000,000

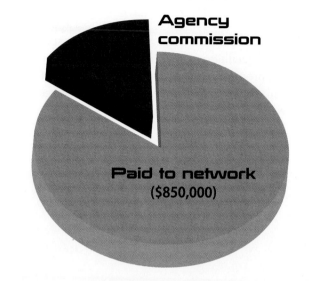

Agency commission

Paid to network
($850,000)

as compensation for all costs in creating advertising/ promotion for the advertiser. (The percentage has traditionally been 15 percent, or 16.67 percent for outdoor media, but in practice, many agencies today charge different amounts.) As shown in Exhibit 2.4, there are three basic steps to calculate an agency's compensation in the commission system:

1. The agency bills the client for the media time or space—in this case, $1 million for television airtime.

2. The agency pays the media 85 percent ($850,000 in the example).

3. The agency keeps a 15 percent commission ($150,000).

In recent years, advertisers and agencies themselves have questioned the wisdom of the commission system. As the chairman of a large full-service agency put it long ago, "It's incenting us to do the wrong thing, to recommend network TV and national magazines and radio when other forms of communication like direct marketing or public relations might do the job better."[40] Still, about half of all advertisers compensate their agencies using a commission system based on media cost.

Markup Charges

Another method of agency compensation is to add a percentage **markup charge** to a variety of services the agency purchases from outside suppliers. In many cases, an agency will turn to outside contractors for art, illustration, photography, printing, research,

and production. The agency then, in agreement with the client, adds a markup charge to these services.

The reason markup charges became prevalent in the industry is that many promotion agencies were providing services that did not use traditional media. Because the traditional commission method was based on media charges, there was no way for these agencies to receive payment for their work. A typical markup on outside services is 17.65 to 20 percent.

Fee Systems

A **fee system** is much like that used by consultants or attorneys, whereby the advertiser and the agency agree on an hourly rate for different services provided. The hourly rate can be based on average salaries within departments or on some agreed-upon hourly rate across all services. This is the most common basis for promotion agency compensation.

Another version of the fee system is a fixed fee, or contract, set for a project between the client and the agency. It is imperative that the agency and the marketer agree on precisely what services will be provided, by what departments in the agency, and over what specified period of time. In addition, the parties must agree on which supplies, materials, travel costs, and other expenses will be reimbursed beyond the fixed fee. Fixed-fee systems have the potential for causing serious rifts in the client-agency relationship because out-of-scope work can easily spiral out of control when so many variables are at play. When such controversies arise, the client-agency relationship is damaged and trust suffers.

Most agencies are vigorously opposed to the fee system. They argue that creative impact cannot be measured in "work hours" but rather must be measured in "the value of the materials the agency is creating for the client."[41]

Pay-for-Results

Recently, many marketers and agencies have been working on compensation programs called **pay-for-results**; these base the agency's fee on the achievement of agreed-upon results. Historically, agencies have not agreed to be evaluated on results because results have often been narrowly defined as sales volume, which is

markup charge
method of agency compensation based on adding a percentage charge to a variety of services the agency purchases from outside suppliers

fee system method of agency compensation whereby the advertiser and agency agree on an hourly rate for services provided

pay-for-results
compensation plan based on an agreement in which fee amounts are tied to a set of results criteria

mainly related to factors outside the agency's control (product features, pricing strategy, and distribution programs—that is, the overall marketing mix, not just advertising or IMC). An agency may agree to be compensated based on achievement of sales levels, but more often (and more appropriately) the main results criteria are communications objectives such as the target audience's brand awareness, brand identification, or knowledge of brand features.

LO 4 External Facilitators

While agencies offer clients many services and are adding more, marketers often need to rely on specialized external facilitators in planning, preparing, and executing promotional campaigns. **External facilitators** are organizations or individuals that provide specialized services to marketers and agencies.

F. Young/Shutterstock.com

ETHICS TRUST—BUT VERIFY

When marketers and their agencies had long histories together, they sealed deals with a handshake. Today, marketers are quick to change partners, so they need a new basis for trust in the client–agency relationship. Enter the auditor. Auditing firms scrutinize all aspects of agency work, from creative services to billing practices. In one assignment, an international ad-agency auditing firm called Firm Decisions found that an agency staffer had billed an average of 17 hours a day, including weekends, for an entire month. One day, she even logged 26 hours. That's not the norm for agency behavior, but it sure does make the auditors look like a wise investment.

Sources: Claire Atkinson, "GM Ad Boss Takes Agencies to Task," *Advertising Age*, June 30, 2003, 1, 26; Erin White, "Making Sure the Work Fits the Bill," *Wall Street Journal*, February 5, 2004, B8.

Marketing and Advertising Research Firms

Many firms rely on outside assistance during the planning phase of advertising. Research firms such as Burke and Simmons can perform original research for marketers, using focus groups, surveys, or experiments to assist in understanding the potential market or consumer perceptions of a product or services. Other research firms, such as SRI International, routinely collect data (from grocery store scanners, for example) and have these data available for a fee.

Advertisers and their agencies also seek measures of promotional program effectiveness after a campaign has run. After an advertisement or promotion has been running for some reasonable amount of time, firms such as Starch INRA Hooper will run recognition tests on print advertisements. Other firms such as Burke offer day-after recall tests of broadcast advertisements. Some firms specialize in message testing to determine whether consumers find advertising messages appealing and understandable.

Consultants

A variety of **consultants** specialize in areas related to the promotional process. Marketers can seek out marketing consultants for assistance in the planning stage. Creative and communications consultants provide insight on issues related to message strategy and message themes. Consultants in event planning and sponsorships offer their expertise to marketers and their agencies. Public relations consultants often work with top management. Media experts can help a marketer determine the proper media mix and efficient media placement.

Three new types of consultants have emerged in recent years:

1. A database consultant works with marketers and agencies to help them identify and then manage databases that allow for the development of IMC programs. Organizations such as Shepard Associates can merge or cross-reference diverse databases from research sources discussed earlier.

2. Consultants specializing in website development and management typically have the creative skills to develop websites and corporate home pages and the technical skills to advise marketers on managing the technical aspects of the user interface.

3. Other consultants work with a firm to integrate information across a wide variety of customer contacts and to organize all this information to achieve customer relationship management (CRM).

In addition, traditional management consultants, such as Accenture and McKinsey, have started to work with agencies on structure and business strategy.[42] These sorts of consultants also can advise on image strategy, market research procedure, and process and account planning. But the combination of traditional consulting and advertising has not always produced compelling results; the typical role of consultants—focusing on marketing, creative, or technical issues—is the more likely role for consultants in the future.

Production Facilitators

External **production facilitators** offer essential services during and after the production process. Production is the area where advertisers and their agencies rely most heavily on external facilitators. All forms of media advertising require special expertise that even the largest full-service agency, much less a marketer, typically does not retain on staff. In broadcast production, directors, production managers, songwriters, camera operators, audio and lighting technicians, and performers are all essential to preparing a professional, high-quality radio or television ad. Production houses can provide the physical facilities, including sets, stages, equipment, and crews, needed for broadcast

> **consultant** individual who specializes in areas related to the promotional process
>
> **production facilitator** organization that offers essential services during and after the production process

Yuri Arcurs/Shutterstock.com

production. Similarly, in preparing print advertising, brochures, and direct-mail pieces, graphic artists, photographers, models, directors, and producers may be hired. In-store promotions is another area where designing and producing materials require the skills of a specialty organization.

Software Firms

An interesting and complex new category of facilitator in advertising and promotion is that of software firms. The technology in the industry, particularly new media technology, has expanded so rapidly that a variety of software firms facilitate the process. Some of these firms are well established and well known, including Microsoft and Oracle. These firms provide software that gathers and analyzes data on the behavior of Web

Software firms like Hyperion are providing marketers with help in audience analysis and broadband communications. As detailed in its ad, Hyperion specializes in gathering customer data from website visits.

surfers, streams audio and video files, and manages relationships with trade partners. The expertise provided by these firms is so esoteric that even the most advanced full-service or digital/interactive agency must seek their assistance.

LO 5 Media Organizations

At the next level in the industry structure are media organizations, which own and manage the media access to consumers. Exhibit 2.5 shows the basic categories of media providers available to marketers:

- *Broadcast media* include television (networks, independent stations, cable, and broadband) and radio (networks and local stations, as well as satellite programming).

  - *Print media* include magazines, newspapers, direct mail, and specialty publications such as handbills and theater programs.

  - *Interactive media* include online computer services, home-shopping broadcasts, interactive broadcast entertainment, kiosks, CDs, Internet, podcasts, smart phones, and e-readers.

  - *Support media* include all those places that advertisers want to put their messages other than mainstream traditional or interactive media. Often referred to as *out-of-home media*, support media include outdoor (billboards, transit ads, and posters); directories such as print and online Yellow Pages; premiums (for example, logos or messages on key chains, calendars, clothing, and pens); point-of-purchase displays; event sponsorship; and placement of the brand in films, video games, and television programs.

  - *Media conglomerates* bring together most or all of these media under one corporate roof. For example, Time Warner, which has been ranked as the world's largest media conglomerate, offers broadcasting, cable, music, film, print publishing, and an Internet presence.[43]

In traditional media, major television networks such as NBC and Fox, as well as national magazines such as *U.S. News & World Report* and *People*, provide advertisers with time and space for their messages at considerable cost. Other media options are more useful for reaching narrowly defined target audiences. Specialty programming on cable television, tightly focused direct-mail pieces, and a well-designed

Exhibit 2.5
Types of Media Organizations

Internet campaign may be better ways to reach a specific audience. One of the new-media options, broadband, lets advertisers target very specific audiences. Internet users can customize their programming by requesting specific broadcasts from various providers.

Media Conglomerates

Broadcast

Support Media

Print

Interactive Media

© Cengage Learning 2011.

Target Audiences

The structure of the promotion industry (Exhibit 2.1) and the flow of communication would obviously be incomplete without an audience: If there's no audience, there's no communication. One interesting thing about the audiences for promotional communications is that, with the exception of household consumers, they are also the marketers that use advertising and IMC.

We all are familiar with the type of advertising directed at us in our role as consumers: ads for toothpaste, sport-utility vehicles, insurance, and on and on.

But business and government audiences are keys to the success of many, many firms that sell only to business and government buyers. While many of these firms rely heavily on personal selling in their promotional mix, many also use a variety of IMC tools. For example, Accenture Consulting uses high-profile television and magazine advertising and sponsors events. Many business and trade sellers regularly need public relations, and most use direct mail to communicate with potential customers as a prelude to a personal selling call.

The Evolution of Promoting Brands

Then

AWF'LY SORRY WORKING LATE AGAIN!

OFFICE WIDOW

Why was Bob neglecting her? Then she learned . . .

Courtesy, Unilever U.S.A., Inc.

Now

© Hugo Philpot/Reuters/Landov.

RA52 PVT

Brand promotion evolves to show consumers that they understand the contemporary social scene.

Learning Outcomes

After studying this chapter, you should be able to:

LO 1   Identify economic changes that gave rise to advertising.

LO 2   Discuss how the relationship between marketers and retailers has changed over time.

LO 3   Describe significant eras of promotion in the United States, including the impact of social change on promotion.

LO 4   Define consumer empowerment and branded entertainment.

LO 5   Identify forces that will continue to affect the evolution of integrated marketing communication.

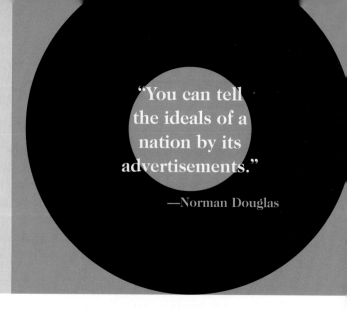

> "You can tell the ideals of a nation by its advertisements."

—Norman Douglas

AFTER YOU
FINISH THIS
CHAPTER
GO TO
PAGE 64
FOR STUDY
TOOLS

When Soap Saved Marriage

The 1935 Lux advertisement shown on the first page of this chapter is undoubtedly curious to contemporary audiences. It is, however, typical of its time and probably made perfect sense to its original audience. In the 1930s, in the middle of the Great Depression, anxiety about losing one's husband—and thus one's economic well-being—to divorce was not unfounded. These ads were targeted to a new generation of stay-at-home housewives potentially insecure about their exclusion from the modern world of their husbands, geographically separated from their usually agrarian parents, and living in a fast-paced and unsure urban environment. These ads went out to women at a time when losing one's source of income (husband) could mean poverty and shame. They were read by women in a society where daily bathing was still relatively new but where self-doubt about personal hygiene was on the rise. Such an ad pushed (maybe even created) just the right buttons. If Lux can "remove perspiration odor from underthings," it might save more than colors and fabrics. It might save affection; it might save marriages. If Bob's romantic indifference continues, Sally soon may be back home with Mom or even on the street. But with Lux on the scene, Bob goes home for dinner.

Although some ads today use the same general strategy to sell deodorants, soaps, and feminine-hygiene products, this ad is not read today as it was in 1935. Ads and other promotional messages are part of their times. To really understand marketing, you must understand that successful advertisements, like all types of brand promotion, convey a perceptive understanding of the contemporary social scene. The makers of this 1930s ad understood, helped create, and used the pressures bearing down on the young married women of that time. Society was changing, and these changes affected Sally and a lot of young women like her. This social change and

What do you think?

The Lux ad shown here is timeless.

2   3   4   5   6   7
STRONGLY DISAGREE   STRONGLY AGREE

GOOD PROMOTION IS **IN TOUCH** WITH ITS TIME.

the associated feelings, including uncertainty and anxiety, gave advertisers a chance to offer new products and services to address these very fears and to leverage society's upheaval to their branded benefit.

There is a valuable lesson here from history: When the sands of culture and society shift beneath consumers' feet, marketing opportunities usually present themselves. Today, Sally likely would have a job and be far less economically vulnerable and socially isolated—not to mention that Sally and Bob would both be bathing more often. So we see the 1930s in this ad in the same way that students of the future will view ads of our time: as interesting, revealing, but still somewhat distorted reflections of daily life in the early 21st century. But ads look enough like life to work, at least sometimes. Good promotion is in touch with its time and constantly looks for social and cultural changes that open up marketing opportunities.

Throughout the decades, marketers have tried many different strategies and approaches, and you can learn a lot from their successes and failures. Just about every strategy used today came about decades ago; only the specifics have changed. Studying advertisements and other promotional efforts will teach you when a given technique is really something new, and when and why it worked. You can see how it leveraged the social forces of its time. Besides being interesting, history is very practical. Hint: When you are interviewing for a job in a marketing position, explain how that marketer's best brand promotions worked.

LO 1 The Rise of Advertising

Before there was brand promotion, there was advertising. In many histories of advertising, the process is portrayed as having originated in ancient times, with even primitive peoples practicing some form of advertising. This is substantively incorrect. Whatever those ancients were doing, they weren't advertising. Although the Romans and others communicated with one another with persuasive intent in buying and selling, they were not using advertising. Advertising is a product of modern times and modern media. It came into being as a result of at least four major factors (see Exhibit 3.1):

1. The rise of capitalism
2. The Industrial Revolution
3. Branding as a way for manufacturers to assert power in distribution channels
4. The rise of modern mass media

Exhibit 3.1
A Foundation for Advertising

Rise of Capitalism

In capitalism, organizations compete for resources, called *capital*, in a free-market environment. Part of the competition for resources involves stimulating demand for the seller's goods or services. When an organization successfully stimulates demand, it attracts capital to the organization in the form of money (or other goods) as payment. One of the tools used to stimulate demand is advertising. So, as the Western world turned to capitalism, it was laying a foundation for advertising to become a prominent part of the business environment.

Industrial Revolution

Another economic force that yielded the need for advertising was the **Industrial Revolution**, a rapid shift from an agricultural to an industrial economy. Beginning around 1750 in England, the revolution spread to North America, where it progressed slowly until the early 1800s, when the War of 1812 in the United States boosted domestic production. The emergence of the principle of interchangeable parts and the perfection of the sewing machine, both in 1850, coupled with the American Civil War a decade later, set the scene for widespread industrialization. In the 1840s, the **principle of limited liability**, which caps an investor's risk in a business venture at only his or her shares in a corporation, rather than all personal assets, gained acceptance and resulted in the accumulation of large amounts of capital to finance the Industrial Revolution.

Several changes associated with the Industrial Revolution made advertising attractive and important. Western societies shifted away from fulfilling material needs through household self-sufficiency and became more dependent on a marketplace as a way of life. The mass-production of goods increased rapidly, so manufacturers needed to stimulate demand, something that advertising can do well.

Other developments that were part of the broad Industrial Revolution contributed to the growth and concentration of populations, providing the marketplaces essential to the widespread use of advertising. A revolution in transportation, most dramatically symbolized by the East–West connection of the United States in 1869 by the railroad, represented the beginnings of the distribution network needed to move mass quantities of goods. Finally, rapid population growth and urbanization began in the 1800s. From 1830 to 1860, the population of the United States nearly tripled, from 12.8 million to 31.4 million. During the same period, the number of cities with more than 20,000 inhabitants grew to 43. Historically, there is a strong relationship between per capita outlays for advertising and an increase in the size of cities.[1] As the potential grew for goods to be produced, delivered, and introduced to large numbers of people residing in concentrated areas, the stage was set for advertising to emerge and flourish.

Industrial Revolution a rapid shift in Western society from an agricultural to an industrial economy, beginning in the mid-18th century

principle of limited liability limitation of an investor's risk in a corporation to his or her investment in the company's shares

branding strategy of developing brand names so that manufacturers can focus consumer attention on a clearly identified item

LO 2 Power in Distribution Channels

Another force behind the emergence and growth of advertising relates to manufacturers' pursuit of power in their channel of distribution. If a manufacturer can persuade shoppers to demand its products, wholesalers and retailers will need to sell those products to comply with their customers' desires. A manufacturer that enjoys this level of power in the channel of distribution not only can force other participants in the channel to stock its products, but it is also in a position to command a higher price. In contrast, retail giants like Walmart and Costco recently have grown so large they can dictate what will be carried in their stores and at what price.

In the 1800s, some manufacturers discovered that they could increase their power in distribution channels by using a strategy of **branding** products. These manufacturers developed brand names so that consumers could focus their attention on a clearly identified item. Manufacturers began branding previously unmarked commodities, such as work clothes and packaged goods. Some of the first branded goods to show up on shopkeepers shelves were Ivory soap (1882) and Maxwell House coffee (1892). Once a product had a brand mark and name that consumers could identify, marketers gained power. Of course, an essential tool in stimulating demand for a brand was advertising.

Today, when Procter & Gamble and Kraft spend billions of dollars each year to stimulate demand for such popular brands as Crest and Velveeta, wholesalers and retailers carry these brands because integrated

marketing communication has stimulated demand and brought consumers into the store to find those brands. This sort of pursuit of power by manufacturers is argued to have caused the widespread use of advertising.[2]

Modern Mass Media

Advertising also is inextricably tied to the rise of mass communication. The invention of the telegraph in 1844 set in motion a communication revolution. The telegraph not only allowed nations to benefit from the inherent efficiencies of rapid communication, but it also did a great deal to engender a sense of national identity. People began to know and care about people and things going on thousands of miles away. This changed commerce and society.[3]

During the same period, publishers launched many new magazines designed for larger and less socially privileged audiences. They made magazines both a viable mass advertising medium and a democratizing influence on society.[4] Advertising in these mass-circulation magazines projected national brands into national consciousness. National magazines made national advertising possible; national advertising made national brands possible.

For the most part, mass media are supported by advertising. Television networks, radio stations, newspapers, magazines, and websites produce shows, articles, films, programs, and Web content, not for the ultimate goal of entertaining or informing, but to make a healthy profit from selling brands through advertising and branded entertainment. Media vehicles sell audiences to make money.

LO 3 Evolution of Promotion

In the years following the emergence of the first published advertisements, promotion has evolved toward today's focus on brands and an integrated effort at marketing and brand communication. Until recently, most of the developments involved changes in the content and methods of advertising. By looking at this evolution in terms of several periods of history (see Exhibit 3.2), we gain insights into the marketing process and the importance of brands.

Preindustrialization (before 1800)

In the 17th century, printed advertisements appeared in newsbooks (the precursor to newspapers).[5] The messages were informational and appeared on the last pages of the tabloid. In America, the first newspaper advertisement is said to have appeared in 1704 in the *Boston News Letter*. Two notices printed under the heading "Advertising" offered rewards for the return of merchandise stolen from an apparel shop and a wharf.[6]

Advertising grew in popularity during the 18th century in Britain and the American colonies. The *Pennsylvania Gazette* was the first newspaper to separate ads with blank lines, which made the ads easier to read and more prominent.[7] As far as we know, the *Gazette* was also the first newspaper to use illustrations in advertisements.

Advertising changed little over the next 70 years. The early 1800s saw the advent of the penny

Exhibit 3.2
Periods of Promotion

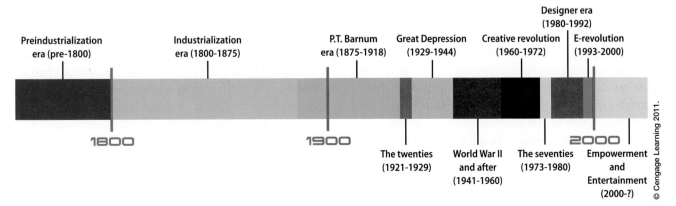

© Cengage Learning 2011.

newspaper, which resulted in widespread distribution of the news media. However, advertisements in penny newspapers were dominated by simple announcements by skilled laborers. As one historian notes, "Advertising was closer to the classified notices in newspapers than to product promotions in our media today."[8]

Industrialization (1800–1875)

In practice, marketers in the mid- to late 1800s were trying to cultivate markets for growing production in the context of an increasing urban population. A middle class, spawned by the economic windfall of regular wages from factory jobs, was beginning to emerge. This newly developing populace with economic means was concentrated geographically in cities more than ever before.

By 1850, circulation of the **dailies**, as newspapers were then called, was estimated at 1 million copies per day. The first advertising agent—thought to be Volney Palmer, who opened shop in Philadelphia—basically worked for the newspapers by soliciting orders for advertising and collecting payment from advertisers.[9] Merchants readily embraced this new opportunity to reach consumers, and at least one newspaper doubled its advertising volume from 1849 to 1850.[10]

With the expansion of newspaper circulation fostered by the railroads, a new era of opportunity emerged for advertising. The practice of advertising was not universally hailed as honorable, however. Without any formal regulation, advertising was considered an embarrassment by many segments of society, including some parts of the business community. At one point, firms that used advertising even risked their credit ratings; banks considered the practice a sign of financial weakness. The negative image wasn't helped much by ads for patent medicines, the first products heavily advertised on a national scale. These advertisements promised cures for every ailment from rheumatism to cancer.

P. T. Barnum Era (1875–1918)

Only when America was well on its way to being an urban, industrialized nation did advertising become a vital and integral part of the social landscape. Shortly after the Civil War in the United States, marketers began using modern advertising—ads that we would recognize as advertising. From about 1875 to 1918, advertising ushered in what has come to be known as **consumer culture**, a way of life centered on consumption.

Advertising became a full-fledged industry in this period. It was the time of advertising legends: Albert Lasker, head of Lord and Thomas in Chicago, possibly the most influential agency of its day; Francis W. Ayer, founder of N. W. Ayer; John E. Powers, the most important copywriter of the period; Earnest Elmo Calkins, champion of advertising design; Claude Hopkins, influential in promoting ads as "dramatic salesmanship"; and John E. Kennedy, creator of "reason why" advertising.[11] These were the founders, visionaries, and artists who played principal roles in the establishment of the advertising business. An interesting side note: Several of the founders of this industry had fathers who shared the very same occupation: minister. These young men would have been exposed to public speaking and the passionate selling of ideas as well as to the new "religion" of modernity: city life, science, progress, unapologetic fun, and public consumption.

By 1900, total sales of patent medicines in the United States had reached $75 million—an early

dailies newspapers published every weekday

consumer culture a way of life centered around consumption

Originally published in The Southern Cultivator, Vol 44, January 1886.

As newspaper circulation grew, so did the use of advertising. Unfortunately, ads like this one—for a patent medicine that supposedly could cure all liver ailments, including cancer—did not help the image of advertising.

Pure Food and Drug Act 1906 U.S. law requiring manufacturers to list the active ingredients of their products on their labels

demonstration of the power of advertising.[12] The stage was set for advertising's modern form. During this period, the first advertising agencies were founded, and the practice of branding products became the norm. Advertising was motivated by the need to sell the vastly increased supply of goods brought on by mass production and by the demands of an increasingly urban population seeking social identity through (among other things) branded products. In earlier times, when shoppers went to the general store and bought soap sliced from a large, locally produced cake, advertising had no place. But with advertising's ability to create meaningful differences between near-identical soaps, advertising suddenly held a very prominent place in early consumer culture. Advertising made unmarked commodities into social symbols and identity markers, which allowed marketers to charge far more money for them. This is the power of brands.

Advertising was completely unregulated in the United States until 1906. In that year, Congress passed the **Pure Food and Drug Act**, which required manufacturers to list the active ingredients of their products on their labels. You still could put some pretty amazing things in products; you just had to tell the consumer. The direct effect of this federal act on advertising was minimal; advertisers could continue to say just about anything—and usually did. But the law probably started to slow some of the more outrageous offenders of truth and ethics. Many advertisements still took on the style of a sales pitch for "snake oil." The tone and spirit of advertising owed more to P. T. Barnum—"There's a sucker born every minute"—than to any other influence. And as Barnum was the famous showman and circus entrepreneur (Barnum and Bailey Circus) of his day, ads of this period were bold, carnivalesque, garish, and often full of dense copy that hurled incredible claims.

Ads of this era have some notable qualities:

- A lot of copy (words)
- Prominence of the product itself and relative lack of real-world context (visuals) in which the advertised product was to be consumed
- Small size
- Little color, few photographs
- Plenty of hyperbole

Ads from the P. T. Barnum era were often packed with fantastic promises, like this claim you could raise ducks profitably anywhere.

During this period, despite some variation and steady evolution, ads generally remained this way until World War I.

Consider the world in which these ads existed. It was a period of rapid urbanization, massive immigration, labor unrest, and significant concerns about the abuses of capitalism. Some of capitalism's excesses and abuses, including deceptive and misleading advertising, were the targets of early reformers. It also was the age of suffrage, the progressive movement, motion pictures, and mass culture. The world was changing rapidly, which was disruptive and unsettling, but advertising was there to offer solutions to the stresses of modern life, no matter how real, imagined, or suggested. Remember, social and cultural change often opens up opportunities for marketers.

The Twenties (1918–1929)

In many ways, the Roaring Twenties began a couple of years early. After World War I, advertising found respectability, fame, and glamour. It was the most modern of all professions and, short of starring in the movies, the most fashionable. According to popular perception, it was where the young, smart, and sophisticated worked and played. During the 1920s, it also

was a place where institutional freedom rang. The prewar movement to reform and regulate advertising was pretty much dissipated by the distractions of the war and advertising's role in the war effort. During World War I, the advertising industry learned a valuable lesson: Donating time and personnel to the common good is not only good civics but smart business.

The 1920s were prosperous times. Most (but not all) enjoyed a previously unequaled standard of living. It was an age of considerable hedonism; the pleasure principle was practiced and appreciated, openly and often. The Victorian Age was over, and a great social experiment in the joys of consumption was under way. Victorian repression and modesty gave way to a more open sexuality and a love affair with modernity. Advertising was made for this burgeoning sensuality; advertising gave people permission to enjoy. Ads of the era exhorted consumers to have a good time and instructed them in how to do it. Consumption not only was respectable but expected. Being a consumer became synonymous with being a citizen—a *good* citizen.

During these good economic times, advertising taught consumers how to be thoroughly modern and how to avoid the pitfalls of this new age. Consumers learned of halitosis from Listerine advertising

and about body odor from Lifebuoy advertising. There happened to be a product with a cure for just about any social anxiety and personal failing, many of which had supposedly been brought on as side effects of modernity. This was perfect for the growth and entrenchment of advertising as an institution: Modern times bring on many wonderful new things, but the new way of life has side effects that, in turn, have to be fixed by even more modern goods and services. For example, modern canned food replaced fresh fruit and vegetables, thus "weakening the gums," causing dental problems—which could be cured by a modern toothbrush. The result was a seemingly endless consumption chain: Needs lead to products, new needs are created by new products, newer products solve newer needs, and so on. This chain of needs is essential to a capitalist economy, which must continue to expand in order to survive. It also makes a necessity of advertising.

Other ads from the 1920s emphasized other modernity themes, such as the division between public workspace, the male domain of the office and the private, "feminine" space of the home. Two separate consumption domains were created, with women placed in charge of the latter, more economically important one. Advertisers figured out that women were responsible for as much as 80 percent of household

These ads from the 1920s show widely divergent roles for men and women. The business world was a male space, and the home was where women's work was done.

{"image_id":"1","caption":"How much do you pay to get clothes clean?"}

Advertising during the 1920s chronicled the state of technology and styles for clothing, furniture, and social functions. Advertising specified social relationships between people and products by depicting the social settings and circumstances into which people and products fit. Consider this ad for Standard Sanitary bathroom fixtures showing a carefully constructed snapshot of domestic life. Note the attention to the social setting into which plumbing fixtures were to fit. Is the ad really about plumbing? Yes, in a very important way, because it demonstrates plumbing in a social context that works for both advertiser and consumer. Modern consumers, consumers who really care about the best for their family, use modern plumbing.

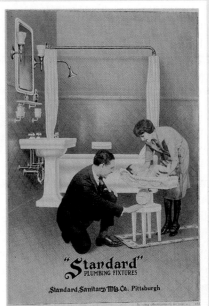

purchases. While 1920s men were out in the "jungle" of the work world, women made most purchase decisions. From this time forward, women became the primary target of brand promotion.

Another important aspect of advertising in the 1920s and beyond was the role played by science and technology. Science and technology were in many ways the new religions of the modern era. Consumers saw ads appealing to the popularity of science in virtually all product categories during this period. Sonatron said its radio tubes were "bombarded with energy," and Pet evaporated milk announced that it was "approved by" the new field of "domestic science."

The style of 1920s ads was more visual than ads of earlier eras. Twenties ads showed slices of life—carefully constructed "snapshots" of social life with the product. In these ads, the relative position, background, and dress of the people using or needing the advertised product were crafted carefully, as they are today. These visual lessons generally were about how to fit in with the "smart" crowd, how to be urbane and modern by using the newest conveniences, and how not to fall victim to the perils and pressures of the new fast-paced modern world.

The J. Walter Thompson advertising agency was the dominant agency of the period. Stanley Resor, Helen Resor, and James Webb Young brought this agency to a leadership position through intelligent management, vision, and great advertising. Helen Resor, the first prominent female advertising executive, was instrumental in J. Walter Thompson's success. Still, the most famous ad person of the era was a man named Bruce Barton. Not only the leader of BBDO, Barton also was a best-selling author, most notably of a 1924 book called *The Man Nobody Knows*,[13] which portrayed Jesus as the archetypal ad man. This blending of Christian and capitalist principles was enormously attractive to a people struggling to reconcile traditional religious thought, which preached against excess, and the new religion of consumption, which preached just the opposite.

Great Depression (1929–1941)

If you weren't there, it's hard to imagine how bad the **Great Depression** was:

By 1932, a quarter of American workers were unemployed. But matters were worse than this suggests, for three quarters of those who had jobs were working part-time—either working short hours, or faced with chronic and repeated layoffs. . . . Millions actually went hungry, not once, but again and again. Millions knew what it was like to eat bread and water for supper, sometimes for days at a stretch. A million people were drifting around the country begging, among them thousands of children, including numbers of girls disguised as boys.[14]

The Depression was brutal, crushing, and mean. It killed people; it broke lives. And it forever changed the way people thought about a great many things: their government, business, money, spending, saving, credit, and, not coincidentally, advertising.

Just as sure as advertising was glamorous in the 1920s, it was villainous in the 1930s. It was part of big business, and big business, big greed, and big lust had gotten America into the great economic depression beginning in 1929—or so the story goes. The public began to see advertising as something that had tempted and seduced them into the excesses for which they were being punished.

Advertisers responded to this feeling by adopting a tough, no-nonsense advertising style. The stylish and highly aesthetic ads of the 1920s gave way to harsher and more cluttered ads. As one historian said, "The new hard-boiled advertising mystique brought a proliferation of 'ugly,' attention-grabbing, picture-dominated copy in the style of the tabloid newspaper."[15] Clients wanted their money's worth, and agencies responded by cramming every bit of copy and image they could into their ads or using obviously inappropriate sex appeals. This type of advertising persisted, quite likely making the relationship between the public and the institution of advertising even worse. (Regrettably, it remains an industry impulse in bad economic times today.) The themes in advertisements traded on the anxieties of the day—losing one's job, being a bad provider, and lack of sex appeal.

Another notable event during these years was the emergence of radio as a significant advertising medium. During the 1930s, the number of radio stations rose from a handful to 814 by the end of the decade, and the number of radio sets in use more than quadrupled to 51 million, just over one radio set per household. Radio was in its heyday as a news and entertainment medium, and it would remain so until the 1950s, when television emerged. Radio offered the ability to create a sense of community in which people thousands of miles apart listened to and became involved with their favorite radio soap opera, so named in reference to the soap sponsors of these shows.

Advertising, like the rest of the country, suffered dark days during this period. Agencies cut salaries and forced staff to work four-day weeks, without pay for the mandatory extra day off. Clients demanded frequent review of work, and agencies were compelled to provide more and more free services to keep accounts. Advertising would emerge from this depression, just as the economy itself did, during World War II. However, the advertising industry never again would reach its pre-Depression status. It became the subject of a well-organized and angry consumerism movement. The U.S. Congress passed real reform in this period. In 1938, the Wheeler-Lea Amendments to the Federal Trade Commission Act declared "deceptive acts of commerce" to be against the law; this was interpreted to include advertising. Between 1938 and 1940, the FTC issued 18 injunctions against advertisers; one of these forced Fleischmann's Yeast "to stop claiming that it cured crooked teeth, bad skin, constipation, and halitosis."[16]

World War II and After (1941–1960)

Many people mark the end of the Depression with the start of America's involvement in World War II in December 1941. During the war, advertising often made direct reference to the war effort, linking the product with patriotism and helping to rehabilitate the tarnished image of advertising. Marketers sold war bonds and encouraged conservation. Of all companies, Coca-Cola probably both contributed to and benefited the most from the company's amazingly successful efforts to get Coca-Cola to the front lines. When the war was over, Coke had bottling plants all over the globe, and returning American GIs were loyal to Coke over competitors such as Pepsi by 4:1.[17]

American Cleaning Institute® (formerly The Soap and Detergent Association).

He had to fight himself so hard...
he didn't put it over

YES, he was his own worst enemy. His appearance was against him and he knew it. Oh why had he neglected the bath that morning, the shave, the change of linen? Under the other fellow's gaze it

was hard to forget that cheap feeling. There's self-respect in soap and water. The clean-cut chap can look any man in the face and tell him the facts—for when you're clean, your appearance fights *for you*.

There's self-respect in SOAP & WATER
PUBLISHED BY THE ASSOCIATION OF AMERICAN SOAP AND GLYCERINE PRODUCERS, INC., TO AID THE WORK OF CLEANLINESS INSTITUTE

Advertising during the 1930s traded on the anxieties of the day.

subliminal
advertising
advertisements alleged to work
on a subconscious level

The war got women to join the workforce in what were non-traditional roles, as seen in the so-called Rosie the Riveter ads. After the war ended in 1945, many women left their jobs (both voluntarily and involuntarily). In her recollections of the 1950s, Wini Breines notes the return to traditional roles:

Almost one-half of all women married while they were still teenagers. Two out of three white women in college dropped out before they graduated.[18]

Following World War II, the economy continued (with a few starts and stops) to improve, and the consumption spree was on again. The first shopping malls were built. This time, however, public sentiment toward advertising was fundamentally different from what it had been following WWI. This time, there was widespread belief that America's successful propaganda experts at the War Department had simply moved over to Madison Avenue and started manipulating consumer minds. Perhaps because there was also great concern about the rise of communism and its use of "mind control," it was natural to believe that advertising was involved in the same type of pursuit, only aimed at purchasing instead of politics. The United States was filled with suspicion on a variety of topics—McCarthyism, the bomb, repressed sexual thoughts (a resurgence of Freudian thought), and even aliens from outer space. Otherwise-normal people were building bomb shelters in their backyards, wondering whether their neighbors were communists and whether listening to rock 'n' roll would make their daughters less virtuous.

In this environment of mass fear, stories began circulating that advertising agencies were doing motivation research and using the "psychological sell," which served only to fuel an underlying suspicion of advertising. Similarly, Americans began to fear they were being seduced by **subliminal advertising** (subconscious advertising) to buy all sorts of things they didn't really want or need. As their homes and garages filled up with their purchases, some consumers blamed advertising—and so a great excuse for lack of self-control was born. A best-selling 1957 book, *The Hidden Persuaders*, bolstered that view by maintaining that slick advertising works on the subconscious.[19] Suspicions about slick advertising persist and are a big business for the "aren't consumers dumb?/aren't

Advertisers often used America's involvement in World War II as a way to link their products with patriotism. That link gave advertising a much-needed image boost.

advertisers evil?" propagandists. Selling fears about advertising always has been good business.

The most incredible story of the period involved a man named James Vicary. According to historian Stuart Rogers, in 1957, Vicary convinced the marketing world, and most of the U.S. population, that he had successfully demonstrated a technique to get consumers to do exactly what advertisers wanted. He claimed to have placed subliminal messages in a motion picture, brought in audiences, and recorded the results. He claimed that the embedded messages of "Eat Popcorn" and "Drink Coca-Cola" had increased sales of popcorn by 57.5 percent and Coca-Cola by 18.1 percent. He held press conferences and took retainer fees from advertising agencies. According to later research, he then skipped town, just ahead of reporters who had figured out that none of his claims was true. He disappeared, leaving no bank accounts and no forwarding address, with about $4.5 million (around $28 million in today's dollars) paid to him by advertising agencies and clients.[20] Vicary probably pulled off the greatest scam in advertising history. Unfortunately, a lot of people still believe in the hype he was selling and that advertisers can actually manipulate unsuspecting people.

Besides fears, the 1950s were about sex, youth culture, rock 'n' roll, and television. In terms of sex, volumes could be written about the paradoxical '50s. This was the time of neo-Freudian pop psychology and *Beach Blanket Bingo*, with sexual innuendo everywhere; at the same time, very conservative pronouncements about sexual mores were giving young people, particularly women, contradictory messages. What's more, young people were advertised to with a singular focus and force never seen before, becoming, as a result, the first "kid" and then "teen" markets. Because of their sheer numbers, they ultimately would constitute an unstoppable youth culture, one that everyone else had to deal with and try to please—the baby boomers. They would, over their parents' objections, buy rock 'n' roll records in numbers large enough to revolutionize the music industry. Now they buy SUVs, mutual funds, and $8,000 bicycles.

And then there was TV. Nothing like it had happened before. Its rise from pre–World War II science experiment to 90 percent penetration in U.S. households occurred during this period. At first, advertisers didn't know what to do with it and did two- and three-minute commercials, typically demonstrations. Of course, they soon began to learn TV's look and language.

This era also saw growth in the U.S. economy and in household incomes. The suburbs emerged, and along with them, there was an explosion of consumption. Technological change was relentless and was a national obsession. Along with the television, the telephone and automatic washer and dryer became common to the American lifestyle. Advertisements of this era were characterized by scenes of modern life, social promises, and reliance on science and technology.

Into all of this, 1950s advertising projected a confused, often harsh, and at other times, sappy presence. It rarely is remembered as advertising's golden age. Two of the most significant advertising personalities of the period were Rosser Reeves of the Ted Bates agency, who is best remembered for his ultra-hard-sell style, and consultant Ernest Dichter, best remembered for his motivational research, which focused on the subconscious and symbolic elements of consumer desire.

Typical advertisements from this contradictory and jumbled period in American advertising show mythic nuclear families, well-behaved children, our "buddy" the atom, the last days of unquestioned faith in science, and rigid (but about to break loose) gender roles, while the rumblings of the sexual revolution of the 1960s were just audible. In a few short years, the atom no longer would be our friend; we would question science; youth would rebel and become a hugely important market; women and African Americans would demand inclusion and fairness; and bullet bras would be replaced with no bras.

In the 1950s, society's view of sex was paradoxical: titillating but innocent. (It's just underwear, and she's alone, just getting dressed.)

Creative Revolution (1960–1972)

The cultural revolution in the 1960s affected just about everything—including advertising. Ads started to take on the themes, the language, and the look of the 1960s. But as an institution, advertising in the United States during the 1960s was actually slow to respond to the massive social revolution going on all around it. While the nation was struggling with civil rights, the Vietnam War, and the sexual revolution, advertising often still was portraying women and other minorities in subservient roles. Advertising agencies remained one of the whitest industries in America, despite images in the ads. In fact, much of the sexual revolution just made women into boy toys in ads. Gays and lesbians, as far as advertising was concerned, didn't exist.

The only thing truly revolutionary about 1960s advertising was the **creative revolution**. This revolution was characterized by the "creatives" (art directors and copywriters) having a bigger say in the management of their agencies and the look and voice of the ads. The emphasis in advertising turned "from ancillary services to the creative product; from science and research to art, inspiration, and intuition."[21]

At first, the look of this revolutionary advertising was clean and minimalist, with simple copy and a sense of self-effacing humor. Later (around 1968 or so), it became self-aware and unabashedly latched itself onto social revolution—including, irony of all ironies, the antimaterialist movement. Advertising admitted being advertising (and even poked fun at itself). More than anything, the creative revolution was about self-awareness, saying, "OK, here's an ad, you know it's an ad—and so do we."

The 1960s was also a time when advertising began to understand that it was all about hip, cool, youth, and rebellion. Whatever became cool, ads had to incorporate into their messages. The '60s cultural revolution soon became ad copy. Everything became rebellion; even an unhip brand like Dodge traded successfully on the "Dodge Rebellion."[22] Even hip anti-advertising sentiment could be used to help sell stuff through advertising. Marketers learned that people (particularly youth) play out their revolutionary phase *through* consumption—you've got to have the right look, the right clothes, the right revolutionary garb. Once advertising learned that it successfully could attach itself to youth, hipness, and revolution, it never went back:

> Every few years, it seems, the cycles of the sixties repeat themselves on a smaller scale, with new rebel youth cultures bubbling their way to a happy replenishing of the various culture industries' depleted arsenal of cool. . . . As adman Merle Steir wrote back in 1967, "Youth has won. Youth must always win. The new naturally replaces the old." And we will have new generations of youth rebellion as certainly as we will have generations of mufflers or toothpaste or footwear.[23]

The creative revolution, and the look it produced, most often is associated with four famous advertising agencies: Leo Burnett in Chicago, Ogilvy & Mather in New York (a little less so), Doyle Dane Bernbach

$1.02 a pound.

Volkswagen of America, Inc.

Through innovative advertising, Volkswagen refuels its original message that cars aren't expensive luxuries. At $1.02 a pound, this Beetle is cheaper than ground round.

in New York (the most), and Wells Rich and Green in New York (deserving of more credit than it gets). They were led in this revolution by agency heads Leo Burnett, David Ogilvy, Bill Bernbach, and Mary Wells.

Of course, it would be wrong to characterize the entire period as a creative revolution. Many ads in the 1960s still reflected traditional values and relied on relatively uncreative executions. Typical of the more traditional ads during the era is a message from Goodyear featuring a helpless and anxious young woman gazing at a flat tire on her car next to the headline "When there's no man around, Goodyear should be."

In the era from 1960 to 1972, advertisers became generally aware of their industry's role in consumer culture: Advertising was an icon of a culture fascinated with consumption. Besides playing a role in encouraging consumption, advertising had become a symbol of consumption itself. The creative revolution did not last long, but advertising was changed forever. After the 1960s, it never again would be quite as naive about its own place in society; it since has become much more self-conscious. In a very significant way, advertising learned how to dodge the criticism of capitalism forever: Hide in plain sight.

The Seventies (1973–1980)

The reelection of Richard Nixon in 1972 marked the real start of the 1970s. America had just suffered through its first lost war, the memory of four student protesters shot and killed by the National Guard at Kent State University in the spring of 1970 was still vivid, Mideast nations appeared to be dictating the energy policy of the United States, and we were, as President Jimmy Carter suggested late in this period, in a national malaise. In this environment, advertising again retreated into the tried-and-true but hackneyed styles of decades before. The creative revolution of the 1960s gave way to a slowing economy and a return to the hard sell.

This period also marked the beginning of the second wave of the American feminist movement. In the 1970s, advertisers actually started to present women in "new" roles and to include people of color. Twenty years later, they would admit gays and lesbians exist.

The '70s were the end of "the '60s" and the end of whatever revolution one wished to speak of. Accounts of this period describe it as a time of excess and self-induced numbness. This was the age of polyester, disco, blow, and driving 55, the era of self-help and selfishness. "Me" became the biggest word in the 1970s. What a great environment for advertising. All of society was telling people that it not only was okay to be selfish, but it was the right thing to do. Selfishness was said to be natural and good. A refrain similar to "Hey, babe, I can't be good to you if I'm not good to me," became a '70s mantra. Of course, being good to oneself often meant buying stuff.

Paradoxically, the '70s also resulted in added regulation and the protection of special audiences.

Andrew Lever/Shutterstock.com

ETHICS DISCOVERING GAY CONSUMERS

One of the first gay-friendly commercials aired by a major corporation showed a couple shopping for a dining room table at IKEA. The 1994 ad, in which the couple debating furniture styles and finishing each other's sentences were two men, broke down a long-standing cultural barrier. It generated controversy but eventually became a touchstone for marketers considering how to appeal to gay and lesbian consumers.

In 2006, IKEA prominently featured a gay couple in another ad, this time with a young child and a golden retriever. The ad for living room furniture closes with the line "Why shouldn't sofas come in flavors, just like families?" Why shouldn't advertisements as well?

Sources: Aparna Kumar, "Commercials: Out of the Closet," *Wired*, May 8, 2001, http://www.wired.com; Stuart Elliott, "Hey, Gay Spender, Marketers Spending Time with You," *New York Times*, June 26, 2006, C8.

Advertising encountered a new round of challenges on several fronts. First, there was growing concern over what effect $200 million a year in advertising had on children. A group of women in Boston formed **Action for Children's Television**, which lobbied the government to limit the amount and content of advertising directed at children. Established regulatory bodies, in particular the **Federal Trade Commission (FTC)** and the industry's **National Advertising Review Board**, demanded higher standards of honesty and disclosure from the advertising industry. Several firms were subjected to legislative mandates and fines because their advertising was judged to be misleading. Most notable among these firms were Warner-Lambert (for advertising that Listerine mouthwash could cure and prevent colds), Campbell's (for putting marbles in the bottom of a soup bowl to bolster its look in ads), and Anacin (for advertising that its aspirin could help relieve tension).

Even as the process of advertising was being restricted by consumer and governmental regulatory challenges, technological advances posed unprecedented opportunities. It was also the birth of what were essentially program-length commercials, particularly in children's television. Product/show blends for toys like Strawberry Shortcake made regulation more difficult: If it's a show about a product, then it's not really an ad (and can't be regulated as an ad)—or is it? This drove regulators crazy, but program-length commercials were incredibly smart marketing.[24] They generally were treated by regulators as shows and opened the door for countless numbers of imitators. The "new" branded entertainment had its real start here, not 30 years later.

While advertising during this period featured more African Americans and women, the effort to adequately represent and serve these consumers was fairly minimal; advertising agency hiring and promotion practices with respect to minorities were formally challenged in the courts. Despite this, two important agencies owned and managed by African Americans emerged and thrived: Thomas J. Burrell founded Burrell Advertising, and Byron Lewis founded Uniworld. Burrell perhaps is best known for ads that rely on the principle of "positive realism." Positive realism is the use of black actors "in authentic, optimistic settings" in which it is evident that "the products are intended for them, not just the general [white] market."[25] (Go to www.littleafrica.com/resources/advertising.htm for a current list of major African-American advertising agencies and resources.)

Another very important person in opening up the promotion industry to minorities was John H. Johnson, founder of *Ebony* magazine. He was in many ways the man who made possible the black American experience in publishing, marketing, and advertising. He opened up enormous opportunities for black entrepreneurs, advertisers, and artists.

The 1970s also signaled a period of growth in communications technology. Consumers began to surround themselves with devices related to communication. The VCR, cable television, and the laserdisc player were all developed during the 1970s. Cable TV claimed 20 million subscribers by the end of the decade. Similarly, cable programming grew in quality, with viewing options such as ESPN and Nickelodeon. As cable subscribers and their viewing options increased, marketers learned how to reach more specific audiences through the diversity of programming on cable systems.

This era saw the beginning of the merger mania that swept the industry throughout the end of the decade and into the next. Most of the major agencies merged with one another and with non-U.S. agencies as well.

In all of this, the look of advertising was about as interesting as it was in the 1950s. Often, advertisements focused on the product itself, rather than on creative technique. At ad agencies, management took control. Among employees used to creative control, the idea of "bottom-liners" struck deep at the soul. But the cultural revolution of the 1960s and 1970s (and the creative revolution) was over. By the end of the 1970s, American culture was really very different, so the ad business changed as well. The youth undercurrent of revolution and rebellion was more cynical and ambivalent about consumption and advertising. These youth were the first generation to grow up on TV advertising.

Photos: top, Zoltan Pataki/Shutterstock.com; bottom, PiotrMaciejewski/Shutterstock.com

Designer Era (1980–1992)

Consumers had a lot of income to spend in the 1980s. By one account, "In 1980, the average American had twice as much real income as his parents had had at the end of WWII."[26] The political, social, business, and advertising landscapes changed in 1980 with the election of Ronald Reagan. The country made a right, and conservative politics were the order of the day. There was, of course, some backlash and many countercurrents, but the conservatives were in the mainstream. Greed was good, stuff was good, and advertising was good.

Many ads from the Designer era are particularly social-class conscious and values conscious. They openly promote consumption but in a conservative way, all wrapped up in "traditional American values." The quintessential 1980s ad may be the 1984 television ad for President Ronald Reagan's reelection campaign, "Morning in America." Other advertisers quickly followed with ads that looked similar to "Morning in America."

At the same time, several new trends in communication technology were emerging, and these led to more creative, bold, and provocative advertising. Television advertising of this period was influenced by the rapid-cut editing style of music videos shown on MTV. George Lois, himself of the 1960s creative revolution, was hired by MTV to save the fledgling network after a dismal first year. After calling a lot of people who were unwilling to take the chance, he got Mick Jagger to proclaim, "I want my MTV." The network turned around, and music television surged into popular consciousness. Most importantly for us, television ads in the 1980s started looking like MTV videos: rapid cuts with a very self-conscious character.

The spread of cable television also provided a media outlet for a new and longer form of promotion, the *infomercial*, discussed in Chapter 10.

The advertising of the 1980s was also affected by the growth and creative impact of British agencies, particularly Saatchi and Saatchi. One lesson Saatchi and Saatchi realized earlier than most was that politics, culture, and products all resonate together. The Saatchi and Saatchi ads of this period were often sophisticated and politically non-neutral. They worked and began to be copied (at least the sensibility) in other places, including the United States.

E-Revolution (1993–2000)

As modern advertising entered its second century, it had become more self-conscious than ever. In the 1990s, self-parody was the inside joke of the day, except everyone was "inside." Winks and nods to the media-savvy audience were becoming pretty common. Advertising was fast, and it was everywhere. Nineties ads were generally more visually oriented and much more self-aware. They said "this is an ad" in their look and feel. They had a young and ironic flavor. Some call them "postmodern."

Even as advertising was getting edgier, marketers were watching their traditional audiences switch off their television sets and lay down their newspapers to explore the Internet. With consumers' eyeballs glued to computer screens, marketers realized they needed to put brand messages online or lose their audience. Until the mid-1990s, the potential for advertising in an Internet Age looked perilous. The first phase of the Web revolution had its scary moments:

- *The setting*: American Association of Advertising Agencies (4As) annual conference, May 1994. *The speaker*: Edwin L. Artzt, then chairman and CEO of Procter & Gamble, the then $40 billion-a-year marketer of consumer packaged goods. *The news*: Artzt dropped a bomb on the advertising industry when he warned that agencies must confront a "new media" future that wouldn't be driven by traditional advertising. Although P&G was spending about $1 billion a year on television advertising, Artzt told the 4As audience, "From where

SOME CIRCLES SHALL REMAIN EXCLUSIVE.

The ultimate recognition from your banker. A gold MasterCard card.

Courtesy of MasterCard.

This MasterCard ad demonstrates the social-class and designer consciousness of the 1980s.

we stand today, we can't be sure that ad-supported TV programming will have a future in the world being created—a world of video-on-demand, pay-per-view, and subscription TV. These are designed to carry no advertising at all."[27] An icy chill filled the room.

- *The setting*: The 4As annual conference, one year later. *The speaker*: William T. Esrey, chairman and CEO of Sprint. *The news*: Esrey gave advertisers another jolt with a point that was somewhat different but equally challenging. He said clients would "hold ad agencies more closely accountable for results than ever before." Again, the challenge would come from technology: "It's . . . because we know the technology is there to measure advertising impact more precisely than you have done in the past."[28]

Esrey's point was that **Interactive media** would allow direct measurement of ad exposure and impact, quickly revealing which advertisements or other brand messages perform well and which do not, and marketers would hold their agencies accountable for results. Exhibit 3.3 shows how this was supposed to work with direct-response advertising online. Well, the precise measurement didn't really work out, but accountability still became the order of the day.

Unsure of what could be delivered and what could be counted, Procter & Gamble hosted an August 1998 Internet "summit" to investigate "the difficulties confronted by marketers using online media to pitch products."[29] Some of these problems were technological: incompatible technical standards, limited bandwidth, and disappointing measurement of audience size and return on investment. Others were the result of naïveté. Marketers such as P&G want to know what they are getting and what it costs when they place an Internet ad. Does anyone notice these ads, or do people click right past them? What would "exposure" in this environment really mean? Is "exposure" really even a meaningful term in the new media ad world? How do you use these new media to build brand relationships? At the end of this summit, P&G reaffirmed its commitment to the Internet.

But history again showed that measurement of bang for buck (return on investment, ROI) in advertising (Internet or not) is very elusive. While better than TV, the Internet fundamentally was unable to yield precise measurements of return on investment in advertisement. Too many variables, too much noise in the system, too many lagged (delayed) effects, and too many uncertainties about who is really online abound.

Phoenix Footwear Group, Inc.

Advertising of the 1990s was highly visual and self-aware. This shoe ad parodies advertising formats with a dog for a model and the statement "Bull terrier wears shoes from Pussyfoot."

That's not a big surprise for those who pay attention to history: Advertising's impact is always tough to measure. Even with all this technology, it still is. Which bump in sales comes from where is still elusive.

Another change in the world of promotion was a challenge to New York's claim as the center of advertising activity. In the United States, the center moved west, with the ascendancy of agencies in California, Minnesota, Oregon, and Washington. In the 1990s, these agencies tended to be more creatively oriented and less interested in numbers-oriented research than those in New York. Other hot or nearly hot ad-shop markets include Minneapolis, Austin, Atlanta, Houston, and Dallas. Outside the United States, London emerged as the key player, with Singapore and Seoul as close seconds.

LO 4 Anxiety and Empowerment (2000–Present)

With this millennium barely into its second decade, American consumers have already weathered two major recessions, and as these words are written, many

Exhibit 3.3
Better Data Online?

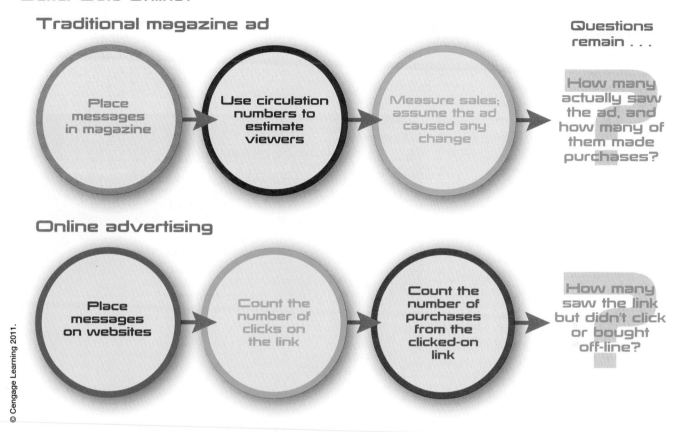

Traditional magazine ad

Place messages in magazine → Use circulation numbers to estimate viewers → Measure sales; assume the ad caused any change

Questions remain . . .

How many actually saw the ad, and how many of them made purchases?

Online advertising

Place messages on websites → Count the number of clicks on the link → Count the number of purchases from the clicked-on link

How many saw the link but didn't click or bought off-line?

© Cengage Learning 2011.

are still doubtful about the economic future. At the same time, the Internet has been fulfilling its potential to empower individual consumers in ways they would not have dreamed of at the start of the e-revolution. Marketers have continued to develop news ways to reach ever more fragmented groups of society in ever more places.

Economic Uncertainty

The first two decades of the 21st century have been scarred by two recessions, each sparked by the bursting of an investment "bubble." The first bubble burst in 2000. This was the dot-com bubble: Thrilled by the seemingly endless potential of the Internet, ambitious entrepreneurs started every kind of online business they could imagine, and investors wanted a piece of every new venture, even business ideas without a significant stream of revenues. Part of the problem was the lack of effective Internet advertising. Even as more consumers made purchases online, sellers of pop-up

advertising and other easy-to-avoid ads couldn't convince marketers that the Internet medium was driving those sales. Investors started deserting companies that couldn't turn a profit, the high-tech sector of the stock market crashed, and a recession followed. The upshot for marketers: today they insist that online media demonstrate a real return on marketing dollars, knowing that consumers won't be wowed by a message just because it is online.

More recently, a collapse in real estate values that started in 2007 began a downward spiral that first was a financial-industry crisis and then spread to the whole economy, becoming what is now popularly known as the Great Recession. This unusually long recession with its persistent unemployment and occasional spikes in gasoline prices has contributed to widespread anxiety. Consumers are looking for ways to stay home, spend less, and increase their security. Opportunities are great for marketers offering coupons and discounts, while marketers of brand-name products scaled back ad budgets, a trend that has devastated many traditional media outlets, including newspapers and magazines. More than ever, marketers need to be skillful in building relationships of trust with today's nervous consumers. To do this, many marketers shifted more of their ad spending to branded entertainment and non-traditional brand promotion.

A growing share of promotion on the Web is undertaken in support of e-business. **E-business** is promotion in which companies selling to business customers (rather than to household consumers) rely on the Internet to send messages and close sales (we'll cover this in detail in Chapter 9).

Consumer Empowerment

In a shaky economic climate, it's no surprise that consumers want to feel in control. Today online brand promotion is catching up to consumers by letting them push the messages. It's all happening with the next generation of Internet use, known as Web 2.0.

Web 2.0 is all about collaboration among Internet users. In terms of brand promotion, this means that consumers can communicate with each other, actually talk back to the marketer with one voice or millions, and even make their own ads and distribute them on media such as YouTube. The promotion industry is accepting the fact that consumers now can do many of the very same things that only big studios, agencies, and distributors could do a decade ago. Consumers now co-create brands. The reactions of consumers (particularly young people) are fused with agency "professional" creative to make ads that are one step from homemade, or in some cases completely homemade—what is typically called **consumer-generated content (CGC)**. Doritos, for example, invited consumers to make their own advertisements and then chose one of those submissions to run during the Super Bowl. This has turned the industry upside down. The industry bible, *Advertising Age*, has declared this era the "post-advertising age." Still, even with these amazing and fundamental changes, it would be an exaggeration to say that advertising is dead or that advertisers have absolutely no power.

Annette Shaff/Shutterstock.com.

Web advertising growth will be fostered by three aspects of technology: interactive, wireless, and broadband. Because of advances in technology, firms like Procter & Gamble continue to invest heavily in these means of sending messages and reaching target customers. P&G has developed and maintains dozens of websites for the company's approximately 300 brands to serve and interact with customers.[30] P&G also has gone beyond just product-oriented sites and has launched "relationship building" sites like Beinggirl, a teen community site. With such a site, the firm can gather data, test new product ideas, and experiment with interactivity. For example, if a website visitor wants to know what nail polish will match the lipstick she just saw in a commercial, she can get an immediate answer. Thus, target audiences do not have to be broadly defined by age or geographic groups—individual households can be

THE DAY OF THE MARKETER'S HEAVY HAND IS PRETTY MUCH OVER.

targeted through direct interaction with the audience member. Also, P&G can reach a global audience through beinggirl.com without the cost and time-consuming effort of placing traditional media ads in dozens of markets. Furthermore, the consumer comes willingly to the advertiser, not the other way around, as in the case of the more intrusive traditional media. Social networking sites such as Facebook have made brand communities and personal identity projects the stuff of e-commerce.

Branded Entertainment

Even as consumer-generated content is blurring the lines between marketers and consumers, the lines

The ultimate in branded entertainment, the BMW Web videos entertain viewers by featuring their cars in short features made by well-known movie directors, including Wong Kar-Wai, Ang Lee, John Frankenheimer, Guy Ritchie, and Alejandro González Iñárritu. The videos have attracted millions of viewers, who watch for more than 15 minutes at a time.

© Hugo Philpott/Reuters/Landov.

between media content and advertiser content are blurring with the use of "branded entertainment." **Branded entertainment** is the blending of integrated marketing communication with entertainment, primarily film, music, and television programming. A subset of branded entertainment is *product placement*, the significant placement of brands within films or television programs. When PlentyOfFish arranged to have its brand show up in Lady Gaga's "Telephone" music video, viewers took notice. The online dating site reported 15 percent growth in use of the site after Gaga's video was released.[31] Branded entertainment takes product placement a quantum leap forward. With branded entertainment, a brand is not just a bit player; it is the star of the program. An early participant in branded entertainment and still a leader in using the technique is BMW. Similarly, along with videos, the U.S. Army offers Web-based computer games at its recruiting site (www.goarmy.com).

Branded entertainment offers the marketer many advantages—among them, not running into the consumer's well-trained resistance mechanisms to ads. When the brand message is part of the entertainment message, viewers of a prerecorded broadcast can't simply fast-forward through the ads.

Another advantage is greater freedom. With branded entertainment, marketers are not subject to all the ad regulations. In an ad, BMW has to use a disclaimer ("closed track, professional driver") when it shows its cars tearing around, but in movies, like *The Italian Job*, no such disclaimer is required. Also, movies have been seen by the courts as artistic speech, not as the less protected "commercial speech." Branded entertainment, therefore, gets more First Amendment protection than ordinary advertising does. This is an important distinction because regulation and legal fights surrounding ads represent a large cost of doing business.

This merger of advertising with music, film, television, and other telecom arenas (such as cell phones) often is referred to as Madison & Vine, a nod to New York's Madison Avenue, the traditional home of the advertising industry, and the famous Hollywood intersection of Hollywood and Vine. Whatever you call it, branded entertainment has opened up enormous real possibilities for what has become a much cluttered and a bit beat-up traditional advertising industry.

branded entertainment embedding brands or brand icons as part of an entertainment property in an effort to connect with consumers in a unique and compelling way

As you can imagine, marketers love the exposure and freedom of using branded entertainment. But not all consumers are wildly enthusiastic about the blurring line between marketing and entertainment. One survey showed that 52 percent of respondents were worried about advertisers influencing entertainment content. But in which real world are no brands visible and being used? We doubt that today's consumers find branded entertainment particularly distracting, particularly if it's done well.

LO 5 Does History Matter?

As intrigued as we are by new technology like Wi-Fi and new media like Web films, we shouldn't jump to the conclusion that everything about promotion will change. So far, it hasn't. Advertising still will be a paid attempt to persuade, and it still will be one of the primary tools in the promotional mix that contribute to revenues and profits by stimulating demand and nurturing brand loyalty. Even though executives at P&G believe there is a whole new world of communication and have developed dozens of websites to take advantage of this new world, the firm still spends about $3.5 billion a year on traditional advertising through traditional media.[32]

It also is safe to argue that consumers still will be highly involved in some product decisions and not so involved in others. That means some messages will be particularly relevant, but others will be completely irrelevant to forming and maintaining beliefs and feelings about brands. To this date, technology (particularly e-commerce) has changed the way people shop, gather information, and make purchases. And while the advance in online advertising continues, net TV revenues are still attractive. Where else are you going to get such an enormous audience with sight and sound?

History is very, very relevant and practiced. You don't have to make the same mistakes over and over. Learn from the past what works and what doesn't. It's a smart thing to do.

STUDY TOOLS
CHAPTER 3

Located at back of the textbook
- **Rip out Chapter in Review Card.**

Located at www.cengagebrain.com
- **Review Key Terms Flashcards (Print or Online).**
- **Complete the Practice Quiz to prepare for tests.**
- **Play "Beat the Clock" and "Quizbowl" to master concepts.**
- **Complete "Crossword Puzzle" to review key terms.**
- **Watch videos on Samsung and Patrick Jean Pixels for real company examples.**
- **For additional examples, go online to learn about the creative revolution (1960–1972), the iPod mini ads, and consumer-generated advertising.**

USE THE TOOLS.

- Rip out the Review Cards in the back of your book to study.

Or Visit CourseMate to:

- Read, search, highlight, and take notes in the Interactive eBook
- Review Flashcards (Print or Online) to master key terms
- Test yourself with Auto-Graded Quizzes
- Bring concepts to life with Games, Videos, and Animations!

Go to CourseMate for **PROMO2** to begin using these tools.
Access at **www.cengagebrain.com**

Complete the Speak Up
survey in CourseMate at
www.cengagebrain.com

f Follow us at
www.facebook.com/4ltrpress

Understanding the Marketing Environment:

Segmentation, Targeting, and Positioning

Q: How do you reach young people who want to wake up with a cup of coffee but aren't used to brewing it at home?

A: Find them online, and show you understand how rough mornings can be.

Learning Outcomes

After studying this chapter, you should be able to:

LO 1 Explain the process of STP marketing.

LO 2 Describe bases for identifying target segments.

LO 3 Discuss criteria for choosing a target segment.

LO 4 Identify the essentials of a positioning strategy.

LO 5 Review the necessary ingredients for creating a brand's value proposition.

> "The more you engage with customers the clearer things become and the easier it is to determine what you should be doing."
>
> —John Russell

How Well Do You "Tolerate Mornings"?

AFTER YOU FINISH THIS CHAPTER GO TO **PAGE 85** FOR **STUDY TOOLS**

You know by now that advertising, in its many forms, always is sponsored for a reason. Generally that reason has something to do with winning new customers or reinforcing the habits of existing customers.[1] However, advertising has no chance of producing a desired result if we are unclear about whom we want to reach. We need a target audience. Folgers targeted net-savvy young adults with the Yellow People movie seen opposite.

One special problem that most companies face is reaching potential customers just as they are experimenting in a product category for the first time. This is a pivotal time when the marketer wants the consumer to have a great experience with the brand. So, for example, if we are Gillette and seek to market anything and everything associated with shaving, we will want one of our shavers in the hands of the consumer the first time he or she shaves. First-time users are not heavy users, but they represent the future. If we don't keep winning these beginners, eventually, we go out of business. Developing advertising campaigns to win with first-time users often is referred to as point-of-entry marketing. More on that later . . .

Folgers does a huge business in the coffee category but can take nothing for granted when it comes to new users. Thus, the marketers of Folgers must launch campaigns to appeal specifically to the next generation of coffee drinkers: young people just learning the coffee habit. Attracted by coffee titans like Starbucks and Dunkin' Donuts, many people get to know coffee in their teens. But when it's time to start brewing coffee at home, Folgers sees its big chance to get in your cupboard.

What do you think?

Before you can sell anything, you have to know what your customer wants.

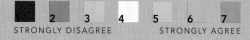

1	2	3	4	5	6	7
STRONGLY DISAGREE					STRONGLY AGREE	

© Olaf Doering/Alamy.

The Folgers brand team launched an advertising initiative aimed to attract just-graduated 20-somethings. When young adults move into the "real world" and take that first job with a new apartment in a strange city, they are primed to develop the coffee habit. Folgers aspires to be the brand of choice for this target as they potentially commit to a morning brew-it-yourself coffee ritual. Mornings are tough, so Folgers realistically aims to make them tolerable. But how does Folgers, your grandparents' brand, connect with a new generation of coffee drinkers? Tried-and-true slogans ("The best part of waking up is Folgers in your cup") and 30-second TV spots just won't do.

Working with its ad agency Saatchi & Saatchi, the Folgers brand team started with the premise that mornings are hard, filled with emails and bosses making demands and those darn "morning people" (who, for some bizarre reason, seem to love sunrises). Folgers exists to help a person tolerate mornings, particularly to tolerate those morning people. A short film was produced to show Folgers as your first line of defense when the fanatical Yellow People try to invade your space first thing in the morning. The film also was designed to generate traffic to toleratemornings.com, which offered other tools (boss-tracker, auto emails, wake-up calls, screensaver) for making mornings better. The campaign also included print ads code-named "Dreamscapes," reflecting that frightful moment just before dawn when the creepy Yellow People are planning their attack.

To distribute the Yellow People film, Folgers spent zero dollars. Rather, the spot was submitted to three websites (Adcritic, Bestadsontv.com, and Boards), where 20-somethings had their way with it. Chatter quickly spread across the blogosphere, website hits increased, and the film soon was posted on YouTube (receiving 4 out of 5 stars and more than 300,000 viewings). This little sample of YouTube comments suggests that the Folgers team was on the right track in their effort to engage new users:

"I now watch this every morning to wake up, cause it's just so damn funny and awesome that it wakes me right up. If I ever get rich, I'm going to hire a bunch of people to dress like happy yellow people and come wake me up with that song every morning."

"I am without speech at the sheer brilliance. If commercials were like this . . . I wouldn't skip them on the DVR."

(COMPANIES) MUST **BE CLEAR** ABOUT WHOM THEY ARE TRYING TO REACH AND ABOUT WHAT THEY CAN SAY THAT WILL **RESONATE WITH CONSUMERS.**

Many companies share the problem we see embedded in the Folgers example: They must be clear about whom they are trying to reach and about what they can say that will resonate with consumers. Companies address this challenge through a process referred to as STP marketing. From their standpoint, the process is critical because it leads to decisions about *whom* they need to advertise to, *what* value proposition they want to present to them, and *how* they plan to reach them with their message.

LO1 STP Marketing

The Folgers example illustrates the process that marketers use to decide whom to advertise to and what to say. The Folgers brand team started with the diverse market of all possible coffee drinkers and then broke the market down by age segments. The team then selected *just-graduated 20-somethings* as its target segment. The **target segment** is the subgroup (of the larger market) chosen as the focal point for the marketing program and advertising campaign.

Markets are segmented; products are positioned. To pursue the target segment, a firm organizes its marketing and advertising efforts around a coherent positioning strategy. **Positioning** is the process of designing and representing one's product or service so that

it will occupy a distinct and valued place in the target customer's mind. **Positioning strategy** involves the selection of key themes or concepts that the organization will feature when communicating this distinctiveness to the target segment. In Folgers's case, the positioning concept is "Tolerate Mornings," expressed in a way that positions Folgers so that just-graduated 20-somethings can relate. Folks on the Folgers team assumed they would not convert this segment with an old-fashioned slogan like "The best part of waking up is Folgers in your cup." Instead, they used a skillful, low-cost approach to getting the message in front of the target: Let YouTube do it!

Planning the Folgers marketing strategy followed the specific sequence illustrated in Exhibit 4.1: *segmenting, targeting,* and *positioning*. This sequence of activities, often referred to as **STP marketing**, represents a sound basis for generating effective advertising.[2] While no formulas or models guarantee success, the STP approach is strongly recommended for markets in which customers' needs and preferences are diverse. In markets with any significant degree of diversity, it is impossible to design one product that would appeal

Exhibit 4.1
STP Marketing

to everyone or one advertising campaign that would communicate with everyone. Organizations that lose sight of this simple premise run into trouble.

In most product categories, different consumers are looking for different things, and the only way for a company to take advantage of the sales potential represented by different customer segments is to develop and market a different brand for each segment. No company has done this better than cosmetics juggernaut Estée Lauder.[3] Lauder has more than a dozen cosmetic brands, each developed for a different target segment.[4] Exhibit 4.2 shows just some of the cosmetics brands that Estée Lauder has marketed to appeal to diverse target segments. Check out the company's current brand lineup at http://www.elcompanies.com.

We offer the Estée Lauder example to make two key points before moving on. First, STP marketing is a lot more complicated than the Folgers case; it involves far more than deciding to target a particular age group. Second, as in the descriptions of the groups served by Estée Lauder, many factors beyond demographics can come into play when marketers identify target segments. Considerations such as attitudes, lifestyles, and basic values all may play a role in describing customer segments.

Compare the ad for the Marines with the ad for Hard Candy lip gloss. Both ran in *Seventeen* magazine, so it is safe to say that both advertisers were trying to reach adolescent girls. But it should be obvious that the advertisers were trying to reach out to very different segments of adolescent females.

Exhibit 4.2
Something for Everyone from Estée Lauder

Estée Lauder	For women with conservative values and upscale tastes
Clinique	A no-nonsense brand that represents functional grooming for Middle America
Bobbi Brown	For the working mom who skillfully manages a career and her family and manages to look good in the process
M.A.C.	For those who want to make a bolder statement (as represented by such spokespersons as Boy George, Missy Elliott, Linda Evangelista, and RuPaul)
Prescriptives	For a hip, urban, multiethnic target segment
Origins	For those who appreciate the connection between Mother Nature and human nature, signaled by earthy packaging and natural ingredients

Beyond STP Marketing

Even when STP marketing yields profitable outcomes, one must presume that success will not last indefinitely. Indeed, an important feature of marketing and advertising—a feature that can make these professions both terribly interesting and terribly frustrating—is their dynamic nature. To paraphrase a

To put it bluntly, it is hard to imagine a marine captain wearing Hard Candy lip gloss.

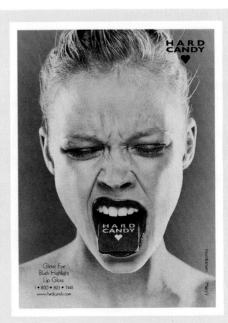

popular saying, shifts happen. Consumer preferences shift, competitors improve their marketing strategies, and technology changes, making a popular product obsolete. Successful marketing strategies need to be modified or even reinvented as shifts occur in the organization's competitive environment.

To maintain the vitality and profitability of its products or services, an organization has two options. The first is to reassess the segmentation strategy. Reassessment may come through a more detailed examination of the current target segment to develop new and better ways of meeting its needs, or the organization may have to adopt new targets and position new brands for them, as Estée Lauder often does.

The second option is to pursue a product differentiation strategy. As defined in Chapter 1, product differentiation focuses the firm's efforts on emphasizing or even creating differences for its brands to distinguish them from competitors' offerings. Advertising plays a critical role as part of the product differentiation strategy because often the consumer will have to be convinced that the intended difference is meaningful. For example, Schick's response to Gillette's Mach3 Turbo was the Schick Quattro with four blades instead of three. But does that fourth blade really deliver a better shave? Following a product differentiation strategy, the role of Schick's advertising is to convince men that that fourth blade is essential for a close shave. But next up is Gillette's Fusion, with five blades to shave you closer than close. And so it goes.

The message is that marketing strategies and the advertising that supports them are never really final. Successes realized through proper application of STP marketing can be short lived in highly competitive markets, where any successful innovation is almost sure to be copied or one-upped by competitors.

Thus, the value-creation process for marketers and advertisers is continuous; STP marketing must be pursued over and over again and may be supplemented with product differentiation strategies.

<div class="sidebar">

market segmentation the breaking down of a large, heterogeneous market into more homogeneous submarkets or segments

heavy users consumers who purchase a product or service much more frequently than others

</div>

LO 2 Identifying Target Segments

The first step in STP marketing involves breaking down large, heterogeneous markets into more manageable submarkets or customer segments. This activity is known as **market segmentation**. It can be accomplished in many ways, but, whatever the method, each segment should have common characteristics that will lead the members of that segment to respond distinctively to a marketing program. For a segment to be really useful, advertisers also must be able to reach that segment with information about the product. Typically, this means that advertisers must be able to identify the media that will allow them to get a message to the segment. For example, teenage males can be reached through product placements in video games and on selected rap, contemporary rock, or country radio stations.

Segmenting by Usage and Commitment

One of the most common ways to segment markets is by consumers' usage patterns or commitment levels. With respect to usage patterns, it is important to recognize that, for most products and services, some users will purchase much more frequently than others. It is common to find that **heavy users** in a category account for the majority of a product's sales and thus become the preferred or primary target segment.[5]

To illustrate, Coffee-mate executives launched a program to get to know their customers better by returning calls to those who had left a complaint or suggestion using the toll-free number printed on the product packaging.[6] As a result, they met Paula Baumgartner, a 44-year-old who consumes four jars of Coffee-mate's mocha-flavored creamer every week (more than 200 jars a year!). Conventional marketing thought holds that it is in Coffee-mate's best interest to get to know heavy users like Paula in great depth and to make them a focal point of the company's marketing strategy.

In spite of its obvious appeal, the heavy-user focus has some potential downsides. For one, devoted users may need no encouragement at all to keep consuming. A heavy-user focus could take attention and resources away from those who do need encouragement to purchase the marketer's brand. Perhaps most important, heavy users may differ significantly from average or infrequent users in terms of their motivations to consume, their approach to the brand, or their image of the brand.

Another segmentation option combines prior usage patterns with commitment levels to identify four fundamental segment types:[7]

- **Nonusers** offer the lowest level of opportunity relative to the other three groups.

- **Brand-loyal users** are a tremendous asset if they are the advertiser's customers, but they are difficult to convert if they are loyal to a competitor.

- **Switchers** or **variety seekers** often buy what is on sale or choose brands that offer discount coupons or other price incentives. Whether they are pursued through price incentives, high-profile advertising campaigns, or both, switchers are a costly target segment. Marketers can spend heavily to get their business, merely to have it disappear quickly when these customers move on.

- **Emergent consumers** are motivated by many different factors, but they share one notable characteristic: Their brand preferences are still under development. In most product categories, there is a gradual but constant influx of first-time buyers. Reasons for this influx include purchase triggers such as college graduation or a new job. Immigration also can be a source of new customers in many product categories.

Each segment represents a unique opportunity for the advertiser. For example, targeting emergents with messages that fit their age or social circumstances may produce only modest effects in the short run, but it eventually may yield a brand loyalty that pays handsome rewards for the discerning organization. Developing advertising campaigns to win with first-time users often is referred to as **point-of-entry marketing**. This was exactly Folgers' rationale in targeting *just-*

Wells Fargo Bank targets students at the University of Arizona with this ad. Why do you think these emergent consumers present a long-term opportunity for Wells Fargo?

graduated 20-somethings. Similarly, banks actively recruit college students, who have limited financial resources in the short term but offer excellent potential as long-term customers.

Segmenting by Demographics

A widely used method for selecting target segments is **demographic segmentation**, which divides consumers according to basic descriptors such as age, gender, race, marital status, income, education, and occupation (see the array of possibilities at http://www.factfinder.census.gov). Demographic information has special value in market segmentation because, if an advertiser knows the demographic characteristics of the target segment, choosing media to efficiently reach that segment is easier.

Demographic information has two specific applications. First, demographics are commonly used to describe or profile segments that have been identified with some other variable. If an organization first had

segmented its market in terms of product usage rates, the next step would be to describe or profile its heavy users in terms of demographic characteristics such as age or income. In fact, one of the most common approaches for identifying target segments is to combine information about usage patterns with demographics.

Mobil Oil Corporation used such an approach in segmenting the market for gasoline buyers and identified five basic segments: Road Warriors, True Blues, Generation F3, Homebodies, and Price Shoppers.[8] Extensive research on more than 2,000 motorists revealed considerable insight about these five segments. At one extreme, Road Warriors spend at least $1,200 per year at gas stations; they buy premium gasoline and snacks and beverages and sometimes opt for a car wash. Road Warriors are generally more affluent, middle-aged males who drive 25,000 to 50,000 miles per year. (Note how Mobil combined information about usage patterns with demographics to provide a detailed picture of the segment.) In contrast, Price Shoppers spend no more than $700 annually at gas stations, are generally less affluent, rarely buy premium, and show no loyalty to particular brands or stations. In terms of relative segment sizes, there are about 25 percent more Price Shoppers on the highways than Road Warriors. If you were the marketing vice president at Mobil, which of these two segments would you target? Second, demographic categories are used frequently as the starting point in market segmentation. This was true in the Folgers example, where young people who recently had graduated from college turned out to be the segment of interest. Demographics also will be a major consideration for targeting by the tourism industry; often, families with young children are the marketer's primary focus. For instance, the Bahamian government launched a program to attract families to its island paradise. But instead of reaching out to mom and dad, Bahamian officials made their appeal to kids by targeting the 2- to 11-year-old viewing audience of Nickelodeon's cable television channel.[9] Marketing to and through children is always complex—and often controversial as well.

Another demographic group that is receiving renewed attention from advertisers is the "woopies,"

or well-off older people. In the United States, consumers over 50 years old control two-thirds of the country's wealth, around $28 trillion. The median net worth of households headed by persons 55 to 64 is 15 times larger than the net worth for households headed by a person under age 35. Put in simple terms, for most 20-year-olds, $100 is a lot of money. For woopies, $100 is change back from the purchase of a $10,000 home theater system. Marketers such as Sony and Virgin Entertainment Group have reconsidered their product offerings with woopies in mind.[10] By 2025, the number of people over 50 will grow by 80 percent to become a third of the U.S. population. Growth in the woopie segment also will be dramatic in other countries, such as Japan and the nations of Western Europe. Still, like any other age segment, older consumers are a diverse group, and the temptation to stereotype must be resisted. Some marketers advocate partitioning older consumers into groups aged 50–64, 65–74, 75–84, and 85 or older, as a means of reflecting important differences in needs. That's a good start, but again, age alone will not tell the whole story.

Segmenting by Geography

Geographic segmentation needs little explanation other than to emphasize how useful geography is in segmenting markets. Geographic segmentation may be conducted within a country by region (for example, the Pacific Northwest versus New England in the United States). Climate and topographical features yield dramatic differences in consumption by region for products such as snow tires and surfboards, but geography also can correlate with other differences that are not so obvious. Eating and food preparation habits, entertainment preferences, recreational activities, and other aspects of lifestyle have been shown to vary along geographic lines. As shown on the U.S. map, even a brand like Hostess Twinkies has its red and blue states.

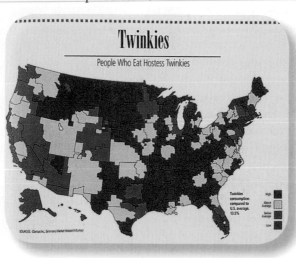

The red regions have the highest consumption of Twinkies.

geodemographic segmentation
market segmentation that identifies neighborhoods sharing common demographic characteristics

psychographics a form of market research that emphasizes the understanding of consumers' activities, interests, and opinions

lifestyle segmentation
market segmentation that identifies consumers sharing similar activities, interests, and opinions

In recent years, skillful marketers have merged information on where people live with the U.S. Census Bureau's demographic data to produce a form of market segmentation known as geodemographic segmentation.[11] **Geodemographic segmentation** identifies neighborhoods (by ZIP codes) around the country that share common demographic characteristics. One such system, known as PRIZM (potential rating index by ZIP marketing), identifies 62 market segments that encompass all the ZIP codes in the United States. Each of these segments has similar lifestyle characteristics and can be found throughout the country. For example, the American Dreams segment is found in many metropolitan neighborhoods and comprises upwardly mobile ethnic minorities, many of whom were foreign-born. This segment's brand preferences differ from those of people belonging to the Rural Industrial segment, who are young families with one or both parents working at low-wage jobs in small-town America.

Systems such as PRIZM are very popular because of the depth of segment description they provide. Also, they can identify where the segment is located precisely (for more details, search for PRIZM at http://www.claritas.com).

Segmenting by Psychographics and Lifestyle

Psychographics is a term that advertisers created in the mid-1960s to refer to a form of research that emphasizes the understanding of consumers' activities, interests, and opinions (AIOs).[12] Many advertising agencies were using demographic variables for segmentation purposes, but they wanted insights into consumers' motivations, which demographic variables did not provide. Psychographics were created as a tool to supplement the use of demographic data. Because a focus on consumers' activities, interests, and opinions often produces insights into differences in the lifestyles of various segments, this approach usually results in **lifestyle segmentation**. Details about the lifestyle of a target segment can be valuable for creating advertising messages that ring true to the consumer.

Lifestyle or psychographic segmentation can be customized with a focus on the issues germane to a single product category, or it may be pursued so that the resulting segments have general applicability to many different product or service categories. An illustration of the former is research conducted for Pillsbury to segment the eating habits of American households.[13] Based on consumer interviews with more than 3,000 people, this study identified five population segments with distinct eating styles:

- **Chase and Grabbits,** at 26 percent of the population, are heavy users of all forms of fast food. These are people who can make a meal out of microwave popcorn; as long as the popcorn keeps hunger at bay and is convenient, this segment is happy with its meal.

- **Functional Feeders,** at 18 percent of the population, are a bit older than the Chase and Grabbits but no less convenience oriented. Because they are more likely to have families, their preferences for convenient foods involve frozen products that are prepared quickly at home. They constantly seek faster ways to prepare the traditional foods they grew up with.

- **Down-Home Stokers,** at 21 percent of the population, involve blue-collar households with modest incomes. They are very loyal to their regional diets, such as meat and potatoes in the Midwest and clam chowder in New England. Fried chicken, biscuits and gravy, and bacon and eggs make this segment the champion of cholesterol.

Fotocrisis/Shutterstock.com

- **Careful Cooks,** at 20 percent of the population, are more prevalent on the West Coast. They have replaced most of the red meat in their diet with pasta, fish, skinless chicken, and mounds of fresh fruit and vegetables. They believe they are knowledgeable about nutritional issues and are willing to experiment with foods that offer healthful options.

- **Happy Cookers,** the remaining 15 percent of the population, are a shrinking segment. These cooks are family oriented and take substantial satisfaction from preparing a complete homemade meal for the family. Young mothers in this segment are aware of nutritional issues but will bend the rules with homemade meat dishes, casseroles, pies, cakes, and cookies.

Even these abbreviated descriptions of Pillsbury's five psychographic segments should make it clear that very different marketing and advertising programs are called for to appeal to each group.

As noted, lifestyle segmentation studies also can be pursued with no particular product category as a focus, and the resulting segments could prove useful for many different marketers. A notable example of this approach is the VALS (originally for "values and lifestyles") system developed by SRI International and now owned and marketed by Strategic Business Insights, an SRI spinoff, of Menlo Park, California.[14] The VALS framework originally had nine potential segments, but in the late 1980s was revised to feature eight segments. The VALS system groups consumers by psychological characteristics and several key demographics instead of using social values as it originally did. As shown in Exhibit 4.3, the segments are organized in terms of resources (including age, income, and education) and primary motivation. For instance, experiencers are relatively affluent and expressive. This enthusiastic and risk-taking group

Exhibit 4.3
VALS™ Segments

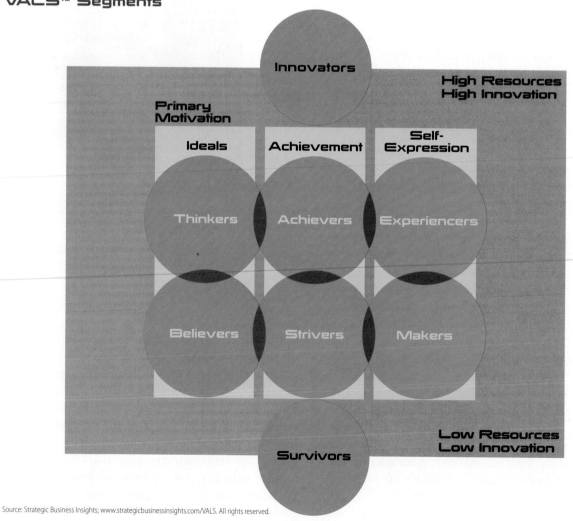

is highly social. Its members look to sports, recreation, exercise, and social activities as outlets for their abundant energies. Strategic Business Insights sells detailed information and marketing recommendations about the eight segments to corporations' new product development and marketing divisions.

Segmenting by Benefits

Another segmentation approach developed by advertising researchers and used extensively over the past 30 years is **benefit segmentation**. In benefit segmentation, target segments are delineated by the various benefit packages that different consumers want from competing products and brands. For instance, different people want different benefits from their automobiles. Some consumers want efficient and reliable transportation; others want speed, excitement, and glamour; and still others want luxury, comfort, and prestige. One product possibly could not serve such diverse benefit segments. Similarly, the two ads for hair care products promise different kinds of benefits to comparable consumers.

Segmenting Business Buyers

Thus far, our discussion of segmentation options has focused on ways to segment **consumer markets**. Consumer markets are the markets for products and services purchased by individuals or households to satisfy their specific needs. Consumer marketing often is compared and contrasted with business-to-business marketing. **Business markets** are the institutional buyers who purchase items to be used in other products and services or to be resold to other businesses or households. Although advertising is more prevalent in consumer markets, products and services such as consulting services and a wide array of business machines are promoted commonly to business customers around the world. Hence, segmentation strategies also are valuable for business-to-business marketers.

Business markets can be segmented using several of the options already discussed.[15] For example, business customers differ in their usage rates and geographic locations, so these variables may be productive bases for segmenting business markets. Additionally, one of the most common approaches uses the Standard Industrial Classification (SIC) codes prepared by the U.S. Census Bureau. SIC information is helpful for

Courtesy of TIGI Bed Head.

Courtesy of TIGI Catwalk.

Bed Head promises a "superstar" look, while Catwalk is all about care for curls: defrizz, define, detangle.

identifying categories of businesses and then pinpointing the precise locations of these organizations.

Some of the more sophisticated segmentation methods used by firms that market to individual consumers do not translate well to business markets.[16] Rarely would there be a place for psychographic or lifestyle segmentation in the business-to-business setting. In business markets, advertisers fall back on simpler strategies that are easier to work with from the perspective of the sales force. Segmentation by a potential customer's stage in the purchase process is

one such strategy. It turns out that first-time prospects, novices, and sophisticates want very different packages of benefits from their vendors, so they should be targeted separately in advertising and sales programs.

LO 3 Prioritizing Target Segments

Whether segmentation is done through usage patterns, demographic characteristics, geographic location, benefit packages, or any combination of options, it typically yields a mix of segments that vary in their attractiveness to the advertiser. In pursuing STP marketing, the advertiser must get beyond this potentially confusing mixture of segments to a selected subset that will become the target for its marketing and advertising programs. Recall the example of Mobil Oil Corporation and the segments of gasoline buyers it identified via usage patterns and demographic descriptors. What criteria should Mobil use to help decide between Road Warriors and Price Shoppers as possible targets?

Perhaps the most fundamental criterion in segment selection revolves around what the members of the segment want versus the organization's ability to provide it. Every organization has distinctive strengths and weaknesses that must be acknowledged when choosing its target segment. The organization may be particularly strong in some aspect of manufacturing. Or perhaps its strength lies in well-trained and loyal service personnel, like those at FedEx, who effectively can implement new service programs initiated for customers, such as next-day delivery "absolutely, positively by 10:30 AM." To serve a target segment, an organization may have to commit substantial resources to acquire or develop the capabilities to provide what that segment wants. If the price tag for these new capabilities is too high, the organization must find another segment.

Another major consideration in segment selection is the segments' size and growth potential. Segment size is a function of the number of people,

households, or institutions in the segment, plus their willingness to spend in the product category. When assessing size, advertisers must keep in mind that the number of people in a segment of heavy users may be relatively small, but the extraordinary usage rates of these consumers can more than make up for their small numbers. In addition to looking for adequate size as of today, marketers often are most interested in devoting resources to segments projected for dramatic growth. As we have seen already, the purchasing power and growth projections for people age 50 and older have made this age segment one that many companies are targeting.

So does bigger always mean better when choosing target segments? The answer is a function of the third major criterion for segment selection. In choosing a target segment, an advertiser must also look at the **competitive field**—companies that compete for the segment's business—and then decide whether it has a particular expertise, or perhaps just a bigger budget, that would allow it to serve the segment more effectively.

Upon considering the competitive field, marketers often determine that smaller is better when selecting target segments. Almost by definition, large segments tend to be established segments already targeted by many companies. Trying to enter the competitive field in a mature segment isn't easy because established competitors (with their many brands) can be expected to respond aggressively with advertising campaigns or price promotions in an effort to repel any newcomer.

Alternatively, large segments simply may be poorly defined segments; that is, marketers may need to break down a large segment into smaller categories before they can understand consumers' needs well enough to serve them effectively. The segment of older consumers—age 50 and older—is huge, but in most instances, it would simply be too big to be valuable as a target. Too much diversity exists in the needs and preferences of this age group, so further segmentation based on other demographic or perhaps psychographic variables is called for before an appropriate target can be located.

Tony Mathews/Shutterstock.com

The smaller-is-better principle has become so popular in choosing target segments that it now is referred to as niche marketing. A **market niche** is a relatively small group of consumers who have a unique set of needs and who typically are willing to pay a premium price to the firm that specializes in meeting those needs.[17] The small size of a market niche often means serving it would not be profitable for more than one organization. Thus, identifying and developing products for market niches reduces the threat of competitors developing imitative products.

Niche marketing will continue to grow in popularity as the mass media splinter into a more complex and narrowly defined array of specialized vehicles. A few decades ago, cable television enabled marketers to target narrow segments such as fitness fanatics and history buffs, and more recently, the Internet has become the vehicle for communicating with people who have very specific concerns and hobbies. For example, people with a particular health issue—such as the 2 percent of the population with celiac disease, who cannot eat foods containing wheat and other sources of gluten—go online to do research and set up support groups. General Mills decided to serve this market niche, so it posted a list of its gluten-free products on its website. Now whenever consumers search for "celiac" or "gluten-free," a link to that list turns up near the top of the results. And when consumers got wind of General Mills' plan to offer gluten-free versions of Betty Crocker baking mixes, they quickly spread the news themselves, using Twitter.[18]

Let's return to the question faced by Mobil Oil Corporation. Who should it target—Road Warriors or Price Shoppers? Road Warriors are a more attractive segment in terms of both segment size and growth potential. Although there are more Price Shoppers in terms of sheer numbers, Road Warriors spend more at the gas station, making them the larger segment from the standpoint of revenue generation. Road Warriors are also more prone to buy extras, such as a sandwich and a coffee, which could be extremely profitable. In contrast, it's hard to win in gasoline retailing by competing on price.

Mobil selected Road Warriors as its target segment and developed a positioning strategy it referred to as "Friendly Serve." Gas prices went up at Mobil stations, but Mobil also improved the gas-purchasing experience. Cleaner restrooms and better lighting yielded sales gains between 2 and 5 percent. Next, more attendants were hired to run between the pump

On the Internet, General Mills found consumers who are hunting for gluten-free products and who spread the word when they find something they like.

Olga Lyubkina/Shutterstock.com.

and the snack bar to get Road Warriors in and out quickly—complete with their sandwich and beverage. Early results indicated that helpful attendants boosted station sales by another 15 to 20 percent.

LO 4 Formulating the Positioning Strategy

If a firm has been careful in segmenting the market and selecting its targets, then a positioning strategy should occur naturally. In addition, as an aspect of positioning strategy, we entertain ideas about how a firm can communicate best to the target segment what it has to offer. This is where advertising plays its vital role. A positioning strategy will include particular ideas or

themes that must be communicated effectively if the marketing program is to succeed.

Positioning Strategies

Any sound positioning strategy includes several essential elements. Effective positioning strategies are based on meaningful commitments of organizational resources to produce substantive value for the target segment. They also are consistent internally and over time, and they feature simple and distinctive themes. Each of these essential elements is described below.

Deliver on the Promise

For a positioning strategy to be effective and remain effective over time, the organization must be committed to creating substantive value for the customer. Take the example of Mobil Oil Corporation and its target segment, the Road Warriors. Road Warriors are willing to pay a little more for gas if it comes with extras such as prompt service or fresh coffee. So Mobil must create an ad campaign that depicts its employees as the brightest, friendliest, most helpful people you'd ever want to meet. The company asks its ad agency to come up with a catchy jingle that will remind people about the great services they can expect at a Mobil station. It spends millions of dollars running these ads over and over. Will it win the enduring loyalty of the Road Warriors? Certainly, a new ad campaign will have to be created to make Road Warriors aware of the new Mobil, but it all falls apart if they drive in with great expectations and the company's people do not live up to them.

Effective positioning begins with substance. In the case of Mobil's "Friendly Serve" strategy, this means keeping restrooms attractive and clean, adding better lighting to all areas of the station, and upgrading the quality of the snacks and beverages available in each station's convenience store. It also means hiring more attendants and training and motivating them to anticipate and fulfill the needs of the harried Road Warrior. Raising service levels at thousands of stations nationwide is expensive and time consuming, but without some substantive change, there can be no hope of retaining the Road Warrior's lucrative business.

There's Magic in Consistency

A positioning strategy also must be consistent internally and consistent over time. Regarding internal consistency, everything must work in combination to reinforce a distinct perception in the consumer's eyes about what a brand stands for. If we have chosen to position our airline as the one that will be known for on-time reliability, then we certainly would invest in things like extensive preventive maintenance and state-of-the-art baggage-handling facilities. There would be no need for exclusive airport lounges as part of this strategy. If our target segment wants reliable transportation, then this should be our obsession. This particular obsession has made Southwest Airlines a formidable competitor, even against much larger airlines, earning profits year after year, even when others have faltered.[19]

A strategy also needs consistency over time. Consumers have perceptual defenses that allow them to screen or ignore most of the ad messages they are exposed to. Breaking through the clutter and establishing what a brand stands for is a tremendous challenge, but it is a challenge made easier by consistent positioning. If year in and year out an advertiser communicates the same basic themes, then the message may get through and shape the way consumers perceive the brand. An example of a consistent approach is the long-running

FOR A POSITIONING STRATEGY TO **BE EFFECTIVE AND REMAIN EFFECTIVE** OVER TIME, THE ORGANIZATION MUST BE COMMITTED TO **CREATING SUBSTANTIVE VALUE** FOR THE CUSTOMER.

"Good Neighbor" ads of State Farm Insurance. While the specific copy changes, the thematic core of the campaign does not change.

Make It Different Simply

Simplicity and distinctiveness are essential to the advertising task. No matter how much substance has been built into a product, it will fail in the marketplace if the consumer doesn't perceive what the product can do. In a world of harried consumers who can be expected to ignore, distort, or forget most of the ads they are exposed to, complicated, imitative messages simply have no chance of getting through. The basic premise of a positioning strategy must be simple and distinctive if it is to be communicated effectively to the target segment.

Verizon is notable for its use of a simple message about the wireless network's reliability. The anonymous but amiable "Verizon test guy" who consistently pops up in the company's marketing materials reassures us that we can trust him to help us use a service that is mysterious but essential in modern times. His "Can you hear me now?" expresses in basic terms what it means for this high-tech service to perform optimally, and the "Good" that always follows that question promises us that Verizon works relentlessly to deliver on its promise.

Most important, the Verizon test guy is more than just an actor in an advertising campaign. He embodies a real job function performed by Verizon workers to deliver on the promise of reliable service. The company in fact hires scores of technicians to drive around service areas in vehicles loaded with computers, antennas, and GPS, testing for dead zones and weaknesses in the cellular network. Their objective is to keep dropped calls and blocked reception below 2 percent of calls.[20]

Positioning Themes

Positioning themes that are simple and distinctive help an organization make internal decisions that yield substantive value for customers, and they assist in the development of focused ad campaigns to break through the clutter of competitors' advertising. Choosing a viable positioning theme is one of the most important decisions that advertisers face. In many ways, the raison d'être for STP marketing is to generate viable positioning themes.

Positioning themes take many forms, and they can benefit from creative breakthroughs. Yet while novelty and creativity are valued in developing positioning themes, some basic principles should be considered when selecting a theme. Whenever possible, it is helpful if the organization can settle on a single premise—such as "Tolerate Mornings"—to reflect its positioning strategy.[21] In addition, three fundamental options should always be considered in selecting a positioning theme: benefit positioning, user positioning, and competitive positioning.[22]

"Friendly Serve" is an example of **benefit positioning**. Notice that it expresses a distinctive customer benefit. This single-benefit focus is the first option that should be considered when formulating a positioning strategy. Consumers purchase products to derive functional, emotional, or self-expressive benefits, so an emphasis on the primary benefit they can expect to receive from a brand is fundamental. While it might seem that more compelling positioning themes would result from promising consumers a wide array

HARD WORK, ATTENTION TO DETAIL, PERSONAL SERVICE. SOUND FAMILIAR? WE LIVE WHERE YOU LIVE.

State Farm® agents are business owners too. That's why they know how to take care of you and your business insurance needs with comprehensive coverage, reasonable rates and monthly payments. Call your State Farm agent to find out if you qualify for up to 30% off your premium.

LIKE A GOOD NEIGHBOR STATE FARM IS THERE.®

Call your neighborhood State Farm Agent, or visit statefarm.com®

Providing Insurance and Financial Services

STATE FARM'S MARKETING CONSISTENTLY COMMUNICATES "LIKE A GOOD NEIGHBOR, STATE FARM IS THERE" BOTH DIRECTLY AND WITH RELATED SLOGANS SUCH AS "WE LIVE WHERE YOU LIVE."

Courtesy, Colgate-Palmolive Company.

When the functional benefits of 24-hour protection and no white residue became commonplace, this deodorant advertiser thought of emotional benefits.

CEO James E. Preston insisted that tie-ins with high-profile social issues can cut through the clutter of rivals' marketing messages.[23] It's not surprising, then, that Avon has been a regular sponsor of important causes, such as the Avon Walk for Breast Cancer. Likewise, Star-Kist has promoted dolphin-safe fishing practices. Even smaller companies with smaller budgets have set up micro-sponsorships, which enable a wide range of brands to help consumers feel better about what they buy.[24]

Self-expressive benefits also can be the bases for effective positioning strategies. With this approach, the purpose of an advertising campaign is to create distinctive images or personalities for brands and then to invite consumers into brand communities.[25] These brand images or personalities can be of value to individuals as they use the brands to make statements about themselves to other people. Feelings of status, pride, and prestige might be derived from the imagery associated with brands such as BMW, Rolex, and Gucci. Brand imagery also can be valued in gift-giving contexts. The woman who gives Calvin Klein's Euphoria for men is expressing something very different than the woman who gives Old Spice. Advertisers help brands acquire meaning and self-expressive benefits to distinguish them beyond their functional forms.

Besides benefit positioning, another fundamental option is **user positioning**. Instead of featuring a benefit or attribute of the brand, this option takes a specific profile of the target user as the focal point of the positioning strategy. In advertising for high-performance Pinarello bicycles, the camera gazes lovingly at the bike's components, attracting serious cyclists who are passionate about the technical features. An ad for novice riders or parents buying for their children might emphasize low price or deliver an emotional appeal.

The third option for a positioning theme is **competitive positioning**. This option sometimes is useful in well-established product categories with a crowded competitive field. The goal is to use an explicit reference to an existing competitor to help define precisely what the brand can do. Often, smaller brands use this approach to carve out a position relative to the market share leader in their category. For instance, many companies selling over-the-counter pain relievers have used market leader Tylenol as an explicit point of reference in their positioning strategies. Excedrin, for

of benefits, keep in mind that multiple-benefit strategies are hard to implement. Not only will they send mixed signals within an organization about what a brand stands for, but they also will place a great burden on advertising to deliver and validate multiple messages.

Functional benefits are the place to start in selecting a positioning theme, but in many mature product categories, the functional benefits provided by the various brands in the competitive field are essentially the same. In these instances, the organization may turn to emotion in an effort to distinguish its brand. Emotional benefit positioning may involve a promise of exhilaration, like "Exciting Armpits," or may feature a way to avoid negative feelings, such as the embarrassment felt in social settings due to bad breath.

Another way to add an emotional benefit in one's positioning is by linking a brand with important causes that provoke intense feelings. Avon Products' former

repositioning
returning to the STP marketing process to arrive at a revised positioning strategy

one, has attempted to position itself as the best option to treat a simple headache, granting that Tylenol might be the better choice to treat the various symptoms of a cold or the flu.

Besides using any of the three fundamental options for creating a positioning strategy, an advertiser can combine these options to create a hybrid strategy in which two or more of them work together. A frequent hybrid is benefit-plus-user positioning. Whether strategies are used alone or in combination, the point is to arrive at a strategy that reflects substance, consistency, simplicity, and distinctiveness.

Repositioning

STP marketing is far from a precise science, so marketers do not always get it right the first time. Furthermore, markets are dynamic. Even when marketers get it right, competitors can react, or consumers' preferences may shift for any number of reasons. Then, what once was a viable positioning strategy must be altered if the brand is to survive. One of the best ways to revive an ailing brand or fix the lackluster performance of a new market entry is to redeploy the STP process to arrive at a revised positioning strategy. This type of effort commonly is referred to as **repositioning**.

Even though repositioning efforts are a fact of life for marketers and advertisers, they present a tremendous challenge. When brands that have been around for some time are forced to reposition, perceptions of the brand that have evolved over the years must be changed through advertising. This problem is common for brands that become popular with one generation but fade as that generation ages and emergent consumers come to view the brand as passé. So, for several years, the makers of Pontiac tried to breathe new life into their brand with catchy ad slogans such as "Luxury with Attitude" and "Fuel for the Soul." Ultimately, none of these efforts could save a brand that had become passé.[26]

In contrast, marketers of many other brands have persuaded consumers to take a fresh look. Mazda found itself in a funk in the '90s when it tried to go head-to-head with Toyota and Honda around dependability and good value. So Mazda's new CEO decided to return the brand to its roots

What elements of this ad signal Xootr's user and competitive position?

as a stylish and fun-to-drive vehicle, targeting the 25 percent of the car-buying market who consider themselves auto enthusiasts. The "Zoom Zoom" theme resulted, and with it the Mazda brand got its groove back.[27]

LO 5 Capturing Your Strategy in a Value Proposition

Marketers have to assess customer segments, target markets, and the competitive field to make decisions about various kinds of positioning themes that might be appropriate in guiding the creation of a campaign. Not only can these tasks get complicated, but as time passes, new people from both the client and agency sides will be brought in to work on the brand team. Before long, team members can lose sight of what the brand used to stand for in the eyes of the target segment. If the people who create the advertising for a brand get confused about the brand's desired identity, then the consumer is bound to get confused as well.

This is a recipe for disaster. We need a way to capture and keep a record of what our brand is supposed to stand for in the eyes of the target segment.

Although there are many ways to capture one's strategy on paper, we recommend doing it by articulating the brand's value proposition. The following definition of a **value proposition** is a natural extension of marketing concepts; it simply consolidates this chapter's emphasis on customer benefits:

A brand's value proposition is a statement of the functional, emotional, and self-expressive benefits delivered by the brand that provide value to customers in the target segment. A balanced value proposition is the basis for brand choice and customer loyalty, and is critical to the ongoing success of a firm.[28]

If a company is crystal clear on what value it believes its brand offers to consumers, and everyone on the brand team shares that clarity, the foundation is in place for creating effective advertising and integrated brand promotion.

Exhibit 4.4 lists the value propositions for two global brands.[29] Notice from these two statements that, over time, many different aspects can be built into the value proposition for a brand. Brands like Nike may offer benefits in all three benefit categories; McDonald's from two of the three. Benefit complexity of this type is extremely valuable when the various benefits reinforce one another. In these examples, this cross-benefit reinforcement is especially strong for Nike, with all levels working together to deliver the desired state of performance excellence.

The job of advertising is to carry the message to the target segment about the value that is offered by the brand. For brands with complex value propositions such as McDonald's and Nike, no single ad could be expected to reflect all aspects of the brand's value. If any given ad is not communicating some selected aspects of the brand's purported value, then we have to ask, why run that ad?

One gains tremendous leverage from the process of STP marketing because it is all about anticipating and servicing customers' wants and needs. But targeting groups for focused advertising and promotion has a controversial side. This is especially true when children are in your target market.

> **value proposition**
> a statement of the functional, emotional, and self-expressive benefits that are delivered by the brand and provide value to customers in the target segment

---

Exhibit 4.4
Value Propositions for Two Popular Brands

McDonald's

Functional benefits	Good-tasting hamburgers, fries, and drinks served fast; extras such as playgrounds, prizes, premiums, and games.
Emotional benefits	Kids—fun via excitement at birthday parties; relationship with Ronald McDonald and other characters; a feeling of special family times. Adults—warmth via time spent enjoying a meal with the kids; admiration of McDonald's social involvement such as McDonald's Charities and Ronald McDonald Houses.

Nike

Functional benefits	High-technology shoe that will improve performance and provide comfort.
Emotional benefits	The exhilaration of athletic performance excellence, feeling engaged, active, and healthy; exhilaration from admiring professional and college athletes as they perform wearing "your brand"—when they win, you win too.
Self-expressive benefits	Using the brand endorsed by high-profile athletes lets your peers know your desire to compete and excel.

GLOBAL MICKEY MOUSE TAKES THE HIGH ROAD

Critics including the American Psychological Association and American Academy of Pediatrics have called for restrictions on advertising to children. One reason is concern that promotion of junk food has contributed to America's obesity crisis. Disney has tried a different route. It launched a companywide initiative to promote healthy eating and eliminate most foods with high fat and sugar content from its theme-park menus and co-promotions with corporate partners. Now most of the foods Disney promotes contain 0 grams of trans fats, and most of the children's meals at its theme parks are sold with healthier sides, such as apples and milk instead of fries and soft drinks.

Sources: Walt Disney Company, "Children and Family," *2008 Corporate Responsibility Report*, Disney corporate website, http://a.media.global.go.com/corporateresponsibility/pdf/Disney_CR_Report_2008.pdf (accessed September 8, 2009), 16–20; and Merissa Marr and Janet Adamy, "Disney Pulls Characters from Junk Food," *Wall Street Journal*, October 17, 2006, D1, D6.

Monkey Business Images/Shutterstock.com

Putting It All Together

To pull together the concepts presented in this chapter, we can use a practical model: the strategic planning triangle proposed by advertising researchers Esther Thorson and Jeri Moore.[30] As shown in Exhibit 4.5, the corners of this triangle represent the segment(s) selected as targets for the campaign, the brand's value proposition, and the array of persuasion tools that will be deployed to achieve campaign goals.

The starting point of STP marketing is identifying who the customers or prospects are and what

they want, so identification and specification of the target segment appear at the top of Thorson and Moore's model. For the campaign to succeed, the client and the agency must reach a consensus about which segments will be targeted. Compelling advertising begins with personal and precise insights about the target segment.

The second important apex in the planning triangle is specification of the brand's value proposition—a statement of the functional, emotional, and/or

ADVERTISING AND INTEGRATED BRAND PROMOTION ALWAYS ENTAILS FINDING THE RIGHT MIX TO DO THE JOB.

Exhibit 4.5
Thorson and Moore's Strategic Planning Triangle

Identify and profile target segment(s)

Consolidate brand's value proposition

Select persuasion tools

Adapted from Esther Thorson and Jeri Moore, *Integrated Communication Synergy of Persuasive Voices*, Mahwah, NJ: Erlbaum, 1996.

self-expressive benefits delivered by the brand. In formulating the value proposition, one should consider both what a brand has stood for or communicated to consumers in the past and what new types of value or additional benefits one wants to claim for the brand. For mature, successful brands, reaffirming the existing value proposition may be the primary objective of any campaign. Launching a new brand provides an opportunity to start from scratch in establishing the value proposition.

The final apex of the planning triangle considers the various persuasion tools that may be deployed as part of the campaign. A description of these tools is yet to come. Chapter 9 looks at the Internet advertising option; Chapter 10 provides a comprehensive look at direct marketing; Chapters 11 and 12 consider support media, sales promotions, and the exciting new arena of branded entertainment; Chapter 13 discusses the public relations function; and Chapter 14 fills out the tool box with personal selling and sales management. The mix of tools used will depend on campaign goals. The point here is simply to reinforce our mantra that advertising and integrated brand promotion always entails finding the right mix to do the job: Knowing the target segment and the value proposition is essential to doing the job right.

STUDY TOOLS
CHAPTER 4

Located at back of the textbook

· **Rip out Chapter in Review Card.**

Located at www.cengagebrain.com

· **Review Key Terms Flashcards (Print or Online).**

· **Complete the Practice Quiz to prepare for tests.**

· **Play "Beat the Clock" and "Quizbowl" to master concepts.**

· **Complete "Crossword Puzzle" to review key terms.**

· **Watch videos on Dagens Industri Zoo and John Smiths UK Diner for real company examples.**

· **For additional examples, go online to learn about taking special care promoting to kids, Estee Lauder brands of cosmetics, and more about Mickey Mouse and the "Disney Magic Selections" products.**

CHAPTER **5** | # Understanding Buyer Behavior and the Communication Process

Branding from *The Simpsons*, outside and inside the store.

Would *Simpsons* fans be more likely to shop at 7-Eleven with the store disguised as the show's Kwik-E-Mart?

© Susan Sheldon.

Learning Outcomes

After studying this chapter, you should be able to:

LO 1 Describe the four stages of consumer decision making.

LO 2 Explain how consumers adapt their decision-making processes based on involvement and experience.

LO 3 Discuss how brand communication influences consumers' psychological states and behavior.

LO 4 Describe the interaction of culture and advertising.

LO 5 Explain how sociological factors affect consumer behavior.

LO 6 Discuss how advertising transmits sociocultural meaning in order to sell things.

"The one thing a brand can never be is just a box on the shelf."

—Martin Davidson[1]

AFTER YOU FINISH THIS CHAPTER GO TO **PAGE 111** FOR **STUDY TOOLS**

Ay Caramba!

In the summer of 2007, 7-Eleven and *The Simpsons* teamed up for a contemporary piece of branded entertainment, cross-promotion, and buzz advertising.[2] In a project arranged by FreshWorks, an Omnicom Group virtual-agency network headed up by Tracy Locke of Dallas, twelve U.S. and Canadian 7-Eleven stores were remodeled, literally overnight, into Kwik-E-Marts from *The Simpsons* television show. The change was total: Professional set designers installed more than a thousand items from the show, including KrustyO's and Buzz Cola. (Duff Beer was not included because promoting beer would clash with the movie's PG rating.) Gracie Films, the production company for *The Simpsons*, failed to persuade 7-Eleven to carry one Kwik-E-Mart staple, month-old hot dogs, but the Squishee was accepted. The new look lasted one month, and then the stores reverted to 7-Elevens.

The goal was to promote the release of *The Simpsons Movie* and, for 7-Eleven, to attract a crop of new customers: die-hard *Simpsons* fans. Some have called this promotion "reverse product placement." Tim Stock, of Scenario DNA, said, "It's pop culture commenting on pop culture commenting on itself." Welcome to 21st-century consumer culture and brand promotion.

Why would a consumer who generally doesn't buy Pepsi at 7-Eleven make a trip to Kwik-E-Mart for a Buzz Cola? How do moviegoers choose between *The Simpsons* and *Spider-Man 3*, another movie released the same summer? The answers are a function of psychological, economic, sociological, anthropological, historical, textual, and other forces. Marketers combine those perspectives to understand consumer behavior. Like all human behavior, the behavior of consumers is complicated, rich, and varied. However, marketers must make it their job to

What do you think?

If brand messages aren't fun, I'll just ignore them.

1   2   3   4   5   6   7

STRONGLY DISAGREE   STRONGLY AGREE

Find out what others think at CourseMate for PROMO2.

consumer behavior activities and decision processes directly involved in obtaining, consuming, and disposing of products and services

need state psychological state arising when one's desired state of affairs differs from one's actual state of affairs

understand consumers if they want to experience sustained success. Sometimes, this understanding comes from comprehensive research efforts. Other times, it comes from years of experience coupled with creative management.

This chapter summarizes the concepts and frameworks we believe are most helpful in understanding **consumer behavior**, using two major perspectives. The first portrays consumers as reasonably systematic decision makers who seek to maximize the benefits they derive from their purchases. The second views consumers as active interpreters of advertising, influenced by their membership in various cultures, societies, and communities. These two perspectives are different ways of looking at the exact same people and many of the exact same behaviors. Both perspectives are valuable to the marketer because no one perspective can adequately explain consumer behavior. Consumers are psychological, social, cultural, historical, and economic beings all at the same time, so understanding their behavior is complex but also exciting.

Monkey Business Images/Shutterstock.com

LO 1 Consumers as Decision Makers

One way to view consumer behavior is as a fairly predictable sequential process culminating with the individual's reaping a set of benefits from a product or service that satisfies the person's perceived needs. In this basic view, we can think of individuals as purposeful decision makers who either weigh and balance alternatives or (typically in complex situations with too much information) resort to simple decision rules of thumb to make the choice easier.

Basic Decision-Making Process

Often, but not always, consumers' decision-making process occurs in a straightforward sequence. Many consumption episodes then might be conceived as a sequence of four basic stages, shown in Exhibit 5.1. Understanding what typically happens at each stage gives the marketer a foundation for understanding consumers, and it also can illuminate opportunities for developing more powerful brand communication.

Need Recognition

A consumer's decision-making process begins when he or she perceives a need. A **need state** arises when one's desired state of affairs differs from one's actual state of affairs.

**Exhibit 5.1
Consumer Decision Making**

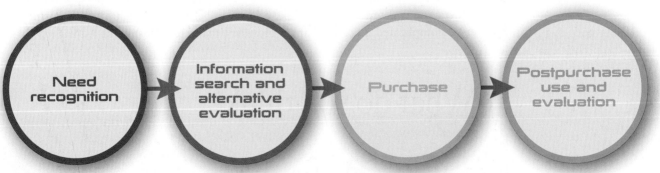

Need recognition → Information search and alternative evaluation → Purchase → Postpurchase use and evaluation

© Cengage Learning 2011.

How is your baby's skin different?

It loses moisture nearly 2X faster than yours. Use JOHNSON'S® Baby Lotion 2X a day to replenish the moisture she needs. Dermatologist tested and the #1 choice of hospitals, it's gentle enough to use both morning and night.

Courtesy, Johnson & Johnson.

Parents feel protective of their babies. This ad promises both functional benefits and emotional rewards for diligent parents.

Williams-Sonoma kitchen gadgetry or other accoutrement to place in their uptown condo, perhaps seeking to validate personal accomplishments and derive status and recognition through consumption and social display. Even though income clearly matters in this regard, it would be a mistake to believe that the poor have no aesthetic concerns. Rather, a variety of needs can be fulfilled through consumption.

One of the marketer's primary jobs is to make the connection between the consumer's need states and the benefits delivered by the marketer's products. Benefits come in different forms:

- Some benefits are "functional"—that is, they derive from the more objective performance characteristics of a product or service. Examples of such **functional benefits** are convenience, reliability, nutrition, durability, and energy efficiency.

- Products also may provide **emotional benefits**; these are not typically found in some tangible feature or objective characteristic of a product. Emotional benefits are more subjective and may be perceived differently from one consumer to the next. Products and services help consumers feel pride, avoid guilt, relieve fear, and experience pleasure. These are powerful consumption motives that advertisers often try to activate. Can you find the emotional benefits promised in the ad for Johnson's Baby Lotion?

Some scholars believe *all* benefits are functional, even emotional ones; in other words, they believe all benefits serve a purpose. But distinguishing the benefit types can be helpful for crafting brand communication.

Marketers must develop a keen appreciation for the kinds of benefits that consumers derive from their brands. Even within the same product category, the benefits promised may vary widely. For instance, the makers of Ernst Benz watches promise that their product delivers precision measurements, whereas advertising for Duby & Schaldenbrand watches emphasizes the feelings of elegance and pride afforded the owner of a prestigious timepiece. To create advertising that resonates with your customers, you must know what benefits they are looking for—or might look for, if you suggest it.

Information Search and Alternative Evaluation

When a consumer has recognized a need, he or she may not be sure about the best way to satisfy that need. For example, if you have a fear of being trapped in a blizzard in North Dakota, a

Need states are accompanied by a mental discomfort or anxiety that motivates action; the severity of this discomfort can be widely variable, depending on the genesis of the need. For example, when you run out of toothpaste, your need state probably involves mild discomfort, but if you're driving on a dark and deserted highway in North Dakota in mid-February and your car breaks down, your need state might approach true desperation.

One way brand communication works is to point to and thereby activate needs that will motivate consumers to buy a company's product or service. For instance, in the fall in northern climates, marketers of snow blowers and boots roll out predictions for another severe winter and encourage consumers to prepare themselves before it's too late. Every change of season brings new needs, large and small, and advertisers are at the ready.

Many factors can influence consumers' need states. A popular model, Maslow's hierarchy of needs, says individuals try to satisfy basic survival needs before addressing "higher-level" needs such as status or a sense of accomplishment. Thus, because they have plenty to eat and a roof over their heads, more-affluent consumers may fret over which new piece of

condo on Miami Beach may be a much better solution than a Jeep or new snow tires. Need recognition simply sets in motion a process that may involve an extensive information search and careful evaluation of alternatives before purchase. Of course, during this search and evaluation, marketers have numerous opportunities to influence the final decision.

Once a need has been recognized, consumers acquire information:

- The consumer's first option for information is an **internal search**, which draws on personal experience and prior knowledge. When a consumer has considerable experience with the product type, attitudes about alternatives may be well established and could determine choice. An internal search also can tap into information that has accumulated in one's memory as a result of repeated advertising exposures, such as "Tide's In, Dirt's Out," or stored judgments, such as a belief that Apple computers are unlikely to crash. Marketers want internal searches to result in their brand being in the "evoked set"—the set of brands (usually two to five) that come to mind when a category is mentioned. The evoked set is usually highly related to the **consideration set**, the set of the brands the

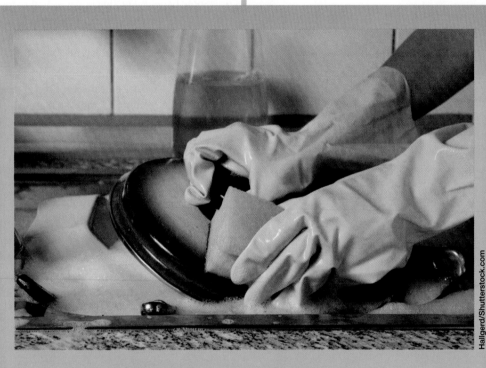

Hallgerd/Shutterstock.com

GLOBAL JOY IN JAPAN

The Japanese marketplace is tough, even for giants like Procter & Gamble. To find an opening for its dishwashing soap, P&G began investigating consumer behavior. Managers videotaped Japanese homemakers as they washed dishes and then talked to them about the chore. They learned that, as Japanese diets added more meat and fried foods, it had become harder to scrub grease stains out of plastic dishes and storage containers, and homemakers were using too much dish soap.

P&G began offering a highly concentrated Joy dish soap formulated for the Japanese market. A TV ad demonstrated how a squirt of Joy could dissolve the grease in a sink full of dirty dishes. Joy rapidly gained market share, largely thanks to the television ads.

Source: Norihiko Shirouzu, "P&G's Joy Makes an Unlikely Splash in Japan," *The Wall Street Journal*, December 10, 1997, B1. Copyright © 1977 Dow Jones & Company, Inc.

consumer will consider for purchase. If your brand is the first one recalled, you have achieved something even better: "top of mind." Many people believe that top-of-mind awareness predicts purchase of inexpensive and low-risk consumer packaged goods. As noted in Chapter 1, the purpose of delayed-response advertising is to generate recognition of and a favorable predisposition toward a brand so that, when consumers enter search mode, that brand will be one they immediately consider.

- If an internal search does not turn up enough information to yield a decision, the consumer proceeds with an **external search**. This search involves visiting retail stores to examine the alternatives, seeking input from friends and relatives about their experiences with the products in question, or perusing professional product evaluations from various sources such as *Consumer Reports* or *Car and Driver*. In addition, when consumers are in an active information-gathering mode, they may be receptive to detailed, informative advertisements delivered through any of the print media, or they may deploy a shopping agent or a search engine to scour the Internet for the best deal or for opinions of other users.

During an internal or external search, consumers are not merely gathering information for its own sake. They have a need that is propelling the process, and their goal is to make a decision that yields benefits for them. Consumers search for and simultaneously are forming attitudes about possible alternatives. This effort, alternative evaluation, is another key phase for the marketer to address.

Alternative evaluation is structured by two variables:

1. The *consideration set* is the subset of brands from a particular product category that becomes the focal point of the consumer's evaluation. Most product categories contain too many brands for all to be considered, so the consumer finds some way to focus the evaluation. For autos, a consumer might consider only cars priced less than $25,000, or only cars that have antilock brakes, or that are foreign-made, or that are sold at dealerships within a five-mile radius of home. Thus, advertising often aims to make consumers aware of the brand and to keep them aware so that the brand has a chance to be part of the consideration set.

2. Next, consumers form evaluations by applying **evaluative criteria**—product attributes or performance characteristics used to compare various brands. Evaluative criteria differ from one product category to the next. Examples include price, texture, warranty terms, service support, color, scent, and carb content.

Marketers need to have an understanding as complete as possible of the evaluative criteria that consumers use to make their buying decisions. They also must know how consumers rate their brand in comparison

with others from the consideration set. This information furnishes a powerful starting point for any promotional campaign.

Purchase

At the third stage of consumers' decision making, a purchase occurs. The consumer has made a decision, and a sale is made. That might sound like the culmination of the decision-making process, but from the marketer's standpoint, it should be only one action in a longer-term relationship. In any product or service category, the consumer is likely to buy again in the future. Therefore, what happens after the sale is very important to marketers. The first purchase is in effect a trial; marketers then want conversion (repeat purchase). They want brand loyalty. Some want to create brand ambassadors—users who will become apostles for the brand, spreading its gospel. At the same time, competitors will be working to persuade consumers to give their brand a try.

external search
gathering product information by visiting retail stores to examine alternatives, seeking input from friends and relatives, or perusing professional product evaluations

evaluative criteria product attributes or performance characteristics on which consumers base their product evaluations

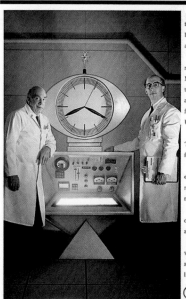

The evaluative criteria for an airline include on-time arrival.

customer satisfaction good feelings that come from a favorable postpurchase experience

cognitive dissonance anxiety or regret that lingers after a difficult decision

Postpurchase Use and Evaluation

The goal for marketers must not be simply to generate a sale; it must be to create satisfied and, ultimately, loyal customers. The data to support this position are astounding. Research shows that about 65 percent of the average company's business comes from its present satisfied customers, so they are essential to retain. In addition, 91 percent of dissatisfied customers again will never buy from the company that disappointed them, so disappointing a customer is a huge mistake.[3] For good or for ill, consumers' evaluations of products in use become a major determinant of which brands will be in the consideration set the next time around.

Customer satisfaction derives from a favorable postpurchase experience. It may develop after a single use, but more likely it will require sustained use. Brand communication can play an important role in inducing customer satisfaction by creating appropriate expectations for a brand's performance or by helping the consumer who already has bought the advertised brand to feel good about it.

Advertising plays an important role in alleviating the **cognitive dissonance** that can occur after a purchase. Cognitive dissonance is the anxiety or regret that lingers after a difficult decision, sometimes called "buyer's remorse." Often, rejected alternatives have attractive features that lead people to second-guess their own decisions. If the marketer's goal is to generate satisfied customers, this dissonance must be resolved in a way that leads consumers to conclude they made the right decision.

When dissonance is expected (it's most likely with high-cost items or products that have many competitors), marketers should reassure buyers by providing detailed information about their brands. Postpurchase reinforcement programs might involve direct mail, email, or other types of personalized contacts with the customer. Nowadays, consumers often search the Internet for other purchasers of the product to tell them they did the right thing. Some marketers sponsor or contribute to online discussion groups and user sites so that they can provide informa-tion aimed at converting buyers into satisfied customers. This postpurchase period represents a great opportunity because the consumer is likely to be attentive and willing to provide information and advice about product use that will increase customer satisfaction.

LO 2 Modes of Decision Making

The decision-making process we've been considering is deliberate and systematic, but as consumers ourselves, we know that some purchase decisions are hasty, impulsive, or even irrational. The time and effort that people put into their purchase decisions can vary dramatically for different types of products. Maybe you buy whatever toothpaste you usually use, agonize a little bit about picking out a Valentine's gift for someone special, and do some thoughtful research to choose a college or a car.

Our decision-making model takes this into account by defining four decision-making modes that help marketers appreciate the richness and complexity of consumer behavior. These four modes are determined by a consumer's degree of involvement and level of experience with the product or service in question (see Exhibit 5.2).

**Exhibit 5.2
Modes of Decision Making**

	Involvement	
	High	**Low**
Low	Extended problem solving	Limited problem solving
High	Brand loyalty	Habit or variety seeking

(Experience)

© Cengage Learning 2011.

In this model, **involvement** refers to the degree of perceived relevance and personal importance accompanying the choice of a certain product or service within a particular context. Many factors have been identified as potential contributors to an individual's level of involvement with a consumption decision:[4]

- Interests and avocations, such as cooking and pet ownership, can enhance involvement levels in related product categories.

- Any time a great deal of risk is associated with a purchase—perhaps as a result of a high price or the need to live with the decision for a long time—involvement tends to be elevated.

- Products and brands that carry important symbolic meaning will generate high involvement. For example, this occurs when owning or using a product helps people reinforce some aspect of their self-image or makes a statement to other people who are important to them. In the case of choosing a Valentine's Day gift, the purchase may carry both great symbolic meaning and real consequences.

- Purchases that tap into deep emotional concerns or motives are associated with high involvement. Marketing messages that appeal to patriotism are aimed at generating or maintaining this kind of involvement.

Together with consumers' degree of experience, their level of involvement determines the way they will use or modify the decision-making process. As shown in Exhibit 5.2, consumers may engage in extended problem solving, limited problem solving, habit or variety seeking, or brand loyalty.

Extended Problem Solving

When consumers are inexperienced in a particular consumption setting yet find the setting highly involving, they are likely to engage in **extended problem solving**. In this mode, consumers go through a deliberate decision-making process that tracks the steps in Exhibit 5.1: explicit need recognition, careful internal and external search, alternative evaluation, purchase, and a lengthy postpurchase evaluation.

Consumers might engage in extended problem solving when choosing a home or a diamond ring. These products are expensive, are publicly evaluated, and can carry a considerable amount of risk in terms of making an uneducated decision. These purchases also tend to be infrequent. Extended problem solving is the exception, not the rule.

Limited Problem Solving

When experience and involvement are both low, consumers are more likely to use **limited problem solving**. In this mode, a consumer is less systematic in his or her decision making. The consumer has a new problem to solve, but the problem is not interesting or engaging, so the information search is limited to trying the first brand encountered. For example, let's say a young couple has just brought home a new baby, and suddenly the parents perceive a very real need for disposable diapers. At the hospital, they received complimentary trial packs of several products, including Pampers disposables. They try the Pampers, find them an acceptable solution to their messy new problem, and take the discount coupon

involvement degree of perceived relevance and personal importance accompanying the choice of a product or service in a particular context

extended problem solving decision-making mode in which inexperienced but highly involved consumers go through a deliberate decision-making process

limited problem solving decision-making mode in which relatively inexperienced and uninvolved consumers are not systematic about decisions

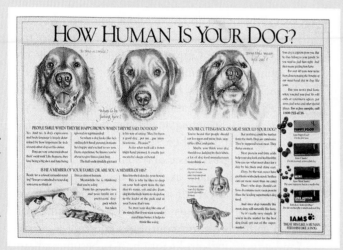

Courtesy, The IAMS Company.

Involvement levels vary not only among product categories but also among individuals for any given product category. People who think of their pets as human take the selection of pet food very seriously. For example, some pet owners will feed their pets only the expensive canned products that look and smell like people food. IAMS understands this and made a special premium dog food for consumers who think of their pets as close to humans. Many other pet owners, however, are perfectly happy with feeding Rover from a 50-pound, economy-size bag of dry dog food.

that came with the sample to their local grocery, where they buy several packages.

In the limited problem-solving mode, consumers often are simply seeking adequate solutions to mundane problems. Also, trying a brand or two may be the most efficient way of collecting information about one's options. Smart marketers realize that trial offers can be a preferred means of collecting information, and they facilitate trial of their brands through free samples, inexpensive "trial sizes," or discount coupons.

Habit or Variety Seeking

In settings where a decision isn't involving and an experienced consumer repurchases from the category over and over again, the mode of purchase is some combination of habit and variety seeking. **Habit** refers to buying a single brand repeatedly as a solution to a simple consumption problem. Habitual purchases are probably the most common decision-making mode. Consumers find a brand of laundry detergent that suits their needs, they run out of the product, and they buy it again. The cycle repeats itself many times per year in an almost mindless fashion. The habit of buying just one brand simplifies life and minimizes the time invested in "nuisance" purchases. A lot of consumption decisions are boring but necessary; habits help us minimize the inconvenience.

In some product categories where a buying habit would be expected, variety seeking may be observed instead. **Variety seeking** refers to the tendency of consumers to switch their selection among various brands in a given category in a seemingly random pattern. Habitual buying can be tedious, and some consumers use variety seeking to fight the boredom. This is not to say that a consumer will buy just any brand; he or she probably selects from two to five brands that provide similar levels of satisfaction. However, from one purchase occasion to the next, the individual will switch brands from within this set, just for the sake of variety.

Variety seeking is most likely in frequently purchased categories where sensory experience, such as taste or smell, accompanies product use. In such categories, no amount of ad spending can overcome the consumer's basic desire for fresh sensory experience.[5] Satiation occurs after repeated use and leaves the consumer looking for a change of pace. Product categories such as soft drinks and alcoholic beverages, snack foods, breakfast cereals, and fast food are prone to variety seeking, so marketers in these categories constantly introduce new possibilities to feed the craving for variety.

Brand Loyalty

In situations typified by high involvement and rich prior experience, **brand loyalty** becomes a major consideration in the purchase decision. Consumers demonstrate brand loyalty when they repeatedly purchase a single brand as their choice to fulfill a specific need. In one sense, brand-loyal purchasers may look as if they have developed a simple buying habit; however, it is important to distinguish brand loyalty from simple habit. Brand loyalty is based on highly favorable attitudes toward the brand and a conscious commitment to find this brand each time the consumer purchases from this category. Conversely, habits are merely consumption simplifiers that are not based on deeply held convictions. Habits can be disrupted through a skillful combination of advertising and sales promotions. Spending advertising dollars to persuade truly brand-loyal consumers to try an alternative can be a great waste of resources.

Brands such as Starbucks and Apple have inspired very loyal consumers. Brand loyalty is something that any marketer aspires to have, but in a world filled with more-savvy consumers and endless product (and advertising) proliferation, it is becoming harder and harder to attain. What causes brand loyalty to emerge? Here are some answers:

- The consumer perceives that one brand simply outperforms all others in providing some critical functional benefit. Apple's computers are known for having little, if any, trouble with computer viruses, and its iPods caught on partly because users found it easy and fun to download music from iTunes.

- Perhaps even more important, brand loyalty can be due to the emotional benefits that accompany certain brands. In one of the strongest indicators for brand loyalty, some loyal consumers have tattooed their bodies with the insignia of their favorite brand. Supposedly, the worldwide leader in brand-name tattoos is Harley-Davidson. What accounts for Harley's fervent following? Do its motorcycles simply perform better? More likely, part of the loyalty comes from the association of the Harley brand with the deep emotional benefit of taking a big bike out on the open road and leaving civilization far behind, as well as feelings of pride, kinship, and community with other Harley riders. Owning a Harley—and perhaps the tattoo—makes a person feel different and special. Harley ads are designed to reaffirm the deep emotional appeal of this product.

Strong emotional benefits might be expected from consumption decisions that we classify as highly involving, and they are major determinants of brand loyalty. Indeed, with so many brands in the marketplace, it is becoming harder and harder to create loyalty for one's brand through functional benefits alone. To break free of this brand-parity problem and provide consumers with enduring reasons to become or stay loyal, marketers are investing more and more effort in communicating the emotional benefits that might be derived from brands in categories as diverse as greeting cards (Hallmark—"When you care enough to send the very best") and vacation hot spots (Las Vegas—"What happens in Vegas, stays in Vegas"). You might go to YouTube and check out one of those Vegas spots or some of the consumer-generated parodies. Many, probably most, companies are exploring ways to use the Internet to create dialogue, manage relations, and even create a community with their customers. To do this, one must look for means to connect with customers at an emotional level.

As we noted earlier in the chapter, a good deal of advertising is designed to ensure recognition and create favorable predispositions toward a brand so that, as consumers search for solutions to their problems, they will think of the brand immediately. The goal of any delayed-response ad is to affect some psychological state that subsequently will influence a purchase. This generally involves some combination of attitudes and beliefs, illustrated in Exhibit 5.3.

- **Attitude** is an overall evaluation of any object, person, or issue that varies along a continuum, such as favorable to unfavorable or positive to negative. Attitudes are learned, and if they are based on substantial experience with the object or issue in question, they can be held with great conviction. Attitudes simplify decision-making; when faced with a choice among several alternatives, we do not need to process new information or analyze the merits of the alternatives. We merely select the alternative we think is the most favorable. Marketers are most interested in one particular class of attitudes, **brand attitudes**, which are summary evaluations that reflect preferences for various products and services.

- **Beliefs** represent the knowledge and feelings a person has accumulated about an object or issue. They can be logical and factual, or biased and self-serving. A person might believe that the Mini Cooper is cute. That belief can serve as a basis for the person's attitude toward Minis. People have many beliefs about various features and attributes of products and brands. Typically, a small number of beliefs—on the order of five to

attitude overall evaluation of any object, person, or issue; varies along a continuum, such as favorable to unfavorable or positive to negative

brand attitudes summary evaluations that reflect preferences for various products or brands

beliefs a person's knowledge and feelings about an object or issue

LO 3 Key Psychological Processes

To complete our picture of the consumer as a fairly thoughtful decision maker, one key issue remains. We need to examine the explicit psychological consequences of brand communication. What do advertisements or other brand messages leave in the minds of consumers that ultimately may influence their behavior?

© Cengage Learning 2011.

**Exhibit 5.3
Beliefs Shape Attitudes**

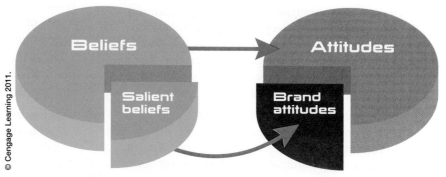

nine—underlie brand attitudes.[6] These beliefs are the critical determinants of an attitude and are referred to as **salient beliefs**.

If we know a person's beliefs, usually it is possible to infer attitude. Someone with many favorable beliefs about a product or brand is likely to have a favorable attitude toward it.

The number of salient beliefs varies between product categories. The loyal Harley owner who proudly displays a tattoo will have many more salient beliefs about his bike than he has about his brand of shaving cream. Also, salient beliefs can be modified, replaced, or extinguished. For example, Nicorette Stop Smoking Gum has advertised a new product, Fruit Chill Gum, that "tastes like a dream." One interpretation of this message is that many people held the belief that earlier versions didn't taste very good, and the ad was seeking to replace that belief and improve attitudes toward the product.

Because belief shaping and reinforcement can be one of the principal goals of brand communication, marketers make belief assessment a focal point in their attempts to understand consumer behavior.

Multi-Attribute Attitude Models (MAAMs)

Multi-attribute attitude models (MAAMs) provide a framework and a set of research procedures for collecting information from consumers to assess their salient beliefs and attitudes about competitive brands. Any MAAMs analysis will feature four fundamental components:

1. *Evaluative criteria* are the attributes or performance characteristics that consumers use in comparing competitive brands. In pursuing a MAAMs analysis, a marketer must identify all evaluative criteria relevant to its product category.

2. *Importance weights* reflect the priority that a particular evaluative criterion receives in the consumer's decision-making process. Importance weights can vary dramatically from one consumer to the next. Some people will merely want good taste from their bowl of cereal, while others will be more concerned about fat and fiber content.

3. The *consideration set* is the group of brands that represents the real focal point for the consumer's decision. For example, the potential buyer of a luxury sedan might be focusing on Acura and Lexus. These and comparable brands would be featured in a MAAMs analysis. If

Losevsky Pavel/Shutterstock.com

another automaker aspired to be part of this consideration set, it could conduct a MAAMs analysis featuring its brand and its major competitors.

4. *Beliefs* represent the consumers' knowledge and feelings about various brands. A MAAMs analysis assesses beliefs about each brand's performance on all relevant evaluative criteria. Beliefs can be matters of fact (a 12-ounce Pepsi has 150 calories) or highly subjective (the Cadillac XLR Roadster is the sleekest, sexiest car on the street). Beliefs may vary widely among consumers.

In conducting a MAAMs analysis, first we must specify the relevant evaluative criteria for our category as well as our direct competitors (see Exhibit 5.4). We then go to consumers and let them tell us what's important and how our brand fares against the competition on the various evaluative criteria. The information generated from this survey research will give us a better appreciation for the salient beliefs that underlie brand attitudes, and it may suggest important opportunities for changing our marketing or advertising to yield more favorable brand attitudes:

- If consumers do not accurately perceive the relative performance of a brand on an important evaluative criterion, brand communication may try to correct the misperception. For example, if Colgate marketers learn that consumers perceive Crest to be far and away the best brand of toothpaste for fighting cavities, when in fact all brands with a fluoride additive perform equally well on cavity prevention, they might try to correct this misperception.

- If a brand is perceived as the best performer on an evaluative criterion that most consumers view as unimportant, the task for brand communication would be to persuade consumers that the brand's benefits are more important than they had thought.

- If consumers don't have favorable attitudes toward a brand, marketers sometimes conclude that the only way to improve attitudes would be through the introduction of a new attribute, which then will be featured in promotional messages. Marketers may add the new attribute or feature to an existing product or develop a new or extended product line.

When marketers use the MAAMs approach, they can improve both brand attitudes and market share. When marketers carefully isolate key evaluative criteria, bring products to the marketplace that perform well on the focal criteria, and develop ads that effectively shape salient beliefs about the brand, the results can be dramatic.

Information Processing and Perceptual Defense

Brand promotion would be easy if consumers would just pay close attention to what marketers say and believe every message, and if competitors weren't so busy spreading their own messages. Of course, these things aren't going to happen. In real life, marketers encounter resistance. One way to think about this problem is to portray the consumer as an information processor who must advance through a series of stages before a brand message can have its intended effect:

1. Pay attention to the message

2. Comprehend the message correctly

3. Accept the message exactly as it was intended

4. Retain the message until it is needed for a purchase decision

Unfortunately, problems can and do occur at any or all of these four stages, completely negating the effect of the brand communication.

The first major obstacle that marketers must overcome if their message is to have its intended effect is the **cognitive consistency** impetus, which stems from the individual consumer. A person tends to maintain a set of beliefs and attitudes over time. These consistent attitudes help him or her make efficient decisions that yield pleasing outcomes. When a consumer is satisfied with these outcomes, there is really no reason to alter the belief system that generated them. New information that challenges existing beliefs can be ignored or disparaged to prevent modification of the present cognitive system.

A second obstacle is **advertising clutter**, which derives from the context in which ads are processed. Even if a person wanted to, it would be impossible to process

cognitive consistency maintenance of a system of beliefs and attitudes over time

advertising clutter volume of similar ads for products or services that presents an obstacle to brand promotion

Exhibit 5.4
Using MAAMs Analysis

© Cengage Learning 2011.

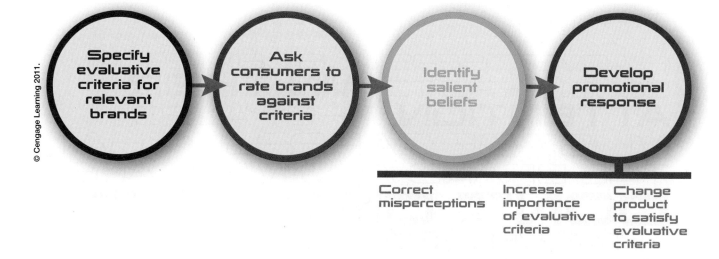

Specify evaluative criteria for relevant brands → Ask consumers to rate brands against criteria → Identify salient beliefs → Develop promotional response

Correct misperceptions | Increase importance of evaluative criteria | Change product to satisfy evaluative criteria

and integrate every marketing message that he or she is exposed to each day. If you pick up today's newspaper, you won't have time to study every ad and read the stories, too. The clutter problem is magnified further by competitive brands making very similar performance claims.[7] Was it Advil, Anacin, Aveda, Aleve, Avia, Aflexa, Aveya, Actonel, Motrin, Nuprin, or Tylenol Gelcaps that promised you 12 hours of relief from your headache? (Can you select the brands from this list that aren't headache remedies?) The simple fact is that each of us is exposed to hundreds, maybe thousands, of ads each day, and no one has the time or inclination to sort through them all. Some industry experts and researchers believe that the simple mass of advertising, the enormous number of ads, is now working very hard against the institution of advertising itself.

Consumers thus employ perceptual defenses to simplify and control their own processing of marketing messages. That means the consumer is in control, and the marketer must find some way to engage the consumer if a message is to have any impact. Of course, the best way to engage consumers is to offer information about a product or service that will address an active need state.

The advertiser's greatest challenge is **selective attention**. Consumers simply ignore most ads. They turn the page, change the station, mute the sound, head for the refrigerator, TiVo past the ad, or just daydream or doze off. Advertisers employ a variety of tactics to catch consumers' attention. Devices for combating selective attention include popular music, celebrity spokespersons, sexy models, rapid scene changes, and anything that is novel. In their never-ending battle for the attention of the consumer, marketers try so hard to be noticed that they often step over the line between novelty and annoyance. In addition, the provocative, attention-attracting devices used to engage consumers often become the focal point of consumers' ad processing. Viewers remember seeing an ad featuring 27 Elvis Presley impersonators, but they can't recall what brand was being advertised or what claims were being made about the brand. If advertisers must entertain consumers to win their attention, they also must be careful that the brand and message don't get lost in the shuffle.

Even when a brand-related message gets attention and the consumer comprehends the message, more resistance will follow if the message is asking the consumer to alter beliefs. At that point, the cognitive consistency impetus kicks in, and cognitive responses can be expected. **Cognitive responses** are the thoughts that occur to individuals at that exact moment when their beliefs and attitudes are being challenged by some form of persuasive communication. Most ads will not provoke enough mental engagement to yield any form of cognitive response, but when these responses occur, the valence of the responses is critical to the acceptance of one's message.

The final stage of information processing involves memory. Traditionally, marketers have tested consumers' memory of advertising messages asking them to recall brand names and points made in advertising copy. However, recent models of human memory provide strong evidence that memory is a much more fluid and interpretive system than we have thought in the past.[8] Human memory is not a mental VCR; it's more likely to combine, delete, add, and rewrite information. Still, it does stand to reason that if a consumer can remember most of your ad, it can benefit your brand.

IF ADVERTISERS MUST ENTERTAIN CONSUMERS TO **WIN THEIR ATTENTION,** THEY ALSO MUST BE CAREFUL THAT THE BRAND AND MESSAGE **DON'T GET LOST** IN THE SHUFFLE.

The Elaboration Likelihood Model (ELM)

Cognitive responses are one of the main components of an influential framework for understanding the impact of advertising: the **elaboration likelihood model (ELM)**. The ELM has been borrowed from social psychology; it gathers the concepts of involvement, information processing, cognitive responses, and attitude formation in a single, integrated framework, which can be applied to advertising settings.[9] It has limitations but applies to many advertising situations and has a certain intuitive appeal. The basic premise of the ELM is that, to understand how a persuasive message may affect a person's attitudes, we must consider his or her motivation and ability to elaborate on the message during processing. For most marketing contexts, motivation and ability will be a function of how involved the person is with the consumption decision in question. When involvement is high, consumers will engage in active mental elaboration during ad processing; when involvement is low, ad processing will be more passive.

As indicated in Exhibit 5.5, the ELM uses the involvement dichotomy to map two distinct routes to attitude change:

1. *Central route to persuasion:* When involvement is high, the consumer tends to draw on prior knowledge and experience and scrutinize or elaborate on the central arguments of the message. The nature of the individual's effortful thinking about the issues at hand can be judged from the cognitive responses to the message. These cognitive responses may be positive or negative, and they can be reactions to specific claims or any element of the ad. Responses are more likely to be positive when messages are designed to reinforce existing beliefs or shape beliefs for a brand that the consumer was unaware of. If the cognitive responses provoked by an ad are primarily negative, the ad has backfired: The consumer is maintaining cognitive consistency by disparaging the ad, and his or her negative thoughts are likely to foster negative evaluation of the brand. However, when the central route induces positive attitudes, they are based on careful thought, so they will come to mind quickly for use in product selection, resist the change efforts of other advertisers, persist in memory without repeated ad exposures, and be excellent predictors of behavior. These properties cannot be expected of attitudes that are formed in the peripheral route.

2. *Peripheral route to persuasion:* For low-involvement contexts, attitude formation tends to follow a more peripheral route, where peripheral cues become the focal point for judging the impact of a brand communication. **Peripheral cues** refer to features of a promotional message other than the actual arguments about the brand's performance. They include an attractive or comical spokesperson, novel imagery, humorous incidents, or a catchy jingle. (Critics of the ELM find this the weakest part of the model: We can all think of ads where the music and pictures are anything but peripheral.

> **elaboration likelihood model (ELM)** social psychological model of the response to a persuasive communication, expressing the response in terms of motivation and ability
>
> **peripheral cues** features of an advertisement other than the actual arguments about the brand's performance

Exhibit 5.5
Routes to Attitude Change

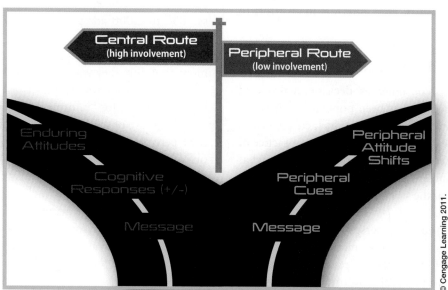

© Cengage Learning 2011.

The model works better with traditional copy-heavy ads.) In the peripheral route, the consumer can still learn from the marketer's communication, but the learning is passive and typically must be achieved by frequent association of the peripheral cue (for example, the Eveready Energizer Bunny) with the brand in question. It even has been suggested that advertises might use classical conditioning principles to facilitate and accelerate this associative learning process.[10] As consumers learn to associate pleasant feelings and attractive images with a brand, their attitude toward the brand should become more positive. However, this is an expensive tactic because any gains made along the peripheral route are short lived and repetition of a message, coupled with a never-ending search for the freshest, most popular peripheral cues, demands huge budgets.

When all brands in a category offer similar benefits, the most fruitful avenue for advertising strategy is likely to be the peripheral route, where the advertiser merely tries to maintain positive or pleasant associations with the brand by constantly presenting it with appealing peripheral cues. Of course, peripheral cues can be more than merely cute, with the right ones adding an undeniable level of "hipness" to aging brands.[11] Selecting peripheral cues can be especially important for mature brands in low-involvement categories, where the challenge is to keep the customer from getting bored.[12] Marketing typical of the peripheral route includes advertising campaigns for high-profile, mature brands such as Budweiser and Doritos. They entertain in an effort to keep you interested.

Limits of Decision-Making Models

The view of the consumer as decision maker and information processor has been popular, but it is not without its limitations and critics. In fact, the critics are getting louder, particularly in the actual practice of integrated marketing communication. Although what goes on in consumers' minds is obviously important, it tells only part of the story of consumer behavior and brand promotion.

The decision-making perspective is reasonably good at explaining how consumers make decisions. For example, it tells us that, in general, consumers tend to use less as opposed to more information. Although consumers *say* more information is best, they tend to *actually use* less. If you think about it, this makes perfect sense. Consumers store and retrieve previously made judgments (e.g., "Honda is the best value") to spare themselves from deciding all over again every time they make a purchase. If this were not true, a trip to the convenience store would take hours.

But in their effort to isolate psychological mechanisms, information-processing academic researchers typically take consumer behavior (and consumers) out of its (their) natural environment in favor of a laboratory. This makes a great deal of sense if your desire is experimental control, the elimination of other possible explanations for a certain effect, or evidence of a mental process. But few consumers actually watch ads and buy products in laboratories. In fact, some critics argue that, under such obviously unrealistic conditions, researchers no longer are studying marketing but only "stimulus material." According to this view, marketing messages really exist *only* in the real social world and natural environment. When removed from that environment, ads are no longer ads in any meaningful sense.

Apply that idea to your own experience: When you watch advertising on television, you usually see 10 ads in a commercial break. You may or may not be paying attention. You might be talking to friends or family, reading, or doing just about anything else. Chances are you are not watching an ad on a computer monitor for class credit. In the real world, where you might see 800 to 2,000 ads per day, many ads just become wallpaper, nothing you really focus on. But in a lab, the degree of focus typically is far greater. Subjects pay more attention; they watch the "ads" differently. More importantly, what the ad means often is completely lost in the quest for "information" being "processed."

The allure of science and its symbols (e.g., labs and their perceived certainty and infallibility of science) is one of the modern period's best-known seductions and comfortable mythologies. The trappings and appearance of science give people (including clients) feelings of certainty and truth, whether it is deserved or appropriate. And, to be fair, the aims of academic experimental research (to advance basic knowledge and theory) often are quite different from the aims of the advertising industry (to make ads that sell things).

Industry critics and more and more academic researchers believe that much of the psychological "information-processing" research (most popular in the industry in the 1950s) has significantly less to do with the promotion and consumption of real goods and services in the real world than with advancing psychological theory—a completely worthy goal for some college professors but not necessarily important to the actual practice of marketing. In the real world of advertising, what matters is real consumers and how they respond to real brand promotion in real environments.

Consumers as Social Beings

For quite some time, at least 40 years, marketers—particularly in the advertising industry—have been moving away from purely psychological approaches. This shift gathered enormous momentum in the 1980s. At that time, U.S. West Coast agencies began adopting what they called "British research," which was really just qualitative research as has been practiced by anthropologists, sociologists, and others for more than a century. It was called "British" because some very hot London agencies had been doing research this way all along. A good example comes from Judie Lannon, then–creative research director at J. Walter Thompson, London, who beautifully sums up this emphasis on meaning:

> And if Advertising contributes to the meaning of inanimate goods, then the study of these values and meanings are of prime importance ... the perspective of research must be what people use advertising for.[13]

meaning what a brand message intends or conveys

This industry trend toward qualitative research and naturalistic methods resonated with a similar move in academic research toward more qualitative field work, and interpretive and textual approaches to the study of human behavior, including consumer behavior. Investigators began to see consumers as more than "information processors" and to see ads as more than socially isolated attempts at attitude manipulation. The truth is most major companies do a lot of qualitative research, often under the heading "consumer insights." In this approach, **meaning** becomes more important than attitudes. Consumers do "process" information, but they also do a whole lot more. Furthermore, "information" itself is a rich and complex textual product, bound by history, society, and culture, and it is interpreted in sophisticated ways by human beings. Brand promotion is not engineering or chemistry; ads are not atoms or molecules. This approach centers on knowing how to use brand promotion to connect with human beings around their consumption practices. That's why advertising agencies hire people who know about material culture (anthropology), demography and social process (sociology), the history of brands and consumption practices (history), memory (psychology), communication, text (literature), and art (what a lot of ads are). Humans and their creations (including ads and branded goods) are not just processors of information; they are that and much more.

© T. O'Guinn.

REAL CONSUMERS DO NOT CONSUME IN A LABORATORY. RATHER, THEY ARE CONNECTED TO ONE ANOTHER THROUGH SOCIAL IDENTITIES, FAMILIES, CULTURES, AND MORE.

Therefore, this second perspective on consumer behavior is concerned with social and cultural processes. It should be considered another part of the larger story of how advertising works, viewing the same consumers' behavior from a different vantage point.

LO 4 Consuming in the Real World

The lives of real consumers include several major components: culture, family, race and ethnicity, geopolitics, gender, and community.

Culture

If you are in the business of brand promotion, you are in the culture business. Culture infuses, works on, is part of, and generally lands on all consumption. **Culture** is what a people do, or "the total life ways of a people, the social legacy the individual acquires from his (her) group."[14] It is the way we eat, groom ourselves, celebrate, and mark our space and assert our position. It is the way things are done. Cultures often are thought of as large and national, but, in reality, cultures usually are smaller and not necessarily geographic, such as *urban hipster culture* or *teen tech-nerd culture*.

Usually it's easier to see and note culture when it's distant and unfamiliar, such as while traveling to another place. Members of a culture find the ways they do things to be perfectly natural. Culture thus is said to be invisible to those who are immersed in it. When everyone around us behaves in a similar fashion, we do not easily think about the existence of some large and powerful force acting on us all. But it's there; this constant background force is the force of culture. The sociocultural perspective offers the tools to help us see the culture that is all around us, as if we were visiting a strange land.

When marketers spend time and money studying why consumers consume certain goods or services, or why they consume them in a certain way, they are considering culture. Culture informs consumers' views about food, the body, gifts, possessions, a sense of self versus others, mating, courtship, death, religion, family, jobs, art, holidays, leisure, satisfaction, work—just about everything. It does this through several types of cultural expression:

- Values
- Rituals
- Stratification (social class), expressed through taste and cultural capital

Values are the defining expressions of culture. Values express in words and deeds what is important to a culture. For example, some cultures value propriety and restrained behavior, while others value open expression. Values are cultural bedrock; they cannot be changed quickly or easily. They thus are different from attitudes, which can be changed through a single advertising campaign or even a single ad. As shown in Exhibit 5.6, values are the foundation for attitudes and behavior. They influence attitudes, which then shape behavior. In this context, effective brand promotion is consistent with a culture's values. Marketers cannot expect to use advertising to change values in any substantive way. Rather, advertising influences values in the same way a persistent drip of water wears down a granite slab—very slowly and through cumulative impact, over years and years.

Typically, advertisers try to associate their product with a cultural value or criticize a competitor for being out of step with one. Advertisements that are out of step with the values of a people likely will be rejected. Many argue that the best (most effective) ads are those that best express and affirm core cultural values. For example, one core American value is said to be individualism, or the predisposition to value the individual over the group. To the extent that this is true, marketers in America can appeal to consumers' sense of individual style or their rugged individualism.

IF YOU ARE IN THE BUSINESS OF **BRAND PROMOTION,** YOU ARE IN THE **CULTURE** **BUSINESS.**

Exhibit 5.6
Culture Shapes Consumer Behavior

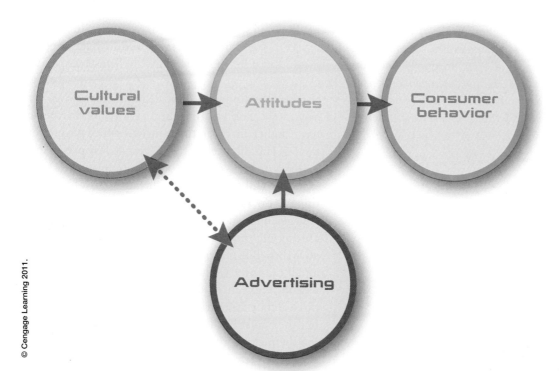

© Cengage Learning 2011.

rituals repeated behaviors that affirm, express, and maintain cultural values

stratification (social class) individuals' relative standing in a social system as produced by systematic inequalities

However, globalization makes the world more homogeneous in media and consumption. The trick for transnational companies is to understand how to adjust for both globalism and local values.

Cultures affirm, express, and maintain their values through rituals. **Rituals** are "often-repeated formalized behaviors involving symbols."[15] Through the practice of rituals, individuals are made part of the culture, and the culture constantly renews and perpetuates itself. For example, ritual-laden holidays such as Thanksgiving and the Fourth of July help perpetuate aspects of American culture through their repeated reenactment (tradition).

As a part of their cultures, consumers participate in rituals. In fact, rituals help intertwine culture and consumption practices in a very real way. For example, Jell-O may have attained the prominence of an "official" American holiday food because of its regular usage as part of the Thanksgiving dinner ritual.[16] If you are a consumer packaged-goods manufacturer, understanding these types of ritual is not a trivial concern at all. Likewise, when a married couple buys a new home, they do all sorts of "unnecessary" things to make it theirs. They clean the carpets even if they were just cleaned; they trim trees that don't need trimming—all to make the new possession theirs and remove any trace of the former owner. These behaviors are not only

important to anthropologists; they also are important to those making and trying to sell products such as rug shampoos or lawn and garden equipment.

Rituals don't have to be the biggest events of the year. There are everyday rituals, such as the way we eat, clean ourselves, and groom. Think about all the habitual things you do from the time you get up in the morning until you crawl into bed at night. These things are done in a certain way; they are not random.[17] Members of a common culture tend to do them one way, and members of other cultures do them other ways. Daily rituals seem inconsequential because they are habitual and routine, and thus "invisible." If, however, someone tried to get you to significantly alter how often you shower or the way you handle a fork, that person would quickly learn just how resistant to change these rituals are.

If a product or service cannot be incorporated into an already-existing ritual, marketers will find it difficult and expensive to affect a change. Conversely, when a marketer can incorporate the consumption of a good or service into an existing ritual, success is much more likely. Clearly, there are important opportunities for marketers who successfully can link their products to consumption rituals.

Stratification (social class) refers to a person's relative standing in a social system as produced by systematic inequalities in measures such as wealth, income, education, power, and status. For example, some members of society exist within a richer group (stratum), others within a less affluent stratum. Race and gender also are unequally distributed across these strata. For example, men generally have higher incomes than women. Thus, a cross-section, or slice, of American society would reveal many different levels (or strata) of the population along these different dimensions. Some combination of these inequalities is what we mean by "social class." Social class is hard to pin down in some contemporary societies. In America, a very large majority of folks with a huge range in income, wealth, and education call themselves "middle class."

Income alone does not define "social class" very accurately. For example, successful plumbers often have higher incomes than unsuccessful lawyers, but their occupation tends to be seen as less prestigious, and the prestige of one's occupation also enters into what we call social class. Education also has something to do with social class, but a person with a little college experience and a lot of inherited wealth probably would rank higher than an insurance agent with an MBA. Bill Gates left Harvard without a degree, and he has pretty high social standing, not to mention wealth. Thus, income, education, and occupation are three important variables for indicating social class, but they must be viewed together. Further complicating the picture, rock stars, professional athletes, and successful actors have high incomes but are generally thought to be somewhat outside the social class system. This is another reason the term "social class" has been falling away.

Members of the same social strata tend to live in similar ways, have similar views and philosophies, and, most critically, tend to consume in somewhat similar ways. Markers of social class would include what one wears, where one lives, and how one speaks. In a consumer society, consumption marks or indicates stratification in a myriad of ways. Stratification-related consumption preferences reflect value differences and ways of seeing the world. Writer John Seabrook notes that we now know social class mostly by "the services you use, where you live, and the control they have over other people's labor."[18] In other words, other than housing, social stratification is marked through consumption by a consumer's ability to afford all sorts of services, particularly those such as housekeepers and personal trainers.

Social class affects consumption through tastes. **Taste** refers to a generalized set or orientation to consumer preferences. We think of upper classes preferring tennis to bowling and eating brie more than Velveeta. Tastes include media habits and, thus, exposure to various advertising media vehicles—for example, *RV Life* versus *Wine Spectator*. Today fashion and taste cycle faster than they once did, and

Target has been one of the most amazing brands, with amazing ads to match over the last few years. The company's ads are almost devoid of words (copy) and are stylish, hip, and self-aware. Throughout the years, Target has made the logo for its store mean more than the labels on many of its products. It is, in our view, the best branding communication of the past few years.

consumers may be more playful in their use of class markers than they once were. For example, Target combined low prices with designer labels in a way that attracted shoppers from various strata. Some have seen this retail success as a democratization of style and taste.

A concept related to taste is *cultural capital*, the value that cultures place on certain consumption practices and objects. For example, a certain consumption practice (say, snowboarding) has a certain capital or value (like money) for some segment of the population. If you own a snowboard (a certain amount of cultural capital), and actually can use it (more cultural capital), and look good while using it (even more capital), then this activity is like cultural currency or cultural money in the bank. You can "spend" it. It gets you things you want. Depending on your cultural group, you might get cultural capital from ordering the right pinot noir, flying first class, or knowing about the funniest new video on YouTube. The value of the cultural capital will depend on which consumer practices are favored within the culture. Advertisers try to figure out which ones are valued more, and why, and how to make their product sought after because it has higher cultural capital and can be sold at a higher price. Does an iPhone have more cultural capital than a BlackBerry? To whom? To what cultural group? To what market segment? Maybe the coolest people don't have any of those things; they are free of their electronic leash. Having good "taste" helps you know which things have high cultural capital.

archetype/Shutterstock.com

Family

Consumer behavior also takes place within the context of families. Advertisers not only want to discern the needs of different kinds of families but also to discover how decisions are made within families. The first is possible; the latter is much more difficult. For a while, consumer researchers tried to determine who in the traditional nuclear family (that is, Mom, Dad, and the kids) made various purchasing decisions. This was largely an exercise in futility. Due to errors in reporting and conflicting perceptions between partners, it became clear that the family purchasing process is anything but clear. While some types of purchases are handled by one family member, many decisions actually are diffuse nondecisions, arrived at through what consumer researcher C. W. Park aptly calls a "muddling-through" process.[19] These "decisions" just get made, and no one really is sure who made them, or even when. For an advertiser to influence such a diffuse and vague process indeed is a challenge.

The consumer behavior of the family is a complex and often subtle type of social negotiation. One person handles this, another one takes care of that. Sometimes specific purchases fall along gender lines, but sometimes they don't. While children may not be the buyers in many instances, they can play important roles as initiators, influencers, and users in many categories, such as cereals, clothing, vacation destinations, fast-food restaurants, and technology (like computers). Still, some advertisers capitalize on the flexibility of this social system by suggesting in their ads who *should* take charge of a given consumption task, and then arming that person with the appearance of expertise so that whoever wants the job can take it and defend his or her purchases.

Families have a lasting influence on the consumer preferences of family members. One of the best predictors of the brands adults use is the ones their parents used. This is true for cars, toothpaste, household cleansers, and many more products. Say you go off to college. You eventually have to do laundry, so you go to the store, and you buy Tide. Why Tide? Well, you're not sure, but you saw it around your house when you lived with your parents, and things seemed to have worked out okay for them, so you buy it for yourself. The habit sticks, and you keep buying it. This is called an **intergenerational effect**.

intergenerational effect choice of products based on what was used in the consumer's childhood household

Marketers often focus on the major or gross differences in types of families because different families have different needs, buy different things, and are reached by different media. *Family* is a very open concept these days. The old-fashioned norm of two parents and a few children is not today's norm. There are a lot of single parents and quite a few second and even third marriages. Many households include members of the extended family (nuclear family plus grandparents, cousins, and others). Also, there are gay and lesbian households with and without children. Even in traditional family structures, roles often change when both parents (or a single parent) take jobs outside the home. For instance, a teenage son or daughter may be given the role of initiator and buyer, while the parent or parents merely serve as influences.

Beyond the basic configuration, advertisers often are interested in knowing details such as the age of the youngest child, the size of the family, and the family income. The age of the youngest child living at home is called a **life stage** variable; it tells an advertiser where the family is in terms of its needs and obligations (that is, toys, investment instruments for college savings, clothing, and vacations). When the youngest child leaves home, the consumption patterns of a family radically change.

Celebrity is a unique sociological concept, and it matters a great deal to advertisers. Twenty-first-century society is all about celebrity. Current thinking is that, in a celebrity-based culture, celebrities help contemporary consumers with identity. Identity in a consumer culture becomes a "fashion accessory" prop for a day—head banger, corporate drudge at work in a cubicle, and so forth. The idea is that contemporary consumers are very good at putting on and taking off, trying on, switching, and trading various identities, in the same way that they have clicked through the channels since they could reach the remote. Sometime during one's mid- to late 20s (at least in the United States), social identity stabilizes dramatically. Therefore, the understanding of the celebrity is more complex and vital than merely thinking in terms of similar attitudes and behaviors such as body image and choice of hairstyles. Some sociologists believe that celebrities have become socialization agents, a role traditionally held by local communities and families. Further, with social media websites such as YouTube and Facebook, the line between mass media and daily contemporary life blurs more all the time. Advertisers generally think this is a good thing because rapid identity shifts are another kind of marketing opportunity.

Race and Ethnicity

Race and ethnicity provide other ways to think about important social groups. Answering the question of how race figures into consumer behavior is very difficult. Our discomfort stems from having, on the one hand, the desire to say, "Race doesn't matter, we're all the same," and on the other hand not wanting (or not being able) to deny the significance of race in terms of reaching ethnic cultures and influencing a wide variety

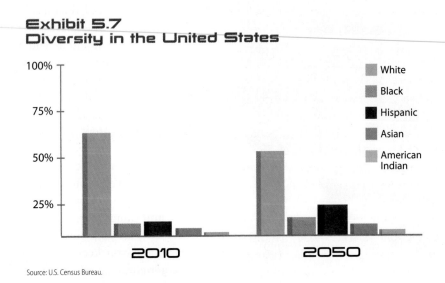

Exhibit 5.7
Diversity in the United States

Source: U.S. Census Bureau.

of behaviors, including consumer behavior. The truth is we are less and less sure what *race* is and what it means. Obviously, a person's pigmentation, in and of itself, has almost nothing to do with preferences for one type of product over another. But because race has mattered in culture, it does still matter in consumer behavior.

The United States, Europe, and much of the world is becoming an increasingly ethnically diverse culture, while at the same time becoming more homogeneous (important exceptions exist) in terms of consumer culture. Exhibit 5.7 compares current and projected racial diversity in the United States. By the middle of the 21st century, whites probably will be very close to only 50 percent of the U.S. population. This demographic reality is very important to advertisers and marketers. However, it wasn't until the mid- to late 1980s that most American corporations made a concerted effort to court African-American consumers, or even to recognize their existence.[20] Efforts to serve the Hispanic consumer have been intermittent and inconsistent.

There probably isn't an area in consumer behavior where research is more inadequate. This probably is because everyone is terrified to discuss it and because most of the findings we do have are suspect. What is attributed to race often is due to another factor that is itself associated with race. For example, consumer behavior textbooks commonly say something to the effect that African Americans and Hispanics are more brand loyal than their Anglo counterparts. Data on the frequency of brand switching is offered, and lo and behold, it does appear that white people switch brands more often. But why? Some ethnic minorities live in areas where there are fewer retail choices. When we statistically remove the effect of income disparities between white people and people of color, we see that the brand-switching effect often disappears. This suggests that brand loyalty is not a function of race but of disposable income and shopping options.

Still, race does inform one's social identity to varying degrees. One is not blind to one's own ethnicity. African Americans, Hispanics, and other ethnic groups have culturally related consumption preferences. Certain brands become associated with racial or ethnic groups. It is not enough, however, for advertisers to say one group is different from another group, or that people prefer one brand over another simply because they are members of a racial or ethnic category. If advertisers really want a good, long-term relationship with their customers, they must acquire, through good consumer research, a deeper understanding of who their customers are and how this identity is affected by culture, felt ethnicity, and race. In short, advertisers must ask why groups of consumers are different or prefer different brands, and they must not settle for an easy answer.

Geopolitics

In spite of increasing globalization and general homogeneity at the level of accepting the basic ethos and trappings of consumer culture, there are some important countercurrents: brands for "us." There are many places in the world where religious-ethnic-political strife is abundant, and this gets played out in consumption domains. An example is Mecca Cola, created to appeal to consumers in parts of the world where the West is not admired. Current issues also have provided the impetus for "green" brands and brands associated with fair labor practices.

Courtesy of Lexus, a division of Toyota USA; ad developed by Team One, El Segundo, CA.

A major political issue today involves the impact of consumption practices on the environment. For people who hate to give up creature comforts but care about the planet, this ad promises that the hybrid Lexus LS 600h L "Gives more to the driver. Takes less from the world."

Gender

Gender is the social expression of sexual biology, sexual choice, or both. Obviously, gender matters in consumption. But are men and women really that different in any meaningful way in their consumption behavior, beyond the obvious? Again, to the extent that gender informs a "culture of gender," the answer is yes. As long as men and women are the products of differential socialization, then they will continue to be different in some significant ways. There is, however, no definitive list of gender differences in consumption because the expression of gender, just like anything else social, depends on the situation and the social circumstances. In the 1920s, advertisers openly referred to women as less logical, more emotional, and the cultural stewards of beauty.[21] (Some say that the same soft, irrational, emotional feminine persona still is invoked in advertising.) Advertising helps construct a social reality, with gender a predominant feature. Not only is it a matter of conscience and social responsibility to be aware of this, but it is good business as well. Advertisers must keep in mind, though, that it's hard to keep the business of people you patronize, insult, or ignore.

Obviously, gender's impact on consumer behavior is not limited to heterosexual men and women. Gay men and lesbians are large and significant markets. Of late, these markets have been targeted by corporate titans such as IBM and United Airlines.[22] Again, these are markets that desire to be acknowledged and served, but not stereotyped and patronized.

Just as marketers discovered working women in the late 1970s, African-American and Hispanic consumers in the 1980s, and then somewhat later Asian Americans, they recently have discovered gays and lesbians. Of course, these people weren't missing. They were there all along. These "discoveries" of forgotten and marginalized social groups create some interesting problems for advertisers. Members of these groups, quite reasonably, want to be served just like any other consumers. Consider what Wally Snyder of the American Advertising Federation said:

Advertising that addresses the realities of America's multicultural population must be created by qualified professionals who understand the nuances of the disparate cultures.

Otherwise, agencies and marketers run the risk of losing or, worse, alienating millions of consumers eager to buy their products or services. Building a business that "looks like" the nation's increasingly multicultural population is no longer simply a moral choice, it is a business imperative.[23]

Attention and representation without stereotyping from a medium and a genre that is known for stereotyping might be a lot to expect, but it's not that much.

Community

Consumers also are members of communities. **Community** is a powerful and traditional sociological concept with a meaning that extends well beyond the idea of a specific geographic place. Communities can be imagined or even virtual. Community members believe that they belong to a group of people who are similar to them in some important way and different from those not in the community. Members of communities often share rituals and traditions, and they feel some sort of responsibility to one another and the community.

Advertisers are becoming increasingly aware of the power of community. Products have social meanings, and community is the quintessential social domain, so consumption is inseparable from the notion of where we live (actually or virtually), and with whom we feel a kinship or a sense of belonging. Communities often exert a great deal of power. A community may be your neighborhood, or it may be people like you with whom you feel a kinship, such as members of social clubs, other consumers who collect the same things you do, or people who have, use, or admire the same brands you do.

Brand communities are groups of consumers who feel a commonality and a shared purpose attached to

Mike Flippo/Shutterstock.com.

a consumer good or service.[24] When owners of vintage Corvettes experience a sense of connectedness by virtue of their common ownership or usage, a brand community exists. When two perfect strangers stand in a parking lot and act like old friends simply because they both own Corvettes, a type of community is revealed.

Most of these communities exist online. Like many other companies, the online T-shirt business Threadless builds a community around its brand. But at Threadless, the community builds the brand, too. Threadless designs come not from big-name stylists but from customers. Anybody who wants to can submit a design; about 125 new submissions come in daily. Entries are posted online, where site visitors rate them on a zero-to-five scale. Each week, the company picks six of the most popular designs to print on T-shirts. Threadless also relies on its online community to be its primary marketing tool. Site visitors are encouraged to upload photos, leave comments, and refer friends. "The bigger and more active the community, the more sales go up," said creative director Jeffrey Kalmikoff. "It's hard to argue with that formula."[25]

The promise of community—not to be alone, to share appreciation and admiration of something or someone, no matter how odd or inappropriate others feel it to be—is fulfilled in online communities. It is a rewarding and embracing social collective centered on a brand. This should not surprise us too much, given how central consumption and branding have become in contemporary society. Brands matter socially, so brands matter.

LO 5 Advertising, Social Rift, and "Revolution"

Thomas Frank, Doug Holt, Heath and Potter, and others have noted that consumers sometimes use their consumption choices to stake out a position in a "revolution" of sorts. Frank traces this to the 1960s cultural revolution (discussed in Chapter 3) and sees it as an opportunity, particularly for youth markets, to provide the costumes and consumable accessories for these "revolutions": certain "looks," such as dressing all in black, that say "I'm part of this political-social group."

More generally, marketers should keep in mind that any time there is a great social movement or a time of rapid change, opportunities galore are opened up to the marketer. When the earth moves under our feet, we feel off balance and in need of reassurance. At those times, branded products often promise that reassurance. In the United States, many people would define the past decade as a time of disruption and change, as people struggle with how to respond to frightening problems such as terrorism and economic uncertainty. How well would you say marketers have responded with reassurance?

LO 6 How Ads Transmit Meaning

Things always stand for other values; and the advertiser is merely making sure the translation is vivid and to the product's advantage.
—Michael Schudson

Advertising can be thought of as a text. It is "read" and interpreted by consumers. You can think of it as being like other texts, books, movies, posters, paintings, and so on. To "get" ads, you have to know something of the cultural code, or they would make no sense. To understand a movie fully, you have to know something about the culture that created it. When you see a foreign film (even in your native tongue), you might not get all the jokes and references because you don't possess the cultural knowledge necessary to "read" the text effectively. Like these other forms, advertisements are sociocultural texts. Ads try to turn already meaningful things into things with very special meaning— carefully projected and crafted meaning concentrated through the mass media with the purpose of selling.

Of course, consumers are free to accept, reject, or adjust that meaning to suit their taste. Marketers say the product they are selling is cool. The consumer might say, "No, it isn't," or "Yeah, it is," or "Well, yeah, but not in the way they think," or "Maybe for you, but not for me." While marketers try very hard to project just the right meaning, it is ultimately consumers who determine the meaning of ads and brands. Likewise, consumers determine what is or is not cool, what has cultural value (capital) to them, and how much.

In this regard, Martin Davidson aptly expressed the advertiser's challenge:

Start work in an ad agency and the first thing they teach you is the difference between a product and a brand. That is because it is advertising's job to turn one into another.[26]

Exhibit 5.8
The Movement of Meaning

Location of meaning Instrument of meaning transfer

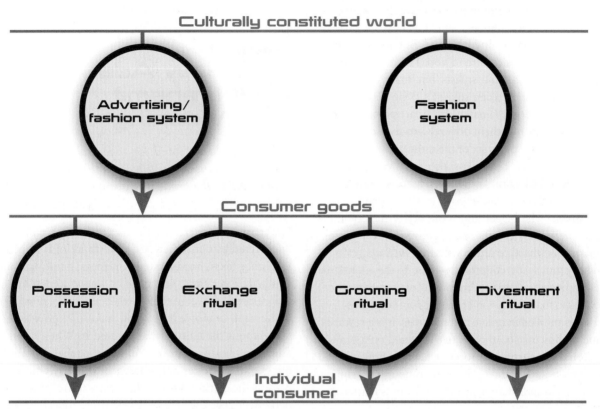

© Cengage Learning 2011.

Yes, ads turn products into brands, and sometimes successful ones. They do this, in large part, by trying to wrap material objects or marketed services with a certain meaning—a meaning that comes from culture.

The key is the link between culture and advertising. Anthropologist Grant McCracken has offered the model in Exhibit 5.8 to explain how advertising (along with other cultural agents) functions in the transmission of meaning. To understand advertising as a mechanism of cultural meaning transfer is to understand a great deal about advertising. In fact, one legitimately could say that advertisers really are in the meaning transfer business. You take meaning that exists in the culture and massage it, shape it, and try to transfer it onto your brand.

Think about McCracken's model as you examine the ad for Ugg. The product—in this case, boots—exists "out there" in the culturally constituted world

(the real social world), but it needs advertising to link it to certain social scenes, certain slices of life. The advertiser places the advertised product and the slice of social life in an ad to get the two to rub off on each other, to intermingle, to become part of the same social scene. In other words, the product is given social meaning by being placed within an ad that represents an idealized context. This slice of life, of course, is the type of social setting in which potential customers might find, or desire to find, themselves. According to McCracken's model, meaning has moved from the world to the product (boots) by virtue of its sharing space within the frame of the advertisement. When advertisers put things within the frame of an ad, they want the reader of the ad to put them together seamlessly, to take them together as part of each other. When a consumer purchases or otherwise incorporates that good or service into his or her own life, the meaning is transferred to the individual consumer. Meaning is thus moved from the world to the product (via advertising) to the individual. When the individual uses the product, that person conveys to others the meaning he or she and the advertisement have given it now. Their use incorporates various rituals that facilitate the movement of meaning from good to consumer. The rituals aren't central to this discussion, but they would be the kinds of activities we already discussed in the section on rituals, such as possession rituals that make a product feel like one's own.

Ads also become part of consumers' everyday landscape, language, and reality. Characters, lines, and references all become part of conversations, thoughts, and—coming full circle—the culture. Children, coworkers, family members, and talk-show hosts all pick up phrases, ideas, slogans, and agendas from ads, and then they replay them, adapt them, and recirculate them as they do with similar elements from movies, books, and other texts. Ads, in many ways, don't exist just within the sociocultural context; they *are* the sociocultural context of our time. If you want to do well in the real world of brand promotion, it's a very good idea to understand that getting the contemporary culture and knowing how to move it into ads is worth its weight in gold.

An Ugg boot is not just any boot. One goal of this advertisement is to create a special meaning for this brand.

STUDY TOOLS
CHAPTER 5

Located at back of the textbook

- **Rip out Chapter in Review Card.**

Located at www.cengagebrain.com

- **Review Key Terms Flashcards (Print or Online).**
- **Complete the Practice Quiz to prepare for tests.**
- **Play "Beat the Clock" and "Quizbowl" to master concepts.**
- **Complete "Crossword Puzzle" to review key terms.**
- **Watch videos on Old Spice and Chevrolet for real company examples.**
- **Additional examples can be found online for use.net groups, GM's promotion of Cadillac, and peripheral cues used in advertising campaigns.**

CHAPTER 6

The Regulatory and Ethical Environment of Promotions

When you go online, hundreds of companies are tracking your every click. Are they serving you or stalking you?

| DOWNLOAD NOW | ABOUT GHOSTERY | PRIVACY POLICY | SUPPORT | GHOSTERY BLOG |

Today's marketers see consumer control as an ethical priority.

Detect

Ghostery sees the invisible web - tags, web bugs, pixels and beacons. Ghostery tracks the trackers and gives you a roll-call of the ad networks, behavioral data providers, web publishers, and other companies interested in your activity.

Learn

After showing you who's tracking you, Ghostery also gives you a chance to learn more about each company it identifies. How they describe themselves, a link to their privacy policies, and a sampling of pages where we've found them are just a click away.

Control

Ghostery allows you to block scripts from companies that you don't trust, delete local shared objects, and even block images and iframes. Ghostery puts your web privacy back in your hands.

DOWNLOAD GHOSTERY FOR FREE

| CONNECT WITH GHOSTERY | FEATURED ON | OUR PROMISE |

 Follow Us On Twitter

 Friend Us on Facebook

 Contact Us

The New York Times

THE GLOBE AND MAIL

The Washington Post

 AOL PC WORLD

NO ADWARE, SPYWARE OR MALWARE...EVER.

Ghostery is free to download and use - plus you have our promise that Ghostery will never be used for advertising. In fact, Ghostery is now part of Evidon, whose mission is to enable a more transparent, trusted environment for consumers and advertisers online.
Learn more »

Learning Outcomes

After studying this chapter, you should be able to:

LO 1 Discuss the impact of promotion on society's well-being.

LO 2 Summarize ethical considerations related to brand promotion campaigns.

LO 3 Describe aspects of advertising regulated by the U.S. government.

LO 4 Summarize the regulatory role of the Federal Trade Commission.

LO 5 Explain the meaning and importance of self-regulation by marketers.

LO 6 Discuss the regulation of direct marketing, sales promotion, and public relations.

> "Never write an advertisement which you wouldn't want your own family to read."
>
> —David Ogilvy

Stalking or Serving?

AFTER YOU FINISH THIS CHAPTER GO TO PAGE 137 FOR STUDY TOOLS

We're all busy these days, so maybe it would be a dream come true to have a talented butler or executive assistant follow us around to help, knowing our tastes and anticipating our priorities. That seems to be how some online marketers view their role: they want to know everything they can about Internet users so they can offer up the most relevant products and promotional messages, sparing consumers the nuisance of sorting through mass-marketing appeals. Some consumers, however, feel more like they're being stalked—if they even notice what's going on.

Suppose you're in the market for a credit card. If you visit Capital One Financial Corporation's website, you might see an offer for a deal that looks pretty good. What you might not realize is that Capital One has other offers but is serving up one or two to you, based on what it thinks it knows about you, even if it's your first visit to the site. Capital One can do this because it subscribes to a data-gathering and analysis service called [x+1]. That service plants software around the Internet to gather data on your computer's activity, cross-referencing it with public records to make inferences about your home ownership, household income, marital status, regular purchases, topics of interest, and more. Then [x+1] uses statistical analysis to make predictions about your interests and activities. While Capital One says it doesn't use information from [x+1] to make lending decisions, it does use the information to tailor its marketing message. If it believes a visitor to its website is likely to be someone with no credit card or a limit below $5,000, the site will serve up an offer tailored for someone with just "average" credit.[1] That's handy if you wouldn't have qualified for a better deal anyway, but if you already have a stellar track record of paying off a credit card, you might not realize you can search the site for a better offer.

What do you think?

On the whole, brand promotion is good for our society.

1 2 3 4 5 6 7
STRONGLY DISAGREE   STRONGLY AGREE

More disturbing to some computer users is that companies—sometimes dozens of them on one website—are collecting data without the user's knowledge. Many people are familiar with cookies, the small files installed by websites that keep track of user information so it's easy to fill out forms or so you can quickly find products you've ordered in the past. Fewer people know about Web bugs, which are image files that are planted on websites and are so small (as small as a pixel) that they go undetected as they gather data. And more recently, major websites have begun using "supercookies," which can recreate users' profiles even if they delete their cookie files.[2] These can study the history of the Web browser's activity to see if the user visited certain kinds of websites, including topics as personal as fertility problems and fixing bad credit. In general, all of these tools operate automatically, without informing the computer user about data being gathered. So if you let your cousin borrow your computer to see if she can get advice on avoiding bankruptcy, when you start using your computer again, you might suddenly start seeing ads offering to help you repair your own credit rating.

For the most part, these activities are legal, at least at the time of this writing. But are they ethical? There are plenty of signs that they make consumers uncomfortable. Web browsers have been designed to help users manage their cookies, and the major browsers have announced efforts to develop "do not track" options that limit the amount of information gathered. Computer users are installing programs such as Ghostery and Abine, which display lists of services tracking your data and allow you to block the tracking.[3] Ethical marketers are addressing this concern, too. Many publish privacy policies and give consumers the choice to opt in to receive promotional messages. Industry trade groups that belong to the Digital Advertising Alliance have set up a program in which participants who run online ads include an icon that takes consumers to a website explaining how data are used to target consumers and how consumers can opt out if they prefer to receive only standard ads. And a group of data-tracking firms are creating a service called the Open Data Partnership, which will allow consumers to read and edit the information the firms have gathered about them.[4] That effort should improve the quality of the data at the same time it soothes ethical concerns.

The challenges of gathering online data from consumers show that the social, ethical, and regulatory aspects of marketing are dynamic and controversial. What is socially responsible or irresponsible, ethically debatable, politically correct, or legal? The answers are changing constantly. As a society changes, so, too, do its perspectives. And marketing, like anything else with social roots and implications, will be affected by these changes.

Many criticisms of promotional campaigns are uninformed, naïve, and simplistic; they fail to consider the complex social and legal environment in which contemporary brand promotion operates. Especially as marketers, we need to distinguish valid critiques of overzealous promotion efforts from irrational criticism based only on intuition and emotion.

LO 1 Social Impact of Brand Promotion

For those who feel that advertising is intrusive, manipulative, and wasteful, the impact of brand promotion on society usually fuels heated debate. From a balanced perspective, however, we can consider the effect of brand promotion on consumers' knowledge, standard of living, and feelings of happiness and well-being, and its potential effects on the mass media. Our approach is to offer the pros and cons on several issues that often arise in discussions of marketing's impact on society (see Exhibit 6.1). These are matters of opinion, with no clear right and wrong answers. As you draw your own conclusions, be analytical and thoughtful. Until you understand and contemplate these issues, you really haven't studied promotion at all.

Education or Intrusion?

Does brand promotion give consumers valuable information, or does it only confuse or entice them? Here's what experts on both sides have to say.

Promotion Informs

Supporters of brand promotion argue that it educates consumers, equipping them with information needed to make informed purchasing decisions. By regularly assessing the information in promotional messages, consumers become more educated about the features, benefits, functions, and value of products. Further, consumers can become more aware of their own tendencies to be persuaded by and rely on certain types of product information. Historically, the view has been that advertising is "clearly an immensely powerful instrument for the elimination of ignorance."[5] That might be a *little* bit overstated, but there's logic to the idea that better-educated consumers enhance their lifestyles and economic power through astute decision making.

A related argument is that brand promotion reduces the amount of time spent in searching for desired products

Exhibit 6.1
Pros and Cons of Brand Promotion

Where would you rate brand promotion on each scale?

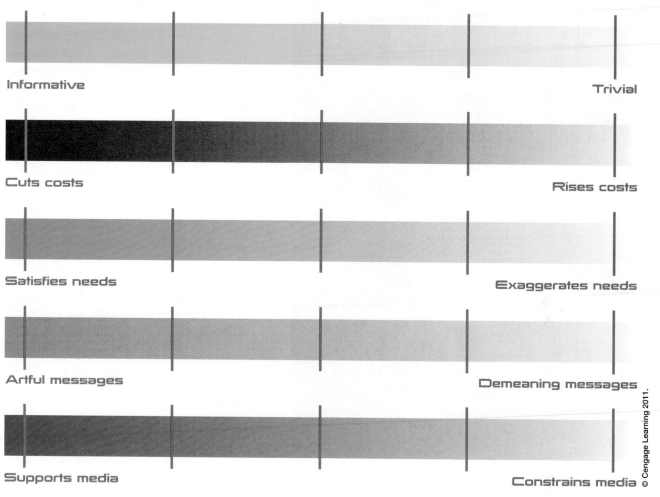

Informative   Trivial

Cuts costs   Rises costs

Satisfies needs   Exaggerates needs

Artful messages   Demeaning messages

Supports media   Constrains media

and services. The large amount of information readily available through advertisements, websites, and other marketing communication helps consumers learn about the potential value of brands; they don't have to travel from store to store, trying to evaluate each one.

Advertising also informs the public about important social issues. Miller Brewing devotes millions of dollars a year to promoting responsible drinking through advertisements. Another brewer, Anheuser-Busch, has developed an integrated marketing campaign designed to combat drunken driving, underage drinking, and binge drinking. Anheuser-Busch has spent more than $500 million on efforts that include the website http://www.beeresponsible.com, which details company policies and programs and also offers statistics about the issue plus links to resources and information. Advertising messages have promoted the use of designated drivers and cab rides home, as well as encouraged parents to discuss responsible

drinking with their children. The firm's "Responsibility Matters" campaign supports community-based programs that promote responsible behavior.[6]

Promotion Is Superficial and Intrusive

Critics argue that brand promotion does not provide good product information at all but only superficial ideas. Some would go so far as to say that advertising messages are biased, limited, and inherently deceptive. This argument is based on an attitude that promotional efforts should provide information related strictly to functional features and performance results—qualities that can be measured and tested brand by brand.

Marketers respond that, in many instances, consumers are interested in more than a physical, tangible material good with performance features and purely functional value. Emotional factors also play an important role in consumer's choices. Thus, critics often dismiss as unimportant or ignore the totality of

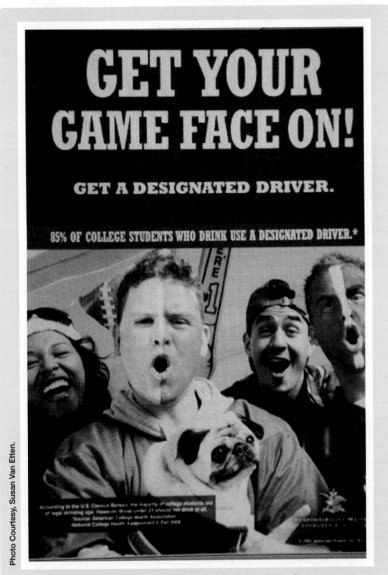

Advertising can be used to inform the public about important social issues. Here, Anheuser-Busch tells possible beer drinkers that they should pick a designated driver *before* they start celebrating.

mere 30-second advertising spot and to make their brands part of consumer lifestyles. The chief marketing officer at American Express said in a keynote speech to a large advertising audience, "We need to adapt to the new landscape by thinking not in day-parts [referring to television advertising schedules] but to mindparts."[8]

Marketers should pay attention to consumers' aggravation with the intrusiveness of promotional messages because clutter and intrusiveness reduce the effectiveness of those messages. According to one expert, "The ability of the average consumer to even remember advertising 24 hours later is at the lowest level in the history of our business."[9] But there is little evidence that marketers will reduce clutter. Another industry expert suggests, "New media have more potential to deliver even more saturation, clutter, and intrusiveness than traditional media, in which case the new media will only worsen marketing resistance."[10]

Lower Costs or Wasted Resources?

Another hotly debated issue is whether brand promotion raises or lowers costs. Opinions on this issue go right to the heart of whether promotional efforts are a good use or a waste of energy and resources.

Lower Product Costs

According to supporters of brand promotion, it helps lower the cost of products in four ways:

1. By stimulating demand, promotion results in economies of scale (as a company produces larger quantities, the cost of each unit falls). As a result, products cost less than if there was less promotion and hence less demand. Presumably, companies with lower production and administrative costs per unit will pass on the savings to consumers.

2. Promotion increases the probability that new products will succeed, so consumers have a greater variety of choices. They can more easily switch to a new offering, so marketers have an incentive to keep costs and prices low.

3. As brand promotion fuels the pressures of competition and the desire to have fresh, marketable brands, firms are motivated to produce improved products and brands and to introduce lower-priced brands.

brand benefits that consumers seek, including emotional, hedonic (pleasure-seeking), or aesthetic benefits. Marketers say they are trying to communicate relevant information for buyers who focus on these qualities.

Critics further contend that brand promotion is not merely unhelpful but so pervasive and intrusive that it is downright annoying. Similarly, consumers are frustrated with brands working their way into entertainment programming. In a different survey, 72 percent of consumers said product placement and integration with entertainment content were allowing advertising to become too pervasive.[7] Are marketers paying attention? Even as consumers say brand promotion is intruding on their lives, big advertisers like American Express are pushing to become more "relevant" to consumers than a

BRAND PROMOTION HELPS CREATE THE ECONOMIC CONDITIONS IN WHICH CONSUMERS HAVE AN ABUNDANCE OF CHOICES. DO YOU FIND SUCH CHOICES EXCITING OR OVERWHELMING?

carroteater/Shutterstock.com

4. The speed and reach of the marketing process aids in the diffusion of innovations. This means that new discoveries can be communicated to a large percentage of the marketplace very quickly. Innovations succeed when the promotional mix communicates their benefits.

All four of these factors can contribute positively to a society's standard of living and quality of life. Brand promotion may be instrumental in bringing about these effects because it serves an important role in demand stimulation and keeping customers informed.

Wasted Resources and Uneven Benefits

One of the traditional criticisms of marketing, especially advertising, is that it represents an inefficient, wasteful process that channels monetary and human resources in a society to the "shuffling of existing total demand," rather than to the expansion of total demand.[11] In this view, a society is no better off with advertising because ads do not stimulate demand—they only shift demand from one brand to another. Advertising thus brings about economic stagnation and a *lower* standard of living, not a higher standard of living.

Similarly, critics argue that brand differences are trivial, so the proliferation of brands does not offer a greater variety of choice but rather a meaningless waste of resources, with confusion and frustration for the consumer.

Some critics go so far as to argue that advertising is a tool of capitalism that only helps widen the gap between rich and poor, creating strife between social classes.

Greater Well-Being or More Dissatisfaction?

Critics and supporters of brand promotion differ significantly in their views about how it affects consumers' happiness and general well-being. This is a complex issue.

Need Creation

A common cry among critics is that brand promotion creates needs and makes people buy things they don't really need or even want. The argument is that consumers are relatively easy to seduce into wanting the next shiny bauble offered by marketers. Critics would say, for example, that any issue of *Seventeen* magazine seems to be intent on teaching young women to covet slim bodies and a glamorous complexion. Cosmetics giants like Estée Lauder and Revlon typically spend from 15 to 30 cents of every dollar of sales to promote their brands as the ultimate solution for those in search of the ideal complexion.

Need Satisfaction

Supporters of brand promotion take a broad understanding of human needs as their starting point. Abraham Maslow, a pioneer in the study of human motivation, conceived that human behavior is motivated by a hierarchy of need states:[12]

- *Physiological needs:* Biological needs that require the satisfaction of hunger, thirst, and basic bodily functions.
- *Safety needs:* The need to provide shelter and protection for the body and to maintain a comfortable existence.

- *Love and belonging needs:* The need for affiliation and affection. A person will strive for both the giving and receiving of love.

- *Esteem needs:* The need for recognition, status, and prestige. In addition to the respect of others, there is a need and desire for self-respect.

- *Self-actualization needs:* Maximum fulfillment of individual capabilities. This highest of the need states is achieved by only a small percentage of people, according to Maslow.

Recognizing that Maslow was describing *basic* human needs and motivations, not consumer needs and motivations, this model supports the idea that in the context of an affluent society, individuals will turn to goods and services to satisfy needs.

Many products directly address the requirements of one or more of Maslow's need states. Food and healthcare products, for example, relate to physiological needs. Home security systems and smoke detectors help address safety needs. Many personal care products promote feelings of self-esteem, confidence, glamour, and romance. In the pursuit of esteem, many consumers buy products they perceive to have status and prestige: expensive jewelry and homes are examples. Although it may be difficult to buy self-actualization, educational pursuits and high-intensity leisure activities (e.g., extreme sports) certainly can foster feelings of pride and accomplishment that contribute to self-actualization. But while marketing messages may be directed at many different forms of need fulfillment, that does not make it powerful enough to *create* basic human needs.

Promotion of Materialism

Critics also claim that brand promotion distorts individuals' wants and aspirations. The long-standing argument is that, in societies characterized by heavy advertising, people seek conformity and engage in status-seeking behavior, both of which are considered materialistic and superficial, because material goods are placed ahead of spiritual and intellectual pursuits.[13] Advertising, which portrays brands as symbols of status, success, and happiness, thus contributes to a society's materialism and superficiality. It creates wants and aspirations that are artificial and self-centered. As a result, societies overemphasize the production of private goods, to the detriment of public goods, such as highways, parks, schools, and infrastructure.[14]

Reflection of Society's Priorities

Although marketing messages undeniably promote the good life, defenders of brand promotion argue that it did not create the American emphasis on materialism. For example, in the United States, major holidays such as Christmas (gifts), Thanksgiving (food), and Easter (candy and clothing) have become festivals of consumption. This is the American way. Historian and social observer Stephen Fox concludes his treatise on the history of American advertising as follows:

> *One may build a compelling case that American culture is—beyond redemption—money-mad, hedonistic, superficial, rushing heedlessly down a railroad track called Progress. Tocqueville and other observers of the young republic described America in these terms in the early 1800s, decades before the development of national advertising. To blame advertising now for these most basic tendencies in American history is to miss the point. . . . The people who have created modern advertising are not hidden persuaders pushing our buttons in the service of some malevolent purpose. They are just producing an especially visible manifestation, good and bad, of the American way of life.[15]*

While we clearly live in the age of consumption, goods and possessions have been used by all cultures throughout history to mark special events, to play significant roles in rituals, and to serve as vessels of special meaning long before there was modern marketing. Still, it is worth asking whether marketing has taken it too far.

Demeaning or Artistic?

Marketers are always on the lookout for creative and novel ways to grab and hold the attention of their audience. Additionally, as we saw in Chapter 4, a marketer has a very specific profile of the target customer in mind when a promotional message is being created. Critics and defenders of marketing practices have reacted to the consequences of grabbing attention and appealing to social groups.

Perpetuating Stereotypes

Advertisements often portray people who look like members of their target audience. Marketers hope that, as a result, people who see the ad will be more prone to relate to it and attend to its message. Critics charge that advertisers trying to portray a target audience end up perpetuating stereotypes, especially in the portrayal of women, the elderly, and ethnic minorities. For example, many ads show women as homemakers or objects of desire, even though women really hold a wide variety of roles in society. The elderly often are shown as helpless or ill, even though many active seniors enjoy a rich lifestyle. Critics contend that advertisers' propensity to feature African-American or Latino athletes in ads is simply a more contemporary form of stereotyping.

Showing Sensitivity

Blatant stereotyping is becoming part of the past. Although advertisements from prior generations show a vivid stereotyping problem, today's images offer more variety. For example, Dove launched its "Campaign for Real Beauty" in September 2004 with advertisements featuring women whose appearances do not conform to the stereotypical and relatively narrow norms of beauty. The ads invited viewers to join in a discussion of beauty issues at http://www.campaignforrealbeauty.com.

Marketers are realizing that a diverse world requires diversity in the social reality that ads represent and help construct. However, many remain dissatisfied with the pace of change. Ads for women's beauty products that offer something other than the body of a supermodel as a valid point of reference are still the exception, not the rule.

Offending Sensibilities

Another criticism of brand promotion messages is that many of them are in poor taste, even offensive. Some would say the trend in American advertising is to be rude, crude, and sometimes lewd, as advertisers struggle to grab attention. Of course, taste is an inherently subjective evaluation. What offends one person is merely satiric to another. What should we call an ad prepared for the Australian market that shows the owner of an older Honda Accord admiring a newer model? The owner's admiration of the new car spurs the old version to lock its doors, rev its motor, and drive off a cliff—with the owner still inside. Critics decry the ad as trivializing suicide—an acute problem among young people, who also are the target market for this ad.[16]

But not all advertising deemed offensive has to be as extreme as this example. Many times, advertisers get caught in a firestorm of controversy because relatively small segments of the population are offended. Do you think the makers of Black Flag bug spray could have expected the reaction to their commercial? A war veterans' group objected to the playing of "Taps" over dead bugs.[17]

Do these advertisers portray women as objects to look at or as human beings? Would you call their messages affirming or offensive? Effective or ineffective?

Richard Avedon for Gianni Versace.

Extract used with kind permission of The Body Shop Int'l PLC UK.

Maybe hypersensitivity to consumer reaction is unnecessary. GoDaddy.com is making a nice living running risqué ads on the Super Bowl every year. In 2006, broadcaster ABC rejected the Web firm's first 13 ad submissions as "tasteless." The still-racy ad that finally ran during that year's Super Bowl created a 15-fold spike in traffic to the firm's website.[18]

In the end, we have to consider whether advertising is truly offensive or whether society is merely pushing the limits of what is appropriate for freedom of speech and expression. Standards for what is acceptable and what is offensive change over time in a culture.

Promising Liberation

Where some see stereotyping and poor taste, others see fulfillment and liberation. In fact, some argue that the consumption glorified by promotional campaigns is actually good for society. Most people sincerely appreciate modern conveniences that liberate us from the fouler facets of everyday life, such as body odor and close contact with dirty diapers. Some observers remind us that, when the Berlin Wall came down, those in East Germany did not immediately run to libraries and churches—they ran to department stores and shops.

Before the modern consumer age, the consumption of many goods was restricted by social class. Modern marketing has helped bring us a "democratization" of goods. In that sense, brand promotion and consumption offer a kind of liberation that should be appreciated and encouraged.

Deceiving with Subliminal Messages

Ever since a crackpot allegedly inserted the phrases "Eat Popcorn" and "Drink Coca-Cola" in a movie back in the 1950s, the world has been terrified that unscrupulous marketers will use subliminal messaging techniques to sell products. Much controversy—and almost a complete lack of understanding—persists about the issue of subliminal (below the threshold of consciousness) communication.[19] Despite rumors you may have heard, no one ever sold anything by putting images of breasts in ice cubes or the word *sex* in the background of an ad. Furthermore, no one at an advertising agency, except the very bored or the very eager to retire, has time to sit around dreaming up such things. Although it makes a great story, hiding pictures in other pictures doesn't get anyone to buy anything.

Recently, the issue has resurfaced as a research topic among neural scientists, but what they seem to be "rediscovering" is that you only can communicate commercial messages to people below the conscious threshold of awareness. People, indeed, can process information transmitted to them subliminally. However, these effects are very short lived and found only in laboratories. And the next effect never has been discovered: You cannot persuade people to act on the information they may have received this way. In other words, subliminal advertising doesn't work. The Svengali-type hocus-pocus that has become advertising mythology simply does not exist.[20] If the rumors are true that some advertisers actually are trying to use subliminal messages in their ads, the best research on the topic would conclude that they're wasting their money.[21]

Bringing Art to the Masses

Some argue that one of the best aspects of advertising is its artistic nature. The pop art movement of the late 1950s and 1960s, particularly in London and New York, was characterized by a fascination with commercial culture. Some of this art critiqued consumer culture and simultaneously celebrated it. Above all, Andy Warhol, himself a commercial illustrator, demonstrated that art was for the people and that the most accessible art was advertising. Art was not restricted to museum walls; it was on Campbell's soup cans, Life Savers candy rolls, and Brillo pads. Advertising is anti-elitist, pro-democratic art. As Warhol said about America, democracy, and Coke:

> *What's great about this country is that America started the tradition where the richest consumers buy essentially the same things as the poorest. . . . A Coke is a Coke and no amount of money can get you a better Coke than the one the bum on the corner is drinking. All the Cokes are the same and all the Cokes are good.*[22]

ADVERTISING GIVES PEOPLE **INVALUABLE EXPOSURE** TO SOCIAL AND POLITICAL ISSUES.

Enabling or Controlling Mass Media?

One final issue that advertisers and their critics debate is the matter of advertising's influence on the mass media. Here again, we find a wide range of viewpoints.

Support for Mass Media

Supporters of brand promotion describe advertising as the best thing that can happen to an informed democracy. Advertising expenditures support magazines, newspapers, and television and radio stations. In 2009, mass-media ad expenditures (counting mainly print and broadcast media) in the United States exceeded $140 billion.[23] If you include online advertising, the number approaches $200 billion. With this support of the media, citizens have access to a variety of information and entertainment sources at low cost. Without advertising support, network television and radio broadcasts would not be free, and newspapers and magazines likely would cost two to four times more. As marketers expand their efforts to reach consumers on social media, their ads are helping to support sites like Facebook and Twitter as well.

Furthermore, advertising gives people invaluable exposure to social and political issues. When noncommercial organizations (like social service organizations) advertise, members of society receive information on important issues. For example, the U.S. government, working in conjunction with the Partnership for a Drug-Free America, launched a multimedia campaign

Advertisements in magazines, in newspapers, and on television lowers the cost to consumers. Ad-free magazines could cost up to four times as much.

to remind the American public of the ruinous power of drugs such as heroin.[24] Over five years, the campaign has spent nearly $1 billion and prepared almost 400 ads, including powerful messages about the ultimate consequence of drug abuse.

ethics moral standards and principles against which behavior is judged

Influence over Programming

Critics argue that marketers who place ads in media have an unhealthy effect on the content of information in the media. The CEO of a firm headed for prosecution was accused of hiring a public relations firm to turn out a series of newspaper articles sympathetic to the CEO's firm.[25] Similarly, there have been several instances of "stealth sponsorship" of newspaper editorials: journalists were being paid by corporations that received favorable treatment in the editorials.[26]

Another type of influence comes indirectly when marketers purchase air time only on programs that draw large audiences. Critics argue that these mass-market programs lower the quality of television because cultural and educational programs, which draw smaller and more selective markets, are dropped in favor of mass-market programs. Watch a few episodes of *Survivor* or *Lost,* and it's hard to argue against the proposition that shallow content indeed is winning out over culture and education.

Similarly, television programmers have difficulty attracting advertisers to shows that may be valuable yet are controversial. Programs about abortion, sexual abuse, or AIDS may have trouble drawing advertisers, who fear the consequences of any association with controversial issues, given the predictable public reaction.

LO 2 Ethical Issues in Promotion

Where the social impact of brand promotion may be negative, ethical questions arise. **Ethics** are moral standards and principles against which behavior is judged. A broad definition of ethical behavior includes honesty, integrity, fairness, and sensitivity to others. In particular situations, however, determining what is ethical or unethical often comes down to personal judgment.

Telling the Truth

Truth in advertising is a legal issue with ethical dimensions. The most fundamental ethical issue has to do with **deception**—making false or misleading statements in a promotional message. The difficulty involves determining just what is deceptive. A manufacturer that claims a laundry product can remove grass stains is exposed to legal sanctions if the product cannot perform the task. In contrast, a manufacturer that claims to have "The Best Laundry Detergent in the World" is perfectly within its rights to employ superlatives. Just what constitutes "The Best" is a subjective determination; it cannot be proved or disproved. The use of superlatives such as "Number One" or "Best in the World" is called **puffery** and is considered legal. The courts have long held that consumers recognize and interpret superlatives as the exaggerated language of advertising.

Various promotional tools often are challenged as being deceptive. Consumers criticize the "small print" that spells out the details of contests or sweepstakes. Similarly, they get angry when the appeal of a "free" gift for listening to a pitch on a resort time-share leads them to a persistent hard sell. A consumer watchdog group is challenging brand placements in television shows as another kind of deception. The group Commercial Alert argues that television networks are deceiving consumers by not disclosing that they are taking money for highlighting brands within their programming.[27]

Another area of debate regarding truth in advertising relates to emotional appeals. It is likely impossible to legislate against emotional appeals such as those made about the beauty- or prestige-enhancing qualities of a brand because these claims are unquantifiable. Because these types of appeals are legal, the ethics of such appeals fall into a gray area. Beauty and prestige, it is argued, are in the eye of the beholder, and such appeals are neither illegal nor unethical. Your challenge is to develop ethical standards and values against which you will judge yourself and the actions of any organization for which you may work.

Targeting Children

The desire to restrict promotional messages aimed at children is based on a wide range of concerns, particularly because children between 2 and 11 years old see about 25,600 advertisements in a year. One concern is that brand promotion teaches superficiality and values founded in material goods and consumption, as we discussed earlier in the broader social context. Another is that children are inexperienced consumers and easy prey for marketers' sophisticated persuasions, so promotion influences children's demands for everything from toys to snack foods. These demands, in turn, create an environment of child-parent conflict. Parents have to say no over and over again to children whose desires are piqued by effective brand promotion. Child psychologists contend that advertising advocates violence, is responsible for child obesity, creates a breakdown in early learning skills, and results in a destruction of parental authority.[28]

A related contention is that many television shows aimed at children constitute program-length commercials. These programs feature commercial products, especially products aimed at children. A movement against this programming began in 1990, when critics counted

Anetta/Shutterstock.com

DO CHILDREN HAVE ENOUGH JUDGMENT AND EXPERIENCE TO MAKE SAFE, HEALTHY PURCHASE DECISIONS? DO MARKETERS HAVE AN OBLIGATION TO PROTECT THEM?

70 programs based on commercial products such as He-Man, the Smurfs, and the Muppets.[29] Special-interest groups have made several attempts to regulate this type of programming aimed at children, but, to date, the Federal Communications Commission permits it.

One of the earliest restrictions on advertising to children came in response to efforts of the special-interest group Action for Children's Television. Before the group disbanded in 1992, it helped get the Children's Television Act passed in 1990. This law restricts advertising on children's programming to 10.5 minutes per hour on weekends and 12 minutes per hour on weekdays.[30] More recently, in an attempt to head off government regulation, big food and beverage marketers—including Kraft and General Mills—signed the Children's Food and Beverage Advertising Initiative. The initiative is a voluntary commitment by firms to address obesity among children. Food and beverage marketers will devote half of their advertising dollars to ads directed to children to promote more healthful eating choices.[31]

Controversial Products

Some people question the wisdom of allowing the promotion of controversial goods and services, such as tobacco, alcoholic beverages, gambling and lotteries, and firearms. Critics charge that makers of tobacco and alcoholic beverages are targeting adolescents with promotional messages and are making dangerous and addictive products appealing.[32] This issue is complex.

Tobacco and Alcohol

Many medical journals have published survey research claiming that advertising "caused" cigarette smoking and alcohol consumption, particularly among teenagers.[33] However, these recent studies contradict research conducted since the 1950s carried out by marketing, communications, psychology, and economics researchers—including assessments of all the available research by the Federal Trade Commission.[34] The earlier studies (as well as several Gallup polls during the 1990s) found that family, friends, and peers—not advertising—are the primary influences on the use of tobacco and alcohol products. Studies published in the late 1990s and early in this decade have reaffirmed the findings of this earlier research.[35] While children at a very early age, indeed, can recognize tobacco advertising characters like Joe Camel, they also recognize as easily the Energizer Bunny (batteries), the Jolly Green Giant (canned vegetables), and Snoopy (life insurance)—all characters associated with adult products. Kids also are aware that

cigarettes cause disease and know that these products are intended for adults. Research in Europe offers the same conclusion: "Every study on the subject [of advertising effects on the use of tobacco and alcohol] finds that children are more influenced by parents and playmates than by the mass media."[36]

Why doesn't advertising cause people to smoke and drink? The simple answer is that advertising just isn't that powerful. Eight out of 10 new products fail, and if advertising were so powerful, no new products would fail. The more detailed answer is that advertising cannot create primary demand in mature product categories. **Primary demand** is demand for an entire product category. With mature products—like milk and alcohol—advertising isn't powerful enough to have that effect. Research across several decades has demonstrated repeatedly that advertising does not create primary demand for tobacco or alcohol.[37]

Although smoking any amount or drinking to excess is certainly not good for you, these behaviors emerge in a complex social context. The vast weight of research evidence over 40 years suggests that advertising is not a significant causal influence on initiation behavior (e.g., smoking, drinking). Rather, advertising plays its most important role in consumers' choice of brands (e.g., Camel, Coors) after they have decided to use a product category (e.g., cigarettes, beer).

Gambling and Lotteries

Another controversial product area is that of gambling and state-run lotteries. What is the purpose of promoting these activities? Informing gamblers and lottery players of the choices available would be selective demand stimulation. Stimulation of demand for engaging in wagering behavior would be primary demand stimulation. Do you consider one more ethical than the other? Your answer might depend on your concern for compulsive gamblers. Some might argue that the state has an obligation to protect vulnerable citizens by restricting the placement or content of lottery advertising. In the late 1990s, as online gambling became widespread, it proved to be a fast and easy way for people to lose their life savings. Stories of out-of-control online gambling were widespread.[38] Even as online gaming revenues approached $1 billion, the federal government in October 2006 banned all online gambling in the United States.[39]

One way to think about vulnerable audiences is to consider the basis for this vulnerability—a consideration that can become complex and emotionally charged. Some might describe gamblers as an audience that is "information poor"—that is, people who tend not to seek out information from a wide range of sources. Others find descriptions of "information poverty" demeaning, patronizing, and paternalistic.

"Junk" Food

Reflecting on the complexity of sorting out the ethics of promoting controversial products, we wrote in a 2003 textbook:

> But consider this as you contemplate the role advertising plays in people's decisions regarding these types of products. Currently, one in three children in the United States is diagnosed as clinically obese. Will parents of these kids begin to sue McDonald's, Coca-Cola, Kellogg's, and General Mills because they advertise food products to children?

As a matter of fact, this is *exactly* what happened. McDonald's and other food companies had to prepare themselves for lawsuits from people claiming food providers "made them fat." The food industry has countered with the proposition that kids are obese because of unconcerned parents, underfunded school systems that have dropped physical activity programs, and sedentary entertainment like home video games.[40]

This issue is troublesome enough that the U.S. government passed legislation barring people from suing food companies for their obesity. In March 2004, the House of Representatives overwhelmingly approved legislation nicknamed the "cheeseburger bill" that would block lawsuits blaming the food industry for making people fat. During the debate on the bill, one of its sponsors said it was about "common sense and personal responsibility."[41]

Many marketers are worried about the intense focus on this global health problem. The chief creative officer of Coca-Cola Company called obesity concerns "our Achilles heel," adding, "It dilutes our marketing and works against us. It's a huge, huge issue."[42]

LO Regulation of Advertising

Advertising is the promotional tool that tends to get the most scrutiny because of its global presence; therefore, much regulation of brand promotion focuses

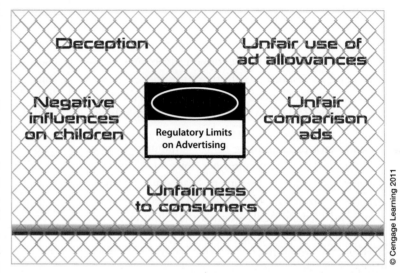

Exhibit 6.2
Don't Go There . . .

Deception

Unfair use of ad allowances

Negative influences on children

Regulatory Limits on Advertising

Unfair comparison ads

Unfairness to consumers

© Cengage Learning 2011

on advertising. Governments, industry groups, and advocacy organizations have identified several types of behavior that advertisers should avoid because they are illegal or socially unacceptable (see Exhibit 6.2).

Like the other topics in this chapter, regulation of advertising can be controversial, and opinions about what does and doesn't need to be regulated can be highly variable. However, while specific cases are in dispute, there is widespread agreement that deception, unfairness, anticompetitive behavior, and exploitation of children are unacceptable.

Deception and Unfairness

Deception in advertising is illegal, but determining whether a specific advertisement or promotional campaign is deceptive can be difficult. The authoritative source for defining deceptive advertising is a policy statement by the Federal Trade Commission (FTC). This policy statement specifies three elements as essential in declaring an ad deceptive:[43]

1. There must be a representation, omission, or practice that is likely to mislead the consumer.

2. This representation, omission, or practice must be judged from the perspective of a consumer acting reasonably in the circumstance.

3. The representation, omission, or practice must be a "material" one, meaning the act or the practice is likely to affect the consumer's conduct or decision with regard to the product or service, and consumer injury is likely as a result.

This definition of deception can lead to diverse interpretations when it is actually applied to advertisements in real life. Fortunately, the FTC offers practical advice for anticipating what can make an ad deceptive; this is available at the Advertising Guidance page of the FTC website (go to http://www.ftc.gov/bcp/menus/resources/guidance/adv.shtm).

According to the FTC, both implied claims and *missing* information can be bases for deeming an ad deceptive. Obviously, the FTC expects any explicit claim made in an ad to be truthful, but it also is on the lookout for ads that deceive through allusion and innuendo or ads that deceive by not telling the whole story.

Many instances of deceptive advertising and packaging have resulted in formal government programs designed to regulate such practices. But there can be complications in regulating puffery. Conventional wisdom has argued that consumers don't actually believe extreme claims and realize advertisers are only trying to attract attention. Some people, however, disagree with this view of puffery and feel it actually represents "soft-core" deception because some consumers may believe exaggerated claims.[44]

In contrast to the definition of deception, the definition of unfairness in advertising has been left relatively vague. In 1994, Congress ended a long-running dispute in the courts and in the advertising industry by approving legislation that defines **unfair advertising** as "acts or practices that cause or are likely to cause substantial injury to consumers, which is not reasonably avoidable by consumers themselves, and not outweighed by the countervailing benefits to consumers or competition."[45] This definition obligates the FTC to assess both the benefits and costs of advertising, and rules out reckless acts on the part of consumers, before a judgment can be rendered that an advertiser has been unfair.

Competitive Issues

Because the large amounts spent on advertising may foster inequities that literally can destroy competition, several advertising practices relating to maintaining fair competition are regulated.

One of these practices is **vertical cooperative advertising**, an advertising technique whereby a manufacturer and dealer (either a wholesaler or retailer) share the expense of advertising. This technique is used commonly in regional or local markets where a manufacturer wants a brand to benefit from a special promotion run by local dealers (recall the co-op advertising example in Chapter 1). There is nothing illegal, per se, about this practice, and it is used regularly. The competitive threat arises when dealers (especially since the advent of first department store chains and now mega retailers like

Walmart and Home Depot) are given bogus cooperative advertising allowances. These allowances require little or no effort or expenditure on the part of the dealer/retailer, so they really represent hidden price concessions. As such, they are a form of unfair competition and are deemed illegal. If an advertising allowance is granted to a dealer, that dealer must demonstrate that the funds are applied specifically to advertising.

Another area of unfair competition is to use comparison ads inappropriately. **Comparison advertisements** are those in which an advertiser makes a comparison between the firm's brand and competitors' brands. The comparison may or may not explicitly identify the competition. Again, comparison ads are completely legal and are used frequently by all sorts of organizations. But if an advertisement is carried out in such a way that the comparison is not fair, then there is an unfair competitive effect. For example, Duracell once ran ads that claimed its "Coppertop" battery outlasted Energizer's heavy-duty battery. While the claim was

unfair advertising
acts by advertisers that cause or are likely to cause substantial injury that is not reasonably avoidable or outweighed by other benefits

vertical cooperative advertising sharing of advertising expense by a manufacturer and dealer (wholesaler or retailer)

comparison advertisements ads that compare the advertiser's brand with competitors' brands

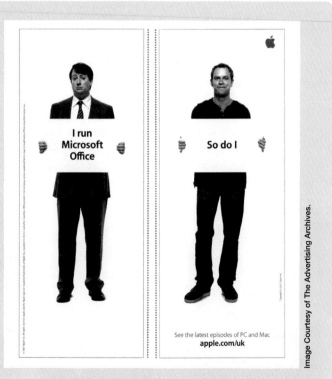

The advertising industry provides marketers with guidelines to ensure that comparison ads, like this one, offer fair comparisons between brands.

technically true, the Coppertop is an alkaline battery and was not being compared to Energizer's alkaline battery. The FTC may require a firm using comparisons to substantiate claims made in an advertisement and prove that the claims do not tend to deceive. It also may require that ads use a disclaimer to help consumers understand comparative product claims. Gillette, makers of Duracell, agreed to include a disclaimer in its Coppertop ads; it later pulled the campaign altogether.[46]

Some firms are so powerful in their use of advertising that **monopoly power** by virtue of their ad spending can become a problem. This issue normally arises in the context of mergers and acquisitions. As an example, the FTC carefully investigated the acquisition of AdMob by Google based on concern that the merger of the two companies would diminish competition in the market for mobile advertising.[47]

Advertising to Children

As we discussed in the area of ethics, critics argue that continually bombarding children with persuasive stimuli can alter their motivation and behavior. Even though government organizations such as the FTC have been active in trying to regulate advertising directed at children, industry and consumer groups have been more successful in securing restrictions. Recall that the group Action for Children's Television persuaded Congress to pass the Children's Television Act, which limits the amount of commercial airtime allowed during children's programs.

The Council of Better Business Bureaus established a Children's Advertising Review Unit and has issued a set of guidelines for advertising directed at children. These guidelines emphasize that advertisers should be sensitive to children's knowledge and sophistication as decision makers. The guidelines also urge advertisers to make a constructive contribution to children's social development by emphasizing positive social standards, such as friendship, kindness, honesty, and generosity. Similarly, the major television networks have set guidelines for advertising aimed at children. The guidelines restrict the use of celebrities, prohibit exhortative language (such as "Go ask Dad"), and restrict the use of animation to one-third of the total time of the commercial.

The Internet era has spawned additional FTC regulation aimed at protecting children and limiting the collection of information from children. The Children's Online Privacy Protection Act (COPPA) regulates websites directed at children under 13. These sites must obtain parental consent before they are allowed to collect information from children. Determined preteens can circumvent the rules by pretending to be older when they fill out information requests, so watchdog groups have asked for stronger regulation. In addition, responding to concerns about ever more intrusive data-gathering techniques, Congress is considering a law to forbid companies from using or sharing with third parties any personal information they have gathered about children under the age of 18.[48]

Who Regulates Advertising?

As you would expect, much of the regulation of advertising involves government scrutiny and control of the advertising process. In addition, consumers themselves and several industry organizations exert regulatory power over advertising. Together, government, industry groups, and consumers shape and restrict the advertising process.

Given the multiple participants, the regulation of advertising turns out to be a highly complex activity. Additionally, although our discussion focuses on regulatory activities in the United States, advertising regulation can vary dramatically from country to country. Chapter 7 provides additional insights on advertising regulation around the world.

LO 4 Federal Government Regulation

Governments have a powerful tool available for regulating advertising: the threat of legal action. In the United States, several federal government agencies have been given the power and responsibility to regulate the advertising process. Seven agencies are most directly involved in advertising regulation:

1. *Federal Trade Commission (FTC):* Controls unfair methods of competition, regulates deceptive advertising, and has various programs for controlling the advertising process.

2. *Federal Communications Commission (FCC):* Prohibits obscenity, fraud, and lotteries on radio and television.

3. *Food and Drug Administration (FDA):* Regulates the advertising of food, drug, cosmetic, and medical products; can require special labeling for hazardous products; prohibits false labeling and packaging.

4. *Securities and Exchange Commission (SEC):* Regulates the advertising of securities and the disclosure of information in annual reports.

5. *U.S. Postal Service (USPS):* Regulates direct-mail advertising and prohibits lotteries, fraud, and misrepresentation; can regulate and impose fines for materials deemed to be obscene.

6. *Bureau of Alcohol, Tobacco, Firearms, and Explosives (ATF):* Regulates advertising for alcoholic beverages; can determine what constitutes misleading advertising in these product categories.

7. *Consumer Finance Protection Agency:* Organizing to regulate home loan and credit card practices and to establish regulations for advertising financial services so they give full and clear disclosure to consumers.

Several other agencies have minor powers in the regulation of advertising, such as the Civil Aeronautics Board (advertising by air carriers), the Patent Office (trademark infringement), and the Library of Congress (copyright protection).

Most active among these agencies is the Federal Trade Commission, which has the most power and is most directly involved in controlling the advertising process. The FTC has been granted legal power through legislative mandates and also has developed programs for regulating advertising.

FTC's Legislative Mandates

The Federal Trade Commission was created by the Federal Trade Commission Act in 1914. The original purpose of the agency was to prohibit unfair methods of competition. In 1916, the FTC concluded that false advertising was one way in which a firm could take unfair advantage of another, and advertising was established as a primary concern of the agency.

It was not until 1938 that the effects of deceptive advertising on consumers became a key issue for the FTC. Until the passage of the Wheeler-Lea

Amendment (1938), the commission primarily was concerned with the direct effect of advertising on competition. The amendment broadened the FTC's powers to include regulation of advertising that was misleading to the public (regardless of the effect on competition). Through this amendment, the agency could order a firm to stop its deceptive practices. The amendment also granted the agency specific jurisdiction over drug, medical device, cosmetic, and food advertising.

Several other acts give the FTC legal powers over advertising. The Robinson-Patman Act (1936) prohibits firms from providing phantom cooperative-advertising allowances as a way to court important dealers. The Wool Products Labeling Act (1939), the Fur Products Labeling Act (1951), and the Textile Fiber Products Identification Act (1958) provided the commission with regulatory power over labeling and advertising for specific products. Consumer protection legislation, which seeks to increase the ability of consumers to make more-informed product comparisons, includes the Fair Packaging and Labeling Act (1966), the Truth in Lending Act (1969), and the Fair Credit Reporting Act (1970). The FTC Improvement Act (1975) expanded the authority of the commission by giving it the power to issue trade regulation rules.

Recent legislation has expanded the FTC's role in monitoring and regulating product labeling and advertising. For example, the 1990 Nutrition Labeling and Education Act (NLEA) requires uniformity in the nutrition labeling of food products and establishes strict rules for claims about the nutritional attributes of food products. The standard "Nutrition Facts" label required by the NLEA appears on everything from breakfast cereals to barbecue sauce.

The Internet has drawn scrutiny from the FTC. Concern for children's privacy led to the Children's Online Privacy Protection Act of 1998, which makes it illegal for operators of websites directed at children—and any website operators who know they are getting information from children—to collect personal information from children.[49] Full disclosure of the website's information gathering (if any) must appear plainly on these websites.

FTC's Regulatory Programs and Remedies

The application of legislation has evolved as the FTC exercises its powers and expands its role as a regulatory agency. This evolution of the FTC has spawned

advertising substantiation program FTC program that ensures advertisers make available to consumers supporting evidence for advertising claims

consent order FTC action asking an advertiser to stop running deceptive or unfair advertising without admitting guilt

cease-and-desist order FTC action requiring an advertiser to stop running an ad so that a hearing can be held to determine whether the ad is deceptive or unfair

affirmative disclosure FTC action requiring that important material determined to be absent from prior ads be included in future ads

corrective advertising FTC action requiring an advertiser to run additional ads to dispel false beliefs created by deceptive advertising

celebrity endorsements advertisements that use an expert or celebrity as spokesperson to endorse the use of a product or service

several regulatory programs and remedies to help enforce legislative mandates in specific situations (see Exhibit 6.3). Not only does FTC enforcement cause advertisers to change advertising when it is found to violate the guidelines, but advertisers and their agencies also try to avoid violating FTC precepts as they plan the content of their ads.

The FTC's **advertising substantiation program** was initiated in 1971 with the intention of ensuring that advertisers make supporting evidence for their claims available to consumers. The program was strengthened in 1972 when the commission forwarded the notion of "reasonable basis" for the substantiation of advertising. This extension suggests not only that advertisers should substantiate their claims but also that the substantiation should provide a reasonable basis for believing the claims are true.[50] Simply put, before a company runs an ad, it must have documented evidence that supports the claim it wants to make in that ad. The kind of evidence required depends on the kind of claim being made. For example, health and safety claims require competent and reliable scientific evidence that has been examined and validated by experts in the field.

The most basic remedies used by the FTC to deal with deceptive or unfair advertising are the consent order and the cease-and-desist order. In a **consent order**, an advertiser accused of running deceptive or unfair advertising agrees to stop running the ads in question, without admitting guilt. For advertisers who do not comply voluntarily, the FTC can issue a **cease-and-desist order**, which generally requires that the advertising in question be stopped within 30 days so that a hearing can be held to determine whether the advertising is deceptive or unfair. For products that have a direct effect on consumers' health or safety (for example, foods), the FTC can issue an immediate cease-and-desist order.

Exhibit 6.3
Remedies Sought by the FTC

© Cengage Learning 2011. Logo: Federal Trade Commission.

If an advertisement is deemed deceptive because it fails to disclose important material facts about a product, the FTC may require another remedy, **affirmative disclosure**. This remedy requires that the important material absent from prior ads be included in subsequent advertisements.

The most extensive remedy for advertising determined to be misleading is **corrective advertising**.[51] If evidence suggests that consumers have developed incorrect beliefs about a brand based on deceptive or unfair advertising, the firm may be required to run corrective ads in an attempt to dispel those faulty beliefs. The commission can specify not only the message content for corrective ads but also the budgetary allocation, the duration of transmission, and the placement of the advertising. The corrective-advertising remedy has been required of Listerine ads that claimed the mouthwash could "cure and prevent colds" (which it couldn't). Although corrective advertising is intended to rectify erroneous beliefs created by deceptive advertising, it hasn't always worked as intended.

Another area of FTC regulation and remedy involves **celebrity endorsements**. For advertisements in which the spokesperson for a product is an expert (someone whose experience or training allows a superior judgment of products), the FTC requires that the endorser's actual qualifications justify his or her status as an expert. In the case of celebrities (such as Sarah Jessica Parker as a spokesperson for Garnier Nutrisse), the celebrity must be an actual user of the product.

When these requirements are not satisfied, the ad is considered deceptive. A variation on celebrity endorsements is paying people to endorse products on blogs; in this situation, the FTC requires the bloggers to disclose the business relationship.

State Regulation

When goods and services are marketed across state lines, any violation of fair practices or existing regulation is a federal government issue. The vast majority of companies are involved in interstate marketing, so state governments do not have extensive policing powers over the promotional activities of firms. However, they do exert control at times.

Typically, one state government organization, the attorney general's office, is responsible for investigating questionable promotional practices. In Texas, for example, the state attorney general's office claimed a demonstration used by Volvo was misleading. In the ad, a monster truck with oversized tires was shown rolling over the roofs of a row of cars, crushing all of them except a Volvo. The problem was, the roof of the Volvo used in the test had been reinforced, while the other cars' roof supports had been weakened.[52]

In 1995, 13 states passed prize notification laws regarding sweepstakes and contests. The laws require marketers to make full disclosure of rules, odds, and retail value of prizes. The states were responding to what they felt was widespread fraud and deception. Some states aggressively prosecuted the sweepstakes companies in court.

Since the 1980s, the National Association of Attorneys General, whose members include the attorneys general from all 50 states, has been active as a group in monitoring advertising and sharing its findings. Overall, however, states will rely on the vigilance of federal agencies to monitor promotional practices and then act against firms with questionable activities.

LO 5 Industry Self-Regulation

The promotion industry has come far in terms of self-control and restraint. Some of this improvement is due to tougher government regulation and some to industry self-regulation. **Self-regulation** is the promotion industry's attempt to police itself. Depending on your viewpoint, you might think of self-regulation as a sign that government intervention is unnecessary or as a cynical attempt by marketers to head off further regulation without necessarily behaving in a socially responsible manner. Most marketers would say that self-regulation is good and creates credibility for, and therefore enhances, promotion itself.

> **self-regulation** the advertising industry's attempt to police itself

A review of all aspects of industry self-regulation suggests that many of these programs are effective. Those whose livelihoods depend on advertising are just as interested as consumers and legislators in maintaining high standards. If advertising deteriorates into an unethical and untrustworthy business activity, the economic vitality of many organizations will be compromised.

Self-regulation of advertising includes voluntary guidelines established by several industry and trade associations and public service organizations. Many organizations have taken on the task of regulating and monitoring promotional activities; here are a few examples, by type of organization:

- *Advertising associations:* American Advertising Federation, American Association of Advertising Agencies, Association of National Advertisers, and Business/Professional Advertising Association
- *Special industry groups:* Council of Better Business Bureaus, National Advertising Division of the National Advertising Review Board
- *Media associations:* American Business Press, Direct Marketing Association, National Association of Broadcasters

MOST MARKETERS WOULD SAY THAT SELF-REGULATION IS GOOD FOR THE PROMOTION COMMUNITY AS A WHOLE.

- *Trade associations:* Pharmaceutical Manufacturers Association, Bank Marketing Association, Motion Picture Association of America

Each of these organizations has established a code of standards.

The purpose of self-regulation by these organizations is to evaluate the content and quality of promotion specific to their industries. The effectiveness of such organizations depends on the cooperation of members and the policing mechanisms used. Each organization exerts an influence on the nature of promotion in its industry. Some are particularly noteworthy in their activities and warrant further discussion.

National Advertising Review Board

One important self-regulation organization is the National Advertising Review Board (NARB). The NARB is the operations arm of the National Advertising Division (NAD) of the Council of Better Business Bureaus. When the Better Business Bureau (BBB) receives complaints from consumers, competitors, or local branches, it forwards them to the NAD. Most such complaints come from competitors.

The NAD maintains a permanent professional staff that works to resolve complaints with the advertiser and its agency. After the NAD conducts a full review of the complaint, if no resolution is achieved, it may forward the issue to the NARB, where it is evaluated by a panel of three advertiser representatives, one agency representative, and one public representative. The panel holds hearings regarding the advertising in question. The advertiser is allowed to present its case. If the panel finds that the advertising is misleading, it will again request changes. If the advertiser does not comply, NARB publicly identifies the advertiser, the complaint against the advertiser, and the panel's findings. Then the case is forwarded to an appropriate government regulatory agency (usually the FTC). This procedure for dealing with complaints is summarized in Exhibit 6.4.

Exhibit 6.4
Handling Complaints to the Better Business Bureau

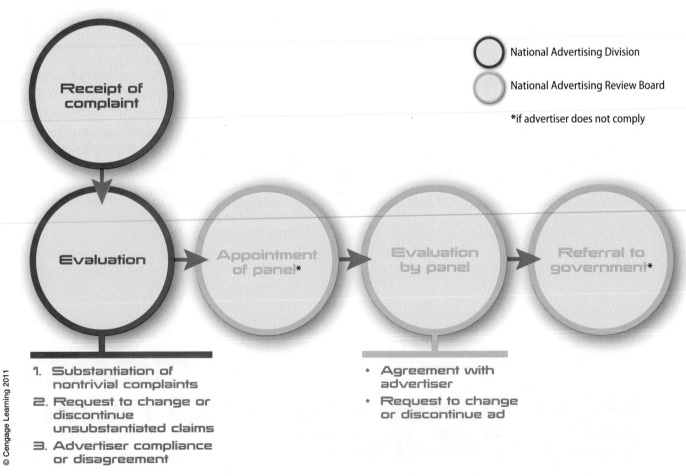

National Advertising Division

National Advertising Review Board

*if advertiser does not comply

Receipt of complaint

Evaluation

Appointment of panel*

Evaluation by panel

Referral to government*

1. Substantiation of nontrivial complaints
2. Request to change or discontinue unsubstantiated claims
3. Advertiser compliance or disagreement

- Agreement with advertiser
- Request to change or discontinue ad

© Cengage Learning 2011

The NAD and NARB are not empowered to impose penalties on advertisers, but the threat of going before the board acts as a deterrent to deceptive and questionable advertising practices. Further, the regulatory process of the NAD and the NARB probably is less costly and time consuming for all parties involved than if every complaint were handled by a government agency.

State and Local Better Business Bureaus

Aside from the national BBB, there are more than 140 separate local bureaus. Each local organization is supported by membership dues paid by area businesses. The three divisions of a local BBB—merchandise, financial, and solicitations—investigate the advertising and selling practices of firms in their areas. A local BBB has the power to forward a complaint to the NAD for evaluation.

Beyond its regulatory activities, the BBB tries to avert problems associated with advertising by counseling new businesses and providing information to advertisers and agencies regarding legislation, potential problem areas, and industry standards.

Advertising Agencies and Associations

It makes sense that advertising agencies and their industry associations would engage in self-regulation. An individual agency is legally responsible for the advertising it produces and is subject to reprisal for deceptive claims. The agency is in a difficult position in that it must monitor not only the activities of its own people but also the information that clients provide to the agency. Should a client direct an agency to use a product appeal that turns out to be untruthful, the agency is still responsible.

The American Association of Advertising Agencies (4As) has no legal or binding power over its agency members, but it can apply pressure when its board feels that industry standards are not being upheld. The 4As also publishes guidelines for its members regarding various aspects of advertising messages. One of the most widely recognized industry standards is the 4As' Creative Code. The code outlines the responsibilities and

potential social impact of advertising and promotes high ethical standards of honesty and decency. You can view the 4As' standards of practice, including the Creative Code, at http://www.aaaa.org.

Media Organizations

Individual media organizations evaluate the advertising they receive for broadcast and publication. The National Association of Broadcasters (NAB) has a policing arm known as the Code Authority, which implements and interprets separate radio and television codes. These codes deal with truth, fairness, and good taste in broadcast advertising. Newspapers historically have been rigorous in their screening of advertising. Many newspapers have internal departments to screen and censor ads believed to be in violation of the newspaper's advertising standards. The magazine industry does not have a formal code, but many individual publications have very high standards.

Direct mail may have a poor image among many consumers, but its industry association, the Direct Marketing Association (DMA), is active in promoting ethical behavior and standards among its members. It has published guidelines for ethical business practices. In 1971, the association established the Direct Mail Preference Service, which allows consumers to have their names removed from most direct-mail lists.

Internet Self-Regulation

Because few federal guidelines have been established for promotion on the Internet (with the exception of antispam legislation), the industry itself has been the governing body. So far, no industry-wide trade association has emerged to offer guidelines or standards. You will see later in this chapter that several special-interest groups are questioning the ethics of some Internet promotional practices. Some people are skeptical that the industry can regulate itself.

The Global Business Dialog on Electronic Commerce (GBDe) is trying to establish itself as a trade association for the online industry. But while it counts some big companies among its 200 members—Time Warner, Daimler AG, Toshiba—not one of the Internet heavyweights, like

consumerism actions of individual consumers to exert power over the marketplace activities of organizations

Amazon.com or Yahoo!, has joined the ranks. The GBDe has drawn up a proposal for dealing with harmful content (pornography), protecting personal information, enforcing copyrights, and handling disputes in e-commerce. But the organization's efforts have not created great enthusiasm. Lester Thurow, the prominent public policy professor from the Massachusetts Institute of Technology, may have pinpointed the problem: "Self-regulation can play a role if you have real regulation that will come piling in if you don't do it."[53]

Consumers as Regulators

Consumers themselves are motivated to act as regulatory agents based on a variety of interests, including product safety, reasonable choice, and the right to information. Advertising tends to be a focus of consumer regulatory activities because it is conspicuous. The primary vehicles for consumer regulatory efforts are consumerism and consumer organizations.

Consumerism, the actions of individual consumers or groups of consumers designed to exert power in the marketplace, is by no means a recent phenomenon. The earliest consumerism efforts can be traced to 17th-century England. In the United States, there have been recurring consumer movements throughout the 20th and into the 21st century. A recent example is the *Adbusters* magazine and website.

In general, these movements have focused on the same issue: Consumers want a greater voice in the whole process of product development, distribution, and information dissemination. Consumers commonly try to create pressures on firms by withholding patronage through boycotts. Some boycotts have been effective. Firms as powerful as Procter & Gamble, Kimberly-Clark, and General Mills all have historically responded to threats of boycotts by pulling advertising from programs consumers found offensive. Advertisers themselves have threatened to withhold advertising

dollars unless they can be assured of decency in programming by producers and networks.[54]

Consumers also seek to bring about regulation through established consumer organizations. The following three organizations are the most prominent:

1. *Consumer Federation of America (CFA;* http://www.consumerfed.org): This organization, founded in 1968, includes more than 200 national, state, and local consumer groups and labor unions as affiliate members. The CFA's goals are to encourage the creation of consumer organizations, provide services to consumer groups, and act as a clearinghouse for information exchange among consumer groups.

2. *Consumers Union* (http://www.consumersunion.org): This nonprofit consumer organization is best known for its publication of *Consumer Reports*. Established in 1936, Consumers Union has as its stated purpose "to provide consumers with information and advice on goods, services, health, and personal finance; and to initiate and cooperate with individual and group efforts to maintain and enhance the quality of life for consumers."[55] This organization supports itself through the sale of publications and accepts no funding, including advertising revenues, from any commercial organization.

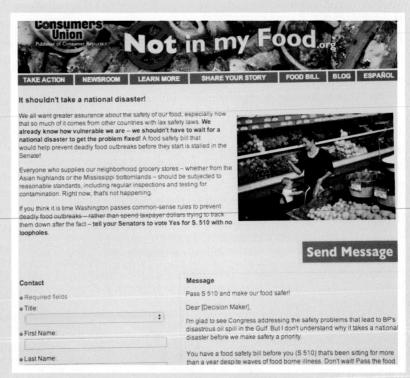

Consumer organizations, including Consumers Union, regulate advertising by influencing legislation and letting marketers know what they will and will not tolerate in products and promotional messages. This Consumers Union Web page is encouraging consumers to press for tougher food-safety standards.

3. *Commercial Alert* (http://www.commercialalert.org): Commercial Alert is headed by Ralph Nader, a historic figure in consumer rights and protection. The organization's stated mission is to keep the commercial culture within its proper sphere and to prevent it from exploiting children and subverting the higher values of family, community, environmental integrity, and democracy.

These three consumer organizations are the most active and potent of the consumer groups, but there are hundreds of such groups organized by geographic location or product category.

Consumers have proven that, when faced with an organized effort, corporations can and will change their practices. In one of the most publicized events in recent times, after Coca-Cola tried modifying its formula, consumers applied pressure and, in part, were responsible for forcing the firm to re-market the original product (as Coca-Cola Classic). If consumers can exert such a powerful and nearly immediate influence on a firm such as Coca-Cola, what other changes might they affect in the market?

LO 6 Regulation of Direct Marketing and E-Commerce

The most pressing regulatory issue facing direct marketing and e-commerce is database development and the privacy debate that accompanies the practice. The crux of the privacy issue has to do with firms' emerging ability to merge offline databases with data about consumers' online search and shopping behavior.

Privacy

E-commerce privacy issues encompass a wide range, from database development to **cookies**, those online tracking markers that advertisers place on a Web surfer's hard drive to track that person's online behavior. The early efforts were seen by some as an invasion of privacy, but they were minor compared with today's use of **behavioral targeting**, the process of database development in which online tracking markers are used to track computer users' online behavior so that brand promotion messages can be very specifically targeted to them. As we described at the beginning of this chapter, behavioral targeting efforts gather extensive and sometimes sensitive data about what people are looking up and doing online. Media and marketers see ever more useful or intrusive (depending on your viewpoint) uses of tracking technology. Facebook has explored creating a kind of digital "calling card" of its members that can gather data about what they do online and then make the data available to marketers who want to target messages based on computer users' interests.[56] And GPS devices in smart phones can tell marketers where consumers are physically located, so they can deliver related text messages. For example, a shopper standing outside a Gap clothing store might get a message about special deals available inside.

Spam

Few of us would argue with the allegation that **spam**, unsolicited commercial messages sent through email, is the scourge of the Internet. A particularly insidious version of spam is **phishing**, efforts by spammers to entice Web users to enter personal information on a website forged to look like a legitimate site. The phisher pretends a bank, government agency, or other organization needs personal data such as an account

Potapov Alexander/Shutterstock.com

Although the spelling of "phishing" is different, it's a lot like trying to catch a fish: the unethical data gatherer dangles a deceptive email, hoping consumers will bite by clicking on a link to a phony website.

number from the person receiving the message—something these organizations would actually never request via email. To put the spam problem in perspective, an estimated 100 billion spam messages are sent every 24 hours worldwide, representing about 86 percent of all email traffic.[57] Spam actually has shut down a company's entire operations.

To cope with the onslaught, individuals and companies use spam-filtering software to stem the flow and take back control of their email systems. Internet service providers have formed a coalition against spammers. In the spring of 2003, Yahoo!, AOL, and MSN announced a joint antispam offensive relying on technological and legal remedies. About the same time, the FTC convened a brainstorming session to determine what, if anything, could be done legally. In 2003, Congress passed the CAN SPAM Act. The act does not outlaw all unsolicited email but rather targets fraudulent, deceptive, and pornographic messages, estimated to make up about two-thirds of all commercial unsolicited email.[58] The most severe prosecution to date has been notorious spammer Alan Soloway, operator of Newport Internet Marketing, which offered "broadcast email" software. Soloway is accused of facilitating the distribution of hundreds of millions of spam emails via hijacked networks.[59]

michaeljung/Shutterstock.com.

ᴇTHICS PAYING FOR PRAISE

"You can't believe anything you see or read." This cynical-sounding quote is from the founder of an interactive ad agency that pays bloggers to write nice things about corporate sponsors. And as Twitter caught on, marketers began paying celebrities such as Greg Grunberg of *Heroes* and Dr. Drew Pinsky from *Celebrity Rehab* thousands of dollars per tweet to mention the companies' products. Agencies will connect marketers with bloggers, letting marketers post details about how they want bloggers to write about their brands. Even though the bloggers are paid for their comments, they still could give an honest opinion. But what do you expect when you read a magazine, newspaper, tweet, or blog? Many readers assume or at least hope advertisers are not directly involved in content decisions.

Sources: Jon Fine, "An Onslaught of Hidden Ads," *BusinessWeek*, June 27, 2005, 24; Associated Press, "GM Ends Boycott of LA Times," August 2, 2005, *Yahoo! News*, http://news.yahoo.com; Liz Moyer, "Managing Ads, Not News," *Forbes*, May 23, 2005, http://www.forbes.com.; Olivia Allin, "Prepare to Cry: What Celebrities Make for Twittvertizing," *ABC News*, January 18, 2010, http://www.abcnews.go.com.

Contests, Sweepstakes, Coupons

Another legal issue in the realm of direct marketing has to do with sweepstakes, contests, and coupons. Because of the success and widespread use of sweepstakes in direct marketing (such as the Publishers Clearing House sweepstakes), Congress has imposed limits on such promotions. The existing limits on direct-mail sweepstakes include the requirement that the phrases "No purchase is necessary to win" and "A purchase will not improve an individual's chance of winning" must be repeated three times in letters to consumers and again on the entry form. In addition, penalties can be imposed on marketers who do not promptly remove consumers' names from mailing lists at the consumers' request.[60]

The online version of sweepstakes and contests also has the attention of the U.S. Congress. Sweepstakes online are similar to traditional sweepstakes, lotteries, games, or contests. For example, visitors to the Lucky-Surf website merely need to register (providing name, home address, email address, and password), pick seven numbers, and then click on a four banner ad to activate an entry in a $1-million-a-day drawing. So far, these online games have avoided both lawsuits and regulation, but they have attracted the attention of policymakers.[61]

Coupons distributed through direct mail, newspapers, magazines, or the Internet require legal protection for the *marketer* more than anything else. Fraud abounds in the area of couponing, aggravated by the fact that approximately 90 percent of the U.S. population uses coupons, redeeming 2.2 billion coupons every year.[62] Phony coupons easily can be reproduced and redeemed well after the firm's promotional campaign ends. Starbucks ended up with a promotional nightmare by not enacting safeguards for a "Free Iced Beverage" coupon it intended for a small email distribution. The coupons were forwarded in huge numbers, and consumers throughout the United States tried to redeem them. Because of the unexpected nationwide demand, Starbucks had to cancel the offer before the coupons' expiration date, frustrating many customers.[63] Safeguards that reduce problems with contests, sweepstakes, and coupons include strict limitations on redemption, geographic limitations, and encrypted bar codes that can be scanned to detect fraud.[64]

Telemarketing

Direct marketing also has run into regulation of telemarketing practices. The first restriction on telemarketing was the Telephone Consumer Fraud and Abuse Prevention Act of 1994 (strengthened by the FTC

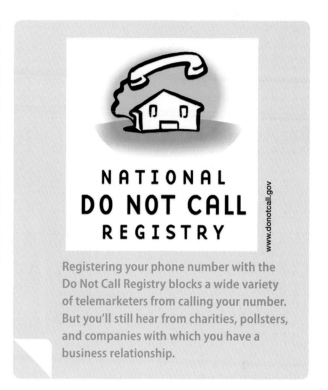

NATIONAL DO NOT CALL REGISTRY

www.donotcall.gov

Registering your phone number with the Do Not Call Registry blocks a wide variety of telemarketers from calling your number. But you'll still hear from charities, pollsters, and companies with which you have a business relationship.

in 1995), which requires telemarketers to state their name, the purpose of the call, and the company they work for. Telemarketers may not call before 8 AM or after 9 PM, nor may they call the same customer more than once every three months. In addition, they cannot use automatic-dialing machines that contain recorded messages, and they must keep a list of consumers who do not want to be called.

Since the 1994 law, much stricter limits have been placed on telemarketers. At the center of new regulation is the Do Not Call Law, which allows consumers to sign up for a Do Not Call Registry (http://www.donotcall.gov). The Federal Trade Commission, the Federal Communications Commission, and states started to enforce the registry on October 1, 2003. When the program was launched, about 60 million phone numbers were registered by consumers as "do not call" numbers.

Under the Do Not Call Law, certain organizations still have rights to continue telemarketing efforts, so even if you have registered with the Do Not Call Registry, you still can get calls from:[65]

- Charities, politicians, pollsters, and market researchers
- Companies you do business with
- Companies that have sold you something or delivered something to you within the previous 18 months
- Businesses *you've* contacted in the past three months
- Companies that obtain your permission to call

Regulation of Sales Promotion

Regulatory issues in sales promotion focus on premium offers, trade allowances, and contests and sweepstakes.

Premium Offers

With respect to **premiums** (an item offered for "free" or at a greatly reduced price with the purchase of another item), the main area of regulation is a requirement that marketers state the fair retail value of the item offered as a premium.

Vladru/Shutterstock.com

Trade Allowances

In the area of trade allowances, marketers need to be familiar with the guidelines set forth in the Robinson-Patman Act of 1936. The Robinson-Patman Act requires marketers to offer similar customers similar prices on similar merchandise. This means that a marketer cannot use special allowances as a way to discount the price to highly attractive customers. This issue was raised earlier in the context of vertical cooperative advertising.

Contests and Sweepstakes

In the previous discussion of e-commerce, we addressed regulation of sweepstakes and contests. Other issues arise as well. The FTC has specified four violations that marketers must avoid to meet regulations for sweepstakes and contests:

1. *Misrepresentations about the value of the prizes being offered:* For example, it is unlawful to state an inflated retail price.

2. *Failure to provide complete disclosure about the conditions necessary to win:* Are certain behaviors required on the part of the contestant?

3. *Failure to disclose the conditions necessary to obtain a prize:* Are certain behaviors required of the contestant after being designated a "winner"?

4. *Failure to ensure that a contest or sweepstakes is not classified as a lottery:* A contest or sweepstakes is a lottery if a prize is offered based on chance and the contestant has to give up something of value in order to play. A lottery is not permitted because it is considered a form of gambling.

Product/Brand Placement

The area of sales promotion receiving attention most recently in the regulatory arena is brand/product placement in television programs and films. In the view of consumer groups, unless television networks and film producers reveal that brands are placed into a program or film for a fee, consumers could be deceived into believing that the product use is natural and real. The industry makes this counterclaim: "There is a paranoia about our business that shouldn't be there. We don't control the storyline, or the brands that are included. The writers and producers do."[66] In reaction to criticism, Philip Morris has gone so far as to run print ads in *Variety* and the *Hollywood Reporter*, urging filmmakers not to put its products in films.[67]

Regulation of Public Relations

Public relations is not bound by the same sorts of laws as other elements of the promotional mix. Because public relations activities deal with public press and public figures, much of the regulation relates to these issues. A firm's public relations activities may place it on either side of legal issues with respect to privacy, copyright infringement, or defamation through slander and libel.

Privacy

The privacy problems facing a public relations firm center on the issue of appropriation. **Appropriation** is the use of pictures or images owned by someone else without permission. If a firm uses a model's photo or a photographer's work in an advertisement or company brochure without permission, then the work has been appropriated without the owner's permission. The same is true of public relations materials prepared for release to the news media or as part of a company's public relations kit.

Copyright Infringement

Copyright infringement can occur when a public relations effort uses written, recorded, or photographic material in public relations materials. Much as with appropriation, written permission must be obtained to use such works.

Defamation

When a communication occurs that damages the reputation of an individual because the information in the communication was untrue, this is called **defamation** (sometimes referred to as "defamation of character"). Defamation can occur in one of two ways:

1. **Slander** is oral defamation. In the context of promotion, it would occur during a television or radio broadcast of an event involving a company and its employees.

2. **Libel** is defamation that occurs in print. It would occur in magazine, newspaper, direct mail, or Internet reports.

Public relations practitioners must protect clients from slanderous or libelous reports about a company's activities. Inflammatory TV "investigative" news programs often are sued for slander and are challenged to prove their allegations about a company and its personnel. The issues concern whether negative comments can be fully substantiated. Erroneous magazine or newspaper reports about a firm also can result in a defamation lawsuit. Less frequently, public relations experts need to defend a client accused of making defamatory remarks.

appropriation use of pictures or images owned by someone else without permission

defamation untrue communication that damages the reputation of an individual

slander oral defamation (for example, during a radio broadcast)

libel defamation that occurs in print (for example, in a magazine story)

STUDY TOOLS CHAPTER 6

Located at back of the textbook

- **Rip out Chapter in Review Card.**

Located at www.cengagebrain.com

- **Review Key Terms Flashcards (Print or Online).**
- **Complete the Practice Quiz to prepare for tests.**
- **Play "Beat the Clock" and "Quizbowl" to master concepts.**
- **Complete "Crossword Puzzle" to review key terms.**
- **Watch videos on Old Spice and Chevrolet for real company examples.**
- **Additional examples are available online including: supermarkets use of databases, ad choices that were not received as well as planned, and subliminal advertising.**

CHAPTER **7** | # The International Market Environment for Brand Promotion

Safeguard needed an engaging way to get its message across to families—that many infectious diseases are preventable through basic hygiene.

Commander Safeguard Pakistan's First Super Hero

Commander Safeguard, the superhero, pitches hand washing to kids. Using a superhero, a popular idea in Pakistan, the brand comes across as the hero as well.

Safeguard *Against Germs*

Website gets schools involved.

www.commandersafeguard.com

© Procter & Gamble. Used by permission.

After studying this chapter, you should be able to:

LO 1 Identify types of audience research that contribute to understanding cultural barriers to effective communication.

LO 2 Describe challenges that complicate integrated marketing communication in international settings.

LO 3 Compare the basic types of agencies that can assist in brand promotion around the world.

LO 4 Discuss the advantages and disadvantages of globalized versus localized promotional campaigns.

> "Any forward-thinking company needs to be thinking globally today."
>
> —Barbara Turf,
> Crate & Barrel[1]

Commander Safeguard Cleans Up

AFTER YOU FINISH THIS CHAPTER GO TO **PAGE 154** FOR **STUDY TOOLS**

In 2003, the Safeguard soap brand was floundering in Pakistan. Amid strong competition from traditional favorites like Unilever's Lifebuoy, the antibacterial claim behind Safeguard's positioning was taking it nowhere. In Pakistan at that time, all antibacterial brands combined held only a skimpy 7 percent share of the bar soap market.

Pakistan had serious public health challenges that are common in less-developed economies. Significantly, 250,000 children were dying every year because of diarrhea. Many of these deaths were preventable through basic hygiene, like hand washing. But no one was getting this message out. A country struggling with poverty, terrorism threats, and a long-standing border war didn't have the resources to devote to public service announcements about hygiene. Dire situations like this one often hold great opportunity. For Safeguard, the challenge was to reach families with a message that many infectious diseases are preventable through basic hygiene; to make the message fun and engaging, especially for children; and to accomplish all this on a shoestring budget that would increase sales for Safeguard.

That sounds like a job for a superhero—someone on the order of Voltron, Captain Planet, or Spiderman, three popular cartoon characters in Pakistan. Inspired by these characters, the marketers of Safeguard launched one of their own: Commander Safeguard. Of course, for every superhero, there has to be a villain. Commander Safeguard's first foe would be Dirtoo, the germ king, whose evil mission was to stalk children at every turn to spoil their health.

Commander Safeguard was introduced to children via a 15-minute cartoon program code-named "Clean Sweep." This programming was delivered as part of

What do you think?

Brands can offer value even in nations with low incomes.

	2	3	4	5	6	7
STRONGLY DISAGREE				STRONGLY AGREE		

a school edutainment program for kids. The aim from the beginning was to fuse entertainment with education to make the program high impact. Commander Safeguard storybooks also were provided for the kids to take home and share with their parents. This engaged both kids and parents around an idea that was fun and lifesaving.

Following an initial favorable response, Safeguard prepared a series of Commander Safeguard adventures for national TV and radio. New villains were invented, representing different infectious diseases, and Commander Safeguard defeated them all. Appealing to the local culture, these messages used Pakistani celebrities in the voiceovers for each episode. Plots included details that Pakistani kids could relate to; for instance, Dirtoo tried to spoil kids' enjoyment of a cricket match by making them all sick. This attention to details gave Commander Safeguard a unique status in Pakistan. He wasn't a borrowed superhero from some other country or culture; he was Pakistan's own superhero.

Safeguard also developed its brand relationship online and in schools. An art gallery hosted at http://www.commandersafeguard.com invited children to post drawings and poems created in school-sponsored Health Day contests to celebrate both good hygiene and Pakistan's first superhero. This popular program benefits from the ongoing support of the Safeguard brand, as well as the Pakistan Medical Association and the Infectious Diseases Society of Pakistan.

This integrated marketing communication (IMC) program helped Safeguard double its sales over the next two years and made Pakistan the fastest-growing Safeguard market in the world. Germ protection became the most important attribute influencing choice of a bar soap. Safeguard became the brand recommended by doctors and the brand associated with a movement to improve the health and hygiene of Pakistan. Eventually, the company began to export this promotion model to other countries, including China and the Philippines, where good hygiene and superheroes also were in short supply.

LO 1 Communicating across Cultures

The remarkable success of Safeguard's IMC effort in Pakistan has many intriguing elements. Some of these elements (superheroes) are familiar in U.S. culture; others (cricket matches) are less familiar. The unanticipated or underappreciated elements of a culture can trip up even the best marketers when they prepare to meet the needs of people in another culture or region. Just as Toyota goofed when it launched its Land Cruiser in China, even the most savvy companies must overcome hurdles as they take their products and brands to new markets.

International brand promotion is brand promotion that reaches across national and cultural boundaries. As with all the promotional efforts you've learned about thus far, it can take many forms, from Internet ads to superhero spokespersons to signage on the sides of buses. In the past, a great deal of international brand promotion was nothing more than translations of domestic advertising. Often these simple translations were ineffective, and sometimes they were even offensive. The day has passed—if there ever was such a day—when marketers based in industrialized nations can simply "do a foreign translation" of their ads. Today, international marketers have learned they must pay greater attention to local cultures. One reason the Safeguard campaign succeeded in Pakistan was that the managers who created it were in that country and totally immersed in the local culture.

As we said in Chapter 5, culture is a set of values, rituals, and behaviors that define a way of life. Culture is typically invisible to those who are immersed in it. Communicating *across* cultures is one of the most difficult of all communication tasks, largely because there is no such thing as culture-free communication. Brand communication is a cultural product; it means nothing outside of culture. Culture surrounds brand communication, informs it, and

Shane White/Shutterstock.com

Photobank/Shutterstock.com

GLOBAL STUMBLING INTO CHINA

With more than one billion people and a fast-growing economy, China is a key business opportunity. It also presents enormous challenges for marketers, including the use of seven major languages (with 80 spoken dialects) and vast differences in climate, income, and lifestyle. Toyota's launch of the Prado Land Cruiser in China illustrates the challenges. A print campaign showed a Prado driving past two large stone lions, which were bowing to the Prado, signifying the respect this vehicle should command. Chinese consumers saw it differently. The name Prado can be translated into Chinese as *badao*, meaning "rule by force" or "overbearing"; the bowing stone lions called to mind Japan's 1937 invasion of China. Toyota pulled the ads and issued an apology.

Sources: Geoffrey Fowler, "China's Cultural Fabric Is a Challenge to Marketers," *Wall Street Journal*, January 21, 2004, B7; Sameena Ahmad, "A Billion Three, but Not for Me," *The Economist*, March 20, 2004, 5, 6; Norihiko Shirouzu, "In Chinese Market, Toyota's Strategy Is Made in USA," *Wall Street Journal*, May 26, 2006, A1, A8; Laurel Wentz, "China's Ad World: A New Crisis Every Day," *Advertising Age*, December 11, 2006, 6; and Dexter Roberts, "Cautious Consumers," *BusinessWeek*, April 30, 2007, 32–34.

gives it meaning. To transport a marketing message across cultural borders, one must respect and understand the influence of culture.

For any kind of message, effective communication depends on shared meaning. The degree of shared meaning is significantly affected by cultural membership. When a marketer in culture A wants to communicate with consumers in culture B, culture B will surround the created message, form its cultural context, and significantly affect how it will be interpreted.

Nevertheless, some products and brands belong to a global consumer culture more than to any one national culture. Such brands travel well, as do their promotional messages, because there already is common cultural ground on which to build effective

Courtesy, LG Electronics, Inc.

Electronics is a product category that lends itself to global brands. For consumers who have the disposable income to afford these products, performance is performance, whether you watch, listen, or play in Montreal, Madrid, or Mexico City. If you're in the market for a plasma TV with a seven-foot screen and high-definition DVR, LG wants you to know it has the product for you, as it does for consumers in Asia, Europe, Latin America, and the rest of the world.

advertising. LG Electronics, headquartered in Seoul, South Korea, markets its products in dozens of countries around the world. Consumers who can afford high-performance electronics value the same performance measures everywhere. But brands like LG are more the exceptions than the rule, and, as "global" as they may be, they still are affected by local culture as to their use and, ultimately, their meaning.

Spotting Cultural Barriers

It's not hard to identify the companies that are making a major commitment to international brand promotion. Just follow the money. In a recent year, *Advertising Age* reported that Procter & Gamble spent more than $1 billion to advertise in China and $300 million in Germany.[2] Other companies with big international budgets include firms as diverse as Volkswagen and L'Oréal. In fact, most companies today consider their markets to extend beyond national boundaries and across cultures. Hence, marketers must come to terms with how they will overcome cultural barriers in trying to communicate with consumers around the world.

Cross-Cultural Blind Spots

Adopting an international perspective often is difficult for marketers. The experience gained over a career and a lifetime creates a cultural "comfort zone." One's own cultural values, experiences, and knowledge serve as a subconscious guide for decision making and behavior.

To succeed in international markets, marketers must overcome two related biases:

1. **Ethnocentrism** is the tendency to view and value things from the perspective of one's own culture.

2. A **self-reference criterion (SRC)** is the unconscious reference to one's own cultural values, experiences, and knowledge as a basis for decisions.

These two closely related biases are primary obstacles to success when conducting marketing and advertising planning that demand a cross-cultural perspective.

A decision maker's SRC and ethnocentrism can inhibit his or her ability to sense important cultural distinctions between markets. This, in turn, can blind advertisers to their own culture's "fingerprints" on the ads they've created. Sometimes these are offensive; at a minimum, they signal "outsider" influence.

Outsiders are sometimes welcome, but they may appear ignorant.

Consider humor, for example. Sense of humor is culturally bounded. For instance, while HBO's relationships-based *Sex in the City* TV show was popular in Germany, the ironic humor of *Seinfeld* was lost on Germans.[3] Marketers often use humor to engage their audiences, so differences in sense of humor can become a huge issue when trying to roll out promotional campaigns across cultures.

Apple ran into "humor problems" with its quirky campaign "Mac vs. PC," in which the character representing a nerdy PC keeps getting embarrassed by a hip Mac. Created in the United States, with droll *Daily Show* commentator John Hodgman personifying the bumbling PC and comic actor Justin Long as the Mac, the campaign had just the right amount of dry humor to tickle American funny bones. But in Japan, direct-comparison ads are viewed as rude and showing a lack of class, so the ads had to be completely revamped. Even in the United Kingdom, where Apple tried to re-create the exchanges using British comedians, the humor seemed to get lost along the way. A local polling firm found that Apple's reputation suffered after the ads started showing in British cinemas and on the Web.[4]

To counteract the confounding influence that ethnocentrism and SRC have on international brand communications, decision makers must be constantly sensitive to their existence and recognize that important differences among cultures are almost certain. Even with cross-cultural research, problems are likely. Without research, problems are inevitable.

Cross-Cultural Audience Research

Analyzing audiences in international markets can be a humbling task. For firms with worldwide product distribution networks, like Nestlé and Unilever, international audience research will require dozens of separate analyses. There really is no way to avoid the task of specific audience analysis. This typically involves research in each country, generally from a local research supplier.

In addition, good secondary resources provide broad-based information about international markets:

- The International Trade Administration (ITA), a division of the U.S. Department of Commerce, helps companies based in the United States develop foreign market opportunities for their products and services. The ITA publishes specialized reports that provide economic and regulatory information about most of the major markets in the world (see http://www.ita.doc.gov).

- The United Nations' *Statistical Yearbook* (http://unstats.un.org/unsd), updated annually, provides general economic and population data for more than 200 countries.

An international audience analysis also will involve evaluation of economic conditions, demographic characteristics, values, customs and rituals, and product use and preferences.

Economic Conditions

From nation to nation, consumers' access to resources varies enormously. As shown by the examples in Exhibit 7.1, gross domestic product (GDP) per capita varies widely. Another way to think about the economic conditions of a potential international audience is to break the world's markets into three broad classes of economic development:

1. **Less-developed countries** represent nearly 75 percent of the world's population. Some of these countries are plagued by drought and civil war, and their economies lack almost all the resources necessary for development: capital, infrastructure, political stability, and trained workers. Many of the products sold in these economies are business products used for building infrastructure (such as heavy construction equipment) or agricultural equipment.

less-developed countries countries whose economies lack most resources necessary for development: capital, infrastructure, political stability, and trained workers

DECISION MAKERS MUST . . . RECOGNIZE THAT IMPORTANT DIFFERENCES AMONG CULTURES ARE ALMOST CERTAIN.

Exhibit 7.1
Wide Differences in Wealth

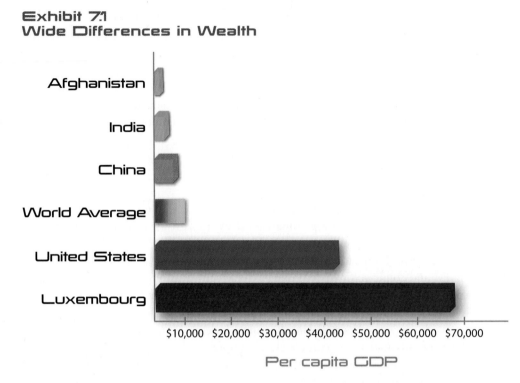

Per capita GDP

Source: Central Intelligence Agency, *The World Factbook*, https://www.cia.gov/library/publications/the-world-factbook, accessed January 27, 2010.

2. **Newly industrialized countries** have economies defined by change: traditional ways of life that endured for centuries are changing, and modern consumer cultures are emerging. This change creates problems for the outside marketer trying to hit a moving target. But many marketers see low-income consumers as an opportunity deserving more attention, partly because some of these countries—Brazil, India, and China—include billions of consumers. When Nestlé Brazil appealed to low-income consumers by shrinking the package size for Bono cookies from 200 to 140 grams and lowering its price, sales jumped 40 percent.[5] But communicating with low-income consumers is an ongoing challenge for the big, multinational firms, in part because their employees and those of their ad agencies are well educated and highly affluent. Understanding the wants and needs of a person in different economic circumstances is difficult.

3. The **highly industrialized countries** of the world have mature economies and high levels of affluence, as indicated by data such as GDP per capita. These countries also have invested heavily over many years in infrastructure—roads, hospitals, airports, power-generating plants, educational institutions, and the Internet. Within this broad grouping, an audience assessment will focus on more-detailed analyses of the market, including the nature and extent of competition, marketing trade channels, lifestyle trends, and market potential. This is the usual method of market analysis in the United States. Brand promotion in these countries often varies based

on unique cultural and lifestyle factors, and consumers are accustomed to seeing a full range of creative appeals for goods and services.

These categories provide a basic understanding of the economic capability of the average consumer in a market and thus help place consumption in the context of economic realities.

Demographic Characteristics

Advertisers must be sensitive to demographic similarities and differences in international markets, along with key trends. Demographics, including size of population, age distribution, income distribution, education levels, occupations, literacy rates, and household size, can dramatically affect the promotional mix prepared for a market. Also, marketing expenditures flow to where the purchasing power resides. Big marketers generally place a higher priority on wealthy nations with their high levels of purchasing power per household, but the sheer number of households in countries like India and China is changing the dynamics of marketing spending.

The world's wealthy nations are, for the most part, getting older,[6] and this also creates the potential for wealth redistribution around the world.[7] It could work this way: While the United States, Japan, and Western

Europe will struggle in the future with pension plan shortfalls and rising health-care costs, countries like Brazil and Mexico have an opportunity to surge ahead economically because of something referred to as the **demographic dividend**. In these developing nations, falling labor costs, a younger and healthier population, and the entry of millions of women into the workforce produce a favorable climate for economic expansion. The experts say these developing nations have about a 30-year window to capitalize on their demographic dividend. Better education for more of their populations will be an essential element in realizing this dividend.

Increases and decreases in the proportion of the population in specific age groups also are closely related to the demand for particular products and services. As populations continue to increase in developing countries, new market opportunities emerge for products and services for teens and young families. Similarly, as advanced-age groups continue to increase in countries with stable population rates, the demand for consumer services such as health care, travel, and retirement planning will increase. Thus, knowing the age segment you want to target is critical for developing effective international marketing.

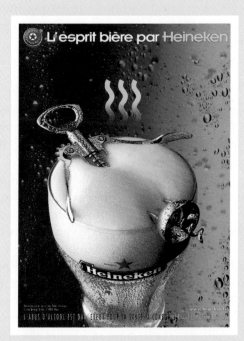

© Heineken Brouwrijen V.V.

Heineken's distinctive red star is a logo known around the world. Here Heineken challenges partygoers in France to choose the bottle opener over the corkscrew for their next celebration.

Information on nations' demographic characteristics is generally available. Both the U.S. Department of Commerce and the United Nations publish annual studies of population for hundreds of countries.

> **demographic dividend** favorable climate for economic expansion in developing nations as a result of falling labor costs, a younger and healthier population, and entry of women into the workforce

Values

Cultural values are enduring beliefs about what is important to the members of a culture. They are the defining bedrock of a culture and an outgrowth of the culture's history and collective experience. (Even though there are many cultures within any given nation, many believe that there still are enough shared values to constitute a meaningful national culture, such as "American culture.") For example, the value of individualism enjoys a long and prominent place in American history and is considered by many to be a core American value. Other cultures seem to value the group or collective more. Even though a "collectivist" country like Japan may be becoming more individualistic, there still is a Japanese tradition that favors the needs of the group over those of the individual. In Japan, organizational loyalty and social interdependence are values that promote a group mentality. Japanese consumers thus are thought to be more sensitive to appeals that feature stability, longevity, and reliability, and they find appeals using competitive comparisons to be rude and inappropriate.[8] Some researchers believe this continuum from individualism to collectivism to be a stable and dependably observed difference among the people of the world, or at least stable enough to serve as a basis for crafting different ads for different cultures.[9]

Customs and Rituals

Among other things, rituals perpetuate a culture's connections to its core values. They seem perfectly natural to members of a culture, and they often can be performed without much thought (in some cases, none at all) regarding their deeper meaning. Rituals are involved in many consumer behaviors, such as grooming, gift giving, or food preparation. Effective cross-cultural advertising not only appreciates the rituals of other cultures but also understands them. This requires in-depth and extended research efforts, explaining the growing popularity of ethnographic studies.[10] Quick marketing surveys rarely do anything in this context except invite disaster.

MÖVENPICK
OF SWITZERLAND

NEU

Am Ende glauben Sie noch,
Sie hätten es selbst gemacht.

MÖVENPICK
OF SWITZERLAND
Birchermüesli

MÖVENPICK
Birchermüesli

MÖVENPICK
Birchermüesli

Das Müesli.

Something as simple as preparing a meal can entail different rituals from one culture to another. In many European countries, a common morning ritual is to create a homemade batch of cereal from natural grains and fresh fruit. In this ad from Switzerland's Mövenpick, the marketer is attempting to align the convenient packaging of its new product with the homemade tradition. The headline reads, "At the end, you'll even think that you made it yourself."

Religion is an obvious expression of values in a culture. In countries adhering to the precepts of the Islamic religion (including most Arab nations), traditional religious beliefs restrict several products, such as alcohol and pork, from being advertised at all. These countries also may forbid advertisements from showing women and may restrict the manner in which children can be portrayed in advertisements. Each market must be evaluated for the extent to which prevalent customs or values translate into product choice and other consumer behaviors.

One of the most devastating mistakes an advertiser can make is to presume that consumers in one culture have the same values and rituals as those in another. A U.S. phone company created an advertisement intended to show its South American audience the practicality of having reliable phone service. In the ad, a wife asks her husband to call a friend to say they will be late for dinner. The problem was, in that culture, wives don't generally ask husbands for help with household tasks, and people generally aren't punctual for social occasions anyway.[11] Further complicating this challenge is the fact that cultures may change. China, for instance, has historically had a culture that values collectivism, or interdependence aimed at the good of the community. But as Chinese young people have moved to the fast-growing cities, taken jobs with multinational corporations, and been exposed to Western culture, they have become more open to individualistic advertising appeals, which relate to personal goals, uniqueness, and independence.[12] The marketer's dilemma in situations like these is how to make ads that reflect real changes in a culture without alienating important segments of consumers by appearing to push the changes.

Product Use and Preferences

Information about product use and preferences is available for many markets. The major markets of North America, Europe, and the Pacific Rim typically are relatively heavily researched. In recent years, A. C. Nielsen has developed an international database on consumer product use in 26 countries. Also, Roper Starch Worldwide has conducted "global" studies on product preferences, brand loyalty, and price sensitivity in 40 countries.

Studies by firms such as Nielsen and Roper document how consumers around the world display different product use characteristics and preferences. One area of great variation is personal-care products. There is no market in the world like the United States, where consumers are preoccupied with the use of personal-care products such as toothpaste, shampoo, deodorant, and mouthwash. Procter & Gamble, maker of brands such as

Crest, Head & Shoulders, Secret, and Scope, among others, learned the hard way in Russia with its Wash & Go shampoo. Wash & Go was a shampoo and conditioner designed for the consumer who prefers the ease, convenience, and speed of one-step washing and conditioning. Russian consumers, accustomed to washing their hair with bar soap, didn't understand the concept of a hair conditioner and didn't perceive a need to make shampooing any more convenient.

Other examples of unique and culture-specific product uses and preferences come from Brazil and France. In Brazil, many women still wash clothes by hand in metal tubs, using cold water. Because of this behavior, Unilever must specially formulate its Umo laundry powder and tout its effectiveness under these washing conditions. In France, men commonly use cosmetics like those used by women in the United States. Advertising, therefore, must be specifically prepared for men and placed in media to reach them with specific male-oriented appeals.

iStockphoto.com/peng wu.

Creative Challenge

Written or spoken language is a basic barrier to cross-cultural communication. Ads written in Japanese are typically difficult for those who speak only Spanish—this much is obvious. But language issues always will be a formidable challenge. We've all heard stories of how some literal translation of an ad said something very different from what was intended. International blunders are a rich part of advertising lore:[13]

• The name *Coca-Cola* in China was first rendered as "Ke-kou-ke-la." Unfortunately, Coke did not discover until after thousands of signs had been printed that the phrase means "bite the wax tadpole" or "female horse stuffed with wax," depending on the dialect. Coke then researched 40,000 Chinese characters and found a close phonetic equivalent, "ko-kou-ko-le," which can be loosely translated as "happiness in the mouth."

• Scandinavian vacuum manufacturer Electrolux used the following in an American ad campaign: "Nothing sucks like an Electrolux."

Nowadays, translation software tools are so readily available for free on the Internet that companies may not even bother to ask an ad agency to provide a translation. Hilarious mistakes that have ensued include the Chinese restaurant sign on which the English "translation" of the restaurant's name was the phrase delivered by the software: "Translate server error."[14]

LO 2 Challenges of International Brand Promotion

Cross-cultural audience research on basic economic, social, and cultural conditions is an essential starting point for planning international promotion. But even with excellent audience analysis, marketers face formidable and unique challenges.

picturing creating representations of things

In addition, less obvious than the issue of language is the role of **picturing** in cross-cultural communication. There is a widely held belief that pictures are less culturally bound than words are and that pictures can speak to many cultures at once. International marketers are increasingly using ads that feature few words and rely on visuals to communicate. This is, as you might expect, a bit more complicated than it sounds. A few human expressions, such as a smile, are widely accepted to mean a positive feeling. Such expressions and their representations, even though culturally connected, have widespread commonality. But cultureless picture meanings are rare.

As a general rule, picturing *is* culturally bound. Photographic two-dimensional representations are not even recognizable as pictures to those who have not learned to interpret such representations. Even in cultures that use such images, different cultures use different conventions or rules to create representations (or pictures). Like words, pictures must be "read" or interpreted, and the "rules" for doing this vary from culture to culture. Assuming that everyone knows what a certain picture means is an example of ethnocentrism. Symbolic representations that seem absolute, common, and harmless in one culture can have varied, unusual, and even threatening meaning in another.

Cross-cultural commonalities are more likely in representations that are part of a far-flung culture of commerce and thus have taken on similar meanings in many (but certainly not all) nations. With sports playing an ever-larger role in international commerce, the sports hero often is used to symbolize common meaning across the world. What do you think? In what markets would Serena Williams be an effective spokesperson? Similarly, other types of celebrities add their star power in marketing campaigns around the world. But few will have common, desirable meaning across all cultures.

Media Challenge

Of all the challenges faced by marketers in international markets, the greatest may be the media challenge. Assumptions about media availability are likely to be faulty in other cultures.

Media Availability and Coverage

Some international markets simply have too few media options. Even in markets where diverse media are available, governments may place severe restrictions on the type of advertising that can be done or the way in which advertising is organized in a certain medium.

Many countries have dozens of subcultures and language dialects within their borders, each with its own newspapers and radio stations. This complicates the problem of deciding which combination of newspapers or radio stations will achieve the desired coverage of the market. Newspapers actually are the most localized medium worldwide, and they require the greatest amount of local market knowledge to be used correctly as an advertising option. Turkey, for example, has hundreds of daily newspapers; the Netherlands has only a handful. Further, many newspapers (particularly regional papers) are positioned in the market based on a particular political philosophy. Advertisers must be aware of this, making certain that their brand's position with the target audience does not conflict with the politics of the medium.

While local differences persist in some media, new media are far less contained by national borders. From CNN to Al Jazeera, media exist in transnational space. Even vehicles strongly associated with a particular country are trying to soften that association. CNN is looking less like a U.S. news agency and more like a global one; if you watch CNN at midday, it's pretty much CNN-Europe. And the Internet is worldwide; search engines and news sites don't really care about national boundaries.

OF ALL THE CHALLENGES FACED BY MARKETERS IN INTERNATIONAL MARKETS, THE GREATEST MAY BE THE **MEDIA CHALLENGE.**

Many global media organizations have large audiences outside their home country. BBC Worldwide TV, based in London, has several million viewers in Asia. The massive population of Asia makes that a continent marketers cannot afford to ignore. India, for example, is growing fast in population and economic development. There, television remains the best media buy due largely to the high population density and the concentration of wealth in the ever-denser urban centers.

Media Costs and Pricing

Confounding the media challenge is the issue of media costs and pricing. As discussed with regard to media availability, some markets have literally hundreds of media options. Whenever the marketer chooses a different medium, separate payment and placement must be made. Additionally, in many markets, media prices are subject to negotiation, no matter what the official rate cards say. The time needed to negotiate these rates is a tremendous cost in and of itself.

Global coverage is an expensive proposition, and both ad rates and the demand for ad space are rising. In some markets, advertising time and space are in such short supply that, regardless of the published rate, a bidding system is used to escalate the prices. Media costs represent the majority of costs in an advertising budget. With the seemingly chaotic buying practices in some international markets, media costs indeed are a great challenge in executing cost-effective marketing campaigns.

Regulatory Challenge

The regulatory restrictions on international advertising are many and varied, reflecting diverse cultural values, market by market. The range and specificity of regulation can be aggravatingly complex. Tobacco and liquor advertising are restricted (typically banned from television) in many countries, including India, where the beer market has been slow to develop in part because there is no beer advertising.[15] With respect to advertising to children, Austria, Canada, Germany, and the United States have specific regulations. Other products and topics monitored or restricted throughout the world are drugs (Austria, Switzerland, Germany, Greece, and the Netherlands), gambling (United Kingdom, Italy, and Portugal), and religion (Germany, United Kingdom, and the Netherlands).

This regulatory complexity continues to grow. For instance, the European Union, the world's largest trading bloc, has strict regulations protecting citizens' privacy, which limit marketers' access to kinds of data readily available in North America. The European Union has recently added location data collected by mobile devices to the kinds of personal data (including names and birthdays) that must be protected. Marketers must obtain users' permission to gather the personal data, keep it anonymous, and delete it after a time limit expires.[16]

Generally, marketers must be sensitive to the fact that advertising regulations, depending on the international market, can impose limitations in the following areas:

- Types of products that can be advertised
- Kinds of data that can be collected from consumers
- Types of message appeals that can be used
- Times during which ads for certain products can appear on television
- Advertisements that target children
- Use of foreign languages (and talent) in advertisements
- Use of national symbols, such as flags and government seals, in advertisements
- Taxes levied against advertising expenditures

In short, just about every aspect of advertising can be regulated, and every country has some peculiarities with respect to ad regulation.

Monkey Business Images/Shutterstock.com

eTHICS ENDING OBESITY BY LIMITING ADS

As in the United States, debate is raging across Europe about who is to blame for increases in childhood obesity and, more importantly, how to reverse the trend. In 2007, U.K. regulator Ofcom announced a sweeping ban on TV ads for foods high in fat, salt, and sugar that are targeted to children under age 16. Britain's health minister, Caroline Flint, announced that the ban would apply to all print, poster, online, and cinema ads. Ofcom developed a nutrient-profiling system to decide which foods are subject to the restrictions. Ads for low-fat cheese, butter, and dark chocolate, among other things, were banned.

Sources: Emma Hall, "Brit Ban on Junk-Food Ads to Cost TV Titans $75 Mil," *Advertising Age*, November 27, 2006, 18; and Emma Hall, "In Europe, the Clash over Junk-Food Ads Heats Up," *Advertising Age*, March 5, 2007, 32.

LO 3 Ad Agencies for International Marketing

An experienced and astute advertising agency can help a marketer deal with the creative, media, and regulatory challenges of international promotion. In Brazil, using a local agency is essential to getting the creative style and tone just right. In Australia, Australian nationals must be involved in certain parts of the production process. In China, the demand is so enormous and the market economy so young that the need for local creative talent far outstrips the supply. However, Chinese agencies are invaluable for helping to navigate bureaucratic controls and drawing on China's rich cultural tradition to develop messages that resonate with consumers.[17]

Marketers looking for an agency to help them prepare and place advertising in other countries have the three basic alternatives shown in Exhibit 7.2. They can use a global agency, an international affiliate, or a local agency.

Global Agencies

The consolidation and mergers taking place in the advertising industry are creating more and more **global agencies**, or worldwide advertising groups. Among the giants are Omnicom Group, WPP Group, Interpublic Group of Companies, Publicis Groupe, and Dentsu. These multibillion-dollar businesses have assembled a network of diverse service providers to deliver integrated marketing communication for clients who demand global reach.

When a marketer uses a global agency for its domestic and international brand promotion, the great advantage of this type of organization is that the global agency will know the marketer's products and current advertising programs before it plans campaigns for other countries. With this knowledge, the agency either can adapt domestic campaigns for international markets or launch entirely new campaigns. Another advantage is that the marketer may select a global agency whose headquarters is nearby or at least in the same country, which can often facilitate planning and preparation of ads. The size of a global agency can be a benefit in terms of economies of scale and political leverage.

Global agencies' greatest disadvantage stems from their distance from the local culture(s). Exporting meaning is never easy. However, most advertising experts recognize this and have procedures for acquiring local knowledge.

International Affiliates

Many agencies do not own and operate worldwide offices but rather have established foreign-market **international affiliates** to handle clients' international advertising needs. Many times, these agencies join a network of foreign agencies or take minority ownership positions in several foreign agencies. The benefit of this arrangement is that the marketer typically has access to a large number of international agencies that can provide local market expertise. These international agencies usually are well established and managed by foreign nationals, giving the marketer a local presence in its international markets while avoiding any resistance to foreign ownership.

global agencies advertising agencies with a worldwide presence

international affiliates foreign-market advertising agencies with which a local agency has established a relationship to handle international advertising needs

**Exhibit 7.2
Take Your Pick**

© Cengage Learning 2011.

The risk of these arrangements is that, while an international affiliate will know the local market, it may be less knowledgeable about the marketer's brands and competitive strategy. The threat is that the real value and relevance of the brand will not be incorporated into the foreign campaign.

Local Agencies

The final option is for an advertiser to choose a **local agency** in every foreign market where brand promotion will be carried out. Local agencies have the same advantages as the affiliate agencies just discussed: They will be knowledgeable about the culture and local market conditions. Such agencies tend to have well-established contacts for market information, production, and media buys.

On the downside, a marketer that chooses this option is open to administrative problems. There is less opportunity for standardization of the creative effort; each agency in each market will feel compelled to provide a unique creative execution. This lack of standardization can be expensive and potentially disastrous for brand imagery when the local agency seeks to make its own creative statement without a good working knowledge of a brand's heritage. Finally, working with local agencies can create internal communication problems, which increases the risk of delays and errors in execution.

LO 4 Globalized versus Localized Campaigns

Planning for brand promotion in international markets also involves the extent to which a campaign will be standardized across markets versus localized for each market. In discussions of this issue, the question often is posed in terms of two options:

1. **Globalized campaigns** use the same message and creative execution across all (or most) international markets. The "Got Milk?" campaign promoting milk consumption looks essentially the same in the United States and in the Spanish-speaking countries of South America. Only the language and choice of models are adjusted for the different locations.

2. **Localized campaigns** involve preparing specific messages and/or creative executions for a particular market.

To decide the degree to which a campaign should be globalized, the marketer must examine both the brand and its overall marketing strategy. The marketer first must consider the extent to which the brand can be standardized across markets and then the extent to which the promotional campaign can be globalized across markets.

The degree to which advertising in international markets can use a common appeal has been a widely debated issue.[18] Those who favor the globalized campaign assume that similarities as well as differences between markets can be taken into account. They argue that standardization of messages should occur whenever possible, adapting the message only when absolutely necessary. For example, Mars's U.S. advertisements for Pedigree dog food have used golden retrievers, while poodles were deemed more effective for the brand's positioning and image in Asia. Otherwise, the advertising campaigns were identical in terms of basic message appeal. Those who argue for the localized approach see each country or region as a unique communication context and claim that the only way to achieve advertising success is to develop separate campaigns for each market.

The two most fundamental arguments for globalized campaigns are based on potential cost savings and creative advantages. Just as organizations seek to gain economies of scale in production, they also look for opportunities to streamline the communication process. Having one standard theme to communicate allows an advertiser to focus on a uniform brand or corporate image worldwide, develop plans more quickly, and make maximum use of good ideas. Thus, while Gillette sells hundreds of different products in more than 200 countries around the

Yuriy Chaban/Shutterstock.com

world, its corporate philosophy of globalization is expressed in its tagline, "Gillette—The Best a Man Can Get," which has been repeated again and again all over the world.

Several trends in the global marketplace are working in combination to create conditions that are supportive of globalized campaigns because they facilitate the creation of a global consumer:

- *Global communications.* Thanks to worldwide cable and satellite networks, television is becoming a truly global communications medium. Almost all of MTVN's 200 European advertisers run English-language-only campaigns in the station's 28-nation broadcast area. These standardized messages themselves homogenize the viewers within these market areas. Similarly, common experience and exposure on the Internet reinforce shared values around the world, especially among young people.

- *Global youth.* Young people around the world have a lot in common. Global communications, global travel, and the demise of communism are argued to have created common norms and values among teenagers around the world.[19] And it's not just teenagers. Toymakers like Mattel, Hasbro, and Lego once worked under the assumption that children around the world would value toys that carried some local flavor. No more. The large toymakers now create and launch standardized products for children worldwide.[20]

- *Common demographic and lifestyle trends.* Demographic and related lifestyle trends that emerged in the 1980s in the United States are manifesting themselves in other countries. More working women, more single-person households, increasing divorce rates, and fewer children per household are widespread demographic phenomena that are affecting common lifestyles worldwide, with marketers sure to follow. For instance, the rising number of working women in Japan caused Ford Motor Company to prepare ads specifically targeted to this audience.

- *The Americanization of consumption values.* Another advantage for U.S. advertisers has been the Americanization of consumption values around the world. American icons have gained popularity worldwide, especially due to the exportation of pop culture fueled by the U.S. entertainment industry. Adulation of Hollywood, high fashion, and celebrities transcends the United States. However, some countries have seen a backlash against American brands in reaction to some high-profile events such as failure to ratify the Kyoto treaty on greenhouse gas emissions, as well as the wars in Afghanistan and Iraq.

Arguments against globalization tend to center on issues relating to local market requirements and cultural constraints within markets. For a globalized campaign to be effective, the target audiences in different countries must understand and place the same level of importance on brand features or attributes.

To win the hearts of teens around the world, Coke speaks a "language" they share: the language of popular music.

In practice, however, people in different markets value different features at different levels of intensity, making a common message inappropriate. Also, if a globalized campaign defies local customs, values, and regulations, or if it ignores the efforts of local competition, then it is unlikely to succeed.

Furthermore, local managers do not always appreciate the value of globalized campaigns. Because they did not help create the campaign, they may drag their feet in implementing it. Without the support of local managers, no globalized campaign can ever achieve its potential.

Developing global brands through standardized campaigns can succeed only when advertisers can find similar needs, feelings, or emotions as a basis for communication across cultures. Take McDonald's as a case in point. The fast-food chain has roughly 30,000 restaurants in more than 100 countries. To accommodate local interests, the company uses Olympic champions as spokespersons in China and excludes beef products from its menu in India. But everywhere it operates, McDonald's stands for being family friendly. That premise resonates from Moscow to Memphis, making McDonald's a legitimate global brand.[21]

Finally, when using a global approach to brand promotion, marketers need to distinguish between strategy and execution. The basic need identified may well be universal, but communication about the product or service that offers satisfaction of the need may be strongly influenced by cultural values in different markets, which may work against globalization.

STUDY TOOLS
CHAPTER 7

Located at back of the textbook

- **Rip out Chapter in Review Card.**

Located at www.cengagebrain.com

- **Review Key Terms Flashcards (Print or Online).**
- **Complete the Practice Quiz to prepare for tests.**
- **Play "Beat the Clock" and "Quizbowl" to master concepts.**
- **Complete "Crossword Puzzle" to review key terms.**
- **Watch videos on Coca-Cola and Eastpack for real company examples.**
- **Additional examples can be found online including: perfume as a global product category, the importance of exploring how your ad will translate in a different language, and the Williams sisters try to revive the Avon brand.**

WHY CHOOSE?

Every 4LTR Press solution comes complete with a visually engaging textbook in addition to an interactive eBook. Go to CourseMate for **PROMO2** to begin using the eBook. Access at **www.cengagebrain.com**

Complete the Speak Up
survey in CourseMate at
www.cengagebrain.com

 Follow us at
www.facebook.com/4ltrpress

and Media Strategies

You're creative if you can make "creepy" an asset.

By defining its target segment, CP+B unleashed a series of offbeat characters to engage these consumers.

You're creative if you get customers to pay to play with your brand.

Photo Courtesy, Susan Van Etten.

"The creative mind
plays with
the objects it loves."

—C. G. Jung[1]

Learning Outcomes

After studying this chapter, you should be able to:

LO 1 Describe characteristics of great creative minds.

LO 2 Contrast the roles of an agency's creative department and its business managers/account executives.

LO 3 Discuss how teams manage tensions and promote creativity in integrated marketing communication.

LO 4 Evaluate your own passion for creativity.

AFTER YOU
FINISH THIS
CHAPTER
GO TO
PAGE 173
FOR STUDY
TOOLS

Creativity Begets a Creepy King

A few years ago, Crispin Porter + Bogusky (CP+B) was the hot little underdog agency working on low-budget but high-buzz campaigns for clients like Mini and IKEA. The business press had fallen in love with CP+B as the so-called prototype of ad agency fused with PR firm.[2] The agency's chief creative force, Alex Bogusky, was seen as the ad industry guru who had figured out how to thrive in a world where 30-second TV ads appeared on everybody's death watch.[3]

In contrast to CP+B, Burger King was in pretty rough shape. Customer traffic was steadily declining, and the product line was in need of some serious excitement. As promotion efforts failed to bring improvement, Burger King hired and fired four ad agencies in the course of four years. Many ad agencies would want to avoid being the unhappy fifth agency—but not feisty CP+B. When it took on the Burger King account, skeptics predicted doom and gloom, especially because CP+B had yet to prove itself with a major mass-market client. Some predicted that CP+B's culture of creativity would be stifled by a client that expected to communicate with customers through 30-second TV spots.

But right from the start, CP+B showed its dexterity with creativity that befuddled the skeptics and maxed out the buzz factor. Success was grounded in an unequivocal focus on the one target segment that everyone agreed Burger King had to win: 18- to 35-year-old males, who are among the heaviest users of fast foods of all kinds. With the target defined, CP+B unleashed a series of offbeat characters to engage these consumers. First came "Subservient Chicken," a viral, online campaign hyping the new TenderCrisp chicken sandwich. Next up was "Blingo," an over-the-top rapper who mocked diet-crazed consumers and pushed the Angus steak burger as the antidote to politically correct fast food.

What do you think?

I consider myself to be a creative person.

1   2   3   4   5   6   7
STRONGLY DISAGREE   STRONGLY AGREE

Find out what others think at CourseMate for PROMO2.   157

ETHICS CP+B'S RECIPE FOR "HOOPLA"

Foto Factory/Shutterstock.com

Many have tried to decode the CP+B model to understand how the agency achieves creative breakthroughs. In a recent book, CP+B's principals say it's just a matter of emulating P. T. Barnum and focusing on the Hoopla:

- *Mutation:* Look for the established rules, and then find a way to violate them.

- *Invention:* Consumers constantly crave new things, so CP+B's Alex Bogusky advises, "Do the opposite of what everybody else does."

- *Candor:* Don't overlook your flaws and limitations; do talk about them—they make the product unique.

- *Mischief:* Pranks and playfully naughty behavior keep people interested and engaged with your message.

- *Connection:* To really connect, stop shouting and get into a conversation. Use interactive media.

- *Pragmatism:* Find little ways to make the product and promotional mix more useful to consumers.

- *Momentum:* Get people—from celebrities to reporters to consumers—talking about your brand.

Sources: Warren Berger, "Dare-Devils," *Business 2.0*, April 2004, 111–116; David Kiley, "The Craziest Ad Guys in America," *BusinessWeek*, May 22, 2006, 73–80; and Crispin Porter + Bogusky with Warren Berger, *Hoopla*, New York: powerHouse Books, 2006.

And, of course, CP+B would resurrect The King, with a new and very strange persona. The King's first job would be to revive the breakfast menu, but ultimately he introduced us to a whole new dimension for evaluating corporate icons: No one does *creepy* better than The King. He also proved to be a selling machine. A holiday promo with Xbox for the adver-games Pocketbike Racer and Big Bumpin set sales records.[4] Not only did more than 2 million people pay $3.99 for a video game, but they also took home a stealth advertisement for Burger King. Keep in mind that purchasers were young-adult males, and they turn on the TV to play games, not to watch programs (and ads).

The offbeat and out-of-the-box characters made a difference. Unlike its predecessors, CP+B did not get fired after one year. More importantly, it really did help turn around the fast-food business for Burger King. Five years into the relationship, Burger King was celebrating 20 consecutive quarters of same-store sales growth, a key performance metric in the fast-food business.[5] The brand was relevant again and had entered the everyday conversations of men 18 to 35.

So in a matter of just a few years, CP+B went from underdog to big dog. For its work with Burger King and other clients, including Domino's and The Gap, CP+B won lots of awards, including the title Agency of the Decade from *Advertising Age*.[6] Even so, professional critics scold the agency for its edgy campaigns, and they piled on when, after a few quarters of declining same-store sales, Burger King switched to a new ad agency and a new food-focused advertising message.[7] Still, criticism is exactly what we should expect. Creative people and creative organizations have to be risk takers. They shake things up. They step on some people's toes. They commonly are boastful, which of course irks their critics even more. They do things differently.

In a discussion of creativity, we should expect stories about great successes and also stories about great failures. But there can be absolutely no doubt that creativity is the secret ingredient in great brand promotion.

LO 1 Why Promotion Needs Creativity

What is it about creativity that makes it such a big deal in the promotion business? Why do big, successful marketing firms like Procter & Gamble send their employees on expensive junkets to the Cannes Lions International Advertising Festival to make connections with the best creative minds in the ad business?

Creativity contributes in numerous ways, but let's start with the pervasive problem of advertising clutter. Everyone hates ad clutter. To try to break through the clutter, advertisers generate more ads, which typically only increase the clutter.[8] If you want your message heard, you'll need a way to stand out from the crowd, and that will require creativity. Research shows that a primary benefit of award-winning, creative ads is that they break through the clutter and get remembered.[9] Part of the challenge is to make sure that the brand gets remembered along with the creativity.

But getting the consumer's attention and being memorable are hardly enough. Going back to Burger King's issues, the problem wasn't that consumers were unaware of Burger King or didn't know they served Whoppers. Rather, Burger King was boring—a syndrome one could expect with many mature brands.[10] The brand needed to become relevant again with its core customers, to get back in their everyday conversations. That's what Subservient Chicken and the creepy King did for Burger King.

Great brands use creativity to make emotional connections with consumers. Brands make emotional connections when they engage consumers through complex sensory experiences and deep emotional episodes.[11] Integrated marketing communication (IMC) in its many forms helps create these experiences, but great creative execution brings it all to life. Believe it or not, marketers can even do this with bathroom tissue. Charmin has embraced the challenge of helping consumers find safe and clean restrooms while away

Charmin's sponsorship of the SitOrSquat mobile-phone app worked because of the creative genius of seeing that Charmin's cuddly mascots can be connected to the prickly situation of needing a restroom. The cute, humorous message appears with the critical locations and ratings, easing tension while linking the ideas of bathrooms, Charmin, and comfort.

iStockphoto.com; Courtesy of Procter & Gamble. Used by permission.

from home. The company sponsors an app developed by SitOrSquat Inc. for mobile devices. The app uses GPS technology to pinpoint public restrooms nearest to the user's location, and it collects user reviews of those restrooms, so you can decide which facilities you're willing to use. While you're using the app, you see Charmin ads and pictures of its lovable bear mascots. For a modest advertising fee, the sponsorship generated more than 500 million media impressions right when bath tissue was at the forefront of consumers' minds.[12]

Creative Minds

Creativity, in its essence, is the same no matter what the domain. People who create, create, whether they write novels, take photographs, ponder the particle physics that drives the universe, craft poetry, write songs, play a musical instrument, dance, make films, design buildings, paint, or make ads.

Creativity is the ability to consider and hold together seemingly inconsistent elements and forces, making a new connection. This ability to step outside of everyday logic, to free oneself of thinking in terms of "the way things are" or "the way things have to be," apparently allows creative people to put things together in a way that, once we see it, makes sense, is interesting, and is creative. To see love and hate as the same entity, to see "round squares," or to imagine time bending like molten steel is to have this ability. Ideas

born of creativity reveal their own logic, and then we all say, "Oh, I see."

Creativity sometimes is seen as a gift—a special way of seeing the world. Throughout the ages, creative people have been seen as special, revered and reviled, loved and hated. They have served as powerful political instruments (for good and evil), and they have been ostracized, imprisoned, and killed for their art. Socrates associated creativity with various forms of madness:

Madness, provided it comes as the gift of heaven, is the channel by which we receive the greatest blessings. . . . [T]he men of old who gave their names saw no disgrace or reproach in madness; otherwise they would not have connected it with the name of the noblest of all arts, the art of discerning the future, and called by our ancestors, madness is a nobler thing than sober sense. . . . [M]adness comes from God, whereas sober sense is merely human.[13]

Extraordinary Examples

Creativity reflects early childhood experiences, social circumstances, and cognitive styles. In one of the best books ever written on creativity, *Creating Minds*, Howard Gardner examines the lives and works of seven of the greatest creative minds of the 20th century: Sigmund Freud, Albert Einstein, Pablo Picasso, Igor Stravinsky, T.S. Eliot, Martha Graham, and Mahatma Gandhi (see Exhibit 8.1).[14] He uncovers fascinating similarities

Exhibit 8.1
Seven Creative Geniuses

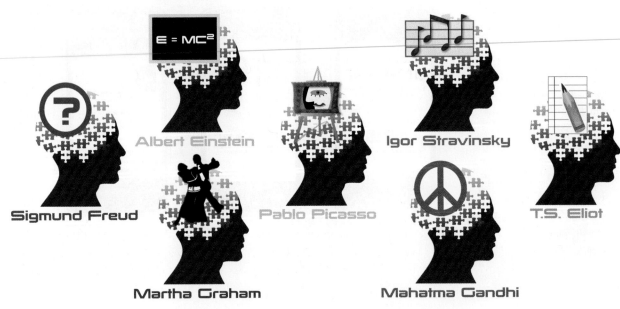

among great creators. All seven of these individuals were "self confident, alert, unconventional, hardworking, and committed obsessively to their work. Social life or hobbies are almost immaterial, representing at most a fringe on the creator's work time."[15]

Apparently, total commitment to one's craft is the rule. This commitment has a downside: "The self confidence merges with egotism, egocentrism, and narcissism: highly absorbed, not only wholly involved in his or her own projects, but likely to pursue them at costs of other individuals."[16] In other words, don't stand between a great creator and his or her work. It's not safe; you'll have tracks down your back.

Not coincidentally, these great creative minds had troubled personal lives and simply did not have time for ordinary people (such as their families). According to Gardner, they generally were not very good to those around them.

All seven of these great creative geniuses also were great self-promoters. Well-recognized creative people typically are not shy about seeking exposure for their work. Apparently, fame in the creative realm rarely comes to the self-effacing and timid.

All seven of these creators were able to see things as a child does. Einstein spent much of his career revolutionizing physics by pursuing in no small way an idea he produced as a child: What would it be like to move along with a strand of pure light? Picasso commented that ultimately much of his greatness came from his ability to paint like a child (along with amazingly superior technical skills). Freud's obsession with and interpretation of his childhood dreams had a significant role in what is one of his most significant works, *The Interpretation of Dreams*.[17] T.S. Eliot's poetry demonstrated imaginative abilities that typically disappear past childhood. The same is true of Martha Graham's modern dance. Even Gandhi's particular form of social action was formulated with a very simple and childlike logic at its base. These artists and creative thinkers never lost the ability to see the ordinary as extraordinary and to maintain their particular form of imagination despite the process of "growing up."

AP/Taco Bell, HO.

¡Yo Quiero Taco Bell!

This ad for Taco Bell is among the famous themes created under Lee Clow's leadership.

These individuals also behaved as children throughout most of their lives. Their social behavior was egocentric and selfish. They expected those around them to be willing to sacrifice at the altar of their gift. Gardner put it this way: "[T]he carnage around a great creator is not a pretty sight, and this destructiveness occurs whether the individual is engaged in solitary pursuit or ostensibly working for the betterment of humankind."[18] They, however, could be extraordinarily charming when it suited their ambitions.

Apparently, the creative mind also desires marginality.[19] Gardner found that his subjects reveled in being outsiders. This marginality seems to have been absolutely necessary to these people and provided them with some requisite energy.

Emotional stability did not mark these creative lives either. All but Gandhi had a major mental breakdown at some point in their lives, and Gandhi suffered from at least two periods of severe depression. Extreme creativity, as the popular myth suggests, seems to come at a psychological price.

Creativity in the Ad Business

While their influence may be more mundane than Gandhi's or Freud's, some individuals who worked in the advertising business have been praised for remarkable careers that revealed sparks of creative genius. One example is Lee Clow, who at the time of this writing was in his sixties and still the main creative force with TBWA/Chiat/Day. His portfolio includes such familiar messages as the Energizer Bunny, billboards for Nike, "Dogs Rule" for Pedigree, the "1984" spot that launched Apple's Mac, and the iPod silhouettes.

Lee Clow is one of the great creative maestros of the modern advertising business. *Ad Age* referred to him simply as "The Dude Who Thought Different."[20] But those who have worked at his side say his real gift is as the synthesizer. Sorting through a wall full of creative ideas in the form of rough sketches, Lee is the guy who knows how to pick a winner: the one simplest marketing idea that is most likely to resonate with consumers, as in "Shift" for Nissan. Some say he is fervent about great creativity; others say he is prone to fits of temper and can be mean to those who don't see things his way.[21] Doesn't that sound a lot like the seven great creators studied by Gardner?

Creativity in Corporations

If determining who or what is creative in the artistic world is difficult, that difficulty is at least as great in the business world. Certainly, no matter how this trait is defined, creativity is viewed in the business world as a positive quality for employees to have. It's been said that creative individuals assume almost mythical status in the corporate world. Everybody needs them, but no one is sure who or what they are. Furthermore, business types often expect that working with creative people will not be easy. Often, they are right.

In any organization, creativity is not tied to a particular job. Someone in a "creative" job in a marketing department or ad agency isn't necessarily a creative thinker. Conversely, someone on the account or business side of a marketing project (a.k.a. "a suit") isn't necessarily uninspired. As the folks at CP+B will tell you, good ideas can come from anyone, anywhere.[22] Tension and conflict (often between the suits and the creatives) occur regularly during the development of marketing campaigns. To get good outcomes, you have to anticipate and manage this conflict in positive ways.

Inherited or Learned?

Can people learn to be creative? This is an important question. The popular answer in a democratic society would be to say that anyone, with enough effort, can be a creative genius. But in the end, the genius of a Picasso or an Einstein is a standard that few of us will be able to achieve. And given some of the costs associated with intense creativity, maybe that's good.

An accurate answer to this question depends on what we mean by *creativity*. Is a person creative because he or she can produce a creative result or because of

ARTIST DAVID ROSS'S "SWIMMING SUITS" SUGGESTS A VIEW OF CORPORATE INDIVIDUALITY AND CREATIVITY THAT OFTEN IS HELD BY ART DIRECTORS AND COPYWRITERS.

the way he or she thinks? While there are numerous elusive elements on the path to being creative, we can learn how to improve our own level of creativity. We all start from a different baseline, but we can learn to be more creative and contribute to the creativity process in developing brand communication. While few of us are destined to become the next Pablo Picasso or even Lee Clow, we need to keep coming back to the point that in the business of brand promotion, we can't do without creative ideas.

LO 2 Agencies, Clients, and the Creative Process

Day to day, many creative pursuits boil down to spending a lot of time trying to get an idea, or the right idea. You turn things over and over in your head, trying to see the light. You try to find that one way of seeing it that makes it all fall into place. Copywriter and author Luke Sullivan says about one-fourth of his job looks like sitting and staring:

> The ad is due in two days. The media space has been bought and paid for. The pressure's building. And your muse is sleeping off a drunk behind a dumpster somewhere. Your pen lies useless. So you talk movies.
>
> That's when the traffic person comes by. Traffic people stay on top of a job as it moves through the agency; which means they also stay on top of you. They'll come by to remind you of the horrid things that happen to snail-assed creative people who don't come through with the goods on time . . .
>
> So you try to get your pen moving. And you begin to work; and working in this business means staring at your partner's shoes.[23]

Sometimes you get lucky and skip that part. A great idea just comes to you, as if by magic.

Every creative pursuit involves this sort of thing. However, the creation of brand promotion, like all creative pursuits, is unique in some respects. The creative personnel in an ad agency are trying to solve a problem, always under time pressure, given to them

by a businessperson. Often the problem is poorly defined, and there are competing agendas. The clients may seem not to be creative at all, and they may seem to be preventing the agency from being creative. Even the agency practice of using a "creative department" makes it seem as if the executives keep all the creativity in some sort of warehouse, so they can find it when they need it, and so it won't get away.

Conflict between Creatives and Management

Brand promotion is produced through a social process. As a social process, it's marked daily by struggles for control and power within departments, between departments, and between agencies and their clients. From the creative side, advertising great William Bernbach is hardly tepid or diplomatic in his observations about management and creativity:

> The majority of businessmen are incapable of original thinking, because they are unable to escape from the tyranny of reason. Their imaginations are blocked.[24]

Most research concerning the contentious environment in advertising agencies places the creative department in a central position within these conflicts. One explanation for the central role of creative departments in conflict is the uncertain nature of that department's product. What do an agency's creative people do? From the outside, they appear to be having a lot of fun while everyone else has to dress formally and focus on how much they can sell.

Creatives versus Clients

Regardless of its participation in conflict, the creative department is an essential part of any agency's success. Creative talent is a primary consideration of potential clients when they select advertising agencies.[25] Creativity is crucial to a positive client–advertiser relationship. Interestingly, clients see creativity as an overall agency trait, whereas agency people place the responsibility for it on the shoulders of the creative department.[26]

However, many clients don't recognize their role in killing the very same breakthrough ideas they claim to be looking for. Anyone who has worked in the creative department of an advertising agency for any length of time has a full quiver of client stories— like the one about the client who wanted to produce a single 30-second spot for his ice cream novelty company. The creative team went to work and brought in a single spot that everyone agreed delivered the strategy perfectly, set up further possible spots in the same campaign, and, in the words of the copywriter, was just damn funny. It was the kind of commercial that you actually look forward to seeing on television. During the storyboard presentation, the client laughed in all the right places and admitted the spot was on strategy.

The client said the agency was trying to force him into a corner where he had to approve the spot, because they didn't show him any alternatives. The agency went back to work. Thirty-seven alternatives were presented during the next six months. Thirty-seven alternatives were killed. Finally, the client approved the first spot from half a year earlier. There was much rejoicing. One week later, he canceled the production, saying he wanted to put the money behind a national coupon drop instead. Then he took the account executive out to lunch and asked why none of the creatives liked him.

It's easy and sometimes fun to blame clients for all of the anxieties and frustrations of the creatives, especially if you've worked in a creative department. You can criticize the clients all you want, and because they aren't in the office next to you, they can't hear you. But, despite the obvious stake that creative departments have in generating superior advertising, no creative ever put $10 million of his or her own money behind a campaign.

Creatives versus Account Services

Indeed, you can't always blame the client. Sometimes the conflicts and problems that preclude wonderful creative work occur within the walls of the advertising agency itself. To say there can be conflict between the creative department and other departments within an agency is a bit like saying there will be conflict when Jerry Springer walks into the studio. In advertising, the conflict often centers on the creative department versus account services.

Conflict arises between the creative department and account services department because the departments do not always share the same ultimate goals for campaigns. Individuals in the creative department see an ad as a vehicle to communicate a personal creative ideology that will further their careers. The account manager, serving as liaison between client and agency, sees the goal of the communication as achieving some predetermined objective in the marketplace.[27]

Another source of conflict is that members of creative groups and members of account services teams have different perspectives due to differing background knowledge. Account managers must be generalists with broad knowledge. Creatives are specialists with great expertise in a single area.[28]

The difficulty of assessing the effectiveness of an advertisement also can create antagonism between the creative department and the research department.[29] Vaughn states that the tumultuous social environment between creative departments and ad testers represents the "historical conflict between art and science."[30] In the world of advertising, people in research departments are put in the unenviable position of judging the creatives—again, "science" judges art. Creatives don't like this, particularly when it's bad science or not science at all. Of course, researchers sometimes are creative themselves and don't typically enjoy being a constraint on those in the creative department.

So why doesn't everybody pull together and love each other within an agency? When a client is unhappy, it fires the agency. Billings and revenue drop. Budgets are cut. And pink slips fly. It's no wonder that conflict occurs. When someone is looking out for his or her job, it's tough not to get involved in struggles over control of the creative product.

Conflict with Account Executives

Account executives (AEs) are the liaison between the agency and the client. Their primary responsibility is to

MANY CLIENTS DON'T RECOGNIZE THEIR ROLE IN KILLING THE VERY SAME **BREAKTHROUGH IDEAS** THEY CLAIM TO BE LOOKING FOR.

WE'D LIKE TO TELL ALL OF TONIGHT'S AWARD HUNGRY, SMART ASS, HOLIER-THAN-THOU ADDY WINNERS EXACTLY WHERE THEY CAN GO.

Foote, Cone & Belding used a bit of sassy tongue-in-cheekiness to signal that résumés were wanted.

make sure that the client is happy. Because clients hold the final power of approval over creative output, the members of the account team see an advertisement as a product they must control before the client sees it.[31] Members of the account team perceive the creatives as experts in the written word or in visual expression. However, they believe that creatives don't understand advertising strategy or business dealings. Members of the creative department resent that.

For AEs to rise in their career even when budget-cutting agencies are eliminating their position,[32] they must excel in the care and feeding of clients. It's a job of negotiation, gentle prodding, and ambassador-ship. For creatives to rise, their work must challenge. It must arrest attention. It must provoke. At times, it must shock. Yet, as we indicated earlier, this kind of effectiveness makes clients nervous. That juggling act of soothing clients, enabling creatives, and winning management's appreciation of their friction-reducing role is an account executive's key challenge.

Meeting the challenge produces the kind of ads that win awards for the creatives. People who win awards are recognized: Their work gets published in *The One Show* and *Communication Arts* and appears on the Clios. They are in demand and are wined and dined by rival agencies. They become famous and, yes, rich by advertising standards. The trick is how to get creatives to want to pursue cool ads that also sell.

So is there any way around the tension and conflict inherent in the people-intensive business of creating integrated marketing communication? John Sweeney, a true expert on advertising creativity, emphasizes that, when creativity is the goal, agency management should establish a clear "vision of advertising and a code of behavior."[33] Managers should reward ideas consistent with that vision but allow flexibility for the creative process and creative ideas to unfold. They should insist that promotional communications be limited to one dominant message but should expect creative staff to try genuinely new ideas, rather than cutting and pasting ideas from other campaigns or other agencies. Whether an agency's work is good or bad is more a matter of structure than talent alone. Given a pool of talented people, managers have to provide some structure that allows them to produce their best work.

LO 3 Coordination, Collaboration, and Creativity

The execution of an IMC campaign is very much like the performance of a symphony orchestra. To produce glorious music, many individuals must make their unique contributions to the performance, but it sounds right only if the maestro brings it all together at the critical moment. Attend a symphony, and get there early so that you can hear each musician warming up. Reflect on the many years of dedicated practice that this individual put in to master that instrument and his or her specific part for tonight's performance. As each musician warms up independently, the sound becomes a collection of hoots and clangs. Mercifully, the maestro finally steps to the podium to quell the cacophony. All is quiet for a moment. Finally, the maestro calls the orchestra into action. As a team, with each person executing a specific assignment defined by the composer, under the direction of the maestro, they make beautiful music.

So it goes in the world of brand promotion. Preparing and executing breakthrough IMC campaigns is a people-intensive business. Many different kinds of expertise will be needed to pull it off, so people must be enlisted to play a variety of roles. But some order must be imposed on the collection of players. Frequently, a maestro will need to step in to give these players a common theme or direction for their work. Lee Clow of TBWA Worldwide once received a conductor's baton as a gift. About the role of maestro, he has said: "I was a pretty good soloist when I joined the orchestra, but I think I'm a much better conductor than I was a soloist. If we can make beautiful music together, that makes me happy. . . . And different people end up getting to do the solos and get the standing ovations."[34]

Coordination and collaboration will be required for executing any kind of promotional effort. Moreover, the creative essence of the campaign can be aided and elevated by skillful use of teams. Teams can generate a synergy that allows them to rise above the talents of their individual members on many kinds of tasks. Even without an Igor Stravinsky, Pablo Picasso, or Martha Graham, a group of diverse and motivated people can be expected to generate big ideas and also put them into action.

Because great brand promotion and great teamwork go hand in hand, we don't just want to hope for a good team; we need to make it happen. Teamwork must be planned for and facilitated. People who lead brand promotion efforts therefore need to understand how winning teams operate.

What We Know about Teams

More and more instructors in all sorts of classes are incorporating teamwork as part of their courses because they know that interpersonal skills are highly valued in the real world of work. In fact, an impressive body of research indicates that teams have become essential to the effectiveness of modern organizations. In their book *The Wisdom of Teams*, consultants Jon Katzenbach and Douglas Smith review many valuable insights about the importance of teams. Here we summarize several of their key conclusions.[35]

James Steidl/Shutterstock.com

- *Teams rule!* There can be little doubt that, in a variety of organizations, teams have become the primary means for getting things done. The growing number of performance challenges faced by most businesses—as a result of more-demanding customers, technological changes, government regulation, and intensifying competition—demand speed and quality in work products that simply are beyond the scope of what an individual can offer. Teams often are the only valid option for getting things done.

- *It's all about performance.* Research shows that teams are effective in organizations where the leadership makes it perfectly clear that teams will be held accountable for performance. Teams are expected to produce results that satisfy the client and yield financial gains.

- *Synergy through teams.* Modern organizations require many kinds of expertise to get the work done. The only reliable way to mix people with different expertise to generate solutions where the whole is greater than the sum of the parts is through team discipline. Research shows that blending expertise from diverse disciplines often produces the most innovative solutions to many different types of business problems.[36] The "blending" must be done through teams.

- *The demise of individualism?* Rugged individualism is the American way. But does a growing reliance on teams in the workplace mean a devaluation of the individual and a greater emphasis on conformity to what the group thinks? Not at all. Left unchecked, an "always look out for number one" mentality can destroy teams. But teams are not incompatible with individual excellence. Effective teams let each individual bring his or her unique contributions to the forefront. When an individual does not have a personal contribution to make, then one can question that person's value to the team.

Péter Gudella/Shutterstock.com

- *Teams promote personal growth.* Teamwork promotes learning for each individual team member. In a team, people learn about their own work styles and observe the work styles of others. This learning makes them more effective team players in their next assignment. Once team principles take hold in an organization, momentum builds.

> **account team** group of people comprising different facets of the promotion industry who work together under a team leader

Leadership of Teams

A critical element in the equation for successful teams is leadership. Leaders do many things for their teams to help them succeed.[37] Teams ultimately must reach a goal to justify their standing, and here is where the leader's job starts. The leader's first job is to help team members build consensus about the goals they hope to achieve and the approach they will take to reach those goals. Without a clear sense of purpose, the team is doomed. Once goals and purpose are agreed upon, then the leader plays a role in ensuring that the work of the team is consistent with the strategy or plan. This is a particularly important role in the context of creating IMC campaigns.

Finally, team leaders must help do the real work of the team. Here the team leader must be careful to contribute ideas without dominating the team. There also are two key things that team leaders should never do: They should not blame or allow specific individuals to fail, and they should never excuse away shortfalls in team performance.[38] Mutual accountability must be emphasized over individual performance.

Applying these principles to brand promotion, think of an agency's **account team** as a bicycle wheel,

TEAMS OFTEN ARE THE ONLY VALID OPTION FOR GETTING THINGS DONE.

with the team leader as the hub of the wheel. Spokes of the wheel reach out to the diverse disciplinary expertise needed in today's world of IMC. The spokes represent team members from direct marketing, public relations, broadcast media, graphic design, interactive, creative, accounting, and so on. The hub connects the spokes and ensures that all of them work in tandem to make the wheel roll smoothly.

To illustrate the multilayered nature of the team approach to IMC, we also can think of each account team member as a hub in his or her very own wheel. For example, the direct-marketing member on the account team is team leader for her own set of specialists charged with preparing direct-marketing materials. Through this type of multilevel "hub-and-spokes" design, agencies can achieve the

Exhibit 8.2
A Creative Brief

← Previous page

| PRODUCTS | FORMS |

CLIENT [   ] **DATE** [   ] **JOB NO.** [   ]

Prepared by [   ]

What is the product or service?

Simple description or name of product or service.

Who/what is the competition?

Provide a snapshot of the brand situation including current position in the category, brand challenges, competitive threats, and future goals.

Who are we talking to?

Clear definition of who the target is both demographically and psychographically. Be as specific as possible in defining the target so the creative can connect target and brand in the most compelling way.

What consumer need or problem do we address?

Describe the unmet consumer need that this product or service fills or how this product addresses a need in a way that's unique.

What does the consumer currently think about us?

Uncover target insights to get at attitudes and behaviors related to broader context as well as specific category and brand. Determine whether insights currently exist or whether new research needs to be conducted.

What one thing do we want them to believe?

Be as single-minded as possible. Write in benefit (functional, emotional, or self-expressive) language. Should differentiate us . . . no other brand in the category can or is currently saying it.

What can we tell them that will make them believe this?

Not a laundry list of available support but the few things that clearly support the "one thing we want them to believe."

What is the tonality of the advertising?

A few adjectives or phrase that captures the tonality and personality of the advertising.

NEXT

Based on Northlich, http://www.northlich.com.

coordination and collaboration essential for effective IMC campaigns.

Fostering Collaboration: The Creative Brief

The **creative brief** is a little document with a huge role in promoting good teamwork and fostering the creative process. It sets up the goal for any promotional effort in a way that gets everyone moving in the same direction, but it should never force or mandate a particular solution. It provides basic guidelines with plenty of room for the creatives to be creative.

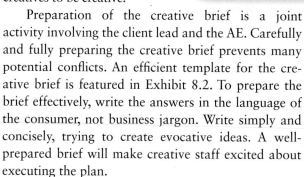

Preparation of the creative brief is a joint activity involving the client lead and the AE. Carefully and fully preparing the creative brief prevents many potential conflicts. An efficient template for the creative brief is featured in Exhibit 8.2. To prepare the brief effectively, write the answers in the language of the consumer, not business jargon. Write simply and concisely, trying to create evocative ideas. A well-prepared brief will make creative staff excited about executing the plan.

Teams Liberate Decision Making

With the right combination of expertise assembled on the account team, a carefully crafted creative brief, and a leader that has the team working well as a unit, what appears to be casual or spur-of-the-moment decision making can turn out to be breakthrough decision making. This is one of the huge benefits of good teamwork. Teams composed of members who trust one another are liberated to be more creative because no one is worried about having his or her best ideas stolen. No one is worried about trying to look good for the boss. What counts is the team. This type of "safe" team environment allows everyone to contribute and lets the whole be greater than the sum of the parts.

creative brief
document that outlines and channels an essential creative idea and objective

Exhibit 8.3
Keys to Creativity

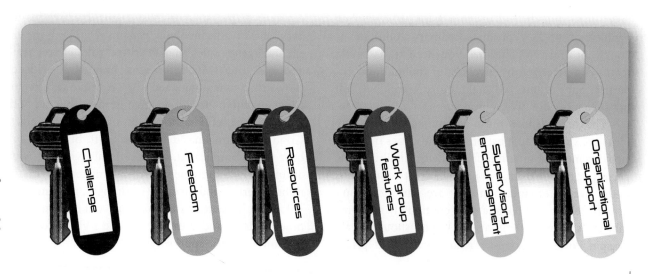

Challenge · Freedom · Resources · Work group features · Supervisory encouragement · Organizational support

Pete Saloutos/Shutterstock.com

Researchers in many fields have tackled the issue of how to foster creativity in the workplace. Teresa Amabile, a researcher at Harvard, has identified what she refers to as the six keys to creativity in any organization (see Exhibit 8.3 on the previous page).[39] According to Amabile, the foundation for creativity is setting up people with just the right amount of challenge and then giving them the freedom to choose a path for meeting it. In the world of brand promotion, the creative brief typically lays out the challenge for a team in a simple framework that should not restrict or dictate solutions in any way.

Resources include time and money. Here again, it is a matter of finding just the right balance. For example, setting deadlines is extremely important, and it's fine to make people stretch themselves, but fabricated deadlines or impossibly short time frames will kill the team's motivation and stifle creativity.

Next is a theme you'll see over and over again in any literature about creativity: Pay careful attention to the design of your teams. Homogeneous teams get tasks done quickly and without a lot of conflict or problems, but they produce ordinary solutions. If you want creative solutions, you need to assemble teams characterized by diversity of thought and expertise. Such teams will make more waves but will produce more creative solutions.

The team leader must communicate that new ideas are valued and must prevent the critics from destroying momentum around new ideas. Finally, no one person or no one team will produce creative solutions if the overall organization they are part of doesn't brand itself as creative and then continually reinforce that message to its employees. As you should recall, Crispin Porter + Bogusky is an agency that prides itself on being creative. It is not shy about making this claim or promoting it to the world. Leaders at all levels of an organization must reinforce the creativity mantra if individual employees in those organizations are to take it seriously.

Along with using these basic tools for promoting creativity, leaders can have some fun bringing out their team members' creative side. In particular, many ad agencies do special things to let their employees know that creativity is job one. Notable perks offered by agencies include on-site yoga and game rooms, espresso bars, celebrity chefs, Halloween parties, movie nights, tai chi classes, and concierge services. The goal is to attract and retain interesting people and keep them happy about their jobs. As one agency leader put it: "We sell ideas, and if your employees are unhappy, you are not going to get a lot of good ideas."[40] Maybe it's as simple as that.

Igniting Creativity in Teams

Account teams, sub-specialist teams, creative teams, and hybrid teams involving persons from both the client and agency sides all play critical roles in preparing and executing IMC campaigns. Impressive evidence shows that, when managed in a proactive way, teams come up with better ideas—that is, ideas that are both creative and useful in the process of building brands.[41] Good teamwork may be serious stuff, but it doesn't have to be complicated, and it certainly will get rowdy at times. The requirements are building teams with the right expertise and diversity of thought, pushing individuals in those teams to challenge and build on each others' ideas, and creating just the right amount of tension to get the sparks flying.

Cognitive Styles

According to the stereotype, business types favor left-brain thinking, and advertising types favor right-brain thinking. Business types like to talk about testing and data and return on investment, while advertising types like to talk about movies and the Cannes Film Festival.[42] While such stereotypes misrepresent individual differences, the old left-brain/right-brain metaphor reminds us that people approach problem solving with different styles; they prefer to think in their own style.

The unique preferences of each person for thinking about and solving a problem are a reflection of **cognitive style**. For instance, some people prefer logical and analytical thinking; others prefer intuitive and nonlinear thinking. Numerous categorization schemes have been developed for classifying people based on their cognitive styles. Psychologist Carl Jung was a pioneer among cognitive stylists. He proposed essential differences among individuals along three dimensions of cognitive style: sensing versus intuiting, thinking versus feeling, and extraverted versus introverted.

These differences affect creativity of teams. The more homogeneous a team is in terms of cognitive styles, the more limited the range of its solutions to a problem will be. Simply stated, diversity of thought nourishes creativity.

Creative Abrasion

Teamwork is not a picnic in the park. That's why it's called team*work*. When teams bring together people with diverse cognitive styles and they truly get engaged in the task, there will be friction. Friction can be both good and bad:[43]

- We can have **creative abrasion**, which is the clash of *ideas*. This can produce new ideas and breakthroughs.

- We can have **interpersonal abrasion**, which is the clash of *people*. This causes communication to shut down and slaughters new ideas.

As we pointed out earlier, teams must have leadership that creates a safe environment, allowing creative abrasion to flourish. At the same time, leaders must be vigilant about defusing interpersonal abrasion. It's a fine line, but getting it right means the difference between creativity and chaos.

Brainstorming and Alien Visitors

A common complaint about meetings is that they bring together people who sit in a conference room and shoot the breeze for an hour, and when it is all over, they discover they just wasted another hour. Groups can waste a lot of time if not managed.

One of the key means for getting groups or teams to generate novel solutions is through the use of a process called brainstorming. **Brainstorming** is an organized approach to idea generation in groups. As suggested by Exhibit 8.4, there is a right way and a

cognitive style an individual's preference for thinking about and solving a problem

creative abrasion clash of ideas, abstracted from the people who propose them, from which new ideas can evolve

interpersonal abrasion clash of people, often resulting from an inability to regard idea feedback as separate from personal feedback, causing communication to shut down

brainstorming organized approach to idea generation in groups

Exhibit 8.4
Eight Rules for Brainstorming

1. Build off each other.	Don't just generate ideas; build off them.
2. Fear drives out creativity.	Be sure no one is teased or embarrassed.
3. Prime individuals before and after.	Give everyone a chance to prepare and learn.
4. Make it happen.	Put ideas into action.
5. It's a skill.	Use a skilled facilitator.
6. Embrace creative abrasion.	Welcome conflicting ideas and viewpoints.
7. Listen and learn.	Focus on learning and building trust.
8. Follow the rules.	If you don't, you're not really brainstorming.

Source: Based on Robert L. Sutton, "The Truth about Brainstorming," *Inside Business Week*, September 25, 2006, 17–21.

wrong way to brainstorm. Follow the rules laid out in Exhibit 8.4, and you can call it brainstorming. Otherwise, you're just shooting the breeze—and probably wasting time.

Adding more diversity to the group fosters creative abrasion; moreover, well-established teams can get stale and stuck in a rut. To ramp up the creative abrasion, you may need a visit from an alien. If you can get one from Pluto or Mars, that's fine, but more likely, this alien will be someone from outside the normal network, either from elsewhere in your organization or from outside the organization entirely. Perhaps the team will need to take a field trip to visit some aliens. Teams that insulate themselves from outside influences run the risk of eventually losing their spark.[44] Tranquility and sameness can be enemies of creativity.

Leadership from the Creative Director

The trust and open communication of effective teams can foster creativity in the preparation of an IMC campaign. Nevertheless, the creativity required for breakthrough campaigns also comes from personal work products generated by individuals laboring on their own. Thus, both personal and team creativity are critical in the preparation of IMC campaigns. The daunting task of facilitating both usually falls in the lap of an agency's creative director.

The position of creative director is very special because, much like the maestro of the symphony orchestra, the creative director must encourage personal excellence but at the same time demand team accountability. We interviewed veteran creative directors to get more insights into the challenge of channeling the creative energies of their teams. All acknowledge that creativity has an intensely personal element, often motivated by the desire to satisfy one's own ego or sense of self. But despite this interpersonal element, team unity has to be a priority. In orchestrating creative teams, these are some good principles to follow:

- Take great care in assigning individuals to a team in the first place. Be sensitive to existing workloads and the proper mix of expertise required to do the job for the client.

- Get to know the cognitive style of each individual. Listen carefully. Because creativity can be an intensely personal matter, one has to know when it is best to leave people alone, versus when one needs to support them in working through the inevitable rejection.

- Make teams responsible to the client. Individuals and teams are empowered when they have sole responsibility for performance outcomes.

- Beware of adversarial and competitive relationships between individuals and between teams. They quickly can lead to mistrust that destroys camaraderie and synergy.

- If the same set of individuals will work on multiple teams over time, rotate team assignments to foster fresh thinking, or bring in some aliens.

Here we see once again that the fundamentals of effective teams—communication, trust, complementary expertise, and leadership—produce the desired performance outcome. There's simply no alternative. Advertising is a team sport.

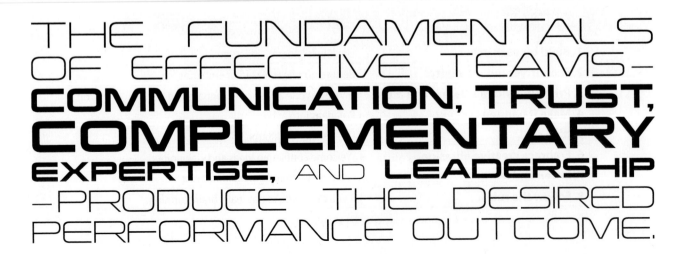

THE FUNDAMENTALS OF EFFECTIVE TEAMS— COMMUNICATION, TRUST, COMPLEMENTARY EXPERTISE, AND LEADERSHIP —PRODUCE THE DESIRED PERFORMANCE OUTCOME.

LO 4 Your Commitment to Creativity

Most of us are not going to model our lives after creative geniuses like Pablo Picasso or Martha Graham. While it's great to have role models to inspire us, it's unrealistic for most of us to aspire to be the next Gandhi or Einstein. But we all can take stock of our own special skills and abilities, and we candidly should assess our own strengths and weaknesses.

For example, we can complete assessments that reveal our own cognitive styles and then compare ourselves to others. And if you want to calibrate your level of creativity, you can search the Internet for "creativity tests" or "creativity assessments," and a host of options will present themselves. Get to know yourself, and think about your skills and abilities.

In addition, if you have any interest in a career in advertising, it would be a good thing to decide right now to make yourself more creative. Although we all may start in different places, becoming more creative is a worthy goal. Yale psychologist Robert Sternberg, who has devoted his professional career to the study of intelligence and creativity, advises his students as follows:

To make yourself more creative, decide now to:

Redefine problems to see them differently from other people;

Be the first to analyze and critique your own ideas, since we all have good ones and bad ones;

Be prepared for opposition whenever you have a really creative idea;

Recognize that it is impossible to be creative without adequate knowledge;

Recognize that too much knowledge can stifle creativity;

Find the standard, safe solution and then decide when you want to take a risk by defying it;

Keep growing and experiencing, and challenging your own comfort zone;

Believe in yourself, especially when surrounded by doubters;

Learn to cherish ambiguity, because from it comes the new ideas;

Remember that research has shown that people are most likely to be creative when doing something they love.[45]

It's good advice.

STUDY TOOLS CHAPTER 8

Located at back of the textbook

- **Rip out Chapter in Review Card.**

Located at www.cengagebrain.com

- **Review Key Terms Flashcards (Print or Online).**
- **Complete the Practice Quiz to prepare for tests.**
- **Play "Beat the Clock" and "Quizbowl" to master concepts.**
- **Complete "Crossword Puzzle" to review key terms.**
- **Watch videos on Ford and John Lewis's Always a Woman for real company examples.**
- **An additional example is available online that explains the outstanding creative work required of an Account Executive in an agency.**

Brand messages on YouTube, Facebook, or Flickr are believed to communicate in a more "social" way, seeming to be more part of "life" and less like corporate commercial-speak.

Marketers combine Web content with traditional media because it is more likely to stick for the Web generation.

Links to YouTube videos are a fun way to engage with the brand.

Photo Courtesy, OmniTerra Images.

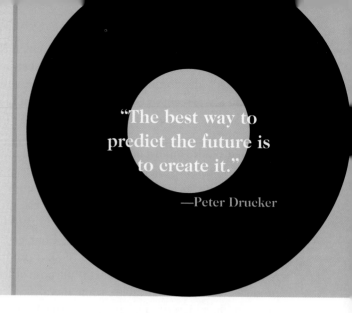

"The best way to
predict the future is
to create it."

—Peter Drucker

Learning Outcomes

After studying this chapter, you should be able to:

LO 1 Summarize the Internet's role in integrated marketing communication (IMC).

LO 2 Describe the nature of the Internet as a medium for communicating promotional messages.

LO 3 Define options for promotion on the Web.

LO 4 Identify the issues involved in establishing a website.

LO 5 List developments likely to shape the future of IMC on the Web.

AFTER YOU
FINISH THIS
CHAPTER
GO TO
PAGE 197
FOR STUDY
TOOLS

Axe Goes Where the Boys Are

When Unilever, one of the world's largest consumer products companies (http://www.unilever.com), wanted a fresh and powerful promotional campaign for its Axe spray deodorant brand for men, the firm turned to London-based advertising agency Bartle Bogle Hegarty (BBH). Unilever wanted a global brand message that would work in all 75 countries where it sold Axe. BBH (http://www.bbh.co.uk) delivered a new phrase that guys would come to know and love as an expression of female attraction for any guy wearing Axe: BomChickaWahWah.[1]

Unilever's brand managers and BBH's creatives released a wave of BomChickaWahWahs around the world through videos of an all-female band singing the phrase (which would show up on YouTube), online games, live performances by the band, and television ads also destined to end up on social-networking sites. Interested guys could learn about, replay, and interact with these messages by visiting Axe's brand-building website at http://www.theaxeeffect.com. The campaign attracted widespread attention, meeting its goal to make the phrase stick in the minds of millions of young guys around the globe.

Marketers combine Web content with traditional media because they expect the Web generation to seek out messages online and attend to those messages more readily than messages sent through magazines or television. Brand messages on YouTube, Facebook, or Flickr are believed to communicate in a more "social" way, seeming to be more part of "life" and less like corporate commercial-speak. When a message catches on and spreads through the networks, it reaches global target markets nearly instantaneously.

What do you think?

If a Web link looks interesting, I'll click on it.

1	2	3	4	5	6	7
STRONGLY DISAGREE				STRONGLY AGREE		

So how does this story end? Did BomChicka-WahWah work? Axe grabbed significant market share in the men's deodorant market around the world, including 8.9 percent in Germany, 13.5 percent in the United States, 17.6 percent in Australia, and 28.6 percent in India.[2]

What's more important in terms of understanding brand promotion is that this story *hasn't* ended. Axe is maintaining its online connection to young men, just varying the message enough to keep the target market interested. More recent visitors to http://www.theaxeeffect.com could go to the Skin Contact page not only for details about that line of skin products but also to pursue their interest in the purpose of those products (soft skin that invites some literal skin contact with the object of one's affection). Tips for getting along with girls are balanced with humorous offerings that keep the tone guy-friendly. Humor also is a feature of Axe's "Double Pits to Chesty" theme, which uses terms from skateboarding to instruct young men that they should apply Axe spray not only to their armpits but also to their chests for a full aromatic impact. That theme offers plenty of material for brand-related action videos (featuring skater and reality TV star Ryan Sheckler) on YouTube. Unilever is keeping a sharp edge on the Axe brand.

LO 1 The Internet's Role in Brand Promotion

The Internet has taken businesses on a wild ride ever since a boom in the 1990s became an investment bubble that burst at the beginning of this century. Despite terrorism, recession, and skepticism, use of the Internet continues to grow. In the United States alone, networked business-to-business Internet transactions exceed $9 trillion annually. Consumer e-commerce exceeds $10 trillion annually, with the majority spent on services.[3]

The Web has become the brand promotion medium it was expected to be. As we talked about in Chapter 2, marketers are incorporating Web promotional messages into their integrated marketing communication (IMC) and channeling money once spent on traditional media over to the Web. Expenditures on Web advertising exceed $30 billion annually.[4]

What to Expect

As the Internet has developed as an option for marketers, many firms like Pepsi (http://www.pepsiworld.com) and BMW (http://www.bmw.com) have been highly successful in folding the Internet into their brand-promotion strategies. A trip to these websites shows that they deliver a lot of information and promotion. But the Internet is more than corporate websites. What is the role of the Internet in brand promotion? A few "truths" have made themselves evident.

First, the Internet will *not* replace all other forms of advertising. Nor is it likely that the biggest spenders on promotion will use the Internet as the *main* method of communicating with their target audiences. Rather, marketers are following the lead of companies like Pepsi, Starbucks, and Ford by using the Internet as a key component of IMC.

Second, all aspects of the Internet are still changing dramatically. In recent years, auction sites like eBay have provided huge opportunities for small business all over the world. Web 2.0, with its emphasis on social networking, provides a whole new way of delivering promotional messages.

Therefore, for marketers today, it's essential to understand the structure of the Internet and its potential as a promotional medium. That understanding prepares marketers to use the Internet as part of effective IMC.

THE WEB HAS BECOME THE BRAND PROMOTION MEDIUM IT WAS EXPECTED TO BE.

boasted 12 advertisers, including AT&T and Club Med; each paid $30,000 for a 12-week run of online ads, with no guarantee of the number or profile of the viewers.

Now the Internet is being accessed worldwide by more than 1.7 billion users.[5] Spending for advertising on the Internet was estimated at about $12 billion in 2005 and is forecast to grow to more than $40 billion by 2012.[6] The medium is used by all forms of companies—large, small, bricks and mortar, virtual, e-commerce, not-for-profit, you name it. Further, the medium is home to millions of websites, and the value of the Internet to individual consumers is growing daily.

Cyberspace: An Overview

The **Internet** is a global collection of computer networks linking both public and private computer systems. It originally was designed by the U.S. military to be a decentralized, highly redundant, and thus reliable communications system in the event of a national emergency. Even if some of the military's computers crashed, the Internet would continue to perform. Today, the Internet comprises computers from government, educational, military, and commercial sources.

In the beginning, the number of computers connected to the Internet roughly doubled every year, from 2 million in 1994 to 5 million in 1995 to about 10 million in 1996. But beginning in 1998, Internet use accelerated, with around 90 million people connected in the United States and Canada, and 155 million people worldwide. Exhibit 9.1 shows that Internet use has become a global phenomenon. The Internet users in these top 10 countries on four continents represent less than half of the estimated worldwide Internet population, which now exceeds 1.8 billion.[7]

The numbers in Exhibit 9.1 mask the potential for further growth, especially in developing nations. Although China is estimated to have the most users, its vast population means it could—and probably will—have far more. The percentage of China's population using the Internet is only 19 percent, and only about 7 percent of India's population uses the Internet. In contrast, almost three out of every four people in the United States and South Korea go online. In Europe, the share of Internet users typically is about one-half to two-thirds of the total population.

How It Started

Technology has the potential to change everything. And *communications* technology (including the Internet) can change fundamental aspects of human existence. By connecting people in real time, the Internet has the potential to deliver not only information but also community, empowerment, and even liberation.

Even though the Internet has experienced some growing pains, it can be truly revolutionary for marketers in terms of its ability to alter the basic nature of communication within a commercial channel. To see this, consider the short history of communication in this channel.

In 1994, marketers began working with Prodigy and CompuServe, the first Internet service providers (ISPs). These marketers hoped to send television commercials online, but the technology at that time made this idea impossible. Still, as more users went online, joining fast-growing ISPs such as America Online and EarthLink, the technology continued to develop. Newer Web browsers, such as Netscape (which replaced the first browser, Mosaic), seemed worth exploring as a way to send commercial messages. The first ads began appearing in *HotWired* magazine (the online version of *Wired* magazine) in October 1994. *HotWired*

Exhibit 9.1
Countries with the Most Internet Users

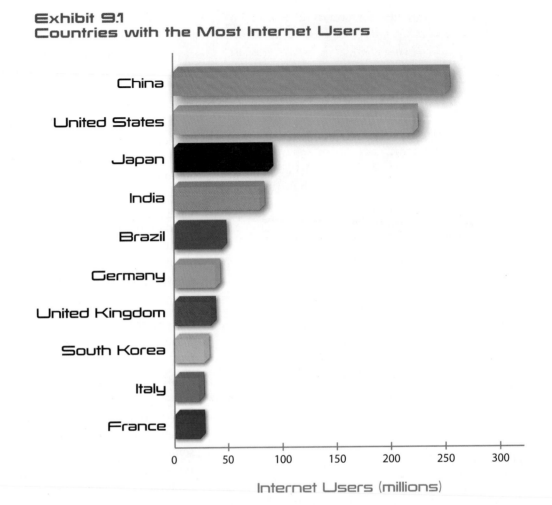

Internet Users (millions)

Source: Data from "Stats—Web Worldwide," *ClickZ*, http://www.clickz.com/stats/web_worldwide, accessed December 1, 2009.

LO 2 Internet Media

Internet media for marketing consist mainly of email (including electronic mailing lists) and the World Wide Web.

Email

Marketers often use email to reach potential and existing customers. A variety of companies collect email addresses and profiles that allow marketers to direct email to a specific group. Widespread, targeted email advertising is facilitated by organizations like Advertising.com (http://www.advertising.com). These organizations target, prepare, and deliver emails to highly specific audiences for advertisers.

Marketers are addressing consumer resistance to email marketing by limiting who receives their messages. **Opt-in email** is commercial email that is sent with the recipient's consent, such as when website visitors give their permission to receive commercial email about topics and products that interest them. Typically, when customers purchase a product online, the order page includes a box for them to check if they want to receive future information about the company and its products. Service providers help OfficeMax, Exxon, and other companies manage their opt-in email promotions. Other firms, including L-Soft (http://www.lsoft.com), offer software for managing electronic mailing lists.

An ethical/social issue we discussed in Chapter 6 is sending uninvited commercial messages to electronic mailing lists or some other compilation of email addresses. These messages are called **spam**, and the practice, called spamming, is notorious. Various estimates suggest 14.5 *billion* spam emails are sent every day worldwide.[8] Few promotional techniques have drawn as much wrath from consumers and regulators. But as annoying as spam seems to be, it also appears to be effective. Those mass emailings can get a 3 to 5 percent response, compared with 1 to 3 percent for offline direct-marketing efforts. Before we write off mass emails, we had better consider the results, not just the public reaction.

World Wide Web

The **World Wide Web (WWW)** is a "web" of information available to most Internet users, and its graphical environment makes navigation simple and exciting. For some people, spending time on the Web is replacing time once devoted to other media, such as print, radio, and television.

Of all the options available for Internet marketers, the Web provides the greatest breadth and depth of opportunity. It allows for detailed and full-color graphics, audio transmission, customized messages, 24-hour availability, and two-way information exchanges between the marketer and customer. There is one great difference between the Web and other cyber-advertising vehicles: The consumer actively searches for the marketer's home page. Of course, Web marketers are attempting to make their pages much easier to find—and harder to avoid.

Surfing the Web

About 75 percent of Americans use the Web.[9] Exhibit 9.2 shows what they're doing. In many cases, the desire for information, entertainment, and personal services leads to **surfing**—gliding from one Web page to another. Users can seek and find sites in a variety of ways: through search engines, through direct links with other sites, and by word-of-mouth.

Surfing is made fast and efficient by search-engine technology. A **search engine** allows an Internet user to surf by typing in a few keywords; the search engine then finds all sites that contain the keywords. Search engines all have the same basic user interface but differ in how they perform the search and in the amount of the Web accessed. The big Internet sites like Yahoo! and Google use search-engine technology to optimize results, so they direct surfers to sites most likely to be of interest.

Portals and Websites

An Internet **portal** is a starting point for Web access and search. Portals can be general, like Yahoo!; vertical (serving a specialized market or industries, such as Jobster, http://www.jobster.com, for employment opportunities); horizontal (providing access and links across industries, such as MSN, http://www.msn.com, with access to a wide area of topics); or community based (such as Latina Online, http://www.latina.com). Portals designed for specific groups are intended to make surfing and searching a bit easier.[10]

In addition to the portals, the Web is dominated by individual company or brand websites. Formally defined, a **website** is a collection of Web pages, images, videos, and other digital content hosted on a Web

> **World Wide Web (WWW)** database of information available online in a graphical environment that simplifies navigation
>
> **surfing** gliding from website to website, guided by hyperlinks, a search engine, or word-of-mouth
>
> **search engine** software tool for finding websites by entering keywords
>
> **portal** website that serves as a starting point for Web access and search
>
> **website** collection of Web pages, images, videos, and other content hosted on a Web server

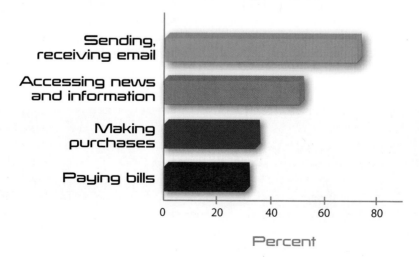

Exhibit 9.2
What Americans Are Doing Online

Source: Based on "Digital Marketing Facts 2010," *Advertising Age*, February 22, 2010, insert.

mash-up combination of websites into a single site for analyzing or comparing information

blog personal journal that is published on a website, frequently updated, and intended for public access

blogger author of a blog

WiFi wireless technology allowing Internet access connections to reach out about 300 feet

WiMax wireless Internet technology capable of a range of 25 to 30 miles

Mi-Fi wireless Internet technology with multi-mile access and ability to access the Internet while the user is moving in a car or train

ultrabroadband wireless Internet technology allowing users to move extremely large files quickly over short distances

server. Typically, an Internet user starts out at a portal and then navigates around a series of websites.

A variation of the standard website is the **mash-up**—a combination of one or more websites into a single site. An example is EveryBlock's Chicago crime section (http://chicago .everyblock.com/crime/), where local crime statistics are overlaid on Google Maps so you can see what crimes have been committed in particular neighborhoods.[11]

Personal Websites and Blogs

Many people have created their own Web pages that list their favorite sites. This is a fabulous way of finding new and interesting sites (as well as feeding a person's narcissism).

Although most people find Web pages via Internet resources, sites also can be discovered through traditional word-of-mouth communications. Internet enthusiasts tend to share their experiences on the Web through discussions in coffeehouses, by reading and writing articles, and via other non-Web venues. There also are mega-search engines, like Dogpile (http://www.dogpile .com), that combine several search engines at once.

Another popular personal use of the Web is the **blog**, a short form for Weblog, referring to a personal journal that frequently is updated and intended for public access. Blogs generally represent the personality of the author (the **blogger**) or the website and its purpose. Topics include brief philosophical musings, favorite hobbies and music, political leanings, commentary on Internet and other social issues, and links to other sites the author favors. The essential characteristics of the blog are its journal form, typically a new entry each day, and its informal style.

Blogs get a lot of publicity, and about 57 million people reported using blogs. However, only about 12 percent of those blog users visit a blog once a week or more frequently—meaning 88 percent of Internet users seldom or never read blogs.[12] Still, big corporations like Procter & Gamble are finding that some of their brands are featured on customer blogs. Marketers in general feel this aspect of the Web holds great potential for peer-to-peer communication, which can be a powerful advocate for brands.[13]

The Mobile Web

The main development that has made the Internet more widely used than ever in recent years is wireless communication technology.

WiFi, which became widely popular in 2004, allows Internet-access connections that reach out about 300 feet. That meant people on the go—whether coffee drinkers at Starbucks or emergency workers at disaster sites—could have wireless access to information through their laptops. But that was just the beginning. People are tapping into WiFi networks with smaller devices like smartphones and tablets (for example, the iPad), and these devices are so portable that even a WiFi network seems too confining. The wireless revolution is coming to the rescue with innovative technologies that push wireless networking into every facet of life from cars to homes to offices to the beach:

1. **WiMax** (Worldwide Interoperability for Microwave Access), like WiFi, creates "hot spots" around a central antenna within which people wirelessly can tap into the Net. But while WiFi creates a hot spot of 300 feet, WiMax has a potential range of 25 to 30 miles. WiMax is well suited to rural areas.

2. **Mi-Fi** (or Mobile-Fi) is similar to WiMax in that it has multi-mile access, but it adds the capability of accessing the Net while the user is moving in a car or a train.

Community portals like Latina Online offer a site that matches surfers' interests in information on a variety of topics from politics to culture to entertainment.

GLOBAL TO RUSSIA WITH WIMAX

Alcatel-Lucent, developers of WiMax technology, recently landed a deal to build a nationwide rural WiMax access network in Russia, the world's most rural country. Alcatel-Lucent will work with Russian telecommunications company Synterra to build the WiMax infrastructure in towns with populations smaller than 100,000. The project is enormous, providing Internet access to more than 40 million Russians without a DSL or cable modem connection to the Internet. This, in turn, will give marketers a vast new market of Russian consumers.

Sources: Dan O'Shea, "Study: WiMax, MobileFi No Threat to DSL," *TelephonyOnline*, June 8, 2004, http://www.telephonyonline.com; Kevin Fitchard, "Alcatel-Lucent to Build WiMax in Russia," *TelephonyOnline*, July 6, 2007, http://www.telephonyonline.com.

3. **Ultrabroadband** allows people to move extremely large files quickly over short distances. On the road, a driver could download a large file from an on-board PC to a handheld computer. Or, at home, you could do a wireless upload of your favorite concert from your PC to your TV. Ultrabroadband is a boon to social network users who want to share photos or use tablet computers to download movies and books.

These technologies will allow marketers to communicate with audiences as they access the Internet through WiMax, WiFi, or Mi-Fi in homes, airports, or restaurants; while relaxing, working, or commuting; alone or with friends, customers, or colleagues. This flexibility makes the communication potential almost limitless.

LO 3 Promotion on the Internet

Brand promotion via the Internet is growing dramatically. Marketers spent $54.7 million for Internet ads in 1995 and just over $8 billion in 2000. After a dip when the economy softened, ad revenues rebounded, reaching somewhere in the range of $23 billion in 2010.[14]

Advantages of Online Promotion

Marketers use more and more Internet advertising not only because the Web represents a new and different technological option. Several unique characteristics

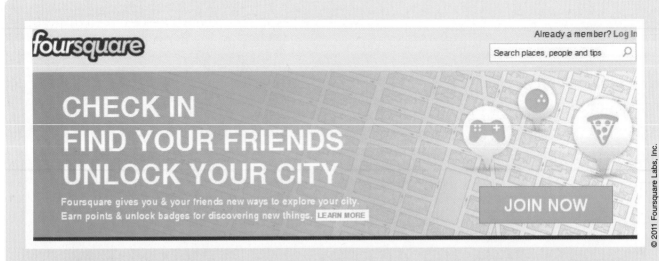

Foursquare helps marketers engage customers by targeting special offers based on their precise location. Consumers can access Foursquare on their mobile devices, and the app provides marketers with the location data. It's a win-win situation, because consumers who use Foursquare are already looking for deals.

of the Internet offer advantages over traditional media options.

Target Market Selectivity

The Web gives marketers a precise way to target market segments. Not only are the segments precisely defined—you can place an ad on the numismatist (coin collecting) society page, for example—but the Internet allows forms of targeting that truly enhance traditional segmentation schemes such as demographics, geographics, and psychographics. Besides focusing on specific interest areas, marketers also can target based on geographic regions (including global), time of day, computer platform, or browser. American Airlines enlisted the help of TM Advertising to track the Web behavior of the readers of *Wall Street Journal* online travel columns and then "followed" those surfers around with American Airlines ads at various other sections. Response to the online advertising increased 115 percent.[15]

Tracking

The Internet allows advertisers to track how users interact with their brands and learn what interests current and potential customers. Display or banner ads and websites also provide the opportunity to measure the response to an ad by means of hits, a measure that is unattainable in traditional media. We'll discuss tracking and measurement in more detail later in the chapter.

Deliverability, Flexibility, and Reach

Online advertising and website content are delivered 24 hours a day, seven days a week, at the convenience of the receiver. Whenever receivers are logged on and active, ads are there. Just as important, a campaign can be tracked on a daily basis and updated, changed, or replaced almost immediately. This is a dramatic difference from traditional media, where changing a campaign might be delayed for weeks, given media schedules and the time needed to produce ads. The Maui Jim sunglasses website (http://www .mauijim.com) is a perfect example of this kind of deliverability and flexibility. It allows consumers to visit the site at any time to dig for information and check out new products. And with wireless options, there will be even more flexibility and deliverability.

Also, behind television and radio, no medium has the reach (use of a medium by audiences) of the Internet. As mentioned earlier, almost three-quarters of U.S. households have Internet access. In addition, the Internet is a global medium unlike any traditional media option. The convenience and, in some cases, affordability of mobile devices such as smartphones and tablets is adding to the numbers of Internet users and the frequency with which people go online to look up directions, send email, and get weather forecasts and news updates— all services where marketers can place their brand messages.[16]

Interactivity

A lofty and often unattainable goal for a marketer is to engage a prospective customer with the brand and the firm. This can be done with Internet advertising in a way that just cannot be accomplished in traditional media. A consumer can go to a company website or click through from a display or banner ad and take a tour of the brand's features and values. A **click-through** is a measure of the number of page elements (hyperlinks) that actually have been requested (that is, "clicked through" from the display or banner ad to the link).

Social media offer perfect examples of this sort of advantage. You can suggest new menu items at My Starbucks Idea (http://www.mystarbucks.com) for your favorite Starbucks location. Then you can tweet your friends to tell them about the experience in 140 characters or less. AARP, the organization for senior citizens, runs a trivia contest at its website to engage consumers with the brand and the organization (http://aarp.promo .eprize.com/trivia). Users can also rate the quizzes—an activity that delivers an extra level of interaction and engagement.

The click-through is an important component of Web advertising for another important reason. If advertisers can attract surfers to the company or brand website, then they have a chance to convert that surfer to a buyer if the site is set up for e-commerce. Researchers are discovering that design components of various Internet ad formats can have an important effect on click-through and, therefore, sales potential.[17]

Integration

Web advertising is the most easily integrated and coordinated with other forms of promotion. In the most basic sense, all traditional media advertising being used by a marketer can carry the website URL (uniform resource locator; basically, the website's address). Web display or banner ads can highlight themes and images from television or print campaigns. Special events or contests can be featured in display or banner ads and on websites. Overall, the integration of Web activities with other components of the marketing mix is one of the easiest integration tasks in IMC, thanks to the flexibility and deliverability of Web advertising.

A great example of integrating consumer Web behavior with another part of the promotional process, personal selling, is the strategy used by Mazda Corp. Mazda's salespeople used to hate the Web because shoppers would come to the showrooms armed with "cost" data on every vehicle, obtained from various websites. Rather than battle consumers, Mazda embraced the fact that car shoppers use the Web to search for pricing information. The company installed Internet kiosks in its showrooms so that customers could look up information right there. One dealership owner found that the Internet access doesn't interfere with selling but rather "helps build trust and close sales faster."[18]

Monkey Business Images/Shutterstock.com.

Cost of Online Promotion

Preparing an ad and placing it on a website once cost a few thousand dollars. But given the huge audiences that now can be reached on the Web and the availability of technology that tracks the number of people who visit a website and click on an ad, the cost has skyrocketed. A banner ad on a leading portal like Yahoo! can cost more than $100,000 per day—about the same as a 30-second television spot on a highly rated network show. Granted, the ad runs all day versus one 30-second insertion, but costs are escalating dramatically.

Measured in terms of **cost per thousand (CPM)**, however, the cost of Web ads for the most part compares favorably with ads placed in traditional media. Most agencies price banner ads on a CPM basis, while a smaller number base their prices on click-throughs.[19]

The real attraction of Internet promotion is not found in raw numbers and CPMs but rather in the expectation of reaching highly desirable, highly segmentable, and highly motivated audiences. The Internet enables niche marketing—that is, reaching only the consumers most likely to buy what the marketer is selling. Marketers can identify segments and deliver almost-customized (or in the case of email, actually customized) messages directly to those customers, one by one.

Types of Internet Promotion

There are several ways for marketers to place their messages on the Web. The most prominent is paid search, and the best known is banner advertising, but many more options exist.

Paid Search

The biggest share of spending on Internet advertising is for **paid search**, the practice of paying websites and portals to place ads in or near relevant search results based on keywords. For example, if you search for "running shoes," links to retailers such as Finish Line and Zappos will be displayed next to the search results as sources for purchasing running shoes. Paid search has grown astronomically, and marketers spend more than $15 billion a year on this type of advertising.[20] The catalyst for growth in paid search is the success of Google, which pushed the concept from its beginning. Paid-search technology can fine-tune a Web user's search to more relevant and specific websites. For example, if an astronomy buff enters the word "saturn" in a search, paid search results would be returned for the planet, not the car company.

Paid search is extremely valued by firms as they try to improve the effectiveness and efficiency of their online promotion. Paid search is not particularly cheap—about 58 cents per verified click for second-tier search sites to about $1.61 on Google.[21]

An important principle for using paid search is that Web users are most likely to read and click on links that appear near the top of their results. To obtain those valued positions, marketers use **search engine optimization (SEO)**. SEO is a process whereby the volume and quality of traffic to a website from search engines is improved based on surfers' profiles.

Display or Banner Ads

When most people think of Internet advertising, they think of **display or banner ads**. These are paid placements of advertising on websites that contain editorial material. Not only do consumers see the ad, but they also can make a quick trip to the marketer's home page by clicking on the ad (the "click-through" defined earlier). Thus, the dual challenge of creating and placing display or banner ads is first to catch people's attention and then to entice them to visit the marketer's website and stay for a while. Research indicates that the ability to create curiosity and provide resolution to that curiosity can have an important impact on learning and brand attitude.[22] The downside of these ads is the enormous clutter. Web users are bombarded by more than 1,800 Web ads daily, and perhaps in reaction, click-through rates have fallen to 0.1 percent.[23]

Display or banner ads such as this one generally invite the viewer to click on a link to expand the ad, learn more about the product, or place an order. Offering something of value, such as a coupon, for clicking can increase the chance of a response.

Photo Courtesy, OmniTerra Images.

A more targeted option is to place banner ads on sites that attract specific market niches. For example, a banner ad for running shoes would be placed on a site that offers information related to running. This option enables marketers to focus more closely on their target audiences. Niche users have particular interests that may represent important opportunities for the right marketer.

A pricing evaluation service for these types of ads is offered by Interactive Traffic. The I-Traffic Index computes a site's advertising value based on traffic, placement and size of ads, ad rates, and evaluations of the site's quality. Firms such as Forrester Research assess the costs of display or banner ads on a variety of sites and provide marketers with an estimate of the audience delivered.

Sponsorship

Marketers can pay to maintain a section of a website, a type of brand promotion known as **sponsorship**. Along with the sponsorship, the marketer also may provide content for a site. On Yahoo!'s home page (http://m.www.yahoo.com), the Yahoo! Movies section and Yahoo! Marketplace section are almost always "sponsored by" a marketer. The Weather Channel website (http://www.weather.com) is another site that attracts sponsors. Public service or not-for-profit websites often try to recruit local sponsors.

In the context of more animated display or banner ads and paid search, it appears that sponsorships are becoming less and less popular. Marketers are spending about $320 million annually on sponsorship.[24]

Pop-Up and Pop-Under Ads

From the Web surfer's perspective, some of the most-hated ads are pop-up Internet ads. The idea is borrowed from TV. A **pop-up ad** is an Internet advertisement that opens in a separate window while a Web page is loading. The more times people click on these ads, the more money can be charged for the privilege of advertising. In a recent study, nearly 80 percent of surfers said pop-ups are annoying, and about 65 percent said display or banner ads were annoying.[25] But like spam, pop-ups are relatively effective, with 2 percent of Web visitors clicking on the pop-up—nearly double the click-through rate for display and banner ads.[26] Many Internet service providers provide pop-up blocking software that greatly reduces an advertiser's ability to get a pop-up onto a user's screen.

A subcategory of pop-up ads is the **splash screen**, also called an interstitial. These appear on a site after a page has been requested but before it has loaded, and they stay onscreen long enough for the message to be registered. So a surfer who wants to go to a certain site must see an ad page first, just as a television viewer must watch a commercial before seeing a favorite show. Interstitials often invite the viewer to link to another, related site.

Pop-under ads are ads that are present "under" the Web user's active window so that they are visible only when the surfer closes that window. Like pop-ups, pop-unders are seen as a nuisance by computer users. Regardless, if the click-through rate is not identifiable or if paid search comes to dominate online advertising (as it may), then pop-up and pop-under ads may become a bit of odd Internet history.

Email Communication

As mentioned earlier, email communication may be the Internet's most advantageous promotional application because it makes the Internet the only mass medium capable of customizing a message for thousands or even millions of receivers. The messages are delivered in a unique way, one at a time. The United States alone has about 200 million email users, and marketers are spending more than $1.6 billion annually on newsletters, direct messaging, and email list rental.

Email from organizations is most effective when Web users have agreed to receive it; this is called opt-in email, as discussed earlier, or **permission marketing**. Some Web firms, such as InetGiant, specialize in developing opt-in lists of Web users who have agreed to accept commercial emails. The data on permission-based emailing versus spamming are compelling. Sixty-six percent of Web users who give their permission to have email sent to them indicate that they either are eager or curious to read the email. This compares with only 15 percent of Web users who receive email through spamming.

Email marketers are turning to some traditional message strategies such as humor to make their messages more palatable and interesting. BitMagic, an

sponsorship payment to maintain a section of a website and perhaps provide content for the site in exchange for being mentioned on the site

pop-up ad Internet advertisement that opens a separate window while a Web page is loading

splash screen Internet ad that appears briefly on a website after a page has been requested but before it has loaded

pop-under ad Internet ad that is displayed "under" the active window, so it appears only after that window is closed

permission marketing sending commercial email only to Web users who have agreed to receive it

viral marketing process of consumers spreading brand messages through email

rich media, video, and audio use of streaming video and audio that plays when the user's mouse passes over an Internet ad

corporate home page website that focuses on a corporation and its products

virtual mall gateway to a group of Internet storefronts where the user gains access to a retailer by clicking on a storefront

Amsterdam-based Web advertising specialty firm, has Web users download software containing a joke, cartoon, or game along with the email message.[27]

Through email and electronic mailing lists, advertisers can encourage viral marketing. **Viral marketing** is the process of consumers marketing to consumers over the Internet through word-of-mouth transmitted through emails and electronic mailing lists. Posting the video of a TV ad or a follow-on to a TV ad can generate viral marketing if consumers find it entertaining. Nike's three-minute "Write the Future" video related to the 2010 World Cup attracted nearly 16 million views on YouTube within three weeks after it was placed.[28]

Rich Media, Video, and Audio

Online marketers also are making their ads more engaging through the use of **rich media, video, and audio**—advanced technology like streaming video or audio that interacts with the user when the user's mouse passes over the ad. For example, if you go to the Yahoo! main page, you may see an ad for a new movie about to be released. As you pass your mouse over the ad, it launches a video clip from the film. Firms such as RealNetworks, NetRadio, and MusicVision insert streaming video into ads for advertisers. The widespread use of MP3 players such as iPods also makes it possible to offer podcasts, or content that users can download to these devices and listen to again and again if they find it interesting or entertaining.

Besides simply making online ads more interesting, streaming audio and video can realize click-through rates of 3.5 percent—hundreds of times greater than click-throughs for display or banner ads. Academic literature supports the proposition that adding animation to Internet ads increases click-through rates, recall, and favorable attitudes toward Web ads.[29]

Corporate Home Pages

A **corporate home page** simply is the website where a business provides current and potential customers with information about the firm and usually its brands in great detail. The best corporate home

Binney & Smith.

In contrast to purely informational or business sites, the Crayola website offers parents, teachers, and kids a variety of educational and entertainment options.

pages not only provide corporate and brand information but also offer other content of interest to site visitors. The Crayola site doesn't have to explain details about its already-famous product. Instead, the website addresses the creative needs of the parents of children who use Crayola crayons. Visitors get craft ideas as they plan parties, look up family travel ideas, download coloring pages and projects, and, of course, create art with computerized Crayolas.

Virtual Malls

A variation on the corporate website is a website placed inside a virtual mall. A **virtual mall** is a gateway to a group of Internet storefronts that provide access to mall sites by simply clicking on a category of store, as shown on the Mall Internet site (http://www.mall-internet.com). This site is set up to lead shoppers to product categories. When a click is made to a product category, Mall Internet offers "featured store" click-throughs that lead to corporate websites and home pages. This additional presence gives stores such as Nordstrom and ESPRIT more exposure.

Widgets

A new piece of technology with potential as an advertising option is a **widget**—a module of software that people can drag and drop onto their personal Web page of their social network (e.g., Facebook) or onto a blog. Widgets look like a website window but carry the power of a full website. Advertisers can create widgets that feature their brands or that direct the widget clicker to an e-commerce site. The advertiser will pay a fee each time a user installs the widget. Southwest Airlines created the "Ding" widget, which features the Southwest logo. After consumers download the widget, it alerts them with a ding whenever special fares become available. Within a year, the widget was downloaded 2 million times.[30]

Second Life and Virtual Worlds

Marketers can interact with consumers within virtual worlds. The most prominent of the virtual worlds is **Second Life**, an online virtual world where participants log into a space and then use their mouse and keyboard to roam landscapes, chat, create virtual homes, or conduct real business. Participants "exist" in Second Life (http://www.secondlife.com) as avatars, or onscreen graphical characters.

The growth of participation in Second Life has attracted the attention of advertisers for three reasons:

1. There are about 2 million active participants in Second Life, and that number is growing.[31]

2. Because participants in Second Life can "own" the objects they create, real commerce is taking place.

3. The landscapes and cityscapes created in Second Life offer an ideal environment for brand promotion. Along with paid search at the Second Life site, you will find merchants with offerings to outfit your "second life."

Real-world marketers can create billboards and branded product use, and avatars can wear branded apparel or use branded items. Several automobile firms have committed to Second Life as a good brand promotion opportunity. Pontiac and Toyota have established virtual dealerships and "sell" some of their most popular youth-oriented brands.[32]

But despite the excitement about brand promotion in virtual worlds, the ultimate potential of this venue as a promotional medium is still in question. One analyst described Second Life as "so popular, no one goes there anymore."[33] This analyst counted "actual" visitors and then repeat visitors to Second Life and found only about 100,000 Americans per week available for targeting by U.S. marketers—and "nobody" visiting virtual islands owned by American Apparel, Reebok, and Scion.[34] Virtual worlds may offer Internet users another social networking venue, but they may not offer marketers a very good message-communication venue.

Video Games

Marketers especially are interested in video games as a way to reach the elusive 18- to 34-year-old male segment that has abandoned many traditional media for digital media. For example, *Need for Speed: Carbon*, an auto-racing game from Electronic Arts, is full of ads. Advertising spending within video games, primarily through embedded billboards and posters, has reached nearly $400 million.[35]

A question remains for marketers to address: How effective is in-game placement? There is some evidence that it helps consumers recall brands. However, there is also evidence that, after repeatedly playing a game, consumers develop a less positive attitude toward the embedded brands.[36]

widget software module that people can add to their blog or their personal page on a social network; may feature a brand or direct the user to an e-commerce site

Second Life online virtual world where participants can roam landscapes and interact, simulating real-world activities, including (often real) business transactions

LO 4 Establishing a Website

It's fairly easy to set up a website, but setting up a commercially viable one is a lot harder and a lot more expensive. The top commercial sites can cost $1 million to develop, about $4.9 million for the initial launch, and about $500,000 to more than $1 million a year to maintain.[37] Setting up an attractive site costs so much because of the need for specialized designers to create the site and, most important, to update it constantly. The basic hardware for a site can be a personal computer, and the software to run the site ranges from free to several thousand dollars, depending on the number of extras needed. A site anticipating considerable traffic will need to plan for higher-capacity connections—and hence, a bigger phone bill.

Still, even small companies that want a Web presence can employ some inexpensive ways of setting up a site and finding hosts to maintain it. Companies like

1&1 Internet (http://www.1and1.com) offer small businesses a wide range of services, including hosting at extremely low cost, maintenance of domain names, website connectivity, email accounts, and some limited e-commerce applications for as little as $9.99 per month. One company that successfully set up and maintains an inexpensive site is Backcountry.com (http://www.backcountry.com). The two founders, former ski bums, started in 2000 with $2,000 and now run the second-largest online outdoor-gear organization, behind REI.[38]

In addition, use of the Web as a key component of a brand building is not reserved for consumer brands. Marketers of business products—from large firms like Caterpillar to small firms like PrintingForLess.com—are discovering the power of the Web in providing customer service and brand building. Plus, the Web is the fastest and most efficient way to reach a global market. The instant you establish a website, any computer user from any part of the globe can access your site and navigate through all the features and information opportunities you care to provide.

© Bartlomiej Magierowski/Shutterstock.com.

GLOBAL THE NEXT NET WAVE

With more than 250 million users, China is the Internet's biggest population. And even though it's already number one, China represents a huge opportunity for future growth: Only one out of five Chinese people is using the Internet. Here are a few firms already surfing this massive Net wave:

- Sina, the most popular portal in the country, has links to online gaming and Yahoo! Auctions.
- NetEase operates a portal called 163.com, earning revenue through online ads, text messages, and games.
- Shanda is China's first indigenous online gaming company.
- TOM Online focuses on mobile Internet services.

Source: Bruce Einhorn, "The Net's Second Superpower," *BusinessWeek*, March 15, 2004, 54–56; "Stats—Web Worldwide," *ClickZ*, http://www.clickz.com/stats/web_worldwide, accessed December 1, 2009.

Another key consideration in website design is interactivity. The interactivity of a site has important consequences, not only for loyalty to a site, but also for intention to purchase items from the site. Research shows that when consumers engage in more human-message (an interactive message) or human-human interaction (like a chat room), there is a more positive attitude toward the site and a higher purchase intention.[39] An excellent example of a highly interactive site is Neutrogena's SkinID site (http://www.skinid.com). Users can enter a wide range of individual characteristics, and the site produces a personalized skin evaluation and recommends the Neutrogena products designed to address the needs identified.

Developing a Domain Name

A **domain name** is a company's unique identity on the Internet, such as www.yourcompany.com. Companies like VeriSign help companies identify, register, and manage Internet names and keywords in both domestic and global markets.

If you are the Gap (http://www.gap.com) or Sony (http://www.sony.com), your domain name is your corporate name, and consumers know how to search for your location. But for thousands of Web startups that provide specialized products and services, selection of a domain name is a dilemma. The name should be descriptive but unique, and intuitive but distinctive. Consultant Dennis Scheyer once recommended that GoToTix.com, a ticketing and entertainment site, stick with its original name because it was intuitive and easy to remember. But the firm insisted on running a consumer contest to rename the company. It eventually chose Acteva.com (and the domain name http://www.acteva.com) because "Act conveys activity. E signifies E-commerce and 'va' has that international flavor." The company has expanded beyond selling tickets and provides online registration and tracking for all sorts of events from fundraisers to corporate meetings.[40]

The suffix of a website name is called the **top-level domain (TLD)**. Until late 2000, there were only five TLDs in the United States: .com, .edu, .org, .gov, and .net. Recently, the Internet Corporation for Assigned Names and Numbers (ICANN), a nonprofit formed in 1998 to coordinate technical management of the domain name system, issued new top-level domains. You can visit ICANN's website at http://www.icann.org to learn about the new TLD extensions available, as well as country-specific TLDs (e.g., .us and .uk). The purpose of releasing new TLDs, such as .tv and .us, is to relieve the pressure on the original top-level domains. But pairing an existing name with a new suffix could create confusion among consumers.

If you have an idea, be sure to register the URL for your company ASAP with a provider like Register.com. The cost can be less than $20 per year, and that price often includes email. Why hurry? Domain names are big business, and folks called "domainers" register every name they can think of, hoping they can resell the right to the name for a tidy sum. The domain http://www.cellphones.com was resold for $4.2 million.[41] An estimated 90,000 domain names are purchased each day, and Internet domain purchasing could become a $10 billion-per-year industry by 2010.[42]

Promoting Websites

After building a website, the next step is promoting it. Several agencies, including Wieden & Kennedy and OgilvyOne, specialize in promoting websites. Several methods are available:

- Feature the website address in traditional media advertising. Most print ads and many radio and TV ads feature the marketer's Web address.

- Register the site with search engines such as Yahoo! and Ask.com. With Yahoo!, because it is a hierarchical search

Photo Courtesy, OmniTerra Images.

engine, pick keywords that commonly are chosen yet describe and differentiate the site.

- Register with online yellow-pages services—for example, SuperPages, (http://www.bigyellow.com)—and with appropriate electronic mailing lists.
- Send press releases to Internet news sites.
- Use email as a form of direct mail.

Security and Privacy Issues

Any Web user can download text, images, and graphics from the Web. Although marketers place trademark and copyright disclaimers in their online messages, trademarks and logos easily can be copied without authorization. Currently, there is no viable policing of this practice. Marketers have taken legal action only against users who have taken proprietary materials and blatantly used them in a fashion that is detrimental to the brand or infringes on the exclusivity of the marketer's own site. This may change.

In Chapter 6, we discussed privacy as an ethical and regulatory issue. It also is a matter of strategic management. Discussions at the highest levels focus on the extent to which regulations should be mandated for gathering and disseminating information about Web use. The concern among marketers is not only regulation but also sensitivity to consumers' concerns about their privacy being violated online.

Privacy is a legitimate concern for Internet users and will likely continue to be one for civil libertarians and regulators as well. But it is not clear that consumers themselves (as opposed to critics or watchdog groups) really care much about privacy. In a survey of U.S. consumers, only 6 percent said they always read a site's privacy policy, and another 15 percent said they sometimes read the policy.[43] Some interesting research has discovered that, for people from countries with "weak rule of law," privacy and security issues affect the perceived value of a website, whereas for people from countries that are high on national identity, privacy and security is less important than the cultural congruity between the site and themselves.[44]

Nevertheless, technology is changing rapidly, and a whole new level of concern and controversy could find its way into the privacy discussions. More consumers are accessing the Internet through wireless technology, which is more readily subject to monitoring. Hacking an in-home or in-firm wireless system without the proper security hardware is as easy as sitting in a car with a laptop and an antenna.

Measuring Effectiveness of Online Promotion

To measure the effectiveness of their online promotion, marketers want information about how many people visit a particular website and, if possible, details about whom those people are. At a minimum, when a user connects with a website, the basic information that can be collected includes the IP address of the computer requesting the page, the page requested, and the time of the request. For an opt-in site that requires registration, the marketer can obtain additional information provided by the user, such as email address, ZIP code, gender, age, and household income. Consumers tend to resist attempts to learn about them via registration. Still, plenty of service providers, described later in this section, are available to guide marketers through Web measurement options.

WE DISCUSSED **PRIVACY** AS AN ETHICAL AND REGULATORY ISSUE. IT IS ALSO A MATTER OF **STRATEGIC MANAGEMENT.**

Web analytics firms such as NextLevel Reporting count and analyze a variety of user data. For example, NextLevel customers can use their smartphones to get daily, weekly, and monthly data about how many unique visitors are coming to their websites, what they are clicking on, and more.

hits number of pages and graphical images requested from a website

page views record of the pages that have been sent to a user's computer; multiscreen pages are counted as one page

visits number of occasions on which a particular user looks up a particular website during a given time period

unique visitors number of people (identified using registration information) who visit a site during a given time period

What Gets Counted

Several terms are used in Web audience measurement. The following are the most meaningful of these measurement factors:

- **Hits** are the number of elements requested from a given page. The number of hits provides almost no indication of actual Web traffic. For instance, a user's request for a page with four graphical images counts as five hits. By including many images, a site quickly can pull up its hit count. Thus, the *Seventeen* magazine site (http://www.seventeen.com) might get 3 million hits a day, placing it among the top websites, but this 3 million hits translates into perhaps only 80,000 visitors daily.

- Another measure of a site's advertising effectiveness is the extent to which visitors click through and request information from an ad, as we have discussed before. Most analysts consider the *click-through* number (and percentage) to be the best measure of Web advertising's effectiveness. An ad that motivates a visitor to click on it and follow the link to more information presumably was viewed and was motivating (more on this later).

- **Page views** are the pages (actually, the number of HTML—hypertext markup language—files) sent to the requesting user's computer. If a downloaded page occupies several screens, there is no indication whether the user examined the entire page. The page-view count also doesn't tell you how many visitors the page actually has: 100,000 page views in a week could be 10 people reading 10,000 pages, 100,000 people reading one page, or any variation in between.

- **Visits** are the number of occasions on which user X interacted with site Y after time Z has elapsed. Usually Z is set to some standard time, such as 30 minutes. If the user interacts with a site and then interacts again more than 30 minutes later, the second interaction would be counted as a new visit.

- **Unique visitors** are the number of different "people" visiting a site (a new user is determined from the user's registration with the site) during a specified period of time. Besides the address, page, and time, a website can find out the referring link address. This allows a website to discover what links are directing people to the site. This

Haywiremedia/Shutterstock.com.

can be extremely helpful in Internet advertising planning. The problem is that what is really counted are unique IP numbers. Many Internet service providers use a dynamic IP number, which changes every time a given user logs in through the service, so you might show up as 30 different unique visitors to a site you visited daily for a month.

To obtain these statistics, marketers use Web analytic software. **Web analytic software** is measurement software that not only provides information on hits, pages, visits, and users but also lets a website track audience traffic within the site. The publisher of the site could determine which pages are popular and expand on them. It also is possible to track people's behavior as they go through the site, thus providing ideas about what people find appealing and unappealing. An example of Web analytic software is MaxInfo's WebC, which lets marketers track what information is viewed, when it is viewed, how often it is viewed, and where users go within a site. A marketer then can modify the content and structure it accordingly. It also can help marketers understand how buyers make purchase decisions in general. But although it is possible to know a lot about users' behavior at sites, it still isn't possible to know what people actually do with website information.[45]

Despite all of these options, there is no industry standard for measuring the effectiveness of one interactive ad placement over another. There also is no standard for comparing Internet with traditional media placements. Moreover, demographic information on who is using the Web is severely limited to consumers who have signed up for opt-in programs and, for example, allow targeted emails to be sent to them. Until these limitations are overcome, many marketers will remain hesitant about spending substantial dollars for advertising on the Web.

Measurement Help

Plenty of companies offer measurement services for interactive media. Exhibit 9.3 lists only some of the companies providing measurement and evaluation services.

With Internet tracking services, an advertiser used to be able to know only how many people see an ad and how many respond to it with a click. But new technologies now allow tracking of mouse movement on Web pages and grouping of shoppers by age, ZIP code, and reading habits. DoubleClick, which places 200 billion ads a month for customers, can provide 50 different types of metrics for an Internet campaign. With mouse tracking, advertisers can know which parts of a banner ad appear to be of interest to visitors and how long they spend on different parts of an ad. With new control monitors, referred to as "dashboards," advertising strategists can check the performance of their online ads in real time. There is so much data available that agencies are hiring teams of analytic people, including PhDs in statistics, to make sense of the data.

The next step is to get inside users' heads. One agency, Tacoda Systems, announced plans to wire a group of Web surfers with brain scanners to see which ads register in their minds.[46] And academics are deep into the evaluation process, researching the effect of animation speed on attention, memory, and impression formation.[47]

Click Fraud

To measure effectiveness, you need to know that measures and data are valid. Unfortunately, sometimes they aren't. One big problem is **click fraud**—clicking on Internet advertising solely to generate illegitimate revenue for the website carrying the ad.[48] Click fraud

takes place when a person is paid to visit websites, or when a computer program roams the Web and imitates a legitimate Web user by "clicking" on ads. Click fraud thus generates a charge per click without there having been actual interest in the ad's link.

Click fraud is a crime and occurs when an advertiser has a pay-per-click agreement with a website. There have been arrests related to click fraud with regard to malicious clicking in order to deplete a competitor's advertising budget. And this is no small problem. Forty percent of Web advertisers claim they have been victims of click fraud.

Google and Yahoo!, prime targets for click scammers, are working to stop click fraud by monitoring Web traffic for repeated clicks or unusual visit patterns from anonymous servers.[49] Yahoo! has named a senior executive to lead the company's effort to combat click fraud in its advertising business. The company also discards as invalid or inferior quality about 12 to 15 percent of clicks on advertisements; in the case of invalid clicks, it will not charge the advertiser. In a similar move, Google said its computers automatically reject up to 10 percent of potential advertising billings resulting from invalid clicks.

Exhibit 9.3
Measurement and Evaluation Services

Arbitron (http://www.arbitron.com)	One of the oldest advertising measurement firms; better known for traditional media (especially radio and television) measures but also specializes in providing data on Internet radio broadcasts.
Audit Bureau of Circulations (http://www.accessabc.com)	For many years, the main print circulation auditing organization; recently established ABC Interactive (ABCI), which offers independent measurement of online activity to ensure that website traffic and ad delivery metrics are reported accurately.
eMarketer (http://www.emarketer.com)	One of the newer entrants in the advertising measurement area; accumulates data from various research sources and provides summary statistics.
Experian Simmons (http://www.smrb.com)	Measures media and purchase behaviors of consumers; offers data on more than 8,000 brands across more than 460 product categories; creates 600 lifestyle profiles linked to every media genre, including information on Web use and product purchase.
Forrester Research (http://www.forrester.com)	Provides a wide range of data analysis, research, and advice for firms using the Internet for promotion and e-commerce.
Lyris HQ (http://www.lyris.com/solutions/lyris-hq/web-analytics/)	Web analytics program that makes it easy for marketers to compile website navigation patterns by users and compute return on investment (ROI) for Web advertising.
Nielsen NetRatings (http://en-us.nielsen.com/tab/product_families/nielsen_netratings)	Probably the highest profile of the data providers, ruling the ratings game for many years; relies on its traditional method of finding consumers who are willing to have their media behavior (in this case, Internet use) monitored by a device attached to their computers.
Ranking.com (http://www.ranking.com)	Performs market research on a statistically, geographically, and demographically significant number of Internet surfers; records these surfers' website visits and calculates rankings for the most-visited websites; one of the very few free sources of Web data research.

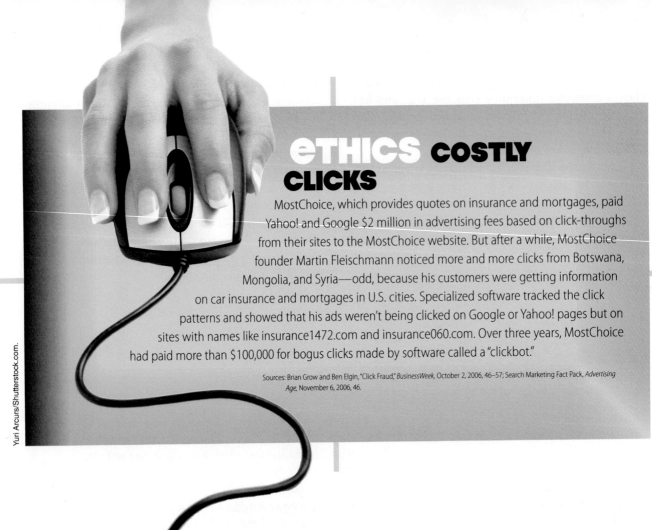

ETHICS COSTLY CLICKS

MostChoice, which provides quotes on insurance and mortgages, paid Yahoo! and Google $2 million in advertising fees based on click-throughs from their sites to the MostChoice website. But after a while, MostChoice founder Martin Fleischmann noticed more and more clicks from Botswana, Mongolia, and Syria—odd, because his customers were getting information on car insurance and mortgages in U.S. cities. Specialized software tracked the click patterns and showed that his ads weren't being clicked on Google or Yahoo! pages but on sites with names like insurance1472.com and insurance060.com. Over three years, MostChoice had paid more than $100,000 for bogus clicks made by software called a "clickbot."

Sources: Brian Grow and Ben Elgin, "Click Fraud," *BusinessWeek*, October 2, 2006, 46–57; Search Marketing Fact Pack, *Advertising Age*, November 6, 2006, 46.

Yuri Arcurs/Shutterstock.com.

Managing the Brand in an E-Community

The Internet, besides giving marketers a medium for communicating with consumers, also gives consumers a new and efficient way to communicate with one another. In fact, the social aspect of the Internet is one of the most important reasons for its success. Via email, blogs, and social-networking Web pages, consumers have a way to interact and form communities. For marketers, this is yet another opportunity: the chance to communicate with consumers in a brand community or e-community.

Communities formed online among users of a particular brand behave much like a community in the traditional sense, such as a small town or ethnic neighborhood. They have their own cultures, rituals, and traditions. Members create detailed Web pages devoted to the brand. Members even feel a sense of duty or moral responsibility to other members of the community. For example, among many Volkswagen drivers, it is a common courtesy to pull over to help

another VW broken down on the side of the road. Harley-Davidson riders feel a similar sense of affinity and desire to help others who use the same brand when they are in trouble.

In addition, the affinity to social-networking sites cannot be underestimated—or ignored. Sites like Facebook attract up to 100 million unique visitors per month.[50] It seems clear that the credibility of these sites appeals to consumers who are weary of the blatant promotional intent of traditional media and commerce-oriented websites.

Because the Internet makes it easier for members of these communities to interact, brand communities are likely to continue to proliferate in coming years. Dealing effectively with these communities will be one of the challenges facing marketers. One approach is to encourage community building on the brand's own website. Harley-Davidson's site (http://www.harley-davidson.com) tries to accomplish e-community interaction. Events around the country, promoted on the site, are a highlight for riders. Another technique for creating a community around the brand is to draw community members to the website by using features like those of Web portals, such as lifestyle and entertainment information.

mobile marketing
communicating with target markets through mobile devices

Building a loyal e-community is a natural step for Harley-Davidson, whose enthusiastic customers look forward to company-sponsored motorcycle events.

LO 5 The Future of Online Promotion

When it comes to the Internet, the future seems to arrive with every new issue of *Fortune* or *Wired*. But we are reasonably confident to say that the future of promotion on the Internet will be linked to technological advances enabling video on the Web and mobile marketing.

Video on the Web

Marketers and advertising agencies are preparing for new opportunities with "broadcast Web." As more Web users have access to broadband (a majority of users in the United States now do), more complex data, including video files, can be streamed to them. The possibilities are attracting all the big players—Microsoft, ABC, and CBS, to name just a few. They all see video streaming as another piece of the Web broadcast puzzle.[51] Does this mean that in the near future every television ad really is a Web ad? Well, maybe it won't be that extreme, but the technology is available to provide direct links to websites for information and purchasing through television ads—a huge opportunity and potential for marketers.

The next evolution in the process is Internet television. Other big players, including Google in partnership with Sony, are introducing services that blend streams from the Internet and broadcast programming on television screens. Hulu has a paid service that delivers broadcast television shows over the Internet to computers, televisions, smartphones, and e-readers. This is no minor trend; by 2010, hundreds of thousands of U.S. households had canceled cable television service and were relying exclusively on online services.[52]

Mobile Marketing

As you saw in the discussion of the World Wide Web, more and more people are making their Internet connections with mobile devices, wherever and whenever they want to gather information or connect with others. As a result, marketing will increasingly be reaching out to people on the go. **Mobile marketing** is communicating with target markets through mobile devices, including smartphones and tablet computers such as iPads. Already, there are more than 100 million mobile Internet subscribers, and spending on mobile advertising is approaching $1 billion per year.[53]

Placing messages on mobile devices gives marketers the opportunity to tailor messages to the user's location—for example, promoting a nearby restaurant or offering a deal at a store around the corner. In Chapter 6, we considered that GPS-based consumer tracking is a privacy issue. But it also is an opportunity to make brand communication more relevant. Companies like Foursquare already have the technology and services in place to allow marketers to beam messages related to your location. Whether campaigns use data collected by GPS, mobile carrier, cell tower triangulation, or personally provided by customers via an opt-in interactive promotion, the most successful campaigns of the future will deliver messages to customers who are already close to the point of sale or in the store where a purchase can be made. Investment in these mobile campaigns is already $400 million annually and expected to surpass $1 billion by 2014.[54]

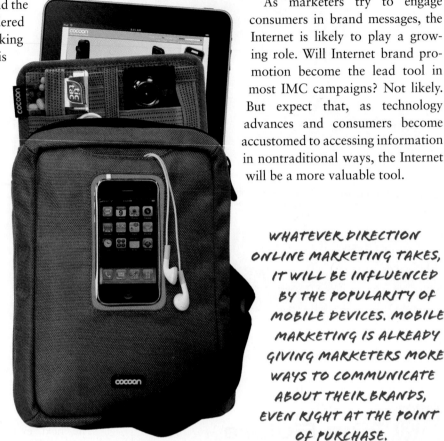

AP Images/PRNewsFoto/Cocoon Innovations, LLC.

As marketers try to engage consumers in brand messages, the Internet is likely to play a growing role. Will Internet brand promotion become the lead tool in most IMC campaigns? Not likely. But expect that, as technology advances and consumers become accustomed to accessing information in nontraditional ways, the Internet will be a more valuable tool.

WHATEVER DIRECTION ONLINE MARKETING TAKES, IT WILL BE INFLUENCED BY THE POPULARITY OF MOBILE DEVICES. MOBILE MARKETING IS ALREADY GIVING MARKETERS MORE WAYS TO COMMUNICATE ABOUT THEIR BRANDS, EVEN RIGHT AT THE POINT OF PURCHASE.

STUDY TOOLS
CHAPTER 9

Located at back of the textbook

- Rip out Chapter in Review Card.

Located at www.cengagebrain.com

- Review Key Terms Flashcards (Print or Online).
- Complete the Practice Quiz to prepare for tests.
- Play "Beat the Clock" and "Quizbowl" to master concepts.
- Complete "Crossword Puzzle" to review key terms.
- Watch videos on **IKEA** and **iPad** for real company examples.
- For additional examples, go online to learn about Web-based contests, music stars getting their start online, and **American Express Webisodes.**

4LTR Press solutions are designed for today's learners through the continuous feedback of students like you. Tell us what you think about **PROMO2** and help us improve the learning experience for future students.

YOUR FEEDBACK MATTERS.

Complete the Speak Up
survey in CourseMate at
www.cengagebrain.com

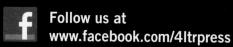 Follow us at
www.facebook.com/4ltrpress

iStockphoto.com/mustafahacalak | © Cengage Learning 2011

CarMax customers were invited to "retweet" a pre-set message on Twitter for this contest.

Can ePrize and CarMax lure you with a contest? That's what they're counting on.

Learning Outcomes

After studying this chapter, you should be able to:

LO 1 Identify purposes served by direct marketing.

LO 2 Explain the popularity of direct marketing.

LO 3 Distinguish a mailing list from a marketing database, and review the applications of each.

LO 4 Describe the media used by direct marketers in delivering messages to consumers.

"Fun without sell gets nowhere but sell without fun tends to become obnoxious."

—Leo Burnett

AFTER YOU FINISH THIS CHAPTER GO TO PAGE 216 FOR STUDY TOOLS

Luring Consumers with ePrizes

When Josh Linkler was young, he bought a lot of Cracker Jack boxes in hopes of finding decoder rings as his sticky surprise. As an adult still intrigued by the decoder mystique, he used it as the big idea for a marketing service. His company, ePrize, has used decoder contests to drive curious customers to the Web, where they can play games online and, in the process, provide information about themselves and their interests.

One of ePrize's recent projects involved CarMax's "Tweet Yourself to a New Ride" sweepstakes. Customers were invited to "retweet" a message on Twitter that was pre-set by the contest rules. If their retweet was selected at the end of the eight-week sweepstakes, the winner would receive $25,000 toward the purchase of any used car at CarMax. In addition, each week the site awarded one winner with a $250 gas card. ePrize again played the key role of running the sweepstakes and collecting consumer information.[1]

In one application, Linkler worked with the Michigan International Speedway to build a database to unlock the secrets of NASCAR fans.[2] It started with mass distribution of e-decoder game pieces through ticket-order envelopes, movie theaters, and Pepsi retailers. The game pieces encouraged NASCAR fans to go online in the hopes of winning prizes like a $10,000 garage makeover from Gladiator Garage Works. First-time players registered by giving their name, address, email, age, and gender. With each return visit, they answered more questions so that they could go deeper into the game. Ultimately, the database was enriched with answers to around 150 demographic and lifestyle questions. There also were questions concerning leisure-time pursuits like camping and fishing, and specific questions like "Do you shop at Cabela's?"

What do you think?

Because I'm on mailing lists, I get information I value.

1	2	3	4	5	6	7
STRONGLY DISAGREE						STRONGLY AGREE

Find out what others think at CourseMate for PROMO2.

Details about NASCAR fans help marketers connect with them via personalized offers that are timely and relevant. For example, Cabela's, a huge outdoor-sports retailer, can target offers to hunters or campers or boaters in the ePrize database. Why are NASCAR fans willing to divulge personal information? Well, some aren't, but Josh Linkler sees it as an issue of value: "If you want consumers to speak to you and provide information, you have to give them something to get them to react."[3]

The same principle has lured consumers to websites for other brand promotion and list-building efforts in which ePrize has played a role. For example, through mailings to local residents coupled with print and radio ads, Fifth Third Bank invited consumers to visit its bank branches and ask a teller for a game piece to enter its "Unlock Your Dreams" sweepstakes.[4] Consumers would go online and enter a code on their game piece to register for the sweepstakes with a grand prize of $250,000 plus smaller prizes. Of course, when they registered, they also provided information about themselves. Similarly, packages of Jelly Belly jelly beans invited candy lovers to go online to an ePrize-run site and enter a contest to choose a new flavor.[5] The winner received not only a cash prize but also fame and a chance to taste the new flavor, acai berry. Of course, Jelly Belly was a winner, too, because it drew 200,000 contestants and many more voters to its website and got them excited about the brand.

Evolution of Direct Marketing

When marketers speak of *direct marketing*, they generally are referring to something like the definition provided by the Direct Marketing Association (DMA): "**Direct marketing** is an interactive system of marketing, which uses one or more advertising media to affect a measurable response and/or transaction at any location."[6] Examined piece by piece, this definition furnishes an excellent basis for understanding the scope of direct marketing:[7]

- *Interactive:* Direct marketing is interactive in that the marketer is attempting to develop an ongoing dialogue with the customer. Direct-marketing programs

Adirondack Country Store; www.adirondackcountrystore.com.

How about a new moose rug or carved loon for your grandparents' cottage up north? You could find them at the Adirondack Country Store in upstate New York, call 1-800-LOON-ADK to request a catalog, or shop online at http://www.adirondackcountrystore.com.

commonly are planned with the notion that one contact will lead to another and then another so that the marketer's message can become more focused and refined with each interaction.

- *Multiple media:* The use of multiple media in direct-marketing programs is an important point for two reasons. First, there is more to direct marketing than direct mail. Second, as we have noted before, a combination of media is likely to be more effective than any one medium alone.

- *Immediate, measurable response:* Another key aspect of direct-marketing programs is that they almost always are designed to produce some form of immediate, measurable response, especially an immediate sale. The customer might be asked to return an order form with check or money order for $189 to get a stylish Klaus Kobec Couture Sports Watch, or to call an 800 number with credit card handy to get 22 timeless hits on a CD called *The Very Best of Tony Bennett*. This emphasis on immediate response enables direct marketers to judge the effectiveness of a particular program.

- *Any location:* When the DMA's definition notes that a direct-marketing transaction can take place "at any location," it means customers do not have to make a trip to a retail store for a direct-marketing program to work. Follow-ups can be made by mail, over the telephone, or on the Internet. At one time, the Internet was expected to provide so much convenience for shoppers that traditional retail stores would fall by the wayside. However, it now seems clear that consumers like the option of contacting companies in many ways (and vice versa).[8] Smart retailers make themselves available in both the physical and virtual worlds.[9] Customers are free then to choose where and how they want to shop.

A Look Back

From Johannes Gutenberg and Benjamin Franklin to Montgomery Ward and Lillian Vernon, the evolution of direct marketing has involved some of the great pioneers in business. The practice of direct marketing today is shaped by the successes of many notable mail-order companies and catalog merchandisers, such as those identified in Exhibit 10.1.[10] Among them, none is more exemplary than L. L. Bean, who founded his company in 1912 on his integrity and $400. His first product was a unique hunting shoe made from a leather top and rubber bottom sewn together. Other outdoor clothing and equipment soon followed in the Bean catalog.

A look at the L.L.Bean catalog of 1917 (black and white, only 12 pages) reveals the fundamental strategy underlying Bean's success. It featured the Maine Hunting Shoe and other outdoor clothing with descriptive copy that was informative, factual, and low key. On the front page was Bean's commitment to quality:

> *Maine Hunting Shoe—guarantee. We guarantee this pair of shoes to give perfect satisfaction in every way. If the rubber breaks or the tops grow hard, return them together with this guarantee tag and we will replace them, free of charge. Signed, L. L. Bean.[11]*

Bean realized that long-term relationships with customers must be based on trust, and his guarantee policy was aimed at developing and sustaining that trust.

As an astute direct marketer, Bean also showed a keen appreciation for the importance of building a good mailing list. For many years, he used his profits to promote his free catalog via advertisements in hunting and fishing magazines. Those replying to the ads received a rapid response and typically became Bean customers. Bean's obsession with building mailing lists is nicely captured by this quote from his friend, Maine native John Gould: "If you drop in just to shake his hand, you get home to find his catalog in your mailbox."[12]

Today, L.L.Bean still is a family-operated business that emphasizes the basic philosophies of its founder, thoughtfully summarized at http://www.llbean.com. Quality products, understated advertising, and sophisticated customer contact and distribution systems sustain the business. Additionally, L.L.Bean's 100 percent satisfaction guarantee still can be found in every Bean catalog. It remains at the heart of the relationship between Bean and its customers.

Exhibit 10.1
Some Direct-Marketing Milestones

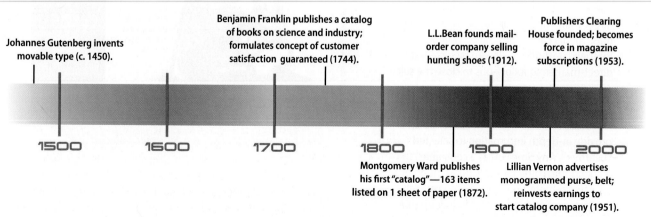

Johannes Gutenberg invents movable type (c. 1450).

Benjamin Franklin publishes a catalog of books on science and industry; formulates concept of customer satisfaction guaranteed (1744).

L.L.Bean founds mail-order company selling hunting shoes (1912).

Publishers Clearing House founded; becomes force in magazine subscriptions (1953).

1500   1600   1700   1800   1900   2000

Montgomery Ward publishes his first "catalog"—163 items listed on 1 sheet of paper (1872).

Lillian Vernon advertises monogrammed purse, belt; reinvests earnings to start catalog company (1951).

Source: Based on Direct Marketing Association, "Grassroots Advocacy Guide for Direct Marketers" (1993).

LO 1 Direct Marketing Today

Direct marketing today is rooted in the legacy of mail-order giants and catalog merchandisers such as L.L.Bean and Publishers Clearing House. Today, however, direct marketing has broken free from its mail-order heritage to become a tool used by all types of organizations throughout the world. Although many types of businesses and not-for-profit organizations are using direct marketing, it is common to find that such direct-marketing programs are not carefully integrated with an organization's other advertising efforts. Integration should be the goal for advertising and direct marketing. Again and again, the evidence supports our thesis that integrated programs are more effective than the sum of their parts.[13]

Because the label "direct marketing" now encompasses many different types of activities, it is important to remember the defining characteristics spelled out in the DMA's definition. Direct marketing involves an attempt to interact or create a dialogue with the customer; multiple media often are employed in the process, and a measurable response is immediately available for assessing a program's impact. With these defining features in mind, we can see that direct-marketing programs are commonly used for three primary purposes:

1. *Close sales:* The most common use of direct marketing is as a tool to close the sale with a customer. This can be done as a stand-alone program, or it can be coordinated with a firm's other promotional efforts. Telecommunications giants such as AT&T and Verizon make extensive use of the advertising and direct-marketing combination. High-profile mass media campaigns build awareness for their latest offer, followed by systematic direct-marketing follow-ups to close the sale.

2. *Cultivate prospects:* Direct-marketing programs also may aim to identify prospects for future contacts and, at the same time, provide in-depth information to selected customers. Any time you as a consumer respond to an offer for more information or for a free sample, you've identified yourself as a prospect and can expect follow-up sales pitches from a direct marketer. StairMaster uses advertising to initiate a dialogue with prospective customers. Ordering the free catalog and video, whether through the 800 number or at the website, begins a process of interactive marketing ultimately designed to produce the sale of another Free-Climber 4600.

3. *Engage customers with the brand:* Direct-marketing programs also are initiated as a means to engage customers, seek their advice, furnish helpful information about using a product, reward customers for using a brand, and in general foster brand loyalty. For instance, the manufacturer of Valvoline motor oil seeks to build loyalty for its brand by encouraging young car owners to join the Valvoline Performance Team.[14] To join the team, young drivers just fill out a questionnaire that enters them into the Valvoline database. Team members receive posters, special offers on racing-team apparel, news about racing events that Valvoline has sponsored, and promotional reminders at regular intervals that reinforce the virtues of Valvoline for the driver's next oil change.

Courtesy of Stairmaster Co., Kirkland, WA.

Most people won't buy a major piece of exercise equipment based on a magazine ad. The marketers at StairMaster know this, and their ad simply aims to start the purchase process by persuading consumers to order a free video.

LO 2 Growing Popularity

With the increasing concern about fragmenting markets and the diminishing effectiveness of traditional media in reaching those markets, we can expect that more and more promotion dollars will be moved into options besides advertising.[15] Direct-marketing programs are capturing some of that spending and growing in popularity for several reasons. Some of these have to do with changes in consumer lifestyles and technological developments that, in effect, create a climate more conducive to the practice of direct marketing. In addition, direct-marketing programs offer unique advantages vis-à-vis conventional mass media advertising.

From the consumer's standpoint, direct marketing's growing popularity might be summarized in a single word: *convenience*. Dramatic growth in the number of dual-income and single-person households has reduced the time people have to visit stores. Direct marketers give consumers access to a growing range of products and services in their homes, thus saving many households' most precious resource: time.

More liberal attitudes about the use of credit and the accumulation of debt also have contributed to the growth of direct marketing. Credit cards are the primary means of payment in most direct-marketing transactions. The widespread availability of credit cards makes it ever more convenient to shop from the comfort of one's home.

Developments in telecommunications also have facilitated the direct-marketing transaction. After getting off to a slow start in the late 1960s, toll-free telephone numbers have exploded in popularity to the point where one can hardly find a product or a catalog that does not include an 800 or 888 number for interacting with the seller. Whether consumers are requesting the StairMaster video or planning an adventure in Wyoming, the preferred mode of access for many consumers has been the 800 number.

Another obvious development having a huge impact on the growth of direct marketing is the computer.

The diffusion of computer technology sweeping through all modern societies has been a tremendous boon to direct marketers. The computer allows firms to track, keep records on, and interact with millions of customers with relative ease. As we will see in an upcoming discussion, the computer power now available for modest dollar amounts is fueling the growth of direct marketing's most potent tool: the marketing database.

And just as the computer has given marketers the tool they need to handle massive databases of customer information, it too has provided convenience-oriented consumers with the tool they need to comparison shop with the point and click of a mouse. What could be more convenient than logging on to the Internet and pulling up a shopping agent like PriceScan.com or MySimon to check prices on everything from toaster ovens to snowboards? Why leave home?

zentilia/Shutterstock.com.

Direct-marketing programs also offer some unique advantages that make them more appealing than what might be described as conventional mass marketing. A general manager of marketing communications with AT&T's consumer services unit put it this way: "We want to segment our market more; we want to learn more about individual customers; we want to really serve our customers by giving them very specific products and services. Direct marketing is probably the most effective way in which we can reach customers and establish a relationship with them."[16] As you might expect, AT&T is one of the organizations that has shifted more and more of its marketing dollars into direct-marketing programs.

The appeal of direct marketing is enhanced further by the persistent emphasis on producing measurable effects. For instance, in direct marketing, it is common for calculations such as **cost per inquiry (CPI)** or **cost per order (CPO)** to be featured in program evaluation. These calculations simply divide the number of responses to a program by that program's cost. When calculated for every program an organization conducts over time, CPI and CPO data tell an organization what works and what doesn't work in its competitive arena.

This emphasis on producing and monitoring measurable effects is realized most effectively through an approach called *database marketing*.[17] Working with a database, direct marketers can target specific customers, track their actual purchase behavior over time, and experiment with different programs for affecting the purchasing patterns of these customers. The programs that produce the best outcomes become the candidates for increased funding in the future.

Finding that waterfall in Wyoming will take some planning, and Wyoming's Office of Travel & Tourism is happy to help. The adventure begins with a request for a vacation packet. This ad provides two options: calling a toll-free number or visiting the tourism office's website.

LO 3 Database Marketing

If any ambiguity remains about what makes direct marketing different from marketing in general, that ambiguity can be erased by the database. The one characteristic of direct marketing that distinguishes it from marketing more generally is its emphasis on database development. Knowing who the best customers are along with what and how often they buy is a direct marketer's secret weapon.[18] This knowledge accumulates in the form of a marketing database.

Databases used as the centerpieces of direct-marketing campaigns take many forms and can contain many different layers of information about customers. At one extreme is the simple mailing list that contains nothing more than the names and addresses of possible customers; at the other extreme is the customized marketing database that augments names and addresses with various additional information about customers' characteristics, past purchases, and product preferences. Understanding this distinction between mailing lists and marketing databases is important for appreciating the scope of database marketing.

Mailing Lists

A **mailing list** simply is a file of names and addresses that an organization might use for contacting prospective or prior customers. Mailing lists are plentiful, easy to access, and inexpensive. For example, CD-ROM phone directories available for a few hundred dollars provide a cheap and easy way to generate mailing lists. More-targeted mailing lists are available from a variety of suppliers. The range of possibilities is mind-boggling, including groupings like the 238,737 subscribers to *Mickey Mouse Magazine*; 102,961 kindergarten teachers; 4,145,194 physical fitness enthusiasts; 117,758 Lord & Taylor credit card purchasers; and a whopping 269 archaeologists.[19]

Each time you subscribe to a magazine, order from a catalog, register your automobile, fill out a warranty card, redeem a rebate offer, apply for credit, join a professional society, or log on to a website, the information you provide goes on another mailing list. These lists are freely bought and sold through many means, including over the Internet. Sites such as Worldata, HDML, and InfoUSA allow marketers to buy names and addresses, or email address lists, for as little as 10 cents per record. What's out there is truly remarkable—go have a look.

> **mailing list** file of names and addresses used for contacting prospects or customers

Monkey Business Images/Shutterstock.com

KNOWING WHO THE BEST CUSTOMERS ARE ALONG WITH WHAT and HOW OFTEN THEY BUY IS A DIRECT MARKETER'S SECRET WEAPON.

Lists fall into two broad categories:

1. **Internal lists** simply are an organization's records of its own customers, subscribers, donors, and inquirers.

2. **External lists** are purchased from a list compiler or rented from a list broker.

At the most basic level, internal and external lists facilitate the two fundamental activities of the direct marketer: Internal lists are the starting point for developing better relationships with current customers, whereas external lists help an organization cultivate new business.

List Enhancement

Name-and-address files, no matter what their source, are merely the starting point for database marketing. The next step in the evolution of a database is mailing-list enhancement. Typically this involves augmenting an internal list by combining it with other, externally supplied lists or databases. External lists can be appended or merged with a house list.

One of the most straightforward list enhancements entails simply adding or appending more names and addresses to an internal list. Proprietary name-and-address files may be purchased from other companies that operate in noncompetitive businesses. With today's computer capabilities, adding these additional households to an existing mailing list is simple. Many well-known companies such as Sharper Image and Hertz sell or rent their customer lists for this purpose.

A second type of list enhancement involves incorporating information from external databases into a house list. Here the number of names and addresses remains the same, but an organization ends up with a more complete description of who its customers are. Typically, this kind of enhancement includes any of four categories of information:

1. *Demographic data:* the basic descriptors of individuals and households available from the U.S. Census Bureau.

Pete Saloutos/Shutterstock.com.

2. *Geodemographic data:* information that reveals the characteristics of the neighborhood in which a person resides.

3. *Psychographic data:* data that allow for a more qualitative assessment of a customer's general lifestyle, interests, and opinions.

4. *Behavioral data:* information about other products and services a customer has purchased. Knowledge about prior purchases can suggest a customer's preferences.

List enhancements that entail merging existing records with new information rely on software that allows the database manager to match records based on some piece of information the two lists share. For example, matches might be achieved by sorting on ZIP codes and street addresses. Many suppliers gather and maintain databases that can be used for list enhancement. One of the biggest is InfoUSA of Papillion, Nebraska (see http://www.infousa.com). With more than 210 million people in its database, and literally dozens of pieces of information about each person, InfoUSA offers exceptional capabilities for list enhancement. Because of the massive size of the InfoUSA database, it has a high match rate (60 to 80 percent) when it is merged with clients' internal lists. A more common match rate between internal and external lists is around 50 percent.

Marketing Databases

Mailing lists come in all shapes and sizes, and when used to enhance internal lists, they can become rich sources of information about customers. But for a mailing list to qualify as a marketing database, it must include one important additional type of information. Although a **marketing database** can be viewed as a natural extension of an internal mailing list, it also includes information collected directly from individual customers (see Exhibit 10.2). Developing a marketing database involves pursuing dialogues with customers and learning about their individual preferences and behavioral patterns. This can be potent information for hatching marketing programs that will hit the mark with consumers.

Aided by the dramatic escalation in processing power that comes from every new generation of computer chip, marketers see the chance to gather and manage more information about every individual who buys, or could buy, from them. Their goal might be portrayed as an attempt to cultivate a kind of cybernetic intimacy with the customer. A marketing database represents an organization's collective memory, which allows the organization to make the kind of personalized offer that once was characteristic of the corner grocer in small-town America. For example, working in conjunction with the Ohio State University Alumni Association, Lands' End created a special autumn promotion to offer OSU football fans all of their favorite gear just in time for the upcoming session. Print ads in the September issue of the OSU alumni magazine set the stage for a special catalog of merchandise mailed to Buckeye faithful. Of course, Lands' End had similar arrangements with other major universities to tap into fall football frenzy. Database marketing at its best delivers consumers an offer that is both relevant and timely. That's cybernetic intimacy.

Database marketing also can yield important efficiencies that contribute to the marketer's bottom line. Cabela's, like many other multichannel retailers, finds it useful to create many targeted versions of its base or master catalogs, with seasonal points of emphasis. Why? The gender- or age-specific versions run about 100 pages, versus more than 1,000 pages for some of its master catalogs. A customer or household receives the targeted versions based on its profile in Cabela's database and the time of year. These streamlined catalogs are a great way to make timely offerings to targeted households in a cost-effective manner. In a nutshell, that's what database marketing is all about.

To summarize the information used by direct marketers, the crucial distinction between a mailing list and a marketing database is that the latter includes direct input from customers. Building a marketing database entails pursuing an ongoing dialogue with customers and continually updating records with new information. Thus, while mailing lists can be rich sources of information for program development, a marketing database has a dynamic quality that sets it apart.

Exhibit 10.2
What Makes a Marketing Database

List Enhancements (demographic, geodemographic, psychographic, and/or behavioral data)

Mailing List (names and addresses)

Consumer Provided Information (e.g., preferences, behavior patterns)

Marketing Database

© Cengage Learning 2011.

Marketing Database Applications

Many different types of customer communication programs are driven by marketing databases. One of the greatest benefits of a database is that it allows an organization to quantify how much business the organization is actually doing with its current best customers. A useful way to isolate the best customers is with a recency, frequency, and monetary (RFM) analysis. An **RFM analysis** asks how recently and how often a specific customer is buying from a company, and how much money he or she is spending per order and over time. With this transaction data, it is a simple matter to calculate the value of every customer to the organization and identify customers that have given the organization the most business in the past. Past behavior is an excellent predictor of future behavior, so yesterday's best customers are likely to be an organization's primary source of future business.

A marketing database can be a powerful tool for organizations that seek to create a genuine relationship with their best customers. The makers of Ben & Jerry's ice cream have used their database in two ways: to find out how customers react to potential new flavors and product ideas, and to involve their customers in social causes.[20] In one program, their goal was to find 100,000 people in their marketing database who would volunteer to work with Ben & Jerry's to support the Children's Defense Fund. Jerry Greenfield, cofounder of Ben & Jerry's, justified the program as follows: "We are not some nameless conglomerate that only looks at how much money we make every year. I think the opportunity to use our business and particularly the power of our business as a force for progressive social change is exciting."[21] Of course, when customers feel genuine involvement with a brand like Ben & Jerry's, they also turn out to be very loyal customers.

Reinforcing and recognizing your best customers is an essential application of the marketing database. This application may be nothing more than a simple follow-up letter that thanks customers for their business or reminds them of the positive features of the brand to reassure them that they made the right choice. Reinforcement also can include discounts and coupons mailed or emailed to regular customers.

Loyal repeat customers tend to be the most profitable, so businesses try to win more sales from their frequent customers. Date of birth is a common piece of information in a marketing database, so customers' birthdays are a great time to contact them. Sunglass Hut International uses a birthday card mailing to stay in a dialogue with its best customers. Of course, everyone likes a birthday present, so Sunglass Hut encloses a Customer Appreciation Check for $20, good at any Sunglass Hut store. According to the company's executives, this promotion, targeted to customers identified from its marketing database, is one of its best investments in advertising.

To recognize and reinforce the behaviors of preferred customers, marketers in many fields are offering frequency-marketing programs that provide concrete rewards to frequent customers. **Frequency-marketing programs** have three basic elements:

1. A *database*, which is the collective memory for the program

2. A *benefit package*, which is designed to attract and retain customers

3. A *communication strategy*, which emphasizes a regular dialogue with the organization's best customers

The casino industry is renowned for its application of frequency-marketing principles, and Harrah's Entertainment has set the standard for program innovation.[22] Harrah's "Total Rewards" program started out as a way for its 27 million members to accumulate points that could be cashed in for free meals and other casino amenities. This simple approach was quickly copied by the competition. Harrah's subsequently upgraded its program on a number of dimensions. Now Harrah's has 10 million active members in its Total Rewards program, and the company knows a lot about each one. The database knows who is a golfer, who likes down pillows, who prefers a room near the elevator, and what games customers play. With that kind of information, Harrah's tailors the direct mail and email it sends to Total Rewards members, who generate 80 percent of Harrah's gaming revenues annually.

Another common application for the marketing database is **cross-selling**. Because most organizations today have many different products or services they hope to sell, one of the best ways to build business is to identify customers who already purchase some of a firm's products and to create marketing programs aimed at these customers but featuring other products. If they have a checking account with us, can we interest them in a credit card? If customers dine in our restaurants on Fridays and Saturdays, with the proper incentives perhaps we can get them to dine with us midweek, when we really need the extra business. A marketing database can provide a myriad of opportunities for cross-selling.

A final application for the marketing database is a natural extension of cross-selling. Once an organization gets to know who its current customers are and what they like about various products, it is in a much stronger position to go out and seek new customers. Knowledge about current customers is especially valuable when an organization is considering purchasing external mailing lists to append to its marketing database. If a firm knows the demographic characteristics of current customers—knows what they like about products, knows where they live, and has insights about their lifestyles and general interests—then the selection of external lists will be much more efficient. The basic premise here simply is to try to find prospects who share many of the same characteristics and interests with current customers. And what's the best vehicle for coming to know the current, best customers? Marketing-database development.

Rosli Othman/Shutterstock.com

Protecting Privacy

One very large dark cloud looms on the horizon for database marketers: consumers' concerns about invasion of privacy. It is easy for marketers to gather extensive information about consumers, and this is making the general public nervous. Many consumers are uneasy about the way their personal information is gathered and exchanged by businesses and the government without their knowledge, participation, or consent. Of course, the Internet only amplifies

zerøknowledge
Internet privacy solutions

I AM NOT A PIECE OF YOUR INVENTORY.

I am not a pair of eyeballs to be captured or a consumer profile to be sold.

I am an individual and you will respect my privacy.

I will not be bartered, traded or sold.

On the Net I am in control.

WWW.ZEROKNOWLEDGE.COM

This ad paints a dark picture of a future in which database marketers go unchecked. The ease of information sharing on the Internet has heightened concern about who is in control of personal information.

these concerns because the Web makes it easier for all kinds of people and organizations to get access to personal information. Nowadays, some databases even merge Internet usage data with financial data such as credit rating, amount in savings, and home value.[23]

In response to public opinion, state and federal lawmakers have proposed and sometimes passed legislation to limit businesses' access to personal information. Additionally, consumers' desire for privacy clearly was the motivation for the launch of the Federal Trade Commission's Do Not Call Registry. The registry has proved to be a very popular idea with consumers, but it has many opponents in business, including the Direct Marketing Association.[24] The DMA has estimated that the list could cost telemarketers on the order of $50 billion in lost sales. What the "do not call" list ultimately will mean for both sides remains to be seen. If you are one of those people who would like to do more to protect the privacy of your personal information, you can start with a visit to http://www.ftc.gov/privacy/protect.shtm.

Many in business are keenly aware of consumers' concerns about the privacy of their personal information. Companies can address customers' concerns about privacy if they remember two fundamental premises of database marketing. First, a primary goal for developing a marketing database is to get to know customers in such a way that an organization can offer them products and services that better meet their needs. The whole point of a marketing database is to keep junk mail to a minimum by targeting only exciting and relevant programs to customers. If customers are offered something of value, they will welcome being in the database.

The second premise is that developing a marketing database is about creating meaningful, long-term relationships with customers. If you want people's trust and loyalty, would you collect personal information from them and then sell it to a third party behind their backs? We hope not! When collecting information from customers, an organization must help them understand why it wants the information and how it will use what it learns. If the organization

is planning to sell this information to a third party, it must get customers' permission. If the organization pledges that the information will remain confidential, it must honor that pledge. Integrity is fundamental to all meaningful relationships, including those involving direct marketers and their customers. Recall that it was his integrity as much as anything else that enabled L. L. Bean to launch his successful career as a direct marketer. It will work for you, too.

LO 4 Media Used in Direct Marketing

Although mailing lists and marketing databases are the focal point for originating most direct-marketing programs, marketers implementing these programs must communicate information and arguments to consumers. As we saw in the definition of direct marketing, the message can be communicated through multiple media, typically with the overriding goal of achieving an immediate, measurable response. The desired response may be an order for services or merchandise, a request for more information, or the acceptance of a free trial offer. Because advertising conducted in direct-marketing campaigns emphasizes an immediate response, it commonly is referred to as **direct-response advertising**.

The direct marketer's prime media are **direct mail** and **telemarketing**. However, all conventional media, including magazines, radio, and television, can be used to deliver direct-response advertising, and many companies are deploying email as an economical means of interacting with customers. In addition, a dramatic transformation of the television commercial—the infomercial— has become especially popular.

Direct Mail

Direct mail has some notable faults as an advertising medium, not the least of which is cost. Reaching a person with a direct-mail piece can cost 15 to 20 times more than reaching that person with a television commercial or newspaper advertisement.[25] Additionally, in a society where people are constantly on the move, mailing lists commonly are plagued by bad addresses. Each bad address represents

advertising dollars wasted. And direct-mail delivery dates, especially for bulk, third-class mailings, can be unpredictable. When precise timing of an advertising message is critical to its success, direct mail can be the wrong choice.

Despite these drawbacks, direct mail is the right choice in some situations. Direct mail's advantages stem from the selectivity of the medium. When an advertiser begins with a database of prospects, direct mail can be the perfect vehicle for reaching those prospects with little waste. Also, direct mail is a flexible medium that allows message adaptations literally on a household-by-household basis. For example, through surveys conducted with its 15 million U.S. subscribers, *Reader's Digest* amassed a huge marketing database detailing the health problems of specific subscribers.[26] In the database were 771,000 people with arthritis, 679,000 people with high blood pressure, 206,000 people with osteoporosis, 460,000 smokers, and so on. Using this information,

Reader's Digest sent its subscribers disease-specific booklets containing advice on coping with their afflictions. The booklets also contained advertisements from drug companies that had tailored messages they wanted to communicate to those with a particular problem. This kind of precise targeting of tailored messages is the hallmark of direct marketing.

Direct mail as a medium also lends itself to testing and experimentation. With direct mail, it is common to test two or more different appeal letters using a modest budget and a small sample of households.

direct-response advertising advertising that asks the receiver of the message to act immediately

direct mail direct-marketing medium that uses the postal service to deliver marketing materials

telemarketing direct-marketing medium that involves using the telephone to deliver a spoken appeal

This postcard for Fleece & Flannel announces the grand opening of a store in Livingston, Montana. In that part of the country, it's perfectly natural to select a fly-fishing guide and guru to serve as your spokeswoman.

The goal is to establish which version yields the largest response. When a winner is decided, that form of the letter is backed by big-budget dollars in launching the organization's primary campaign.

Additionally, direct mail allows marketers to use a substantial array of formats. Marketers can mail large, expensive brochures, CDs, or DVDs. They can use pop-ups, foldouts, scratch-and-sniff strips, or a simple, attractive postcard. If a product can be described in a limited space with minimal graphics, there really is no need to get fancy with the direct-mail piece. The double postcard (DPC) format has an established track record of outperforming more expensive and elaborate direct-mail packages.[27] Moreover, if an organization follows U.S. Postal Service guidelines carefully in mailing DPCs, the pieces can go out as first-class mail for reasonable rates. Because the Postal Service supplies address corrections on all first-class mail, using DPCs usually turns out to be a winner on either CPI or CPO measures, and DPCs can be an effective tool for cleaning up the bad addresses in a mailing list.

Telemarketing

As with direct mail, telemarketing contacts can be targeted selectively, the impact of programs is easy to track, and experimentation with different scripts and delivery formats is simple and practical. Because telemarketing involves live, person-to-person dialogue, no medium produces better response rates.

BECAUSE TELEMARKETING IS **POWERFUL AND HIGHLY INTRUSIVE,** IT MUST BE USED WITH DISCRETION.

Telemarketing also shares many of direct mail's limitations. It is very expensive on a cost-per-contact basis, and just as names and addresses go bad as people move, so do phone numbers. Furthermore, telemarketing lacks direct mail's flexibility in terms of delivery options. When you reach people in their home or workplace, you have a limited amount of time to convey information and request some form of response.

The biggest concern with telemarketing is that it probably is the direct marketer's most invasive tool. Because telemarketing is powerful and highly intrusive, it must be used with discretion. High-pressure telephone calls at inconvenient times can alienate customers. Telemarketing will give the best results over the long run if it is used to maintain constructive dialogues with existing customers and qualified prospects.

Email

Perhaps the most controversial tool deployed of late by direct marketers has been unsolicited or "bulk" email. Commonly referred to as spam, this junk email can get you in big trouble with consumers. In a worst-case scenario, careless use of the email tool

Ivan Ponomarev/Shutterstock.com.

eTHICS MeeT A FORMeR SPAM QUeeN

Everybody hates spam—even Laura Betterly, and she once referred to herself as the "spam queen" (she meant it ironically, she explained later). Betterly used to make her living by delivering bulk email; her company, Data Resources Consulting (DRC), reportedly sent out as many as 60 million email messages a month. DRC also sold email addresses to other bulk emailers. At least for a time, the business was profitable. Betterly said DRC could make money when as few as 100 people responded to a mailing of 10 million. (For direct mail, marketers typically look for a response of 2 percent or better.) Betterly has acknowledged that commercial email messages aren't always welcome but insists that DRC aimed to stay on the right side of the law.

Sources: Mylene Mangalindan, "Web Vigilantes Give Spammers a Big Dose of Their Medicine," *Wall Street Journal*, May 19, 2003, A1, A13; Mylene Mangalindan, "For Bulk E-Mailer, Pestering Millions Offers a Path to Profit," *Wall Street Journal*, November 13, 2002, A1, A17; Laura Betterly, "It's 2006—E-mail Is Dead," *Laura Betterly Official Blog: Rants of a Marketing Executive*, September 22, 2005, http://laurabetterly. blogspot.com.

can earn one's company the label of a "spammer," and because of the community-oriented character of the Internet, this then can be a continuing source of negative buzz.

But is this drawback discouraging companies from deploying this tool? Hardly. According to recent studies, 97 percent of all emails received by business email servers are essentially spam.[28] Given spam's bad reputation and the fact that better filtering tools are blocking much of it from users anyway, it does make you wonder, why does anyone do it? The ethics box tackles this weighty question.

One school of thought says some consumers are not averse to receiving targeted email advertisements, and as the Internet continues to evolve as an increasingly commercial medium, companies that observe proper etiquette on the Net will be rewarded through customer loyalty.[29] The key is to get the consumer's permission to send information about specific products or services; as discussed in Chapter 9, they must opt in. Consequently, many e-marketing service providers claim to have constructed email lists of consumers who have opted in for all manner of products and services. Others now promise large lists of consumers who have agreed to receive commercial emails; for two examples, visit http://www.infousa.com and http://www.yesmail.com. The future of direct marketing may be in reaching people who already have said yes.

Our advice is to stay away from the low-cost temptations of bulk email. The quickest way to get flamed and damage your brand name is to start sending out bulk emails to people who do not want to hear from you. Instead, through database development, ask your customers for permission to contact them via email. Honor their requests. Don't abuse the privilege by selling their email addresses to other companies, and when you do contact them, have something important to say. Seth Godin, whose 1999 book *Permission Marketing* really launched the opt-in mindset, puts it this way: "The best way to make your [customer] list worthless is to sell it. The future is, this list is mine and it's a secret."[30] Perhaps you can imagine L. L. Bean feeling exactly the same way about his customer list 95 years ago.

Other Media

As direct marketers try to convey their appeals for a customer response, they have experimented with many other methods. In magazines, a popular device

This magazine ad for Oreck floor vacuums, which ran in *Bon Appetit,* delivers the basics of direct marketing: an introduction to the product plus three ways to respond: a toll-free number, website address, and coupon with a mailing address. Throwing in a free iron gives consumers an extra incentive to act.

for executing a direct marketer's agenda is the bind-in insert card. If you thumb through a copy of any magazine, you will see how effective these light-cardboard inserts are at stopping the reader and calling attention to themselves. Insert cards not only promote their product, but they also provide tempting offers like $25 off your next order at Coldwater Creek or a free sample of Skoal smokeless tobacco.

When AT&T introduced the first 800 number in 1967, it simply could not have known how important this service would become to direct marketing. Newspaper ads from *The Wall Street Journal* provide toll-free numbers for requesting everything from really cheap online trading services (800-619-SAVE) to leasing a Learjet 40 (800-FLEXJET). If you watch late-night TV, you may know the 800 number to call to order that Snuggie for you and your dog (sales to date: people, 18 million; dogs, 2 million).[31] Finally, magazine ads are commonly used to provide an 800 number to initiate contact with customers. As these diverse examples indicate, toll-free numbers make it possible to use nearly any medium for direct-response purposes.

Infomercials

The infomercial is a novel form of direct-response advertising that merits special mention. An **infomercial** fundamentally is just a long television advertisement made possible by the lower cost of ad space on many cable and satellite channels. Infomercials range in length from 2 to 60 minutes, but the common length is 30 minutes. Although producing an infomercial is more like producing a television program than it is like producing a 30-second commercial, infomercials are all about selling.

There appear to be several keys to successful use of this unique vehicle (see Exhibit 10.3).[32] A critical element is testimonials from satisfied users. Celebrity testimonials can help catch a viewer as he or she is channel surfing past the program, but celebrities aren't necessary—and, of course, they add to the production costs. Whether testimonials are from celebrities or from folks just like us, without them, your chances of producing a profitable infomercial diminish hugely.

> **infomercial** long advertisement that looks like a talk show or product demonstration

Exhibit 10.3
Elements of a Successful Infomercial

© Cengage Learning 2011. Photo: VVO/Shutterstock.com.

Bratwustle/Shutterstock.com

Another requirement for successful infomercials arises from the fact that viewers are not likely to stay tuned for the full 30 minutes. An infomercial is a 30-minute direct-response sales pitch, not a classic episode of *South Park* or *The Simpsons*. Therefore, the call to action should not come just at the end of the infomercial; most of the audience could be long gone by minute 28 into the show. For a 30-minute infomercial, a good rule of thumb is to divide the program into three 10-minute increments, with a close at the end of each segment. Each closing should feature

the 800 number or Web address that allows the viewer to order the product or request more information.

Finally, an organization should not offer information to the customer unless it can deliver speedy follow-up. The goal in pursuing leads generated by an infomercial should be a same-day response.

Many different types of products and services have been marketed using infomercials via Internet extensions such as http://www.iqvc.com. Self-help videos, home exercise equipment, kitchen appliances, and Annette Funicello Collectible Bears all have had success with the infomercial. Although it is easy to associate the infomercial with gadgets such as the Ronco Showtime Rotisserie & BBQ (yours for just four easy payments of $39.95!), many familiar brands have experimented with this medium. Brand marketers such as Quaker State, Disney, and even Mercedes-Benz have used infomercials to help inform consumers about their offerings.[33]

How can we explain the growing appeal of the infomercial for all manner of marketers? Data generated by TiVo's StopWatch service are revealing.[34] They show that bare-bones, direct-response ads for products like Perfect Pushup exercise equipment are among the least likely to be zapped. That kind of result will get a lot of scrutiny from all corners of the brand promotion business.

STUDY TOOLS
CHAPTER 10

Located at back of the textbook
- **Rip out Chapter in Review Card.**

Located at www.cengagebrain.com
- **Review Key Terms Flashcards (Print or Online).**
- **Complete the Practice Quiz to prepare for tests.**
- **Play "Beat the Clock" and "Quizbowl" to master concepts.**
- **Complete "Crossword Puzzle" to review key terms.**
- **Watch videos on Pizza Hut and Pedigree UK for real company examples.**
- **For additional examples, go online to learn about Lester Wunderman and the invention of "direct marketing."**

THE IN-CROWD

Share your 4LTR Press story on Facebook at
www.facebook.com/4ltrpress for a chance to win.

To learn more about the In-Crowd opportunity 'like' us on Facebook.

Promotion and Point of Purchase

"Free" is a price few can resist. It also is a great sales promotion for McDonald's.

McDonald's credits free coffee giveaways with boosting breakfast revenues.

Learning Outcomes

After studying this chapter, you should be able to:

LO 1 Explain the importance and growth of sales promotion.

LO 2 Describe the main sales promotion techniques used in the consumer market.

LO 3 Describe the main sales promotion techniques used in the trade channel and business markets.

LO 4 Identify the risks to the brand of using sales promotion.

LO 5 Understand the role and techniques of point-of-purchase advertising.

LO 6 Describe the role of support media in a comprehensive integrated marketing communication plan.

"If your advertising goes unnoticed, everything else is academic."

—William Bernbach

Free Drinks!

AFTER YOU FINISH THIS CHAPTER GO TO PAGE 243 FOR STUDY TOOLS

As competition between fast-food chains continually intensifies, each brand is struggling to become consumers' favorite. Menus are tweaked, new stores are opened at convenient spots, ad campaigns are rolled out, and prices are slashed. So how can you persuade a jaded consumer to try *your* place? How about giving away the product?

Big, powerful fast-food operations like Wendy's, KFC, and McDonald's have found that price discounts sometimes can cheapen brand image and condition consumers to look for deals. In contrast, they can get positive attention and boost traffic by picking an item to give away for free. Wendy's launched a 25-city, six-month "taste tour" offering free hamburgers. KFC gave out free Colonel's Crispy Strips supported by a full-page ad in *USA Today*. During the first week of the sampling, the chain saw its highest sales for the strips. McDonald's launched Free Coffee Mondays as a way to lure consumers from Starbucks and demonstrate that its new premium coffee is just as good. McDonald's has credited coffee giveaways with boosting breakfast revenues.[1]

The Sonic Drive-In chain has drawn in new and repeat customers with a once-a-year Free Float Night. From 8 P.M. until midnight on Free Float Night, customers can order a root beer float at no charge. The first year Sonic tried the event, the chain of 3,500 drive-ins exceeded its goal of 3 million free floats, and in the second year, it gave away more than 5 million.[2] What's in it for Sonic? First, the company believes consumers will be charmed by its old-fashioned drive-in ambience. Second, customers who show up for a free float tend to order—and pay for—burgers and fries as well. The promotion also dovetails with the chain's effort to position itself

What do you think?

I'll try anything if it's free.

1 2 3 4 5 6 7
STRONGLY DISAGREE   STRONGLY AGREE

as a place to purchase a wide variety of delicious drinks, using the slogan "Your Ultimate Drink Stop." And giving something away for a short time, rather than issuing coupons or announcing a sale, stimulates sales in a way that doesn't cause consumers to expect a price break the rest of the year.

Of course, freebies have their downside. One problem, of course, is that not everyone who shows up for something free also places a paid order or returns for another visit at full price. At the same time, the extra work of serving people for free requires plenty of employees, who may struggle to provide the restaurant's usual level of service. A Sonic vice president admitted that sales per customer and customer satisfaction levels suffer while the company is running one of these promotions.[3] Sonic tries to counter that challenge on Free Float Nights by getting employees in on the excitement. Employees have worn silly hats to keep up an atmosphere of fun as they hand out the free drinks.

Most likely, fast-food restaurants will keep the free trials coming. Although this kind of sampling always has been useful in attracting consumer attention and making consumers feel good about getting "something for free," sampling is valuable for building sales at existing units in the absence of opportunities to build new stores. Attractive real estate is getting scarcer, so new-unit growth has slowed considerably. Rather than building new stores, companies are trying to build traffic—and revenues—at existing stores by enticing old and new customers with free food and drink.

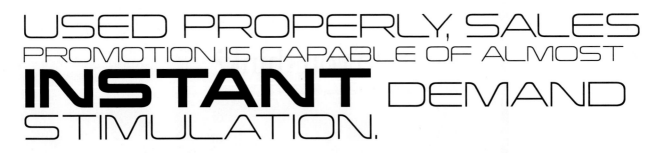

Iznogood/Shutterstock.com.

LO 1 Role of Sales Promotion

Sales promotion, such as the free trials offered by Sonic and other fast-food restaurants, often is a key component within an integrated marketing communication (IMC) campaign. Sales promotions can attract attention and give new energy to the overall marketing effort. Used properly, sales promotion is capable of almost instant demand stimulation, like the kind that contests and sweepstakes can create.

Formally defined, **sales promotion** is the use of incentive techniques that create a perception of greater brand value among consumers, the trade, and business buyers. The "message" in a sales promotion features price reduction, free samples, a prize, or some other incentive for consumers to try a brand or for a retailer to feature the brand in a store. The intent is to generate a short-term increase in sales by motivating trial use, encouraging larger purchases, or stimulating repeat purchases.

Based on the audience for the message, sales promotion falls into three categories:

1. **Consumer-market sales promotion** includes methods of inducing household consumers to purchase a firm's brand rather than a competitor's brand. Examples are coupons and samples. These incentives reduce price, offer a reward, or encourage a trip to the retailer.

2. **Trade-market sales promotion** is aimed at motivating distributors, wholesalers, and retailers to stock and feature a firm's brand in their store merchandising programs. Examples include allowances (a type of discount) and specially designed displays to feature the brand.

USED PROPERLY, SALES PROMOTION IS CAPABLE OF ALMOST **INSTANT** DEMAND STIMULATION.

3. **Business-market sales promotion** is designed to cultivate buyers in large corporations who are making purchase decisions about a wide range of products including computers, office supplies, and consulting services. Techniques used for business buyers are similar to the trade-market techniques.

Later in the chapter, we will identify and describe specific sales promotion techniques.

Importance of Sales Promotion

Sales promotion has proven to be a popular complement to mass-media advertising because it accomplishes things advertising cannot. Sales promotion is designed to affect demand differently than advertising does. Whereas most advertising is designed to build brand awareness, image, and preference over the long run, sales promotion primarily is aimed at eliciting an immediate purchase from a customer group. Samples, rebates, and similar techniques offer household consumers, trade buyers, or business buyers an immediate incentive to choose one brand over another. Even longer-term efforts, such as airline frequent-flyer programs, not only provide an affiliation value for a brand but also offer practical benefits for repeat purchases, thus stimulating sales.

The goals for sales promotion and those of advertising are compared in Exhibit 11.1. While mass-media advertising is designed to build a brand image over time, sales promotion is conspicuous and designed to make things happen in a hurry. When a firm determines that a more immediate response is called for—whether the target customer is a household, business buyer, distributor, or retailer—sales promotions try to provide that incentive.

The importance of sales promotion in the United States should not be underestimated. Sales promotion may not seem as stylish and sophisticated as mass-media advertising, but expenditures on this tool are impressive. In recent years, sales promotion expenditures have grown at an annual rate of about 4 to 8 percent, compared with about a 3 to 5 percent rate for advertising. Spending on sales promotion efforts in the United States alone now exceeds $300 billion annually. The rapid growth is occurring as big consumer products firms shift dollars out of media advertising and into promotions.[4]

It is important to realize that full-service advertising agencies specializing in advertising planning, creative preparation, and media placement typically do not prepare sales promotion materials for clients. These activities normally are assigned to sales promotion agencies that specialize in coupons, premiums, displays, or other forms of sales promotion and point-of-purchase techniques that require specific skills and creative preparation.

The development and management of an effective sales promotion program requires a major commitment by a firm. During any given year, it is typical that as much as 30 percent of brand management time is spent on designing, implementing, and overseeing sales promotions.

business-market sales promotion
promotion designed to cultivate buyers making purchase decisions in corporations

Exhibit 11.1
Complementary Roles

Sales Promotion
- Stimulates short-term demand
- Encourages brand switching
- Induces trial use
- Promotes price orientation
- Obtains immediate, often measurable results

Advertising
- Cultivates long-term demand
- Encourages brand loyalty
- Encourages repeat purchases
- Promotes images/feature orientation
- Obtains long-term effects, often difficult to measure

© Cengage Learning 2011.

Growing Use of Sales Promotion

Many marketers have shifted the emphasis of their promotional spending during the past decade. Much of the shift has been away from mass-media advertising. Some has made its way to the Internet, as we saw in Chapter 9, and more spending has found its way to consumer, trade, and business sales promotions. Currently, the budget allocation on average stands at about 17.5 percent for advertising, 54 percent for trade and business promotions, and 28.5 percent for consumer promotions.[5]

There are several reasons why many marketers have been shifting funds from mass-media advertising to sales promotions:

- *Demand for greater accountability:* In an era of cost cutting and shareholder scrutiny, companies are demanding greater accountability across all functions, including marketing. When activities are evaluated for their contribution to sales and profits, it often is difficult to draw specific conclusions regarding the effects of advertising. But the more immediate effects of sales promotions typically are easier to document. Various studies show that only 18 percent of TV advertising campaigns produced a short-term positive return on investment on promotional dollars.[6] Conversely, point-of-purchase in-store displays have been shown to positively affect sales by as much as 35 percent in some product categories.[7]

- *Short-term orientation:* Several factors have created a short-term orientation among managers. These include a bottom-line mentality and pressures from stockholders to increase quarter-by-quarter revenue and profit per share. Many organizations are developing marketing plans—with rewards and punishments for manager performance—based on short-term revenue generation. As a result, companies are seeking tactics that can have short-term effects. For example, McDonald's credits its "Play to Win" game with boosting store sales up to 15 percent during the game's promotion period.[8]

- *Consumer response to promotions:* Shoppers are demanding greater value across all purchase situations, and that trend is battering overpriced brands.[9] For shoppers who search for extra value in every purchase, coupons and other sales promotions increase the value of a brand. Historically, consumers report that coupons, price, and good value for their money influence 75 to 85 percent of their brand choices.[10]

(However, this does not necessarily mean consumers are choosing the *lowest*-priced item. The analysis suggests that sales promotion techniques act as an incentive to purchase the brand using a promotion, even if another brand has a lower basic price.)

- *Proliferation of brands:* Each year, thousands of new brands are introduced into the consumer market, creating a mind-dulling maze for consumers. Consider this case of brand proliferation: in one 12-month period, Coca-Cola's new head of marketing launched *1,000* new drinks or new variations of existing brands worldwide (has anybody tried Coca-Cola Blak?).[11] At any point in time, consumers are typically able to choose from about 60 spaghetti sauces, 100 snack chips, 50 laundry detergents, 90 cold remedies, and 60 disposable-diaper varieties. Gaining attention in this blizzard of brands is no easy task. Marketers turn to sales promotions to gain some attention.

- *Increased power of retailers:* Big retailers like Home Depot and Walmart now dominate retailing in the United States. These powerful retailers have responded quickly and accurately to the new environment for retailing, where consumers are demanding more and better products and services at lower prices. Because of these consumer demands, retailers are, in turn, demanding more deals from manufacturers. Many of the deals are delivered in terms of trade-oriented sales promotions,

Photo by Jeff Greenberg/Thomson Learning (now Cengage Learning).

When consumers are shopping for pasta sauce in today's supermarkets, they face a dizzying array of choices. Getting them to pay attention to any one brand is quite a challenge for marketers. Sales promotions like coupons in advertising or signs in the store are aimed at helping consumers choose the marketer's brand.

Martin Muránsky/Shutterstock.com

eTHICS NEW TOOLS FOR BIG BROTHER?

Marketers want to know if their brand messages on supermarket shelves and product packages are getting through, and retailers are eager to provide data that will help. Some stores are going so far as to install surveillance technology that records, say, how long it takes you to select that box of Cheerios. Data on product inspection and store movement can be combined with sales figures and data from store loyalty cards to analyze shoppers' behavior. Privacy experts worry that the data will also let marketers pinpoint—without shoppers' knowledge—what individuals are doing and buying.

Sources: Emily Bryson York, "They Learned It by Watching You," *Advertising Age*, March 15, 2010, pp. 1, 19; Stephanie Rosenbloom, "Buyer Beware: You May Be on Tape," *New York Times*, March 23, 2010, pp. A1, A10.

such as point-of-purchase displays and co-op advertising allowances. In the end, manufacturers use more and more sales promotions to gain and maintain good relations with the powerful retailers—a critical link to the consumer. And retailers use the tools of sales promotion as competitive strategies against each other. Manufacturers are coming up with clever ways to provide value to retailers and thus maintain the balance of power.

• *Media clutter:* A nagging and traditional problem in the advertising process is clutter. Many advertisers target the same customers because their research has led them to

the same conclusion about whom to target. As a result, advertising media are cluttered with ads seeking the attention of the same people. When consumers encounter a barrage of ads, they tune out (remember the discussion in Chapter 5). And clutter is getting worse, not better, across all media—including the Internet, where pop-ups, pop-unders, and banners decorate nearly every website.[12] One way to break through the clutter effectively is to feature a sales promotion. In print ads, the featured deal often is a coupon. In television and radio advertising, sweepstakes, premium, and rebate offers can attract viewers' and listeners' attention.

LO 2 Consumer Sales Promotion

U.S. consumer product firms have made a tremendous commitment to sales promotion in their overall marketing plans. During the 1970s, consumer goods marketers allocated only about 30 percent of their budgets to sales promotion, with about 70 percent allocated to mass-media advertising. Now, at many consumer goods firms, the percentages are just the opposite, with nearly 75 percent of budgets spent on various forms of promotion and point-of-purchase materials. With this level of investment in mind, let's examine the objectives for sales promotion in the consumer market and the range of techniques available.

Objectives

To help ensure the proper application of sales promotion, specific strategic objectives should be set. As illustrated in Exhibit 11.2, several basic objectives can be pursued with sales promotion in the consumer market.

When a firm wants to attract new users, sales promotion can reduce the consumer's risk of trying something new. Offering a rebate or free sample may stimulate trial purchase. Peet's Coffee & Tea has attempted to stimulate trial use by creating a sampler pack available at a special price. This promotion tries to get consumers to try a brand, not a product category, because coffee is a mature product. As described in Chapter 1, promotion for mature products typically emphasizes selective demand stimulation—that is, brand choice among people who already use the product category.

Sales promotion also seeks to stimulate repeat purchases. For example, a program in which consumers accumulate points with repeated purchases can keep them loyal to a particular brand. The most prominent frequency programs are found in the airline and hotel industries.

Besides stimulating more frequent purchases, sales promotion can stimulate larger purchases. Two-for-one sales can motivate consumers to stock

Exhibit 11.2
Objectives for Consumer-Market Sales Promotion

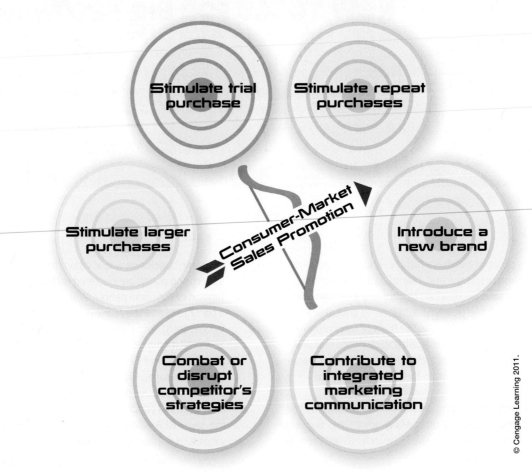

Stimulate trial purchase

Stimulate repeat purchases

Stimulate larger purchases

Introduce a new brand

Combat or disrupt competitor's strategies

Contribute to integrated marketing communication

Consumer-Market Sales Promotion

© Cengage Learning 2011.

Exhibit 11.3
Where the Money Goes

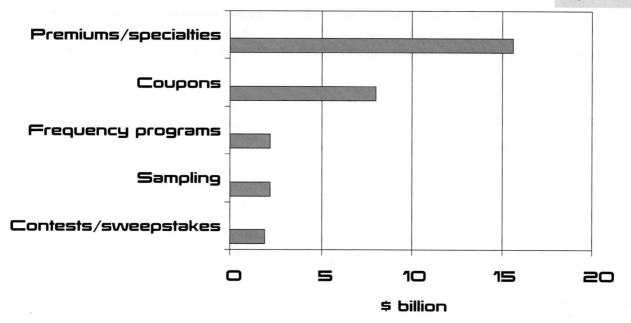

Annual spending for selected promotion types

$ billion

Sources: Richard Alan Nelson and Rick Ebel, "2009 PPAI Sales Volume Study: The Only Direction to Go Is Up," *Promotional Products Business*, July 2010, p. 8; Patricia O'Dell, "Spending Up by a Nose," *Promo*, December 1, 2009, http://promomagazine.com; Patricia O'Dell, "Steady Growth," *Promo*, December 1, 2009, http://promomagazine.com; Patricia O'Dell, "Faithful Following," *Promo*, December 1, 2009, http://promomagazine.com.

up on a brand. Shampoo often is double-packaged to offer a value to consumers while reducing inventory or increasing cash flow.

Because sales promotion can attract attention and motivate trial purchase, it commonly is used for introducing a new brand. In one of the most successful uses of sales promotions to introduce a new brand, Curad introduced its kid-size bandage by distributing 7.5 million sample packs in McDonald's Happy Meal sacks. Initial sales of the bandages exceeded forecasts by 30 percent.

Because sales promotions often motivate consumers to buy in larger quantities or try new brands, they can be used to disrupt competitors' marketing strategies. If a firm knows that one of its competitors is launching a new brand or initiating a new advertising campaign, it can severely compromise competitors' efforts with a well-timed sales promotion. In an effort to address increasing competition from newspaper TV supplements and cable-guide magazines, *TV Guide* magazine ran a sweepstakes in several regional markets. Winners won $200 shopping sprees in supermarkets—precisely where 65 percent of its sales are realized.

In conjunction with advertising, direct marketing, public relations, and other programs being carried out by a firm, sales promotion can add yet another type of communication to the promotional mix. Sales

promotions suggest an additional value—a different message within the firm's IMC effort.

Techniques

A variety of techniques are used to stimulate demand and attract attention in the consumer market. Exhibit 11.3 shows how marketers allocate their spending among some of the major alternatives.

Coupons

A **coupon** entitles a buyer to a designated reduction in price for a product or service. Coupons are the oldest and most widely used form of sales promotion. The first use of a coupon is traced to around 1895, when the C. W. Post Company used a penny-off coupon as a way to get people to try its Grape-Nuts cereal. Annually, about 350 billion coupons are distributed to American consumers, and consumers redeem about 3 billion of them. Redemption rates range from 2 percent for gum purchases to nearly 45 percent for disposable diaper purchases.[13]

Most coupons are distributed in free-standing inserts, those stacks of colorful ads stuffed into newspapers. But marketers—especially small businesses with a local clientele—are generating a lot of buzz by offering coupon deals online, including daily-deal websites like Groupon and LivingSocial. In a typical arrangement, the marketer uses the service to announce an offer (say, a $30 service for $15), and if a preset minimum number of consumers request a coupon, it becomes available for them to print out. The amount the consumer pays is split between the merchant and the couponing site. Some of the deals have generated such a surge of interest and sales that the resulting publicity is immeasurable. The downside, obviously, is that an offer attractive enough to create excitement cuts into profits, and the low-paying customers with coupons may crowd out more profitable ones without ever becoming repeat customers. After such experiences, marketers have become savvier about making offers that don't torpedo their ability to operate at a profit.[14]

As a sales promotion tool, coupons offer several advantages:

- Marketers can give a discount to price-sensitive consumers while selling the product at full price to other consumers.

- Coupon-redeeming customers may use a competitive brand, so the coupon can induce brand switching.

- Marketers can control the timing and distribution of coupons, so retailers are not implementing price discounts in a way that might damage brand image.

- Coupons effectively stimulate repeat purchases. Once a consumer has purchased a brand, an in-package coupon can induce the consumer to buy it again.

- Coupons can get regular users to trade up within a brand array. For example, users of low-priced disposable diapers may be willing to try the premium version of a brand with a coupon.

On the downside, coupon use involves some administrative burdens and risks. Couponing entails careful administration and associated costs. There are costs for producing and distributing the coupons and for retailer and manufacturer handling. The total cost for handling, processing, and distributing coupons typically equals about two-thirds of the coupon's face value. Marketers must track these costs against the amount of product sold with and without coupon redemption.

Risks include uncertainty about timing, reduced profitability, and fraud. While the marketer controls when coupons are distributed, consumers control the timing of redemption. Some consumers redeem coupons immediately; depending on the expiration date, others may hold them for months. If the consumers who redeem coupons already are regular users of the brand, coupons merely reduce a firm's profitability.

Fraud is a chronic and serious problem with couponing. The problem relates directly to misredemption practices. Three types of misredemption cost firms money:

1. Redemption of coupons by consumers who do not purchase the couponed brand

2. Redemption of coupons by salesclerks and store managers without consumer purchases

3. Illegal collection or copying of coupons by individuals who sell them to unethical store merchants, who in turn redeem the coupons without the accompanying consumer purchases.

Jim Barber/Shutterstock.com.

Price-Off Deals

Another straightforward sales promotion technique is the **price-off deal**, which offers consumers cents or even dollars off merchandise at the point of purchase through specially marked packages. The typical price-off deal is a 10 to 25 percent price reduction. The reduction is taken from the manufacturer's profit margin rather than the retailer's.

Manufacturers like the price-off technique because it is controllable. Also, when consumers at the point of purchase judge the offer, they may make a positive price comparison against competitors' products. Consumers like a price-off deal because it is straightforward and automatically increases the value of a known brand. Regular users tend to stock up on an item during a price-off deal.

Retailers are less enthusiastic about this technique. Price-off promotions can create inventory and pricing problems. Also, most price-off deals are snapped up by regular customers, so the retailer often doesn't benefit from new business.

Premiums and Advertising Specialties

Premiums are items offered free, or at a reduced price, with the purchase of another item. Many firms offer a related product, such as a free granola bar packed inside a box of granola cereal. Service firms, such as a car wash or dry cleaner, may use a two-for-one offer to persuade consumers to try the service.

Two options are available for the use of premiums.

1. A **free premium** gives consumers an item at no cost; the item either is included in the package of a purchased item or mailed to the consumer after proof of purchase is verified. The most frequently used free premium is an additional package of the original item or a free related item placed in the package (e.g., free conditioner with shampoo purchase).

2. A **self-liquidating premium** requires a consumer to pay most of the cost of the item received as a premium. For example, Snapple can offer a "Snapple cooler" with the purchase of six bottles of Snapple for $6.99 (which equals the cost of the cooler to Snapple). Self-liquidating premiums are particularly effective with loyal customers. However, they must be used cautiously. Unless the premium is related to a value-building

strategy for a brand, it can focus consumer attention on the premium rather than the benefits of the brand. If consumers buy a brand only to get a great-looking T-shirt at $4.99, then they won't purchase the brand again until another great premium becomes available.

Advertising specialties have three key elements: a *message* placed on a *useful item* that is *given to consumers* with no obligation. Popular advertising specialties are baseball caps, T-shirts, coffee mugs, computer mouse pads, pens, and calendars. Advertising specialties allow a firm to tout its company or brand name with a target customer in an ongoing fashion.

free premium sales promotion that gives consumers an item at no cost by including the item in the package or mailing it after proof of purchase is verified

self-liquidating premium sales promotion that requires a consumer to pay most of the cost of the item received as a premium

advertising specialties sales promotion consisting of a message placed on useful items given to consumers with no obligation

Companies like Cook Advertising Specialties put logos on a wide variety of products. Marketers use these as specialties—giving them away to potential customers as a way to spread awareness of a brand and good feelings about it.

Photo Courtesy, Susan Van Etten.

contest sales promotion in which consumers compete for prizes based on skill or ability

sweepstakes sales promotion in which winners are awarded prizes based on chance

sampling sales promotion technique that offers consumers a trial opportunity

Contests and Sweepstakes

No other sales promotion technique can match contests and sweepstakes in drawing attention to a brand. Technically, there are important differences between contests and sweepstakes:

- In a **contest**, consumers compete for prizes based on skill or ability. Winners are determined by a panel of judges or based on which contestant comes closest to a predetermined criterion for winning, such as picking the total points scored in the Super Bowl. Contests tend to be somewhat expensive to administer because each entry must be judged.

- A **sweepstakes** is a promotion in which winners are determined purely by chance. Consumers need only to enter their names in the sweepstakes as a criterion for winning. Often consumers enter by filling out official entry forms, but instant-winner scratch-off cards are another method that tends to attract customers. Many retailers use scratch-off-card sweepstakes as a way of building and maintaining store traffic. Sweepstakes also can be designed so that repeated trips to the retail outlet are necessary to gather a complete set of winning cards.

Contests and sweepstakes create excitement and generate interest for a brand. For them to be effective, marketers must design them in such a way that consumers perceive value in the prizes and find playing the games intrinsically interesting. British Airways ran a contest with the theme "The World's Greatest Offer," in which it gave away thousands of free airline tickets to London and other European destinations. Besides increasing awareness, contests like these create a database of interested customers and potential customers. The company can send these people information on future programs and other premium offers.

Contests and sweepstakes also pose several challenges:

- They are subject to government regulations and restrictions. The design and administration of a contest or sweepstakes must comply with federal and state laws, and each state may have slightly different regulations. The legal problems are complex enough that most firms hire agencies specializing in contests and sweepstakes to administer the programs.

- Consumers may focus more on the game itself than on the brand being promoted. This technique thus fails to build long-term consumer affinity for a brand.

- In the context of a game, it is hard to get any meaningful message across. The consumer's interest is focused on the game, not on any feature of the brand.

- Administration of a contest or sweepstakes is complex enough that the risk of errors is fairly high and can create negative publicity.[15]

- For a firm trying to develop a quality or prestige image for a brand, contests and sweepstakes may contradict this goal.

Sampling and Trial Offers

Getting consumers to simply try a brand can have a powerful effect on future decision making. **Sampling** is a sales promotion technique designed to provide a consumer with an opportunity to use a brand on a trial basis with little or no risk. Most consumer product companies use sampling in some manner. Surveys have shown that consumers are very favorable toward

GWImages/Shutterstock.com.

OFFERING SHOPPERS FREE SAMPLES GIVES THEM A WAY TO EXPERIENCE THE PRODUCT'S BENEFITS FIRSTHAND, WITH NO COST IF THEY ARE DISSATISFIED. OFTEN MARKETERS HAND OUT COUPONS ALONG WITH THE SAMPLES IN ORDER TO MAKE A PURCHASE EVEN MORE ATTRACTIVE.

sampling, with 43 percent indicating they would consider switching brands if they liked a free sample that was being offered.[16]

Sampling can involve any of six techniques:

1. **In-store sampling** takes place at the point of purchase, where consumers may be swayed by a direct encounter with the brand. It is popular for food products and cosmetics. In-store demonstrators often hand out coupons along with samples.

2. **Door-to-door sampling** involves delivering samples to the homes of the target segment. This is extremely expensive because of labor costs, but it can be effective if the marketer has information that locates the target segment in a well-defined geographic area.

3. **Mail sampling** delivers samples through the postal service, which allows the marketer to target certain ZIP-code markets. A drawback is that the sample must be small enough that mailing it is economically feasible. Cox Target Media has developed a mailer that contains multiple samples related to a specific industry—like car-care products—and that can reach highly targeted market segments.[17]

4. **Newspaper sampling**—distributing samples in newspapers—has become very popular; 42 percent of consumers report having received samples of health and beauty products in this manner.[18] Much like mail sampling, newspaper samples allow specific geographic and geodemographic targeting.

5. **On-package sampling**, a technique in which the sample item is attached to another product package, is useful for brands targeted to current customers. Attaching a small bottle of Ivory conditioner to a regular-sized container of Ivory shampoo is a logical sampling strategy.

6. **Mobile sampling** is carried out by logo-emblazoned vehicles that dispense samples, coupons, and premiums to consumers at shopping centers, fairgrounds, and recreational areas.

Sampling is particularly useful for new products but should not be reserved for new products alone. It can be used successfully for established brands with weak market share in specific geographic areas. Ben & Jerry's "Stop & Taste the Ice Cream" tour gave away more than a million scoops of ice cream in high-traffic urban areas in order to reestablish a presence for the brand in weak markets.[19]

Sampling has its downside. Unless the brand has a clear value and benefit over the competition, a trial of the brand is unlikely to persuade consumers to switch brands. This is especially true for convenience goods because consumers perceive a high degree of similarity among brands, even after trying them. To develop a perception of benefit and superiority, marketers may have to combine sampling with advertising. In addition, sampling is expensive, especially if a significant quantity of a product, such as shampoo or laundry detergent, must be given away for consumers to appreciate a brand's value. Finally, sampling can be a very imprecise process. Even when using specialized agencies to handle sampling programs, marketers cannot completely ensure that the product is reaching the target audience.

Trial offers have the same goal as sampling—to induce trial use of a brand—but are used for more expensive items. Appliances and consumer electronics are typical of items offered on a trial basis. Trial offers can be free for low-priced products. The trial period can be as brief as a day to as long as 90 days for more expensive items like vacuum cleaners or computer software. The expense to the firm, of course, can be formidable. Segments chosen for this sales promotion technique must have high sales potential.

Phone and Gift Cards

A new and increasingly popular form of sales promotion is to offer phone and gift cards. This technique could be classified as a premium offer, but it has enough unique features to warrant separate classification as a sales promotion technique. The use of phone and gift cards is fairly straightforward. Manufacturers or retailers offer either free or for-purchase debit cards that provide the holder with a preset spending limit or minutes of phone time. The cards are designed to be colorful and memorable.

A wide range of marketers, including luxury car manufacturers like Lexus and retailers like the Gap, have made effective use of phone and gift cards. A significant benefit for marketers is that gift card holders tend to use them freely to pay the full retail price for items, so retailers and brand marketers earn higher profit margins from gift card purchases.[20]

Rebates

A **rebate** is a money-back offer requiring a buyer to mail in a form requesting the money back from the manufacturer, rather than from the retailer (as in

in-store sampling sampling that occurs at the point of purchase

door-to-door sampling sampling in which samples are brought to the homes of the target segment in a well-defined geographic area

mail sampling sampling in which samples are delivered through the postal service

newspaper sampling sampling in which samples are distributed in newspapers to allow specific geographic and geodemographic targeting

on-package sampling sampling in which a sample item is attached to another product's package

mobile sampling sampling carried out using logo-emblazoned vehicles where samples are dispensed at malls or other high-traffic areas

trial offers sales promotion in which expensive items are offered on a trial basis to induce consumers to try a brand

rebate money-back offer requiring a buyer to mail in a form requesting the money back from the manufacturer

couponing). The rebate technique has been refined throughout the years and now is used by a wide variety of marketers. More than 400 million rebates are offered each year for products as diverse as computers (Dell) and mouthwash (Warner-Lambert).[21] Rebates are well suited to increasing the quantity purchased, so they commonly are tied to multiple purchases. For example, if you buy a 10-pack of Kodak film, you can mail in a rebate coupon worth $2.

Marketers like rebates because relatively few consumers take advantage of the rebate offer after buying a brand. By one estimate, only 60 percent of buyers ever bother to fill out and then mail in the rebate request—resulting in an extra $2 billion in revenue for manufacturers and retailers that offer rebates.[22]

Frequency (Continuity) Programs

One of the most popular consumer-market sales promotion techniques has been frequency programs. **Frequency programs**, also referred to as continuity programs, offer consumers discounts or free product rewards for repeat purchase or patronage of a brand or company. These programs were pioneered by airlines. Frequent-flyer programs such as Delta Air Lines' SkyMiles, frequent-stay programs such as Marriott's Honored Guest Award Rewards program, and frequent-renter programs such as Hertz's #1 Club are examples of such loyalty-building activities. But frequency programs are not reserved for the travel industry. Chart House Enterprises, a chain of 65 upscale restaurants, successfully launched a frequency program for diners, who earned points for every dollar spent. Frequent diners were issued "passports," which were stamped at each visit. Within two years, the program had more than 300,000 members.

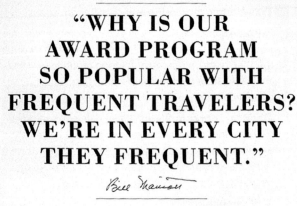

"WHY IS OUR AWARD PROGRAM SO POPULAR WITH FREQUENT TRAVELERS? WE'RE IN EVERY CITY THEY FREQUENT."

Bill Marriott

As a business traveler you earn free vacations faster with Marriott's Honored Guest Award program. With over 250 locations worldwide, we're doing business wherever you're doing business. To join the program call 1-800-648-8024. For reservations, call your travel agent or 1-800-228-9290.

Marriott
HOTELS · RESORTS · SUITES
WE MAKE IT HAPPEN FOR YOU

©1994 Marriott International, Inc.

Frequency (continuity) programs build customer loyalty and offer opportunities for building a large, targeted database for other promotions.

LO 3 Sales Promotion to the Trade and Business Buyers

Sales promotions also can be directed at members of the trade—wholesalers, distributors, and retailers—and business markets. For example, Hewlett-Packard designs sales promotion programs for its retailers, like Circuit City, to ensure that the HP line gets proper attention and display. HP also develops sales promotion campaigns aimed at business buyers like Accenture or IHC HealthCare. Firms spend big money to attract business to their brands with sales promotions. Recent estimates put business-to-business sales promotions at more than $44 billion annually.[23]

Objectives

The purpose of sales promotion as a tool does not change from the consumer market to the trade or business markets. It still is intended to stimulate demand in the short term and help push the product through the distribution channel or cause business buyers to act more immediately and positively toward the marketer's brand.

Effective trade and business market promotions can generate enthusiasm for a product and contribute positively to the loyalty distributors show for a brand. In the business market, sales promotions can mean the difference between landing a very large order and missing out entirely on a revenue opportunity. With the proliferation of new brands and brand extensions, manufacturers need to stimulate enthusiasm and loyalty among members of the trade and get the attention of business buyers suffering from information overload.

As in the consumer market, trade market sales promotions should be undertaken with specific objectives in mind. Generally speaking, when marketers devise incentives for the trade market, they are executing a **push strategy**: using sales promotions to help push a brand into the distribution channel until it ultimately reaches the consumer. These promotions have the four primary objectives shown in Exhibit 11.4.

Obtain Initial Distribution

The proliferation of brands in the consumer market generates fierce competition for shelf space. Sales promotion incentives can help a firm gain initial distribution and shelf placement. Like consumers deciding what to buy, members of the trade allocating shelf space need a reason to choose one brand over another. A well-conceived promotion may sway them.

Bob's Candies, a small family-owned business in Albany, Georgia, is the largest candy cane manufacturer in the United States. But Bob's old-fashioned candy was having trouble keeping distributors. To reverse the trend, Bob's designed a new name, logo, and packaging for the candy canes. It mailed each scheduled attendee at the All-Candy Expo trade show three strategically timed postcards with the teaser question "Wanna Be Striped?" The mailing got a 25 percent response rate, and booth visitations at the trade show were a huge success.[24]

Increase Order Size

One of the struggles in the channel of distribution is over the location of inventory. Manufacturers prefer that members of the trade maintain large inventories

Exhibit 11.4
Objectives for Trade-Market Sales Promotion

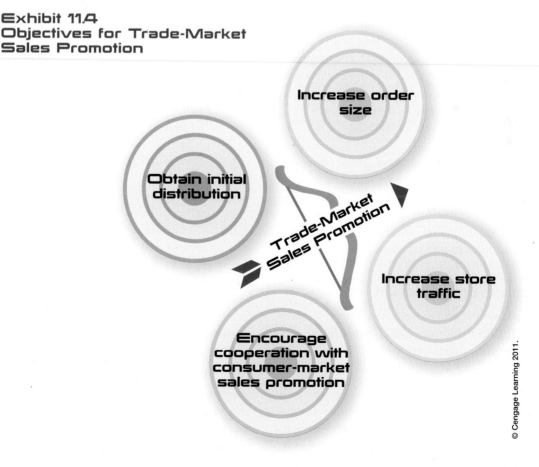

© 8781118005/Shutterstock.com

push money trade incentive in which retail salespeople are offered monetary rewards for featuring a marketer's brand

so that the manufacturer can reduce inventory-carrying costs. Members of the trade would rather place frequent, small orders and carry little inventory. Sales promotion can encourage wholesalers and retailers to order in larger quantities, shifting the inventory burden to the trade channel.

Encourage Cooperation with Consumer-Market Sales Promotions

A sales promotion in the consumer market won't fly if there is little cooperation in the channel. Implementation of the promotion may require that wholesalers maintain larger inventories and retailers provide special displays or handling. When Toys "R" Us ran a "scan and win" promotion, the retailer ran out of several popular toys during the critical holiday buying season because distributors (and Toys "R" Us) were unprepared for the magnitude of consumers' response. To guard against such problems, marketers often run trade promotions simultaneously with consumer promotions.

Increase Store Traffic

Retailers can increase store traffic through special promotions or events. Door-prize drawings or live radio broadcasts from the store are common sales promotions aimed at increasing traffic. Burger King has become a leader in building traffic at its 6,500 outlets with special promotions tied to Disney movie debuts. Beginning in 1991 with a *Beauty and the Beast* tie-in promotion, Burger King has set records for generating store traffic with premium giveaways. The *Pocahontas* campaign distributed 55 million toys and glasses.

Manufacturers also can design sales promotions that increase store traffic for retailers. A promotion that generates a lot of interest within a target audience can drive consumers to retail outlets.

Techniques: Trade Market

The sales promotion techniques used with the trade emphasize financial incentives and support for the retailers' sales and advertising efforts.

Incentives

Incentives to members of the trade include tactics that resemble those used in the consumer market. Awards in the form of travel, gifts, or cash bonuses for

reaching targeted sales levels can induce retailers and wholesalers to give a firm's brand added attention. The Volvo national sales manager put together an incentive program for dealerships, in which the leading U.S. dealership won a trip to the Super Bowl and dinner with Hall of Fame footballer Lynn Swann.[25] But the incentive does not have to be large or expensive to be effective. Weiser Lock offered its dealers a Swiss Army knife with every dozen cases of locks ordered. The program was a huge success. A follow-up promotion featuring a Swiss Army watch was an even bigger hit.

Another form of trade incentive is known as push money. **Push money** is carried out through a program in which retail salespeople are offered a monetary reward for featuring a marketer's brand with shoppers. The program is quite simple. If a salesperson sells a particular brand, the salesperson will be paid an extra $50 or $75 "bonus."

One risk with incentive programs for the trade is that salespeople can be so motivated to win an award or extra push money that they may try to sell the brand to every customer, whether it fits that customer's needs or not. Also, a firm must carefully manage such programs to minimize ethical dilemmas. An incentive technique can look like a bribe unless it is carried out in a highly structured and open fashion.

Allowances

Various forms of allowances are offered to retailers and wholesalers with the purpose of increasing the attention given to a firm's brands. Allowances typically are made available to wholesalers and retailers about every four weeks during a quarter. Several types of allowances are common:

- **Merchandise allowances**, in the form of free products packed with regular shipments, are payments to the trade for setting up and maintaining displays. The payments typically are far less than manufacturers would have to spend to maintain the displays themselves.

- **Slotting fees** are direct cash payments to induce food chains to stock an item. They are popular because of the high demand for shelf space in recent years, especially in supermarkets. The proliferation of new products has made shelf space so precious that these fees run in the hundreds of thousands of dollars per product.

- **Bill-back allowances** give retailers a monetary incentive for featuring a marketer's brand in advertising or in-store displays. If a retailer chooses to participate in an advertising campaign or a display bill-back program, the marketer requires the retailer to verify the services performed and provide a bill for the services.

- **Off-invoice allowances** allow wholesalers and retailers to deduct a set amount from the invoice they receive for merchandise. This program really is only a price reduction offered to the trade on a particular marketer's brand. The price reduction increases the margin (and profits) a wholesaler or retailer realizes on the off-invoiced brand.

One risk with allowances is monitoring the extent to which retailers actually use the allowance to cover extra effort to feature a brand or else to reduce prices charged to consumers. Procter & Gamble, which spends more than $2 billion per year on trade promotions, has implemented controls to ensure that displays and other merchandising of the firm's brands are actually occurring.[26]

Sales Training

An increasingly popular trade promotion is to provide training for retail store personnel. This method is used for consumer durables and specialty goods, such as home theater systems and exercise equipment. The complexity of these products has made it important for manufacturers to ensure that the proper factual information and persuasive themes are reaching consumers at the point of purchase. For personnel at large stores, manufacturers can hold special classes that feature product information, demonstrations, and training about sales techniques.

Several training tools are available to marketers. They may provide training videos and brochures, or they may send sales trainers into stores to work side by side with store personnel. The use of trainers is costly but can be very effective because it offers one-on-one attention.

Co-op Advertising

Cooperative advertising as a trade promotion technique is referred to as vertical cooperative advertising and involves providing dollars directly to retailers for featuring the company's brand in local advertising. Such efforts also are called vendor co-op programs.

merchandise allowances trade-market sales promotion in which free products are packed with regular shipments as payment to the trade for setting up and maintaining displays

slotting fees trade-market sales promotion in which manufacturers make direct cash payments to retailers to ensure shelf space

bill-back allowances monetary incentive provided to retailers for featuring a marketer's brand in advertising or in-store displays

off-invoice allowance program allowing wholesalers and retailers to deduct a set amount from the invoice they receive for merchandise

cooperative advertising sharing of advertising expenses between national advertisers and local merchants

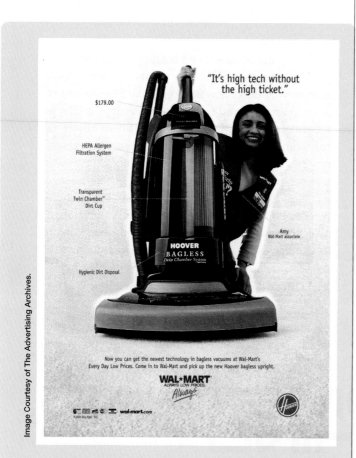

Here is a classic example of co-op advertising. Hoover, the manufacturer, is being featured by Walmart, a retailer, in this magazine ad.

Marketers try to control the content of this co-op advertising in two ways. They may set strict specifications for the size and content of the ad and then ask for verification that such specifications have been met. Or they may send retailers the template for an ad, into which retailers merely insert the names and locations of their stores.

Techniques: Business Market

The discussion of sales promotion often focuses only on consumer and trade techniques, but it is a major oversight to leave the business market out of the discussion. The Promotional Product Association estimates that several billion dollars a year in sales promotion is targeted to the business buyer.[27]

Trade Shows

Trade shows are events where several related products from many manufacturers are displayed and demonstrated to members of a trade. At a typical trade show, company representatives staff a booth that displays the company's products or service programs. The representatives are there to explain the products and services and perhaps make an important contact for the sales force. Literally every industry has trade shows. For example, Comdex, the annual trade show of the computer and electronics industry, is held in Las Vegas and attracts more than a quarter of a million business buyers.

Advertisers are finding that a trade show is an efficient way to reach interested current and potential buyers with the brand right at hand for discussion and actual use. The Promotional Products Association reports that, when trade show visitors receive a promotional item from a firm at a trade show booth, more than 70 percent of them remember the name of the company that gave them the item.[26] Trade shows can be critically important to a small firm that cannot afford advertising and has a sales staff too small to reach all its potential customers. At trade shows, salespeople can make far more contacts than they could with direct sales calls.

Trade shows also are an important route for reaching potential wholesalers and distributors. But the proliferation of trade shows has been so extensive in recent years that the technique really is more oriented to business buyers.

Business Gifts

By some estimates, nearly half of corporate America gives business gifts. These gifts are given as part of building and maintaining a close working relationship with suppliers. Business gifts that are part of a promotional program may include small items like logo golf balls, jackets, or small items of jewelry. Extravagant gifts or expensive trips that might be construed as "buying business" are not included in this category of business-market sales promotion.

Premiums and Advertising Specialties

As mentioned in the context of promoting to consumers, a key chain or mouse pad bearing a brand name and slogan can be an inexpensive but useful form of sales promotion. A significant portion of the $14 billion market for premiums and advertising specialties is directed to business buyers. Even though business buyers are professionals, they are not immune to the value perceptions created by an advertising specialty; getting something for nothing appeals to business buyers as much as it does to consumers. Will a business buyer choose one consulting firm over another to get a sleeve of golf balls? Probably not. But advertising specialties can create awareness and increase customer satisfaction.

Trial Offers

Trial offers are particularly well suited to the business market. Because many business products and services have a high cost and require a significant time

GETTING SOMETHING FOR NOTHING APPEALS TO BUSINESS BUYERS AS MUCH AS IT DOES TO CONSUMERS.

commitment to a brand (because these products and services have a long life), trial offers give buyers a way to lower the risk of making a commitment to a brand. A trial offer also can attract new customers who need a reason to try something new. An opportunity to try a new product for 30 days with no financial risk can be compelling.

Frequency Programs

The extensive travel associated with many business professions makes frequency programs an ideal form of sales promotion for the business market. Airline, hotel, and restaurant frequency programs are dominated by the business market traveler. In addition, retailers of business products—for example, Staples and OfficeMax—have programs designed to reward the loyalty of the business buyer. Costco has teamed with American Express to offer business buyers an exclusive Costco/American Express credit card. Among the card's benefits is a rebate at the end of the year based on the level of buying: the greater the dollar amount of purchases, the greater the percentage rebate.

LO 4 Risks of Sales Promotion

Although sales promotion can help marketers achieve important sales objectives, marketers must carefully consider some significant risks associated with sales promotion:

- *Creating a price orientation:* Because most sales promotions rely on some sort of price incentive or giveaway, the marketer risks having its brand perceived as cheap, with low price being its primary value or benefit. Creating this perception defeats the purpose of integrated marketing communication. If advertising messages highlighting the value of a brand are contradicted by a price emphasis in sales promotions, the market receives mixed signals.

- *Borrowing from future sales:* Sales promotions typically are short-term tactics designed to reduce inventories, increase cash flow, or show periodic boosts in market share. The downside is that a firm simply may be borrowing from future sales. Consumers or trade buyers who would have purchased the brand any way may be motivated to stock up at the lower price. Then, during the next few periods of measure-

ment, sales will decline. This can play havoc with the measurement and evaluation of the effect of advertising campaigns or other image-building communications. If consumers are responding to sales promotions, it may be impossible to tease out the effects of advertising.

- *Alienating customers:* When a firm relies heavily on sweepstakes or frequency programs to build loyalty among customers, particularly its best customers, any change in the program risks alienating these customers. Airlines suffered just such a fate when they tried to adjust the mileage levels needed for awards in their frequent-flyer programs. Ultimately, many of the airlines had to give concessions to their most frequent flyers.

- *Time and expense:* Sales promotions are costly and time consuming. The marketer and retailer must handle promotional materials and protect against fraud and waste in the process. In recent years, funds allocated to sales promotions are taking dollars away from advertising. Advertising is a long-term, franchise-building process that should not be compromised for short-term gains.

- *Legal considerations:* As the popularity of sales promotions, particularly contests and premiums, has grown, legal scrutiny has intensified at the federal and state levels. Legal experts advise marketers planning promotions that use coupons, games, sweepstakes, and contests to check into lottery laws, copyright laws, state and federal trademark laws, prize notification laws, right-of-privacy laws, tax laws, and the regulations of the Federal Trade Commission and Federal Communications Commission. To stay out of legal trouble with sales promotions, marketers carefully and clearly should state the rules and conditions related to the program so that consumers are fully informed.

Mikael Damkier/Shutterstock.com.

point-of-purchase (P-O-P) advertising advertising that appears in the retail setting

SHOPPERS OFTEN MAKE PRODUCT SELECTIONS BASED ON WHAT THEY SEE IN THE STORE.

LO 5 Point-of-Purchase Advertising

One of the fastest-growing categories of brand promotion in today's marketplace is **point-of-purchase (P-O-P) advertising**: materials used in the retail setting to attract shoppers' attention to a brand, convey primary brand benefits, or highlight pricing information. P-O-P displays also may feature price-off deals or other consumer sales promotions. A corrugated-cardboard dump bin and an attached header card featuring the brand logo or related brand information can be produced for pennies per unit. When the bin is filled with products and placed as a freestanding display at retail, sales gains usually follow.

Marketers clearly believe in the power of P-O-P. From 1981 to 2008, marketers' annual expenditures on point-of-purchase (P-O-P) advertising rose from $5.1 billion to more than $20 billion per year.[29] Why this dramatic growth? P-O-P is the only medium that places advertising, products, and a consumer together in the same place at the same time. According to research conducted by the trade association Point of Purchase Advertising International (http://www.popai.com), 70 percent of all product selections involve some final deliberation by consumers at the point of purchase.[30] Additionally, in an early study on the effects of P-O-P sponsored by Kmart and Procter & Gamble, P-O-P advertising boosted the sales of coffee, paper towels, and toothpaste by 567 percent, 773 percent, and 119 percent, respectively.[31]

Effective deployment of P-O-P advertising requires careful coordination with the marketer's sales force. Gillette found this out when it realized it was wasting money on a lot of P-O-P materials and displays that retailers simply ignored.[32] Gillette sales reps, who visit about 20,000 stores per month, are in a position to know what retailers will and will not use. Gillette's marketing executives finally woke up to this fact when their sales reps told them, for example, that 50 percent

Your lucky photo/Shutterstock.com

of the shelf signs being shipped to retailers from three separate suppliers were going directly to retailers' garbage bins. Reps helped redesign new display cards that mega-retailers such as Walmart approved for their stores and immediately put into use. Now, any time Gillette launches a new P-O-P program, it tracks its success carefully.[33] Having a sales force that can work with retailers to develop and deliver effective P-O-P programs is a critical element for achieving integrated marketing communication.

P-O-P Objectives

The objectives of point-of-purchase advertising are similar to those for sales promotion. The goal is to create a short-term impact on sales while preserving the long-term image of the brand being developed and maintained by advertising. Specifically, the objectives for sales promotion are as follows:

- Draw consumers' attention to a brand in the retail setting.
- Maintain purchase loyalty among brand-loyal users.
- Stimulate increased or varied usage of the brand.
- Stimulate trial use by users of competitive brands.

These objectives are self-explanatory. The key to the effective use of P-O-P is to maintain the brand image being developed by advertising.

P-O-P Advertising Formats

A myriad of displays and presentations are available to marketers. P-O-P materials generally fall into two categories:

1. **Short-term promotional displays** are used for six months or less.

2. **Permanent long-term displays** are intended to provide point-of-purchase presentation for more than six months.

Within these two categories, marketers have a wide range of choices, defined in Exhibit 11.5.[34] This array of in-store options gives marketers a way to attract shoppers' attention, induce purchase, and provide reinforcement for key messages being

Exhibit 11.5
Options for P-O-P Advertising

Window and door signage	Any sign that identifies and/or advertises a company or brand or gives directions to the consumer.
Counter/shelf unit	Smaller display designed to fit on counters or shelves.
Floor stand	Any P-O-P unit that stands independently on the floor.
Shelf talker	Printed card or sign designed to mount on or under a shelf.
Mobile/banner	Advertising sign suspended from the ceiling of a store or hung across a large wall area.
Cash register	P-O-P signage or small display mounted near a cash register and designed to sell impulse items such as lip balm or candy.
Full-line merchandiser	Unit that provides the only selling area for a manufacturer's line; often located as an end-of-aisle display.
End-of-aisle display/gondola	Usually large display of products placed at the end of an aisle.
Dump bin	Large bin with graphics or other signage attached.
Illuminated sign	Lighted signage used outside or in store to promote a brand or the store.
Motion display	Any P-O-P unit that has moving elements to attract attention.
Interactive unit	Computer-based kiosk where shoppers get information such as tips on recipes or how to use the brand; also can be a unit that flashes and dispenses coupons.
Overhead merchandiser	Display rack that stocks product and is placed above the cash register. The cashier can reach the product for the consumer. The front of an overhead merchandiser usually carries signage.
Cart advertising	Any advertising message adhered to a shopping cart.
Aisle directory	Sign delineating contents of a store aisle; also provides space for a brand message.
Retail digital signage	Video displays that typically have been ceiling- or wall-mounted and now are being moved to end-of-aisle caps or given strategic shelf placement to relay special pricing or new-product introductions; newest P-O-P device available.

Source: Information on retail digital signage from Dale Smith, "Coming Down to Eye Level," *Marketing at Retail*, June 2007, 28–31.

conveyed through other components of the promotional plan.

Retailers are increasingly looking to P-O-P displays as ways to differentiate and provide ambience for their individual stores. Therefore, the kind of displays valued by Whole Foods versus Walgreens versus Target (to name just a few) often will vary considerably. The marketer's field sales force will be critical in developing the right P-O-P alternative for each retailer stocking that marketer's products. Without retailers' cooperation, P-O-P advertising cannot work its magic.

P-O-P with Mobile Marketing

Mobile marketing, introduced in Chapter 9, offers another place for point-of-purchase messages: the consumer's smartphone or other mobile device. When marketers use applications on these devices to keep track of customers' locations, they can send a message to each customer who is at or near a place to buy the brand. In fact, this kind of location marketing has been called "the new point-of-purchase."[35]

Marketers are still exploring the full breadth of the potential for location marketing, including consumers' attitudes toward the practice. But the possibilities are compelling. Imagine you're on your way home from work, and as you approach your supermarket, you get a text alerting you that your favorite brand of soft drink (according to the amount you buy when using your store loyalty card) just happens to be on sale. Companies like Placecast "geo-fence" retail locations, so that for consumers who opt in, Placecast will send offers to mobile devices when the consumers are within a predetermined radius of the retailers. In initial tests of the system, more than three-quarters of participating consumers said their likelihood of visiting a store or restaurant increased with using geo-fencing.[36]

P-O-P for Trade and Business Buyers

Even though we have focused on using point-of-purchase advertising as a technique to attract consumers, this promotional tool also is strategically valuable to marketers trying to secure the cooperation of the trade and appeal to business markets. Product displays and information

sheets often encourage retailers to support one distributor or manufacturer's brand over another. P-O-P promotions can help win precious shelf space and exposure in a retail setting. From a retailer's perspective, a P-O-P display can enhance the atmosphere of the store and make the shopping experience easier for customers. Brand manufacturers and distributors obviously share that interest. When a retailer can move a particular brand off the shelf, that ability adds to the manufacturer's and distributor's sales.

Also, as store retailers combat the threat of losing business to online shopping, they are trying to enliven the retail environment. Point-of-purchase displays are part of the strategy. Distributors and retailers are trying to create a better and more satisfying shopping experience. The president of a large display company says, "We're trying to bring more of an entertainment factor to our P-O-P programs."[37]

LO 6 Support Media

Marketers use **support media** to reinforce or supplement a message being delivered via some other media vehicle. Support media are especially productive when used to deliver a message near the time or place where consumers are actually contemplating product selections—for example, a billboard ad on or near a store where the brand is sold. Because these media can be tailored to local markets, they can have value to any organization that wants to reach consumers in a particular venue, neighborhood, or metropolitan area.

iStockphoto.com/Marcello Bortolino

Outdoor Signs and Billboards

Billboards, posters, and outdoor signs perhaps are the oldest advertising form. Posters first appeared in North America during the Revolutionary War, not as promotional pieces, but as a way to keep the civilian population informed about the war's status. In the 1800s, they became a promotional tool, with circuses and politicians among the first to adopt this new medium. Today, the creative challenge posed by outdoor advertising is as it always has been: to grab attention and communicate with minimal verbiage and striking imagery.

riding the boards
assessing possible locations for
billboard advertising

Courtesy of Horst Salons.

Minimal verbiage is one key to success with billboard advertising. This example easily meets that standard.

Total spending on outdoor advertising in the United States has been holding fairly steady in recent years at about $6 billion per year.[38] The product categories that rely most heavily on outdoor advertising are local services (like gas stations), real estate and insurance companies, hotels, financial institutions, and automobile dealers and services.[39]

Pros and Cons

Outdoor advertising offers several distinct advantages:[40]

- It can achieve wide exposure of a message in specific local markets.
- Billboards are attention getting because of their size and features such as special lighting and moving elements. Billboards created for a store in Minneapolis even wafted a mint scent throughout the city as part of a candy promotion for Valentine's Day.[41]
- The medium offers around-the-clock exposure for the marketer's message.
- It is well suited to showing off a brand's distinctive packaging or logo.

Billboards and outdoor signs are especially effective when they reach viewers with a message that speaks to a need or desire that is immediately relevant. For instance, fast-food restaurants use billboards along major freeways to tell hungry travelers where to exit to enjoy a Whopper or Big Mac.

Billboards have obvious drawbacks. Long and complex messages simply make no sense on billboards; some experts suggest that billboard copy should be limited to no more than six words. Additionally, the impact of billboards can vary dramatically depending on their location, and assessing locations is tedious and time consuming. To assess locations, companies may have to send individuals to the site to see if the location is desirable. This activity, known in the industry as **riding the boards**, can be a major investment of time and money. Moreover, the Institute of Outdoor Advertising has rated billboards as expensive relative to several other media alternatives.[42] Considering that billboards are constrained to short messages, often in the background, and not the primary focus of anyone's attention, their costs may be prohibitive for many marketers.

New Developments

Despite the cost issue and frequent criticism that billboards represent a form of visual pollution, advocates for this medium contend that important technological advances will make outdoor advertising an increasingly attractive alternative in the future. The first of these advances, which offers the prospect of changing what largely has been a static medium to a dynamic medium with previously unimagined possibilities, is that digital and wireless technologies have found their way to billboards. Google and Microsoft are experimenting with digital technology to make billboards a more targeted medium.[43] Digital billboard displays let advertisers rotate their messages on a board at different times during the day. This capability is especially appealing to local marketers—like television stations and food sellers—whose businesses are time sensitive. Coca-Cola purchased giant LED screens in over two dozen markets so it can run its own ads on them exclusively. It uses different sets of messages at different times of day (for example, advertising Minute Maid juice in the morning and Coke in the afternoon), and messages related to local or seasonal promotions are rotated into the mix at appropriate times in targeted locations.[44]

Another key development entails a testing system to profile the people who see a billboard in any given day.[45] For the past 70 years, the only information available for assessing the impact of billboard advertising came from raw traffic counts. But recently, Nielsen Outdoor, part of the company known for rating television viewership, has developed a system using GPS satellites to track minute-by-minute movements in the "impact zone" of a billboard. Drivers in the Nielsen panel are paid a small stipend to have their latitude and longitude recorded by

GPS every 20 seconds. Using demographic data provided by panel members, Nielsen can advise marketers about the characteristics of persons who viewed a billboard at any given time.

Measuring how many people see an outdoor ad has always been difficult. When people see outdoor signs and billboards, they are generally busy with other activities. One measurement solution is offered by the Traffic Audit Bureau: the Eyes On system combines results from traffic pattern studies, video monitoring, and travel surveys to estimate demographic and ethnographic data on audiences "likely to see" an outdoor ad.[46]

Out-of-Home Media Advertising

Along with billboard advertising, advertising venues that reach primarily local audiences away from home and work are collectively called **out-of-home media advertising**. This is a popular advertising form around the world. Out-of-home ads appear in many venues, including backs of buildings, subway tunnels, and sports stadiums.

The major forms of out-of-home media advertising are billboards and **transit advertising**—ads placed inside and on the outside of mass-transit vehicles, at terminals, and on station platforms. Transit ads may even envelop mass-transit vehicles. One of the latest

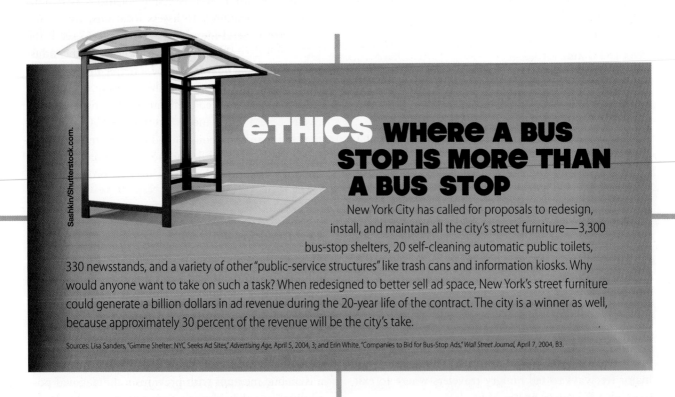

Sashkin/Shutterstock.com.

ETHICS WHERE A BUS STOP IS MORE THAN A BUS STOP

New York City has called for proposals to redesign, install, and maintain all the city's street furniture—3,300 bus-stop shelters, 20 self-cleaning automatic public toilets, 330 newsstands, and a variety of other "public-service structures" like trash cans and information kiosks. Why would anyone want to take on such a task? When redesigned to better sell ad space, New York's street furniture could generate a billion dollars in ad revenue during the 20-year life of the contract. The city is a winner as well, because approximately 30 percent of the revenue will be the city's take.

Sources: Lisa Sanders, "Gimme Shelter: NYC Seeks Ad Sites," *Advertising Age*, April 5, 2004, 3; and Erin White, "Companies to Bid for Bus-Stop Ads," *Wall Street Journal*, April 7, 2004, B3.

Happy Berliners enjoy their Cokes at three degrees Celsius while waiting for the U-bahn (subway).

aerial advertising
advertising that involves airplanes pulling signs or banners, as well as skywriting and blimps

cinema advertising
ads that run in movie theaters before the film and other brand messages that appear off-screen within a theater

innovations in out-of-home media is taxi-top electronic billboards that deliver customized messages by neighborhood, using wireless Internet technology.[47]

Transit advertising is especially valuable when a marketer wishes to target adults who live and work in major metropolitan areas. The medium reaches people as they travel to and from work, week after week, so it offers an excellent means for repetitive message exposure. In large metro areas such as New York City, with its 200 miles of subways and 3 million subway riders, transit ads can reach many individuals in a cost-efficient manner. Even the once-utilitarian bus stop also has become big business.

When working with this medium, an advertiser may find it most appropriate to buy space on just those train or bus lines that consistently haul people belonging to the demographic segment being targeted. This type of demographic matching of vehicle with target audience derives more value from limited ad budgets. Transit advertising also can be appealing to local merchants because their messages may reach a passenger as he or she is traveling to a store to shop.

Transit advertising works best for building or maintaining brand awareness. But, as with billboards, it is not suitable for lengthy or complex messages. Also, transit ads can easily go unnoticed in the hustle and bustle of daily life. People traveling to and from work via a mass-transit system are one of the hardest audiences to engage with a brand message. They may be bored, exhausted, absorbed by their thoughts, or occupied by another medium. Given the static nature of a transit poster, its message may not be able to break through to a harried commuter.

When advertisers can't break through on the ground or under the ground, they always can look to the sky. **Aerial advertising** involves airplanes pulling signs or banners, skywriting, or those majestic blimps. Aerial billboards pulled by small planes or jet helicopters equipped with screeching loudspeakers also have proliferated in recent years, as advertisers look for new ways to connect with consumers.[48]

For several decades, Goodyear had blimps all to itself; now the availability of smaller, less-expensive blimps has made this medium more popular to advertisers. Virgin Lightships has created a fleet of small blimps that can be rented for advertising purposes for around $200,000 per month that include huge full-color LED screens that can display brand images, advertising, and live TV broadcast feeds.[49]

Cinema advertising includes ads that run in movie theaters before the film and other brand messages that appear off-screen within a theater. Off-screen messages may include samples, concession-based advertising (such as an ad on a popcorn box), and ads posted or played in lobbies. Although consumers often complain that they dislike watching ads before a film they have paid to see, surveys have found that 63 percent of moviegoers don't mind the ads before the film.[50]

Directory Advertising

Yellow Pages advertising plays an important role in the media mix for many types of organizations, as evidenced by the $16 billion spent in this medium annually.[51] A wealth of current facts and figures about this media option are available from the Yellow Pages Association's website, http://www.buyyellow.com.

A phone directory can play a unique and important role in consumers' decision-making processes. While most support media keep the brand name or key product information in front of a consumer, Yellow Pages advertising helps people follow through on their decision to buy. By providing the information that consumers need to actually find a particular product or service, the Yellow Pages can serve as the final link in a buying decision. Because of their availability and consumers' familiarity with this advertising tool, Yellow Pages directories provide an excellent means to supplement awareness-building and interest-generating campaigns that a marketer might be pursuing through other media.

On the downside, the proliferation and fragmentation of phone directories can make this medium challenging. Many metropolitan areas are covered by multiple directories, some of which are specialty directories designed to serve specific neighborhoods, ethnic groups, or interest groups. Selecting the right set of directories to get full coverage of large sections of the country can be a daunting task. Thus, of the $16 billion spent in this medium annually, less than $2 billion is from advertisers looking for national coverage.[52] Additionally, working in this medium requires long lead times and ties the marketer into a yearlong message. Throughout the course of a year, information in a Yellow Pages ad can easily become dated.

There also is limited flexibility for creative execution in the traditional paper format.

Growth of the Internet once was viewed as a major threat to providers of paper directories. Websites such as Switchboard (http://www.switchboard.com) and Superpages (http://www.superpages.com) provide online access to Yellow Pages–style databases that allow individualized searches at one's desktop. Other high-profile players such as Yahoo! and AOL also have developed online directories as components of their service offerings. But, as it turns out, consumers still want their old-style Yellow Pages; market research has established that people who spend the most time on the Internet searching for addresses and phone numbers are the same people who make heavy use of paper directories.[53] When people are in an information-gathering mode, they commonly use multiple media. So, thus far, the Internet has been more of an opportunity than a threat for Yellow Pages publishers.

Packaging

In the simplest terms, **packaging** is the container or wrapping for a product. Although the brand package is not a "medium" in the classic sense, we are treating it as an element of support media because it carries important brand information, and that information carries a message. Classic quotes from consultants

CRAYONS HAS DEVELOPED A PACKAGE FOR ITS ALL-NATURAL FRUIT JUICE DRINK THAT REFLECTS THE BRAND'S QUALITY AND EXCITEMENT.

© Crayons, Inc.

describe packaging as "the last five seconds of marketing" and "the first moment of truth."[54]

Although the basic purpose of packaging seems fairly obvious, it also can make a strong positive contribution to the promotional effort. One of the best incidents demonstrating the power of packaging was Dean Foods' creation of the "Milk Chug," the first stylish, single-serving milk package. Officials of Dean Foods noted that "one thing milk didn't have was the 'cool' factor like Pepsi and Coke."[55] Twelve months after introduction of the new package, sales of white milk increased 25 percent, and chocolate and strawberry flavors saw increases of as much as 50 percent.

As we noted in the discussion of point-of-purchase advertising, more than two-thirds of supermarket purchases involve in-store decisions. For consumers in that important stage of their purchase decision, packaging adds another chance for a brand message. That gives packaging a role in promotional strategy and an important place in IMC.

Packaging provides several strategic benefits to the brand manufacturer. First, the package carries the brand name and logo and communicates the name and symbol to a consumer. In the myriad of products displayed at the retail level, a well-designed package can attract a buyer's attention and induce the shopper to more carefully examine the product. Several firms attribute renewed success of their brands to changes in package design. Kraft Dairy Group believes that significant package changes helped its Breyer's ice cream brand make inroads in markets west of the Mississippi. A package consulting firm came up with a package with a black background, a radically different look for an ice cream product.

Packaging helps create a perception of value for the product (and the "value" message is a key part of IMC). When consumers are buying image, the package must reflect the appropriate image. The color, design, and shape of a package have been found to affect consumer perceptions of a brand's quality, value, and image.[56] Perrier, one of the most expensive bottled waters on the market, has an aesthetically pleasing bottle compared with the rigid plastic packages of its competitors.

STUDY TOOLS CHAPTER 11

Located at back of the textbook
- **Rip out Chapter in Review Card.**

Located at www.cengagebrain.com
- **Review Key Terms Flashcards (Print or Online).**
- **Complete the Practice Quiz to prepare for tests.**
- **Play "Beat the Clock" and "Quizbowl" to master concepts.**
- **Complete "Crossword Puzzle" to review key terms.**
- **Watch videos on Gap and Nordstrom Rack for real company examples.**
- **For additional examples, go online to learn about Web-based incentive programs, the impact of P-O-P advertising, and the packaging of products.**

Sponsorship, Product Placements, and Branded Entertainment

Problem: How to tell busy young professionals that Fresh Mixers handily travel from cupboard to work to microwave.

Solution: Engage them online while they're at their desks.

> "A brand is a living entity—and it is enriched or undermined cumulatively over time, the product of a thousand small gestures."
>
> —Michael Eisner

AFTER YOU FINISH THIS CHAPTER GO TO PAGE 261 FOR STUDY TOOLS

Branding the Lunch Break

Picture the dilemma of today's young, health-conscious working professionals. After a long day on the job, they arrive home feeling hungry but too tired to cook. Marketers for years have been offering a solution as close as the nearest freezer: brands like Lean Cuisine and Healthy Choice sell frozen entrees that promise a healthful meal without the work of boiling pasta or chopping vegetables. These products offer a solution at home that doesn't translate so well into lunch at work, for the simple reason that frozen products need to stay frozen until it's time to heat and eat them. Healthy Choice cooked up a way around this shortcoming: shelf-stable pasta- and rice-based entrees called Fresh Mixers. The busy worker can toss a Fresh Mixers box into a backpack or briefcase, pull it out at lunchtime, and zap it in the handiest microwave.

The marketing question for Healthy Choice was how to educate workers about shelf-stable foods in general (that you find them next to the canned goods, not in the freezer case) and Fresh Mixers in particular (that you can enjoy such tasty offerings as Sesame Teriyaki Chicken without leaving your desk for more than a few minutes to heat them). Given that the brand's target market was professionals between the ages of 25 and 35, the company knew these consumers were heavy users of the Internet. Also, in today's fast-paced workplace, young professionals tend to grab lunch at their desks while multitasking—perhaps taking a quick break from the grind to surf the Web or see what friends are up to.

With this profile in mind, the promoters of Fresh Mixers decided to get the brand in front of their target market where and when they're hungry: in their cubicles at lunchtime. The brand's ad agency, Bridge Worldwide, assembled a great team that included Second City Communications, which applies the famed comedy troupe's talents to serving businesses, and MSN's Branded Entertainment and Experience

What do you think?

I notice who sponsors the concerts or events I attend.

1 2 3 4 5 6 7
STRONGLY DISAGREE   STRONGLY AGREE

Find out what others think at CourseMate for PROMO2.

Madison & Vine
convergence of advertising and entertainment; reference to the names of streets that represent each industry

Team (BEET), which has expertise in distributing entertainment online. Second City created an improv comedy series called "Working Lunch," in which skits poke fun at tedious office meetings as actors respond to directions arriving in real time via online polls about what should happen next. BEET arranged to have "Working Lunch" air at noon in every U.S. time zone.

All of this entertainment was presented on a "Working Lunch" website, which prominently displayed the Healthy Choice Fresh Mixers brand. Brief messages such as "Not in the freezer section" spread the word about how to buy the product. And perhaps most significantly, a lot of the action in the skits took place at the office microwave, as the characters prepared and enjoyed the sponsor's meals.

Healthy Choice used several measures to determine that giving consumers a lunchtime laugh translates into marketing success. It counted the people who saw the site: more than 5 million viewers in just 3-1/2 weeks of live programming, including more than a million repeat visitors. The company also compared attitudes and brand knowledge of site visitors with those of a control population. Consumers who visited the "Working Lunch" website were more aware of Fresh Mixers and more likely to know about features such as ease of preparation and no need for refrigeration. They also declared stronger intent to buy the brand.[1]

Meet Me at Madison & Vine

The "Working Lunch" videos exemplify the novel means that marketers are using to create meaningful connections with consumers because traditional mass media are no longer enough. Marketers are always on the lookout for new venues where they can advance their messages. Nowadays, as more and more people get engrossed in games on their mobile devices, this involves finding ways for consumers to earn "points" in brand-related activities. For example, FarmVille announced plans for its first branded virtual crop, and players of SCVNGR can earn a badge and points for visiting a Tesla dealer and taking pictures of the Tesla roadster.[2]

The array of tools and tactics that marketers are using to create unique experiences with consumers is so wide that it is not always obvious what these innovations have in common. The dynamic nature of this subject matter also means that the rules for success are hard to pin down. But within this dynamic environment we find the central premise that the fields of advertising, branding, and entertainment are converging. More than ever, brand builders want to be embedded in the entertainment that their target consumers enjoy. They are pursuing this goal with integrated marketing communication (IMC) that includes event sponsorship, product placement in entertainment media, and branded entertainment.

As indicated by "Working Lunch" videos with viewer input, the Folgers Yellow People on YouTube (see Chapter 4), and many other examples we've provided in this book, marketers around the world are receptive to many possibilities for brand building, and the list continues to grow. Think about what these examples have in common. Whether they're chuckling at lunchtime videos or playing FarmVille, consumers are engaged with these brands as part of some entertainment activity. Advertising, branding, and entertainment are converging at an accelerating rate, and the resulting linkage now has its own catchphrase: **Madison & Vine**, which refers to two renowned avenues representing the advertising and entertainment industries, respectively.

Why the accelerating convergence? One reason is the erosion in the effectiveness of traditional broadcast media. Many forces have been undermining old-school media. People have an ever-expanding set of options to fill their leisure time, from playing video games to surfing the Web to social networking. Among people who still do watch television, some are

BRAND BUILDERS WANT TO BE EMBEDDED IN THE ENTERTAINMENT THAT THEIR TARGET CONSUMERS ENJOY.

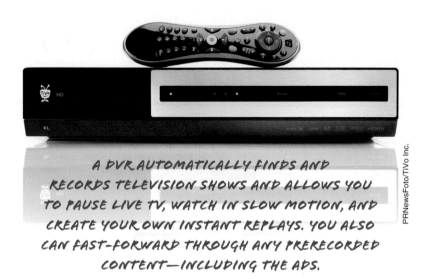

A DVR AUTOMATICALLY FINDS AND RECORDS TELEVISION SHOWS AND ALLOWS YOU TO PAUSE LIVE TV, WATCH IN SLOW MOTION, AND CREATE YOUR OWN INSTANT REPLAYS. YOU ALSO CAN FAST-FORWARD THROUGH ANY PRERECORDED CONTENT—INCLUDING THE ADS.

PRNewsFoto/TiVo Inc.

buying digital video recorders (DVRs) that can make TV ads optional. For example, a DVR offers an array of features, but in the minds of many, the best feature is that it lets you skip commercials. The share of U.S. households with a DVR has passed the one-third mark, and about half of these consumers are skipping the ads when they watch recorded shows.[3]

In the "**Chaos Scenario**" predicted by *Advertising Age*'s Bob Garfield, a mass exodus from the traditional broadcast media is coming. According to Garfield, it will work something like this: Advertisers' dollars stop flowing to traditional media because audience fragmentation and ad-avoidance hardware are undermining their value. With reduced funds available, the networks will have less to invest in the quality of their programs, leading to further reductions in the size of their audiences. This then causes even faster advertiser defections and on and on in what Garfield calls an "inexorable death spiral" for traditional media.[4] He predicts a brave new world where "marketing—and even branding—are conducted without much reliance on the 30-second [television] spot or the glossy [magazine] spread."[5] Nudged along by the recent recession, Garfield's Advertising Armageddon looks to be arriving ahead of schedule.[6]

As the old model collapses, billions of advertising dollars will be freed up to move to other brand-building tools. As discussed in Chapter 9, online advertising in its many forms will continue to surge because of this new money. But according to a 2007 Trendwatch survey, the brand-building options preferred by marketers as a replacement for old-school advertising involve sponsored events and experiential marketing.[7]

Event sponsorship, product placements, and branded entertainment are surging in popularity not only because advertisers *must* find new ways to connect with their consumers. These tools and tactics also can work in numerous ways to assist with a brand-building agenda. In theory, they can foster brand awareness and even liking through a process known as mere exposure.[8] In addition, the meaning-transfer process discussed in Chapter 5 can change people's perceptions of the brand. That is, the fun and excitement of a Panama City beach at spring break can become part of your feelings about the brands that were there with you. The brand evokes that pleasant memory. Similarly, consumers' sense of self may be influenced by the events they attend (as in a NASCAR race or a sporting event), and brands associated with such venues may assist in embellishing and communicating that sense of self.[9]

LO 1 Event Sponsorship

One of the time-tested and increasingly popular means for reaching targeted groups of consumers on their terms is event sponsorship. **Event sponsorship** involves a marketer providing financial support to help fund an event, such as a rock concert, tennis tournament, or hot-dog-eating contest. In return, that marketer acquires the rights to display a brand name, logo, or advertising message on-site at the event. If the event is covered on TV, the marketer's brand and logo most likely will receive exposure with the television audience as well.

Event sponsorship can take varied forms. The events can be international in scope, as in the 2008 Summer Olympics in Beijing with big-name sponsors like Adidas and Visa. Or they may have a distinctive local flavor, like the Flying Pig Marathon. Events like the Summer Olympics or the Flying Pig Marathon provide a captive audience, may receive radio and television coverage, and often are reported in the print media. Hence, event sponsorship can yield face-to-face contact with real consumers and receive simultaneous and follow-up publicity—all good things for a brand.

Event sponsorship continues to produce impressive results, so even in a tough economy, marketers continue embrace it. After a long growth surge, spending on events by North American companies has stagnated, but on a global scale, event spending has continued to grow, approaching $50 billion.[10]

Who Sponsors Events?

General Motors, one of the world's foremost old-school ad spenders, typifies the trend to events. GM has experimented with events that get consumers in direct contact with its vehicles or that associate the GM

Cincinnati Flying Pig Marathon; Photographer: Mark Bowen.

Even though there are no gold medals at the Flying Pig Marathon in Cincinnati (a.k.a. Porkopolis), crossing the "finish swine" at the head of the pack still is cause for a bit of snorting. Events like this one provide sponsorship opportunities for Mercy Health Partners, a regional office of the accounting firm Ernst & Young, and other companies with a local presence.

name with causes or activities of interest to its target customers. For example, GM has sponsored a scholarship program for the Future Farmers of America and a week of fashion shows in New York City. GM also has launched a movie theater on wheels that travels to state fairs, fishing contests, and auto races to show its 15-minute "movie" about the Silverado pickup truck. Like many marketers large and small, GM has been shifting more and more of its budget out of the "measured" media and into events and the Web.[11]

The list of companies participating in various forms of event sponsorships seems to grow every year. Jeep, Best Buy, and a host of other companies have sponsored tours and special appearances for recording artists such as Faith Hill and Tim McGraw. Searching for a connection with younger audiences, companies including McDonald's and Coca-Cola have been hunting for rising musical stars to sponsor; their finds have included IB Fokuz, DJ Kaskade, and Ingrid Michaelson.[12] Soon after ESPN launched the X Games to attract younger viewers, a host of sponsors signed on, including Taco Bell and Activision. These brands were looking for benefits through association with something new and hip through a process that anthropologist Grant McCracken has labeled the movement of meaning (see Chapter 5).[13]

Professional soccer has become one of the darlings of the sports business because of the valuable marketing opportunities it supports. For example, Manchester United of the English Premier Soccer League surpasses the New York Yankees in its ability to generate revenues. In this world of big-time sports, global companies like Pepsi and Vodafone pay huge amounts to have their names linked to the top players and teams. Nike's marketing VP calls the FIFA World Cup "the No. 1 event in all of sports."[14]

Because sports sponsorships come in all shapes and sizes, including organizations like Professional Bull Riders and the World Hunting Association, marketers have diverse opportunities to associate their brands with the distinctive images of various participants, sports, and even nations (for example, in the case of Olympic teams).[15]

Choosing an Event

A major sweet spot in event sponsorship comes when an event's participants overlap significantly with the marketer's target audience. It's even better when the event also has big numbers of fans and/or participants.

Another consideration is the marketer's budget. Marketers stand to gain the most if they support an

It's hard to compete with the Nikes and Reeboks of the world when it comes to sports sponsorship. The dollars spent in this regard are prohibitive for some companies. But if sponsoring a team from a small country, such as track and field athletes in Jamaica, seems like a long shot, consider that Puma has sponsored Jamaican runner Usain Bolt, who set three world records at the 2008 Summer Olympics.

event as its exclusive sponsor, but exclusivity can be extremely pricey. One solution is to sponsor smaller events. Sometimes marketers can find a small neighborhood event with passionate supporters just waiting to be noticed. Consider, for example, the World Bunco Association (WBA), chartered in 1996. Bunco is a dice game, usually played in groups of 8, 12, or 16. It's especially popular with middle-aged women. Bunco is a game of chance, so it leaves players with a lot of time for eating, drinking, and intimate conversation. Approximately 14 million women in the United States have played Bunco, and 4.6 million play regularly. Six out of 10 women say recommendations from their Bunco group influence their buying decisions.[16]

For marketers, the question is whether this group of women has a need that its products can meet. For the makers of Prilosec, the answer is a firm yes. About a third of regular Bunco players suffer from frequent heartburn, and 70 percent of frequent heartburn suffers are women. So in 2005, the makers of Prilosec OTC®, an over-the-counter heartburn medication, discovered Bunco and went to work learning about the women who play it regularly. Besides attending Bunco parties, they explored these consumers' other interests by listening to country music, camping in RVs, and watching NASCAR races. Bunco seemed like a great fit. Prilosec's marketers entered into a partnership with the World Bunco Association to sponsor the first Bunco World Championship in 2006. With a $50,000 first prize, associated fund-raising for the National Breast Cancer Foundation, and a lot of favorable word-of-mouth from regional Bunco tournaments, the World Championships caught on fast. Before long, cable TV caught Bunco fever and began covering the championship matches, where the Prilosec OTC purple tablecloths made it a branded experience.

Prilosec OTC's sponsorship of the Bunco World Championship illustrates an ideal scenario. There is excellent overlap between the lifestyles of event enthusiasts and benefits of the sponsoring product. Supporting Bunco allows Prilosec OTC to connect with its core customer in a fun and meaningful way, and the unique connection between Prilosec OTC and Bunco fosters brand loyalty and favorable word-of-mouth. The marketing director for Prilosec OTC said business has responded "phenomenally" on all measures as a result of its Bunco sponsorships.

Assessing Results

In the early days of event sponsorship, it often wasn't clear what an organization was receiving in return for its sponsor's fee. Even today, many critics contend that sponsorships, especially those of the sporting kind, can be ego-driven and thus a waste of money.[17] Company presidents are human, and they like to associate with sports stars and celebrities. This is fine, but when sponsorship of a golf tournament is motivated mainly by a CEO's desire to play in the same foursome as Annika Sorenstam, the company is really just throwing money away.

More often today, however, companies have found ways to make a case for the effectiveness of their sponsorship dollars (see Exhibit 12.1). Boston-based financial-services company John Hancock has been a pioneer in developing detailed estimates of the advertising equivalencies of its sponsorships. John

Hancock began sponsoring a college football bowl game in 1986 and soon after had a means to judge the value of its sponsor's fee. Hancock employees scoured magazine and newspaper articles about their bowl game to determine name exposure in print media. Next, they factored in the exact number of times the John Hancock name was mentioned in pregame promos and during the television broadcast. Early on, Hancock executives estimated they received the equivalent of $5.1 million in advertising exposure for their $1.6 million sponsorship fee. However, as the television audience for the John Hancock bowl dwindled in subsequent years, Hancock's estimates of the bowl's value also plunged. Hancock then moved its sports sponsorship dollars into other events, such as the Olympics, the Boston Marathon, and Major League Baseball.

Media Impressions

As marketers find better ways to gauge the effectiveness of marketing dollars spent, they generally are willing to spend more on any IMC tool.[18] In the realm of event sponsorship, Nielsen Media Research has developed a measurement it calls the Sponsorship Scorecard to give marketers a read on the impact of their signage in sports stadiums. Nielsen keeps track of when a sponsor's sign is shown on TV or the sponsor is mentioned on TV, and then it matches up those broadcast impressions with data it gathers on audience size for the broadcast to find the television audience for the sponsorship messages. In one assessment for Fleet Bank in Boston's Fenway Park, Nielsen calculated that Fleet signage received 84 impressions of at least five seconds each during a telecast of a Red Sox/Yankees baseball game. Based on the size of the TV audience for the game at the times when those impressions occurred, Nielsen determined that the images and mentions of Fleet's sponsorship generated a total of 418 million impressions among adults age 18 and over.[19]

In the John Hancock and Fleet Bank examples, marketers evaluated the effectiveness of their sponsorship spending by using a popular approach: **media impressions**, counting the number of instances in which a product or brand is exposed to consumers through media coverage, rather than paid advertising. Marketers use media impressions as a metric because it lets them directly compare sponsorship spending with spending in the traditional measured media.

**Exhibit 12.1
When Event Sponsorship Is a Winner**

Enough media impressions

Stronger brand loyalty

Targeted consumers in audience

© Cengage Learning 2011.

Brand Loyalty

Adding to their appeal, sponsorships can furnish a unique opportunity to foster brand loyalty. When marketers connect their brand with the potent emotional experiences often found at rock concerts, in soccer stadiums, at the Bunco table, or on Fort Lauderdale beaches in March, positive feelings may attach to the sponsor's brand and linger well beyond the duration of the event. Therefore, judging whether your brand is receiving this loyalty dividend is another important aspect of sponsorship assessment.

Getting a good read on the return from one's sponsorship dollars requires a mix of qualitative and quantitative approaches.[20] On the quantitative side, marketers will need, at a minimum, good data on the number and types of consumers who are making direct contact with their brands at any given event. Technology provides useful tools like tablet-size wireless computers that allow data collection and input by those scouting the event. Also, as attendees exit, marketers can conduct a survey asking their impressions of the various brands sponsoring the event and the all-important question for predicting loyalty: Is this a brand you will recommend to a friend or family member?

Sponsorships yield their greatest benefit when they foster a relationship or deep connection between

Lijuan Guo/Shutterstock.com

GLOBAL WHERE COKE WAS A GOOD SPORT

Coca-Cola's sponsorship at the 2010 Winter Olympics in Vancouver was a major platform on which Coke could position itself as a global good citizen. Although selling beverages at a major event sounds like a recipe for a mountain of trash, Coke vowed to produce zero waste. The fabric for all staff uniforms was made from recycled bottles, and every athlete received a T-shirt made from recycled-bottle fabric. Beverages were delivered by electric cart. Recycling bins were widely available. Impressed by these and other efforts, the Vancouver Organizing Committee awarded Coke a Sustainability Star.

Source: Natalie Zmuda, "Big Red Goes Completely Green at Olympics," *Advertising Age*, February 1, 2010.

leveraging using any collateral communication or activity to reinforce the link between a brand and an event

the target consumer and the sponsoring company or brand. This connection is created when the consumer's passion for the event in question (say, World Cup soccer) becomes associated with a sponsoring brand (such as Adidas or Heineken). Although traditional evaluation tools like exit surveys and media impressions are important in assessing the value of sponsorships, they cannot reveal deep connections. Careful listening is key to uncovering these connections.

Three areas of questioning can provide important insights for evaluating the relationship-building benefits of event sponsorship:

1. This qualitative research process should begin by exploring attendees' subjective experience of an event. Do they have strong feelings about the events they attend? What is it that ignites their passion for an event?

2. Next, it is critical to explore whether fans really understand the role of the sponsor. Most fans know little about the benefits that sponsors provide; research has shown that the more they know, the more the sponsor benefits. Auto-racing fans have the greatest understanding of the sponsor's role, which helps explain the eagerness of companies to get involved as sponsors of this sport.

3. Marketers need to probe the issue of connection: What specific brands do people connect with specific events, and how have their opinions of those brands been affected, if at all?

Tapping emotional connections requires sophisticated listening. Keen listening in these areas will help reveal whether sponsorships are deepening a brand's relevance and meaning in event goers' lives.

Audience Characteristics

Because various types of events attract well-defined target audiences, marketers also should monitor event participants to ensure the messages are reaching their desired target. Consider the marketing needs of JBL Electronics in reaching young consumers. JBL has teamed up with Trek Bikes to sponsor nationwide mountain-biking events. These so-called gravity sports are particularly attractive to skeptical teens, who reject traditional broadcast advertising and are starting to reject other forms of promotion. Their support of these sports at least puts JBL and Trek on the radar screen for this demanding audience.

Leveraging the Sponsorship

Marketers tend to justify event sponsorship by calculating the number of viewers who will be exposed to a brand either at the event or through media coverage of the event, and then assessing whether the sponsorship provides a cost-effective way of reaching the target segment. This approach assesses sponsorship benefits in direct comparison with traditional advertising media. However, some experts maintain that the benefits of sponsorship can be fundamentally different from anything that traditional media might provide.

In particular, marketers can benefit from finding ways to leverage the sponsorship. **Leveraging** or activating a sponsorship refers to any collateral communication or activity reinforcing the link between a brand and an event.[21]

Events can be leveraged as ways to entertain important clients, recruit new customers, motivate the firm's salespeople, and generally enhance employee morale. Events provide unique opportunities for face-to-face contact with key customers. Marketers commonly use this point of contact to distribute specialty-advertising items so that attendees will have a branded memento to remind them of the rock concert or their New York City holiday. Marketers also may use this opportunity to sell premiums such as T-shirts and hats, administer consumer surveys as part of their marketing research efforts, or distribute product samples. As you will see in the next chapter, a firm's event participation also may be the basis for public relations activities that then generate additional media coverage. Exhibit 12.2 provides a checklist of guidelines for selecting the right events and maximizing their benefits for the brand.

LO 2 Product Placements

As the fields of advertising, branding, and entertainment converge, marketers aspire to embed their brands in any form of entertainment that their target consumers enjoy. And while event sponsorship has been around for decades, brand builders also are looking elsewhere. Indeed, in today's world of integrated marketing communication, no show seems to be off limits. Brands now can be found whenever and wherever consumers are being entertained—whether at a sporting event, in a movie theater, on the Internet, or in front of a TV set or video game console.

This effort takes the form of **product placement**, the practice of placing any branded product into the content and execution of an established entertainment vehicle. These placements are purposeful and paid for by the marketer to expose and/or promote a brand. Product placement has come a long way since E.T. nibbled on Reese's Pieces in the movie *E.T. the Extra-Terrestrial*. But that product (or brand) placement foreshadowed much that has followed.

Product Placement Media

Product placement agencies work with marketers to build bridges to the entertainment industry. Working collaboratively, agents, marketers, producers, and writers find ways to incorporate the marketer's brand as part of the show. The show can be of almost any kind. Movies, short films on the Internet, and reality TV are great venues for product placements. Video games, novels, and magazines (or mag-a-logs) offer great potential.

Television

Television viewers have grown accustomed to product placements. Soap operas and reality shows have helped make product placements seem the norm on TV, and the tactic is spreading like wildfire. On Time Warner's WB network, a shiny orange Volkswagen Beetle convertible played an important role in the teen superhero drama *Smallville*. The final episode of NBC's long-running comedy *Frasier* included a special moment where Niles gave his brother a little gift to cheer him up. That gift? Pepperidge Farm Mint Milano cookies. The branded "special moment," like that one on *Frasier*, will only become more commonplace.[22]

There's even a school of thought contending that product placements can be television's savior.[23]

product placement sales promotion technique of getting a marketer's product featured in movies and television shows

Exhibit 12.2
Checklist for Event Sponsorship

- ☐ Pick an event that matches the brand.
- ☐ Pick an event that draws your target audience—not only a big audience, but the right audience.
- ☐ Deliver a few key messages, and repeat them often.
- ☐ Develop your event participation in terms of a plot or story with a beginning, middle, and end.
- ☐ Make participation exclusive by issuing invitations to a select group.
- ☐ Make participation relevant to your target group—not only about selling.
- ☐ Use the Internet to promote your event and share your story with those who couldn't be there.
- ☐ Integrate your event sponsorship with your other brand communications.

Source: MARKETING NEWS: REPORTING ON MARKETING AND ITS ASSOCIATION by Laura Shuler. Copyright 1999 by AMERICAN MARKETING ASSOCIATION.

Recall Bob Garfield's Chaos Scenario, discussed previously in this chapter, with its "inexorable death spiral" for the traditional media like TV. Concern that consumers won't watch ads on TV is a primary rationale for turning the programming itself into an ad vehicle. When contestants get rewarded with a Pringles snack on an episode of *Survivor*, that brand in effect is receiving an implicit endorsement. There's no telling where this trend is headed, but it's hard to put the genie back into the bottle, so maybe TV will be saved.

Rafael Ramirez Lee/Shutterstock.com

Movies

The car chase is a classic component of many action/adventure movies, and, in recent years, it has been seized as a platform for launching new automotive brands.[24] If you'd like to immerse yourself in a superb example of branded entertainment, rent the DVD of *The Italian Job,* a movie released in 2003 starring the lovable Mini Cooper. The Mini proves to be the perfect getaway car, as it deftly maneuvers in and out of tight spots throughout the movie. BMW has been a pioneer in the product-placement genre, starting with its Z3 placement in the 1995 James Bond thriller *Goldeneye.*

Of course, automakers aren't the only companies that have discovered product placements in movies and films. White Castle and the Weather Channel—to name just two—have joined the party as well. The 2006 movie *Talladega Nights: The Ballad of Ricky Bobby,* starring Will Ferrell, featured a cornucopia of product placements for everything from Applebee's to Wonder Bread.[25]

All this activity is supported by research indicating that persons under 25 years old are most likely to notice product placements in films and also are willing to try products they see in movies and films.[26] As we have emphasized, young consumers are increasingly difficult to reach via traditional broadcast media. Because they are likely to get their fill of product placements at the movies, in the near term, this looks like a good tactic for reaching an age cohort that can be hard to reach.

Video Games

According to Forrester Research, 100 million U.S. households have at least some gaming capability.[27] Moreover, most analysts conclude that around 40 percent of the hard-core players are in the 18-to-34 age cohort—highly sought after by advertisers because of their discretionary spending but expensive to reach via conventional media. For these consumers and media users, video games not only are an attractive entertainment option but also a form of entertainment where players rarely wander off during a commercial break. Nielsen research has established that the majority of players see brand placements as adding to the quality of play, and because brand exposures in games are repetitive, they affect purchase intent more than old-style media do.

With all those focused eyeballs in play, is it any wonder that marketers want to be involved? Billboard ads and virtual products have become standard fare in games like True Crime: Streets of L.A., starring Puma-wearing Nick Kang. And Tony Hawk must be a Jeep fan, because Wranglers, Grand Cherokees, and Liberties are always on the scene in his games.

The next big thing for marketers is Web-enabled consoles that allow more dynamic ad placements and precise tracking of where and how often players pause to take a closer look.[28] Whether you call these efforts "game-vertising" or "adver-gaming," you can expect to see more of brands as varied as LG Mobile, Ritz Bits, and Old Spice in the virtual world.

Requirements for Success

As the business of product placements has evolved, an activity that once was rare, haphazard, and opportunistic has become more systematic and, in many cases, even strategic. Even though product placement will never be as tidy as crafting and running a 30-second

One way video games differ from TV shows is that the players don't wander off to get a snack during commercial breaks. The product placements are an accepted part of the games, making the game environments appear more authentic.

authenticity quality of genuineness or naturalness

TV spot, numerous case histories help us identify factors that can improve the marketer's odds for success.[29]

First, product placements will add the greatest value when they are integrated with other elements of a promotional plan. As with event sponsorship, the idea is to leverage the placement of the brand message. Marketers should avoid isolated product placement opportunities and create connections to other elements of the IMC plan. For instance, a placement combined with a well-timed public relations campaign can yield synergy: novel product placements create great media buzz. Research suggests that brands can gain the most from product placements when consumers are engaged enough to make the brands part of their daily conversation.[30] So to get people talking about your brand, give them something to talk about. Favorable word-of-mouth is a great asset for a brand and helps build sales momentum. This can make product placements just right as a way to complement advertising initiatives that attend the launch of a new product.

Another factor affecting the value of any placement has to do with the elusive concept of **authenticity**— the quality of being perceived as genuine and natural. As marketers and their agents look for more and more chances to write their brands into the script of shows, it is to be expected that some of these placements will come off as phony. For example, when Eva Longoria plugs a new Buick at a shopping mall during an episode of *Desperate Housewives,* the scene looks phony and contrived. No way would Longoria or her character in this TV show ever stoop to such an unflattering activity. Conversely, when Kramer argues with a homeless man in the show *Seinfeld* about returning

his Tupperware containers, the spoof is perfect and adds to the comedic moment. Brands should be embedded in the entertainment, not detract from it. This often is a difficult goal to achieve.

Marketers foster success with product placements by developing deep relationships with the key players in this dynamic business. You need to have the right people looking for the right opportunities that fit with the strategic objectives established for the brand. This, too, is not a new idea. Advertising in particular, like marketing in general, is a team sport; the best team wins most of its games. You want to be part of a team where the various members understand each other's goals and are working to support one another. Good teams take time to develop. They also move product placement from an opportunistic and haphazard endeavor to one that supports integrated marketing communication.

Measuring Success

As with event sponsorship, a major challenge of product placements is how to measure the success or return on investment of the activity. The collective wisdom seems to be that calculating media impressions for placements does not tell the whole story regarding their value. Product placements can vary dramatically in the value they offer to the marketer.

One key item to look for is the celebrity connection in the placement.[31] When Tom Cruise puts on Wayfarer shades in one of his movies, the implied endorsement drives sales of the product.[32] Astute users of product placements are always looking for plot connections that could be interpreted by the audience as an implied brand endorsement from the star of the show.

LO 3 Branded Entertainment

Branded entertainment is a natural extension and outgrowth of product placement. It raises the stakes—and the potential payout. With product placement, the question is "What shows are in development that we might fit our brand into?" With branded entertainment, marketers create their own shows, so they don't have to find a place for their brand. This, of course, guarantees that the brand will be one of the stars in the show, as in the case of the Old Spice car on your TV at the Lowe's Motor Speedway.

For a stock-car racing fan, there is nothing quite like being at the Lowe's Motor Speedway on the evening of the Coca-Cola 600, NASCAR's longest night. Being there live is a rare treat, so the NASCAR Sprint Cup Series gets plenty of coverage on television, making it among the most popular televised sporting events in North America.[33] Although NASCAR is all about the drivers and the race, every race also is a colossal celebration of brands. The cars themselves carry the logos of something like 800 NASCAR sponsors. The announcers keep you informed throughout via the Old Spice Lap Leaders update and the Visa Race Break. We are told that Home Depot is the "Official Home Improvement Warehouse of NASCAR" and UPS is the "Official Delivery Service of NASCAR." At commercial breaks, Budweiser and Miller duel via advertisements, and we rejoin the race to follow the Budweiser or Miller Lite car around the track. None of this comes as any surprise because NASCAR openly and aggressively bills itself as the best marketing opportunity in sports. Said another way, a NASCAR race is a fantastic example of branded entertainment.

It's not hard to understand why Gillette or Budweiser would be willing to shell out millions of dollars to be a featured brand in the NASCAR Sprint Cup Series. Same could be said for the Old Spice team. Huge television audiences will yield hundreds of thousands of media impressions, especially for the cars (and brands) leading the race. A hundred thousand fans in the stands will make your brand a focal point, and many will visit a branded showcase before or after the race to meet car and driver. In addition, general industry research indicates that NASCAR fans are unusually loyal to the brands that sponsor cars and have no problem with marketers plastering logos over their cars and drivers. Indeed, many NASCAR fans wear those logos proudly. Moreover, the data say race fans are three times more likely to purchase a product promoted by their favorite NASCAR driver, relative to the fans of all other sports.[34] One NASCAR marketing executive put it this way: "Our teams and drivers have done a wonderful job communicating to fans that the more Old Spice they buy, the faster Tony Steward is going to go."[35] Obviously, this entails impressing and connecting with consumers in a most compelling way, making the Tide car or the Lowe's car a great symbol of branded entertainment.

NASCAR truly is a unique brand-building "vehicle," with numerous marketing opportunities for brands large and small.[36] But we use it here as an exemplar of something that is bigger, more pervasive, and growing in popularity as a way to support and build brands. Although it has been called many things,

[BRANDED ENTERTAINMENT] GUARANTEES THE BRAND WILL BE ONE OF **THE STARS** OF THE SHOW.

There's something special about the relationship between fans and their brands at a NASCAR event. Each race truly is a celebration, with brands as costars of the show. Fans are loyal to both NASCAR and its many sponsors.

we have settled on the label **branded entertainment** to describe the development and support of any entertainment property (e.g., TV show, theme park, short film, movie, or video game) where a primary objective is to feature one's brand or brands in an effort to impress and connect with consumers in a unique and compelling way.

What distinguishes branded entertainment from product placement is that, in branded entertainment, the entertainment would not exist without the marketers' support, and in many instances, marketers themselves create the entertainment property. BMW's efforts in product placement versus branded entertainment provide a perfect example. The appearance of the Z3 in the 1995 James Bond thriller *Goldeneye* is a nice example of product placement. But BMW did not stop there. In 2001, BMW and its ad agency Fallon Minneapolis decided it was time to make their own movies with BMW vehicles as the star of the show. The result was a series of original, Web-distributed short films like *Beat the Devil,* starring Clive Owen, James Brown, Marilyn Manson, and most especially, the BMW Z4. The success of these custom-made BMW films helped launch the new era of branded entertainment.

Many have followed BMW's lead in developing their own forms of entertainment as a means to feature brands.[37] Goen Group has developed a reality show, the *Million Dollar Makeover Challenge,* starring its diet pill Trimspa. *The Fairway Gourmet,* featured on PBS stations, promoted images of the good life, courtesy of the Hawaii Visitors & Convention Bureau. By creating shows themselves (often with their ad agencies), marketers seek to attract a specific target audience with a carefully tailored story that shows their brands at their best. This is quite different from trying to find a special place for one's brand in an existing show. As others have suggested, "Clients often enter the (general) realm of entertainment marketing via small product placements that eventually develop into larger promotional programs."[38] On the path of brand building, it is natural to evolve from the simple product placement to the more elaborate enterprise of branded entertainment.

Returning to the NASCAR example, today's NASCAR racing circuit could not exist without big brands like Gillette and Tide sponsoring racing teams and their drivers. Without the brands, there would be no NASCAR. As exemplified by a NASCAR race, in today's world of brand building, it often is impossible to disentangle the brand building from the entertainment. That's a great scenario for brand builders because, among other things, it makes their efforts TiVo-proof.

branded entertainment embedding a brand in any entertainment property to impress and connect with consumers

Challenges of Product Placement and Branded Entertainment

The surging popularity of product placement and branded entertainment is understandable, considering how well they help marketers reach an otherwise unreachable audience with messages that stand out and connect with consumers. However, to make the most of these opportunities, marketers must be able to overcome some obstacles to success, collaborate with the entertainment industry, and coordinate product placements and branded entertainment with the rest of their promotional mix.

Obstacles Ahead

No one can really say how rapidly marketing dollars will flow into these options in the next decade because several complicating and countervailing forces could hinder that flow (see Exhibit 12.3).

One of the obvious countervailing forces is instant oversaturation. As when any promotional tactic becomes popular, especially if it becomes a fad, overuse by marketers can result in jaded consumers and a cluttered media environment. As stated by a former marketing vice president at General Motors, "Any reasonable observer today has to see most of the marketing world is chasing a handful of product-placement deals. This is problematic and limiting. There just aren't enough bona fide hits to go around."[39] Some will argue that creative collaboration can always yield new opportunities for branded entertainment, but you have to acknowledge at some point that yet another motion picture featuring another hot

automobile will start to feel stale. Indeed, we already may be there.

A related problem involves the current processes and systems for matching brands with entertainment properties. Traditional media provide a well-established path for reaching consumers. Marketers like that predictability. Branded entertainment is a new and often unpredictable path. As noted by a senior executive at Fallon Minneapolis, a pioneer in branded entertainment with BMW Films, "For every success you have several failures, because you're basically using a machete to cut through the jungle . . . with branded entertainment, every time out, it's new."[40] Lack of predictability causes the process to break down.

In some cases, marketers and filmmakers don't appreciate one another's needs. Consider the soured relationship between General Motors and Warner Bros. over the promotion of the film *Matrix Reloaded*. GM's Cadillac division abandoned a big-budget TV campaign associated with the sequel when it couldn't get the talent cooperation or film footage it wanted. Samsung, Heineken, and Coke also complained in public about poor treatment from Warner Bros. These kinds of high-profile squabbles make big news and leave marketers wondering whether the branded-entertainment path is really worth all the aggravation.[41]

Exhibit 12.3
Obstacles to Overcome

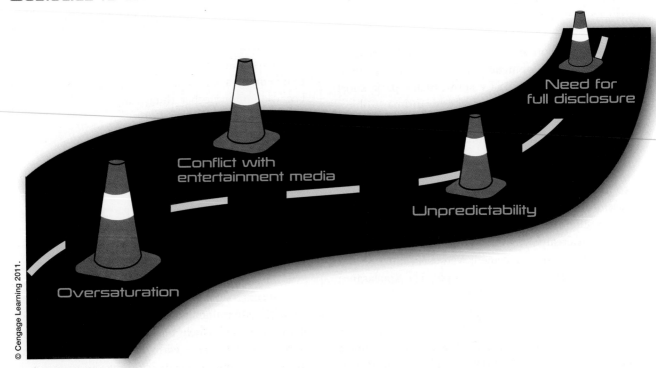

© Cengage Learning 2011.

Oversaturation

Conflict with entertainment media

Unpredictability

Need for full disclosure

Finally, there is concern about playing it straight with consumers. Ralph Nader's Commercial Alert consumer advocacy group has filed a complaint with the Federal Trade Commission and the Federal Communication Commission alleging that TV networks deceive the public by failing to disclose the details of product-placement deals.[42] The group's basic argument seems to be that, because most product placements are in fact "paid advertisements," consumers should be advised as such. It is conceivable that a federal agency will call for some form of disclosure when fees have been paid to place brands in U.S. TV shows, although now that the practice has become prevalent, we expect that consumers already perceive there is money changing hands behind the scenes. Consumers generally are pretty savvy about this sort of thing. On the global front, opinions about this issue vary from country to country.

Collaborating with the Media

Marketers have much in common with media companies and entertainers: They do what they do for business reasons. And they have and will continue to do business together. Smart marketers recognize this as they go about their business of trying to reach consumers with a positive message on behalf of their brands. Thus, while branded entertainment is enjoying a huge surge of popularity recently, it has been around for decades.

No firm has managed this collaboration better throughout the years than Procter & Gamble. In 1923, P&G was on the cutting edge of branded entertainment in the then-new medium of radio. To promote its shortening product Crisco, the company helped create a new radio program called *Crisco Cooking Talks.* This 15-minute program featured recipes and advice to encourage cooks to find more uses for Crisco. Although it was a good start, P&G's market research soon indicated that listeners wanted something more entertaining than just a recipe show. So a new form of entertainment was created just for radio: the soap opera. These dramatic series used a storyline that encouraged listeners to tune in day after day. *Guiding Light,* P&G's most enduring soap opera, started on the radio in 1937. In 1952, *Guiding Light* made a successful transition to television. It ran until 2009, thus earning the distinction of being the longest-running show in the history of electronic media.[43] And, of course, P&G has become a dominant seller of soap—and many other products as well.

IN THE 1920S, P&G WAS AN INNOVATOR IN THE MEDIUM OF RADIO, TRYING TO REACH CONSUMERS ON BEHALF OF BRANDS LIKE CRISCO SHORTENING AND IVORY SOAP.

Today, P&G's consumer has changed, the soap opera has lost much of its traditional appeal, and new forms of integrated marketing communication are necessary. P&G works with partners like NBC Digital Networks and Starcom MediaVest Group to ensure that its brands are embedded in the entertainment venues preferred by its targeted consumers. A great example is the integration of P&G's CoverGirl brand in the CW network's *America's Next Top Model,* hosted by former CoverGirl model Tyra Banks. This CoverGirl/*Top Model* relationship exemplifies many best practices for branded entertainers.

An enduring relationship is clearly something to strive for. Long-term relationships beget trust, and when partners trust each other, they also look out for each other. So even though P&G does not have direct control over the content of *Top Model,* it is able to ask for brand inserts and sometimes influence the show's content because of the relationship. However, P&G has learned not to push too hard to get its brand featured. That can detract from the entertainment value of the programming, which wouldn't help anyone. To maintain the right balance, the CoverGirl brand receives strong integration into the plot in only three episodes per season. But online communication at the brand's website invites audience participation every week.

Authenticity of the brand integration is always desirable, and CoverGirl definitely gets that on *Top Model*. For example, each season, the three finalists must prepare to be photographed for a magazine ad. This is, after all, what models get paid to do: appear in ads. So it's perfectly natural that this is part of the show, and it's perfectly natural that the magazine ad will be for CoverGirl, a brand that stands for "enhancing your natural beauty." The content of the show and the essence of the brand become intertwined, with an implied endorsement from *America's Next Top Model*. It doesn't get any better in the world of brand building.

Like many other marketers, P&G Productions is also moving to the Internet to create original content. P&G's recent Webisodes have included a series titled *A Parent Is Born*, an online documentary that follows Suzie and Steve on their emotional journey to parenthood.[44] Each 5-minute episode tracks one stage of that journey, such as finding out the sex of their baby or attending childbirth class. The people who would most likely want to watch this kind of story would be expectant parents—the prime prospects for the series sponsor, Pampers. Producing this kind of series is relatively inexpensive, and the brand has control over the content.

LO 4 Coordinating IMC Efforts

As the choices for delivering messages to a target audience continue to evolve and as marketers constantly search for cost-effective ways to break through the clutter and connect with consumers, promotion portfolios are including everything from advertising in restrooms to sponsoring a marathon. Simply put, marketers have a vast and ever-expanding array of options for delivering messages to their potential customers. The keys to success for any promotional campaign are choosing the right set of options to engage a target segment and then coordinating the placement of messages to ensure coherent and timely communication.

Many factors work against coordination. As integrated marketing communication (IMC) has become more complex, organizations often become reliant on diverse functional specialists. For example, an organization might have separate managers for advertising, event sponsorship, branded entertainment, and Web development. Specialists, by definition, focus on their specialty and can lose sight of what others in the organization are doing.[45] Specialists also want their own budgets and typically argue for more funding for their particular area. This competition for budget dollars often yields rivalries and animosities that work against coordination. Never underestimate the power of competition for the budget. It is exceedingly rare to find anyone who will volunteer to take less of the budget so that someone else can have more.

Coordination is further complicated by the potential for a lack of agreement about who is responsible for achieving integration.[46] Should the client accept this responsibility, or should integration be the responsibility of a "lead" agency? Ad agencies often see themselves in this lead role but have not played it to anyone's satisfaction.[47] In one

EDHAR/Shutterstock.com.

vision of the ideal arrangement, the lead agency plays the role of an architect and general contractor.[48] The campaign architect is charged with drawing up a plan that is media neutral and then hiring subcontractors to deliver aspects of the project that the agency itself is ill suited to handle. The plan also must be profit neutral—that is, the budget must go to the subcontractors who can deliver the work called for in the master plan. Here again, the question becomes, will the agency in the role of architect/general contractor really spread the wealth, even if doing so means the agency would forfeit wealth? Whether or not it will, one principle holds: When there is doubt about who is accountable for delivering an integrated campaign, the campaign is unlikely to be well integrated.

The objective underlying the need for coordination is to achieve a synergistic effect. Individual media can work in isolation, but advertisers get more for their dollars if various media and IMC tools build on one another and work together. Even savvy marketers like American Express are challenged by the need for coordination, especially as they cut back on their use of the 30-second TV spot and venture into diverse IMC tools. For instance, to launch its Blue card, AmEx employed an innovative mix, starting with Blue-labeled water bottles given away at health clubs and Blue ads printed on millions of popcorn bags. The company sponsored a Sheryl Crow concert in New York's Central Park and transformed L.A.'s House of Blues jazz club into the "House of Blue," with performances by Elvis Costello, Stevie Wonder, and Counting Crows. Print ads and TV also have been used to back the Blue, but AmEx's spending in these traditional media was down by more than 50 percent relative to previous campaigns. Making diverse components like these work together and speak to the targeted consumer with a single voice is the essence of IMC. AmEx appears to have found a good formula: the Blue card was the most successful new-product launch in the company's history.[49]

The coordination challenge does not end here. For example, added complexity—and opportunities—come from additional options, such as personal selling, public relations, and social media. These activities entail additional contacts with a target audience, and they should reinforce the other brand messages.

STUDY TOOLS
CHAPTER 12

Located at back of the textbook

- **Rip out Chapter in Review Card.**

Located at www.cengagebrain.com

- **Review Key Terms Flashcards (Print or Online).**
- **Complete the Practice Quiz to prepare for tests.**
- **Play "Beat the Clock" and "Quizbowl" to master concepts.**
- **Complete "Crossword Puzzle" to review key terms.**
- **Watch videos on Cannes Film Festival and BMW for real company examples.**
- **For additional examples, go online to learn about brand placement in TV shows, movies, and video games.**

Public Relations, Influencer Marketing, Social Media, and Corporate Advertising

Miss Sprint Cup isn't just a friendly face at the races; she's also communicating with race fans online.

Miss Sprint Cup's insider status (symbolized by the driver's suit) makes her an influencer if you're a NASCAR fan.

AP Photo/Brandon Wade

Learning Outcomes

After studying this chapter, you should be able to:

LO 1 Discuss the role of public relations as part of a strategy for integrated marketing communication (IMC).

LO 2 Identify the objectives and tools of public relations.

LO 3 Describe basic strategies for PR activities.

LO 4 Summarize how companies use influencer marketing programs.

LO 5 Describe how marketers use social media to promote brands.

LO 6 Discuss the applications and objectives of corporate advertising.

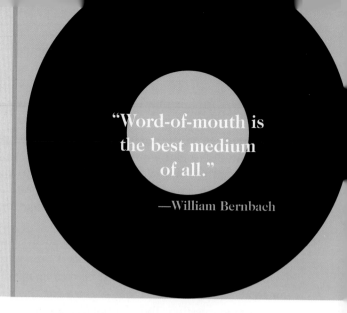

"Word-of-mouth is the best medium of all."

—William Bernbach

AFTER YOU FINISH THIS CHAPTER GO TO PAGE 281 FOR STUDY TOOLS

Your Friend from NASCAR

You might not have known it, but there's a pretty young woman working for NASCAR who would like you to join her social network. We're referring to Miss Sprint Cup, who for the past few years has traveled weekly to NASCAR Sprint Cup Series races. Wearing a Sprint-branded driver's suit, she (or, more accurately, they—three women share the title) stirs up excitement by interviewing drivers, hanging out in the pit area, attending victory celebrations, and interacting with fans. The general manager of NASCAR Sprint Cup sponsorship thinks of her this way: "Here's a woman living a lifestyle that fans would die to be part of—hanging out in the garage area, meeting drivers and pre-race festivities."[1]

Her marketing impact is greatest online, however. Sprint set up Facebook and Twitter accounts where Miss Sprint Cup communicates in real time with racing fans. She has more than 100,000 fans on Facebook and more than 10,000 Twitter followers. While attending an event on race weekends, she updates her Facebook status and sends tweets to her followers about 20 times. Every time she posts, fans send in more than 100 responses, almost all of them positive.

Miss Sprint Cup promotes more than the races or the NASCAR brand; she also promotes the racing sponsors. And she's far too subtle to post an advertising message. Instead, she uses her position as a NASCAR insider to gain an audience for casual remarks that just happen to mention the brands. So to promote the BlackBerry brand, she would carry a BlackBerry Tour to a race, take a picture, and upload it with a caption that includes a mention of the device. Consumers want to hear from Miss Sprint Cup, based on their existing personal interests, so they'll pay attention. And if they want to emulate her, they will want to use a BlackBerry Tour, too.

What do you think?

When my friends care about something, so do I.

STRONGLY DISAGREE   STRONGLY AGREE

The idea of sending brand messages through social media, such as Twitter posts or YouTube videos, is that Internet users will attend to the messages more naturally than to traditional advertising. These brand messages come across more as a part of everyday life than as a corporate attempt to manipulate. Best of all for marketers, if messages are especially entertaining, inspirational, or informative, consumers will even pass them along to family and friends.

The impact of promotional efforts such as Miss Sprint Cup's presence on social media is even greater when they are part of integrated marketing, in which marketers use multiple tools, selected for the target segment in question. Today, a popular approach is to combine paid messages such as advertising with public relations to build buzz in social media so that consumers themselves are spreading the brand messages. It's an effort that brings together so many different activities—activating social media, engaging mainstream media, choosing spokespeople, orchestrating teamwork, and much more—that some see a convergence in the talents required of today's marketers, advertisers, and public relations professionals.[2]

LO 1   Public Relations

The classic role of **public relations** is to foster goodwill between a firm and its many constituent groups. These constituent groups include customers, stockholders, suppliers, employees, government entities, citizen action groups, and the general public. The firm's public relations function seeks to highlight positive events like outstanding quarterly sales and profits (to stockholders) or noteworthy community service programs (to government entities and the general public). As well, PR is used strategically for "damage control" when adversity strikes.

Additionally, public relations has entered an exciting new era. New PR techniques have fostered a bolder, more aggressive role for public relations in brand promotion campaigns. The traditional functions of managing goodwill and engaging in damage control still are important, but societal forces support a growing role for PR activities as part of IMC campaigns:

- Increasingly sophisticated and connected consumers are talking to each other more and more about brands. Stephen Brown, a prolific and provocative writer on the subject of branding, says today's world is different from the heyday of mass marketing.[3] It is intensely commercial. TV shows feature stories about marketing and consumer psychology, stand-up comics perform skits about shopping routines and brand strategies, and documentaries like *Who Killed the Electric Car?* and *Walmart: The High Cost of Low Price* make great anti-brand entertainment. Industry gossip, executive screw-ups, and product critiques are bloggers' standard fodder. It is a brand-obsessed world.

- The consumer increasingly is in control, using tools like blogs, podcasts, YouTube, RSS feeds, and whatever will be invented next week to exert that control across the Internet.[4] Marketers must monitor the current buzz about their brands and become part of the dialogue in an effort to rescue or revive their brands. In contrast, mass-media advertising was never a dialogue.

- Although marketers have always believed that the most powerful influence in any consumer's decision is the recommendations of friends and family, they only are beginning to figure out what to do about it. In his bestseller *The Tipping Point*, Malcolm Gladwell makes the case that "mavens" and "connectors" are critically important in fostering social epidemics. If marketers locate these mavens and connectors, and give them useful information or interesting stories about a brand, these people may spread the news through their networks. The sharing is intensified online, where one connected person can spread the word to thousands of friends or followers with the simple click of a mouse.

NEW PR TECHNIQUES HAVE FOSTERED A BOLDER, MORE AGGRESSIVE ROLE FOR PUBLIC RELATIONS.

COMPANY REPRESENTATIVES MAKE AN EFFORT TO COMMUNICATE EFFECTIVELY WITH THE NEWS MEDIA BECAUSE NEWS STORIES ARE AN IMPORTANT WAY TO SPREAD BELIEVABLE INFORMATION ABOUT THE COMPANY AND ITS BRANDS.

R. Gino Santa Maria/Shutterstock.com

Given that people talk about brands, the marketer's challenge then is to give them interesting things to talk about, bringing a brand into the conversation in a positive way. In that context, PR is about more than managing goodwill; it can involve many ways to get a brand into the day-to-day conversations of key consumers. Maytag has used PR expertise in a proactive way to build its brand. Its nationwide contest to select the next Maytag Repairman generated 2,000 candidates and a lot of buzz in the conventional media and across the Internet. Maytag's vice president of marketing described the effort as a $500,000 campaign that generated $10 million of value and attributed its success to integrating PR expertise into the planning process for the brand early and often.[5]

In today's dynamic marketplace, with multitudes of online and offline conversations about brands, a brand builder needs to influence at least some of those conversations. It's a reasonable goal when you consider that the biggest source of content for online chatter about brands is advertising, especially TV ads.[6] At the same time, ads get the biggest results when they get conversations going, online or face-to-face. To achieve this, the necessary integration takes a strong team effort, and it is becoming increasingly clear that PR expertise must be well represented on any brand promotion team.[7]

Damage Control

As consumers become more informed and connected, bad news about companies and brands travels faster and lingers longer. And, of all the promotional tools, public relations is the only one that can provide damage control in response to bad publicity. Such public relations problems can arise either from a firm's own activities or from external forces outside the firm's control.

The bad news that turns into a need for damage control can take many forms. For Taco Bell, it was an Internet video of rats running amok at its Greenwich Village restaurant.[8] You can close the restaurant, but that video is out there still. Johnson & Johnson walked into a PR firestorm by suing the Red Cross for logo infringement.[9] That's a hard case to win in the court of public opinion, but it's definitely a self-inflicted

wound for J&J. Marketers themselves have been the source of trouble at KFC by dreaming up popular promotions but failing to coordinate them with store managers. When you offer a discount coupon but don't have a product to back it up, everyone gets agitated—that is, everyone except your competitors.[10]

Companies need to learn how to handle the bad news. No company is immune. But while many public relations episodes must be reactive, a firm can be prepared with public relations materials to conduct an orderly and positive relations-building campaign with its constituents.

LO 2 PR Objectives

Even though reacting to a crisis is a necessity, it is more desirable to be proactive. The key is to have a structured approach to public relations, including a clear understanding of objectives for PR. Public relations can address any combination of six primary objectives:

1. *Promoting goodwill:* This image-building function highlights industry events or community activities that reflect favorably on a firm. When Pepsi launched a program to support school music programs, the firm garnered widespread goodwill.

2. *Promoting a product or service:* Companies can spread "news" about its brands to increase public awareness of the brands. Large pharmaceutical firms such as Merck and GlaxoSmithKline issue press releases when they discover new drugs or achieve FDA approval.

3. *Preparing internal communications:* By disseminating information and correcting misinformation within a firm, public relations can reduce the impact of rumors and increase employee morale. Internal communications about major changes such as layoffs or mergers can dispel rumors circulating among employees.

4. *Counteracting negative publicity:* With PR's damage-control function, the attempt is not to cover up negative events but rather to prevent the negative publicity from damaging the image of a firm and its brands. When a lawsuit was filed against NEC alleging that one of its cell phones had caused cancer, McCaw Cellular Communications used PR activities to inform the public (especially cell phone users) of scientific knowledge that argued against the claims in the lawsuit.

5. *Lobbying:* The PR function can help a firm communicate with government officials and influence pending legislation. Microsoft reportedly spent $4.6 billion on lobbying efforts when antitrust violations were leveled at the company.

6. *Giving advice and counsel:* Helping management determine what (if any) position to take on public issues, preparing employees for public appearances, and helping management anticipate public reactions are ways that PR can deliver advice and counsel.

PR Tools

There are several means by which a firm can pursue its PR objectives. The goal is to gain as much control over the process as possible by integrating public relations with other brand communications.

Press Releases

Disseminating information that makes for good news stories puts the firm in a position to take advantage of free media coverage. To obtain that coverage, companies put that information in press releases sent to media outlets. In general, several kinds of topics are suitable for press releases:

- New products
- New scientific discoveries
- New personnel
- New corporate facilities
- Innovative corporate practices, such as energy-saving programs or employee benefit programs
- Annual shareholder meetings
- Charitable and community-service activities

Editors prefer information that focuses on technical or how-to features along with in-depth case studies about company successes and failures.

The drawback of press releases is that marketers don't control how the media use the message. A firm often doesn't know if or when the information will appear in the news. Also, journalists are free to edit or interpret a news release, which may alter its intended message. Marketers try to reduce these liabilities by cultivating relationships with editors at publications likely to have the most impact.

Feature Stories

Although a firm cannot write a feature story for a news medium, it can invite journalists to do an exclusive story on the firm when there is a particularly noteworthy event. A feature story, as opposed to a news release, offers a single journalist the opportunity to do a fairly lengthy piece with exclusive rights to the information. Compared with a press release, a feature story is more controllable. Jupiter Communications, a research organization that tracks Internet usage and generates statistics about the Internet, has a simple philosophy about using feature stories as a public relations tool. Says Jupiter's CEO, "It is our goal to get every research project we do covered somewhere. We know this is the cheapest, and maybe most effective, way to market ourselves."[11]

Company Newsletters

In-house publications, such as newsletters, can disseminate positive information about a firm to its employees. As members of the community, employees are proud of their firm's achievements. The company also can distribute newsletters to important constituents in the community, such as government officials, the chamber of commerce, or the tourism bureau. Suppliers often enjoy reading about an important customer, so newsletters can be mailed to this group as well. These newsletters were traditionally printed and mailed or passed out, but firms increasingly are distributing company news online via email or posting newsletters on their websites.

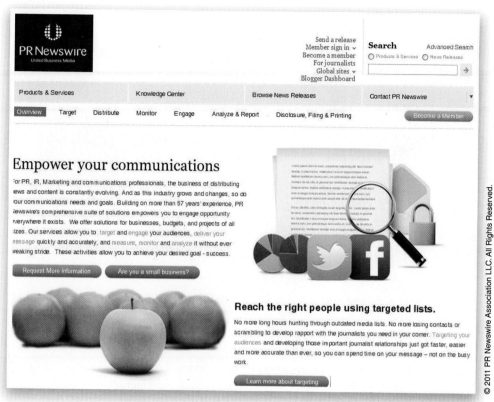

PR Newswire is the global leader in innovative communications and marketing services, enabling organizations to connect and engage with their target audiences worldwide. Pioneering the commercial news distribution industry over 56 years ago, PR Newswire's suite of services are used by many of the world's top organizations. From news dissemination to audience intelligence, engagement, measurement, and compliance services, PR Newswire's offerings provide a comprehensive solution for communications success. For more information about PR Newswire, visit www.prnewswire.com.

Interviews and Press Conferences

Interviews with key executives or staged press conferences can be highly effective public relations tools. Often they are warranted in a crisis-management situation. Firms also call press conferences to announce important scientific breakthroughs or to explain the details of a corporate expansion or a new product launch. No one did this better than Steve Jobs each and every time Apple had big news about a new product. The press conference has an air of credibility because it uses a news format to present salient information.

Sponsored Events

As was discussed in Chapter 12, sponsoring events can be aimed at supporting public relations. Sponsorship opportunities can run the gamut from community events to mega-events such as the Olympics. At the local level, prominent display of the corporate name and logo shows residents that the organization is dedicated to supporting its community.

Many sponsored events are fund-raisers. Raising funds for nonprofit organizations gives corporations a positive image. For many years, Chevrolet has sponsored college scholarships through the NCAA by choosing the best offensive and defensive player in televised football games. The scholarships are announced with much fanfare at the end of the game.

Publicity

Essentially, **publicity** is "free" media exposure about a firm's activities or brands. The public relations function monitors and manages publicity, though it cannot control what journalists choose to say or report. Organizations must be prepared to take advantage of events that generate good publicity and to counter events that are potentially damaging to their reputation.

ETHICS PUBLICITY GETS SCARY

To generate publicity for the Cartoon Network show *Aqua Teen Hunger Force,* Turner Broadcasting arranged for its street operatives Sean Stevens and Peter Berdovsky to place 40 blinking black boxes in public places around Boston. Unfortunately, while the campaign's creators saw the blinking lights as a humorous outline of a cartoon character making an obscene gesture, a few Bostonians saw possible bombs and alerted the police. Stevens and Berdovsky were arrested and charged with a felony: placing a hoax device with the intent to cause anxiety. For 48 hours, the Boston affair upstaged the Super Bowl. Was it great publicity for a cartoon show—or just irresponsible fear mongering?

Sources: Andrew Hampp, "Lite-Brites, Big City and a Whole Load of Trouble," *Advertising Age,* February 5, 2007, 1, 34; and Jennifer Levitz and Emily Steel, "Boston Stunt Draws Legal, Ethical Fire," *The Wall Street Journal,* February 2, 2007, B3.

---

proactive public relations strategy
PR strategy that is dictated by marketing objectives, seeks publicity, and takes the offense

The appeal of publicity—when the information is positive—is that it tends to carry heightened credibility. Publicity from stories on television and radio and in newspapers and magazines assumes an air of believability because of the credibility of the media context. Not-for-profit organizations often use publicity in the form of news and public-interest stories to gain widespread visibility at little or no cost.

Publicity is not always entirely out of the company's control. For instance, during the Academy Awards, a bracelet worn by actress Julia Roberts caused a stir. After Roberts won the award for best actress, she waved to the cameras, and suddenly the whole world wanted to know about the snowflake-design Van Cleef & Arpels bracelet adorning her right (waving) wrist. For the designers, that wasn't just a lucky break. The episode had been carefully planned by Van Cleef's PR agency, Ted, Inc., which lobbied hard to convince

Roberts that the bracelet and matching earrings were stunning with her dress, knowing that if she won the Oscar, she would be highly photographed.[12]

Is there truth to the old saying "There's no such thing as bad publicity"? Stirring up a controversy is a sure way to get publicity, and many companies and their brands thrive on publicity. In most cases, a brand benefits from being in the news. But controversy can backfire if it generates ill will.

LO 3 PR Strategies

Although there are many ways to use public relations as part of a firm's overall IMC effort, the options fall into two basic categories of PR strategies:

1. **Proactive public relations strategy** is guided by marketing objectives, seeks to publicize a company and its brands, and takes an offensive rather than defensive posture in the public relations process.

2. **Reactive public relations strategy** is dictated by influences outside the control of a company, focuses on problems to be solved rather than on opportunities, and requires a company to take defensive measures.

These two strategies involve different orientations to public relations.

Proactive Strategy

In developing a proactive PR strategy, a firm acknowledges opportunities to use public relations to accomplish something positive. Companies often rely heavily on their PR firms to help them put together a proactive strategy. Such a strategy aims to ensure that positive messages such as employee achievements, corporate contributions to the community, and the organization's social and environmental programs do not go unnoticed by important constituents.

To implement a proactive strategy, a firm needs to develop a comprehensive PR program. Such a program has two key components:

1. A **public relations audit** identifies the firm's characteristics or aspects of its activities that are positive and newsworthy. Those conducting the audit gather information much as they would for developing an advertising strategy: by questioning customers and collecting company information such as descriptions of company products and services, market performance of brands, profitability, goals for products, market trends, new product introductions, important suppliers, important customers, employee programs and facilities, community programs, and charitable activities.

2. Once the firm is armed with information from a public relations audit, it develops a structured **public relations plan**. This plan identifies the objectives and activities related to the firm's PR communications. The components of a public relations plan are described in Exhibit 13.1.

A proactive public relations strategy can make an important supportive contribution to a firm's IMC effort. Carefully placing positive information targeted to potentially influential constituents—such as members of the community or stockholders—supports the overall goal of enhancing the image, reputation, and perception of a firm and its brands.

Reactive Strategy

A reactive PR strategy may seem like a contradiction in terms, but as stated earlier, firms must implement a reactive strategy when events outside their control create negative publicity. Coca-Cola reined in negative publicity by acting swiftly after an unfortunate incident in Europe. Seven days after a bottling problem caused teens in Belgium and France to become sick after drinking Coke, the firm pulled all Coca-Cola products from the market and issued an apology from the CEO.[13] Coca-Cola's quick actions could not prevent a decline in product sales. That would call for new marketing programs tailored to meet the needs of consumers on a country-by-country basis. The

Council for Biotechnology Information

Biotechnology is helping him protect the land and preserve his family's heritage.

"I'm raising a better soybean crop that helps me conserve the topsoil, keep my land productive and help this farm support future generations of my family." —Rod Gangwish, farmer

Biotechnology is helping Rod Gangwish to grow a type of soybean that requires less tilling of the soil. That helps him preserve precious topsoil and produce a crop with less impact on the land. Preserving topsoil today means a thriving farm for generations to come. Biotechnology allows farmers to choose the best combination of ways to help grow their crops. It helps cotton farmers use fewer chemicals to protect their crops against certain pests. And, it's helping provide ways for developing countries to better feed a growing population. And, in the future, it can help farmers grow better quality, more nutritious food. Biotechnology is also enhancing lives in other ways, helping to create more effective treatments for diseases such as leukemia and diabetes. Biotechnology is helping create solutions that are improving lives today, and solutions that could improve our world tomorrow. If you're interested in learning more, visit our Web site or call the number below for a free brochure about biotechnology and agriculture.

COUNCIL FOR BIOTECHNOLOGY INFORMATION

good ideas are growing

1-800-980-8660
www.whybiotech.com

The biotechnology industry is subject to controversy regarding the use of genetically altered food and seed products. In this advertisement, the Council for Biotechnology Information, an industry group, attempts to take a proactive approach to dealing with the controversy by presenting a positive image and information.

Exhibit 13.1
Components of a PR Plan

Situation analysis	Summary of information obtained from the public relations audit, often broken down by category, such as product performance or community activity
Program objectives	Objectives stemming from the current situation and set for both short-term and long-term opportunities; generally focus on reputation, such as the credibility of product performance (e.g., placing products in verified, independent tests) or the stature of the firm's research and development efforts (article in a prestigious trade publication)
Program rationale	Identification of the PR program's role relative to the other brand promotion efforts; articulates an integrated marketing communication perspective
Communications vehicles	Specification of the tools (e.g., press releases, interviews, newsletters) to be used to implement the PR plan
Message content	Development of the PR message based on research such as focus groups and in-depth interviews

© Cengage Learning 2011.

programs relied heavily on IMC strategies including free samples, dealer incentive programs, and beach parties featuring sound and light shows, DJs, and cocktail bars with free Cokes to win back the critical teen segment.[14] In the end, this integrated effort restored trust and rebuilt the business across Europe.

It is difficult to organize for and provide structure around reactive PR. Because the events that trigger a reactive effort are unpredictable and uncontrollable, a firm simply must be prepared to act quickly and thoughtfully. Two steps help firms implement a reactive public relations strategy:

1. *Public relations audit:* The public relations audit prepared for the proactive strategy helps a firm prepare its reactive strategy. The information in the audit helps the company issue public statements based on current and accurate data.

2. *Identification of vulnerabilities:* To be ready for a reactive strategy, companies need to recognize their *vulnerabilities*—areas of weakness in their operations or products that can damage relationships with important constituents. If aspects of a firm's operations are vulnerable to criticism, such as environmental issues related to manufacturing processes, then the PR function should be prepared to discuss the issues in a broad range of forums with various constituents.

When these steps don't uncover vulnerabilities, companies will be taken by surprise. Surprises are just about inevitable for Walmart's PR staff. Considering

that the company operates more than 3,750 stores in the United States and serves 140 million shoppers a week, odds are that some of the things that go wrong will go wrong at Walmart. Still, it's hard to imagine how to prepare for some of the incidents that Walmart has been asked to comment on, such as the nutria (a rodent) that scared a shopper in Louisiana so badly that she ran over her foot with a shopping cart, breaking bones, or the case of the man in Virginia who allegedly donned a cow costume, stole 26 gallons of milk, and handed them out in the store's parking lot.[15] That's not even counting the births, marriages, and deaths that have taken place inside various Walmart stores. In a company that is so enormous and deals with the public every day, PR staffers simply have to think fast and expect challenges.

Keeping PR Integrated

Public relations, as much as every other method of brand promotion, must be part of an integrated and synergistic effort to communicate with diverse audiences. If a company fails to recognize PR activities as a component of the firm's overall communication effort, misinformation or disinformation may compromise the impact of advertising or other efforts at marketing communication. The coordination of public relations and other elements of an integrated program is a matter of recognizing and identifying the PR

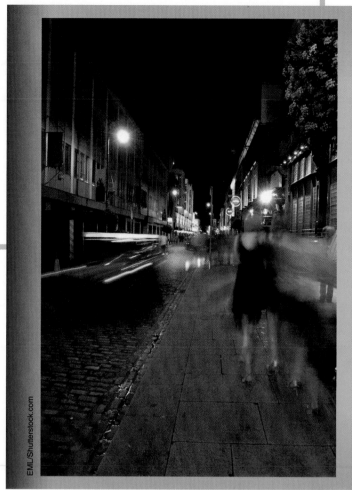

GLOBAL
GUINNESS AS CULTURAL ICON

Guinness has attracted tourists to its St. James's Gate Brewery in Dublin, Ireland, for more than a century. But as visitor traffic grew to thousands per year, the reception area could no longer handle the volume. Goals for a new reception/visitor area included preserving the tradition of the brand, accommodating devotees who flocked to Dublin to connect with the brand's "spiritual home," and appealing to younger Irish consumers, who have been tempted by new beers and other drinks. The solution: a new seven-story structure called the Guinness Storehouse, which preserved and incorporated the five-story Market Street Storehouse, a Guinness storage facility in the early 1900s. It's now Ireland's number one fee-paying tourist spot.

Source: Arundhati Parmar, "Guinness Intoxicates," *Marketing News*, November 10, 2003, 4, 6.

process as critical to the overall IMC effort and getting the right players on the team. At Guinness, for example, marketers understand that the historical nature of the 250-year-old brand of stout beer is essential to the brand's appeal. Therefore, preserving the brewery as a tourist attraction is as much a brand promotion effort as its advertising and sales promotions.

LO 4 Influencer Marketing

If public relations is the discipline devoted to monitoring and managing how people view us, then it also can be thought of as a discipline devoted to monitoring and managing what consumers are saying to one another about us. Moreover, because consumers have become increasingly predisposed to talk about our brands anyway, it seems prudent to follow the advice of Bonnie

Raitt, who in her album *Luck of the Draw* sings in her 1990s blues-rock hit, "Let's give them something to talk about!"

The idea of giving people something to talk about underlies the evolution of influencer marketing. As defined by Northlich, a leader in influencer marketing programming, **influencer marketing** refers to a series of personalized marketing techniques directed at individuals or groups who have the credibility and capability to drive positive word-of-mouth in a broader and salient segment of the population. Whether these influential people are professionals or peers, marketing to them so that they influence others can provide one of the most valued assets for any brand builder—an advocacy message from a trusted source.[16] Think of influencer marketing as systematic seeding of conversations involving a consumer, an influencer, and a brand.

influencer marketing series of personalized marketing techniques directed at individuals or groups with the credibility and capability to drive positive word-of-mouth in a market segment

Professional Influencers

If you're a pet owner, you've probably made many visits to the vet. And perhaps you asked your vet about the best products to feed your puppy or kitten. If so, you know what comes next. Not only is the vet ready to talk about proper feeding, he or she may offer you product samples or brochures describing the benefits of a particular brand of pet food. Coincidence? Not at all. The makers of IAMS, Eukanuba, and Hill's Science Diet know that vets are key influencers in the decision about what to feed one's pet, especially for devoted pet owners who don't mind paying a little extra to get the best. These brands target vets with influencer marketing programs aimed at earning their recommendation.

Many professionals are in a similar position. Your doctor, auto mechanic, and hair stylist all have the credibility to influence product choices in their specific areas of expertise. Sometimes the opportunity is obvious, as with vets recommending pet food. But more and more, creative programming takes influencer programming into new territory. An excellent example is how Select Comfort targets various types of healthcare professionals with an influencer program for its Sleep Number bed. For instance, Select Comfort targets occupational therapists (OTs), who provide therapy to individuals with serious physical challenges, helping them learn to carry out basic tasks of living. But are OTs experts on sleep? It doesn't matter. Many of their patients are likely to value their opinions, and all healthcare professionals commonly hear complaints from their patients about having trouble sleeping.

Obviously, if you're Select Comfort, you'd like the OT to encourage patients to have a look at the Sleep Number bed. Select Comfort starts by giving OTs firsthand experience with the product. Special promotions encourage OTs to purchase Sleep Number beds for their own bedrooms. Next, Select Comfort buys mailing lists from OT professional associations and journals in order to build a marketing database. When an OT expresses interest in the Sleep Number bed, Select Comfort sends the therapist an advocacy kit containing brochures and other helpful materials. Marketers at Select Comfort cannot control what the OT tells patients about the Sleep Number bed, but they can make available materials that will make becoming an advocate easy if the OT believes it is justified.

Professionals in any field of endeavor take their role seriously, so influencer programs directed to them must be handled with great care. When developing programs for professionals, keep in mind that their time is money, so any program that wastes their time will be a waste of money. Valuable tactics include encouraging professionals to try the product themselves and delivering messages that are up-to-date and help the professional learn important benefits of the brand. For example, healthcare professionals' concerns will be better addressed through clinical studies than celebrity endorsements. Additionally, programs directed at professionals require a long-term commitment. Professionals will advocate only for brands they trust, and marketers needs patience and persistence to earn that trust.

Peer-to-Peer Programs

Peer-to-peer programs typically have a very different tone than programs for professionals. In peer-to-peer programs, the objective is to give influencers something fun or provocative to talk about. A great guiding principle for peer-to-peer programs is "Do something remarkable" to get people talking about your brand.[17] To promote Virgin Mobile's "Nothing to Hide" campaign, Richard Branson descended into Times Square on a giant cell phone while performing a striptease act. To promote a book launch,

David Davis/Shutterstock.com

PROFESSIONALS WILL ADVOCATE ONLY FOR BRANDS THEY TRUST.

BzzAgent links marketing clients with consumers willing to write passionately about brands online.

German publisher Eichborn attached tiny banners to 200 flies and let them buzz around at a book fair.[18]

But today's practice of influencer marketing amounts to more than publicity stunts. For one thing, peer-to-peer programs are shaped by the experience and sophistication of organizations like Northlich and Keller Fay Group, which assist clients with influencer programming. Keller Fay has developed a tracking system that can estimate the number of word-of-mouth conversations taking place daily. Another key supplier is Nielsen BuzzMetrics, which provides services for tracking word-of-mouth activity across the Internet. And with billions of conversations every day, a lot of brand builders, from Kodak to Kashi, want to be involved.[19]

One area where we see dramatic advancements in influencer marketing on the peer-to-peer side involves identifying and cultivating connectors. Procter & Gamble has been building a connector database, focusing on women who have large social networks. P&G searches for them over the Internet at sites like iVillage.com and is always looking for referrals. (It seems connectors like the idea of being the first to receive new product samples and to feel that their voice is being heard by a big company.) One of P&G's connectors is Donna Wetherell, an outgoing mom who works at a customer-service call center, where she knows about 300 coworkers by name. She likes to talk about shopping and many different brands. She always seems to have a lot of extra coupons for the brands she likes—her coworkers call her the coupon lady. Donna is only one of 600,000 connectors that P&G has enrolled in its influencer program, called Vocalpoint.[20]

Once a company has developed a connector database, the influencer program gets back to basics: giving the connectors something to talk about. But it's not always simple to get consumers talking about a product like dishwashing detergent, so companies that sell such products have to start by finding a motivation to talk. P&G execs assert, "We do tremendous research behind it to give them a reason to care."[21] Just as with professional programs, you can't force someone to be an advocate for your brand. You can identify people who have big social networks, but they're not going to compromise their relationships with others by sharing dull stories or phony information. You must give them something interesting to talk about.

As marketers gain experience in influencer marketing, they are demystifying what once was mysterious: word-of-mouth marketing. A pioneer in this regard is Andy Sernovitz, who founded the Word-of-Mouth Marketing Association (WOMMA) in 2004. The WOMMA website, http://www.womma.org, is a great resource for learning more about influencer marketing. In his book *Word of Mouth Marketing: How Smart Companies Get People Talking*, Sernovitz draws on numerous cases for a wide variety of brands to offer up success principles for those who desire favorable word-of-mouth. Turns out it's as simple as the Five *T*s, spelled out in Exhibit 13.2. And applying the Five *T*s nowadays tends to take marketers into the new realm of social media.

LO 5   Social Media

Today, more people are using community websites like Facebook and MySpace than are using email.[22] These social-networking sites have revolutionized the way marketers think about mediated communication. From the earliest work on brand communities, Muniz and O'Guinn noted that communication about brands in these communities has three nodes, rather than the

Exhibit 13.2
Five "T"s of Peer-to-Peer Influence

Talkers	Find and get to know the people who are predisposed to talk about brands in general and/or your brand in particular.
Topics	Give the talkers something to talk about—not a marketing message or mission statement but a mystery or engaging story or breaking news. For example, Apple's Steve Jobs created interest with suspenseful product announcements and an implied promise that the next great thing is just around the corner.
Tools	Make good use of the tools that promote conversations. A story on a blog is more portable than a story on a corporate Web page.
Taking part	Instead of one-way communication, think in terms of dialogue. Listen to the conversations already taking place. You have to be tuned in if you ever want to join the conversation.
Tracking	Word-of-mouth on the Internet is very measurable. Keep track of what people are saying about your brand and why they are saying it.

Sources: Andy Sernovitz, *Word of Mouth Marketing: How Smart Companies Get People Talking* (Chicago: Kaplan Publishing, 2006); and Michael Krauss, "To Generate Buzz, Do Remarkable Things," *Marketing News*, December 15, 2006.

social media websites where users create and share information about themselves, brands, and other mutual interests

traditional two (see Exhibit 13.3). In other words, not only do consumers interact with the brand, as they do when viewing an ad or entering a sweepstakes, but they also talk to each other about brands they care about. Thanks to the Internet, these brand-related interactions happen instantaneously, at almost no cost, and with huge numbers of participants.

These three-way online communications take place using what marketers call **social media**—websites where users create and share information about themselves, brands, and other mutual interests. The applications of social media continue to multiply, but the following are some of the most relevant to marketers:[23]

- Social networking on sites such as Facebook and MySpace

- Business networking on sites such as LinkedIn

- Works sharing on sites such as YouTube (for videos) and Flickr (for photos)

- Blogs, which may be sponsored by users (Cnet.com) or companies (Apple.com)

- Microblogging—sending short messages to subscribers (Twitter)

- Commerce communities, such as Amazon and Craigslist

- Social bookmarking—used for recommending content (for example, Digg and Reddit)

- Collaborative projects, such as Wikipedia

An important implication of social media is that marketers no longer generate all the important brand communications. Rather, consumers are making and distributing brand material—even ads—on the Internet. These may be celebrating beloved brands or mocking brands or brand messages that consumers find ridiculous. Consumer-generated content costs marketers nothing and offers them no control over the message. Several marketers have told of receiving a lot of great feedback for an Internet ad and calling their ad agency with congratulations, only to be told that the agency has no idea what the marketer is talking about. The ad turns out to have been made by some 14-year-old kid in Ohio.

Shaping the Message

Social media's impact on the marketing environment can be a little bit frightening: Nasty product reviews or satirical versions of the company's ads are only

Exhibit 13.3
New Brand Relationships with Social Media

Traditional Relationship:
Brand to Customer

New Relationship:
Brand Community

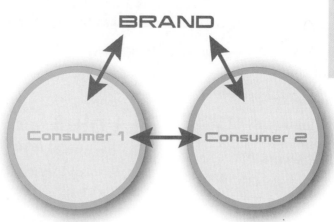

© Cengage Learning 2011.

two of the possible new publicity nightmares. But for marketers who can shape the messages spread online, social media also present a tremendous opportunity.[24]

One way marketers can shape conversations about their brands is by creating venues online for consumers to gather around a brand-related interest or value. Procter & Gamble has set up Facebook pages for its brands, and on those pages during the 2010 Olympics, P&G posted links to a YouTube video of its sponsorship advertisement.[25] To facilitate this sort of activity, YouTube offers a media kit for setting up an Advertising Brand Channel and guidelines for posting ad campaigns directly on the site.

Marketers also can invite consumer feedback via social media. Toyota invites drivers, automobile enthusiasts, and journalists to post replies to its Open Road Blog. The Red Robin restaurant chain invites customers to complete satisfaction surveys. Those who give the restaurant high ratings are asked to post a recommendation on their Facebook pages; about one out of five agrees to do so.[26] Because the wording of the recommendations comes from the individual consumers, these brand messages come across as more natural and sincere than a company-generated message. Of course, you also have to be prepared for negative feedback. When someone complains, be ready to offer an apology, a coupon, or a way to fix problems.

Participants in social media want to feel like they are collaborating with others, not just being sold to. Marketers can become trusted participants in the conversation by sharing valuable information, such as tips for using their products, details about ingredients and prices, solutions to product-related problems, or

general advice on brand-related topics, say, health or parenting. Videos and podcasts should be entertaining as well as informative; for example, instead of only saying your product is durable, make a video showing how it withstands tough conditions. Another way to talk about subjects consumers care about is to get involved in a social cause that matters to targeted consumers. Marketers also can personalize messages by taking advantage of the fact that many social-media venues provide information about participants—say, a profile on LinkedIn or a status message that tells where an individual is located or even what mood the person is in.[27]

Marketers using social media are to some extent relying on consumers to spread the word. Therefore, they should be careful to create messages that will be conveyed accurately. That means brand advantages should be clear, memorable, and easy to describe.

Buzz and Viral Marketing

Marketers often turn to social media to create buzz and stimulate viral marketing. Both of these objectives rely on word-of-mouth communication:

- **Buzz marketing** involves creating an event or experience that yields conversations that include the brand.

- **Viral marketing** is the process of consumers marketing to consumers via the Web (e.g., via blogs or forwarding YouTube links) or through personal contact stimulated by a firm marketing a brand.

Both buzz and viral marketing strategies target a handful of carefully chosen trendsetters or connectors as influencers, letting them spread the word.[28]

Following potential users' comments posted online helped IBM decide how to communicate its brand message for Lotus software. The company learned that people didn't talk about technology and features but about what they were trying to do with the software. IBM used the insights to develop its "Lotus Knows" theme.

Then, once the word is out, spreading it becomes a collaborative activity, no longer under the marketer's control. To be sure that the word gets spread at all, marketers must have a message with social value: interesting content, valuable brand features, and a website where consumers can get actively involved with the brand.[29] One company that gets this right is Procter & Gamble with its Old Spice brand promotion. P&G created a fun, memorable character, its Old Spice Guy, the idealized "man your man could smell like," launched him in a Super Bowl ad, and posted the ad on YouTube, where hundreds of people were watching it within hours of the big game. A few months later, the main social media campaign got going. Visitors to Old Spice social media pages were invited to submit questions, and a small production team quickly filmed Old Spice Guy delivering witty answers, which were posted on YouTube. Consumers also can visit Old Spice's Facebook page to read wall posts reflecting Old Spice Guy's over-the-top lifestyle and to post their comments. These and other interactive projects have generated millions of views and turned consumers into fans of the brand.[30]

The offline components of buzz marketing programs often are fielded in major cities because places like New York and London are where you find the most trendsetters. Consider this scene at the cafés on Third Street Promenade in and around Los Angeles. A gang of sleek, impossibly attractive bikers pulls up, and guess what, they seem *genuinely* interested in getting to know you over an iced latte—their treat! Sooner or later, the conversation turns to their Vespa scooters glinting in the sun, and they eagerly pull out a pad and jot down an address and phone number—for the nearest Vespa dealer. The scooter-riding, latte-drinking models are on the Vespa payroll, and they're paid to create buzz about the scooters by engaging hip café dwellers in conversation.[31]

Generating buzz is important because it gets the brand noticed and sparks interest in trying the product. But for long-term success, marketers have to turn buzz into brand loyalty and sales. For that, they have to incorporate social-media messages into a broader IMC campaign. Threadless created buzz with its collaborative process for generating T-shirt designs: Anyone can post a design idea at the Threadless website, and then site visitors vote for their favorites, which are printed on shirts for sale. To sustain interest, Threadless has added sales promotion to its brand communications; the company sends gift codes and premiums to its followers on Twitter. Similarly, Batter Blaster generated a lot of buzz when it launched its innovative product, organic

THE CHANCE TO WATCH AND INTERACT WITH THE OH-SO-PERFECT OLD SPICE GUY HAS SENT MILLIONS OF VIEWERS TO YOUTUBE AND OTHER SOCIAL MEDIA HOSTED BY THE OLD SPICE BRAND.

Image Courtesy of The Advertising Archives.

corporate advertising advertising intended to establish a favorable attitude toward a company as a whole

pancake batter sold in aerosol cans. Consumers fell in love with Batter Blaster, blogged about it, and posted videos about it on YouTube. To keep interest high, the company has added sampling and event sponsorship to its integrated marketing communication.[32]

Measuring Results

Maybe you're not in total control of your message on social media, but as a marketer, you still need to know whether the time and effort of social media are worthwhile. And in a sign that social media are firmly entrenched in the promotional mix, research services now are offering marketers performance metrics akin to those for other media. For example, Nielsen Buzz-Metrics tracks more than a million blogs, social networks, and other consumer-generated online content to provide clients with information such as where conversations about the brand are taking place, what people are saying about the brand, and when threats to the brand's reputation are developing. Radian6 scans more than 100 million websites, including blogs, Twitter, and public Facebook groups to find messages, videos, and photos related to clients' brands. It delivers statistics such as the volume of comments, reach of messages, and type of consumer sentiment. Data also can be integrated with Web analytics software to measure how much traffic is being driven to the marketer's website from the social media—and even who is driving the most traffic and how much of that traffic leads to sales or subscriptions at the website.

One advantage of services like Radian6 and BuzzMetrics is that they offer real-time tracking and reporting. Online messages move fast—that's the thrill and terror of viral marketing—so if marketers don't like what's being said, they have to jump into the conversation immediately. Marketers also can watch social-media activity when they engage in other types of brand communication, such as an ad campaign or press release, to see whether those efforts are generating the desired buzz. If not, they can tweak their efforts right away.

This kind of immediate feedback rewards marketers for being flexible and responsive. Consider how data on social media helped Dell with its launch of the Mini 9 notebook computer. The buzz started almost immediately after a blogger spotted Michael Dell carrying a prototype at a technology conference four months before the product was to be released. As Dell marketers followed messages posted to technology blogs, forums, and social-networking sites, they selectively posted bits of information and corrected errors. They learned what consumers were expecting and used the information to adjust the product design and marketing messages. When the Mini 9 was released, Dell was ready with an on-target product and marketing campaign, and the buzz had reached a state of intense excitement that drove high demand. In addition, Dell's efforts to track social-media traffic helped the company identify key influencers, whom the company can target for roles in future brand communication.[33]

LO 6 Corporate Advertising

When social media are used to create buzz about the company as a whole, rather than a particular brand or product, the effort falls under the umbrella of corporate advertising. **Corporate advertising** is designed to establish a favorable attitude toward a company as a whole, rather than to promote the benefits of a specific brand. It typically uses major media to communicate a unique, broad-based message that is distinct from the company's product-specific brand building and contributes to the development of an overall image for a firm.

Corporate advertising often addresses the firm's trustworthiness and reputation. As consumers are becoming increasingly informed and sophisticated, they demand a higher standard of conduct from the companies they patronize. When a company has established trust and integrity, it has an easier time building productive relationships with consumers.

Scope of Corporate Advertising

Highly regarded and successful firms use corporate advertising to enhance the image of the firm and affect consumers' attitudes. The use of corporate advertising

Delight in everyday perfection.

ELKAY.
elkay.com

specialty collection sinks. Style that endures.

© Elkay Manufacturing

Quality System ISO 9001 Certified ©2003 Elkay

Firms often use corporate advertising as a way to generate name recognition and a positive image for the firm. Here Elkay, a high-end manufacturer of sinks and other plumbing fixtures, touts the company name, rather than any specific features of a brand.

is gaining favor worldwide. Firms with the stature of General Electric and Toyota are investing in corporate ad campaigns. Billions of dollars are spent annually to buy media space and time for these campaigns.

Interestingly, most corporate campaigns run by consumer-goods manufacturers are undertaken by firms in the shopping-goods category, such as appliance and auto marketers. Studies also have found that larger firms are much more prevalent users of corporate advertising than smaller firms are. Presumably, these larger firms have broader communications programs and more money to invest in advertising, which allows the use of corporate campaigns.

In terms of media, magazines and television are well suited to corporate advertising. Corporate advertising appearing in magazines has the advantage of being able to target particular constituent groups with image- or issue-related messages. Magazines also provide the space for lengthy copy, which often is needed to achieve corporate advertising objectives. Television is a popular choice for corporate campaigns because the creative opportunities provided by television can deliver a powerful, emotional message.

Objectives of Corporate Advertising

The objectives for corporate advertising should be focused. In fact, corporate advertising shares similar purposes with proactive public relations. Here are some of the possibilities for a corporate campaign:

- To build the image of the firm among customers, shareholders, the financial community, and/or the general public
- To boost employee morale or attract new employees
- To communicate an organization's views on social, political, or environmental issues
- To better position the firm's products against competition, particularly foreign competition
- To play a role in the company's overall advertising and IMC strategy, providing a platform for more brand-specific campaigns

Corporate advertising is not always targeted at consumers. Rather, the effort can target a broad range of constituents. For example, when Glaxo Wellcome and SmithKline Beecham merged to form a $73 billion pharmaceutical behemoth, the newly created firm, known as GlaxoSmithKline, launched an international print campaign aimed at investors who had doubts about the viability of the new corporate structure. The campaign was all about image

Exhibit 13.4
Varieties of Corporate Advertising

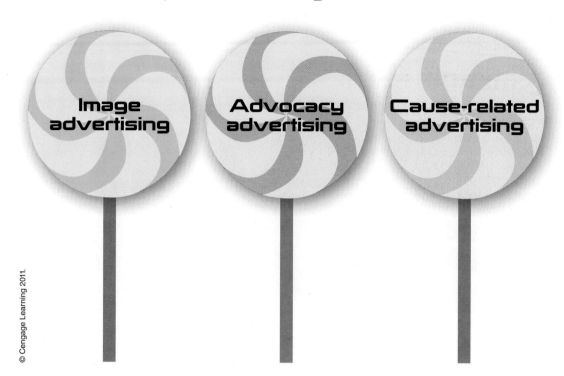

advocacy advertising advertising that attempts to influence public opinion about social, political, or environmental issues of concern to the advertiser

cause-related marketing marketing messages that identify corporate sponsorship of philanthropic activities

and led with the theme "Disease does not wait. Neither will we."[34]

Types of Corporate Advertising

Corporate advertising campaigns are dominated by three basic types: image advertising, advocacy advertising, and cause-related advertising (see Exhibit 13.4). In addition, green marketing is an important special case that could fall within any of these.

Image Advertising

The majority of corporate advertising efforts focus on enhancing the overall image of a firm among important constituents—typically customers, employees, and the general public. When IBM promotes itself as the firm providing "Solutions for a small planet" or when General Mills says it is engaged in "Nourishing Lives," the goal is to enhance the overall image of the firm.

Bolstering a firm's image may not result in immediate effects on sales, but as we saw in Chapter 5, attitude can play an important directive force in consumer decision making. When a firm can enhance its overall image, it may well affect consumer predisposition in brand choice.[35]

Energy giant Shell Oil developed a series of television, print, online, and outdoor ads to tout its efforts to develop cleaner sources of energy. The ads announce that Shell is "ready to help tackle the challenge of the new energy future."[36] Launched in 2010, just as oil from a BP-owned oil rig was gushing into the Gulf of Mexico, the campaign also implied that where BP (whose corporate message was "Beyond Petroleum") had stumbled, Shell intended to succeed. Only time will tell whether Shell will deliver on that bold promise.

Advocacy Advertising

Advocacy advertising attempts to establish an organization's position on important social or political issues. Advocacy advertising attempts to influence public opinion on issues of concern to a firm. Typically, the issue featured in an advocacy campaign is directly relevant to the business operations of the organization. For example, Burt's Bees advocates for a Natural Standard for Personal Care Products. This message is perfectly aligned with its business model, which is based on developing and selling products that feature natural ingredients.

Cause-Related Marketing

Cause-related marketing features a firm's affiliation with an important social or societal cause (for example, reducing poverty, increasing literacy, conserving

General Electric's Ecoimagination program is based on the assumption that conserving the planet's resources also is good business. GE isn't shy about promoting that theme through corporate advertising, such as this message about its commitment to wind energy.

Photo Courtesy, OmniTerra Images.

energy, protecting the environment, and curbing drug abuse). The goal of cause-related marketing can be to enhance the image of the firm by associating it with important social issues; this tends to work best when the firm confronts an issue that truly connects to its business. Anheuser-Busch's efforts to promote the control of teenage drinking, described in Chapter 6, are a good example. This campaign helps establish the firm as a responsible marketer of alcoholic beverages, while also helping society deal with an important problem.

Cause-related marketing often features philanthropic activities funded by a company. Each year, *Promo Magazine* publishes an extensive list of charitable, philanthropic, and environmental organizations that have formal programs in which corporations may participate. Most of the programs suggest a minimum donation for corporate sponsorship and specify how the organization's resources will be mobilized in conjunction with the sponsor's other resources.

Cause-related marketing is becoming increasingly common. One reason for the increase is that research supports the wisdom of such expenditures. In a consumer survey conducted by Cone, a Boston-based brand strategy firm, 91 percent of respondents said they have a more favorable impression of companies that support good causes; respondents also said the causes a company supports can be a valid reason for switching brands.[37] Other studies indicate that support of good causes can translate into brand preference—and, importantly, that consumers will judge a firm's motives for the support.[38] If the firm's support is perceived as disingenuous, cause-related expenditures are largely wasted.

One also would like to think that the trend toward greater use of cause-related marketing is fueled by a desire to do the right thing. For instance, Whirlpool Corporation is a Habitat Cornerstone Partner and has assisted in the massive rebuilding effort needed in the wake of Hurricane Katrina. Jeff Terry, who manages the program of donations and volunteering on behalf of Whirlpool, says of the experience: "The first time you do this work, it will change your life."[39] Sure, Whirlpool's participation in this program brings the company a lot of favorable publicity, but its people's hearts also appear to be in the right place. That makes the program a win/win activity for everyone involved.

The range of firms participating in cause-related marketing programs continues to grow. Pedigree has built its dog food brand through a commitment to finding homes for orphan animals, with free food and grant support given to rescue shelters. PepsiCo's Refresh Project gives away small grants to businesses and nonprofits that do good for their communities in a variety of ways. Consumers get involved with the brand by voting online for the causes they want Pepsi to support.[40]

Green Marketing

Among the many causes backed by companies, one area in particular seems to offer opportunities: concern for protecting and sustaining the natural environment. Corporate communication efforts that embrace a cause or a program in support of the environment are popularly known as **green marketing**. Such efforts include Timberland's use of shoe boxes made out of 100 percent recycled materials and the "Dawn Saves Wildlife" program sponsored by Procter & Gamble. General Electric's "Ecoimagination" campaign is another high-profile exemplar of this movement. In funding this corporate campaign, GE has taken the stance that it simply is a good business strategy to seek real solutions to problems like air pollution and fossil-fuel dependency.[41]

The green marketing movement has been on again and off again, especially in the United States. In the early 1990s, Jacquelyn Ottman's book *Green Marketing* predicted that going green would be a marketing revolution. It didn't come to pass, at least not in the United States. However, many signs now suggest that this time around, green marketing really will take hold as a major opportunity for businesses, maybe just in time to save our planet. Most informed people now accept the inconvenient truth that our addiction to fossil fuels is putting the planet at risk. Surveys show that environmental issues are of major concern to consumers, and a formidable segment is acting on this concern.[42] The green movement looks sustainable this time around.

In addition, the Internet again is changing the game. Companies no longer can pay lip service to environmental causes but hide their true motives. Websites like Green Seal and EnviroLink can assist in determining who really is doing what to protect the environment. Motivated, well-informed consumers are hard to fool, so it doesn't pay to make token gestures on behalf of the planet. When it comes to getting it right with green (or any other) marketing, firms just need to follow the one immutable law of branding: Underpromise and overdeliver.

> **green marketing**
> corporate communication efforts to promote a cause or program in support of the environment

STUDY TOOLS
CHAPTER 13

Located at back of the textbook
- **Rip out Chapter in Review Card.**

Located at www.cengagebrain.com
- **Review Key Terms Flashcards (Print or Online).**
- **Complete the Practice Quiz to prepare for tests.**
- **Play "Beat the Clock" and "Quizbowl" to master concepts.**
- **Complete "Crossword Puzzle" to review key terms.**
- **Watch videos on Red The Lazarus Effect and JCPenny for real company examples.**
- **For additional examples, go online to learn about green initiatives and buzz builders.**

PRO

Personal Selling
and Sales
Management

Sant's salespeople talk to its clients—other salespeople—in their language and about their goals.

Sant Corporation has developed software to help sales teams create more effective sales presentations.

Learning Outcomes

After studying this chapter, you should be able to:

LO 1   Explain why personal selling is important in brand promotion.

LO 2   Describe the activities besides selling performed by salespeople.

LO 3   Summarize the role of setting objectives for personal selling.

LO 4   Outline the steps involved in personal selling.

LO 5   Describe factors that contribute to a new environment for personal selling.

LO 6   Define the responsibilities of sales force management.

"Character is the salesman's stock in trade. It is he who must first sell himself."

—George Matthew Adams

Selling to Salespeople

AFTER YOU FINISH THIS CHAPTER GO TO PAGE 305 FOR STUDY TOOLS

If choosing a brand of jeans or a computer takes effort, consider the challenges faced by business managers. Their purchase decisions may be multiplied by thousands or even millions of units. Their choices affect the company's bottom line, its image, and its ability to satisfy customers. No wonder, then, that these customers want to talk to a human being—a salesperson—who can help them sort through their options.

That kind of marketing works great as long as salespeople speak their customers' language. But companies that sell highly technical products, such as software systems or manufacturing equipment, often rely on people with great technical expertise, who may not readily see situations from their business-oriented customers' point of view. Enter Sant Corporation. Founded by Tom Sant, a former English professor and writing consultant, the company has developed software that helps sales teams create more effective presentations.

A typical sales presentation starts with background about the salesperson's company. In contrast, Sant Corporation's products help salespeople analyze customers' needs and build each presentation around a desired outcome, such as cutting inventory costs, showing how the salesperson's products or services can help the customer reach the desired outcome.[1] The Sant software bases its guidance on academic research into communication persuasiveness. This frees technically oriented salespeople to focus on contributing their knowledge about their customers and their company's products. In addition, the software makes the creation of presentations more efficient by automatically producing standard data, graphs, and background information, such as prewritten statements of the selling company's strengths. Sant Corporation also provides consulting services to help its clients use the software effectively and improve their writing skills.

What do you think?

Salespeople succeed when they put the customer first.

1   2   3   4   5   6   7
STRONGLY DISAGREE   STRONGLY AGREE

Find out what others think at CourseMate for PROMO2.   283

Of course, Sant Corporation needs its own sales force, too. Dozens of employees at the Cincinnati-based company contact leads, applying the company's own expertise to explain how Sant can help clients close sales. They also follow up to make sure clients are satisfied.

Sant's salespeople keep up with all this information by using customer relationship management software from Salesforce.com. The Salesforce software includes a database of easily retrievable information important to salespeople:

- Details about prospects, including tasks and deadlines for moving a prospect to a contract for software and services

- Data about customers, including products purchased, so that salespeople can identify additional services to offer

- Results from customer surveys so that salespeople can follow up with unhappy clients

- Types of problems and how they were resolved so that salespeople can quickly identify solutions that have worked in the past

- Reports and research sharing employees' knowledge so that salespeople can learn from one another and better inform their clients with the most up-to-date versions of documents

Since Sant Corporation began using the Salesforce.com software, it has shrunk the time needed to provide customer support and has enjoyed dramatic growth in revenues and customer satisfaction.[2]

LO 1 Personal Selling

Despite the conspicuousness of advertising, sales promotion, sponsorships, and other tools in the promotional mix, personal selling is the most important force for communication in many corporations. Along with the Sant Corporation, firms as diverse as Xerox and Nordstrom rely primarily on personal selling for contacting customers, communicating, and closing sales. Formally defined, **personal selling** is the face-to-face communication and persuasion process. It includes many activities such as the ones described in the example of the Sant Corporation: assessing customer needs, communicating with them about how the salesperson's company can address those needs, and following up to make sure they are satisfied. Effective salespeople are careful listeners, skilled problem solvers, and persuasive writers and

Simon van den Berg/Shutterstock.com

speakers who are knowledgeable about their products and their customers.

Personal selling is a key part of many firms' activities. Some companies spend hundreds of dollars for each face-to-face sales call. Compensation paid to these salespeople can range up to more than $140,000 a year for a top-notch sales engineer or financial-services sales agent with in-depth knowledge of customers' needs. Another measure of the importance of personal selling is the number of people employed in the profession. The most recent statistics from the U.S. Department of Labor put the number of people employed in sales jobs at over 8 percent of the civilian labor force in the United States. And, as Exhibit 14.1 shows, the various categories of salespeople (except travel agents) are expected to grow through 2018 at least as fast as the overall growth in the number of jobs.[3]

There are good reasons why personal selling is the dominant component in the promotional mix for many firms. First, face-to-face communication is potent; it often generates action. And in many decision contexts, only a qualified and well-trained salesperson can address the questions and concerns of a potential buyer. Companies are especially dependent on personal selling if their products are higher priced, complicated to use, require demonstration, are tailored to

Exhibit 14.1
Number of Sales Jobs: Current and Projected

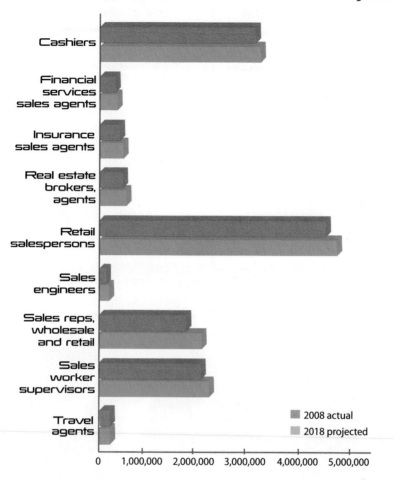

Source: Bureau of Labor Statistics, *Occupational Outlook Handbook: 2010–11*, http://data.bls.gov.

users' needs, involve a trade-in, or are judged at the point of purchase. For these products, a salesperson helps consumers and business buyers make a decision and obtain value from their purchases.

LO 2 What Salespeople Do

Often, salespeople are responsible for more than the selling effort; they also may implement various aspects of marketing strategy. In a very real sense, the sales force is the embodiment of the firm's entire marketing program. The responsibilities of salespeople have expanded to include the following activities:

- *Market analysis:* Because of their direct contact with customers, salespeople can provide information related to trends in overall demand. Regular contact with buyers

who also are buying competitors' products may help salespeople detect and report on competitors' activities.

- *Sales forecasting:* Salespeople can give marketing planners estimates of sales potential for the short and long term, based on the competitiveness of the firm's products and conditions in their customers' industries.

- *New product ideas:* Close contact with customers allows the sales force to detect unmet needs in the market and contribute ideas for new products.

- *Buyer behavior analysis:* The salesperson is in the best position to analyze buyer behavior. In negotiating sales with customers, the salesperson learns the criteria upon which buyers base their decisions. Salespeople feed this information to marketing strategists, who adjust the marketing and promotion mixes.

- *Communication:* To effectively inform and persuade customers, salespeople must be experts in communication methods. No matter how well the marketing mix is conceived, the sales force has to inform customers about the satisfaction to be gained from the brand.

customer relationship management (CRM) continual effort to cultivate and maintain long-term relationships with customers by emphasizing customer needs

- *Sales coordination:* The salesperson must coordinate the firm's many marketing and sales activities with the buyer.

- *Customer service:* When customers need service after a purchase, they turn first to the salesperson. Salespeople can coordinate product delivery, installation, training, and financing.

- *Customer relationship management:* Salespeople play an important role in building long-term relationships with customers—an effort referred to as **customer relationship management (CRM)**. For that reason, Merck spends 12 months training its sales representa-

tives, not only in knowledge of pharmaceuticals, but also in trust-building techniques. Its reps must take regular refresher courses as well. Similarly, General Electric stationed its own engineers full time at Praxair, a user of GE electrical equipment, to help the firm boost productivity.[4] Furthermore, CRM is a key strategy for gaining competitive advantage in foreign markets.[5]

Extending the idea of CRM, salespeople are instrumental in ensuring total customer satisfaction. Playing a role in marketing strategy, they do not simply approach customers with the intention of making a sale. Rather, they serve as problem solvers in partnership with customers. By accepting the role of analyzing customer needs and proposing solutions, the sales force

Sean Prior/Shutterstock.com

GLOBAL CRM WITHOUT BORDERS

CRM for a global sales team presents challenges beyond single-country programs. The first is to learn what sales reps need. When Information Systems Marketing developed a CRM for a German biotech company, it formed two teams—one made up of American and Australian reps with a European group leader, and the other consisting of European and Japanese reps with an American project leader—to identify the features needed. Also, companies must learn what kinds of sales relationships customers prefer in each foreign market. This reflects each country's political and social conditions, trade regulations, and business customs.

Sources: Erika Rasmusson, "Going Global with CRM," *Sales and Marketing Management*, May 2000, 96; and Lambeth Hochwald, "Are You Smart Enough to Sell Globally?" *Sales and Marketing Management*, July 1998, 53–56.

helps determine ways in which a firm can provide total customer satisfaction not only through the personal-selling process but with the entire marketing mix.

Types of Personal Selling

Although every salesperson is engaged in personal communication, there are quite different types of selling. As summarized in Exhibit 14.2, the communication requirements vary according to whether the salesperson is engaged in order taking, creative selling, or supportive communication.

Order Taking

The least complex type of personal selling is **order taking**, which involves accepting orders for merchandise or scheduling services either in written form or over the telephone. Order takers deal mostly with existing customers (who are lucrative because it costs less to generate revenue from this group). Order takers also deal with new customers, so they must be trained well enough to answer any questions a new customer might have about products or services. Order takers are responsible for communicating with buyers in a way that maintains a quality relationship. This type of selling rarely warrants in-depth analysis of the customer or involves communicating large amounts of information, but a careless approach to the job can turn off loyal customers, damaging their relationship with the company and the brand.

Order takers may work inside the company or call on customers:

1. A retail clerk who simply takes payment for products or services is an *inside order taker.* Examples are the person who runs the cash register at a supermarket and the people working the phones at an L.L.Bean catalog center. The buyer already has chosen the product or service and merely uses the salesperson to make payment.

2. An *outside order taker* typically calls on business buyers or members of the trade channel and performs relatively routine tasks related to orders for inventory replenishment or catalog orders. The customer accounts have been established, and the salesperson merely services them on a regular basis.

Although order takers do not engage in many of the marketing activities discussed earlier, they are an important link between the firm and the market. They help bring about customer satisfaction through their courteous, timely, and attentive service.

Creative Selling

To conduct **creative selling**—the type of selling where customers rely heavily on the salesperson for technical information, advice, and service—salespeople need considerable effort and expertise. Situations where creative selling takes place include retail stores,

order taking practice of accepting and processing customer information for prearranged purchase or scheduling services a customer will purchase

creative selling assisting and persuading customers regarding purchase decisions (typically for specialty goods or high-priced items)

Exhibit 14.2
Three Types of Selling

Order taking
- Answering questions
- Being courteous

Creative selling
- Providing technical information and advice
- Analyzing and solving problems

Supportive communications
- Providing background information
- Monitoring satisfaction

© Cengage Learning 2011. Photos: left, Kristian Sekulic/Shutterstock.com; center, Patrick Hermans/Shutterstock.com; right, NY-P/Shutterstock.com.

presentations aimed at selling services to business clients, and the sale of large industrial installations and component parts. At the retail level, stores that sell higher-priced items and specialty goods have a fully trained sales staff and emphasize customer and product knowledge. The services of an insurance agent, stockbroker, media representative, or real estate agent represent another type of creative selling. These salespeople provide services customized to the unique needs and circumstances of each buyer.

The most complex and demanding creative-selling positions serve the business-to-business market. Many of these salespeople have advanced degrees in technical areas like chemical engineering, computer science, or mechanical engineering. Business salespeople who deal in large-dollar purchases and complex corporate decisions for capital equipment, specialized component parts, or raw materials often are called on to analyze the customer's product and production needs and carry this information back to the firm so that product design and supply schedules can be tailored for each customer. At MCI, sales representatives can spend weeks inside a customer's organization determining the precise mix of hardware and communications services needed to solve customer problems.

Three types of creative selling in the business market are worth particular attention:

1. In **team selling**, a group of people from different functional areas within the organization call on a particular customer. A sales engineer might analyze the customer's operations and design a product; a financial expert could work out a purchase or lease agreement that fits the customer's financial situation; and a service representative could participate to ensure that delivery, installation, and training are carried out. Sales teams often are used to sell communications equipment, computer installations, and manufacturing equipment. At IBM, a marketing strategist, salespeople, and financial experts operated as a team that consulted with customers such as G. Heilemann Brewing and Gulfstream Aerospace. After interviewing clients, touring facilities, analyzing operations, and studying the customer's information systems, the team modeled the client's company to show its financial performance with and without investments in IBM software. The effort greatly simplified purchase decisions for IBM's clients.[6]

2. **Seminar selling** is designed to reach a group of customers, rather than an individual customer, with information about the firm's products or services. The focus of seminar selling is not an immediate sale. Rather, the intent is to educate customers and potential customers about various aspects of a company's market offerings. Seminar selling is a good way to begin developing relationships with potential customers without the pressures of trying to close a sale.

3. **System selling** entails selling a set of interrelated components that fulfill all or a majority of a customer's needs in a product or service area. System selling has emerged in response to customers' desire for "system buying." In particular, large industrial and government buyers often seek out one or a few suppliers that can provide a full range of products and services needed in an area. System selling offers the convenience of buying from one source. Systems selling reflects the CRM aspects of selling discussed earlier. Large government purchases in China and Eastern Europe for huge infrastructure projects like sea ports, airports, and communications systems demand that project engineering firms like Bechtel employ just such a system-selling approach.

altrendo images/Jupiterimages

Creative-selling tasks call for high levels of preparation, expertise, and close contact with the customer and are primary to the process of relationship building. This sort of personal selling assumes that the sales function is part of a comprehensive marketing strategy. Some widely used creative-selling positions include *account representatives*, who sell to large, established accounts (typically wholesalers and retailers), and *sales engineers*, who use their technical training to help customers identify needs for products such as software systems and manufacturing equipment.

Supportive Communications

When a sales force is deployed with the purpose of supportive communications, it is not charged directly with generating sales. Rather, people in this sales area aim to give customers information, offer services, and generally create goodwill. Salespeople involved in supportive communications try to ensure that buyers are satisfied with the firm's products and services. Supportive communications takes place with two types of salespeople:

1. A **missionary salesperson** calls on accounts to monitor buyers' satisfaction and update their needs. They may provide some product information after a purchase. Many firms carry out missionary sales through tele-marketing techniques, which use telephone and computer (voicemail and email) communications.

2. A **detail salesperson** introduces new products and provides product information to potential buyers without trying to make an immediate sale. Detail salespeople are widely used by large pharmaceutical firms to introduce new prescription drugs to physicians and provide information about the drugs' application and efficacy.

LO 3 Personal-Selling Objectives

The appropriate overall objective for any element of the promotional mix, including personal selling, is to communicate. In general, the message conveys the brand's value and benefits. Also, because several of the types of personal selling involve culminating a sale, reaching a sales objective is primary. Because a salesperson is typically present when a contract is signed or an order is placed, the direct effect of personal selling on sales is more identifiable than the effect of other elements of the promotional mix. Besides these basics, every encounter with potential buyers may be approached with specific objectives in mind.

Note that these objectives are external in their orientation: each focuses on the buyer. The emphasis is to understand the buyer's needs and use that understanding to provide information on how the firm can satisfy those needs. If these objectives are accomplished, the probability of a sale increases greatly.

> **missionary salesperson**
> salesperson who calls on accounts to monitor buyers' satisfaction and update their needs
>
> **detail salesperson**
> salesperson who introduces new products and provides product information without aiming for an immediate sale

Create a Competitive Advantage

Buyers ultimately will choose the product they perceive as best suited to their needs. It is up to the salesperson to quickly understand what is best from the buyer's perspective. Different buyers value different attributes of a product—functional, emotional, or self-expressive. Further, their assessment of value will factor in the services offered—delivery, installation, and repair services, for example. The salesperson must identify what is valued and then pursue the objective of demonstrating to the buyer that the firm's products and services match the buyer's needs more closely than what competitors offer. In this way, the salesperson conveys a competitive advantage that differentiates the firm's products and services from the competition.

Treat Each Buyer as Unique

The salesperson also may grant the potential buyer unique status. To do this, the salesperson manages the communication process to ensure that a buyer does not feel like he or she is being "sold." Rather, the buyer comes away from the contact feeling as if he or she made a voluntary decision to buy.

An important part of accomplishing this objective is to listen attentively. Good listening skills allow the salesperson to grant a buyer unique status by actually learning the buyer's individual needs and desires. Also, the salesperson can shape the communication specifically to each buyer's unique desire for information, thus making full use of personal communication's primary advantage: tailoring the message to each receiver.

ONE OF THE **GREATEST CHALLENGES** FACING A SALESPERSON IS DETERMINING HOW HIS OR HER FIRM IS **UNIQUELY CAPABLE OF SATISFYING** CUSTOMER NEEDS.

Manage Relationships for Mutual Benefit

One of the greatest challenges facing a salesperson is determining how his or her firm is uniquely capable of satisfying customer needs. Matching what the firm is capable of doing with what a buyer desires allows both parties to enter a buying–selling relationship that is mutually beneficial.

To achieve this objective, the salesperson must determine the basis on which the firm can satisfy the buyers:

- Product superiority
- Service superiority
- Price superiority
- Source (company) superiority
- People superiority

The buyer's expression of his or her needs can reveal which of these is most highly valued in the purchase decision. Then the salesperson can emphasize the firm's unique capabilities in terms of satisfying the customer.

Over time, loyalty develops between organizations as firms rely on each other and fulfill promises. Several firms offer specialized sales force training designed to prepare salespeople for the task of managing the buying–selling relationship for mutual benefit.

Control the Communication

Both buyer and seller benefit if the communication process is managed efficiently. The salesperson is in the best position to bring about effective and efficient information exchange by controlling the communication. If a salesperson can control the content and direction of the encounter, the potential buyer will be able to learn quickly and accurately what a firm has to offer.

The father of a teenager recently told how he was wowed by a Nordstrom shoe salesman who controlled the content and direction of communication to yield a sale that pleased everyone involved.[7] Instead of the usual "Can I help you?" the salesman greeted the father and son by asking an open-ended question, "What brings you into the store today?" This initiated a genuine dialogue as the father explained that the son wanted to branch out beyond wearing athletic shoes to buy a pair of Top-Siders, then popular at his school. The salesman took this opening to learn more from the son about which styles he liked and where he planned to wear them. His next act to control the communication involved his choice of shoes to bring out from the stockroom: not just the pair that the son pointed out, but also a couple of extra styles for the boy to try on when the first pair weren't as comfortable as expected. Having the alternatives close at hand kept the son engaged in shopping when he otherwise might have given up after his first choice proved disappointing. Once the Top-Siders were selected, the salesman noted the "good use" the son had gotten from his thoroughly worn-out sneakers and invited him to see the latest offerings in athletic shoes as well. Was the father upset? No, he is a salesman, too, and he was so impressed that he didn't mind paying for two pairs of shoes for his son that day.

LO 4 The Selling Process

Objectives for personal selling are achievable only in the context of a well-conceived and well-executed sales effort. Therefore, the selling effort must be organized into a sequence of well-defined activities. Every organization has its own perspective on the steps required for effective personal selling. Generally, a well-conceived process involves the activities depicted in Exhibit 14.3.

Preparation

Preparation for personal selling involves gathering relevant information about current customers, potential customers, product characteristics and applications, product choice criteria, corporate support activities (such as advertising and trade channel support), and competitors' products and activities. Further, the salesperson analyzes economic and demographic trends that affect customers. A firm can greatly aid its salespeople in preparing for sales calls by maintaining an effective marketing information system (MkIS). This contains data about purchasing behavior in the market as well as records relating to past behavior of current customers.

For example, a well-prepared salesperson may recognize that potential business buyers of drilling equipment have a general dissatisfaction with suppliers' ability to deliver on a dependable schedule. In general, dependable delivery is a primary motive in business buyer behavior. Armed with such knowledge, the salesperson can approach a prospect with a sales presentation that highlights the reliability and dependability of the firm's distribution and delivery program.

Another important aspect of preparation is to recognize the extent to which the buying decision will be an individual decision versus a group buying decision. With individual buyers, the salesperson can tailor a very specific sales presentation to that person. Group buying decisions may involve representatives from several different functional areas in the firm as well as pure administrators (like purchasing agents). Communication at the group level must recognize the information needs of a wide range of constituents. Some

Exhibit 14.3
How to Sell: Steps in the Process

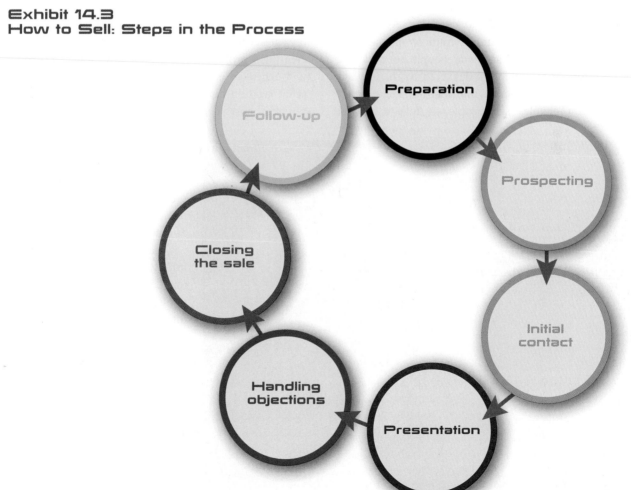

experts recommend that salespeople encourage multiple decision makers within their customer firms. If the salesperson relies on one contact to champion a specific brand or project, the sale will die if that person leaves the firm or team making the buying decision.[8]

Overall, well-prepared salespeople know their firms' capabilities in all areas of the marketing mix, competitors' strengths and weaknesses, effects of the external environment, and customer choice criteria. With this information, they can deliver a relevant and persuasive message. This preparation phase is so important that Ken Morse, director of MIT's Entrepreneurship Center and a former salesman, used to spend up to eight hours preparing for a 15-minute sales call.[9]

Prospecting

Growth in a company's revenues depends partly on the sales force cultivating new customers. Therefore, salespeople must prospect for new accounts. Successful prospecting depends on generating leads—names of new potential buyers.

Current customers are an excellent source of leads because the salesperson benefits from a personal "introduction" to a potential customer. Advertising can create leads—for example, coupons in magazine ads or Internet ads that invite people to click for more information, which is delivered to them when they provide basic contact information. The contact information enables salespeople to follow up via phone or email and, if appropriate, set up a face-to-face meeting. In addition, the firm may purchase leads from companies that specialize in creating databases of firms in different industries. These lists can help the firm identify potential customers in well-defined target areas, and existing lists offer time and cost savings. Of course, these same lists are readily available to competitors.[10]

Telemarketing has increased the efficiency of the use of leads. Some firms maintain a full staff or outsource a call center operation to qualify sales leads. Leads then can be classified as either high or low potential, and salespeople can avoid unproductive, expensive in-person sales calls for leads that seem to hold little promise.

Leads are the most valuable and effective source of prospecting, but salespeople also use cold calls as a prospecting method. Here, the salesperson either telephones or visits a potential customer with whom there has been no previous contact. Compared with the use of leads, cold calling is inefficient and rarely profitable.

Initial Contact

During the initial contact with a potential customer, the salesperson must begin to address the objectives of creating a profitable competitive advantage, according uniqueness to each buyer, and developing the buyer–seller relationship. Merely "stopping by" to call on a potential customer with vague notions of what might be accomplished is wasteful. The potential customer is likely to view such a call as an intrusion. A professional, well-planned, purposeful, and brief initial contact can establish the salesperson as a new and important source.

Reasonable activities in an initial contact can include leaving comprehensive information about the firm and its products, introducing the buyer to corporate selling programs, and gathering information about the buyer's organization and product needs.

Presentation

The presentation is an important focal point of the personal-selling process. On rare occasions, it

Johann Helgason/Shutterstock.com

Effective presentations focus on customer needs, rather than rattling off a canned speech.

canned presentation
recitation of a prepared sales pitch

attention-interest-desire-action (AIDA) structured presentation aimed at capturing attention, identifying features of interest, defining desirable benefits, and requesting action in the form of a purchase

need satisfaction
sales presentation that begins with assessment of each buyer's need state and then adjusts the selling effort to that need state

will occur during the initial contact. Normally, it is a separately scheduled phase in the process. Presentations require great skill and preparation.

There are several ways in which a presentation can be carried out. Some firms will require a **canned presentation**, meaning the salesperson recites, nearly verbatim, a prepared sales pitch. The canned-presentation approach ensures that important selling points are covered and also can enhance the performance of marginally skilled salespeople. However, the canned presentation undermines fundamental advantages of personal communication: tailoring the message to the buyer's unique needs and being able to respond to buyer feedback. Further, such an approach presumes (often incorrectly) that every buyer faces a similar buying situation.

An often implemented but marginally useful approach is **attention-interest-desire-action (AIDA)**. In this form of presentation, the salesperson carefully structures the selling contact so that the presentation first gains the buyer's attention and then stimulates interest in the firm's offering by touting product and service attributes. Next, in an effort to stimulate the buyer's desire, the salesperson demonstrates how the firm's offering fulfills the buyer's needs. Finally, the salesperson attempts to close the sale (the buyer's action). This approach is considered marginally effective because it grants the buyer very little participa-

tion in the process. The salesperson dominates (not only controls) the communication, leading the buyer through the various stages of the AIDA system. Experienced buyers, after years of being subjected to this technique, find it tiresome and obvious.

A far more sophisticated and informed approach to the presentation is referred to as **need satisfaction**.[11] With this customer-oriented approach, the salesperson assesses each buyer's need state during every sales encounter and then adjusts the selling effort to that need state. The approach considers the following possible need states:

- *Need development:* Potential customers are beginning to recognize the types of problems that exist in their organizations. The salesperson does very little talking and almost exclusively monitors feedback during the presentation. The salesperson concentrates on according uniqueness to the buyer.

- *Need awareness:* The buyer can articulate specific needs in his or her organization. The salesperson can help define the buyer's needs relative to which of the firm's products and services address those needs.

- *Need fulfillment:* The buyer is fully aware of what products and services are needed, and the salesperson assumes a dominant communication role by demonstrating how the firm and its products can fulfill the needs. With this sort of buyer, the salesperson concentrates on creating a differential competitive advantage.

The superiority of the need satisfaction approach is that it explicitly recognizes that a sales presentation will emphasize different information depending on how developed the buyer's need recognition is. Occasionally, a salesperson can lead a buyer through all the need stages in a single presentation, but, more often, buyers are already at different levels, and the salesperson has to adjust the presentation accordingly. Besides emphasizing the buyer's needs and state of mind, this approach takes full advantage of direct feedback and tailoring the message according to that feedback.

Besides choosing presentation content, salespeople can select from three basic presentation formats:

1. *Face-to-face presentations* take place when the salesperson and the prospect(s) are together, in person. This format allows the salesperson to present materials or product examples and to demonstrate the product. Analysts suggest that face-to-face presentations are critical for recruiting new customers and maintaining good relationships with existing customers.[12] Often referred to as **consultive selling**, face-to-face sales presentations can be used by the sales force to create significant value for customers by helping them define their problems and design unique solutions.

2. *Telemarketing* is a process whereby salespeople make their sales and information presentations over the telephone. With telemarketing, companies can reach many more customers and more often than they can with consultive selling. For small accounts that wouldn't warrant a face-to-face presentation because of expense, telemarketing offers a way to maintain relationships. An efficient way to develop and maintain a global presence is to establish call centers that can reach a worldwide customer base regularly and efficiently.[13]

3. *Videoconferencing* and *telepresence* are technologies in which participants in different locations use Internet connections to talk and share images with one another. With videoconferencing, a digital camera records a video of the participant at each location and transmits it to other participants' computer screens. Telepresence is a new technology that displays the background of an identical room for all the participants, so the high-definition screen display creates an illusion of being in the same place. Participants can also share documents in real time over the Internet. These technologies merge advantages of face-to-face selling (seeing customers' faces and showing them pictures) and telemarketing (saving the cost and time of travel). They are not a perfect substitute for face-to-face interaction, however, because the participants lack the warmth of a real physical presence and the ability to make direct eye contact.[14]

Sean Prior/Shutterstock.com

CRITICAL TO [CLOSING A SALE] IS THAT THE SALESPERSON ACTUALLY ASK FOR THE ORDER.

Handling Objections

During a presentation, especially with buyers in the need fulfillment stage, objections are likely to surface. The most serious objections relate to the buyer's perception that the firm's product is not well suited to the need being discussed.

The salesperson must be prepared to deal with objections. This is a highly sensitive situation that requires great skill. The salesperson must counter objections without seeming argumentative. Objections cannot be met with defensiveness or brushed aside as insignificant or irrational. Again, the buyer must be accorded unique-

ness, so *every* objection is legitimate and reasonable. The best method for handling objections is to probe for the exact nature of the obstacle and then try to lead the buyer to proposing a solution. This effort creates an alliance with the buyer so that seller and buyer can work in partnership to solve the customer's problem.

Closing the Sale

After the presentation, or perhaps several presentations, the salesperson must try to close the sale. Closing the sale is generally regarded as the most difficult part of the personal-selling process—for good reason. The salesperson is asking a buyer to incur costs—monetary, time, risk, opportunity, and, potentially, anxiety costs. The salesperson must ensure that the buyer perceives an opportunity to obtain satisfaction that will exceed the costs. This is another reason why the need-satisfaction approach to the presentation can be so effective.

A variety of techniques have been recommended for closing a sale. Critical to the process is that the salesperson actually ask for the order! Amazingly, according to surveys, about 60 percent of the time, salespeople never ask for the order.[15] There are several ways to ask, but the best approach is a straightforward close. The salesperson senses when to ask for an order in a straightforward, courteous manner—no tricks, no presumptions, no innuendo. If a salesperson has successfully achieved the objective of developing a buying–selling relationship for mutual profit, then a buyer will find this method most acceptable. This is the technique used by Ken Libman, founder of the architecture, engineering, and construction firm Libman Wolf Couples. Libman closes an astonishing 80 percent of all the new business he competes for. He explains his success by saying, "I understand people; I put myself in their shoes."[16]

Ewa Walicka/Shutterstock.com

Follow-Up

Two distinct and important activities occur after a sale has been made. First, the salesperson must ensure that all commitments of the negotiated sale are fulfilled. The salesperson can monitor shipping dates, installation, financing, and any training required.

In addition, the salesperson should prepare to deal with buyer post-purchase behavior. The salesperson makes the purchase more satisfying and lays the foundation for future sales when he or she relieves any regrets, doubts, or second thoughts the buyer may be experiencing. Salespeople can help buyers release these concerns through direct communication, either written or oral. Salespeople at Nordstrom department stores send customers a handwritten and personalized note expressing appreciation for the purchase and encouraging them to contact the salesperson for any future clothing needs. Dealing with post-purchase also includes inquiring about needs for related items. Many consumers, out of enthusiasm or newly recognized needs, will purchase items that complement an initial purchase.

help qualify leads and to relieve the sales force of repeated calls on existing customers.

Sales Force Automation

A second major change is new technology that enables **sales force automation (SFA)**, which is the incorporation of computers, cell phones, personal digital assistants (PDAs), the Internet, and other technologies to improve the efficiency and effectiveness of personal selling. Firms like Salesforce.com provide sales automation software to help integrate the various technologies for communication among the sales force, the firm, and customers.[17]

SFA has made the personal-selling process database driven. Salespeople now rely on marketing information systems to store and help them find knowledge about customers, markets, and company products. They can prepare for sales calls by entering prices and forecasts, update their forecasts as orders are booked, and retrieve product data or presentations during meetings with customers. Salespeople can connect to these databases at their home office or on the road via their laptop, cell phone, or PDA.

LO 5 Selling in a New Environment

Changes in the broad business environment have created a significantly new environment for personal selling.

Better Planning

First, the increased sophistication of marketing planning has greatly altered activities of salespeople. More precise segmentation of markets means the efforts of the sales force are more tightly focused on specific types of customers. Enhanced marketing planning also enables salespeople to respond more quickly to customer requests because the marketing effort is more narrowly defined on a customer-by-customer basis. Also, promotional campaigns rely more on telemarketing to

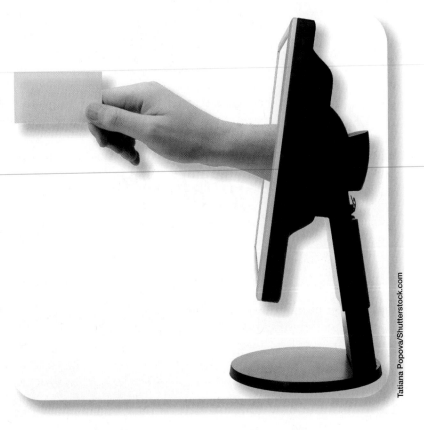

Tatiana Popova/Shutterstock.com

In this way, salespeople can stay connected to their company's data sources on a global basis.[18]

Communication technology provides salespeople with an arsenal of tools that greatly enhance the ability to manage information. Judicious use of such devices is paramount, however. If the only contacts a customer has with a sales representative are voicemail and email messages, the lack of personal attention can strain an otherwise healthy relationship. These tools aid efficiency but are not substitutes for personal contact and customer service.

Many of these tools are more useful and more efficient because of Internet technology. Experts see the Internet bringing value to personal selling in several areas:[19]

- Building customer loyalty
- Saving customers money
- Increasing the speed of the sales process
- Improving customer relationships with more frequent communication
- Lowering the sales cost

But using the Internet also introduces a major threat to the selling process if firms fail to consider the impact of their Web strategies on compensation and incentive plans. If salespeople see the company's website as competing with them, they will discourage customers from using it. To avoid this problem, compensation arrangements should balance the desired efficiency of Internet promotion against the need to motivate salespeople. This issue was part of the reasoning behind Dell Computer's decision to give sales reps full commission on sales generated through the Internet.[20]

One of the best ways for salespeople to flourish in the Internet-based world of sales is to be completely knowledgeable about what the Internet can and cannot do in the personal-selling process. This means knowing when face-to-face communication is needed and what to focus on during those communications.[21]

More-Demanding Buyers

Salespeople now deal with more-demanding buyers. While salespeople have benefited from readily available and larger amounts of information, so have buyers. Customers can easily look up and compare product reviews and prices for many kinds of products before they talk to a salesperson.

Along with more information, today's buyers have higher expectations of products and the firms that provide them. Competitive pressures to satisfy customers have escalated the average level of product performance and service, so sellers have to perform to higher standards. Household and business customers will expect the salesperson to provide timely and high-quality service and respond to specific requests.

sales management responsibility for the personal-selling effort, met by evaluating needs, setting objectives and budgets, structuring and hiring the sales force, training and motivating salespeople, and evaluating their performance

LO 6 Sales Management

Whereas salespeople are responsible for managing their own individual efforts, the sales management team is responsible for the overall performance of the entire sales force. **Sales management** involves responsibility for the many activities related to the personal-selling effort, from analyzing needs, through hiring and motivating salespeople, to evaluating their work. Exhibit 14.4 identifies the manager's areas of responsibility for ensuring that the sales force is effectively designed and efficiently deployed to carry out its role in the organization. Notice that these areas of responsibility are depicted in a circular fashion. No phase of the management process takes priority over the others.

Notice also that the activities in Exhibit 14.4 are different from actually selling. As obvious as it sounds, sales managers are charged with managing; in practice, research suggests that they often see themselves more as superstar salespeople who lead by example. Interviews with salespeople and sales managers have suggested that managers can best fulfill their responsibility by communicating expectations, building salespeople's confidence, developing their abilities, and motivating them to excel.[22] These activities fit well with the manager's areas of responsibility.

Situation Analysis

Managers of the sales process must engage in a comprehensive situation analysis of the conditions in which the sales effort will take place. This analysis has two parts:

Exhibit 14.4
What Sales Managers Do

Circles showing cycle: Situation analysis → Setting objectives → Budgeting → Structuring sales force → Hiring salespeople → Training → Motivating → Evaluating performance → (back to Situation analysis)

© Cengage Learning 2011.

1. An *external situation analysis* identifies trends in the industry, technological advances in product categories, economic conditions that may affect the firm's customers, competitors' activities, and the choice criteria emphasized by buyers. It also includes an evaluation of the markets within which the firm has a significant competitive advantage, as well as the potential for new products and markets. For example, when Apple Computer and IBM were competing to sell personal computers in schools and colleges—a target market emphasized by Apple—Apple conducted surveys of these customers to see what they wanted in new software and hardware. Teams of employees visited universities on "camping trips" to pick the brains of students and faculty."[23] Apple's sales management incorporated that information into planning for the sales effort.

2. An *internal situation analysis* entails assessing the strengths and weaknesses of the sales force and corpo-

rate support for the selling effort. The manager evaluates sales force performance in the context of the firm's overall marketing mix. (Note that, in Exhibit 14.4, performance evaluation feeds directly into situation analysis.) The manager also examines sales force knowledge and training relative to the competition. Corporate support for the sales force includes product development and positioning activities that give the product an advantage, pricing incentives that help salespeople make attractive offers, inventory levels and delivery schedules that enable the company to keep promises, and integrated marketing communication that stimulates demand.

Sales Objectives

Sales managers must set objectives at various levels. At the broadest level, the objective is the total sales for the company. This type of sales objective is determined by sales forecasts that draw on projections of total industry sales and the firm's estimate of its share of those sales.

The next level of specificity is the desired level of sales by territory or product category. Here, different geographic territories or product groups are evaluated for conditions that may affect the firm's ability to generate sales during a given time period. Quarterly and annual sales objectives are set for territories and product categories.

The most specific level of objectives is the amount of sales to be generated by each salesperson, typically expressed as sales quotas. The most common way of specifying a sales quota is to state it as a percentage of the prior year's sales (usually greater than 100 percent). In setting sales quotas, the manager considers the effects of new products, competitors' activities, economic conditions, and nonselling tasks that the salesperson is expected to carry out.[24]

Budgets

Establishing a budget for the personal-selling effort requires painstaking effort. The budget includes a variety of expenses:

- Salaries and benefits
- Incentive programs—bonuses, awards
- Recruiting costs
- Training costs
- Travel expenses
- Promotional materials—samples, catalogs, product brochures

Salaries, benefits, recruiting, training, and travel expenses are self-explanatory. Promotional materials are materials from the promotional mix used by salespeople to support the selling effort. For example, an auto parts sales rep may have a catalog of several thousand items to give customers so that they can easily place orders. The coordination of marketing communications materials is managed in consultation with the marketing manager. In the best spirit of integrated marketing communication (IMC), any promotional program that might affect the salesperson's job must be carefully coordinated with the sales effort.

The methods of establishing a budget for personnel are defined and compared in Exhibit 14.5.

Sales Force Structure

The sales management must determine how the sales force will be structured to achieve the sales goals. The structure uses some form of three basic options:

1. *Structured by product lines:* Salespeople are assigned to handle specific products. Structuring the sales force around product lines is helpful when products are technologically complex because salespeople will need special training and experience to sell the products. Pharmaceutical firms that manufacture both prescription and over-the-counter drug items often have a separate sales force for each product line based on the complexity of the product.

2. *Structured by type of customer:* Customer groups can be segmented based on order size, position in the channel, or product use characteristics. For example, some salespeople might call on wholesalers, whereas others call on retailers, or salespeople might be assigned to particular industry groups so that they can specialize in how their products meet different needs.

3. *Structured by geographic territory:* When salespeople are assigned to geographic territories, each salesperson calls on all types of customers in the area and is prepared to sell the firm's entire product line. This structure is most appropriate for standardized items that are sold to a variety of customers. Stanley Tools, for example, can have its sales force call on hardware stores, home improvement centers, and discount retailers with the firm's entire line of hammers, screwdrivers, wrenches, and the like.

The choice or combination of these structures depends on the nature of the product and the nature of the market.

SALESPEOPLE MAY COVER A GEOGRAPHIC TERRITORY AS WIDE AS SEVERAL CITIES OR STATES. MANAGERS SET SALES OBJECTIVES FOR EACH TERRITORY.

Darrin Henry/Shutterstock.com

Exhibit 14.5
Ways to Budget Selling Expenses

Method	Description	Pros and Cons
Percentage-of-sales approach	Multiply a product line's sales volume by a predetermined percentage; the result is the sales budget for that product line	Easy to use; fails to recognize unique challenges or opportunities facing the sales force
Competitive-parity approach	Base the size of the budget (particularly salary, benefit, and bonus programs) on what other firms in the industry are doing	Attempts to avoid falling behind competitors; fails to account for differences in companies' objectives; can easily result in over- or underpaying salespeople
Objective-and-task method	Assess the objectives established for the overall selling effort, specify tasks for the sales force, define the required compensation and incentive programs, and then match the budget to the costs associated with these requirements	Most effective method because it relates activities to costs; the only rational and reasonable basis for establishing a budget

© Cengage Learning 2011.

Hiring Salespeople

Decisions about sales force structure help managers determine how many and what kinds of salespeople to hire. The hiring process includes defining job requirements, recruiting candidates, and making selections.

Job Requirements

Sales managers must prepare complete job descriptions and identify the qualifications an individual must have for each sales job. A *job description* identifies all the selling and nonselling tasks to be performed by the salesperson. Nonselling tasks include paperwork and service activities such as maintaining point-of-purchase displays, coordinating and monitoring delivery, and arranging financing or training for the customer.

The tasks included in a job description translate directly into the *qualifications* of the individuals needed to fill positions—the combination of skills and training that relate to effective performance. Highly technical selling jobs require people with relevant technical training. When job descriptions include significant nonselling tasks, salespeople need skills in those kinds of activities.

In determining what qualifications are most directly related to success, many firms draw on their experience with current sales personnel, including personal characteristics of successful salespeople. Research suggests that a successful salesperson is a good listener, enjoys social events, feels socially satisfied, and is relatively individualistic. Top salespeople also tend to be more disciplined, aggressive, and creative than unsuccessful salespeople.[25]

Recruiting

A firm with well-written job descriptions and statements of qualifications can begin to recruit people to meet staffing needs. The recruiting effort should be a continuous process. A manager who begins to recruit only when a need arises may feel so pressed for time that he or she is tempted to accept unqualified or inappropriate people.

Managers can turn to various sources to generate a pool of qualified applicants. These include college and university campuses, employment agencies, and advertisements in newspapers, trade journals, and online. Many companies recruit internally by moving salespeople among products or divisions. Procter & Gamble regularly moves salespeople among its Noxell, Revlon, and Richardson-Vicks divisions.[26]

RESEARCH SUGGESTS THAT A SUCCESSFUL SALESPERSON IS A GOOD LISTENER, ENJOYS SOCIAL EVENTS, FEELS SOCIALLY SATISFIED, AND IS RELATIVELY INDIVIDUALISTIC.

Effective recruiting understands the value that applicants bring to the recruiting process. In tight labor markets, firms need to battle for top recruits. Winning the recruiting war will depend largely on offering top candidates what they want. According to Development Dimensions International, a recruiting research firm, employers say that successful recruiting depends on corporate reputation, benefits package, potential for advancement, corporate culture, salary scale, and stock options, in that order.[27] Notice that corporate culture and reputation rank higher than salary in the minds of modern recruits.

Screening and Evaluation

When recruiting efforts produce job applicants, the firm must screen and evaluate them. Typical methods include reviewing résumés, administering psychological tests designed to identify personality and motivation characteristics related to job success, and conducting personal interviews. At Capital One Financial, managers have applied the company's data-driven approach to its hiring process. The Capital One system relies on a battery of tests that measure everything from data analysis skills to reliability.[28]

Interviews should aim to identify traits, such as personal appearance and verbal skills, that are not evident from résumés and test results. To economize, more and more firms screen candidates through telephone or videoconference interviews. Videoconferencing is playing a part in the interview process because firms can get feedback about candidates faster and from more parts of the organization. People in different departments or offices can tune in to the videoconference or view a video posted on a secure website.[29]

Training

Training is a critical sales management responsibility, whether salespeople are new or experienced. Because the selling effort is integral to achieving corporate revenue objectives, the firm must have a well-planned training program.

Content and Methods

The content of the training program will depend on the sales force structure, type of product, tasks involved, and sales objectives. Every salesperson needs adequate knowledge about the products and the choice criteria used by customers. Beyond these basics, popular topics for training include industry trends and economic conditions affecting the firm's market. Companies that use team selling need to provide training in team building, team managing, and team membership skills. Seminar selling, which requires the ability to communicate to a diverse group of participants, also requires the development of unique skills. And companies that use sales force automation tools must train the sales force in the use of those tools, including the hardware and software used.[30]

Plans for training include the techniques to use. Options include role playing, classroom lectures, videotaping of presentations, computer simulations, tours of corporate facilities, and other possibilities.

Duration

Plans for training should identify how long it will take to properly train salespeople. At Procter & Gamble, the training period lasts 12 to 18 months; at State Farm, training is a two-year stint. New employees hired to

cal installations, for example), Home Depot trains the staff in effective selling techniques like listening to customers' needs and walking customers through the store to find the materials they require.[32]

Location

The broad choice with regard to training location is whether the trainees will learn in a classroom setting or go out into the field to learn. Classrooms offer a low-pressure environment where there are few consequences for mistakes. Training in the field allows salespeople to encounter actual selling situations under the tutelage of an experienced salesperson. The drawbacks of training in the field are the mistakes a trainee might make with customers and the time drain on the salespeople who conduct the training.

Nowadays, classroom training isn't confined to actual classrooms, as a growing number of firms post training materials on the Web. For example, Fisher Scientific, a New Hampshire–based chemical company, uses the Internet to teach the majority of its salespeople in the privacy of their homes, cars, hotel rooms, or wherever else they bring their laptops. To get updates on pricing or to refresh themselves on a technical product feature, salespeople log on to the Web and select from a lengthy list of subjects in which they might need training or support. They can get information on a new product, take an exam, or post messages for product experts.[33]

Sales training should not be reserved for new salespeople. As the external environment changes, as the firm develops new products and customer knowledge, and as experts develop new selling techniques, members of the existing sales staff can benefit enormously from regular training sessions.

Motivation

Perhaps the most challenging responsibility of sales management is to motivate salespeople to do their best. The motivation effort includes decisions about how to compensate salespeople, but money is far from the only motivator that matters. The amount of satisfaction and sense of personal achievement individuals feel from performing tasks also are important to motivation.

work in Apple's stores receive classroom training in customer service, followed by a few weeks in which they shadow an experienced coworker who observes their customer interactions.[31] The duration of training depends on the complexity of the selling task and the company's product line, as well as the trainees' background and experience.

Personnel

Many firms rely on experts outside the firm to conduct some or all of their training programs. Universities and colleges of business often have corporate training programs, many of which concentrate on selling tasks. Outsourcing the training program to specialized firms can be a much more effective way of achieving training goals than trying to do all the training in-house.

At some firms, sales managers and highly successful members of the current sales staff act as trainers. Occasionally, upper-level management will participate as well. Home Depot founder Bernie Marcus helped prepare the sales training program for his home improvement products chain and often participates in training sessions. Besides giving the sales staff extensive technical training (how to lay tile and do electri-

Photo Courtesy, OmniTerra Images.

COMPANIES THAT NEED SALES TRAINING OFTEN TURN TO TRAINING SPECIALISTS. NEWLANDS SALES CONSULTING SPECIALIZES IN TRAINING REAL ESTATE BROKERS AND AGENTS. ITS SERVICES INCLUDE GROUP SEMINARS IN SELLING SKILLS, CLASSES IN AN AGENCY'S OFFICES, AND EVEN ONE-ON-ONE COACHING.

Compensation

For paying salespeople, three basic compensation alternatives are available: straight salary, straight commission, and some combination of the two. Exhibit 14.6 indicates the factors influencing the use of salary and commission alternatives. Straight salary is most effective when the sales staff is highly skilled, the selling effort is drawn out over a long period, salespeople are expected to carry out time-consuming nonselling tasks, or a team selling approach is being used. As the selling task becomes less complex and requires fewer service activities, then the commission approach is more feasible. Many firms use a combination plan because many selling efforts include features from both ends of the spectrum.

If a firm relies on a commission compensation program but the selling task strongly warrants a salary arrangement, salespeople work so hard to generate sales and, therefore, income for themselves that they do not attend to important nonselling activities. Such a conflict of interest usually spells disaster for the firm. Customers are dissatisfied and will seek alternative suppliers. In contrast, Apple instructs the salespeople at its stores that their purpose is not to sell, but to help customers solve problems. To keep the focus on problem solving, the company pays salespeople an hourly wage with no commission.[34]

CHAPTER 14: PERSONAL SELLING AND SALES MANAGEMENT | 303

Exhibit 14.6
Salaries or Commissions? How to Choose

Salary for . . .
- High-cost products
- Long planning intervals
- Technical selling
- Well-structured tasks
- Many service functions

Commissions for . . .
- Low-cost products
- Few service functions
- Need for motivation
- Little supervision
- Financially weak firm

Task Clarity

Salespeople will be more motivated when their realm of responsibility is well defined. Further, they will engage in more goal-oriented behavior when they clearly know the criteria upon which they will be evaluated. Clear criteria show salespeople that they have attainable goals to pursue. This motivational approach seems to work especially well with today's employees, who expect a more cooperative relationship with managers.

Tasks are defined precisely for sales associates at Apple stores. To ensure a high level of customer service and protect the golden reputation of the Apple brand, the company trains store salespeople in helping customers define and solve problems. It details how to deliver service beginning with a "personalized warm welcome," through listening and suggesting solutions, to ending the transaction "with a fond farewell and an invitation to return."[35] Employees also know that whenever they sell a device, they are expected to sell a service package for it. Every action that can affect the quality of the shopping experience has a standard. Salespeople may not, for example, correct customers who mispronounce the name of an item. Knowing just how to act helps the salespeople make Apple stores a prime destination that sells far more in dollars per square foot than Best Buy or even prestige jeweler Tiffany & Company.

Recognition of Goal Attainment

The organization also should recognize goal achievement by its salespeople. Short-term goal attainment, such as exceeding sales quotas, should be rewarded with incentive pay, such as bonuses or stock options. Attainment of longer-term goals, such as market or customer development, should be rewarded with status-enhancing recognition, such as promotions or job titles. Recognition also comes in the form of feedback. By launching a website where its 9,000 salespeople could check on their goal attainment, IBM found it could effectively keep its sales force focused on the company's goals. The site also gave the sales reps immediate feedback on how their performance was matching up against objectives. Brad Brown from the sales consulting firm Reward Strategies says that such systems are "important in terms of keeping salespeople motivated and focused on selling. These tools give reps instantaneous access to where they are versus their goals—it's like knowing the score of a ball game."[36]

Job Enrichment

Managers also can motivate salespeople with job-enriching experiences. Many firms send salespeople to professional conferences. Paid attendance at sales-training programs is a similar reward. The firm also

can consider allowing salespeople to participate in corporate planning sessions with management personnel. This can give the sales force a sense of "ownership" in the corporate strategies they will be asked to support. Of course, the most job-enriching experience is to offer people new tasks, responsibilities, and projects. When employees feel as if they are constantly being challenged, they will be more motivated and likely to stay with a firm.[37]

Yuri Arcurs/Shutterstock.com

Perquisites

Along with money, sales professionals often appreciate being rewarded with "perks." A new car every year or so, membership at a health club, dinner at fine restaurants, or season tickets to sporting events are all legitimate business expenses that salespeople can enjoy while doing business.

Flexibility is another kind of perk. Compensation experts have been advising firms to try to let people, as much as is legally and organizationally possible, design their own compensation packages. Whereas one person may be very focused on salary, another may be far more motivated by a flexible work schedule.

Evaluation

Evaluating the performance of salespeople draws directly on the objectives set for the personal-selling process and the sales objectives. Managers can judge performance based on several objective and subjective criteria described in the next chapter. The criteria used should be consistent with the way the firm conducts the overall assessment of the IMC effort.

STUDY TOOLS CHAPTER 14

Located at back of the textbook

- **Rip out Chapter in Review Card.**

Located at www.cengagebrain.com

- **Review Key Terms Flashcards (Print or Online).**
- **Complete the Practice Quiz to prepare for tests.**
- **Play "Beat the Clock" and "Quizbowl" to master concepts.**
- **Complete "Crossword Puzzle" to review key terms.**
- **Watch videos on Porsche and Bogusky On Creativity for real company examples.**
- **For additional examples, go online to learn about Internet-based sales management, Dell's support system, and setting sales quotas.**

CHAPTER 15

Measuring the Effectiveness of Brand Promotions

Read further to find out how Unilever measured the effectiveness of its Dove promotional efforts.

The Campaign for Real Beauty enhanced Dove's visibility. Dove made it its mission to "make women feel more beautiful every day."

discover the beauty treatment for your underarms.
Dove deodorant has a unique combination of ingredients found in a face cream: **Omega 6, hydrating glycerol and 1/4 moisturising cream.** The result? Soft, smooth and evenly toned underarms and of course 24 hour protection. **Dove Deodorant.**

Image Courtesy of The Advertising Archives

Learning Outcomes

After studying this chapter, you should be able to:

LO 1 Discuss issues that shape the evaluation of brand promotion.

LO 2 Describe how marketers measure the effectiveness of advertising.

LO 3 Identify measures of effectiveness for Internet advertising, direct marketing, sales promotion, point of purchase, sponsorships, public relations, and corporate advertising.

LO 4 Explain how sales managers evaluate salespeople and the personal-selling effort.

LO 5 Describe the process of evaluating the effectiveness of IMC campaigns.

"The idea that business is just a numbers affair has always struck me as preposterous."

—Richard Branson

Research and the Campaign for Real Beauty

AFTER YOU FINISH THIS CHAPTER GO TO PAGE 326 FOR STUDY TOOLS

The Campaign for Real Beauty was one of the most successful and controversial advertising campaigns of all time. The effort enhanced Dove's visibility and contributed to record profits for Unilever, Dove's parent company. Unilever's managers attributed much of the increased sales of Dove to the innovative advertising campaign, which featured the theme "Real Beauty."

The Dove Campaign for Real Beauty (CFRB) began in the United Kingdom in 2004 to respond to Dove's declining sales as a result of a crowded market. Unilever approached Edelman, its PR agency, for a solution. Together, they conceived a campaign that focused not on the product but on a way to make women feel beautiful regardless of their age and size. According to Unilever, sales of the products featured in the ads increased by 600 percent in the first two months of the campaign.

In 2005, the CFRB was brought to the United States and Canada. CFRB aimed not only to increase sales of Dove beauty products but also to target women of all ages and shapes. According to the CFRB website (www.dove.us/#/cfrb/), "The Dove Campaign for Real Beauty is a global effort that is intended to serve as a starting point for societal change and act as a catalyst for widening the definition and discussion of beauty. The campaign supports the Dove mission: To make women feel more beautiful every day by challenging today's stereotypical view of beauty and inspiring women to take great care of themselves."

What do you think?

You know brand promotion is working if sales are strong.

1   2   3   4   5   6   7

STRONGLY DISAGREE   STRONGLY AGREE

promotion research marketing research focused on the development and performance of promotional materials

reliability tendency to generate consistent findings over time

validity relevance in terms of actually answering the questions being investigated

trustworthiness quality of deserving confidence

meaningfulness in promotion research, practical applicability of conclusions to the promotional effort

Dove commissioned The Real Truth About Beauty study as a way to explore what beauty means to women. The following statistics are a sampling of results from the study:

- Only 2 percent of these women describe themselves as "beautiful"

- About three-quarters of them rate their beauty as "average"

- Almost half of them think their weight is "too high"

Larry Koffler, the senior vice president of consumer brands at Edelman, maintained that the research was vital to the campaign: "Without having a foundation in the global research study, which showed that the image of beauty was unattainable, we wouldn't have had the credibility in creating the materials, in pitching stories and being able to answer some of the folks that didn't agree with the campaign."

After the initial study, Dove commissioned two more studies, one in 2005 and one in 2006. The additional information furthered Dove's research about women's perceptions of beauty across several cultures.[1]

Unilever's experience highlights the importance of measuring the effectiveness of a promotional effort. Managers may be tempted to make decisions based on their experience in a product category and marketing discipline. But applying this experience to a particular target segment often cannot fully meet the challenge of judging how best to craft a message and assess its effectiveness. By drawing on research, marketers can better identify which tools are working best. In a world of multimillion-dollar (or even billion-dollar) promotional budgets, managers are held responsible for verifying the effectiveness of all that spending. As you will see in this chapter, many issues are involved in measuring the effectiveness of the whole array of promotional options, and many measurement tools are available for meeting the challenge.

iofoto/Shutterstock.com

LO 1 Issues in Measuring Effectiveness

Several issues must be addressed regarding the process of measuring the effectiveness of the promotional tools and the overall integrated marketing communication (IMC) effort. The most basic of these is the scope of promotion research. **Promotion research** is a specialized form of marketing research that focuses on the development and performance of promotional materials.

Research comes into the promotional process at several points. It helps strategists understand who will be the audience members for the promotional message and which buttons to push. It also provides information for making go or no-go decisions, determining when to pull a promotion that is worn out (as Goodyear did), and evaluating the performance of an advertising or promotion agency.

Another issue is how to decide whether the promotion research itself is doing its job. Research is not magic or truth, although it sometimes seems to be confused with such. When research is used to make important promotional decisions, marketers need to consider whether that research meets some basic criteria:

- **Reliability**: Does the method generate consistent findings over time?

- **Validity**: Is the information generated relevant to the research questions being investigated? In other words, does the research investigate what it seeks to investigate?

- **Trustworthiness**: Knowing how the data were collected, can the marketer trust the data, and to what extent? This term usually is applied to qualitative data.

- **Meaningfulness**: Just what does a piece of research really mean (if anything)? This can be the hardest question to answer.

It is important for marketing professionals to take a moment (or several) to consider the limitations inherent in their data and in their interpretations.

Screen grab courtesy of Jaguar Cars North America 2001

In the research method illustrated here, consumers in a theater watch an advertisement frame by frame and turn dials to indicate electronically how much they like each part of the advertisement. The researcher graphs average responses of the audience and superimposes these results over the ad so that marketers can see which parts of the ad generated the most interest (the highest points on the graph). Such results are interesting to marketers, but they don't measure how consumers normally see advertising or tell what qualities of the ad consumers liked or disliked.

account planning system in which an agency assigns a coequal account planner to work alongside the account executive and analyze research data, staying with projects on a continuous basis

naturalistic inquiry broad-based research method that relies on qualitative data collection, including video and audio recordings and photography

Research can result from logic and adaptive decision making, or it may be driven by custom and history. In the best case, reliable, valid, trustworthy, and meaningful tests are appropriately applied. In the worst case, tests in which few still believe continue to thrive because they represent "the way we have always done things." More typically, industry practice falls somewhere in between. The pressure of history and the felt need for normative data (allowing comparisons with the past) partially obscure questions of appropriateness and validity. In this environment, the best test is not always done, and the right questions are not always asked.

Research Systems

Jon Steel, director of Account Planning and vice chairman of Goodby, Silverstein, and Partners, has called account planning "the biggest thing to hit American advertising since Doyle Dane Bernbach's Volkswagen campaign."[2] That is stretching it a bit, but account planning is a big story in the industry, so it's important to compare its role with traditional promotion research.

Account planning is a system in which an agency assigns a coequal account planner to work with the brand's account executive and analyze research data

for projects on an ongoing basis. It differs from traditional promotion research mostly in three ways:

1. In terms of organization, the assignment of an account planner to work as coequal with the account executive on a given client's business contrasts with the traditional approach of depending on a separate research department's occasional involvement. The planner is assigned to a single client and stays with the project on a continuous basis. In the traditional system, the research department gets involved from time to time as needed, and members of the research department work on several clients' materials.

2. This organizational structure puts research and measurement in a different, more prominent role. Researchers (or "planners") seem to be more actively involved throughout the entire promotional process and seem to have a bigger impact on it as well. Advertising and promotion agencies that practice account planning tend to do more developmental research and less evaluative or measurement research.

3. "Planning agencies" tend to do more qualitative and naturalistic research than their more traditional counterparts, which use quantitative techniques and models to measure effectiveness. **Naturalistic inquiry** is a broad-based research approach that relies on data collection methods that are more qualitative than quantitative and that use video and audio recordings and photography in an effort to investigate an issue more holistically.

Issues in Message Evaluation

At the heart of any successful promotional campaign is the message that will be used to engage a target audience and give audience members a reason to believe in the brand. The various types of advertising have the most elaborate message development and execution. But direct-marketing materials, sales promotion appeals, and public relations have message content, too. Even sponsorships send a message about the brand's image projected by the firm's affiliation with the event. For example, what sort of message does it send to an audience if a firm is a sponsor of a World Wrestling Federation event as opposed to being the sponsor of a fund-raiser for a children's hospital?

Given the image effects and the meaning consumers take from messages, it should come as no surprise that much of the research conducted by promotion agencies and their clients involves testing messages. Message-testing research may be conducted before a promotional campaign is executed (a pretest) or after a promotional campaign is placed (a post-test). There is no one right way to test messages used in a campaign, so experts offer conflicting advice about how to execute this type of measure of effectiveness. This di-

versity of opinion stems from multiple and sometimes competing testing criteria or outright confusion about what a promotion must do to be considered effective.

Motives and Expectations

What do marketers and agencies want out of their message tests? The answer, of course, depends on who you ask. Generally speaking, the account team wants some assurance that the promotional message does essentially what it's supposed to do. Many times, the team simply wants whatever the client wants. The client typically wants to see some numbers, generally meaning **normative test scores**; in other words, the client wants to see how well a particular advertisement or promotion scored against average campaigns of its type that were tested previously.

Whenever people begin looking at the numbers, there is a danger that trivial statistical differences can be made monumental. Other times, the required measure is simply inappropriate. Still other times, managers wishing to keep their jobs simply give clients whatever they ask for. If clients want to see that consumers can recall an ad for the brand, then the ad will mention the brand more often, even to the point of silliness. If the client craves sales, this can be achieved with a big package of short-term sales promotions, even if these erode the brand's image and long-term profitability.

Based on the content of this advertisement, which of the assessment criteria do you think the marketer was most interested in?

AND NOW FOR OUR NEXT ACT. HEADLIGHTS THAT SEE AROUND CORNERS.

These tactics may not make good campaigns, but they boost scores and, presumably, make the client happy for a while.

Despite the politics involved, message-testing research probably is helpful most of the time. Properly conducted, such research can yield important data that management can use to determine the suitability of a promotional effort. It's far better to shelve an expensive direct-mail piece or proposed sponsorship than to execute a campaign that will produce little good and may even do harm.

Dimensions of Message Assessment

Marketers judge the effectiveness of promotional messages against many standards. In fact, they need to avoid using only sales as the single measure for judging messages. Certainly, inquiries or sales are a valid measure of a direct-action message that implores receivers to call in and order today. But especially in other situations, an immediate uptick in sales may not be an appropriate measure of success.

Picking the right criteria is not always easy, but it is the essence of effective message evaluation. A message can be judged along many dimensions and with several criteria. Four possibilities are widely used:

1. *Imparting knowledge:* It commonly is assumed that a promotional message generates thoughts, some of which are later retrieved and then influence a purchase. Some messages are judged to be effective if they leave this knowledge about the brand, whether in the form of a jingle, a product symbol, or merely brand-name recognition at the point of purchase. When McDonald's launched the "Two all-beef patties, special sauce, lettuce, cheese, pickles, onions on a sesame seed bun" Big Mac campaign, people had the jingle stuck in their heads for weeks! Generally, when knowledge generation is the marketer's primary concern, marketers use tests of recall and recognition.

2. *Shaping attitudes:* Attitudes can tell us a lot about where a brand stands in the consumer's eyes. Attitudes can be influenced by what people both know and feel about a brand, so they are a summary evaluation that ties together the influence of many different factors. Marketers thus may view shaping or changing attitudes as a key dimension of advertising effectiveness. Message-testing research frequently is structured around questions related to attitudes. If a researcher asks how much you like or dislike Tide versus Bold versus Wisk laundry detergent, the research is focusing on a summary evaluation of attitude toward the brands.

3. *Attaching emotions:* Marketers always have had a special interest in emotions. Ever since the 1920s, there has been a belief that feelings may be more important than thoughts as a reaction to certain messages, and this belief has spurred interest in developing better measures of the feelings generated by promotional messages.[3] Measures of emotions include paper-and-pencil assessments and dial-turning devices where those receiving a message turn a dial in either a positive or negative direction to indicate their emotional response to the message. Participants' responses are tracked by computer and can be aggregated and superimposed over the message during playback to allow brand managers to see the pattern of emotional reactions generated.

4. *Legitimizing the brand:* Legitimizing a brand within its target audience means receivers embrace the message as meaningful and relevant to their view of the world. Thus, in a **resonance test**, the goal is to determine to what extent the message resonates or rings true with target-audience members.[4] The questions become, Does this message match consumers' own experiences? Does it produce an affinity reaction? Do consumers who view it say, "'Yeah, that's right; I feel just like that"? Do consumers receive the message and make it their own?[5]

> **resonance test**
> message assessment aimed at determining the extent to which a message rings true with target audience members

LO 2 Effectiveness of Advertisements

Maybe because advertising is so conspicuous, or because of the billions of dollars spent on production, or because it relies so much on creative execution, advertising has been and continues to be the subject of more measurement effort than any other promotional tool, even on a global scale.

Throughout many years, many different methods to measure the effectiveness of advertising have been developed. In general, these methods take the form of pretest evaluations of advertising effectiveness, pilot testing of ads in the marketplace, and post-test evaluations of advertising effectiveness in the marketplace during or after a campaign.

Pretest Evaluations

Because so much time, effort, and expense are involved in the development of advertising messages, most organizations pretest their messages to gauge consumer reaction *before* advertisements are placed. The goal

communication test pretest message research aimed at measuring whether a message is communicating something close to what is desired

is to save the firm the expense (or embarrassment) of running ads that will not achieve the desired objectives. A variety of tools may be used in pretesting.

Communication Tests

A **communication test** simply investigates whether a message is communicating something close to what is desired. Communication tests usually are done in a group setting, with data coming from a combination of pencil-and-paper questionnaires and group discussion.

Communication tests are done with one major goal in mind: to avoid a major disaster from communicating something the creators of the ad are too close to see even if it is obvious to consumers seeing the ad—for example, an unintended double entendre or unexpected interpretation of the visual imagery in an ad in different parts of the world. Cadillac embarrassed itself with an unfortunate bit of film introducing the Cadillac Catera. In an effort to show consumers the handling capability of the "Cadillac that Zigs," one ad demonstrated the car's ability to pass on a curvy road—right over a double yellow line. A communication test might have caught this unfortunate oversight.

Marketers should balance the risk of an error in an ad against the possibility of nitpicking. Test respondents tend to feel responsible for being helpful, so they may try too hard to see things. Well-trained and experienced researchers must be counted on to draw a proper conclusion from the testing.

Ronen/Shutterstock.com

GLOBAL NIELSEN'S GLOBAL VIEW

ACNielsen Corporation has expanded services for international marketers through its Nielsen Media International division in order to give global marketers a method for measuring the results of multicountry programs. The company's offerings include measurement of international television audiences and global Internet advertising and sales. Nielsen can provide marketers with data from dozens of international markets.

Source: Juliana Koranteng, "ACNielsen Shoots for Global Growth," *Ad Age International*, December 1999, 29.

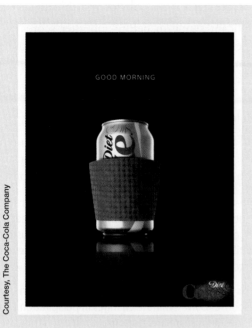

Courtesy, The Coca-Cola Company

GOOD MORNING

In this ad, Diet Coke is relying on only one picture and two words to get its point across. Do readers get it, or is Coke too clever? A communication test can answer that question.

Magazine Dummies

Dummy advertising vehicles are mock-ups of magazines that contain editorial content and advertisements, as a real magazine would. Inserted in the dummy vehicle are one or more test advertisements. Consumers representing the target audience are asked to read through the magazine as they normally would. The test usually is administered in consumers' homes, so it has some sense of realism. Once the reading is completed, the consumers are asked questions about the content of *both* the magazine and the advertisements as a way to divert heightened attention away from only the ads. Questions typically relate to recall of the test ads and feelings toward the ad and the featured brand. This method is most valuable for comparing alternative messages.

Theater Tests

Advertisements also are tested in small theaters, usually set up in or near shopping malls. Members of the theater audience have an electronic device through which they can express how much they like or dislike the advertisements shown. Simulated shopping trips also can be a part of these **theater tests**.

The problem with theater tests is that it is difficult to determine whether the respondent is really

expressing feelings toward the ad or the brand being advertised. Given the artificial and demanding conditions of the test, experienced researchers again are needed to interpret the results.

This form of message pretesting has become quite common in the United States, so considerable data are available for judging the validity of this approach. Analyses of these data by John Philip Jones, a professor of communications at Syracuse University, are very supportive.[6] According to Jones, even if this form of message pretesting yields some incorrect predictions about ads' potential effectiveness (as it occasionally will), a marketer's success rate will improve relative to what would be realized without this sort of testing.

Thought Listings

Advertising generates thoughts (cognitions) during and after exposure. Message research that tries to identify specific thoughts that may be generated by an ad is referred to as **thought listing** or cognitive response analysis. Typically, researchers have groups of individuals watch the commercial and, as soon as it is over, ask these audience members to write down all the thoughts that were in their minds while watching the commercial. The hope is that this will capture what the ad meant to the audience members and how they reacted to it.

The usual way to analyze these responses is to compile simple percentages or box scores of word counts. Marketers might find the ratio of favorable to unfavorable thoughts or count the number of times subjects' reactions to an ad included a self-relevant connection, such as "That would be good for me" or "That looks like something I'd like."

Attitude Change Studies

The typical **attitude change study** uses a before-and-after ad exposure design, frequently in a theater test setting. Researchers recruit people from the target market and ask about their preexposure attitudes toward the advertised brand and competitors' brands. Then the subjects are exposed to the test ad and some dummy ads. Following this exposure, subjects' attitudes are

dummy advertising vehicles mock-ups of magazines that contain editorial content and advertisements, including ads being tested

theater tests pretest message research in which subjects view ads played in small theaters and record their reactions

thought listing pretest message research that tries to identify specific thoughts that may be generated by an ad

attitude change study message research that uses a before-and-after ad exposure design

physiological measures interpretation of biological feedback from subjects exposed to an ad

eye-tracking systems physiological measure that monitors eye movements across advertisements

psychogalvanometer device that measures galvanic skin response, or minute changes in perspiration that may suggest arousal

voice response analysis physiological assessment in which computers measure inflections in subjects' voices

measured again. The goal, of course, is to gauge the potential of specific ad versions to change brand attitudes.

To test attitude change with print ads, test ads contained in test magazines can be dropped off at the participants' homes. Inserting the test ads into the magazines makes the competitive environment for communication more realistic. To measure attitudes before and after exposure, the researchers ask subjects to choose from a variety of potential prizes being offered in a drawing. The subjects select from the same alternatives when the magazines are dropped off and again the next day. Attitude change studies in radio are rare, perhaps because most people consider radio to be most useful for building awareness and recall, not for attitude change.

The reliability of these procedures is fairly high, but questions remain about meaningfulness. The change is measured after only one or two ad exposures in an unnatural viewing environment. Many marketers believe that commercials don't register

their impact until after three or four exposures. Still, a significant swing in before-and-after scores with a single exposure suggests that something is going on, and some of this effect might be expected when the ad reaches the target audience.

Physiological Measures

Several message pretests use physiological measurement devices. **Physiological measures** detect how consumers react to messages, based on their physical responses:

- **Eye-tracking systems** monitor eye movements across print ads. With one such system, respondents wear a gogglelike device that records (on a computer system) pupil dilations, eye movements, and length of view by sectors within a print advertisement.

- A **psychogalvanometer** measures galvanic skin response (GSR)—minute changes in perspiration, which suggest arousal related to some stimulus (in this case, an advertisement).

- A new physiological measurement, borrowed from NASA research, employs brain wave tracking technology. This research is being applied to measure how effective banner ads are in causing an emotional response in Web users and how that response might translate into click-throughs and brand recall.[7]

- **Voice response analysis** measures inflections in the voice when consumers are discussing an ad and identifies patterns that indicate excitement and other physiological states. Deviations from a flat response are claimed to be meaningful.

Other, less frequently used physiological measures record heart rate, blood pressure, and muscle contraction.

All physiological measures suffer from the same drawbacks. Even though we may be able to detect a physiological response to an advertisement, there is no way to determine whether the response is to the ad or the brand, or which part of the advertisement was responsible for the response. In some sense, even the positive–negative dimension is obscured. Is excitement, increased heart

ASL Applied Science Laboratories

781.275.4000
Tell Us What You Think | New to Eye Tracking?

Products · Applications · Eye Tracking Services · Company · Resource Center · Partners · News and Events · Support · Contact Us

EYE TRACKING SERVICES

Overview

Mobile Eye and Eye Tracking Services

Eye Tracking Services

ASL Launches New Eye Tracking Services with its Unique Mobile Eye Technology.

The technology of eye tracking is emerging as one of the most potent tools in the hands of market researchers. It can add an objective dimension in assessing the impact of consumer shopping behavior, packaging design and product placement. Until now, eye tracking has been limited to virtual or artificial environments. To truly gain insight into the consumers' thinking and attitudes natural environments need to be tested. Imagine placing yourself in the 'shoes' of the consumer while they shop? Go where they go, see what they see!

Now you can...with the ASL Mobile Eye – a revolutionary new eye tracking technology from the eye tracking experts. This technological breakthrough is revolutionizing the use of eye tracking and opening up new worlds of applications and discovery in many different industries and disciplines. The Mobile Eye is wearable and portable and combines highly accurate point of gaze with audio capability to record what the respondents are saying as they view their environment. Envision the powerful insights you could provide your clients in addition to your standard qualitative methodologies.

Eye Tracking measures how consumers interact with:
In-store shopping
Packaging Design
Point-of-Sale Displays
Outdoor Advertising
Product Placement
Color Design

MARKETERS OFTEN BELIEVE THAT HARD SCIENCE TECHNIQUES, SUCH AS MEASURING PHYSIOLOGICAL RESPONSES, LEND LEGITIMACY TO EFFORTS AT MESSAGE EVALUATION.

Ads with an engaging story line, such as this buzz-generating television ad for the Volkswagen Passat, tend to be easily recalled by consumers.

rate, a change in blood pressure, or muscle contraction the result of a positive or negative reaction? Without being able to correlate specific effects with other dimensions of an ad, physiological measures are of minimal benefit. Thus, these measures tell us little beyond the simple degree of arousal attributable to an ad. For most marketers, this minimal benefit usually doesn't justify the expense and intrusion involved.

Pilot Testing

Before committing to the expense of a major campaign, marketers often take their message-testing programs into the field. Pursuing message evaluation with experimentation in the marketplace is known as **pilot testing**.

The fundamental options for pilot testing fall into one of three classes:

1. **Split-cable transmission** allows testing of two versions of an advertisement through direct transmission to two separate samples of similar households within a single, well-defined market area. This method heightens realism by providing exposure in a natural setting. The frequency and timing of transmission can be carefully controlled. The advertisements then are compared in terms of exposure, recall, and persuasion.

2. **Split-run distribution** applies similar principles to the print medium. One version of an advertisement is placed in every other copy of a magazine, and a second version is placed in the other magazines. To use direct response as a

test measure, researchers can design ads with a reply card, coupons, or a toll-free number. The realism of this method is a great advantage in the testing process. Expense is, of course, a major drawback.

3. **Split-list experiments** test the effectiveness of various aspects of direct-mail advertising pieces. Multiple versions of a direct-mail piece are prepared and sent to various segments of a mailing list. The version that produces the most sales is deemed superior.

The advantage of all the pilot-testing methods is the natural setting within which the test takes place. A major disadvantage is that competitive or other environmental influences in the market cannot be controlled and may affect the performance of an advertisement without being detected by the researcher.

Post-Testing

Post-test message tracking assesses the performance of advertisements during or after the launch of an advertising campaign. Common measures of an ad's

pilot testing message evaluation that consists of experimentation in the marketplace

split-cable transmission pilot testing of two versions of an advertisement through direct transmission to separate sample households

split-run distribution pilot testing in which different versions of an advertisement are placed in magazines and direct responses to each advertisement are compared

split-list experiments pilot testing in which multiple versions of a direct-mail piece are sent to segments of a mailing list and responses to each version are compared

post-test message tracking assessment of an ad's performance during or after the launch of an ad campaign

recall test test of how much the viewer of an ad remembers of the message

recognition tests tests in which audience members are asked whether they recognize an ad or something in an ad

performance are recall, recognition, awareness and attitude, and behavior-based measures.

Overall, post-testing is appealing because of the strong desire to track the continuing effectiveness of advertising in a real-world setting. However, the problems of expense, delay of feedback, and inability to separate sources of effect are compromises that need to be understood and evaluated when using this form of message testing.

Recall Testing

Building on the basic idea that, if an ad is to work, it has to be remembered, the most common method of advertising research is the **recall test**, which aims to see how much, if anything, the viewer of an ad remembers of the message. Recall is used in the testing of print, television and radio, and some supportive communications like billboard advertising.

In television, the basic procedure is to recruit a group of individuals from the target market who will be watching a certain channel during a certain time on a test date. They simply are asked to watch the show. A day after exposure, the testing company phones the individuals, identifies which ones actually saw the ad, and asks those subjects what they can recall. In analyzing the transcribed interview, researchers code responses into various categories representing levels of recall. For radio advertising, recall testing follows similar procedures.

In a typical print recall test, consumers are recruited from the target market and given a magazine containing the ads to be tested. The participants are told that they should look at the magazine and will be telephoned the following day and asked some questions. During the telephone interview, the participants answer questions about ads they remember

seeing. The analysis determines the percentage that showed evidence of actually remembering the ad. Other tests go into more detail by actually bringing the ad back to the respondent and asking about various components of the ad, such as the headline and body copy.

Some research indicates there is little relation between recall scores and sales effectiveness.[8] Remembering an ad does not necessarily make you want to buy a particular brand. For example, although the "Got Milk?" ad campaign is hugely popular and widely familiar, milk consumption in the United States continued to decline throughout the campaign.

Recognition Testing

Recognition tests ask subjects whether they remember having seen particular advertisements and whether they can name the company sponsoring each of those ads. For print advertising, the actual advertisement is shown to respondents, and for television advertising, a script with accompanying photos is shown. Recognition is a much easier task than recall because respondents are cued by the very stimulus they are supposed to remember, and they aren't asked to do anything more than say yes or no.

In a typical recognition test, subscribers to a relevant magazine are contacted and asked if an interview can be set up in their home. The readers must have at least glanced at the issue to qualify. The readers are shown each target ad and asked if they remember seeing the ad, if they read or saw enough of the ad to notice the brand name, and if they claim to have read at least 50 percent of the copy. This testing usually is conducted only a few days after the current issue becomes available.

The history of recognition scores is longer than that of any other testing method, so there are normative data on many types of ads. The biggest problem

CONSUMERS DON'T WATCH NEW TELEVISION COMMERCIALS THE WAY THEY WATCH NEW, EAGERLY AWAITED FEATURE FILMS.

with this test is that of a yeah-saying bias; many people say they recognize an ad that in truth they haven't actually seen. Respondents probably believe they are telling the truth, but marketers whose brands have similar features tend to prepare ads that are astonishingly similar.

Recognition tests suffer from two other problems. First, because direct interviewing is involved, the test is expensive. Second, because respondents are given visual aids, the risk of overestimation threatens the meaningfulness of the collected data.

Awareness and Attitude Tracking

Tracking studies measure the change in an audience's brand awareness and attitude before and after an advertising campaign. This common type of advertising research is almost always conducted as a survey. Members of the target market are surveyed on a fairly regular basis to detect any changes. Any change in awareness or attitude usually is attributed (rightly or wrongly) to the advertising effort.

The problem with this type of test is the inability to isolate the effect of advertising on awareness and attitude amid a myriad of other influences—media reports, observation, friends, competitive advertising, and so forth.

Behavior-Based Measures

Other post-testing tries to get beyond what is in the heads of audience members and see how they respond in the marketplace. The usual assumption in planning these behavior-based post-test measures is that the sole "behavior" to measure is sales. Even though measuring sales often is reasonable, other measures of behavior may be relevant to an advertising campaign's effectiveness. For example, the goal of an ad campaign may be to drive traffic to the firm's website—certainly a meaningful and obtainable behavioral measure of advertising effectiveness. It's a measure that must have given pause to E*Trade after it ran well-liked ads during Super Bowl 2000. In the week following ad exposure, unique visitors to the E*Trade site *fell* 5.5 percent.[9] More positively, the Census Bureau ran an ad campaign with the theme "It's Your Future. Don't Leave It Blank" to stem the tide of steadily declining response rates for mailing back census forms. Following the campaign, a 66 percent mail-in rate was an improvement over previous censuses and 5 percentage points higher than the Census Bureau had expected.[10]

So, even though sales may be the most obvious behavioral measure of the effectiveness of advertising, there certainly are other behaviors that would suggest advertising has had an intended effect. Marketers need to be sensitive to behavioral measures other than sales that are related to the effectiveness of advertising.

Practical Limitations

None of the methods for measuring the effectiveness of advertising is perfect. All of them pose challenges to reliability, validity, trustworthiness, and meaningfulness. One reason is that consumers don't watch new television commercials the way they watch new, eagerly awaited feature films, nor do they listen to radio spots the way they listen to a symphony, or read magazine ads as carefully as a Steinbeck novel. Rather, we watch TV while we eat and study, we use radio as a background noise, and we skim through magazines looking for content.[11] Although the traditional methods of advertising evaluation have their strengths, more naturalistic methods—where researchers observe consumers observing advertising—are clearly recommended.

LO 3 Identifying Measures of Effectiveness

Internet Advertising

Unlike advertising in traditional media, Internet ads are evaluated by measuring individuals' Web-surfing activity. The information a website typically gets when a user connects with a site is the Internet Protocol (IP) address identifying the site requesting the page, the IP address for the page requested, and the

log analysis software measurement software that provides data about online consumer behavior, including hits, pages, visits, and users, as well as audience traffic within a website

time of the request. If a registered user signs in at the site, then additional information provided by the user (for example, email address or age) also is identifiable. The challenge with gathering information from registrations is that consumers may be wary of registering because they want to protect their privacy or limit email from marketers.

Common Measurements

Chapter 9 introduced widely used measures of Web audience size and activity:

- *Hits*—the number of times a given element is requested from a given page—provide almost no indication of actual Web traffic. For instance, a user's request for a page containing four graphical images counts as five hits. Thus, by inflating the number of images, a site can pull up its hit count quickly.

- A *click-through*—the number of page elements (hyperlinks) that have been requested—typically is equal to 1 to 2 percent of hits. The click-through number (and percentage) is the best measure of the effectiveness of banner advertising. Clicks on a link in an ad suggest that the ad was viewed and was motivating.

- *Page views*—the pages (actually the number of HTML files) sent to the requesting site—indicate what information was requested but not whether the requester examined the entire page. Also, this measure doesn't reveal the number of visitors: "100,000 page views in a week could be ten people reading 10,000 pages, or 100,000 people reading one page, or any variation in between."[12]

- *Visits*—the number of occasions in which a user interacted with a site in a given time period (say, 30 minutes)—is a rough count of website traffic. If a user interacts with the site at 8:30 p.m., then takes a phone call, and interacts with the site again at 9:45 p.m., this counts as two visits.

- *Unique visitors*—the number of different people visiting a site during a specified time period—is the most reasonable measure of visits to a site. A new user is determined from the user's registration with the site. Besides the address, page, and time, a website can find out the referring link address, which provides insight into which links people are taking to the site. Knowing which links bring people to the site can be helpful in planning online advertising. However, this method identifies visitors by their IP numbers, and many Internet service providers use a dynamic IP number, which is different every time a given user logs in through the service.

Web Measurement Tools

Marketers continue to seek new measurement systems that verify and justify their Web advertising investments. One such tool is **log analysis software**, measurement software that not only provides information on hits, pages, visits, and users, but also lets a website track audience traffic within the site. A site could determine which pages are popular and expand on them. It also is possible to track the behavior of people as they go through the site, thus providing inferential information on what people find appealing and unappealing. A marketer then can modify the content and structure accordingly, as well as gain a deeper understanding of how buyers make purchase decisions.[13] However, these tools still can't identify what people actually do with website information.

There is no industry standard for measuring the effectiveness of one interactive ad placement over another. There also is no standard for comparing Internet with traditional media placements. But the increasing use of social media is providing an avenue for overcoming one weakness of Web measurement, a lack of data about the Internet users who visit a page where ads are displayed. When computer users sign up for social media, they provide data about themselves, and when they use the social media, the site can measure who is engaged with which brand messages.

Facebook, for example, has partnered with Nielsen to conduct research on the effectiveness of social media advertising. Nielsen can readily compute reach and frequency from Facebook's profile data, and Facebook also conducts online polls that deliver data on ad recall, brand awareness, and intent to purchase. Facebook gives Nielsen aggregated data (for example, by age group and sex), rather than responses for individual users. Overall, early results show that an ad on Facebook inviting users to "become a fan" of a brand increases consumers' recall, awareness, and intent to purchase. Importantly for marketers, the impact is far greater if the ad also provides a social context by listing friends who have become fans, and the impact is greatest when the user's home page displays a newsfeed statement that friends have become fans—an "organic" brand message that doesn't look like an ad.[14]

Nielsen NetRatings and comScore Media Metrix have invoked older technology to develop measures of Web ad effectiveness. They use sampling to draw a representative set of families, install tracking software on the computers of households that agree to participate in a panel, and then use the software to collect data about the households' online activities. These data are projected to the universe of Internet users. The figure that has become the standard is the *reach,* which here represents the percentage of users who visit a site in any one-month period. Of course, this method has some systematic biases, such as undercounting of workplace surfing.

As a measure of Web use, reach is weighted toward the superficial: It favors sprawling sites with vast collections of largely unrelated pages (for instance, About.com) over well-focused sites that collect specific groups of users with shared interests. For marketers, then, the more valuable sites may not be the ones with the largest reach but the ones that attract individuals who are in the marketer's target audience and have a very great interest in the website's subject matter.

Measurement and Payment

Internet marketers pay for ads in several ways, but they all, in one way or another, depend on the measurement of activity related to website visits where ads appear. Many pay in terms of impressions, a measure intended to represent the number of times a page with the ad on it is viewed. In reality, impressions are roughly equivalent to hits, which are opportunities to view.

Prices may be stated as flat fees (so many dollars for so many impressions) or as pay-per-click, which in effect is the same as impressions. Others pay a price per click-through. Other advertisers will buy on cost per lead (documented business leads) or cost per actual sale (a rare arrangement).

Direct Marketing

Direct marketing (including e-commerce) is by far the easiest promotional technique to measure for effectiveness. By its very nature, direct marketing is designed to stimulate action. In some cases, the action is a request for information. In many cases, direct-marketing promotions offer an opportunity to place an inquiry or respond directly through a website, reply card, or toll-free phone number. An appeal that implores a behavioral response on the part of receivers allows for **inquiry/direct-response measures**. These measures are quite straightforward. Promotions that generate a high number of inquiries, such as orders or website visits, are deemed effective. Additional analyses may compare the number of inquiries or responses with the number of sales generated.

Aside from measuring only the number of inquiries or sales, direct marketing allows for a more refined evaluation. Because these tools primarily are database driven for targeting audiences, the responses similarly can be partitioned with respect to the nature of respondents. That is, marketers can compare one promotional campaign against another based on who responded, what region of the country the responses came from, and how quickly the responses occurred. For example, in telemarketing, various scripts can be tested to see if any one particular message helps phone solicitors exceed the historical average. Marketers can tailor different types of messages to different target markets depending on historical response data.

Finally, the data-rich nature of direct marketing also allows for a profitability analysis of these tools. Because of the fairly direct correlation with sales, a return on investment is quite easily calculated for direct-marketing campaigns.

With direct marketing, the basic measure of success is the number of the desired responses obtained. How would J.C. Penney Corporation measure the success of this direct-marketing message?

ballot method

ballot method
pretest of sales promotion in which consumers are given a list of promotional options and asked to rank their preferences

Sales Promotion and Point of Purchase

The approach to measuring the effectiveness of sales promotion is similar to measuring the effectiveness of advertising. Marketers can evaluate sales promotion through pretesting and post-testing using techniques similar to those used for advertising.

Pretesting Sales Promotion

The options for pretesting sales promotion vary somewhat depending on whether the efforts are aimed at consumers or the trade channel.

Consumer Sales Promotion When a sales promotion is aimed at consumers, marketers pretest it by measuring consumers' perception of the value of a promotion. They test the perceived value of different levels of cents-off coupons, premiums, giveaways, frequency programs, or contests. For example, researchers might ask consumers to compare the perceived value of a 50-cents-off coupon for a brand they never use versus paying 50 cents more for a brand they have been using regularly and find satisfying. Similarly, they might ask them whether they would consider switching brands to enter a contest or sweepstakes. When it comes to premiums or bonus packs, it's relatively easy to predict a brand-loyal customer's perception of value: more of a preferred brand at less cost. But for a consumer contemplating trial use, getting an additional quantity of an unknown brand may be perceived as a liability because there is the risk the brand will not offer sufficient satisfaction.

Marketers can pretest each of the possibilities by using standard and fairly simple research methods like focus groups or a ballot method. A **ballot method** consists of mailing target consumers a list of promotional options and asking them to rank their preferences; the consumer then mails the ballot back to the firm.

Sales Promotion in the Trade Channel Two issues arise with respect to pretesting sales promotion in the trade channel. First, the effectiveness of consumer-oriented sales promotions is greatly compromised if members of the trade channel are not excited about the promotion and do not support it. If trade partners don't maintain sweepstakes entries, coupons, or premium packs, the effectiveness of a sales promotion effort will be undermined. The best approach for pretesting consumer promotions with the trade channel is to meet with trade channel managers and work out the details of the execution with them.

The second issue in pretesting sales promotion in the channel has to do with trade-oriented sales promotions—that is, promotions directed at the channel members themselves. Here, the techniques used to pretest sales promotions with consumers are valuable as well. A survey of key retail partners, asking what they would perceive as an energizing and high-value promotion, will provide important feedback. Getting a read on the channel's perceptions of value can mean the difference between motivating channel members and creating a program they will totally ignore.

Post-Testing Sales Promotion

Post-testing sales promotion is largely a matter of generating a quantified measure of the performance of a sales promotion device. In the broadest sense, for any sales promotion tool, changes in sales can be used as a measure of effectiveness. Other measures will be suitable

CREATISTA/Shutterstock.com

Exhibit 15.1
Measures for Post-Testing Sales Promotion

Type of Promotion	Suitable Measures
Contests and sweepstakes	Changes in sales; number of entries
Coupons	Changes in sales; number of coupons redeemed
Rebates	Changes in sales; number of rebate forms submitted
Trade promotions	Changes in sales

© Cengage Learning 2011.

for certain promotional tools (see Exhibit 15.1). For example, Nestlé distributed coupon inserts for its Ortega salsa in Sunday papers slated to reach 50 million consumers. A reasonable measure of effectiveness would be tracking the redemption rate of that particular coupon.[15]

In terms of working with trade channel partners, relying on sales measures time period by time period will allow a comparison of the effects of any sales promotion program. And you can be sure that the trade itself is focused on sales as a measure of a promotion's success. When Procter & Gamble introduced the Swiffer sweeper/duster, some retailers resisted carrying the brand because of the high price: $18 for the mop. But one supermarket buyer who had decided against carrying the product because of the high price said he might have to bow to consumer demand if P&G promotions were successful.[16] Some retailers are fairly aggressive at devising sales promotion programs and having ways of measuring their effectiveness.

As program manager for J. Rice Communications in Santa Ana, California, Nicole Del Prato has spent most of her marketing career helping business clients ensure that their trade show marketing supports their entire communications plan. Before each show, questionnaires and surveys are used to benchmark the awareness of each client's target audience. Preshow mailings sent to conference attendees, encouraging them to visit the client's booth, often contain offers that can be redeemed at the trade show, providing a way to track their effectiveness at drawing customers. During the show, in-booth profiling questionnaires and drawings help determine visitor interest levels and planned buying activity. After the show, Del Prato and her staff conduct surveys to see how much actual buying activity resulted from the show.

Point of Purchase

The success of point-of-purchase (P-O-P) materials is measured almost exclusively on the basis of sales effects. Because the context for P-O-P materials offers little opportunity for "message" execution per se, changes in sales are a legitimate and appropriate measure of effectiveness. Also, because this promotional communication takes place at the point of behavior, the display material should play a role in catalyzing a sale.

Sponsorship and Supportive Communications

Sponsorship probably shouldn't even be measured. Sponsoring an event or community activity is meant to enhance the image of a brand and ultimately create a more positive attitude—which, in the long term, may have an effect on sales. But in an era of accountability, managers usually are pressed to come up with some measure of effectiveness for their sponsorship spending. Some simple quantitative measures are available:

- If the sponsorship is an event, the number of people attending the event is easily obtained.

- If the event is televised, the number of viewers of the event gives a proxy measure of exposure to the brand.

Managers at John Hancock Insurance counted the number of times the company logo appeared on the television screen and the number of times the company name was mentioned during the telecast of a sponsored college football game. They then came up with a fairly elaborate model to translate those exposures into the equivalent of advertising dollars.[17]

Several research firms offer services to calculate the effects of sponsorship. Some specialize in performing sales audits in event areas, conduct exit interviews with attendees, and offer economic-impact studies.[18] Others try to identify the impact of an event on the firm's image, and some have tried to calculate the effects on sales—but with fairly strained methodologies.[19]

Testing the effectiveness of supportive communications should rely on recall of the messages that appear in the major support media, including billboards, transit, and aerial ads. A basic approach for testing recall is to conduct a survey before and after a message has run. For example, researchers might make random phone calls in an area and ask, "Who was the 22nd and 24th president of the United States?" Researchers then would place a test message on a billboard or bus board or blimp stating simply, "Grover Cleveland was the 22nd and 24th president of the United States." After the message has run for some designated time—usually two to four weeks—another random sample of households is surveyed. The difference in knowledge then is attributed to recall of the message. Although that may seem to be a simple enough test of effectiveness, it does have a significant flaw: The message in this example is so strange to passersby that it may be an artificial measure of effectiveness.

There are, however, some supportive communication tools that can be tracked directly for effectiveness. John Deere relies heavily on a wide range of promotional tools to communicate with both its commercial and consumer target audiences. In one recent consumer promotion, the firm mailed videotapes to a select consumer target group. The promotion not only doubled the response rate of previous campaigns (measured by inquiries), but it also was credited with doubling sales—an obviously measurable result.[20]

PR and Corporate Advertising

One attitude about measuring the effects of public relations and corporate advertising is that it really shouldn't even be tried. Because the primary objectives of public relations and corporate advertising are long-term image effects, trying to measure the effect of such programs at any one time seems pointless. For example, just what would you be measuring if

The effects of corporate advertising campaigns like this one for Apple Computer are extremely hard to measure. Why?

© Michael Newman/PhotoEdit, Inc.

you attempted to measure the effectiveness of the Apple advertising shown here? This outdoor advertising above a car wash doesn't focus any product that Apple sold. You couldn't just count the sales of iPods or iPads to measure its success. Rather, this eye-catching display evokes an appreciation of creative brilliance. It links creativity to Apple's brand and its products. But to what extent and within what time frame—after a week, after five months? Just what would the measurement be? Herein lies the problem with measuring the effects of public relations and corporate advertising.

But in an environment where promotional budgets are subject to heavy scrutiny, attempts are made to measure the effects of these types of subtle promotional efforts. One easy measure of the effects of public relations merely is to count the number of media exposures created by the PR program. Public relations firms often present clients with a "clippings" book showing all the media that carried stories about the company, its employees, its products, or its events. But equating placement with exposure is a tenuous link at best.

Another measure of the effects of either public relations or corporate advertising would be to measure changes in awareness or attitude. This would require original research that measures awareness and attitude before and then after a campaign has been carried out. Of course, it is likely that a firm will be running a wide range of promotional activities along with the PR and corporate campaign. This being the case, it would be almost impossible to separately measure the effects of public relations or corporate advertising from the other elements of the promotional mix.

Given the broad and subtle effects of public relations and corporate advertising, it may be advisable to save the expense of the measurement process and have faith that these are important and useful forms of promotion and are doing their behind-the-scenes job. Should such a perspective meet with resistance from managers, the best recommendation is to carry out pre- and postcampaign attitude and opinion tests and regularly monitor the image of the firm and each brand.

LO 4 Effectiveness of Personal Selling

Measuring the performance of salespeople draws directly on the objectives set for the personal-selling process and sales objectives discussed in Chapter 14. There are several objective and subjective criteria upon which sales staff members can be judged.[21] Exhibit 15.2 identifies these criteria.

The objective criteria need to be carefully applied. For example, the total dollar volume of sales must be judged against the order size and expenses generated. A salesperson or an entire sales force might be rated highly on total dollar volume at the expense of many, repeated small orders at great cost to the firm. Also, depending on the specific objectives and the selling tasks involved, the nonselling tasks may be critical to long-range plans even if they slow short-term growth in sales. Customer satisfaction also is critical. As part of the process of relationship building, quantifiable customer satisfaction criteria can be of value to both management and the salesperson.

Exhibit 15.2
Performance Criteria for Salespeople

© Cengage Learning 2011.

Subjective criteria can be difficult to define and measure accurately. Sales managers must be flexible and allow individual styles to manifest themselves. The strength of any particular salesperson may lie in his or her unique style. Suppression of individual differences may be inefficient and demoralizing.

Measuring the effectiveness of sales personnel is important for two reasons. First, salespeople need feedback on which they can base future efforts. An evaluation exercise itself can motivate the sales staff. The evaluation also is the basis on which management will make annual salary and bonus decisions. Second, the measurement of effectiveness is a primary source of information for an internal situation analysis. It helps managers determine strengths and weaknesses in the sales staff, changes that need to be made in the nature of the selling task, and the level of corporate support needed for the sales staff.

LO 5 Effectiveness of the IMC Program

Marketers attempting to measure the effectiveness of the overall IMC program have tried several approaches. One merely is to measure each of the promotional tools used in a campaign, weighing each one independently. This fragmented process makes no attempt to account for the synergies that are the hallmark of IMC in the first place. The purpose of creating and executing an integrated campaign is to enhance the impact of the communication. Logically, then, marketers would want to measure the full impact of that effort. But the limitations of measurement methodologies make that task difficult.

Consider the complexity of measuring the overall effect of IBM's $30 million campaign called "Business Intelligence." The goal was to establish IBM as a leader in developing solutions to gather, analyze, and manage data about a company's customers. The campaign had many dimensions:[22]

- Print ads ran in high-profile publications, including *Business Week* and *Forbes,* to build widespread awareness.

- Print ads also were placed in "vertical market" magazines that specifically targeted decision makers in the banking, retail, and insurance industries.

- Radio ads were run in the top 10 North American markets.

- Television commercials were run during prime-time programs to build awareness.

- Direct-mail pieces were sent to 250,000 executives in three target industries. A week after the initial mailing, an additional 10,000 special mailers were sent to key companies in the targeted industries.

- Public relations initiatives included using IBM employees and local PR agencies to target analysts and industry publications.

- Banner ads were run on approximately 40 websites, including several vertical industry sites and IT-related sites.

THE PURPOSE OF . . . AN INTEGRATED CAMPAIGN IS TO **ENHANCE THE IMPACT** OF THE COMMUNICATION. LOGICALLY, THEN, MARKETERS WOULD WANT TO **MEASURE** THE FULL IMPACT.

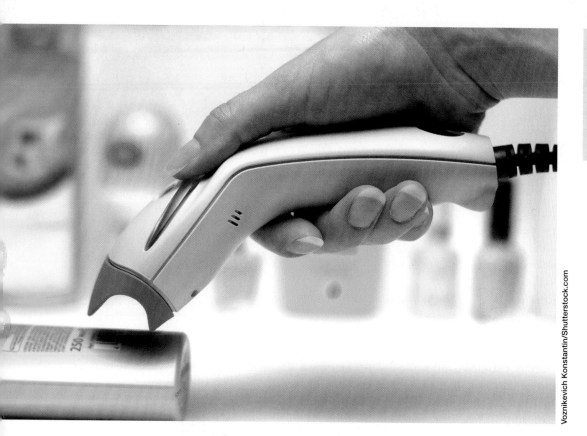

single-source tracking measures

post-test message tracking that uses a combination of scanner data and devices that monitor television-viewing behavior to collect information about brand purchases, coupon use, and television ad exposure

This campaign targeted a broad market, a narrow market, executives, IT managers, and more. The methodologies available pale in comparison to IMC campaigns like IBM's.

Despite the methodological challenges, there are some recommendations on how to proceed. One of these is to use **single-source tracking measures**, which identify the extent to which a sample of consumers potentially has been exposed to multiple promotional messages and the effect those messages have had on their behaviors. Researchers create a respondent pool of households with known demographics. They use devices attached to the households' televisions to monitor viewing behavior. Checkout scanners read the universal product codes (UPCs) on product packages and coupons. Data about shoppers' viewing behavior and data about coupon use and brand purchases are combined so that marketers can gauge the impact of brand promotion on consumers' actual purchases.

The main problem with these measures is that it is impossible to determine what aspects of advertising had positive effects on consumers. And although such a system is sophisticated, it really focuses on only two promotional tools: television advertising and couponing. Researchers are developing methods that try to integrate more forms of research in a final assessment.

Some of these approaches synthesize tracking data with mall-intercept and consumer survey research.[23]

Another approach is offered by industry practitioners Helen Katz and Jacques Lendrevie.[24] Katz and Lendrevie offer a measurement program that segments total exposures of an integrated program. Their orientation is that, regardless of the promotional tools used in the promotional mix, communication will occur in up to three ways:

1. *Media exposure:* Consumers may be exposed to the brand through traditional media, including advertising in all media, public relations and publicity that appear in mass media, and media exposure from any sales promotion announced through placement in major media (for example, free-standing inserts in the Sunday paper).

2. *Product (brand) impressions:* The target audience receives information and forms impressions based on exposure to the brand itself.[25] This includes in-store and in-home contact with the product, as well as contact with the product on the street, while visiting friends and acquaintances, or in the workplace. Incidental exposure such as passing by a McDonald's and seeing the store sign and logo also would be counted as a brand impression. Although the authors do not mention event sponsorship, personal exposure to a brand message as a result of a sponsorship presumably would be included as well.

3. *Personal contacts:* A variety of personal contacts create brand impressions. Examples include interactions with salespeople at dealerships, conversations with friends, contact with opinion leaders, or the professional advice of a doctor, pharmacist, or hairstylist. These can affect brand knowledge and awareness.

Kristian Sekulic/Shutterstock.com

For the evaluation program to be worthwhile, marketers must somehow measure each kind of communication. The developers of this model offer some tenuous and hypothetical approaches to measuring brand impressions and personal contacts.[26]

Overall, the challenge of measuring the effectiveness of the total IMC effort is extremely difficult. Communication is a complex process that varies across times and places and from individual to individual. Testimony to the difficulty in measuring the effectiveness of the IMC effort is the almost total lack of literature devoted to the discussion.[27] Consider this lack of literature a sign of just how complex and fascinating the topic of integrated marketing communication is and will continue to be.

STUDY TOOLS
CHAPTER 15

Located at back of the textbook

- **Rip out Chapter in Review Card.**

Located at www.cengagebrain.com

- **Review Key Terms Flashcards (Print or Online).**
- **Complete the Practice Quiz to prepare for tests.**
- **Play "Beat the Clock" and "Quizbowl" to master concepts.**
- **Complete "Crossword Puzzle" to review key terms.**
- **Watch videos on Starling, SXSW, and Wolfram Alpha for real company examples.**
- **For additional examples, go online to learn about Internet audience tracking and measuring the effects of IMC programs.**

Endnotes

Chapter 1

1. Jessi Hempel, "The MySpace Generation," *BusinessWeek*, December 15, 2005, 86–94.
2. Robert Levine, "Reaching the Unreachables," *Business 2.0*, October 2005, 109–116.
3. "Question of the Week, Ad Infinitum," *BusinessWeek*, November 20, 2006, 18.
4. To see current "Madison and Vine" campaign strategies, go to http://www.adage.com/madisonandvine.
5. Emily Bryson York, "How Heinz Satisfies Moms' Hunger for Comfort Food," *Advertising Age*, September 7, 2009, Business & Company Resource Center, http://galenet.galegroup.com (interview with Brian Hansberry).
6. A special issue of the *Journal of Advertising*, Vol. 34, No. 4, Winter 2005, featuring research and perspectives on IMC; contains several articles that focus on the integrated brand promotion aspects of IMC.
7. John Gaffney, "Most Innovative Campaign," *Business 2.0*, May 2002, 98–99.
8. U.S. Census Bureau, "Population of the United States 2009," FactFinder, http://factfinder.census.gov, accessed February 10, 2010.
9. "2009 Survey of Buying Power," *Sales and Marketing Management*, 2009, 18.
10. This definition of marketing was approved in 1995 by the American Marketing Association (http://www.marketingpower.com) and remains the official definition offered by the organization.
11. Peter D. Bennett, *Dictionary of Marketing Terms*, 2nd ed., Chicago: American Marketing Association, 1995, 4.
12. Interbrand, "Best Global Brands: 2009 Rankings," http://www.interbrand.com.
13. Michael Myser, "Marketing Made Easy," *Business 2.0*, June 2006, 43–45.
14. "Research and Markets Offers Report: Wireless Telecommunications Services," *Wireless News*, October 17, 2010, Business & Company Resource Center, http://galenet.galegroup.com; and CTIA, "Wireless Quick Facts," http://www.ctia.org, accessed July 26, 2011.
15. Jack Neff, "Snuggie," *Advertising Age*, November 16, 2009, 25.
16. Douglas W. Vorhies, "Brand Extension Helps Parent Gain Influence," *Marketing News*, January 20, 2003, 25. This concept was verified in academic research as well. See Franziska Volckner and Henrik Sattler, "Drivers of Brand Extension Success," *Journal of Marketing* 70, April 2006, 18–34.
17. Kevin L. Keller, *Strategic Brand Management: Building, Measuring, and Managing Brand Equity*, Upper Saddle River, NJ: Prentice Hall, 1998, 2.
18. Kevin L. Keller, "Conceptualizing, Measuring, and Managing Customer-Based Brand Equity," *Journal of Marketing*, 57, January 1993, 4.
19. Stephanie Thompson, "Kraft Counters Unilever Launch," *Advertising Age*, August 25, 2003, 4.
20. Franziska Volckner and Henrik Sattler, "Drivers of Brand Extension Success," *Journal of Marketing*, 70, April 2006, 18–34.
21. Peter F. Drucker, *People and Performance: The Best of Peter Drucker*, New York: HarperCollins, 1997, 90.
22. The research study is reported in Robert G. Docters, Michael R. Reopel, Jeanne-Mey Sun, and Stephen M. Tanney, *Winning the Profit Game: Smarter Pricing, Smarter Branding*, New York: McGraw-Hill, 2004; the information on Louis Vuitton was taken from Carol Matlack et al., "The Vuitton Machine," *BusinessWeek*, March 22, 2004, 98–102.
23. U.S. Bureau of the Census, *Statistical Abstract of the United States: 1995*, 115th ed., Washington, D.C.: U.S. Government Printing Office, 1995; "Got Results?" *Marketing News*, March 2, 1998, 1.
24. For an excellent summary of decades of research on the topic, see Mark S. Abion and Paul W. Farris, *The Advertising Controversy: Evidence of the Economic Effects of Advertising*, Boston: Auburn House, 1981; and J. C. Luik and M. S. Waterson, *Advertising and Markets*, Oxfordshire, England: NTC Publications, 1996.
25. Kerry Capell, "How Philips Got Brand Buzz," *BusinessWeek*, July 31, 2006, http://www.businessweek.com, accessed August 1, 2006.
26. There are several historical treatments of how advertising is related to demand. See, for example, Neil H. Borden, *The Economic Effects of Advertising*, Chicago: Richard D. Irwin, 1942, 187–189; and John Kenneth Galbraith, *The New Industrial State*, Boston: Houghton Mifflin, 1967, 203–207.
27. This fundamental argument about the effect of advertising on competition was identified and well articulated many years ago by Colston E. Warn, "Advertising: A Critic's View," *Journal of Marketing*, 26(4), October 1962, 12.
28. "100 Leading National Advertisers," *Advertising Age*, June 25, 2007, 5–14.
29. For a historical perspective on culture, consumers, and the meaning of goods, see Ernest Ditcher, *Handbook of Consumer Motivations*, New York: McGraw-Hill, 1964, 6. For a contemporary view, see David Glen Mick and Claus Buhl, "A Meaning-Based Model of Advertising Experiences," *Journal of Consumer Research*, 19, December 1992, 312–338.

Chapter 2

1. Matthew Creamer, "Caught in the Clutter Crossfire: Your Brand," *Advertising Age*, April 2, 2007, 1, 35.
2. Robert D. Hof, "The Power of Us," *BusinessWeek*, June 20, 2005, 74–82.
3. "Worldwide Ad Spending by Region 2008," *Advertising Age* Data Center, http://adage.com/globalmareters09/#302.
4. Bob Garfield, "The Chaos Scenario 2.0: The Post Advertising Age," *Advertising Age*, March 26, 2007, 1, 12–14.
5. Erick Schonfeld, "Tuning Up Big Media," *Business 2.0*, April 6, 2006, 61–63.
6. Dean Foust and Brian Grow, "Coke: Wooing the TiVo Generation," *BusinessWeek*, March 1, 2004, 77–78.
7. Beth Snyder Bulik, "Ad Dollars Flow into Online Games," *Advertising Age*, March 26, 2007, 10.
8. Jon Fine, "Now, an Ad from Our Network," *BusinessWeek*, November 27, 2006, 26.
9. Tom Lowry, "The Dilemma Vexing Big Media," *BusinessWeek*, July 3, 2006, 94–98.
10. "Ad Spending Heads into Tepid Recovery," *Advertising Age*, December 28, 2009, 8; Brian Steinberg, "Marketers Say TV Spending Will Drop; Nets Stay Bullish; Let the Deals Begin," *Advertising Age*, February 8, 2010, 3.
11. Tim Bradshaw, "Adverts Make a Seismic Shift to Digital," *Financial Times*, June 29, 2009, http://www.ft.com.
12. David Ho, "FCC Votes to Ease Media Ownership Rules," *Washington Post*, available at http://news.yahoo.com, accessed June 2, 2003.
13. Nat Ives, "Special Report: More Than Magazines," *Advertising Age*, March 12, 2007, S1–S6.
14. Matthew Boyle, "Brand Killers," *Fortune*, April 11, 2003, 89–100.
15. Bob Horowitz, "No Mere 30-Second Spot," *Atlanta Journal-Constitution*, February 6, 2011, Business & Company Resource Center, http://galenet.galegroup.com.
16. Jack Neff, "J&J Jolts 'Old Media' with $250M Spend Shift," *Advertising Age*, March 19, 2007, 1, 29.
17. Betsy Streisand, "Why Great American Brands Are Doing Lunch," *Business 2.0*, September 2003, 146–150.
18. Brian Stelter, "The Myth of Fast-Forwarding Past the Ads," *New York Times*, December 20, 2010, http://www.nytimes.com; and Sav Evangelou and Lindsey Clay, "Media: Double Standards," *Campaign*, June 17, 2011, Business & Company Resource Center, http://galenet.galegroup.com.
19. Stelter, "The Myth of Fast-Forwarding."
20. David Kiley, "Learning to Love the Dreaded TiVo," *BusinessWeek*, April 17, 2006, 88.

21. "A World of Connections," *The Economist*, January 10, 2010, 3; and Spencer E. Ante, "The Real Value of Tweets," *Bloomberg Businessweek*, January 18, 2010, 31.
22. Jean Halliday, "Honda Feels the Love on Facebook," *Advertising Age*, October 26, 2009, 53.
23. Garrik Schmitt, "Can Creativity Be Crowd-sourced?" *Advertising Age*, April 16, 2009, http://adage.com/digitalnext.
24. "100 Leading National Advertisers," *Advertising Age*, June 22, 2009, S-4.
25. Ibid.
26. Bradley Johnson, "Top 100 Spending Up 3.1% to $105 Billion," *Advertising Age*, June 25, 2007, S-2.
27. The 2006 ranking for the U.S. government was 29th at $1.13 billion annual spending on advertising. "100 Leading National Advertisers," *Advertising Age*, June 25, 2007, S-4.
28. Bob Garfield, "Army Ad Strong—If You Totally Forget We're at War," *Advertising Age*, November 13, 2006, 57.
29. "World's 50 Largest Agency Companies," *Advertising Age* Datacenter, http://adage.com/datacenter.
30. Bradley Johnson, "Diller Leads Top Execs in 2005 Pay," *Advertising Age*, December 4, 2006, S-2.
31. David Kiley, "The Craziest Ad Guys in America," *BusinessWeek*, May 22, 2006, 72–80.
32. Hillary Chura and Kate MacArthur, "Cramer-Krasselt Thinks Small," *Advertising Age*, September 11, 2000, 32.
33. Martin Sorell, "Agencies Face New Battle Grounds," *Advertising Age*, April 13, 1998, 22.
34. Jonah Bloom, "Zimmerman's Virtual Agency Marks the Rise of Machines," *Advertising Age*, January 15, 2007, 15.
35. Jack Neff, "P&G Boosts Design's Role in Marketing," *Advertising Age*, February 9, 2004, 1, 52.
36. Betsy Streisand, "Why Great American Brands Are Doing Lunch," *Business 2.0*, September 2003, 146–150.
37. Jon Steel, *Truth, Lies & Advertising: The Art of Account Planning,* New York: John Wiley & Sons, 1998, 42.
38. Tobi Elkin, "Motorola Tenders Brand Challenge," *Advertising Age*, August 14, 2000, 14.
39. Rupal Parekh, "TBWA's Answer to Client Squeeze: Anoint a Chief Compensation Officer," *Advertising Age*, February 8, 2010, 1, 21.
40. Patricia Sellers, "Do You Need Your Ad Agency?" *Fortune*, November 15, 1993, 148.
41. Lisa Sanders and Alice Z. Cuneo, "Fed-Up Agencies Quit Punching the Clock," *Advertising Age*, January 27, 2007.
42. Matthew Creamer, "March of the Management Consultants," *Advertising Age*, June 5, 2006, 1, 58.
43. Clair Atkinson, "AOL Sees Future in Ad Networks," *Advertising Age*, December 11, 2006, 4.

Chapter 3

1. Julian Simon, *Issues in the Economics of Advertising*, Urbana: University of Illinois Press, 1970, 41–51.
2. Vincent P. Norris, "Advertising History—According to the Textbooks," *Journal of Advertising* 9(3), 1980, 3–12.

3. James W. Carey, *Communication as Culture: Essays on Media and Society,* Winchester, MA: Unwin Hyman, 1989.
4. Christopher P. Wilson, "The Rhetoric of Consumption: Mass-Market Magazines and the Demise of the Gentle Reader, 1880–1920," in *The Culture of Consumption: Critical Essays in American History, 1880–1980*, eds. Richard Weightman Fox and T. J. Jackson Lears, New York: Pantheon, 1983, 39–65.
5. Frank Presbrey, *The History and Development of Advertising,* Garden City, NY: Doubleday, Doran & Co., 1929, 7.
6. Ibid., 11.
7. Ibid., 40.
8. James P. Wood, *The Story of Advertising,* New York: Ronald, 1958, 45–46.
9. Daniel Pope, *The Making of Modern Advertising and Its Creators,* New York: William Morrow, 1984, 14.
10. Cited in Stephen Fox, *The Mirror Makers: A History of American Advertising and Its Creators,* New York: William Morrow, 1984, 14.
11. Ibid.
12. Presbrey, *The History and Development of Advertising,* 16.
13. Bruce Barton, *The Man Nobody Knows,* New York: Bobbs-Merrill, 1924.
14. James Lincoln Collier, *The Rise of Selfishness in America,* New York: Oxford University Press, 1991, 162.
15. Ibid., 303–304.
16. Fox, *The Mirror Makers*, 168.
17. Mark Pendergrast, *For God, Country & Coca-Cola: The Definitive History of the Great American Soft Drink and the Company That Makes It,* New York: Basic Books, 2003.
18. Wini Breines, *Young, White and Miserable: Growing Up Female in the Fifties,* Boston: Beacon, 1992.
19. Vance Packard, *The Hidden Persuaders,* New York: D. McKay, 1957. With respect to the effects of "subliminal advertising," researchers have shown that, while subliminal communication is possible, subliminal persuasion, in the typical real-world environment, remains all but impossible. As it was discussed as mind control in the 1950s, it remains a joke. See Timothy E. Moore, "Subliminal Advertising: What You See Is What You Get," *Journal of Marketing* 46, Spring 1982, 38–47.
20. Stuart Rogers, "How a Publicity Blitz Created the Myth of Subliminal Advertising," *Public Relations Quarterly,* Winter 1992–1993, 12–17.
21. Fox, *The Mirror Makers*, 218.
22. Thomas Frank, *The Conquest of Cool: Business Culture, Counterculture, and the Rise of Hip Consumerism,* Chicago: University of Chicago Press, 1997.
23. Ibid., 235.
24. Tom Engelhardt, "The Shortcake Strategy," in *Watching Television*, ed. Todd Gitlin, New York: Pantheon, 1986, 68–110.
25. Marty Westerman, "Death of the Frito Bandito," *American Demographics*, March 1989, Business & Company Resource Center, http://galenet.galegroup.com.
26. Collier, *The Rise of Selfishness in America*, 230.
27. This quote and information from this section can be found in Steve Yahn, "Advertising's Grave New World," *Advertising Age*, May 16, 1994, 53.

28. Kevin Goodman, "Sprint Chief Lectures Agencies on Future," *Wall Street Journal*, April 28, 1995, B6.
29. Stuart Elliot, "Procter and Gamble Calls Internet Marketing Executives to Cincinnati for a Summit Meeting," *New York Times*, August 19, 1998, D3, available at http://www.nytimes.com.
30. Beth Snyder Bulik, "Procter & Gamble's Great Web Experiment," *Business 2.0*, November 28, 2000, 48–54.
31. Andrew Hampp and Emily Bryson, "How Miracle Whip, Plenty of Fish Tapped Lady Gaga's 'Telephone,'" *Advertising Age*, March 13, 2010.
32. "100 Leading National Advertisers," *Advertising Age*, June 28, 2004, S4.

Chapter 4

1. Christie L. Nordhielm, *Marketing Management: The Big Picture*, Hoboken, NJ: John Wiley & Sons, 2006.
2. For more on STP marketing, see Philip Kotler, *Marketing Management*, Upper Saddle River, NJ: Prentice Hall, 2003, Chs. 10, 11.
3. Nina Munk, "Why Women Find Lauder Mesmerizing," *Fortune*, May 25, 1998, 96–106.
4. See, for example, Stephanie Thompson, "Gager Mixes Art, Commerce to Boost M.A.C. Sales, Image," *Advertising Age*, April 12, 2004, 60.
5. Steve Hughes, "Small Segments, Big Payoff," *Advertising Age*, January 15, 2007, 17.
6. Deborah Ball, "Toll-Free Tips: Nestle Hotlines Yield Big Ideas," *Wall Street Journal*, September 3, 2004, A7.
7. This four-way scheme is detailed in David W. Stewart, "Advertising in Slow-Growth Economies," *American Demographics,* September 1994, 40–46.
8. Allanna Sullivan, "Mobil Bets Drivers Pick Cappuccino over Low Prices," *Wall Street Journal*, January 30, 1995, B1.
9. Sally Beatty, "Nickelodeon Sets $30 Million Ad Deal with the Bahamas," *Wall Street Journal*, March 14, 2001, B6.
10. Kelly Greene, "Marketing Surprise: Older Consumers Buy Stuff, Too," *Wall Street Journal*, April 6, 2004, A1, A12.
11. Amy Merrick, "Counting on the Census," *Wall Street Journal*, February 14, 2001, B1.
12. Michael R. Solomon, *Consumer Behavior,* Upper Saddle River, NJ: Pearson Prentice Hall, 2007, 215–219.
13. Rebecca Piirto, *Beyond Mind Games: The Marketing Power of Psychographics,* Ithaca, NY: American Demographics Books, 1991, 222–223.
14. Ibid.; see Chs. 3, 5, and 8 for an extensive discussion of the VALS system.
15. Kotler, *Marketing Management*, 296–298.
16. Thomas S. Robertson and Howard Barich, "A Successful Approach to Segmenting Industrial Markets," *Planning Forum,* November/December 1992, 5–11.
17. Kotler, *Marketing Management*, 280–281.
18. Emily York, "Social Media Allows Giants to Exploit Niche Markets," *Advertising Age*, July 13, 2009, 3, 25.
19. Dan Reed, "Continental, Southwest Airlines Land Profits," *USA Today*, January 21, 2010, http://www.usatoday.com.

20. Darren Garnick, "The Working Stiff: There Really Is a 'Verizon Guy,'" *Boston Herald*, October 29, 2008, Business & Company Resource Center, http://galenet.galegroup.com; and Richard Mullins, "Goodbye Chad, Hello Verizon Test Guy," *Tampa Tribune*, January 8, 2009, Business & Company Resource Center, http://galenet.galegroup.com.

21. A more elaborate case for the importance of a single, consistent positioning premise is provided in Ries and Trout's classic, *Positioning: The Battle for Your Mind,* New York: Warner Books, 1982.

22. Other positioning options are discussed in Philip Kotler and Kevin Lane Keller, *A Framework for Marketing Management,* Upper Saddle River, NJ: Pearson Prentice Hall, 2007, Ch. 9.

23. Geoffrey Smith and Ron Stodghill, "Are Good Causes Good Marketing?" *Business Week*, March 21, 1994, 64–65.

24. Natalie Zmuda and Emily York, "Cause Effect: Brands Rush to Save the World One Deed at a Time," *Advertising Age*, March 1, 2010, 1, 22.

25. Albert M. Muniz Jr. and Thomas C. O'Guinn, "Brand Community," *Journal of Consumer Research* 27, 2001, 412–432.

26. Jean Halliday, "Looking Back on 83 Years of Pontiac Advertising," *Advertising Age*, May 4, 2009, 14.

27. Jean Halliday, "Mazda Repositioning Begins to Show Results," *Advertising Age*, January 6, 2003, 4.

28. This definition is adapted from David Aaker, *Building Strong Brands*, New York: Free Press, 1996, Ch. 3.

29. These examples are adapted from Aaker, *Building Strong Brands*, Ch. 3.

30. Esther Thorson and Jeri Moore, *Integrated Communication: Synergy of Persuasive Voices,* Mahwah, NJ: Erlbaum, 1996.

Chapter 5

1. Martin Davidson, "Objects of Desire: How Advertising Works," in Martin Davidson, *The Consumerist Manifesto: Advertising in Postmodern Times,* London: Routledge, 1992, 23–60.

2. Kate MacArthur, "Marriage of Convenience: 7-Eleven, 'Simpsons,'" *Advertising Age*, July 16, 2007.

3. Terry G. Vavra, *Aftermarketing: How to Keep Customers for Life through Relationship Marketing,* Homewood, IL: Business One Irwin, 1992, 13.

4. Michael R. Solomon, *Consumer Behavior,* Upper Saddle River, NJ: Prentice Hall, 2004, Ch. 4.

5. Shirley Leung, "Fast-Food Firms' Big Budgets Don't Buy Consumer Loyalty," *Wall Street Journal,* July 24, 2003, B4.

6. Icek Ajzen and Martin Fishbein, *Understanding Attitudes and Predicting Social Behavior,* Englewood Cliffs, NJ: Prentice Hall, 1980, 63.

7. Clutter creates a variety of problems that compromise the effectiveness of advertising. For instance, research has shown that clutter interferes with basic memory functions, inhibiting a person's ability to keep straight which brands are making what claims. For more details, see Anand Kumar and Shanker Krishnan, "Memory Interference in Advertising: A Replication and Extension," *Journal of Consumer Research,* 30, March 2004, 602–612.

8. Joel Schwarz, "Bugs at Disney? Not on Your Life, Doc," *University Week* (University of Washington), July 5, 2001, http://depts.washington.edu/uweek/archives/2001.07.JUL_05/_article5.html; Kathryn A. Braun-LaTour, Michael S. LaTour, Jacqueline E. Pickrell, and Elizabeth F. Loftus, "How and When Advertising Can Influence Memory for Consumer Experience," *Journal of Advertising,* 33, Winter 2004, 7–25.

9. For an expanded discussion of these issues, see Richard E. Petty, John T. Cacioppo, Alan J. Strathman, and Joseph R. Priester, "To Think or Not to Think: Exploring Two Routes to Persuasion," in *Persuasion: Psychological Insights and Perspectives,* eds. Sharon Shavitt and Timothy C. Brock, Boston: Allyn & Bacon, 1994, 113–147.

10. For additional discussion of this issue, see Frances K. McSweeney and Calvin Bierley, "Recent Developments in Classical Conditioning," *Journal of Consumer Research* 11, September 1984, 619–631.

11. Associations like Jay-Z with Heineken, Missy Elliott with Gap, and Queen Latifah with Cover Girl illustrate the influence of Russell Simmons in bringing hip-hop into the advertising mainstream. (See "The CEO of Hip Hop," *Business Week,* October 27, 2003, 91–98.) It is fair to say that Simmons found great success by lining up hip-hop icons as peripheral cues for all sorts of big-name advertisers.

12. The rationale for cultivating brand interest for mature brands is discussed more fully in Karen A. Machleit, Chris T. Allen, and Thomas J. Madden, "The Mature Brand and Brand Interest: An Alternative Consequence of Ad-Evoked Affect," *Journal of Marketing* 57, October 1993, 72–82.

13. Davidson, "Objects of Desire."

14. Gordon Marshall, ed., *The Concise Oxford Dictionary of Sociology,* New York: Oxford University Press, 1994, 104–105.

15. Ibid., 452.

16. Melanie Wallendorf and Eric J. Arnould, "We Gather Together: Consumption Rituals of Thanksgiving Day," *Journal of Consumer Research,* 18, No. 1, June 1991, 13–31.

17. For a great review, see Cele C. Otnes and Tina M. Lowrey, eds., *Contemporary Consumption Rituals: A Research Anthology,* Mahwah, NJ: Lawrence Erlbaum, 2004.

18. John Seabrook, "Sunday in Soho," in *Nobrow: The Culture of Marketing—The Marketing of Culture,* New York: Knopf, 2000, 161–175, available at http://www.booknoise.net/johnseabrook/stories/culture/nobrow/index.html. See also Jennifer Steinhauer, "When the Joneses Wear Jeans: Signs of Status Are Harder to Spot, but Look Again," in *Class Matters,* ed. Correspondents of the *New York Times,* New York: Times Books, 2005, 134–145.

19. C. Whan Park, "Joint Decisions in Home Purchasing: A Muddling-Through Process," *Journal of Consumer Research* 9, September 1982, 151–162.

20. Jannette L. Dates, "Advertising," in *Split Image: African Americans in the Mass Media,* eds. Jannette L. Dates and William Barlow, Washington, DC: Howard University Press, 1990, 421–454.

21. Roland Marchand, *Advertising: The American Dream,* Berkeley: University of California Press, 1984, 25.

22. Laura Koss-Feder, "Out and About: Firms Introduce Gay-Specific Ads for Mainstream Products, Services," *Marketing News,* May 25, 1998, 1, 20.

23. Wally Snyder, "Advertising's Ethical and Economic Imperative," *American Advertising,* Fall 1992, 28.

24. Albert Muniz Jr. and Thomas O'Guinn, "Brand Community," *Journal of Consumer Research* 27, 2001, 412–432.

25. Mark Weingarten, "Designed to Grow," *Business 2.0,* June 2007, 35; Rob Walker, "Consumed: Mass Appeal," *New York Times Magazine,* July 8, 2007, 16.

26. Davidson, "Objects of Desire."

Chapter 6

1. Emily Steel and Julia Angwin, "The Web's Cutting Edge, Anonymity in Name Only," *The Wall Street Journal,* August 4, 2010, http://online.wsj.com.

2. Julia Angwin, "Latest in Web Tracking: Stealthy 'Supercookies,'" *The Wall Street Journal,* August 18, 2011, http://online.wsj.com.

3. Dan Frakes, "Mac Gems," *Macworld,* August 2011, 16; and Jeff Gelles, "How to Get Online Ads to Quit Following You Around," *Philadelphia Inquirer,* February 24, 2011, http://www.philly.com.

4. Joelle Tessler, "Internet Ads Pose Privacy Challenges," *Houston Chronicle,* August 1, 2011, Business & Company Resource Center, http://galenet.galegroup.com; "Reset Thinking for a New Era Online," *DM News,* June 21, 2010, 14; and Emily Steel, "Some Data-Miners Ready to Reveal What They Know," *The Wall Street Journal,* December 3, 2010, http://online.wsj.com.

5. George J. Stigler, "The Economics of Information," *Journal of Political Economy,* June 1961, 213–220.

6. Anheuser-Busch, "Responsibility Matters," corporate social responsibility Web page, http://www.beeresponsible.com, accessed May 26, 2007.

7. Clair Atkinson, "Ad Intrusion Up, Say Consumers," *Advertising Age,* January 6, 2003, 1, 19.

8. Hank Kim, "Just Risk It," *Advertising Age,* February 9, 2004, 1, 51.

9. Matthew Creamer, "Caught in the Clutter Crossfire: Your Brand," *Advertising Age,* April 2, 2007, 1, 35.

10. Ibid., 35.

11. Richard Caves, *American Industry: Structure, Conduct, Performance,* Englewood Cliffs, NJ: Prentice-Hall, 1964, 102.

12. A. H. Maslow, *Motivation and Personality,* New York: Harper & Row, 1970.

13. Vance Packard, *The Status Seekers,* New York: David McKay, 1959.

14. This argument was first offered by authors George Katona, *The Mass Consumption Society,* New York: McGraw-Hill, 1964, 54–61; and John Kenneth Galbraith, *The Affluent Society,* Boston: Houghton Mifflin, 1958.

15. Fox, *The Mirror Makers: A History of American Advertising and Its Creators,* New York: William Morrow, 1984, 330.

16. Normandy Madden, "Honda Pulls Suicide Car Ad from Australian TV Market," *Advertising Age,* September 22, 2003, 3.

17. Kevin Goldman, "From Witches to Anorexics, Critical Eyes Scrutinize Ads for Political Correctness," *Wall Street Journal,* May 19, 1994, B1, B10.

18. Georgia Flight, "Hits and Misses," *Business 2.0,* April 2006, 140.

19. Don E. Schultz, "Subliminal Ad Notions Still Resonate Today," *Marketing News,* March 15, 2007, 5, 9.

20. Murphy, Monahan, and Zajonc, "Additivity of Nonconscious Affect: Combined Effects of Priming and Exposure," *Journal of Personality and Social Psychology 69,* 1995, 589–602.

21. Timothy E. Moore, "Subliminal Advertising: What You See Is What You Get," *Journal of Marketing,* 46, Spring 1982, 38–47; Timothy E. Moore, "The Case against Subliminal Manipulation," *Psychology and Marketing,* 5, No. 4, Winter 1988, 297–317.

22. Andy Warhol, *The Philosophy of Andy Warhol: From A to B and Back Again,* New York: Harcourt Brace Jovanovich, 1975, 101.

23. "100 Leading National Advertisers," *Advertising Age,* June 22, 2009, S1.

24. B. G. Gregg, "Tax Funds Bankroll New Anti-Drug Ads," *Cincinnati Enquirer,* July 10, 1998, A1, A17.

25. Jay Reeves, "Scrushy Said to Pay for Positive Stories," *Associated Press,* January 19, 2006, www.news.yahoo.com, accessed January 20, 2006.

26. Eamon Javers, "This Opinion Brought to You by . . . ," *Business Week,* January 30, 2006, 35.

27. Claire Atkinson, "Watchdog Group Hits TV Product Placement," *Advertising Age,* October 6, 2003, 12.

28. Richard Linnett, "Psychologists Protest Kids' Ads," *Advertising Age,* September 11, 2000, 4.

29. Patrick J. Sheridan, "FCC Sets Children's Ad Limits," *1990 Information Access Company,* 119, No. 20, 1990, 33.

30. Laura Bird, "NBC Special Is One Long Prime-Time Ad," *Wall Street Journal,* January 21, 1994, B1, B4.

31. Stephanie Thompson and Ira Teinowitz, "Big Food's Big Deal Not Such a Big Concession," *Advertising Age,* November 20, 2006, 1, 29.

32. Kathleen Deveny, "Joe Camel Ads Reach Children, Research Finds," *Wall Street Journal,* December 11, 1991, B1, B6.

33. See, for example, Joseph R. DiFranza et al., "RJR Nabisco's Cartoon Camel Promotes Camel Cigarettes to Children," *Journal of the American Medical Association,* 266, No. 22, 1991, 3168–3153.

34. For a summary of more than 60 articles that address the issue of alcohol and cigarette advertising and the lack of a relationship between advertising and cigarette and alcohol industry demand, see Mark Frankena et al., "Alcohol, Consumption, and Abuse," Bureau of Economics, Federal Trade Commission, March 5, 1985. For a similar listing of research articles where the same conclusions were drawn during congressional hearings on the topic, see "Advertising of Tobacco Products," hearings before the Subcommittee on Health and the Environment, Committee on Energy and Commerce, and House of Representatives, 99th Congress, July 18 and August 1, 1986, No. 99–167.

35. For examples of the more recent studies that reaffirm peers and family rather than advertising as the basis for smoking initiation, see Charles R. Taylor and P. Greg Bonner, "Comment on 'American Media and the Smoking-Related Behaviors of Asian Adolescents,'" *Journal of Advertising Research,* December 2003, 419–430; Bruce Simons Morton, "Peer and Parent Influences on Smoking and Drinking among Early Adolescents," *Journal of Health Education and Behavior* (February 2000); and Karen H. Smith and Mary Ann Stutz, "Factors That Influence Adolescents to Smoke," *Journal of Consumer Affairs,* 33, No. 2, Winter 1999, 321–357.

36. With regard to cartoon characters, see, for example, Lucy L. Henke, "Young Children's Perceptions of Cigarette Brand Advertising: Awareness, Affect and Target Market Identification," *Journal of Advertising,* 24, No. 4, Winter 1995, 13–27; and Richard Mizerski, "The Relationship between Cartoon Trade Character Recognition and Attitude toward the Product Category," *Journal of Marketing,* 59, October 1995, 58–70. The evidence in Europe is provided by Jeffrey Goldstein, "Children and Advertising—the Research," *Commercial Communications,* July 1998, 4–8.

37. For research on this topic across several decades, see Richard Schmalensee, *The Economics of Advertising,* Amsterdam and London: North-Holland, 1972; Mark S. Albion and Paul W. Farris, *The Advertising Controversy,* Boston: Auburn House, 1981; and Michael J. Waterson, "Advertising and Tobacco Consumption: An Analysis of the Two Major Aspects of the Debate," *International Journal of Advertising,* 9, 1990, 59–72.

38. Ira Singer et al., "The Underground Web," *Business Week,* September 2, 2002, 67–74.

39. Bloomberg News, "Frank Eyes Restoring Web Gaming," *Boston Globe,* March 17, 2007, accessed at www.boston.com/news.

40. Mercedes M. Cardona, "Marketers Bite Back as Fat Fight Flares Up," *Advertising Age,* March 1, 2004, 3, 35.

41. Rep. Ric Keller (R-Fla.), quoted in Joanne Kenen, "U.S. House Backs Ban on Obesity Lawsuits," *Yahoo Finance,* March 10, 2004, http://biz.yahoo.com/rc/040310/congress_obesity_3.html.

42. Stephanie Thompson and Kate MacArthur, "Obesity Fear Frenzy Grips Food Industry," *Advertising Age,* April 23, 2007, 1, 46.

43. One of the best discussions of the FTC's definition of deception was offered many years ago by Gary T. Ford and John E. Calfee, "Recent Developments in FTC Policy on Deception," *Journal of Marketing,* 50, July 1986, 82–103.

44. Ivan Preston, *The Great American Blow Up,* Madison: University of Wisconsin Press, 1975, 4.

45. Christy Fisher, "How Congress Broke Unfair Ad Impasse," *Advertising Age,* August 22, 1994, 34. For additional discussion of the FTC's definition of unfairness, see Ivan Preston, "Unfairness Developments in FTC Advertising Cases," *Journal of Public Policy and Marketing,* 14, No. 2, 1995, 318–321.

46. Daniel Golden and Suzanne Vranica, "Duracell's Duck Will Carry Disclaimer," *Wall Street Journal,* February 7, 2002, B2.

47. Ville Heiskanen, "Google's AdMob Deal Criticized," *Business Week,* December 28, 2009, http://www.businessweek.com.

48. Anthony D. Miyazaki, Andrea J. S. Stanaland, and May O. Lwin, "Self-Regulatory Safeguards and the Online Privacy of Preteen Children," *Journal of Advertising* 38(4), Winter 2009, 80; and Steve Stecklow and Julia Angwin, "House Releases 'Do Not Track' Bill," *The Wall Street Journal,* May 7, 2011, http://online.wsj.com.

49. The full text and specifications of the Children's Online Privacy Protection Act can be found at http://www.ftc.gov/ogc/coppa1.htm.

50. For a discussion of the origins and intent of the FTC's advertising substantiation program and its extension to require reasonable basis, see Debra L. Scammon and Richard J. Semenik, "The FTC's 'Reasonable Basis' for Substantiation of Advertising: Expanded Standards and Implications," *Journal of Advertising,* 12(1), 1983, 4–11.

51. The history and intent of the corrective-advertising concept and several of its applications are provided by Debra L. Scammon and Richard J. Semenik, "Corrective Advertising: Evolution of the Legal Theory and Application of the Remedy," *Journal of Advertising,* 11(1), 1982, 10–20.

52. Steven W. Colford and Raymond Serafin, "Scali Pays for Volvo Ad: FTC," *Advertising Age,* August 26, 1991, 4.

53. Neal Boudette, "Internet Self-Regulation Seen Lacking Punch," *Yahoo Finance,* September 14, 1999, http://biz.yahoo.com.

54. "Upstaged Advertisers Riled by Bowl Stunt," *Advertising Age* (*Advertising Age* Roundup), February 9, 2004, 1.

55. This statement of purpose can be found inside the cover of any issue of *Consumer Reports.*

56. Douglas MacMillan, "Why Facebook Wants Your ID," *Bloomberg Businessweek,* January 4, 2010, 92–93.

57. Maria Namestnikova, "Spam Evolution," February 2010, March 22, 2010, www.viruslist.com.

58. "Senate Approves Antispam Bill," *Reuters News Service,* October 22, 2003, http://news.reuters.com.

59. Elaine Porterfield, "First Arrest under Spam Law Could Dent E-Mail Flood," *Reuters News Service,* May 31, 2007.

60. Ira Teinowitz, "Congress Nears Accord on Sweepstakes Limits," *Advertising Age,* August 9, 1999, 33.

61. James Heckman, "Online, but Not on Trial, though Privacy Looms Large," *Marketing News,* December 6, 1999, 8.

62. Promotion Marketing Association, "The Promotion Marketing Association Coupon Council Reports an Increase in Coupon Activity in 2009," March 26, 2010, http://www.pmalink.org.

63. Melissa Allison, "Starbucks Coupon Gets out of Hand," *Seattle Times,* August 31, 2006, available at http://archives.seattletimes.nwsource.com/web.

64. Ibid.

65. Lorraine Woellert, "The Do-Not-Call Law Won't Stop the Calls," *Business Week,* September 29, 2003, 89.

66. Atkinson, "Watchdog Group Hits TV Product Placement," 12.

67. Rich Thomaselli, "Philip Morris: No Smoking in Movies," *Advertising Age,* November 20, 2006, 3, 27.

Chapter 7

1. Monee Fields-White, "Expanding Her Turf," *Crain's Chicago Business,* October 19, 2009, Business & Company Resource Center, http://galenet.gale group.com.
2. "Global Marketers: Top 10 Global Marketers by Country," *Advertising Age,* December 8, 2008.
3. Matthew Karnitschnig, "Comedy Central Export Aims for Local Laughs," *Wall Street Journal,* March 2, 2007, B1.
4. Gregory Fowler, "Mac and PC's Overseas Adventures," *Wall Street Journal,* March 1, 2007, B1.
5. Antonio Regalado, "Marketers Pursue the Shallow-Pocketed," *Wall Street Journal,* January 26, 2007, B3.
6. Clay Chandler, "Changing Places," *Fortune,* September 18, 2006, 61–64.
7. Gautam Naik, "Leveraging the Age Gap," *Wall Street Journal,* February 27, 2003, B1, B4.
8. Johny Johansson, "The Sense of Nonsense: Japanese TV Advertising," *Journal of Advertising,* March 1994, 17–26.
9. S. Han and S. Shavitt, "Persuasion and Culture: Advertising Appeals in Individualistic and Collectivistic Societies," *Journal of Experimental Social Psychology,* 30, 1994, 326–350.
10. Spencer Ante, "The Science of Desire," *BusinessWeek,* June 5, 2006, 98–106.
11. Jiri Stejskal, "Save Money and Save Face: Hire a Professional Translator," *Corporate Logo .com,* January 29, 2009, accessed at http://www.beckyblackley.com.
12. Jing Zhang, "The Persuasiveness of Individualistic and Collectivistic Advertising Appeals among Chinese Generation-X Consumers," *Journal of Advertising* 39(3), Fall 2010, 69–80.
13. Robert Kirby, "Kirby: Advertising Translates into Laughs," *Salt Lake Tribune,* http://www .sltrib.com, accessed February 24, 1998.
14. Stejskal, "Save Money and Save Face."
15. Nandini Lakshman, "The Great Indian Beer Rush," *BusinessWeek,* April 23, 2007, 50.
16. John W. Miller, "EU to Say Location Data Private," *The Wall Street Journal,* May 13, 2011, http://online.wsj.com.
17. "Why China's Distinctive Creative Aesthetic Has Been Slow to Peak," *Advertising Age,* June 19, 2011, http://adage.com.
18. For contrasting points of view, compare Douglas B. Holt, John A. Quelch, and Earl L. Taylor, "How Global Brands Compete," *Harvard Business Review,* September 2004, 68–75; with Darrell K. Rigby and Vijay Vishwanath, "Localization: The Revolution in Consumer Markets," *Harvard Business Review,* April 2006, 82–92.
19. Arundhati Parmar, "Global Youth United," *Marketing News,* October 28, 2002, 1, 49.
20. Lisa Bannon, "One-Toy-Fits-All: How Industry Learned to Love the Global Kid," *Wall Street Journal,* April 29, 2003, A1, A12.
21. Michael Fielding, "Walk the Line," *Marketing News,* September 1, 2006, 8–10.

Chapter 8

1. Carl G. Jung, cited in Astrid Fitzgerald, *An Artist's Book of Inspiration: A Collection of Thoughts on Art, Artists, and Creativity,* New York: Lindisfarne, 1996, 58.

2. Warren Berger, "Dare-Devils," *Business 2.0,* April 2004, 111–116.
3. Matthew Creamer, "Crispin Ups Ante," *Advertising Age,* January 10, 2005, S-1, S-2.
4. Kate MacArthur, "BK Sets High Score with Its Adver-games," *Advertising Age,* January 8, 2007, 3, 31.
5. Emily York, "Economy, Rivals No Match for BK's Marketing," *Advertising Age,* May 5, 2008, 4, 58.
6. "Ad Age's Best of the Decade—Agencies," *Advertising Age,* December 14, 2009, 6.
7. Eloy Trevino and Scott Davis, "There's Nothing New in Desperate Marketing," *Advertising Age,* April 23, 2007, 22; Annie Gasparro, "Burger King Removes Mascot from Throne," *The Wall Street Journal,* August 20, 2011, http://online.wsj.com; Alicia Kelso, "Burger King's New Ad Campaign Is Spot On," *QSR Web,* August 23, 2011, http://www.qsrweb. com; Marc E. Babej, "Burger King Decapitates Its 'King' Mascot," *Forbes,* August 19, 2011, http://www.forbes.com.
8. Matthew Creamer, "Caught in the Clutter Crossfire: Your Brand," *Advertising Age,* April 2, 2007, 1, 35.
9. Brian Till and Daniel Baack, "Recall and Persuasion: Does Creative Advertising Matter?" *Journal of Advertising,* Fall 2005, 47–57.
10. Karen Machleit, Chris Allen, and Thomas Madden, "The Mature Brand and Brand Interest," *Journal of Marketing,* October 1993, 72–82.
11. Marc Gobe, *Emotional Branding: The New Paradigm for Connecting Brands to People,* New York: Allworth, 2001.
12. Procter & Gamble, "Charmin Launches Global Sponsorship with SitOrSquat Website and Mobile Phone Application," news release, March 24, 2009, http://www.prnewswire .com; Mickey Kham, "P&G's Charmin Brand Runs First Mobile Sponsorship," *Mobile Marketer,* April 10, 2009, http://mobilemarketer. com; Suzanne Vranica, "Babies and Tigers: Best and Worst Ads of 2009," *The Wall Street Journal,* December 21, 2009, B1, B6.
13. Socrates, quoted in Plato, *Phaedrus and the Seventh and Eighth Letters,* trans. Walter Hamilton, Middlesex, England: Penguin, 1970, 46–47, cited in Kay Redfield Jamison, *Touched with Fire: Manic-Depressive Illness and the Artistic Temperament,* New York: Free Press, 1993, 51.
14. Howard Gardner, *Creating Minds: An Anatomy of Creativity Seen through the Lives of Freud, Einstein, Picasso, Stravinsky, Eliot, Graham, and Gandhi,* New York: Basic Books, 1993.
15. Ibid., 364.
16. Ibid.
17. Ibid., 145; Sigmund Freud, *The Interpretation of Dreams,* in *The Basic Writings of Sigmund Freud,* ed. A. A. Brill, New York: Modern Library, 1900/1938.
18. Gardner, *Creating Minds,* 369.
19. Ibid.
20. Alice Cuneo, "The Dude Who Thought Different," *Advertising Age,* July 31, 2006, 1, 25.
21. Ibid.
22. Berger, "Dare-Devils."
23. Luke Sullivan, "Staring at Your Partner's Shoes," in *Hey Whipple, Squeeze This: A Guide to Creating Great Ads,* New York: Wiley, 1998, 20–22.
24. William Bernbach, quoted in Thomas Frank, *The Conquest of Cool: Business Culture, Consumer*

Culture, and the Rise of Hip Consumerism, Chicago: University of Chicago Press, 1997.
25. D. West, "Restricted Creativity: Advertising Agency Work Practices in the U.S., Canada, and the U.K.," *Journal of Creative Behavior,* 27, No. 3, 1993, 200–213; D. C. West, "Cross-National Creative Personalities, Processes, and Agency Philosophies," *Journal of Advertising Research,* 33, No. 5, 1993, 53–62.
26. P. C. Michell, "Accord and Discord in Agency-Client Perceptions of Creativity," *Journal of Advertising Research,* 24, No. 5, 1984, 9–24.
27. Elizabeth Hirschman, "The Effect of Verbal and Pictorial Advertising Stimuli on Aesthetic, Utilitarian, and Familiarity Perceptions," *Journal of Advertising,* 1985, 27–34.
28. B. G. Vanden Berg, S. J. Smith, and J. W. Wickes, "Internal Agency Relationships: Account Service and Creative Personnel," *Journal of Advertising,* 15, No. 2, 1986, 55–60.
29. A. J. Kover and S. M. Goldberg, "The Games Copywriters Play: Conflict, Quasi-Control, a New Proposal," *Journal of Advertising Research,* 25, No. 4, 1995, 52–62.
30. R. L. Vaughn, "Point of View: Creatives versus Researchers—Must They Be Adversaries?" *Journal of Advertising Research,* 22, No. 6, 1983, 45–48.
31. Kover and Goldberg, "The Games Copywriters Play."
32. Jeremy Mullman, "Think Twice before Axing Account Management," *Advertising Age,* April 26, 2010, 8.
33. John Sweeney, "Assuring Poor Creative," in Thomas C. O'Guinn, Chris T. Allen, and Richard J. Semenik, *Advertising and Integrated Brand Promotion,* Mason, OH: South-Western Cengage Learning, 2009, 325–326.
34. Cuneo, "The Dude Who Thought Different," 25.
35. Jon R. Katzenbach and Douglas K. Smith, *The Wisdom of Teams: Creating the High-Performance Organization,* Boston: Harvard Business School Press, 1993.
36. Dorothy Leonard and Susaan Straus, "Putting Your Company's Whole Brain to Work," *Harvard Business Review,* July–August 1997: 111–121.
37. Katzenbach and Smith, *The Wisdom of Teams,* Ch. 7.
38. Ibid., 144.
39. Teresa Amabile, "How to Kill Creativity," *Harvard Business Review,* Fall 1998, 77–87. See also Jaafar El-Murad and Douglas C. West, "The Definition and Measurement of Creativity: What Do We Know?" *Journal of Advertising Research,* June 2004, 188–201.
40. Brooke Capps, "Playtime, Events, Perks Go Long Way in Team Building," *Advertising Age,* January 15, 2007, 30.
41. Jacob Goldenberg, David Mazursky, and Sorin Solomon, "The Fundamental Templates of Quality Ads," *Marketing Science,* 18, No. 3, 1999, 333–351.
42. Dale Buss, "Bridging the Great Divide in Marketing Thinking," *Advertising Age,* March 26, 2007, 18–19.
43. Dorothy Leonard and Walter Swap, *When Sparks Fly: Igniting Creativity in Groups,* Boston: Harvard Business School Press, 1999.
44. Ibid.
45. Robert J. Sternberg, "Creativity as a Decision," *American Psychologist,* May 2002, 376; and Robert J. Sternberg, "Identifying and Developing Creative Giftedness," *Roeper Review,* 23, No. 2, 2000, 60–65.

Chapter 9

1. Steve Hamm, "Children of the Web," *BusinessWeek,* July 2, 2007, 51–58.
2. Ibid., 56.
3. U.S. Census Bureau, "E-Stats," May 26, 2011, http://www.census.gov/estats.
4. Forrester Research, "U.S. Interactive Marketing Forecast, 2009–2014," July 30, 2009, 7; "Digital Marketing Facts 2010," *Advertising Age,* February 22, 2010.
5. Miniwatts Marketing Group, "Internet World Stats," http://www.internetworldstats.com, accessed June 15, 2010.
6. Forrester Research, "U.S. Interactive Marketing Forecast."
7. "Stats—Web Worldwide," *ClickZ,* http://www.clickz.com/showPage.html?page=stats/web_worldwide, accessed December 1, 2009.
8. "Spam Statistics and Facts," *Spam Laws,* http://www.spamlaws.com/spam-stats.html, accessed June 15, 2010.
9. "Digital Marketing Facts 2010."
10. Om Malik, "Growing in the Shadow of Google," *Business 2.0,* December 2006, 40.
11. Robert D. Hof, "Mix, Match, and Mutate," *BusinessWeek,* July 25, 2005, 72–74.
12. Digital Marketing & Media Fact Pack, *Advertising Age,* April 23, 2007, 21.
13. Nancy Einhart, "Clean Sweep of the Market," *Business 2.0,* March 2003, 56.
14. "Digital Marketing Facts 2010."
15. Kris Oser, "Targeting Web Behavior Pays, American Airlines Study Finds," *Advertising Age,* May 17, 2004, 8.
16. *Mobile Marketing Association,* "Mobile Internet Usage Continues to Climb," Public Research, January 6, 2010, http://www.mmaglobal.com.
17. Kelli S. Burns and Richard J. Lutz, "The Function of Format," *Journal of Advertising,* 35, No. 1, Spring 2006, 53–63.
18. Bob Parks, "Let's Remake a Dealership," *Business 2.0,* June 2004, 65–67.
19. Fuyuan Shen, "Banner Advertisement Pricing, Measurement, and Pretesting Practices: Perspectives from Interactive Agencies," *Journal of Advertising,* 31, No. 3, Fall 2002, 59–68.
20. Abbey Klaassen, "Search Marketing," *Advertising Age,* November 2, 2009, 16.
21. Ibid., 33.
22. Satya Menon and Dilip Soman, "Managing the Power of Curiosity for Effective Web Advertising Strategies," *Journal of Advertising,* 31, No. 3, Fall 2002, 1–14.
23. Rita Chang, "Travelocity Offers Hope in Evolution of Display Advertising," *Advertising Age,* October 26, 2009, 14.
24. "Digital Marketing Facts 2010."
25. The statistics referenced here were from a Forrester Research survey cited in Digital Marketing & Media Fact Pack, *Advertising Age,* April 23, 2007, 45.
26. Stephen Baker, "Pop-Up Ads Had Better Start Pleasing," *BusinessWeek,* December 8, 2003, 40.
27. Kathryn Kranhold, "Internet Advertisers Use Humor in Effort to Entice Web Surfers," *Wall Street Journal,* August 17, 1999, B9.
28. Michael Learmonth, "Nike Breaks Own Viral Record with World Cup Ad," *Advertising Age,* May 27, 2010, http://www.adage.com.
29. Heather Green and Ben Elgin, "Do E-Ads Have a Future?" *BusinessWeek e.biz,* January 22, 2001, 46–49; and S. Shyam Sundar and Sriram Kalyanaraman, "Arousal, Memory, and Impression Formation Effects of Animation Speed in Web Advertising," *Journal of Advertising,* 33, No.1, Spring 2004, 7–17.
30. Bob Garfield, "Widgets Are Made for Marketing, so Why Aren't More Advertisers Using Them?" *Advertising Age,* December 1, 2008, 26.
31. Robert D. Hof, "My Virtual Life," *BusinessWeek,* May 1, 2006, 72–80. A visit to Second Life on July 23, 2007, showed 8,310,736 total residents; 1,548,131 logged in within the last 60 days; 33,940 online at the moment; and $1,761,092 spent in the past 24 hours.
32. Peter Valdes-Dapena, "Real Cars Drive into Second Life," CNNMoney.com, November 18, 2006, accessed at http://www.cnn.com.
33. Frank Rose, "Lonely Planet," *Wired,* August 2007, 140–145.
34. Ibid., 142.
35. Entertainment Software Association, "Industry Facts," 2008, http://www.theesa.com/facts, accessed June 18, 2010.
36. Verolien Cauberghe and Patrick De Pelsmacker, "Advergames: The Impact of Brand Prominence and Game Repetition on Brand Responses," *Journal of Advertising* 39(1), Spring 2010, 5–18.
37. Lynn Ward, "Hidden Costs of Building an E-Commerce Site," *E-Commerce Times,* April 28, 2003, http://www.ecommercetimes.com.
38. Duff McDonald, "A Website as Big (and Cheap) as the Great Outdoors," *Business 2.0,* October 2003, 70–71.
39. Hanjun Ko, Chang-Hoan Cho, and Marilyn S. Roberts, "Internet Uses and Gratifications," *Journal of Advertising,* 34, No. 2, Summer 2005, 57–70.
40. Laurie Freeman, "Domain-Name Dilemma Worsens," *Advertising Age,* November 8, 1999, 100.
41. Paul Sloan, "Masters of Their Domain," *Business 2.0,* December 2005, 138–144.
42. Adam Goldman, "Domain Names: 21st Century Real Estate," *Associated Press,* July 22, 2007, accessed at http://biz.yahoo.com.
43. Ann Harrison, "Privacy? Who Cares," *Business 2.0,* June 12, 2001, 48–49.
44. Jan-Benedict, E. M. Steenkamp, and Inge Geyskens, "How Country Characteristics Affect the Perceived Value of Web Sites," *Journal of Marketing,* 70, No. 3, July 2006, 136–150.
45. Definitions in this section adapted from Brian Getting, "Web Analytics: Understanding Visitor Behavior," *Practical eCommerce,* January 2006, 8.
46. Stephen Baker, "Wiser about the Web," *BusinessWeek,* March 27, 2006, 55.
47. Sundar and Kalyanaraman, "Arousal, Memory, and Impression Formation Effects."
48. Brian Grow and Ben Elgin, "Click Fraud," *BusinessWeek,* October 2, 2006, 46–57.
49. Burt Helm, "How Do You Clock the Clicks?" *BusinessWeek,* March 13, 2006, 44; and Reuters News Service, "Yahoo Taps Click Fraud Watchdog," March 22, 2007, accessed at http://www.cnnmoney.com.
50. Peter Corbett, "Facebook Demographics and Statistics Report June 2010—Privacy Concerns Don't Stop Growth," iStrategyLabs blog, June 8, 2010, http://www.istrategylabs.com.
51. John Kuczala, "Online Video Ads Get Ready to Grab You," *Business 2.0,* May 2005, 25.
52. James Templeton, "Internet Products Ready to Challenge TV," *San Francisco Chronicle,* July 4, 2010, http://www.sfgate.com.
53. Mobile Marketing Association, "Mobile Internet Usage Continues to Climb."
54. "Location Based Mobile Marketing Poised for Expansion," *Mobile Marketer,* February 24, 2010, http://www.mobilestorm.com.

Chapter 10

1. Interactive Promotions Brand Marketing by ePrize, http://eprize.com/portfolio, accessed February 16, 2010. CarMax's Tweet Yourself to a New Ride Sweepstakes, http://www.carmax.com/enUS/tweetstakes/default.html, accessed February 16, 2010.
2. Kris Oser, "Speedway Effort Decodes NASCAR Fans," *Advertising Age,* May 17, 2004, 150.
3. Ibid.
4. Anthony Malakian, "Ad Beat: Scratch and Win Customers," *Banking Wire,* November 26, 2008, Business & Company Resource Center, http://galenet.galegroup.com.
5. Amy Johannes, "Jelly Belly Names Illinois Man Winner of Flavor Contest," *Promo,* September 16, 2008, Business & Company Resource Center, http://galenet.galegroup.com.
6. Bob Stone, *Successful Direct Marketing Methods,* Lincolnwood, IL: NTC Business Books, 1994.
7. The discussion to follow builds on that of Stone, *Successful Direct Marketing Methods.*
8. Louise Lee, "Catalogs, Catalogs, Everywhere," *BusinessWeek,* December 4, 2006, 32–34; Elisabeth Sullivan, "Direct to Digital," *Marketing News,* November 5, 2009, 25.
9. Allanna Sullivan, "From a Call to a Click," *Wall Street Journal,* July 17, 2000, R30.
10. See Edward Nash, "The Roots of Direct Marketing," *Direct Marketing Magazine,* February 1995, 38–40; Cara Beardi, "Lillian Vernon Sets Sights on Second Half-Century," *Advertising Age,* March 19, 2001, 22.
11. Allison Cosmedy, *A History of Direct Marketing,* New York: Direct Marketing Association, 1992, 6.
12. Ibid.
13. Daniel Klein, "Disintegrated Marketing," *Harvard Business Review,* March 2003, 18, 19; Michael Fielding, "Spread the Word," *Marketing News,* February 15, 2005, 19, 20; and Michael Fielding, "Direct Mail Still Has Its Place," *Marketing News,* November 1, 2006, 31, 33.

14. Nash, "The Roots of Direct Marketing."
15. Anthony Bianco, "The Vanishing Mass Market," *Business Week,* July 12, 2004, 61–68.
16. Gary Levin, "AT&T Exec: Customer Access Goal of Integration," *Advertising Age,* October 10, 1994, S1.
17. Like many authors, Winer contends that direct marketing starts with the creation of a database. See Russell Winer, "A Framework for Customer Relationship Management," *California Management Review,* Summer 2001, 89–105.
18. Ibid.
19. *The 2001 Mailing List Catalog,* New York: Hugo Dunhill Mailing Lists, 2001.
20. Murray Raphel, "What's the Scoop on Ben & Jerry?" *Direct Marketing Magazine,* August 1994, 23, 24.
21. Ibid.
22. Michael Bush, "Why Harrah's Loyalty Effort Is Industry's Gold Standard," *Advertising Age,* October 5, 2009, 8.
23. Michael Learmonth, "Holy Grail of Targeting Is Fuel for Privacy Battle," *Advertising Age,* March 22, 2010, 1, 21.
24. Ira Teinowitz and Ken Wheaton, "Do Not Market," *Advertising Age,* March 12, 2007, 1, 44.
25. Stone, *Successful Direct Marketing Methods.*
26. Sally Beatty, "Drug Companies Are Minding Your Business," *Wall Street Journal,* April 17, 1998, B1, B3.
27. Michael Edmondson, "Postcards from the Edge," *Marketing Tools,* May 1995, 14.
28. Mathew Schwartz, "U.S. Extends Spam Lead," *Information Week,* July 14, 2010, http://www.informationweek.com.
29. Cara Beardi, "Opt-In Taken to Great Heights," *Advertising Age,* November 6, 2000, S54; and Michael Battisto, "Preparation Yields Spam-Free E-Mail Lists," *Marketing News,* February 17, 2003, 17.
30. Jodi Mardesich, "Too Much of a Good Thing," *Industry Standard,* March 19, 2001, 85.
31. Katherine Rosman, "As Seen on TV . . . and in Aisle 5," *The Wall Street Journal,* January 28, 2010, D1, D4.
32. Thomas Mucha, "Stronger Sales in Just 28 Minutes," *Business 2.0,* June 2005, 56–60; and Elizabeth Holmes, "Golf-Club Designer Hopes to Repeat TV Success," *Wall Street Journal,* January 30, 2007, B4.
33. Evantheia Schibsted, "Ab Rockers, Ginsu Knives, E320s," *Business 2.0,* May 29, 2001, 46–49; Jack Neff, "Wait, There's More! DRTV Is Gaining Mainstream Appeal," *Advertising Age,* March 23, 2009, 17.
34. Brian Steinberg, "How to Stop Them from Skipping: TiVo Tells All," *Advertising Age,* July 16, 2007, 1, 33.

Chapter 11

1. Kate MacArthur, "Give It Away: Fast Feeders Favor Freebies," *Advertising Age,* June 18, 2007, 10.
2. "Float Night Surpasses Oklahoma City-Based Sonic's Expectations," *Daily Oklahoman (Oklahoma City),* June 5, 2009, Business & Company Resource Center, http://galenet.galegroup.com; and Sonic Corp., "Summer at Sonic Starts with Free Root Beer Floats," News Release, May 29, 2009, http://www.sonicdrivein.com.
3. Pamela Parseghian, "Panel: Unique Promotions Add Value to Guest Experience," *Nation's Restaurant News,* October 26, 2009, 44.
4. Bradley Johnson, "Leading National Advertisers Report: Spending up 3.1% to $105 Billion," *Advertising Age,* June 25, 2007, S-2.
5. 2004 Industry Trends Report, *Promo Magazine.*
6. Jack Neff, "TV Doesn't Sell Packaged Goods," *Advertising Age,* May 24, 2004, 1, 30.
7. Cara Beardi, "POP Ups Sales Results," *Advertising Age,* July 23, 2001, 27.
8. Kate MacArthur, "McD's Sees Growth, but Are Ads a Factor?" *Advertising Age,* November 24, 2003, 3, 24.
9. Jack Neff, "Black Eye in Store for Big Brands," *Advertising Age,* April 30, 2001, 1, 34.
10. *Cox Direct 20th Annual Survey of Promotional Practices,* Chart 22, 1998, 37.
11. Dean Foust, "Queen of Pop," *Business Week,* August 7, 2006, 44–45.
12. Matthew Creamer, "Caught in the Clutter Crossfire: Your Brand," *Advertising Age,* April 2, 2007, 1, 35.
13. "Coupon Use Skyrocketed in 2009," *Promo,* January 27, 2010, http://promomagazine.com.
14. Elizabeth Holmes, "Burned by Daily-Deal Craze, Small Businesses Get Savvy," *The Wall Street Journal,* March 24, 2011, http://online.wsj.com.
15. Barry M. Benjamin, "Plan Ahead to Limit Potential Disasters," *Marketing News,* November 10, 2003, 15.
16. *Cox Direct 20th Annual Survey of Promotional Practices,* 1998, 28.
17. Cara Beardi, "Cox's Introz Mailer Bundles Samples in Industry," *Advertising Age,* November 2000, 88.
18. *Cox Direct 20th Annual Survey of Promotional Practices,* 1998, 27.
19. Betsy Spethmann, "Branded Moments," *Promo Magazine,* September 2000, 84.
20. Louise Lee, "What's Roiling the Selling Season," *Business Week,* January 10, 2005, 38.
21. Brian Grow, "The Great Rebate Runaround," *Business Week,* December 5, 2005, 34–38.
22. Ibid., 34.
23. 2007 Marketing Fact Book, *Marketing News,* July 15, 2007, 32.
24. Lee Duffey, "Sweet Talk: Promotions Position Candy Company," *Marketing News,* March 30, 1998, 11.
25. Ron Donoho, "It's Up! It's Good!" *Sales and Marketing Management,* April 2003, 43–47.
26. Jack Neff, "P&G Trims Fat off Its $2B Trade-Promotion System," *Advertising Age,* June 5, 2006, 8.
27. Data available at Promotional Products Association International website at http://www.ppa.org, accessed on August 5, 2007.
28. Ibid.
29. Ibid; Patricia O'Dell, "Shopping Trip," *Promo,* December 1, 2009, http://promomagazine.com.
30. Data on point-of-purchase decision making cited in O'Dell, "Shopping Trip."
31. Data cited in Lisa Z. Eccles, "P-O-P Scores with Marketers," *Advertising Age,* September 26, 1994.
32. Nicole Crawford, "Keeping P-O-P Sharp," *Promo Magazine,* January 1998, 52, 53.
33. Neff, "P&G Trims Fat off Its $2B Trade-Promotion System."
34. Retailer Guide to Maximizing In-Store Advertising Effectiveness, Washington, DC: Point of Purchase Advertising International, 1999, 5–7.
35. Kunur Patel, "Forget Foursquare: Why Location Marketing Is the New Point-of-Purchase," *Advertising Age,* March 22, 2010, pp. 1, 19.
36. Ibid.
37. 2004 Industry Trends Report, *Promo Magazine.*
38. Richard Alan Nelson and Rick Ebel, "2009 PPAI Sales Volume Study: The Only Direction to Go Is Up," *Promotional Products Business,* July 2010, p. 8.
39. Data on outdoor advertising categories obtained from Outdoor Advertising Association of America website, http://www.oaaa.org, accessed on August 4, 2007.
40. Jack Z. Sissors and Lincoln Bumba, *Advertising Media Planning,* Lincolnwood, IL: NTC Business Books, 1996.
41. Ronald Grover, "Billboards Aren't Boring Anymore," *Business Week,* September 21, 1998, 88–89.
42. Sissors and Bumba, *Advertising Media Planning.*
43. Andrew Hampp, "What Are Online Giants Doing in Out-of-Home?" *Advertising Age,* January 29, 2007, 30.
44. Natalie Zmuda, "Coca-Cola Gets Hands-On with Its Own Digital Billboards," *Advertising Age,* February 18, 2010, p. 12.
45. Lisa Sanders, "Nielsen Outdoor Tracks Demo Data," *Advertising Age,* May 31, 2004, 14.
46. Andrew Hampp, "Outdoor Ad Industry Finally Gets Its Improved Metrics," *Advertising Age,* March 30, 2010, p. 6.
47. Stephen Freitas, "Evolutionary Changes in the Great Outdoors," *Advertising Age,* June 9, 2003, C4.
48. Barry Newman, "Sky-Borne Signs Are on the Rise as Most Ad Budgets Take a Dive," *Wall Street Journal,* August 27, 2002, B3.
49. Brad Bartz, "Face of Outdoor Advertising Changes with New Airship Design," *Space Daily,* May 15, 2006, http://spacedaily.com.
50. Center for Media Research, "Catch a Commercial at the Movies," Research Brief, October 29, 2007, http://www.mediapost.com; Jack Loechner, "After the Popcorn, before the Show," Center for Media Research Research Brief, June 18, 2010, http://www.mediapost.com.
51. 2007 Marketing Fact Book, *Marketing News,* July 15, 2007, 29.
52. Lisa Sanders, "Major Marketers Turn to Yellow Pages," *Advertising Age,* March 8, 2004, 4, 52.

53. Bradley Johnson, "Yellow Pages Deals Red Hot as Telecom Industry Regroups," *Advertising Age,* January 6, 2003, 4, 20.

54. Don Hootstein, "Standing Out in the Aisles," *Marketing at Retail,* June 2007, 22–24.

55. Catherine Arnold, "Way Outside the Box," *Marketing News,* June 23, 2003, 13–14.

56. Robert L. Underwood and Julie L. Ozanne, "Is Your Package an Effective Communicator? A Normative Framework for Increasing the Communicative Competence of Packaging," *Journal of Marketing Communications,* December 1998, 207–219.

Chapter 12

1. Ann-Christine Diaz, "Best Non-TV Campaigns," *Advertising Age,* December 14, 2009, 14.

2. Kunur Patel, "All the World's a Game, and Brands Want to Play Along," *Advertising Age,* May 31, 2010, 4.

3. Bill Carter, "DVR, Once TV's Mortal Foe, Helps Ratings," *New York Times,* November 2, 2009, http://www.nytimes.com; and Brooke Gladstone, "TV's Unlikely Ally," *On the Media,* November 6, 2009, http://www.onthemedia.org (interview of Bill Carter).

4. Bob Garfield, "The Post Advertising Age," *Advertising Age,* March 26, 2007, 1, 12–14.

5. Ibid.

6. Bob Garfield, "Future May Be Brighter, but It's Apocalypse Now," *Advertising Age,* March 23, 2009, 26–27.

7. Dan Lippe, "Events Trail Only Ads in Alignment with Brands," *Advertising Age,* March 19, 2007, S-2.

8. Bettina Cornwell, Clinton Weeks, and Donald Roy, "Sponsor-Linked Marketing: Opening the Black Box," *Journal of Advertising,* Summer 2005, 21–42.

9. Chris Allen, Susan Fournier, and Felicia Miller, "Brands and Their Meaning Makers," in *Handbook of Consumer Psychology* Hillsdale, NJ: LEA Publishing, 2007, Ch. 31.

10. Jack Neff, "Specialists Thrive in Fast-Growing Events Segment," *Advertising Age,* March 19, 2007, S-2, S-4; and "Event & Sponsorship Spending," *AMA Marketing Fact Book,* July 15, 2007, 31.

11. Emily Steel, "Measured Media Lose in Spending Cuts," *Wall Street Journal,* March 14, 2007, B3; and Mike Spector and Gina Chon, "The Great Texas Truck Fair," *Wall Street Journal,* October 20, 2006, B1, B10.

12. Emily York, "McDonald's, Pepsi and Coca-Cola Troll for Up-and-Coming Artists," *Advertising Age,* June 7, 2010, 3, 38.

13. Grant McCracken, "Culture and Consumption: A Theoretical Account of the Structure and Movement of the Cultural Meaning of Consumer Goods," *Journal of Consumer Research,* June 1986, 71–84.

14. Jeremy Mullman, "World Cup Kicks Off International Marketing Games on Epic Scale," *Advertising Age,* May 17, 2010, 4.

15. Jim Hanas, "Going Pro: What's with All These Second-Tier Sports?" *Advertising Age,* January 29, 2007, S-3.

16. Ellen Byron, "An Old Dice Game Catches On Again, Pushed by P&G," *Wall Street Journal,* January 30, 2007, A1, A13.

17. Amy Hernandez, "Research Studies Gauge Sponsorship ROI," *Marketing News,* May 12, 2003, 16; and Ian Mount, "Exploding the Myths of Stadium Naming," *Business 2.0,* April 2004, 82, 83.

18. Kate Fitzgerald, "Events No Longer Immune to Marketer Demand for ROI," *Advertising Age,* March 19, 2007, S-3.

19. Rich Thomaselli, "Nielsen to Measure Sports Sponsorship," *Advertising Age,* May 3, 2004, 14.

20. The ideas in this section are drawn from Julie Zdziarski, "Evaluating Sponsorships," *Promo Magazine,* March 2001, 92, 93; and Fitzgerald, "Events No Longer Immune."

21. Cornwell, Weeks, and Roy, "Sponsor-Linked Marketing."

22. Brian Steinberg and Suzanne Vranica, "Prime-Time TV's New Guest Stars: Products," *Wall Street Journal,* January 12, 2004, B1, B4; Brian Steinberg, "Frasier Finale: Amid Nostalgia, A Product Plug," *Wall Street Journal,* May 12, 2004, B1, B2; and Grover, "Can Mad Ave. Make Zap-Proof Ads?"

23. Marc Graser, "TV's Savior?" *Advertising Age,* February 6, 2006, S-1, S-2.

24. Marc Graser, "Automakers: Every Car Needs a Movie," *Advertising Age,* December 11, 2006, 8.

25. Kate Kelly and Brian Steinberg, "Sony's 'Talladega Nights' Comedy Is Product-Plug Rally," *Wall Street Journal,* July 28, 2006, A9, A12.

26. Emma Hall, "Young Consumers Receptive to Movie Product Placements," *Advertising Age,* March 29, 2004, 8; Federico de Gregorio and Yongjun Sung, "Understanding Attitudes toward and Behaviors in Response to Product Placement," *Journal of Advertising,* Spring 2010, 83–96.

27. David Kiley, "Rated M for Mad Ave," *Business Week,* February 27, 2006, 76, 77.

28. John Gaudiosi, "In-Game Ads Reach the Next Level," *Business 2.0,* July 2007, 36, 37.

29. See also Cristel Russell and Michael Belch, "A Managerial Investigation into the Product Placement Industry," *Journal of Advertising Research,* March 2005, 73–92.

30. De Gregorio and Sung, "Understanding Attitudes toward and Behaviors in Response to Product Placement."

31. James Karrah, Kathy McKee, and Carol Pardun, "Practitioners' Evolving Views on Product Placement Effectiveness," *Journal of Advertising Research,* June 2003, 138–149.

32. Christina Passariello, "Ray-Ban Hopes to Party Like It's 1983 by Re-launching Its Wayfarer Shades," *Wall Street Journal,* October 27, 2006, B1, B4.

33. Tom Lowry, "The Prince of NASCAR," *Business Week,* February 23, 2004, 91–98; and Rich Thomaselli, "How NASCAR Plans to Get Back on the Fast Track," *Advertising Age,* February 12, 2007, 3, 26,

34. Rich Thomaselli, "Nextel Link Takes NASCAR to New Level," *Advertising Age,* October 27, 2003, S-7.

35. Lisa Napoli, "A New Era in Stock-Car Racing," *New York Times,* July 14, 2003, available at http://www.nytimes.com.

36. Rich Thomaselli, "Hitch a Ride with NASCAR for Under $5M," *Advertising Age,* November 6, 2006, 4, 80.

37. Burt Helm, "Bet You Can't TiVo Past This," *Business Week,* April 24, 2006, 38, 40; and Louise Story, "Brands Produce Their Own Shows," *New York Times,* November 10, 2006, available at http://www.nytimes.com.

38. Cristel Russell and Michael Belch, "A Managerial Investigation into the Product Placement Industry," *Journal of Advertising Research,* March 2005, 82, 83.

39. Phil Guarascio, "Decision Time at Mad + Vine," *Advertising Age,* September 1, 2003, 15.

40. Kate MacArthur, "Branded Entertainment, Marketing Tradition Tussle," *Advertising Age,* May 10, 2004, 6.

41. T. L. Stanley, "Sponsors Flee Matrix Sequel," *Advertising Age,* October 13, 2003, 1, 71.

42. Claire Atkinson, "Watchdog Group Hits TV Product Placements," *Advertising Age,* October 6, 2003, 12.

43. Davis Dyer, Frederick Dalzell, and Rowena Olegario, *Rising Tide: Lessons from 165 Years of Brand Building at Procter & Gamble,* Boston: Harvard Business School Publishing, 2004; Jack Neff, "Last P&G Produced Soap Opera to End," *Advertising Age,* December 8, 2009, http://adage.com.

44. Andrew Hampp, "How Madison & Vine Moved to Silicon Valley," *Advertising Age,* March 15, 2010, 4.

45. Don E. Schultz, Stanley I. Tannenbaum, and Robert F. Lauterborn, *Integrated Marketing Communications,* Lincolnwood, IL: NTC Business Books, 1993; and Daniel Klein, "Disintegrated Marketing," *Harvard Business Review,* March 2003, 18–19.

46. Laura Q. Hughes and Kate MacArthur, "Soft Boiled: Clients Want Integrated Marketing at Their Disposal, but Agencies Are (Still) Struggling to Put the Structure Together," *Advertising Age,* May 28, 2001, 3, 54; Claire Atkinson, "Integration Still a Pipe Dream for Many," *Advertising Age,* March 10, 2003, 1, 47; and Burt Helm, "Struggles of a Mad Man: Saatchi & Saatchi CEO Kevin Roberts," *Business Week,* December 3, 2007, 44–50.

47. Joe Cappo, *The Future of Advertising,* Chicago: McGraw-Hill, 2003, Ch. 8.

48. Ibid., 153, 154.

49. Suzanne Vranica, "For Big Marketers Like AmEx, TV Ads Lose Starring Role," *Wall Street Journal,* May 17, 2004, B1, B3.

Chapter 13

1. Matthew Schwartz, "NASCAR: Driving Social Media," *Advertising Age Integrated Marketing Guide,* November 16, 2009, C3, C13.

2. Matthew Schwartz, "New Influence," *Advertising Age,* October 26, 2009, S4–S5; Michael Bush, "Growth of Social Media Shifts PR Chiefs toward Center of Marketing Departments," *Advertising Age,* September 21, 2009, 7.

3. Stephen Brown, "Ambi-brand Culture," in *Brand Culture,* New York: Routledge, 2006, 50–66.

4. Frank Rose, "Let the Seller Beware," *Wall Street Journal,* December 20, 2006, D10; Jack Neff, "Lever's CMO Throws Down the Social Media Gauntlet," *Advertising Age,* April 13, 2009, 1, 20.

5. Jeffrey Davidoff, "Want Great PR? Get Your Agencies to Share the Load," *Advertising Age,* August 13, 2007, 12–13.

6. Simon Dumenco, "In Praise of the Original Social Media: Good Ol' Television," *Advertising Age,* May 17, 2010, 30; Ed Keller, "All Media Are Social," *MediaBizBloggers,* July 15, 2010, http://www.mediabizbloggers.com; Jack Neff, "Future of Advertising? Print, TV, Online Ads," *Advertising Age,* June 1, 2009, 3.

7. Claire Stammerjohan, Charles M. Wood, Yuhmiin Chang, and Esther Thorson, "An Empirical Investigation of the Interaction Between Publicity, Advertising, and Previous Brand Attitudes and Knowledge," *Journal of Advertising,* Winter 2005, 55–67; Jonah Bloom, "With PR on the Rise, Here's a Refresher Course in the Basics," *Advertising Age,* May 11, 2009, 22.

8. Kate MacArthur, "Taco Hell: Rodent Video Signals New Era in PR Crises," *Advertising Age,* February 26, 2007, 1, 46.

9. Jack Neff, "J&J Targets Red Cross, Blunders into PR Firestorm," *Advertising Age,* August 13, 2007, 1, 22.

10. Emily York, "Grilled Chicken a Kentucky Fried Fiasco," *Advertising Age,* May 11, 2009, 1, 30.

11. Andy Cohen, "The Jupiter Mission," *Sales and Marketing Management,* April 2000, 56.

12. Beth Snyder Bulik, "Well-Heeled Heed the Need for PR," *Advertising Age,* June 11, 2001, S2.

13. Kathleen V. Schmidt, "Coke's Crisis," *Marketing News,* September 27, 1999, 1, 11.

14. Amie Smith, "Coke's European Resurgence," *Promo Magazine,* December 1999, 91.

15. Miguel Bustillo, "Today's Special at Wal-Mart: Something Weird," *The Wall Street Journal,* July 8, 2011, http://online.wsj.com.

16. Robert Berner, "I Sold It Through the Grapevine," *BusinessWeek,* May 29, 2006, 32–34.

17. Michael Krauss, "To Generate Buzz, Do Remarkable Things," *Marketing News,* December 15, 2006, 6.

18. "Pretty Fly Campaign," *Advertising Age,* October 29, 2009, http://adage.com.

19. Michael Bush, "How Marketers Use Online Influencers to Boost Branding Efforts," *Advertising Age,* December 21, 2009, http://adage.com.

20. Berner, "I Sold It Through the Grapevine."

21. Ibid., 34.

22. Jessica E. Vascellaro, "Why Email No Longer Rules," *Wall Street Journal,* October 12, 2009, http://online.wsj.com.

23. W. Glynn Mangold and David J. Faulds, "Social Media: The New Hybrid Element of the Promotion Mix," *Business Horizons,* 52, 2009, 357–365.

24. Ibid., 361–364; and Diana Ransom, "How to Channel Your Twitter Voice," *Wall Street Journal,* October 29, 2009, http://online.wsj.com.

25. Jack Neff, "Once Skeptics, Brands Drink the Facebook Kool-Aid," *Advertising Age,* February 22, 2010, 40.

26. Emily Bryson York, "Red Robin Calls in a Facebook Favor from 1,500 Fans," *Advertising Age,* September 28, 2009, Business & Company Resource Center, http://galenet.galegroup.com.

27. Vascellaro, "Why Email No Longer Rules."

28. Gerry Khermouch and Jeff Green, "Buzz-z-z Marketing," *BusinessWeek,* July 30, 2001, 50–56.

29. Taddy Hall, "10 Essential Rules for Brands in Social Media," *Advertising Age,* March 22, 2010, 6.

30. Dave Smith, "Five Marketing Lessons from Old Spice," *Inc.,* August 18, 2011, http://www.inc.com.

31. Khermouch and Green, "Buzz-z-z Marketing."

32. Raymund Flandez, "Entrepreneurs Strive to Turn Buzz into Loyalty," *Wall Street Journal,* July 21, 2009, http://online.wsj.com.

33. Radian6, "Dell: Free Range Marketing," Case Studies, Radian6 website, accessed December 31, 2009.

34. David Goetzl, "GlaxoSmithKline Launches Print Ads," *Advertising Age,* January 8, 2001, 30.

35. For an exhaustive assessment of the benefits of corporate advertising, see David M. Bender, Peter H. Farquhar, and Sanford C. Schulert, "Growing from the Top," *Marketing Management,* Winter–Spring 1996, 10–19, 24.

36. Michael Bush, "Shell Breaks Industry Silence with Aggressive Campaign," *Advertising Age,* June 28, 2010, 10.

37. Stephanie Thompson, "Raising Awareness, Doubling Sales," *Advertising Age,* October 2, 2006, 4.

38. Michael J. Barone, Anthony D. Miyazaki, and Kimberly A. Taylor, "The Influence of Cause-Related Marketing on Consumer Choice," *Journal of the Academy of Marketing Science,* 28(2), 2000, 248–262.

39. James Tenser, "The New Samaritans," *Advertising Age,* June 12, 2006, S-1, S-6.

40. Bob Liodice, "Ten Companies with Social Responsibility at the Core," *Advertising Age,* April 19, 2010, 88; Natalie Zmuda and Emily York, "Cause Effect: Brands Rush to Save World One Good Deed at a Time," *Advertising Age,* March 1, 2010, 1, 22.

41. Kathryn Kranhold, "GE's Environment Push Hits Business Realities," *Wall Street Journal,* September 14, 2007, A1, A10.

42. Mya Frazier, "Going Green? Plant Deep Roots," *Advertising Age,* April 30, 2007, 1, 54–55.

Chapter 14

1. Jenny Callison, "Firm Refines Sales Pitches," *Cincinnati Enquirer,* February 10, 2006, http://cincinnati.com; and R. Dennis Green, "Professor of Persuasion—Dr. Tom Sant," *APMP Journal,* Fall/Winter 2003, 8–14.

2. Jessica Tsai, "Selling to the Sales Experts," *Customer Relationship Management,* November 2009, 46–47; and "The Sant Corporation Runs Its Entire Business in the Cloud with Salesforce.com," *Marketing Weekly News,* August 29, 2009, Business & Company Resource Center, http://galenet.galegroup.com.

3. Bureau of Labor Statistics, "Paid to Persuade: Careers in Sales," *Occupational Outlook Quarterly,* Summer 2011, 24–33; Bureau of Labor Statistics, *Occupational Outlook Handbook: 2010–11,* http://data.bls.gov.

4. Michele Marchetti, "What a Sales Call Costs," *Sales and Marketing Management,* September 2000, 80.

5. Erika Rasmusson, "Going Global with CRM," *Sales and Marketing Management,* May 2000, 96.

6. Patricia Sellers, "How IBM Teaches Techies to Sell," *Fortune,* June 6, 1988, 146.

7. Tim Wackel, "Schooled by a Shoe Salesman," *Sales and Marketing Management,* March 24, 2011, http://www.salesandmarketing.com.

8. William Weeks, "Buying Decisions a Group Effort," *Marketing News,* December 6, 1999, 22.

9. Ann Harrington, "I'll Take That Pitch with a Dash of Politesse," *Fortune,* June 12, 2000, 334.

10. Jamie Teschner, "Skill Workshop: Prospecting," *Selling Power,* March 2000, 34.

11. This section is based on an excellent discussion in Gary M. Grikscheit, Harold C. Cash, and Cliff E. Young, *Handbook of Personal Selling,* New York: John Wiley & Sons, 1993, Ch. 1.

12. Neil Rackham, "The Other Revolution in Sales," *Sales and Marketing Management,* March 2000, 34–36.

13. Erika Rasmusson, "Global Sales on the Line," *Sales and Marketing Management,* March 2000, 76–81.

14. Elizabeth Lux, "Screen Presence," *The Wall Street Journal,* May 25, 2010, http://online.wsj.com; John Cusano and Ravi Mahotra, "Direct Sales, Agent Model Might Converge in P&C Distribution Future," *National Underwriter Property & Casualty,* October 4, 2010, 30–31.

15. Joseph P. Vaccaro, "Best Salespeople Know Their ABCs (Always Be Closing)," *Marketing News,* March 28, 1998, 10.

16. Erika Rasmusson, "Image Is Everything," *Sales and Marketing Management,* December 1999, 25.

17. Tim R. Furey, "Sales Rep Not Dead, Just Redefined," *Marketing News,* December 6, 1999, 16.

18. Janet Guyon, "The World Is Your Office," *Fortune,* June 12, 2000, 227–234.

19. Rochelle Garner, "The E-Commerce Connection," *Sales and Marketing Management,* January 1999, 40–46.

20. Dana James, "Hit the Bricks," *Marketing News,* September 13, 1999, 1, 15.

21. Garner, "The E-Commerce Connection."

22. Jason Jordan, "From Sales Star to Sales Supporter," *Sales and Marketing Management,* February 26, 2009, Business & Company Resource Center, http://galenet.galegroup.com.

23. Barbara Buell et al., "Apple: New Team, New Strategy," *BusinessWeek,* October 15, 1991, 93.

24. Michele Marchetti, "How High Can Your Reps Go?" *Sales and Marketing Management,* September 1998, 101.

25. Bradley D. Lockman and John H. Hallaq, "Who Are Your Successful Salespeople?" *Journal of the Academy of Marketing Science,* Fall 1982, 463–468; and Timothy J. Trow, "The Secret of a Good Hire: Profiling," *Sales and Marketing Management,* May 1990, 44.

26. Patricia Sellers, "How to Remake Your Sales Force," *Fortune,* May 4, 1992; and Erin Strout, "Finding Your Company's Top Talent," *Sales and Marketing Management,* May 2000, 113.

27. Geoffrey Brewer, "How to Win Today's Recruiting Wars," *Sales and Marketing Management,* March 2000, 85.

28. Mike McNamee, "We Try to Minimize Face-to-Face Interviews," *Business Week,* November 22, 1999, 176.

29. Dan Hanover, "Hiring Gets Cheaper and Faster," *Sales and Marketing Management,* March 2000, 87.

30. Jack Retterer, "Successful Sales Automation Calls for Incorporating People," *Marketing News,* November 8, 1999, 12.

31. Yukari Iwatani Kane and Ian Sherr, "Secrets from Apple's Genius Bar: Full Loyalty, No Negativity," *The Wall Street Journal,* June 15, 2011, http://online.wsj.com.

32. Walecia Konrad, "Cheerleading, and Clerks Who Know Awls from Augers," *Business Week,* August 3, 1992, 51.

33. Melinda Ligos, "Point, Click, and Sell," *Sales and Marketing Management,* May 1999, 51–56.

34. Kane and Sherr, "Secrets from Apple's Genius Bar."

35. Ibid.

36. Michele Marchetti, "Helping Reps Count Every Penny," *Sales and Marketing Management,* July 1998.

37. Ibid.

Chapter 15

1. Information on Unilever's development of the Campaign for Real Beauty is adapted from Melinda Brodbeck and Erin Evans "Public Relations Problems and Cases: 'Dove Campaign for Real Beauty' Case Study," March 5, 2007; Jack Neff, "Study: Stick to Skinny Models for Fat Profits" *Advertising Age,* August 4, 2008; and The Campaign for Real Beauty website (www.dove.us/#/cfrb/), accessed February 15, 2010.

2. Jon Steel, *Truth, Lies & Advertising: The Art of Account Planning,* New York: John Wiley & Sons, 1998, Jacket.

3. Stuart J. Agres, Julie A. Edell, and Tony M. Dubitsky (eds.), *Emotion in Advertising,* Westport, CT: Quorum Books, 1990; see especially Chapters 7 and 8.

4. Bruce F. Hall, "A New Model for Measuring Advertising Effectiveness," *Journal of Advertising Research* 42, April 2002, 23–31; David Glenn Mick and Claus Buhl, "A Meaning-Based Model of Advertising Experiences," *Journal of Consumer Research,* 19, December 1992, 317–338.

5. Linda Scott, "The Bridge from Text to Mind: Adapting Reader Response Theory for Consumer Research," *Journal of Consumer Research* 21, December 1994, 461–486.

6. John Philip Jones, "Advertising Pre-Testing: Will Europe Follow America's Lead?" *Commercial Communications,* June 1997, 21–26.

7. Jennifer Gilbert, "Capita Taps Brain Waves to Study Web Ads' Potency," *Advertising Age,* February 14, 2000, 55.

8. Rajeev Batra, John G. Meyers, and David A. Aaker, *Advertising Management,* 5th ed., Upper Saddle River, NJ: Prentice Hall, 1996, 469.

9. Jennifer Gilbert, "Top 10 Ads Score Raves, Not Hits Post-Super Bowl," *Advertising Age,* February 7, 2000, 63. See also Donald E. Bruzzone, "Tracking Super Bowl Commercials Online," *ARF Workshop Proceedings,* October 2001, 35–47.

10. Ira Teinowitz, "Census Bureau Counts Ad Effort a Success," *Advertising Age,* May 22, 2000, 8.

11. James Lull, "How Families Select Television Programs: A Mass Observational Study," *Journal of Broadcasting* 26, No. 4, 1982, 801–811.

12. For an article that focuses exclusively on the measurement issue, see Scott Rosenberg, "Let's Get This Straight: Reach for the Hits," *Salon,* February 5, 1999, http://www.salon.com; see also Allan L. Baldinger, "Integrated Communication and Measurement: The Case for Multiple Measures," in Esther Thorson and Jeri Moore, eds., *Integrated Communications,* Mahwah, NJ: Lawrence Erlbaum, 1996, 271–283.

13. Eric Johnson, "Microsoft Developing Oscar's Website," *Marketing Doctoral Consortium,* Wharton Business School, August 1995.

14. "Nielsen, Facebook Partner for Studies," *Sales & Marketing Management,* July 31, 2010, http://www.salesandmarketing.com; Jon Gibs and Sean Bruich, "Nielsen/Facebook Report: The Value of Social Media Ad Impressions," *Nielsen Wire,* April 20, 2010, http://blog.nielsen.com/nielsenwire/; Facebook, "What is the Nielsen Partnership with Facebook and How Does It Affect Me?" Facebook Help Center, http://www.facebook.com/help/.

15. Stephanie Thompson, "Nestlé Tries Fresh Approach for Premium Ortega Salsa," *Advertising Age,* February 21, 2000, 16.

16. Jack Neff, "P&G Introduces Trio of Products in DMB&B Boon," *Advertising Age,* May 22, 2000, 77.

17. Angeline G. Close, R. Zachary Finney, Russell Z. Lacey, and Julie Z. Sneath, "Engaging the Consumer through Event Marketing: Linking Attendees with the Sponsor, Community, and Brand," *Journal of Advertising Research* 46, December 2006, 420–433.

18. B. Spethmann, "Sponsorships Sing a Profitable Tune in Concert with Event Promotions," *Brandweek,* January 1, 1994, 20.

19. Scott Hume, "Sports Sponsorship Value Measured," *Advertising Age,* June 3, 1996, 46.

20. Amanda Beeler, "Deere Goes Beyond Famed Brand to Cultivate Ties with Customers," *Advertising Age,* May 22, 2000.

21. For an extensive discussion of sales force evaluation procedures and criteria, see Mark W. Johnson and Greg Marshall, *Sales Force Management,* 10th ed., Burr Ridge, IL: McGraw-Hill Higher Education, 2011, Ch. 13.

22. Chad Kaydo, "Big Blue's Media Blitz," *Sales and Marketing Management,* December 1999, 80.

23. Michael Hess and Robert Mayer, "Integrate Behavioral and Survey Data," *Marketing News,* January 3, 2000, 22.

24. Helen Katz and Jacques Lendrevie, "In Search of the Holy Grail: First Steps in Measuring Total Exposures of an Integrated Communications Program," in Thorson and Moore, eds., *Integrated Communications,* Mahwah, NJ: Lawrence Erlbaum, 1996, 259–270.

25. We presume the authors really mean "brand" rather than "product" impressions. It does Honda or Adidas little good if consumers encounter automobiles or sport shoes as a product category. The intent of the authors here would clearly seem to be that consumers encounter the "brand" in question, not the broad product category.

26. Katz and Lendrevie, "In Search of the Holy Grail," 266–268.

27. Although there is extensive literature on measuring the effectiveness of *individual* elements of the promotional mix, aside from the Katz and Lendrevie article discussed here, the author was able to locate only *one* other article that focuses exclusively on the measurement issue: Allan L. Baldinger, "Integrated Communication and Measurement: The Case for Multiple Measures," in Thorson and Moore, eds., *Integrated Communications,* 271–283.

Glossary

account executive liaison between an advertising agency and its clients

account planner person in an advertising agency who synthesizes all relevant consumer research and uses it to design an advertising strategy

account planning system in which an agency assigns a coequal account planner to work alongside the account executive and analyze research data, staying with projects on a continuous basis

account services team of managers that identifies the benefits a brand offers its target audiences and the best competitive position, and then develops a promotion plan

account team group of people comprising different facets of the promotion industry who work together under a team leader

Action for Children's Television group formed during the 1970s to lobby the government to limit the amount and content of advertising to children

advertisement a specific message that an organization has placed to persuade an audience

advertising a paid, mass-mediated attempt to persuade

advertising agency organization of professionals who provide creative and business services related to planning, preparing, and placing advertisements

advertising campaign a series of coordinated promotional efforts, including advertisements, that communicate a single theme or idea

advertising clutter volume of similar ads for products or services that presents an obstacle to brand promotion

advertising specialties sales promotion consisting of a message placed on useful items given to consumers with no obligation

advertising substantiation program FTC program that ensures advertisers make available to consumers supporting evidence for advertising claims

advocacy advertising advertising that attempts to influence public opinion about social, political, or environmental issues of concern to the advertiser

aerial advertising advertising that involves airplanes pulling signs or banners, as well as skywriting and blimps

affirmative disclosure FTC action requiring that important material determined to be absent from prior ads be included in future ads

appropriation use of pictures or images owned by someone else without permission

attention-interest-desire-action (AIDA) structured presentation aimed at capturing attention, identifying features of interest, defining desirable benefits, and requesting action in the form of a purchase

attitude overall evaluation of any object, person, or issue; varies along a continuum, such as favorable to unfavorable or positive to negative

attitude change study message research that uses a before-and-after ad exposure design

audience a group of individuals who may receive and interpret promotional messages

authenticity quality of genuineness or naturalness

ballot method pretest of sales promotion in which consumers are given a list of promotional options and asked to rank their preferences

behavioral targeting the process of database development in which online tracking markers are used to track computer users' online behavior so that brand promotion messages can be very specifically targeted to them

beliefs a person's knowledge and feelings about an object or issue

benefit positioning a positioning option that features a distinctive customer benefit

benefit segmentation market segmentation that identifies the various benefit packages consumers want from a product category

bill-back allowances monetary incentive provided to retailers for featuring a marketer's brand in advertising or in-store displays

blog personal journal on a website that is frequently updated and intended for public access

blogger author of a blog

brainstorming organized approach to idea generation in groups

brand a name, term, sign, symbol, or any other feature that identifies one seller's good or service as distinct from those of other sellers

brand advertising advertising that communicates a brand's features, values, and benefits

brand attitudes summary evaluations that reflect preferences for various products or brands

brand community group of consumers who feel a commonality and shared purpose grounded in or attached to a consumer good or service

brand equity positive associations with a brand in the minds of consumers

brand extension an adaptation of an existing brand to a new product area

brand loyalty decision-making mode in which consumers repeatedly choose to buy the same brand of a product to fulfill a specific need

brand-loyal users a market segment made up of consumers who repeatedly buy the same brand of a product

branded entertainment embedding brands or brand icons as part of an entertainment property in an effort to connect with consumers in a unique and compelling way

branding strategy of developing brand names so manufacturers can focus consumer attention on a clearly identified item

business markets the institutional buyers who purchase items to be used in other products and services or to be resold to other businesses or households

business-market sales promotion promotion designed to cultivate buyers making purchase decisions in corporations

buzz marketing creation of events or experiences that yield conversations that include the brand or product

canned presentation recitation of a prepared sales pitch

cause-related marketing marketing messages that identify corporate sponsorship of philanthropic activities

cease-and-desist order FTC action requiring an advertiser to stop running an ad so a hearing can be held to determine whether the ad is deceptive or unfair

celebrity sociological category of famous individuals who shape identity for others

celebrity endorsements advertisements that use an expert or celebrity as spokesperson to endorse the use of a product or service

Chaos Scenario exodus of ad revenue from traditional broadcast media in reaction to audience fragmentation and tools for ad avoidance; causes media cutbacks, followed by further reductions in audience size and even less advertising

cinema advertising ads that run in movie theaters before the film and other brand messages that appear off-screen within a theater

click fraud act of clicking on Internet ads solely to generate revenue for the website carrying the ads

click-through measure of the number of hyperlinks that users click on, especially links from advertisements to the advertiser's website

client or **sponsor** the organization that pays for advertising

cognitive consistency maintenance of a system of beliefs and attitudes over time

cognitive dissonance anxiety or regret that lingers after a difficult decision

cognitive responses thoughts that occur at the exact moment when beliefs and attitudes are being challenged by a message

cognitive style an individual's preference for thinking about and solving a problem

commission system method of agency compensation based on the amount of money the advertiser spends on the media

communication test pretest message research aimed at measuring whether a message is communicating something close to what is desired

community group of people loosely joined by a common characteristic or interest

comparison advertisements ads that compare the advertiser's brand with competitors' brands

competitive field the companies that compete for a segment's business

competitive positioning a positioning option that uses an explicit reference to an existing competitor to help define precisely what a brand can do

consent order FTC action asking an advertiser to stop running deceptive or unfair advertising without admitting guilt

consideration set subset of brands from a product category that becomes the focal point of a consumer's evaluation

consultant individual who specializes in areas related to the promotional process

consultive selling face-to-face selling in which salespeople help customers define problems and design solutions

consumer behavior activities and decision processes directly involved in obtaining, consuming, and disposing of products and services

consumer culture a way of life centered around consumption

consumer markets the markets for products and services purchased by individuals or households to satisfy their specific needs

consumer sales promotion sales promotion that is aimed at consumers and focuses on price-off deals, coupons, sampling, rebates, and premiums

consumer-generated content (CGC) advertisements made partly or completely by the product's end users, typically with the aid of Internet tools

consumer-market sales promotion sales promotions designed to induce consumers to purchase a firm's brand rather than a competitor's

consumerism actions of individual consumers to exert power over the marketplace activities of organizations

contest sales promotion in which consumers compete for prizes based on skill or ability

cookies online tracking markers that advertisers place on a web surfer's hard drive to track that person's online behavior

cooperative advertising sharing of advertising expenses between national advertisers and local merchants

cooperative promotion (co-op promotion) sharing of promotion expenses between national advertisers and local merchants

corporate advertising advertising intended to establish a favorable attitude toward a company

corporate home page website that focuses on a corporation and its products

corrective advertising FTC action requiring an advertiser to run additional ads to dispel false beliefs created by deceptive advertising

cost per inquiry (CPI) number of inquiries generated by a direct-marketing program divided by the program's cost

cost per order (CPO) number of orders generated by a direct-marketing program divided by that program's cost

cost per thousand (CPM) dollar cost of reaching 1,000 members of an audience

coupon sales promotion that entitles a buyer to a designated reduction in price for a product or service

creative abrasion clash of ideas, abstracted from the people who propose them, from which new ideas can evolve

creative boutique advertising agency that emphasizes copywriting and artistic services

creative brief document that outlines and channels an essential creative idea and objective

creative revolution shift toward greater influence of "creatives" in advertising agencies during the 1960s

creative selling assisting and persuading customers regarding purchase decisions (typically for specialty goods or high-priced items)

creative services group in an advertising agency that develops the message to be delivered through advertising, sales promotion, direct marketing, event sponsorship, or public relations

creativity ability to consider and hold together seemingly inconsistent elements and forces, making a new connection

cross-selling marketing programs aimed at selling additional products to existing customers

crowdsourcing online distribution of tasks to groups (crowds) of experts, enthusiasts, or general consumers

culture a group's characteristic ways of behaving

customer relationship management (CRM) continual effort to cultivate and maintain long-term relationships with customers by emphasizing customer needs

customer satisfaction good feelings that come from a favorable postpurchase experience

dailies newspapers published every weekday

database agency agency that helps customers construct databases of target customers, merge databases, develop promotional materials, and execute direct-marketing campaigns

deception making false or misleading statements in a promotional message

defamation untrue communication that damages the reputation of an individual

delayed-response promotion promotion that relies on imagery and message themes to emphasize a brand's benefits and positive qualities to encourage customers to purchase the product at a later date

demographic dividend favorable climate for economic expansion in developing nations as a result of falling labor costs, a younger and healthier population, and entry of women into the workforce

demographic segmentation market segmentation that divides consumers according to basic descriptors such as age, gender, race, marital status, income, education, and occupation

designer specialist involved in execution of creative ideas and efforts by designing logos and other visual promotional pieces

detail salesperson salesperson who introduces new products and provides product information without aiming for an immediate sale

differentiation creation of a perceived difference, in the consumer's mind,

between an organization's brand and the competition's

digital/interactive agency advertising agency that helps clients prepare communications for new media (for example, the Internet and interactive kiosks)

direct mail direct-marketing medium that uses the postal service to deliver marketing materials

direct marketing interactive marketing system that uses multiple media to generate a transaction or other measurable response at any location

direct-marketing agency or **direct-response agency** agency that maintains large databases of mailing lists and may design direct-marketing campaigns

direct-response advertising advertising that asks the receiver of the message to act immediately

direct-response promotion promotion that asks the receiver of the message to act immediately

display or banner ads advertisements placed on websites that contain editorial material

domain name unique URL that establishes a Web location

door-to-door sampling sampling in which samples are brought to the homes of the target segment in a well-defined geographic area

dummy advertising vehicles mock-ups of magazines that contain editorial content and advertisements, including ads being tested

e-business promotion in which companies selling to business customers rely on the Internet to send messages and close sales

economies of scale lower per-unit production costs resulting from larger volume

elaboration likelihood model (ELM) social psychological model of the response to a persuasive communication, expressing the response in terms of motivation and ability

emergent consumers a market segment made up of the gradual but constant influx of first-time buyers

emotional benefits benefits not typically found in a product's tangible features or objective characteristics

ethics moral standards and principles against which behavior is judged

ethnocentrism tendency to view and value things from the perspective of one's own culture

evaluative criteria product attributes or performance characteristics on which consumers base their product evaluations

event sponsorship financial support for an event, given in exchange for the right to display a brand name, logo, or promotional message at the event

event-planning agency agency that finds locations, secures dates, and assembles a team of people to pull off a promotional event

extended problem solving decision-making mode in which inexperienced but highly involved consumers go through a deliberate decision-making process

external facilitator organization or individual that provides specialized services to advertisers and agencies

external lists mailing lists purchased from a list compiler or rented from a list broker; used for cultivating new business

external position competitive niche pursued by a brand

external search gathering product information by visiting retail stores to examine alternatives, seeking input from friends and relatives, or perusing professional product evaluations

eye-tracking systems physiological measure that monitors eye movements across advertisements

Federal Trade Commission (FTC) government regulatory agency most directly involved in overseeing the advertising industry

fee system method of agency compensation whereby the advertiser and agency agree on an hourly rate for services provided

free premium sales promotion that gives consumers an item at no cost by including the item in the package or mailing it after proof of purchase is verified

frequency programs sales promotion that offers consumers discounts or rewards for repeat purchases

frequency-marketing programs direct-marketing programs that provide concrete rewards to frequent customers

fulfillment center operation that ensures consumers receive products ordered in response to direct marketing

full-service agency advertising agency that includes an array of advertising professionals to meet all the promotional needs of clients

functional benefits benefits that come from a product's objective performance characteristics

gender social expression of sexual biology or sexual choice

geodemographic segmentation market segmentation that identifies neighborhoods sharing common demographic characteristics

global agencies advertising agencies with a worldwide presence

global promotion developing and placing messages with a common theme and presentation in all markets around the world where the brand is sold

globalized campaigns promotional campaigns that use the same message and creative execution across all or most international markets

government officials and employees advertising audience that includes employees of government organizations at the federal, state, and local levels

Great Depression a period (1929–1941 in the United States) of a severe economic decline affecting the vast majority of people in many countries

green marketing corporate communication efforts to promote a cause or program in support of the environment

gross domestic product (GDP) the total value of goods and services produced within an economic system

habit decision-making mode in which consumers buy a single brand repeatedly as a solution to a simple consumption problem

heavy users consumers who purchase a product or service much more frequently than others

highly industrialized countries countries with a high GDP and a high standard of living

hits number of pages and graphical images requested from a website

household consumers the most conspicuous audience for advertising

in-house agency advertising department of a marketer's own firm

in-store sampling sampling that occurs at the point of purchase

Industrial Revolution a rapid shift in Western society from an agricultural to an industrial economy, beginning in the mid-eighteenth century

inelasticity of demand low sensitivity to price increases; may result from brand loyalty

influencer marketing series of personalized marketing techniques directed at individuals or groups with the credibility and capability to drive positive word of mouth in a market segment

infomercial long advertisement that looks like a talk show or product demonstration

inquiry/direct-response measures post-test message tracking in which an advertisement calls for a direct response and the number of responses is counted

integrated marketing communication (IMC) the use of a wide range of promotional tools working together to create widespread brand exposure

interactive media media that allow consumers to call up games, entertainment, shopping, and educational programs on a subscription or pay-per-view basis

intergenerational effect choice of products based on what was used in the consumer's childhood household

internal lists organization's records of its customers and inquirers; used for developing better customer relationships

internal position niche a brand occupies with regard to the company's other, similar brands

internal search search for product information that draws on personal experience and prior knowledge

international affiliates foreign-market advertising agencies with which a local agency has established a relationship to handle international advertising needs

international brand promotion the preparation and placement of brand communication in different national and cultural markets

international promotion preparation and placement of messages in different national and cultural markets

Internet global collection of computer networks linking public and private computer systems to connect more than a billion users

interpersonal abrasion clash of people, often resulting from an inability to regard idea feedback as separate from personal feedback, causing communication to shut down

involvement degree of perceived relevance and personal importance accompanying the choice of a product or service in a particular context

less-developed countries countries whose economies lack most resources necessary for development: capital, infrastructure, political stability, and trained workers

leveraging using any collateral communication or activity to reinforce the link between a brand and an event

libel defamation that occurs in print (for example, in a magazine story)

life stage circumstance that changes a family's consumption patterns

lifestyle segmentation market segmentation that identifies consumers sharing similar activities, interests, and opinions

limited problem solving decision-making mode in which relatively inexperienced and uninvolved consumers are not systematic about decisions

local agency advertising agency in a foreign market hired because of its knowledge of the culture and local market conditions

local promotion promotion directed to an audience in a single trading area (a city or state)

localized campaigns promotional campaigns that involve different messages and creative executions for each foreign market served

log analysis software measurement software that provides data about online consumer behavior, including hits, pages, visits, and users, as well as audience traffic within a website

logo graphic mark that identifies a company

Madison & Vine convergence of advertising and entertainment; reference to the names of streets that represent each industry

mail sampling sampling in which samples are delivered through the postal service

mailing list file of names and addresses used for contacting prospects or customers

market niche a relatively small group of consumers with a unique set of needs and the willingness to pay a premium price to a firm that meets those needs

market segmentation breaking down a large, heterogeneous market into submarkets that are more homogeneous

marketer business, not-for-profit, or government organization that uses advertising and other promotional techniques to communicate with target markets to stimulate awareness of and demand for its brands

marketing the process of conceiving, pricing, promoting, and distributing ideas, goods, and services to create exchanges that benefit customers and companies

marketing database mailing list with added information collected directly from individual customers

marketing mix the blend of the four responsibilities of marketing (conception, pricing, promotion, and distribution) used for a particular idea, product, or service

markup charge method of agency compensation based on adding a percentage charge to a variety of services the agency purchases from outside suppliers

mash-up combination of websites into a single site for analyzing or comparing information

meaning what a brand message intends or conveys

meaningfulness in promotion research, practical applicability of conclusions to the promotional effort

media impressions instances in which a product or brand is exposed to consumers through media coverage, rather than paid advertising

media planning and buying services services that are related to media planning or buying and are provided by advertising agencies or specialized media-buying organizations

media specialist organization that specializes in buying media time and space and that offers media strategy consulting to agencies and advertisers

members of a trade channel advertising audience that includes retailers, wholesalers, and distributors

members of business organizations advertising audience that buys business and industrial goods and services

merchandise allowances trade-market sales promotion in which free products are packed with regular shipments as payment to the trade for setting up and maintaining displays

Mi-Fi wireless Internet technology with multi-mile access and ability to access the Internet while the user is moving in a car or train

missionary salesperson salesperson who calls on accounts to monitor buyers' satisfaction and update their needs

mobile marketing communicating with target markets through mobile devices

mobile sampling sampling carried out using logo-emblazoned vehicles where samples are dispensed at malls or other high-traffic areas

monopoly power a company's ability, either through advertising or in some other way, to prevent rivals from competing

multi-attribute attitude models (MAAMs) framework and set of procedures for collecting information from consumers to assess their salient beliefs and attitudes about competing brands

National Advertising Review Board body formed by the advertising industry to oversee its practices

national promotion promotion directed to all geographic areas of one nation

naturalistic inquiry broad-based research method that relies on qualitative data collection, including video and audio recordings and photography

need satisfaction sales presentation that begins with assessment of each buyer's need state and then adjusts the selling effort to that need state

need state psychological state arising when one's desired state of affairs differs from one's actual state of affairs

newly industrialized countries countries where traditional ways of life are changing into modern consumer cultures

newspaper sampling sampling in which samples are distributed in newspapers to allow specific geographic and geodemographic targeting

nonusers a market segment made up of consumers who do not use a particular product or service

normative test scores scores determined by testing an ad and then comparing the scores with those of previously tested campaigns of the same type

off-invoice allowance program allowing wholesalers and retailers to deduct a set amount from the invoice they receive for merchandise

on-package sampling sampling in which a sample item is attached to another product's package

opt-in email messages sent to website visitors who have given permission to receive commercial email about particular topics or products

order taking practice of accepting and processing customer information for prearranged purchase or scheduling services a customer will purchase

out-of-home media advertising advertising venues that reach local audiences away from home and work

packaging a product's container or wrapping, which conveys product information and user appeal

page views record of the pages that have been sent to a user's computer; multiscreen pages are counted as one page

paid search the practice of paying search engines and portals to place ads near relevant search results

pay-for-results compensation plan based on an agreement in which fee amounts are tied to a set of results criteria

peripheral cues features of an advertisement other than the actual arguments about the brand's performance

permanent long-term displays P-O-P materials intended for presentation for more than six months

permission marketing sending commercial email only to Web users who have agreed to receive it

personal selling process of face-to-face communication and persuasion

phishing efforts by spammers to entice Web users to enter personal information on a website forged to look like a legitimate site

physiological measures interpretation of biological feedback from subjects exposed to an ad

picturing creating representations of things

pilot testing message evaluation that consists of experimentation in the marketplace

point-of-entry marketing advertising strategy designed to win the loyalty of consumers whose brand preferences are under development

point-of-purchase (P-O-P) advertising advertising that appears in the retail setting

pop-under ad Internet ad that is displayed "under" the active window, so it appears only after that window is closed

pop-up ad Internet advertisement that opens a separate window while a Web page is loading

portal website that serves as a starting point for Web access and search

positioning the process of designing and representing a product or service to occupy a distinct and valued place in the target customer's mind

positioning strategy the key themes or concepts that an organization features when communicating a product's or service's distinctiveness to a target segment

post-test message tracking assessment of an ad's performance during or after the launch of an ad campaign

premiums items that feature a sponsor's logo and are offered free or at a reduced price with the purchase of another item

price-off deal type of sales promotion that offers consumers money off merchandise at the point of purchase through specially marked packages

primary demand demand for an entire product category

primary demand stimulation promotion aimed at creating demand for a product category

principle of limited liability limitation of an investor's risk in a corporation to his or her investment in the company's shares

proactive public relations strategy PR strategy that is dictated by marketing objectives, seeks publicity, and takes the offense

product placement sales promotion technique of getting a marketer's product featured in movies and television shows

production facilitator organization that offers essential services during and after the production process

production services team in an agency that takes creative ideas and turns them into advertisements, direct-mail pieces, or events materials

professionals advertising audience that includes workers with special training or certification

promotion the communications process in marketing that is used to create a favorable predisposition toward a brand of product or service

promotion agency specialized agency that handles promotional efforts

promotion research marketing research focused on the development and performance of promotional materials

promotional mix a blend of communications tools used to carry out the promotion process and communicate directly with an audience

psychogalvanometer device that measures galvanic skin response, or minute changes in perspiration that may suggest arousal

psychographics a form of market research that emphasizes the understanding of consumers' activities, interests, and opinions

public relations function that provides communications to foster goodwill between a firm and its constituent groups

public relations audit internal study that identifies aspects of the firm or its activities that are positive and newsworthy

public relations firm firm that handles an organization's needs regarding relationships with the local community, competitors, industry associations, and government organizations

public relations plan plan that identifies the objectives and activities of a firm's PR communications

publicity unpaid-for media exposure about a firm's activities or its products and services

puffery use of superlatives like "number one" and "best in the world" in promotional messages

Pure Food and Drug Act 1906 U.S. law requiring manufacturers to list the active ingredients of their products on their labels

push money trade incentive in which retail salespeople are offered monetary rewards for featuring a marketer's brand

push strategy sales promotion strategy in which marketers devise incentives to encourage purchases by members of the trade, moving product into the distribution channel

reactive public relations strategy PR strategy that is dictated by influences outside the company's control, focuses on solving problems, and requires defensive measures

rebate money-back offer requiring a buyer to mail in a form requesting the money back from the manufacturer

recall test test of how much the viewer of an ad remembers of the message

recognition tests tests in which audience members are asked whether they recognize an ad or something in an ad

regional promotion promotion concentrated on a large, but not national, region

reliability tendency to generate consistent findings over time

repositioning returning to the STP marketing process to arrive at a revised positioning strategy

resonance test message assessment aimed at determining the extent to which a message rings true with target audience members

RFM analysis analysis of how recently and frequently a customer bought from an organization, and how much the customer spent

rich media, video, and audio use of streaming video and audio that plays when the user's mouse passes over an Internet ad

riding the boards assessing possible locations for billboard advertising

rituals repeated behaviors that affirm, express, and maintain cultural values

sales force automation (SFA) integration of computers, communication technology, and the Internet to improve the efficiency and effectiveness of personal selling

sales management responsibility for the personal-selling effort, met by evaluating needs, setting objectives and budgets, structuring and hiring the sales force, training and motivating salespeople, and evaluating their performance

sales promotion use of innovative techniques that create a perception of greater brand value among consumers or distributors

salient beliefs the few beliefs that are the critical determinants of an attitude

sampling sales promotion technique that offers consumers a trial opportunity

search engine software tool for finding websites by entering keywords

search engine optimization (SEO) process for improving the volume and quality of traffic to a website from a search engine's results pages

Second Life online virtual world where participants can roam landscapes and interact, simulating real-world activities, including (often real) business transactions

selective attention processing of only a few messages among many encountered

selective demand stimulation promotion aimed at stimulating demand for a specific brand

self-liquidating premium sales promotion that requires a consumer to pay most of the cost of the item received as a premium

self-reference criterion (SRC) unconscious reference to one's own cultural values, experiences, and knowledge as a basis for decisions

self-regulation the advertising industry's attempt to police itself

seminar selling education of customer or prospect groups to inform them about the firm's products or services

short-term promotional displays P-O-P materials used for six months or less

single-source tracking measures post-test message tracking that uses a combination of scanner data and devices that monitor television-viewing behavior to collect information about brand purchases, coupon use, and television ad exposure

slander oral defamation (for example, during a radio broadcast)

slotting fees trade-market sales promotion in which manufacturers make direct cash payments to retailers to ensure shelf space

social media highly accessible Web-based media that allow the sharing of information among individuals and between individuals and groups

spam uninvited commercial messages sent to electronic mailing lists or online discussion groups

splash screen Internet ad that appears briefly on a website after a page has been requested but before it has loaded

split-cable transmission pilot testing of two versions of an advertisement through direct transmission to separate sample households

split-list experiments pilot testing in which multiple versions of a direct-mail piece are sent to segments of a mailing list and responses to each version are compared

split-run distribution pilot testing in which different versions of an advertisement are placed in magazines and direct responses to each advertisement are compared

sponsorship payment to maintain a section of a website and perhaps provide content for the site in exchange for being mentioned on the site

STP marketing developing a strategy through segmenting, targeting, and positioning

stratification (social class) individuals' relative standing in a social system as produced by systematic inequalities

subliminal advertising advertisements alleged to work on a subconscious level

support media media used to reinforce a message being delivered via some other media vehicle

surfing gliding from website to website, guided by hyperlinks, a search engine, or word of mouth

sweepstakes sales promotion in which winners are awarded prizes based on chance

switchers or variety seekers a market segment made up of consumers who often buy what is on sale or choose brands that offer price incentives

symbolic value nonliteral meaning of a product or service, as perceived by consumers

system selling selling a set of interrelated components that fulfill a majority of a customer's needs in a product or service area

target audience a particular group of consumers singled out for an advertising or promotion campaign

target segment the subgroup (of the larger market) chosen as the focal point for a marketing program and advertising campaign

taste a generalized set or orientation to consumer preferences

team selling sales effort by a team of salespeople representing different functions

telemarketing direct-marketing medium that involves using the telephone to deliver a spoken appeal

theater tests pretest message research in which subjects view ads played in small theaters and record their reactions

thought listing pretest message research that tries to identify specific thoughts that may be generated by an ad

top-level domain (TLD) suffix that follows a website name

trade journals magazines that publish technical articles for members of a trade

trade reseller organization in the marketing channel of distribution that buys products to resell to customers

trade shows events where several related products from many manufacturers are displayed and demonstrated to members of the trade

trade-market sales promotion sales promotion that is designed to motivate distributors, wholesalers, and retailers to stock and feature a firm's brand in their merchandising programs

transit advertising advertising that appears as interior and exterior displays on mass-transit vehicles and at terminal and station platforms

trial offers sales promotion in which expensive items are offered on a trial basis to induce consumers to try a brand

trustworthiness quality of deserving confidence

ultrabroadband wireless Internet technology allowing users to move extremely large files quickly over short distances

unfair advertising acts by advertisers that cause or are likely to cause substantial injury that is not reasonably avoidable or outweighed by other benefits

unique visitors number of people (identified using registration information) who visit a site during a given time period

user positioning a positioning option that focuses on a specific profile of the target user

validity relevance in terms of actually answering the questions being investigated

value perception that a product or service provides satisfaction beyond the cost incurred to acquire it

value proposition a statement of the functional, emotional, and self-expressive benefits that are delivered by the brand and provide value to customers in the target segment

values defining expressions of what is important to a culture

variety seeking decision-making mode in which consumers switch their selection among various brands in a category in a random pattern

vertical cooperative advertising sharing of advertising expense by a manufacturer and dealer (wholesaler or retailer)

viral marketing process of consumers marketing to consumers over the Internet through word of mouth

viral marketing process of consumers spreading brand messages through email

virtual mall gateway to a group of Internet storefronts where the user gains access to a retailer by clicking on a storefront

visits number of occasions on which a particular user looks up a particular website during a given time period

voice response analysis physiological assessment in which computers measure inflections in subjects' voices

Web analytic software software that measures hits, pages, visits, and users, and allows a website to track audience traffic on the site

website collection of Web pages, images, videos, and other content hosted on a Web server

widget software module that people can add to their blog or their personal page on a social network; may feature a brand or direct the user to an e-commerce site

WiFi wireless technology allowing Internet access connections to reach out about 300 feet

WiMax wireless Internet technology capable of a range of 25 to 30 miles

World Wide Web (WWW) database of information available online in a graphical environment that simplifies navigation

Company Index

Subject Index

Directory advertising,
241–242
Direct-response advertising,
211
Direct-response agency, 34
Direct-response promotion,
18
Discomfort, need states
and, 89
Displays
for point-of-purchase
advertising, 236
sales promotions and,
221
Display ads, 184–185
Distribution channels,
47–48
DJ Kaskade, 248
Domain names, 189
Do Not Call Law, 135
Do Not Call Registry, 135,
210
Door-to-door sampling,
229
Double postcard (DPC), 212
Down-Home Stokers, 74
Dummy advertising
vehicles, 313

E

Ebony, 58
E-business, 62
E-commerce
Internet and, 177
regulation of, 133–137
E-communities, 194–195
Economies of scale, 17
price and, 20
promotion and, 116
800 numbers, 215
with infomercials, 216
Einstein, Albert, 160–161
Elaboration likelihood
model (ELM), 99–100
Eliot, T.S., 160–161
Email, 178–179, 185–186
for direct marketing,
213–214
Emergent consumers, 72
Emotional benefits, 81,
83, 89
creativity and, 159–160
decision-making and, 95
event sponsorships and,
252
message assessment and,
311
E-revolution, 59–60
Esrey, William T., 60
Esteem needs, 118

Ethics, 112–137
on advertising to
children, 126
on alcohol and tobacco,
123
on competitive
advertising, 126
on deceptive advertising,
124–125
on telemarketing, 135
Ethnicity, 106–107.
See also African
Americans; Hispanics
Ethnocentrism, 141
European Union, 149
Evaluative criteria, 91
in multi-attribute
attitude models, 96
Event-planning agency,
34–35
Event sponsorship,
247–252
audience for, 252
brand loyalty and,
251–252
emotional benefits and,
252
leverage of, 252
media impressions and,
250
for promotion, 5
public relations and,
267
relationship building
with, 252
Extended problem solving,
93
External facilitators, 29,
40–42
External lists, 206
External position, 16–17
External search, 91
External situation analysis,
298
Eye-tracking systems,
314

F

Face-to-face presentations,
294
Fair Credit Reporting Act,
127
Fair labor, 107
Fair Packing and Labeling
Act, 127
The Fairway Gourmet,
257
Family, consumer behavior
and, 105–106
Feature stories, 266

Federal Communications
Commission (FCC),
25, 127
on advertising to
children, 123
on product placement,
259
Federal government. *See
also specific agencies
and laws*
advertising by, 31
contests/sweepstakes
and, 228
regulation by, 126–129
Federal Trade Commission
(FTC), 58, 127–129
on advertising to
children, 126
on alcohol and tobacco,
123
on competitive
advertising, 126
on deceptive advertising,
124–125
Do not Call Registry
from, 210
on product placement,
259
on telemarketing, 135
Federal Trade Commission
Act, 53, 127
Fee systems, 39
Feminism, 57
First Amendment, 63
Flexibility, with Internet,
182
Food and Drug
Administration (FDA),
127
France, 178
Frank, Thomas, 109
Franklin, Benjamin, 201
Frasier, 253
Fraud
click fraud, 192–194
with coupons, 226
Free premium, 227
Frequency-marketing
programs, 209
Frequency programs, 230,
235
Freud, Sigmund, 160
Frost, Geoffrey, 37–38
FTC Improvement Act, 127
Fulfillment center, 34
Full-service agency, 32, 36
Functional benefits, 80–81,
83, 89
Functional Feeders, 74
Fur Products Labeling Act,
127

Future Farmers of America,
248
Future sales, 235

G

Galvanic skin response
(GSR), 314
Gambling, 123–124
Gandhi, Mahatma,
160–161
Garfield, Bob, 247, 254
Gates, Bill, 104
Gays, 55, 57
Gender. *See also* Women
consumer behavior and,
108
stratification and, 104
Geodemographics
for mailing lists, 206
segmentation by, 74
Geography
of audience, 11–12
segmenting by, 73–74
Geopolitics, 107
Germany, 178
Ghostery, 114
Gift cards, 229
Gladwell, Malcolm, 264
Global agencies, 151
Global Business Dialog on
Electronic Commerce
(GBDe), 131–132
Globalized campaigns,
152–153
Global promotion, 11
Godin, Seth, 214
Goldeneye, 254, 257
Goodman, Shira, 14
Goodwill, 266
Government. *See also*
Federal government;
Local governments;
State governments
advertising by, 31
officials and employees
of, 11
GPS, 80, 133, 160
mobile marketing and,
196
Graham, Martha, 160, 166,
173
Great Depression,
52–53
Great Recession, 61–62
Green brands, 107
Greenfield, Jerry, 208
Green marketing, 281
Gross domestic product
(GDP), 19, 143–144
Gutenberg, Johannes, 201

GLOSSARY TERMS

promotion the communications process in marketing that is used to create a favorable predisposition toward a brand of product or service

promotional mix a blend of communications tools used to carry out the promotion process and to communicate directly with an audience

advertising a paid, mass-mediated attempt to persuade

client or **sponsor** the organization that pays for advertising

integrated marketing communication (IMC) the use of a wide range of promotional tools working together to create widespread brand exposure

advertisement a specific message that an organization has placed to persuade an audience

advertising campaign a series of coordinated promotional efforts, including advertisements, that communicate a single theme or idea

audience a group of individuals who may receive and interpret promotional messages

target audience a particular group of consumers singled out for an advertising or promotion campaign

household consumers the most conspicuous audience for advertising

members of business organizations advertising audience that buys business and industrial goods and services

members of a trade channel advertising audience that includes retailers, wholesalers, and distributors

professionals advertising audience that includes workers with special training or certification

trade journals magazines that publish technical articles for members of a trade

government officials and employees advertising audience that includes employees of government organizations at the federal, state, and local levels

CHAPTER SUMMARY

LO 1 Define promotion and integrated marketing communication (IMC).

Promotion is the communications process in marketing that is used to create a favorable predisposition toward a brand of product or service, an idea, or even a person. Promotional efforts are combined into a promotional mix that includes tools such as advertising, direct marketing, public relations, and personal selling. One of the most widely used tools is advertising, which is distinguished by its three essential elements: paid sponsorship, use of mass media, and the intent to persuade. The promotional mix will be most effective if the elements are integrated to achieve particular goals, and the realities of promotion in the 21st century demand that these goals be centered on brand. As a result, marketers have been turning toward the use of integrated marketing communication (IMC). IMC is the process of using a wide range of promotional tools working together to build and maintain brand awareness, identity, and preference.

LO 2 Discuss a basic model of communication.

Promotion occurs through various forms of communication, and advertising involves a particular type: mass-mediated communication. A model of mass-mediated communication that helps explain how advertising works show this type of communication as a process where people, institutions, and messages interact. This model has two major components—production and reception—each of which is a quasi-independent process. Between these are the mediating (interpretation) processes of accommodation and negotiation. According to this model, consumers create their own meanings when they interpret advertisements.

[Exhibit 1.2]
Mass-Mediated Communication

© Cengage Learning 2011.

LO 3 Describe the different ways of classifying audiences for promotion and IMC.

In the language of promotion, an audience is a group of individuals who receive and interpret advertisements and other promotional messages sent from companies. Broad audience categories are household consumers, members of business organizations, members of a trade channel, professionals, and government officials and employees. Audiences also may be defined by the scope of their location as global, international, national, regional, or local. Besides directing advertisements to audience groups at these levels, marketers may engage in cooperative advertising, a team effort in which producers and retailers work together on messages about a brand and where it is available for sale.

global promotion developing and placing messages with a common theme and presentation in all markets around the world where the brand is sold

international promotion preparation and placement of messages in different national and cultural markets

national promotion promotion directed to all geographic areas of one nation

regional promotion promotion concentrated on a large, but not national, region

local promotion promotion directed to an audience in a single trading area (a city or state)

cooperative promotion (co-op promotion) sharing of promotion expenses between national advertisers and local merchants

marketing the process of conceiving, pricing, promoting, and distributing ideas, goods, and services to create exchanges that benefit customers and companies

marketing mix the blend of the four responsibilities of marketing (conception, pricing, promotion, and distribution) used for a particular idea, product, or service

brand a name, term, sign, symbol, or any other feature that identifies one seller's good or service as distinct from those of other sellers

brand extension an adaptation of an existing brand to a new product area

brand loyalty decision-making mode in which consumers repeatedly buy the same brand to fulfill a specific need

brand equity positive associations with a brand in the minds of consumers

market segmentation breaking down a large, heterogeneous market into submarkets that are more homogeneous

differentiation creation of a perceived difference, in the consumer's mind, between an organization's brand and the competition's

positioning designing a product or service to occupy a distinct and valued place in the target consumer's mind and then communicating this distinctiveness

external position competitive niche pursued by a brand

Explain the key role of IMC as a business process.

LO 4

As organizations carry out marketing activities, IMC helps them do so in a way that achieves profitability and other goals. It provides a way to coordinate promotional activities, which are a key part of the marketing mix—the blend of strategic emphasis on product, pricing, promotion, and distribution. In IMC, the role of promotional tools is to communicate a brand's value, including product features, convenience, and emotional benefits through information and persuasion, introduction of new offerings, cultivation of brand loyalty among consumers and the trade, and creation of a brand's image and meaning. In these ways, IMC contributes to building brand awareness and brand equity. IMC also helps marketers implement market segmentation, differentiation, and positioning. All these efforts enhance revenues and profits. In addition, IMC involves selection of options such as primary versus selective demand stimulation, direct- versus delayed-response advertising, and promotion of the company or the brand.

[Exhibit 1.3]
The Marketing Mix

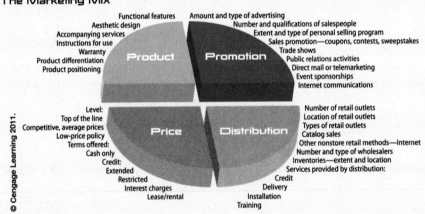

© Cengage Learning 2011.

Use the skills you've learned in this chapter to get started on the brand campaign card at the end of the book.

internal position niche a brand occupies with regard to the company's other, similar brands

economies of scale lower per-unit production costs resulting from larger volume

inelasticity of demand low sensitivity to price increases; may result from brand loyalty

primary demand stimulation promotion aimed at creating demand for a product category

selective demand stimulation promotion aimed at stimulating demand for a specific brand

direct-response promotion promotion that asks the receiver of the message to act immediately

delayed-response promotion promotion that relies on

imagery and message themes to emphasize a brand's benefits and positive qualities to encourage customers to purchase the product at a later date

brand advertising advertising that communicates a brand's features, values, and benefits

corporate advertising advertising intended to establish a favorable attitude toward a company

gross domestic product (GDP) the total value of goods and services produced within an economic system

value perception that a product or service provides satisfaction beyond the cost incurred to acquire it

symbolic value nonliteral meaning of a product or service, as perceived by consumers

Visit CourseMate for PROMO2 at www.cengagebrain.com for additional study tools.

CHAPTER 1

GLOSSARY TERMS

blog personal journal on a website that is frequently updated and intended for public access

social media highly accessible Web-based media that allow the sharing of information among individuals and between individuals and groups

crowdsourcing online distribution of tasks to groups (crowds) of experts, enthusiasts, or general consumers

marketer business, not-for-profit, or government organization that uses advertising and other promotional techniques to communicate with target markets to stimulate awareness of and demand for its brands

client organization that pays for advertising

trade reseller organization in the marketing channel of distribution that buys products to resell to customers

advertising agency organization of professionals who provide creative and business services related to planning, preparing, and placing advertisements

full-service agency advertising agency that includes an array of advertising professionals to meet all the promotional needs of clients

creative boutique advertising agency that emphasizes copywriting and artistic services

digital/interactive agency advertising agency that helps clients prepare communications for new media (for example, the Internet and interactive kiosks)

in-house agency advertising department of a marketer's own firm

media specialist organization that specializes in buying media time and space and that offers media strategy consulting to agencies and advertisers

promotion agency specialized agency that handles promotional efforts

CHAPTER SUMMARY

LO 1 Discuss important trends transforming the promotion industry.

Recent years have seen dramatic changes in the promotion industry. The proliferation of media from cable television to the Internet has created new advertising options, and giant media conglomerates are expected to control a majority of these television, radio, and Internet properties. Media proliferation has led to increasing media clutter and fragmentation, reducing the effectiveness of advertisements. As a result, marketers are using sales promotions, event sponsorships, and public relations to enhance the advertising effort. Finally, today's consumers have greater control over the information they receive about brands. New technology applications from blogs to TiVo empower consumers and diminish the role of promotion.

LO 2 Describe the promotion industry's size, structure, and participants.

Spending on promotional efforts exceeds a trillion dollars a year. The industry serves marketers, which are organizations that have a message they wish to communicate to a target audience. Typically, a marketer hires advertising and promotion agencies to launch and manage a campaign. Often, other external facilitators are brought in to perform specialized functions, such as assisting in the production of promotional materials or managing databases for efficient direct-marketing campaigns. These external facilitators also include consultants with whom advertisers and their agencies may confer regarding advertising and IMC strategy decisions. Promotional campaigns use some type of media to reach target markets, so marketers and their agencies work with media companies that have time or space to sell.

[Exhibit 2.1]
Structure of the Promotion Industry

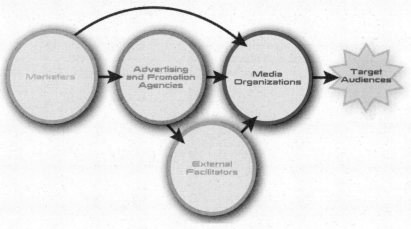

© Cengage Learning 2011.

direct-marketing agency or **direct-response agency** agency that maintains large databases of mailing lists and may design direct-marketing campaigns

database agency agency that helps customers construct databases of target customers, merge databases, develop promotional materials, and execute direct-marketing campaigns

fulfillment center operation that ensures consumers receive products ordered in response to direct marketing

infomercial long advertisement that resembles a talk show or product demonstration

consumer sales promotion sales promotion that is aimed at consumers and focuses on price-off deals, coupons, sampling, rebates, and premiums

trade-market sales promotion sales promotion that is designed to motivate distributors, wholesalers, and retailers to stock and feature a firm's brand in their merchandising programs

event-planning agency agency that finds locations, secures dates, and assembles a team of people to pull off a promotional event

designer specialist involved in execution of creative ideas and efforts by designing logos and other visual promotional pieces

logo graphic mark that identifies a company

public relations firm firm that handles an organization's needs regarding relationships with the local community, competitors, industry associations, and government organizations

account services team of managers that identifies the benefits a brand offers its target audiences and the best competitive position, and then develops a promotion plan

account planner person in an advertising agency who synthesizes all relevant consumer research and uses it to design an advertising strategy

creative services group in an advertising agency that develops the message to be delivered through advertising, sales promotion, direct marketing, event sponsorship, or public relations

LO 3 Summarize what advertising and promotion agencies do and how they are compensated.

Advertising and promotion agencies offer diverse services with respect to planning, preparing, and executing advertising and IMC campaigns. These services include market research and marketing planning, the creation and production of ad materials, the buying of media time or space for ad placement, and traffic management to keep production on schedule. Some advertising agencies offer a full array of services under one roof; others such as creative boutiques develop a particular expertise and win clients with their specialized skills. Promotion agencies specialize in one or more of the other forms of promotion beyond advertising. New-media agencies serve the Internet and other new-media needs of marketers. Clients pay agencies for services rendered based on commissions, markups, fee systems, and pay-for-results programs.

LO 4 Identify experts who help plan and execute integrated marketing communication campaigns.

Marketing and advertising research firms help advertisers and their agencies understand the market environment. Other external facilitators consult on marketing strategy, event planning, or retail display. Perhaps the most widely used facilitators specialize in production of promotional materials. In advertising, outside facilitators are used for the production of broadcast and print advertising. In promotions, designers and planners assist in creation and execution of promotional mix tools. Software firms fill a new role in the industry by providing expertise in tracking and analyzing consumer usage of new media technology.

LO 5 Discuss the role played by media organizations in IMC campaigns.

Media organizations are the essential link in delivering advertising and IMC messages to target audiences. Traditional media organizations include television, radio, newspaper, and magazines. Interactive media include the Internet, CD-ROMs, electronic kiosks, and less widely known communications companies. Media conglomerates control several different aspects of the communications system, such as cable broadcasting and Internet connections.

Use the skills you've learned in this chapter to get started on the brand campaign card at the end of the book.

production services team in an agency that takes creative ideas and turns them into advertisements, direct-mail pieces, or events materials

media planning and buying services services that are related to media planning or buying and are provided by advertising agencies or specialized media-buying organizations

commission system method of agency compensation based on the amount of money the advertiser spends on the media

markup charge method of agency compensation based on adding a percentage charge to a variety of services the agency purchases from outside suppliers

fee system method of agency compensation whereby the advertiser and agency agree on an hourly rate for services provided

pay-for-results compensation plan based on an agreement in which fee amounts are tied to a set of results criteria

external facilitator organization or individual that provides specialized services to advertisers and agencies

consultant individual who specializes in areas related to the promotional process

production facilitator organization that offers essential services during and after the production process

GLOSSARY TERMS

Industrial Revolution a rapid shift in Western society from an agricultural to an industrial economy, beginning in the mid-18th century

principle of limited liability limitation of an investor's risk in a corporation to his or her investment in the company's shares

branding strategy of developing brand names so that manufacturers can focus consumer attention on a clearly identified item

dailies newspapers published every weekday

consumer culture a way of life centered around consumption

Pure Food and Drug Act 1906 U.S. law requiring manufacturers to list the active ingredients of their products on their labels

Great Depression a period (1929–1941 in the United States) of a severe economic decline affecting the vast majority of people in many countries

subliminal advertising advertisements alleged to work on a subconscious level

creative revolution shift toward greater influence of "creatives" in advertising agencies during the 1960s

Action for Children's Television group formed during the 1970s to lobby the government to limit the amount and content of advertising to children

Federal Trade Commission (FTC) government regulatory agency most directly involved in overseeing the advertising industry

National Advertising Review Board body formed by the advertising industry to oversee its practices

interactive media media that allow consumers to call up games, entertainment, shopping, and educational programs on a subscription or pay-per-view basis

CHAPTER SUMMARY

LO 1 Identify economic changes that gave rise to advertising.

Advertising as we know it today is connected with the emergence of capitalistic economic systems. In such systems, business organizations must compete for survival in a freemarket setting. In this setting, it is natural that a firm would embrace a tool that assists it in persuading potential customers to choose its products over those offered by others. The explosion in production capacity that marked the Industrial Revolution added to the importance of demand-stimulation tools. Mass moves of consumers to cities and modern times helped create, along with advertising, consumer culture.

[Exhibit 3.1]
A Foundation for Advertising

© Cengage Learning 2011. Photo: iStockphoto .com/Jason Titzer.

LO 2 Discuss how the relationship between marketers and retailers has changed over time.

Marketing and branding play a key role in the ongoing power struggle between manufacturers and their retailers. Retailers have power in the marketplace deriving from the fact that they are closer to the customer. To assert more power in distribution channels, U.S. manufacturers began branding their products in the late 1800s. They used advertising to build awareness of and desire for their brands. Customers who are loyal to brands demand that retailers carry those brands and will pay a premium price for those brands. Lately, big retailers have been reclaiming some of the power by negotiating large purchases from manufacturers at lower prices.

LO 3 Describe significant eras of promotion in the United States, including the impact of social change on promotion.

Social and economic trends, along with technological developments, are major determinants of the marketing messages used in advertising and other forms of promotion. Before the Industrial Revolution, advertising's presence in the United States was barely noticeable. With an explosion in economic growth around the turn of the century, modern advertising was born: The "P. T. Barnum era" and the 1920s established advertising as a major force in the U.S. economic system. With the Great Depression and World War II, cynicism and paranoia regarding advertising began to grow. This concern led to refinements in practice and more careful regulation of advertising in the 1960s and 1970s. Consumption was again in vogue during the designer era of the 1980s.

consumer-generated content (CGC) advertisements made partly or completely by the product's end users, typically with the aid of Internet tools

e-business promotion in which companies selling to business customers rely on the Internet to send messages and close sales

branded entertainment embedding brands or brand icons as part of an entertainment property in an effort to connect with consumers in a unique and compelling way

The new communication technologies that emerged in the 1990s era seem certain to affect significant changes in future practice. In the 21st century, two recessions and the emergence of online social networking have been steering consumers and marketers into new media and more interactive brand communications.

[Exhibit 3.2]
Periods of Promotion

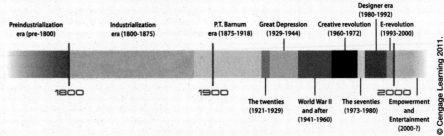

[Exhibit 3.3]
Better Data Online?

LO 4 **Define consumer empowerment and branded entertainment.**

Economic downturns and consumer anxiety, along with technological developments, have hastened consumers' exit from traditional media and made them less prone to snap up brand-name products. Marketers have had to get more creative in reaching them and building trust through other means. In the Web 2.0 era, consumers are joining in the creation of brand-related messages. This consumer-generated content can build excitement for brands but also requires that marketers cede some control to their customers. Interactive media not only allow marketers to reach consumers in the digital realm but also let them gauge consumers' attitudes. While the use of services like TiVo demonstrates a consumer backlash against the ubiquity of advertising, marketers can still grab attention and interest with branded entertainment, which blends marketing messages with entertainment in movies, music, and television programming. Communicating about brands through branded entertainment gives marketers freedom to work outside the constraints of traditional advertising.

LO 5 **Identify forces that will continue to affect the evolution of integrated marketing communication.**

History is practical. Consumers will always be affected by social and cultural change, and marketers will always convey messages about how they can help people cope with life's challenges. Learning how marketers addressed societal changes effectively in the past offers useful lessons for IMC opportunities in the future.

Use the skills you've learned in this chapter to get started on the brand campaign card at the end of the book.

Visit CourseMate for PROMO2 at www.cengagebrain.com **for additional study tools.**

GLOSSARY TERMS

target segment the subgroup (of the larger market) chosen as the focal point for a marketing program and advertising campaign

positioning the process of designing and representing a product or service to occupy a distinct and valued place in the target customer's mind

positioning strategy the key themes or concepts that an organization features when communicating a product's or service's distinctiveness to a target segment

STP marketing developing a strategy through segmenting, targeting, and positioning

market segmentation the breaking down of a large, heterogeneous market into more homogeneous submarkets or segments

heavy users consumers who purchase a product or service much more frequently than others

nonusers a market segment made up of consumers who do not use a particular product or service

brand-loyal users a market segment made up of consumers who repeatedly buy the same brand of a product

switchers or **variety seekers** a market segment made up of consumers who often buy what is on sale or choose brands that offer price incentives

emergent consumers a market segment made up of the gradual but constant influx of first-time buyers

point-of-entry marketing advertising strategy designed to win the loyalty of consumers whose brand preferences are under development

demographic segmentation market segmentation that divides consumers according to basic descriptors such as age, gender, race, marital status, income, education, and occupation

CHAPTER SUMMARY

LO 1 **Explain the process of STP marketing.**

STP marketing is the process of segmenting, targeting, and positioning. Marketers pursue this set of activities to formulate marketing strategies for their brands. STP marketing also provides a strong foundation for the development of advertising campaigns. While no single approach can guarantee success in marketing and advertising, STP marketing should be considered when customers in a category have heterogeneous wants and needs.

[Exhibit 4.1]
STP Marketing

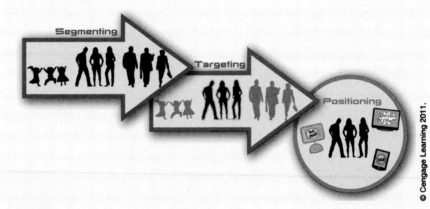

© Cengage Learning 2011.

LO 2 **Describe bases for identifying target segments.**

In market segmentation, the goal is to break down a heterogeneous market into more manageable subgroups or segments. Markets can be segmented on the basis of usage patterns and commitment levels, demographics, geography, psychographics, lifestyles, benefits sought, SIC codes, or stages in the purchasing process. Different bases are typically applied for segmenting consumer versus business-to-business markets.

LO 3 **Discuss criteria for choosing a target segment.**

In STP marketing, after segment identification, an organization must settle on one or more segments as a target for its marketing and advertising efforts. Several criteria are useful in establishing a target segment: the organization's ability to serve the segment in question, the size of the

Monkey Business Images/Shutterstock.com

Targeting children raises ethical concerns. Disney met the challenge by setting standards for healthful food options in its parks.

geodemographic segmentation market segmentation that identifies neighborhoods sharing common demographic characteristics

psychographics a form of market research that emphasizes the understanding of consumers' activities, interests, and opinions

lifestyle segmentation market segmentation that identifies consumers sharing similar activities, interests, and opinions

benefit segmentation market segmentation that identifies the various benefit packages consumers want from a product category

consumer markets the markets for products and services purchased by individuals or households to satisfy their specific needs

business markets the institutional buyers who purchase items to be used in other products and services or to be resold to other businesses or households

competitive field the companies that compete for a segment's business

market niche a relatively small group of consumers with a unique set of needs and the willingness to pay a premium price to a firm that meets those needs

benefit positioning a positioning option that features a distinctive customer benefit

user positioning a positioning option that focuses on a specific profile of the target user

competitive positioning a positioning option that uses an explicit reference to an existing competitor to help define precisely what a brand can do

repositioning returning to the STP marketing process to arrive at a revised positioning strategy

value proposition a statement of the functional, emotional, and self-expressive benefits that are delivered by the brand and provide value to customers in the target segment

segment and its growth potential, and the intensity of the competition the firm is likely to face in the segment. Often, small segments known as market niches can be quite attractive because they will not be hotly contested by numerous competitors.

LO 4 **Identify the essentials of a positioning strategy.**

The P in STP marketing refers to the positioning strategy, which should guide all marketing and advertising activities undertaken in pursuit of the target segment. Effective positioning strategies should be linked to the substantive benefits offered by the brand. They are also consistent internally and over time, and they feature simple and distinctive themes. Options for positioning strategies include benefit positioning, user positioning, and competitive positioning.

LO 5 **Review the necessary ingredients for creating a brand's value proposition.**

Many complex considerations underlie marketing and advertising strategies, so it is useful to summarize the essence of one's strategy with a device such as a value proposition. A value proposition is a statement of the brand's various benefits (functional, emotional, and self-expressive) that create value for the customer. These benefits as a set justify the price of the product or service. Clear expression of the value proposition is critical for developing advertising that sells.

[Exhibit 4.4]
Value Propositions for Two Popular Brands

McDonald's

Functional benefits	Good-tasting hamburgers, fries, and drinks served fast; extras such as playgrounds, prizes, premiums, and games.
Emotional benefits	Kids—fun via excitement at birthday parties; relationship with Ronald McDonald and other characters; a feeling of special family times. Adults—warmth via time spent enjoying a meal with the kids; admiration of McDonald's social involvement such as McDonald's Charities and Ronald McDonald Houses.

Nike

Functional benefits	High-technology shoe that will improve performance and provide comfort.
Emotional benefits	The exhilaration of athletic performance excellence, feeling engaged, active, and healthy; exhilaration from admiring professional and college athletes as they perform wearing "your brand"—when they win, you win too.
Self-expressive benefits	Using the brand endorsed by high-profile athletes lets your peers know your desire to compete and excel.

© Cengage Learning 2011.

Use the skills you've learned in this chapter to get started on the brand campaign card at the end of the book.

5 Understanding Buyer Behavior and the Communication Process

GLOSSARY TERMS

consumer behavior activities and decision processes directly involved in obtaining, consuming, and disposing of products and services

need state psychological state arising when one's desired state of affairs differs from one's actual state of affairs

functional benefits benefits that come from a product's objective performance characteristics

emotional benefits benefits not typically found in a product's tangible features or objective characteristics

internal search search for product information that draws on personal experience and prior knowledge

consideration set subset of brands from a product category that becomes the focal point of a consumer's evaluation

external search gathering product information by visiting retail stores to examine alternatives, seeking input from friends and relatives, or perusing professional product evaluations

evaluative criteria product attributes or performance characteristics on which consumers base their product evaluations

customer satisfaction good feelings that come from a favorable postpurchase experience

cognitive dissonance anxiety or regret that lingers after a difficult decision

involvement degree of perceived relevance and personal importance accompanying the choice of a product or service in a particular context

extended problem solving decision-making mode in which inexperienced but highly involved consumers go through a deliberate decision-making process

limited problem solving decision-making mode in which relatively inexperienced and uninvolved consumers are not systematic about decisions

habit decision-making mode in which consumers buy a single brand repeatedly as a solution to a simple consumption problem

CHAPTER SUMMARY

LO 1
Describe the four stages of consumer decision making.

Marketers need a keen understanding of their consumers as a basis for effective brand communication. This understanding begins with a view of consumers as systematic decision makers who follow a predictable process in making choices among products and brands. The process begins when consumers perceive a need, and it proceeds with a search for information that will help in making an informed choice. The search-and-evaluation stage is followed by purchase. Then, in postpurchase use and evaluation, customer satisfaction is ultimately determined.

[Exhibit 5.1]
Consumer Decision Making

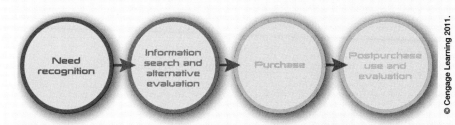

Need recognition → Information search and alternative evaluation → Purchase → Postpurchase use and evaluation

© Cengage Learning 2011.

LO 2
Explain how consumers adapt their decision-making processes based on involvement and experience.

Some purchases are more important to people than others, a fact that adds complexity to consumer behavior. To accommodate this complexity, marketers think about the level of involvement that attends any given purchase. High or low involvement and experience with a product or service category determine the mode of consumer decision making: extended problem solving, limited problem solving, habit or variety seeking, or brand loyalty.

LO 3
Discuss how brand communication influences consumers' psychological states and behavior.

Brand messages are developed to influence the way people think about products and brands, specifically their beliefs and brand attitudes. Marketers use multi-attribute attitude models (MAAMs) to help them ascertain the beliefs and attitudes of target consumers. However, consumers employ perceptual defenses to ignore or distort most of the commercial messages to which they are exposed. When consumers are not motivated to process an advertiser's message thoughtfully, the marketer may need to feature peripheral cues as part of the message.

LO 4
Describe the interaction of culture and advertising.

Advertisements are cultural products, and culture provides the context in which an ad will be interpreted. Marketers who overlook the influence of culture are bound to struggle in their attempt to communicate with the target audience. Culture is based on values, which are enduring beliefs that shape more-transitory psychological states, such as brand attitudes. Within a culture, individuals share patterns of behavior, or rituals. Violating cultural values and rituals is a sure way to squander advertising dollars.

variety seeking decision-making mode in which consumers switch their selection among various brands in a category in a random pattern

brand loyalty decision-making mode in which consumers repeatedly choose to buy the same brand of a product to fulfill a specific need

attitude overall evaluation of any object, person, or issue; varies along a continuum, such as favorable to unfavorable or positive to negative

brand attitudes summary evaluations that reflect preferences for various products or brands

beliefs a person's knowledge and feelings about an object or issue

salient beliefs the few beliefs that are the critical determinants of an attitude

multi-attribute attitude models (MAAMs) framework and set of procedures for collecting information from consumers to assess their salient beliefs and attitudes about competing brands

cognitive consistency maintenance of a system of beliefs and attitudes over time

advertising clutter volume of similar ads for products or services that presents an obstacle to brand promotion

selective attention processing of only a few messages among many encountered

cognitive responses thoughts that occur at the exact moment when beliefs and attitudes are being challenged by a message

elaboration likelihood model (ELM) social psychological model of the response to a persuasive communication, expressing the response in terms of motivation and ability

peripheral cues features of an advertisement other than the actual arguments about the brand's performance

meaning what a brand message intends or conveys

culture a group's characteristic ways of behaving

values defining expressions of what is important to a culture

rituals repeated behaviors that affirm, express, and maintain cultural values

Advertising and other elements of the promotional mix turn products into brands when they wrap brands with cultural meaning. Brands with high cultural capital are worth more. In these ways, brands are co-created by consumers and marketers.

LO 5 — Explain how sociological factors affect consumer behavior.

Consumer behavior is an activity each person undertakes before a broad audience of other consumers. Brand promotion helps the transfer of meaning. Gender, ethnicity, and race are important influences on consumption. Who consumers are—their identity—is changeable; through what they buy and use, consumers rapidly and frequently change aspects of who they are. Celebrities are particularly important in this regard.

LO 6 — Discuss how advertising transmits sociocultural meaning in order to sell things.

Advertising transfers a desired meaning to the brand by placing the brand within a carefully constructed social world represented in an ad, or "slice of life." Marketers paint a picture of the ideal social world, with all the meanings they want to impart to their brand. The brand is placed carefully in that picture, and the two (the constructed social world and the brand) rub off on each other, becoming a part of each other. Meaning thus is transferred from the ad's constructed social world to the brand.

[Exhibit 5.8]
The Movement of Meaning

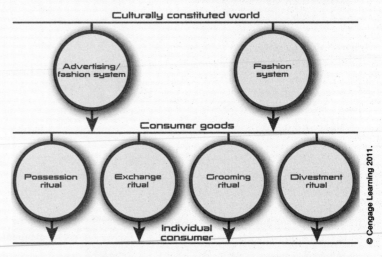

Use the skills you've learned in this chapter to get started on the brand campaign card at the end of the book.

stratification (social class) individuals' relative standing in a social system as produced by systematic inequalities

taste a generalized set or orientation to consumer preferences

intergenerational effect choice of products based on what was used in the consumer's childhood household

life stage circumstance that changes a family's consumption patterns

celebrity sociological category of famous individuals who shape identity for others

gender social expression of sexual biology or sexual choice

community group of people loosely joined by a common characteristic or interest

brand community group of consumers who feel a commonality and shared purpose grounded in or attached to a consumer good or service

Visit CourseMate for PROMO2 at www.cengagebrain.com for additional study tools.

The Regulatory and Ethical Environment of Promotions

GLOSSARY TERMS

ethics moral standards and principles against which behavior is judged

deception making false or misleading statements in a promotional message

puffery use of superlatives like "number one" and "best in the world" in promotional messages

primary demand demand for an entire product category

unfair advertising acts by advertisers that cause or are likely to cause substantial injury that is not reasonably avoidable or outweighed by other benefits

vertical cooperative advertising sharing of advertising expense by a manufacturer and dealer (wholesaler or retailer)

comparison advertisements ads that compare the advertiser's brand with competitors' brands

monopoly power a company's ability, either through advertising or in some other way, to prevent rivals from competing

advertising substantiation program FTC program that ensures advertisers make available to consumers supporting evidence for advertising claims

consent order FTC action asking an advertiser to stop running deceptive or unfair advertising without admitting guilt

cease-and-desist order FTC action requiring an advertiser to stop running an ad so that a hearing can be held to determine whether the ad is deceptive or unfair

affirmative disclosure FTC action requiring that important material determined to be absent from prior ads be included in future ads

corrective advertising FTC action requiring an advertiser to run additional ads to dispel false beliefs created by deceptive advertising

CHAPTER SUMMARY

LO 1 Discuss the impact of promotion on society's well-being.

On the positive side, promotional efforts are said to benefit society by lowering costs to increase the standard of living, fostering innovation, providing revenues to mass media, delivering a constant flow of information valued by consumers, and informing about political and social issues. At the same time, critics have said promotional expenditures are wasteful and intrusive, messages often are offensive to society and frustrating to those who can't afford a lavish lifestyle, and advertisements rarely furnish useful information but instead perpetuate superficial stereotypes. For many years, some critics have been concerned that advertisers are controlling consumers with subliminal advertising messages—a claim that is not well supported.

LO 2 Summarize ethical considerations related to brand promotion campaigns.

Ethical considerations that frequently arise involve truthfulness, concern for the impact of promotional messages on children, and the promotion of controversial products and practices such as firearms, gambling, alcohol, and cigarettes. Ethical standards are a matter for personal reflection; for example, there are many shades of gray between purely fact-based ads and intentional efforts to deceive by withholding information or lying. However, it certainly is the case that unethical people can create unethical advertising. But there also are many safeguards against such behavior, including the corporate and personal integrity of advertisers.

LO 3 Describe aspects of advertising regulated by the U.S. government.

In the United States, advertisers may not engage in deceptive or unfair practices, including bogus cooperative advertising allowances, unfair comparison advertising, and the exercise of monopoly power. The government places limits on the amount of advertising aimed at children on television, and industry groups have developed guidelines for the content of ads targeting children.

[Exhibit 6.2]
Don't Go There . . .

Deception

Unfair use of ad allowances

Negative influences on children

DANGER
Regulatory Limits on Advertising

Unfair comparison ads

Unfairness to consumers

© Cengage Learning 2011

celebrity endorsements advertisements that use an expert or celebrity as spokesperson to endorse the use of a product or service

self-regulation the advertising industry's attempt to police itself

consumerism actions of individual consumers to exert power over the marketplace activities of organizations

cookies online tracking markers that advertisers place on a Web surfer's hard drive to track that person's online behavior

behavioral targeting the process of database development in which online tracking markers are used to track computer users' online behavior so that brand promotion messages can be very specifically targeted to them

spam unsolicited commercial messages sent through email

phishing efforts by spammers to entice Web users to enter personal information on a website forged to look like a legitimate site

premiums items that feature a sponsor's logo and are offered free or at a reduced price with the purchase of another item

appropriation use of pictures or images owned by someone else without permission

defamation untrue communication that damages the reputation of an individual

slander oral defamation (for example, during a radio broadcast)

libel defamation that occurs in print (for example, in a magazine story)

LO 4 Summarize the regulatory role of the Federal Trade Commission.

In the United States, the Federal Trade Commission (FTC) was established in 1914 and has been especially active in trying to deter deception and unfairness in advertising. The FTC has developed regulatory remedies, such as the advertising substantiation program. When the FTC determines that advertising is unfair or deceptive, it may issue a consent or cease-and-desist order, or require affirmative disclosure or corrective advertising. The FTC also has issued guidelines for the use of celebrity endorsements and for endorsements by bloggers.

[Exhibit 6.3]
Remedies Sought by the FTC

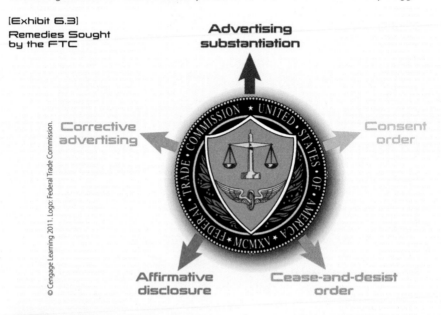

© Cengage Learning 2011. Logo: Federal Trade Commission.

LO 5 Explain the meaning and importance of self-regulation by marketers.

Some of the most important controls on advertising involve voluntary self-regulation by marketing professionals. For example, the American Association of Advertising Agencies has issued guidelines for promoting fairness and accuracy when using comparative advertisements. Many other organizations, such as the Better Business Bureau, the National Association of Broadcasters, and the Direct Marketing Association, participate in the process to help ensure fairness and assess consumer complaints about advertising and promotion.

LO 6 Discuss the regulation of direct marketing, sales promotion, and public relations.

In direct marketing and e-commerce, the primary concern has to do with consumer privacy. Laws and regulations, including the Do Not Call Registry and the CAN SPAM Act, restrict the ways in which companies can contact consumers with a sales offer. Other restrictions are aimed at ensuring that contests and sweepstakes do not amount to gambling opportunities. In sales promotions, premium offers, trade allowances, and offline contests and sweepstakes are subject to regulation. Firms must state the fair value of "free" premiums, trade allowances must follow the guidelines of fair competition, and contests and sweepstakes must follow strict rules specified by the FTC. The regulation of public relations efforts requires that privacy be protected and that firms avoid copyright infringement and defamation.

Use the skills you've learned in this chapter to get started on the brand campaign card at the end of the book.

Visit CourseMate for PROMO2 at www.cengagebrain.com for additional study tools.

CHAPTER 7

CHAPTER IN REVIEW

The International Market Environment for Brand Promotion

GLOSSARY TERMS

international brand promotion the preparation and placement of brand communication in different national and cultural markets

ethnocentrism tendency to view and value things from the perspective of one's own culture

self-reference criterion (SRC) unconscious reference to one's own cultural values, experiences, and knowledge as a basis for decisions

less-developed countries countries whose economies lack most resources necessary for development: capital, infrastructure, political stability, and trained workers

newly industrialized countries countries where traditional ways of life are changing into modern consumer cultures

highly industrialized countries countries with a high GDP and a high standard of living

demographic dividend favorable climate for economic expansion in developing nations as a result of falling labor costs, a younger and healthier population, and entry of women into the workforce

picturing creating representations of things

global agencies advertising agencies with a worldwide presence

international affiliates foreign-market advertising agencies with which a local agency has established a relationship to handle international advertising needs

local agency advertising agency in a foreign market hired because of its knowledge of the culture and local market conditions

globalized campaigns promotional campaigns that use the same message and creative execution across all or most international markets

CHAPTER SUMMARY

LO 1 Identify types of audience research that contribute to understanding cultural barriers to effective communication.

All of us wear cultural blinders, so we must overcome substantial barriers in trying to communicate with people from other countries. This is a major problem for international marketers as they seek to promote their brands around the world. To overcome this problem and avoid errors in advertising planning, marketers need to conduct cross-cultural audience analysis. Such analyses involve evaluation of economic conditions, demographic characteristics, customs, values, rituals, and product use and preferences in the target countries.

[Exhibit 7.1]
Wide Differences in Wealth

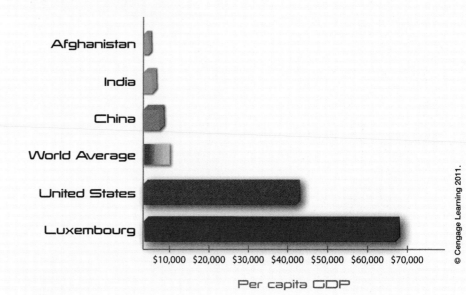

Afghanistan
India
China
World Average
United States
Luxembourg

$10,000 $20,000 $30,000 $40,000 $50,000 $60,000 $70,000

Per capita GDP

© Cengage Learning 2011.

LO 2 Describe challenges that complicate integrated marketing communication in international settings.

Worldwide marketers face three distinctive challenges in executing their campaigns. The first is a creative challenge that derives from differences in experience and meaning among cultures. Even the pictures featured in an ad may be translated differently from one country to the next. Media availability, media coverage, and media costs vary dramatically around the world, adding a second complication to

Monkey Business Images/Shutterstock.com

localized campaigns promotional campaigns that involve different messages and creative executions for each foreign market served

international brand promotion. Finally, the amount and nature of advertising regulations vary dramatically from country to country, sometimes forcing a complete reformulation of a promotional campaign.

LO 3 **Compare the basic types of agencies that can assist in brand promotion around the world.**

Advertising agencies offer marketers the expertise needed to develop and execute brand promotion campaigns in international markets. Marketers can choose to work with global agencies, an international affiliate of the agency they use in their home country, or local agencies in the targeted market. Each of these agency types brings different advantages and disadvantages on evaluative dimensions such as geographic proximity, economies of scale, political leverage, awareness of the client's strategy, and knowledge of the local culture.

[Exhibit 7.2]
Take Your Pick

© Cengage Learning 2011.

LO 4 **Discuss the advantages and disadvantages of globalized versus localized promotional campaigns.**

A final concern for international brand promotion entails the degree of customization a marketer should attempt in campaigns designed to cross national boundaries. Globalized campaigns involve little customization among countries, whereas localized campaigns feature heavy customization for each market. Standardized messages bring cost savings and create a common brand image worldwide, but they may miss the mark with consumers in different nations. As consumers around the world become more similar, globalized campaigns may become more prevalent. Teenagers in many countries share similar values and lifestyles and thus make a natural target for globalized campaigns.

Use the skills you've learned in this chapter to get started on the brand campaign card at the end of the book.

Visit CourseMate for PROMO2 at www.cengagebrain.com **for additional study tools.**

GLOSSARY TERMS

creativity ability to consider and hold together seemingly inconsistent elements and forces, making a new connection

account executive liaison between an advertising agency and its clients

account team group of people comprising different facets of the promotion industry who work together under a team leader

creative brief document that outlines and channels an essential creative idea and objective

cognitive style an individual's preference for thinking about and solving a problem

creative abrasion clash of ideas, abstracted from the people who propose them, from which new ideas can evolve

interpersonal abrasion clash of people, often resulting from an inability to regard idea feedback as separate from personal feedback, causing communication to shut down

brainstorming organized approach to idea generation in groups

CHAPTER SUMMARY

LO 1 **Describe characteristics of great creative minds.**

How we recognize and define creativity in marketing rests on our understanding of the achievements of acknowledged creative geniuses from the worlds of art, literature, music, science, and politics. A look at great creative minds—such as Picasso, Gandhi, Freud, Eliot, Stravinsky, Graham, and Einstein—reveals shared sensibilities including a strikingly exuberant self-confidence, (childlike) alertness, unconventionality, and an obsessive commitment to their work. However, self-confidence at some point becomes crass self-promotion, and an unconstrained childlike ability to see the world as forever new eventually devolves into childish self-indulgence. In spite of creativity's downside, it is essential. Without creativity, there can be no brand promotion.

[Exhibit 8.1]
Seven Creative Geniuses

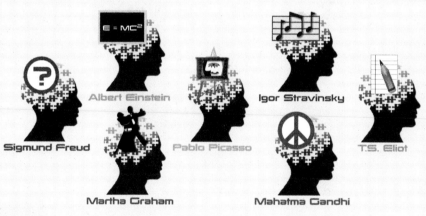

© Cengage Learning 2011.

LO 2 **Contrast the roles of an agency's creative department and its business managers/account executives.**

The significant effort required to get the right idea, coupled with the client's apparent ease in dismissing that idea, underlies the contentiousness between an agency's creative staff and its account executives and clients. Creatives provoke. Managers restrain. Ads that win awards for creative excellence don't necessarily fulfill a client's business goals. All organizations deal with the competing agendas of one department versus another, but in advertising agencies, this competition plays out at an amplified level. The difficulty of assessing the effectiveness of brand promotion only adds to the problem. Advertising researchers are in the unenviable position of judging the creatives, pitting "science" against art. In spite of these tensions, creativity is essential to the vitality of brands. Creativity makes a brand, and creativity reinvents established brands in new and desired ways.

LO 3 **Discuss how teams manage tensions and promote creativity in integrated marketing communication.**

There are many sources of conflict and tension in the creation of a promotional mix. Many organizations attempt to address this challenging issue through systematic utilization of teams. Teams, when effectively managed, will produce outputs that are greater than the sum of their individual parts. Teams need to be managed to promote creative abrasion but limit interpersonal abrasion. They need guidance from a maestro (like a Lee Clow or Alex Bogusky). Use of a creative brief can get teams headed in the right direction and preempt many forms of conflict.

[Exhibit 8.3]
Keys to Creativity

© Cengage Learning 2011.

LO 4 **Evaluate your own passion for creativity.**

Self-assessment is an important part of learning and growing. Now is the perfect time to be thinking about yourself and your passion for creativity. If marketing, especially brand promotion, interests you, then improving your own creative abilities should be a lifelong quest. Now is the time to decide to become more creative.

[Exhibit 8.4]
Eight Rules for Brainstorming

1. Build off each other.	Don't just generate ideas: build off them.
2. Fear drives out creativity.	Be sure no one is teased or embarrassed.
3. Prime individuals before and after.	Give everyone a chance to prepare and learn.
4. Make it happen.	Put ideas into action.
5. It's a skill.	Use a skilled facilitator.
6. Embrace creative abrasion.	Welcome conflicting ideas and viewpoints.
7. Listen and learn.	Focus on learning and building trust.
8. Follow the rules.	If you don't, you're not really brainstorming.

Source: Based on Robert L. Sutton, "The Truth about Brainstorming," *Inside Business Week*, September 25, 2006, 17–21.

Use the skills you've learned in this chapter to get started on the brand campaign card at the end of the book.

GLOSSARY TERMS

Internet global collection of computer networks linking public and private computer systems to connect more than a billion users

opt-in email messages sent to website visitors who have given permission to receive commercial email about particular topics or products

spam uninvited commercial messages sent to electronic mailing lists or online discussion groups

World Wide Web (WWW) database of information available online in a graphical environment that simplifies navigation

surfing gliding from website to website, guided by hyperlinks, a search engine, or word-of-mouth

search engine software tool for finding websites by entering keywords

portal website that serves as a starting point for Web access and search

website collection of Web pages, images, videos, and other content hosted on a Web server

mash-up combination of websites into a single site for analyzing or comparing information

blog personal journal that is published on a website, frequently updated, and intended for public access

blogger author of a blog

WiFi wireless technology allowing Internet access connections to reach out about 300 feet

WiMax wireless Internet technology capable of a range of 25 to 30 miles

Mi-Fi wireless Internet technology with multi-mile access and ability to access the Internet while the user is moving in a car or train

ultrabroadband wireless Internet technology allowing users to move extremely large files quickly over short distances

CHAPTER SUMMARY

LO 1 Summarize the Internet's role in integrated marketing communication (IMC).

The Internet will be important but is unlikely to replace other forms of brand promotion or even to become the main method of communicating with target audiences. Internet technologies and opportunities are changing dramatically. For example, small businesses are selling through auction sites, social networking provides a new way of delivering promotional messages, and new venues like mobile devices offer communication opportunities very different from traditional message delivery. Finally, the Internet's structure and potential as an advertising medium offer ways for marketers to create and deliver messages that are significantly different from those in traditional mass media.

LO 2 Describe the nature of the Internet as a medium for communicating promotional messages.

The Web offers target market selectivity—targeting that is more finely tuned than traditional segmentation schemes such as demographics, geographics, and psychographics. Marketers can focus on very specific interest areas or geographic regions, time of day, or computer platform. The Internet also allows advertisers to track how users interact with their brands and learn what interests current and potential customers. In addition, online content is delivered 24 hours a day, seven days a week, at the convenience of the receiver. A campaign can be tracked on a daily basis and updated, changed, or replaced almost immediately. Furthermore, the Internet is immediately a global medium unlike any traditional media option. Another benefit is interactivity: A marketer can engage a prospective customer to a degree that just cannot be accomplished in traditional media. Finally, Web promotion is the most easily integrated and coordinated with other forms of promotion.

[Exhibit 9.2]
What Americans Are Doing Online

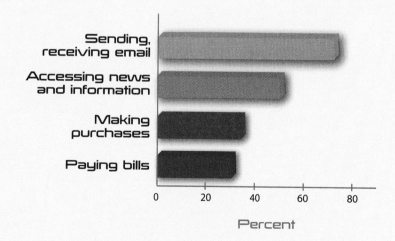

Source: Based on Digital Marketing & Media Fact Pack, *Advertising Age*, April 23, 2007, 32.

click-through measure of the number of hyperlinks that users click on, especially links from advertisements to the advertiser's website

cost per thousand (CPM) dollar cost of reaching 1,000 members of an audience

paid search the practice of paying search engines and portals to place ads near relevant search results

search engine optimization (SEO) process for improving the volume and quality of traffic to a website from a search engine's results pages

display or banner ads advertisements placed on websites that contain editorial material

sponsorship payment to maintain a section of a website and perhaps provide content for the site in exchange for being mentioned on the site

pop-up ad Internet advertisement that opens a separate window while a Web page is loading

splash screen Internet ad that appears briefly on a website after a page has been requested but before it has loaded

pop-under ad Internet ad that is displayed "under" the active window, so it appears only after that window is closed

permission marketing sending commercial email only to Web users who have agreed to receive it

viral marketing process of consumers spreading brand messages through email

rich media, video, and audio use of streaming video and audio that plays when the user's mouse passes over an Internet ad

corporate home page website that focuses on a corporation and its products

virtual mall gateway to a group of Internet storefronts where the user gains access to a retailer by clicking on a storefront

widget software module that people can add to their blog or their personal page on a social network; may feature a brand or direct the user to an e-commerce site

Second Life online virtual world where participants can roam landscapes and interact, simulating real-world activities, including (often real) business transactions

LO 3 Define options for promotion on the Web.

Web advertising includes paid search (placement of ads in or near relevant search results), display or banner ads (placed on sites containing editorial material), and pop-up or pop-under ads (which appear as a Web page is loading or after a page has loaded). Internet ads can use rich media, video, and audio (which include music and video clips) and widgets (software that people can drag and drop onto their personal Web page or blog). Marketers also can engage users with their brands through website sponsorship, email messages, and their corporate home pages. They can offer brand information and purchase opportunities in a virtual mall (a gateway to a group of Internet storefronts). And they can place billboards or branded business opportunities in video games or in a virtual world such as Second Life.

LO 4 Identify the issues involved in establishing a website.

Three issues are key to successfully establishing and maintaining a site on the World Wide Web: developing a domain name, promoting the website, and providing adequate security and privacy.

LO 5 List developments likely to shape the future of IMC on the Web.

The future of IMC on the Web will be linked to technological advances enabling video on the Web and mobile marketing. More access to broadband means more content can be streamed to users. The technology is available for using the Internet to watch TV shows (with ads) and to link from ads to marketers' websites. Also, wireless technology is giving consumers access to the Web while they are on the go. Marketers can precisely target consumers based on their location and send relevant messages to their mobile devices.

Use the skills you've learned in this chapter to get started on the brand campaign card at the end of the book.

domain name unique URL that establishes a Web location

top-level domain (TLD) suffix that follows a website name

hits number of pages and graphical images requested from a website

page views record of the pages that have been sent to a user's computer; multiscreen pages are counted as one page

visits number of occasions on which a particular user looks up a particular website during a given time period

unique visitors number of people (identified using registration information) who visit a site during a given time period

Web analytic software software that measures hits, pages, visits, and users, and allows a website to track audience traffic on the site

click fraud act of clicking on Internet ads solely to generate revenue for the website carrying the ads

mobile marketing communicating with target markets through mobile devices

GLOSSARY TERMS

direct marketing interactive marketing system that uses multiple media to generate a transaction or other measurable response at any location

cost per inquiry (CPI) number of inquiries generated by a direct-marketing program divided by the program's cost

cost per order (CPO) number of orders generated by a direct-marketing program divided by that program's cost

mailing list file of names and addresses used for contacting prospects or customers

internal lists organization's records of its customers and inquirers; used for developing better customer relationships

external lists mailing lists purchased from a list compiler or rented from a list broker; used for cultivating new business

marketing database mailing list with added information collected directly from individual customers

RFM analysis analysis of how recently and frequently a customer bought from an organization, and how much the customer spent

frequency-marketing programs direct-marketing programs that provide concrete rewards to frequent customers

cross-selling marketing programs aimed at selling additional products to existing customers

direct-response advertising advertising that asks the receiver of the message to act immediately

direct mail direct-marketing medium that uses the postal service to deliver marketing materials

telemarketing direct-marketing medium that involves using the telephone to deliver a spoken appeal

infomercial long advertisement that looks like a talk show or product demonstration

CHAPTER SUMMARY

LO 1 Identify purposes served by direct marketing.

Many types of organizations are increasing their expenditures on direct marketing. These expenditures serve three primary purposes: direct marketing offers potent tools for closing sales with customers, identifying prospects for future contacts, and offering information and incentives that help foster brand loyalty.

[Exhibit 10.1]
Some Direct-Marketing Milestones

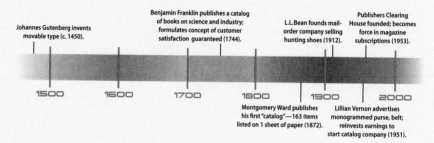

Source: Based on Direct Marketing Association, "Grassroots Advocacy Guide for Direct Marketers" (1993).

LO 2 Explain the popularity of direct marketing.

The growing popularity of direct marketing can be attributed to several factors. Direct marketers make consumption convenient: Credit cards, 800 numbers, and the Internet take the hassle out of shopping. Additionally, today's computing power, which allows marketers to build and mine large customer information files, has enhanced direct marketing's impact. The emphasis on producing and tracking measurable outcomes also is well received by marketers in an era when everyone is trying to do more with less.

LO 3 Distinguish a mailing list from a marketing database, and review the applications of each.

A mailing list is a file of names and addresses of current or potential customers, such as lists that might be generated by a credit card company or a catalog retailer. Internal lists are valuable for creating relationships with current customers, and external lists are useful in generating new customers. A marketing database is a natural extension of the internal list, but it also includes information about individual customers and their specific preferences and purchasing patterns. A marketing database allows organizations to identify and focus their efforts on their best customers. Recognizing and reinforcing preferred customers can be a potent strategy for building loyalty. Cross-selling opportunities also emerge once a database is in place. In addition, as one gains keener information about the motivations of current best customers, insights usually emerge about how to attract new customers.

[Exhibit 10.2]
What Makes a Marketing Database

© Cengage Learning 2011.

LO 4 **Describe the media used by direct marketers in delivering messages to consumers.**

Direct-marketing programs emanate from mailing lists and databases, but there still is a need to deliver a message to the customer. Direct mail and telemarketing are the most common means used in executing direct-marketing programs. Email has emerged as a low-cost alternative. Because the advertising done as part of direct-marketing programs typically requests an immediate response from the customer, it is known as direct-response advertising. Conventional media such as television, newspapers, magazines, and radio also can be used to request a direct response by offering an 800 number or a Web address to facilitate customer contact.

Use the skills you've learned in this chapter to get started on the brand campaign card at the end of the book.

GLOSSARY TERMS

sales promotion use of innovative techniques that create a perception of greater brand value among consumers or distributors

consumer-market sales promotion sales promotions designed to induce consumers to purchase a firm's brand rather than a competitor's

trade-market sales promotion sales promotion designed to motivate distributors, wholesalers, and retailers to stock and feature a firm's brand

business-market sales promotion promotion designed to cultivate buyers making purchase decisions in corporations

coupon sales promotion that entitles a buyer to a designated reduction in price for a product or service

price-off deal type of sales promotion that offers consumers money off merchandise at the point of purchase through specially marked packages

premiums items that feature a sponsor's logo and are offered free or at a reduced price with the purchase of another item

free premium sales promotion that gives consumers an item at no cost by including the item in the package or mailing it after proof of purchase is verified

self-liquidating premium sales promotion that requires a consumer to pay most of the cost of the item received as a premium

advertising specialties sales promotion consisting of a message placed on useful items given to consumers with no obligation

contest sales promotion in which consumers compete for prizes based on skill or ability

sweepstakes sales promotion in which winners are awarded prizes based on chance

sampling sales promotion technique that offers consumers a trial opportunity

in-store sampling sampling that occurs at the point of purchase

CHAPTER SUMMARY

LO 1
Explain the importance and growth of sales promotion.

Sales promotions use incentives to motivate action by consumers, members of the trade channel, and business buyers. They serve different purposes than mass-media advertising does, and many companies spend more on sales promotions than on advertising. Reasons for greater reliance on promotions include pressure on marketing managers to account for their spending and meet sales objectives in short time frames, along with deal-prone shoppers, brand proliferation, the increasing power of large retailers, and media clutter.

LO 2
Describe the main sales promotion techniques used in the consumer market.

Coupons, price-off deals, phone and gift cards, and premiums provide obvious incentives for purchase. Contests, sweepstakes, and product placements can be excellent devices for stimulating brand interest. A variety of sampling techniques are available to get a product into the hands of the target audience. Rebates and frequency programs provide rewards for repeat purchase.

[Exhibit 11.2]
Objectives for Consumer-Market Sales Promotion

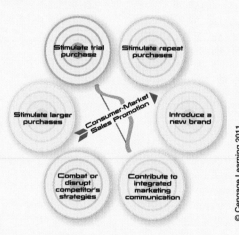

© Cengage Learning 2011.

LO 3
Describe the main sales promotion techniques used in the trade channel and business markets.

Sales promotions directed at the trade are a necessity in obtaining initial distribution of a new brand. For established brands, they can be a means to increase distributors' order quantities or obtain retailers' cooperation in implementing a consumer-directed promotion. Incentives, allowances, sales training programs, and cooperative advertising programs can motivate distributors' support for a brand. In the business market, professional buyers are attracted by various sales promotion techniques. Frequency (continuity) programs are very valuable in the travel industry and have spread to business-product advertisers. Trade shows efficiently reach a large number of highly targeted business buyers. Other tools that have proven successful include gifts, premiums, advertising specialties, and trial offers.

[Exhibit 11.4]
Objectives for Trade-Market Sales Promotion

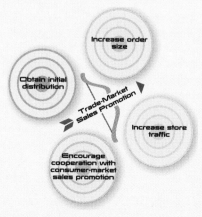

© Cengage Learning 2011.

door-to-door sampling sampling in which samples are brought to the homes of the target segment in a well-defined geographic area

mail sampling sampling in which samples are delivered through the postal service

newspaper sampling sampling in which samples are distributed in newspapers to allow specific geographic and geodemographic targeting

on-package sampling sampling in which a sample item is attached to another product's package

mobile sampling sampling carried out using logo-emblazoned vehicles where samples are dispensed at malls or other high-traffic areas

trial offers sales promotion in which expensive items are offered on a trial basis to induce consumers to try a brand

rebate money-back offer requiring a buyer to mail in a form requesting the money back from the manufacturer

frequency programs sales promotion that offers consumers discounts or rewards for repeat purchases

push strategy sales promotion strategy in which marketers devise incentives to encourage purchases by members of the trade, moving product into the distribution channel

push money trade incentive in which retail salespeople are offered monetary rewards for featuring a marketer's brand

merchandise allowances trade-market sales promotion in which free products are packed with regular shipments as payment to the trade for setting up and maintaining displays

slotting fees trade-market sales promotion in which manufacturers make direct cash payments to retailers to ensure shelf space

bill-back allowances monetary incentive provided to retailers for featuring a marketer's brand in advertising or in-store displays

off-invoice allowance program allowing wholesalers and retailers to deduct a set amount from the invoice they receive for merchandise

cooperative advertising sharing of advertising expenses between national advertisers and local merchants

trade shows events where several related products from many manufacturers are

LO 4 Identify the risks to the brand of using sales promotion.

Offering constant deals for a brand can erode brand equity, and sales resulting from a promotion simply may be borrowing from future sales. Constant deals also can create a customer mind-set that leads consumers to abandon a brand as soon as a deal is retracted. Sales promotions are expensive to administer and fraught with legal complications. Sales promotions yield their most positive results when carefully integrated with the overall advertising plan.

LO 5 Understand the role and techniques of point-of-purchase advertising.

Point-of-purchase (P-O-P) advertising refers to materials used in the retail setting to attract shoppers' attention to a firm's brand, convey primary brand benefits, or highlight pricing information. P-O-P can reinforce a consumer's brand preference or change a consumer's brand choice in the retail setting. P-O-P displays may feature price-off deals or other consumer and business sales promotions. A myriad of displays and presentations are available in two categories: short-term promotional displays (used for six months or less) and permanent long-term displays (used for more than six months). With location marketing, a marketer uses GPS to target consumers by their precise location and sends point-of-purchase messages to their mobile devices. In trade and business markets, P-O-P displays encourage retailers to support one manufacturer's brand over another; they also can be used to gain preferred shelf space and exposure in a retail setting.

LO 6 Describe the role of support media in a comprehensive integrated marketing communication plan.

The traditional support media include billboard, out-of-home media, and directory advertising. Billboards and transit advertising are excellent means for carrying simple messages into specific metropolitan markets. Street furniture is popular as a placard for brand builders around the world. Aerial and cinema advertising also can be great ways to break through the clutter and target specific geographic markets in a timely manner. Directory advertising, primarily the Yellow Pages directories, can be a sound investment because it helps a committed customer locate an advertiser's product. Finally, packaging can be considered support media because the package carries important information for consumer choice at the point of purchase, including the brand logo and "look and feel" of the brand.

Use the skills you've learned in this chapter to get started on the brand campaign card at the end of the book.

displayed and demonstrated to members of the trade

point-of-purchase (P-O-P) advertising advertising that appears in the retail setting

short-term promotional displays P-O-P materials used for six months or less

permanent long-term displays P-O-P materials intended for presentation for more than six months

support media media used to reinforce a message being delivered via some other media vehicle

riding the boards assessing possible locations for billboard advertising

out-of-home media advertising advertising venues that reach

local audiences away from home and work

transit advertising advertising that appears as interior and exterior displays on mass-transit vehicles and at terminal and station platforms

aerial advertising advertising that involves airplanes pulling signs or banners, as well as skywriting and blimps

cinema advertising ads that run in movie theaters before the film and other brand messages that appear off-screen within a theater

packaging a product's container or wrapping, which conveys product information and user appeal

Visit CourseMate for PROMO2 at www.cengagebrain.com for additional study tools.

GLOSSARY TERMS

Madison & Vine convergence of advertising and entertainment; reference to the names of streets that represent each industry

Chaos Scenario exodus of ad revenue from traditional broadcast media in reaction to audience fragmentation and tools for ad avoidance; causes media cutbacks, followed by further reductions in audience size and even less advertising

event sponsorship financial support for an event, given in exchange for the right to display a brand name, logo, or promotional message at the event

media impressions instances in which a product or brand is exposed to consumers through media coverage, rather than paid advertising

leveraging using any collateral communication or activity to reinforce the link between a brand and an event

product placement sales promotion technique of getting a marketer's product featured in movies and television shows

authenticity quality of genuineness or naturalness

branded entertainment embedding a brand in any entertainment property to impress and connect with consumers

CHAPTER SUMMARY

LO 1 **Explain the popularity of event sponsorship as a means of brand promotion.**

The list of companies sponsoring events grows with each passing year, and the events include a wide variety of activities. Of these activities, sports attract the most sponsorship dollars. Sponsorship can help build brand familiarity, can promote brand loyalty by connecting a brand with powerful emotional experiences, and in most instances allows a marketer to reach a well-defined target audience. Events also can facilitate face-to-face contacts with key customers, and they present opportunities to distribute product samples, sell premiums, and conduct consumer surveys.

[Exhibit 12.1]
When Event Sponsorship Is a Winner

Enough media impressions

Stronger brand loyalty

Targeted consumers in audience

© Cengage Learning 2011.

[Exhibit 12.2]
Checklist for Event Sponsorship

- Pick an event that matches the brand.
- Pick an event that draws your target audience—not only a big audience, but the right audience.
- Deliver a few key messages, and repeat them often.
- Develop your event participation in terms of a plot or story with a beginning, middle, and end.
- Make participation exclusive by issuing invitations to a select group.
- Make participation relevant to your target group—not only about selling.
- Use the Internet to promote your event and share your story with those who couldn't be there.
- Integrate your event sponsorship with your other brand communications.

Source: Based on Laura Shuler, "Make Sure to Deliver When Staging Events," *Marketing News*, September 13, 1999, 12.

LO 2 Summarize the uses and appeal of product placements.

Product placements have surged in popularity, and there are many reasons to believe that marketers will continue to commit resources to this activity. Like any other brand promotion tactic, product placements offer the most value when they are connected to other elements of the promotional plan. One common use of the placement is to help create excitement for the launch of a new product. Implicit celebrity endorsements and authenticity are key issues to consider when judging placement opportunities. High-quality placements are most likely to result from great collaboration among marketers, agents, producers, and writers.

LO 3 Describe benefits and challenges of connecting with entertainment properties to build a brand.

Brand builders want to connect with consumers, and to do so, they are connecting with the entertainment business. Although not everyone can afford a NASCAR sponsorship, in many ways, NASCAR sets the standard for celebrating brands in an entertaining setting. Many marketers, such as BMW and Unilever, are developing their own entertainment properties to feature their brands. However, the rush to participate in branded-entertainment ventures raises the risk of oversaturation and consumer backlash, or at least consumer apathy. As with any tool, while it is new and fresh, good things happen. When it gets old and stale, advertisers will turn to the next big thing.

[Exhibit 12.3]
Obstacles to Overcome

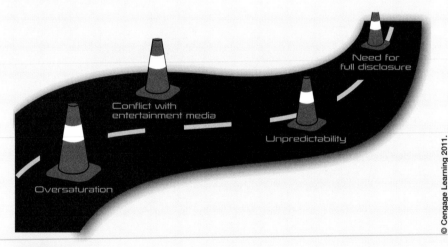

Oversaturation

Conflict with entertainment media

Unpredictability

Need for full disclosure

© Cengage Learning 2011.

LO 4 Discuss challenges presented by the ever-increasing variety of communication and branding tools.

The tremendous variety of media options represents a monumental challenge for a marketer wishing to speak to customers with a single voice. Achieving this single voice is critical for breaking through the clutter of the modern marketing environment. However, the functional specialists required for working in the various media have their own biases and subgoals, which can get in the way of integration.

Use the skills you've learned in this chapter to get started on the brand campaign card at the end of the book.

13 Public Relations, Influencer Marketing, Social Media, and Corporate Advertising

GLOSSARY TERMS

public relations function that provides communications to foster goodwill between a firm and its constituent groups

publicity unpaid-for media exposure about a firm's activities or its products and services

proactive public relations strategy PR strategy that is dictated by marketing objectives, seeks publicity, and takes the offense

reactive public relations strategy PR strategy that is dictated by influences outside the company's control, focuses on solving problems, and requires defensive measures

public relations audit internal study that identifies aspects of the firm or its activities that are positive and newsworthy

public relations plan plan that identifies the objectives and activities of a firm's PR communications

influencer marketing series of personalized marketing techniques directed at individuals or groups with the credibility and capability to drive positive word-of-mouth in a market segment

social media websites where users create and share information about themselves, brands, and other mutual interests

buzz marketing creation of events or experiences that yield conversations that include the brand or product

viral marketing process of consumers marketing to consumers over the Internet through word-of-mouth

corporate advertising advertising intended to establish a favorable attitude toward a company as a whole

advocacy advertising advertising that attempts to influence public opinion about social, political, or environmental issues of concern to the advertiser

cause-related marketing marketing messages that identify corporate sponsorship of philanthropic activities

CHAPTER SUMMARY

LO 1 **Discuss the role of public relations as part of a strategy for integrated marketing communication (IMC).**

Public relations focuses on communications that can foster goodwill between a firm and constituent groups such as customers, stockholders, employees, government entities, and the general public. Businesses use PR activities to highlight positive events associated with the organization and to engage in damage control when adversity strikes. Public relations has entered a new era, as changing corporate demands and new techniques have fostered a bolder, more aggressive role for PR in IMC campaigns.

LO 2 **Identify the objectives and tools of public relations.**

An active PR effort can serve many objectives, such as building goodwill and counteracting negative publicity. Public relations activities also may be orchestrated to support the launch of new products or communicate with employees on matters of interest to them. The PR function also may be instrumental to the firm's lobbying efforts and in preparing executives to meet with the press. The primary tools of public relations are press releases, feature stories, company newsletters, interviews and press conferences, and participation in the firm's event sponsorship decisions and programs.

LO 3 **Describe basic strategies for PR activities.**

When companies perceive public relations as a source of opportunity for shaping public opinion, they are likely to pursue a proactive PR strategy. With a proactive strategy, a firm strives to build goodwill with key constituents via aggressive programs. The foundation for these proactive programs is a rigorous public relations audit and a comprehensive public relations plan. The plan should include an explicit statement of objectives to guide the overall effort. In many instances, however, PR activities take the form of damage control, which places the firm in a reactive mode. Although a reactive strategy may seem a contradiction in terms, organizations can be prepared to react to bad news. Organizations that understand their inherent vulnerabilities can prepare themselves to react quickly and effectively in the face of hostile publicity.

[Exhibit 13.1]
Components of a PR Plan

Situation analysis	Summary of information obtained from the public relations audit, often broken down by category, such as product performance or community activity
Program objectives	Objectives stemming from the current situation and set for both short-term and long-term opportunities; generally focus on reputation, such as the credibility of product performance (e.g., placing products in verified, independent tests) or the stature of the firm's research and development efforts (article in a prestigious trade publication)
Program rationale	Identification of the PR program's role relative to the other brand promotion efforts; articulates an integrated marketing communication perspective
Communications vehicles	Specification of the tools (e.g., press releases, interviews, newsletters) to be used to implement the PR plan
Message content	Development of the PR message based on research such as focus groups and in-depth interviews

© Cengage Learning 2011.

green marketing corporate communication efforts to promote a cause or program in support of the environment

LO 4
Summarize how companies use influencer marketing programs.

Given that consumers are predisposed to talk about brands and what they say is vital to the well-being of those brands, it is no surprise that marketers are pursuing strategies to influence the conversation. Influencer marketing refers to tools and techniques directed at driving positive word-of-mouth about a brand. In professional programs, important gatekeepers may be a focal point. Peer-to-peer programs look for the connectors who spread influential messages. In both types of program, the marketer is challenged to give the influencers a meaningful or provocative topic that they will want to talk about.

LO 5
Describe how marketers use social media to promote brands.

Social media are websites where users create and share information. Examples include social-networking sites, works-sharing sites, blogs, and microblogging (Twitter). To engage in brand communication via social media, marketers need to enter a community conversation that includes listening as well as transmitting messages. They can shape conversations by creating venues, seeking feedback, providing valued information, and crafting messages that are simple enough to convey accurately. Often, marketers' use of social media is aimed at creating buzz and stimulating viral marketing.

[Exhibit 13.3]
New Brand Relationships with Social Media

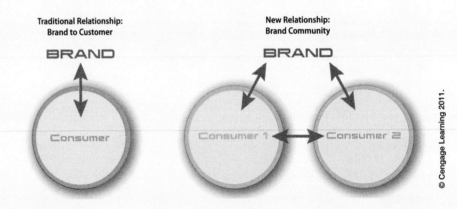

Traditional Relationship: Brand to Customer

BRAND

Consumer

New Relationship: Brand Community

BRAND

Consumer 1 ⟷ Consumer 2

© Cengage Learning 2011.

LO 6
Discuss the applications and objectives of corporate advertising.

Corporate advertising, rather than supporting an organization's specific brands, aims to build the general reputation of the organization in the eyes of key constituents. This form of advertising serves goals such as enhancing the firm's image and building credibility for its line of products. Corporate advertising also may serve the objectives of improving employee morale, building shareholder confidence, or denouncing competitors. Corporate ad campaigns may take the form of image advertising, advocacy advertising, or cause-related advertising. Corporate advertising may be orchestrated in such a way as to be newsworthy, so it must be carefully coordinated with the organization's PR programs.

Use the skills you've learned in this chapter to get started on the brand campaign card at the end of the book.

Visit CourseMate for PROMO2 at www.cengagebrain.com for additional study tools.

CHAPTER 13

GLOSSARY TERMS

personal selling process of face-to-face communication and persuasion

customer relationship management (CRM) continual effort to cultivate and maintain long-term relationships with customers by emphasizing customer needs

order taking practice of accepting and processing customer information for prearranged purchase or scheduling services a customer will purchase

creative selling assisting and persuading customers regarding purchase decisions (typically for specialty goods or high-priced items)

team selling sales effort by a team of salespeople representing different functions

seminar selling education of customer or prospect groups to inform them about the firm's products or services

system selling selling a set of interrelated components that fulfill a majority of a customer's needs in a product or service area

missionary salesperson salesperson who calls on accounts to monitor buyers' satisfaction and update their needs

detail salesperson salesperson who introduces new products and provides product information without aiming for an immediate sale

canned presentation recitation of a prepared sales pitch

attention-interest-desire-action (AIDA) structured presentation aimed at capturing attention, identifying features of interest, defining desirable benefits, and requesting action in the form of a purchase

need satisfaction sales presentation that begins with assessment of each buyer's need state and then adjusts the selling effort to that need state

consultive selling face-to-face selling in which salespeople help customers define problems and design solutions

CHAPTER SUMMARY

LO 1 **Explain why personal selling is important in brand promotion.**
Household consumers and business buyers frequently are confronted with purchase decisions that are facilitated by interaction with a salesperson. This especially is true for products that are higher priced and complicated to use, require demonstration, are tailored to users' needs, involve a trade-in, or are judged at the point of purchase. In many decision contexts, only a qualified and well-trained salesperson can address a potential buyer's questions and concerns.

LO 2 **Describe the activities besides selling performed by salespeople.**
The modern salesperson resembles a one-person marketing strategy program. Aside from the direct tasks of personal selling, salespeople contribute to the overall marketing effort by providing information relevant to market analysis, sales forecasting, ideas for new product development, and analysis of buyer behavior. Salespeople also participate in brand communications, sales coordination, customer service, and customer relationship management (CRM).

LO 3 **Summarize the role of setting objectives for personal selling.**
A salesperson in a contemporary selling environment doesn't only sell but rather manages a set of buying–selling relationships between the buyer and seller for mutual benefit. One of the greatest challenges facing a salesperson is determining how his or her firm is uniquely capable of satisfying customer needs. Matching what the firm is capable of doing with what a buyer desires allows both parties to enter a buying–selling relationship that is mutually beneficial. The salesperson must determine which features of a firm's products and services are most attractive and potentially satisfying.

[Exhibit 14.3]
How to Sell: Steps in the Process

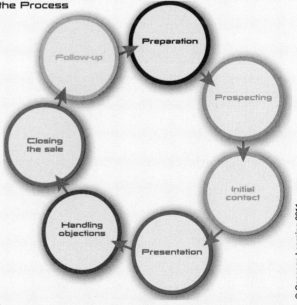

© Cengage Learning 2011.

sales force automation (SFA) integration of computers, communication technology, and the Internet to improve the efficiency and effectiveness of personal selling

sales management responsibility for the personal-selling effort, met by evaluating needs, setting objectives and budgets, structuring and hiring the sales force, training and motivating salespeople, and evaluating their performance

Based on the buyer's expression of needs, a salesperson can determine what is most highly valued in the purchase decision. Through such a determination, the salesperson can emphasize the firm's unique capabilities in satisfying the customer. Negotiations can emphasize the firm's ability to provide superior satisfaction on the desired factors.

LO 4 **Outline the steps involved in personal selling.**

A well-conceived personal-selling process involves seven distinct steps: preparation, prospecting, initial contact, presentation, handling objections, closing the sale, and follow-up.

LO 5 **Describe factors that contribute to a new environment for personal selling.**

The key factors that have contributed to a new environment for personal selling are more sophisticated marketing planning techniques, information technologies (both hardware and software), communication technologies, the Internet, and a trend for customers to be more demanding and knowledgeable. The technological changes have enabled companies to benefit from greater use of sales force automation (SFA).

LO 6 **Define the responsibilities of sales force management.**

Sales force management includes the following areas of responsibility: conducting a situation analysis, setting sales objectives, establishing a budget for selling activities, identifying the proper sales force structure based on the situation analysis and budget, hiring salespeople (identifying job requirements and recruiting, screening, and evaluating candidates), training salespeople, motivating the sales force (including the use of compensation and recognition programs), and evaluating the performance of salespeople.

[Exhibit 14.4]
What Sales Managers Do

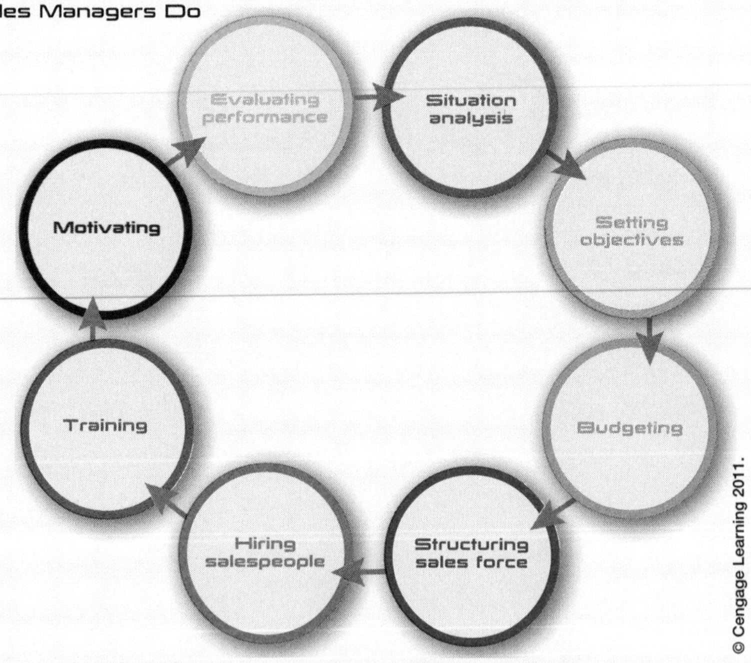

Evaluating performance · Situation analysis · Setting objectives · Budgeting · Structuring sales force · Hiring salespeople · Training · Motivating

© Cengage Learning 2011.

Use the skills you've learned in this chapter to get started on the brand campaign card at the end of the book.

Visit CourseMate for PROMO2 at www.cengagebrain.com **for additional study tools.**

GLOSSARY TERMS

promotion research marketing research focused on the development and performance of promotional materials

reliability tendency to generate consistent findings over time

validity relevance in terms of actually answering the questions being investigated

trustworthiness quality of deserving confidence

meaningfulness in promotion research, practical applicability of conclusions to the promotional effort

account planning system in which an agency assigns a coequal account planner to work alongside the account executive and analyze research data, staying with projects on a continuous basis

naturalistic inquiry broad-based research method that relies on qualitative data collection, including video and audio recordings and photography

normative test scores scores determined by testing an ad and then comparing the scores with those of previously tested campaigns of the same type

resonance test message assessment aimed at determining the extent to which a message rings true with target audience members

communication test pretest message research aimed at measuring whether a message is communicating something close to what is desired

dummy advertising vehicles mock-ups of magazines that contain editorial content and advertisements, including ads being tested

theater tests pretest message research in which subjects view ads played in small theaters and record their reactions

thought listing pretest message research that tries to identify specific thoughts that may be generated by an ad

CHAPTER SUMMARY

LO 1 Discuss issues that shape the evaluation of brand promotion.

First among the issues to consider when exploring the measurement of promotion's effectiveness is the scope of promotion research. It is a specialized form of marketing research that helps marketers learn who audience members are and which messages will work most effectively. A second issue is that marketers must determine whether research meets the criteria of reliability, validity, trustworthiness, and meaningfulness. In addition, the research effort may be carried out piecemeal by experts in particular tasks or managed through an ongoing process of account planning. Finally, marketers must assess marketers' motives and expectations and define criteria for the assessment—that is, whether the message imparts knowledge, shapes attitudes, attaches feelings and emotions, or legitimizes the brand.

LO 2 Describe how marketers measure the effectiveness of advertising.

Advertising is measured more than other promotional tools because it is conspicuous and expensive to prepare. It is measured in three main ways: (1) Pretest evaluations use communication tests, magazine dummies, theater tests, thought listings, attitude change studies, and physiological measures to measure the effectiveness of advertising before a campaign launches, (2) Marketplace pilot testing uses split-cable transmission for TV ads, split-run distribution for print ads, and split-list distribution for direct mail to measure effectiveness in real market conditions, and (3) Post-testing, which occurs after a campaign is running, tests recall and recognition and tracks awareness and attitude.

[Exhibit 15.1]
Measures for Post-Testing Sales Promotion

Type of Promotion	Suitable Measures
Contests and sweepstakes	Changes in sales; number of entries
Coupons	Changes in sales; number of coupons redeemed
Rebates	Changes in sales; number of rebate forms submitted
Trade promotions	Changes in sales

© Cengage Learning 2011.

LO 3 Identify measures of effectiveness for Internet advertising, direct marketing, sales promotion, point of purchase, sponsorships, public relations, and corporate advertising.

Internet advertising is judged by counting visits to websites, hits on banner ads, unique visitors, impressions formed and expressions of liking on social media. Direct marketing is relatively easy to evaluate by measuring the responses (sales or inquiries) that are the primary intention for the campaign. Sales promotions can be pretested by asking customers to rate alternative promotions and post-tested by measuring changes in sales or number or responses. Point-of-purchase promotion also is judged mainly by changes in sales. Sponsorships can be measured by the number of people attending an event or viewing a televised event. Rough measures for public relations and corporate advertising are surveys of attitude changes and counts of the number of exposures.

attitude change study message research that uses a before-and-after ad exposure design

physiological measures interpretation of biological feedback from subjects exposed to an ad

eye-tracking systems physiological measure that monitors eye movements across advertisements

psychogalvanometer device that measures galvanic skin response, or minute changes in perspiration that may suggest arousal

voice response analysis physiological assessment in which computers measure inflections in subjects' voices

pilot testing message evaluation that consists of experimentation in the marketplace

split-cable transmission pilot testing of two versions of an advertisement through direct transmission to separate sample households

split-run distribution pilot testing in which different versions of an advertisement are placed in magazines and direct responses to each advertisement are compared

split-list experiments pilot testing in which multiple versions of a direct-mail piece are sent to segments of a mailing list and responses to each version are compared

post-test message tracking assessment of an ad's performance during or after the launch of an ad campaign

recall test test of how much the viewer of an ad remembers of the message

recognition tests tests in which audience members are asked whether they recognize an ad or something in an ad

log analysis software measurement software that provides data about online consumer behavior, including hits, pages, visits, and users, as well as audience traffic within a website

inquiry/direct-response measures post-test message tracking in which an advertisement calls for a direct response and the number of responses is counted

ballot method pretest of sales promotion in which consumers are given

LO 4 Explain how sales managers evaluate salespeople and the personal-selling effort.

Measuring the performance of salespeople draws directly on the objectives set for the personal-selling process and sales objectives. Sales staff can be judged on several objective and subjective criteria. The objective criteria include quantifiable variables such as sales volume, profits or orders generated, and activities including sales calls and nonselling activities. Subjective criteria describe how a salesperson manages time and account relationships—for example, preparedness, product knowledge, and team relationships. Measurement of salespeople's performance provides a basis for evaluating the success of the overall personal-selling effort.

[Exhibit 15.2]
Performance Criteria for Salespeople

© Cengage Learning 2011.

LO 5 Describe the process of evaluating the effectiveness of IMC campaigns.

One approach to measuring the effectiveness of the overall IMC program is to measure each of the promotional tools used in a campaign as if it were independent of the others. This fragmented approach fails to account for the synergies that are the hallmark of IMC campaigns. Another approach is to use single-source tracking measures, which identify the extent to which a sample of consumers potentially has been exposed to multiple promotional messages. A third alternative proposed by practitioners suggests measuring media exposures, product (brand) impressions, and personal contacts as a basis for determining the overall effect of an IMC program. However, measuring the interaction of all elements of the promotional mix elements is extremely complicated and may be beyond the methodological tools available at this time.

Use the skills you've learned in this chapter to complete the brand campaign card at the end of the book.

a list of promotional options and asked to rank their preferences

single-source tracking measures post-test message tracking that uses a combination of scanner data and devices that monitor television-viewing behavior to collect information about brand purchases, coupon use, and television ad exposure

GLOSSARY TERMS

SWOT analysis assessment of the strengths, weaknesses, opportunities, and threats facing a firm and its brand, so that a strategy will capitalize on strengths and opportunities while avoiding or overcoming weaknesses and threats

brand promotion plan document that specifies the thinking, tasks, and timetable needed to conceive and implement the brand promotion effort

PLANNING A BRAND CAMPAIGN

Marketers and their agencies (see Chapters 2 and 8) engage in many activities to plan a successful brand campaign:

- Studying the firm's marketing plan to identify objectives and activities that will affect decisions about brand promotion

- Conducting SWOT analyses (see next page) to evaluate what promotional activities and messages are possible and desirable, given the resources and needs at hand

- Researching the target audience to identify messages that might be well received (see Chapters 5 and 7)

- Defining objectives for the campaign—for example, a desired level of sales, trial use, or awareness of the brand

- Identifying appropriate media for reaching the target audience in an integrated marketing campaign (see Chapters 1 and 9 through 14)

- Preparing a brand promotion plan (see next page), including objectives, budgets, activities, and schedules

- Creating brand promotion messages for each medium

- Testing messages and revising them as necessary to achieve promotional objectives (see Chapter 15)

- Measuring the effectiveness of the campaign (see Chapter 15) and adjusting media and messages if needed

To build a brand campaign, use a calendar to schedule the activities.

[Exhibit CIR16.1]
Brand Campaign Calendar

Time Period	Activities Scheduled
Month 1	
Month 2	
Month 3	
Month 4	
Month 5	
Month 6	
Month 7	
Month 8	
Month 9	
Month 10	
Month 11	
Month 12	

© Cengage Learning 2011.

Sharon L. Jonz/Getty Images.

KEY QUESTIONS

- What message will best convey the brand's value proposition (see Chapter 4)?

- Who is in the brand's target audience (see Chapter 4)? What do we know about those potential and current customers?

- What media do people in our target audience use? Where do they encounter our brand or competitors' brands?

- Will the message we want to send be most effective in a particular format—for example, conveyed creatively on television or easily shared on the Internet?

- Are our brand message and brand promotion strategy legal and ethical (see Chapter 6)?

- Will customers in different geographic areas respond differently to our message (see Chapter 7)?

- How many times will the target audience need to be exposed to our message for us to meet our objectives? To reach that level of exposure, how should we schedule our message delivery?

- Will our sales force need training to present the new campaign message? If so, how much training?

- If our firm can't afford our original marketing plan, how can we achieve our objectives on a tighter budget?

SWOT ANALYSIS

A **SWOT analysis** assesses four types of information:

1. *Strengths:* What advantages do the firm and its brand already possess, relative to other companies and brands?

2. *Weaknesses:* In what areas are the firm and its brand at a disadvantage, relative to other companies and brands?

3. *Opportunities:* What developments and needs in the market might be addressed by the firm's product line and brand? Opportunities may arise from changes in technology, laws, social norms, customer needs, or any other source of a new demand in the marketplace.

4. *Threats:* What changes in the market might make it harder for the firm and its brand to meet customer needs? The same areas of change that produce opportunities may also create threats.

After identifying and describing the strengths, weaknesses, opportunities, and threats facing the firm and its brand, planners develop objectives aimed at building on the strengths and opportunities while overcoming or avoiding the weaknesses and threats.

Applying SWOT analysis to brand promotion, marketers generally develop messages that emphasize the brand's strengths and downplay its weaknesses (although, as described in the opening story in Chapter 8, a creative message can sometimes have fun with weaknesses such as the high fat content of a company's sandwiches or the creepiness of its mascot). Also, marketers generally examine the target audience to find opportunities and threats that will help them define a relevant and convincing message.

BRAND PROMOTION PLAN

The **brand promotion plan** specifies the thinking, tasks, and timetable needed to conceive and implement the brand promotion effort. It describes the decisions made in planning the brand campaign. A complete plan contains all the elements shown in the following table.

[Exhibit CIR16.2]
Elements of a Brand Promotion Plan

Introduction	Summary of objectives and tactics for executing the plan
Situation analysis	Historical background and description of the industry, market, and competition
Objectives	Goals of the plan, stated specifically enough to indicate how to tell when the plan succeeded
Budget	Amount that each part of the plan is expected to cost
Strategy	Type of media and promotional tools to be used in achieving the objectives
Execution	Details about how the firm will carry out the plan, including responsibilities and deadlines
Evaluation	Methods to be used in measuring the outcome of the brand campaign and determining whether it succeeded or must be revised

© Cengage Learning 2011.